Literature

Reading, Reacting, Writing

Second Canadian Edition

Literature
Reading, Reacting, Writing

Laurie G. Kirszner
University of the Sciences in Philadelphia

Stephen R. Mandell
Drexel University

Candace Fertile
Camosun College

NELSON / **EDUCATION**

NELSON / EDUCATION

Literature: Reading, Reacting, Writing
Second Canadian Edition

by Laurie G. Kirszner, Stephen R. Mandell,
and Candace Fertile

**Associate Vice President,
Editorial Director:**
Evelyn Veitch

Editor-in-Chief:
Anne Williams

Marketing Manager:
Sandra Green

Developmental Editor:
Linda Sparks

Permissions Coordinator:
Kristiina Bowering

Senior Production Editor:
Julie van Veen

Copy Editor:
Liba Berry

Proofreader:
Wayne Herrington

Production Coordinator:
Ferial Suleman

Design Director:
Ken Phipps

Interior Design Modifications:
Katherine Strain

Cover Design:
Peter Papayanakis

Cover Image:
Don Farrall/Getty Images

Compositor:
Carol Magee

Printer:
Webcom

**Library and Archives Canada
Cataloguing in Publication**

Kirszner, Laurie G.
    Literature : reading, reacting,
writing / Laurie G. Kirszner,
Stephen R. Mandell, Candace
Fertile. — 2nd Canadian ed.

Includes bibliographical rferences
and index.
ISBN 0-17-640706-5

1. English language—Rhetoric.
2. Literature—History and
criticism—Theory, etc. 3.
Criticism—Authorship. 4. Academic
writing. 5. College readers.
I. Fertile, Candace Evelyn, 1954–
II. Mandell, Stephen R. III. Title.

PE1479.C7K57 2006   808'.0427
C2006-900572-9

◆ ◆ ◆

Brief Contents

Brief Contents

Detailed Contents

FICTION

◈ **CHAPTER 3**   **READING AND WRITING ABOUT FICTION   40**

◇ CHAPTER 12   READING AND WRITING ABOUT
POETRY   599

◇ **CHAPTER 13   VOICE   618**

◊ CHAPTER 14   WORD CHOICE, WORD ORDER   **654**

❖ **CHAPTER 17   SOUND   730**

◆ CHAPTER 19   SYMBOL, ALLEGORY, ALLUSION,
MYTH   791

DRAMA

Preface

Trying to turn an American anthology of literature into a text suitable for Canadian students presents several opportunities and one overwhelming drawback—the sheer abundance of excellent Canadian works meant that I had to leave out wonderful stories, poems, and plays. As a drawback, this one is welcome. The opportunities I faced mainly lay in how to incorporate a representative selection from the vast array possible. The social, political, and cultural context of Canada is different from that of the United States, although the countries do have much in common. The model of the Canadian mosaic versus the American melting pot may be a cliché, but the forces that have gone into the history of Canada have resulted in different attitudes about culture. Canada's (politically) entrenched views on multiculturalism have their roots in the two formative European sensibilities: French and English. And once other groups settled in Canada, and a recognition of the Aboriginal peoples already residing in the Americas was finally made, the nature of being Canadian became more fluid and open.

The vastness of the Canadian landscape and the extreme variations in geography and climate are also factors in the selection of material. In addition, an editor can get caught up in considering gender, race, place, sexual orientation, and politics, among other points. I also had to think about which selections would be useful in an introductory anthology. And, naturally, I had certain restrictions from the publisher. Finally, my goal was to create a book with enough range to indicate the wealth of Canadian literature in the context of other literatures, a goal consistent with the aims of Laurie G. Kirszner and Stephen R. Mandell when they were writing the first edition of *Literature: Reading, Reacting, Writing*—to include works that represent a varied assortment of cultures and viewpoints and to weave together old and new, past and present. I hope this anthology will enable students to read widely and thoughtfully, and I hope students will be encouraged to move beyond this anthology to other literary riches.

PEDAGOGICAL FEATURES

To introduce students to some of the complex issues involved in the study of literature, we begin with a chapter called "Understanding Literature." After surveying traditional literary themes, we summarize the reasons why many believe that the traditional canon needs to be revised. We then discuss the processes of interpreting and evaluating literature, placing special emphasis on how readers' personal experiences affect meaning. Finally, we examine the role of literary criticism and consider how it can offer students perspectives that can help them to expand their literary horizons.

Fulfilling its commitment to emphasizing writing about literature, the text includes student papers. To help students to see writing about literature as a process of exploring and testing ideas, of growing into a point of view or critical stance, and of participating in an ongoing critical debate, we include writing instruction.

In Chapter 2, we discuss the process of gathering and arranging ideas, drafting, and so on, and explain and illustrate how these concepts apply specifically to writing about literature. Then, within each of the text's three major sections, we follow the writing process of a student as he or she writes about a particular literary work in a particular genre: Madeleine Thien's story "Simple Recipes" (p. 45); two poems, Robert Hayden's "Those Winter Sundays" and Seamus Heaney's "Digging" (pp. 573–74); and Susan Glaspell's play *Trifles* (p. 948). We believe that these chapters will prepare students to explore the literary works in this anthology with confidence and creativity.

Other features enhance and strengthen the text's emphasis on reading and writing about literary works. Each of the eighteen chapters based on an element of literature (plot, setting, point of view, and so on) contains a checklist designed to help students generate, explore, focus, and organize ideas for writing about works of literature. The text also includes an appendix, "Documenting Sources," which explains and illustrates the most up-to-date information on MLA documentation style (including the 2003 guidelines on how to document electronic sources) and contains two additional source-based student papers, one on Eudora Welty's "A Worn Path," and the other on Alice Munro's "Boys and Girls." It also includes a second appendix, "Using Literary Criticism in Your Writing."

Throughout the text, Reading and Reacting questions, including suggestions for journal entries, follow many selections, and suggestions for paper topics are included at the end of each chapter. The reading and reacting questions ask students to interpret and evaluate what they have read, with many of the journal entries encouraging students to make connections—between two works, between two genres, between two themes, or between a given work and their own lives and experiences. This edition also includes a Related Works feature that enables students to make connections among works and among genres—connections they can explore in discussion and in writing.

Two additional features are designed to introduce students to the voices of literary critics. Most chapters open with a collection of quotations pertaining to the chapter's focus—point of view, imagery, staging, and so on. These quotations provide an accessible introduction to literary criticism. In addition, a critical perspective question (included in sets of Reading and Reacting questions) asks students to respond to an analytical, interpretative, or evaluative comment a critic has made about the work being considered, thus encouraging students to apply their own critical-thinking skills not just to the particular work but also to literary criticism of that work.

Each of the features described above encourages students both to appreciate works representing diverse literary subjects, styles, and perspectives and to recognize their own critical abilities by reading, reacting to, and writing about these works. If this anthology can encourage students to respond spontaneously and enthusiastically to what they read and to see their responses as involving them in an ongoing and stimulating (if sometimes unpredictable) dialogue—with their peers, with critics, with their instructors, with themselves, and with the work itself—then we will have accomplished our purpose.

To assist users of *Literature: Reading, Reacting, Writing,* Second Canadian Edition, the following ancillary material is available from Nelson:

- **Instructor's Resource Guide**—discussion and activities for every story, poem, and play in the anthology; thematic table of contents; semester and quarter syllabi; articles on evolution of the literary canon and reader-response theory. (ISBN 0-17-625168-5)

ACKNOWLEDGMENTS

◆ ◆ ◆

As this text is a Canadian version of an American book that has been through several editions, my first thanks must go to the editors who have preceded me in the creation of *Literature: Reading, Reacting, Writing*: Laurie G. Kirszner of the University of the Sciences in Philadelphia and Stephen R. Mandell of Drexel University. Along with their students and colleagues, these editors have designed a flexible anthology that meets the needs of first-year university and college students. The framework of the text is clear and pedagogically attractive. My task has been made easy by the work that has been done before me.

I would also like to thank Anne Williams, Editor-in-Chief, Linda Sparks, Developmental Editor, and Julie van Veen, Senior Production Editor, at Nelson for their patience, encouragement, and confidence. Various reviewers have also been instrumental in the preparation of the Canadian edition of *Literature: Reading, Reacting, Writing*. Thanks to Liba Berry for copy editing this edition. Wayne Herrington is to be commended for his keen eye, dedication, excellent suggestions, and patience while proofreading the text. A project of this magnitude reflects the accumulated efforts of a skilled team, and I am grateful for all the help I have been given. Many thanks are also due to Jon C. Stott, Raymond E. Jones, and Rick Bowers: authors of the footnotes this edition uses from the *Harbrace Anthology of Literature*.

Nelson would like to thank the following reviewers for their insightful comments: Lee Easton, Mount Royal College; Kathryn McArthur, University of Waterloo; Peter Laurie, Sir Sandford Fleming College; Aicha Gaboune, Northern Lakes College; Anita Arvast, Georgian College; Greg Doran, University of Prince Edward Island; Paul Malott, College of the North Atlantic; and Susan Briggs, Douglas College.

Candace Fertile

Authors Represented with Multiple Works

INTRODUCTION TO LITERATURE

CHAPTER 1

Understanding Literature

WHAT IS LITERATURE?

◆ ◆ ◆

IMAGINATIVE LITERATURE

Imaginative literature begins with a writer's need to convey a personal vision to readers. Even when writers use factual material—historical documents, newspaper stories, or personal experience, for example—their primary purpose is to present a unique view of experience, one that has significance beyond the moment. (As the poet Ezra Pound said, "Literature is the news that *stays* news.") To convey their views of experience, writers of imaginative literature often manipulate facts—changing dates, inventing characters, and putting words into their mouths. For example, in writing "Stones" (p. 135), Timothy Findley drew on the disastrous World War II battle at Dieppe, France. In August 1942, an amphibious raid by 1,000 British and 5,000 Canadian troops resulted in the deaths of two-thirds of the Allied troops. Findley used details of the raid, in particular the confusion and near-certain death the men were facing, along with details of setting, such as the stones on the beach. He invents the characters of David Max and his family and develops the story by showing the effect that Dieppe had on David Max, his wife, and children. Max's inability to order his men to advance into a massacre is perhaps understandable. The tanks could not move on the stones of the beach, and the soldiers were being mown down, but Max's failure to lead his men only added to the suffering. His own retreat is cowardly, and he is haunted for the rest of his life by that day. Findley uses the factual backdrop of the Dieppe raid to show the devastation of war on both soldiers and their families at home. The imaginative creation of the Max family and how the various members cope with David Max's changed personality as a result of Dieppe show Findley's skill in putting historical events to use in fiction.

Imaginative literature is more likely than other types of writing to include words chosen not only because they communicate the writer's ideas, but also because they are memorable. Using vivid imagery and evocative comparisons, writers of imaginative literature often stretch language to its limits. By relying on the multiple connotations of words and images, a work of imaginative literature encourages readers to see the possibilities of language and to move beyond the factual details of an event. Consider, for example, how William Wordsworth uses language in the following lines from his poem "Composed upon Westminster Bridge, September 3, 1802" (p. 896):

> This City now doth, like a garment, wear
> The beauty of the morning; silent, bare,
> Ships, towers, domes, theatres, and temples lie
> Open unto the fields, and to the sky;
>   All bright and glittering in the smokeless air.

Wordsworth does not try to present a picture of London that is topographically or sociologically accurate. Instead, by comparing the city at dawn to a person wearing a beautiful garment, Wordsworth creates a striking picture that has its own kind of truth. By using a vivid, original comparison, the poet is able to suggest the oneness of the city, nature, and himself—an idea that is not easily communicated.

Even though imaginative literature can be divided into types called **genres**—fiction, poetry, and drama—the nature of literary genres varies from culture to culture. In fact, some literary forms that Western readers take for granted are alien to other literary traditions. For example, the sonnet, although fairly common in the West, is not a conventional literary form in Chinese or Arabic poetry. Similarly, the most popular theatrical entertainment in Japan since the mid-seventeenth century, the kabuki play, has no exact counterpart in the West. (In a kabuki play, which includes stories, scenes, dances, music, acrobatics, and elaborate costumes and stage settings, all of the actors are men, some of whom play the parts of females. Many of the kabuki plays have little plot and seem to be primarily concerned with spectacle. One feature of this form of drama is a walkway that extends from the stage through the audience to the back of the theatre.)

Conventions of narrative organization and character development can also vary considerably from culture to culture, especially in literature derived from oral traditions. For example, narrative organization can vary widely depending on the cultural source of the story. Events may be arranged spatially instead of chronologically: first a story presents all the events that happened in one place, then it presents everything that happened in another location, and so on. Similarly, character development may have a different importance in some traditional African and Native North American stories than it does in short fiction from other cultures. In fact, a character's name, description, and personality can change dramatically (and without warning) during the course of a story.

Despite such differences, the imaginative literature of all cultures can have similar effects on readers: memorable characters, vivid descriptions, imaginative use of language, and intricately developed plots can fascinate and delight. Literature can take readers where they have never been before and, in so doing, can create a sense of wonder and adventure.

At another level, however, readers can find more than just pleasure or escape in literature. Beyond transporting readers out of their lives and times, literature can enable readers to see their lives and times more clearly. Whether a work of imaginative literature depicts a young boy as he experiences disillusionment for the first time, as in James Joyce's "Araby" (p. 267), or examines the effect of discrimination on a black African who is looking for an apartment, as in Wole Soyinka's "Telephone Conversation" (p. 8), it can help readers to understand their own experiences and those of others. In this sense, literature offers readers increased insight and awareness. As the Chilean poet Pablo Neruda said, works of imaginative literature fulfill "the most ancient rites of our conscience in the awareness of being human and of believing in a common destiny."

CONVENTIONAL THEMES

The **theme** of a work of literature is its central or dominant idea. This idea is seldom stated explicitly. Instead, it is conveyed through the selection and arrangement of details; through the emphasis of certain words, events, or images; and through the actions and reactions of characters.

Although one central theme may dominate a literary work, most works explore a number of different themes. For example, the central theme of Mordecai Richler's *The Apprenticeship of Duddy Kravitz* might be the importance of moral and ethical considerations in the attainment of one's goals and ambitions. The main character, Duddy Kravitz, is very shrewd and clever, but his lack of moral principles contributes to his final failure. The novel sketches Duddy's involvement in corrupt activities from an early age to his highly suspect real estate deals later on as a young man. However, *The Apprenticeship of Duddy Kravitz* also examines other themes. Throughout his novel, Richler explores many of the ideas that prevailed in Canadian society in the 1940s and 1950s, such as anti-Semitism, and also looks at the dissolution of the traditional family structure.

A literary work can explore any theme, but certain themes have recurred so frequently over the years that they have become conventions. One theme frequently explored in literature, a character's loss of innocence, appears in the biblical story of Adam and Eve and later finds its way into works such as Nathaniel Hawthorne's 1835 short story "Young Goodman Brown" (p. 307) and James Joyce's 1914 short story "Araby" (p. 267). Another conventional theme—the conflict between an individual's values and the values of society—is examined in the ancient Greek play *Antigone* by Sophocles. Almost two thousand years later, Norwegian playwright Henrik Ibsen deals with the same theme in *A Doll House* (p. 1013).

Other themes often examined in literary works include the individual's quest for spiritual enlightenment, the *carpe diem* ("seize the day") theme, the making of the artist, the nostalgia for a vanished past, the disillusionment of adulthood, the pain of love, the struggle of women for equality, the conflict between parents and children, the clash between civilization and the wilderness, the evils of unchecked ambition, the inevitability of fate, the impact of the past on the present, the conflict between human beings and machines, and the tension between the ideal and the actual realms of experience.

Nearly every culture explores similar themes, but writers from different cultures may develop these themes differently. A culture's history, a particular region's geography, or a country's social structure can suggest unique ways of developing conventional themes. In addition, the assumptions, concerns, values, ideals, and beliefs of a particular country or society—or of a particular group within that society—can help to determine the themes writers choose to explore and the manner in which they do so.

In Canadian literature, for instance, familiar themes include the loss of innocence, rites of passage, childhood epiphanies, the ability (or inability) to form relationships, the struggle to survive in an inhospitable environment, the attempt to fit into a cultural landscape that is frequently shifting, and the opportunities available for a wide variety of experiences. Canadian writers of colour, in addition to exploring these themes, may also express their frustration with racism or celebrate their cultural identities. Even when they explore more conventional themes, writers of colour may choose to do so in the context of their own experience. For example, the theme of loss of innocence may be presented as a first encounter with racial prejudice; a conflict between the individual and society may be presented as a conflict between a minority view and the values of the dominant group; and the theme of failure or aborted relationships may be explored in a work about cultural misunderstandings.

Another point to keep in mind is that modern works of literature sometimes treat conventional themes in new ways. For example, in *1984* George Orwell explores the negative consequences of unchecked power by creating a nightmare world in which technology controls and dehumanizes a population. Even though Orwell's novel is set in an imaginary future (it was written in 1948), its theme echoes ideas frequently examined in the plays of both Sophocles and Shakespeare.

THE LITERARY CANON

Originally the term *canon* referred to the authoritative or accepted list of books that made up the Christian Bible. Recently, the term **literary canon** has come to denote a group of works generally agreed upon by writers, teachers, and critics to be worth reading and studying. Over the years, as standards have changed, the definition of "good" literature has also changed, and the literary canon has been modified accordingly. For example, at various times, critics have characterized Shakespeare's plays as mundane, immoral, commonplace, and brilliant. The eighteenth-century critic Samuel Johnson said of Shakespeare that "in his comick scenes he is seldom very successful" and in tragedy "his performance seems constantly to be worse, as his labor is more." Many people find it difficult to believe that a writer whose name today is synonymous with great literature could ever have been judged so harshly. But like all aesthetic works, the plays of Shakespeare affect individuals in different periods of history and in different societies in different ways.

Lately, educators and literary scholars have charged that the traditional literary canon, like a restricted club, admits some authors and excludes all others. This fact is borne out, they say, by an examination of the literature curriculum that until recently was standard at many North American universities. This curriculum typically began with Homer, Plato, Dante, and Chaucer, progressed to Shakespeare, Milton, the eighteenth-century novel, the Romantics, and the Victorians, and ended with some of the "classics" of modern British and American literature. Most of the authors of these works are white and male, and their writing primarily reflects only Western values.

During the past two decades, however, many universities have expanded the traditional canon by including more works by women, people of colour, and writers from a variety of cultures. These additions, studied alongside works representing the traditional canon, have opened up the curriculum and redefined the standards by which literature is judged.

An example of a literary work that might challenge the traditional canon is the brief story "All about Suicide" by Luisa Valenzuela, an Argentinean writer. An experimental story, moving freely in time, bending the facts, and speaking directly to readers, "All about Suicide" is part of a large and growing genre of literature that purposely violates standard literary expectations to make its point—in this case, a point about the political realities of Argentina in the 1960s.

> ◊ ◊ ◊

LUISA VALENZUELA
(1938–   )

All about Suicide
(1967)

Translated by Helen Lane

Ismael grabbed the gun and slowly rubbed it across his face. Then he pulled the trigger and there was a shot. Bang. One more person dead in the city. It's getting to be a vice. First he grabbed the revolver that was in a desk drawer, rubbed it gently across his face, put it to his temple, and pulled the trigger. Without saying a word. Bang. Dead.

Let's recapitulate: the office is grand, fit for a minister. The desk is ministerial too, and covered with a glass that must have reflected the scene, the shock. Ismael knew where the gun was, he'd hidden it there himself. So he didn't lose any time, all he had to do was open the right-hand drawer and stick his hand in. Then he got a good hold on it and rubbed it over his face with a certain pleasure before putting it to his temple and pulling the trigger. It was something almost sensual and quite unexpected. He hadn't even had time to think about it. A trivial gesture, and the gun had fired.

There's something missing: Ismael in the bar with a glass in his hand thinking over his future act and its possible consequences.

We must go back farther if we want to get at the truth: Ismael in the cradle crying because his diapers are dirty and nobody is changing him.

5   Not that far.

Ismael in the first grade fighting with a classmate who'll one day become a minister, his friend, a traitor.

No, Ismael in the ministry without being able to tell what he knew, forced to be silent. Ismael in the bar with the glass (his third) in his hand, and the irrevocable decision: better death.

Ismael pushing the revolving door at the entrance to the building, pushing the swinging door leading to the office section, saying good morning to the guard, opening the door of his office. Once in his office, seven steps to his desk. Terror, the act of opening the drawer, taking out the revolver, and rubbing it across his face, almost a single gesture and very quick. The act of putting it to his temple and pulling the trigger—another act, immediately following the previous one. Bang. Dead. And Ismael coming out of his office (the other man's office, the minister's) almost relieved, even though he can predict what awaits him.

◆

The Nigerian poet and playwright Wole Soyinka is another writer whose works are not part of the traditional canon. The subject of the following poem may not seem "relevant" to European audiences, and the language ("pillar-box," "omnibus") may not be clear to Canadians. Still, as a reading of the poem demonstrates, Soyinka's work makes a moving plea for individual rights and self-determination—a theme that transcends boundaries of time and place.

◊ ◊ ◊

WOLE SOYINKA
(1934–   )

Telephone Conversation
(1962)

The price seemed reasonable, location
Indifferent. The landlady swore she lived
Off premises. Nothing remained
But self-confession. "Madam," I warned
5   "I hate a wasted journey—I am—African."
Silence. Silenced transmission of

Pressurized good-breeding. Voice, when it came,
Lip-stick coated, long gold-rolled
Cigarette-holder pipped. Caught I was, foully.
10 "HOW DARK?" . . . I had not misheard . . .
    "ARE YOU LIGHT
OR VERY DARK?" Button B. Button A. Stench
Of rancid breath of public-hide-and-speak.
Red booth. Red pillar-box. Red double-tiered
15 Omnibus squelching tar. It *was* real! Shamed
By ill-mannered silence, surrender
Pushed dumbfoundment to beg simplification.
Considerate she was, varying the emphasis—
"ARE YOU DARK? OR VERY LIGHT?" Revelation came.
20 "You mean—like plain or milk chocolate?"
Her assent was clinical, crushing in its light,
Impersonality. Rapidly, wave-length adjusted,
I chose, "West African sepia"—and as an afterthought,
"Down in my passport." Silence for spectroscopic
25 Flight of fancy, till truthfulness clanged her accent
Hard on the mouthpiece. "WHAT'S THAT?" conceding
"DON'T KNOW WHAT THAT IS." "Like brunette."
"THAT'S DARK, ISN'T IT?" "Not altogether.
Facially, I am brunette, but madam, you should see
30 The rest of me. Palm of my hand, soles of my feet
Are a peroxide blond. Friction, caused—
Foolishly madam—by sitting down, has turned
My bottom raven black—One moment madam!"—sensing
Her receiver rearing on the thunder clap
35 About my ears—"Madam," I pleaded, "Wouldn't you rather
See for yourself?"

Certainly canon revision is not without problems—for example, the possibility of including a work more for political or sociological reasons than for literary merit. Nevertheless, if the debate about the literary canon has accomplished anything, it has revealed that the canon is not fixed and that many works formerly excluded deserve to be included.

THINKING CRITICALLY
◊ ◊◊ ◊

INTERPRETING LITERATURE

When you *interpret* a literary work, you explore its possible meanings. One commonly held idea about reading a literary work is that its meaning lies buried somewhere within it, waiting to be unearthed. This reasoning suggests that a clever reader has only to discover the author's intent to find out what a story or poem means, and that the one actual meaning of a work is hidden between the lines, unaffected by a reader's experiences or interpretations. More recently, however, a different model of the reading process— one that takes into consideration the reader as well as the work he or she is interpreting—has emerged.

Many contemporary critics see the reading process as *interactive*. In other words, meaning is created through the reader's interaction with a text. The meaning of a particular work comes alive in the imagination of an individual reader, and no reader can determine a work's meaning without considering his or her own reaction to the text. Meaning, therefore, is created partly by what is supplied by a work and partly by what is supplied by the reader.

The most obvious meaning a work supplies is factual, the information that enables a reader to follow the plot of a story, the action of a play, or the development of a poem. For instance, the work itself will provide factual details about the setting; the characters' names, ages, and appearances; the sequence of events; and the emotions and attitudes of a poem's speaker, a story's narrator, or the characters in a play or story. This factual information cannot be ignored: if a play's stage directions identify its setting as nineteenth-century Norway or the forest of Arden, that is where it is set.

In addition to facts, a work also conveys the social, political, class, and gender attitudes of the writer. Thus, a work may have an overt feminist or working-class bias or a subtle political agenda; it may confirm or challenge contemporary attitudes; it may communicate a writer's nostalgia for a vanished past or his or her outrage at a corrupt present; it may take an elitist, distant view of characters and events or present a sympathetic perspective. A reader's understanding of these attitudes will contribute to his or her interpretation of the work.

Finally, a work also includes assumptions about literary conventions. A poet, for example, may have definite ideas about whether a poem should be rhymed or unrhymed or about whether a particular subject is appropriate or inappropriate for poetic treatment. Therefore, a knowledge of the literary conventions of a particular period or the preferences of a particular writer can provide a starting point for your interpretation of literature.

As a reader you also bring to a work your own personal perspectives. Your experiences, your beliefs, your ideas about the issues discussed in the work, and your assumptions about literature colour your interpretations. In fact, virtually every literary work has somewhat different meanings to different people, depending on their age, gender, nationality, political and religious beliefs, ethnic background, social and economic class, education, knowledge, and experiences. Depending on your race, where you live, your biases, and the nature of your experience, a story about racial discrimination can strike you as accurate and realistic, exaggerated and unrealistic, or understated and restrained.

In a sense, then, the process of determining meaning is like a conversation, one in which both you and the text have a voice. Sometimes, by clearly dictating the terms of the discussion, the text determines the direction of the conversation; at other times, by using your knowledge and experience to interpret the text, you dominate. Thus, because every reading of a literary work is actually an interpretation, it is a mistake to look for a single "correct" reading.

The poem "Ode on a Grecian Urn" (p. 852) by the English Romantic poet John Keats illustrates how a single work can have more than one interpretation. Readers may interpret the poem as being about death and the static immobility of sculpture: the Grecian urn, passed down through centuries to the time of the speaker's viewing, exists outside of time in the human sense; it does not age, it does not die. At the same time, the figures on the vase are free from time, but they are frozen in time. It is, however, the final two lines of the poem that have been the most difficult to interpret. After the urn answers the enigmatic phrase "Beauty is truth, truth beauty," one cannot say for certain who "speaks" the concluding line "that is all / Ye know on earth, and all ye need to know." Could it be the speaker addressing the urn, or could it be the urn addressing mankind? If it is the speaker addressing the urn, then it would appear that the speaker has become aware of the urn's limits: the urn may not need to know anything apart from the equation of truth and beauty, but the difficulties of life make it impossible for this simple phrase to articulate anything about human knowledge. If, however, it is the urn speaking to mankind, then the last line of the poem holds a crucial message: despite all the complications of human life, all that human beings need to know is that beauty and truth are the same. When reading a work of literature, then, keep in mind that the meaning of the text is not fixed. Your best strategy is to open yourself up to the text's possibilities and explore the full range of your responses.

As you read, do not be afraid to take chances and develop unusual or creative interpretations of a work. A "safe" reading of a work is likely to result in a dull paper that simply states the obvious, but an aggressive or "strong" reading of a work—one that challenges generally held assumptions—can lead to interesting and intellectually challenging conclusions. Even if your reading differs from established critics' interpretations, you should not automatically assume it has no merit. Your own special knowledge of the material discussed in the text—a regional practice, an ethnic custom, an attitude toward gender—may give you a unique perspective from which to view the work. Whatever interpretation you make, be sure that you support it with specific references to the text. If your interpretation is based on your own experiences, explain those experiences and relate them clearly to the work you are discussing. As long as you can make a reasonable case, you have the right (and perhaps the obligation) to present your ideas. By doing so you may provide your fellow students and your instructor with new insight into the work.

Remember, however, that some interpretations are *not* reasonable. You may contribute ideas based on your own perspectives, but you cannot ignore or contradict evidence in the text to suit your own biases. As you read and reread a text, continue to question and reexamine your judgments. The conversation between you and the text should be a dialogue, not a mono-logue or a shouting match.

Evaluating Literature

When you *evaluate* a work of literature, you do more than interpret it; you make a judgment about it. You reach conclusions—not simply about whether the work is good or bad, but also about how effectively the work presents itself to you, the reader. To evaluate a work, you *analyze* it, breaking it apart and considering its individual elements. As you evaluate a work of literature, remember that different works are designed to fulfill different needs—entertainment, education, or enlightenment, for example. Before you begin to evaluate a work, be sure you understand its purpose; then, follow the guidelines discussed below.

Begin your evaluation by considering how various literary elements function within a work. Fiction may be divided into chapters and use flashbacks and foreshadowing; plays may be divided into scenes and acts and include dialogue and special staging techniques; poems may be arranged in regularly ordered groups of lines and use poetic devices such as rhyme and metre. Understanding the choices writers make about these and other literary elements can help you make judgments about the work. For example, why does Madeleine Thien use a first-person narrator (*I*) in her story "Simple Recipes" (p. 45)? Would the story have been different had it been told in the third person by a nar-rator who was not a participant? Naturally, you cannot focus on every aspect of a particular story, poem, or play. But you can and should focus on those that play a major role in determining your responses to a work. For this reason the unusual stanzaic form in E. E. Cummings's poem "Buffalo Bill's" (p. 829) should be of special interest to you.

As you read, then, you should ask questions. Do the characters in a short story seem real, or do they seem like cardboard cutouts? Are the images in a poem original and thought-provoking, or are they clichéd? Are the stage directions of a play sketchy or very detailed? The answers to these questions will help you to shape your response.

As you continue your evaluation, decide whether or not the literary elements of a work interact to achieve a common goal. Well-crafted literary works are aesthetically pleasing, fitting together in a way that conceals the craft of the writer. Good writers are like master cabinetmakers; their skill disguises the actual work that has gone into the process of creation. Consider the following stanza from the 1862 poem "Echo" by Christina Rossetti:

Come to me in the silence of the night;
   Come to me in the speaking silence of a dream;

Come with soft round cheeks and eyes as bright
As sunlight on a stream;
Come back in tears,
O memory, hope, love of finished years.

Throughout this stanza Rossetti repeats words (<u>Come</u> to me. . . . / <u>Come</u> with soft. . . . / <u>Come</u> back. . . .) and initial consonants (<u>s</u>peaking <u>s</u>ilence / <u>s</u>unlight on a <u>s</u>tream) to create an almost hypnotic mood. The rhyme scheme (*night/bright, dream/stream,* and *tears/years*) reinforces the mood by creating a musical undercurrent that extends throughout the poem. Thus, this stanza is effective because its repeated words and sounds work together to create a single lyrical effect.

The chorus in *Oedipus the King* by Sophocles (p. 1293) also illustrates how the elements of a well-crafted work of literature function together. In ancient Greece plays were performed by masked male actors who played both male and female roles. A chorus of fifteen men would remain in a central circle called the *orchestra* and comment on and react to the action taking place around them. The chorus expresses the moral judgment of the community and acts as a guide for the audience. Once modern audiences grow accustomed to the presence of the chorus, it becomes an integral part of the play. It neither distracts the audience nor intrudes upon the action. In fact, eliminating the chorus would diminish the impact of the play.

Next, consider whether a work reinforces or calls into question your ideas about the world.
The 1992 short story "Flight Paths of the Emperor" by Steven Heighton (p. 354) may lead readers to examine their assumptions about cross-cultural experiences. The story presents a young Canadian couple living in Japan. Nick and Sandra face their own relationship as they are coping with the differences in Japanese and Canadian customs. When Nick and Sandra have to leave Japan unexpectedly, Nick's boss believes he should stay and fulfill his contract. But Nick believes that he and Sandra must go home because of his mother-in-law's impending death. Nick's boss is used to seeing foreign teachers leave before their time is up, and she does not have any sympathy for Nick's situation. Conflicting ideas of duty shape the story and encourage readers to consider the meaning of duty, to a job, to a family member, to a marriage. The differences between Japan and Canada emphasize the different feelings and approaches Nick and Sandra have to their families and to each other.

Works of popular fiction—those aimed at a mass audience—usually do little more than reassure readers that what they believe is correct. Catering to people's prejudices, or to their desires (for wealth or success, for example), or to their fears, these works serve as escapes from life. Serious fiction, however, often goes against the grain, challenging cherished beliefs and leading readers to reexamine long-held assumptions. For instance, in the 1985 story "Inland Passage" (p. 150), Jane Rule explores the need for contact between two women who have recently lost loved ones. Comfort comes in a way that may be seen as unexpected for some readers.

Then, consider whether or not a work is intellectually challenging.   The extended comparison between a draftsperson's compass and two people in love in "A Valediction: Forbidding Mourning" by the seventeenth-century English poet John Donne (p. 710) illustrates how effectively an image can communicate complex ideas to readers. Compressed into this comparison are ideas about the perfection of love, the pain of enforced separation, and the difference between sexual and spiritual love. As intellectually challenging as the extended comparison is, it is nonetheless accessible to the careful reader. After all, many people have used a compass to draw a circle and, therefore, are able to understand the relationship between the two points of the compass and the two lovers.

A fine line exists, however, between works that are intellectually challenging and those that are simply obscure. An *intellectually challenging* work makes readers think; it requires some effort on their part to unlock ideas that enrich and expand their understanding of themselves and the world. Although complex, the work gives readers a sense that they have gained something by putting forth the effort to interpret it. An *obscure* work, however, exists solely to display a writer's erudition or intellectual idiosyncrasies. Allusions to other works and events are so numerous and confusing that the work seems more like a private code than an effort to enlighten readers. Consider the following excerpt from "Canto LXXVI" by the twentieth-century American poet Ezra Pound:

> Le Paradis n'est pas artificiel
>> States of mind are inexplicable to us.
>>> δακρύων δακρύων δακρύων
> L.   P. gli onesti
>> J'ai eu pitié des autres
> probablement pas assez, and at moments that suited my own
>> convenience
>>> Le paradis n'est pas artificiel,
>>>> l'enfer non plus.
> Came Eurus as comforter
> and at sunset la pastorella dei suini
>> driving the pigs home, benecomata dea
>>> under the two-winged cloud
>>> as of less and more than a day

This passage contains lines in French, Greek, and Italian; a reference to Eurus, the ancient Greek personification of the east wind; and the initials L.P. (Loomis Pound?). Admittedly, it demands a lot from readers; the question is whether the reward is worth the effort.

No hard and fast rule exists for determining whether a work is intellectually challenging or simply obscure. Just as a poem has no fixed meaning, it also has no fixed value. Some readers would say that the preceding passage is good, even great, poetry. Others would argue that these lines do not yield enough pleasure and insight to justify the work needed to analyze them. As a reader, you must draw your own conclusions and justify them in a clear and reasonable way. Do not assume that just because a work is difficult, it is obscure. (Nor should you assume that all difficult works are great literature or that all accessible literature is trivial.) Some of the most beautiful and inspiring literary works demand a great deal of effort from readers. Most readers would agree, however, that the time spent exploring such works yields tremendous rewards.

Finally, consider whether a work gives you pleasure.   One of the primary reasons that literature endures is that it gives readers enjoyment. As subjective as this assessment is, it is a starting point for critical judgment. When readers ask themselves what they liked about a work, why they liked it, or what they learned, they begin the process of evaluation. Although this process is largely uncritical, it can lead to an involvement with the work and to a critical response. When you encounter great literature, with all its complexities, you may lose sight of the idea of literature as a source of pleasure. But literature should touch you on a deep emotional or intellectual level, and if it does not—despite its technical perfection—it fails to achieve one of its primary aims.

THE FUNCTION OF LITERARY CRITICISM

Sometimes your personal reactions and knowledge cannot give you enough insight into a literary work. For example, archaic language, obscure references, historical allusions, and textual inconsistencies can make reading a work particularly difficult. Similarly, an intellectual or philosophical movement such as Darwinism, Marxism, naturalism, structuralism, or feminism may influence a work, and if this is the case, you will need some knowledge of the movement before you can interpret the work. In addition, you may not have the background to appreciate the technical or historical dimension of a work. To widen the context of your reading, you may choose to read **literary criticism**—books and journal articles written by experts who describe, analyze, interpret, or evaluate a work of literature. Reading literary criticism enables you not only to expand your knowledge of a particular work, but also to participate in the public dialogue about literature. In a sense, you become part of a community of scholars who share their ideas and who are connected to one another through their writing.

Literary criticism is written by experts, but this fact does not mean you must always accept it. You have to evaluate literary criticism just as you do any new opinion that you encounter. Not all criticism is sound, timely, or responsible (and not all literary criticism is pertinent to your assignment or useful for your purposes). Some critical comments will strike you as plausible, whereas others will seem unfounded or biased. Quite often two critics will reach strikingly different conclusions about the quality or significance of the same work or writer or will interpret a character, a symbol, or even the entire work quite differently.

Critics may disagree, but even conflicting ideas can help you to reach your own conclusions about a work. It is up to you to sort out the various opinions and decide which have merit and which do not.

✓ CHECKLIST: EVALUATING LITERARY CRITICISM

- ✓ What is the main point of the book or article you are reading?
- ✓ Does the critic supply enough examples to support his or her conclusions?
- ✓ Does the critic acknowledge and refute the most obvious arguments against his or her position?
- ✓ Does the critic ignore any information in the text that might call his or her conclusions into question?
- ✓ Does the critic present historical information? Biographical information? Literary information? How does this information shed light on significant aspects of the work or works being discussed?
- ✓ Does the critic hold any beliefs that might interfere with his or her critical judgment?
- ✓ Does the critic seem to slant the facts, or does he or she offer a fair and objective reading of the text?
- ✓ Does the critic support his or her conclusions with references to other sources? Does he or she document these sources? Does the critical article or book contain a list of works cited? Are these works current?
- ✓ Do other critics mention the critical book or article you are reading? Do they accept or challenge its conclusions?

With your instructor's help, you might also try to answer these questions:

- ✓ Does the critic identify with a particular critical school of thought—deconstruction or Marxism, for example? What ideas does this school of thought hold?
- ✓ Is the critic well known and respected or unknown?
- ✓ Does the critic take into consideration the most important critical books and articles on his or her subject? Are there works that should have been mentioned but that were not? Do these gaps cast doubts on the critic's conclusions?
- ✓ Is the critical work's publication date of any significance?

CHAPTER 2

Reading and Writing about Literature

READING LITERATURE
◊ ◊ ◊

The process of writing about literature starts the moment you begin to read, when you begin interacting with a work and start to discover ideas about it. This process of **active reading** helps you to interpret what you read and, eventually, to develop your ideas into a clear and logical paper.

Most readers are passive; that is, they expect the text to give them everything they need, and they don't expect to contribute much to the reading process. Active readers, however, participate in the reading process—thinking about what they read, asking questions, and challenging ideas. Active reading is excellent preparation for the discussion and writing you will do in college literature classes. And, because it helps you understand and appreciate the works you read, active reading will continue to be of value to you long after your formal classroom study of literature has ended.

Three strategies in particular—*previewing, highlighting,* and *annotating*—will help you to become a more effective reader. Remember, though, that reading and responding to what you read is not an orderly process—or even a sequential one. You will most likely find yourself doing more than one thing at a time—annotating at the same time you highlight, for example. For the sake of clarity, however, we discuss each active reading strategy separately in the pages that follow.

PREVIEWING

You begin the active reading process by **previewing** a work to get a general idea of what to look for later, when you read it more carefully.

Start with the work's most obvious physical characteristics. For example, how long is a short story? How many acts and scenes does a play have? Is a poem divided into stanzas? The answers to these and similar questions will help you begin to notice more subtle aspects of the work's form. For example, previewing may reveal that a contemporary short story is presented entirely in a question-and-answer format, that it is organized as diary entries, or that it is divided into sections by headings. Previewing may identify poems that seem to lack formal structure, such as bp Nichol's unconventional "Blues" (p. 788); those written in traditional forms (such as sonnets) or in experimental forms, such as the numbered list of questions and answers in Denise Levertov's "What Were They Like?" (p. 591); or concrete poems such as George Herbert's "Easter Wings" (p. 787). Your awareness of these and other distinctive features at this point may help you gain insight into a work later on.

Perhaps the most physically distinctive element of a work is its title. Not only can the title give you a general idea of what the work is about, as a straightforward title like "The Cask of Amontillado" does, but it can also isolate (and thus call attention to) a word or phrase that emphasizes an important idea. For example, the title of Joan MacLeod's *The Shape of a Girl* (p. 1348) immediately draws our attention to the physical appearance of a girl and what immense importance that can have. A title can also be an allusion to another work. Thus, *The Sound and the Fury,* the title of a novel by William Faulkner, alludes to a speech from Shakespeare's *Macbeth* that reinforces the major theme of the novel. Finally, a title can introduce a symbol that will gain meaning in the course of a work—as stones do in Timothy Findley's "Stones" (p. 135).

Other physical elements—such as paragraphing, capitalization, italics, and punctuation—can also provide clues about how to read a work. In William Faulkner's short story "Barn Burning" (p. 234), for instance, previewing would help you to notice passages in italic type, indicating the protagonist's thoughts, which occasionally interrupt the narrator's story.

Finally, previewing can enable you to see some of the more obvious stylistic and structural features of a work—the point of view used in a story, how many characters a play has and where it is set, or the repetition of certain words or lines in a poem, for example. Such features may or may not be important; at this stage, your goal is to observe, not to analyze or evaluate.

Previewing is a useful strategy not because it provides answers but because it suggests questions to ask later, as you read more closely. For instance, *why* does Faulkner use italics in "Barn Burning," and *why* does Herbert shape his poem on the page as he does? Elements such as those described may be noticeable as you preview, but they will gain significance as you read more carefully and review your notes.

HIGHLIGHTING

When you go on to read a work closely, you will notice additional, sometimes more subtle, elements that you may want to examine further. At this point, you should begin **highlighting**—physically marking the text to identify key details and to note relationships among ideas.

What should you highlight? As you read, ask yourself whether repeated words or phrases form a pattern, as they do in D. H. Lawrence's short story "The Rocking-Horse Winner" (p. 370), in which the sentence *"There must be more money!"* appears again and again. Because this sentence appears so frequently, and because it appears at key points in the story, it helps to reinforce the story's theme—that money cannot replace or buy love. Repeated words and phrases are particularly important in poetry. In Dylan Thomas's "Do Not Go Gentle into That Good Night" (p. 571), for example, the repetition of two of the poem's nineteen lines four times each enhances the poem's rhythmic, almost monotonous, cadence. As you read, highlight your text to identify such repeated words and phrases. Later on, you can consider *why* they are repeated.

During the highlighting stage, also pay particular attention to images that occur repeatedly in a work, keeping in mind that such repeated images may form patterns that can help you to interpret the work. When you reread the work, you can begin to determine what pattern the images form and perhaps decide how this pattern enhances the work's ideas. When highlighting Robert Kroetsch's "Meditation on Tom Thomson" (p. 684), for instance, you might identify the related images of nature and death. Later, you can consider their significance.

 # CHECKLIST: USING HIGHLIGHTING SYMBOLS

- ✓ Underline important ideas that you should read again.
- ✓ Box or circle repeated words, phrases, or images.
- ✓ Put question marks beside confusing passages, unfamiliar references, or words that need to be defined.
- ✓ Draw lines or arrows to connect related ideas or images.
- ✓ Number incidents that occur in sequence.
- ✓ Set off a long portion of the text with a vertical line in the margin.
- ✓ Place stars beside particularly important ideas.

The following poem by Earle Birney has been highlighted by a student preparing to write about it. Notice how the student uses highlighting symbols to help him identify stylistic features, key points, and patterns of repetition that he may want to examine later.

◊ ◊ ◊

EARLE BIRNEY
(1904–1995)

Bushed
(1951–52)

He invented a rainbow but lightning struck it
shattered it into the (lake-lap) of a mountain
*so big his mind slowed when he looked at it

Yet he built a shack on the shore
5 learned to roast porcupine belly and
wore the quills on his hatband

At first he was out with the dawn
whether it yellowed bright as wood-columbine?
or was only a fuzzed moth in a flannel of storm
10 But he found the mountain was (clearly alive)
sent messages whizzing down every hot morning
(boomed proclamations) at noon and spread out
(a white guard) of goat
before (falling asleep) on its feet at sundown

15 When he tried his eyes on the lake   ospreys
would fall like valkyries?
choosing the cut-throat
*He took then to waiting
till the night smoke rose from the boil of the sunset

20 But the moon carved unknown totems?
out of the lakeshore
owls in the beardusky woods derided him
moosehorned cedars circled his swamps and tossed
their antlers up to the stars
25 then he knew   though the mountain slept   the winds
were shaping its peak to an arrowhead
*poised

And now he could only
bar himself in and wait
30*for the great flint to come singing into his heart

The student identifies unusual words and constructions. He puts question
marks by words he wants to look up. When he rereads the poem, his highlighting will make it easier for him to react to and interpret the writer's ideas.

ANNOTATING

At the same time you highlight a text, you also **annotate** it, recording your reactions as marginal notes. In these notes you may define new words, identify allusions, identify patterns of language or imagery, summarize plot relationships, list a work's possible themes, suggest a character's motivation, examine the possible significance of particular images or symbols, or record questions that occur to you as you read. Ideally, your annotations will help you find ideas to write about.

The following paragraph from John Updike's 1961 short story "A&P" (p. 122) was highlighted and annotated by a student in an introduction to literature course who was writing an essay in response to the question "Why does Sammy quit his job?":

Action doesn't seem to be the result of thought. Sammy reacts to the girl's embarrassment.

Lengel sighs and begins to look very patient and old and gray. He's been a friend of my parents for years. "Sammy, you don't want to do this to your Mom and Dad," he tells me. It's true, I don't. But it seems to me that once you begin a gesture it's fatal not to go through with it. I fold the apron, "Sammy" stitched in red on the pocket, and put it on the counter, and drop the bow tie on top of it. The bow tie is theirs, if you've ever wondered. "You'll feel this for the rest of your life," Lengel says, and I know that's true, too, but remembering how he made the pretty girl blush makes me so scrunchy inside I punch the No Sale tab and the machine whirs "pee-pul" and the drawer splats out. One advantage to this scene taking place in summer, I can follow this up with a clean exit, there's no fumbling around getting your coat and galoshes, I just saunter into the electric eye in my white shirt that my mother ironed the night before, and the door heaves itself open, and outside the sunshine is skating around on the asphalt.

*

*

* Need for a clean exit— reinforce immatu[re] romantic ideas.

Romantic cowboy, but his mother irons his shirt. Irony.

Because the instructor had discussed the story in class and given the class a specific assignment, the student's annotations are quite focused. In addition to highlighting important information, she notes her reactions to the story and tries to interpret Sammy's actions. Sometimes, however, you annotate a work before you have decided on a topic—in fact, the process of reading and responding to your text can help you to focus on a topic. In the absence of a topic, your annotations are likely to be less focused, so you will probably need to repeat the process when your paper's direction is clearer.

WRITING ABOUT LITERATURE
❖ ❖ ❖

Writing about literature—or about anything else, for that matter—is an idiosyncratic process during which many activities occur at once: as you write, you think of ideas; as you think of ideas, you clarify the focus of your essay; and as you clarify your focus, you reshape your paragraphs and sentences and refine your word choice. Even though this process sounds chaotic, it has three stages: *planning, drafting,* and *revising and editing.*

PLANNING AN ESSAY
Considering Your Audience

Sometimes—for example, in a journal entry—you write primarily for yourself. At other times, however, you write for others. As you write an essay, you should consider the special requirements of that **audience.** Is your audience your classmates or your instructor? Can you assume your readers are familiar with your paper's topic and with any technical terms you will use, or will they need brief plot summaries or definitions of key terms? If your audience is your instructor, remember that he or she is a representative of a larger academic audience and therefore expects accurate information; standard English; correct grammar, mechanics, and spelling; logical arguments; and a certain degree of stylistic fluency. In addition, your instructor expects you to support your statements with specific information, to express yourself clearly and explicitly, and to document your sources. In short, your instructor wants to see how clearly you think and whether you are able to arrange your ideas into a well-organized, coherent essay.

In addition to being a member of a general academic audience, your instructor is also a member of a particular community of scholars—in this case, those who study literature. By writing about literature, you engage in a dialogue with this community. For this reason, you should adhere to the specific **conventions**—procedures that by habitual use have become accepted practice—its members follow. Many of the conventions that apply specifically to writing about literature—matters of style, format, and the like—will be discussed in this book. (The Editing Checklist on page 37 addresses some of these conventions.)

Understanding Your Purpose

Sometimes you write with a single **purpose** in mind; at other times, a writing assignment may suggest more than one purpose. In general terms, you may write for any of the following reasons:

Writing to Respond   When you write to *respond,* your goal is to discover and express your reactions to a work. To record your responses you engage in relatively informal activities, such as brainstorming, listing, and journal writing (see pp. 26–28). As you write, you explore your own ideas, forming and reforming your impressions of the work.

Writing to Interpret   When you write to *interpret,* your aim is to explain a work's possible meanings. To do so, you may summarize, give examples, or compare and contrast the work to other works or to your own experiences. Then, you may go on to analyze the work, studying each of its elements in turn, putting complex statements in your own words, defining difficult concepts, or placing ideas in context.

Writing to Evaluate   When you write to *evaluate,* your purpose is to assess a work's literary merits. You may consider not only its aesthetic appeal, but also its ability to retain that appeal over time and across national or cultural boundaries. As you write, you use your own critical sense and the opinions of experts in the field to help you make judgments about the work.

Choosing a Topic

When you write an essay about literature, you develop and support an idea about a literary work or works. Before you begin your writing, you should make certain that you understand your assignment. Do you know how much time you have to complete your essay? Are you expected to rely on your own ideas, or are you able to consult outside sources? Is your essay to focus on a specific work or on a particular element of literature? Do you have to write on an assigned topic, or are you free to choose a topic? About how long should your essay be? Do you understand exactly what the assignment is asking you to do?

Sometimes your assignment limits your options by telling you what you should discuss:

◊   Write an essay in which you analyze Margaret Atwood's use of irony in her poem "Death of a Young Son by Drowning."

◊   Discuss Hawthorne's use of allegory in his short story "Young Goodman Brown."

◊   Write a short essay in which you explain the narrator's final comment in Alice Munro's "Boys and Girls."

At other times, however, your instructor will give you few guidelines other than a paper's length and format. In such situations, where you must choose a topic on your own, you can often find a topic by brainstorming or by writing journal entries. As you engage in these activities, however, keep in mind that you have many options for writing papers about literature:

◇ You can compare two works of literature. ("Related Works" listed at the end of each set of "Reading and Reacting" questions in the text suggest possible connections.)

◇ You can compare two characters or discuss some trait those characters share.

◇ You can trace a common subject—jealousy, revenge, power, coming of age—in several works.

◇ You can consider how a common subject—war, love, nature—is treated in several works.

◇ You can examine a single element in one or more works—for instance, plot, point of view, or character development.

◇ You can focus on a single aspect of that element, such as the use of flashbacks, the effect of a shifting narrative perspective, or the role of a minor character.

◇ You can apply a critical theory to a work of literature—for instance, apply a feminist perspective to Jane Rule's "Inland Passage."

◇ You can examine connections between an issue treated in a work of literature—for instance, spousal abuse in Susan Glaspell's *Trifles*— and that same issue as it is treated in sociological or psychological journals or in the popular press.

◇ You can examine some aspect of history or biography and consider its impact on a literary work—for instance, the influence of World War I on Wilfred Owen's poems.

◇ You can explore a problem within a work and propose a possible solution—for example, consider Montresor's actual reason for killing Fortunato in Edgar Allan Poe's "The Cask of Amontillado."

Any of the preceding options may lead you to an interesting topic. Remember, however, that you will still have to narrow the scope of your topic so that it fits within the limits of your assignment.

Finding Something to Say

Once you have a topic, you have to find something to say about it. The information you collected when you highlighted and annotated will help you formulate the statement that will be the central idea of your essay and find ideas that can support that statement.

You can use a variety of different strategies to find supporting material:

◇ You can discuss ideas with others—friends, classmates, instructors, or parents, for example.

◇ You can ask questions.

◇ You can do research, either in the library or on the Internet.

◇ You can *freewrite*—that is, keep writing on your topic for a given period of time without pausing to consider style, structure, or content.

Three additional strategies—*brainstorming, keeping a journal,* and *listing*—are especially helpful.

Brainstorming   When you **brainstorm,** you record ideas—single words, phrases, or sentences; statements or questions; quotations, paraphrases, summaries, or your own ideas—as they occur to you, moving as quickly as possible. Your starting point may be a general assignment, a particular work (or works) of literature, a specific topic, or even a thesis statement; in fact, you can brainstorm at any stage of the writing process (alone or in a group), and you can repeat this activity as often as you like.

The brainstorming notes that follow were made by a student preparing to write a paper on the relationships between children and parents in four poems. She began by brainstorming about each poem and went on to consider thematic relationships among the poems. These notes are her preliminary reactions to one of the four poems she planned to study, Adrienne Rich's "A Woman Mourned by Daughters" (p. 567):

```
Memory: then and now

    Then: leaf, straw, dead insect (= light); ignored

    Now: swollen, puffed up, weight (= heavy); focus of

        attention. controls their movements.

✱Kitchen = a "universe"

    Teaspoons, goblets, etc. = concrete representations

        of mother; also = obligations, responsibilities

        (like plants and father)

    (weigh on them, keep

    them under her spell)

Milestones of past: weddings, being fed as children

"You breathe upon us now"

    PARADOX? (Dead, she breathes, has weight, fills house

and sky. Alive, she was a dead insect, no one paid

attention to her.)
```

Keeping a Journal   A journal can be a notebook, a small notepad, or a computer file. You can use a journal to find ideas—and, later, to help you to find a topic or a thesis. In a **journal** you expand your marginal annotations, recording your responses to works you have read, noting questions, exploring emerging ideas, experimenting with possible paper topics, trying to paraphrase or summarize difficult concepts, or speculating about a work's ambiguities. A journal is the place to take chances, to try out ideas that may initially seem frivolous or irrelevant; here you can think on paper (or on a computer screen) until connections become clear or ideas crystallize. You can also use your journal as a convenient place to collect your brainstorming notes and, later, your lists of related ideas.

As she prepared to write a paper analyzing the role of Laertes in *Hamlet* (p. 1093), a student explored ideas in the following journal entry:

> Laertes is a protective brother to Ophelia, but he doesn't consider her feelings. He tends to be a hot head and flares into anger before he knows what's going on. He provides a good contrast to Hamlet because Laertes doesn't care how his revenge is accomplished.

This journal entry, which represents the student's preliminary explorations, can help her to decide on a specific direction for her essay.

Seeing Connections

Listing   After you have actively read a work, you should have a good many underlinings and marginal notes. Some of this material will be useful, and some will be irrelevant. **Listing** is the process of reviewing your notes, deciding which ideas are most interesting, and arranging related ideas into lists. Listing enables you to discover patterns: to see repeated images, similar characters, recurring words and phrases, and interrelated themes or ideas. Identifying these patterns can help you to decide which points to make in your paper and what information you will use to support these points. A student preparing a paper about D. H. Lawrence's short story "The Rocking-Horse Winner" (p. 370) made the following list of related details:

> Secrets
>   Mother can't feel love
>   Paul gambles
>   Paul gives mother money
>   Family lives beyond means
>   Paul gets information from horse

```
Religion
      Gambling becomes like a religion
      They all worship money
      Specific references: "serious as a church"; "It's as
      if he had it from heaven"; "secret, religious voice"
Luck
      Father is unlucky
      Mother is desperate for luck
      Paul is lucky (ironic)
```

This kind of listing can be a very helpful preliminary organizing strategy, but remember that the lists you make now do not necessarily reflect the order or emphasis of ideas in your paper. As your thoughts become more focused, you will add, delete, and rearrange material.

Deciding on a Thesis

Whenever you are ready, you should try to express the main idea of your emerging essay in a tentative **thesis statement**—an idea, often expressed in a single sentence, that the rest of your essay supports. This idea should emerge logically out of your highlighting, annotating, brainstorming notes, journal entries, and lists. Eventually, you will write a **thesis-and-support** paper: stating your thesis in your introduction, supporting the thesis in the body paragraphs of your essay, and reinforcing the thesis or summarizing your points in your conclusion.

An effective thesis statement tells readers what your essay will discuss and how you will approach your material. Consequently, it should be precisely worded, making its point clear to your readers, and it should contain no vague words or inexact diction that will make it difficult for readers to follow your discussion. Although the statement "The use of sound in Tennyson's poem 'The Eagle' is interesting" is accurate, it does not convey a precise idea to your readers because the words *sound* and *interesting* are not specific. A more effective thesis statement would be "Unity in 'The Eagle' is achieved by Tennyson's use of alliteration, assonance, and rhyme throughout the poem." In addition to being specific, your thesis statement should give your readers an accurate sense of the scope and direction of your essay. It should not make promises that you do not intend to fulfill or contain extraneous details that might confuse your readers. If, for example, you are going to write a paper about the dominant image in a poem, your thesis should not imply that you will focus on the poem's setting or tone.

Remember that as you organize your ideas and as you write, you will probably modify and sharpen your tentative thesis. Sometimes you will even begin planning your essay with one thesis in mind and end it with an entirely different idea. If this happens, be sure to revise your support paragraphs so that they are consistent with your changes and so that the points you include support your new thesis. If you find that your thoughts about your topic are changing, don't be concerned; remember that this is how the writing process works.

Preparing an Outline

Once you have decided on a tentative thesis and have some idea of how you will support it, you can begin to plan your essay's structure. Quite often, an outline can help you to shape your essay. Not all writers outline, but many do because it helps them to clarify their ideas and the relationship of these ideas to one another. Realizing, however, that they will discover many new ideas as they write, these writers seldom take the time to prepare a detailed formal outline, preferring instead to make a scratch outline that lists just the major points they plan to discuss.

A **scratch outline** is perhaps the most useful kind of outline for a short paper. An informal list of the main points you will discuss in your essay, a scratch outline is more focused than a simple list of related points because it presents ideas in the order in which they will be introduced. As its name implies, however, a scratch outline lacks the detail and the degree of organization of a more formal outline. The main purpose of a scratch outline is to give you a sense of the shape and order of your paper and thus enable you to begin writing. A student writing a short essay on Marlene Nourbese Philip's use of irony in her poem "Blackman Dead" (p. 621) used the following scratch outline as a guide:

```
Speaker's Attitude
     Angry
     Ironic
     Cynical
     Critical
Use of Diction
     Formal
     Dialect
Use of Allusions
     Donne
     Winstons
Use of Repetition
     "blackman dead"
     "deserved to die"
     "red roads of silence"
```

Once this outline was complete, the student was ready to write a first draft.

DRAFTING AN ESSAY

Your first draft is a preliminary version of your paper, something to react to and revise. Still, before you actually begin drafting your paper, you should review the material you have collected to support your thesis.

First, make sure you have collected enough information to support your thesis.   The points you make are only as convincing as the evidence you present to support them. As you read and took notes, you collected examples from the work or works about which you are writing—summaries, paraphrases, or quoted lines of narrative, verse, or dialogue—to back up your statements. Just how many of these examples you need to use in your draft depends on the breadth of your thesis and how skeptical you believe your audience to be. In general, the more inclusive your thesis, the more material you need to support it. For example, if you were supporting the rather narrow thesis that the speech of a certain character in the second scene of a play was wooden or awkward, only a few examples would be needed. However, if you wanted to support the inclusive thesis that Nora and Torvald Helmer in Henrik Ibsen's 1879 play *A Doll House* (p. 1013) are trapped in their roles, you would need to present a wide range of examples.

Second, see if the work includes any details that contradict your thesis.   Before you begin writing, you should test the validity of your thesis by looking for details that contradict it. For example, if you plan to support the thesis that in *A Doll House* Ibsen makes a strong case for the rights of women, you should look for counterexamples. Can you find subtle hints in the play that suggest women should remain locked in their traditional roles and continue to defer to their fathers and husbands? If so, you will want to modify your thesis accordingly.

Finally, consider whether you need to use literary criticism to help you support your thesis. You could, for example, strengthen the thesis that *A Doll House* challenged contemporary attitudes about marriage by including the information that when the play first opened, Ibsen was convinced by an apprehensive theatre manager to write another ending. In the new ending, Ibsen had Nora decide, after she stopped briefly to look in at her sleeping children, that she could not leave her family. Sometimes information from another source can even lead you to change your thesis. For example, after reading *A Doll House,* you might have decided that Ibsen's purpose was to make a strong case for the rights of women. In class, however, you might learn that Ibsen repeatedly said that his play was about the rights of all human beings, not just of women. This information could lead you to a thesis that suggests Torvald is just as trapped in his role as Nora is in hers. Naturally, Ibsen's interpretation of his work does not invalidate your first judgment, but it does suggest another conclusion that is worth investigating.

After you have carefully evaluated the completeness, relevance, and validity of your supporting material, you can begin drafting your essay, using your scratch outline as your guide. Your goal is to get your ideas down on paper, so you should write quickly. Once you have a draft, you will be able to examine the connections among ideas and to evaluate preliminary versions of your paragraphs and sentences. Your focus in this draft should be on the body of your essay; this is not the time to worry about constructing the "perfect" introduction and conclusion. In fact, many writers, knowing that their ideas will change as they write, postpone writing these paragraphs until a later draft, preferring instead to begin with just their tentative thesis. As you write, remember that your first draft is naturally going to be rough and will probably not be as clear as you would like it to be; still, it will enable you to see the ideas you have outlined begin to take shape.

REVISING AND EDITING AN ESSAY

As soon as you begin to draft your essay, you begin the process of revision. When you **revise,** you literally "re-see" your draft and, in many cases, you go on to reorder and rewrite substantial portions of your essay. Before you are satisfied with your essay, you will probably write several drafts, each more closely focused and more coherent than the previous one.

Strategies for Revision

Two strategies can help you to revise your drafts: *peer review* and *a dialogue with your instructor.*

Peer review is a process in which students assess each other's work-in-progress. This activity may be carried out in informal sessions, during which one student comments on another's draft, or it may be a formal process in which a student responds to specific questions on a form supplied by the instructor. In either case, one student's reactions can help another student revise.

A **dialogue with your instructor**—in conference or by e-mail— can give you a sense of how to proceed with your revision. Establishing such an oral or written dialogue can help you learn how to respond critically to your own writing, and your reactions to your instructor's comments on any draft can help you to clarify your essay's goals. (If your instructor is not available, try to schedule a conference with a writing centre tutor, if your school offers this service.) Using your own responses as well as those of your classmates and your instructor, you can write drafts that are increasingly more consistent with these goals.

The Revision Process

As you move through successive drafts, the task of revising your essay will be easier if you follow a systematic process. As you read and react to your essay, begin by assessing the effectiveness of the larger elements—thesis and support, for instance—and proceed to examine increasingly smaller elements.

Thesis Statement First, reconsider your **thesis statement.** Is it carefully and precisely worded? Does it provide a realistic idea of what your essay will cover? Does it make a point that is worth supporting? It is not enough, for instance, to base an essay about literature on a vague thesis.

> **Vague:** Images in Alistair MacLeod's "The Boat" are important to understanding the protagonist's guilt.

> **Vague:** Dickens's characters are a lot like those of Addison and Steele.

To give focus and direction to your essay, a thesis statement must be more pointed and more specific:

> **Revised:** The prevailing images of the sea in Alistair MacLeod's "The Boat" reveal the haunting legacy and familial obligations that the protagonist must confront.

> **Revised:** With their extremely familiar, almost caricature-like physical and moral traits, many of Charles Dickens's minor characters reveal that he owes a debt to the "characters" created by the seventeenth-century essayists Joseph Addison and Richard Steele for the newspaper The Spectator.

Support Next, assess the appropriateness of your **supporting ideas** and consider whether you present enough support for your thesis and whether all the details you include are relevant to that thesis. Make sure you have supported all points with specific, concrete examples from the work or works you are discussing, briefly summarizing key events, quoting dialogue or description, describing characters or settings, or paraphrasing important ideas. Make certain, however, that your own ideas control the essay and that you have not substituted plot summary for analysis and interpretation. Your goal is to draw a conclusion about one or more works and to support that conclusion with pertinent details. If a plot detail supports a point you wish to make, include a *brief* summary of the event or series of events, showing its relevance by explicitly connecting the summary to the point you are making. In the following excerpt from a paper on a short story by James

Joyce, the first sentence summarizes a key event and the second sentence explains its significance:

> At the end of "Counterparts," when Farrington returns home after a day of frustration and abuse at work, his reaction is to strike out at his son Tom. This act shows that although he and his son are similarly victimized, Farrington is also the counterpart of his tyrannical boss.

Topic Sentences Now, turn your attention to the **topic sentences** that present the main idea of each body paragraph, making sure that they are clearly worded and that they communicate the direction of your ideas and the precise relationships of ideas to one another.

Be especially careful to avoid abstractions and vague generalities in topic sentences:

> **Vague:** One similarity revolves around the dominance of the men by women. *(What exactly is the similarity?)*
>
> **Revised:** In both stories, a man is dominated by a woman.
>
> **Vague:** There is one reason for the fact that Jay Gatsby remains a mystery. *(What is the reason?)*
>
> **Revised:** Because <u>The Great Gatsby</u> is narrated by the outsider Nick Carraway, Jay Gatsby himself remains a mystery.

When revising topic sentences that are intended to move readers from one point (or section of your paper) to another, be sure the relationship between the ideas they link is clear:

> **Relationship between ideas unclear:** Now the poem's imagery will be discussed.
>
> **Revised:** Another reason for the poem's effectiveness is its unusual imagery.
>
> **Relationship between ideas unclear:** The sheriff's wife is another interesting character.
>
> **Revised:** Like her friend Mrs. Hale, the sheriff's wife has mixed feelings about what Mrs. Wright has done.

Introductions and Conclusions   When you are satisfied with the body of your essay, you can go on to examine your paper's *introduction* and *conclusion*.

The **introduction** of an essay about literature should identify the works to be discussed and indicate the emphasis of the discussion to follow. Depending on your purpose and on your paper's topic, you may want to provide some historical background or biographical information or to briefly discuss the work in relation to other, similar works. Like all introductions, the one you write for an essay about literature should create interest in your topic and include a clear thesis statement.

The following introduction, although adequate for a first draft, is in need of revision:

> Revenge, which is defined as "the chance to retal-
> iate, get satisfaction, take vengeance, or inflict damage
> or injury in return for an injury, insult, etc.," is a
> major component in many of the stories we have read. The
> stories that will be discussed here deal with a variety
> of ways to seek revenge. In my essay, I will show some of
> these differences.

Although the student clearly identifies her paper's topic, she does not identify the works she will discuss or the particular point she will make about revenge. Her tired opening strategy, a dictionary definition, is not likely to create interest in her topic, and her announcement of her intention in the last sentence is awkward and unnecessary. The following revision is much more effective:

> In Edgar Allan Poe's "The Cask of Amontillado" Montresor
> vows revenge on Fortunato for an unspecified "insult"; in
> William Faulkner's "A Rose for Emily" Emily uses violence
> to avoid a personal disappointment. Both of these stories
> present characters who seek revenge, and both stories end
> in murder. However, the murderers' motivations are pre-
> sented very differently. In "A Rose for Emily" the nar-
> rator is unaware of the significance of many events, and
> his ignorance helps to create sympathy for the murderer.
> In "The Cask of Amontillado," where the narrator is the
> murderer himself, Montresor's inability to offer a con-
> vincing motive turns the reader against him.

In your **conclusion** you restate your thesis or sum up your essay's main points; then, you make a graceful exit.

The concluding paragraph that follows is acceptable for a first draft, but it communicates little information:

> Although the characters of Montresor and Emily were created by different authors at different times, they do have similar motives and goals. However, they are portrayed very differently.

The following revision reinforces the essay's main point, effectively incorporating a brief quotation from "The Cask of Amontillado" (p. 227):

> In fact, then, what is significant is not whether or not each murderer's act is justified, but rather how each murderer, and each victim, is portrayed by the narrator. Montresor--driven by a thirst to avenge "a thousand injuries" as well as a final insult--is shown to be sadistic and unrepentant; in "A Rose for Emily" Emily is seen as an object of pity.

Sentences and Words Now, focus on the individual sentences and words of your essay. Begin by evaluating your **transitions,** the words and phrases that link sentences and paragraphs. Be sure that every necessary transitional element has been supplied and that each word or phrase you have selected accurately conveys the exact relationship (sequence, contradiction, and so on) between ideas. When you are satisfied with the clarity and appropriateness of your paper's transitions, consider sentence variety and word choice.

First, be sure you have varied your sentence structure. You will bore your readers if all your sentences begin the same way ("The story. . . . "; "The story. . . . "), or if they are all about the same length. In addition, make sure that all the words you select accurately communicate your ideas and that you have not used vague, inexact diction. For example, saying that a character is *bad* is a lot less effective than characterizing him or her as *ruthless, conniving,* or *malicious.* Finally, eliminate subjective expressions, such as *I think, in my opinion, I believe, it seems to me,* and *I feel.* These phrases weaken your essay by suggesting that its ideas are "only" opinions and have no objective validity.

Using and Documenting Sources Make certain that all references to sources are integrated smoothly and documented appropriately (see Appendix A, "Documenting Sources").

CHECKLIST: USING SOURCES

✓ Acknowledge all sources, including the work or works under discussion, using the documentation style of the Modern Language Association (MLA).

✓ Combine paraphrases, summaries, and quotations with your own interpretations, weaving quotations smoothly into your paper. Introduce the words or ideas of others with a phrase that identifies their source ("According to Timothy Findley's biographer, . . . "), and end with appropriate parenthetical documentation.

✓ Use quotations *only* when something vital would be lost if you did not reproduce the author's exact words.

✓ Integrate short quotations (four lines or less of prose or three lines or less of poetry) smoothly into your paper. (Use a slash to separate lines of poetry.) Be sure that you enclose quotations in quotation marks.

✓ Set off quotations of more than four lines of prose or three lines of poetry by indenting ten spaces (approximately 2.5 cm) from the left-hand margin. Double-space, and do not use quotation marks. If you are quoting a single paragraph, do not indent the first line.

✓ Use ellipses—three spaced periods—to indicate material omitted within a quotation ("MacLeod revised his story often . . . that summer."). Use ellipses after end punctuation to indicate an omission at the end of a sentence ("He frequently spent days without writing. . . . "). Use a single line of periods to indicate that you have omitted a line of poetry.

✓ Use brackets to indicate that you have added words to a quotation ("[Nanabush] is a modern-day Trickster."). Use brackets to alter a quotation so that it fits grammatically into your sentence (Clarke says that Highway "offer[s] audiences a mixed view of a reserve.").

✓ Place commas and periods *inside* the quotation marks (According to Robert Coles, the child "could make others smile.").

✓ Place punctuation marks other than commas and periods *outside* the quotation marks (What does Frost mean when he says "a poem must ride on its own melting"?). If the punctuation marks are part of the quoted material, place them inside the quotation marks (In "Mending Wall," Frost asks, "*Why* do they make good neighbors?").

✓ When citing a part of a short story or novel, supply the page number (143); for a poem, supply the line numbers (3–5); for a play, supply the act, scene, and line numbers (2.2.17–22).

✓ Include a Works Cited list (unless your instructor tells you otherwise).

Editing

Once you have finished revising, you **edit**—that is, you make certain that your paper's grammar, punctuation, spelling, and mechanics are correct. Always run a spell check—but remember that you still have to proofread carefully for errors that the spell checker will not identify. These include homophones (*brake* incorrectly used instead of *break*), typos that create correctly spelled words (*work* instead of *word*), and proper nouns that may not be in your computer's dictionary. If you use a grammar checker, remember that grammar programs may identify potential problems—long sentences, for example—but may not be able to determine whether or not a particular long sentence is grammatically correct (let alone stylistically pleasing). Always keep a style handbook as well as a dictionary nearby so that you can double check any problems a spell checker or grammar checker highlights in your writing.

As you edit, pay particular attention to the mechanical conventions of literary essays, some of which are addressed in the Editing Checklist below. When your editing is complete, give your essay a descriptive title; before you retype or reprint it, be sure that its format conforms to your instructor's requirements.

 # EDITING CHECKLIST: CONVENTIONS OF WRITING ABOUT LITERATURE

- ✓ Use present-tense verbs when discussing works of literature: "The character of Mrs. Mallard's husband *is* not developed. . . . "
- ✓ Use past-tense verbs only when discussing historical events ("Owen's poem conveys the destructiveness of World War I, which at the time the poem *was* written *was* considered to be . . ."), when presenting historical or biographical data ("Her first novel, which *was* published in 1811 when Austen *was* thirty-six, . . ."), or when identifying events that occurred prior to the time of the story's main action ("Miss Emily is a recluse; since her father *died* she has lived alone except for a servant.").
- ✓ Support all points with specific, concrete examples from the work you are discussing, briefly summarizing key events, quoting dialogue or description, describing characters or setting, or paraphrasing ideas.
- ✓ Avoid unnecessary plot summary. Your goal is to draw a conclusion about one or more works and to support that conclusion with pertinent details. If a plot detail supports a point you wish to make, a *brief* summary is acceptable. But plot summary is no substitute for analysis.

✓ Use *literary terms* accurately. For example, be careful not to confuse *narrator* or *speaker* with *author;* feelings or opinions expressed by a narrator or character do not necessarily represent those of the author. You should not say, "In the poem's last stanza, *Frost* expresses his indecision" when you mean that the poem's *speaker* is indecisive.

✓ Underline titles of novels and plays; place titles of short stories and poems within quotation marks.

✓ Refer to authors of literary works by their full names (*Margaret Atwood*) in your first reference to them and by their last names (*Atwood*) in subsequent references. Never refer to authors by their first names, and never use titles that indicate marital status (*Flannery O'Connor* or *O'Connor,* never *Flannery* or *Miss O'Connor*).

FICTION

CHAPTER 3

Reading and Writing about Fiction

UNDERSTANDING FICTION

◇ ◇ ◇

A **narrative** tells a story by presenting events in some logical or orderly way. Works of narrative fiction originate in the imagination of the author, not in history or fact. Certainly some fiction—historical or autobiographical fiction, for example—focuses on real people and actual events, but the way the characters interact and how the plot unfolds are the author's invention.

Even before they know how to read, most people have learned how narratives are structured. Once children can tell a story, they also know how to exaggerate, how to add or delete details, how to rearrange events, and how to bend facts—in other words, how to fictionalize a narrative to achieve a desired effect. This kind of informal, personal narrative is similar in many ways to the more structured literary narratives included in this anthology.

Our earliest examples of narrative fiction are stories and songs that came out of a prehistoric oral tradition. These stories, embellished with each telling, were often quite long, embodying the history, the central myths, and the religious beliefs of the cultures in which they originated. Eventually transcribed, these extended narratives became **epics**—long narrative poems about heroic figures whose actions determine the fate of a nation or an entire race. Homer's *Iliad* and *Odyssey*, the ancient Babylonian *Epic of Gilgamesh,* the Hindu *Bhagavad Gita,* and the Anglo-Saxon *Beowulf* are examples. Many of the tales of the Old Testament also came out of this tradition. The setting of an epic is vast—sometimes worldwide or cosmic, including heaven and hell—and the action commonly involves a battle or a perilous journey. Quite often divine beings participate in the action and influence the outcome of events, as they do in the Trojan War in the *Iliad* and in the founding of Rome in Vergil's *Aeneid.*

Folktales and **fairy tales** also come out of an oral tradition. These tales, which developed along with other narrative forms, have influenced works as diverse as Chaucer's *The Canterbury Tales* and D. H. Lawrence's "The Rocking-Horse Winner" (p. 370). The folktales and fairy tales that survive (such as "Cinderella" and Aesop's *Fables*) are contemporary versions of old, even ancient, tales that can be traced back centuries through many different cultures. Folktales and fairy tales share certain characteristics. First, they feature simple characters who illustrate a quality or trait that can be summed up in a few words. Much of the appeal of "Cinderella," for example, depends on the contrast between the selfish, sadistic stepsisters and poor, gentle, victimized Cinderella. In addition, the folktale or fairy tale has an obvious theme or moral—good triumphing over evil, for instance. The stories move directly to their conclusions, never interrupted by ingenious or unexpected twists of plot. (Love is temporarily thwarted, but the prince eventually finds Cinderella and marries her.) Finally, these tales are anchored not in specific times or places but in "Once upon a time" settings, green worlds of prehistory filled with royalty, talking animals, and magic.

During the Middle Ages, the **romance** supplanted the epic. Written initially in verse but later in prose, the romance replaced the epic's gods and central heroic figures with knights, kings, and damsels in distress. Events were controlled by enchantments rather than by the will of divine beings. *Sir Gawain and the Green Knight* and other tales of King Arthur and the Knights of the Round Table are examples of romances. Eventually the romance gave way to other types of narratives. Short prose tales, such as those collected in Giovanni Boccaccio's *The Decameron,* originated in fourteenth-century Italy, and the **picaresque,** an episodic, often satirical work about a rogue or rascal, such as Miguel de Cervantes's *Don Quixote,* emerged in seventeenth-century Spain. The **pastoral romance,** a prose tale set in an idealized rural world, and the **character,** a brief satirical sketch illustrating a type of personality, both became popular in Renaissance England.

From these diverse sources emerged the **novel.** The English writer Daniel Defoe is commonly given credit for writing the first novel in 1719. His *Robinson Crusoe* is an episodic narrative similar to a picaresque but unified by a central character and a single setting. By the nineteenth century, the novel reached a high point in its development, replacing other kinds of extended narratives. Because of its ability to present a wide range of characters in realistic settings and to develop them in depth, the novel appealed to members of the rising middle class, who seemed to have an insatiable desire to see themselves portrayed. Writers such as George Eliot, Charles Dickens, William Thackeray, and Charlotte and Emily Brontë appealed to this desire by creating large fictional worlds populated by many different characters who reflected the complexity—and at times the melodrama—of Victorian society. From these roots, the novel as a literary form continued to develop throughout the twentieth century.

THE SHORT STORY

Like the novel, the short story evolved from the various forms of narrative discussed earlier. Because the short story comes from so many different sources from all over the world, it is difficult to determine where it originated. In the United States, Nathaniel Hawthorne and Edgar Allan Poe, along with France's Guy de Maupassant and Russia's Anton Chekhov, took the form seriously and helped create its success.

Whereas the novel is an extended piece of narrative fiction, the **short story** is limited in length and scope. These limitations account for the characteristics that distinguish the short story from longer prose forms. Unlike the novelist, the short story writer cannot devote a great deal of space to developing a highly complex plot or a large number of characters. As a result, the short story begins close to or at the height of action and develops only one character in depth. Usually concentrating on a single incident, the writer develops a character by showing his or her responses to events. (This attention to character development, as well as its detailed description of setting, is what distinguishes the short story from earlier short narrative forms, such as folktales and fairy tales.) In many contemporary stories, a character experiences an **epiphany,** a moment of illumination in which something hidden or not understood becomes immediately clear. Examples of epiphany are found in this anthology in James Joyce's "Araby," John Updike's "A&P," and Sinclair Ross's "A Field of Wheat."

Today the term *short story* is applied to a wide variety of prose narratives: short stories such as Madeleine Thien's "Simple Recipes" (p. 45), which runs about eight pages; **short short stories,** such as Luisa Valenzuela's "All about Suicide" (p. 7), which are under five pages in length; and long stories, such as Herman Melville's "Bartleby the Scrivener" (p. 460). Stories ranging from 80 to 120 pages, such as Joseph Conrad's *Heart of Darkness,* may more accurately be called short novels or **novellas.**

As the stories in this anthology show, the possibilities of the short story are infinite. A short story may be comic or tragic; its subject may be growing up, marriage, crime and punishment, war, sexual awakening, death, or any number of other human concerns. The setting can be an imaginary world, the old West, rural North America, the jungles of Uruguay, nineteenth-century Russia, pre-communist China, or modern Egypt. The story may have a conventional form, with a definite beginning, middle, and end, or it may be structured as a letter, as a diary entry, or even as a collection of random notes. The narrator of a story may be trustworthy or unreliable, involved in the action or a disinterested observer, sympathetic or deserving of scorn, extremely ignorant or highly insightful, limited in vision or able to see inside the minds of all the characters. The conventions of short fiction are constantly changing.

READING FICTION

◊ ◊ ◊

As you read more works of short fiction, you will begin paying careful attention to elements such as plot; character; setting; point of view; style, tone, and language; symbol and allegory; and theme. The following guidelines, designed to help you explore works of fiction, focus on issues that will be examined in depth in chapters to come.

◊ Look at the **plot** of the story. How do the events in the story relate to one another, and how do they relate to the story as a whole? What conflicts occur in the story, and how are these conflicts developed or resolved? Does the story include any noteworthy plot devices, such as flashbacks or foreshadowing? (See Chapter 4.)

◊ Analyze the **characters** of the story. What are their most striking traits? How do these individuals interact with one another? What motivates them? Are the characters fully developed, or are they stereotypes whose sole purpose is to express a single trait (good, evil, generosity) or to move the plot along? (See Chapter 5.)

◊ Identify the **setting** of the story. At what time period and in what geographic location does the action of the story occur? How does the setting affect the characters of the story? How does it determine the relationships among the characters? How does the setting affect the plot? Does the setting create a mood for the story? In what way does the setting reinforce the central ideas that the story examines? (See Chapter 6.)

◊ Examine the narrative **point of view** of the story. What person or persons are telling the story? Is the story told in the first person (*I* or *we*) or in the third person (*he, she,* or *they*)? Does the narrator see from various perspectives, or is the story restricted to the perspective of one person—a major character, a minor character, or just an observer? How much does the narrator know about the events in the story? Does the narrator present an accurate or inaccurate picture of events? Does the narrator understand the full significance of the story he or she is telling? (See Chapter 7.)

◊ Analyze the **style, tone,** and **language** of the story. Does the writer make any unusual use of diction or syntax? Does the writer use imaginative figures of speech? Patterns of imagery? What styles or levels of speech are associated with particular characters? What words or phrases are repeated throughout the work? Is the story's style plain or elaborate? Does the narrator's tone reveal his or her attitude toward characters or events? Are there any discrepancies between the narrator's attitude and the attitude of the author? Is the tone of the story playful, humorous, ironic, satirical, serious, sombre, solemn, bitter, condescending, formal, informal—or does the tone suggest some other attitude? (See Chapter 8.)

◇ Focus on **symbolism** and **allegory.** Does the author use any objects or ideas symbolically? What characters or objects in the story are part of an *allegorical framework?* How does an object establish its symbolic or allegorical significance in the story? Does the same object have different meanings at different places in the story? Are the symbols or *allegorical figures* conventional or unusual? At what points in the story do symbols or allegorical figures appear? (See Chapter 9.)

◇ Identify the **themes** of the story. What is the central theme? How is this idea or concept expressed in the work? What elements of the story develop the central theme? How do character, plot, setting, point of view, and symbols reinforce the central theme? How does the title of the story contribute to readers' understanding of the central theme? What other themes are explored? (See Chapter 10.)

ACTIVE READING

Lucy Jay, a student in an introduction to literature course, was assigned to write a three- to five-page essay on a topic of her choice, focusing on any short story in this literature anthology, without consulting outside sources. After considering a number of possible choices, Lucy selected Madeleine Thien's "Simple Recipes," which appears on the pages that follow.

◆ **MADELEINE THIEN** (1977–   ) represents a new breed of young Canadian writers on the rise. She is a graduate of the University of British Columbia's creative writing program, a hotbed of new Canadian literary talent. Thien won the Asian Canadian Writer's Workshop for the manuscript of her first book, *Simple Recipes*. Her parents are of Chinese-Malaysian descent, immigrated to Canada in the 1960s, but divorced when she was a teenager—an event that has affected her deeply. Her writing focuses on the dissolution of the immigrant family and draws heavily from her experiences as an Asian-Canadian. Her stories are about learning to live with grief and moving beyond it; her characters are in search of hope when they see that the hope in others has been extinguished. She has published a children's book, *The Chinese Violin* (2001), which is also an animated short film for the National Film Board of Canada. Her first published adult novel is *Certainty* (2006).

MADELEINE THIEN

Simple Recipes
(2001)

There is a simple recipe for making rice. My father taught it to me when I was a child. Back then, I used to sit up on the kitchen counter watching him, how he sifted the grains in his hands, sure and quick, removing pieces of dirt or sand, tiny imperfections. He swirled his hands through the water and it turned cloudy. When he scrubbed the grains clean, the sound was as big as a field of insects. Over and over, my father rinsed the rice, drained the water, then filled the pot again.

The instructions are simple. Once the washing is done, you measure the water this way—by resting the tip of your index finger on the surface of the rice. The water should reach the bend of your first knuckle. My father did not need instructions or measuring cups. He closed his eyes and felt for the waterline.

Sometimes I still dream my father, his bare feet flat against the floor, standing in the middle of the kitchen. He wears old buttoned shirts and faded sweatpants drawn at the waist. Surrounded by the gloss of the kitchen counters, the sharp angles of the stove, the fridge, the shiny sink, he looks out of place. This memory of him is so strong, sometimes it stuns me, the detail with which I can see it.

Every night before dinner, my father would perform this ritual—rinsing and draining, then setting the pot in the cooker. When I was older, he passed this task on to me but I never did it with the same care. I went through the motions, splashing the water around, jabbing my finger down to measure the water level. Some nights the rice was a mushy gruel. I worried that I could not do so simple a task right. "Sorry," I would say to the table, my voice soft and embarrassed. In answer, my father would keep eating, pushing the rice into his mouth as if he never expected anything different, as if he noticed no difference between what he did so well and I so poorly. He would eat every last mouthful, his chopsticks walking quickly across the plate. Then he would rise, whistling, and clear the table, every motion so clean and sure, I would be convinced by him that all was well in the world.

•••

5 My father is standing in the middle of the kitchen. In his right hand he holds a plastic bag filled with water. Caught inside the bag is a live fish.

The fish is barely breathing, though its mouth opens and closes. I reach up and touch it through the plastic bag, trailing my fingers along the gills, the soft, muscled body, pushing my finger overtop the eyeball. The fish looks straight at me, flopping sluggishly from side to side.

My father fills the kitchen sink. In one swift motion he overturns the bag and the fish comes sailing out with the water. It curls and jumps. We watch it closely, me on my tiptoes, chin propped up on the counter. The fish is the length of my arm from wrist to elbow. It floats in place, brushing up against the sides of the sink.

I keep watch over the fish while my father begins the preparations for dinner. The fish folds its body, trying to turn or swim, the water nudging overtop. Though I ripple tiny circles around it with my fingers, the fish stays still, bobbing side-to-side in the cold water.

For many hours at a time, it was just the two of us. While my mother worked and my older brother played outside, my father and I sat on the couch, flipping channels. He loved cooking shows. We watched *Wok with Yan*, my father passing judgement on Yan's methods. I was enthralled when Yan transformed orange peels into swans. My father sniffed. "I can do that," he said. "You don't have to be a genius to do that." He placed a sprig of onion in water and showed me how it bloomed like a flower. "I know many tricks like this," he said. "Much more than Yan."

10   Still, my father made careful notes when Yan demonstrated Peking Duck. He chuckled heartily at Yan's punning. "Take a wok on the wild side!" Yan said, pointing his spatula at the camera.

"Ha ha!" my father laughed, his shoulders shaking. "*Wok* on the wild side!"

In the mornings, my father took me to school. At three o'clock, when we came home again, I would rattle off everything I learned that day. "The brachiosaurus," I informed him, "eats only soft vegetables."

My father nodded. "That is like me. Let me see your forehead." We stopped and faced each other in the road. "You have a high forehead," he said, leaning down to take a closer look. "All smart people do."

I walked proudly, stretching my legs to match his steps. I was overjoyed when my feet kept time with his, right, then left, then right, and we walked like a single unit. My father was the man of tricks, who sat for an hour mining a watermelon with a circular spoon, who carved the rind into a castle.

15   My father was born in Malaysia and he and my mother immigrated to Canada several years before I was born, first settling in Montreal, then finally in Vancouver. While I was born into the persistence of the Vancouver rain, my father was born in the wash of a monsoon country. When I was young, my parents tried to teach me their language but it never came easily to me. My father ran his thumb gently over my mouth, his face kind, as if trying to see what it was that made me different.

My brother was born in Malaysia but when he immigrated with my parents to Canada the language left him. Or he forgot it, or he refused it, which is also common, and this made my father angry. "How can a child forget a language?" he would ask my mother. "It is because the child is lazy. Because the child chooses not to remember." When he was twelve years old, my brother stayed away in the afternoons. He drummed the soccer ball up and down the back alley, returning home only at dinner time. During the day, my mother worked as a sales clerk at the Woodward's store downtown, in the building with the red revolving W on top.

In our house, the ceilings were yellowed with grease. Even the air was heavy with it. I remember that I loved the weight of it, the air that was dense with the smell of countless meals cooked in a tiny kitchen, all those good smells jostling for space.

The fish in the sink is dying slowly. It has a glossy sheen to it, as if its skin is made of shining minerals. I want to prod it with both hands, its body tense against the pressure of my fingers. If I hold it tightly, I imagine I will be able to feel its fluttering heart. Instead, I lock eyes with the fish. *You're feeling verrrry sleepy*, I tell it. *You're getting verrrry tired.*

Beside me, my father chops green onions quickly. He uses a cleaver that he says is older than I am by many years. The blade of the knife rolls forward and backward, loops of green onion gathering in a pyramid beside my father's wrist. When he is done, he rolls his sleeve back from his right hand, reaches in through the water and pulls the plug.

20   The fish in the sink floats and we watch it in silence. The water level falls beneath its gills, beneath its belly. It drains and leaves the sink dry. The fish is lying on its side, mouth open and its body heaving. It leaps sideways and hits the sink. Then up again. It curls and snaps, lunging for its own tail. The fish sails into the air, dropping hard. It twitches violently.

My father reaches in with his bare hands. He lifts the fish out by the tail and lays it gently on the counter. While holding it steady with one hand, he hits the head with the flat of the cleaver. The fish falls still, and he begins to clean it.

•••

In my apartment, I keep the walls scrubbed clean. I open the windows and turn the fan on whenever I prepare a meal. My father bought me a rice cooker when I first moved into my own apartment, but I use it so rarely it stays in the back of the cupboard, the cord wrapped neatly around its belly. I have no longing for the meals themselves, but I miss the way we sat down together, our bodies leaning hungrily forward while my father, the magician, unveiled plate after plate. We laughed and ate, white steam fogging my mother's glasses until she had to take them off and lay them on the table. Eyes closed, she would eat, crunchy vegetables gripped in her chopsticks, the most vivid green.

•••

My brother comes into the kitchen and his body is covered with dirt. He leaves a thin trail of it behind as he walks. The soccer ball, muddy from outside, is encircled in one arm. Brushing past my father, his face is tense.

Beside me, my mother sprinkles garlic onto the fish. She lets me slide one hand underneath the fish's head, cradling it, then bending it backwards so that she can fill the fish's insides with ginger. Very carefully, I turn the fish over. It is firm and slippery, and beaded with tiny, sharp scales.

25 At the stove, my father picks up an old teapot. It is full of oil and he pours the oil into the wok. It falls in a thin ribbon. After a moment, when the oil begins crackling, he lifts the fish up and drops it down into the wok. He adds water and the smoke billows up. The sound of the fish frying is like tires on gravel, a sound so loud it drowns out all other noises. Then my father steps out from the smoke. "Spoon out the rice," he says as he lifts me down from the counter.

My brother comes back into the room, his hands muddy and his knees the colour of dusty brick. His soccer shorts flutter against the backs of his legs. Sitting down, he makes an angry face. My father ignores him.

Inside the cooker, the rice is flat like a pie. I push the spoon in, turning the rice over, and the steam shoots up in a hot mist and condenses on my skin. While my father moves his arms delicately over the stove, I begin dishing the rice out: first for my father, then my mother, then my brother, then myself. Behind me the fish is cooking quickly. In a crockery pot, my father steams cauliflower, stirring it round and round.

My brother kicks at a table leg.

"What's the matter?" my father asks.

30 He is quiet for a moment, then he says, "Why do we have to eat fish?"

"You don't like it?"

My brother crosses his arms against his chest. I see the dirt lining his arms, dark and hardened. I imagine chipping it off his body with a small spoon.

"I don't like the eyeball there. It looks sick."

My mother tuts. Her nametag is still clipped to her blouse. It says *Woodward's*, and then, *Sales Clerk*. "Enough," she says, hanging her purse on the back of the chair. "Go wash your hands and get ready for supper."

35 My brother glares, just for a moment. Then he begins picking at the dirt on his arms. I bring plates of rice to the table. The dirt flies off his skin, speckling the tablecloth. "Stop it," I say crossly.

"*Stop it*," he says, mimicking me.

"Hey!" My father hits his spoon against the counter. It *pings*, high-pitched. He points at my brother. "No fighting in this house."

My brother looks at the floor, mumbles something, and then shuffles away from the table. As he moves farther away, he begins to stamp his feet.

Shaking her head, my mother takes her jacket off. It slides from her shoulders. She says something to my father in the language I can't understand. He merely shrugs his shoulders. And then he replies, and I think his words are so familiar, as if they are words I should know, as if maybe I did know them once but then I forgot them. The language that they speak is full of soft vowels, words running together so that I can't make out the gaps where they pause for breath.

40 My mother told me once about guilt. Her own guilt she held in the palm of her hands, like an offering. But your guilt is different, she said. You do not need to hold on to it. Imagine this, she said, her hands running along my

forehead, then up into my hair. Imagine, she said. Picture it, and what do you see?

A bruise on the skin, wide and black.

A bruise, she said. Concentrate on it. Right now, it's a bruise. But if you concentrate, you can shrink it, compress it to the size of a pinpoint. And then, if you want to, if you see it, you can blow it off your body like a speck of dirt.

She moved her hands along my forehead.

I tried to picture what she said. I pictured blowing it away like so much nothing, just these little pieces that didn't mean anything, this complicity that I could magically walk away from. She made me believe in the strength of my own thoughts, as if I could make appear what had never existed. Or turn it around. Flip it over so many times you just lose sight of it, you lose the tail end and the whole thing disappears into smoke.

45 My father pushes at the fish with the edge of his spoon. Underneath, the meat is white and the juice runs down along the side. He lifts a piece and lowers it carefully onto my plate.

Once more, his spoon breaks skin. Gingerly, my father lifts another piece and moves it towards my brother.

"I don't want it," my brother says.

My father's hand wavers. "Try it," he says, smiling. "Take a wok on the wild side."

"No."

50   My father sighs and places the piece on my mother's plate. We eat in silence, scraping our spoons across the dishes. My parents use chopsticks, lifting their bowls and motioning the food into their mouths. The smell of food fills the room.

Savouring each mouthful, my father eats slowly, head tuned to the flavours in his mouth. My mother takes her glasses off, the lenses fogged, and lays them on the table. She eats with her head bowed down, as if in prayer.

Lifting a stem of cauliflower to his lips, my brother sighs deeply. He chews, and then his face changes. I have a sudden picture of him drowning, his hair waving like grass. He coughs, spitting the mouthful back onto his plate. Another cough. He reaches for his throat, choking.

My father slams his chopsticks down on the table. In a single movement, he reaches across, grabbing my brother by the shoulder. "I have tried," he is saying. "I don't know what kind of son you are. To be so ungrateful." His other hand sweeps by me and bruises into my brother's face.

My mother flinches. My brother's face is red and his mouth is open. His eyes are wet.

55   Still coughing, he grabs a fork, tines aimed at my father, and then in an unthinking moment, he heaves it at him. It strikes my father in the chest and drops.

"I hate you! You're just an asshole, you're just a fucking asshole chink!" My brother holds his plate in his hands. He smashes it down and his food scatters across the table. He is coughing and spitting. "I wish you weren't my father! I wish you were dead."

My father's hand falls again. This time pounding downwards. I close my eyes. All I can hear is someone screaming. There is a loud voice. I stand awkwardly, my hands covering my eyes.

"Go to your room," my father says, his voice shaking.

And I think he is talking to me so I remove my hands.

60   But he is looking at my brother. And my brother is looking at him, his small chest heaving.

A few minutes later, my mother begins clearing the table, face weary as she scrapes the dishes one by one over the garbage.

I move away from my chair, past my mother, onto the carpet and up the stairs.

Outside my brother's bedroom, I crouch against the wall. When I step forward and look, I see my father holding the bamboo pole between his hands. The pole is smooth. The long grains, fine as hair, are pulled together, at intervals, jointed. My brother is lying on the floor, as if thrown down and dragged there. My father raises the pole into the air.

I want to cry out. I want to move into the room between them, but I can't.

65   It is like a tree falling, beginning to move, a slow arc through the air.

The bamboo drops silently. It rips the skin on my brother's back. I cannot hear any sound. A line of blood edges quickly across his body.

The pole rises and again comes down. I am afraid of bones breaking.

My father lifts his arms once more.

On the floor, my brother cries into the carpet, pawing at the ground. His knees folded into his chest, the crown of his head burrowing down. His back is hunched over and I can see his spine, little bumps on his skin.

70   The bamboo smashes into bone and the scene in my mind bursts into a million white pieces.

My mother picks me up off the floor, pulling me across the hall, into my bedroom, into bed. Everything is wet, the sheets, my hands, her body, my face, and she soothes me with words I cannot understand because all I can hear is screaming. She rubs her cool hands against my forehead. "Stop," she says. "Please stop," but I feel loose, deranged, as if everything in the known world is ending right here.

In the morning, I wake up to the sound of oil in the pan and the smell of French toast. I can hear my mother bustling around, putting dishes in the cupboards.

No one says anything when my brother doesn't come down for breakfast. My father piles French toast and syrup onto a plate and my mother pours a glass of milk. She takes everything upstairs to my brother's bedroom.

As always, I follow my father around the kitchen. I track his footprints, follow behind him and hide in the shadow of his body. Every so often, he reaches down and ruffles my hair with his hands. We cast a spell, I think. The way we move in circles, how he cooks without thinking because this is the task that comes to him effortlessly. He smiles down at me, but when he does this, it somehow breaks the spell. My father stands in place, hands dropping to his sides as if he has forgotten what he was doing mid-motion. On the walls, the paint is peeling and the floor, unswept in days, leaves little pieces of dirt stuck to our feet.

75   My persistence, I think, my unadulterated love, confuse him. With each passing day, he knows I will find it harder to ignore what I can't comprehend, that I will be unable to separate one part of him from another. The unconditional quality of my love for him will not last forever, just as my brother's did not. My father stands in the middle of the kitchen, unsure. Eventually, my mother comes downstairs again and puts her arms around him and holds him, whispering something to him, words that to me are meaningless and incomprehensible. But she offers them to him, sound after sound, in a language that was stolen from some other place, until he drops his head and remembers where he is.

Later on, I lean against the door frame upstairs and listen to the sound of a metal fork scraping against a dish. My mother is already there, her voice rising and falling. She is moving the fork across the plate, offering my brother pieces of French toast.

I move towards the bed, the carpet scratchy, until I can touch the wooden bed-frame with my hands. My mother is seated there, and I go to her, reaching my fingers out to the buttons on her cuff and twisting them over to catch the light.

"Are you eating?" I ask my brother.

He starts to cry. I look at him, his face half hidden in the blankets.

80   "Try and eat," my mother says softly.

He only cries harder but there isn't any sound. The pattern of sunlight on his blanket moves with his body. His hair is pasted down with sweat and his head moves forward and backward like an old man's.

At some point I know my father is standing at the entrance of the room but I cannot turn to look at him. I want to stay where I am, facing the wall. I'm afraid that if I turn around and go to him, I will be complicit, accepting a portion of guilt, no matter how small that piece. I do not know how to prevent this from happening again, though now I know, in the end, it will break us apart. This violence will turn all my love to shame and grief. So I stand there, not looking at him or my brother. Even my father, the magician, who can make something beautiful out of nothing, he just stands and watches.

A face changes over time, it becomes clearer. In my father's face, I have seen everything pass. Anger that has stripped it of anything recognizable, so that it is only a face of bones and skin. And then, at other times, so much pain that it is unbearable, his face so full of grief it might dissolve. How to reconcile all that I know of him and still love him? For a long time, I thought it was not possible. When I was a child, I did not love my father because he was complicated, because he was human, because he needed me to. A child does not know yet how to love a person that way.

How simple it should be. Warm water running over, the feel of the grains between my hands, the sound of it like stones running along the pavement. My father would rinse the rice over and over, sifting it between his fingertips, searching for the impurities, pulling them out. A speck, barely visible, resting on the tip of his finger.

85   If there were some recourse, I would take it. A cupful of grains in my open hand, a smoothing out, finding the impurities, then removing them piece by piece. And then, to be satisfied with what remains.

Somewhere in my memory, a fish in the sink is dying slowly. My father and I watch as the water runs down.

◆

Previewing

Lucy Jay began the reading process by previewing her text. A quick glance showed her that it was quite short (under ten pages), that it was written in the first person ("My father taught it to me when I was a child"), that it included dialogue, as well as narrative, and that it had an apparently straightforward title.

Highlighting and Annotating

As she reread the story, Lucy highlighted words and ideas that she thought might be useful to her, indicated possible connections among ideas, and noted questions and comments as they occurred to her. During this process, she considered the meaning of the term *simple recipes*, and she paid close attention to the narrator's voice. The highlighted and annotated passage that follows illustrates her responses to the first three paragraphs of the story:

Title?

There is a ⟨simple⟩ recipe for making rice. <u>My father taught it to me</u>   *pt of view*

child → adult   when I was a child. <u>Back then</u>, I used to sit up on the kitchen counter

watching him, how he sifted the grains in his hands, sure and quick,

<u>removing pieces of dirt or sand, tiny imperfections.</u> He swirled his hands   *like he tries with his son?*

repetition of simple   through the water and it turned cloudy. When he scrubbed the grains

clean, the sound was as big as a field of insects. Over and over, my father

rinsed the rice, drained the water, then filled the pot again.

The instructions are (simple.) Once the washing is done, you measure the water this way—by resting the tip of your index finger on the surface of the rice. The water should reach the bend of your first knuckle. My father did not need instructions or measuring cups. He closed his eyes and felt for the waterline.

shift in point of view

Sometimes I still dream my father, his bare feet flat against the floor, standing in the middle of the kitchen. He wears old buttoned shirts and faded sweatpants drawn at the waist. Surrounded by the gloss of the kitchen counters, the sharp angles of the stove, the fridge, the shiny sink, he looks out of place. This memory of him is so strong, sometimes it stuns me, the detail with which I can see it.

sound

dream about? or create?

detail vs. dream

Lucy's highlighting and annotating suggested some interesting possibilities for her paper. First, Lucy noticed that the story reveals both the narrator's childhood innocence and her adult feelings. The highlighting also identified stylistic features, such as the concrete detail ("the gloss of the kitchen counters") and the repetition of the word *simple*. Lucy also noticed that contrast is significant in the passage and the whole story: the contrast between what is simple and what is not, between two cultures, between two generations, and between the genders of male and female. Lucy concluded that the title is extremely important and is both straightforward and ironic. She also thought the rice was symbolic.

WRITING ABOUT FICTION

◊ ◊ ◊

PLANNING AN ESSAY

At this stage, Lucy had not thought of a definite topic, but she knew she would write on "Simple Recipes." However, her previewing, highlighting, and annotating had revealed some ideas about style, point of view, and perhaps theme. Because the assignment was for a short paper (750–1,000 words), she decided to try to focus on one element.

Choosing a Topic

Lucy decided to explore topics in her journal. Her journal entry is as follows:

```
    The style is simple, like the title, but maybe the
simplicity hides something else. Words are chosen for
```

```
meaning and sound--alliteration is used ("father . . .
feet flat"). When the narrator thinks of her father she
uses the words strong and stunned. Maybe these words refer
to what happens with her brother and the beating. Contrast
is used to show the difference between the dirty and
clean rice and also between the softness of the father
and the "sharp angles" in the kitchen. Contrast is also
shown between the perspective of the child and the adult
who is recounting the story. What does cleaning and
cooking the rice really mean? Why do the son and daughter
respond in different ways to their father's food?
```

Lucy had many scattered things to say about the story, but she needed to tie her ideas together. She considered an essay on point of view, but decided that was too limited for what she wanted to explore. She finally decided to examine the symbolism of the words of the title "Simple Recipes," and she thought she could touch on point of view and style in her explanation of symbolism. She wrote a journal entry on symbolism.

```
    The washing and cooking of the rice symbolize the
father's way of doing things, his culture and background.
As an immigrant to Canada, he has had to cope with many
changes, but the washing of the rice provides a link
between his past and present. For his children, especially
his son, the rice and food (especially the fish) are
relics of the past. The son rejects his father's food
(very important symbolic action). The daughter does not
reject her father's food, but she too is drifting away
from her father's culture as she cannot make the rice as
well as her father can. The rice is a staple of the par-
ents' Malaysian background, but it does not mean the same
thing for the children. The "simple recipe" of making rice
cannot be applied to culture or nationality. Canada has
many immigrants (nearly everyone), and the difficulty of
the transition to a new home and culture is symbolized by
the rice and fish in this story.
```

Finding Something to Say

Brainstorming Once Lucy decided to write about symbolism, she moved on to brainstorming about her topic, focusing on the most important—and most obvious—symbol: the rice. She wrote:

```
Rice = white, needs to be cleaned to have the specks of
dirt (black) washed away by repeated rinsing. Things have
```

to be done properly, according to the father--the washing
of the rice symbolizes that idea. Daughter doesn't wash it
as well.

Maybe father sees Canadian culture as something that
needs to be washed away from his children. Rice is small
like the children are small.

Fish = alive, needs to be killed violently, also in
water, and also son rejects the meal. Wants different
food. (food a marker of a culture)

Wok with Yan = father watches on television but is critical, mixing of cultures

Language = son has forgotten or "refused" parents' language; daughter has tried to learn but fails

Dirt = son tracks in dirt from soccer and spreads it on
the tablecloth

Bruise = mother says daughter can make it go away like a
speck of dirt

Fork = son throws fork (western implement) at father (who
uses chopsticks)

Bamboo pole = used to beat son, symbol of past

French toast = mother tries to cheer up son with a
western dish

Woodward's = mother works there; father at home; store now
out of business

Seeing Connections

Listing When she looked over her brainstorming notes in search of an orga-
nizational scheme for her paper, Lucy saw that she had plenty of information about food and utensils, language, and violence. An obvious option was
to discuss each item one at a time. But Lucy knew she had to find a common
element among the separate items, a thematic connection that would relate
them to one another. When she noticed that all the items related to changes
in culture, she realized she could write about the changes that families
undergo when they immigrate from one country to another. She experimented with this possibility in the following lists of related details:

Rice: pure clean rice symbolizes pure culture of father;
dirt specks symbolize infiltration of another culture

Fish: whole live fish symbolizes father's culture; son's
refusal to eat shows his shift away from father's culture

French toast: mother tries to console son with western food

Chopsticks: parents use, but children use forks

Language: neither child knows language of parents; parents can speak without children knowing content; puns on "Wok with Yan"--combines food and language

Violence: the fish is killed with a violent blow, the son throws his fork at his father, and the father beats the son with the bamboo pole

Lucy's lists confirm that the meanings of the items are related and are interdependent as symbols. The food and utensils with which the food is eaten indicate the changes between the generations in terms of culture. The connection between food and language is made with the television show *Wok with Yan*. And most important, the incremental violence shows the breakdown in cultural values from father to son.

Deciding on a Thesis

With her ideas organized into lists that indicated some relationships among them, Lucy began to see a central idea for her essay. She expressed this idea in a tentative thesis, a sentence that she could use to guide her essay's first draft (for a full discussion of this stage of the writing process, see "Deciding on a Thesis," p. 28, in Chapter 2):

The key symbols in the story indicate the changes occurring in the family as the younger generation moves away from the cultural beliefs of the older generation.

Preparing an Outline

Even though her essay was to be short, Lucy prepared a scratch outline that mapped out an arrangement for her ideas. She decided to discuss the three types of food (rice, fish, French toast) and what they signify. She decided to discuss them in the order in which they appear in the story because that order shows a significant change in cultural values.

Rice
    Malaysia
    Father's world
    Attention to detail
    Staple food
    Daughter makes lousy rice

Fish
    In water like the rice
    Necessary protein
    Special dish--live, must be killed with cleaver

Son comes to table and sheds dirt, refuses to eat
fish, dislikes eyeball (being examined?)
Son throws fork (not chopstick) at father

French toast
Mother tries to help son eat French toast, syrup and milk
--Canadian food--with a fork--signifies that immigrants
have to cope with new cultures and find a way to integrate them into their lives.

DRAFTING AN ESSAY

Guided by her scratch outline, her thesis statement, and her notes, Lucy
wrote the following first draft. Because her notes included ideas not
included in her scratch outline, and because she discovered new ideas and
connections as she wrote, the draft does not follow the scratch outline
exactly.

first draft

Symbols in "Simple Recipes"

"Simple Recipes" is a story rich in symbols. It is also a story about change. Different symbols show how the lives of the immigrant family are being changed as the children move away from their parents' culture and try to fit into their home in Canada. The most important symbol in the story is food.

The most important symbol in the story is the fish. The father prepares the fish in a traditional manner, bringing it home live, and keeping it in water in the sink until he is ready to cook it. The daughter is fascinated by the fish. "I keep watch over the fish while my father begins the preparations for dinner. The fish folds its body, trying to turn or swim, the water nudging overtop. Though I ripple tiny circles around it with my fingers, the fish stays still, bobbing side-to-side in the cold water" (46). The small actions of the girl cannot change the fate of the fish--it is trapped and will be consumed. While the daughter is engaged in the kitchen with her father, the son is outside playing soccer. He has no interest in cooking and is much less obedient than his sister. When the family gathers for dinner, the son comes to the table covered with dirt. "The dirt flies off his skin, speckling the tablecloth" (48). The boy's disrespect is quickly challenged, and he goes to wash, but the specks of dirt symbolize that the son is bringing something new and unwanted into the family home.

When the son returns to the table and refuses to eat the fish, the split in the family widens. The father believes the boy spits some food onto his plate. Really, the boy is choking, but the father sees it as willful disrespect. The father hits his son, and then the son throws a fork at his father. Even the boy's choice of weapon shows his move away from his family background. His parents use chopsticks. The violence

continues with the son's verbal assault on his father,
an assault containing a vicious racial slur: "You're
just an asshole, you're just a fucking asshole chink!"
(50). In retaliation, the father beats his son, and
uses a "bamboo pole" (50), an instrument of his culture. The beating is brutal, and the narrator loses
her ability to understand her mother's soothing words
because she is making so much noise screaming. The
daughter says, " . . . I feel loose, deranged, as if
everything in the known world is ending right here"
(50). Certainly the connection between father and son
has been severed, and that break foreshadows the break
between daughter and father.

The title refers to the narrator's father's
method of making rice. The recipe is simple, but it
is important to follow the father's steps to get the
rice to turn out the way it should be. The father
takes much care in washing the rice "he sifted the
grains in his hands, sure and quick, removing pieces
of dirt or sand, tiny imperfections" (45). When the
daughter, who is also the narrator, tries to make the
rice, she is not always successful. She doesn't prepare the rice in the same way, and the rice is not as
good as it is when her father makes it. "When I was
older, he passed this task on to me but I never did
it with the same care. . . . Some nights the rice was
a mushy gruel" (45). But the father doesn't seem to
mind that his daughter makes lousy rice; the two of
them are very close, and the daughter shares her
father's fondness for cooking shows, especially Wok
with Yan, a Canadian show with a Chinese chef. Rice
symbolizes the parents' origins. It is a staple food
in their home country of Malaysia, and the care the
father takes in preparing it indicates his respect for
his background and traditions. The daughter's lack of
care suggests a disregard of values regarding the food
and the culture of her parents.

The cultural divide between the father and son is made clear by the final item of food mentioned in the story: the French toast. This breakfast symbolizes the Canadian culture, not the Chinese culture of the parents. Like rice, bread is a staple food in many cultures. The father makes the French toast and pours syrup over it (another Canadian custom). The mother pours a glass of milk, not a standard beverage in Chinese culture, but a basic one in Canada, and the mother is the parent who takes the meal to the son. As the mother tries to encourage her son to eat, the father and daughter are in the kitchen. "With each passing day, he knows I will find it harder to ignore what I can't comprehend, that I will be unable to separate one part of him from another. The unconditional quality of my love for him will not last forever, just as my brother's did not" (51). When the mother returns to the kitchen, she whispers to her husband "in a language that was stolen from some other place, until he drops his head and remembers where he is" (51). The different foods the family eats--the rice, fish, and French toast--symbolize the shift in cultures. The changing utensils, from chopsticks to forks for the children, reinforce this change.

Because the narrator is remembering childhood experiences from the vantage point of adulthood, she can understand more clearly the pain felt and the damage done in a family trying to cope with massive changes in cultural beliefs. The adult woman can make the connection between the "simple" recipe of making rice and the simple recipe for love. The conclusion of the story expands the symbolic meaning of the title "Simple Recipes" to include not only the creation of food, but also the creation of love. The final image in the story of the fish in the sink suggests that reconciliation is not possible. "Somewhere in my memory,

> a fish in the sink is dying slowly. My father and I watch as the water runs down" (52). Just as the water disappears down the drain, so has the son's love for his father, and the narrator does not mention her brother after the incident of the beating. "Simple Recipes" uses the symbolism of food to show the painful cultural changes and losses an immigrant family may endure in coming to a country in search of a better life.

First Draft: Commentary

As Lucy reviewed her first draft, she made some changes in content, style, and organization. She deleted wordiness and repetition; added more specific references, including quotations, from the story; sharpened transitions and added clearer topic sentences; and reorganized paragraphs to make logical and causal connections more obvious.

Discussions with classmates in a peer review group and with her instructor gave her some additional insights. The students' major criticism was that the order of the ideas was wrong: while the fish may be the trigger for the father's rage, the idea of the importance of food needs to be established. They also suggested that more could be made of the French toast, given the nature of Canada's history. In general, the students thought Lucy had a good idea and just needed to work on the organization of her paper.

Lucy's instructor agreed with the students' criticism that the symbol of the fish needs to be discussed after the symbol of the rice. The instructor also suggested that Lucy sharpen her use of language, that she be more clear and concise. The instructor also reminded Lucy that she must introduce her quotations so that they fit smoothly (and grammatically) into Lucy's sentences and paragraphs. The instructor agreed with the students' view that Lucy had a good idea, and he said that Lucy had dealt with a volatile subject in a respectful and sensitive manner. He suggested that Lucy give a little more development to the character of the father so that the reader can see the father as more than a man who beats his son. He also suggested that Lucy pay more attention to the importance of language in the story.

REVISING AND EDITING AN ESSAY

The revisions Lucy decided to make are reflected in her second draft.

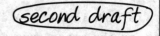

Symbols in "Simple Recipes"

"Simple Recipes" is a story rich in symbols. It is also a story about change. Different symbols show how the lives of the immigrant family are being changed as the children move away from their parents' culture and try to fit into their home in Canada. The most important symbols in the story are food and language.

The title refers to the narrator's father's method of making rice. The recipe is simple, but it's important to follow the father's steps to get the rice to turn out the way it should be. The father takes much care in washing the rice: "he sifted the grains in his hands, sure and quick, removing pieces of dirt or sand, tiny imperfections" (45). When the daughter, who is also the narrator, tries to make the rice, she is not always successful. She doesn't prepare the rice in the same way, and the rice is not as good as it is when her father makes it. "When I was older, he passed this task on to me but I never did it with the same care. . . . Some nights the rice was a mushy gruel" (45). But the father doesn't seem to mind that his daughter makes lousy rice; the two of them are very close, and the daughter shares her father's fondness for cooking shows, especially Wok with Yan, a Canadian show with a Chinese chef who makes puns. Rice symbolizes the parents' origins. It is a staple food in their home country of Malaysia, and the care the father takes in preparing it indicates his respect for his background and traditions. The daughter's lack of care suggests her values are slipping regarding the food and the culture of her parents.

Another important symbol in the story is the fish. The father prepares the fish in a traditional manner, bringing it home live, and keeping it in water

in the sink until he is ready to cook it. The daughter
is fascinated by the fish: "I keep watch over the fish
while my father begins the preparations for dinner.
The fish folds its body, trying to turn or swim, the
water nudging overtop. Though I ripple tiny circles
around it with my fingers, the fish stays still, bobbing side-to-side in the cold water" (46). The small
actions of the girl cannot change the fate of the
fish--it is trapped and will be consumed. While the
daughter is engaged in the kitchen with her father,
the son is outside playing soccer. He has no interest
in cooking and is much less pliable than his sister.
When the family gathers for dinner, the son comes to
the table covered with dirt. "The dirt flies off his
skin, speckling the tablecloth" (48). The boy's disrespect is quickly challenged, and he goes to wash,
but the image of the specks of dirt is eerily similar
to that of the specks in the rice that the father
cleans.

When the son returns to the table and refuses to
eat the fish, the father tries to make a joke from his
favourite television program. "'Take a wok on the wild
side'" (49), he tells his son, trying to encourage his
son to eat the fish. But the joke doesn't work, and
the father then mistakes his son's choking for willful
disrespect. That error leads to trauma. The father
hits his son, and then the son throws a fork at his
father. Even the boy's choice of weapon shows his move
away from his family background. His parents use chopsticks. The violence continues with the son's verbal
assault on his father, an assault containing a vicious
racial slur: "You're just an asshole, you're just a
fucking asshole chink!" (50). In retaliation, the
father beats his son, and uses a "bamboo pole" (50),
an instrument of his culture. The beating is brutal,
and the narrator loses her ability to understand her

mother's soothing words because she is making so much noise screaming. The daughter says, " . . . I feel loose, deranged, as if everything in the known world is ending right here" (50). Certainly the connection between father and son has been severed, and that break foreshadows the break between daughter and father.

The cultural divide between the father and son is made clear by the final item of food mentioned in the story: the French toast. This breakfast symbolizes the Canadian culture, not the Chinese culture of the parents. Like rice, bread is a staple food in many cultures, and the making of the bread into "French" toast suggests two of the founding cultures of Canada. The father makes the French toast and pours syrup over it (another Canadian custom). The mother pours a glass of milk, not a standard beverage in Chinese culture, but a basic one in Canada, and the mother is the parent who takes the meal to the son. As the mother tries to encourage her son to eat, the father and daughter are in the kitchen. The narrator reflects: "With each passing day, he knows I will find it harder to ignore what I can't comprehend, that I will be unable to separate one part of him from another. The unconditional quality of my love for him will not last forever, just as my brother's did not" (51). The different foods the family eats--the rice, fish, and French toast--symbolize the shift in cultures. The changing utensils, from chopsticks to forks for the children, reinforce this change.

When the mother returns to the kitchen, she whispers to her husband "in a language that was stolen from some other place, until he drops his head and remembers where he is" (51). The language the family members use also symbolizes their shifting cultures. The parents whisper in a language the children don't know. The son knew the language once, but since moving to Canada, he has forgotten, something his father cannot understand. The daughter, who was born in Canada, has tried to learn the language but has failed. When the son lashes out at his father, he uses vulgar English. And when her brother is being beaten, the narrator loses all language and is left with screaming to show her pain. Like food, language shows the differences in attitude about culture among the family.

Because the narrator is remembering childhood experiences from the vantage point of adulthood, she can understand more clearly the pain felt and the damage done in a family trying to cope with massive changes in cultural beliefs. The adult woman can make the connection between the "simple" recipe of making rice and the simple recipe for love. The conclusion of the story expands the symbolic meaning of the title "Simple Recipes" to not only include the creation of food, but also the creation of love. The final image in the story of the fish in the sink suggests that reconciliation is not possible. "Somewhere in my memory, a fish in the sink is dying slowly. My father and I watch as the water runs down" (52). Just as the water disappears down the drain, so has the son's love for his father, and the narrator does not mention her brother after the incident of the beating. "Simple Recipes" uses the symbolism of food to show the painful cultural changes and losses an immigrant family may endure in coming to a country in search of a better life.

Second Draft: Commentary

Lucy felt satisfied with her second draft, although she knew there were many more points she could make about the story. But she did not want to make the essay too long according to the guidelines of the assignment. She thought she had a good thesis and clear topic sentences for the paragraphs.

She thought the overall development was more coherent than it was in her first draft.

She thought she was ready to tackle smaller items, such as style, grammar, mechanics, spelling, punctuation, and format. She planned to eliminate contractions, to check all verb tenses carefully, to work quotations into her text more smoothly, and to revise the language of her introduction and conclusion. As she made her revisions, she planned to scrutinize this draft carefully, aiming to make the final paper as concise as she could.

Lucy Jay   Jay 1

English 1013

Professor Johnson

1 March 2007

Symbols in "Simple Recipes"

"Simple Recipes" by Madeleine Thien is a story rich in symbols that represent change. The narrator, the daughter of the family, shows how the lives of her parents, brother, and herself are being changed as the children move away from their Malaysian parents' culture and try to fit into their home in Canada. The most important symbols in the story are food and language.

The title can refer to the narrator's father's method of making rice, an important food in the family's diet. The recipe is simple, but the father's steps must be followed to produce the rice correctly. The father takes much care in washing the rice: "he sifted the grains in his hands, sure and quick, removing pieces of dirt or sand, tiny imperfections" (45). When the daughter tries to make the rice, she is not always successful. She does not prepare the rice as her father does, and the rice is not as good as it is when her father makes it. She says, "When I was older, he passed this task on to me but I never did it with the same care. . . . Some nights the rice was a mushy gruel" (45). But the father seems not to mind his daughter's substandard rice; the two of them are very close, and the daughter shares her father's fondness for cooking shows, especially <u>Wok with Yan</u>, a Canadian show with a Chinese chef who makes puns. Rice symbolizes the parents' origins. It is a staple food in their home country of Malaysia, and the care the father takes in preparing it indicates his respect for his background and traditions. The daughter's lack of care suggests her values are slipping regarding the food and the culture of her parents.

Opening paragraph identifies work and author. It also delineates the thesis of the essay.

Topic sentence identifies a key symbol.

Parenthetical documentation identifies source of quotation.

Jay 2

Topic
sentence
identifies
another key
symbol.

Another important symbol is a fish. The father prepares a fish in the traditional manner, bringing it home live, and keeping it in water in the sink until he is ready to cook it. The daughter is fascinated by the fish: "I keep watch over the fish while my father begins the preparations for dinner. The fish folds its body, trying to turn or swim, the water nudging overtop. Though I ripple tiny circles around it with my fingers, the fish stays still, bobbing side-to-side in the cold water" (46). The small actions of the girl cannot change the fate of the fish: it is trapped and will be consumed. While the daughter is engaged in the kitchen with her father, the son is outside playing soccer. He has no interest in cooking and is much less interested in his father's cooking than his sister is. When the family gathers for dinner, the son comes to the table covered with dirt. "The dirt flies off his skin, speckling the tablecloth" (48). The boy's disrespect is quickly challenged, and he goes to wash, but the image of the specks of dirt is eerily similar to that of the specks in the rice that the father cleans.

Paragraph
develops
subtopic
from symbol
of fish.

When the son returns to the table and refuses to eat the fish, the father tries to make a joke from his favourite television program. "'Take a wok on the wild side'" (49), he tells his son, trying to encourage his son to eat the fish. But the joke fails, and the father then mistakes his son's choking for willful disrespect. That error leads to trauma. The father hits his son, and then the son throws a fork at his father. Even the boy's choice of weapon shows his move away from his family background. His parents use chopsticks while the children use forks. The violence continues with the son's verbal assault on his father, an assault containing a vicious racial slur: "You're just an asshole, you're just a fucking asshole chink!"

Jay 3

(50). In retaliation, the father beats his son, and uses a "bamboo pole" (50), an instrument of his culture. The beating is brutal, and the narrator loses her ability to understand her mother's soothing words because she is making so much noise screaming. The daughter says, " . . . I feel loose, deranged, as if everything in the known world is ending right here" (50). Certainly the connection between father and son has been severed, and that break foreshadows the break between daughter and father.

The cultural divide between the father and son is made clear by the final item of food mentioned in the story: the French toast. This breakfast symbolizes the Canadian culture, not the Chinese culture of the parents. Like rice, bread is a staple food in many cultures, and the making of the bread into "French" toast suggests two of the founding cultures of Canada. The father makes the French toast and pours syrup over it (another Canadian custom). The mother pours a glass of milk, a standard beverage in Canada but not in Chinese culture, and the mother takes the meal to the son. As the mother tries to encourage her son to eat, the father and daughter are in the kitchen. The narrator reflects: "With each passing day, he knows I will find it harder to ignore what I can't comprehend, that I will be unable to separate one part of him from another. The unconditional quality of my love for him will not last forever, just as my brother's did not" (51). The different foods of the family--the rice, fish, and French toast--symbolize the shift in cultures. The changing utensils, from chopsticks to forks for the children, also symbolize the change in culture.

In conjunction with food, language also symbolizes the changes in the family. When the mother returns to the kitchen from giving her son the French

Topic sentence identifies another key symbol.

Topic sentence identifies another key symbol, different from previously discussed ones but thematically connected.

Jay 4

toast, she whispers to her husband "in a language that was stolen from some other place, until he drops his head and remembers where he is" (51). The language of the family members reflects shifting cultures. The parents whisper in a language the children don't know. The son knew the language once, but since moving to Canada, he has forgotten it, something his father cannot understand. The daughter, who was born in Canada, has tried to learn the language but has failed. When the son lashes out at his father, he uses vulgar English. And when her brother is being beaten, the narrator loses all language and is left with screaming to show her pain. Like food, language shows the differences in attitude about culture among the family.

Conclusion

Because the narrator is remembering childhood experiences from the vantage point of adulthood, she can understand more clearly the pain felt and the damage done in a family trying to cope with massive changes in cultural beliefs. The adult woman can make the connection between the "simple" recipe of making rice and the simple recipe for love. The conclusion of the story expands the symbolic meaning of the title "Simple Recipes" to include not only the creation of food, but also the perpetuation of love. Both food and language are ways to demonstrate love. The final image in the story of the fish in the sink suggests that reconciliation is not possible. As the narrator says, "Somewhere in my memory, a fish in the sink is dying slowly. My father and I watch as the water runs down" (52). Just as the water disappears down the drain, so has the son's love for his father, and the narrator does not mention her brother after the incident of the beating. But in her maturity, the daughter has learned about the simple recipe for love. She says, "When I

Jay 5

was a child, I did not love my father because he was
complicated, because he was human, because he needed
me to. A child does not know yet how to love a person
that way" (52). Evidently she learns to love her
father that way, despite the violent treatment of her
brother. But the brother does not. "Simple Recipes"
uses the symbolism of food and language to show the
painful cultural changes and losses an immigrant
family may endure in coming to a country in search of
a better life. Instead of that better life, an immigrant family may find itself torn apart by the changes
in culture.

Final Draft: Commentary

As she revised and edited her second draft, Lucy made changes in word
choice and sentence structure. She edited to eliminate errors in mechanics,
punctuation, and spelling. She used a spell check program, but she also went
through the essay carefully because a spell check does not catch any wrong
words, only those spelled incorrectly. She added the name of the author to
her opening sentence. She tried to make sure that quotations were accurate
and smoothly introduced. (Because students were permitted to write papers
only about works in this anthology, the instructor did not require a Works
Cited page.) Finally, Lucy checked all her references against page numbers of
the story, so readers would be able to return to her source if necessary to
check the quotations.

CHAPTER 4

Plot

◆ ◆ ◆

It's a truism that there are only two basic plots in fiction: one, somebody takes a trip; two, a stranger comes to town.

LEE SMITH, *New York Times Book Review*

The beginning of an action always presents us with a situation in which there is some element of instability, some conflict; in the middle of an action there is a period of readjustment of forces in the process of seeking a new kind of stability; in the end of an action, some point of stability is reached, the forces that have been brought into play have been resolved.

CLEANTH BROOKS AND ROBERT PENN WARREN, *Understanding Fiction*

The simplest way to tell a story, equally favoured by tribal bards and parents at bedtime, is to begin at the beginning, and go on until you reach the end, or your audience falls asleep. But even in antiquity, storytellers perceived the interesting effects that could be obtained by deviating from chronological order. . . . A shift of narrative focus back in time may change our interpretation of something which happened much later in the chronology of the story, but which we have already experienced as readers of the text. This is a familiar device of cinema, the flashback.

DAVID LODGE, *The Art of Fiction*

So much for endings. Beginnings are always more fun. True connoisseurs, how-ever, are known to favor the stretch in between, since it's the hardest to do anything with.

That's about all that can be said for plots, which anyway are just one thing after another, a what and a what and a what.

Now try How and Why.

MARGARET ATWOOD, "Happy Endings"

I like stories that end rather than merely stop, stories that somehow assure me that their stopping point is the best moment for all progress to cease.

RICHARD FORD (quoted in *New York Times Book Review*)

◇ ◇ ◇

Alfred Hitchcock's 1951 film *Strangers on a Train,* based on a suspense novel by Patricia Highsmith, offers an intriguing premise: two men, strangers, each can murder someone the other wishes dead; because they have no apparent connection to their victims, both can escape suspicion. Many people would describe this ingenious scheme as the film's "plot," but in fact it is simply the gimmick around which the complex plot revolves. Certainly a clever twist can be an important ingredient of a story's plot, but plot is more than "what happens"; it is how what happens is presented. **Plot** is the way in which a story's events are arranged; it is shaped by causal connections—historical, social, and personal—by the interaction between characters, and by the juxtaposition of events. In *Strangers on a Train,* as in many well-developed works of fiction, the plot that unfolds is complex, with one character directing the events and determining their order while the other character is drawn into the action against his will. The same elements that enrich the plot of the film—unexpected events, conflict, suspense, flashbacks, foreshadowing—can also enrich the plot of a work of short fiction.

CONFLICT

◇ ◇ ◇

Readers' interest and involvement are heightened by a story's **conflict,** the struggle between opposing forces that emerges as the action develops. This conflict is a clash between the **protagonist,** a story's principal character, and an **antagonist,** someone or something presented in opposition to the protagonist. Sometimes the antagonist is a villain; more often, he or she simply represents a conflicting point of view or advocates a course of action different from the one the protagonist follows. Sometimes the antagonist is not a character at all but a situation (for instance, war or poverty) or an event (a natural disaster, such as a flood or a storm, for example) that challenges the protagonist. In other stories, the protagonist may struggle against a supernatural force, or the conflict may occur within a character's mind. It may, for example, be a struggle between two moral choices, such as whether to stay at home and care for an aging parent or to leave and make a new life.

STAGES OF PLOT

◇ ◇ ◇

A work's plot explores one or more conflicts, moving from *exposition* through a series of *complications* to a *climax* and, finally, to a *resolution.*

In a story's **exposition** the writer presents the basic information readers need to understand the events that follow. Typically, the exposition sets the story in motion: it establishes the scene, introduces the major characters, and perhaps suggests the major events or conflicts to come. Sometimes a single sentence can present exposition clearly and economically, giving readers information vital to their understanding of the plot that will unfold.

For example, the opening sentence of Shirley Jackson's "The Lottery" (p. 319)—"The morning of June 27th was clear and sunny, with the fresh warmth of a full-summer day; the flowers were blossoming profusely and the grass was richly green"—introduces the picture-perfect setting that is essential to the story's irony. At other times, as in Alistair MacLeod's "The Boat" (p. 447), a more fully developed section establishes the story's setting, introduces the main characters, and suggests possible conflicts. In some experimental stories a distinct exposition component may be absent, as it is in Luisa Valenzuela's "All about Suicide" (p. 7).

As the plot progresses, the story's conflict unfolds through a series of complications that will eventually lead readers to the story's climax. The action may include several crises. A **crisis** is a peak in the story's action, a moment of considerable tension or importance; the **climax** is the point of greatest tension or importance, the scene that presents a story's decisive action or event.

The final stage of plot, the **resolution,** or **denouement** (French for "untying of the knot"), draws the action to a close and accounts for all remaining loose ends. Sometimes this resolution is achieved with the help of a **deus ex machina** (Latin for "a god from a machine"), an intervention of some force or agent previously extraneous to the story—for example, the appearance of a long-lost relative or a fortuitous inheritance, the discovery of a character's true identity, a last-minute rescue by a character not previously introduced. Usually, however, the resolution is more plausible: all the events lead logically and convincingly (although not necessarily predictably) to the resolution. Sometimes the ending of a story is indefinite— that is, readers are not quite sure what the protagonist will do, or what will happen next. This kind of resolution, although it may leave some readers feeling cheated, has its advantages: it mirrors the complexity of life, where closure rarely occurs, and it can draw readers into the action as they try to understand the significance of the story's ending or to decide how conflicts should have been resolved.

ORDER AND SEQUENCE
◆ ◆ ◆

A writer may present a story's events in strict chronological order, with each event presented in the sequence in which it actually took place. More often, however, especially in relatively modern fiction, writers do not present events chronologically. Instead, they present incidents out of expected order, or in no apparent order. For example, a writer may choose to begin **in medias res** (Latin for "in the midst of things"), starting with an event and going back in time to explain preceding events, as Mavis Gallant does in "The Ice Wagon Going Down the Street" (p. 98). Or, a writer can decide to begin a work of fiction at the end and then move back to reconstruct events that led up to the final outcome, as William Faulkner does in "A Rose for Emily" (p. 90). Many sequences are possible as the writer manipulates events to create interest, suspense, confusion, wonder, or some other effect.

Writers who wish to depart from strict chronological order use *flashbacks* and *foreshadowing*. A **flashback** moves out of sequence to examine an event or situation that occurred before the time in which the story's action takes place. A character can remember an earlier event, or a story's narrator can re-create an earlier situation. For example, in Madeleine Thien's "Simple Recipes" (p. 45), the adult narrator looks back on events that occurred when she was a child and then jumps to the present to consider the effect of the past. In Edgar Allan Poe's "The Cask of Amontillado" (p. 227), the entire story is told as a flashback. Flashbacks are valuable because they can substitute for or supplement formal exposition by presenting background vital to the readers' understanding of a story's events. One disadvantage of flashbacks is that, because they interrupt the natural flow of events, they may be intrusive or distracting. Such distractions, however, can be an advantage if the writer wishes to reveal events gradually and subtly or to obscure causal links.

Foreshadowing is the introduction early in a story of situations, events, characters, or objects that hint at things to come. A chance remark, a natural occurrence, or a seemingly trivial event is eventually revealed to have great significance. For example, a dark cloud passing across the sky can foreshadow future problems. In this way, foreshadowing allows a writer to hint provocatively at what is to come, so that readers only gradually become aware of a particular detail's role in a story. Thus, foreshadowing helps readers sense what will occur and grow increasingly involved as they see the likelihood (or even the inevitability) of a particular outcome.

In addition to employing conventional techniques like flashbacks and foreshadowing, writers may experiment with sequence by substantially tampering with—or even dispensing with—chronological order. An example is the scrambled chronology of "A Rose for Emily." In such instances the experimental form enhances interest and encourages readers to become involved with the story as they work to untangle or reorder the events and determine their logical and causal connections.

A FINAL NOTE
◇ ◇ ◇

In popular fiction, plot is likely to dominate the story, as it does, for example, in mystery or adventure stories, which tend to lack fully developed characters, complex themes, and elaborately described settings. In richer, more complicated works of fiction, however, plot is often more complex and less obvious.

CHECKLIST: WRITING ABOUT PLOT

✓ What happens in the story?

✓ Where does the story's formal exposition section end? What do readers learn about characters in this section? What do readers learn about setting? What possible conflicts are suggested here?

✓ What is the story's central conflict? What other conflicts are presented? Who is the protagonist? Who (or what) serves as the antagonist?

✓ Identify the story's crisis or crises.

✓ Identify the story's climax.

✓ How is the story's central conflict resolved? Is this resolution plausible? Satisfying?

✓ Which portion of the story constitutes the resolution? Do any problems remain unresolved? Does any uncertainty remain? If so, does this uncertainty strengthen or weaken the story? Would another ending be more effective?

✓ How are the story's events arranged? Are they presented in chronological order? What events are presented out of logical sequence? Does the story use foreshadowing? Flashbacks? Are the causal connections between events clear? Logical? If not, can you explain why?

◆ **KATE CHOPIN** (1851–1904) must, in a sense, be considered a contemporary writer. Her honest, sexually frank stories (many of which had been out of print for more than half a century) were rediscovered in the 1960s and 1970s, influencing a new generation of writers. Though she was a popular contributor of stories and sketches to the magazines of her day, Chopin scandalized many critics with her outspoken novel *The Awakening* (1899), in which a woman seeks sexual and emotional fulfillment with a man who is not her husband. The book was removed from the shelves of the public library in St. Louis, where Chopin was born.

Chopin was born Katherine O'Flaherty, the daughter of a wealthy Irish-born merchant and his aristocratic Creole wife. Educated at convent schools, she was married at nineteen to Oscar Chopin, a Louisiana cotton broker, who took her to live first in New Orleans and later on a plantation at Cloutierville, near Natchitoches, in central Louisiana, where it is said that she offended members of polite society by drinking beer and crossing her legs—at the knees. Chopin's representations of the Cane River region and its people in two volumes of short stories—*Bayou Folk* (1894) and *A Night in Arcadie* (1897)—are the foundation of her reputation as a local colourist.

Resemblances have been noted between these stories and certain works of Guy de Maupassant, which Chopin had translated from French to English.

A busy wife and mother, Chopin seems to have begun writing only after she returned to St. Louis following her husband's sudden death in 1883. "The Story of an Hour" depicts a brief event in a woman's life, but in this single hour, Chopin reveals both a lifetime's emotional torment and the momentary joy of freedom.

KATE CHOPIN

The Story of an Hour
(1894)

Knowing that Mrs. Mallard was afflicted with a heart trouble, great care was taken to break to her as gently as possible the news of her husband's death.

It was her sister Josephine who told her, in broken sentences, veiled hints that revealed in half concealing. Her husband's friend Richards was there, too, near her. It was he who had been in the newspaper office when intelligence of the railroad disaster was received, with Brently Mallard's name leading the list of "killed." He had only taken the time to assure himself of its truth by a second telegram, and had hastened to forestall any less careful, less tender friend in bearing the sad message.

She did not hear the story as many women have heard the same, with a paralyzed inability to accept its significance. She wept at once, with sudden, wild abandonment, in her sister's arms. When the storm of grief had spent itself she went away to her room alone. She would have no one follow her.

There stood, facing the open window, a comfortable, roomy armchair. Into this she sank, pressed down by a physical exhaustion that haunted her body and seemed to reach into her soul

5   She could see in the open square before her house the tops of trees that were all aquiver with the new spring life. The delicious breath of rain was in the air. In the street below a peddler was crying his wares. The notes of a distant song which some one was singing reached her faintly, and countless sparrows were twittering in the eaves.

There were patches of blue sky showing here and there through the clouds that had met and piled one above the other in the west facing her window.

She sat with her head thrown back upon the cushion of the chair, quite motionless, except when a sob came up into her throat and shook her, as a child who has cried itself to sleep continues to sob in its dreams.

She was young, with a fair, calm face, whose lines bespoke repression and even a certain strength. But now there was a dull stare in her eyes, whose gaze was fixed away off yonder on one of those patches of blue sky. It was not a glance of reflection, but rather indicated a suspension of intelligent thought.

There was something coming to her and she was waiting for it, fearfully. What was it? She did not know; it was too subtle and elusive to name. But she felt it, creeping out of the sky, reaching toward her through the sounds, the scents, the color that filled the air.

10   Now her bosom rose and fell tumultuously. She was beginning to recognize this thing that was approaching to possess her, and she was striving to beat it back with her will—as powerless as her two white slender hands would have been.

When she abandoned herself a little whispered word escaped her slightly parted lips. She said it over and over under her breath: "Free, free, free!" The vacant stare and the look of terror that had followed it went from her eyes. They stayed keen and bright. Her pulses beat fast, and the coursing blood warmed and relaxed every inch of her body.

She did not stop to ask if it were not a monstrous joy that held her. A clear and exalted perception enabled her to dismiss the suggestion as trivial.

She knew that she would weep again when she saw the kind, tender hands folded in death; the face that had never looked save with love upon her, fixed and gray and dead. But she saw beyond that bitter moment a long procession of years to come that would belong to her absolutely. And she opened and spread her arms out to them in welcome.

There would be no one to live for during those coming years; she would live for herself. There would be no powerful will bending her in that blind persistence with which men and women believe they have a right to impose a private will upon a fellow creature. A kind intention or a cruel intention made the act seem no less a crime as she looked upon it in that brief moment of illumination.

15   And yet she had loved him—sometimes. Often she had not. What did it matter! What could love, the unsolved mystery, count for in face of this possession of self-assertion which she suddenly recognized as the strongest impulse of her being.

"Free! Body and soul free!" she kept whispering.

Josephine was kneeling before the closed door with her lips to the keyhole, imploring for admission. "Louise, open the door! I beg; open the door—you will make yourself ill. What are you doing, Louise? For heaven's sake open the door."

"Go away. I am not making myself ill." No; she was drinking in a very elixir of life through that open window.

Her fancy was running riot along those days ahead of her. Spring days, and summer days, and all sorts of days that would be her own. She breathed a quick prayer that life might be long. It was only yesterday she had thought with a shudder that life might be long.

20   She arose at length and opened the door to her sister's importunities. There was a feverish triumph in her eyes, and she carried herself unwittingly like a goddess of Victory. She clasped her sister's waist, and together they descended the stairs. Richards stood waiting for them at the bottom.

Some one was opening the front door with a latchkey. It was Brently Mallard who entered, a little travel-stained, composedly carrying his grip-sack and umbrella. He had been far from the scene of the accident, and did not even know there had been one. He stood amazed at Josephine's piercing cry; at Richards' quick motion to screen him from the view of his wife.

But Richards was too late.

When the doctors came they said she had died of heart disease—of joy that kills.

READING AND REACTING

1. The story's basic exposition is presented in its first two paragraphs. What additional information about character or setting would you like to know? Why do you suppose the writer does not supply this information?

2. "The Story of an Hour" is a very economical story, with little action or dialogue. Is this a strength or a weakness? Explain.

3. When "The Story of an Hour" was first published in *Vogue* magazine in 1894, the magazine's editors titled it "The Dream of an Hour." A film version, echoing the last words of the story, is called *The Joy That Kills*. Which of the three titles do you believe most accurately represents what happens in the story?

4. Did Brently Mallard abuse his wife? Did he love her? Did she love him? Exactly why was she so relieved to be rid of him? Can you answer any of these questions with certainty?

5. What is the nature of the conflict in this story? Who, or what, do you see as Mrs. Mallard's antagonist?

6. What emotions does Mrs. Mallard experience during the hour she spends alone in her room? What events do you imagine take place during this same period outside her room? Outside her house?

7. Do you find the story's ending satisfying? Believable? Contrived?

8. Was the story's ending unexpected, or were you prepared for it? What elements foreshadowed this ending?

9. **JOURNAL ENTRY** Rewrite the story's ending, substituting a few paragraphs of your own for the last three paragraphs of the story.

10. **CRITICAL PERSPECTIVE** Writing in the *Southern Literary Journal*, Cynthia Griffin Wolff observes that before the 1960s, many critics had a "tendency to dismiss Chopin's fiction as little more than local color," viewing her as essentially a regional writer. Accordingly, they saw her major contribution to literature as the accurate depiction of setting, customs, and manners in the Louisiana bayou. Other critics, according to Wolff, believe Chopin's major contribution is her surprise or "trick" conclusions, endings that are not what readers expect.

    Which do you see as more important to "The Story of an Hour," the setting or the ending? Do you believe that the story has something to offer beyond these two elements, or do you agree with those critics who would see Chopin as "only" a local colourist or the creator of clever plot twists?

Related Works: "The Yellow Wall-Paper" (p. 189), "The Boat" (p. 447), "Women" (p. 786), *A Doll House* (p. 1013).

◊ **NADINE GORDIMER** (1923–   ), winner of the 1991 Nobel Prize in literature, has been publishing short stories, essays, and novels about South Africa, her native country, since she was fifteen. Gordimer once explained that after growing up as a middle-class child of Jewish immigrants, becoming a politically aware writer in South Africa was like "peeling an onion. You're sloughing off all the conditioning that you've had since you were a child." The prevailing attitude of her extensive work has evolved from cautious optimism to pessimism in accord with the changing nature of Africa in her lifetime. *New York Times* book critic Michiko Kakutani suggests that in the attempt to illustrate that apartheid debases the lives of both blacks and whites, "she has mapped out the social, political and emotional geography of that troubled land with extraordinary passion and precision." Though Gordimer's work was often banned in her own country because of its condemnation of apartheid, she continues to live in Johannesburg.

Gordimer's novels include *The Lying Days* (1953), *A Guest of Honour* (1970), *Burger's Daughter* (1979), *July's People* (1981), *None to Accompany Me* (1994), *The House Gun* (1998), and *Get a Life* (2005). Her short stories have been collected in such volumes as *Face to Face* (1949), *Jump and Other Stories* (1981), *Why Haven't You Written?* (1992), and *Loot* (2003). *Writing and Being* (2002) explores experience and narrative creativity.

◊ ◊ ◊

NADINE GORDIMER

Town and Country Lovers
(1980)

Dr. Franz-Josef von Leinsdorf is a geologist absorbed in his work; wrapped up in it, as the saying goes—year after year the experience of his work enfolds him, swaddling him away from the landscapes, the cities and the people, wherever he lives: Peru, New Zealand, the United States. He's always been like that, his mother could confirm from their native Austria. There, even as a handsome small boy he presented only his profile to her: turned away to his bits of rock and stone. His few relaxations have not changed much since then. An occasional skiing trip, listening to music, reading poetry—Rainer Maria Rilke once stayed in his grandmother's hunting lodge in the forests of Styria and the boy was introduced to Rilke's poems while very young.

Layer upon layer, country after country, wherever his work takes him— and now he has been almost seven years in Africa. First the Côte d'Ivoire, and for the past five years, South Africa. The shortage of skilled manpower brought about his recruitment here. He has no interest in the politics of the countries he works in. His private preoccupation-within-the-preoccupation of his work has been research into underground water-courses, but the mining company that employs him in a senior though not executive capacity is interested only in mineral discovery. So he is much out in the field—which is the veld, here—seeking new gold, copper, platinum and uranium deposits. When he is at home—on this particular job, in this particular country, this city—he lives in a two-roomed flat in a suburban block with a landscaped garden, and does his shopping at a supermarket conveniently across the street. He is not married—yet. That is how his colleagues, and the typists and secretaries at the mining company's head office, would define his situation. Both men and women would describe him as a good-looking man, in a foreign way, with the lower half of the face dark and middle-aged (his mouth is thin and curving, and no matter how close-shaven his beard shows like fine shot embedded in the skin round mouth and chin) and the upper half contradictorily young, with deep-set eyes (some would say grey, some black), thick eyelashes and brows. A tangled gaze: through which concentration and gleaming thoughtfulness perhaps appear as fire and langour. It is this that the women in the office mean when they remark he's not unattractive. Although the gaze seems to promise, he has never invited any of them to go out with him. There is the general assumption he probably has a girl who's been picked for him, he's bespoken by one of his own kind, back home in Europe where he comes from. Many of these well-educated Europeans have no intention of becoming permanent immigrants; neither the remnant of white colonial life nor idealistic involvement with Black Africa appeals to them.

One advantage, at least, of living in underdeveloped or half-developed countries is that flats are serviced. All Dr. von Leinsdorf has to do for himself is buy his own supplies and cook an evening meal if he doesn't want to go to a restaurant. It is simply a matter of dropping in to the supermarket on his way from his car to his flat after work in the afternoon. He wheels a trolley up and down the shelves, and his simple needs are presented to him in the form of tins, packages, plastic-wrapped meat, cheeses, fruit and vegetables, tubes, bottles . . . At the cashiers' counters where customers must converge and queue there are racks of small items uncategorized, for last-minute purchase. Here, as the coloured girl cashier punches the adding machine, he picks up cigarettes and perhaps a packet of salted nuts or a bar of nougat. Or razor-blades, when he remembers he's running short. One evening in winter he saw that the cardboard display was empty of the brand of blades he preferred, and he drew the cashier's attention to this. These young coloured girls are usually pretty unhelpful, taking money and punching their machines in a manner that asserts with the time-serving obstinacy of the half-literate the limit of any responsibility towards customers, but this one ran an alert glance over the selection of razor-blades, apologized that she was not allowed to leave her post, and said she would see that the stock was replenished "next time." A day or two later she recognized him, gravely, as he took his turn before her counter—"I ahssed them, but it's out of stock. You can't get it. I did ahss about it." He said this didn't matter. "When it comes in, I can keep a few packets for you." He thanked her.

He was away with the prospectors the whole of the next week. He arrived back in town just before nightfall on Friday, and was on his way from car to flat with his arms full of briefcase, suitcase and canvas bags when someone stopped him by standing timidly in his path. He was about to dodge round unseeingly on the crowded pavement but she spoke. "We got the blades in now. I didn't see you in the shop this week, but I kept some for you when you come. So . . ."

5   He recognized her. He had never seen her standing before, and she was wearing a coat. She was rather small and finely-made, for one of them. The coat was skimpy but no big backside jutted. The cold brought an apricot-graining of warm colour to her cheekbones, beneath which a very small face was quite delicately hollowed, and the skin was smooth, the subdued satiny colour of certain yellow wood. That crêpey hair, but worn drawn back flat and in a little knot pushed into one of the cheap wool chignons that (he recognized also) hung in the miscellany of small goods along with the razor-blades, at the supermarket. He said thanks, he was in a hurry, he'd only just got back from a trip—shifting the burdens he carried, to demonstrate. "Oh shame." She acknowledged his load. "But if you want I can run in and get it for you quickly. If you want."

He saw at once it was perfectly clear that all the girl meant was that she would go back to the supermarket, buy the blades and bring the packet to him there where he stood, on the pavement. And it seemed that it was this certainty that made him say, in the kindly tone of assumption used for an obliging underling, "I live just across there—*Atlantis*—that flat building. Could you drop them by for me—number seven-hundred-and-eighteen, seventh floor—"

She had not before been inside one of these big flat buildings near where she worked. She lived a bus- and train-ride away to the West of the city, but this side of the black townships, in a township for people her tint. There was a pool with ferns, not plastic, and even a little waterfall pumped electrically over rocks, in the entrance of the building *Atlantis*; she didn't wait for the lift marked goods but took the one meant for whites and a white woman with one of those sausage-dogs on a lead got in with her but did not pay her any attention. The corridors leading to the flats were nicely glassed-in, not draughty.

He wondered if he should give her a twenty-cent piece for her trouble—ten cents would be right for a black; but she said, "Oh no—please, here—" standing outside his open door and awkwardly pushing back at his hand the change from the money he'd given her for the razor-blades. She was smiling, for the first time, in the dignity of refusing a tip. It was difficult to know how to treat these people, in this country; to know what they expected. In spite of her embarrassing refusal of the coin, she stood there, completely unassuming, fists thrust down the pockets of her cheap coat against the cold she'd come in from, rather pretty, thin legs neatly aligned, knee to knee, ankle to ankle.

"Would you like a cup of coffee or something?"

10 He couldn't very well take her into his study-cum-living-room and offer her a drink. She followed him to his kitchen, but at the sight of her pulling out the single chair to drink her cup of coffee at the kitchen table, he said, "No—bring it in here—" and led the way into the big room where, among his books and his papers, his files of scientific correspondence (and the cigar boxes of stamps from envelopes), his racks of records, his specimens of minerals and rocks, he lived alone.

It was no trouble to her; she saved him the trips to the supermarket and brought him his groceries two or three times a week. All he had to do was leave a list and the key under the doormat, and she would come up in her lunch-hour to collect them, returning to put his supplies in the flat after work. Sometimes he was home and sometimes not. He bought a box of chocolates and left it, with a note, for her to find; and that was acceptable, apparently, as a gratuity.

Her eyes went over everything in the flat although her body tried to conceal its sense of being out of place by remaining as still as possible, holding its contours in the chair offered her as a stranger's coat is set aside and remains exactly as left until the owner takes it up to go. "You collect?"

"Well, these are specimens—connected with my work."

"My brother used to collect. Miniatures. With brandy and whiskey and that, in them. From all over. Different countries."

15 The second time she watched him grinding coffee for the cup he had offered her she said, "You always do that? Always when you make coffee?"

"But of course. Is it no good, for you? Do I make it too strong?"

"Oh it's just I'm not used to it. We buy it ready—you know, it's in a bottle, you just add a bit to the milk or water."

He laughed, instructive: "That's not coffee, that's a synthetic flavouring. In my country we drink only real coffee, fresh, from the beans—you smell how good it is as it's being ground?"

She was stopped by the caretaker and asked what she wanted in the building. Heavy with the *bona fides* of groceries clutched to her body, she said she was working at number 718, on the seventh floor. The caretaker did not tell her not to use the whites' lift; after all, she was not black; her family was very light-skinned.

20 There was the item "grey button for trousers" on one of his shopping lists. She said as she unpacked the supermarket carrier "Give me the pants, so long, then," and sat on his sofa that was always gritty with fragments of pipe tobacco, sewing in and out through the four holes of the button with firm, fluent movements of the right hand, gestures supplying the articulacy missing from her talk. She had a little yokel's, peasant's (he thought of it) gap between her two front teeth when she smiled that he didn't much like, but, face ellipsed to three-quarter angle, eyes cast down in concentration

with soft lips almost closed, this didn't much matter. He said, watching her sew, "You're a good girl"; and touched her.

She remade the bed every late afternoon when they left it and she dressed again before she went home. After a week there was a day when late after-noon became evening, and they were still in the bed.

"Can't you stay the night?"

"My mother," she said.

"Phone her. Make an excuse." He was a foreigner. He had been in the country five years, but he didn't understand that people don't usually have telephones in their houses, where she lived. She got up to dress. He didn't want that tender body to go out in the night cold and kept hindering her with the interruption of his hands; saying nothing. Before she put on her coat, when the body had already disappeared, he spoke. "But you must make some arrangement."

25   "Oh my mother!" Her face opened to fear and vacancy he could not read.

He was not entirely convinced the woman would think of her daughter as some pure and unsullied virgin . . . "Why?"

The girl said, "S'e'll be scared. S'e'll be scared we get caught."

"Don't tell her anything. Say I'm employing you." In this country he was working in now there were generally rooms on the roofs of flat build-ings for tenants' servants.

She said: "That's what I told the caretaker."

30   She ground fresh coffee beans every time he wanted a cup while he was working at night. She never attempted to cook anything until she had watched in silence while he did it the way he liked, and she learned to repro-duce exactly the simple dishes he preferred. She handled his pieces of rock and stone, at first admiring the colours—"It'd make a beautiful ring or a necklace, ay." Then he showed her the striations, the formation of each piece, and explained what each was, and how, in the long life of the earth, it had been formed. He named the mineral it yielded, and what that was used for. He worked at his papers, writing, writing, every night, so it did not matter that they could not go out together to public places. On Sundays she got into his car in the basement garage and they drove to the country and picnicked away up in the Magaliesberg,[1] where there was no one. He read or poked about among the rocks; they climbed together, to the mountain pools. He taught her to swim. She had never seen the sea. She squealed and shrieked in the water, showing the gap between her teeth, as—it crossed his mind—she must do when among her own people. Occasionally he had to go out to dinner at the houses of colleagues from the mining company; she sewed and listened to the radio in the flat and he found her in bed, warm and already asleep, by the time he came in. He made his way into her body

---

[1] A mountain range north of Johannesburg.

without speaking; she made him welcome without a word. Once he put on evening dress for a dinner at his country's consulate; watching him brush one or two fallen hairs from the shoulders of the dark jacket that sat so well on him, she saw a huge room all chandeliers and people dancing some dance from a costume film—stately, hand-to-hand. She supposed he was going to fetch, in her place in the car, a partner for the evening. They never kissed when either left the flat; he said, suddenly, kindly, pausing as he picked up cigarettes and keys, "Don't be lonely." And added, "Wouldn't you like to visit your family sometimes, when I have to go out?"

He had told her he was going home to his mother in the forests and mountains of his country near the Italian border (he showed her on the map) after Christmas. She had not told him how her mother, not knowing there was any other variety, assumed he was a medical doctor, so she had talked to her about the doctor's children and the doctor's wife who was a very kind lady, glad to have someone who could help out in the surgery as well as the flat.

She remarked wonderingly on his ability to work until midnight or later, after a day at work. She was so tired when she came home from her cash register at the supermarket that once dinner was eaten she could scarcely keep awake. He explained in a way she could understand that while the work she did was repetitive, undemanding of any real response from her intelligence, requiring little mental or physical effort and therefore unrewarding, his work was his greatest interest, it taxed his mental capacities to their limit, exercised all his concentration, and rewarded him constantly as much with the excitement of a problem presented as with the satisfaction of a problem solved. He said later, putting away his papers, speaking out of a silence: "Have you done other kinds of work?" She said, "I was in a clothing factory before. Sportbeau shirts; you know? But the pay's better in the shop."

Of course. Being a conscientious newspaper-reader in every country he lived in, he was aware that it was only recently that the retail consumer trade in this one had been allowed to employ coloureds as shop assistants; even punching a cash register represented advancement. With the continuing shortage of semi-skilled whites a girl like this might be able to edge a little farther into the white-collar category. He began to teach her to type. He was aware that her English was poor, even though, as a foreigner, in his ears her pronunciation did not offend, nor categorize her as it would in those of someone of his education whose mother tongue was English. He corrected her grammatical mistakes but missed the less obvious ones because of his own sometimes exotic English usage—she continued to use the singular pronoun "it" when what was required was the plural "they." Because he was a foreigner (although so clever, as she saw) she was less inhibited than she might have been by the words she knew she misspelled in her typing. While she sat at the typewriter she thought how one day she would type notes for him, as well as making coffee that way he liked it, and taking him inside her body without saying anything, and sitting (even if only through the empty streets of quiet Sundays) beside him in his car, like a wife.

On a summer night near Christmas—he had already bought and hidden a slightly showy but nevertheless good watch he thought she would like—there was a knocking at the door that brought her out of the bathroom and him to his feet, at his work-table. No one ever came to the flat at night; he had no friends intimate enough to drop in without warning. The summons was an imperious banging that did not pause and clearly would not stop until the door was opened.

35 She stood in the open bathroom doorway gazing at him across the passage into the living-room; her bare feet and shoulders were free of a big bath-towel. She said nothing, did not even whisper. The flat seemed to shake with the strong unhurried blows.

He made as if to go to the door, at last, but now she ran and clutched him by both arms. She shook her head wildly; her lips drew back but her teeth were clenched, she didn't speak. She pulled him into the bedroom, snatched some clothes from the clean laundry laid out on the bed and got into the wall-cupboard, thrusting the key at his hand. Although his arms and calves felt weakly cold he was horrified, distastefully embarrassed at the sight of her pressed back crouching there under his suits and coat; it was horrible and ridiculous. *Come out!* he whispered. *No! Come out!* She hissed: *Where? Where can I go?*

Never mind! Get out of there!

He put out his hand to grasp her. At bay, she said with all the force of her terrible whisper, baring the gap in her teeth: *I'll throw myself out the window.*

She forced the key into his hand like the handle of a knife. He closed the door on her face and drove the key home in the lock, then dropped it among the coins in his trouser pocket.

40 He unslotted the chain that was looped across the flat door. He turned the serrated knob of the Yale lock. The three policemen, two in plain clothes, stood there without impatience although they had been banging on the door for several minutes. The big dark one with an elaborate moustache held out in a hand wearing a plaited gilt ring some sort of identity card.

Dr. von Leinsdorf said quietly, the blood coming strangely back to legs and arms, "What is it?"

The sergeant told him they knew there was a coloured girl in the flat. They had had information; "I been watching this flat three months, I know."

"I am alone here." Dr. von Leinsdorf did not raise his voice.

"I know, I know who is here. Come—" And the sergeant and his two assistants went into the living-room, the kitchen, the bathroom (the sergeant picked up a bottle of after-shave cologne, seemed to study the French label) and the bedroom. The assistants removed the clean laundry that was laid upon the bed and then turned back the bedding, carrying the sheets over to be examined by the sergeant under the lamp. They talked to one another in Afrikaans, which the Doctor did not understand. The sergeant himself looked under the bed, and lifted the long curtains at the window. The wall cupboard was of the kind that has no knobs; he saw that it was locked and began to ask in Afrikaans, then politely changed to English, "Give us the key."

45   Dr. von Leinsdorf said, "I'm sorry, I left it at my office—I always lock and take my keys with me in the mornings."

"It's no good, man, you better give me the key."

He smiled a little, reasonably. "It's on my office desk."

The assistants produced a screwdriver and he watched while they inserted it where the cupboard doors met, gave it quick, firm but not forceful leverage. He heard the lock give.

She had been naked, it was true, when they knocked. But now she was wearing a long-sleeved T-shirt with an appliquéd butterfly motif on one breast, and a pair of jeans. Her feet were still bare; she had managed, by feel, in the dark, to get into some of the clothing she had snatched from the bed, but she had no shoes. She had perhaps been weeping behind the cupboard door (her cheeks looked stained) but now her face was sullen and she was breathing heavily, her diaphragm contracting and expanding exaggeratedly and her breasts pushing against the cloth. It made her appear angry; it might simply have been that she was half-suffocated in the cupboard and needed oxygen. She did not look at Dr. von Leinsdorf. She would not reply to the sergeant's questions.

50   They were taken to the police station where they were at once separated and in turn led for examination by the district surgeon. The man's underwear was taken away and examined, as the sheets had been, for signs of his seed. When the girl was undressed, it was discovered that beneath her jeans she was wearing a pair of men's briefs with his name on the neatly-sewn laundry tag; in her haste, she had taken the wrong garment to her hiding-place.

Now she cried, standing there before the district surgeon in a man's underwear.

He courteously pretended not to notice. He handed briefs, jeans and T-shirt round the door, and motioned her to lie on a white-sheeted high table where he placed her legs apart, resting in stirrups, and put into her where the other had made his way so warmly a cold hard instrument that expanded wider and wider. Her thighs and knees trembled uncontrollably while the doctor looked into her and touched her deep inside with more hard instruments, carrying wafers of gauze.

When she came out of the examining room back to the charge office, Dr. von Leinsdorf was not there; they must have taken him somewhere else. She spent what was left of the night in a cell, as he must be doing; but early in the morning she was released and taken home to her mother's house in the coloured township by a white man who explained he was the clerk of the lawyer who had been engaged for her by Dr. von Leinsdorf. Dr. von Leinsdorf, the clerk said, had also been bailed out that morning. He did not say when, or if she would see him again.

A statement made by the girl to the police was handed in to Court when she and the man appeared to meet charges of contravening the Immorality Act in a Johannesburg flat on the night of — December, 19——. *I lived with the white man in his flat. He had intercourse with me sometimes. He gave me tablets to take to prevent me becoming pregnant.*

55   Interviewed by the Sunday papers, the girl said, "I'm sorry for the sadness brought to my mother." She said she was one of nine children of a female laundry worker. She had left school in Standard Three because there was no money at home for gym clothes or a school blazer. She had worked as a machinist in a factory and a cashier in a supermarket. Dr. von Leinsdorf taught her to type his notes.

Dr. Franz-Josef von Leinsdorf, described as the grandson of a baroness, a cultured man engaged in international mineralogical research, said he accepted social distinctions between people but didn't think they should be legally imposed. "Even in my own country it's difficult for a person from a higher class to marry one from a lower class."

The two accused gave no evidence. They did not greet or speak to each other in Court. The Defence argued that the sergeant's evidence that they had been living together as man and wife was hearsay. (The woman with the dachshund, the caretaker?) The magistrate acquitted them because the State failed to prove carnal intercourse had taken place on the night of — December, 19——.

The girl's mother was quoted, with photograph, in the Sunday papers: "I won't let my daughter work as a servant for a white man again."

READING AND REACTING

1. How is the introduction—paragraphs 1–3—related to the relationship of Dr. von Leinsdorf and the young woman and the eventual outcome?
2. List the tasks that the young woman performs for Dr. von Leinsdorf.
3. The story's events are presented in strict chronological order. Give some examples of words and phrases that move readers from one time period to another. Why is chronological order so important?
4. What effect does the race law in South Africa have on the couple and their behaviour? What is the effect of Dr. von Leinsdorf's comment in paragraph 56 about the difficulty of marriage between people of different classes?
5. What is Dr. von Leinsdorf's attitude to the woman? What is hers to him?
6. How important is lying to the story?
7. What aspects of the society are criticized in the story?
8. What is the significance of education, and what does it reveal about the young woman?
9. **JOURNAL ENTRY** "Town and Country Lovers" is set in South Africa. Could it have been set in Canada?

10. **CRITICAL PERSPECTIVE** In an interview conducted in the early 1980s, Gordimer spoke about her education and about the town in which she lived:

> When I got to university, it was through mixing with other people who were writing or painting that I got to know black people as equals. In a general and inclusive, nonracial way, I met people who lived in the world of ideas, in the world that interested me passionately.
>
> In the town where I lived, there was no mental food of this kind at all. I'm often amazed to think how they live, those people, and what an oppressed life it must be, because human beings *must* live in the world of ideas. This dimension in the human psyche is very important. It was there, but they didn't know how to express it. Conversation consisted of trivialities. For women, household matters, problems with children. The men would talk about golf or business or horseracing or whatever their practical interests were. Nobody ever talked about, or even around, the big things—life and death.

Focusing on Gordimer's characterization of the conversation in her town as consisting of "trivialities" rather than of "the big things," consider how her description of that town might apply to "Town and Country Lovers."

Related Works: "The Rocking-Horse Winner" (p. 370), "Gretel in Darkness" (p. 620), "Cinderella" (p. 646)

◈ **WILLIAM FAULKNER** (1897–1962), winner of the 1949 Nobel Prize in literature and the 1955 and 1963 Pulitzer prizes for fiction, was an unabashedly "Southern" writer whose work continues to transcend the regional label. His nineteen novels, notably *The Sound and the Fury* (1929), *As I Lay Dying* (1930), *Light in August* (1932), *Absalom, Absalom!* (1936), and *The Reivers* (1962), explore a wide range of human experience—from high comedy to tragedy—as seen in the life of one community, Faulkner's fictional "Yoknapatawpha County" (modelled on the area around Faulkner's own hometown of Oxford, Mississippi). Faulkner's Yoknapatawpha stories— a fascinating blend of complex Latinate prose and primitive Southern dialect—paint an extraordinary portrait of a community bound together by ties of blood, by a shared belief in moral "verities," and by an old grief (the Civil War). Faulkner's grandfather raised "Billy" on Civil War tales and local legends, including many about the "Old Colonel," the writer's great-grandfather, who was a colourful Confederate officer. But Faulkner was no Margaret Mitchell. Like Mitchell's *Gone with the Wind,* his stories elegize the agrarian virtues of the Old South, but they look unflinchingly at that world's tragic flaw: the "peculiar institution" of slavery.

Local legends and gossip frequently served as the spark for Faulkner's stories. As John B. Cullen, writing in *Old Times in Faulkner Country,* notes, "A

Rose for Emily," Faulkner's first nationally published short story, was based on the tale of Oxford's aristocratic "Miss Mary" Neilson, who married Captain Jack Hume, the charming Yankee foreman of a street-paving crew, over her family's shocked protests. But Hume didn't meet the fate of "Miss Emily's" lover. He lived on to a ripe old age and lovingly cared for his wife during her final illness. According to Cullen, one of Faulkner's neighbours said he created his story "out of fears and rumors"—the dire predictions of what *might* happen if Mary Neilson married her Yankee.

◊ ◊ ◊

WILLIAM FAULKNER

A Rose for Emily
(1930)

I

When Miss Emily Grierson died, our whole town went to her funeral: the men through a sort of respectful affection for a fallen monument, the women mostly out of curiosity to see the inside of her house, which no one save an old manservant—a combined gardener and cook—had seen in at least ten years.

It was a big, squarish frame house that had once been white, decorated with cupolas and spires and scrolled balconies in the heavily lightsome style of the seventies, set on what had once been our most select street. But garages and cotton gins had encroached and obliterated even the august names of that neighborhood; only Miss Emily's house was left, lifting its stubborn and coquettish decay above the cotton wagons and the gasoline pumps—an eyesore among eyesores. And now Miss Emily had gone to join the representatives of those august names where they lay in the cedar-bemused cemetery among the ranked and anonymous graves of Union and Confederate soldiers who fell at the battle of Jefferson.

Alive, Miss Emily had been a tradition, a duty, and a care; a sort of hereditary obligation upon the town, dating from that day in 1894 when Colonel Sartoris, the mayor—he who fathered the edict that no Negro woman should appear on the streets without an apron—remitted her taxes, the dispensation dating from the death of her father on into perpetuity. Not that Miss Emily would have accepted charity. Colonel Sartoris invented an involved tale to the effect that Miss Emily's father had loaned money to the town, which the town, as a matter of business, preferred this way of repaying. Only a man of Colonel Sartoris' generation and thought could have invented it, and only a woman could have believed it.

When the next generation, with its more modern ideas, became mayors and aldermen, this arrangement created some little dissatisfaction. On the first of the year they mailed her a tax notice. February came, and there was no reply. They wrote her a formal letter, asking her to call at the sheriff's office at her convenience. A week later the mayor wrote her himself, offering to call or to send his car for her, and received in reply a note on paper of an archaic shape, in a thin, flowing calligraphy in faded ink, to the effect that she no longer went out at all. The tax notice was also enclosed, without comment.

5   They called a special meeting of the Board of Aldermen. A deputation waited upon her, knocked at the door through which no visitor had passed since she ceased giving china-painting lessons eight or ten years earlier. They were admitted by the old Negro into a dim hall from which a stairway mounted into still more shadow. It smelled of dust and disuse—a close, dank smell. The Negro led them into the parlor. It was furnished in heavy, leather-covered furniture. When the Negro opened the blinds of one window, they could see that the leather was cracked; and when they sat down, a faint dust rose sluggishly about their thighs, spinning with slow motes in the single sun-ray. On a tarnished gilt easel before the fireplace stood a crayon portrait of Miss Emily's father.

They rose when she entered—a small, fat woman in black, with a thin gold chain descending to her waist and vanishing into her belt, leaning on an ebony cane with a tarnished gold head. Her skeleton was small and spare; perhaps that was why what would have been merely plumpness in another was obesity in her. She looked bloated, like a body long submerged in motionless water, and of that pallid hue. Her eyes, lost in the fatty ridges of her face, looked like two small pieces of coal pressed into a lump of dough as they moved from one face to another while the visitors stated their errand.

She did not ask them to sit. She just stood in the door and listened quietly until the spokesman came to a stumbling halt. Then they could hear the invisible watch ticking at the end of the gold chain.

Her voice was dry and cold. "I have no taxes in Jefferson. Colonel Sartoris explained it to me. Perhaps one of you can gain access to the city records and satisfy yourselves."

"But we have. We are the city authorities, Miss Emily. Didn't you get a notice from the sheriff, signed by him?"

10   "I received a paper, yes," Miss Emily said. "Perhaps he considers himself the sheriff . . . I have no taxes in Jefferson."

"But there is nothing on the books to show that, you see. We must go by the—"

"See Colonel Sartoris. I have no taxes in Jefferson."

"But, Miss Emily—"

"See Colonel Sartoris." (Colonel Sartoris had been dead almost ten years.) "I have no taxes in Jefferson. Tobe!" The Negro appeared. "Show these gentlemen out."

II

15 So she vanquished them, horse and foot, just as she had vanquished their fathers thirty years before about the smell. That was two years after her father's death and a short time after her sweetheart—the one we believed would marry her—had deserted her. After her father's death she went out

very little; after her sweetheart went away, people hardly saw her at all. A few of the ladies had the temerity to call, but were not received, and the only sign of life about the place was the Negro man—a young man then—going in and out with a market basket.

"Just as if a man—any man—could keep a kitchen properly," the ladies said; so they were not surprised when the smell developed. It was another link between the gross, teeming world and the high and mighty Griersons.

A neighbor, a woman, complained to the mayor, Judge Stevens, eighty years old.

"But what will you have me do about it, madam?" he said.

"Why, send her word to stop it," the woman said. "Isn't there a law?"

20   "I'm sure that won't be necessary," Judge Stevens said. "It's probably just a snake or a rat that nigger of hers killed in the yard. I'll speak to him about it."

The next day he received two more complaints, one from a man who came in diffident deprecation. "We really must do something about it, Judge. I'd be the last one in the world to bother Miss Emily, but we've got to do something." That night the Board of Aldermen met—three graybeards and one younger man, a member of the rising generation.

"It's simple enough," he said. "Send her word to have her place cleaned up. Give her a certain time to do it in, and if she don't . . ."

"Dammit, sir," Judge Stevens said, "will you accuse a lady to her face of smelling bad?"

So the next night, after midnight, four men crossed Miss Emily's lawn and slunk about the house like burglars, sniffing along the base of the brick-work and at the cellar openings while one of them performed a regular sowing motion with his hand out of a sack slung from his shoulder. They broke open the cellar door and sprinkled lime there, and in all the out-buildings. As they recrossed the lawn, a window that had been dark was lighted and Miss Emily sat in it, the light behind her, and her upright torso motionless as that of an idol. They crept quietly across the lawn and into the shadow of the locusts that lined the street. After a week or two the smell went away.

25   That was when people had begun to feel really sorry for her. People in our town, remembering how old lady Wyatt, her great-aunt, had gone completely crazy at last, believed that the Griersons held themselves a little too high for what they really were. None of the young men were quite good enough for Miss Emily and such. We had long thought of them as a tableau, Miss Emily a slender figure in white in the background, her father a sprad-dled silhouette in the foreground, his back to her and clutching a horse-whip, the two of them framed by the back-flung front door. So when she got to be thirty and was still single, we were not pleased exactly, but vindicated; even with insanity in the family she wouldn't have turned down all of her chances if they had really materialized.

When her father died, it got about that the house was all that was left to her; and in a way, people were glad. At last they could pity Miss Emily.

Being left alone, and a pauper, she had become humanized. Now she too would know the old thrill and the old despair of a penny more or less.

The day after his death all the ladies prepared to call at the house and offer condolence and aid, as is our custom. Miss Emily met them at the door, dressed as usual and with no trace of grief on her face. She told them that her father was not dead. She did that for three days, with the ministers calling on her, and the doctors, trying to persuade her to let them dispose of the body. Just as they were about to resort to law and force, she broke down, and they buried her father quickly.

We did not say she was crazy then. We believed she had to do that. We remembered all the young men her father had driven away, and we knew that with nothing left, she would have to cling to that which had robbed her, as people will.

III

She was sick for a long time. When we saw her again, her hair was cut short, making her look like a girl, with a vague resemblance to those angels in colored church windows—sort of tragic and serene.

30 The town had just let the contracts for paving the sidewalks, and in the summer after her father's death they began the work. The construction company came with niggers and mules and machinery, and a foreman named Homer Barron, a Yankee—a big, dark, ready man, with a big voice and eyes lighter than his face. The little boys would follow in groups to hear him cuss the niggers, and the niggers singing in time to the rise and fall of picks. Pretty soon he knew everybody in town. Whenever you heard a lot of laughing anywhere about the square, Homer Barron would be in the center of the group. Presently we began to see him and Miss Emily on Sunday afternoons driving in the yellow-wheeled buggy and the matched team of bays from the livery stable.

At first we were glad that Miss Emily would have an interest, because the ladies all said, "Of course a Grierson would not think seriously of a Northerner, a day laborer." But there were still others, older people, who said that even grief could not cause a real lady to forget *noblesse oblige*[1]—without calling it *noblesse oblige*. They just said, "Poor Emily. Her kinsfolk should come to her." She had some kin in Alabama; but years ago her father had fallen out with them over the estate of old lady Wyatt, the crazy woman, and there was no communication between the two families. They had not even been represented at the funeral.

And as soon as the old people said, "Poor Emily," the whispering began. "Do you suppose it's really so?" they said to one another. "Of course it is. What else could . . ." This behind their hands; rustling of craned silk and satin behind jalousies closed upon the sun of Sunday afternoon as the thin, swift clop-clop-clop of the matched team passed: "Poor Emily."

---

[1] The obligation of those of high birth or rank to behave in an honourable fashion.

She carried her head high enough—even when we believed that she was fallen. It was as if she demanded more than ever the recognition of her dignity as the last Grierson; as if it had wanted that touch of earthiness to reaffirm her imperviousness. Like when she bought the rat poison, the arsenic. That was over a year after they had begun to say "Poor Emily," and while the two female cousins were visiting her.

"I want some poison," she said to the druggist. She was over thirty then, still a slight woman, though thinner than usual, with cold, haughty black eyes in a face the flesh of which was strained across the temples and about the eye-sockets as you imagine a lighthouse-keeper's face ought to look. "I want some poison," she said.

35   "Yes, Miss Emily. What kind? For rats and such? I'd recom—"

"I want the best you have. I don't care what kind."

The druggist named several. "They'll kill anything up to an elephant. But what you want is—"

"Arsenic," Miss Emily said. "Is that a good one?"

"Is . . . arsenic? Yes, ma'am. But what you want—"

40   "I want arsenic."

The druggist looked down at her. She looked back at him, erect, her face like a strained flag. "Why, of course," the druggist said. "If that's what you want. But the law requires you to tell what you are going to use it for."

Miss Emily just stared at him, her head tilted back in order to look him eye for eye, until he looked away and went and got the arsenic and wrapped it up. The Negro delivery boy brought her the package; the druggist didn't come back. When she opened the package at home there was written on the box, under the skull and bones: "For rats."

IV

So the next day we all said, "She will kill herself"; and we said it would be the best thing. When she had first begun to be seen with Homer Barron, we had said, "She will marry him." Then we said, "She will persuade him yet," because Homer himself had remarked—he liked men, and it was known that he drank with the younger men in the Elks' Club—that he was not a marrying man. Later we said, "Poor Emily" behind the jalousies as they passed on Sunday afternoon in the glittering buggy, Miss Emily with her head high and Homer Barron with his hat cocked and a cigar in his teeth, reins and whip in a yellow glove.

Then some of the ladies began to say that it was a disgrace to the town and a bad example to the young people. The men did not want to interfere, but at last the ladies forced the Baptist minister—Miss Emily's people were Episcopal—to call upon her. He would never divulge what happened during that interview, but he refused to go back again. The next Sunday they again drove about the streets, and the following day the minister's wife wrote to Miss Emily's relations in Alabama.

45   So she had blood-kin under her roof again and we sat back to watch developments. At first nothing happened. Then we were sure that they were

to be married. We learned that Miss Emily had been to the jeweler's and ordered a man's toilet set in silver, with the letters H. B. on each piece. Two days later we learned that she had bought a complete outfit of men's clothing, including a nightshirt, and we said, "They are married." We were really glad. We were glad because the two female cousins were even more Grierson than Miss Emily had ever been.

So we were not surprised when Homer Barron—the streets had been finished some time since—was gone. We were a little disappointed that there was not a public blowing-off, but we believed that he had gone on to prepare for Miss Emily's coming, or to give her a chance to get rid of the cousins. (By that time it was a cabal, and we were all Miss Emily's allies to help circumvent the cousins.) Sure enough, after another week they departed. And, as we had expected all along, within three days Homer Barron was back in town. A neighbor saw the Negro man admit him at the kitchen door at dusk one evening.

And that was the last we saw of Homer Barron. And of Miss Emily for some time. The Negro man went in and out with the market basket, but the front door remained closed. Now and then we would see her at a window for a moment, as the men did that night when they sprinkled the lime, but for almost six months she did not appear on the streets. Then we knew that this was to be expected too; as if that quality of her father which had thwarted her woman's life so many times had been too virulent and too furious to die.

When we next saw Miss Emily, she had grown fat and her hair was turning gray. During the next few years it grew grayer and grayer until it attained an even pepper-and-salt iron-gray, when it ceased turning. Up to the day of her death at seventy-four it was still that vigorous iron-gray, like the hair of an active man.

From that time on her front door remained closed, save for a period of six or seven years, when she was about forty, during which she gave lessons in china-painting. She fitted up a studio in one of the downstairs rooms, where the daughters and granddaughters of Colonel Sartoris' contemporaries were sent to her with the same regularity and in the same spirit that they were sent to church on Sundays with a twenty-five-cent piece for the collection plate. Meanwhile her taxes had been remitted.

50   Then the newer generation became the backbone and the spirit of the town, and the painting pupils grew up and fell away and did not send their children to her with boxes of color and tedious brushes and pictures cut from the ladies' magazines. The front door closed upon the last one and remained closed for good. When the town got free postal delivery, Miss Emily alone refused to let them fasten the metal numbers above her door and attach a mailbox to it. She would not listen to them.

Daily, monthly, yearly we watched the Negro grow grayer and more stooped, going in and out with the market basket. Each December we sent her a tax notice, which would be returned by the post office a week later, unclaimed. Now and then we would see her in one of the downstairs windows—she had evidently shut up the top floor of the house—like the carven torso of an idol in a niche, looking or not looking at us, we could never tell which. Thus she passed from generation to generation—dear, inescapable, impervious, tranquil, and perverse.

And so she died. Fell ill in the house filled with dust and shadows, with only a doddering Negro man to wait on her. We did not even know she was sick; we had long since given up trying to get any information from the Negro. He talked to no one, probably not even to her, for his voice had grown harsh and rusty, as if from disuse.

She died in one of the downstairs rooms, in a heavy walnut bed with a curtain, her gray head propped on a pillow yellow and moldy with age and lack of sunlight.

V

The Negro met the first of the ladies at the front door and let them in, with their hushed, sibilant voices and their quick, curious glances, and then he disappeared. He walked right through the house and out the back and was not seen again.

55   The two female cousins came at once. They held the funeral on the second day, with the town coming to look at Miss Emily beneath a mass of bought flowers, with the crayon face of her father musing profoundly above the bier and the ladies sibilant and macabre; and the very old men—some in their brushed Confederate uniforms—on the porch and the lawn, talking of Miss Emily as if she had been a contemporary of theirs, believing that they had danced with her and courted her perhaps, confusing time with its mathematical progression, as the old do, to whom all the past is not a diminishing road but, instead, a huge meadow which no winter ever quite touches, divided from them now by the narrow bottle-neck of the most recent decade of years.

Already we knew that there was one room in that region above stairs which no one had seen in forty years, and which would have to be forced. They waited until Miss Emily was decently in the ground before they opened it.

The violence of breaking down the door seemed to fill this room with pervading dust. A thin, acrid pall as of the tomb seemed to lie everywhere upon this room decked and furnished as for a bridal: upon the valance curtains of faded rose color, upon the rose-shaded lights, upon the dressing table, upon the delicate array of crystal and the man's toilet things backed with tarnished silver, silver so tarnished that the monogram was obscured. Among them lay collar and tie, as if they had just been removed, which, lifted, left upon the surface a pale crescent in the dust. Upon a chair hung the suit, carefully folded; beneath it the two mute shoes and the discarded socks.

The man himself lay in the bed.

For a long while we just stood there, looking down at the profound and fleshless grin. The body had apparently once lain in the attitude of an embrace, but now the long sleep that outlasts love, that conquers even the grimace of love, had cuckolded him. What was left of him, rotted beneath what was left of the nightshirt, had become inextricable from the bed in which he lay; and upon him and upon the pillow beside him lay that even coating of the patient and biding dust.

60   Then we noticed that in the second pillow was the indentation of a head. One of us lifted something from it, and leaning forward, that faint and invisible dust dry and acrid in the nostrils, we saw a long strand of iron-gray hair.

READING AND REACTING

1. Arrange these events in the sequence in which they actually occur: Homer's arrival in town, the aldermen's visit, Emily's purchase of poison, Colonel Sartoris's decision to remit Emily's taxes, the development of the odour around Emily's house, Emily's father's death, the arrival of Emily's relatives, Homer's disappearance. Then, list the events in the sequence in which they are presented in the story. Why do you suppose Faulkner presents these events out of their actual chronological order?

2. Despite the story's confusing sequence, many events are foreshadowed. Give some examples of this technique. How does foreshadowing enrich the story?

3. Where does the exposition end and the movement toward the story's climax begin? Where does the resolution stage begin?

4. Emily is clearly the story's protagonist. In the sense that he opposes her wishes, Homer is the antagonist. What other characters—or what larger forces—are in conflict with Emily?

5. Explain how each of these phrases moves the story's plot along: "So she vanquished them, horse and foot . . ." (15); "After a week or two the smell went away" (24); "And that was the last we saw of Homer Barron" (47); "And so she died" (52); "The man himself lay in the bed" (58).

6. The narrator of the story is an observer, not a participant. Who might this narrator be? How do you suppose the narrator might know so much about Emily? Why do you think the narrator uses *we* instead of *I*?

7. Some critics have suggested that Miss Emily Grierson is a kind of symbol of the Old South, the last defender of its outdated ideas of chivalry, formal manners, and tradition. Do you think this inter-pretation is justified? Would you characterize Miss Emily as a champion or a victim of the values her town tries to preserve?

8. **JOURNAL ENTRY** When asked at a seminar at the University of Virginia about the meaning of the title "A Rose for Emily," Faulkner replied, "Oh, it's simply the poor woman had no life at all. Her father had kept her more or less locked up and then she had a lover who was about to quit her, she had to murder him. It was just 'A Rose for Emily'—that's all." In another interview,

asked the same question, he replied, "I pitied her and this was a salute, just as if you were to make a gesture, a salute, to anyone; to a woman you would hand a rose, as you would lift a cup of *sake* to a man." What do you make of Faulkner's responses? Can you offer other possible interpretations of the title's significance?

9. **CRITICAL PERSPECTIVE** In his essay "William Faulkner: An American Dickens," literary critic Leslie A. Fiedler characterizes Faulkner as "primarily . . . a sentimental writer; not a writer with the occasional vice of sentimentality, but one whose basic mode of experience is sentimental." He continues, "In a writer whose very method is self-indulgence, that sentimentality becomes sometimes downright embarrassing." Fiedler also notes Faulkner's "excesses of maudlin feelings and absurd indulgences in overripe rhetoric."

Do you think these criticisms apply to "A Rose for Emily"? If so, does the "vice of sentimentality" diminish the story, or do you agree with Fiedler—who calls Faulkner a "supereminently good 'bad' writer"—that the author is able to surmount these excesses?

Related Works: "Her First Ball" (p. 129), "Boys and Girls" (p. 504), "Porphyria's Lover" (p. 640), *Trifles* (p. 948)

◆ **MAVIS GALLANT** (1922–   ) was born in Montreal. She attended seventeen different schools in Canada and the United States and moved to Paris in 1950, where she has resided since. She has published two novels, *Green Water, Green Sky* (1959) and *A Fairly Good Time* (1970). Her short stories are often published in *The New Yorker,* and Gallant has several collections of short stories to her credit, including *The Other Paris* (1956); *The End of the World and Other Stories* (1973); *Home Truths: Selected Canadian Stories* (1981), which won a Governor General's Award; and the highly acclaimed *The Selected Stories* (1996). She has published over 100 stories, and many deal with the problems of lonely children and expatriates. She has written drama (*What Is To Be Done?* premiered by Tarragon Theatre in 1982) and many works of nonfiction. Gallant was made a Companion of the Order of Canada in 1993.

◊ ◊ ◊

MAVIS GALLANT

The Ice Wagon Going Down the Street
(1964)

Now that they are out of world affairs and back where they started, Peter Frazier's wife says, "Everybody else did well in the international thing except us."

"You have to be crooked," he tells her.

"Or smart. Pity we weren't."

It is Sunday morning. They sit in the kitchen, drinking their coffee, slowly, remembering the past. They say the names of people as if they were magic. Peter thinks, *Agnes Brusen*, but there are hundreds of other names. As a private married joke, Peter and Sheilah wear the silk dressing gowns they bought in Hong Kong. Each thinks the other a peacock, rather splendid, but they pretend the dressing gowns are silly and worn in fun.

5   Peter and Sheilah and their two daughters, Sandra and Jennifer, are visiting Peter's unmarried sister, Lucille. They have been Lucille's guests seventeen weeks, ever since they returned to Toronto from the Far East. Their big old steamer trunk blocks a corner of the kitchen, making a problem of the refrigerator door; but even Lucille says the trunk may as well stay where it is, for the present. The Fraziers' future is so unsettled; everything is still in the air.

Lucille has given her bedroom to her two nieces, and sleeps on a camp cot in the hall. The parents have the living-room divan. They have no privileges here; they sleep after Lucille has seen the last television show that interests her. In the hall closet their clothes are crushed by winter overcoats. They know they are being judged for the first time. Sandra and Jennifer are waiting for Sheilah and Peter to decide. They are waiting to learn where these exotic parents will fly to next. What sort of climate will Sheilah consider? What job will Peter consent to accept? When the parents are ready, the children will make a decision of their own. It is just possible that Sandra and Jennifer will choose to stay with their aunt.

The peacock parents are watched by wrens. Lucille and her nieces are much the same—sandy-colored, proudly plain. Neither of the girls has the father's insouciance or the mother's appearance—her height, her carriage, her thick hair, and sky-blue eyes. The children are more cautious than their parents; more Canadian. When they saw their aunt's apartment they had been away from Canada nine years, ever since they were two and four; and Jennifer, the elder, said, "Well, now we're home." Her voice is nasal and flat. Where did she learn that voice? And why should this be home? Peter's answer to anything about his mystifying children is, "It must be in the blood."

On Sunday morning Lucille takes her nieces to church. It seems to be the only condition she imposes on her relations: the children must be decent. The girls go willingly, with their new hats and purses and gloves and coral bracelets and strings of pearls. The parents, ramshackle, sleepy, dim in the brain because it is Sunday, sit down to their coffee and privacy and talk of the past.

"We weren't crooked," says Peter. "We weren't even smart."

10   Sheilah's head bobs up; she is no drowner. It is wrong to say they have nothing to show for time. Sheilah has the Balenciaga.[1] It is a black afternoon

---

[1] A dress designed by Spanish couturier Cristobal Balenciaga. His creations were noted for their elegance.

dress, stiff and boned at the waist, long for the fashions of now, but neither Sheilah nor Peter would change a thread. The Balenciaga is their talisman, their treasure; and after they remember it they touch hands and think that the years are not behind them but hazy and marvelous and still to be lived.

The first place they went to was Paris. In the early 'fifties the pick of the international jobs was there. Peter had inherited the last scrap of money he knew he was ever likely to see, and it was enough to get them over: Sheilah and Peter and the babies and the steamer trunk. To their joy and astonishment they had money in the bank. They said to each other, "It should last a year." Peter was fastidious about the new job; he hadn't come all this distance to accept just anything. In Paris he met Hugh Taylor, who was earning enough smuggling gasoline to keep his wife in Paris and a girl in Rome. That impressed Peter, because he remembered Taylor as a sour scholarship student without the slightest talent for life. Taylor had a job, of course. He hadn't said to himself, I'll go over to Europe and smuggle gasoline. It gave Peter an idea; he saw the shape of things. First you catch your fish. Later, at an international party, he met Johnny Hertzberg, who told him Germany was the place. Hertzberg said that anyone who came out of Germany broke now was too stupid to be here, and deserved to be back home at a desk. Peter nodded, as if he had already thought of that. He began to think about Germany. Paris was fine for a holiday, but it had been picked clean. Yes, Germany. His money was running low. He thought about Germany quite a lot.

That winter was moist and delicate; so fragile that they daren't speak of it now. There seemed to be plenty of everything and plenty of time. They were living the dream of a marriage, the fabric uncut, nothing slashed or spoiled. All winter they spent their money, and went to parties, and talked about Peter's future job. It lasted four months. They spent their money, lived in the future, and were never as happy again.

After four months they were suddenly moved away from Paris, but not to Germany—to Geneva. Peter thinks it was because of the incident at the Trudeau wedding at the Ritz. Paul Trudeau was a French-Canadian Peter had known at school and in the Navy. Trudeau had turned into a snob, proud of his career and his Paris connections. He tried to make the difference felt, but Peter thought the difference was only for strangers. At the wedding reception Peter lay down on the floor and said he was dead. He held a white azalea in a brass pot on his chest, and sang, "Oh, hear us when we cry to Thee for those in peril on the sea." Sheilah bent over him and said, "Peter, darling, get up. Pete, listen, every single person who can do something for you is in this room. If you love me, you'll get up."

"I do love you," he said, ready to engage in a serious conversation. "She's so beautiful," he told a second face. "She's nearly as tall as I am. She was a model in London. I met her over in London in the war. I met her there in the war." He lay on his back with the azalea on his chest, explaining their history. A waiter took the brass pot away, and after Peter had been hauled to his feet he knocked the waiter down. Trudeau's bride, who was freshly out of an Ursuline convent, became hysterical; and even though Paul Trudeau and Peter were old acquaintances, Trudeau never spoke to him again. Peter says now that French-Canadians always have that bit of spite. He says Trudeau asked the Embassy to interfere. Luckily, back home there were still a few people to whom the name "Frazier" meant something, and it was to these people that Peter appealed. He wrote letters saying that a French-Canadian combine was preventing his getting a decent job, and could anything be done? No one answered directly, but it was clear that what they settled for was exile to Geneva: a season of meditation and remorse, as he explained to Sheilah, and it was managed tactfully, through Lucille. Lucille wrote that a friend of hers, May Fergus, now a secretary in Geneva, had heard about a job. The job was filing pictures in the information service of an international agency in the Palais des Nations. The pay was so-so, but Lucille thought Peter must be getting fed up doing nothing.

15   Peter often asks his sister now who put her up to it—what important person told her to write that letter suggesting Peter go to Geneva?

"Nobody," says Lucille. "I mean, nobody in the way *you* mean. I really did have this girl friend working there, and I knew you must be running through your money pretty fast in Paris."

"It must have been somebody pretty high up," Peter says. He looks at his sister admiringly, as he has often looked at his wife.

Peter's wife had loved him in Paris. Whatever she wanted in marriage she found that winter, there. In Geneva, where Peter was a file clerk and they lived in a furnished flat, she pretended they were in Paris and life was still the same. Often, when the children were at supper, she changed as though she and Peter were dining out. She wore the Balenciaga, and put candles on the card table where she and Peter ate their meal. The neckline of the dress was soiled with make-up. Peter remembers her dabbing on the make-up with a wet sponge. He remembers her in the kitchen, in the soiled Balenciaga, patting on the make-up with a filthy sponge. Behind her, at the kitchen table, Sandra and Jennifer, in buttonless pajamas and bunny slippers, ate their supper of marmalade sandwiches and milk. When the children were asleep, the parents dined solemnly, ritually, Sheilah sitting straight as a queen.

It was a mysterious period of exile, and he had to wait for signs, or signals, to know when he was free to leave. He never saw the job any other way. He forgot he had applied for it. He thought he had been sent to Geneva because of a misdemeanor and had to wait to be released. Nobody pressed him at work. His immediate boss had resigned, and he was alone for months in a room with two desks. He read the *Herald-Tribune,* and tried to discover how things were here—how the others ran their lives on the pay they were officially getting. But it was a closed conspiracy. He was not dealing with adventurers now but civil servants waiting for pension day. No one ever answered his questions. They pretended to think his questions were a form of wit. His only solace in exile was the few happy weekends he had in the late spring and early summer. He had met another old acquaintance, Mike Burleigh. Mike was a serious liberal who had married a serious heiress. The Burleighs had two guest lists. The first was composed of stuffy people they felt obliged to entertain, while the second was made up of their real friends, the friends they wanted. The real friends strove hard to become stuffy and dull and thus achieve the first guest list, but few succeeded. Peter went on the first list straight away. Possibly Mike didn't understand, at the beginning, why Peter was pretending to be a file clerk. Peter had such an air—he might have been sent by a universal inspector to see how things in Geneva were being run.

20   Every Friday in May and June and part of July, the Fraziers rented a sky-blue Fiat and drove forty miles east of Geneva to the Burleighs' summer house. They brought the children, a suitcase, the children's tattered picture books, and a token bottle of gin. This, in memory, is a period of water and water birds; swans, roses, and singing birds. The children were small and still belonged to them. If they remember too much, their mouths water, their stomachs hurt. Peter says, "It was fine while it lasted." Enough. While it lasted Sheilah and Madge Burleigh were close. They abandoned their husbands and spent long summer afternoons comparing their mothers and praising each other's skin and hair. To Madge, and not to Peter, Sheilah opened her Liverpool childhood with the words "rat poor." Peter heard about it later, from Mike. The women's friendship seemed to Peter a bad beginning. He trusted women but not with each other. It lasted ten weeks. One Sunday, Madge said she needed the two bedrooms the Fraziers usually occupied for a party of sociologists from Pakistan; and that was the end. In November, the Fraziers heard that the summer house had been closed, and that the Burleighs were in Geneva, in their winter flat; they gave no sign. There was no help for it, and no appeal.

Now Peter began firing letters to anyone who had ever known his late father. He was living in a mild yellow autumn. Why does he remember the streets of the city dark, and the windows everywhere black with rain? He remembers being with Sheilah and the children as if they clung together while just outside their small shelter it rained and rained. The children slept in the bedroom of the flat because the window gave on the street and they could breathe air. Peter and Sheilah had the living-room couch. Their window was not a real window but a square on a well of cement. The flat seemed damp as a cave. Peter remembers steam in the kitchen, pools under the sink, sweat on the pipes. Water streamed on him from the children's clothes, washed and dripping overhead. The trunk, upended in the children's room, was not quite unpacked. Sheilah had not signed her name to this life; she had not given in. Once Peter heard her drop her aitches. "You kids are lucky," she said to the girls. "I never 'ad so much as a sit-down meal. I ate chips out of a paper or I 'ad a butty[2] out on the stairs." He never asked her what a butty was. He thinks it means bread and cheese.

---

[2] Slang for "sandwich," especially in Liverpool; e.g., a jam butty.

The day he heard "You kids are lucky" he understood they were becoming in fact something they had only *appeared* to be until now—the shabby civil servant and his brood. If he had been European he would have ridden to work on a bicycle, in the uniform of his class and condition. He would have worn a tight coat, a turned collar, and a dirty tie. He wondered then if coming here had been a mistake, and if he should not, after all, still be in a place where his name meant something. Surely Peter Frazier should live where "Frazier" counts? In Ontario even now when he says "Frazier" an absent look comes over his hearer's face, as if its owner were consulting an interior guide. What is Frazier? What does it mean? Oil? Power? Politics? Wheat? Real estate? The creditors had the house sealed when Peter's father died. His aunt collapsed with a heart attack in somebody's bachelor apartment, leaving three sons and a widower to surmise they had never known her. Her will was a disappointment. None of that generation left enough. One made it: the granite Presbyterian immigrants from Scotland. Their children, a generation of daunted women and maiden men, held still. Peter's father's crowd spent: they were not afraid of their fathers, and their grandfathers were old. Peter and his sister and his cousins lived on the remains. They were left the rinds of income, of notions, and the memories of ideas rather than ideas intact. If Peter can choose his reincarnation, let him be the oppressed son of a Scottish parson. Let Peter grow up on cuffs and iron principles. Let him make the fortune! Let him flee the manse! When he was small his patrimony was squandered under his nose. He remembers people dancing in his father's house. He remembers seeing and nearly understanding adultery in a guest room, among a pile of wraps. He thought he had seen a murder; he never told. He remembers licking glasses wherever he found them—on window sills, on stairs, in the pantry. In his room he listened while Lucille read Beatrix Potter. The bad rabbit stole the carrot from the good rabbit without saying please, and downstairs was the noise of the party—the roar of the crouched lion. When his father died he saw the chairs upside down and the bailiff's chalk marks. Then the doors were sealed.

He has often tried to tell Sheilah why he cannot be defeated. He remembers his father saying, "Nothing can touch us," and Peter believed it and still does. It has prevented his taking his troubles too seriously. "Nothing can be as bad as this," he will tell himself. "It is happening to me." Even in Geneva, where his status was file clerk, where he sank and stopped on the level of the men who never emigrated, the men on the bicycles—even there he had a manner of strolling to work as if his office were a pastime, and his real life a secret so splendid he could share it with no one except himself.

In Geneva Peter worked for a woman—a girl. She was a Norwegian from a small town in Saskatchewan. He supposed they had been put together because they were Canadians; but they were as strange to each other as if "Canadian" meant any number of things, or had no real meaning. Soon after Agnes Brusen came to the office she hung her framed university degree on the wall. It was one of the gritty, prideful gestures that stand for push, toil, and family sacrifice. He thought, then, that she must be one of a family of immigrants for whom education is everything. Hugh Taylor had told him that in some families the older children never marry until the youngest have finished school. Sometimes every second child is sacrificed and made to work for the education of the next born. Those who finish college spend years paying back. They are white-hot Protestants, and they live with a load of work and debt and obligation. Peter placed his new colleague on scraps of information. He had never been in the West.

25   She came to the office on a Monday morning in October. The office was overheated and painted cream. It contained two desks, the filing cabinets, a map of the world as it had been in 1945, and the Charter of the United Nations left behind by Agnes Brusen's predecessor. (She took down the Charter without asking Peter if he minded, with the impudence of gesture you find in women who wouldn't say boo to a goose; and then she hung her college degree on the nail where the Charter had been.) Three people brought her in—a whole committee. One of them said, "Agnes, this is Pete Frazier. Pete, Agnes Brusen. Pete's Canadian, too, Agnes. He knows all about the office, so ask him anything."

Of course he knew all about the office: he knew the exact spot where the cord of the venetian blind was frayed, obliging one to give an extra tug to the right.

The girl might have been twenty-three: no more. She wore a brown tweed suit with bone buttons, and a new silk scarf and new shoes. She clutched an unscratched brown purse. She seemed dressed in going-away presents. She said, "Oh, I never smoke," with a convulsive movement of her hand, when Peter offered his case. He was courteous, hiding his disappointment. The people he worked with had told him a Scandinavian girl was arriving, and he had expected a stunner. Agnes was a mole: she was small and brown, and round-shouldered as if she had always carried parcels or younger children in her arms. A mole's profile was turned when she said goodbye to her committee. If she had been foreign, ill-favored though she was, he might have flirted a little, just to show that he was friendly; but their being Canadian, and suddenly left together, was a sexual damper. He sat down and lit his own cigarette. She smiled at him, questioningly, he thought, and sat as if she had never seen a chair before. He wondered if his smoking was annoying her. He wondered if she was fidgety about drafts, or allergic to anything, and whether she would want the blind up or down. His social compass was out of order because the others couldn't tell Peter and Agnes apart. There was a world of difference between them, yet it was she who had been brought in to sit at the larger of the two desks.

While he was thinking this she got up and walked around the office, almost on tiptoe, opening the doors of closets and pulling out the filing trays. She looked inside everything except the drawers of Peter's desk. (In any case, Peter's desk was locked. His desk is locked wherever he works. In Geneva he went into Personnel one morning, early, and pinched his application form. He had stated on the form that he had seven years' experience in public relations and could speak French, German, Spanish, and Italian. He has always collected anything important about himself—anything useful. But he can never get on with the final act, which is getting rid of the information. He has kept papers about for years, a constant source of worry.)

"I know this looks funny, Mr. Ferris," said the girl. "I'm not really snooping or anything. I just can't feel easy in a new place unless I know where everything is. In a new place everything seems so hidden."

30   If she had called him "Ferris" and pretended not to know he was Frazier, it could only be because they had sent her here to spy on him and see if he had repented and was fit for a better place in life. "You'll be all right here," he said. "Nothing's hidden. Most of us haven't got brains enough to have secrets. This is Rainbow Valley." Depressed by the thought that they were having him watched now, he passed his hand over his hair and looked outside to the lawn and the parking lot and the peacocks someone gave the Palais des Nations years ago. The peacocks love no one. They wander about the parked cars looking elderly, bad-tempered, mournful, and lost.

Agnes had settled down again. She folded her silk scarf and placed it just so, with her gloves beside it. She opened her new purse and took out a notebook and a shiny gold pencil. She may have written

> Duster for desk
> Kleenex
> Glass jar for flowers
> Air-Wick because he smokes
> Paper for lining drawers

because the next day she brought each of these articles to work. She also brought a large black Bible, which she unwrapped lovingly and placed on the left-hand corner of her desk. The flower vase—empty—stood in the middle, and the Kleenex made a counterpoise for the Bible on the right.

When he saw the Bible he knew she had not been sent to spy on his work. The conspiracy was deeper. She might have been dispatched by ghosts. He knew everything about her, all in a moment: he saw the ambition, the terror, the dry pride. She was the true heir of the men from Scotland; she was at the start. She had been sent to tell him, "You can begin, but not begin again." She never opened the Bible, but she dusted it as she dusted her desk, her chair, and any surface the cleaning staff had overlooked. And Peter, the first days, watching her timid movements, her insignificant little face, felt, as you feel the approach of a storm, the charge of moral certainty round her, the belief in work, the faith in undertakings, the bread of the Black Sunday. He recognized and tasted all of it: ashes in the mouth.

After five days their working relations were settled. Of course, there was the Bible and all that went with it, but his tongue had never held the taste of ashes long. She was an inferior girl of poor quality. She had nothing in her favor except the degree on the wall. In the real world, he would not have invited her to his house except to mind the children. That was what he said to Sheilah. He said that Agnes was a mole, and a virgin, and that her tics and mannerisms were sending him round the bend. She had an infuriating habit of covering her mouth when she talked. Even at the telephone she put up her hand as if afraid of losing anything, even a word. Her voice was nasal and flat. She had two working costumes, both dull as the wall. One was the brown suit, the other a navy-blue dress with changeable collars. She dressed for no one; she dressed for her desk, her jar of flowers, her Bible, and her box of Kleenex. One day she crossed the space between the two desks and stood over Peter, who was reading a newspaper. She could have spoken to him from her desk, but she may have felt that being on her feet gave her authority. She had plenty of courage, but authority was something else.

"I thought—I mean, they told me you were the person . . ." She got on with it bravely: "If you don't want to do the filing or any work, all right, Mr. Frazier. I'm not saying anything about that. You might have poor health or your personal reasons. But it's got to be done, so if you'll kindly show me about the filing I'll do it. I've worked in Information before, but it was a different office, and every office is different."

35 "My dear girl," said Peter. He pushed back his chair and looked at her, astonished. "You've been sitting there fretting, worrying. How insensitive of me. How trying for you. Usually I file on the last Wednesday of the month, so you see, you just haven't been around long enough to see a last Wednesday. Not another word, please. And let us not waste another minute." He emptied the heaped baskets of photographs so swiftly, pushing "Iran—Smallpox Control" into "Irish Red Cross" (close enough), that the girl looked frightened, as if she had raised a whirlwind. She said slowly, "If you'll only show me, Mr. Frazier, instead of doing it so fast, I'll gladly look after it, because you might want to be doing other things, and I feel the filing should be done every day." But Peter was too busy to answer, and so she sat down, holding the edge of her desk.

"There," he said, beaming. "All done." His smile, his sunburst, was wasted, for the girl was staring round the room as if she feared she had not inspected everything the first day after all; some drawer, some cupboard, hid a monster. That evening Peter unlocked one of the drawers of his desk and took away the application form he had stolen from Personnel. The girl had not finished her search.

"How could you *not* know?" wailed Sheilah. "You sit looking at her every day. You must talk about *something*. She must have told you."

"She did tell me," said Peter, "and I've just told you."

It was this: Agnes Brusen was on the Burleighs' guest list. How had the Burleighs met her? What did they see in her? Peter could not reply. He knew that Agnes lived in a bed-sitting room with a Swiss family and had her meals with them. She had been in Geneva three months, but no one had ever seen her outside the office. "You *should* know," said Sheilah. "She must have something, more than you can see. Is she pretty? Is she brilliant? What is it?"

40   "We don't really talk," Peter said. They talked in a way: Peter teased her and she took no notice. Agnes was not a sulker. She had taken her defeat like a sport. She did her work and a good deal of his. She sat behind her Bible, her flowers, and her Kleenex, and answered when Peter spoke. That was how he learned about the Burleighs—just by teasing and being bored. It was a January afternoon. He said, "*Miss* Brusen. Talk to me. Tell me everything. Pretend we have perfect rapport. Do you like Geneva?"

"It's a nice clean town," she said. He can see to this day the red and blue anemones in the glass jar, and her bent head, and her small untended hands.

"Are you learning beautiful French with your Swiss family?"

"They speak English."

"Why don't you take an apartment of your own?" he said. Peter was not usually impertinent. He was bored. "You'd be independent then."

45   "I am independent," she said. "I earn my living. I don't think it proves anything if you live by yourself. Mrs. Burleigh wants me to live alone too. She's looking for something for me. It mustn't be dear. I send money home."

Here was the extraordinary thing about Agnes Brusen: she refused the use of Christian names and never spoke to Peter unless he spoke first, but she would tell anything, as if to say, "Don't waste time fishing. Here it is."

He learned all in one minute that she sent her salary home, and that she was a friend of the Burleighs. The first he had expected; the second knocked him flat.

"She's got to come to dinner," Sheilah said. "We should have had her right from the beginning. If only I'd known! But *you* were the one. You said she looked like—oh, I don't even remember. A Norwegian mole."

She came to dinner one Saturday night in January, in her navy-blue dress, to which she had pinned an organdy gardenia. She sat upright on the edge of the sofa. Sheilah had ordered the meal from a restaurant. There was lobster, good wine, and a *pièce-montée*[3] full of kirsch and cream. Agnes refused the lobster; she had never eaten anything from the sea unless it had been sterilized and tinned, and said so. She was afraid of skin poisoning. Someone in her family had skin poisoning after having eaten oysters. She touched her cheeks and neck to show where the poisoning had erupted. She sniffed her wine and put the glass down without tasting it. She could not eat the cake because of the alcohol it contained. She ate an egg, bread and butter, a sliced tomato and drank a glass of ginger ale. She seemed unaware she was creating disaster and pain. She did not help clear away the dinner plates. She sat, adequately nourished, decently dressed, and waited to learn why she had been invited here—that was the feeling Peter had. He folded

---

[3] Show-piece.

the card table on which they had dined, and opened the window to air the room.

50   "It's not the same cold as Canada, but you feel it more," he said, for something to say.

"Your blood has gotten thin," said Agnes.

Sheilah returned from the kitchen and let herself fall into an armchair. With her eyes closed she held out her hand for a cigarette. She was performing the haughty-lady act that was a family joke. She flung her head back and looked at Agnes through half-closed lids; then she suddenly brought her head forward, widening her eyes.

"Are you skiing madly?" she said.

"Well, in the first place there hasn't been any snow," said Agnes. "So nobody's doing any skiing so far as I know. All I hear is people complaining because there's no snow. Personally, I don't ski. There isn't much skiing in the part of Canada I come from. Besides, my family never had that kind of leisure."

55   "Heavens," said Sheilah, as if her family had every kind.

I'll bet they had, thought Peter. On the dole.

Sheilah was wasting her act. He had a suspicion that Agnes knew it was an act but did not know it was also a joke. If so, it made Sheilah seem a fool, and he loved Sheilah too much to enjoy it.

"The Burleighs have been wonderful to me," said Agnes. She seemed to have divined why she was here, and decided to give them all the information they wanted, so that she could put on her coat and go home to bed. "They had me out to their place on the lake every weekend until the weather got cold and they moved back to town. They've rented a chalet for the winter, and they want me to come there, too. But I don't know if I will or not. I don't ski, and, oh, I don't know—I don't drink, either, and I don't always see the point. Their friends are too rich and I'm too Canadian."

She had delivered everything Sheilah wanted and more: Agnes was on the first guest list and didn't care. No, Peter corrected; doesn't know. Doesn't care and doesn't know.

60   "I thought with you Norwegians it was in the blood, skiing. And drinking," Sheilah murmured.

"Drinking, maybe," said Agnes. She covered her mouth and said behind her spread fingers, "In our family we were religious. We didn't drink or smoke. My brother was in Norway in the war. He saw some cousins. Oh," she said, unexpectedly loud, "Harry said it was just terrible. They were so poor. They had flies in their kitchen. They gave him something to eat a fly had been on. They didn't have a real toilet, and they'd been in the same house about two hundred years. We've only recently built our own home, and we have a bathroom and two toilets. I'm from Saskatchewan," she said. "I'm not from any other place."

Surely one winter here had been punishment enough? In the spring they would remember him and free him. He wrote Lucille, who said he was lucky to have a job at all. The Burleighs had sent the Fraziers a second-guest list Christmas card. It showed a Moslem refugee child weeping outside a tent. They treasured the card and left it standing long after the others had been given the children to cut up. Peter had discovered by now what had gone wrong in the friendship—Sheilah had charged a skirt at a dressmaker to Madge's account. Madge had told her she might, and then changed her mind. Poor Sheilah! She was new to this part of it—to the changing humors of independent friends. Paris was already a year in the past. At Mardi Gras the Burleighs gave their annual party. They invited everyone, the damned and the dropped, with the prodigality of a child at prayers. The invitation said "in costume," but the Fraziers were too happy to wear a disguise. They might not be recognized. Like many of the guests they expected to meet at the party, they had been disgraced, forgotten, and rehabilitated. They would be anxious to see one another as they were.

On the night of the party, the Fraziers rented a car they had never seen before and drove through the first snowstorm of the year. Peter had not driven since last summer's blissful trips in the Fiat. He could not find the switch for the windshield wiper in this car. He leaned over the wheel. "Can you see on your side?" he asked. "Can I make a left turn here? Does it look like a one-way?"

"I can't imagine why you took a car with a right-hand drive," said Sheilah.

65   He had trouble finding a place to park; they crawled up and down unknown streets whose curbs were packed with snow-covered cars. When they stood at last on the pavement, safe and sound, Peter said, "This is the first snow."

"I can see that," said Sheilah. "Hurry, darling. My hair."

"It's the first snow."

"You're repeating yourself," she said. "Please hurry, darling. Think of my poor shoes. My *hair*."

She was born in an ugly city, and so was Peter, but they have this difference: she does not know the importance of the first snow—the first clean thing in a dirty year. He would have told her then that this storm, which was wetting her feet and destroying her hair, was like the first day of the English spring, but she made a frightened gesture, trying to shield her head. The gesture told him he did not understand her beauty.

70   "Let me," she said. He was fumbling with the key, trying to lock the car. She took the key without impatience and locked the door on the driver's side; and then, to show Peter she treasured him and was not afraid of wasting her life or her beauty, she took his arm and they walked in the snow down a street and around a corner to the apartment house where the

Burleighs lived. They were, and are, a united couple. They were afraid of the party, and each of them knew it. When they walk together, holding arms, they give each other whatever each can spare.

Only six people had arrived in costume. Madge Burleigh was disguised as Manet's "Lola de Valence,"[4] which everyone mistook for Carmen. Mike was an Impressionist painter, with a straw hat and a glued-on beard. "I am all of them," he said. He would rather have dressed as a dentist, he said, welcoming the Fraziers as if he had parted from them the day before, but Madge wanted him to look as if he had created her. "You know?" he said.

"Perfectly," said Sheilah. Her shoes were stained and the snow had softened her lacquered hair. She was not wasted; she was the most beautiful woman here.

About an hour after their arrival, Peter found himself with no one to talk to. He had told about the Trudeau wedding in Paris and the pot of azaleas, and after he mislaid his audience he began to look round for Sheilah. She was on a window seat, partly concealed by a green velvet curtain. Facing her, so that their profiles were neat and perfect against the night, was a man. Their conversation was private and enclosed, as if they had in minutes covered leagues of time and arrived at the place where everything was implied, understood. Peter began working his way across the room, toward his wife, when he saw Agnes. He was granted the sight of her drowning face. She had dressed with comic intention, obviously with care, and now she was a ragged hobo, half tramp, half clown. Her hair was tucked up under a bowler hat. The six costumed guests who had made the same mistake—the ghost, the gypsy, the Athenian maiden, the geisha, the Martian, and the apache—were delighted to find a seventh; but Agnes was not amused; she was gasping for life. When a waiter passed with a crowded tray, she took a glass without seeing it; then a wave of the party took her away.

Sheilah's new friend was named Simpson. After Simpson said he thought perhaps he'd better circulate, Peter sat down where he had been. "Now look, Sheilah," he began. Their most intimate conversations have taken place at parties. Once at a party she told him she was leaving him; she didn't, of course. Smiling, blue-eyed, she gazed lovingly at Peter and said rapidly, "Pete, shut up and listen. That man. The man you scared away. He's a big wheel in a company out in India or someplace like that. It's gorgeous out there. Pete, the *servants*. And it's warm. It never never snows. He says there's heaps of jobs. You pick them off the trees like . . . orchids. He says it's even easier now than when we owned all those places, because now the poor pets can't run anything and they'll pay *fortunes*. Pete, he says it's warm, it's heaven, and Pete, they pay."

---

[4] A painting by Edouard Manet (1832–83) of the Spanish dancer whom he and Baudelaire admired as being *"un bijou rose et noir."* "Carmen": entrancing but heartless Spanish *femme fatale*, the heroine of Bizet's renowned opera of the same name (1875).

75   A few minutes later, Peter was alone again and Sheilah part of a closed, laughing group. Holding her elbow was the man from the place where jobs grew like orchids. Peter edged into the group and laughed at a story he hadn't heard. He heard only the last line, which was, "Here comes another tunnel." Looking out from the tight laughing ring, he saw Agnes again, and he thought, I'd be like Agnes if I didn't have Sheilah. Agnes put her glass down on a table and lurched toward the doorway, head forward. Madge Burleigh, who never stopped moving around the room and smiling, was still smiling when she paused and said in Peter's ear, "Go with Agnes, Pete. See that she gets home. People will notice if Mike leaves."

"She probably just wants to walk around the block," said Peter. "She'll be back."

"Oh, stop thinking about yourself, for once, and see that that poor girl gets home," said Madge. "You've still got your Fiat, haven't you?"

He turned away as if he had been pushed. Any command is a release, in a way. He may not want to go in that particular direction, but at least he is going somewhere. And now Sheilah, who had moved inches nearer to hear what Madge and Peter were murmuring, said, "Yes, go, darling," as if he were leaving the gates of Troy.[5]

Peter was to find Agnes and see that she reached home: this he repeated to himself as he stood on the landing, outside the Burleighs' flat, ringing for the elevator. Bored with waiting for it, he ran down the stairs, four flights, and saw that Agnes had stalled the lift by leaving the door open. She was crouched on the floor, propped on her fingertips. Her eyes were closed.

80   "Agnes," said Peter. "*Miss* Brusen, I mean. That's no way to leave a party. Don't you know you're supposed to curtsey and say thanks? My God, Agnes, anybody going by here just now might have seen you! Come on, be a good girl. Time to go home."

She got up without his help and, moving between invisible crevasses, shut the elevator door. Then she left the building and Peter followed, remembering he was to see that she got home. They walked along the snowy pavement, Peter a few steps behind her. When she turned right for no reason, he turned, too. He had no clear idea where they were going. Perhaps she lived close by. He had forgotten where the hired car was parked, or what it looked like; he could not remember its make or its color. In any case, Sheilah had the key. Agnes walked on steadily, as if she knew their destination, and he thought, Agnes Brusen is drunk in the street in Geneva and dressed like a tramp. He wanted to say, "This is the best thing that ever happened to you, Agnes; it will help you understand how things are for some of the rest of us." But she stopped and turned and, leaning over a low hedge, retched on a frozen lawn. He held her clammy forehead and rested his hand on her arched back, on muscles as tight as a fist. She straightened up and drew a breath but the cold air made her cough. "Don't breathe too deeply," he said. "It's the worst thing you can do. Have you got a handkerchief?" He

---

[5] An allusion to the flight of the Trojans during the destruction of Troy by the Greeks.

passed his own handkerchief over her wet weeping face, upturned like the face of one of his little girls. "I'm out without a coat," he said, noticing it. "We're a pair."

"I never drink," said Agnes. "I'm just not used to it." Her voice was sweet and quiet. He had never seen her so peaceful, so composed. He thought she must surely be all right, now, and perhaps he might leave her here. The trust in her tilted face had perplexed him. He wanted to get back to Sheilah and have her explain something. He had forgotten what it was, but Sheilah would know. "Do you live around here?" he said. As he spoke, she let herself fall. He had wiped her face and now she trusted him to pick her up, set her on her feet, take her wherever she ought to be. He pulled her up and she stood, wordless, humble, as he brushed the snow from her tramp's clothes. Snow horizontally crossed the lamplight. The street was silent. Agnes had lost her hat. Snow, which he tasted, melted on her hands. His gesture of licking snow from her hands was formal as a handshake. He tasted snow on her hands and then they walked on.

"I never drink," she said. They stood on the edge of a broad avenue. The wrong turning now could lead them anywhere; it was the changeable avenue at the edge of towns that loses its houses and becomes a highway. She held his arm and spoke in a gentle voice. She said, "In our house we didn't smoke or drink. My mother was ambitious for me, more than for Harry and the others." She said, "I've never been alone before. When I was a kid I would get up in the summer before the others, and I'd see the ice wagon going down the street. I'm alone now. Mrs. Burleigh's found me an apartment. It's only one room. She likes it because it's in the old part of town. I don't like old houses. Old houses are dirty. You don't know who was there before."

"I should have a car somewhere," Peter said. "I'm not sure where we are."

85 He remembers that on this avenue they climbed into a taxi, but nothing about the drive. Perhaps he fell asleep. He does remember that when he paid the driver Agnes clutched his arm, trying to stop him. She pressed extra coins into the driver's palm. The driver was paid twice.

"I'll tell you one thing about us," said Peter. "We pay everything twice." This was part of a much longer theory concerning North American behavior, and it was not Peter's own. Mike Burleigh had held forth about it on summer afternoons.

Agnes pushed open a door between a stationer's shop and a grocery, and led the way up a narrow inside stair. They climbed one flight, frightening beetles. She had to search every pocket for the latchkey. She was shaking with cold. Her apartment seemed little warmer than the street. Without speaking to Peter she turned on all the lights. She looked inside the kitchen and the bathroom and then got down on her hands and knees and looked under the sofa. The room was neat and belonged to no one. She left him standing in this unclaimed room—she had forgotten him—and closed a door behind her. He looked for something to do—some useful action he could repeat to Madge. He turned on the electric radiator in the fireplace. Perhaps Agnes wouldn't thank him for it; perhaps she would rather undress in the cold. "I'll be on my way," he called to the bathroom door.

She had taken off the tramp's clothes and put on a dressing gown of orphanage wool. She came out of the bathroom and straight toward him. She pressed her face and rubbed her cheek on his shoulder as if hoping the contact would leave a scar. He saw her back and her profile and his own face in the mirror over the fireplace. He thought, This is how disasters happen. He saw floods of sea water moving with perfect punitive justice over reclaimed land; he saw lava covering vineyards and overtaking dogs and stragglers. A bridge over an abyss snapped in two and the long express train, suddenly V-shaped, floated like snow. He thought amiably of every kind of disaster and thought, This is how they occur.

Her eyes were closed. She said, "I shouldn't be over here. In my family we didn't drink or smoke. My mother wanted a lot from me, more than from Harry and the others." But he knew all that; he had known from the day of the Bible, and because once, at the beginning, she had made him afraid. He was not afraid of her now.

90   She said, "It's no use staying here, is it?"

"If you mean what I think, no."

"It wouldn't be better anywhere."

She let him see full on her blotched face. He was not expected to do anything. He was not required to pick her up when she fell or wipe her tears. She was poor quality, really—he remembered having thought that once. She left him and went quietly into the bathroom and locked the door. He heard taps running and supposed it was a hot bath. He was pretty certain there would be no more tears. He looked at his watch: Sheilah must be home, now, wondering what had become of him. He descended the beetles' staircase and for forty minutes crossed the city under a windless fall of snow.

The neighbor's child who had stayed with Peter's children was asleep on the living-room sofa. Peter woke her and sent her, sleepwalking, to her own door. He sat down, wet to the bone, thinking, I'll call the Burleighs. In half an hour I'll call the police. He heard a car stop and the engine running and a confusion of two voices laughing and calling goodnight. Presently Sheilah let herself in, rosy-faced, smiling. She carried his trenchcoat over her arm. She said, "How's Agnes?"

95   "Where were you?" he said. "Whose car was that?"

Sheilah had gone into the children's room. He heard her shutting their window. She returned, undoing her dress, and said, "Was Agnes all right?"

"Agnes is all right. Sheilah, this is about the worst . . ."

She stepped out of the Balenciaga and threw it over a chair. She stopped and looked at him and said, "Poor old Pete, are you in love with Agnes?" And then, as if the answer were of so little importance she hadn't time for it, she locked her arms around him and said, "My love, we're going to Ceylon."

Two days later, when Peter strolled into his office, Agnes was at her desk. She wore the blue dress, with a spotless collar. White and yellow freesias were symmetrically arranged in the glass jar. The room was hot, and the spring snow, glued for a second when it touched the window, blurred the view of parked cars.

100   "Quite a party," Peter said.

She did not look up. He sighed, sat down, and thought if the snow held he would be skiing at the Burleighs' very soon. Impressed by his kindness to Agnes, Madge had invited the family for the first possible weekend.

Presently Agnes said, "I'll never drink again or go to a house where people are drinking. And I'll never bother anyone the way I bothered you."

"You didn't bother me," he said. "I took you home. You were alone and it was late. It's normal."

"Normal for you, maybe, but I'm used to getting home by myself. Please never tell what happened."

105   He stared at her. He can still remember the freesias and the Bible and the heat in the room. She looked as if the elements had no power. She felt neither heat nor cold. "Nothing happened," he said.

"I behaved in a silly way. I had no right to. I led you to think I might do something wrong."

"*I* might have tried something," he said gallantly. "But that would be my fault and not yours."

She put her knuckle to her mouth and he could scarcely hear. "It was because of you. I was afraid you might be blamed, or else you'd blame yourself."

"There's no question of any blame," he said. "Nothing happened. We'd both had a lot to drink. Forget about it. Nothing *happened*. You'd remember if it had."

110   She put down her hand. There was an expression on her face. Now she sees me, he thought. She had never looked at him after the first day. (He has since tried to put a name to the look on her face; but how can he, now, after so many voyages, after Ceylon, and Hong Kong, and Sheilah's nearly leaving him, and all their difficulties—the money owed, the rows with hotel managers, the lost and found steamer trunk, the children throwing up the foreign food?) She sees me now, he thought. What does she see?

She said, "I'm from a big family. I'm not used to being alone. I'm not a suicidal person, but I could have done something after that party, just not to see any more, or think or listen or expect anything. What can I think when I see these people? All my life I heard, Educated people don't do this, educated people don't do that. And now I'm here, and you're all educated people, and you're nothing but pigs. You're educated and you drink and do everything wrong and you know what you're doing, and that makes you worse than pigs. My family worked to make me an educated person, but they didn't know you. But what if I didn't see and hear and expect anything any more? It wouldn't change anything. You'd all be still the same. Only *you* might have thought it was your fault. You might have thought you were to blame. It could worry you all your life. It would have been wrong for me to worry you."

He remembered that the rented car was still along a snowy curb somewhere in Geneva. He wondered if Sheilah had the key in her purse and if she remembered where they'd parked.

"I told you about the ice wagon," Agnes said. "I don't remember everything, so you're wrong about remembering. But I remember telling you that. That was the best. It's the best you can hope to have. In a big family, if you want to be alone, you have to get up before the rest of them. You get up early in the morning in the summer and it's you, you, once in your life alone in the universe. You think you know everything that can happen . . . Nothing is ever like that again."

He looked at the smeared window and wondered if this day could end without disaster. In his mind he saw her falling in the snow wearing a tramp's costume, and he saw her coming to him in the orphanage dressing gown. He saw her drowning face at the party. He was afraid for himself. The story was still unfinished. It had to come to a climax, something threatening to him. But there was no climax. They talked that day, and afterward nothing else was said. They went on in the same office for a short time, until Peter left for Ceylon; until somebody read the right letter, passed it on for the right initials; and the Fraziers began the Oriental tour that should have made their fortune. Agnes and Peter were too tired to speak after that morning. They were like a married couple in danger, taking care.

But what were they talking about that day, so quietly, such old friends? They talked about dying, about being ambitious, about being religious, about different kinds of love. What did she see when she looked at him— taking her knuckle slowly away from her mouth, bringing her hand down to the desk, letting it rest there? They were both Canadians, so they had this much together—the knowledge of the little you dare admit. Death, near-death, the best thing, the wrong thing—God knows what they were telling each other. Anyway, nothing happened.

When, on Sunday mornings, Sheilah and Peter talk about those times, they take on the glamor of something still to come. It is then he remembers Agnes Brusen. He never says her name. Sheilah wouldn't remember Agnes. Agnes is the only secret Peter has from his wife, the only puzzle he pieces together without her help. He thinks about families in the West as they were fifteen, twenty years ago—the iron-cold ambition, and every member pushing the next one on. He thinks of his father's parties. When he thinks of his father he imagines him with Sheilah, in a crowd. Actually, Sheilah and Peter's father never met, but they might have liked each other. His father admired good-looking women. Peter wonders what they were doing over there in Geneva—not Sheilah and Peter, *Agnes* and Peter. It is almost as if they had once run away together, silly as children, irresponsible as lovers. Peter and Sheilah are back where they started. While they were out in world affairs picking up microbes and debts, always on the fringe of disaster, the fringe of a fortune, Agnes went on and did—what? They lost each other. He thinks of the ice wagon going down the street. He sees something he has never seen in his life—a Western town that belongs to Agnes. Here is Agnes—small, mole-faced, round-shouldered because she has always carried a younger child. She watches the ice wagon and the trail of ice water in a morning invented for her: hers. He sees the weak prairie trees and the shadows on the sidewalk. Nothing moves except the shadows and the ice wagon and the changing amber of the child's eyes. The child is Peter. He has seen the grain of the cement sidewalk and the grass in the cracks, and the dust, and the dandelions at the edge of the road. He is there. He has taken the morning that belongs to Agnes, he is up before the others, and he knows everything. There is nothing he doesn't know. He could keep the morning, if he wanted to, but what can Peter do with the start of a summer day? Sheilah is here, it is a true Sunday morning, with its dimness and headache and remorse and regrets, and this is life. He says, "We have the Balenciaga." He touches Sheilah's hand. The children have their aunt now, and he and Sheilah have each other. Everything works out, somehow or other. Let Agnes have the start of the day. Let Agnes think it was invented for her. Who wants to be alone in the universe? No, begin at the beginning: Peter lost Agnes. Agnes says to herself somewhere, Peter is lost.

READING AND REACTING

1. What is the significance of the Balenciaga dress?
2. Sheilah and Peter consider each other to be a "peacock," while their daughters are "wrens." How does the bird symbolism help to create character?
3. Why is Peter such a failure at his career attempts? Why does he think he should be successful?
4. Why is the third-person narrative effective in this story? How would the story change if it were told from the perspective of one of the characters in first-person?
5. What role does alcohol play in the story?
6. How is Agnes different from Peter and Sheilah, and why is she a success at her job?
7. The narrator comments that "Agnes is the only secret Peter has from his wife, the only puzzle he pieces together without her help" (116). Why does Peter keep his thoughts about Agnes a secret from his wife?
8. **JOURNAL ENTRY** Consider the importance of social status in the story and how it affects the various characters' abilities to move forward with their lives. Will Peter and Sheilah ever achieve the social goals they desire?
9. **CRITICAL PERSPECTIVE** In *The Canadian Encyclopedia* (online), Donna Coates makes the following observation about Mavis Gallant's work: "Gallant's vibrant, flawless prose, often presented in a detached ironic tone, carries a highly visual quality, and her

sharply delineated characters are routinely set within a truthfully rendered specific time and place." Identify examples of visual impact and details of setting.

◊ WRITING SUGGESTIONS: PLOT

1. Write a sequel to "The Story of an Hour," telling the story in the voice of Brently Mallard. Use flashbacks to provide information about his view of the Mallards' marriage.
2. Find a newspaper story that has a disturbing conclusion. Then write a story like Faulkner's in which you retell the story's events from the perspective of an eyewitness and using flashbacks.
3. "The Story of an Hour" includes a *deus ex machina,* an outside force or agent that suddenly appears to change the course of events. Consider the possible effects of a *deus ex machina* on the other stories in this chapter. What might this outside force be in each story? How might it change the story's action? How plausible would such a dramatic turn of events be in each case?
4. Like Emily in "A Rose for Emily," the narrator of "The Yellow Wall-Paper" (Chapter 6) is a privileged, protected woman driven to the edge of madness by events she cannot control. Despite similarities in the two women's situations, however, their tragic stories are resolved in very different ways. What factors account for the two stories' different outcomes?
5. Imagine that Peter and Sheilah inherit a fortune. What will they do with their lives? Will they stay in Canada? Will they go to a new country with their children? Will they find the social success that has eluded them?

CHAPTER 5

Character

◊ ◊ ◊

I always start with the main character or, as it may be, characters. Usually there are a number of people who have been inhabiting my head for a number of years before I begin on a novel, and their dilemmas grow out of what they are, where they come from.

MARGARET LAURENCE, *Eleven Canadian Novelists*

Making false biography, false history, concocting a half-imaginary existence out of the actual drama of my life *is* my life. There has to be some pleasure in this job, and that's it. To go around in disguise. To act a character. To pass one-self off as what one is not. To *pretend*. . . . You don't necessarily, as a writer, have to abandon your biography completely to engage in an act of impersonation. It may be more intriguing when you don't.

PHILIP ROTH, *Writers at Work*, 7th ed.

Much of what a writer learns he learns simply by imitation. Making up a scene, he asks himself at every step. "Would she really say that?" or "Would he really throw the shoe?" He plays the scene through in his imagination, taking all the parts, being absolutely fair to everyone involved (mimicking each in turn, as Aristotle pointed out, and never sinking to stereotype for even the most minor characters), and when he finishes the scene he understands by sympathetic imitation what each character has done throughout and why the fight, or accident, or whatever, developed as it did.

JOHN GARDNER, *On Moral Fiction*

◊ ◊ ◊

A **character** is a fictional representation of a person—usually (but not necessarily) a psychologically realistic depiction. **Characterization** is the way writers develop characters and reveal those characters' traits to readers. Writers may portray characters through their actions, through their reactions to situations or to other characters, through their physical appearance, through their speech and gestures and expressions, and even through their names.

Generally speaking, characters are developed in two ways. First, readers can be *told* about characters. Third-person narrators can give us information about what characters are doing and thinking, what experiences they have had, what they look like, how they are dressed, and so on. Sometimes they also offer analysis of and judgments about a character's behaviour. Similarly, first-person narrators can tell us about themselves or about other characters. Thus, Sammy in John Updike's "A&P" (p. 122) tells us that he lives with his parents and that he disapproves of the supermarket's customers. He also tells us what various characters are wearing and describes their actions, attitudes, and gestures. (For more information about first-person narrators, see Chapter 7, "Point of View.")

Alternatively, a character's personality traits and motivation may be *revealed* through actions, dialogue, or thoughts. For instance, Sammy's vivid fantasies and his disapproval of his customers' lives suggest to readers that he is something of a nonconformist; however, Sammy himself does not actually tell us this information.

ROUND AND FLAT CHARACTERS
◇ ◇ ◇

In his influential 1927 work *Aspects of the Novel*, English novelist E. M. Forster classifies characters as **round** (well developed, closely involved in and responsive to the action) or **flat** (barely developed or stereotypical). In an effective story, the major characters will usually be complex and fully developed; if they are not, readers will not care what happens to them. In much fiction, readers are encouraged to become involved with the characters, even to identify with them. This empathy is possible only when we know something about the characters—their strengths and weaknesses, for example, or their likes and dislikes. We must know at least enough to understand why characters act the way they do. In some cases, of course, a story can be effective even when its central characters are not well developed. Sometimes, in fact, a story's effectiveness is enhanced by an *absence* of character development. For example, the fact that the narrator's grandmother is not developed fully in Alice Munro's "Boys and Girls" (p. 504) may reveal an important point about one of the important themes of the text.

Readers often expect characters to behave as "real people" in their situation might behave. Real people are not perfect, and realistic characters cannot be perfect either. The flaws that are revealed as round characters are developed—greed, gullibility, naiveté, shyness, a quick temper, or a lack of insight or judgment or tolerance or even intelligence—make them believable. In modern fiction, the protagonist is seldom if ever the noble "hero"; more often, he or she is at least partly a victim, someone to whom some unpleasant things happen, and someone who is sometimes ill-equipped to cope with events.

Unlike major characters, minor characters are frequently not well developed. Often they are flat, perhaps acting as *foils* for the protagonist. A **foil** is a supporting character whose role in the story is to highlight a major character by presenting a contrast with him or her. For instance, in "A&P," Stokesie, another young checkout clerk, is a foil for Sammy. Because he is a little older than Sammy and shows none of Sammy's imagination, restlessness, or nonconformity, Stokesie suggests what Sammy might become if he were to continue to work at the A&P. Some flat characters are **stock characters,** easily identifiable types who behave so consistently that readers can readily recognize them. The kindly old priest, the tough young bully, the ruthless business executive, and the reckless adventurer are all stock characters. Some flat characters can even be **caricatures,** characterized by a single dominant trait, such as miserliness, or even by one physical trait, such as nearsightedness.

Dynamic and Static Characters

◇ ◇ ◇

Characters may also be classified as either *dynamic* or *static*. **Dynamic** characters grow and change in the course of a story, developing as they react to events and to other characters. In "A&P," for instance, Sammy's decision to speak out in defence of the girls—as well as the events that lead him to do so—changes him. His view of the world has changed at the end of the story, and as a result his position in the world will change too. A **static** character may face the same challenges a dynamic character might face but will remain essentially unchanged: a static character who was selfish and arrogant will remain selfish and arrogant, regardless of the nature of the story's conflict. In the fairy tale "Cinderella," for example, the title character is as sweet and good-natured at the end of the story—despite her mistreatment by her family—as she is at the beginning. Her situation may have changed, but her character has not.

Whereas round characters tend to be dynamic, flat characters tend to be static. But even a very complex, well-developed major character may be static; sometimes, in fact, the point of a story may hinge on a character's inability to change. A familiar example is the title character in William Faulkner's "A Rose for Emily" (p. 90), who lives a wasted, empty life, at least in part because she is unwilling or unable to accept that the world around her and the people in it have changed.

A story's minor characters are often static; their growth is not usually relevant to the story's development. Moreover, we usually do not learn enough about a minor character's traits, thoughts, actions, or motivation to determine whether or not the character changes significantly.

MOTIVATION

◊ ◊ ◊

Because round characters are complex, they are not always easy to understand. They may act differently in similar situations, just as real people do.
They wrestle with decisions, resist or succumb to temptation, make mistakes, ask questions, search for answers, hope and dream, rejoice and
despair. What is important is not whether we approve of a character's
actions but whether those actions are *plausible*—whether the actions make
sense in light of what we know about the character. We need to see a character's **motivation**—the reasons behind his or her behaviour—or we will
not believe or accept that behaviour. For instance, given Sammy's age, his
dissatisfaction with his job, and his desire to impress the young woman he
calls Queenie, the decision he makes at the end of the story is perfectly plausible. Without having established his motivation, Updike could not have
expected readers to accept Sammy's actions.

Even when readers get to know a character, they still are not able to predict how a complex, round character will behave in a given situation; only
a flat character is predictable. The tension that develops as readers wait to
see how a character will act or react, and thus how a story's conflict will be
resolved, is what holds readers' interest and keeps them involved as a story's
action unfolds.

 ## CHECKLIST: WRITING ABOUT CHARACTER

- ✓ Who is the story's protagonist? Who is the antagonist? Who are the other major characters?
- ✓ Who are the minor characters? What roles do they play in the story? How would the story be different without them?
- ✓ What do the major characters look like? Is their physical appearance important?
- ✓ What are the major characters' most noticeable traits?
- ✓ What are the major characters' likes and dislikes? Their strengths and weaknesses?
- ✓ What are we told about the major characters' backgrounds and prior experiences? What can we infer?
- ✓ Are characters developed for the most part through the narrator's comments and descriptions or through the characters' actions and dialogue?
- ✓ Are the characters round or flat?
- ✓ Are the characters dynamic or static?

✓ Does the story include any stock characters? Any caricatures? Does any character serve as a foil?

✓ Do the characters act in a way that is consistent with how readers expect them to act?

✓ With which characters are readers likely to be most (and least) sympathetic?

✦ **JOHN UPDIKE** (1932–   ) is a prolific writer of novels, short stories, essays, poems, plays, and children's tales. Updike's earliest ambition was to be a cartoonist for *The New Yorker.* He attended Harvard hoping to draw cartoons for *The Lampoon,* studied drawing and fine art at Oxford, and in 1955 went to work for *The New Yorker*—not as a cartoonist, but as a "Talk of the Town" reporter. Updike left *The New Yorker* after three years to write full-time but (over forty years later) is still contributing stories, reviews, and essays to the magazine. Among his novels are *Rabbit, Run* (1960), *The Centaur* (1963), *Rabbit Redux* (1971), *Rabbit Is Rich* (1981), *The Witches of Eastwick* (1985), *Rabbit at Rest* (1990), *Memories of the Ford Administration* (1992), *Brazil* (1994), *In the Beauty of the Lilies* (1996), and *Toward the End of Time* (1997). His most recent novel is *Terrorist* (2006). Updike has also published *Collected Poems 1953–1993* (1993), a collection of stories titled *The Afterlife and Other Stories* (1994), and *Still Looking: Essays on American Art* (2005).

In early stories such as "A&P" (1961), Updike draws on memories of his childhood and teenage years for the sort of "small" scenes and stories for which he quickly became famous. "There is a great deal to be said about almost anything," Updike comments in an interview in *Contemporary Authors.* "All people can be equally interesting. . . . Now either nobody is a hero or everybody is. I vote for everybody. My subject is the American Protestant small-town middle class. I like middles. It is in middles that extremes clash. . . . "

"What John Updike does for a living," writes John Romano in the *New York Times Book Review,* "is remind us of the human costliness of an everyday situation." In "A&P," there is cost, and a small triumph—and a young man's growing awareness of the "hard" world ahead.

✧ ✧ ✧

JOHN UPDIKE

A&P
(1961)

In walks these three girls in nothing but bathing suits. I'm in the third check-out slot, with my back to the door, so I don't see them until they're over by the bread. The one that caught my eye first was the one in the plaid green two-piece. She was a chunky kid, with a good tan and a sweet broad soft-looking can with those two crescents of white just under it, where the sun never seems to hit, at the top of the backs of her legs. I stood there with my hand on a box of HiHo crackers trying to remember if I rang it up or not. I ring it up again and the customer starts giving me hell. She's one of these cash-register-watchers, a witch about fifty with rouge on her cheekbones and no eyebrows, and I know it made her day to trip me up. She'd been watching cash registers for fifty years and probably never seen a mistake before.

By the time I got her feathers smoothed and her goodies into a bag—she gives me a little snort in passing, if she'd been born at the right time they would have burned her over in Salem—by the time I get her on her way the girls had circled around the bread and were coming back, without a push-cart, back my way along the counters, in the aisle between the check-outs and the Special bins. They didn't even have shoes on. There was this chunky one, with the two-piece—it was bright green and the seams on the bra were still sharp and her belly was still pretty pale so I guessed she just got it (the suit)—there was this one, with one of those chubby berry-faces, the lips all bunched together under her nose, this one, and a tall one, with black hair that hadn't quite frizzed right, and one of these sunburns right across under the eyes, and a chin that was too long—you know, the kind of girl other girls think is very "striking" and "attractive" but never quite makes it, as they very well know, which is why they like her so much—and then the third one, that wasn't quite so tall. She was the queen. She kind of led them, the other two peeking around and making their shoulders round. She didn't look around, not this queen, she just walked straight on slowly, on these long white prima-donna legs. She came down a little hard on her heels, as if she didn't walk in her bare feet that much, putting down her heels and then letting the weight move along to her toes as if she was testing the floor with every step, putting a little deliberate extra action into it. You never know for sure how girls' minds work (do you really think it's a mind in there or just a little buzz like a bee in a glass jar?) but you got the idea she had talked the other two into coming in here with her, and now she was showing them how to do it, walk slow and hold yourself straight.

She had on a kind of dirty-pink—beige maybe, I don't know—bathing suit with a little nubble all over it and, what got me, the straps were down. They were off her shoulders looped loose around the cool tops of her arms, and I guess as a result the suit had slipped a little on her, so all around the top of the cloth there was this shining rim. If it hadn't been there you wouldn't have known there could have been anything whiter than those shoulders. With the straps pushed off, there was nothing between the top of the suit and the top of her head except just her, this clean bare plane of the top of her chest down from the shoulder bones like a dented sheet of metal tilted in the light. I mean, it was more than pretty.

She had sort of oaky hair that the sun and salt had bleached, done up in a bun that was unravelling, and a kind of prim face. Walking into the A&P

with your straps down, I suppose it's the only kind of face you *can* have. She held her head so high her neck, coming up out of those white shoulders, looked kind of stretched, but I didn't mind. The longer her neck was, the more of her there was.

5   She must have felt in the corner of her eye me and over my shoulder Stokesie in the second slot watching, but she didn't tip. Not this queen. She kept her eyes moving across the racks, and stopped, and turned so slow it made my stomach rub the inside of my apron, and buzzed to the other two, who kind of huddled against her for relief, and they all three of them went up the cat-and-dog-food-breakfast-cereal-macaroni-rice-raisins-seasonings-spreads-spaghetti-soft-drinks-crackers-and-cookies aisle. From the third slot I look straight up this aisle to the meat counter, and I watched them all the way. The fat one with the tan sort of fumbled with the cookies, but on second thought she put the packages back. The sheep pushing their carts down the aisle—the girls were walking against the usual traffic (not that we have one-way signs or anything)—were pretty hilarious. You could see them, when Queenie's white shoulders dawned on them, kind of jerk, or hop, or hiccup, but their eyes snapped back to their own baskets and on they pushed. I bet you could set off dynamite in an A&P and the people would by and large keep reaching and checking oatmeal off their lists and muttering "Let me see, there was a third thing, began with A, asparagus, no, ah, yes, applesauce!" or whatever it is they do mutter. But there was no doubt, this jiggled them. A few houseslaves in pin curlers even looked around after pushing their carts past to make sure what they had seen was correct.

You know, it's one thing to have a girl in a bathing suit down on the beach, where what with the glare nobody can look at each other much anyway, and another thing in the cool of the A&P, under the fluorescent lights, against all those stacked packages, with her feet paddling along naked over our checkerboard green-and-cream rubber-tile floor.

"Oh Daddy," Stokesie said beside me. "I feel so faint."

"Darling," I said. "Hold me tight." Stokesie's married, with two babies chalked up on his fuselage already, but as far as I can tell that's the only difference. He's twenty-two, and I was nineteen this April.

"Is it done?" he asks, the responsible married man finding his voice. I forgot to say he thinks he's going to be manager some sunny day, maybe in 1990 when it's called the Great Alexandrov and Petrooshki Tea Company or something.

10   What he meant was, our town is five miles from a beach, with a big summer colony out on the Point, but we're right in the middle of town, and the women generally put on a shirt or shorts or something before they get out of the car into the street. And anyway these are usually women with six children and varicose veins mapping their legs and nobody, including them, could care less. As I say, we're right in the middle of town, and if you stand at our front doors you can see two banks and the Congregational church and the newspaper store and three real-estate offices and about twenty-seven old freeloaders tearing up Central Street because the sewer broke

again. It's not as if we're on the Cape; we're north of Boston and there's people in this town haven't seen the ocean for twenty years.

The girls had reached the meat counter and were asking McMahon something. He pointed, they pointed, and they shuffled out of sight behind a pyramid of Diet Delight peaches. All that was left for us to see was old McMahon patting his mouth and looking after them sizing up their joints. Poor kids, I began to feel sorry for them, they couldn't help it.

Now here comes the sad part of the story, at least my family says it's sad but I don't think it's sad myself. The store's pretty empty, it being Thursday afternoon, so there was nothing much to do except lean on the register and wait for the girls to show up again. The whole store was like a pinball machine and I didn't know which tunnel they'd come out of. After a while they come around out of the far aisle, around the light bulbs, records at dis- count of the Caribbean Six or Tony Martin Sings or some such gunk you wonder they waste the wax on, sixpacks of candy bars, and plastic toys done up in cellophane that fall apart when a kid looks at them anyway. Around they come, Queenie still leading the way, and holding a little gray jar in her hand. Slots Three through Seven are unmanned and I could see her wondering between Stokes and me, but Stokesie with his usual luck draws an old party in baggy gray pants who stumbles up with four giant cans of pineapple juice (what do these bums do with all that pineapple juice? I've often asked myself) so the girls come to me. Queenie puts down the jar and I take it into my fingers icy cold. Kingfish Fancy Herring Snacks in Pure Sour Cream: 49. Now her hands are empty, not a ring or a bracelet, bare as God made them, and I wonder where the money's coming from. Still with that prim look she lifts a folded dollar bill out of the hollow at the center of her nubbled pink top. The jar went heavy in my hand. Really, I thought that was so cute.

Then everybody's luck begins to run out. Lengel comes in from haggling with a truck full of cabbages on the lot and is about to scuttle into that door marked manager behind which he hides all day when the girls touch his eye. Lengel's pretty dreary, teaches Sunday school and the rest, but he doesn't miss that much. He comes over and says, "Girls, this isn't the beach."

Queenie blushes, though maybe it's just a brush of sunburn I was noticing for the first time, now that she was so close. "My mother asked me to pick up a jar of herring snacks." Her voice kind of startled me, the way voices do when you see the people first, coming out so flat and dumb yet kind of tony, too, the way it ticked over "pick up" and "snacks." All of a sudden I slid right down her voice into her living room. Her father and the other men were standing around in ice-cream coats and bow ties and the women were in sandals picking up herring snacks on toothpicks off a big plate and they were all holding drinks the color of water with olives and sprigs of mint in them. When my parents have somebody over they get lemonade and if it's a real racy affair Schlitz in tall glasses with "They'll Do It Every Time" cartoons stencilled on.

15 "That's all right," Lengel said. "But this isn't the beach." His repeating this struck me as funny, as if it had just occurred to him, and he had been thinking all these years the A&P was a great big dune and he was the head lifeguard. He didn't like my smiling—as I say he doesn't miss much—but he concentrates on giving the girls that sad Sunday-school-superintendent stare.

Queenie's blush is no sunburn now, and the plump one in plaid, that I liked better from the back—a really sweet can—pipes up, "We weren't doing any shopping. We just came in for the one thing."

"That makes no difference," Lengel tells her, and I could see from the way his eyes went that he hadn't noticed she was wearing a two-piece before. "We want you decently dressed when you come in here."

"We *are* decent," Queenie says suddenly, her lower lip pushing, getting sore now that she remembers her place, a place from which the crowd that runs the A&P must look pretty crummy. Fancy Herring Snacks flashed in her very blue eyes.

"Girls, I don't want to argue with you. After this come in here with your shoulders covered. It's our policy." He turns his back. That's policy for you. Policy is what the kingpins want. What the others want is juvenile delinquency.

20 All this while, the customers had been showing up with their carts but, you know, sheep, seeing a scene, they had all bunched up on Stokesie, who shook open a paper bag as gently as peeling a peach, not wanting to miss a word. I could feel in the silence everybody getting nervous, most of all Lengel, who asks me, "Sammy, have you rung up this purchase?"

I thought and said "No" but it wasn't about that I was thinking. I go through the punches, 4, 9, GROC, TOT—it's more complicated than you think, and after you do it often enough, it begins to make a little song, that you hear words to, in my case "Hello *(bing)* there, you *(gung)* hap-py *pee*-pul *(splat)*!"—the *splat* being the drawer flying out. I uncrease the bill, tenderly as you may imagine, it just having come from between the two smoothest scoops of vanilla I had ever known were there, and pass a half and a penny into her narrow pink palm, and nestle the herrings in a bag and twist its neck and hand it over, all the time thinking.

The girls, and who'd blame them, are in a hurry to get out, so I say "I quit" to Lengel quick enough for them to hear, hoping they'll stop and watch me, their unsuspected hero. They keep right on going, into the electric eye; the door flies open and they flicker across the lot to their car, Queenie and Plaid and Big Tall Goony-Goony (not that as raw material she was so bad), leaving me with Lengel and a kink in his eyebrow.

"Did you say something, Sammy?"

"I said I quit."

25 "I thought you did."

"You didn't have to embarrass them."

"It was they who were embarrassing us."

I started to say something that came out "Fiddle-de-doo." It's a saying of my grandmother's, and I know she would have been pleased.

"I don't think you know what you're saying," Lengel said.

30   "I know you don't," I said. "But I do." I pull the bow at the back of my apron and start shrugging it off my shoulders. A couple customers that had been heading for my slot begin to knock against each other, like scared pigs in a chute.

Lengel sighs and begins to look very patient and old and gray. He's been a friend of my parents for years. "Sammy, you don't want to do this to your Mom and Dad," he tells me. It's true, I don't. But it seems to me that once you begin a gesture it's fatal not to go through with it. I fold the apron, "Sammy" stitched in red on the pocket, and put it on the counter, and drop the bow tie on top of it. The bow tie is theirs, if you've ever wondered. "You'll feel this for the rest of your life," Lengel says, and I know that's true, too, but remembering how he made that pretty girl blush makes me so scrunchy inside I punch the No Sale tab and the machine whirs "pee-pul" and the drawer splats out. One advantage to this scene taking place in summer, I can follow this up with a clean exit, there's no fumbling around getting your coat and galoshes, I just saunter into the electric eye in my white shirt that my mother ironed the night before, and the door heaves itself open, and outside the sunshine is skating around the asphalt.

I look around for my girls, but they're gone, of course. There wasn't anybody but some young married screaming with her children about some candy they didn't get by the door of a powder-blue Falcon station wagon. Looking back in the big windows, over the bags of peat moss and aluminum lawn furniture stacked on the pavement, I could see Lengel in my place in the slot, checking the sheep through. His face was dark gray and his back stiff, as if he'd just had an injection of iron, and my stomach kind of fell as I felt how hard the world was going to be to me hereafter.

READING AND REACTING

1. Summarize the information Sammy gives readers about his tastes and background. Why is this exposition vital to the story's development?
2. List some of the most obvious physical characteristics of the A&P's customers. How do these characteristics make them foils for Queenie and her friends?
3. What is it about Queenie and her friends that appeals to Sammy?
4. Is Queenie a stock character? Explain.
5. What rules and conventions are customers expected to follow in a supermarket? How does the behaviour of Queenie and her friends violate these conventions?
6. Is the supermarket setting vital to the story? Could the story have been set in a car wash? In a fast-food restaurant?

7. How accurate are Sammy's judgments about the other characters? How might the characters be portrayed if the story were told by Lengel?

8. Given what you learn about Sammy during the course of the story, what do you see as his *primary* motivation for quitting his job? What other factors motivate him?

9. **JOURNAL ENTRY** Where do you think Sammy will find himself in ten years? Why?

10. **CRITICAL PERSPECTIVE** In her 1976 book *The Necessary Blackness,* critic Mary Allen observes, "Updike's most tender reverence is reserved for women's bodies. The elegant style with which he describes female anatomy often becomes overwrought, as his descriptions do generally. But it always conveys wonder."

    In what passages in "A&P" does Updike (through Sammy) convey this sense of wonder? Do you think today's audience, reading the story over forty years after Updike wrote it, and more than twenty-five years after Allen's essay was published, would still see such passages as conveying "tender reverence"? Or do you think readers might now see Sammy (and, indeed, Updike) as sexist? How do you see these passages?

Related Works: "Araby" (p. 267), "Boys and Girls" (p. 504), *The Shape of a Girl* (p. 1348)

◊ **KATHERINE MANSFIELD** (1888–1923), one of the pioneers of the modern short story, was born in New Zealand and educated in England. Very much a "modern young woman," she began living on her own in London at the age of nineteen, soon publishing stories and book reviews in many of the most influential literary magazines of the day. One of these she edited with critic John Middleton Murry, whom she married in 1918.

A short story writer of great versatility, Mansfield produced sparkling social comedies for popular consumption as well as more intellectually and technically complex works intended for "perceptive readers." According to one critic, her best works "[w]ith delicate plainness . . . present elusive moments of decision, defeat, and small triumph." Her last two story collections—*Bliss and Other Stories* (1920) and *The Garden Party and Other Stories* (1922)—were met with immediate critical acclaim, but Mansfield's career was cut short in 1923 when she died of complications from tuberculosis at the age of thirty-five.

KATHERINE MANSFIELD

Her First Ball
(1922)

Exactly when the ball began Leila would have found it hard to say. Perhaps her first real partner was the cab. It did not matter that she shared the cab with the Sheridan girls and their brother. She sat back in her own little corner of it, and the bolster on which her hand rested felt like the sleeve of an unknown young man's dress suit; and away they bowled, past waltzing lampposts and houses and fences and trees.

"Have you really never been to a ball before, Leila? But, my child, how too weird—" cried the Sheridan girls.

"Our nearest neighbor was fifteen miles," said Leila softly, gently opening and shutting her fan.

Oh, dear, how hard it was to be indifferent like the others! She tried not to smile too much; she tried not to care. But every single thing was so new and exciting . . . Meg's tuberoses, Jose's long loop of amber, Laura's little dark head, pushing above her white fur like a flower through snow. She would remember forever. It even gave her a pang to see her cousin Laurie throw away the wisps of tissue paper he pulled from the fastening of his new gloves. She would like to have kept those wisps as a keepsake, as a remembrance. Laurie leaned forward and put his hand on Laura's knee.

5   "Look here, darling," he said. "The third and the ninth as usual, Twig?"

Oh, how marvellous to have a brother! In her excitement Leila felt that if there had been time, if it hadn't been impossible, she couldn't have helped crying because she was an only child, and no brother had ever said "Twig?" to her; no sister would ever say, as Meg said to Jose that moment, "I've never known your hair go up more successfully than it has tonight!"

But, of course, there was no time. They were at the drill hall already; there were cabs in front of them and cabs behind. The road was bright on either side with moving fan-like lights, and on the pavement gay couples seemed to float through the air; little satin shoes chased each other like birds.

"Hold on to me, Leila; you'll get lost," said Laura.

"Come on, girls, let's make a dash for it," said Laurie.

10   Leila put two fingers on Laura's pink velvet cloak, and they were somehow lifted past the big gold lantern, carried along the passage, and pushed into the little room marked "Ladies." Here the crowd was so great there was hardly space to take off their things; the noise was deafening. Two

benches on either side were stacked high with wraps. Two old women in white aprons ran up and down tossing fresh armfuls. And everybody was pressing forward trying to get at the little dressing table and mirror at the far end.

A great quivering jet of gas lighted the ladies' room. It couldn't wait; it was dancing already. When the door opened again and there came a burst of tuning from the drill hall, it leaped almost to the ceiling.

Dark girls, fair girls were patting their hair, tying ribbons again, tucking handkerchiefs down the front of their bodices, smoothing marble-white gloves. And because they were all laughing it seemed to Leila that they were all lovely.

"Aren't there any invisible hairpins?" cried a voice. "How most extraordinary! I can't see a single invisible hairpin."

"Powder my back, there's a darling," cried some one else.

15   "But I must have a needle and cotton. I've torn simply miles and miles of the frill," wailed a third.

Then, "Pass them along, pass them along!" The straw basket of programs was tossed from arm to arm. Darling little pink-and-silver programs, with pink pencils and fluffy tassels. Leila's fingers shook as she took one out of the basket. She wanted to ask someone, "Am I meant to have one too?" but she had just time to read: "Waltz 3. *Two, Two in a Canoe*. Polka 4. *Making the Feathers Fly*," when Meg cried, "Ready, Leila?" and they pressed their way through the crush in the passage towards the big double doors of the drill hall.

Dancing had not begun yet, but the band had stopped tuning, and the noise was so great it seemed that when it did begin to play it would never be heard. Leila, pressing close to Meg, looking over Meg's shoulder, felt that even the little quivering colored flags strung across the ceiling were talking. She quite forgot to be shy; she forgot how in the middle of dressing she had sat down on the bed with one shoe off and one shoe on and begged her mother to ring up her cousins and say she couldn't go after all. And the rush of longing she had had to be sitting on the veranda of their forsaken upcountry home, listening to the baby owls crying "More pork" in the moonlight, was changed to a rush of joy so sweet that it was hard to bear alone. She clutched her fan, and, gazing at the gleaming, golden floor, the azaleas, the lanterns, the stage at one end with its red carpet and gilt chairs and the band in a corner, she thought breathlessly, "How heavenly; how simply heavenly!"

All the girls stood grouped together at one side of the doors, the men at the other, and the chaperones in dark dresses, smiling rather foolishly, walked with little careful steps over the polished floor towards the stage.

"This is my little country cousin Leila. Be nice to her. Find her partners; she's under my wing," said Meg, going up to one girl after another.

20   Strange faces smiled at Leila—sweetly, vaguely. Strange voices answered, "Of course, my dear." But Leila felt the girls didn't really see her. They were

looking towards the men. Why didn't the men begin? What were they waiting for? There they stood, smoothing their gloves, patting their glossy hair and smiling among themselves. Then, quite suddenly, as if they had only just made up their minds that that was what they had to do, the men came gliding over the parquet. There was a joyful flutter among the girls. A tall, fair man flew up to Meg, seized her program, scribbled something; Meg passed him on to Leila. "May I have the pleasure?" He ducked and smiled. There came a dark man wearing an eyeglass, then cousin Laurie with a friend, and Laura with a little freckled fellow whose tie was crooked. Then quite an old man—fat, with a big bald patch on his head—took her program and murmured, "Let me see, let me see!" And he was a long time comparing his program, which looked black with names, with hers. It seemed to give him so much trouble that Leila was ashamed. "Oh, please don't bother," she said eagerly. But instead of replying the fat man wrote something, glanced at her again. "Do I remember this bright little face?" he said softly. "Is it known to me of yore?" At that moment the band began playing; the fat man disappeared. He was tossed away on a great wave of music that came flying over the gleaming floor, breaking the groups up into couples, scattering them; sending them spinning. . . .

Leila had learned to dance at boarding school. Every Saturday afternoon the boarders were hurried off to a little corrugated iron mission hall where Miss Eccles (of London) held her "select" classes. But the difference between that dusty-smelling hall—with calico texts on the walls, the poor terrified little woman in a brown velvet toque with rabbit's ears thumping the cold piano, Miss Eccles poking the girls' feet with her long white wand—and this was so tremendous that Leila was sure if her partner didn't come and she had to listen to that marvellous music and to watch the others sliding, gliding over the golden floor, she would die at least, or faint, or lift her arms and fly out of one of those dark windows that showed the stars.

"Ours, I think—" Some one bowed, smiled, and offered her his arm; she hadn't to die after all. Some one's hand pressed her waist, and she floated away like a flower that is tossed into a pool.

"Quite a good floor, isn't it?" drawled a faint voice close to her ear.

"I think it's most beautifully slippery," said Leila.

25 "Pardon!" The faint voice sounded surprised. Leila said it again. And there was a tiny pause before the voice echoed. "Oh, quite!" and she was swung round again.

He steered so beautifully. That was the great difference between dancing with girls and men, Leila decided. Girls banged into each other, and stamped on each other's feet; the girl who was gentleman always clutched you so.

The azaleas were separate flowers no longer; they were pink and white flags streaming by.

"Were you at the Bells' last week?" the voice came again. It sounded tired. Leila wondered whether she ought to ask him if he would like to stop.

"No, this is my first dance," said she.

30   Her partner gave a little gasping laugh. "Oh, I say," he protested.

"Yes, it is really the first dance I've ever been to." Leila was most fervent. It was such a relief to be able to tell somebody. "You see, I've lived in the country all my life up until now. . . ."

At that moment the music stopped, and they went to sit on two chairs against the wall. Leila tucked her pink satin feet under and fanned herself, while she blissfully watched the other couples passing and disappearing through the swing doors.

"Enjoying yourself, Leila?" asked Jose, nodding her golden head.

Laura passed and gave her the faintest little wink; it made Leila wonder for a moment whether she was quite grown up after all. Certainly her partner did not say very much. He coughed, tucked his handkerchief away, pulled down his waistcoat, took a minute thread off his sleeve. But it didn't matter. Almost immediately the band started, and her second partner seemed to spring from the ceiling.

35   "Floor's not bad," said the new voice. Did one always begin with the floor? And then, "Were you at the Neaves' on Tuesday?" And again Leila explained. Perhaps it was a little strange that her partners were not more interested. For it was thrilling. Her first ball! she was only at the beginning of everything. It seemed to her that she had never known what the night was like before. Up till now it had been dark, silent, beautiful very often— oh, yes—but mournful somehow. Solemn. And now it would never be like that again—it had opened dazzling bright.

"Care for an ice?" said her partner. And they went through the swing doors, down the passage, to the supper room. Her cheeks burned, she was fearfully thirsty. How sweet the ices looked on little glass plates, and how cold the frosted spoon was, iced too! And when they came back to the hall there was the fat man waiting for her by the door. It gave her quite a shock again to see how old he was; he ought to have been on the stage with the fathers and mothers. And when Leila compared him with her other partners he looked shabby. His waistcoat was creased, there was a button off his glove, his coat looked as if it was dusty with French chalk.

"Come along, little lady," said the fat man. He scarcely troubled to clasp her, and they moved away so gently, it was more like walking than dancing. But he said not a word about the floor. "Your first dance, isn't it?" he murmured.

"How *did* you know?"

"Ah," said the fat man, "that's what it is to be old!" He wheezed faintly as he steered her past an awkward couple. "You see, I've been doing this kind of thing for the last thirty years."

40   "Thirty years?" cried Leila. Twelve years before she was born!

"It hardly bears thinking about, does it?" said the fat man gloomily. Leila looked at his bald head, and she felt quite sorry for him.

"I think it's marvellous to be still going on," she said kindly.

"Kind little lady," said the fat man, and he pressed her a little closer, and hummed a bar of the waltz. "Of course," he said, "you can't hope to last anything like as long as that. No-o," said the fat man, "long before that you'll be sitting up there on the stage, looking on, in your nice black velvet. And these pretty arms will have turned into little short fat ones, and you'll beat time with such a different kind of fan—a black bony one." The fat man seemed to shudder. "And you'll smile away like the poor old dears up there, and point to your daughter, and tell the elderly lady next to you how some dreadful man tried to kiss her at the club ball. And your heart will ache, ache"— the fat man squeezed her closer still, as if he really was sorry for that poor heart—"because no one wants to kiss you now. And you'll say how unpleasant these polished floors are to walk on, how dangerous they are. Eh, Mademoiselle Twinkletoes?" said the fat man softly.

Leila gave a light little laugh, but she did not feel like laughing: Was it— could it all be true? It sounded terribly true. Was this first ball only the beginning of her last ball after all? At that the music seemed to change; it sounded sad, sad it rose upon a great sigh. Oh, how quickly things changed! Why didn't happiness last for ever? For ever wasn't a bit too long.

45   "I want to stop," she said in a breathless voice. The fat man led her to the door.

"No," she said. "I won't go outside. I won't sit down. I'll just stand here, thank you." She leaned against the wall, tapping with her foot, pulling up her gloves and trying to smile. But deep inside her a little girl threw her pinafore over her head and sobbed. Why had he spoiled it all?

"I say, you know," said the fat man, "you mustn't take me seriously, little lady."

"As if I should!" said Leila, tossing her small dark head and sucking her underlip. . . .

Again the couples paraded. The swing doors opened and shut. Now new music was given out by the bandmaster. But Leila didn't want to dance any more. She wanted to be home, or sitting on the veranda listening to those baby owls. When she looked through the dark windows at the stars, they had long beams like wings. . . .

50   But presently a soft, melting, ravishing tune began, and a young man with curly hair bowed before her. She would have to dance, out of politeness, until she could find Meg. Very stiffly she walked into the middle; very haughtily she put her hand on his sleeve. But in one minute, in one turn, her feet glided, glided. The lights, the azaleas, the dresses, the pink faces, the velvet chairs, all became one beautiful flying wheel. And when her next partner bumped her into the fat man and he said, "Par*don*," she smiled at him more radiantly than ever. She didn't even recognize him again.

READING AND REACTING

1. Why in paragraph 43 does the older man tell Leila that she "can't hope to last anything like as long as that"?
2. Why does the story end with Leila's not even recognizing the older man with whom she had danced?

3. What is the significance of the dance in cultural and social terms?
4. What do Leila's comments about the floor reveal about her?
5. Why is Leila so much more excited about the ball than her cousins?
6. What do some details of the setting reveal about her?
7. Are the mothers who are sitting on the stage having an unpleasant time, as the man suggests to Leila?
8. What is the significance of the baby owls and the sound they make?
9. **JOURNAL ENTRY** Compare your first experience at an adult event with Leila's.
10. **CRITICAL PERSPECTIVE** Critic Gillian Boddy, in *Katherine Mansfield: The Woman, The Writer*, offers the following analysis of Mansfield's fiction:

> The story evolves through the characters' minds. The external narrator is almost eliminated. As so often in her work, the reader is dropped into the story and simply confronted by a particular situation. There is no preliminary establishing and identification of time and place. The reader is immediately involved; it is assumed that he or she has any necessary prerequisite knowledge and is, in a sense, part of the story too.

Do you see this absence of conventional exposition as a problem in "Her First Ball"? Do you think the story would be more effective if Mansfield had supplied more preliminary information about setting and character? Or do you believe that what Boddy calls Mansfield's "concentration on a moment or episode" is a satisfactory substitute for the missing exposition, effectively shifting interest from "what *happens*" to "*why* it happens"?

Related Works: "Soldier's Home" (p. 273), "Rooming Houses Are Old Women" (p. 705), "The Stenographers" (p. 795)

◈ **TIMOTHY FINDLEY** (1932–2002), born and educated in Toronto, began his artistic life as an actor and appeared in Ontario's first Stratford Festival in 1953. Findley himself wrote four plays, one of which, *Sir John A.—Himself!* (1978), chronicles formative events in the life of Canada's first prime minister. With the publication of *The Wars* (1977), Findley won international acclaim. The book tells the story of Robert Ross, a young Canadian officer in World War I, whose feat of freeing horses trapped in a burning barn stands out as an act of defiance against authority. Throughout his works, Findley examines writing and language as constructions that convey social conventions. The nature of madness is also a central concern in Findley's writing. Timothy Findley died in Provence, France, on June 20, 2002.

TIMOTHY FINDLEY

Stones
(1988)

We lived on the outskirts of Rosedale, over on the wrong side of Yonge Street. This was the impression we had, at any rate. Crossing the streetcar tracks put you in another world.

One September, my sister, Rita, asked a girl from Rosedale over to our house after school. Her name was Allison Pritchard and she lived on Cluny Drive. When my mother telephoned to see if Allison Pritchard could stay for supper, Mrs. Pritchard said she didn't think it would be appropriate. That was the way they talked in Rosedale: very polite; oblique and cruel.

Over on our side—the west side—of Yonge Street, there were merchants—and this, apparently, made the difference to those whose houses were in Rosedale. People of class were not meant to live in the midst of commerce.

Our house was on Gibson Avenue, a cul-de-sac with a park across the road. My bedroom window faced a hockey rink in winter and a football field in summer. Cy, my brother, was a star in either venue. I was not. My forte, then, was the tricycle.

5 Up at the corner, there was an antique store on one side and a variety shop on the other. In the variety shop, you could spend your allowance on penny candy, Eskimo pies and an orange drink I favoured then called *Stubby*. *Stubby* came in short, fat bottles and aside from everything else—the thick orange flavour and the ginger in the bubbles—there was something wonderfully satisfying in the fact that it took both hands to hold it up to your lips and tip it down your throat.

Turning up Yonge Street, beyond the antique store, you came to The Women's Bakery, Adam's Grocery, Oskar Schickel, the butcher and Max's Flowers. We were Max's Flowers. My mother and my father wore green aprons when they stood behind the counter or went back into the cold room where they made up wreaths for funerals, bouquets for weddings and corsages for dances at the King Edward Hotel. Colonel Matheson, retired, would come in every morning on his way downtown and pick out a boutonnière from the jar of carnations my mother kept on the counter near the register. Once, when I was four, I caused my parents untold embarrassment by pointing out that Colonel Matheson had a large red growth on the end of his nose. The "growth" was nothing of the sort, of course, but merely the result of Colonel Matheson's predilection for gin.

Of the pre-war years, my overall memory is one of perfect winters, heavy with snow and the smell of coal- and wood-smoke mingling with the smell of bread and cookies rising from The Women's Bakery. The coal-smoke came from our furnaces and the wood-smoke—mostly birch and maple—came to us from the chimneys of Rosedale, where it seemed that every house must have a fireplace in every room.

Summers all smelled of grass being cut in the park and burning tar from the road crews endlessly patching the potholes in Yonge Street. The heat of these summers was heroic and the cause of many legends. Mister Schickel, the butcher, I recall once cooked an egg on the sidewalk outside his store. My father, who was fond of Mister Schickel, made him a bet of roses it could not be done. I think Mister Schickel's part of the bet was pork chops trimmed of excess fat. When the egg began to sizzle, my father slapped his thigh and whistled and he sent my sister, Rita, in to get the flowers. Mister Schickel, however, was a graceful man and when he placed his winnings in the window of his butcher shop, he also placed a card that read: *Thanks to Max's Flowers one dozen roses.*

The Great Depression held us all in thrall, but its effects on those of us who were used to relative poverty—living on the west side on Yonge Street—were not so debilitating as they were on the far side in Rosedale. The people living there regarded money as something you had—as opposed to something you went out and got—and they were slower to adjust to what, for them, was the unique experience of deprivation.

10   I remember, too, that there always seemed to be a tramp at the door: itinerants asking if—for the price of a meal, or the meal itself—they could carry out the ashes, sweep the walks or pile the baskets and pails in which my father brought his flowers from the market and the greenhouse.

Our lives continued in this way until about the time I was five—in August of 1939. Everyone's life, I suppose, has its demarcation lines—its latitudes and longitudes passing through time. Some of these lines define events that everyone shares—others are confined to personal—even to secret lives. But the end of summer 1939 is a line drawn through the memory of everyone who was then alive. We were all about to be pitched together into a melting pot of violence from which a few of us would emerge intact and the rest of us would perish.

My father joined the army even before the war had started. He went downtown one day and didn't come back till after suppertime. I noticed that he hadn't taken the truck but had ridden off on the streetcar. I asked my mother why he had worn his suit on a weekday and she replied *because today is special*. But that was all she said.

At the table, eating soufflé and salad, my brother, Cy—who was nine years old that summer—talked about the World's Fair in New York City and pictures he'd seen of the future in magazines. The Great World's Fair was a subject that had caught all our imaginations with its demonstrations of new appliances, aeroplanes and motor cars. Everything was "streamlined" in 1939; everything designed with swept-back lines as if we were all preparing to shoot off into space. Earlier that summer, the King and Queen of England had come to Canada, riding on a streamlined train whose blue-painted engine was sleek and slim as something in a silver glove. In fact, the King and Queen had arrived in Toronto just up Yonge Street from where we lived. We got permission from the Darrow family, who lived over Max's Flowers, to stand on the roof and watch the parade with its Mounties in scarlet and its Black Watch Band and the King and Queen, all blue and white and smiling, sitting in an open Buick called a *McLaughlin—built*, according to Cy, *right here in Canada!* For one brief moment while all these symbols of who we were went marching past, the two communities—one on either side of Yonge Street—were united in a surge of cheering and applause. But after the King and Queen were gone, the ribbon of Yonge Street divided us again. It rained.

Now, Cy and Rita were arguing over the remnants in the soufflé dish. Cy held the classic belief that what was in the dish was his by virtue of his being the eldest child. He also held the classic belief that girls were meant to be second in everything. Rita, who was always hungry but never seemed to gain an ounce, held none of these beliefs and was capable of fighting Cy for hours on end when our parents weren't present. With Mother at the table, however, the argument was silenced by her announcement that the soufflé dish and all the delicious bits of cheese and egg that clung to its sides would be set aside for our father.

15 Then—or shortly thereafter—our father did indeed arrive, but he said he wasn't hungry and he wanted to be left alone with Mother.

In half an hour the children were called from the kitchen where we had been doing the dishes and scooping up the remains of the meal. I—the child my mother called *The Rabbit*—had been emptying the salad bowl, stuffing my mouth with lettuce, tomatoes and onion shards and nearly choking in the process. We all went into the sitting-room with food on our lips and tea towels in our hands: Father's three little Maxes—Cy and Rita and Ben. He looked at us then, as he always did, with a measure of pride he could never hide and a false composure that kept his lips from smiling, but not his eyes. I look back now on that moment with some alarm when I realize my father was only twenty-seven years old—an age I have long survived and doubled.

"Children, I have joined the army," he said—in his formal way, as if we were his customers. "I am going to be a soldier."

Our mother had been weeping before we entered the room, but she had dried her eyes because she never allowed us to witness her tears. Now, she was smiling and silent. After a moment, she left the room and went out through the kitchen into the garden where, in the twilight, she found her favourite place and sat in a deck-chair amidst the flowers.

Cy, for his part, crowed with delight and yelled with excitement. He wanted to know if the war would last until he was a man and could join our father at the front.

20 Father, I remember, told him the war had not yet begun and the reason for his enlistment was precisely so that Cy and I could not be soldiers. "There will be no need for that," he said.

Cy was immensely disappointed. He begged our father to make the war go on till 1948, when he would be eighteen.

Our father only laughed at that.

"The war," he said, "will be over in 1940."

I went out then and found our mother in the garden.

25 "What will happen to us while he's away?" I asked.

"Nothing," she said. And then she said: "come here."

I went and leaned against her thigh and she put her arm around my shoulder and I could smell the roses somewhere behind us. It was getting dark.

"Look up there," she said. "The stars are coming out. Why don't you count them?"

This was her way of distracting me whenever my questions got out of hand. Either she told me to count the stars or go outside and dig for China. *There's a shovel in the shed,* she would tell me. *You get started and I will join you.* Just as if we would be in China and back by suppertime.

30 But that night in August, 1939, I wasn't prepared to bite. I didn't want to dig for China and I didn't want to count the stars. I'd dug for China so many times and had so many holes in the yard that I knew I would never arrive; it was much too far and, somehow, she was making a fool of me. As for the stars: "I counted them last night," I told her. "And the night before."

"Oh?" she said—and I felt her body tense, though she went on trying to inject a sense of ease when she spoke. "So tell me," she said. "How many are there?"

"Twelve," I said.

"Ah," she said. And sighed. "Just twelve. I thought there might be more than twelve."

"I mean twelve zillion," I said with great authority.

35 "Oh," she said. "I see. And you counted them all?"

"Unh-hunh."

For a moment she was quiet. And then she said: "what about that one there?"

One week later, the war began. But my father had already gone.

On the 14th of February, 1943, my father was returned. He came back home from the war. He did this on a Sunday and I recall the hush that fell upon our house, as indeed it seemed to have fallen over all the city. Only the sparrows out in the trees made sound.

40 We had gone downtown to the Exhibition Grounds to meet him. The journey on the streetcar took us over an hour, but Mother had splurged and hired a car and driver to take us all home. The car, I remember, embarrassed me. I was afraid some friend would see me being driven—sitting up behind a chauffeur.

A notice had come that told us the families of all returning soldiers would be permitted to witness their arrival. I suspect the building they used for this was the one now used to house the Royal Winter Fair and other equestrian events. I don't remember what it was called and I'm not inclined to inquire. It was enough that I was there that once—and once remains enough.

We sat in the bleachers, Cy and Rita and Mother and me, and there was a railing holding us back. There must have been over a thousand people waiting to catch a glimpse of someone they loved—all of them parents, children or wives of the men returning. I was eight years old that February—almost nine and feeling I would never get there. Time was like a field of clay and all the other children I knew appeared to have cleared it in a single bound while I was stuck in the mud and barely able to lift my feet. I hated being eight and dreaded being nine. I wanted to be ten—the only dignified age a child could be, it seemed to me. Cy, at ten, had found a kind of silence I admired to the point of worship. Rita, who in fact was ten that year and soon to be eleven, had also found a world of silence in which she kept her self secreted—often behind closed doors. Silence was a sign of valour.

The occasion was barely one for public rejoicing. The men who were coming home were mostly casualties whose wounds, we had been warned, could be distressing and whose spirit, we had equally been warned, had been damaged in long months of painful recuperation. Plainly, it was our job to lift their spirits and to deny the severity of their wounds. Above all else, they must not be allowed to feel they could not rejoin society at large. A man with no face must not be stared at.

Our father's wounds were greater by far than we had been told. There was not a mark on his body, but—far inside—he had been destroyed. His mind had been severely damaged and his spirit had been broken. No one had told me what this might have made of him. No one had said *he may never be kind again*. No one had said *he will never sleep again without the aid of alcohol*. No one had said *he will try to kill your mother*. No one had said *you will not be sure it's him when you see him*. Yet all these things were true.

45   I had never seen a military parade without a band. The effect was eerie and upsetting. Two or three officers came forward into the centre of the oval. Somebody started shouting commands and a sergeant-major, who could not yet be seen, was heard outside the building counting off the steps.

I wanted drums. I wanted bugles. Surely this ghostly, implacable sound of marching feet in the deadening sand was just a prelude to everyone standing up and cheering and the music blaring forth. But, no. We all stood up, it is true, the minute the first of the columns rounded the wooden corner of the bleachers and came into sight. But no one uttered a sound. One or two people threw their hands up over their mouths—as if to stifle cries—but most of us simply stood there—staring in disbelief.

Nurses came with some of the men, supporting them. Everyone was pale in the awful light—and the colours of their wounds and bruises were garish and quite unreal. There was a predominance of yellow flesh and dark maroon scars and of purple welts and blackened scabs. Some men wore bandages—some wore casts and slings. Others used canes and crutches to support themselves. A few had been the victims of fire, and these wore tight, blue skull-caps and collarless shirts and their faces and other areas of uncovered skin were bright with shining ointments and dressings.

It took a very great while for all these men and women—perhaps as many as two hundred of them—to arrive inside the building and make their way into the oval. They were being lined up in order of columns—several long lines, and each line punctuated here and there with attendant nurses. The voices of the sergeant-major and of the adjutant who was taking the parade were swallowed up in the dead acoustics, and—far above us—pigeons and sparrows moved among the girders and beams that supported the roof. I still had not seen Father.

At last, because my panic was spreading out of control, I tugged my mother's elbow and whispered that I couldn't see him. Had there been a mistake and he wasn't coming at all?

50   "No," she told me—looking down at me sideways and turning my head with her ungloved fingers. "There he is, there," she said. "But don't say anything, yet. He may not know we're here."

My father's figure could only be told because of his remarkable height. He was six feet four and had always been, to me, a giant. But now his height seemed barely greater than the height of half a dozen other men who were gathered out in the sand. His head was bowed, though once or twice he lifted his chin when he heard the commands. His shoulders, no longer squared, were rounded forward and dipping towards his centre. His neck was so thin I thought that someone or something must have cut over half of it away. I studied him solemnly and then looked up at my mother.

She had closed her eyes against him because she could not bear to look.

Later on that night, when everyone had gone to bed but none of us had gone to sleep, I said to Cy: "what is it?"

"What?"

55   "That's happened to Dad . . ."

Cy didn't answer for a moment and then he said: "Dieppe."

I didn't understand. I thought it was a new disease.

We were told the next day not to mention at school that our father had come back home. Nothing was said about why it must be kept a secret. That was a bitter disappointment. Other children whose fathers had returned from overseas were always the centre of attention. Teachers, beaming smiles and patting heads, would congratulate them just as if they had won a prize. Classmates pestered them with questions: What does he look like? Have you seen his wounds? How many Germans did he kill? But we had none of this. All we got was: *what did you do on the weekend?*

Nothing.

60   All day Monday, Father remained upstairs. Our parents' bedroom was on the second floor directly over the sitting-room. Also, directly underneath the bedroom occupied by Cy and me. We had heard our mother's voice long

into the night, apparently soothing him, telling him over and over again that everything was going to be all right.

We could not make out her words, but the tone of her voice was familiar. Over time, she had sat with each of us, deploying her comforts in all the same cadences and phrases, assuring us that pains and aches and sicknesses would pass.

Because we could not afford to lose the sale of even one flower—neither the single rose bought once a week by Edna Holmes to cheer her ailing sister, nor the daily boutonnière of Colonel Matheson—our mother had persuaded Mrs. Adams, the grocer's wife, to tend the store while she "nipped home" once every hour to see to Father's needs. It was only later that we children realized what those needs entailed. He was drinking more or less constantly in every waking hour, and our mother's purpose was first to tempt him with food—which he refused—and then to make certain that his matches and cigarettes did not set fire to the house.

On the Wednesday, Father emerged from his shell around two o'clock in the afternoon. We were all at school, of course, and I have only the account of what follows from my mother. When she returned at two, Mother found that Father had come down into the hallway, fully dressed in civilian clothes. He had already donned his greatcoat when she arrived. She told me that, at first, he had seemed to be remarkably sober. He told her he wanted to go outside and walk in the street. He wanted to go and see the store, he said.

"But you can't wear your greatcoat, David," she told him.

65 "Why?"

"Because you're in civilian dress. You know that's not allowed. A man was arrested just last week."

"I wasn't here last week," said my father.

"Nevertheless," my mother told him, "this man was arrested because it is not allowed."

"But I'm a soldier!" my father yelled.

70 My mother had to play this scene with all the care and cunning she could muster. The man who had been arrested had been a deserter. All that winter, desertions had been increasing and there had been demonstrations of overt disloyalty. People had shouted *down with the King!* and had booed the Union Jack. There were street gangs of youths who called themselves *Zombies* and they hung around the Masonic Temple on Yonge Street and the Palais Royale at Sunnyside. Some of these young men were in uniform, members of the Home Guard: reserves who had been promised, on joining up, they would not be sent overseas. They may have disapproved of the war, but they did not disapprove of fighting. They waited outside the dancehalls, excessively defensive of their manhood, challenging the servicemen who were dancing inside to *come out fighting and show us your guts!* Men had been killed in such encounters and the encounters had been increasing. The government was absolutely determined to stamp these incidents out before they spread across the country. These were the darkest hours of the war and

morale, both in and out of the Forces, was at its lowest ebb. If my father had appeared on the street with his military greatcoat worn over his civilian clothes, it would have been assumed he was a *Zombie* or a deserter and he would have been arrested instantly. Our neighbours would have turned him in, no matter who he was. Our patriotism had come to that.

"I don't have a civilian overcoat," my father said. "And don't suggest that I put on my uniform, because I won't. My uniform stinks of sweat and I hate it."

"Well, you aren't going out like that," my mother said. "That's all there is to it. Why not come to the kitchen and I'll fix you a sandwich. . . ."

"I don't want a goddamned sandwich," my father yelled at her. "I want to see the store!"

At this point, he tore off his greatcoat and flung it onto the stairs. And then, before my mother could prevent him, he was out the door and running down the steps.

75 My mother—dressed in her green shop apron and nothing but a scarf to warm her—raced out after him.

What would the neighbours think? What would the neighbours say? How could she possibly explain?

By the time she had reached the sidewalk, my father had almost reached the corner. But, when she got to Yonge Street, her fears were somewhat allayed. My father had not gone into Max's Flowers but was standing one door shy of it, staring into the butcher's window.

"What's going on here?" he said, as my mother came abreast of him.

Mother did not know what he meant.

80 "Where is Mister Schickel, Lily?" he asked her.

She had forgotten that, as well.

"Mister Schickel has left," she told him—trying to be calm—trying to steer my father wide of the butcher's window and in towards their own front stoop.

"Left?" my father shouted. "He's only just managed to pay off his mortgage! And who the hell is this imposter, Reilly?"

"Reilly?"

85 "Arthur Reilly the bloody butcher!" My father pointed at and read the sign that had replaced *Oskar Schickel, Butcher* in the window.

"Mister Reilly has been there most of the winter, David. Didn't I write and tell you that?" She knew very well she hadn't.

My father blinked at the meagre cuts of rationed meat displayed beyond the glass and said: "what happened to Oskar, Lily? Tell me."

And so, she had to tell him, like it or not.

Mister Schickel's name was disagreeable—stuck up there on Yonge Street across from Rosedale—and someone from Park Road had thrown a stone through the window.

90 There. It was said.

"But Oskar wasn't a German," my father whispered. "He was a Canadian."

"But his name was German, David."

My father put his fingers against the glass and did not appear to respond to what my mother had said.

At last, my mother pulled at his arm. "Why not come back home," she said. "You can come and see the shop tomorrow."

95   My father, while my mother watched him, concentrated very hard and moved his finger over the dusty glass of Oskar Schickel's store.

"What are you doing, David?"

"Nothing," said my father. "Setting things right, that's all."

Then he stepped back and said to her: "now—we'll go home."

What he had written was:

100   *Oskar Schickel: Proprietor in absentia.*

Mother said that Mrs. Reilly rushed outside as soon as they had reached the corner and she washed the window clean.

This was the only remaining decent thing my father did until the day he died.

The rest was all a nightmare.

I had never seen Dieppe. I had seen its face in photographs. I had read all the books and heard all the stories. The battle, of which my father had been a victim, had taken place in August of 1942—roughly six months before he was returned to us. Long since then, in my adult years, I have seen that battle, or seen its parts, through the medium of documentary film. It was only after Cy and Rita had vetted these films that I was able to watch. Till then, I had been afraid I would catch my father's image unawares—fearful that somehow our eyes would meet in that worst of moments. I couldn't bear the thought of seeing him destroyed. So, I had seen all this—the photographs, the books, the films—but I had never seen the town of Dieppe itself until that day in May of 1987 when I took my father's ashes there to scatter them.

105   Before I can begin this ending, I have to make it clear that the last thing I want to provoke is the sentimental image of a wind-blown stretch of rocky beach with a rainbow of ashes arching over the stones and blowing out to sea. If you want that image, let me tell you that had been the way it was when Cy, my brother, and Rita, my sister, and I went walking, wading into the ocean south of Lunenburg, Nova Scotia—where our mother had been born—to cast her ashes into the air above the Atlantic. Then there was almost music and we rejoiced because our mother had finally gained her freedom from a life that had become intolerable. But in Dieppe, when I shook my father's ashes out of their envelope, there was no rejoicing. None.

I felt, in fact, as if I had brought the body of an infidel into a holy place and laid it down amongst the true believers. Still, this was what my father had wanted—and how could I refuse him? Neither Cy nor Rita would do it for him. *Gone,* they had said. *Good riddance.*

And so it fell to me.

I was always the least informed. I was always the most inquisitive. During my childhood, nobody told me—aside from the single word *Dieppe*—what it was that had happened to my father. And yet, perhaps because I knew the least and because I was the youngest and seemed the most naïve and willing, it was more than often me he focused on.

His tirades would begin in silence—the silence we had been warned of when he first returned. He would sit at the head of the table, eating a piece of fish and drinking from a glass of beer. The beer was always dark in colour. Gold.

110   Our dining-room had a window facing west. Consequently, winter sunsets in particular got in his eyes.

Curtain, he would say at his plate—and jab his fork at me.

If I didn't understand because his mouth was full, my mother would reach my sleeve and pull it with her fingers. *The curtain, Ben*, she would say. *Your father's eyes*.

Yes, ma'am. Down I'd get and pull the curtain.

Then, no sooner would I be reseated than my father—still addressing his plate—would mumble *lights*. And I would rise and turn on the lights. Then, when I was back at last in my chair, he would look at me and say, without apparent rancour, *why don't you tell me to shove the goddamn curtain up my ass?*

115   You will understand my silence in response to this if you understand that—before he went away—the worst my father had ever said in our presence had been *damn* and *hell*. The ultimate worst had been *Christ!* when he'd nearly sliced his finger off with a knife. Then, however, he hadn't known that anyone was listening. And so, when he started to talk this way—and perhaps especially at table—it paralyzed me.

Cy or Mother would sometimes attempt to intervene, but he always cut them off with something worse than he'd said to me. Then he would turn his attention back in my direction and continue. He urged me to refuse his order, then to upbraid him, finally to openly defy him—call him the worst of the words he could put in my mouth and hit him. Of course, I never did any of these things, but the urging, the cajoling and ultimately the begging never ceased.

One night, he came into the bedroom where I slept in the bunk-bed over Cy and he shouted at me *why don't you fight back?* Then he dragged my covers off and threw me onto the floor against the bureau. All this was done in the dark, and after my mother had driven me down in the truck to the Emergency Ward of Wellesley Hospital, the doctors told her that my collar-bone was broken. I heard my mother saying *yes, he fell out of bed*.

Everyone—even I—conspired to protect him. The trouble was, my father had no wish to protect himself. At least, it seemed that way until a fellow veteran of Dieppe turned up one day in the shop and my father turned on him with a pair of garden shears and tried to drive him back onto Yonge Street. Far from being afraid of my father, the other man took off his jacket and threw it in my father's face and all the while he stood there, the man was yelling at my father: *Coward! Coward! Yellow Bastard!*

Then, he turned around and walked away. The victor.

120   Thinking for sure the police would come, my mother drew the blind and closed the shop for the rest of the day.

But that was not the end of it. She gathered us together out on the porch and Cy was told to open a can of pork and beans and to make what our mother called a *passel of toast*. He and Rita and I were to eat this meal in the kitchen, after which Cy, who'd been handed a dollar bill my mother had lifted from the till, was to take us down to the Uptown Theatre where an Abbott and Costello film was playing. All these ordinary things we did. Nonetheless, we knew that our father had gone mad.

It was summer then and when the movie was over, I remember Cy and Rita and I stood on the street and the sidewalks gave off heat and the air around us smelled of peanuts and popcorn and Cy said: "I don't think it's safe to go home just yet." For almost an hour, we wandered on Yonge Street, debating what we should do and, at last, we decided we would test the waters by going and looking at the house and listening to see if there was any yelling.

Gibson Avenue only has about twenty houses, most of them semi-detached—and all of them facing south and the park. The porches and the stoops that night were filled with our neighbours drinking beer from coffee cups and fanning themselves with paper plates and folded bits of the *Daily Star*. They were drinking out of cups—you could smell the beer—because the law back then forbade the public consumption, under any circumstance, of alcohol. Whatever you can hide does not exist.

Passing, we watched our neighbours watching us—the Matlocks and the Wheelers and the Conrads and the Bolts—and we knew they were thinking *there go the Max kids and David Max, their father, tried to kill a man today in his store with gardening shears. . . .*

125   "Hello, Cy."

"Hello."

"Ben. Rita."

"Hi."

"Good-night . . . ."

130   We went and stood together on the sidewalk out in front of our house.

Inside, everything seemed to be calm and normal. The lights were turned on in their usual distribution—most of them downstairs. The radio was playing. Someone was singing *Praise the Lord and Pass the Ammunition*.

Cy went up the steps and turned the handle. He was brave—but I'd always known that. Rita and I were told to wait on the porch.

Two minutes passed—or five—or ten—and finally Cy returned. He was very white and his voice was dry, but he wasn't shaking and all he said was: "you'd best come in. I'm calling the police."

Our father had tried to kill our mother with a hammer. She was lying on the sofa and her hands were broken because she had used them trying to fend off the blows.

135   Father had disappeared. The next day, he turned himself in because, as he told the doctors, he had come to his senses. He was kept for a year and a half—almost until the war was over—at the Asylum of the Insane on Queen Street. None of us children was allowed to visit him there—but our mother went to see him six months after he had been committed. She told me they sat in a long, grey room with bars on all the windows. My father wore a dressing gown and hadn't shaved. Mother said he couldn't look her in the eyes. She told him that she forgave him for what he had done. But my father never forgave himself. My mother said she never saw his eyes again.

Two weeks after our father had tried to kill our mother, a brick was thrown through the window of Max's Flowers. On the brick, a single word was printed in yellow chalk.
   Murderer.
   Mother said: "there's no way around this, now. I'm going to have to explain."
   That was how we discovered what had gone wrong with our father at Dieppe.

140   Our mother had known this all along, and I still have strong suspicions Cy had found it out and maybe Rita before our mother went through the formal procedure of sitting us down and telling us all together. Maybe they had thought I was just too young to understand. Maybe Cy and maybe Rita hadn't known. Maybe they had only guessed. At any rate, I had a very strong sense that I was the only one who received our mother's news in a state of shock.
   Father had risen, since his enlistment in 1939, all the way up from an NCO to the rank of captain. Everyone had adored him in the army. He was what they called a natural leader. His men were particularly fond of him and they would, as the saying goes, have followed him anywhere. Then came Dieppe. All but a handful of those who went into battle there were Canadians. This was our Waterloo. Our Gettysburg.
   There isn't a single history book you can read—there isn't a single man who was there who won't tell you—there isn't a single scrap of evidence in any archive to suggest that the battle of Dieppe was anything but a total and appalling disaster. Most have called it a slaughter.
   Dieppe is a port and market town on the coast of Normandy in northern France. In 1942, the British High Command had chosen it to be the object of a practice raid in preparation for the invasion of Europe. The allies on every front were faltering, then. A gesture was needed, and even the smallest of victories would do.
   And so, on the 19th of August, 1942, the raid on Dieppe had taken place—and the consequent carnage had cost the lives of over a thousand Canadians. Over two thousand were wounded or taken prisoner. Five thousand set out; just over one thousand came back.
145   My father never left his landing craft.

He was to have led his men ashore in the second wave of troops to follow the tanks—but, seeing the tanks immobilized, unable to move because the beaches were made of stone and the stones had jammed the tank tracks—and seeing the evident massacre of the first wave of troops whose attempt at storming the shore had been repulsed by machine-gun fire from the cliffs above the town—my father froze in his place and could not move. His men—it is all too apparent—did not know what to do. They had received no order to advance and yet, if they stayed, they were sitting ducks.

In the end, though a handful escaped by rushing forward into the water, the rest were blown to pieces when their landing craft was shelled. In the meantime, my father had recovered enough of his wits to crawl back over the end of the landing craft, strip off his uniform and swim out to sea where he was taken on board a British destroyer sitting offshore.

The destroyer, H.M.S. *Berkley,* was ultimately hit and everyone on board, including my father—no one knowing who he was—was transferred to another ship before the *Berkley* was scuttled where she sat. My father made it all the way back to England, where his burns and wounds were dressed and where he debated taking advantage of the chaos to disappear, hoping that, in the long run, he would be counted among the dead.

His problem was, his conscience had survived. He stayed and, as a consequence, he was confronted by survivors who knew his story. He was dishonourably discharged and sent home to us. Children don't understand such things. The only cowards they recognize are figures cut from comic books or seen on movie screens.

150 Fathers cannot be cowards.

It is impossible.

His torment and his grief were to lead my father all the way to the grave. He left our mother, in the long run, though she would not have wished him to do so and he lived out his days in little bars and back-street beer parlours, seeking whatever solace he could find with whores and derelicts whose stories might have matched his own. The phone would ring and we would dread it. Either it was him or news of him—either his drunken harangue or the name of his most recent jail.

He died in the Wellesley Hospital, the place where I was born—and when he was dying he asked to see his children. Cy and Rita "could not be reached," but I was found—where he'd always found me—sitting within yelling distance. Perhaps this sounds familiar to other children—of whatever age—whose parents, whether one of them or both of them, have made the mistake of losing faith too soon in their children's need to love.

I would have loved a stone.

155 If only he had known.

He sensed it, maybe, in the end. He told me he was sorry for everything—and meant it. He told me the names of all his men and he said he had walked with them all through hell, long since their deaths, to do them honour. He hoped they would understand him, now.

I said they might.

He asked if his ashes could be put with theirs.

Why not, I thought. *A stone among stones.*

160   The beaches at Dieppe can throw you off balance. The angle at which they slope into the water is both steep and dangerous. At high tide you can slide into the waves and lose your footing before you've remembered how to swim. The stones are treacherous. But they are also beautiful.

My father's ashes were contraband. You can't just walk about with someone's remains, in whatever form, in your suitcase. Stepping off the *Sealink* ferry, I carried my father in an envelope addressed to myself in Canada. This was only in case I was challenged. There was hardly more than a handful of him there. I had thrown the rest of him into the English Channel as the coast of Normandy was coming into view. It had been somewhat more than disconcerting to see the interest his ashes caused amongst the gulls and other sea birds. I had hoped to dispose of him in a private way, unnoticed. But a woman with two small children came and stood beside me at the railing and I heard her explain that *this nice gentleman is taking care of our feathered friends.* I hoped that, if my father was watching, he could laugh. I had to look away.

The ferry arrived in the early afternoon and—once I had booked myself into La Présidence Hotel—I went for a walk along the promenade above the sea-wall. It being May, the offshore breeze was warm and filled with the faintest scent of apple trees in bloom.

I didn't want to relive the battle. I hadn't come to conjure ghosts. But the ghosts and the battle are palpable around you there, no matter what your wishes are. The sound of the tide rolling back across the stones is all the cue you need to be reminded of that summer day in 1942. I stood that evening, resting my arms along the wall and thinking *at last, my father has come ashore.*

In the morning, before the town awoke, I got up in the dark and was on the beach when the sun rose inland beyond the cliffs. I wore a thick woollen sweater, walking shorts and a pair of running shoes. The envelope was in my pocket.

165   The concierge must have thought I was just another crazy North American off on my morning run. He grunted as I passed and I pretended not to know that he was there. Out on the beach, I clambered over retaining walls and petrified driftwood until I felt I was safely beyond the range of prying eyes.

The stones at Dieppe are mostly flint—and their colours range from white through yellow to red. The red stones look as if they have been washed in blood and the sight of them takes your breath away. I hunkered down above them, holding all that remained of my father in my fist. He felt like a powdered stone—pummelled and broken.

I let him down between my fingers, feeling him turn to paste—watching him divide and disappear.

He is dead and he is gone.

Weekends, our parents used to take us walking under the trees on Crescent Road. This was on the Rosedale side of Yonge Street. My brother Cy and I were always dressed in dark blue suits whose rough wool shorts would chafe against our thighs. Our knee socks—also blue—were turned down over thick elastic garters. Everything itched and smelled of Sunday. Cy had cleats on his shoes because he walked in such a way as to wear his heels *to the bone*, as my mother said—and causing much expense. The cleats made a wondrous clicking noise and you could always hear him coming. I wanted cleats, but I was refused because, no matter how I tried, I couldn't walk like that.

170   The houses sat up neat as pins beyond their lawns—blank-eyed windows, steaming chimneys—havens of wealth and all the mysteries of wealth.

Father often walked behind us. I don't know why. Mother walked in front with Rita. Rita always wore a dress that was either red or blue beneath her princess coat and in the wintertime she wore a sort of woollen cloche that was tied with a knitted string beneath her chin. Her Mary Jane shoes were just like Shirley Temple's shoes—which, for a while, was pleasing to Rita; then it was not. Rita always had an overpowering sense of image.

After the advent of our father's return, she said from the corner of her mouth one Sunday as we walked on Crescent Road that she and Cy and I had been named as if we were manufactured products: *Cy Max Office Equipment*; *Rita Max Household Appliances* and *Ben Max Watches*. This, she concluded, was why our father had always walked behind us. Proudly, he was measuring our performance. Now, he had ceased to walk behind us and our mother led us forward dressed in black.

Tick. Tick. Tick. That's me. The Ben Max Watch.

I have told our story. But I think it best—and I like it best—to end with all of us moving there beneath the trees in the years before the war. Mister and Mrs. David Max out walking with their children any Sunday afternoon in any kind of weather but the rain.

175   Colonel Matheson, striding down his walk, is caught and forced to grunt acknowledgement that we are there. He cannot ignore us, after all. We have seen him every weekday morning, choosing his boutonnière and buying it from us.

READING AND REACTING

1. The prevailing symbol in the story is stones. Explain the different stones and their possible meaning.
2. Why does Ben take his father's ashes to Dieppe?
3. Why do Rita and Cy reject their father?
4. David Max thinks of himself as a coward. Do you think that assessment is fair?

5. The war experience changes life for the whole Max family, but it ruins David's life. Is "Stones" an antiwar story?
6. Why does Findley use flashbacks to tell the story?
7. Why is Ben a good choice to be the narrator?
8. **JOURNAL ENTRY** David Max uses alcohol to try to cope with his pain. Why is he unsuccessful?
9. **CRITICAL PERSPECTIVE** In *Timothy Findley*, Diana Brydon makes the following comment: "In the short story 'Stones,' Findley's narrator explains that for Canadians, 'This [Dieppe] was our Waterloo. Our Gettysburg.' . . . Findley, along with most Canadians, is well aware of the importance of both world wars in creating a sense of Canadian national identity." Do you agree with Brydon? How did the world wars contribute to a sense of Canadian identity, if in fact they did so?

Related Works: "Barn Burning" (p. 234), "Boys and Girls" (p. 504), "Fathers and Sons" (p. 569), "Dulce et Decorum Est" (p. 695)

⟡ **JANE RULE** (1931–   ) was born and raised in the United States. While teaching English at a private school in Massachusetts, Rule met Helen Sonthoff, with whom she lived in British Columbia from 1956 until Sonthoff's death in 2000. Rule is best known for her writing on lesbian themes. She depicts love between women as an acceptable form of human expression and intimacy. Her 1964 novel *Desert of the Heart* is set in Reno, Nevada, where two women overcome their fears and prejudices and start living together. The book was the basis for the 1986 film *Desert Hearts*. Rule has been a prolific writer of short stories, published in three collections: *Themes for Diverse Instruments* (1975), *Outlander* (1981), and *Inland Passage and Other Stories* (1985). In 1985, she published a collection of essays and opinions called *A Hot-Eyed Moderate*. Rule declared her retirement from writing in 1990 due in part to severe arthritis.

⟡ ⟡ ⟡

JANE RULE

Inland Passage
(1985)

"The other lady . . ." the ship's steward began.

"We're not together," a quiet but determined female voice explained from the corridor, one hand thrust through the doorway insisting that he take her independent tip for the bag he had just deposited on the lower bunk.

There was not room for Troy McFadden to step into the cabin until the steward had left.

"It's awfully small," Fidelity Munroe, the first occupant of the cabin, confirmed, shrinking down into her oversized duffle coat.

5 "It will do if we take turns," Troy McFadden decided. "I'll let you settle first, shall I?"

"I just need a place to put my bag."

The upper bunk was bolted against the cabin ceiling to leave headroom for anyone wanting to sit on the narrow upholstered bench below.

"Under my bunk," Troy McFadden suggested.

There was no other place. The single chair in the cabin was shoved in under the small, square table, and the floor of the minute closet was taken up with life jackets. The bathroom whose door Troy McFadden opened to inspect, had a coverless toilet, sink and triangle of a shower. The one hook on the back of the door might make dressing there possible. When she stepped back into the cabin, she bumped into Fidelity Munroe, crouching down to stow her bag.

10 "I'm sorry," Fidelity said, standing up, "But I can get out now."

"Let's both get out."

They sidled along the narrow corridor, giving room to other passengers in search of their staterooms.

Glancing into one open door, Troy McFadden said, "At least we have a window."

"Deck?" Fidelity suggested.

15 "Oh, yes."

Neither had taken off her coat. They had to shoulder the heavy door together before they could step out into the moist sea air. Their way was blocked to the raised prow of the ship where they might otherwise have watched the cars, campers, and trucks being loaded. They turned instead and walked to the stern of the ferry to find rows of wet, white empty benches facing blankly out to sea.

"You can't even see the Gulf Islands this morning," Troy McFadden observed.

"Are you from around here?"

"Yes, from North Vancouver. We should introduce ourselves, shouldn't we?"

20 "I'm Fidelity Munroe. Everyone calls me Fido."

"I'm Troy McFadden, and nearly everyone calls me Mrs. McFadden."

They looked at each other uncertainly, and then both women laughed.

"Are you going all the way to Prince Rupert?" Fidelity asked.

"And back, just for the ride."

25 "So am I. Are we going to see a thing?"

"It doesn't look like it," Troy McFadden admitted. "I'm told you rarely do on this trip. You sail into mist and maybe get an occasional glimpse of forest or the near shore or an island. Mostly you seem to be going nowhere."

"Then why . . . ?"

"For that reason, I suppose," Troy McFadden answered, gathering her fur collar more closely around her ears.

"I was told it rarely gets rough," Fidelity Munroe offered.

30   "We're in open sea only two hours each way. All the rest is inland passage."

"You've been before then."

"No," Troy McFadden said. "I've heard about it for years."

"So have I, but I live in Toronto. There you hear it's beautiful."

"*Mrs.* Munroe?"

35   "Only technically," Fidelity answered.

"I don't think I can call you Fido."

"It's no more ridiculous than Fidelity once you get used to it."

"Does your mother call you Fido?"

"My mother hasn't spoken to me for years," Fidelity Munroe answered.

40   Two other passengers, a couple in their agile seventies, joined them on the deck.

"Well . . . ." Troy McFadden said, in no one's direction, "I think I'll get my bearings."

She turned away, a woman who did not look as if she ever lost her bearings.

You're not really old enough to be my mother, Fidelity wanted to call after her, *Why take offense?* But it wasn't just that remark. Troy McFadden would be as daunted as Fidelity by such sudden intimacy, the risk of its smells as much as its other disclosures. She would be saying to herself, *I'm too old for this. Why on earth didn't I spend the extra thirty dollars?* Or she was on her way to the purser to see if she might be moved, if not into a single cabin then into one with someone less . . . more . . .

Fidelity looked down at Gail's much too large duffle coat, her own jeans and hiking boots. Well, there wasn't room for the boots in her suitcase, and, ridiculous as they might look for walking the few yards of deck, they might be very useful for exploring the places the ship docked.

45   *Up yours, Mrs. McFadden, with your fur collar and your expensive, sensible shoes and matching bag. Take up the whole damned cabin!*

All Fidelity needed for this mist-bound mistake of a cruise was a book out of her suitcase. She could sleep in the lounge along with the kids and the Indians, leave the staterooms (what a term!) to the geriatrics and Mrs. McFadden.

Fidelity wrenched the door open with her own strength, stomped back along the corridor like one of the invading troops, and unlocked and opened the cabin door in one gesture. There sat Troy McFadden, in surprised tears.

"I'm sorry . . ." Fidelity began, but she could not make her body retreat.

Instead she wedged herself around the door and closed it behind her. Then she sat down beside Troy McFadden, took her hand, and stared quietly at their unlikely pairs of feet. A shadow passed across the window. Fidelity looked up to meet the eyes of another passenger glancing in. She reached up with her free hand and pulled the small curtain across the window.

50   "I simply can't impose . . ." Troy finally brought herself to say.

"Look," Fidelity said, turning to her companion, "I may cry most of the way myself . . . it doesn't matter."

"I just can't make myself . . . walk into those public rooms . . . alone."

"How long have you been alone?" Fidelity asked.

"My husband died nearly two years ago . . . there's no excuse."

55   "Somebody said to me the other day, 'Shame's the last stage of grief.' 'What a rotten arrangement then,' I said. 'To be ashamed for the rest of my life.'"

"You've lost your husband?"

Fidelity shook her head, "Years ago. I divorced him."

"You hardly look old enough . . ."

"I know, but I am. I'm forty-one. I've got two grown daughters."

60   "I have two sons," Troy said. "One offered to pay for this trip just to get me out of town for a few days. The other thought I should lend him the money instead."

"And you'd rather have?"

"It's so humiliating," Troy said.

"To be alone?"

"To be afraid."

65   The ship's horn sounded.

"We're about to sail," Troy said. "I didn't even have the courage to get off the ship, and here I am, making you sit in the dark . . ."

"Shall we go out and get our bearings together?"

"Let me put my face back on," Troy said.

Only then did Fidelity let go of her hand so that she could take her matching handbag into the tiny bathroom and smooth courage back into her quite handsome and appealing face.

70   Fidelity pulled her bag out from under the bunk, opened it and got out her own sensible shoes. If she was going to offer this woman any sort of reassurance, she must make what gestures she could to be a bird of her feather.

The prow of the ship had been lowered and secured, and the reverse engines had ceased their vibrating by the time the two women joined the bundled passengers on deck to see, to everyone's amazement, the sun breaking through, an ache to the eyes on the shining water.

Troy McFadden reached for her sunglasses. Fidelity Munroe had forgotten hers.

"This is your captain," said an intimate male voice from a not very loud speaker just above their heads. "We are sailing into a fair day."

The shoreline they had left remained hidden in clouds crowded up against the Vancouver mountains, but the long wooded line of Galiano Island and beyond it to the west the mountains of Vancouver Island lay in a clarity of light.

75   "I'm hungry," Fidelity announced. "I didn't get up in time to have breakfast."

"I couldn't eat," Troy confessed.

When she hesitated at the entrance to the cafeteria, Fidelity took her arm firmly and directed her into the short line that had formed.

"Look at that!" Fidelity said with pleasure. "Sausages, ham, bacon, pancakes. How much can we have?"

"As much as you want," answered the young woman behind the counter.

80   "Oh, am I ever going to pig out on this trip!"

Troy took a bran muffin, apple juice and a cup of tea.

"It isn't fair," she said as they unloaded their contrasting trays at a window table. "My husband could eat like that, too, and never gain a pound."

Fidelity, having taken off her coat, revealed just how light-bodied she was.

"My kids call me bird bones. They have their father to thank for being human size. People think I'm their little brother."

85   "Once children tower over you, being their mother is an odd business," Troy mused.

"That beautiful white hair must help," Fidelity said.

"I've had it since I was twenty-five. When the boys were little, people thought I was their grandmother."

"I suppose only famous people are mistaken for themselves in public," Fidelity said, around a mouthful of sausage; so she checked herself and chewed instead of elaborating on that observation.

"Which is horrible in its way, too, I suppose," Troy said.

90   Fidelity swallowed. "I don't know. I've sometimes thought I'd like it: Mighty Mouse[1] fantasies."

She saw Troy try to smile and for a second lose the trembling control of her face. She hadn't touched her food.

"Drink your juice," Fidelity said, in the no-nonsense, cheerful voice of motherhood.

Troy's dutiful hand shook as she raised the glass to her lips, but she took a sip. She returned the glass to the table without accident and took up the much less dangerous bran muffin.

"I would like to be invisible," Troy said, a rueful apology in her voice.

95   "Well, we really are, aren't we?" Fidelity asked. "Except to a few people."

"Have you traveled alone a lot?"

"No," Fidelity said, "just about never. I had the girls, and they're still only semi-independent. And I had a friend, Gail. She and I took trips together. She died last year."

"I'm so sorry."

"Me, too. It's a bit like being a widow, I guess, except, nobody expects it to be. Maybe that helps."

100   "Did you live with Gail?"

"No, but we thought maybe we might . . . someday."

Troy sighed.

"So here we both are at someday," Fidelity said. "Day one of someday and not a bad day at that."

They both looked out at the coast, ridge after ridge of tall trees, behind which were sudden glimpses of high peaks of snow-capped mountains.

105   Back on the deck other people had also ventured, dressed and hatted against the wind, armed with binoculars for sighting of eagles and killer whales, for inspecting the crews of fishing boats, tugs, and pleasure craft.

---

[1] Cartoon character who uses super powers in his battles with cats.

"I never could use those things," Fidelity confessed. "It's not just my eyes. I feel like that woman in the Colville[2] painting."

"Do you like his work?" Troy asked.

"I admire it," Fidelity said. "There's something a bit sinister about it: all those figures seem prisoners of normality. That woman at the shore, about to get into the car . . ."

"With the children, yes," Troy said. "They seem so vulnerable."

110 "Here's Jonathan Seagull!" a woman called to her binocular-blinded husband, "Right here on the rail."

"I loathed that book," Troy murmured to Fidelity.

Fidelity chuckled. "In the first place, I'm no friend to seagulls."

Finally chilled, the two women went back inside. At the door to the largest lounge, again Troy hesitated.

"Take my arm," Fidelity said, wishing it and she were more substantial.

115 They walked the full length of that lounge and on into the smaller space of the gift shop where Troy was distracted from her nerves by postcards, travel books, toys and souvenirs.

Fidelity quickly picked up half a dozen postcards.

"I'd get home before they would," Troy said.

"I probably will, too, but everybody likes mail."

From the gift shop, they found their way to the forward lounge where tv sets would later offer a movie, on into the children's playroom, a glassed-in area heavily padded where several toddlers tumbled and stumbled about.

120 "It's like an aquarium," Fidelity said.

"There aren't many children aboard."

"One of the blessings of traveling in October," Fidelity said. "Oh, I don't feel about kids the way I do about seagulls, but they aren't a holiday."

"No," Troy agreed. "I suppose I really just think I miss mine."

Beyond the playroom they found the bar with only three tables of pre-lunch drinkers. Troy looked in, shook her head firmly and retreated.

125 "Not a drinker?" Fidelity asked.

"I have a bottle of scotch in my case," Troy said. "I don't think I could ever . . . alone . . ."

"Mrs. McFadden," Fidelity said, taking her arm, "I'm going to make a hard point. You're not alone. You're with me, and we're both old enough to be grandmothers, and we're approaching the turn of the 21st not the 20th century, and I think we both could use a drink."

Troy McFadden allowed herself to be steered into the bar and settled at a table, but, when the waiter came, she only looked at her hands.

"Sherry," Fidelity decided. "Two sherries," and burst out laughing.

130 Troy looked over at her, puzzled.

"Sherry is my idea of what you would order. I've never tasted it in my life."

"You're quite right," Troy said. "Am I such a cliché?"

---

[2] Twentieth-century Canadian artist whose paintings depict everyday events and scenes.

"Not a cliché, an ideal. I don't know, maybe they're the same thing when it comes down to it. You have style. I really admire that. If I ever got it together enough to have shoes and matching handbag, I'd lose one of the shoes."

"Is that really your coat?" Troy asked.

135   Fidelity looked down at herself. "No, it belonged to Gail. It's my Linus blanket."

"I've been sleeping in my husband's old pajamas. I had to buy a night-gown to come on this trip," Troy confided. "I think it's marvelous the way you do what you want."

Fidelity bit her lip and screwed her face tight for a moment. Then she said, "But I don't want to cry any more than you do."

The waiter put their sherries before them, and Fidelity put a crumpled ten dollar bill on the table.

"Oh, you should let me," Troy said, reaching for her purse.

140   "Next round," Fidelity said.

Troy handled her glass more confidently than she had at breakfast, and, after her first sip, she said with relief, "Dry."

"This is your captain," the intimate male voice asserted again. "A pod of killer whales is approaching to starboard."

Fidelity and Troy looked out the window and waited. No more than a hundred yards away, a killer whale broke the water, then another, then another, their black backs arching, their bellies unbelievably white.

"They don't look real," Fidelity exclaimed.

145   Then one surfaced right alongside the ferry, and both women caught their breath.

"This trip is beginning to feel less like somebody else's day dream," Fidelity said. "Just look at that!"

For some moments after the whales had passed, the women continued to watch the water, newly interested in its possibilities for surprise. As if as a special reward for their attention, an enormous bird dropped out of the sky straight into the sea, then lifted off the water with a strain of great wings, a flash of fish in its talons.

"What on earth was that?" Fidelity cried.

"A bald eagle catching a salmon," Troy replied.

150   The ship had slowed to navigate a quite narrow passage between the mainland and a small island, its northern crescent shore fingered with docks, reached by flights of steps going back up into the trees where the glint of windows and an occasional line of roof could be seen.

"Do people live there all year long?" Fidelity asked.

"Not many. They're summer places mostly."

"How do people get there?"

"Private boats or small planes."

155   "Ain't the rich wealthy?" Fidelity sighed.

Troy frowned.

"Did I make a personal remark by mistake?"

"Geoff and I had a place when the boys were growing up. We didn't have money, but he earned a good deal . . . law. He hadn't got around to thinking about . . . retiring. I'm just awfully grateful the boys had finished their education. It scares me to think what it might have been like if it had happened earlier. You just don't think . . . we didn't anyway. Oh, now that I've sold the house, I'm perfectly comfortable. When you're just one person . . ."

"Well, on this trip with the food all paid for, I'm going to eat like an army," Fidelity said. "Let's have lunch."

160   Though the ship wasn't crowded, there were more people in the cafeteria than there had been for breakfast.

"Let's not sit near the Jonathan Seagulls," Fidelity said, leading the way through the tables to a quiet corner where they could do more watching than being watched. Troy had chosen a seafood salad that Fidelity considered a first course to which she added a plate of lamb chops, rice and green beans.

"I really don't believe you could eat like that all the time," Troy said.

"Would if I could."

Fidelity tried not to let greed entirely overtake her, yet she needed to eat quickly not to leave Troy with nothing to do.

165   "See those two over there?" Fidelity said, nodding to a nondescript pair of middle-aged women. "One's a lady cop. The other's her prisoner."

"How did you figure that out?"

"Saw the handcuffs. That's why they're sitting side by side."

"They're both right handed," Troy observed critically.

"On their ankles."

170   "What's she done?"

"Blown up a mortgage company," Fidelity said.

"She ought to get a medal."

"A fellow anarchist, are you?"

"Only armchair," Troy admitted modestly.

175   "Mrs. McFadden, you're a fun lady. I'm glad we got assigned to the same shoe box."

"Do call me Troy."

"Only if you call me Fido."

"Will you promise not to bark?"

"No," Fidelity said and growled convincingly at a lamb chop but quietly enough not to attract attention.

180   "Fido, would it be both antisocial and selfish of me to take a rest after lunch?"

"Of course not," Fidelity said. "I'll just come up and snag a book."

"Then later you could have a rest."

"I'm not good at them," Fidelity said. "I twitch and have horrible dreams if I sleep during the day. But, look, I do have to know a few intimate things about you, like do you play bridge or Scrabble or poker because I don't, but I could probably scout out some people who do . . ."

"I loathe games," Troy said. "In any case, please don't feel responsible for me. I do feel much better, thanks to you."

185   A tall, aging fat man nodded to Troy as they left the cafeteria and said, "Lovely day."

"Don't panic," Fidelity said out of the side of her mouth. "I bite too, that is, unless you're in the market for a shipboard romance."

"How about you?" Troy asked wryly.

"I'm not his type."

"Well, he certainly isn't mine!"

190   Fidelity went into the cabin first, struggled to get her case out from under the bunk and found her book, Alice Walker's[3] collection of essays.

"Is she good?" Troy asked, looking at the cover.

"I think she's terrific, but I have odd tastes."

"Odd?"

"I'm a closet feminist."

195   "But isn't that perfectly respectable by now?" Troy asked.

"Nothing about me is perfectly respectable."

"You're perfectly dear," Troy said and gave Fidelity a quick, hard hug before she went into the cabin.

Fidelity paused for a moment outside the closed door to enjoy that affectionate praise before she headed off to find a window seat in the lounge where she could alternately read and watch the passing scene. An occasional deserted Indian village was now the only sign of habitation on the shores of this northern wilderness.

The book lay instead neglected in her lap, and the scenery became a transparency through which Fidelity looked at her inner landscape, a place of ruins.

200   A man whose wife had died of the same cancer that had killed Gail said to Fidelity, "I don't even want to take someone out to dinner without requiring her to have a thorough physical examination first."

The brutality of that remark shocked Fidelity because it located in her her own denied bitterness, that someone as lovely and funny and strong as Gail could be not only physically altered out of recognition but so horribly transformed humanly until she seemed to have nothing left but anger, guilt, and fear, burdens she tried to shift, as she couldn't her pain, onto Fidelity's shoulders, until Fidelity found herself praying for Gail's death instead of her life. Surely she had loved before she grew to dread the sight of Gail, the daily confrontations with her appalled and appalling fear. It was a face looking into hell Fidelity knew did not exist, and yet her love had failed before it. Even now it was her love she mourned rather than Gail, for without it she could not go back to the goodness between them, believe in it and go on.

She felt herself withdraw from her daughters as if her love for them might also corrupt and then fail them. In the way of adolescents they both noticed and didn't, excused her grief and then became impatient with it. They were anyway perched at the edge of their own lives, ready to be free of her.

"Go," she encouraged them, and they did.

"I guess I only think I miss them," Troy said. Otherwise this convention of parent abandonment would be intolerable, a cruel and unusual punishment for all those years of intimate attention and care.

---

[3] Feminist African-American writer (see page 326).

205 And here she was, temporarily paired with another woman as fragile and shamed by self-pity as she was. At least they wouldn't be bleeding all over the other passengers. If they indulged in pitying each other, well, what was the harm in it?

Fidelity shifted uncomfortably. The possibility of harm was all around her.

"Why did you marry me then?" she had demanded of her hostile husband.

"I felt *sorry* for you," he said.

"That's a lie!"

210 "It's the honest truth."

So pity, even from someone else, is the seed of contempt.

Review resolutions for this trip: be cheerful, eat, indulge in Mighty Mouse fantasies, and enjoy the scenery.

An island came into focus, a large bird perched in a tree, another eagle no doubt, and she would not think of the fish except in its surprised moment of flight.

"This is your captain speaking . . ."

215 Fidelity plugged her ears and also shut her eyes, for even if she missed something more amazing than whales, she wanted to see or not see for herself.

"Here you are," Troy said. "What on earth are you doing?"

"Do you think he's going to do that all through the trip?" Fidelity demanded.

"Probably not after dark."

"Pray for an early sunset."

220 It came, as they stood watching it on deck, brilliantly red with promise, leaving the sky christened with stars.

"Tell me about these boys of yours," Fidelity said as they sat over a pre-dinner drink in the crowded bar. "We've spent a whole day together without even taking out our pictures. That's almost unnatural."

"In this den of iniquity," Troy said, glancing around, "I'm afraid people will think we're exchanging dirty post-cards."

"Why oh why did I leave mine at home?"

Fidelity was surprised that Troy's sons were not better looking than they were, and she suspected Troy was surprised at how much better looking her daughters were than she had any right to expect. It's curious how really rare a handsome couple is. Beauty is either too vain for competition or indifferent to itself. Troy would have chosen a husband for his character. Fidelity had fallen for narcissistic good looks, for which her daughters were her only and lovely reward.

225 "Ralph's like his father," Troy said, taking back the picture of her older son, "conservative with some attractive independence of mind. So many of our friends had trouble with first children and blame it on their own inexperience. Geoff used to say, 'I guess the more we knew, the worse we did.'"

"What's the matter with Colin?" Fidelity asked.

"I've never thought there was anything the matter with him," Troy said, "except perhaps the world. Geoff didn't like his friends or his work (Colin's an actor). It was the only hard thing between Geoff and me, but it was very hard."

The face Fidelity studied was less substantial and livelier than Ralph's, though it was easy enough to tell that they were brothers.

"We ought to pair at least two of them off, don't you think?" Fidelity suggested flippantly. "Let's see. Is it better to put the conservative, responsible ones together, and let the scallywags go off and have fun, or should each kite have a tail?"

230   "Colin won't marry," Troy said. "He's homosexual."

Fidelity looked up from the pictures to read Troy's face. Her dark blue eyes held a question rather than a challenge.

"How lucky for him that you're his mother," Fidelity said. "Did you realize that I am, too?"

"I wondered when you spoke about your friend Gail," Troy said.

"Sometimes I envy people his age," Fidelity said. "There's so much less guilt, so much more acceptance."

235   "In some quarters," Troy said. "Geoff let it kill him."

"How awful!"

"That isn't true," Troy said. "It's the first time I've ever said it out loud, and it simply isn't true. But I've been so afraid Colin thought so, so angry, yes, *angry*. I always thought Geoff would finally come round. He was basically a fair-minded man. Then he had a heart attack and died. If he'd had any warning, if he'd had time . . ."

Fidelity shook her head. She did not want to say how easily that might have been worse. Why did people persist in the fantasy that facing death brought out the best in people when so often it did just the opposite?

"How does Colin feel about his father?"

240   "He always speaks of him very lovingly, remembering all the things he did with the boys when they were growing up. He never mentions those last, awful months when Geoff was remembering the same things but only so that he didn't have to blame himself."

"Maybe Colin's learning to let them go," Fidelity suggested.

"So why can't I?" Troy asked.

There was Fidelity's own question in Troy's mouth. *It's because they're dead*, she thought. *How do you go about forgiving the dead for dying*? Then, because she had no answer, she simply took Troy's hand.

"Is that why your mother doesn't speak to you?" Troy asked.

245   "That and a thousand other things," Fidelity said. "It used to get to me, but, as my girls have grown up, I think we're all better off for not trying to please someone who won't be pleased. Probably it hasn't anything to do with me, just luck, that I like my kids, and they like me pretty well most of the time."

"Did they know about you and Gail?"

"Did and didn't. We've never actually talked about it. I would have, but Gail was dead set against it. I didn't realize just how much that had to do with her own hang-ups. Once she was gone, there didn't seem to be much point, for them."

"But for you?"

"Would you like another drink?" Fidelity asked as she signaled the waiter and, at Troy's nod, ordered two. "For myself, I'd like to tell the whole damned world, but I'm still enough of my mother's child to hear her say, 'Another one of your awful self-indulgences' and to think maybe she has a point."

250 "It doesn't seem to me self-indulgent to be yourself," Troy said.

Fidelity laughed suddenly. "Why that's exactly what it is! Why does everything to do with the self have such a bad press: self-pity, self-consciousness, self-indulgence, self-satisfaction, practices of selfish people, people being themselves?"

"The way we are," Troy said.

"Yes, and I haven't felt as good about myself in months."

"Nor I," Troy said, smiling.

255 "Are we going to watch the movie tonight, or are we going to go on telling each other the story of our lives?"

"We have only three days," Troy said. "And this one is nearly over."

"I suppose we'd better eat before the cafeteria closes."

They lingered long over coffee after dinner until they were alone in the room, and they were still there when the movie goers came back for a late night snack. Troy yawned and looked at her watch.

"Have we put off the evil hour as long as we can?" Fidelity asked.

260 "You're going to try to talk me out of the lower bunk."

"I may be little, but I'm very agile," Fidelity claimed.

The top bunk had been made up, leaving only a narrow corridor in which to stand or kneel, as they had to to get at their cases. Troy took her nightgown and robe and went into the bathroom. Fidelity changed into her flannel tent and climbed from the chair to the upper bunk, too close to the ceiling for sitting. She lay on her side, her head propped up on her elbow.

It occurred to her that this cabin was the perfect setting for the horrible first night of a honeymoon and she was about to tell Troy so as she came out of the bathroom but she looked both so modest and so lovely that an easy joke seemed instead tactless.

"I didn't have the courage for a shower," Troy confessed. "Really, you know, we're too old for this."

265 "I think that's beginning to be part of the fun."

When they had both settled and turned out their lights, Fidelity said, "Good night, Troy."

"Good night, dear Fido."

Fidelity did not expect to sleep at once, her head full of images and revelations, but the gentle motion of the ship lulled her, and she felt herself letting go and dropping away. When she woke, it was morning, and she could hear the shower running.

"You did it!" Fidelity shouted as Troy emerged fully dressed in a plum and navy pant suit, her night things over her arm.

270 "I don't wholeheartedly recommend it as an experience, but I do feel better for it."

Fidelity followed Troy's example. It seemed to her the moment she turned on the water, the ship's movement became more pronounced, and she had to hang onto a bar which might have been meant for a towel rack to keep her balance, leaving only one hand for the soaping. By the time she was through, the floor was awash, and she had to sit on the coverless toilet to pull on her grey and patchily soggy trousers and fresh wool shirt.

"We're into open water," Troy said, looking out their window.

"Two hours, you said?"

"Yes."

275   "I think I'm going to be better off on deck," Fidelity admitted, her normally pleasurable hunger pangs suddenly unresponsive to the suggestion of sausages and eggs. "Don't let me keep you from breakfast."

"What makes you think I'm such an old sea dog myself?"

Once they were out in the sun and air of a lovely morning, the motion of the open sea was exciting. They braced themselves against the railing and plunged with the ship, crossing from the northern tip of Vancouver Island to the mainland.

A crewman informed them that the ship would be putting in at Bella Bella to drop off supplies and pick up passengers.

"Will there be time to go ashore?" Fidelity asked.

280   "You can see everything there is to see from here," the crewman answered.

"No stores?"

"Just the Indian store . . . for the Indians," he said, as he turned to climb to the upper deck.

"A real, lived-in Indian village!" Fidelity said. "Do you want to go ashore?"

"It doesn't sound to me as if we'd be very welcome," Troy said.

285   "Why not?"

"You're not aware that we're not very popular with the Indians?"

Fidelity sighed. She resented, as she always did, having to take on the sins and clichés of her race, nation, sex, and yet she was less willing to defy welcome at an Indian village than she was at the ship's bar.

They were able to see the whole of the place from the deck, irregular rows of raw wood houses climbing up a hill stripped of trees. There were more dogs than people on the dock. Several family groups, cheaply but more formally dressed than most of the other passengers, boarded.

"It's depressing," Fidelity said.

290   "I wish we knew how to expect something else and make it happen."

"I'm glad nobody else was living on the moon," Fidelity said, turning sadly away.

The Indian families were in the cafeteria where Troy and Fidelity went for their belated breakfast. The older members of the group were talking softly among themselves in their own language. The younger ones were chatting with the crew in a friendly enough fashion. They were all on their way to a great wedding in Prince Rupert that night and would be back on board ship when it sailed south again at midnight.

"Do you work?" Troy suddenly asked Fidelity as she put a large piece of ham in her mouth.

Fidelity nodded as she chewed.

295 "What do you do?"

"I'm a film editor," Fidelity said.

"Something as amazing as that, and you haven't even bothered to tell me?"

"It's nothing amazing," Fidelity said. "You sit in a dark room all by your-self, day after day, trying to make a creditable half hour or hour and a half out of hundreds of hours of film."

"You don't like it at all?"

300 "Oh, well enough," Fidelity said. "Sometimes it's interesting. Once I did a film on Haida carving that was shot up here in the Queen Charlottes, one of the reasons I've wanted to see this part of the country."

"How did you decide to be a film editor?"

"I didn't really. I went to art school. I was going to be a great painter. Mighty Mouse fantasy number ten. I got married instead. He didn't work; so I had to. It was a job, and after a while I got pretty good at it."

"Did he take care of the children?"

"My mother did," Fidelity said, "until they were in school. They've had to be pretty independent."

305 "Oh, Fido, you've done so much more with your life than I have."

"Got divorced and earned a living because I had to. Not exactly things to brag about."

"But it's ongoing, something of your own to do."

"I suppose so," Fidelity admitted, "but you know, after Gail died, I looked around me and realized that, aside from my kids, I didn't really have any friends. I worked alone. I lived alone. I sometimes think now I should quit, do something entirely different. I can't risk that until the girls are really independent, not just playing house with Mother's off-stage help. Who knows? One of them might turn up on my doorstep as I did on my mother's."

"I'd love a job," Troy said, "but I'd never have the courage . . ."

310 "Of course you would," Fidelity said.

"Are you volunteering to take me by the hand as you did yesterday and say to the interviewer, 'This is my friend, Mrs. McFadden. She can't go into strange places by herself'?"

"Sure," Fidelity said. "I'll tell you what, let's go into business together."

"What kind of business?"

"Well, we could run a selling gallery and lose our shirts."

315 "Or a bookstore and lose our shirts . . . I don't really have a shirt to lose."

"Let's be more practical. How about a gay bar?"

"Oh, Fido," Troy said, laughing and shaking her head.

The ship now had entered a narrow inland passage, moving slowly and carefully past small islands. The captain, though he still occasionally pointed out a deserted cannery, village or mine site, obviously had to pay more attention to the task of bringing his ship out of this narrow reach in a nearly silent wilderness into the noise and clutter of the town of Prince Rupert.

A bus waited to take those passengers who had signed up for a tour of the place, and Troy and Fidelity were among them. Their driver and guide was a young man fresh from Liverpool, and he looked on his duty as bizarre, for what was there really to see in Prince Rupert but one ridge of rather expensive houses overlooking the harbor and a small neighborhood of variously tasteless houses sold to fishermen in seasons when they made too much money so that they could live behind pretentious front doors on unemployment all the grey winter long. The only real stop was a small museum of Indian artifacts and old tools. The present Indian population was large and poor and hostile.

320 "It's like being in Greece," Fidelity said, studying a small collection of beautifully patterned baskets. "Only here it's been over for less than a hundred years."

They ate delicious seafood at an otherwise unremarkable hotel and then skipped an opportunity to shop at a mall left open in the evening for the tour's benefit, business being what it was in winter. Instead they took a taxi back to the ship.

"I think it's time to open my bottle of scotch," Troy suggested.

They got ice from a vending machine and went back to their cabin, where Fidelity turned the chair so that she could put her feet up on the bunk and Troy could sit at the far end with her feet tucked under her.

"Cozy," Troy decided.

325 "I wish I liked scotch," Fidelity said, making a face.

By the time the steward came to make up the bunks, returning and new passengers were boarding the ship. Troy and Fidelity out on deck watched the Indians being seen off by a large group of friends and relatives who must also have been to the wedding. Fidelity imagined them in an earlier time getting into great canoes to paddle south instead of settling down to a few hours' sleep on the lounge floor. She might as well imagine herself and Troy on a sailing ship bringing drink and disease.

A noisy group of Australians came on deck.

"You call this a ship?" they said to each other. "You call those cabins?"

They had traveled across the States and had come back across Canada, and they were not happily prepared to spend two nights in cabins even less comfortable than Fidelity's and Troy's.

330 "Maybe the scenery will cheer them up," Fidelity suggested as they went back to their cabin.

"They sound to me as if they've already had more scenery than they can take."

True enough. The Australians paced the decks like prisoners looking at the shore only to evaluate their means of escape, no leaping whale or plummeting eagle compensation for this coastal ferry which had been described in their brochures as a "cruise ship." How different they were from the stoically settled Indians who had quietly left the ship at Bella Bella shortly after dawn.

Fidelity and Troy stayed on deck for the open water crossing to Port Hardy on Vancouver Island, went in only long enough to get warm, then back out into the brilliant sun and sea wind to take delight in every shape of island, contour of hill, the play of light on the water, the least event of sea life until even their cloud of complaining gulls seemed part of the festival of their last day.

"Imagine preferring something like The Love Boat,"[4] Troy said.

335   "Gail and I were always the ferry, barge, and freighter types," Fidelity said.

Film clips moved through her mind, Gail sipping ouso in a café in Athens, Gail hailing a cab in London, Gail . . . a face she had begun to believe stricken from her memory was there in its many moods at her bidding.

"What is it?" Troy asked.

"Some much better reruns in my head," Fidelity said, smiling. "I guess it takes having fun to remember how often I have."

"What time is your plane tomorrow?" Troy asked.

340   The question hit Fidelity like a blow.

"Noon," she managed to say before she excused herself and left Troy for the first time since she had pledged herself to Troy's need.

Back in their cabin, sitting on the bunk that was also Troy's bed, Fidelity was saying to herself, "You're such an idiot, such an idiot, such an idiot!"

Two and a half days playing Mighty Mouse better than she ever had in her life, and suddenly she was dissolving into a maudlin fool, into tears of a sort she hadn't shed since her delayed adolescence.

"I can't want her. I just can't," Fidelity chanted.

345   It was worse than coming down with a toothache, breaking out in boils, this stupid, sweet desire which she simply had to hide from a woman getting better and better at reading her face unless she wanted to wreck the last hours of this lovely trip.

Troy shoved open the cabin door.

"Did I say something . . . ?"

Fidelity shook her head, "No, just my turn, I guess."

"You don't want to miss your last dinner, do you?"

350   "Of course not," Fidelity said, trying to summon up an appetite she could indulge in.

They were shy of each other over dinner, made conversation in a way they hadn't needed to from the first few minutes of their meeting. The strain of it made Fidelity both long for sleep and dread the intimacy of their cabin where their new polite reserve would be unbearable.

"Shall we have an early night?" Troy suggested. "We have to be up awfully early to disembark."

As they knelt together, getting out their night things, Troy said, mocking their awkward position, "I'd say a prayer of thanks if I thought there was anybody up there to pray to."

---

[4] Television series in which passengers on a cruise ship often discover romance.

Fidelity *was* praying for whatever help there was against her every instinct.

355   "I'm going to find it awfully hard to say good-bye to you, Fido."

Fidelity had to turn then to Troy's lovely, vulnerable face.

"I just can't . . ." Fidelity began.

Then, unable to understand that it could happen, Fidelity was embracing Troy, and they moved into love-making as trustingly as they had talked.

At six in the morning, when Troy's travel alarm went off, she said, "I don't think I can move."

360   Fidelity, unable to feel the arm that lay under Troy, whispered, "We're much too old for this."

"I was afraid you thought I was," Troy said as she slowly and painfully untangled herself, "and now I'm going to prove it."

"Do you know what I almost said to you the first night?" Fidelity asked, loving the sight of Troy's naked body in the light of the desk lamp she'd just turned on. "I almost said, 'what a great setting for the first horrible night of a honeymoon.'"

"Why didn't you?"

"You were so lovely, coming out of the bathroom," Fidelity explained, knowing it wasn't an explanation.

365   "You were wrong," Troy said, defying her painful stiffness to lean down to kiss Fidelity.

"Young lovers would skip breakfast," Fidelity said.

"But you're starved."

Fidelity nodded, having no easy time getting out of bed herself.

It occurred to her to disturb the virgin neatness of her own upper bunk only because it would have been the first thing to occur to Gail, a bed ravager of obsessive proportions. If it didn't trouble Troy, it would not trouble Fidelity.

370   As they sat eating, the sun rose over the Vancouver mountains, catching the windows of the apartment blocks on the north shore.

"I live over there," Troy said.

"Troy?"

"Will you invite me to visit you in Toronto?"

"Come with me."

375   "I have to see Colin . . . and Ralph. I could be there in a week."

"I was wrong about those two over there," Fidelity said. "They sit side by side because they're lovers."

"And you thought so in the first place," Troy said.

Fidelity nodded.

"This is your captain speaking . . ."

380   Because he was giving them instructions about how to disembark, Fidelity did listen but only with one ear, for she had to keep her own set of instructions clearly in her head. She, of course, had to see her children, too.

READING AND REACTING

1. What are the main character traits of Troy McFadden? What is her most positive trait? Least positive?
2. What are the main character traits of Fidelity Munroe? What is her most positive trait? Least positive?
3. Why are the two women going on the boat trip?
4. What significance is there in Troy McFadden's comment that scenery is rarely visible, that "[m]ostly you seem to be going nowhere"?
5. What event makes the women decide to try to be closer to each other emotionally?
6. Jane Rule uses a great deal of dialogue in the story. Do you think it is effective or would more exposition reveal the characters more effectively?
7. **JOURNAL ENTRY** Becoming intimate with someone is often frightening because of a variety of reasons. What are some of these reasons?

Related Works: "Araby" (p. 267), "Opening Night" (p. 542), "Wanting" (p. 707)

◆ WRITING SUGGESTIONS: CHARACTER

1. Focusing on an unconventional character in a past setting, "A Rose for Emily" (p. 90) explores what constitutes proper behaviour. Examine how Emily's need for contact overcomes her sense of social convention and morality.
2. In "A&P" (p. 122), "The Yellow Wall-Paper" (p. 189), and "A Garden of Her Own" (p. 202), characters struggle against rules, authority figures, and inflexible social systems. Choose two of these stories, and compare and contrast the struggles in which the characters are engaged.
3. Write an essay in which you contrast the character of Fidelity Munroe with the character of Phoenix Jackson in "A Worn Path" (p. 397). Consider how each character interacts with those around her as well as how each seems to see her role or mission in the world.
4. Contrast the character of John in "A Field of Wheat" (p. 173) and David Max in "Stones" (p. 135). Consider how each man copes with his role as father and husband and how he relates to the circumstances in which he finds himself.
5. Sammy, Lois in "Death by Landscape" (p. 335), and the narrator of "Boys and Girls" (p. 504) all use their active imaginations to create scenarios to help them get through the day. None of them is able to sustain the illusion, however. As a result, all three find out how harsh reality can be. What steps could these three characters take to fit more comfortably into the worlds they inhabit? *Should* they take such steps? Are they able to do so?

Chapter 6

Setting

◆ ◆ ◆

I think that the sense of place is extremely important to most writers.
Certainly it is to me. I identify very strongly with places where I have lived,
where I have been, where I have invested some part of my being. . . . The earth
was here before I was. When I came, I simply identified place by living in it or
looking at it. One does create place in the same way that the storyteller creates
himself, creates his listener. The writer creates a place.

N. Scott Momaday, *Ancestral Voices*

I once complained to a writer friend that every time I start a new story my goal
is to write it in fast, tight, clean, clear prose—*The Old Man and the Sea; The Bridge
of San Luis Rey*—but that once I get into the job, prose springs up all around me
like a jungle: new people get into the act, the story becomes more complex and
mysterious than I'd anticipated, all of the world seems to want to be part of the
action. Less puzzled by this than I, my friend suggested that things could not be
otherwise. "You were born and raised in a temperate rainforest. You have a rainforest brain—fecund and complex as a jungle. Don't fight it. So long as you're
writing about Vancouver Island, this is not only inevitable but appropriate. . . ."

Jack Hodgins, *A Passion for Narrative*

We all know that the weather affects our moods. The [writer] is in the happy
position of being able to invent whatever weather is appropriate to the mood
he or she wants to evoke.

Weather is therefore frequently a trigger for the effect John Ruskin called the
pathetic fallacy, the projection of human emotions onto phenomena in the natural world. "All violent feelings . . . produce in us a falseness in our impressions
of external things, which I would generally characterize as the pathetic fallacy,"
he wrote. As the name implies, Ruskin thought it was a bad thing, a symptom
of the decadence of modern (as compared to classical) art and literature, and it
is indeed often the occasion of overblown, self-indulgent writing. But used with
intelligence and discretion it is a rhetorical device capable of moving and powerful effects, without which fiction would be much the poorer.

David Lodge, *The Art of Fiction*

◆ ◆ ◆

The **setting** of a work of fiction establishes its historical, geographical, and physical location. *Where* a work is set—on a tropical island, in a dungeon, at a crowded party, in a tent in the woods—influences our interpretation of the story's events and characters. *When* a work takes place—during the French Revolution, during the Vietnam War, today, or in the future—is equally important. Setting, however, is more than just the approximate time and place in which the work is set; setting also encompasses a wide variety of physical and cultural elements.

Clearly, setting is more important in some works than in others. In some stories, no particular time or place is specified, or even suggested, perhaps because the writer does not consider a specific setting to be important or because the writer wishes the story's events to seem timeless and universal. In Ursula K. Le Guin's "The Ones Who Walk Away from Omelas" (p. 442), the setting is fantastical—an imaginative otherworld. In other stories, a writer may provide only minimal information about setting, telling readers little more than where and when the action takes place. Sometimes, however, a particular setting may be vital to the story, perhaps influencing characters' behaviour, as it does in Charlotte Perkins Gilman's "The Yellow Wall-Paper" (p. 189). In such cases, of course, setting must be fully described.

Sometimes a story's central conflict is between the protagonist and the setting—for example, Alice in Wonderland; a Northerner in the U.S. South; a naive, unsophisticated North American tourist in an old European city; a sane person in a mental hospital; a moral person in a corrupt environment; an immigrant in a new world; or a city dweller in the country. This conflict helps to define the characters as well as drive the plot. (A conflict between events and setting—for example, the intrusion of nuclear war into a typical suburban neighbourhood, the intrusion of modern social ideas into an old-fashioned world, or the intrusion of a brutal, senseless murder into a peaceful English village—can also enrich a story.)

HISTORICAL SETTING
◊ ◊ ◊

A particular historical period, and the events associated with it, can be important in a story; therefore, some familiarity with a period can be useful (or even essential) to readers who wish to understand a story fully. Historical context establishes a social, cultural, economic, and political environment. Knowing, for instance, that "The Yellow Wall-Paper" was written in the late nineteenth century, when doctors treated women as delicate and dependent creatures, helps to explain the narrator's emotional state. Likewise, it may be important to know that a story is set during a particularly volatile (or static) political era, during a time of permissive (or repressive) attitudes toward sex, during a war, or during a period of economic prosperity or recession. Any one of these factors may determine—or help to explain—characters' actions. Historical events or cultural norms may, for instance, limit or expand a character's options, and our knowledge of history may reveal to us a character's incompatibility with his or her milieu. For example, in "A Rose for Emily" (p. 90), the townspeople are dismayed by Emily's relationship with Homer Barron because she is a Southerner and he is a Northerner. The Civil War had split the United States, and for a "Southern belle" to be friendly with a Yankee was simply not acceptable.

Knowing the approximate year or historical period during which a story takes place can explain forces that act on characters, help to account for their behaviour, clarify circumstances that influence the story's action, and help to justify a writer's use of plot devices that might otherwise seem improbable. For instance, stories set before the development of modern transportation and communication systems may hinge on plot devices readers would not accept in a modern story. Thus, in "Paul's Case," a 1904 story by Willa Cather, a young man who steals a large sum of money in Pittsburgh is able to spend several days enjoying it before the news of the theft reaches New York, where he has fled. In other stories we see such outdated plot devices as characters threatened by diseases that have now been eradicated (and subjected to outdated medical or psychiatric treatment). In addition, characters may be constrained by social conventions different from those that operate in our own society.

GEOGRAPHICAL SETTING
◊ ◊ ◊

In addition to knowing when a work takes place, readers need to know *where* it takes place. Knowing whether a story is set in Canada, in Europe, or in a developing nation can help to explain anything from why language and customs are unfamiliar to us to why characters act in ways we find improbable. Even in stories set in our own country, regional differences may account for differences in plot development and characters' motivation. For example, the fact that Sinclair Ross's "A Field of Wheat" (p. 173) is set on the prairies during the drought and depression of the 1930s accounts for the characters' near obsession with the weather and their wheat crop.

The size of the town or city in which a story takes place may also be important. In a small town, for example, a character's problems are more likely to be subject to intense scrutiny by other characters, as they are in stories of small-town life such as Shirley Jackson's "The Lottery" (p. 319). In a large city, characters may be more likely to be isolated and anonymous, like Vijai in Shani Mootoo's "A Garden of Her Own" (p. 202). Characters may also be alienated by their big-city surroundings, as the narrator is in James Joyce's "Araby" (p. 267).

Of course, a story may not have a recognizable geographical setting; its location may not be specified, and it may even be set in a fantasy world. Such settings may free writers from the constraints placed on them by familiar environments, allowing them to experiment with situations and characters, unaffected by readers' expectations or associations with familiar settings.

PHYSICAL SETTING

◊ ◊ ◊

The *time of day* can clearly influence a story's mood as well as its development. The gruesome murder described in Edgar Allan Poe's "The Cask of Amontillado" (p. 227) takes place in an appropriate setting: not just underground, but in the darkness of night. Conversely, the horrifying events of Shirley Jackson's "The Lottery" take place in broad daylight, contrasting dramatically with the darkness of the society that permits—and even participates in—such events. Many stories, of course, move through several time periods as the action unfolds, and changes in time may also be important. For instance, the approach of evening, or of dawn, can signal the end of a crisis in the plot.

Whether a story is set primarily *inside* or *out-of-doors* may also be significant. The characters may be physically constrained by a closed-in setting or liberated by an expansive landscape. Some interior settings may be psychologically limiting. For instance, the narrator in "The Yellow Wall-Paper" feels suffocated by her room, whose ugly wallpaper comes to haunt her. In many of Poe's stories, the central character is trapped, physically or psychologically, in a confined, suffocating space. In other stories, an interior setting may serve a symbolic function. For instance, in "A Rose for Emily" the house is for Miss Emily a symbol of the South's past glory as well as a refuge, a fortress, and a hiding place. Similarly, a building or house may represent society, with its rules and norms and limitations. In John Updike's "A&P" (p. 122), for instance, the supermarket establishes social as well as physical limits. This is also the case in Katherine Mansfield's "Her First Ball" (p. 129), where a ballroom serves as the setting for a young girl's initiation into the rules and realities of adult society.

Conversely, an outdoor setting can free a character from social norms of behaviour, as it does for the father in Alistair MacLeod's "The Boat" (p. 447). An outdoor setting can also expose characters to physical dangers, such as untamed wilderness, uncharted seas, and frighteningly empty open spaces.

Weather can be another important aspect of setting. A storm can threaten a character's life or just make the character—and readers—*think* danger is present, distracting us from other, more subtle threats. Extreme weather conditions can make characters act irrationally or uncharacteristically, as in "A Field of Wheat," where a storm changes a family's life and the dynamic of John and Martha. In numerous stories set in hostile landscapes, where extremes of heat and cold influence the action, weather may pose a test for characters.

The various physical attributes of setting combine to create a story's **atmosphere** or **mood.** In "The Cask of Amontillado," for example, several factors work together to create the eerie, intense atmosphere appropriate to the story's events: it is night; it is the hectic carnival season; and the catacombs are dark, damp, and filled with the bones of the narrator's ancestors. The atmosphere that is created in a story can reflect a character's mental state—for example, darkness and isolation can reflect a character's depression, whereas an idyllic, peaceful atmosphere can express a character's joy. A story's atmosphere may also *influence* the characters' reactions or state of mind, causing them to react one way in a crowded, busy, hectic atmosphere but to react very differently in a peaceful rural atmosphere. At the same time, the mood or atmosphere that is created often helps to convey a story's central theme—as the ironic contrast between the atmosphere and the events that unfold communicates the theme of "The Lottery."

 # CHECKLIST: WRITING ABOUT SETTING

✓ Is the setting specified or unidentified? Is it fully described or just sketched in?

✓ Is the setting just background, or is it a key force in the story?

✓ How does the setting influence the characters? Does it affect (or reflect) their emotional state? Does it help to explain their motivation?

✓ Are any characters in conflict with their environment?

✓ Are any situations set in sharp contrast to the setting?

✓ How does the setting influence the story's plot? Does it cause characters to act?

✓ Does the setting add irony to the story?

✓ In what time period does the story take place? How can you tell? What social, political, or economic characteristics of the historical period might influence the story?

✓ In what geographical location is the story set? Is this location important to the story?

✓ At what time of day is the story set? Is time important to the development of the story?

✓ Is the story set primarily indoors or out-of-doors? What role does this aspect of the setting play in the story?

✓ What role do weather conditions play in the story?

✓ Is the story's general atmosphere dark or bright? Clear or murky? Tumultuous or calm? Gloomy or cheerful?

✓ Does the atmosphere change as the story progresses? Is this change significant?

◈ **Sinclair Ross** (1908–1996) was born on a homestead near Prince Albert, Saskatchewan. He worked for a bank throughout his life and served in the Canadian army during World War II. Although his job as a banker moved him to Winnipeg and then Montreal, much of Ross's writing deals with life on the Canadian prairies. His four novels—*As For Me and My House* (1941), *The Well* (1958), *Whir of Gold* (1970), and *Sawbones Memorial* (1974)—and eighteen short stories take place in both rural and urban settings. They focus on artistic, often alienated, young men and boys, who undergo struggles to nurture their creativity and individuality in the face of social pressures to conform to gender expectations. His early short stories examine the psychological effects of isolation, backbreaking toil, and harsh elements that characterized life on the prairies during the early years of settlement and the Great Depression. Ross lived in Greece and Spain for some years after his retirement from his job as a banker in 1968. He died of advanced Parkinson's disease in Vancouver.

↑ ◈ ◈

SINCLAIR ROSS

A Field of Wheat
(1935, 1968)

It was the best crop of wheat that John had ever grown; sturdy, higher than the knee, the heads long and filling well; a still, heat-hushed mile of it, undulating into a shimmer of summer-colts and crushed horizon blue. Martha finished pulling the little patch of mustard that John had told her about at noon, stood a minute with her shoulders strained back to ease the muscles that were sore from bending, then bunched up her apron filled with the yellow-blossomed weeds and started towards the road. She walked carefully, placing her feet edgeways between the rows of wheat to avoid trampling and crushing the stalks. The road was only a few rods distant, but several times she stopped before reaching it, holding her apron with one hand and with the other stroking the blades of grain that pressed close against her skirts, luxuriant and tall. Once she looked back, her eyes shaded, across the wheat to the dark fallow land beside it. John was there; she could see the long, slow-settling plume of dust thrown up by the horses and the harrow-cart. He was a fool for work, John. This year he was farming the whole section of land without help, managing with two outfits of horses, one for the morning and one for the afternoon; six, and sometimes even seven hours a shift.

It was John who gave such allure to the wheat. She thought of him hunched black and sweaty on the harrow-cart, twelve hours a day, smothering in dust, shoulders sagged wearily beneath the glare of sun. Her fingers touched the stalks of grain again and tightened on a supple blade until they made it squeak like a mouse. A crop like this was coming to him. He had had his share of failures and set-backs, if ever a man had, twenty times over.

Martha was thirty-seven. She had clinched with the body and substance of life; had loved, borne children—a boy had died—and yet the quickest aches of life, travail, heartbrokenness, they had never wrung as the wheat wrung. For the wheat allowed no respite. Wasting and unending it was struggle, struggle against wind and insects, drought and weeds. Not an heroic struggle to give a man courage and resolve, but a frantic, unavailing one. They were only poor, taunted, driven things; it was the wheat that was invincible. They only dreaded, built bright futures; waited for the first glint of green, watched timorous and eager while it thickened, merged, and at last leaned bravely to a ripple in the wind; then followed every slip of cloud into the horizon, turned to the wheat and away again. And it died tantalizingly sometimes, slowly: there would be a cool day, a pittance of rain.

Or perhaps it lived, perhaps the rain came, June, July, even into August, hope climbing, wish-patterns painted on the future. And then one day a clench and tremble to John's hand; his voice faltering, dull. Grasshoppers perhaps, sawflies or rust; no matter, they would grovel for a while, stand back helpless, then go on again. Go on in bitterness and cowardice, because there was nothing else but going-on.

5   She had loved John, for these sixteen years had stood close watching while he died—slowly, tantalizingly, as the parched wheat died. He had grown unkempt, ugly, morose. His voice was gruff, contentious, never broke into the deep, strong laughter that used to make her feel she was living at the heart of things. John was gone, love was gone; there was only wheat.

She plucked a blade; her eyes travelled hungrily up and down the field. Serene now, all its sting and torment sheathed. Beautiful, more beautiful than Annabelle's poppies, than her sunsets. Theirs—all of it. Three hundred acres ready to give perhaps a little of what it had taken from her—John, his love, his lips unclenched.

Three hundred acres. Bushels, thousands of bushels, she wouldn't even try to think how many. And prices up this year. It would make him young again, lift his head, give him spirit. Maybe he would shave twice a week as he used to when they were first married, buy new clothes, believe in himself again.

She walked down the road towards the house, her steps quickening to the pace of her thoughts until the sweat clung to her face like little beads of oil. It was the children now, Joe and Annabelle: this winter perhaps they could send them to school in town and let them take music lessons. Annabelle, anyway. At a pinch Joe could wait a while; he was only eight. It wouldn't take Annabelle long to pick up her notes; already she played hymn tunes by ear on the organ. She was bright, a real little lady for manners; among town people she would learn a lot. The farm was no place to bring her up. Running wild and barefoot, what would she be like in a few years? Who would ever want to marry her but some stupid country lout?

John had never been to school himself; he knew what it meant to go through life with nothing but his muscles to depend upon; and that was it, dread that Annabelle and Joe would be handicapped as he was, that was what had darkened him, made him harsh and dour. That was why he

breasted the sun and dust a frantic, dogged fool, to spare them, to help them
to a life that offered more than sweat and debts. Martha knew. He was a
slow, inarticulate man, but she knew. Sometimes it even vexed her, brought
a wrinkle of jealousy, his anxiety about the children, his sense of responsibility where they were concerned. He never seemed to feel that he owed her
anything, never worried about her future. She could sweat, grow flat-footed
and shapeless, but that never bothered him.

10   Her thoughts were on their old, trudging way, the way they always went;
but then she halted suddenly, and with her eyes across the wheat again
found freshening promise in its quiet expanse. The children must come first,
but she and John—mightn't there be a little of life left for them too? A man
was young at thirty-nine. And if she didn't have to work so hard, if she could
get some new clothes, maybe some of the creams and things that other
women had. . . .

As she passed through the gate, Annabelle raced across the yard to meet
her. "Do you know what Joe's done? He's taken off all his clothes and he's
in the trough with Nipper!" She was a lanky girl, sunburned, barefoot, her
face oval and regular, but spoiled by an expression that strained her mouth
and brows into a reproachful primness. It was Martha who had taught her
the expression, dinning manners and politeness into her, trying to make her
better than the other girls who went to the country school. She went on, her
eyes wide and aghast, "And when I told him to come out he stood right up,
all bare, and I had to come away."

"Well, you tell him he'd better be out before I get there."

"But how can I tell him? He's all bare."

Then Joe ran up, nothing on but little cotton knee-pants, strings of
green scum from the water-trough still sticking to his face and arms. "She's
been peekin'." He pointed to Annabelle. "Nipper and me just got into the
trough to get cooled off, and she wouldn't mind her own business."

15   "Don't you tell lies about me." Annabelle pounced on him and slapped
his bare back. "You're just a dirty little pig anyway, and the horses don't
want to drink after you've been in the trough."

Joe squealed, and excited by the scuffle Nipper yelped and spattered
Martha with a spray of water from his coat and tail. She reached out to cuff
him, missed, and then to satisfy the itch in her fingers seized Joe and boxed
his ears. "You put your shirt on and then go and pick peas for supper. Hurry
now, both of you, and only the fat ones, mind. No, not you, Annabelle."
There was something about Annabelle's face, burned and countrified, that
changed Martha's mind. "You shell the peas when he gets them. You're in
the sun too much as it is."

"But I've got a poppy out and if he goes to the garden by himself he'll
pick it—just for spite." Annabelle spun round, and leaving the perplexity in
her voice behind her, bolted for the garden. The next minute, before Martha
had even reached the house, she was back again triumphant, a big fringed
pink and purple poppy in her hand. Sitting down on the doorstep to admire
the gaudy petals, she complained to herself, "They go so fast—the first little
wind blows them all away." On her face, lengthening it, was bitten deeply

the enigma of the flowers and the naked seed-pods. Why did the beauty flash and the bony stalks remain?

Martha had clothes to iron, and biscuits to bake for supper; Annabelle and Joe quarrelled about the peas until she shelled them herself. It was hot—heat so intense and breathless that it weighed like a solid. An ominous darkness came with it, gradual and unnoticed. All at once she turned away from the stove and stood strained, inert. The silence seemed to gather itself, hold its breath. She tried to speak to Nipper and the children, all three sprawled in a heap alongside the house, but the hush over everything was like a raised finger, forbidding her.

A long immobile minute; suddenly a bewildering awareness that the light was choked; and then, muffled, still distant, but charged with resolution, climaxing the stillness, a slow, long brooding heave of thunder.

20   Martha darted to the door, stumbled down the step and around the corner of the house. To the west there was no sky, only a gulf of blackness, so black that the landscape seemed slipping down the neck of a funnel. Above, almost overhead, a heavy, hard-lined bank of cloud swept its way across the sun-white blue in august, impassive fury.

"Annabelle!" She wanted to scream a warning, but it was a bare whisper. In front of her the blackness split—an abrupt, unforked gash of light as if angry hands had snatched to seal the rent.

"Annabelle! Quick—inside—!" Deep in the funnel shaggy thunder rolled, emerged and shook itself, then with hurtling strides leaped up to drum and burst itself on the advancing peak of cloud.

"Joe, come back here!" He was off in pursuit of Nipper, who had broken away from Annabelle when she tried to pull him into the house. "Before I warm you!"

Her voice broke. She stared into the blackness. There it was—the hail again—the same white twisting little cloud against the black one—just as she had seen it four years ago.

25   She craned her neck, looking to see whether John was coming. The wheat, the acres and acres of it, green and tall, if only he had put some insurance on it. Damned mule—just work and work. No head himself and too stubborn to listen to anyone else.

There was a swift gust of wind, thunder in a splintering avalanche, the ragged hail-cloud low and close. She wheeled, with a push sent Annabelle toppling into the house, and then ran to the stable to throw open the big doors. John would turn the horses loose—surely he would. She put a brace against one of the doors, and bashed the end into the ground with her foot. Surely—but he was a fool—such a fool at times. It would be just like him to risk a runaway for the sake of getting to the end of the field.

The first big drops of rain were spitting at her before she reached the house. Quietly, breathing hard, she closed the door, numb for a minute, afraid to think or move. At the other side of the kitchen Annabelle was tussling with Joe, trying to make him go down cellar with her. Frightened a little by her mother's excitement, but not really able to grasp the imminence of danger, she was set on exploiting the event; and to be compelled to seize her little brother and carry him down cellar struck her imagination as a superb way of crystallizing for all time the dreadfulness of the storm and her own dramatic part in it. But Martha shouted at her hoarsely, "Go and get pillows. Here, Joe, quick, up on the table." She snatched him off his feet and set him on the table beside the window. "Be ready now when the hail starts, to hold the pillow tight against the glass. You, Annabelle, stay upstairs at the west window in my room."

The horses were coming, all six at a break-neck gallop, terrified by the thunder and the whip stripes John had given them when he turned them loose. They swept past the house, shaking the earth, their harness jangling tinny against the brattle[1] of thunder, and collided headlong at the stable door.

John, too; through Joe's legs Martha caught sight of his long, scarecrow shape stooped low before the rain. Distractedly, without purpose, she ran upstairs two steps at a time to Annabelle. "Don't be scared, here comes your father!" Her own voice shook, craven. "Why don't you rest your arms? It hasn't started yet."

30   As she spoke there was a sharp, crunching blow on the roof, its sound abruptly dead, sickening, like a weapon that has sunk deep into flesh. Wildly she shook her hands, motioning Annabelle back to the window, and started for the stairs. Again the blow came; then swiftly a stuttered dozen of them.

She reached the kitchen just as John burst in. With their eyes screwed up against the pommelling roar of the hail they stared at each other. They were deafened, pinioned, crushed. His face was a livid blank, one cheek smeared with blood where a jagged stone had struck him. Taut with fear, her throat aching, she turned away and looked through Joe's legs again. It was like a furious fountain, the stones bouncing high and clashing with those behind them. They had buried the earth, blotted out the horizon; there was nothing but their crazy spew of whiteness. She cowered away, put her hands to her ears.

Then the window broke, and Joe and the pillow tumbled off the table before the howling inrush of the storm. The stones clattered on the floor and bounded up to the ceiling, lit on the stove and threw out sizzling steam. The wind whisked pots and kettles off their hooks, tugged at and whirled the sodden curtains, crashed down a shelf of lamps and crockery. John pushed Martha and Joe into the next room and shut the door. There they found Annabelle huddled at the foot of the stairs, round-eyed, biting her nails in terror. The window she had been holding was broken too; and she had run away without closing the bedroom door, leaving a wild tide of wind upstairs to rage unchecked. It was rocking the whole house, straining at the walls. Martha ran up to close the door, and came down whimpering.

There was hail heaped on the bed, the pictures were blown off the walls and broken, the floor was swimming; the water would soak through and spoil all the ceilings.

John's face quietened her. They all crowded together, silent, averting their eyes from one another. Martha wanted to cry again, but dared not. Joe,

---

[1] Sharp rattling sound as of a series of blows or of something bursting.

awed to calmness, kept looking furtively at the trickle of blood on his father's face. Annabelle's eyes went wide and glassy as suddenly she began to wonder about Nipper. In the excitement and terror of the storm they had all forgotten him.

35 When at last they could go outside they stumbled over his body on the step. He had run away from Joe before the storm started, crawled back to the house when he saw John go in, and crouching down against the door had been beaten lifeless. Martha held back the children, while John picked up the mangled heap and hurried away with it to the stable.

Neither Joe nor Annabelle cried. It was too annihilating, too much like a blow. They clung tightly to Martha's skirts, staring across the flayed yard and garden. The sun came out, sharp and brilliant on the drifts of hail. There was an icy wind that made them shiver in their thin cotton clothes. "No, it's too cold on your feet." Martha motioned them back to the step as she started towards the gate to join John. "I want to go with your father to look at the wheat. There's nothing anyway to see."

Nothing but the glitter of sun on hailstones. Nothing but their wheat crushed into little rags of muddy slime. Here and there an isolated straw standing bolt upright in headless defiance. Martha and John walked to the far end of the field. There was no sound but their shoes slipping and rattling on the pebbles of ice. Both of them wanted to speak, to break the atmosphere of calamity that hung over them, but the words they could find were too small for the sparkling serenity of wasted field. Even as waste it was indomitable. It tethered them to itself, so that they could not feel or comprehend. It had come and gone, that was all; before its tremendousness and havoc they were prostrate. They had not yet risen to cry out or protest.

It was when they were nearly back to the house that Martha started to whimper. "I can't go on any longer; I can't, John. There's no use, we've tried." With one hand she clutched him and with the other held her apron to her mouth. "It's driving me out of my mind. I'm so tired—heart-sick of it all. Can't you see?"

He laid his big hands on her shoulders. They looked at each other for a few seconds, then she dropped her head weakly against his greasy smock. Presently he roused her. "Here come Joe and Annabelle!" The pressure of his hands tightened. His bristly cheek touched her hair and forehead. "Straighten up, quick, before they see you!"

40 It was more of him than she had had for years. "Yes, John, I know—I'm all right now." There was a wistful little pull in her voice as if she would have had him hold her there, but hurriedly instead she began to dry her eyes with her apron. "And tell Joe you'll get him another dog."

Then he left her and she went back to the house. Mounting within her was a resolve, a bravery. It was the warming sunlight, the strength and nearness of John, a feeling of mattering, belonging. Swung far upwards by the rush and swell of recaptured life, she was suddenly as far above the desolation of the storm as a little while ago she had been abject before it. But in the house she was alone; there was no sunlight, only a cold wind through the broken window; and she crumpled again.

She tried to face the kitchen, to get the floor dried and the broken lamps swept up. But it was not the kitchen; it was tomorrow, next week, next year. The going on, the waste of life, the hopelessness.

Her hands fought the broom a moment, twisting the handle as if trying to unscrew the rusted cap of a jar; then abruptly she let it fall and strode outside. All very fine for John: he'd talk about education for Joe and Annabelle, and she could worry where the clothes were to come from so that they could go clean and decent even to the country school. It made no difference that she had wanted to take out hail insurance. He was the one that looked after things. She was just his wife; it wasn't for her to open her mouth. He'd pat her shoulder and let her come back to this. They'd be brave, go on again, forget about the crop. Go on, go on—next year and the next—go on till they were both ready for the scrap-heap. But she'd had enough. This time he'd go on alone.

Not that she meant it. Not that she failed to understand what John was going through. It was just rebellion. Rebellion because their wheat was beaten to the ground, because there was this brutal, callous finish to everything she had planned, because she had will and needs and flesh, because she was alive. Rebellion, not John at all—but how rebel against a summer storm, how find the throat of a cloud?

45 So at a jerky little run she set off for the stable, for John. Just that she might release and spend herself, no matter against whom or what, unloose the fury that clawed within her, strike back a blow for the one that had flattened her.

The stable was quiet, only the push of the hay as the horses nosed through the mangers, the lazy rub of their flanks and hips against the stall partitions; and before its quietness her anger subsided, took time for breath. She advanced slowly, almost on tiptoe, peering past the horses' rumps for a glimpse of John. To the last stall, back again. And then there was a sound different from the stable sounds. She paused.

She had not seen him the first time she passed because he was pressed against one of the horses, his head pushed into the big deep hollow of its neck and shoulder, one hand hooked by the fingers in the mane, his own shoulders drawn up and shaking. She stared, thrust out her head incredulously, moved her lips, but stood silent. John sobbing there, against the horse. It was the strangest, most frightening moment of her life. He had always been so strong and grim; had just kept on as if he couldn't feel, as if there were a bull's hide over him, and now he was beaten.

She crept away. It would be unbearable to watch his humiliation if he looked up and saw her. Joe was wandering about the yard, thinking about Nipper and disconsolately sucking hailstones, but she fled past him, head down, stricken with guilty shame as if it were she who had been caught broken and afraid. He had always been so strong, a brute at times in his strength, and now—

Now—why now that it had come to this, he might never be able to get a grip of himself again. He might not want to keep on working, not if he were really beaten. If he lost heart, if he didn't care about Joe and Annabelle any more. Weeds and pests, drought and hail—it took so much fight for a man to hold his own against them all, just to hold his own, let alone make headway.

⁵⁰ "Look at the sky!" It was Annabelle again, breathless and ecstatic. "The far one—look how it's opened like a fan!"

Withdrawn now in the eastern sky the storm clouds towered, gold-capped and flushed in the late sunlight, high still pyramids of snowiness and shadow. And one that Annabelle pointed to, apart, the farthest away of them all, this one in bronzed slow splendour spread up mountains high to a vast, plateau-like summit.

Martha hurried inside. She started the fire again, then nailed a blanket over the broken window and lit the big brass parlour lamp—the only one the storm had spared. Her hands were quick and tense. John would need a good supper tonight. The biscuits were water-soaked, but she still had the peas. He liked peas. Lucky that they had picked them when they did. This winter they wouldn't have so much as an onion or potato.

READING AND REACTING

1. What is the effect of the hailstorm on John and Martha? Do they have different reactions? Do their reactions change?
2. How much influence does the setting of the story have on the characters' ability to maintain hope? Consider both the parents and the children.
3. John and Martha come from different social classes. How does that difference affect their outlook and their lives?
4. What historical perspective is helpful when reading this story?
5. Why does John hide his despair from Martha?
6. Why is Nipper killed?
7. Why does Martha want her children to have an education?
8. **JOURNAL ENTRY** What does the story offer in terms of human beings' ability to overcome great obstacles? What is necessary to be able to move forward after a devastating setback?
9. **CRITICAL PERSPECTIVE** In the Introduction to the New Canadian Library edition of *The Lamp at Noon and Other Stories*, in which "A Field of Wheat" appears, Margaret Laurence says:

   > The isolation is virtually complete. It is in this extreme con-dition of human separateness and in the extremes of summer drought and winter blizzard that Ross's characters grapple with their lives and their fate, a fate partially imposed on them by an uncaring and fickle natural order and partly com-pelled by their own spiritual inheritance, the pride and deter-mination which enable them to refuse defeat, but which also cut them off from nearly all real contact with others.

   How is isolation demonstrated in "A Field of Wheat"? Is there any way to overcome it? Is the isolation necessary for survival?

Related Works: "Death by Landscape" (p. 335), "The Boat" (p. 447), "The Way the Weather Chose to Be Born" (p. 838)

◆ **TILLIE OLSEN** (1912 or 1913–   ) is known for her works of fiction about working-class Americans. Her short stories and one novel are inhabited by those she called the "despised people"—coal miners, farm labourers, packinghouse butchers, and housewives. Olsen was born in Nebraska into a working-class family. Though she has been described as a Depression-era dropout, Olsen has observed that she educated herself, with libraries as her college. According to an account in her nonfiction work *Silences* (1978), Olsen was at age fifteen inspired to write about working-class people when she read Rebecca Harding Davis's *Life in the Iron Mills,* a tale of the effects of industrialization upon workers, in an 1861 issue of *Atlantic Monthly* bought for ten cents in a junk shop.

Shortly after she left high school, she was jailed for helping to organize packinghouse workers. Motivated by her experiences, she began to write a novel, *Yonnondio.* Under her maiden name, Tillie Lerner, she published two poems, a short story, and part of her novel in the 1930s. After her marriage, she did not publish again for twenty-two years, spending her time raising four children and working at a variety of jobs. The collection of short stories *Tell Me a Riddle* (1961), which includes "I Stand Here Ironing" (originally titled "Help Her to Believe"), was published when she was fifty. Her only other work of fiction is *Yonnondio* (1974), which she pieced together from drafts she wrote in the 1930s and edited for publication in 1974.

Because she believed her own career was "ruined" by the passage of time when she could not write because of other responsibilities, she focuses on encouraging young writers by lecturing or reading her own works to writers' groups and holding writer-in-residency or visiting professorships at several major universities. She is also known for her efforts to rediscover long-forgotten works by other working-class women. In 1984, she edited *Mother to Daughter, Daughter to Mother: Mothers on Mothering,* a collection of poems, letters, short fiction, and diary excerpts written by famous and not-so-famous women. Olsen lives in San Francisco.

T I L L I E   O L S E N

I Stand Here Ironing
(1961)

I stand here ironing, and what you asked me moves tormented back and forth with the iron.

"I wish you would manage the time to come and talk with me about your daughter. I'm sure you can help me understand her. She's a youngster who needs help and whom I'm deeply interested in helping."

"Who needs help." . . . Even if I came, what good would it do? You think because I am her mother I have a key, or that in some way you could use me as a key? She has lived for nineteen years. There is all that life that has happened outside of me, beyond me.

And when is there time to remember, to sift, to weigh, to estimate, to total? I will start and there will be an interruption and I will have to gather it all together again. Or I will become engulfed with all I did or did not do, with what should have been and what cannot be helped.

5 She was a beautiful baby. The first and only one of our five that was beautiful at birth. You do not guess how new and uneasy her tenancy in her now-loveliness. You did not know her all those years she was thought homely, or see her poring over her baby pictures, making me tell her over and over how beautiful she had been—and would be, I would tell her—and was now, to the seeing eye. But the seeing eyes were few or nonexistent. Including mine.

I nursed her. They feel that's important nowadays. I nursed all the children, but with her, with all the fierce rigidity of first motherhood, I did like the books then said. Though her cries battered me to trembling and my breasts ached with swollenness, I waited till the clock decreed.

Why do I put that first? I do not even know if it matters, or if it explains anything.

She was a beautiful baby. She blew shining bubbles of sound. She loved motion, loved light, loved color and music and textures. She would lie on the floor in her blue overalls patting the surface so hard in ecstasy her hands and feet would blur. She was a miracle to me, but when she was eight months old I had to leave her daytimes with the woman downstairs to whom she was no miracle at all, for I worked or looked for work and for Emily's father, who "could no longer endure" (he wrote in his good-bye note) "sharing want with us."

I was nineteen. It was the pre-relief, pre-WPA[1] world of the depression. I would start running as soon as I got off the streetcar, running up the stairs, the place smelling sour, and awake or asleep to startle awake, when she saw me she would break into a clogged weeping that could not be comforted, a weeping I can hear yet.

10 After a while I found a job hashing at night so I could be with her days, and it was better. But it came to where I had to bring her to his family and leave her.

It took a long time to raise the money for her fare back. Then she got chicken pox and I had to wait longer. When she finally came, I hardly knew her, walking quick and nervous like her father, looking like her father, thin, and dressed in a shoddy red that yellowed her skin and glared at the pock-marks. All the baby loveliness gone.

She was two. Old enough for nursery school they said, and I did not know then what I know now—the fatigue of the long day, and the lacerations of group life in the kinds of nurseries that are only parking places for children.

Except that it would have made no difference if I had known. It was the only place there was. It was the only way we could be together, the only way I could hold a job.

---

[1] Works Progress Administration, created in 1935 as part of President Franklin D. Roosevelt's New Deal program. The purpose of the WPA (renamed the Works Projects Administration in 1939) was to provide jobs for the unemployed during the Great Depression.

And even without knowing, I knew. I knew the teacher that was evil because all these years it has curdled into my memory, the little boy hunched in the corner, her rasp, "why aren't you outside, because Alvin hits you? that's no reason, go out, scaredy." I knew Emily hated it even if she did not clutch and implore "don't go Mommy" like the other children, mornings.

15   She always had a reason why we should stay home. Momma, you look sick. Momma, I feel sick. Momma, the teachers aren't there today, they're sick. Momma, we can't go, there was a fire there last night. Momma, it's a holiday today, no school, they told me.

But never a direct protest, never rebellion. I think of our others in their three-, four-year-oldness—the explosions, the tempers, the denunciations, the demands—and I feel suddenly ill. I put the iron down. What in me demanded that goodness in her? And what was the cost, the cost to her of such goodness?

The old man living in the back once said in his gentle way: "You should smile at Emily more when you look at her." What was in my face when I looked at her? I loved her. There were all the acts of love.

It was only with the others I remembered what he said, and it was the face of joy, and not of care or tightness or worry I turned to them—too late for Emily. She does not smile easily, let alone almost always as her brothers and sisters do. Her face is closed and sombre, but when she wants, how fluid. You must have seen it in her pantomimes, you spoke of her rare gift for comedy on the stage that rouses laughter out of the audience so dear they applaud and applaud and do not want to let her go.

Where does it come from, that comedy? There was none of it in her when she came back to me that second time, after I had had to send her away again. She had a new daddy now to learn to love, and I think perhaps it was a better time.

20   Except when we left her alone nights, telling ourselves she was old enough.

"Can't you go some other time, Mommy, like tomorrow?" she would ask. "Will it be just a little while you'll be gone? Do you promise?"

The time we came back, the front door open, the clock on the floor in the hall. She rigid awake. "It wasn't just a little while. I didn't cry. Three times I called you, just three times, and then I ran downstairs to open the door so you could come faster. The clock talked loud. I threw it away, it scared me what it talked."

She said the clock talked loud again that night I went to the hospital to have Susan. She was delirious with the fever that comes before red measles, but she was fully conscious all the week I was gone and the week after we were home when she could not come near the new baby or me.

She did not get well. She stayed skeleton thin, not wanting to eat, and night after night she had nightmares. She would call for me, and I would rouse from exhaustion to sleepily call back: "You're all right, darling, go to sleep, it's just a dream," and if she still called, in a sterner voice, "now go to sleep, Emily, there's nothing to hurt you." Twice, only twice, when I had to get up for Susan anyhow, I went in to sit with her.

25   Now when it is too late (as if she would let me hold and comfort her like I do the others) I get up and go to her at once at her moan or restless stirring. "Are you awake, Emily? Can I get you something?" And the answer is always the same: "No, I'm all right, go back to sleep, Mother."

They persuaded me at the clinic to send her away to a convalescent home in the country where "she can have the kind of food and care you can't manage for her, and you'll be free to concentrate on the new baby." They still send children to that place. I see pictures on the society page of sleek young women planning affairs to raise money for it, or dancing at the affairs, or decorating Easter eggs or filling Christmas stockings for the children.

They never have a picture of the children so I do not know if the girls still wear those gigantic red bows and the ravaged looks on the every other Sunday when parents can come to visit "unless otherwise notified"—as we were notified the first six weeks.

Oh it is a handsome place, green lawns and tall trees and fluted flower beds. High up on the balconies of each cottage the children stand, the girls in their red bows and white dresses, the boys in white suits and giant red ties. The parents stand below shrieking up to be heard and the children shriek down to be heard, and between them the invisible wall: "Not to Be Contaminated by Parental Germs or Physical Affection."

There was a tiny girl who always stood hand in hand with Emily. Her parents never came. One visit she was gone. "They moved her to Rose Cottage," Emily shouted in explanation. "They don't like you to love anybody here."

30   She wrote once a week, the labored writing of a seven-year-old. "I am fine. How is the baby. If I write my leter nicly I will have a star. Love." There never was a star. We wrote every other day, letters she could never hold or keep but only hear read—once. "We simply do not have room for children to keep any personal possessions," they patiently explained when we pieced one Sunday's shrieking together to plead how much it would mean to Emily, who loved so to keep things, to be allowed to keep her letters and cards.

Each visit she looked frailer. "She isn't eating," they told us.

(They had runny eggs for breakfast or mush with lumps, Emily said later, I'd hold it in my mouth and not swallow. Nothing ever tasted good, just when they had chicken.)

It took us eight months to get her released home, and only the fact that she gained back so little of her seven lost pounds convinced the social worker.

I used to try to hold and love her after she came back, but her body would stay stiff, and after a while she'd push away. She ate little. Food sickened her, and I think much of life too. Oh she had physical lightness and brightness, twinkling by on skates, bouncing like a ball up and down up and down over the jump rope, skimming over the hill; but these were momentary.

35   She fretted about her appearance, thin and dark and foreign-looking at a time when every little girl was supposed to look or thought she should look a chubby blonde replica of Shirley Temple. The doorbell sometimes rang for her, but no one seemed to come and play in the house or be a best friend. Maybe because we moved so much.

There was a boy she loved painfully through two school semesters. Months later she told me how she had taken pennies from my purse to buy him candy. "Licorice was his favorite and I brought him some every day, but he still liked Jennifer better'n me. Why, Mommy?" The kind of question for which there is no answer.

School was a worry to her. She was not glib or quick in a world where glibness and quickness were easily confused with ability to learn. To her overworked and exasperated teachers she was an overconscientious "slow learner" who kept trying to catch up and was absent entirely too often.

I let her be absent, though sometimes the illness was imaginary. How different from my now-strictness about attendance with the others. I wasn't working. We had a new baby, I was home anyhow. Sometimes, after Susan grew old enough, I would keep her home from school, too, to have them all together.

Mostly Emily had asthma, and her breathing, harsh and labored, would fill the house with a curiously tranquil sound. I would bring the two old dresser mirrors and her boxes of collections to her bed. She would select beads and single earrings, bottle tops and shells, dried flowers and pebbles, old post-cards and scraps, all sorts of oddments; then she and Susan would play Kingdom, setting up landscapes and furniture, peopling them with action.

40   Those were the only times of peaceful companionship between her and Susan. I have edged away from it, that poisonous feeling between them, that terrible balancing of hurts and needs I had to do between the two, and did so badly, those earlier years.

Oh there are conflicts between the others too, each one human, needing, demanding, hurting, taking—but only between Emily and Susan, no, Emily toward Susan that corroding resentment. It seems so obvious on the surface, yet it is not obvious. Susan, the second child, Susan, golden- and curly-haired and chubby, quick and articulate and assured, everything in appearance and manner Emily was not; Susan, not able to resist Emily's precious things, losing or sometimes clumsily breaking them; Susan telling jokes and riddles to company for applause while Emily sat silent (to say to me later: that was *my* riddle, Mother, I told it to Susan); Susan, who for all the five years' difference in age was just a year behind Emily in developing physically.

I am glad for that slow physical development that widened the difference between her and her contemporaries, though she suffered over it. She was too vulnerable for that terrible world of youthful competition, of preening and parading, of constant measuring of yourself against every other, of envy, "If I had that copper hair," "If I had that skin. . . . " She tormented herself enough about not looking like the others, there was enough of the unsureness, the having to be conscious of words before you speak, the constant caring—what are they thinking of me? without having it all magnified by the merciless physical drives.

Ronnie is calling. He is wet and I change him. It is rare there is such a cry now. That time of motherhood is almost behind me when the ear is not one's own but must always be racked and listening for the child cry, the child call. We sit for a while and I hold him, looking out over the city spread in charcoal with its soft aisles of light. *"Shoogily,"* he breathes and curls closer. I carry him back to bed, asleep. *Shoogily*. A funny word, a family word, inherited from Emily, invented by her to say: *comfort*.

In this and other ways she leaves her seal, I say aloud. And startle at my saying it. What do I mean? What did I start to gather together, to try and make coherent? I was at the terrible, growing years. War years. I do not remember them well. I was working, there were four smaller ones now, there was not time for her. She had to help be a mother, and housekeeper, and shopper. She had to set her seal. Mornings of crisis and near hysteria trying to get lunches packed, hair combed, coats and shoes found, everyone to school or Child Care on time, the baby ready for transportation. And always the paper scribbled on by a smaller one, the book looked at by Susan then mislaid, the homework not done. Running out to that huge school where she was one, she was lost, she was a drop; suffering over the unpreparedness, stammering and unsure in her classes.

45 There was so little time left at night after the kids were bedded down. She would struggle over books, always eating (it was in those years she developed her enormous appetite that is legendary in our family) and I would be ironing, or preparing food for the next day, or writing V-mail to Bill, or tending the baby. Sometimes, to make me laugh, or out of her despair, she would imitate happenings or types at school.

I think I said once: "Why don't you do something like this in the school amateur show?" One morning she phoned me at work, hardly understandable through the weeping: "Mother, I did it. I won, I won; they gave me first prize; they clapped and clapped and wouldn't let me go."

Now suddenly she was Somebody, and as imprisoned in her difference as she had been in anonymity.

She began to be asked to perform at other high schools, even in colleges, then at city and statewide affairs. The first one we went to, I only recognized her that first moment when thin, shy, she almost drowned herself into the curtains. Then: Was this Emily? The control, the command, the convulsing and deadly clowning, the spell, then the roaring, stamping audience, unwilling to let this rare and precious laughter out of their lives.

Afterwards: You ought to do something about her with a gift like that— but without money or knowing how, what does one do? We have left it all to her, and the gift has as often eddied inside, clogged and clotted, as been used and growing.

50 She is coming. She runs up the stairs two at a time with her light graceful step, and I know she is happy tonight. Whatever it was that occasioned your call did not happen today.

"Aren't you ever going to finish the ironing, Mother? Whistler painted his mother in a rocker. I'd have to paint mine standing over an ironing board." This is one of her communicative nights and she tells me everything and nothing as she fixes herself a plate of food out of the icebox.

She is so lovely. Why did you want me to come in at all? Why were you concerned? She will find her way.

She starts up the stairs to bed. "Don't get me up with the rest in the morning." "But I thought you were having midterms." "Oh, those," she comes back in, kisses me, and says quite lightly, "in a couple of years when we'll all be atom-dead they won't matter a bit."

She has said it before. She *believes* it. But because I have been dredging the past, and all that compounds a human being is so heavy and meaningful in me, I cannot endure it tonight.

55   I will never total it all. I will never come in to say: She was a child seldom smiled at. Her father left me before she was a year old. I had to work her first six years when there was work, or I sent her home and to his relatives. There were years she had care she hated. She was dark and thin and foreign-looking in a world where the prestige went to blondeness and curly hair and dimples, she was slow where glibness was prized. She was a child of anxious, not proud, love. We were poor and could not afford for her the soil of easy growth. I was a young mother, I was a distracted mother. There were other children pushing up, demanding. Her younger sister seemed all that she was not. There were years she did not want me to touch her. She kept too much in herself, her life was such she had to keep too much in herself. My wisdom came too late. She has much to her and probably little will come of it. She is a child of her age, of depression, of war, of fear.

Let her be. So all that is in her will not bloom—but in how many does it? There is still enough left to live by. Only help her to know—help make it so there is cause for her to know—that she is more than this dress on the ironing board, helpless before the iron.

READING AND REACTING

1. "I Stand Here Ironing" focuses on incidents that took place in the "pre-relief, pre-WPA world of the depression" (9). In light of social, political, and economic changes that have occurred since the 1930s, do you think the events the story presents could occur today? Explain.

2. In what sense is the image of a mother at an ironing board appropriate for this story?

3. The narrator is overwhelmed by guilt. What does she believe she has done wrong? What, if anything, do *you* think she has done wrong? Do you think she has been a good mother? Why or why not?

4. Who, or what, do you blame for the narrator's problems? For example, do you blame Emily's father? The Depression? The social institutions and "experts" to which the narrator turns?

5. Do you see the narrator as a victim limited by the times in which she lives? Do you agree with the narrator that Emily is "a child of her age, of depression, of war, of fear"? Or do you believe both women have some control over their own destinies, regardless of the story's historical setting?

6. What do you think the narrator wants for her daughter? Do you think her goals for Emily are realistic ones?

7. Paragraph 28 describes the physical setting of the convalescent home to which Emily was sent. What does this description add to the story? Why do you suppose there is no physical description of the apartment in which Emily lived as a child? How do you picture this apartment?
8. To whom do you think the mother is speaking in this story?
9. **Journal Entry** Put yourself in Emily's position. What do you think she would like to tell her mother?
10. **Critical Perspective** Writing in *The Red Wheelbarrow*, psychologist Robert Coles discusses the complex family relationships depicted in "I Stand Here Ironing" and reaches an optimistic conclusion:

> But the child did not grow to be a mere victim of the kind so many of us these days are rather eager to recognize—a hopeless tangle of psychopathology. The growing child, even in her troubled moments, revealed herself to be persistent, demanding, and observant. In the complaints we make, in the "symptoms" we develop, we reveal our strengths as well as our weaknesses. The hurt child could summon her intelligence, exercise her will, smile and make others smile.

Do you agree with Coles's psychological evaluation of Emily? Do you find the story's ending as essentially uplifting as he seems to? Why or why not?

Related Works: "A Field of Wheat" (p. 173), "Everyday Use" (p. 327), "Those Winter Sundays" (p. 573).

◆ **Charlotte Perkins Gilman** (1860–1935) was a prominent feminist and social thinker at the turn of the last century. Her essays, lectures, and nonfiction works—such as *Women and Economics* (1898), *Concerning Children* (1900), and *The Man-Made World* (1911)—are forceful statements of Gilman's opinions on women's need for economic independence and social equality. In the main, Gilman's fiction is a didactic expression of her social views. She is probably best known for three utopian feminist novels: *Moving the Mountain* (1911), *Herland* (1915; unpublished until 1978), and *With Her in Ourland* (1916). Gilman's fictional works are full of humour and satire: in *Herland,* for instance, a male sociologist (wandering in by accident from the outside world) is chagrined to find that the women of "Herland" want him for a friend, not a lover.

Although "The Yellow Wall-Paper" (1892) is not typical of Gilman's other fiction, it is considered her artistic masterpiece. The terse, clinical precision of the writing, conveying the tightly wound and distraught mental state of the narrator, is particularly chilling when it is read with a knowledge of Gilman's personal history. In the 1880s, she met and married a young artist, Charles Walter Stetson. Following the birth of their daughter, she grew increasingly depressed and turned to a noted Philadelphia neurologist for help. Following the traditions of the time, he prescribed complete bed rest and mental inactivity—a treatment that, Gilman said later, drove her "so near the borderline of utter mental ruin that I could see over." "The Yellow Wall-Paper" is not simply a psychological study. Like most of Gilman's work, it makes a point—this time about the dangers of women's utter dependence on a male interpretation of their needs.

⊹ ⊹ ⊹

CHARLOTTE PERKINS GILMAN

The Yellow Wall-Paper
(1892)

It is very seldom that mere ordinary people like John and myself secure ancestral halls for the summer.

A colonial mansion, a hereditary estate, I would say a haunted house, and reach the height of romantic felicity—but that would be asking too much of fate!

Still I will proudly declare that there is something queer about it.

Else, why should it be let so cheaply? And why have stood so long untenanted?

5   John laughs at me, of course, but one expects that in marriage.

John is practical in the extreme. He has no patience with faith, an intense horror of superstition, and he scoffs openly at any talk of things not to be felt and seen and put down in figures.

John is a physician, and *perhaps*—(I would not say it to a living soul, of course, but this is dead paper and a great relief to my mind—) *perhaps* that is one reason I do not get well faster.

You see he does not believe I am sick!

And what can one do?

10   If a physician of high standing, and one's own husband, assures friends and relatives that there is really nothing the matter with one but temporary nervous depression—a slight hysterical tendency—what is one to do?

My brother is also a physician, and also of high standing, and he says the same thing.

So I take phosphates or phosphites[1]—whichever it is, and tonics, and journeys, and air, and exercise, and am absolutely forbidden to "work" until I am well again.

Personally, I disagree with their ideas.

Personally, I believe that congenial work, with excitement and change, would do me good.

15   But what is one to do?

---

[1] Both terms refer to salts of phosphorous acid. The narrator, however, means "phosphate," a carbonated beverage of water, flavouring, and a small amount of phosphoric acid.

I did write for a while in spite of them; but it *does* exhaust me a good deal—having to be so sly about it, or else meet with heavy opposition.

I sometimes fancy that in my condition if I had less opposition and more society and stimulus—but John says the very worst thing I can do is to think about my condition, and I confess it always makes me feel bad.

So I will let it alone and talk about the house.

The most beautiful place! It is quite alone, standing well back from the road, quite three miles from the village. It makes me think of English places that you read about, for there are hedges and walls and gates that lock, and lots of separate little houses for the gardeners and people.

20 There is a *delicious* garden! I never saw such a garden—large and shady, full of box-bordered paths, and lined with long grape-covered arbors with seats under them.

There were greenhouses, too, but they are all broken now.

There was some legal trouble, I believe, something about the heirs and co-heirs; anyhow, the place has been empty for years.

That spoils my ghostliness, I am afraid, but I don't care—there is something strange about the house—I can feel it.

I even said so to John one moonlight evening, but he said what I felt was a *draught*, and shut the window.

25 I get unreasonably angry with John sometimes. I'm sure I never used to be so sensitive. I think it is due to this nervous condition.

But John says if I feel so, I shall neglect proper self-control; so I take pains to control myself—before him, at least, and that makes me very tired.

I don't like our room a bit. I wanted one downstairs that opened on the piazza and had roses all over the window, and such pretty old-fashioned chintz hangings! But John would not hear of it.

He said there was only one window and not room for two beds, and no near room for him if he took another.

He is very careful and loving, and hardly lets me stir without special direction.

30 I have a schedule prescription for each hour in the day; he takes all care from me, and so I feel basely ungrateful not to value it more.

He said we came here solely on my account, that I was to have perfect rest and all the air I could get. "Your exercise depends on your strength, my dear," said he, "and your food somewhat on your appetite; but air you can absorb all the time." So we took the nursery at the top of the house.

It is a big, airy room, the whole floor nearly, with windows that look all ways, and air and sunshine galore. It was nursery first and then playroom and gymnasium, I should judge; for the windows are barred for little children, and there are rings and things in the walls.

The paint and paper look as if a boys' school had used it. It is stripped off—the paper—in great patches all around the head of my bed, about as far as I can reach, and in a great place on the other side of the room low down. I never saw a worse paper in my life.

One of those sprawling flamboyant patterns committing every artistic sin.

35   It is dull enough to confuse the eye in following, pronounced enough to constantly irritate and provoke study, and when you follow the lame uncertain curves for a little distance they suddenly commit suicide—plunge off at outrageous angles, destroy themselves in unheard of contradictions.

    The color is repellent, almost revolting; a smouldering unclean yellow, strangely faded by the slow-turning sunlight.

    It is a dull yet lurid orange in some places, a sickly sulphur tint in others.

    No wonder the children hated it! I should hate it myself if I had to live in this room long.

    There comes John, and I must put this away,—he hates to have me write a word.

40   We have been here two weeks, and I haven't felt like writing before, since that first day.

    I am sitting by the window now, up in this atrocious nursery, and there is nothing to hinder my writing as much as I please, save lack of strength.

    John is away all day, and even some nights when his cases are serious.

    I am glad my case is not serious!

    But these nervous troubles are dreadfully depressing.

45   John does not know how much I really suffer. He knows there is no *reason* to suffer, and that satisfies him.

    Of course it is only nervousness. It does weigh on me so not to do my duty in any way!

    I meant to be such a help to John, such a real rest and comfort, and here I am a comparative burden already!

    Nobody would believe what an effort it is to do what little I am able,— to dress and entertain, and order things.

    It is fortunate Mary is so good with the baby. Such a dear baby!

50   And yet I *cannot* be with him, it makes me so nervous.

    I suppose John never was nervous in his life. He laughs at me so about this wall-paper!

    At first he meant to repaper the room, but afterwards he said that I was letting it get the better of me, and that nothing was worse for a nervous patient than to give way to such fancies.

    He said that after the wall-paper was changed it would be the heavy bedstead, and then the barred windows, and then that gate at the head of the stairs, and so on.

    "You know the place is doing you good," he said, "and really, dear, I don't care to renovate the house just for a three months' rental."

55   "Then do let us go downstairs," I said, "there are such pretty rooms there."

    Then he took me in his arms and called me a blessed little goose, and said he would go down cellar, if I wished, and have it whitewashed into the bargain.

    But he is right enough about the beds and windows and things.

    It is an airy and comfortable room as any one need wish, and, of course, I would not be so silly as to make him uncomfortable just for a whim.

I'm really getting quite fond of the big room, all but that horrid paper.

60   Out of one window I can see the garden, those mysterious deep-shaded arbors, the riotous old-fashioned flowers, and bushes and gnarly trees.

Out of another I get a lovely view of the bay and a little private wharf belonging to the estate. There is a beautiful shaded lane that runs down there from the house. I always fancy I see people walking in these numerous paths and arbors, but John has cautioned me not to give way to fancy in the least. He says that with my imaginative power and habit of story-making, a nervous weakness like mine is sure to lead to all manner of excited fancies, and that I ought to use my will and good sense to check the tendency. So I try.

I think sometimes that if I were only well enough to write a little it would relieve the press of ideas and rest me.

But I find I get pretty tired when I try.

It is so discouraging not to have any advice and companionship about my work. When I get really well, John says we will ask Cousin Henry and Julia down for a long visit; but he says he would as soon put fireworks in my pillow-case as to let me have those stimulating people about now.

65   I wish I could get well faster.

But I must not think about that. This paper looks to me as if it knew what a vicious influence it had!

There is a recurrent spot where the pattern lolls like a broken neck and two bulbous eyes stare at you upside down.

I get positively angry with the impertinence of it and the everlastingness. Up and down and sideways they crawl, and those absurd, unblinking eyes are everywhere. There is one place where two breadths didn't match, and the eyes go all up and down the line, one a little higher than the other.

I never saw so much expression in an inanimate thing before, and we all know how much expression they have! I used to lie awake as a child and get more entertainment and terror out of blank walls and plain furniture than most children could find in a toy-store.

70   I remember what a kindly wink the knobs of our big, old bureau used to have, and there was one chair that always seemed like a strong friend.

I used to feel that if any of the other things looked too fierce I could always hop into that chair and be safe.

The furniture in this room is no worse than inharmonious, however, for we had to bring it all from downstairs. I suppose when this was used as a playroom they had to take the nursery things out, and no wonder! I never saw such ravages as the children have made here.

The wall-paper, as I said before, is torn off in spots, and it sticketh closer than a brother—they must have had perseverance as well as hatred.

Then the floor is scratched and gouged and splintered, the plaster itself is dug out here and there, and this great heavy bed which is all we found in the room, looks as if it had been through the wars.

75   But I don't mind it a bit—only the paper.

There comes John's sister. Such a dear girl as she is, and so careful of me! I must not let her find me writing.

She is a perfect and enthusiastic housekeeper, and hopes for no better profession. I verily believe she thinks it is the writing which made me sick!

But I can write when she is out, and see her a long way off from these windows.

There is one that commands the road, a lovely shaded winding road, and one that just looks off over the country. A lovely country, too, full of great elms and velvet meadows.

80   This wall-paper has a kind of sub-pattern in a different shade, a particularly irritating one, for you can only see it in certain lights, and not clearly then.

But in the places where it isn't faded and where the sun is just so—I can see a strange, provoking, formless sort of figure, that seems to skulk about behind that silly and conspicuous front design.

There's sister on the stairs!

Well, the Fourth of July is over! The people are all gone and I am tired out. John thought it might do me good to see a little company, so we just had mother and Nellie and the children down for a week.

Of course I didn't do a thing. Jennie sees to everything now.

85   But it tired me all the same.

John says if I don't pick up faster he shall send me to Weir Mitchell[2] in the fall.

But I don't want to go there at all. I had a friend who was in his hands once, and she says he is just like John and my brother, only more so!

Besides, it is such an undertaking to go so far.

I don't feel as if it was worth while to turn my hand over for anything, and I'm getting dreadfully fretful and querulous.

90   I cry at nothing, and cry most of the time.

Of course I don't when John is here, or anybody else, but when I am alone.

And I am alone a good deal just now. John is kept in town very often by serious cases, and Jennie is good and lets me alone when I want her to.

So I walk a little in the garden or down that lovely lane, sit on the porch under the roses, and lie down up here a good deal.

I'm getting really fond of the room in spite of the wall-paper. Perhaps *because* of the wall-paper.

95   It dwells in my mind so!

I lie here on this great immovable bed—it is nailed down, I believe—and follow that pattern about by the hour. It is as good as gymnastics, I assure you. I start, we'll say, at the bottom, down in the corner over there where it has not been touched, and I determine for the thousandth time that I *will* follow that pointless pattern to some sort of a conclusion.

I know a little of the principle of design, and I know this thing was not arranged on any laws of radiation, or alternation, or repetition, or symmetry, or anything else that I ever heard of.

---

[2] Silas Weir Mitchell (1829–1914)—a Philadelphia neurologist-psychologist who introduced the "rest cure" for nervous diseases.

It is repeated, of course, by the breadths, but not otherwise.

Looked at in one way each breadth stands alone, the bloated curves and flourishes—a kind of "debased Romanesque" with *delirium tremens*[3] go waddling up and down in isolated columns of fatuity.

100 But, on the other hand, they connect diagonally, and the sprawling outlines run off in great slanting waves of optic horror, like a lot of wallowing seaweeds in full chase.

The whole thing goes horizontally, too, at least it seems so, and I exhaust myself in trying to distinguish the order of its going in that direction.

They have used a horizontal breadth for a frieze, and that adds wonderfully to the confusion.

There is one end of the room where it is almost intact, and there, when the crosslights fade and the low sun shines directly upon it, I can almost fancy radiation after all,—the interminable grotesque seems to form around a common center and rush off in headlong plunges of equal distraction.

It makes me tired to follow it. I will take a nap I guess.

105 I don't know why I should write this.

I don't want to.

I don't feel able.

And I know John would think it absurd. But I *must* say what I feel and think in some way—it is such a relief!

But the effort is getting to be greater than the relief.

110 Half the time now I am awfully lazy, and lie down ever so much.

John says I mustn't lose my strength, and has me take cod liver oil and lots of tonics and things, to say nothing of ale and wine and rare meat.

Dear John! He loves me very dearly, and hates to have me sick. I tried to have a real earnest reasonable talk with him the other day, and tell him how I wish he would let me go and make a visit to Cousin Henry and Julia.

But he said I wasn't able to go, nor able to stand it after I got there; and I did not make out a very good case for myself, for I was crying before I had finished.

It is getting to be a great effort for me to think straight. Just this nervous weakness I suppose.

115 And dear John gathered me up in his arms, and just carried me upstairs and laid me on the bed, and sat by me and read to me till it tired my head.

He said I was his darling and his comfort and all he had, and that I must take care of myself for his sake, and keep well.

He says no one but myself can help me out of it, that I must use my will and self-control and not let any silly fancies run away with me.

There's one comfort, the baby is well and happy, and does not have to occupy this nursery with the horrid wall-paper.

---

[3] Mental confusion caused by alcohol poisoning and characterized by physical tremors and hallucinations.

If we had not used it, that blessed child would have! What a fortunate escape! Why, I wouldn't have a child of mine, an impressionable little thing, live in such a room for worlds.

120   I never thought of it before, but it is lucky that John kept me here after all, I can stand it so much easier than a baby, you see.

Of course I never mention it to them any more—I am too wise,—but I keep watch of it all the same.

There are things in that paper that nobody knows but me, or ever will.

Behind that outside pattern the dim shapes get clearer every day.

It is always the same shape, only very numerous.

125   And it is like a woman stooping down and creeping about behind that pattern. I don't like it a bit. I wonder—I begin to think—I wish John would take me away from here!

It is so hard to talk with John about my case, because he is so wise, and because he loves me so.

But I tried it last night.

It was moonlight. The moon shines in all around just as the sun does.

I hate to see it sometimes, it creeps so slowly, and always comes in by one window or another.

130   John was asleep and I hated to waken him, so I kept still and watched the moonlight on that undulating wall-paper till I felt creepy.

The faint figure behind seemed to shake the pattern, just as if she wanted to get out.

I got up softly and went to feel and see if the paper *did* move, and when I came back John was awake.

"What is it, little girl?" he said. "Don't go walking about like that—you'll get cold."

I thought it was a good time to talk, so I told him that I really was not gaining here, and that I wished he would take me away.

135   "Why, darling!" said he, "our lease will be up in three weeks, and I can't see how to leave before.

"The repairs are not done at home, and I cannot possibly leave town just now. Of course if you were in any danger, I could and would, but you really are better, dear, whether you can see it or not. I am a doctor, dear, and I know. You are gaining flesh and color, your appetite is better, I feel really much easier about you."

"I don't weigh a bit more," said I, "nor as much; and my appetite may be better in the evening when you are here, but it is worse in the morning when you are away!"

"Bless her little heart!" said he with a big hug, "she shall be as sick as she pleases! But now let's improve the shining hours by going to sleep, and talk about it in the morning!"

"And you won't go away?" I asked gloomily.

140   "Why, how can I, dear? It is only three weeks more and then we will take a nice little trip of a few days while Jennie is getting the house ready. Really dear you are better!"

"Better in body perhaps—" I began, and stopped short, for he sat up straight and looked at me with such a stern, reproachful look that I could not say another word.

"My darling," said he, "I beg of you, for my sake and for our child's sake, as well as for your own, that you will never for one instant let that idea enter your mind! There is nothing so dangerous, so fascinating, to a temperament like yours. It is a false and foolish fancy. Can you not trust me as a physician when I tell you so?"

So of course I said no more on that score, and we went to sleep before long. He thought I was asleep first, but I wasn't, and lay there for hours trying to decide whether that front pattern and the back pattern really did move together or separately.

On a pattern like this, by daylight, there is a lack of sequence, a defiance of law, that is a constant irritant to a normal mind.

145   The color is hideous enough, and unreliable enough, and infuriating enough, but the pattern is torturing.

You think you have mastered it, but just as you get well underway in following, it turns back-somersault and there you are. It slaps you in the face, knocks you down, and tramples upon you. It is like a bad dream.

The outside pattern is a florid arabesque, reminding one of a fungus. If you can imagine a toadstool in joints, an interminable string of toadstools, budding and sprouting in endless convolutions—why, that is something like it.

That is, sometimes!

There is one marked peculiarity about this paper, a thing nobody seems to notice but myself, and that is that it changes as the light changes.

150   When the sun shoots in through the east window—I always watch for that first long, straight ray—it changes so quickly that I never can quite believe it.

That is why I watch it always.

By moonlight—the moon shines in all night when there is a moon—I wouldn't know it was the same paper.

At night in any kind of light, in twilight, candlelight, lamplight, and worst of all by moonlight, it becomes bars! The outside pattern I mean, and the woman behind it is as plain as can be.

I didn't realize for a long time what the thing was that showed behind, that dim sub-pattern, but now I am quite sure it is a woman.

155   By daylight she is subdued, quiet. I fancy it is the pattern that keeps her so still. It is so puzzling. It keeps me quiet by the hour.

I lie down ever so much now. John says it is good for me, and to sleep all I can.

Indeed he started the habit by making me lie down for an hour after each meal.

It is a very bad habit I am convinced, for you see I don't sleep.

And that cultivates deceit, for I don't tell them I'm awake—O no!

160   The fact is I am getting a little afraid of John.

He seems very queer sometimes, and even Jennie has an inexplicable look.

It strikes me occasionally, just as a scientific hypothesis,—that perhaps it is the paper!

I have watched John when he did not know I was looking, and come into the room suddenly on the most innocent excuses, and I've caught him several times *looking at the paper!* And Jennie too. I caught Jennie with her hand on it once.

She didn't know I was in the room, and when I asked her in a quiet, a very quiet voice, with the most restrained manner possible, what she was doing with the paper—she turned around as if she had been caught stealing, and looked quite angry—asked me why I should frighten her so!

165 Then she said that the paper stained everything it touched, that she had found yellow smooches on all my clothes and John's, and she wished we would be more careful!

Did not that sound innocent? But I know she was studying that pattern, and I am determined that nobody shall find it out but myself!

Life is very much more exciting now than it used to be. You see I have something more to expect, to look forward to, to watch. I really do eat better, and am more quiet than I was.

John is so pleased to see me improve! He laughed a little the other day, and said I seemed to be flourishing in spite of my wall-paper.

I turned it off with a laugh. I had no intention of telling him it was *because* of the wall-paper—he would make fun of me. He might even want to take me away.

170 I don't want to leave now until I have found it out. There is a week more, and I think that will be enough.

I'm feeling ever so much better! I don't sleep much at night, for it is so interesting to watch developments; but I sleep a good deal in the daytime.

In the daytime it is tiresome and perplexing.

There are always new shoots on the fungus, and new shades of yellow all over it. I cannot keep count of them, though I have tried conscientiously.

It is the strangest yellow, that wall-paper! It makes me think of all the yellow things I ever saw—not beautiful ones like buttercups, but old foul, bad yellow things.

175 But there is something else about that paper—the smell! I noticed it the moment we came into the room, but with so much air and sun it was not bad. Now we have had a week of fog and rain, and whether the windows are open or not, the smell is here.

It creeps all over the house.

I find it hovering in the dining-room, skulking in the parlor, hiding in the hall, lying in wait for me on the stairs.

It gets into my hair.

Even when I go to ride, if I turn my head suddenly and surprise it—there is that smell!

180   Such a peculiar odor, too! I have spent hours in trying to analyze it, to find what it smelled like.

It is not bad—at first, and very gentle, but quite the subtlest, most enduring odor I ever met.

In this damp weather it is awful, I wake up in the night and find it hanging over me.

It used to disturb me at first. I thought seriously of burning the house—to reach the smell.

But now I am used to it. The only thing I can think of that it is like is the *color* of the paper! A yellow smell.

185   There is a very funny mark on this wall, low down, near the mopboard. A streak that runs round the room. It goes behind every piece of furniture, except the bed, a long, straight, even *smooch*, as if it had been rubbed over and over.

I wonder how it was done and who did it, and what they did it for. Round and round and round—round and round and round!—it makes me dizzy!

I really have discovered something at last.

Through watching so much at night, when it changes so, I have finally found out.

The front pattern *does* move—and no wonder! The woman behind shakes it!

190   Sometimes I think there are a great many women behind, and sometimes only one, and she crawls around fast, and her crawling shakes it all over.

Then in the very bright spots she keeps still, and in the very shady spots she just takes hold of the bars and shakes them hard.

And she is all the time trying to climb through. But nobody could climb through that pattern—it strangles so; I think that is why it has so many heads.

They get through, and then the pattern strangles them off and turns them upside down, and makes their eyes white!

If those heads were covered or taken off it would not be half so bad.

195   I think that woman gets out in the daytime!

And I'll tell you why—privately—I've seen her!

I can see her out of every one of my windows!

It is the same woman, I know, for she is always creeping, and most women do not creep by daylight.

I see her in that long shaded lane, creeping up and down. I see her in those dark grape arbors, creeping all around the garden.

200   I see her on that long road under the trees, creeping along, and when a carriage comes she hides under the blackberry vines.

I don't blame her a bit. It must be very humiliating to be caught creeping by daylight!

I always lock the door when I creep by daylight. I can't do it at night, for I know John would suspect something at once.

And John is so queer now, that I don't want to irritate him. I wish he would take another room! Besides, I don't want anybody to get that woman out at night but myself.

I often wonder if I could see her out of all the windows at once.

205 But, turn as fast as I can, I can only see out of one at one time.

And though I always see her, she *may* be able to creep faster than I can turn!

I have watched her sometimes away off in the open country, creeping as fast as a cloud shadow in a high wind.

If only that top pattern could be gotten off from the under one! I mean to try it, little by little.

I have found out another funny thing, but I shan't tell it this time! It does not do to trust people too much.

210 There are only two more days to get this paper off, and I believe John is beginning to notice. I don't like the look in his eyes.

And I heard him ask Jennie a lot of professional questions about me. She had a very good report to give.

She said I slept a good deal in the daytime.

John knows I don't sleep very well at night, for all I'm so quiet!

He asked me all sorts of questions, too, and pretended to be very loving and kind.

215 As if I couldn't see through him!

Still, I don't wonder he acts so, sleeping under this paper for three months.

It only interests me, but I feel sure John and Jennie are secretly affected by it.

Hurrah! This is the last day, but it is enough. John to stay in town over night, and won't be out until this evening.

Jennie wanted to sleep with me—the sly thing! But I told her I should undoubtedly rest better for a night all alone.

220 That was clever, for really I wasn't alone a bit! As soon as it was moonlight and that poor thing began to crawl and shake the pattern, I got up and ran to help her.

I pulled and she shook, I shook and she pulled, and before morning we had peeled off yards of that paper.

A strip about as high as my head and half around the room.

And then when the sun came and that awful pattern began to laugh at me, I declared I would finish it to-day!

We go away to-morrow, and they are moving all my furniture down again to leave things as they were before.

225 Jennie looked at the wall in amazement, but I told her merrily that I did it out of pure spite at the vicious thing.

She laughed and said she wouldn't mind doing it herself, but I must not get tired.

How she betrayed herself that time!

But I am here, and no person touches this paper but me,—not *alive!*

She tried to get me out of the room—it was too patent! But I said it was so quiet and empty and clean now that I believed I would lie down again and sleep all I could; and not to wake me even for dinner—I would call when I woke.

230 So now she is gone, and the servants are gone, and the things are gone, and there is nothing left but that great bedstead nailed down, with the canvas mattress we found on it.

We shall sleep downstairs to-night, and take the boat home tomorrow.

I quite enjoy the room, now it is bare again.

How those children did tear about here!

This bedstead is fairly gnawed!

235 But I must get to work.

I have locked the door and thrown the key down into the front path.

I don't want to go out, and I don't want to have anybody come in, till John comes.

I want to astonish him.

I've got a rope up here that even Jennie did not find. If that woman does get out, and tries to get away, I can tie her!

240 But I forgot I could not reach far without anything to stand on!

This bed will *not* move!

I tried to lift and push it until I was lame, and then I got so angry I bit off a little piece at one corner—but it hurt my teeth.

Then I peeled off all the paper I could reach standing on the floor. It sticks horribly and the pattern just enjoys it! All those strangled heads and bulbous eyes and waddling fungus growths just shriek with derision!

I am getting angry enough to do something desperate. To jump out of the window would be admirable exercise, but the bars are too strong even to try.

245 Besides I wouldn't do it. Of course not. I know well enough that a step like that is improper and might be misconstrued.

I don't like to *look* out of the windows even—there are so many of those creeping women, and they creep so fast.

I wonder if they all come out of that wall-paper as I did?

But I am securely fastened now by my well-hidden rope—you don't get *me* out in the road there!

I suppose I shall have to get back behind the pattern when it comes night, and that is hard!

250 It is so pleasant to be out in this great room and creep around as I please!

I don't want to go outside. I won't, even if Jennie asks me to.

For outside you have to creep on the ground, and everything is green instead of yellow.

But here I can creep smoothly on the floor, and my shoulder just fits in that long smooch around the wall, so I cannot lose my way.

255

Why there's John at the door!

It is no use, young man, you can't open it!

How he does call and pound!

Now he's crying for an axe.

It would be a shame to break down that beautiful door!

"John dear!" said I in the gentlest voice, "the key is down by the front steps, under a plantain leaf!"

260

That silenced him for a few moments.

Then he said—very quietly indeed, "Open the door, my darling!"

"I can't," said I. "The key is down by the front door under a plantain leaf!"

And then I said it again, several times, very gently and slowly, and said it so often that he had to go and see, and he got it of course, and came in. He stopped short by the door.

"What is the matter?" he cried. "For God's sake, what are you doing!"

265

I kept on creeping just the same, but I looked at him over my shoulder.

"I've got out at last," said I, "in spite of you and Jane. And I've pulled off most of the paper, so you can't put me back!"

Now why should that man have fainted? But he did, and right across my path by the wall, so that I had to creep over him every time!

READING AND REACTING

1. The story's narrator, who has recently given birth, is suffering from what her husband, a doctor, calls "temporary nervous depression—a slight hysterical tendency" (10). What is the relationship between this depression and the story's setting?

2. Describe the house and grounds. How do they affect the narrator's mood?

3. What aspects of the room in which the narrator lives upset her? Why?

4. Describe the wallpaper. What does the narrator actually see in it, and what does she imagine? How can you tell the difference?

5. What do the following comments reveal about the narrator's situation: "John laughs at me, of course, but one expects that in marriage" (5); "I must put this away,—he hates to have me write a word" (39); "He laughs at me so about this wall-paper" (51); "Then he took me in his arms and called me a blessed little goose" (56)?

6. What has probably caused the narrator's depression? What factors aggravate it? How much insight does the narrator seem to have into her situation?

7. How does the narrator's mood change as the story progresses? How do her descriptions of her setting change?

8. **JOURNAL ENTRY** Do you think a present-day physician or psychiatrist would give the narrator different advice? Do you think a present-day woman would respond differently to advice from her husband or doctor? Explain.

9. **CRITICAL PERSPECTIVE** "The Yellow Wall-Paper" was originally seen by some as a ghost story, and even anthologized as such. More recently, critics have tended to interpret the story from a feminist perspective, focusing on the way in which the nameless narrator is victimized by the men around her and by the values of the Victorian society which they uphold. In the essay "An Unnecessary Maze of Sign-Reading," Mary Jacobus concludes that the overwhelmingly feminist perspective of recent criticism, although certainly valuable and enlightening, has overlooked other promising critical possibilities—for example, "the Gothic and uncanny elements present in the text."

If you were teaching "The Yellow Wall-Paper," would you present it as a feminist story or as a chilling Gothic ghost story? Do you think interpreting the story as a Gothic horror tale precludes a feminist reading, or do you see the two interpretations as compatible?

Related Works: "The Story of an Hour" (p. 77), "A Garden of Her Own" (p. 202), "Barbie Doll" (p. 872), *A Doll House* (p. 1013)

◆ **SHANI MOOTOO** (1958–   ) was born in Dublin and raised in Trinidad from the age of three months. She moved to Canada when she was nineteen and studied fine arts at the University of Western Ontario. She is a painter and video producer in addition to being a writer. Her first collection of short stories, *Out on Main Street*, was published in 1993, and her first novel, *Cereus Blooms at Night*, in 1996. Her most recent book is a novel, *He Drown She in the Sea* (2005). In an interview with Robert Gougeon, online at the Writer's Café, she calls herself a "political person, an agenda-driven writer." Mootoo currently lives in Edmonton.

◆ ◇ ◇

SHANI MOOTOO

A Garden of Her Own
(1993)

A north-facing balcony meant that no sunlight would enter there. A deep-in-the-heart-of-the-forest green pine tree, over-fertilized opulence extending its midriff, filled the view from the balcony.

There was no window, only a glass sliding door which might have let fresh air in and released second- or third-hand air and the kinds of odours that build phantoms in stuffy apartments. But it remained shut. Not locked, but stuck shut from decades of other renters' black, oily grit and grime which had collected in the grooves of the sliding door's frame.

Vijai knew that it would not budge up, down or sideways. For the amount of rent the husband paid for this bachelor apartment, the landlord could not be bothered. She opened the hallway door to let the cooking lamb fat and garlic smells drift out into the hallway. She did not want them to burrow into the bed sheets, into towels and clothes crammed into the dented cream-coloured metal space-saver cupboard that she had to share with the husband. It was what all the other renters did too; everyone's years of oil—sticky, burnt, over-used, rancid oil—and of garlic, onions and spices formed themselves into an impenetrable nose-singeing, skin-stinging presence that lurked menacingly in the hall. Instead of releasing the lamb from the husband's apartment, opening the door allowed this larger phantom to barge its way in.

Vijai, engulfed, slammed the door shut. She tilted her head to face the ceiling and breathed in hard, searching for air that had no smell, no weight. The husband was already an hour late for dinner. She paced the twelve strides, back and forth, from the balcony door to the hall door, glancing occasionally at the two table settings, stopping to straighten his knife, his fork, the napkin, the flowers, his knife, his fork, the napkin, the flowers. Her arms and legs tingled weakly and her intestines filled up with beads of acid formed out of unease and fear. Seeing a smear of her fingerprint on the husband's knife, she picked it up and polished it on her T-shirt until it gleamed brilliantly, and she saw in it her mother's eyes looking back at her.

5   Sunlight. I miss the sunlight—yellow light and a sky ceiling miles high. Here the sky sits on my head, heavy grey with snow and freezing rain. I miss being able to have doors and windows opened wide, never shut except sometimes in the rainy season. Rain, rain, pinging on, winging off the galvanized tin roof. But always warm rain. No matter how much it rained, it was always warm.

And what about the birds? Flying in through the windows how often? Two, three times a week? Sometimes even twice in a single day. In the shimmering heat you could see them flying slowly, their mouths wide open as if crying out soundlessly. They would actually be flicking their tongues at the still air, gulping and panting, looking for a window to enter and a curtain rod to land on to cool off. But once they had cooled off and were ready to fly off again, they could never seem to focus on the window to fly through and they would bang themselves against the walls and the light shade until they fell, panicked and stunned. I was the one who would get the broom and push it gently up toward one of these birds after it looked like it had cooled off, and prod, prod, prod until it hopped onto the broom and then I would lower it and reach from behind and cup the trembling in my hand. I can, right now, feel the life, the heat in the palm of my hand from the little body, and the fright in its tremble. I would want to hold on to it, even think of placing it in a cage and looking after it, but something always held me back. I would put my mouth close to its ears and whisper calming shh shh shhhhs, and then take it, pressed to my chest, out the back door and open my hand and wait for it to take its time fluffing out right there in my open hand before flying away.

But here? There are hardly any birds here, only that raucous, aggressive old crow that behaves as if it owns the scraggly pine tree it sits in across the street. This street is so noisy! Every day, all day and all night long, even on Sundays, cars whiz by, ambulances and fire trucks pass screaming, and I think to myself thank goodness it couldn't be going for anyone I know. I don't know anyone nearby.

Too much quiet here, too shut off. Not even the sound of children playing in the street, or the sound of neighbours talking to each other over fences, conversations floating in through open windows, open bricks. Here even when doors are open people walk down hallways with their noses straight ahead, making a point of not glancing to even nod hello.

Oh! This brings all kinds of images to my mind: the coconut tree outside my bedroom brushing, scraping, swishing against the wall. Green-blue iridescent lizards clinging, upside down, to the ceiling above my bed.

10 And dinner time. Mama's voice would find me wherever I was. "Vijai, go and tell Cheryl to put food on the table, yuh father comin home just now." Standing in one place, at the top of her meagre voice she would call us one by one: "Bindra, is dinner time. Bindra, why you so harden, boy? Dinner gettin cold. Turn off that TV right now! Shanti, come girl, leave what you doin and come and eat. Vashti, go and tell Papa dinner ready, and then you come and sit down." Sitting down, eating together. Talking together. Conversations with no boundaries, no false politeness, no need to impress Mama or Papa.

But that's not how it was always. Sometimes Papa didn't come home till long after suppertime. Mama would make us eat but she would wait for him. Sometimes he wouldn't come for days, and she would wait for him then too.

But there were always flowers from the garden on the table. Pink and yellow gerberas, ferns, ginger lilies. That was your happiness, eh Mama? the garden, eh? And when there were blossoms you and I would go outside together. You showed me how to angle the garden scissors so that the plant wouldn't hurt for too long. We would bring in the bundle of flowers and greenery with their fresh-cut garden smell and little flying bugs and spiders, and you would show me how to arrange them for a centrepiece or a corner table or a floor piece. The place would look so pretty! Thanks for showing that to me, Mama.

Mama, he's never brought me any flowers. Not even a dandelion.

I don't want him to ask how much these cost. Don't ask me who sent them. No one sent them; I bought them myself. With my own money. My own money.

15 He's never given me anything. Only money for groceries.

Late. Again.

I jabbed this lamb with a trillion little gashes and stuffed a clove of garlic in each one with your tongue, your taste buds in mind. I spent half the day cooking this meal and you will come late and eat it after the juices have hardened to a candle-wax finish, as if it were nothing but a microwave dinner.

I want a microwave oven.

Mama, why did you wait to eat? If I were to eat now would you, Papa, he think I am a bad wife? Why did you show me this, Mama?

20   I must not nag.

Vijai remained sleeping until the fan in the bathroom woke her. It sputtered raucously, like an airplane engine starting up, escalating in time to fine whizzing, lifting off into the distance.

Five-thirty, Saturday morning.

She had fretted through most of the night, twisting, arching her body, drawing her legs up to her chest, to the husband's chest, rolling, and nudging him, hoping that he would awaken to pull her body into his and hold her there. She wanted to feel the heat of his body along the length of hers, his arms pressing her to him. Or his palm placed flat on her lower belly, massaging, touching her. He responded to her fidgeting once and she moved closer to encourage him, but he turned his naked back to her and continued his guttural exhaling, inhaling, sounding exactly like her father.

Eventually Vijai's eyes, burning from salty tears that had spilled and dampened the pillow under her cheek, fluttered shut and she slept, deep and dreamless, until the fan awakened her.

25   When the sound of the shower water snapping at the enamel tub was muffled against his body, she pulled herself over to lie in and smell his indentation in the tired foam mattress. She inhaled, instead, the history of the mattress: unwashed hair, dying skin, old and rancid sweat—not the smell she wanted to nestle in. Neither would the indentation cradle her; she could feel the protruding shape of the box-spring beneath the foam.

She debated whether to get up and thanklessly make his toast and tea, or pretend not to have awakened, the potential for blame nagging at her. She slid back to her side of his bed, the other side of the line that he had drawn down the middle with the cutting edge of his outstretched hand. Vijai pulled her knees to her chest and hugged them. When the shower stopped she hastily straightened herself out and put her face inside the crack between the bed and the rough wall. Cold from the wall transferred itself onto her cheek, and layers upon layers of human smells trapped behind cream-coloured paint pierced her nostrils.

Vijai was aware of the husband's every move as she lay in his bed. Water from the kitchen tap pounded the sink basin, then attacked the metal floor of the kettle, gradually becoming muffled and high-pitched as the kettle filled up. He always filled it much more than was necessary for one cup of tea, which he seldom drank. The blow dryer. First on the highest setting, then dropped two notches to the lowest, and off. The electric razor. Whizzing up and down his cheek, circling his chin, the other cheek, grazing his neck. Snip, snip and little dark half-moon hair from his nostrils and his sideburns cling to the rim of the white sink basin. Wiping up, scrubbing, making spotless these areas, and others, before he returns, are her evidence that she is diligent, that she is, indeed, her mother's daughter.

At this point in the routine she always expects a handsome aftershave cologne to fill the little bachelor apartment, to bring a moment of frivolity and romance into the room. In one favourite version of her memories, this is what normally happened in her parents' bedroom at precisely this point. But the husband would only pat on his face a stinging watery liquid with the faintest smell of lime, a smell that evaporated into nothingness the instant it touched his skin.

She held herself tensely, still in the crack between the bed and the wall, as he made his way into the dark corner that he called the bedroom. The folding doors of the closet squeaked open. A shirt slid off a hanger, leaving it dangling and tinkling against the metal rod. Vijai heard the shirt that she had ironed (stretched mercilessly tight across the ironing board, the tip of the iron with staccato spurts of steam sniffing out the crevice of every seam, mimicking the importance with which her mother had treated this task) being pulled against his body and his hands sliding down the stiff front as he buttoned it.

30 Then there was a space empty of his sounds. The silence made the walls of her stomach contract like a closed-up accordion. Her body remained rigid. Her heart sounded as if it had moved right up into her ears, thundering methodically, and that was all that she could hear. She struggled with herself to be calm so that she could know where he was and what he was doing. Not knowing made her scalp want to unpeel itself. Then, the bed sagged as he kneeled on it, leaned across and brushed his mouth on the back of her head. His full voice had no regard for her sleep or the time of morning. He said, "Happy Birthday. I left twenty dollars on the table for you. Buy yourself a present."

The thundering subsided and her heart rolled and slid, rolled and slid, down, low down, and came to rest between her thighs. She turned over with lethargic elegance, as if she were just waking up, stretching out her back like a cat, but the apartment door was already being shut and locked from the outside.

The streets here are so wide! I hold my breath as I walk across them, six lanes wide. What if the light changes before I get to the other side? You have to walk so briskly, not only when you're crossing a wide street but even on the sidewalk. Otherwise people pass you and then turn back and stare at you, shaking their heads. And yet I remember Mama telling us that fast walking, hurrying, was very unladylike.

I yearn for friends. My own friends, not his, but I'm afraid to smile at strangers. So often we huddled up in Mama's big bed and read the newspapers about things that happened to women up here—we read about women who suddenly disappeared and months later their corpses would be found, having been raped and dumped. And we also read about serial murders. The victims were almost always women who had been abducted from the street by strangers in some big North American city. Mama and Papa warned me, when

I was leaving to come up here, not to make eye contact with strangers because I wouldn't know whose eyes I might be looking into or what I was encouraging, unknowingly. It's not like home, they said, where everybody knows everybody.

No bird sounds—there are not quite so many different kinds of birds here. Yes, Papa, yes, I can just hear you saying to stop this nonsense, all this thinking about home, that I must think of here as my home now, but I haven't yet left you and Mama. I know now that I will never fully leave, nor will I ever truly be here. You felt so close, Papa, when you phoned this morning and asked like you have every past year, how was the birthday girl. You said that in your office you often look at the calendar pictures of autumn fields of bales of hay, lazy rivers meandering near brick-red farm-houses, and country roads with quaint white wooden churches with red steeples, and you think that that's what my eyes have already enjoyed.

35   "It's all so beautiful, Papa," I said, and knowing you, you probably heard what I wasn't saying. Thanks for not pushing further. I couldn't tell you that he is working night and day to "make it," to "get ahead," to live like the other men he works with. That he is always thinking about this, and every-thing else is frivolous right now, so we haven't yet been for that drive in the country to see the pictures in the calendars pinned on the wall above your desk. He doesn't have time for dreaming, but I must dream or else I find it difficult to breathe.

At home the fence around our house and the garden was the furthest point that I ever went to on my own. From the house, winding in and out of the dracaenas and the philodendrons that I planted with Mama many Julys ago, feeling the full, firm limbs of the poui, going as far as the hibiscus and jas-mine fence, and back into the house again. Any further away from the house than that and the chauffeur would be driving us! And now? Just look at me! I am out in a big city on my own. I wish you all could see me. I wish we could be doing this together.

Papa, you remember, don't you, when you used to bring home maga-zines from your office and I would flip through them quickly looking for full-page pictures of dense black-green tropical mountains, or snow-covered bluish-white ones? Ever since those first pictures I have dreamt of moun-tains, of touching them with the palms of my hands, of bicycling in them, and of hiking. Even though I never canoed on a river or a big lake with no shores, I know what it must feel like! I can feel what it is to ride rapids like they do in *National Geographic* magazines. Cold river spray and drenchings, sliding, tossing, crashing! I still dream of bicycling across a huge continent. I used to think, if only I lived in North America! But here I am, in this place where these things are supposed to happen, in the midst of so much possi-bility, and for some reason my dreams seem even further away, just out of reach. It's just not quite as simple as being here.

This land stretches on in front of me, behind me and forever. My back feels exposed, naked, so much land behind, and no fence ahead.

Except that I must cook dinner tonight.

40   What if I just kept walking and never returned! I could walk far way, to another province, change my name, cut my hair. After a while I would see my face on a poster in a grocery store, along with all the other missing persons. The problem is that then I wouldn't even be able to phone home and speak with Mama or Papa or Bindra and Vashti without being tracked and caught, and then who knows what.

Well, this is the first birthday I've ever spent alone. But next time we speak on the phone I will be able to tell you that I went for a very long walk. Alone.

I think I will do this every day—well, maybe every other day, and each time I will go a new route and a little further. I will know this place in order to own it, but still I will never really leave you.

Mama, Papa, Vashti, Bindra, Shanti,

Mama, Papa, Vashti, Bindra, Shanti.

45   Mama. Papa. Vashti. Bindra. Shanti.

Twenty-four years of Sundays, of eating three delightfully noisy, lengthy meals together, going to the beach or for long drives with big pots of rice, chicken and peas, and chocolate cake, singing "Michael Row Your Boat Ashore," and "You Are My Sunshine," doing everything in tandem with her brother and sisters and Mama and Papa. This particular characteristic of Sundays was etched deeply in her veins. (Not all Sundays were happy ones but recently she seems to have forgotten that.)

It would be her twenty-fourth Sunday here, the twenty-fourth week of marriage.

The only Sunday since the marriage that the husband had taken off and spent in his apartment was six weeks ago, and since he needed to spend that day alone Vijai agreed to go to the library for at least three hours. Before she left the house she thought she would use the opportunity to take down recipes for desserts, but once she began walking down the street she found herself thinking about rivers and mountains. She bypassed the shelves with all the cooking books and home-making magazines and found herself racing toward valleys, glaciers, canoeing, rapids and the like. She picked up a magazine about hiking and mountaineering, looked at the equipment advertisements, read incomprehensible jargon about techniques for climbing.

After about forty minutes, not seeing herself in any of the magazines, she became less enthusiastic, and eventually frustrated and bored. She looked at her watch every fifteen minutes or so and then she started watching the second hand go around and counting each and every second in her head. When three hours had passed she remembered that she had said at least three hours, and she walked home slowly, stopping to window-shop and checking her watch until an extra twenty minutes had passed.

50   The strength of her determination that they not spend this Sunday apart warded off even a hint of such a suggestion from the husband. What she really wanted to do was to go for the long drive up to a glacier in the nearby

mountains. That way she would have him to herself for at least five hours. But he had worked several twelve-hour shifts that week and needed to rest in his apartment.

She went to the grocery store, to the gardening section, and bought half a dozen packages of flower seeds, half a dozen packages of vegetable seeds, bags of soil, fertilizer, a fork and spade, a purple plastic watering can, and a score of nursery trays. She brought it all home in a taxi. Enough to keep her busy and in his apartment for an entire Sunday. She was becoming adept at finding ways to get what she wanted.

He never asked and Vijai did not tell that from her allowance she had paid a man from the hardware store to come over and fix the balcony sliding door. She stooped on the balcony floor scooping earth into nursery trays. He sat reading the newspaper, facing the balcony in his big sagging gold arm-chair that he had bought next-door at a church basement sale for five dol-lars. She was aware that he was stealing glances at her as she bent over her garden-in-the-making.

I wore this shirt, no bra, am stopping, bending over here to reveal my breasts to you. *Look at them! Feel something!*

I might as well be sharing this apartment with a brother, or a roommate.

55   She feels his hands on her waist, leading her from behind to the edge of his bed. Her body is crushed under his as he slams himself against her, from behind, grunting. She holds her breath, taut against his weight and the pain, but she will not disturb his moment. She hopes that the next moment will be hers. She waits with the bed sheet pulled up to her chin. The toilet flushes and, shortly after, she hears newspaper pages being turned in the sagging five-dollar gold armchair.

Later, deep-sleep breathing and low snoring from the bedroom fills the apartment, dictating her movements. She sits on the green-and-yellow shag carpet, leaning against the foot of the husband's armchair, in front of the snowy black-and-white television watching a French station turned down low enough not to awaken him. Something about listening to a language that she does not understand comforts her, gives her companionship in a place where she feels like a foreigner. She is beginning to be able to repeat advertisements in French.

READING AND REACTING

1. Why is a garden so important to Vijai?
2. What is the nature of Vijai's marriage?
3. Vijai's acquisition of French indicates what about her way of life?
4. **JOURNAL ENTRY** Imagine you are Vijai and write a letter to your husband.
5. **CRITICAL PERSPECTIVE** In the Introduction to *The Penguin Anthology of Stories by Canadian Women*, Denise Chong comments: "The plot that interested me was life lived in the chaos and uncertainty of

everyday happenings and relationships." Mootoo's story is included in Chong's anthology. Using Chong's requirements for inclusion, identify the specific reasons for this story's inclusion.

◆ WRITING SUGGESTIONS: SETTING

1. Both "Inland Passage" (p. 150) and "The Yellow Wall-Paper" use rich language to create a mood that dominates the story. Analyze this use of language in one of the two stories—or compare two short passages, one from each story. How does language create and enrich each story's setting?

2. In all of the stories in this chapter, social constraints determined by the story's setting limit a woman's options. Explore the options each woman might reasonably exercise in order to break free of the limits that social institutions impose on her.

3. In stories in which setting is a strong presence, the danger always exists that the writer will neglect character development in favour of atmosphere. Does this problem occur in any of the stories in this chapter? Explain your answer.

4. Write an essay in which you consider how any one of the four stories in this chapter would be different if its historical, geographical, or physical setting were changed to a setting of your choice. In your essay, examine the changes (in plot development as well as in the characters' conflicts, reactions, and motivation) that might be caused by the change in setting.

5. Select a story from another chapter, and write an essay in which you consider how setting affects its plot—for example, how it creates conflict or crisis, how it forces characters to act, or how it determines how the plot is resolved.

CHAPTER 7

Point of View

◊ ◊ ◊

In dealing with point-of-view the [writer] must always deal with the individual work: which particular character shall tell this particular story, or part of a story, with what precise degree of reliability, privilege, freedom to comment, and so on. . . . Even if the [writer] has decided on a narrator who will fit one of the critic's classifications—"omniscient," "first-person," "limited omniscient," "objective," . . . and so on—his troubles have just begun. He simply cannot find answers to his immediate, precise, practical problems by referring to statements that the "omniscient is the most flexible method," or "the objective the most rapid or vivid," or whatever. Even the soundest of generalizations at this level will be of little use to him.

WAYNE C. BOOTH, "Distance and Point of View"

As some observers have noted, ethnic minority writers have an experience of at least two cultures, one functional and mainstream, the other perhaps more suppressed and rooted in historical memory. This awareness of duality, the potential conflict arising from the friction between the two worlds and the powerful influence of the secondary culture lurking offstage account for what is fresh and energetic and unique about much of this literature. Chinese-Canadian writers are no exception. There may well be a growing and more receptive audience for this kind of fare, but not simply because it is "multicultural" and injects some adrenalin into the body of the Canadian literary tradition. We read to experience alternate realities and perceptions and to be entertained. If the writing is true, it strikes a common chord in all of us, and we gain a deeper satisfaction because it stimulates our imagination and challenges our moral judgement. Otherwise, it will not endure, and no amount of novelty or exotic ornament can preserve it.

BENNETT LEE, *Many Mouthed Birds: Contemporary Writing by Chinese Canadians*

◊ ◊ ◊

All stories are told, or narrated, by someone, and one of the first choices writers make is who tells the story. This choice determines the story's **point of view**—the angle or vantage point from which events are presented. The implications of this choice are far reaching. Consider for a moment the following scenario. Five people witness a crime and are questioned by the police. Their stories agree on certain points: a crime was committed, a body was found, and the crime occurred at noon. But in other ways their stories are different. The man who fled the scene was either tall or of average height; his hair was either dark or light; he either was carrying an object or was empty handed. The events that led up to the crime and even the description of the crime itself are markedly different depending on who tells the story. Thus, the perspective from which a story is told determines what details are included in the story and how they are arranged—in short, the plot. In addition, the perspective of the narrator affects the story's style, language, and themes.

The narrator of a work of fiction is not the same as the author—even when a writer uses the first-person *I*. Writers create narrators, often with personalities and opinions far different from theirs, to tell their stories. (The technical term **persona**—which literally means "mask"—is used to denote this narrator.) By assuming this mask, a writer expands the creative possibilities of a work.

When deciding on a point of view for a work of fiction, a writer can choose to tell the story either in the *first person* or in the *third person*.

FIRST-PERSON NARRATOR
◆ ◆ ◆

Sometimes the narrator is a character who uses the **first person** *I* (or sometimes *we*) to tell the story. Often this narrator is a major character—Sammy in John Updike's "A&P" (p. 122) and the boy in James Joyce's "Araby" (p. 267), for example—who tells his or her own story and is the focus of that story. Sometimes, however, a first-person narrator may tell a story that is primarily about someone else. Such a narrator may be a minor character who plays a relatively small part in the story or simply an observer who reports events experienced or related by others. The narrator of William Faulkner's "A Rose for Emily" (p. 90), for example, is an unidentified witness to the story's events. By using *we* (instead of *I*), this narrator speaks on behalf of all the town's residents, expressing their shared views of their neighbour, Emily Grierson:

> We did not say she was crazy then. We believed she had to do that. We remembered all the young men her father had driven away, and we knew that with nothing left, she would have to cling to that which had robbed her, as people will.

Writers gain a number of advantages when they use a first-person narrator. First, they are able to present incidents very convincingly. Readers are more willing to accept a statement like "My sister changed a lot after that day" than they are to accept the impersonal observations of a third-person narrator. The first-person narrator also simplifies a writer's task of selecting details. Only the events and details that the narrator could actually have seen or experienced can be introduced into the story.

Another major advantage of first-person narrators is that their restricted view can create **irony**—a discrepancy between what is said and what readers believe to be true. Irony may be *dramatic, situational,* or *verbal.* **Dramatic irony** occurs when a narrator or character perceives less than readers do. **Situational irony** occurs when what happens is at odds with what readers are led to expect; **verbal irony** occurs when the narrator says one thing but actually means another.

UNRELIABLE NARRATORS

Sometimes first-person narrators may be self-serving, mistaken, confused, unstable, or even mad. These **unreliable narrators,** whether intentionally or unintentionally, misrepresent events and misdirect readers. In Edgar Allan Poe's "The Cask of Amontillado" (p. 227), for example, the narrator, Montresor, tells his story to justify a crime he committed fifty years before. Montresor's version of what happened is not accurate, and perceptive readers know it: his obvious self-deception, his sadistic manipulation of Fortunato, his detached description of the cold-blooded murder, and his lack of remorse lead readers to question his sanity (and, therefore, to distrust his version of events). This distrust creates an ironic distance between readers and narrator.

The narrator of Charlotte Perkins Gilman's "The Yellow Wall-Paper" (p. 189) is also an unreliable narrator. Suffering from "nervous depression," she unintentionally distorts the facts when she says that the shapes in the wallpaper of her bedroom are changing and moving. Moreover, she does not realize what is wrong with her or why, or how her husband's "good intentions" are hurting her. Readers, however, see the disparity between the narrator's interpretation of events and their own, and this irony enriches their understanding of the story.

Some narrators are unreliable because they are naive. Because they are immature, sheltered, or innocent of evil, these narrators may not be aware of the full significance of the events they are relating. Having the benefit of experience, readers interpret events differently from the way these narrators do. When we read a passage by a child narrator—such as the following one from J. D. Salinger's novel *The Catcher in the Rye*—we are aware of the narrator's innocence, and we know his interpretation of events is flawed:

> Anyway, I keep picturing all these little kids playing some game in this big field of rye and all. Thousands of little kids, and nobody's around— nobody big, I mean—except me. And I'm standing on the edge of some crazy cliff. What I have to do, I have to catch everybody if they start to

> go over the cliff—I mean if they're running and they don't look where they're going I have to come out from somewhere and catch them. I'd just be the catcher in the rye. . . .

The irony in the preceding passage comes from our knowledge that the naive narrator, Holden Caulfield, cannot stop children from growing up. Ultimately, they all fall off the "crazy cliff" and mature into adults. Although he is not aware of the futility of trying to protect children from the dangers of adulthood, readers know that his efforts are doomed from the start.

A naive narrator's background can also limit his or her ability to understand a situation. The narrator in James Joyce's "Araby" is initially naive, but Joyce shows readers the boy's painful realization of lost chances and impossibilities.

Keep in mind that there is a difference between an unreliable narrator and a narrator whose perspective is limited. All first-person narrators are, by definition, limited because they present a situation as only one person sees it. In "Stones" by Timothy Findley (p. 135), Ben Max, the narrator, does not understand what happened to his father at Dieppe. As a child, he is confused by the enormous change in his father, and he struggles to understand the events while loving his father unconditionally. No character, of course, has all the information the story's author has.

As a reader focusing on a story's point of view, you should look for discrepancies between a narrator's view of events and your own sense of what has happened. Discovering that a story has an unreliable narrator enables you not only to question the truth of the narrative but also to recognize the irony in the narrator's version of events. By doing so, you are able to gain a better sense of the story and of the writer's purpose.

Third-Person Narrator

♦ ♦ ♦

Writers can also use **third-person** narrators, who are not characters in the story. These narrators fall into three categories.

Omniscient

Some third-person narrators are **omniscient** (all-knowing) narrators, moving at will from one character's mind to another. One advantage of omniscient narrators is that they are objective; they have none of the naiveté, dishonesty, gullibility, or mental instability that can characterize first-person narrators. In addition, because omniscient narrators are not characters in the story, their perception is not limited to what any one character can observe or comprehend. As a result, they can present a more inclusive overview of events and characters than first-person narrators can. In short, because omniscient narrators speak from outside a character, they are reliable; they maintain an objective distance from events, giving readers an accurate version of what happened. The narrator of Mavis Gallant's "The Ice Wagon Going Down the Street" (p. 98) gives such an overview:

> Peter's wife had loved him in Paris. Whatever she wanted in marriage she found that winter, there. In Geneva, where Peter was a file clerk and they lived in a furnished flat, she pretended they were in Paris and life was still the same. Often, when the children were at supper, she changed as though she and Peter were dining out. She wore the Balenciaga, and put candles on the card table where she and Peter ate their meal. The neckline of the dress was soiled with make-up. Peter remembers her dabbing on the make-up with a wet sponge. He remembers her in the kitchen, in the soiled Balenciaga, patting on the make-up with a filthy sponge. Behind her, at the kitchen table, Sandra and Jennifer, in buttonless pajamas and bunny slippers, ate their supper of marmalade sandwiches and milk. When the children were asleep, the parents dined solemnly, ritually, Sheilah sitting straight as a queen.

Occasionally, omniscient narrators move not only in and out of the minds of the characters but also in and out of a persona (representing the voice of the author) that speaks directly to readers. This experimental narrative technique was popular with writers during the eighteenth century, when the novel was a new literary form. It permitted writers to present themselves as masters of artifice, able to know and control all aspects of experience. Few contemporary writers would give themselves the licence that Henry Fielding does in the following passage from *Tom Jones*:

> And true it was that [Mr. Alworthy] did many of these things; but had he done nothing more I should have left him to have recorded his own merit on some fair freestone over the door of that hospital. Matters of a much more extraordinary kind are to be the subject of this history, or I should grossly misspend my time in writing so voluminous a work; and you my sagacious friend, might with equal profit and pleasure travel through some pages which certain droll authors have been facetiously pleased to call *The History of England*.

LIMITED OMNISCIENT

Third-person narrators can have **limited omniscience**, focusing on only what a single character experiences. In other words, events are limited to one character's perspective, and nothing is revealed that the character does not see, hear, feel, or think. Limited omniscient narrators, like all third-person narrators, have certain advantages over first-person narrators. When a writer uses a first-person narrator, the narrator's personality and speech colour the story, creating a personal or even idiosyncratic narrative. Also, the first-person narrator's character flaws or lack of knowledge may limit his or her awareness of the significance of events. Limited omniscient narrators are more flexible: they take readers into a particular character's mind just as a first-person narrator does, but without the first-person narrator's subjectivity, self-deception, or naiveté. In the following example from Sinclair Ross's "A Field of Wheat"

(p. 173), the limited omniscient narrator presents the story from the point of view of Martha:

> She had loved John, for these sixteen years had stood close watching while he died—slowly, tantalizingly, as the parched wheat died. He had grown unkempt, ugly, morose. His voice was gruff, contentious, never broke into the deep, strong laughter that used to make her feel she was living at the heart of things. John was gone, love was gone; there was only wheat.

While we see both Martha and John in the story, we see the actions largely through Martha.

DRAMATIC

Finally, third-person narrators can tell a story from a **dramatic** (or *objective*) point of view, remaining entirely outside the characters' minds. With dramatic narrators, events unfold the way they would in a play or a movie. Narrators tell the story only by reproducing dialogue and recounting events. They do not present the characters' thoughts or explain their motivation. Thus, they allow readers to interpret the actions of the characters without any interference. Shirley Jackson uses a dramatic point of view for much of "The Lottery" (p. 319):

> Mrs. Hutchinson craned her neck to see through the crowd and found her husband and children standing near the front. She tapped Mrs. Delacroix on the arm as a farewell and began to make her way through the crowd. The people separated good-humoredly to let her through; two or three people said, in voices just loud enough to be heard across the crowd, "Here comes your Missus, Hutchinson," and "Bill, she made it after all."

The story's narrator is distant, seemingly emotionless, and this perspective is consistent with the author's purpose: for Jackson, the matter-of-fact attitude of the narrator conflicts with the actions in the story.

Writers choose the point of view that best enables them to achieve their objectives. If they want to create an intimate, subjective portrait of a character, they will employ a first-person narrator. If they want to have a great deal of freedom in telling their story, they will use an omniscient narrator. A limited omniscient narrator enables writers to maintain the focus on a single individual while commenting on the action. And finally, the dramatic point of view allows writers to remove the narrator from the story and present events in a distant, emotionless way. A useful exercise to see how point of view works is to take a passage from a short story and rewrite it using a different point of view.

SELECTING AN APPROPRIATE POINT
OF VIEW: REVIEW

FIRST-PERSON NARRATOR (*I* OR *WE*)

◇ *Major character telling his or her own story* "Every morning I lay on the floor in the front parlour watching her door." (James Joyce, "Araby")

◇ *Minor character as witness or nonparticipant* "And so she died. . . . We did not even know she was sick; we had long since given up trying to get information. . . . " (William Faulkner, "A Rose for Emily")

THIRD-PERSON NARRATOR (*HE, SHE, IT,* OR *THEY*)

◇ *Omniscient—able to move at will from character to character and comment about them* "In Geneva Peter worked for a woman—a girl. She was a Norwegian from a small town in Saskatchewan. He supposed they had been put together because they were Canadians . . ." (Mavis Gallant, "The Ice Wagon Going Down the Street")

◇ *Limited Omniscient—restricts focus to a single character* "The wagon went on. He did not know where they were going." (William Faulkner, "Barn Burning")

◇ *Dramatic (Objective)—simply reports the dialogue and the actions of characters* "The morning of June 27th was clear and sunny, with the fresh warmth of a full-summer day; the flowers were blossoming profusely and the grass was richly green." (Shirley Jackson, "The Lottery")

 CHECKLIST: WRITING ABOUT
POINT OF VIEW

✓ What is the dominant point of view from which the story is told?

✓ Is the narrator of the story a participant in the story or just a witness?

✓ Does the story's point of view create irony?

✓ If the story has a first-person narrator, is the narrator reliable or unreliable? Are there any inconsistencies in the narrator's presentation of the story?

✓ How do you explain any distortions of fact that you detect? Do you think these distortions are intentional or unintentional?

✓ If the story has a third-person narrator, is he or she omniscient? Does he or she have limited omniscience? Is the narrator objective?

✓ What are the advantages of the story's point of view? How does the point of view accomplish the author's purpose?

✓ Does the point of view remain consistent throughout the story, or does it shift?

✓ How might a different point of view change the story?

◈ **Thomas King** (1943–   ) was born in California of Greek and Cherokee ancestry but has lived and worked for most of his adult life in Canada. His stories often draw on the oral traditions of different North American Native peoples. Many of them contain witty characters that are modern versions of mythic trickster figures that have traditionally inhabited Native folklore. His novel *Green Grass, Running Water* (1993) locates stories of everyday life and political resistance in the Native community within a legend of creation told by a coyote. King's works include *Medicine River*, a novel (1989), *One Good Story, That One*, a collection of short stories (1993), and *Truth and Bright Water*, a novel (1999). His most recent works include *Truth About Stories: A Native Narrative* (2003), the Massey lectures for 2003; *A Short History of Indians in Canada* (2005), a collection of short stories; and *The Red Power Murders: A DreadfulWater Mystery* (2006).

◈   ◈   ◈

THOMAS   KING

Borders
(1993)

When I was twelve, maybe thirteen, my mother announced that we were going to go to Salt Lake City to visit my sister who had left the reserve, moved across the line, and found a job. Laetitia had not left home with my mother's blessing, but over time my mother had come to be proud of the fact that Laetitia had done all of this on her own.

"She did real good," my mother would say.

Then there were the fine points to Laetitia's going. She had not, as my mother liked to tell Mrs. Manyfingers, gone floating after some man like a balloon on a string. She hadn't snuck out of the house, either, and gone to Vancouver or Edmonton or Toronto to chase rainbows down alleys. And she hadn't been pregnant.

"She did real good."

5   I was seven or eight when Laetitia left home. She was seventeen. Our father was from Rocky Boy on the American side.

"Dad's American," Laetitia told my mother, "so I can go and come as I please."

"Send us a postcard."

Laetitia packed her things, and we headed for the border. Just outside of Milk River, Laetitia told us to watch for the water tower.

"Over the next rise. It's the first thing you see."

10   "We got a water tower on the reserve," my mother said. "There's a big one in Lethbridge, too."

"You'll be able to see the tops of the flagpoles, too. That's where the border is."

When we got to Coutts, my mother stopped at the convenience store and bought her and Laetitia a cup of coffee. I got an Orange Crush.

"This is real lousy coffee."

"You're just angry because I want to see the world."

15 "It's the water. From here on down, they got lousy water."

"I can catch the bus from Sweetgrass. You don't have to lift a finger."

"You're going to have to buy your water in bottles if you want good coffee."

There was an old wooden building about a block away, with a tall sign in the yard that said "Museum." Most of the roof had been blown away. Mom told me to go and see when the place was open. There were boards over the windows and doors. You could tell that the place was closed, and I told Mom so, but she said to go and check anyway. Mom and Laetitia stayed by the car. Neither one of them moved. I sat down on the steps of the museum and watched them, and I don't know that they ever said anything to each other. Finally, Laetitia got her bag out of the trunk and gave Mom a hug.

I wandered back to the car. The wind had come up, and it blew Laetitia's hair across her face. Mom reached out and pulled the strands out of Laetitia's eyes, and Laetitia let her.

20 "You can still see the mountain from here," my mother told Laetitia in Blackfoot.

"Lots of mountains in Salt Lake," Laetitia told her in English.

"The place is closed," I said. "Just like I told you."

Laetitia tucked her hair into her jacket and dragged her bag down the road to the brick building with the American flag flapping on a pole. When she got to where the guards were waiting, she turned, put the bag down, and waved to us. We waved back. Then my mother turned the car around, and we came home.

We got postcards from Laetitia regular, and, if she wasn't spreading jelly on the truth, she was happy. She found a good job and rented an apartment with a pool.

25 "And she can't even swim," my mother told Mrs. Manyfingers.

Most of the postcards said we should come down and see the city, but whenever I mentioned this, my mother would stiffen up.

So I was surprised when she bought two new tires for the car and put on her blue dress with the green and yellow flowers. I had to dress up, too, for my mother did not want us crossing the border looking like Americans. We made sandwiches and put them in a big box with pop and potato chips and some apples and bananas and a big jar of water.

"But we can stop at one of those restaurants, too, right?"

"We maybe should take some blankets in case you get sleepy."

30 "But we can stop at one of those restaurants, too, right?"

The border was actually two towns, though neither one was big enough to amount to anything. Coutts was on the Canadian side and consisted of the convenience store and gas station, the museum that was closed and boarded up, and a motel. Sweetgrass was on the American side, but all you could see was an overpass that arched across the highway and disappeared into the prairies. Just hearing the names of these towns, you would expect that Sweetgrass, which is a nice name and sounds like it is related to other places such as Medicine Hat and Moose Jaw and Kicking Horse Pass, would be on the Canadian side, and that Coutts, which sounds abrupt and rude, would be on the American side. But this was not the case.

Between the two borders was a duty-free shop where you could buy cigarettes and liquor and flags. Stuff like that.

We left the reserve in the morning and drove until we got to Coutts.

"Last time we stopped here," my mother said, "you had an Orange Crush. You remember that?"

35   "Sure," I said. "That was when Laetitia took off."

"You want another Orange Crush?"

"That means we're not going to stop at a restaurant, right?"

My mother got a coffee at the convenience store, and we stood around and watched the prairies move in the sunlight. Then we climbed back in the car. My mother straightened the dress across her thighs, leaned against the wheel, and drove all the way to the border in first gear, slowly, as if she were trying to see through a bad storm or riding high on black ice.

The border guard was an old guy. As he walked to the car, he swayed from side to side, his feet set wide apart, the holster on his hip pitching up and down. He leaned into the window, looked into the back seat, and looked at my mother and me.

40   "Morning, ma'am."

"Good morning."

"Where you heading?"

"Salt Lake City."

"Purpose of your visit?"

45   "Visit my daughter."

"Citizenship."

"Blackfoot," my mother told him.

"Ma'am?"

"Blackfoot," my mother repeated.

50   "Canadian?"

"Blackfoot."

It would have been easier if my mother had just said "Canadian" and been done with it, but I could see she wasn't going to do that. The guard wasn't angry or anything. He smiled and looked towards the building. Then he turned back and nodded.

"Morning, ma'am."

"Good morning."

55   "Any firearms or tobacco?"

"No."

"Citizenship?"

"Blackfoot."

He told us to sit in the car and wait, and we did. In about five minutes, another guard came out with the first man. They were talking as they came, both men swaying back and forth like two cowboys headed for a bar or a gunfight.

60   "Morning, ma'am."

"Good morning."

"Cecil tells me you and the boy are Blackfoot."

"That's right."

"Now, I know that we got Blackfeet on the American side and the Canadians got Blackfeet on their side. Just so we can keep our records straight, what side do you come from?"

65   I knew exactly what my mother was going to say, and I could have told them if they had asked me.

"Canadian side or American side?" asked the guard.

"Blackfoot side," she said.

It didn't take them long to lose their sense of humour, I can tell you that. The one guard stopped smiling altogether and told us to park our car at the side of the building and come in.

We sat on a wood bench for about an hour before anyone came over to talk to us. This time it was a woman. She had a gun, too.

70   "Hi," she said. "I'm Inspector Pratt. I understand there is a little misunderstanding."

"I'm going to visit my daughter in Salt Lake City," my mother told her. "We don't have any guns or beer."

"It's a legal technicality, that's all."

"My daughter's Blackfoot, too."

The woman opened a briefcase and took out a couple of forms and began to write on one of them. "Everyone who crosses our border has to declare their citizenship. Even Americans. It helps us keep track of the visitors we get from the various countries."

75   She went on like that for maybe fifteen minutes, and a lot of the stuff she told us was interesting.

"I can understand how you feel about having to tell us your citizenship, and here's what I'll do. You tell me, and I won't put it down on the form. No-one will know but you and me."

Her gun was silver. There were several chips in the wood handle and the name "Stella" was scratched into the metal butt.

We were in the border office for about four hours, and we talked to almost everyone there. One of the men bought me a Coke. My mother brought a couple of sandwiches in from the car. I offered a part of mine to Stella, but she said she wasn't hungry.

I told Stella that we were Blackfoot and Canadian, but she said that didn't count because I was a minor. In the end, she told us that if my mother didn't declare her citizenship, we would have to go back where we came from. My mother stood up and thanked Stella for her time. Then we got back in the car and drove to the Canadian border, which was only about a hundred yards away.

80   I was disappointed. I hadn't seen Laetitia for a long time, and I had never been to Salt Lake City. When she was still at home, Laetitia would go on and on about Salt Lake City. She had never been there, but her boyfriend Lester Tallbull had spent a year in Salt Lake at a technical school.

"It's a great place," Lester would say. "Nothing but blondes in the whole state."

Whenever he said that, Laetitia would slug him on his shoulder hard enough to make him flinch. He had some brochures on Salt Lake and some maps, and every so often the two of them would spread them out on the table.

"That's the temple. It's right downtown. You got to have a pass to get in."

"Charlotte says anyone can go in and look around."

85   "When was Charlotte in Salt Lake? Just when the hell was Charlotte in Salt Lake?"

"Last year."

"This is Liberty Park. It's got a zoo. There's good skiing in the mountains."

"Got all the skiing we can use," my mother would say. "People come from all over the world to ski at Banff. Cardston's got a temple, if you like those kinds of things."

"Oh, this one is real big," Lester would say. "They got armed guards and everything."

90   "Not what Charlotte says."

"What does she know?"

Lester and Laetitia broke up, but I guess the idea of Salt Lake stuck in her mind.

The Canadian border guard was a young woman, and she seemed happy to see us.

"Hi," she said. "You folks sure have a great day for a trip. Where are you coming from?"

95   "Standoff."

"Is that in Montana?"

"No."

"Where are you going?"

"Standoff."

100   The woman's name was Carol and I don't guess she was any older than Laetitia. "Wow, you both Canadians?"

"Blackfoot."

"Really? I have a friend I went to school with who is Blackfoot. Do you know Mike Harley?"

"No."

"He went to school in Lethbridge, but he's really from Browning."

105   It was a nice conversation and there were no cars behind us, so there was no rush.

"You're not bringing any liquor back, are you?"

"No."

"Any cigarettes or plants or stuff like that?"

"No."

110   "Citizenship?"

"Blackfoot."

"I know," said the woman, "and I'd be proud of being Blackfoot if I were Blackfoot. But you have to be American or Canadian."

When Laetitia and Lester broke up, Lester took his brochures and maps with him, so Laetitia wrote to someone in Salt Lake City, and, about a month later, she got a big envelope of stuff. We sat at the table and opened up all the brochures, and Laetitia read each one out loud.

"Salt Lake City is the gateway to some of the world's most magnificent skiing."

115 "Salt Lake City is the home of one of the newest professional basketball franchises, the Utah Jazz."

"The Great Salt Lake is one of the natural wonders of the world."

It was kind of exciting seeing all those colour brochures on the table and listening to Laetitia read all about how Salt Lake City was one of the best places in the entire world.

"That Salt Lake City place sounds too good to be true," my mother told her.

"It has everything."

120 "We got everything right here."

"It's boring here."

"People in Salt Lake City are probably sending away for brochures of Calgary and Lethbridge and Pincher Creek right now."

In the end, my mother would say that maybe Laetitia should go to Salt Lake City, and Laetitia would say that maybe she would.

We parked the car to the side of the building and Carol led us into a small room on the second floor. I found a comfortable spot on the couch and flipped through some back issues of *Saturday Night* and *Alberta Report*.

125 When I woke up, my mother was just coming out of another office. She didn't say a word to me. I followed her down the stairs and out to the car. I thought we were going home, but she turned the car around and drove back towards the American border, which made me think we were going to visit Laetitia in Salt Lake City after all. Instead she pulled into the parking lot of the duty-free store and stopped.

"We going to see Laetitia?"

"No."

"We going home?"

Pride is a good thing to have, you know. Laetitia had a lot of pride, and so did my mother. I figured that someday, I'd have it, too.

130 "So where are we going?"

Most of that day, we wandered around the duty-free store, which wasn't very large. The manager had a name tag with a tiny American flag on one side and tiny Canadian flag on the other. His name was Mel. Towards evening, he began suggesting that we should be on our way. I told him we had nowhere to go, that neither the Americans nor the Canadians would let us in. He laughed at that and told us that we should buy something or leave.

The car was not very comfortable, but we did have all that food and it was April, so even if it did snow as it sometimes does on the prairies, we wouldn't freeze. The next morning my mother drove to the American border.

It was a different guard this time, but the questions were the same. We didn't spend as much time in the office as we had the day before. By noon, we were back at the Canadian border. By two we were back in the duty-free shop parking lot.

The second night in the car was not as much fun as the first, but my mother seemed in good spirits, and, all in all, it was as much an adventure as an inconvenience. There wasn't much food left and that was a problem, but we had lots of water as there was a faucet at the side of the duty-free shop.

135 One Sunday, Laetitia and I were watching television. Mom was over at Mrs. Manyfingers's. Right in the middle of the programme, Laetitia turned off the set and said she was going to Salt Lake City, that life around here was too boring. I had wanted to see the rest of the programme and really didn't care if Laetitia went to Salt Lake City or not. When Mom got home, I told her what Laetitia had said.

What surprised me was how angry Laetitia got when she found out that I had told Mom.

"You got a big mouth."

"That's what you said."

"What I said is none of your business."

140 "I didn't say anything."

"Well, I'm going for sure, now."

That weekend, Laetitia packed her bags, and we drove her to the border.

Mel turned out to be friendly. When he closed up for the night and found us still parked in the lot, he came over and asked us if our car was broken down or something. My mother thanked him for his concern and told him that we were fine, that things would get straightened out in the morning.

"You're kidding," said Mel. "You'd think they could handle the simple things."

145 "We got some apples and a banana," I said, "but we're all out of ham sandwiches."

"You know, you read about these things, but you just don't believe it. You just don't believe it."

"Hamburgers would be even better because they got more stuff for energy."

My mother slept in the back seat. I slept in the front because I was smaller and could lie under the steering wheel. Late that night, I heard my mother open the car door. I found her sitting on her blanket leaning against the bumper of the car.

"You see all those stars," she said. "When I was a little girl, my grand-mother used to take me and my sisters out on the prairies and tell us stories about all the stars."

150 "Do you think Mel is going to bring us any hamburgers?"

"Every one of those stars has a story. You see that bunch of stars over there that look like a fish?"

"He didn't say no."

"Coyote went fishing, one day. That's how it all started." We sat out under the stars that night, and my mother told me all sorts of stories. She was serious about it, too. She'd tell them slow, repeating parts as she went, as if she expected me to remember each one.

Early the next morning, the television vans began to arrive, and guys in suits and women in dresses came trotting over to us, dragging microphones and cameras and lights behind them. One of the vans had a table set up with orange juice and sandwiches and fruit. It was for the crew, but when I told them we hadn't eaten for a while, a really skinny blonde woman told us we could eat as much as we wanted.

155 They mostly talked to my mother. Every so often one of the reporters would come over and ask me questions about how it felt to be an Indian without a country. I told them we had a nice house on the reserve and that my cousins had a couple of horses we rode when we went fishing. Some of the television people went over to the American border, and then they went to the Canadian border.

Around noon, a good-looking guy in a dark blue suit and an orange tie with little ducks on it drove up in a fancy car. He talked to my mother for a while, and, after they were done talking, my mother called me over, and we got into our car. Just as my mother started the engine, Mel came over and gave us a bag of peanut brittle and told us that justice was a damn hard thing to get, but that we shouldn't give up.

I would have preferred lemon drops, but it was nice of Mel anyway.

"Where are we going now?"

"Going to visit Laetitia."

160 The guard who came out to our car was all smiles. The television lights were so bright they hurt my eyes, and, if you tried to look through the wind-shield in certain directions, you couldn't see a thing.

"Morning, ma'am."

"Good morning."

"Where you heading?"

"Salt Lake City."

165 "Purpose of your visit?"

"Visit my daughter."

"Any tobacco, liquor, or firearms?"

"Don't smoke."

"Any plants or fruit?"

170 "Not any more."

"Citizenship?"

"Blackfoot."

The guard rocked back on his heels and jammed his thumbs into his gun belt. "Thank you," he said, his fingers patting the butt of the revolver. "Have a pleasant trip."

My mother rolled the car forward, and the television people had to scramble out of the way. They ran alongside the car as we pulled away from the border, and, when they couldn't run any farther, they stood in the middle of the highway and waved and waved and waved.

175   We got to Salt Lake City the next day. Laetitia was happy to see us, and, that first night, she took us out to a restaurant that made really good soups. The list of pies took up a whole page. I had cherry. Mom had chocolate. Laetitia said that she saw us on television the night before and, during the meal, she had us tell her the story over and over again.

Laetitia took us everywhere. We went to a fancy ski resort. We went to the temple. We got to go shopping in a couple of large malls, but they weren't as large as the one in Edmonton, and Mom said so.

After a week or so, I got bored and wasn't at all sad when my mother said we should be heading back home. Laetitia wanted us to stay longer, but Mom said no, that she had things to do back home and that, next time, Laetitia should come up and visit. Laetitia said she was thinking about moving back, and Mom told her to do as she pleased, and Laetitia said that she would.

On the way home, we stopped at the duty-free shop, and my mother gave Mel a green hat that said "Salt Lake" across the front. Mel was a funny guy. He took the hat and blew his nose and told my mother that she was an inspiration to us all. He gave us some more peanut brittle and came out into the parking lot and waved at us all the way to the Canadian border.

It was almost evening when we left Coutts. I watched the border through the rear window until all you could see were the tops of the flag-poles and the blue water tower, and then they rolled over a hill and disappeared.

READING AND REACTING

1. Why does Thomas King use the first-person narrative of a young boy? What is gained or lost by this choice?
2. What different views of race and nationality are presented by the story?
3. Why is the mother so insistent on replying "Blackfoot" every time she is asked for her nationality?
4. Apart from the border between Canada and the United States, what other borders are suggested in the story?
5. What role does technology play in the plot and theme of the story?
6. How does King incorporate humour into the story? Why does he?

7. We are told the narrator is twelve or thirteen. Do his language and interests appear consistent with those of a boy that age? Give examples.

8. **JOURNAL ENTRY** Have you ever experienced difficulty crossing a border? What would you do if you were in the mother's position? The son's?

Related Works: "Town and Country Lovers" (p. 80), "The Loons" (p. 249), "Theme for English B" (p. 849), *The Rez Sisters* (p. 1248), *The Ecstasy of Rita Joe* (p. 1376)

◆ **EDGAR ALLAN POE** (1809–1849) profoundly influenced many corners of the literary world. His tales of psychological terror and the macabre, his hauntingly musical lyric poems, and his writings on the craft of poetry and short-story writing affected the development of symbolic fiction, the modern detective story, and the Gothic horror tale. In most of Poe's horror tales (as in "The Cask of Amontillado"), readers vicariously "live" the story through the first-person narrator who tells the tale.

Poe was born in 1809, the son of a talented English-born actress who, deserted by her actor husband, died of tuberculosis before her son's third birthday. Though Poe was raised in material comfort by foster parents in Richmond, Virginia, his life was increasingly uncertain: his foster mother loved him, but her husband became antagonistic. He kept the young Poe so short of money at the University of Virginia (and later at West Point) that Poe resorted to gambling to raise money for food and clothing. Finally, debt-ridden, he left school altogether.

Poe found work as a magazine editor, gaining recognition as a perceptive (if sometimes vitriolic) literary critic. In 1836, he married his frail thirteen-year-old cousin, Virginia Clemm. Poe produced many of his most famous stories and poems in the next few years, working feverishly to support his tubercular wife; but although his stories were widely admired, financial success never came. His wife died in 1847. Less than two years after her death, Poe was found barely conscious in a Baltimore street after a mysterious disappearance; three days later, he was dead at age forty.

EDGAR ALLAN POE

The Cask of Amontillado
(1846)

The thousand injuries of Fortunato I had borne as I best could, but when he ventured upon insult I vowed revenge. You, who so well know the nature of my soul, will not suppose, however, that I gave utterance to a threat. *At length* I would be avenged; this was a point definitely settled—but the very definitiveness with which it was resolved precluded the idea of risk. I must not only punish but punish with impunity. A wrong is unredressed when retribution overtakes its redresser. It is equally unredressed when the avenger fails to make himself felt as such to him who has done the wrong.

It must be understood that neither by word nor deed had I given Fortunato cause to doubt my good will. I continued, as was my wont, to smile in his face, and he did not perceive that my smile *now* was at the thought of his immolation.

He had a weak point—this Fortunato—although in other regards he was a man to be respected and even feared. He prided himself on his connoisseurship in wine. Few Italians have the true virtuoso spirit. For the most part their enthusiasm is adopted to suit the time and opportunity, to practise imposture upon the British and Austrian *millionaires*. In painting and gemmary, Fortunato, like his countrymen, was a quack, but in the matter of old wines he was sincere. In this respect I did not differ from him materially;—I was skillful in the Italian vintages myself, and bought largely whenever I could.

It was about dusk, one evening during the supreme madness of the carnival season, that I encountered my friend. He accosted me with excessive warmth, for he had been drinking much. The man wore motley.[1] He had on a tight-fitting parti-striped dress, and his head was surmounted by the conical cap and bells. I was so pleased to see him that I thought I should never have done wringing his hand.

5   I said to him—"My dear Fortunato, you are luckily met. How remarkably well you are looking to-day. But I have received a pipe[2] of what passes for Amontillado,[3] and I have my doubts."

"How?" said he. "Amontillado? A pipe? Impossible! And in the middle of the carnival!"

"I have my doubts," I replied; "and I was silly enough to pay the full Amontillado price without consulting you in the matter. You were not to be found, and I was fearful of losing a bargain."

"Amontillado!"

"I have my doubts."

10   "Amontillado!"

"And I must satisfy them."

"Amontillado!"

"As you are engaged, I am on my way to Luchresi. If any one has a critical turn it is he. He will tell me—"

"Luchresi cannot tell Amontillado from Sherry."

15   "And yet some fools will have it that his taste is a match for your own."

"Come, let us go."

"Whither?"

"To your vaults."

---

[1] The many-coloured attire of a court jester.

[2] In the United States and England, a cask containing a volume equal to 126 gallons.

[3] A pale, dry sherry; literally, a wine "from Montilla" (Spain).

"My friend, no; I will not impose upon your good nature. I perceive you have an engagement. Luchresi—"

20   "I have no engagement;—come."

"My friend, no. It is not the engagement, but the severe cold with which I perceive you are afflicted. The vaults are insufferably damp. They are encrusted with nitre."[4]

"Let us go, nevertheless. The cold is merely nothing. Amontillado! You have been imposed upon. And as for Luchresi, he cannot distinguish Sherry from Amontillado."

Thus speaking, Fortunato possessed himself of my arm; and putting on a mask of black silk and drawing a *roquelaire*[5] closely about my person, I suffered him to hurry me to my palazzo.

There were no attendants at home; they had absconded to make merry in honor of the time. I had told them that I should not return until the morning, and had given them explicit orders not to stir from the house. These orders were sufficient, I well knew, to insure their immediate disappearance, one and all, as soon as my back was turned.

25   I took from their sconces two flambeaux, and giving one to Fortunato, bowed him through several suites of rooms to the archway that led into the vaults. I passed down a long and winding staircase, requesting him to be cautious as he followed. We came at length to the foot of the descent, and stood together upon the damp ground of the catacombs of the Montresors.

The gait of my friend was unsteady, and the bells upon his cap jingled as he strode.

"The pipe," he said.

"It is farther on," said I; "but observe the white web-work which gleams from these cavern walls."

He turned towards me, and looked into my eyes with two filmy orbs that distilled the rheum of intoxication.

30   "Nitre?" he asked at length.

"Nitre," I replied. "How long have you had that cough?"

"Ugh! ugh! ugh!—ugh! ugh! ugh!—ugh! ugh! ugh!—ugh! ugh! ugh!— ugh! ugh! ugh!"

My poor friend found it impossible to reply for many minutes.

"It is nothing," he said at last.

35   "Come," I said, with decision, "we will go back; your health is precious. You are rich, respected, admired, beloved; you are happy, as once I was. You are a man to be missed. For me it is no matter. We will go back; you will be ill, and I cannot be responsible. Besides, there is Luchresi—"

"Enough," he said; "the cough is a mere nothing; it will not kill me. I shall not die of a cough."

---

[4] Mineral deposits.
[5] A short cloak.

"True—true," I replied; "and, indeed, I had no intention of alarming you unnecessarily—but you should use all proper caution. A draught of this Médoc[6] will defend us from the damps."

Here I knocked off the neck of a bottle which I drew from a long row of its fellows that lay upon the mould.

"Drink," I said, presenting him the wine.

40 He raised it to his lips with a leer. He paused and nodded to me familiarly, while his bells jingled.

"I drink," he said, "to the buried that repose around us."

"And I to your long life."

He again took my arm, and we proceeded.

"These vaults," he said, "are extensive."

45 "The Montresors," I replied, "were a great and numerous family."

"I forget your arms."

"A huge human foot d'or, in a field azure; the foot crushes a serpent rampant whose fangs are imbedded in the heel."

"And the motto?"

"Nemo me impune lacessit."[7]

50 "Good!" he said.

The wine sparkled in his eyes and the bells jingled. My own fancy grew warm with the Médoc. We had passed through long walls of piled skeletons, with casks and puncheons[8] intermingling, into the inmost recesses of the catacombs. I paused again, and this time I made bold to seize Fortunato by an arm above the elbow.

"The nitre!" I said; "see, it increases. It hangs like moss upon the vaults. We are below the river's bed. The drops of moisture trickle among the bones. Come, we will go back ere it is too late. Your cough—"

"It is nothing," he said; "let us go on. But first, another draught of the Médoc."

I broke and reached him a flagon of De Grâve.[9] He emptied it at a breath. His eyes flashed with a fierce light. He laughed and threw the bottle upwards with a gesticulation I did not understand.

55 I looked at him in surprise. He repeated the movement—a grotesque one.

"You do not comprehend?" he said.

"Not I," I replied.

"Then you are not of the brotherhood."

"How?"

60 "You are not of the masons."[10]

"Yes, yes," I said; "yes, yes."

---

[6] A claret from the Médoc, near Bordeaux, France.

[7] "No one insults me with impunity"; this is the legend of the royal arms of Scotland.

[8] Barrel.

[9] Correctly, "Graves," a light wine from the Bordeaux area.

[10] Freemasons (members of a secret fraternity). The trowel is a symbol of their alleged origin as a guild of stonemasons.

"You? Impossible! A mason?"

"A mason," I replied.

"A sign," he said, "a sign."

65   "It is this," I answered, producing from beneath the folds of my *roque-laire* a trowel.

"You jest," he exclaimed, recoiling a few paces. "But let us proceed to the Amontillado."

"Be it so," I said, replacing the tool beneath the cloak and again offering him my arm. He leaned upon it heavily. We continued our route in search of the Amontillado. We passed through a range of low arches, descended, passed on, and descending again, arrived at a deep crypt, in which the foulness of the air caused our flambeaux rather to glow than flame.

At the most remote end of the crypt there appeared another less spacious. Its walls had been lined with human remains, piled to the vault overhead, in the fashion of the great catacombs of Paris. Three sides of this interior crypt were still ornamented in this manner. From the fourth side the bones had been thrown down, and lay promiscuously upon the earth, forming at one point a mound of some size. Within the wall thus exposed by the displacing of the bones, we perceived a still interior crypt or recess, in depth about four feet, in width three, in height six or seven. It seemed to have been constructed for no especial use within itself, but formed merely the interval between two of the colossal supports of the roof of the catacombs, and was backed by one of their circumscribing walls of solid granite.

It was in vain that Fortunato, uplifting his dull torch, endeavored to pry into the depth of the recess. Its termination the feeble light did not enable us to see.

70   "Proceed," I said; "herein is the Amontillado. As for Luchresi—"

"He is an ignoramus," interrupted my friend, as he stepped unsteadily forward, while I followed immediately at his heels. In an instant he had reached the extremity of the niche, and finding his progress arrested by the rock, stood stupidly bewildered. A moment more and I had fettered him to the granite. In its surface were two iron staples, distant from each other about two feet, horizontally. From one of these depended a short chain, from the other a padlock. Throwing the links about his waist, it was but the work of a few seconds to secure it. He was too much astounded to resist. Withdrawing the key I stepped back from the recess.

"Pass your hand," I said, "over the wall; you cannot help feeling the nitre. Indeed, it is *very* damp. Once more let me *implore* you to return. No? Then I must positively leave you. But I must first render you all the little attentions in my power."

"The Amontillado!" ejaculated my friend, not yet recovered from his astonishment.

"True," I replied; "the Amontillado."

75   As I said these words I busied myself among the pile of bones of which I have before spoken. Throwing them aside, I soon uncovered a quantity of building stone and mortar. With these materials and with the aid of my trowel, I began vigorously to wall up the entrance of the niche.

I had scarcely laid the first tier of the masonry when I discovered that the intoxication of Fortunato had in a great measure worn off. The earliest indication I had of this was a low moaning cry from the depth of the recess. It was *not* the cry of a drunken man. There was a long and obstinate silence. I laid the second tier, and the third, and the fourth; and then I heard the furious vibrations of the chain. The noise lasted for several minutes, during which, that I might hearken to it with the more satisfaction, I ceased my labors and sat down upon the bones. When at last the clanking subsided, I resumed the trowel, and finished without interruption the fifth, the sixth, and the seventh tier. The wall was now nearly upon a level with my breast. I again paused, and holding the flambeaux over the mason-work, threw a few feeble rays upon the figure within.

A succession of loud and shrill screams, bursting suddenly from the throat of the chained form, seemed to thrust me violently back. For a brief moment I hesitated, I trembled. Unsheathing my rapier, I began to grope with it about the recess; but the thought of an instant reassured me. I placed my hand upon the solid fabric of the catacombs, and felt satisfied. I reapproached the wall; I replied to the yells of him who clamoured. I re-echoed, I aided, I surpassed them in volume and in strength. I did this, and the clamourer grew still.

It was now midnight, and my task was drawing to a close. I had completed the eighth, the ninth and the tenth tier. I had finished a portion of the last and the eleventh; there remained but a single stone to be fitted and plastered in. I struggled with its weight; I placed it partially in its destined position. But now there came from out the niche a low laugh that erected the hairs upon my head. It was succeeded by a sad voice, which I had difficulty in recognizing as that of the noble Fortunato. The voice said—

"Ha! ha! ha!—he! he! he!—a very good joke, indeed—an excellent jest. We will have many a rich laugh about it at the palazzo—he! he! he!—over our wine—he! he! he!"

80   "The Amontillado!" I said.

"He! he! he!—he! he! he!—yes, the Amontillado. But is it not getting late? Will not they be awaiting us at the palazzo, the Lady Fortunato and the rest? Let us be gone."

"Yes," I said, "let us be gone."

"For the love of God, Montresor!"

"Yes," I said, "for the love of God."

85   But to these words I hearkened in vain for a reply. I grew impatient. I called aloud—

"Fortunato!"

No answer. I called again—

"Fortunato!"

No answer still. I thrust a torch through the remaining aperture and let it fall within. There came forth in return only a jingling of the bells. My heart grew sick; it was the dampness of the catacombs that made it so. I hastened to make an end of my labour. I forced the last stone into its position;

I plastered it up. Against the new masonry I re-erected the old rampart of bones. For the half of a century no mortal has disturbed them. *In pace requiescat!*[11]

READING AND REACTING

1. Montresor cites a "thousand injuries" and an "insult" as his motivation for murdering Fortunato. Given what you learn about the two men during the course of the story, what do you suppose the "injuries" and "insult" might be?
2. Do you find Montresor to be a reliable narrator? If not, what makes you distrust his version of events?
3. What is Montresor's concept of personal honour? Is it consistent or inconsistent with the values of contemporary society? How relevant are the story's ideas about revenge and guilt to present-day society? Explain.
4. Does Fortunato ever understand why Montresor hates him? What is Fortunato's attitude toward Montresor?
5. What is the significance of Montresor's family coat of arms and motto? What is the significance of Fortunato's costume?
6. In what ways does Montresor manipulate Fortunato? What weaknesses does Montresor exploit?
7. Why does Montresor wait fifty years to tell his story? How would the story be different if he had told it the next morning?
8. Why does Montresor wait for a reply before he puts the last stone in position? What do you think he wants Fortunato to say?
9. **JOURNAL ENTRY** Do you think the use of a first-person point of view makes you more sympathetic toward Montresor than you would be if his story were told by a third-person narrator? Why or why not?
10. **CRITICAL PERSPECTIVE** In his discussion of this story in *Edgar Allan Poe: A Study of the Short Fiction,* Charles E. May says, "We can legitimately hypothesize that the listener is a priest and that Montresor is an old man who is dying and making final confession. . . . "

    Do you agree or disagree with May's hypothesis? Do you think that Montresor has atoned for his sin? Who else could Montresor be talking to?

Related Works: "A Rose for Emily" (p. 90), "The Love Song of J. Alfred Prufrock" (p. 833), *Trifles* (p. 948)

---

[11] "May he rest in peace."

◆ **WILLIAM FAULKNER** (1897–1962) (biography on p. 89). "Barn Burning" (1939) marks the first appearance of the Snopes clan in Faulkner's fiction. These crafty and unappealing tenant farmers and traders run roughshod over the aristocratic families of Yoknapatawpha County in three Faulkner novels: *The Hamlet* (1940), *The Town* (1957), and *The Mansion* (1959). According to Ben Wasson in *Count No 'Count,* Faulkner once told a friend that "somebody said I was a genius writer. The only thing I'd claim genius for is thinking up that name *Snopes*." In Southern literary circles, at least, the name "Snopes" still serves as a shorthand term for the graceless and greedy (but frequently successful) opportunists of the "New South."

WILLIAM FAULKNER

Barn Burning
(1939)

The store in which the Justice of the Peace's court was sitting smelled of cheese. The boy, crouched on his nail keg at the back of the crowded room, knew he smelled cheese, and more: from where he sat he could see the ranked shelves close-packed with the solid, squat, dynamic shapes of tin cans whose labels his stomach read, not from the lettering which meant nothing to his mind but from the scarlet devils and the silver curve of fish— this, the cheese which he knew he smelled and the hermetic meat[1] which his intestines believed he smelled coming in intermittent gusts momentary and brief between the other constant one, the smell and sense just a little of fear because mostly of despair and grief, the old fierce pull of blood. He could not see the table where the Justice sat and before which his father and his father's enemy (*our enemy* he thought in that despair; *ourn! mine and hisn both! He's my father!*) stood, but he could hear them, the two of them that is, because his father had said no word yet:

"But what proof have you, Mr. Harris?"

"I told you. The hog got into my corn. I caught it up and sent it back to him. He had no fence that would hold it. I told him so, warned him. The next time I put the hog in my pen. When he came to get it I gave him enough wire to patch up his pen. The next time I put the hog up and kept it. I rode down to his house and saw the wire I gave him still rolled on to the spool in his yard. I told him he could have the hog when he paid me a dollar pound fee. That evening a nigger came with the dollar and got the hog. He was a strange nigger. He said, 'He say to tell you wood and hay kin burn.' I said, 'What?' 'That whut he say to tell you,' the nigger said. 'Wood and hay kin burn.' That night my barn burned. I got the stock out but I lost the barn."

"Where is the nigger? Have you got him?"

---

[1] Canned meat.

5   "He was a strange nigger, I tell you. I don't know what became of him."

"But that's not proof. Don't you see that's not proof?"

"Get that boy up here. He knows." For a moment the boy thought too that the man meant his older brother until Harris said, "Not him. The little one. The boy," and, crouching, small for his age, small and wiry like his father, in patched and faded jeans even too small for him, with straight, uncombed, brown hair and eyes gray and wild as storm scud, he saw the men between himself and the table part and become a lane of grim faces, at the end of which he saw the Justice, a shabby, collarless, graying man in spectacles, beckoning him. He felt no floor under his bare feet; he seemed to walk beneath the palpable weight of the grim turning faces. His father, stiff in his black Sunday coat donned not for the trial but for the moving, did not even look at him. *He aims for me to lie,* he thought, again with that frantic grief and despair. *And I will have to do hit.*

"What's your name, boy?" the Justice said.

"Colonel Sartoris Snopes," the boy whispered.

10   "Hey?" the Justice said. "Talk louder. Colonel Sartoris? I reckon anybody named for Colonel Sartoris in this country can't help but tell the truth, can they?" The boy said nothing. *Enemy! Enemy!* he thought; for a moment he could not even see, could not see that the Justice's face was kindly nor discern that his voice was troubled when he spoke to the man named Harris: "Do you want me to question this boy?" But he could hear, and during those subsequent long seconds while there was absolutely no sound in the crowded little room save that of quiet and intent breathing it was as if he had swung outward at the end of a grape vine, over a ravine, and at the top of the swing had been caught in a prolonged instant of mesmerized gravity, weightless in time.

"No!" Harris said violently, explosively. "Damnation! Send him out of here!" Now time, the fluid world, rushed beneath him again, the voices coming to him again through the smell of cheese and sealed meat, the fear and despair and the old grief of blood:

"This case is closed. I can't find against you, Snopes, but I can give you advice. Leave this country and don't come back to it."

His father spoke for the first time, his voice cold and harsh, level, without emphasis: "I aim to. I don't figure to stay in a country among people who . . ." he said something unprintable and vile, addressed to no one.

"That'll do," the Justice said. "Take your wagon and get out of this country before dark. Case dismissed."

15   His father turned, and he followed the stiff black coat, the wiry figure walking a little stiffly from where a Confederate provost's man's[2] musket ball had taken him in the heel on a stolen horse thirty years ago, followed the two backs now, since his older brother had appeared from somewhere in the crowd, no taller than the father but thicker, chewing tobacco steadily, between the two lines of grim-faced men and out of the store and across the

---

[2] Military policeman.

worn gallery and down the sagging steps and among the dogs and half-
grown boys in the mild May dust, where as he passed a voice hissed:

"Barn burner!"

Again he could not see, whirling; there was a face in a red haze, moon-
like, bigger than the full moon, the owner of it half again his size, he leaping
in the red haze toward the face, feeling no blow, feeling no shock when his
head struck the earth, scrabbling up and leaping again, feeling no blow this
time either and tasting no blood, scrabbling up to see the other boy in full
flight and himself already leaping into pursuit as his father's hand jerked
him back, the harsh, cold voice speaking above him: "Go get in the wagon."

It stood in a grove of locusts and mulberries across the road. His two
hulking sisters in their Sunday dresses and his mother and her sister in calico
and sunbonnets were already in it, sitting on and among the sorry residue
of the dozen and more movings which even the boy could remember—the
battered stove, the broken beds and chairs, the clock inlaid with mother-of-
pearl, which would not run, stopped at some fourteen minutes past two
o'clock of a dead and forgotten day and time, which had been his mother's
dowry. She was crying, though when she saw him she drew her sleeve across
her face and began to descend from the wagon. "Get back," the father said.

"He's hurt. I got to get some water and wash his . . ."

20   "Get back in the wagon," his father said. He got in too, over the tail-
gate. His father mounted to the seat where the older brother already sat and
struck the gaunt mules two savage blows with the peeled willow, but
without heat. It was not even sadistic; it was exactly that same quality which
in later years would cause his descendants to overrun the engine before putting a motor car into motion, striking and reining back in the same movement. The wagon went on, the store with its quiet crowd of grimly watching
men dropped behind; a curve in the road hid it. *Forever* he thought. *Maybe
he's done satisfied now, now that he has . . .* stopping himself, not to say it
aloud even to himself. His mother's hand touched his shoulder.

"Does hit hurt?" she said.

"Naw," he said. "Hit don't hurt. Lemme be."

"Can't you wipe some of the blood off before hit dries?"

"I'll wash to-night," he said. "Lemme be, I tell you."

25   The wagon went on. He did not know where they were going. None of
them ever did or ever asked, because it was always somewhere, always a
house of sorts waiting for them a day or two days or even three days away.
Likely his father had already arranged to make a crop on another farm before
he . . . Again he had to stop himself. He (the father) always did. There was
something about his wolf-like independence and even courage when the
advantage was at least neutral which impressed strangers, as if they got from
his latent ravening ferocity not so much a sense of dependability as a feeling
that his ferocious conviction in the rightness of his own actions would be of
advantage to all whose interest lay with his.

That night they camped, in a grove of oaks and beeches where a spring
ran. The nights were still cool and they had a fire against it, of a rail lifted
from a nearby fence and cut into lengths—a small fire, neat, niggard almost,

a shrewd fire; such fires were his father's habit and custom always, even in freezing weather. Older, the boy might have remarked this and wondered why not a big one; why should not a man who had not only seen the waste and extravagance of war, but who had in his blood an inherent voracious prodigality with material not his own, have burned everything in sight? Then he might have gone a step farther and thought that that was the reason: that niggard blaze was the living fruit of nights passed during those four years in the woods hiding from all men, blue or gray, with his strings of horses (captured horses, he called them). And older still, he might have divined the true reason: that the element of fire spoke to some deep main-spring of his father's being, as the element of steel or of powder spoke to other men, as the one weapon for the preservation of integrity, else breath were not worth the breathing, and hence to be regarded with respect and used with discretion.

But he did not think this now and he had seen those same niggard blazes all his life. He merely ate his supper beside it and was already half asleep over his iron plate when his father called him, and once more he followed the stiff back, the stiff and ruthless limp, up the slope and on to the starlit road where, turning, he could see his father against the stars but without face or depth—a shape black, flat, and bloodless as though cut from tin in the iron folds of the frockcoat which had not been made for him, the voice harsh like tin and without heat like tin:

"You were fixing to tell them. You would have told him." He didn't answer. His father struck him with the flat of his hand on the side of the head, hard but without heat, exactly as he had struck the two mules at the store, exactly as he would strike either of them with any stick in order to kill a horse fly, his voice still without fear or anger: "You're getting to be a man. You got to learn. You got to learn to stick to your own blood or you ain't going to have any blood to stick to you. Do you think either of them, any man there this morning, would? Don't you know all they wanted was a chance to get at me because they knew I had them beat? Eh?" Later, twenty years later, he was to tell himself, "If I had said they wanted only truth, justice, he would have hit me again." But now he said nothing. He was not crying. He just stood there. "Answer me," his father said.

"Yes," he whispered. His father turned.

30   "Get on to bed. We'll be there tomorrow."

Tomorrow they were there. In the early afternoon the wagon stopped before a paintless two-room house identical almost with the dozen others it had stopped before even in the boy's ten years, and again, as on the other dozen occasions, his mother and aunt got down and began to unload the wagon, although his two sisters and his father and brother had not moved.

"Likely hit ain't fitten for hawgs," one of the sisters said.

"Nevertheless, fit it will and you'll hog it and like it," his father said. "Get out of them chairs and help your Ma unload."

The two sisters got down, big, bovine, in a flutter of cheap ribbons; one of them drew from the jumbled wagon bed a battered lantern, the other a worn broom. His father handed the reins to the older son and began to climb stiffly over the wheel. "When they get unloaded, take the team to the barn and feed them." Then he said, and at first the boy thought he was still speaking to his brother: "Come with me."

35   "Me?" he said.

"Yes," his father said. "You."

"Abner," his mother said. His father paused and looked back—the harsh level stare beneath the shaggy, graying, irascible brows.

"I reckon I'll have a word with the man that aims to begin tomorrow owning me body and soul for the next eight months."

They went back up the road. A week ago—or before last night, that is—he would have asked where they were going, but not now. His father had struck him before last night but never before had he paused afterward to explain why; it was as if the blow and the following calm, outrageous voice still rang, repercussed, divulging nothing to him save the terrible handicap of being young, the light weight of his few years, just heavy enough to prevent his soaring free of the world as it seemed to be ordered but not heavy enough to keep him footed solid in it, to resist it and try to change the course of its events.

40   Presently he could see the grove of oaks and cedars and the other flowering trees and shrubs, where the house would be, though not the house yet. They walked beside a fence massed with honeysuckle and Cherokee roses and came to a gate swinging open between two brick pillars, and now, beyond a sweep of drive, he saw the house for the first time and at that instant he forgot his father and the terror and despair both, and even when he remembered his father again (who had not stopped) the terror and despair did not return. Because, for all the twelve movings, they had sojourned until now in a poor country, a land of small farms and fields and houses, and he had never seen a house like this before. *Hit's big as a courthouse* he thought quietly, with a surge of peace and joy whose reason he could not have thought into words, being too young for that: *They are safe from him. People whose lives are a part of this peace and dignity are beyond his touch, he no more to them than a buzzing wasp: capable of stinging for a little moment but that's all; the spell of this peace and dignity rendering even the barns and stable and cribs which belong to it impervious to the puny flames he might contrive* . . . this, the peace and joy, ebbing for an instant as he looked again at the stiff black back, the stiff and implacable limp of the figure which was not dwarfed by the house, for the reason that it had never looked big anywhere and which now, against the serene columned backdrop, had more than ever that impervious quality of something cut ruthlessly from tin, depthless, as though, sidewise to the sun, it would cast no shadow. Watching him, the boy remarked the absolutely undeviating course which his father held and saw the stiff foot come squarely down in a pile of fresh droppings where a horse had stood in the drive and which his father could have avoided by a simple change of stride. But it ebbed only for a moment, though he could not have thought this into words either, walking on in the spell of the house, which he could even want but without envy, without sorrow, certainly never with that ravening and jealous rage which unknown

to him walked in the ironlike black coat before him: *Maybe he will feel it too. Maybe it will even change him now from what maybe he couldn't help but be.*

They crossed the portico. Now he could hear his father's stiff foot as it came down on the boards with clocklike finality, a sound out of all proportion to the displacement of the body it bore and which was not dwarfed either by the white door before it, as though it had attained to a sort of vicious and ravening minimum not to be dwarfed by anything—the flat, wide, black hat, the formal coat of broadcloth which had once been black but which had now that friction-glazed greenish cast of the bodies of old house flies, the lifted sleeve which was too large, the lifted hand like a curled claw. The door opened so promptly that the boy knew the Negro must have been watching them all the time, an old man with neat grizzled hair, in a linen jacket, who stood barring the door with his body, saying, "Wipe yo foots, white man, fo you come in here. Major ain't home nohow."

"Get out of my way, nigger," his father said, without heat too, flinging the door back and the Negro also and entering, his hat still on his head. And now the boy saw the prints of the stiff foot on the doorjamb and saw them appear on the pale rug behind the machinelike deliberation of the foot which seemed to bear (or transmit) twice the weight which the body compassed. The Negro was shouting "Miss Lula! Miss Lula!" somewhere behind them, then the boy, deluged as though by a warm wave by a suave turn of carpeted stair and a pendant glitter of chandeliers and a mute gleam of gold frames, heard the swift feet and saw her too, a lady—perhaps he had never seen her like before either—in a gray, smooth gown with lace at the throat and an apron tied at the waist and the sleeves turned back, wiping cake or biscuit dough from her hands with a towel as she came up the hall, looking not at his father at all but at the tracks on the blond rug with an expression of incredulous amazement.

"I tried," the Negro cried, "I tole him to . . ."

"Will you please go away?" she said in a shaking voice. "Major de Spain is not at home. Will you please go away?"

45   His father had not spoken again. He did not speak again. He did not even look at her. He just stood stiff in the center of the rug, in his hat, the shaggy iron-gray brows twitching slightly above the pebble-colored eyes as he appeared to examine the house with brief deliberation. Then with the same deliberation he turned; the boy watched him pivot on the good leg and saw the stiff foot drag round the arc of the turning, leaving a final long and fading smear. His father never looked at it, he never once looked down at the rug. The Negro held the door. It closed behind them, upon the hysteric and indistinguishable woman-wail. His father stopped at the top of the steps and scraped his boot clean on the edge of it. At the gate he stopped again. He stood for a moment, planted stiffly on the stiff foot, looking back at the house. "Pretty and white, ain't it?" he said. "That's sweat. Nigger sweat. Maybe it ain't white enough yet to suit him. Maybe he wants to mix some white sweat with it."

Two hours later the boy was chopping wood behind the house within which his mother and aunt and the two sisters (the mother and aunt, not the two girls, he knew that; even at this distance and muffled by walls the flat loud voices of the two girls emanated an incorrigible idle inertia) were setting up the stove to prepare a meal, when he heard the hooves and saw the linen-clad man on a fine sorrel mare, whom he recognized even before he saw the rolled rug in front of the Negro youth following on a fat bay carriage horse—a suffused, angry face vanishing, still at full gallop, beyond the corner of the house where his father and brother were sitting in the two tilted chairs; and a moment later, almost before he could have put the axe down, he heard the hooves again and watched the sorrel mare go back out of the yard, already galloping again. Then his father began to shout one of the sisters' names, who presently emerged backward from the kitchen door dragging the rolled rug along the ground by one end while the other sister walked behind it.

"If you ain't going to tote, go on and set up the wash pot," the first said.

"You, Sarty!" the second shouted. "Set up the wash pot!" His father appeared at the door, framed against that shabbiness, as he had been against that other bland perfection, impervious to either, the mother's anxious face at his shoulder.

"Go on," the father said. "Pick it up." The two sisters stooped, broad, lethargic; stooping, they presented an incredible expanse of pale cloth and a flutter of tawdry ribbons.

50 "If I thought enough of a rug to have to git hit all the way from France I wouldn't keep hit where folks coming in would have to tromp on hit," the first said. They raised the rug.

"Abner," the mother said. "Let me do it."

"You go back and git dinner," his father said. "I'll tend to this."

From the woodpile through the rest of the afternoon the boy watched them, the rug spread flat in the dust beside the bubbling wash-pot, the two sisters stooping over it with that profound and lethargic reluctance, while the father stood over them in turn, implacable and grim, driving them though never raising his voice again. He could smell the harsh homemade lye[3] they were using; he saw his mother come to the door once and look toward them with an expression not anxious now but very like despair; he saw his father turn, and he fell to with the axe and saw from the corner of his eye his father raise from the ground a flattish fragment of field stone and examine it and return to the pot, and this time his mother actually spoke: "Abner. Abner. Please don't. Please, Abner."

Then he was done too. It was dusk; the whippoorwills had already begun. He could smell coffee from the room where they would presently eat the cold food remaining from the mid-afternoon meal, though when he entered the house he realized they were having coffee again probably because there was a fire on the hearth, before which the rug now lay spread over the backs of the two chairs. The tracks of his father's foot were gone.

---

[3] A soap made from wood ashes and water, unsuitable for washing fine fabrics.

Where they had been were now long, water-cloudy scoriations resembling the sporadic course of a Lilliputian mowing machine.

55   It still hung there while they ate the cold food and then went to bed, scattered without order or claim up and down the two rooms, his mother in one bed, where his father would later lie, the older brother in the other, himself, the aunt, and the two sisters on pallets on the floor. But his father was not in bed yet. The last thing the boy remembered was the depthless, harsh silhouette of the hat and coat bending over the rug and it seemed to him that he had not even closed his eyes when the silhouette was standing over him, the fire almost dead behind it, the stiff foot prodding him awake. "Catch up the mule," his father said.

When he returned with the mule his father was standing in the black door, the rolled rug over his shoulder. "Ain't you going to ride?" he said.

"No. Give me your foot."

He bent his knee into his father's hand, the wiry, surprising power flowed smoothly, rising, he rising with it, on to the mule's bare back (they had owned a saddle once; the boy could remember it though not when or where) and with the same effortlessness his father swung the rug up in front of him. Now in the starlight they retraced the afternoon's path, up the dusty road rife with honeysuckle, through the gate and up the black tunnel to the drive to the lightless house, where he sat on the mule and felt the rough warp of the rug drag across his thighs and vanish.

"Don't you want me to help?" he whispered. His father did not answer and now he heard again that stiff foot striking the hollow portico with that wooden and clocklike deliberation, that outrageous overstatement of the weight it carried. The rug, hunched, not flung (the boy could tell that even in the darkness) from his father's shoulder struck the angle of wall and floor with a sound unbelievably loud, thunderous, then the foot again, unhurried and enormous; a light came on in the house and the boy sat, tense, breathing steadily and quietly and just a little fast, though the foot itself did not increase its beat at all, descending the steps now; now the boy could see him.

60   "Don't you want to ride now?" he whispered. "We kin both ride now," the light within the house altering now, flaring up and sinking. *He's coming down the stairs now*, he thought. He had already ridden the mule up beside the horse block; presently his father was up behind him and he doubled the reins over and slashed the mule across the neck, but before the animal could begin to trot the hard, thin arm came round him, the hard, knotted hand jerking the mule back to a walk.

In the first red rays of the sun they were in the lot, putting plow gear on the mules. This time the sorrel mare was in the lot before he heard it at all, the rider collarless and even bareheaded, trembling, speaking in a shaking voice as the woman in the house had done, his father merely looking up once before stooping again to the hame[4] he was buckling, so that the man on the mare spoke to his stooping back:

---

[4] Harness.

"You must realize you have ruined that rug. Wasn't there anybody here, any of your women . . ." he ceased, shaking, the boy watching him, the older brother leaning now in the stable door, chewing, blinking slowly and steadily at nothing apparently. "It cost a hundred dollars. But you never had a hundred dollars. You never will. So I'm going to charge you twenty bushels of corn against your crop. I'll add it in your contract and when you come to the commissary you can sign it. That won't keep Mrs. de Spain quiet but maybe it will teach you to wipe your feet off before you enter her house again."

Then he was gone. The boy looked at his father, who still had not spoken or even looked up again, who was now adjusting the loggerhead in the hame.

"Pap," he said. His father looked at him—the inscrutable face, the shaggy brows beneath which the gray eyes glinted coldly. Suddenly the boy went toward him, fast, stopping as suddenly. "You done the best you could!" he cried. "If he wanted hit done different why didn't he wait and tell you how? He won't git no twenty bushels! He won't git none! We'll gether hit and hide hit! I kin watch . . ."

65   "Did you put the cutter back in that straight stock like I told you?"

"No, sir," he said.

"Then go do it."

That was Wednesday. During the rest of that week he worked steadily, at what was within his scope and some which was beyond it, with an industry that did not need to be driven nor even commanded twice; he had this from his mother, with the difference that some at least of what he did he liked to do, such as splitting wood with the half-size axe which his mother and aunt had earned, or saved money somehow, to present him with at Christmas. In company with the two older women (and on one afternoon, even one of the sisters), he built pens for the shoat and the cow which were a part of his father's contract with the landlord, and one afternoon, his father being absent, gone somewhere on one of the mules, he went to the field.

They were running a middle buster now, his brother holding the plow straight while he handled the reins, and walking beside the straining mule, the rich black soil shearing cool and damp against his bare ankles, he thought *Maybe this is the end of it. Maybe even that twenty bushels that seems hard to have to pay for just a rug will be a cheap price for him to stop forever and always from being what he used to be;* thinking, dreaming now, so that his brother had to speak sharply to him to mind the mule: *Maybe he even won't collect the twenty bushels. Maybe it will all add up and balance and vanish—corn, rug, fire; the terror and grief, the being pulled two ways like between two teams of horses—gone, done with for ever and ever.*

70   Then it was Saturday; he looked up from beneath the mule he was harnessing and saw his father in the black coat and hat. "Not that," his father said. "The wagon gear." And then, two hours later, sitting in the wagon bed behind his father and brother on the seat, the wagon accomplished a final

curve, and he saw the weathered paintless store with its tattered tobacco- and patent-medicine posters and the tethered wagons and saddle animals below the gallery. He mounted the gnawed steps behind his father and brother, and there again was the lane of quiet, watching faces for the three of them to walk through. He saw the man in spectacles sitting at the plank table and he did not need to be told this was a Justice of the Peace; he sent one glare of fierce, exultant, partisan defiance at the man in collar and cravat now, whom he had seen but twice before in his life, and that on a galloping horse, who now wore on his face an expression not of rage but of amazed unbelief which the boy could not have known was at the incred- ible circumstance of being sued by one of his own tenants, and came and stood against his father and cried at the Justice: "He ain't done it! He ain't burnt . . ."

"Go back to the wagon," his father said.

"Burnt?" the Justice said. "Do I understand this rug was burned too?"

"Does anybody here claim it was?" his father said. "Go back to the wagon." But he did not, he merely retreated to the rear of the room, crowded as that other had been, but not to sit down this time, instead, to stand pressing among the motionless bodies, listening to the voices:

"And you claim twenty bushels of corn is too high for the damage you did to the rug?"

75 "He brought the rug to me and said he wanted the tracks washed out of it. I washed the tracks out and took the rug back to him."

"But you didn't carry the rug back to him in the same condition it was in before you made the tracks on it."

His father did not answer, and now for perhaps half a minute there was no sound at all save that of breathing, the faint, steady suspiration of com- plete and intent listening.

"You decline to answer that, Mr. Snopes?" Again his father did not answer. "I'm going to find against you, Mr. Snopes. I'm going to find that you were responsible for the injury to Major de Spain's rug and hold you liable for it. But twenty bushels of corn seems a little high for a man in your circumstances to have to pay. Major de Spain claims it cost a hundred dol- lars. October corn will be worth about fifty cents. I figure that if Major de Spain can stand a ninety-five dollar loss on something he paid cash for, you can stand a five-dollar loss you haven't earned yet. I hold you in damages to Major de Spain to the amount of ten bushels of corn over and above your contract with him, to be paid to him out of your crop at gathering time. Court adjourned."

It had taken no time hardly, the morning was but half begun. He thought they would return home and perhaps back to the field, since they were late, far behind all other farmers. But instead his father passed on behind the wagon, merely indicating with his hand for the older brother to follow with it, and crossed the road toward the blacksmith shop opposite, pressing on after his father, overtaking him, speaking, whispering up at the harsh, calm face beneath the weathered hat: "He won't git no ten bushels neither. He won't git one. We'll . . ." until his father glanced for an instant down at him, the face absolutely calm, the grizzled eyebrows tangled above the cold eyes, the voice almost pleasant, almost gentle:

80   "You think so? Well, we'll wait till October anyway."

The matter of the wagon—the setting of a spoke or two and the tightening of the tires—did not take long either, the business of the tires accomplished by driving the wagon into the spring branch behind the shop and letting it stand there, the mules nuzzling into the water from time to time, and the boy on the seat with the idle reins, looking up the slope and through the sooty tunnel of the shed where the slow hammer rang and where his father sat on an upended cypress bolt, easily, either talking or listening, still sitting there when the boy brought the dripping wagon up out of the branch and halted it before the door.

"Take them on to the shade and hitch," his father said. He did so and returned. His father and the smith and a third man squatting on his heels inside the door were talking, about crops and animals; the boy, squatting too in the ammoniac dust and hoof-parings and scales of rust, heard his father tell a long and unhurried story out of the time before the birth of the older brother even when he had been a professional horsetrader. And then his father came up beside him where he stood before a tattered last year's circus poster on the other side of the store, gazing rapt and quiet at the scarlet horses, the incredible poisings and convolutions of tulle and tights and the painted leers of comedians, and said, "It's time to eat."

But not at home. Squatting beside his brother against the front wall, he watched his father emerge from the store and produce from a paper sack a segment of cheese and divide it carefully and deliberately into three with his pocket knife and produce crackers from the same sack. They all three squatted on the gallery and ate, slowly, without talking; then in the store again, they drank from a tin dipper tepid water smelling of the cedar bucket and of living beech trees. And still they did not go home. It was a horse lot this time, a tall rail fence upon and along which men stood and sat and out of which one by one horses were led, to be walked and trotted and then cantered back and forth along the road while the slow swapping and buying went on and the sun began to slant westward, they—the three of them—watching and listening, the older brother with his muddy eyes and his steady, inevitable tobacco, the father commenting now and then on certain of the animals, to no one in particular.

It was after sundown when they reached home. They ate supper by lamplight, then, sitting on the doorstep, the boy watched the night fully accomplish, listening to the whippoorwills and the frogs, when he heard his mother's voice: "Abner! No! No! Oh, God. Oh, God. Abner!" and he rose, whirled, and saw the altered light through the door where a candle stub now burned in a bottle neck on the table and his father, still in the hat and coat, at once formal and burlesque as though dressed carefully for some shabby and ceremonial violence, emptying the reservoir of the lamp back into the five-gallon kerosene can from which it had been filled, while the mother tugged at his arm until he shifted the lamp to the other hand and flung her back, not savagely or viciously, just hard, into the wall, her hands flung out against the wall for balance, her mouth open and in her face the same quality of hopeless despair as had been in her voice. Then his father saw him standing in the door.

85 "Go to the barn and get that can of oil we were oiling the wagon with," he said. The boy did not move. Then he could speak.

"What . . ." he cried. "What are you . . ."

"Go get that oil," his father said. "Go."

Then he was moving, running, outside the house, toward the stable: this the old habit, the old blood which he had not been permitted to choose for himself, which had been bequeathed him willy nilly and which had run for so long (and who knew where, battening on what of outrage and savagery and lust) before it came to him. *I could keep on,* he thought. *I could run on and on and never look back, never need to see his face again. Only I can't. I can't,* the rusted can in his hand now, the liquid sploshing in it as he ran back to the house and into it, into the sound of his mother's weeping in the next room, and handed the can to his father.

"Ain't you going to even send a nigger?" he cried. "At least you sent a nigger before!"

90 This time his father didn't strike him. The hand came even faster than the blow had, the same hand which had set the can on the table with almost excruciating care flashing from the can toward him too quick for him to follow it, gripping him by the back of his shirt and on to tiptoe before he had seen it quit the can, the face stooping at him in breathless and frozen ferocity, the cold, dead voice speaking over him to the older brother who leaned against the table, chewing with that steady, curious, sidewise motion of cows:

"Empty the can into the big one and go on. I'll catch up with you."

"Better tie him to the bedpost," the brother said.

"Do like I told you," the father said. Then the boy was moving, his bunched shirt and the hard, bony hand between his shoulderblades, his toes just touching the floor, across the room and into the other one, past the sisters sitting with spread heavy thighs in the two chairs over the cold hearth, and to where his mother and aunt sat side by side on the bed, the aunt's arms about his mother's shoulders.

"Hold him," the father said. The aunt made a startled movement. "Not you," the father said. "Lennie. Take hold of him. I want to see you do it." His mother took him by the wrist. "You'll hold him better than that. If he gets loose don't you know what he is going to do? He will go up yonder." He jerked his head toward the road. "Maybe I'd better tie him."

95 "I'll hold him," his mother whispered.

"See you do then." Then his father was gone, the stiff foot heavy and measured upon the boards, ceasing at last.

Then he began to struggle. His mother caught him in both arms, he jerking and wrenching at them. He would be stronger in the end, he knew

that. But he had no time to wait for it. "Lemme go!" he cried. "I don't want
to have to hit you!"

"Let him go!" the aunt said. "If he don't go, before God, I am going up
there myself!"

"Don't you see I can't?" his mother cried. "Sarty! Sarty! No! No! Help
me, Lizzie!"

100   Then he was free. His aunt grasped at him but it was too late. He
whirled, running, his mother stumbled forward on to her knees behind him,
crying to the nearest sister: "Catch him, Net! Catch him!" But that was too
late too, the sister (the sisters were twins, born at the same time, yet either
of them now gave the impression of being, encompassing as much living
meat and volume and weight as any other two of the family) not yet having
begun to rise from the chair, her head, face, alone merely turned, presenting
to him in the flying instant an astonishing expanse of young female features
untroubled by any surprise even, wearing only an expression of bovine
interest. Then he was out of the room, out of the house, in the mild dust of
the starlit road and the heavy rifeness of honeysuckle, the pale ribbon
unspooling with terrific slowness under his running feet, reaching the gate
at last and turning in, running, his heart and lungs drumming, on up the
drive toward the lighted house, the lighted door. He did not knock, he burst
in, sobbing for breath, incapable for the moment of speech; he saw the
astonished face of the Negro in the linen jacket without knowing when the
Negro had appeared.

"De Spain!" he cried, panted. "Where's . . ." then he saw the white man
too emerging from a white door down the hall. "Barn!" he cried. "Barn!"

"What?" the white man said. "Barn?"

"Yes!" the boy cried. "Barn!"

"Catch him!" the white man shouted.

105   But it was too late this time too. The Negro grasped his shirt, but the
entire sleeve, rotten with washing, carried away, and he was out that door
too and in the drive again, and had actually never ceased to run even while
he was screaming into the white man's face.

Behind him the white man was shouting, "My horse! Fetch my horse!"
and he thought for an instant of cutting across the park and climbing the
fence into the road, but he did not know the park nor how high the vine-
massed fence might be and he dared not risk it. So he ran on down the drive,
blood and breath roaring; presently he was in the road again though he
could not see it. He could not hear either: the galloping mare was almost
upon him before he heard her, and even then he held his course, as if the
very urgency of his wild grief and need must in a moment more find him
wings, waiting until the ultimate instant to hurl himself aside and into the
weed-choked roadside ditch as the horse thundered past and on, for an
instant in furious silhouette against the stars, the tranquil early summer
night sky which, even before the shape of the horse and rider vanished,
stained abruptly and violently upward: a long, swirling roar incredible and
soundless, blotting the stars, and he springing up and into the road again,

running again, knowing it was too late yet still running even after he heard the shot and, an instant later, two shots, pausing now without knowing he had ceased to run, crying "Pap! Pap!", running again before he knew he had begun to run, stumbling, tripping over something and scrabbling up again without ceasing to run, looking backward over his shoulder at the glare as he got up, running on among the invisible trees, panting, sobbing, "Father! Father!"

At midnight he was sitting on the crest of a hill. He did not know it was midnight and he did not know how far he had come. But there was no glare behind him now and he sat now, his back toward what he had called home for four days anyhow, his face toward the dark woods which he would enter when breath was strong again, small, shaking steadily in the chill darkness, hugging himself into the remainder of his thin, rotten shirt, the grief and despair now no longer terror and fear but just grief and despair. *Father. My father*, he thought. "He was brave!" he cried suddenly, aloud but not loud, no more than a whisper: "He was! He was in the war! He was in Colonel Sartoris' cav'ry!" not knowing that his father had gone to that war a private in the fine old European sense, wearing no uniform, admitting the authority of and giving fidelity to no man or army or flag, going to war as Malbrouck[5] himself did: for booty—it meant nothing and less than nothing to him if it were enemy booty or his own.

The slow constellations wheeled on. It would be dawn and then sunup after a while and he would be hungry. But that would be tomorrow and now he was only cold, and walking would cure that. His breathing was easier now and he decided to get up and go on, and then he found that he had been asleep because he knew it was almost dawn, the night almost over. He could tell that from the whippoorwills. They were everywhere now among the dark trees below him, constant and inflectioned and ceaseless, so that, as the instant for giving over to the day birds drew nearer and nearer, there was no interval at all between them. He got up. He was a little stiff, but walking would cure that too as it would the cold, and soon there would be the sun. He went on down the hill, toward the dark woods within which the liquid silver voices of the birds called unceasing—the rapid and urgent beating of the urgent and quiring heart of the late spring night. He did not look back.

READING AND REACTING

1. Is the third-person narrator of "Barn Burning" omniscient, or is his omniscience limited? Explain.
2. What is the point of view of the italicized passages? What do we learn from them? Do they create irony? How would the story have been different without these passages?

---

[5] A character in a popular eighteenth-century nursery rhyme about a famous warrior.

3. "Barn Burning" includes a great deal of dialogue. How would you characterize the level of diction of this dialogue? What information about various characters does it provide?

4. What conflicts are presented in "Barn Burning"? Which, if any, are resolved in the story? Are the conflicts avoidable? Explain.

5. Why does Abner Snopes burn barns? Do you think his actions are justified? Explain your reasoning.

6. What role does the American Civil War play in "Barn Burning"? What does Abner Snopes's behaviour during the war tell readers about his character?

7. In Books 1 and 2 of Samuel in the Old Testament, Abner was a relative of King Saul and commander in chief of his armies. Abner supported King Saul against David and was killed as a result of his own jealousy and rage. What, if any, significance is there in the fact that Faulkner names Ab Snopes, loyal to no man, fighter "for booty, and father of the Snopes clan," after this mighty biblical leader?

8. Why does Sarty Snopes insist that his father was brave? How does your knowledge of events unknown to the boy affect your reactions to this statement?

9. **JOURNAL ENTRY** How would the story be different if it were told from Ab's point of view? From Sarty's? From the point of view of Ab's wife? From the point of view of a member of a community in which the Snopeses have lived?

10. **CRITICAL PERSPECTIVE** Critic Edmond L. Volpe argues in his article "'Barn Burning': A Definition of Evil" that "Barn Burning" is not really about the class conflict between the sharecropping Snopeses and landowners like the de Spains:

> The story is centered upon Sarty's emotional dilemma. His conflict would not have been altered in any way if the person whose barn Ab burns had been a simple poor farmer, rather than an aristocratic plantation owner. . . . Sarty's struggle is against the repressive and divisive force his father represents. The boy's anxiety is created by his awakening sense of his own individuality. Torn between strong emotional attachment to the parent and his growing need to assert his own identity, Sarty's crisis is psychological and his battle is being waged far below the level of his intellectual and moral awareness.

Do you believe "Barn Burning" is, as Volpe suggests, essentially a coming-of-age story, or do you believe it is a story of class conflict?

Related Works: "A&P" (p. 122), "Stones" (p. 135), "Araby" (p. 267), "A Worn Path" (p. 397)

◆ **MARGARET LAURENCE** (1926–1987), born in the small prairie town of Neepawa, Manitoba, decided at a young age that she wanted to be a writer, and she contributed to school and college magazines to help her achieve this goal. Some of her earliest published works were based on her experiences living with her family in East and West Africa during the 1950s. After returning to Canada, she began working on a novel that would eventually be called *The Stone Angel* (1964), one of the most important novels in Canadian literary history. *The Stone Angel*, together with *A Jest of God* (1966), *The Fire-Dwellers* (1969), *A Bird in the House* (1970), and *The Diviners* (1974), is dominated by the fictional town of Manawaka, which is based on Neepawa—the town of her youth—but is also a combination of all small Canadian prairie towns. Humour and irony, as well as colourful everyday speech, exist in her work. Laurence often portrays people's hypocritical efforts to maintain their respectability. Her characters constantly test the stifling social norms that govern their lives.

MARGARET LAURENCE

The Loons
(1966)

Just below Manawaka, where the Wachakwa River ran brown and noisy over the pebbles, the scrub oak and grey-green willow and chokecherry bushes grew in a dense thicket. In a clearing at the centre of the thicket stood the Tonnerre family's shack. The basis of this dwelling was a small square cabin made of poplar poles and chinked with mud, which had been built by Jules Tonnerre some fifty years before, when he came back from Batoche[1] with a bullet in his thigh, the year that Riel was hung and the voices of the Metis entered their long silence.[2] Jules had only intended to stay the winter in the Wachakwa Valley, but the family was still there in the thirties, when I was a child. As the Tonnerres had increased, their settlement had been added to, until the clearing at the foot of the town hill was a chaos of lean-tos, wooden packing cases, warped lumber, discarded car tyres, ramshackle chicken coops, tangled strands of barbed wire and rusty tin cans.

The Tonnerres were French halfbreeds, and among themselves they spoke a *patois* that was neither Cree nor French. Their English was broken and full of obscenities. They did not belong among the Cree of the Galloping Mountain reservation, further north, and they did not belong among the Scots-Irish and Ukrainians of Manawaka, either. They were, as my Grandmother MacLeod would have put it, neither flesh, fowl, or good salt herring. When their men were not working at odd jobs or as section

---

[1] Near Prince Albert, Saskatchewan, in 1885, the site of a major battle in the Northwest Rebellion.

[2] Louis Riel was the leader of the Métis people, who were of mixed white and Native blood.

hands on the C.P.R., they lived on relief. In the summers, one of the Tonnerre youngsters, with a face that seemed totally unfamiliar with laughter, would knock at the doors of the town's brick houses and offer for sale a lard-pail full of bruised wild strawberries, and if he got as much as a quarter he would grab the coin and run before the customer had time to change her mind. Sometimes old Jules, or his son Lazarus, would get mixed up in a Saturday-night brawl, and would hit out at whoever was nearest, or howl drunkenly among the offended shoppers on Main Street, and then the Mountie would put them for the night in the barred cell underneath the Court House, and the next morning they would be quiet again.

Piquette Tonnerre, the daughter of Lazarus, was in my class at school. She was older than I, but she had failed several grades, perhaps because her attendance had always been sporadic and her interest in schoolwork negligible. Part of the reason she had missed a lot of school was that she had had tuberculosis of the bone, and had once spent many months in hospital. I knew this because my father was the doctor who had looked after her. Her sickness was almost the only thing I knew about her, however. Otherwise, she existed for me only as a vaguely embarrassing presence, with her hoarse voice and her clumsy limping walk and her grimy cotton dresses that were always miles too long. I was neither friendly nor unfriendly towards her. She dwelt and moved somewhere within my scope of vision, but I did not actually notice her very much until that peculiar summer when I was eleven.

"I don't know what to do about that kid," my father said at dinner one evening. "Piquette Tonnerre, I mean. The damn bone's flared up again. I've had her in hospital for quite a while now, and it's under control all right, but I hate like the dickens to send her home again."

5   "Couldn't you explain to her mother that she has to rest a lot?" my mother said.

"The mother's not there," my father replied. "She took off a few years back. Can't say I blame her. Piquette cooks for them, and she says Lazarus would never do anything for himself as long as she's there. Anyway, I don't think she'd take much care of herself, once she got back. She's only thirteen, after all. Beth, I was thinking—what about taking her up to Diamond Lake with us this summer? A couple of months rest would give that bone a much better chance."

My mother looked stunned.

"But Ewen—what about Roddie and Vanessa?"

"She's not contagious," my father said. "And it would be company for Vanessa."

10   "Oh dear," my mother said in distress, "I'll bet anything she has nits in her hair."

"For Pete's sake," my father said crossly, "do you think Matron would let her stay in the hospital for all this time like that? Don't be silly, Beth."

Grandmother MacLeod, her delicately featured face as rigid as a cameo, now brought her mauve-veined hands together as though she were about to begin a prayer.

"Ewen, if that half-breed youngster comes along to Diamond Lake, I'm not going," she announced. "I'll go to Morag's for the summer."

I had trouble in stifling my urge to laugh, for my mother brightened visibly and quickly tried to hide it. If it came to a choice between Grandmother MacLeod and Piquette, Piquette would win hands down, nits or not.

15   "It might be quite nice for you, at that," she mused. "You haven't seen Morag for over a year, and you might enjoy being in the city for a while. Well, Ewen dear, you do what you think best. If you think it would do Piquette some good, then we'll be glad to have her, as long as she behaves herself."

So it happened that several weeks later, when we all piled into my father's old Nash, surrounded by suitcases and boxes of provisions and toys for my ten-month-old brother, Piquette was with us and Grandmother MacLeod, miraculously, was not. My father would only be staying at the cottage for a couple of weeks, for he had to get back to his practice, but the rest of us would stay at Diamond Lake until the end of August.

Our cottage was not named, as many were, "Dew Drop Inn" or "Bide-a-Wee," or "Bonnie Doon." The sign on the roadway bore in austere letters only our name, MacLeod. It was not a large cottage, but it was on the lakefront. You could look out the windows and see, through the filigree of the spruce trees, the water glistening greenly as the sun caught it. All around the cottage were ferns, and sharp-branched raspberry bushes, and moss that had grown over fallen tree trunks. If you looked carefully among the weeds and grass, you could find wild strawberry plants which were in white flower now and in another month would bear fruit, the fragrant globes hanging like miniature scarlet lanterns on the thin hairy stems. The two grey squirrels were still there, gossiping at us from the tall spruce beside the cottage, and by the end of the summer they would again be tame enough to take pieces of crust from my hands. The broad moose antlers that hung above the back door were a little more bleached and fissured after the winter, but otherwise everything was the same. I raced joyfully around my kingdom, greeting all the places I had not seen for a year. My brother, Roderick, who had not been born when we were here last summer, sat on the car rug in the sunshine and examined a brown spruce cone, meticulously turning it round and round in his small and curious hands. My mother and father toted the luggage from car to cottage, exclaiming over how well the place had wintered, no broken windows, thank goodness, no apparent damage from storm-felled branches or snow.

Only after I had finished looking around did I notice Piquette. She was sitting on the swing, her lame leg held stiffly out, and her other foot scuffing the ground as she swung slowly back and forth. Her long hair hung black and straight around her shoulders, and her broad coarse-featured face bore no expression—it was blank, as though she no longer dwelt within her own skull, as though she had gone elsewhere. I approached her very hesitantly.

"Want to come and play?"

20   Piquette looked at me with a sudden flash of scorn.

"I ain't a kid," she said.

Wounded, I stamped angrily away, swearing I would not speak to her for the rest of the summer. In the days that followed, however, Piquette began to interest me, and I began to want to interest her. My reasons did not appear bizarre to me. Unlikely as it may seem, I had only just realised that the Tonnerre family, whom I had always heard called half-breeds, were actually Indians, or as near as made no difference. My acquaintance with Indians was not extensive. I did not remember ever having seen a real Indian, and my new awareness that Piquette sprang from the people of Big Bear and Poundmaker,[3] of Tecumseh,[4] of the Iroquois who had eaten Father Brebeuf's heart[5]—all this gave her an instant attraction in my eyes. I was a devoted reader of Pauline Johnson[6] at this age, and sometimes would orate aloud and in an exalted voice, *West Wind, blow from your prairie nest; Blow from the mountains, blow from the west*—and so on. It seemed to me that Piquette must be in some way a daughter of the forest, a kind of junior prophetess of the wilds, who might impart to me, if I took the right approach, some of the secrets which she undoubtedly knew—where the whippoorwill made her nest, how the coyote reared her young, or whatever it was that it said in Hiawatha.

I set about gaining Piquette's trust. She was not allowed to go swimming, with her bad leg, but I managed to lure her down to the beach—or rather, she came because there was nothing else to do. The water was always icy, for the lake was fed by springs, but I swam like a dog, thrashing my arms and legs around at such speed and with such an output of energy that I never grew cold. Finally, when I had had enough, I came out and sat beside Piquette on the sand. When she saw me approaching, her hand squashed flat the sand castle she had been building, and she looked at me sullenly, without speaking.

"Do you like this place?" I asked, after a while, intending to lead on from there into the question of forest lore.

Piquette shrugged. "It's okay. Good as anywhere."

"I love it," I said. "We come here every summer."

"So what?" Her voice was distant, and I glanced at her uncertainly, wondering what I could have said wrong.

"Do you want to come for a walk?" I asked her. "We wouldn't need to go far. If you walk just around the point there, you come to a bay where great big reeds grow in the water, and all kinds of fish hang around there. Want to? Come on."

She shook her head.

"Your dad said I ain't supposed to do no more walking than I got to."

I tried another line.

---

[3] Nineteenth-century Cree chiefs who supported Louis Riel.
[4] Shawnee chief, allied with the British in the War of 1812.
[5] Jesuit missionary killed by Iroquois in 1649.
[6] Early-twentieth-century Mohawk writer.

"I bet you know a lot about the woods and all that, eh?" I began respect-fully.

Piquette looked at me from her large dark unsmiling eyes.

"I don't know what in hell you're talkin' about," she replied. "You nuts or somethin'? If you mean where my old man, and me, and all them live, you better shut up, by Jesus, you hear?"

35 I was startled and my feelings were hurt, but I had a kind of dogged per-severance. I ignored her rebuff.

"You know something, Piquette? There's loons here, on this lake. You can see their nests just up the shore there, behind those logs. At night, you can hear them even from the cottage, but it's better to listen from the beach. My dad says we should listen and try to remember how they sound, because in a few years when more cottages are built at Diamond Lake and more people come in, the loons will go away."

Piquette was picking up stones and snail shells and then dropping them again.

"Who gives a good goddamn?" she said.

It became increasingly obvious that, as an Indian, Piquette was a dead loss. That evening I went out by myself, scrambling through the bushes that overhung the steep path, my feet slipping on the fallen spruce needles that covered the ground. When I reached the shore, I walked along the firm damp sand to the small pier that my father had built, and sat down there. I heard someone else crashing through the undergrowth and the bracken, and for a moment I thought Piquette had changed her mind, but it turned out to be my father. He sat beside me on the pier and we waited, without speaking.

40 At night the lake was like black glass with a streak of amber which was the path of the moon. All around, the spruce trees grew tall and close-set, branches blackly sharp against the sky, which was lightened by a cold flick-ering of stars. Then the loons began their calling. They rose like phantom birds from the nests on the shore, and flew out onto the dark still surface of the water.

No one can ever describe that ululating sound, the crying of the loons, and no one who has heard it can ever forget it. Plaintive, and yet with a quality of chilling mockery, those voices belonged to a world separated by aeons from our neat world of summer cottages and the lighted lamps of home.

"They must have sounded just like that," my father remarked, "before any person ever set foot here."

Then he laughed. "You could say the same, of course, about sparrows, or chipmunks, but somehow it only strikes you that way with the loons."

"I know," I said.

45 Neither of us suspected that this would be the last time we would ever sit here together on the shore, listening. We stayed for perhaps half an hour, and then we went back to the cottage. My mother was reading beside the fireplace. Piquette was looking at the burning birch log, and not doing any-thing.

"You should have come along," I said, although in fact I was glad she had not.

"Not me," Piquette said. "You wouldn' catch me walkin' way down there jus' for a bunch of squawkin' birds."

Piquette and I remained ill at ease with one another. I felt I had somehow failed my father, but I did not know what was the matter, nor why she would not or could not respond when I suggested exploring the woods or playing house. I thought it was probably her slow and difficult walking that held her back. She stayed most of the time in the cottage with my mother, helping her with the dishes or with Roddie, but hardly ever talking. Then the Duncans arrived at their cottage, and I spent my days with Mavis, who was my best friend. I could not reach Piquette at all, and I soon lost interest in trying. But all that summer she remained as both a reproach and a mystery to me.

That winter my father died of pneumonia, after less than a week's illness. For some time I saw nothing around me, being completely immersed in my own pain and my mother's. When I looked outward once more, I scarcely noticed that Piquette Tonnerre was no longer at school. I do not remember seeing her at all until four years later, one Saturday night when Mavis and I were having Cokes in the Regal Café. The jukebox was booming like tuneful thunder, and beside it, leaning lightly on its chrome and its rainbow glass, was a girl.

50   Piquette must have been seventeen then, although she looked about twenty. I stared at her, astounded that anyone could have changed so much. Her face, so stolid and expressionless before, was animated now with a gaiety that was almost violent. She laughed and talked very loudly with the boys around her. Her lipstick was bright carmine, and her hair was cut short and frizzily permed. She had not been pretty as a child, and she was not pretty now, for her features were still heavy and blunt. But her dark and slightly slanted eyes were beautiful, and her skin-tight skirt and orange sweater displayed to enviable advantage a soft and slender body.

She saw me, and walked over. She teetered a little, but it was not due to her once-tubercular leg, for her limp was almost gone.

"Hi, Vanessa." Her voice still had the same hoarseness. "Long time no see, eh?"

"Hi," I said. "Where've you been keeping yourself, Piquette?"

"Oh, I been around," she said. "I been away almost two years now. Been all over the place—Winnipeg, Regina, Saskatoon. Jesus, what I could tell you! I come back this summer, but I ain't stayin'. You kids goin' to the dance?"

55   "No," I said abruptly, for this was a sore point with me. I was fifteen, and thought I was old enough to go to the Saturday-night dances at the Flamingo. My mother, however, thought otherwise.

"Y'oughta come," Piquette said. "I never miss one. It's just about the on'y thing in this jerkwater town that's any fun. Boy, you couldn' catch me stayin' here. I don' give a shit about this place. It stinks."

She sat down beside me, and I caught the harsh over-sweetness of her perfume.

"Listen, you wanna know something, Vanessa?" she confided, her voice only slightly blurred. "Your dad was the only person in Manawaka that ever done anything good to me."

I nodded speechlessly. I was certain she was speaking the truth. I knew a little more than I had that summer at Diamond Lake, but I could not reach her now any more than I had then. I was ashamed, ashamed of my own timidity, the frightened tendency to look the other way. Yet I felt no real warmth towards her—I only felt that I ought to, because of that distant summer and because my father had hoped she would be company for me, or perhaps that I would be for her, but it had not happened that way. At this moment, meeting her again, I had to admit that she repelled and embarrassed me, and I could not help despising the self-pity in her voice. I wished she would go away. I did not want to see her. I did not know what to say to her. It seemed that we had nothing to say to one another.

60   "I'll tell you something else," Piquette went on. "All the old bitches an' biddies in this town will sure be surprised. I'm gettin' married this fall—my boyfriend, he's an English fella, works in the stockyards in the city there, a very tall guy, got blond wavy hair. Gee, is he ever handsome. Got this real classy name. Alvin Gerald Cummings—some handle, eh? They call him Al."

For the merest instant, then, I saw her. I really did see her, for the first and only time in all the years we had both lived in the same town. Her defiant face, momentarily, became unguarded and unmasked, and in her eyes there was a terrifying hope.

"Gee, Piquette —" I burst out awkwardly, "that's swell. That's really wonderful. Congratulations—good luck—I hope you'll be happy —"

As I mouthed the conventional phrases, I could only guess how great her need must have been, that she had been forced to seek the very things she so bitterly rejected.

When I was eighteen, I left Manawaka and went away to college. At the end of my first year, I came back home for the summer. I spent the first few days in talking non-stop with my mother, as we exchanged all the news that somehow had not found its way into letters—what had happened in my life and what had happened here in Manawaka while I was away. My mother searched her memory for events that concerned people I knew.

65   "Did I ever write you about Piquette Tonnerre, Vanessa?" she asked one morning.

"No, I don't think so," I replied. "Last I heard of her, she was going to marry some guy in the city. Is she still there?"

My mother looked perturbed, and it was a moment before she spoke, as though she did not know how to express what she had to tell and wished she did not need to try.

"She's dead," she said at last. Then, as I stared at her, "Oh, Vanessa, when it happened, I couldn't help thinking of her as she was that summer— so sullen and gauche and badly dressed. I couldn't help wondering if we could have done something more at that time—but what could we do? She used to be around in the cottage there with me all day, and honestly, it was all I could do to get a word out of her. She didn't even talk to your father very much, although I think she liked him, in her way."

"What happened?" I asked.

70   "Either her husband left her, or she left him," my mother said. "I don't know which. Anyway, she came back here with two youngsters, both only babies—they must have been born very close together. She kept house, I guess, for Lazarus and her brothers, down in the valley there, in the old Tonnerre place. I used to see her on the street sometimes, but she never spoke to me. She'd put on an awful lot of weight, and she looked a mess, to tell you the truth, a real slattern, dressed any old how. She was up in court a couple of times—drunk and disorderly, of course. One Saturday night last winter, during the coldest weather, Piquette was alone in the shack with the children. The Tonnerres made home brew all the time, so I've heard, and Lazarus said later she'd been drinking most of the day when he and the boys went out that evening. They had an old woodstove there—you know the kind, with exposed pipes. The shack caught fire. Piquette didn't get out, and neither did the children."

I did not say anything. As so often with Piquette, there did not seem to be anything to say. There was a kind of silence around the image in my mind of the fire and the snow, and I wished I could put from my memory the look that I had seen once in Piquette's eyes.

I went up to Diamond Lake for a few days that summer, with Mavis and her family. The MacLeod cottage had been sold after my father's death, and I did not even go to look at it, not wanting to witness my long-ago kingdom possessed now by strangers. But one evening I went down to the shore by myself.

The small pier which my father had built was gone, and in its place there was a large and solid pier built by the government, for Galloping Mountain was now a national park, and Diamond Lake had been re-named Lake Wapakata, for it was felt that an Indian name would have a greater appeal to tourists. The one store had become several dozen, and the settlement had all the attributes of a flourishing resort—hotels, a dance-hall, cafés with neon signs, the penetrating odours of potato chips and hot dogs.

I sat on the government pier and looked out across the water. At night the lake at least was the same as it had always been, darkly shining and bearing within its black glass the streak of amber that was the path of the moon. There was no wind that evening, and everything was quiet all around me. It seemed too quiet, and then I realized that the loons were no longer here. I listened for some time, to make sure, but never once did I hear that long-drawn call, half mocking and half plaintive, spearing through the stillness across the lake.

75   I did not know what had happened to the birds. Perhaps they had gone away to some far place of belonging. Perhaps they had been unable to find

such a place, and had simply died out, having ceased to care any longer whether they lived or not.

I remembered how Piquette had scorned to come along, when my father and I sat there and listened to the lake birds. It seemed to me now that in some unconscious and totally unrecognised way, Piquette might have been the only one, after all, who had heard the crying of the loons.

READING AND REACTING

1. What are the advantages of using a first-person narrator in this story? How might a third-person omniscient narrator change the story?
2. How does Laurence introduce other perspectives into the story? What do these different perspectives contribute to the narrative?
3. Why does the story cover so much time? Why are there gaps in the time-line?
4. Imagine that the story is told from a different first-person narrator. What would change if Piquette were the narrator instead of Vanessa?
5. What is the significance of the loons?
6. Why is Vanessa fascinated with Piquette?
7. What kind of man is Dr. MacLeod?
8. **JOURNAL ENTRY** What conclusions can be drawn about the influence of family on the values and opportunities for a young person?

Related Works: "Simple Recipes" (p. 45), "Borders" (p. 218), "Everyday Use" (p. 327)

◆ WRITING SUGGESTIONS: POINT OF VIEW

1. How would Poe's "The Cask of Amontillado" be different if it were told by a minor character who observed the events? Rewrite the story from this point of view—or tell the story that precedes the story, explaining the thousand injuries and the insult.
2. Assume that you are the mother in "Borders" and that you are keeping a journal of your travels. Write the journal entries for the time on the trip. Include your impressions of Mel and the border guards. Make sure you include your interpretation of the events—especially your son's reaction to the situation.
3. Both "The Cask of Amontillado" and "Barn Burning" deal with crimes that essentially go unpunished and with the emotions that accompany these crimes. In what sense does each story's use of point of view shape its treatment of the crime in question? For instance, how does point of view determine how much readers know about the motives for the crime, the crime's basic circumstances, and the extent to which the crime is justified?

4. Tell the story in "The Loons" from Piquette's point of view.
5. "Barn Burning" is, among other things, a story about a child's conflict with his parent's values. Write an essay in which you compare "Barn Burning" with another work that explores this theme—for example, "Digging" (p. 574) or *Hamlet* (p. 1093).

CHAPTER 8

Style, Tone, and Language

◊ ◊ ◊

A word is intrinsically powerful. If you believe in the power of words, you can bring about physical change in the universe. This is a notion of language that is ancient and it is valid to me. For example, the words of a charm or a spell are formulaic. They are meant to bring about physical change. The person who utters such a formula believes beyond any shadow of doubt that his utterance is going to have this or that actual effect. Because he believes in it and because words are what they are, it is true. It is true. . . . Every day we produce magical results with words.

N. SCOTT MOMADAY, *Ancestral Voices*

INTERVIEWER: You describe seemingly fantastic events in such minute detail that it gives them their own reality. Is this something you have picked up from journalism?

GARCÍA MÁRQUEZ: That's a journalistic trick which you can also apply to literature. For example, if you say that there are elephants flying in the sky, people are not going to believe you. But if you say that there are four hundred and twenty-five elephants in the sky, people will probably believe you. . . . I remember particularly the story about the character who is surrounded by yellow butterflies. . . . I discovered that if I didn't say the butterflies were yellow, people would not believe it. . . . The problem for every writer is credibility. Anybody can write anything so long as it's believed.

GABRIEL GARCÍA MÁRQUEZ, *Writers at Work,* 6th ed.

. . . Words, words, words . . . I can't leave them alone; I am obsessed. I move through the city watching for signs with letters missing ("Beef live with onions" advertises a cheap café near Granville and Broadway, "ELF SERVE" says a gas station out on Hastings) and I am always on the lookout for messages within words: can you see the harm in pharmacy, the dent in accident, the over in lover? In short, I play.

AUDREY THOMAS, "Basmati Rice," in *Canadian Literature*

◊ ◊ ◊

One of the qualities that gives a work of literature its individual personality is its **style,** the way in which a writer selects and arranges words to say what he or she wants to say. Style encompasses elements such as word choice; syntax; sentence length and structure; and the presence, frequency, and prominence of imagery and figures of speech. Closely related to style is **tone,** the attitude of the narrator or author of a work toward the subject matter, characters, or audience. Word choice and sentence structure help to create a work's tone, which may be intimate or distant, bitter or affectionate, straightforward or cautious, supportive or critical, respectful or condescending. (Tone may also be **ironic;** see Chapter 7, "Point of View," for a discussion of irony.)

Style offers almost limitless possibilities to a writer. Creative use of language (unusual word choice, word order, or sentence structure, for instance) can enrich a story and add to its overall effect. Sometimes style can help to create an atmosphere that enhances the setting or communicates the story's theme. In other cases, style can reveal a character's mental state. For instance, the precise details of John Updike's "A&P" (p. 122) show Sammy's intelligence and boredom: "She kept her eyes moving across the racks, and stopped, and turned so slow it made my stomach rub the inside of my apron, and buzzed to the other two, who kind of huddled against her for relief, and they all three of them went up the cat-and-dog-food-breakfast-cereal-macaroni-rice-raisins-seasonings-spreads-spaghetti-soft-drinks-crackers-and-cookies aisle." Sammy's description of the three girls and the food aisle shows his powers of observation and his inventiveness with language. The aisle is a blur of products, strung together, nothing outstanding. Finally, style can expand a story's possibilities through its very inventiveness. For example, James Joyce's innovative **stream-of-consciousness** style mimics thought, allowing ideas to run into one another as random associations are made, so that readers may follow and participate in the thought processes of the narrator. Here is a stream-of-consciousness passage from Joyce's experimental novel *Ulysses:*

> frseeeeeeeefronnnng train somewhere whistling the strength those engines have in them like big giants and the water rolling all over and out of them all sides like the end of Loves old sweet sonnnng the poor men that have to be out all the night from their wives and families in those roasting engines stifling it was today. . . .

The following passage from Dionne Brand's "Tamarindus Indica" (p. 383) illustrates the power of creative language to enrich a story:

> *Tamarindus indica.* He sat under this tree every day. A tree perhaps brought here from Africa in the seventeenth century. Probably brought here by his great-great-grandmother, as a seed in the pocket of her coarse dress. Probably held in her mouth as a comfort. Perhaps then geminating in her bowels. How the tree came to stand in his path he

really did not know. And if it had been his great-great-grandmother, she would have brought a silk cotton tree, its high wing-like buttresses webbing out in embraces. His great-great-grandmother, however, had not passed down into memory but he had heard that silk cotton blew all the way here from Africa and that is how he thought of any ancestry before Marie Ursule, who was his great-grandmother.

The language in this passage suggests the passage of time and the web of family—the tree has roots just as Samuel has roots extending back through his family tree. The disjointed prose with its fragments mirrors the disjointed family; Samuel sits under the tree trying to understand his place in the world. The repetition of "perhaps" and "probably" attests to the uncertain status of a man descended from people brought in slavery from Africa to the Americas.

Use of stylistic devices that place emphasis on the sounds and rhythm of words and sentences also enriches works of fiction. Consider the use of such techniques in the following sentence from James Joyce's "Araby" (p. 267):

> The light from the lamp opposite our door caught the white curve of her neck, lit up her hair that rested there and, falling, lit up the hand upon the railing.

Here the narrator is describing his first conversation with a girl who fascinates him, and the lush, lyrical, almost musical language reflects his enchantment. Note in particular the **alliteration** (<u>l</u>ight/<u>l</u>amp; <u>c</u>aught/<u>c</u>urve; <u>h</u>air/<u>h</u>and), the repetition (lit up/lit up), and the rhyme (lit up her *hair*/that rested *there*) and **near rhyme** (falling/railing); these poetic devices connect the words of the sentence into a smooth, rhythmic whole. Another example of this emphasis on sound may be found in the measured **parallelism** of this sentence from Nathaniel Hawthorne's "Young Goodman Brown" (p. 307):

> But, irreverently consorting with these grave, reputable, and pious people, these elders of the church, these chaste dames and dewy virgins, there were men of dissolute lives and women of spotted fame, wretches given over to all mean and filthy vice, and suspected even of horrid crimes.

Although many stylistic options are available to writers, style must be consistent with the writer's purpose and with the effect he or she hopes to create. Just as writers may experiment with point of view or manipulate events to create a complex plot, so they can adjust style to suit particular narrators, characters, settings, or themes. Two elements with which writers frequently experiment are *level of diction,* and *imagery* and *figurative language.*

LEVEL OF DICTION
◇ ◇ ◇

The level of diction—how formal or informal a story's language is—can suggest a good deal about those who use the language, thus providing insights into the story's theme.

FORMAL DICTION

Formal diction is characterized by elaborate, complex sentences; a learned vocabulary; and a serious, objective, detached tone. The speaker avoids contractions, shortened word forms (like *phone*), regional expressions, and slang, and he or she may use *one* or *we* in place of *I*. At its most extreme, formal language may be stiff and stilted, far removed from everyday speech.

Formal diction, whether used by a narrator or by a character, may indicate erudition, a high educational level, a superior social or professional position, or emotional detachment. When one character's language is significantly more formal than others', he or she may seem old-fashioned or stuffy; when language is inappropriately elevated or complex, it may reveal the character to be pompous or ridiculous; when a narrator's language is noticeably more formal than that of the characters, the narrator may seem superior or even condescending. Thus, level of diction reveals a good deal about characters and about the narrator's attitude toward them.

The following passage from "Young Goodman Brown" illustrates formal style:

> Another verse of the hymn arose, a slow and mournful strain, such as the pious love, but joined to words which expressed all that our nature can conceive of sin, and darkly hinted at far more. Unfathomable to mere mortals is the lore of fiends. Verse after verse was sung, and still the chorus of the desert swelled between, like the deepest tone of a mighty organ. And, with the final peal of that dreadful anthem, there came a sound, as if the roaring wind, the rushing streams, the howling beasts, and every other voice of the unconverted wilderness were mingling and according with the voice of guilty man, in homage to the prince of all. The four blazing pines threw up a loftier flame, and obscurely discovered shapes and visages of horror on the smoke-wreaths, above the impious assembly. At the same moment, the fire on the rock shot redly forth, and formed a glowing arch above its base, where now appeared a figure. With reverence be it spoken, the apparition bore no slight similitude, both in garb and manner, to some grave divine of the New England churches.

The complex and syntactically varied sentences, learned vocabulary ("unfathomable," "impious," "similitude"), and absence of colloquialisms suit Hawthorne's purpose well, re-creating the formal language of the earlier era in which the story is set. The third-person narrator is controlled and distant.

INFORMAL DICTION

Informal diction, consistent with everyday speech, is characterized by slang, contractions, colloquial expressions like *you know* and *I mean,* shortened word forms, incomplete sentences, and a casual, conversational tone. A first-person narrator may use informal style, or characters may speak informally; in either case, informal style tends to narrow the distance between readers and text.

Informal language can range from the straightforward contemporary style of Piquette's dialogue in "The Loons" ("Who gives a good goddamn?") to the regionalisms and dialect employed in Flannery O'Connor's "A Good Man Is Hard to Find" ("aloose"; "you all"; "britches"). In "The Loons" (p. 249), Piquette's self-consciously slangy, conversational style tells readers a good deal about her background and sense of self; in "A Good Man Is Hard to Find" (p. 280), the characters' speech patterns and diction reveal the region in which they live and their social class. In other stories, a character's use of obscenities may suggest his or her crudeness or adolescent bravado, and use of racial or ethnic slurs suggests that a character is insensitive and bigoted.

The following passage from John Updike's "A&P" illustrates informal style:

> She had sort of oaky hair that the sun and salt had bleached, done up in a bun that was unravelling, and a kind of prim face. Walking into the A&P with your straps down, I suppose it's the only kind of face you *can* have. She held her head so high her neck, coming out of those white shoulders, looked kind of stretched, but I didn't mind. The longer her neck was, the more of her there was.

In the preceding passage, the first-person narrator uses a conversational style, including colloquialisms ("sort of," "I suppose," "kind of"), contractions ("it's," "didn't"), and the imprecise, informal *you* ("Walking into the A&P with *your* straps down . . . "). The narrator uses neither elaborate sentences nor learned diction.

IMAGERY AND FIGURATIVE LANGUAGE
◊ ◊ ◊

IMAGERY

Imagery—words and phrases that describe what is seen, heard, smelled, tasted, or touched—can have a significant impact in a story. A pattern of repeated imagery can help to convey a particular impression about a character or situation, or a writer may use such a pattern to communicate or reinforce a story's theme. For example, the theme of newly discovered sexuality can be conveyed through repeated use of words and phrases suggesting blooming or ripening.

In Steven Heighton's "Flight Paths of the Emperor" (p. 354), the narrator's description of Nick's feelings about his wife uses rich visual imagery:

> On New Year's Eve they had made love with a tentative, awakening ardour, like shy lovers giving themselves for the first time; and feeling the generous warmth of her breasts and large body around him he had been sure he could never love another woman. But the next morning she was silent, sullen, their ecstatic communion a victim of poor sleep, anxious dreams or some abrupt recognition. Now that Dorothy was flagrantly well, the energy Sandra had conjured to support her seemed to vanish. The sheen passed from her eyes, the bloom from her cheeks. She moved heavily within her skin, her body had a sad, abandoned look, as if she herself had left and caught a flight to a far-off country. Again Nick felt a nagging urge to escape her, a desire for the youthful, conspicuous good looks that asked so little effort and promised eternal life. There were times Nick thought he knew the future, and times he thought he understood the past. He always turned out to be wrong. On the train to Ōsaka, faced with the prospect of an early return, resurrecting old grievances and finding them undecayed, he'd foreseen with absolute clarity the death of his marriage. On the flight home and on New Year's Eve— and even the night before at dinner, teamed with Sandra against a flagging stepmother—he'd been equally sure they would survive. How many times he had flown between the two extremes, a trapped commuter who never seemed to touch down. And he knew, if he knew anything at all, that he would never touch down.

By describing Nick's married state as that of a "trapped commuter," Heighton shows that Nick is constantly in flux—his feelings alternate between those of security and loss. The image of travel to depict the relationship is particularly relevant as Nick and Sandra leave Canada for Japan and then return.

FIGURATIVE LANGUAGE

Figures of speech—such as *similes, metaphors,* and *personification*—can enrich a story, subtly revealing information about characters and themes. (See Chapter 16 for more information about figures of speech.)

By using **metaphors** and **similes**—figures of speech that compare two dissimilar items—writers can indicate a particular attitude toward characters and events. Thus, Flannery O'Connor's many grotesque similes in "A Good Man Is Hard to Find" help to dehumanize her characters; the children's mother, for instance, has a face "as broad and innocent as a cabbage." In Tillie Olsen's "I Stand Here Ironing" (p. 181), an extended metaphor in which a mother compares her daughter to a dress waiting to be ironed expresses the mother's attitude toward her daughter, effectively suggesting to readers the daughter's vulnerability. Similes and metaphors are used freely in Jane Rule's "Inland Passage" (p. 150), from the title to the specific detail of the attraction Fidelity feels for Troy: "It was worse than coming down with a toothache, breaking out in boils, this stupid sweet desire which she simply had to hide from a woman getting better and better at reading her face unless she wanted to wreck the last hours of this lovely trip." The figures of speech capture the pleasure and pain of desire.

Personification—a figure of speech, closely related to metaphor, that endows inanimate objects or abstract ideas with life or with human characteristics—is used in "Araby," where houses, "conscious of decent lives within them, gazed at one another with brown imperturbable faces." This use of figurative language expands readers' vision of the story's setting and gives a dreamlike quality to the passage. (Other figures of speech, such as **hyperbole** and **understatement,** can also enrich works of fiction. See Chapter 16, "Figures of Speech," for further information.)

Allusions—references to familiar historical or literary personages or events—may also expand readers' understanding and appreciation of a work. An allusion widens a work's context by bringing it into the context of a related subject or idea. For instance, Wole Soyinka's frequent references to political figures and events in "Future Plans" (p. 803) enable readers who recognize the references to gain a deeper understanding of the speaker's position on various political and social issues. Literary and biblical allusions may be used in much the same way.

A FINAL NOTE

◊ ◊ ◊

In analyzing the use of language in a work of fiction, you may occasionally encounter obscure allusions, foreign words and phrases, unusual comparisons, and unfamiliar regional expressions—particularly in works treating cultures and historical periods other than your own. Frequently such language will be clarified by the context, or by explanatory notes in your text; when it is not, you should consult a dictionary, encyclopedia, or other reference work.

CHECKLIST: WRITING ABOUT STYLE, TONE, AND LANGUAGE

✓ Is the story's tone intimate? Distant? Ironic? How does the tone advance the writer's purpose?

✓ Does the writer make any unusual creative use of diction, word order, or sentence structure?

✓ Does the style emphasize the sound and rhythm of language? For example, does the writer use alliteration and assonance? Repetition and parallelism? What do such techniques add to the story?

✓ Is the level of diction generally formal, informal, or somewhere in between?

✓ Is there a difference between the style of the narrator and the style of the characters' speech? If so, what is the effect of this difference?

✓ Do any of the story's characters use regionalisms, colloquial language, or nonstandard speech? If so, what effect does this language have?

✓ What do different characters' levels of diction reveal about them?

✓ What kind of imagery predominates? Where, and why, is imagery used?

✓ Does the story develop a pattern of imagery? How does this pattern of imagery relate to the story's themes?

✓ Does the story use simile and metaphor? Personification? What is the effect of these figures of speech?

✓ Do figures of speech reinforce the story's themes? Reveal details about characters?

✓ Does the story make any historical, literary, or religious allusions? What do these allusions contribute to the story?

✓ What unfamiliar, obscure, or foreign words, phrases, or images are used in the story? What is the effect of these words or expressions?

◈ **JAMES JOYCE** (1884–1941) was born in Dublin but lived his entire adult life in self-imposed exile from his native Ireland. Though his parents sent him to schools that trained young men for the priesthood, Joyce saw himself as a religious and artistic rebel, and he fled to Paris soon after graduation in 1902. Recalled briefly to Dublin by his mother's fatal illness, Joyce returned to the Continent in 1904, taking with him an uneducated Irish country girl named Nora Barnacle, who became his wife in 1931. In dreary quarters in Trieste, Zurich, and Paris, Joyce struggled to support a growing family, sometimes teaching classes in Berlitz language schools.

Though Joyce never again lived in Ireland, he continued to write about Dublin. Publication of *Dubliners* (1914), a collection of short stories that included "Araby," was delayed for seven years because the Irish publisher feared libel suits from local citizens who were thinly disguised as characters in the stories. Joyce's autobiographical *Portrait of the Artist as a Young Man* (1916) tells of a young writer's rejection of family, church, and country. *Ulysses* (1922), the comic tale of eighteen hours in the life of a wandering Dublin advertising salesman, was banned when the U.S. Post Office brought charges of obscenity against the book, and it remained banned in the United States and England for more than a decade. In *Ulysses*, Joyce begins a revolutionary journey away from traditional techniques of plot and characterization to the interior monologues and stream-of-consciousness style that mark his last great novel, *Finnegans Wake* (1939).

JAMES JOYCE

Araby
(1914)

North Richmond Street, being blind,[1] was a quiet street except at the hour when the Christian Brothers' School set the boys free. An uninhabited house of two storeys stood at the blind end, detached from its neighbours in a square ground. The other houses of the street, conscious of decent lives within them, gazed at one another with brown imperturbable faces.

The former tenant of our house, a priest, had died in the back drawing-room. Air, musty from having been long enclosed, hung in all the rooms, and the waste room behind the kitchen was littered with old useless papers. Among these I found a few paper-covered books, the pages of which were curled and damp: *The Abbot,* by Walter Scott, *The Devout Communicant* and *The Memoirs of Vidocq.*[2] I liked the last best because its leaves were yellow. The wild garden behind the house contained a central apple-tree and a few straggling bushes under one of which I found the late tenant's rusty bicycle-pump. He had been a very charitable priest; in his will he had left all his money to institutions and the furniture of his house to his sister.

When the short days of winter came dusk fell before we had well eaten our dinners. When we met in the street the houses had grown sombre. The space of sky above us was the colour of ever-changing violet and towards it the lamps of the street lifted their feeble lanterns. The cold air stung us and we played till our bodies glowed. Our shouts echoed in the silent street. The career of our play brought us through the dark muddy lanes behind the houses where we ran the gauntlet of the rough tribes from the cottages, to the back doors of the dark dripping gardens where odours arose from the ashpits, to the dark odorous stables where a coachman smoothed and combed the horse or shook music from the buckled harness. When we returned to the street light from the kitchen windows had filled the areas. If my uncle was seen turning the corner we hid in the shadow until we had seen him safely housed. Or if Mangan's sister came out on the doorstep to call her brother in to his tea we watched her from our shadow peer up and down the street. We waited to see whether she would remain or go in and, if she remained, we left our shadow and walked up to Mangan's steps resignedly. She was waiting for us, her figure defined by the light from the half-opened door. Her brother always teased her before he obeyed and I

---

[1] A dead-end street.

[2] Sir Walter Scott (1771–1832)—an English Romantic novelist; *The Devout Communicant*—a variant title for *Pious Meditations,* written by an eighteenth-century English Franciscan friar, Pacifus Baker; *The Memoirs of Vidocq*—an autobiography of François-Jules Vidocq (1775–1857), a French soldier of fortune turned police agent.

stood by the railings looking at her. Her dress swung as she moved her body and the soft rope of her hair tossed from side to side.

Every morning I lay on the floor in the front parlour watching her door. The blind was pulled down to within an inch of the sash so that I could not be seen. When she came out on the doorstep my heart leaped. I ran to the hall, seized my books and followed her. I kept her brown figure always in my eye and, when we came near the point at which our ways diverged, I quickened my pace and passed her. This happened morning after morning. I had never spoken to her, except for a few casual words, and yet her name was like a summons to all my foolish blood.

5   Her image accompanied me even in places the most hostile to romance. On Saturday evenings when my aunt went marketing I had to go to carry some of the parcels. We walked through the flaring streets, jostled by drunken men and bargaining women, amid the curses of labourers, the shrill litanies of shop-boys who stood on guard by the barrels of pigs' cheeks, the nasal chanting of street-singers, who sang a *come-all-you* about O'Donovan Rossa,[3] or a ballad about the troubles in our native land. These noises converged in a single sensation of life for me: I imagined that I bore my chalice safely through a throng of foes. Her name sprang to my lips at moments in strange prayers and praises which I myself did not understand. My eyes were often full of tears (I could not tell why) and at times a flood from my heart seemed to pour itself out into my bosom. I thought little of the future. I did not know whether I would ever speak to her or not or, if I spoke to her, how I could tell her of my confused adoration. But my body was like a harp and her words and gestures were like fingers running upon the wires.

One evening I went into the back drawing-room in which the priest had died. It was a dark rainy evening and there was no sound in the house. Through one of the broken panes I heard the rain impinge upon the earth, the fine incessant needles of water playing in the sodden beds. Some distant lamp or lighted window gleamed below me. I was thankful that I could see so little. All my senses seemed to desire to veil themselves and, feeling that I was about to slip from them, I pressed the palms of my hands together until they trembled, murmuring: *"O love! O love!"* many times.

At last she spoke to me. When she addressed the first words to me I was so confused that I did not know what to answer. She asked me was I going to *Araby.* I forgot whether I answered yes or no. It would be a splendid bazaar, she said she would love to go.

"And why can't you?" I asked.

While she spoke she turned a silver bracelet round and round her wrist. She could not go, she said, because there would be a retreat that week in her convent.[4] Her brother and two other boys were fighting for their caps and I

---

[3] Any popular song beginning "Come all you gallant Irishmen . . ."; O'Donovan Rossa was an Irish nationalist who was banished in 1870 for advocating violent rebellion against the British.

[4] A week devoted to prayer and meditation in her convent school.

was alone at the railings. She held one of the spikes, bowing her head towards me. The light from the lamp opposite our door caught the white curve of her neck, lit up her hair that rested there and, falling, lit up the hand upon the railing. It fell over one side of her dress and caught the white border of a petticoat, just visible as she stood at ease.

10 "It's well for you," she said.

"If I go," I said, "I will bring you something."

What innumerable follies laid waste my waking and sleeping thoughts after that evening! I wished to annihilate the tedious intervening days. I chafed against the work of school. At night in my bedroom and by day in the classroom her image came between me and the page I strove to read. The syllables of the word *Araby* were called to me through the silence in which my soul luxuriated and cast an Eastern enchantment over me. I asked for leave to go to the bazaar on Saturday night. My aunt was surprised and hoped it was not some Freemason[5] affair. I answered few questions in class. I watched my master's face pass from amiability to sternness; he hoped I was not beginning to idle. I could not call my wandering thoughts together. I had hardly any patience with the serious work of life which, now that it stood between me and my desire, seemed to me child's play, ugly monotonous child's play.

On Saturday morning I reminded my uncle that I wished to go to the bazaar in the evening. He was fussing at the hallstand, looking for the hat-brush, and answered me curtly:

"Yes, boy, I know."

15 As he was in the hall I could not go into the front parlour and lie at the window. I left the house in bad humour and walked slowly towards the school. The air was pitilessly raw and already my heart misgave me.

When I came home to dinner my uncle had not yet been home. Still it was early. I sat staring at the clock for some time and, when its ticking began to irritate me, I left the room. I mounted the staircase and gained the upper part of the house. The high cold empty gloomy rooms liberated me and I went from room to room singing. From the front window I saw my companions playing below in the street. Their cries reached me weakened and indistinct and, leaning my forehead against the cool glass, I looked over at the dark house where she lived. I may have stood there for an hour, seeing nothing but the brown-clad figure cast by my imagination, touched discreetly by the lamplight at the curved neck, at the hand upon the railings and at the border below the dress.

When I came downstairs again I found Mrs. Mercer sitting at the fire. She was an old garrulous woman, a pawnbroker's widow, who collected used stamps for some pious purpose. I had to endure the gossip of the tea-table. The meal was prolonged beyond an hour and still my uncle did not come. Mrs. Mercer stood up to go: she was sorry she couldn't wait any longer, but

---

[5] At the time the story takes place, Catholics in Ireland thought the Masonic Order was a threat to the church.

it was after eight o'clock and she did not like to be out late, as the night air was bad for her. When she had gone I began to walk up and down the room, clenching my fists. My aunt said:

"I'm afraid you may put off your bazaar for this night of Our Lord."

At nine o'clock I heard my uncle's latchkey in the halldoor. I heard him talking to himself and heard the hallstand rocking when it had received the weight of his overcoat. I could interpret these signs. When he was midway through his dinner I asked him to give me the money to go to the bazaar. He had forgotten.

20   "The people are in bed and after their first sleep now," he said.

I did not smile. My aunt said to him energetically:

"Can't you give him the money and let him go? You've kept him late enough as it is."

My uncle said he was very sorry he had forgotten. He said he believed in the old saying: "All work and no play makes Jack a dull boy." He asked me where I was going and, when I had told him a second time he asked me did I know *The Arab's Farewell to his Steed*.[6] When I left the kitchen he was about to recite the opening lines of the piece to my aunt.

I held a florin tightly in my hand as I strode down Buckingham Street towards the station. The sight of the streets thronged with buyers and glaring with gas recalled to me the purpose of my journey. I took my seat in a third-class carriage of a deserted train. After an intolerable delay the train moved out of the station slowly. It crept onward among ruinous houses and over the twinkling river. At Westland Row Station a crowd of people pressed to the carriage doors; but the porters moved them back, saying that it was a special train for the bazaar. I remained alone in the bare carriage. In a few minutes the train drew up beside an improvised wooden platform. I passed out on to the road and saw by the lighted dial of a clock that it was ten minutes to ten. In front of me was a large building which displayed the magical name.

25   I could not find any sixpenny entrance and, fearing that the bazaar would be closed, I passed in quickly through a turnstile, handing a shilling to a weary-looking man. I found myself in a big hall girdled at half its height by a gallery. Nearly all the stalls were closed and the greater part of the hall was in darkness. I recognised a silence like that which pervades a church after a service. I walked into the centre of the bazaar timidly. A few people were gathered about the stalls which were still open. Before a curtain, over which the words *Café Chantant*[7] were written in coloured lamps, two men were counting money on a salver. I listened to the fall of the coins.

Remembering with difficulty why I had come I went over to one of the stalls and examined porcelain vases and flowered tea-sets. At the door of the stall a young lady was talking and laughing with two young gentlemen. I remarked their English accents and listened vaguely to their conversation.

---

[6] A sentimental poem by Caroline Norton (1808–1877) that tells the story of a nomad's heartbreak after selling his much-loved horse.

[7] A Paris café featuring musical entertainment.

"O, I never said such a thing!"

"O, but you did!"

"O, but I didn't!"

30   "Didn't she say that?"

"Yes. I heard her."

"O, there's a . . . fib!"

Observing me the young lady came over and asked me did I wish to buy anything. The tone of her voice was not encouraging; she seemed to have spoken to me out of a sense of duty. I looked humbly at the great jars that stood like eastern guards at either side of the dark entrance to the stall and murmured:

"No, thank you."

35   The young lady changed the position of one of the vases and went back to the two young men. They began to talk of the same subject. Once or twice the young lady glanced at me over her shoulder.

I lingered before her stall, though I knew my stay was useless, to make my interest in her wares seem the more real. Then I turned away slowly and walked down the middle of the bazaar. I allowed the two pennies to fall against the sixpence in my pocket. I heard a voice call from one end of the gallery that the light was out. The upper part of the hall was now completely dark.

Gazing up into the darkness I saw myself as a creature driven and derided by vanity; and my eyes burned with anguish and anger.

READING AND REACTING

1. How would you characterize the story's level of diction? Is this level appropriate for a story about a young boy's experiences? Explain.

2. Identify several examples of figurative language in the story. Where is Joyce most likely to use this kind of language? Why?

3. What words and phrases express the boy's extreme idealism and romantic view of the world? In what way does such language help to communicate the story's major theme?

4. In paragraph 4, the narrator says, "her name was like a summons to all my foolish blood." In the story's last sentence he sees himself as "a creature driven and derided by vanity." What other expressions does he use to describe his feelings? How would you characterize these feelings?

5. How does word choice illustrate the contrast between the narrator's day-to-day life and the exotic promise of the bazaar?

6. What does each of the italicized words suggest: "We walked through the *flaring* streets" (5); "I heard the rain *impinge* upon the earth" (6); "I *chafed* against the work of school" (12); "I found myself in a big hall *girdled* at half its height by a gallery" (25)? What other examples of unusual word choice can you identify in the story?

7. What is it about the events in this story that causes the narrator to remember them years later?

8. Identify words and phrases in the story that are associated with religion. What purpose do these references to religion serve?

9. **JOURNAL ENTRY** Rewrite a brief passage from this story in the voice of the young boy. Use informal style, simple figures of speech, and vocabulary appropriate for a child.

10. **CRITICAL PERSPECTIVE** In *Notes on the American Short Story Today*, Richard Kostelanetz discusses the epiphany, one of Joyce's most significant contributions to literature:

> In Joyce's pervasively influential theory of the short story we remember, the fiction turned upon an epiphany, a moment of revelation in which, in [critic] Harry Levin's words, "amid the most encumbered circumstances it suddenly happens that the veil is lifted, the . . . mystery laid bare, and the ultimate secret of things made manifest." The epiphany, then, became a technique for jelling the narrative and locking the story's import into place. . . . What made this method revolutionary was the shifting of the focal point of the story from its end . . . to a spot within the body of the text, usually near (but not at) the end.

Where in "Araby" does the story's epiphany occur? Does it do all that Kostelanetz believes an epiphany should do? Or do you think that, at least in the case of "Araby," the epiphany may not be as significant a force as Kostelanetz suggests?

Related Works: "A&P" (p. 122), "Inland Passage" (p. 150), "The Loons" (p. 249), "Shall I Compare Thee to a Summer's Day?" (p. 701)

◊ **ERNEST HEMINGWAY** (1898–1961) grew up in Oak Park, Illinois, and after high school graduation began his writing career as a cub reporter on the *Kansas City Star*. While working as a volunteer ambulance driver in World War I, eighteen-year-old Hemingway was wounded. As Hemingway himself told the story, he was hit by machine-gun fire while carrying an Italian soldier to safety. (Hemingway biographer Michael Reynolds, however, reports that Hemingway was wounded when a mortar shell fell and killed the man next to him.) In 1922, Hemingway and his first wife (he married four times) moved to Paris, where he taught Ezra Pound how to box, let Gertrude Stein mind the baby, and talked literary shop with expatriate writers F. Scott Fitzgerald and James Joyce. He was, said Joyce, "a big, powerful peasant, as strong as a buffalo . . . and ready to live the life he writes about." In fact, this public image of the "man's man"—the war correspondent, the deep-sea fisherman, the hunter on safari—was one Hemingway carefully created for himself.

Success came early, with publication of the short story collection *In Our Time* (1925) and his first and most acclaimed novel, *The Sun Also Rises*

(1926), a portrait of a postwar "lost generation" of Americans adrift in Europe. Hemingway's novels make fiction and art out of the reality of his own life. *A Farewell to Arms* (1929) harks back to his war experiences; *For Whom the Bell Tolls* (1940) emerged out of his experiences as a journalist in Spain during the Spanish Civil War. Late in life, he made his home in Key West, Florida, and then in Cuba, where he wrote *The Old Man and the Sea* (1952). Hemingway's heroes embody the writer's own belief that although life may be followed by *nada*, or nothingness, strong individuals can embrace life and live it with dignity and honour. In 1961, plagued by poor health and mental illness—and perhaps by the difficulty of living up to his own image—Hemingway took his own life.

According to novelist and critic Anthony Burgess, Hemingway changed the sound of English prose by struggling to write a "true simple declarative sentence." His spare, unadorned style "sounds easy now, chiefly because Hemingway has shown us how to do it, but it was not easy at a time when 'literature' still meant fine writing in the Victorian sense. . . . " Hemingway was awarded the 1954 Nobel Prize in literature.

⋄ ⋄ ⋄

ERNEST HEMINGWAY

Soldier's Home
(1925)

Krebs went to the war from a Methodist college in Kansas. There is a picture which shows him among his fraternity brothers, all of them wearing exactly the same height and style collar. He enlisted in the Marines in 1917 and did not return to the United States until the second division returned from the Rhine in the summer of 1919.

There is a picture which shows him on the Rhine with two German girls and another corporal. Krebs and the corporal look too big for their uniforms. The German girls are not beautiful. The Rhine does not show in the picture.

By the time Krebs returned to his home town in Oklahoma the greeting of heroes was over. He came back much too late. The men from the town who had been drafted had all been welcomed elaborately on their return. There had been a great deal of hysteria. Now the reaction had set in. People seemed to think it was rather ridiculous for Krebs to be getting back so late, years after the war was over.

At first Krebs, who had been at Belleau Wood, Soissons, the Champagne, St. Mihiel, and in the Argonne, did not want to talk about the war at all. Later he felt the need to talk but no one wanted to hear about it. His town had heard too many atrocity stories to be thrilled by actualities. Krebs found that to be listened to at all he had to lie, and after he had done this twice he, too, had a reaction against the war and against talking about it. A distaste for everything that had happened to him in the war set in because of the lies he had told. All of the times that had been able to make him feel cool and clean inside himself when he thought of them; the times so long back when he had done the one thing, the only thing for a man to do, easily and naturally, when he might have done something else, now lost their cool, valuable quality and then were lost themselves.

5   His lies were quite unimportant lies and consisted in attributing to himself things other men had seen, done or heard of, and stating as facts certain apocryphal incidents familiar to all soldiers. Even his lies were not sensational at the pool room. His acquaintances, who had heard detailed accounts of German women found chained to machine guns in the Argonne forest and who could not comprehend, or were barred by their patriotism from interest in, any German machine gunners who were not chained, were not thrilled by his stories.

Krebs acquired the nausea in regard to experience that is the result of untruth or exaggeration, and when he occasionally met another man who had really been a soldier and they talked a few minutes in the dressing room at a dance he fell into the easy pose of the old soldier among other soldiers: that he had been badly, sickeningly frightened all the time. In this way he lost everything.

During this time, it was late summer, he was sleeping late in bed, getting up to walk down town to the library to get a book, eating lunch at home, reading on the front porch until he became bored and then walking down through the town to spend the hottest hours of the day in the cool dark of the pool room. He loved to play pool.

In the evening he practised on his clarinet, strolled down town, read and went to bed. He was still a hero to his two young sisters. His mother would have given him breakfast in bed if he had wanted it. She often came in when he was in bed and asked him to tell her about the war, but her attention always wandered. His father was non-committal.

Before Krebs went away to the war he had never been allowed to drive the family motor car. His father was in the real estate business and always wanted the car to be at his command when he required it to take clients out into the country to show them a piece of farm property. The car always stood outside the First National Bank building where his father had an office on the second floor. Now, after the war, it was still the same car.

10   Nothing was changed in the town except that the young girls had grown up. But they lived in such a complicated world of already defined alliances and shifting feuds that Krebs did not feel the energy or the courage to break into it. He liked to look at them, though. There were so many good-looking young girls. Most of them had their hair cut short. When he went away only little girls wore their hair like that or girls that were fast. They all wore sweaters and shirt waists with round Dutch collars. It was a pattern. He liked to look at them from the front porch as they walked on the other side of the street. He liked to watch them walking under the shade of the trees. He liked the round Dutch collars above their sweaters. He liked their silk stockings and flat shoes. He liked their bobbed hair and the way they walked.

When he was in town their appeal to him was not very strong. He did not like them when he saw them in the Greek's ice cream parlor. He did not want them themselves really. They were too complicated. There was something else. Vaguely he wanted a girl but he did not want to have to work to get her. He would have liked to have a girl but he did not want to have to spend a long time getting her. He did not want to get into the intrigue and the politics. He did not want to have to do any courting. He did not want to tell any more lies. It wasn't worth it.

He did not want any consequences. He did not want any consequences ever again. He wanted to live along without consequences. Besides he did not really need a girl. The army had taught him that. It was all right to pose as though you had to have a girl. Nearly everybody did that. But it wasn't true. You did not need a girl. That was the funny thing. First a fellow boasted how girls mean nothing to him, that he never thought of them, that they could not touch him. Then a fellow boasted that he could not get along without girls, that he had to have them all the time, that he could not go to sleep without them.

That was all a lie. It was all a lie both ways. You did not need a girl unless you thought about them. He learned that in the army. Then sooner or later you always got one. When you were really ripe for a girl you always got one. You did not have to think about it. Sooner or later it would come. He had learned that in the army.

Now he would have liked a girl if she had come to him and not wanted to talk. But here at home it was all too complicated. He knew he could never get through it all again. It was not worth the trouble. That was the thing about French girls and German girls. There was not all this talking. You couldn't talk much and you did not need to talk. It was simple and you were friends. He thought about France and then he began to think about Germany. On the whole he had liked Germany better. He did not want to leave Germany. He did not want to come home. Still, he had come home. He sat on the front porch.

15   He liked the girls that were walking along the other side of the street. He liked the look of them much better than the French girls or the German girls. But the world they were in was not the world he was in. He would like to have one of them. But it was not worth it. They were such a nice pattern. He liked the pattern. It was exciting. But he would not go through all the talking. He did not want one badly enough. He liked to look at them all, though. It was not worth it. Not now when things were getting good again.

He sat there on the porch reading a book on the war. It was a history and he was reading about all the engagements he had been in. It was the most interesting reading he had ever done. He wished there were more maps. He looked forward with a good feeling to reading all the really good histories when they would come out with good detail maps. Now he was really learning about the war. He had been a good soldier. That made a difference.

One morning after he had been home about a month his mother came into his bedroom and sat on the bed. She smoothed her apron.

"I had a talk with your father last night, Harold," she said, "and he is willing for you to take the car out in the evenings."

"Yeah?" said Krebs, who was not fully awake. "Take the car out? Yeah?"

20 "Yes. Your father has felt for some time that you should be able to take the car out in the evenings whenever you wished but we only talked it over last night."

"I'll bet you made him," Krebs said.

"No. It was your father's suggestion that we talk the matter over."

"Yeah. I'll bet you made him." Krebs sat up in bed.

"Will you come down to breakfast, Harold?" his mother said.

25 "As soon as I get my clothes on," Krebs said.

His mother went out of the room and he could hear her frying something downstairs while he washed, shaved and dressed to go down into the dining-room for breakfast. While he was eating breakfast his sister brought in the mail.

"Well, Hare," she said. "You old sleepy-head. What do you ever get up for?"

Krebs looked at her. He liked her. She was his best sister.

"Have you got the paper?" he asked.

30 She handed him *The Kansas City Star* and he shucked off its brown wrapper and opened it to the sporting page. He folded *The Star* open and propped it against the water pitcher with his cereal dish to steady it, so he could read while he ate.

"Harold," his mother stood in the kitchen doorway, "Harold, please don't muss up the paper. You father can't read his *Star* if it's been mussed."

"I won't muss it," Krebs said.

His sister sat down at the table and watched him while he read.

"We're playing indoor[1] over at school this afternoon," she said. "I'm going to pitch."

35 "Good," said Krebs. "How's the old wing?"

"I can pitch better than lots of the boys. I tell them all you taught me. The other girls aren't much good."

"Yeah?" said Krebs.

"I tell them all you're my beau. Aren't you my beau, Hare?"

"You bet."

40 "Couldn't your brother really be your beau just because he's your brother?"

"I don't know."

"Sure you know. Couldn't you be my beau, Hare, if I was old enough and if you wanted to?"

"Sure. You're my girl now."

"Am I really your girl?"

45 "Sure."

"Do you love me?"

---

[1] Indoor: that is, a softball game.

"Uh, huh."

"Will you love me always?"

"Sure."

50   "Will you come over and watch me play indoor?"

"Maybe."

"Aw, Hare, you don't love me. If you loved me, you'd want to come over and watch me play indoor."

Krebs's mother came into the dining-room from the kitchen. She carried a plate with two fried eggs and some crisp bacon on it and a plate of buckwheat cakes.

"You run along, Helen," she said. "I want to talk to Harold."

55   She put eggs and bacon down in front of him and brought in a jug of maple syrup for the buckwheat cakes. Then she sat down across the table from Krebs.

"I wish you'd put down the paper a minute, Harold," she said.

Krebs took down the paper and folded it.

"Have you decided what you are going to do yet, Harold?" his mother said, taking off her glasses.

"No," said Krebs.

60   "Don't you think it's about time?" His mother did not say this in a mean way. She seemed worried.

"I hadn't thought about it," Krebs said.

"God has some work for every one to do," his mother said. "There can be no idle hands in His Kingdom."

"I'm not in His Kingdom," Krebs said.

"We are all of us in His Kingdom."

65   Krebs felt embarrassed and resentful as always.

"I've worried about you so much, Harold," his mother went on. "I know the temptations you must have been exposed to. I know how weak men are. I know what your own dear grandfather, my own father, told us about the Civil War and I have prayed for you. I pray for you all day long, Harold."

Krebs looked at the bacon fat hardening on his plate.

"Your father is worried, too," his mother went on. "He thinks you have lost your ambition, that you haven't got a definite aim in life. Charley Simmons, who is just your age, has a good job and is going to be married. The boys are all settling down; they're all determined to get somewhere; you can see that boys like Charley Simmons are on their way to being really a credit to the community."

Krebs said nothing.

70   "Don't look that way, Harold," his mother said. "You know we love you and I want to tell you for your own good how matters stand. Your father does not want to hamper your freedom. He thinks you should be allowed to drive the car. If you want to take some of the nice girls out riding with you, we are only too pleased. We want you to enjoy yourself. But you are going to have to settle down to work, Harold. Your father doesn't care what you start in at. All work is honorable as he says. But you've got to make a start at

something. He asked me to speak to you this morning and then you can stop in and see him at his office."

"Is that all?" Krebs said.

"Yes. Don't you love your mother, dear boy?"

"No," Krebs said.

His mother looked at him across the table. Her eyes were shiny. She started crying.

75   "I don't love anybody," Krebs said.

It wasn't any good. He couldn't tell her, he couldn't make her see it. It was silly to have said it. He had only hurt her. He went over and took hold of her arm. She was crying with her head in her hands.

"I didn't mean it," he said. "I was just angry at something. I didn't mean I didn't love you."

His mother went on crying. Krebs put his arm on her shoulder.

"Can't you believe me, Mother?"

80   His mother shook her head.

"Please, please, Mother. Please believe me."

"All right," his mother said chokily. She looked up at him. "I believe you, Harold."

Krebs kissed her hair. She put her face up to him.

"I'm your mother," she said. "I held you next to my heart when you were a tiny baby."

85   Krebs felt sick and vaguely nauseated.

"I know, Mummy," he said. "I'll try and be a good boy for you."

"Would you kneel and pray with me, Harold?" his mother asked.

They knelt down beside the dining-room table and Krebs's mother prayed.

"Now, you pray, Harold," she said.

90   "I can't," Krebs said.

"Try, Harold."

"I can't."

"Do you want me to pray for you?"

"Yes."

95   So his mother prayed for him and then they stood up and Krebs kissed his mother and went out of the house. He had tried so to keep his life from being complicated. Still, none of it had touched him. He had felt sorry for his mother and she had made him lie. He would go to Kansas City and get a job and she would feel all right about it. There would be one more scene maybe before he got away. He would not go down to his father's office. He would miss that one. He wanted his life to go smoothly. It had just gotten going that way. Well, that was all over now, anyway. He would go over to the schoolyard and watch Helen play indoor baseball.

Reading and Reacting

1. The title "Soldier's Home" is both ironic and ambiguous. What are the meanings suggested by the title?

2. The word "lie" is repeated. Identify the various uses of the word and its significance in the particular context.
3. Characterize the tone of the story.
4. Consider the length of Hemingway's sentences. Is there a connection between length and/or complexity of the sentences and their context?
5. Does Krebs love his mother? Why does he say he doesn't?
6. The story contrasts being silent and talking, and neither satisfies Krebs. Why not?
7. The story is written in third person, with sections of dialogue. Is the story dramatic, or is the narrative limited omniscient? Is there a combination? What is the effect of the narrative point of view?
8. Identify examples of figurative language used in the story. How does the presence or absence of such language help to convey the story's theme?
9. **JOURNAL ENTRY** Pretend that you are Krebs and you are telling your mother as honestly as possible how you feel about your experience.
10. **CRITICAL PERSPECTIVE** In *The Writer's Art of Self-Defense*, Jackson J. Benson states, "Blindness versus awareness is Hemingway's most pervasive theme, and it is borne on a rippling wave of irony into almost everything he writes."

    How do the contrasting perspectives of the son and mother in "Soldier's Home" express this theme? Which one is "blind," and which one is "aware"? How do their words reveal their knowledge or lack of knowledge?

Related Works: "Stones" (p. 135), "Borders" (p. 218), "Dulce et Decorum Est" (p. 695), *The Shape of a Girl* (p. 1348)

◆ **(MARY) FLANNERY O'CONNOR** (1925–1964) was born to a prosperous Catholic family in Savannah, Georgia, and spent most of her adult life on a farm near the town of Milledgeville. She left the South to study writing at the University of Iowa, moving to New York to work on her first novel, *Wise Blood* (1952). On a train going south for Christmas, O'Connor fell desperately ill; she was diagnosed as having lupus, the immune system disease that killed her father and would cause O'Connor's death when she was only thirty-nine years old.

While her mother ran the farm, O'Connor spent mornings writing and afternoons wandering the fields with cane or crutches. Her short story collection *A Good Man Is Hard to Find* (1955) and an excellent French translation of *Wise Blood* established her international reputation, which was solidified with the publication of a second novel, *The Violent Bear It Away* (1960), and a posthumously published book of short stories, *Everything That Rises Must Converge* (1965).

O'Connor delighted in local reaction to her grotesque, often grisly stories: "Ask her," the men at the hardware store prodded her uncle, "why she don't write about some nice people." O'Connor, said a friend, believed that an artist "should face all the truth down to the worst of it." Yet however dark, O'Connor's stories are infused with grim humour and a fierce belief in the possibility of spiritual redemption, even for her most tortured characters. A line from her short story "A Good Man Is Hard to Find" says much about what O'Connor perceived about both natural things and her characters: "The trees were full of silver-white sunlight and the meanest of them sparkled." In O'Connor's work, the "meanest" things and people can sparkle, touched by a kind of holy madness and beauty.

◊ ◊ ◊

FLANNERY O'CONNOR

A Good Man Is Hard to Find
(1955)

The grandmother didn't want to go to Florida. She wanted to visit some of her connections in east Tennessee and she was seizing at every chance to change Bailey's mind. Bailey was the son she lived with, her only boy. He was sitting on the edge of his chair at the table, bent over the orange sports section of the *Journal*. "Now look here, Bailey," she said, "see here, read this," and she stood with one hand on her thin hip and the other rattling the newspaper at his bald head. "Here this fellow that calls himself The Misfit is aloose from the Federal Pen and headed toward Florida and you read here what it says he did to these people. Just you read it. I wouldn't take my children in any direction with a criminal like that aloose in it. I couldn't answer to my conscience if I did."

Bailey didn't look up from his reading so she wheeled around then and faced the children's mother, a young woman in slacks, whose face was as broad and innocent as a cabbage and was tied around with a green headkerchief that had two points on the top like a rabbit's ears. She was sitting on the sofa, feeding the baby his apricots out of a jar. "The children have been to Florida before," the old lady said. "You all ought to take them somewhere else for a change so they would see different parts of the world and be broad. They never have been to east Tennessee."

The children's mother didn't seem to hear her but the eight-year-old boy, John Wesley, a stocky child with glasses, said, "If you don't want to go to Florida, why dontcha stay at home?" He and the little girl, June Star, were reading the funny papers on the floor.

"She wouldn't stay at home to be queen for a day," June Star said without raising her yellow head.

5   "Yes and what would you do if this fellow, The Misfit, caught you?" the grandmother asked.

"I'd smack his face," John Wesley said.

"She wouldn't stay at home for a million bucks," June Star said. "Afraid she'd miss something. She has to go everywhere we go."

"All right, Miss," the grandmother said. "Just remember that the next time you want me to curl your hair."

June Star said her hair was naturally curly.

10   The next morning the grandmother was the first one in the car, ready to go. She had her big black valise that looked like the head of a hippopotamus in one corner, and underneath it she was hiding a basket with Pitty Sing, the cat, in it. She didn't intend for the cat to be left alone in the house for three days because he would miss her too much and she was afraid he might brush against one of the gas burners and accidentally asphyxiate himself. Her son, Bailey, didn't like to arrive at a motel with a cat.

She sat in the middle of the back seat with John Wesley and June Star on either side of her. Bailey and the children's mother and the baby sat in front and they left Atlanta at eight forty-five with the mileage on the car at 55890. The grandmother wrote this down because she thought it would be interesting to say how many miles they had been when they got back. It took them twenty minutes to reach the outskirts of the city.

The old lady settled herself comfortably, removing her white cotton gloves and putting them up with her purse on the shelf in front of the back window. The children's mother still had on slacks and still had her head tied up in a green kerchief, but the grandmother had on a navy blue straw sailor hat with a bunch of white violets on the brim and a navy blue dress with a small white dot in the print. Her collars and cuffs were white organdy trimmed with lace and at her neckline she had pinned a purple spray of cloth violets containing a sachet. In case of an accident, anyone seeing her dead on the highway would know at once that she was a lady.

She said she thought it was going to be a good day for driving, neither too hot nor too cold, and she cautioned Bailey that the speed limit was fifty-five miles an hour and that the patrolmen hid themselves behind billboards and small clumps of trees and sped out after you before you had a chance to slow down. She pointed out interesting details of the scenery: Stone Mountain; the blue granite that in some places came up to both sides of the highway; the brilliant red clay banks slightly streaked with purple; and the various crops that made rows of green lace-work on the ground. The trees were full of silver-white sunlight and the meanest of them sparkled. The children were reading comic magazines and their mother had gone back to sleep.

"Let's go through Georgia fast so we won't have to look at it much," John Wesley said.

15   "If I were a little boy," said the grandmother, "I wouldn't talk about my native state that way. Tennessee has the mountains and Georgia has the hills."

"Tennessee is just a hillbilly dumping ground," John Wesley said, "and Georgia is a lousy state too."

"You said it," June Star said.

"In my time," said the grandmother, folding her thin veined fingers, "children were more respectful of their native states and their parents and everything else. People did right then. Oh look at the cute little pickaninny!" she said and pointed to a Negro child standing in the door of a shack. "Wouldn't that make a picture, now?" she asked and they all turned and looked at the little Negro out of the back window. He waved.

"He didn't have any britches on," June Star said.

20   "He probably didn't have any," the grandmother explained. "Little niggers in the country don't have things like we do. If I could paint, I'd paint that picture," she said.

The children exchanged comic books.

The grandmother offered to hold the baby and the children's mother passed him over the front seat to her. She set him on her knee and bounced him and told him about the things they were passing. She rolled her eyes and screwed up her mouth and stuck her leathery thin face into his smooth bland one. Occasionally he gave her a faraway smile. They passed a large cotton field with five or six graves fenced in the middle of it, like a small island. "Look at the graveyard!" the grandmother said, pointing it out. "That was the old family burying ground. That belonged to the plantation."

"Where's the plantation?" John Wesley asked.

"Gone With the Wind," said the grandmother. "Ha. Ha."

25   When the children finished all the comic books they had brought, they opened the lunch and ate it. The grandmother ate a peanut butter sandwich and an olive and would not let the children throw the box and the paper napkins out the window. When there was nothing else to do they played a game by choosing a cloud and making the other two guess what shape it suggested. John Wesley took one the shape of a cow and June Star guessed a cow and John Wesley said, no, an automobile, and June Star said he didn't play fair, and they began to slap each other over the grandmother.

The grandmother said she would tell them a story if they would keep quiet. When she told a story, she rolled her eyes and waved her head and was very dramatic. She said once when she was a maiden lady she had been courted by a Mr. Edgar Atkins Teagarden from Jasper, Georgia. She said he was a very good-looking man and a gentleman and that he brought her a watermelon every Saturday afternoon with his initials cut in it, E. A. T. Well, one Saturday, she said, Mr. Teagarden brought the watermelon and there was nobody at home and he left it on the front porch and returned in his buggy to Jasper, but she never got the watermelon, she said, because a nigger boy ate it when he saw the initials, E. A. T.! This story tickled John Wesley's funny bone and he giggled and giggled but June Star didn't think it was any good. She said she wouldn't marry a man that just brought her a watermelon on Saturday. The grandmother said she would have done well to marry Mr. Teagarden because he was a gentleman and had bought Coca-Cola stock when it first came out and that he died only a few years ago, a very wealthy man.

They stopped at The Tower for barbecued sandwiches. The Tower was a part stucco and part wood filling station and dance hall set in a clearing outside of Timothy. A fat man named Red Sammy Butts ran it and there were signs stuck here and there on the building and for miles up and down the highway saying, TRY RED SAMMY'S FAMOUS BARBECUE. NONE LIKE FAMOUS RED SAMMY'S! RED SAM! THE FAT BOY WITH THE HAPPY LAUGH. A VETERAN! RED SAMMY'S YOUR MAN!

Red Sammy was lying on the bare ground outside The Tower with his head under a truck while a gray monkey about a foot high, chained to a small chinaberry tree, chattered nearby. The monkey sprang back into the tree and got on the highest limb as soon as he saw the children jump out of the car and run toward him.

Inside, The Tower was a long dark room with a counter at one end and tables at the other and dancing space in the middle. They all sat down at a board table next to the nickelodeon and Red Sam's wife, a tall burnt-brown woman with hair and eyes lighter than her skin, came and took their order. The children's mother put a dime in the machine and played "The Tennessee Waltz," and the grandmother said that tune always made her want to dance. She asked Bailey if he would like to dance but he only glared at her. He didn't have a naturally sweet disposition like she did and trips made him nervous. The grandmother's brown eyes were very bright. She swayed her head from side to side and pretended she was dancing in her chair. June Star said play something she could tap to so the children's mother put in another dime and played a fast number and June Star stepped out onto the dance floor and did her tap routine.

30   "Ain't she cute?" Red Sam's wife said, leaning over the counter. "Would you like to come be my little girl?"

"No I certainly wouldn't," June Star said. "I wouldn't live in a broken-down place like this for a million bucks!" and she ran back to the table.

"Ain't she cute?" the woman repeated, stretching her mouth politely.

"Aren't you ashamed?" hissed the grandmother.

Red Sam came in and told his wife to quit lounging on the counter and hurry up with these people's order. His khaki trousers reached just to his hip bones and his stomach hung over them like a sack of meal swaying under his shirt. He came over and sat down at a table nearby and let out a combination sigh and yodel. "You can't win," he said. "You can't win," and he wiped his sweating red face off with a gray handkerchief. "These days you don't know who to trust," he said. "Ain't that the truth?"

35   "People are certainly not nice like they used to be," said the grandmother.

"Two fellers come in here last week," Red Sammy said, "driving a Chrysler. It was a old beat-up car but it was a good one and these boys looked all right to me. Said they worked at the mill and you know I let them fellers charge the gas they bought? Now why did I do that?"

"Because you're a good man!" the grandmother said at once.

"Yes'm, I suppose so," Red Sam said as if he were struck with this answer.

His wife brought the orders, carrying the five plates all at once without a tray, two in each hand and one balanced on her arm. "It isn't a soul in this green world of God's that you can trust," she said. "And I don't count nobody out of that, not nobody," she repeated, looking at Red Sammy.

40 "Did you read about that criminal, The Misfit, that's escaped?" asked the grandmother.

"I wouldn't be a bit surprised if he didn't attact this place right here," said the woman. "If he hears about it being here, I wouldn't be none surprised to see him. If he hears it's two cent in the cash register, I wouldn't be at all surprised if he . . ."

"That'll do," Red Sam said. "Go bring these people their Co'-Colas," and the woman went off to get the rest of the order.

"A good man is hard to find," Red Sammy said. "Everything is getting terrible. I remember the day you could go off and leave your screen door unlatched. Not no more."

He and the grandmother discussed better times. The old lady said that in her opinion Europe was entirely to blame for the way things were now. She said the way Europe acted you would think we were made of money and Red Sam said it was no use talking about it, she was exactly right. The children ran outside into the white sunlight and looked at the monkey in the lacy chinaberry tree. He was busy catching fleas on himself and biting each one carefully between his teeth as if it were a delicacy.

45 They drove off again into the hot afternoon. The grandmother took cat naps and woke up every few minutes with her own snoring. Outside of Toombsboro she woke up and recalled an old plantation that she had visited in this neighborhood once when she was a young lady. She said the house had six white columns across the front and that there was an avenue of oaks leading up to it and two little wooden trellis arbors on either side in front where you sat down with your suitor after a stroll in the garden. She recalled exactly which road to turn off to get to it. She knew that Bailey would not be willing to lose any time looking at an old house, but the more she talked about it, the more she wanted to see it once again and find out if the little twin arbors were still standing. "There was a secret panel in this house," she said craftily, not telling the truth but wishing that she were, "and the story went that all the family silver was hidden in it when Sherman came through but it was never found . . ."

"Hey!" John Wesley said. "Let's go see it! We'll find it! We'll poke all the woodwork and find it! Who lives there? Where do you turn off at? Hey Pop, can't we turn off there?"

"We never have seen a house with a secret panel!" June Star shrieked. "Let's go to the house with the secret panel! Hey Pop, can't we go see the house with the secret panel!"

"It's not far from here, I know," the grandmother said. "It wouldn't take over twenty minutes."

Bailey was looking straight ahead. His jaw was as rigid as a horseshoe. "No," he said.

50 The children began to yell and scream that they wanted to see the house with the secret panel. John Wesley kicked the back of the front seat and June Star hung over her mother's shoulder and whined desperately into her ear that they never had any fun even on their vacation, that they could never do what THEY wanted to do. The baby began to scream and John Wesley kicked the back of the seat so hard that his father could feel the blows in his kidney.

"All right!" he shouted and drew the car to a stop at the side of the road. "Will you all shut up? Will you all just shut up for one second? If you don't shut up, we won't go anywhere."

"It would be very educational for them," the grandmother murmured.

"All right," Bailey said, "but get this: this is the only time we're going to stop for anything like this. This is the one and only time."

"The dirt road that you have to turn down is about a mile back," the grandmother directed. "I marked it when we passed."

55 "A dirt road," Bailey groaned.

After they had turned around and were headed toward the dirt road, the grandmother recalled other points about the house, the beautiful glass over the front doorway and the candle-lamp in the hall. John Wesley said that the secret panel was probably in the fireplace.

"You can't go inside this house," Bailey said. "You don't know who lives there."

"While you all talk to the people in front, I'll run around behind and get in a window," John Wesley suggested.

"We'll all stay in the car," his mother said.

60 They turned onto the dirt road and the car raced roughly along in a swirl of pink dust. The grandmother recalled the times when there were no paved roads and thirty miles was a day's journey. The dirt road was hilly and there were sudden washes in it and sharp curves on dangerous embankments. All at once they would be on a hill, looking down over the blue tops of trees for miles around, then the next minute, they would be in a red depression with the dust-coated trees looking down on them.

"This place had better turn up in a minute," Bailey said, "or I'm going to turn around."

The road looked as if no one had traveled on it in months.

"It's not much farther," the grandmother said and just as she said it, a horrible thought came to her. The thought was so embarrassing that she turned red in the face and her eyes dilated and her feet jumped up, upsetting her valise in the corner. The instant the valise moved, the newspaper top she had over the basket under it rose with a snarl and Pitty Sing, the cat, sprang onto Bailey's shoulder.

The children were thrown to the floor and their mother, clutching the baby, was thrown out the door onto the ground; the old lady was thrown into the front seat. The car turned over once and landed right-side-up in a gulch off the side of the road. Bailey remained in the driver's seat with the cat—gray-striped with a broad white face and an orange nose—clinging to his neck like a caterpillar.

65   As soon as the children saw they could move their arms and legs, they scrambled out of the car, shouting, "We've had an ACCIDENT!" The grandmother was curled up under the dashboard, hoping she was injured so that Bailey's wrath would not come down on her all at once. The horrible thought she had had before the accident was that the house she had remembered so vividly was not in Georgia but in Tennessee.

Bailey removed the cat from his neck with both hands and flung it out the window against the side of a pine tree. Then he got out of the car and started looking for the children's mother. She was sitting against the side of the red gutted ditch, holding the screaming baby, but she only had a cut down her face and a broken shoulder. "We've had an ACCIDENT!" the children screamed in a frenzy of delight.

"But nobody's killed," June Star said with disappointment as the grandmother limped out of the car, her hat still pinned to her head but the broken front brim standing up at a jaunty angle and the violet spray hanging off the side. They all sat down in the ditch, except the children, to recover from the shock. They were all shaking.

"Maybe a car will come along," said the children's mother hoarsely.

"I believe I have injured an organ," said the grandmother, pressing her side, but no one answered her. Bailey's teeth were clattering. He had on a yellow sport shirt with bright blue parrots designed in it and his face was as yellow as the shirt. The grandmother decided that she would not mention that the house was in Tennessee.

70   The road was about ten feet above and they could see only the tops of the trees on the other side of it. Behind the ditch they were sitting in there were more woods, tall and dark and deep. In a few minutes they saw a car some distance away on top of a hill, coming slowly as if the occupants were watching them. The grandmother stood up and waved both arms dramatically to attract their attention. The car continued to come on slowly, disappeared around a bend and appeared again, moving even slower, on top of the hill they had gone over. It was a big black battered hearse-like automobile. There were three men in it.

It came to a stop just over them and for some minutes, the driver looked down with a steady expressionless gaze to where they were sitting, and didn't speak. Then he turned his head and muttered something to the other two and they got out. One was a fat boy in black trousers and a red sweat shirt with a silver stallion embossed on the front of it. He moved around on the right side of them and stood staring, his mouth partly open in a kind of loose grin. The other had on khaki pants and a blue striped coat and a gray hat pulled down very low, hiding most of his face. He came around slowly on the left side. Neither spoke.

The driver got out of the car and stood by the side of it, looking down at them. He was an older man than the other two. His hair was just beginning to gray and he wore silver-rimmed spectacles that gave him a scholarly look. He had a long creased face and didn't have on any shirt or undershirt. He had on blue jeans that were too tight for him and was holding a black hat and a gun. The two boys also had guns.

"We've had an ACCIDENT!" the children screamed.

The grandmother had the peculiar feeling that the bespectacled man was someone she knew. His face was as familiar to her as if she had known him all her life but she could not recall who he was. He moved away from the car and began to come down the embankment, placing his feet carefully so that he wouldn't slip. He had on tan and white shoes and no socks, and his ankles were red and thin. "Good afternoon," he said. "I see you all had you a little spill."

75   "We turned over twice!" said the grandmother.

"Oncet," he corrected. "We seen it happen. Try their car and see will it run, Hiram," he said quietly to the boy with the gray hat.

"What you got that gun for?" John Wesley asked. "Watcha gonna do with that gun?"

"Lady," the man said to the children's mother, "would you mind calling them children to sit down by you? Children make me nervous. I want all you all to sit down right together there where you're at."

"What are you telling US what to do for?" June Star asked.

80   Behind them the line of woods gaped like a dark open mouth. "Come here," said their mother.

"Look here now," Bailey began suddenly, "we're in a predicament! We're in . . ."

The grandmother shrieked. She scrambled to her feet and stood staring. "You're The Misfit!" she said. "I recognized you at once!"

"Yes'm," the man said, smiling slightly as if he were pleased in spite of himself to be known, "but it would have been better for all of you, lady, if you hadn't of reckernized me."

Bailey turned his head sharply and said something to his mother that shocked even the children. The old lady began to cry and The Misfit reddened.

85   "Lady," he said, "don't you get upset. Sometimes a man says things he don't mean. I don't reckon he meant to talk to you thataway."

"You wouldn't shoot a lady, would you?" the grandmother said and removed a clean handkerchief from her cuff and began to slap at her eyes with it.

The Misfit pointed the toe of his shoe into the ground and made a little hole and then covered it up again. "I would hate to have to," he said.

"Listen," the grandmother almost screamed, "I know you're a good man. You don't look a bit like you have common blood. I know you must come from nice people!"

"Yes mam," he said, "finest people in the world." When he smiled he showed a row of strong white teeth. "God never made a finer woman than my mother and my daddy's heart was pure gold," he said. The boy with the red sweat shirt had come around behind them and was standing with his gun at his hip. The Misfit squatted down on the ground. "Watch them children, Bobby Lee," he said. "You know they make me nervous." He looked at the six of them huddled together in front of him and he seemed to be embarrassed as if he couldn't think of anything to say. "Ain't a cloud in the sky," he remarked, looking up at it. "Don't see no sun but don't see no cloud neither."

90   "Yes, it's a beautiful day," said the grandmother. "Listen," she said, "you shouldn't call yourself The Misfit because I know you're a good man at heart. I can just look at you and tell."

"Hush!" Bailey yelled. "Hush! Everybody shut up and let me handle this!" He was squatting in the position of a runner about to sprint forward but he didn't move.

"I pre-chate that, lady," The Misfit said and drew a little circle in the ground with the butt of his gun.

"It'll take a half a hour to fix this here car," Hiram called, looking over the raised hood of it.

"Well, first you and Bobby Lee get him and that little boy to step over yonder with you," The Misfit said, pointing to Bailey and John Wesley. "The boys want to ast you something," he said to Bailey. "Would you mind stepping back in them woods there with them?"

95   "Listen," Bailey began, "we're in a terrible predicament! Nobody realizes what this is," and his voice cracked. His eyes were as blue and intense as the parrots in his shirt and he remained perfectly still.

The grandmother reached up to adjust her hat brim as if she were going to the woods with him but it came off in her hand. She stood staring at it and after a second she let it fall on the ground. Hiram pulled Bailey up by the arm as if he were assisting an old man. John Wesley caught hold of his father's hand and Bobby Lee followed. They went off toward the woods and just as they reached the dark edge, Bailey turned and supporting himself against a gray naked pine trunk, he shouted, "I'll be back in a minute, Mamma, wait on me!"

"Come back this instant!" his mother shrilled but they all disappeared into the woods.

"Bailey Boy!" the grandmother called in a tragic voice but she found she was looking at The Misfit squatting on the ground in front of her. "I just know you're a good man," she said desperately. "You're not a bit common!"

"Nome, I ain't a good man," The Misfit said after a second as if he had considered her statement carefully, "but I ain't the worst in the world neither. My daddy said I was a different breed of dog from my brothers and sisters. 'You know,' Daddy said, 'it's some that can live their whole life out without asking about it and it's others has to know why it is, and this boy is one of the latters. He's going to be into everything!'" He put on his black hat and looked up suddenly and then away deep into the woods as if he were embarrassed again. "I'm sorry I don't have on a shirt before you ladies," he said, hunching his shoulders slightly. "We buried our clothes that we had on when we escaped and we're just making do until we can get better. We borrowed these from some folks we met," he explained.

100   "That's perfectly all right," the grandmother said. "Maybe Bailey has an extra shirt in his suitcase."

"I'll look and see terrectly," The Misfit said.

"Where are they taking him?" the children's mother screamed.

"Daddy was a card himself," The Misfit said. "You couldn't put anything over on him. He never got in trouble with the Authorities though. Just had the knack of handling them."

"You could be honest too if you'd only try," said the grandmother. "Think how wonderful it would be to settle down and live a comfortable life and not have to think about somebody chasing you all the time."

105   The Misfit kept scratching in the ground with the butt of his gun as if he were thinking about it. "Yes'm, somebody is always after you," he murmured.

The grandmother noticed how thin his shoulder blades were just behind his hat because she was standing up looking down on him. "Do you ever pray?" she asked.

He shook his head. All she saw was the black hat wiggle between his shoulder blades. "Nome," he said.

There was a pistol shot from the woods, followed closely by another. Then silence. The old lady's head jerked around. She could hear the wind move through the tree tops like a long satisfied insuck of breath. "Bailey Boy!" she called.

"I was a gospel singer for a while," The Misfit said. "I been most everything. Been in the arm service, both land and sea, at home and abroad, been twict married, been an undertaker, been with the railroads, plowed Mother Earth, been in a tornado, seen a man burnt alive oncet," and he looked up at the children's mother and the little girl who were sitting close together, their faces white and their eyes glassy; "I even seen a woman flogged," he said.

110   "Pray, pray," the grandmother began, "pray, pray . . ."

"I never was a bad boy that I remember of," The Misfit said in an almost dreamy voice, "but somewheres along the line I done something wrong and got sent to the penitentiary. I was buried alive," and he looked up and held her attention to him by a steady stare.

"That's when you should have started to pray," she said. "What did you do to get sent to the penitentiary that first time?"

"Turn to the right, it was a wall," The Misfit said, looking up again at the cloudless sky. "Turn to the left, it was a wall. Look up it was a ceiling, look down it was a floor. I forget what I done, lady. I set there and set there, trying to remember what it was I done and I ain't recalled it to this day. Oncet in a while, I would think it was coming to me, but it never come."

"Maybe they put you in by mistake," the old lady said vaguely.

115   "Nome," he said. "It wasn't no mistake. They had the papers on me."

"You must have stolen something," she said.

The Misfit sneered slightly. "Nobody had nothing I wanted," he said. "It was a head-doctor at the penitentiary said what I had done was kill my daddy but I known that for a lie. My daddy died in nineteen ought nineteen of the epidemic flu and I never had a thing to do with it. He was buried in the Mount Hopewell Baptist churchyard and you can go there and see for yourself."

"If you would pray," the old lady said, "Jesus would help you."

"That's right," The Misfit said.

120   "Well then, why don't you pray?" she asked trembling with delight suddenly.

"I don't want no hep," he said. "I'm doing all right by myself."

Bobby Lee and Hiram came ambling back from the woods. Bobby Lee was dragging a yellow shirt with bright blue parrots in it.

"Thow me that shirt, Bobby Lee," The Misfit said. The shirt came flying at him and landed on his shoulder and he put it on. The grandmother couldn't name what the shirt reminded her of. "No, lady," The Misfit said while he was buttoning it up, "I found out the crime don't matter. You can do one thing or you can do another, kill a man or take a tire off his car, because sooner or later you're going to forget what it was you done and just be punished for it."

The children's mother had begun to make heaving noises as if she couldn't get her breath. "Lady," he asked, "would you and that little girl like to step off yonder with Bobby Lee and Hiram and join your husband?"

125   "Yes, thank you," the mother said faintly. Her left arm dangled helplessly and she was holding the baby, who had gone to sleep, in the other. "Hep that lady up, Hiram," The Misfit said as she struggled to climb out of the ditch, "and Bobby Lee, you hold onto that little girl's hand."

"I don't want to hold hands with him," June Star said. "He reminds me of a pig."

The fat boy blushed and laughed and caught her by the arm and pulled her off into the woods after Hiram and her mother.

Alone with The Misfit, the grandmother found that she had lost her voice. There was not a cloud in the sky nor any sun. There was nothing around her but woods. She wanted to tell him that he must pray. She opened and closed her mouth several times before anything came out. Finally she found herself saying, "Jesus, Jesus," meaning, Jesus will help you, but the way she was saying it, it sounded as if she might be cursing.

"Yes'm," The Misfit said as if he agreed. "Jesus thown everything off balance. It was the same case with Him as with me except He hadn't committed any crime and they could prove I had committed one because they had the papers on me. Of course," he said, "they never shown me my papers. That's why I sign myself now. I said long ago, you get you a signature and sign everything you do and keep a copy of it. Then you'll know what you done and you can hold up the crime to the punishment and see do they match and in the end you'll have something to prove you ain't been treated right.

I call myself The Misfit," he said, "because I can't make what all I done wrong fit what all I gone through in punishment."

130   There was a piercing scream from the woods, followed closely by a pistol report. "Does it seem right to you, lady, that one is punished a heap and another ain't punished at all?"

"Jesus!" the old lady cried. "You've got good blood! I know you wouldn't shoot a lady! I know you come from nice people! Pray! Jesus, you ought not to shoot a lady. I'll give you all the money I've got!"

"Lady," The Misfit said, looking beyond her far into the woods, "there never was a body that give the undertaker a tip."

There were two more pistol reports and the grandmother raised her head like a parched old turkey hen crying for water and called, "Bailey Boy, Bailey Boy!" as if her heart would break.

"Jesus was the only One that ever raised the dead," The Misfit continued, "and He shouldn't have done it. He thown everything off balance. If He did what He said, then it's nothing for you to do but thow away everything and follow Him, and if He didn't, then it's nothing for you to do but enjoy the few minutes you got left the best way you can—by killing somebody or burning down his house or doing some other meanness to him. No pleasure but meanness," he said and his voice became almost a snarl.

135   "Maybe He didn't raise the dead," the old lady mumbled, not knowing what she was saying and feeling so dizzy that she sank down in the ditch with her legs twisted under her.

"I wasn't there so I can't say He didn't," The Misfit said. "I wisht I had of been there," he said, hitting the ground with his fist. "It ain't right I wasn't there because if I had of been there I would of known. Listen, lady," he said in a high voice, "if I had of been there I would of known and I wouldn't be like I am now." His voice seemed about to crack and the grandmother's head cleared for an instant. She saw the man's face twisted close to her own as if he were going to cry and she murmured, "Why you're one of my babies. You're one of my own children!" She reached out and touched him on the shoulder. The Misfit sprang back as if a snake had bitten him and shot her three times through the chest. Then he put his gun down on the ground and took off his glasses and began to clean them.

Hiram and Bobby Lee returned from the woods and stood over the ditch, looking down at the grandmother who half sat and half lay in a puddle of blood with her legs crossed under her like a child's and her face smiling up at the cloudless sky.

Without his glasses, The Misfit's eyes were red-rimmed and pale and defenseless-looking. "Take her off and thow her where you thown the others," he said, picking up the cat that was rubbing itself against his leg.

"She was a talker, wasn't she?" Bobby Lee said, sliding down the ditch with a yodel.

140   "She would of been a good woman," The Misfit said, "if it had been somebody there to shoot her every minute of her life."

"Some fun!" Bobby Lee said.

"Shut up, Bobby Lee," The Misfit said. "It's no real pleasure in life."

READING AND REACTING

1. How are the style and tone of the narrator's voice different from those of the characters? What, if anything, is the significance of this difference?

2. Figurative language in this story sometimes creates unflattering, even grotesque, pictures of the characters. Find several examples of such negative figures of speech. Why do you think the author uses them?

3. What does the grandmother's use of the words *pickaninny* and *nigger* reveal about her? How are readers expected to reconcile this language with her very proper appearance and her preoccupation with manners? How does her use of these words affect your reaction to her?

4. Explain the **irony** in this statement: "In case of an accident, anyone seeing her dead on the highway would know at once that she was a lady" (12).

5. How does The Misfit's dialect characterize him?

6. What does the allusion to *Gone with the Wind* (24) contribute to the story?

7. How do the style and tone of the two-paragraph description of the three men in the car (71–72) help to prepare readers for the events that follow?

8. When The Misfit tells the grandmother about his life, his language takes on a measured, rhythmic quality: "Been in the arm service, both land and sea, at home and abroad, been twict married, been an undertaker, been with the railroads, plowed Mother Earth, been in a tornado, seen a man burnt alive oncet, . . ." (109). Find other examples of parallelism and rhythmic repetition in this character's speech. How does this style help to develop The Misfit's character?

9. **JOURNAL ENTRY** Why do you think the grandmother tells The Misfit she recognizes him? Why does she fail to realize the danger of her remark?

10. **CRITICAL PERSPECTIVE** In a discussion of "A Good Man Is Hard to Find," Martha Stephens is critical of the story's ending, commenting that "the failure of the final scene—and hence of the story—seems to result from the fact that a tonal shift that occurs midway through the story finally runs out of control." The "tonal shift" to which she refers is the abrupt movement from grotesque comedy to senseless, shocking tragedy. Stephens asks:

> What *is* the reader to think or feel about anything in the massacre scene? There is pain and shock but much that mocks that pain and shock—the heavy comedy, for instance, indeed one might say the almost burlesque treatment, of the three killers. There is the feeling that though we cannot help but pity the tormented family, the story continues to demand our contempt for them. One feels that somehow the central experi-

ence of the story—in spite of the affecting, the chilling details surrounding these deaths, in spite even of the not altogether abusive treatment of the grandmother in Part One—will elude anyone who gives way to these feelings of pain and pity. If the writer's task is, as Conrad said, to make us "see," what is here to be seen? Surely not that life is wholly senseless and contemptible and that our fitting end is in senseless pain.

Do you agree that the story's ending is unsatisfactory? Does the violence "make us 'see,'" or is it just gratuitous? Explain.

Related Works: "The Cask of Amontillado" (p. 227), "The Lottery" (p. 319), "Richard Cory" (p. 877)

⟩ **SHEILA WATSON** (1909–1998) is the author of *The Double Hook* (1959), which is widely considered to be Canada's first modern novel. Watson was born and lived much of her early childhood in New Westminster, British Columbia. After she finished her studies at the University of British Columbia, Watson worked in a series of short-term teaching posts that took her across much of Canada. She completed her doctoral studies at the University of Toronto under the direction of Marshall McLuhan, a pioneering theorist in the study of the media, in 1965. *The Double Hook* is a highly poetic book incorporating a cyclical narrative structure that depicts the struggles of a small group of people living in isolation. In addition to *The Double Hook*, Watson wrote a second novel, *Deep Hollow Creek*, in the 1930s, but this novel was not published until 1992. This book is semi-autobiographical and is based on her experiences as a teacher in the interior of British Columbia. The following story, "Antigone," is taken from her collection of short stories entitled *Four Stories*.

⟩ ⟩ ⟩

SHEILA WATSON

Antigone[1]
(1984)

My father ruled a kingdom on the right bank of the river. He ruled it with a firm hand and a stout heart though he was often more troubled than Moses,[2] who was simply trying to bring a stubborn and moody people under God's yoke. My father ruled men who thought they were gods or the instruments

---

[1] In Greek mythology, Antigone is the daughter of Oedipus and Jocasta. She is sentenced to death by Creon (her uncle) because she defies his order not to bury her brother Polynices, whom Creon considered an enemy. Antigone hangs herself, and Haemon, Creon's son, who loves Antigone, also commits suicide.

[2] Hebrew prophet who wrote down the Ten Commandments on tablets of stone.

of gods or, at very least, god-afflicted and god-pursued. He ruled Atlas[3] who held up the sky, and Hermes[4] who went on endless messages, and Helen[5] who'd been hatched from an egg, and Pan[6] the gardener, and Kallisto[7] the bear, and too many others to mention by name. Yet my father had no thunderbolt, no trident, no helmet of darkness. His subjects were delivered bound into his hands. He merely watched over them as the hundred-handed ones watched over the dethroned Titans so that they wouldn't bother Hellas again.

Despite the care which my father took to maintain an atmosphere of sober common sense in his whole establishment, there were occasional outbursts of self-indulgence which he could not control. For instance, I have seen Helen walking naked down the narrow cement path under the chestnut trees for no better reason, I suppose, than that the day was hot and the white flowers themselves lay naked and expectant in the sunlight. And I have seen Atlas forget the sky while he sat eating the dirt which held him up. These were things which I was not supposed to see.

If my father had been as sensible through and through as he was thought to be, he would have packed me off to boarding school when I was old enough to be disciplined by men. Instead he kept me at home with my two cousins who, except for the accident of birth, might as well have been my sisters. Today I imagine people concerned with our welfare would take such an environment into account. At the time I speak of most people thought us fortunate—especially the girls whose father's affairs had come to an unhappy issue. I don't like to revive old scandal and I wouldn't except to deny it; but it takes only a few impertinent newcomers in any community to force open cupboards which have been decently sealed by time. However, my father was so busy setting his kingdom to rights that he let weeds grow up in his own garden.

As I said, if my father had had all his wits about him he would have sent me to boarding school—and Antigone and Ismene too. I might have fallen in love with the headmaster's daughter and Antigone might have learned that no human being can be right always. She might have found out besides that from the seeds of eternal justice grow madder flowers than any which Pan grew in the gardens of my father's kingdom.

5 Between the kingdom which my father ruled and the wilderness flows a river. It is this river which I am crossing now. Antigone is with me.

How often can we cross the same river, Antigone asks.

---

[3] In Greek mythology, Atlas is the Titan who is punished for his participation in the Revolt of the Titans and must hold up the sky by himself.

[4] In Greek mythology, Hermes is the messenger of the gods, and he is usually depicted with wings on his sandals.

[5] In Greek mythology, Zeus visits Leda in the form of a swan, and their union results in an egg out of which hatches Helen.

[6] Pan is the Greek god of shepherds and flocks.

[7] In Greek mythology, Kallisto was changed into a bear to protect her or as punishment.

Her persistence annoys me. Besides, Heraklitos[8] made nonsense of her question years ago. He saw a river too—the Inachos, the Kephissos, the Lethaios. The name doesn't matter. He said: See how quickly the water flows. However agile a man is, however nimbly he swims, or runs, or flies, the water slips away before him. See, even as he sets down his foot the water is displaced by the stream which crowds along in the shadow of its flight.

But after all, Antigone says, one must admit that it is the same kind of water. The oolichans[9] run in it as they ran last year and the year before. The gulls cry above the same banks. Boats drift towards the Delta and circle back against the current to gather up the catch.

At any rate, I tell her, we're standing on a new bridge. We are standing so high that the smell of mud and river weeds passes under us out to the straits. The unbroken curve of the bridge protects the eye from details of river life. The bridge is fool-proof as a clinic's passport to happiness.

10   The old bridge still spans the river, but the cat-walk with its cracks and knot-holes, with its gap between planking and handrail has been torn down. The centre arch still grinds open to let boats up and down the river, but a child can no longer be walked on it or swung out on it beyond the water-gauge at the very centre of the flood.

I've known men who scorned any kind of bridge, Antigone says. Men have walked into the water, she says, or, impatient, have jumped from the bridge into the river below.

But these, I say, didn't really want to cross the river. They went Persephone's[10] way, cradled in the current's arms, down the long halls under the pink feet of the gulls, under the booms and towlines, under the soft bellies of the fish.

Antigone looks at me.

There's no coming back, she says, if one goes far enough.

15   I know she's going to speak of her own misery and I won't listen. Only a god has the right to say: Look what I suffer. Only a god should say: What more ought I to have done for you that I have not done?

Once in winter, she says, a man walked over the river.

Taking advantage of nature, I remind her, since the river had never frozen before.

Yet he escaped from the penitentiary, she says. He escaped from the guards walking round the walls or standing with their guns in the sentry-boxes at the four corners of the enclosure. He escaped.

Not without risk, I say. He had to test the strength of the ice himself. Yet safer perhaps than if he had crossed by the old bridge where he might have slipped through a knot-hole or tumbled out through the railing.

---

[8] Greek philosopher (c. 500 BCE) who believed that the world is constantly changing. He said "you cannot step twice into the same river."

[9] An oolichan (or eulachon) is a small fish of the Pacific North-West. It is prized for its oil.

[10] In Greek mythology, Persephone is the queen of the underworld.

20   He did escape, she persists, and lived forever on the far side of the river in the Alaska tea and bulrushes. For where, she asks, can a man go farther than to the outermost edge of the world?

The habitable world, as I've said, is on the right bank of the river. Here is the market with its market stalls—the coops of hens, the long-tongued geese, the haltered calf, the bearded goat, the shoving pigs, and the empty bodies of cows and sheep and rabbits hanging on iron hooks. My father's kingdom provides asylum in the suburbs. Near it are the convent, the churches, and the penitentiary. Above these on the hill the cemetery looks down on the people and on the river itself.

It is a world spread flat, tipped up into the sky so that men and women bend forward, walking as men walk when they board a ship at high tide. This is the world I feel with my feet. It is the world I see with my eyes.

I remember standing once with Antigone and Ismene in the square just outside the gates of my father's kingdom. Here from a bust set high on a cairn the stone eyes of Simon Fraser[11] look from his stone face over the river that he found.

It is the head that counts, Ismene said.

25   It's no better than an urn, Antigone said, one of the urns we see when we climb to the cemetery above.

And all I could think was that I didn't want an urn, only a flat green grave with a chain about it.

A chain won't keep out the dogs, Antigone said.

But his soul could swing on it, Ismene said, like a bird blown on a branch in the wind.

And I remember Antigone's saying: The cat drags its belly on the ground and the rat sharpens its tooth in the ivy.

30   I should have loved Ismene, but I didn't. It was Antigone I loved. I should have loved Ismene because, although she walked the flat world with us, she managed somehow to see it round.

The earth is an oblate spheroid, she'd say. And I knew that she saw it there before her comprehensible and whole like a tangerine spiked through and held in place while it rotated on the axis of one of Nurse's steel sock needles. The earth was a tangerine and she saw the skin peeled off and the world parcelled out into neat segments, each segment sweet and fragrant in its own skin.

It's the head that counts, she said.

In her own head she made diagrams to live by, cut and fashioned after the eternal patterns spied out by Plato as he rummaged about in the sewing basket of the gods.

I should have loved Ismene. She would live now in some prefabricated and perfect chrysolite by some paradigm which made love round and whole. She would simply live and leave destruction in the purgatorial ditches outside her own walled paradise.

---

[11] (1776–1862), fur trader and explorer.

35   Antigone is different. She sees the world flat as I do and feels it tip beneath her feet. She has walked in the market and seen the living animals penned and the dead hanging stiff on their hooks. Yet she defies what she sees with a defiance which is almost denial. Like Atlas she tries to keep the vaulted sky from crushing the flat earth. Like Hermes she brings a message that there is life if one can escape to it in the brush and the bulrushes in some dim Hades beyond the river. It is defiance not belief and I tell her that this time we walk the bridge to a walled cave where we can deny death no longer.

      Yet she asks her question still. And standing there I tell her that Heraklitos has made nonsense of her question. I should have loved Ismene for she would have taught me what Plato meant when he said in all earnest that the union of the soul with the body is in no way better than dissolution. I expect that she understood things which Antigone is too proud to see.

      I turn away from her and flatten my elbows on the high wall of the bridge. I look back at my father's kingdom. I see the terraces rolling down from the red-brick buildings with their barred windows. I remember hands shaking the bars and hear fingers tearing up paper and stuffing it through the meshes. Diktynna,[12] mother of nets and high leaping fear. O Artemis,[13] mistress of wild beasts and wild men.

      The inmates are beginning to come out on the screened verandas. They pace up and down in straight lines or stand silent like figures which appear at the same time each day from some depths inside a clock.

      On the upper terrace Pan the gardener is shifting sprinklers with a hooked stick. His face is shadowed by the brim of his hat. He moves as economically as an animal between the beds of lobelia and geranium. It is high noon.

40   Antigone has cut out a piece of sod and has scooped out a grave. The body lies in a coffin in the shade of the magnolia tree. Antigone and I are standing. Ismene is sitting between two low angled branches of the monkey puzzle tree. Her lap is filled with daisies. She slits the stem of one daisy and pulls the stem of another through it. She is making a chain for her neck and a crown for her hair.

      Antigone reaches for a branch of the magnolia. It is almost beyond her grip. The buds flame above her. She stands on a small fire of daisies which smoulder in the roots of the grass.

      I see the magnolia buds. They brood above me, whiteness feathered on whiteness. I see Antigone's face turned to the light. I hear the living birds call to the sun. I speak private poetry to myself: Between four trumpeting angels at the four corners of the earth a bride stands before the altar in a gown as white as snow.

      Yet I must have been speaking aloud because Antigone challenges me: You're mistaken. It's the winds the angels hold, the four winds of the earth.

---

[12] In Greek mythology, Diktynna is a Cretan goddess.

[13] In Greek mythology, Artemis is a goddess of wildlife and is associated with women. She is identified with Britomartis, who is identified with Diktynna.

After the just are taken to paradise the winds will destroy the earth. It's a funeral, she says, not a wedding.

She looks towards the building.

45 Someone is coming down the path from the matron's house, she says.

I notice that she has pulled one of the magnolia blossoms from the branch. I take it from her. It is streaked with brown where her hands have bruised it. The sparrow which she has decided to bury lies on its back. Its feet are clenched tight against the feathers of its breast. I put the flower in the box with it.

Someone is coming down the path. She is wearing a blue cotton dress. Her cropped head is bent. She walks slowly carrying something in a napkin.

It's Kallisto the bear, I say. Let's hurry. What will my father say if he sees us talking to one of his patients?

If we live here with him, Antigone says, what can he expect? If he spends his life trying to tame people he can't complain if you behave as if they were tame. What would your father think, she says, if he saw us digging in the Institution lawn?

50 Pan comes closer. I glower at him. There's no use speaking to him. He's deaf and dumb.

Listen, I say to Antigone, my father's not unreasonable. Kallisto thinks she's a bear and he thinks he's a bear tamer, that's all. As for the lawn, I say quoting my father without conviction, a man must have order among his own if he is to keep order in the state.

Kallisto has come up to us. She is smiling and laughing to herself. She gives me her bundle.

Fish, she says.

I open the napkin.

55 Pink fish sandwiches, I say.

For the party, she says.

But it isn't a party, Antigone says. It's a funeral.

For the funeral breakfast, I say.

Ismene is twisting two chains of daisies into a rope. Pan has stopped pulling the sprinkler about. He is standing beside Ismene resting himself on his hooked stick. Kallisto squats down beside her. Ismene turns away, preoccupied, but she can't turn far because of Pan's legs.

> *Father said we never should*
> *Play with madmen in the wood.*

I look at Antigone.

60 It's my funeral, she says.

I go over to Ismene and gather up a handful of loose daisies from her lap. The sun reaches through the shadow of the magnolia tree.

It's my funeral, Antigone says. She moves possessively toward the body.

An ant is crawling into the bundle of sandwiches which I've put on the ground. A file of ants is marching on the sparrow's box.

I go over and drop daisies on the bird's stiff body. My voice speaks ritual words: Deliver me, O Lord, from everlasting death on this dreadful day. I tremble and am afraid.

65 The voice of a people comforts me. I look at Antigone. I look her in the eye.

It had better be a proper funeral then, I say.

Kallisto is crouched forward on her hands. Tears are running down her cheeks and she is licking them away with her tongue.

My voice rises again: I said in the midst of my days, I shall not see—

Antigone just stands there. She looks frightened, but her eyes defy me with their assertion.

70 It's my funeral, she says. It's my bird. I was the one who wanted to bury it.

She is looking for a reason. She will say something which sounds eternally right.

Things have to be buried, she says. They can't be left lying around anyhow for people to see.

Birds shouldn't die, I tell her. They have wings. Cats and rats haven't wings.

Stop crying, she says to Kallisto. It's only a bird.

75 It has a bride's flower in its hand, Kallisto says.

We shall rise again, I mutter, but we shall not all be changed.

Antigone does not seem to hear me.

Behold, I say in a voice she must hear, in a moment, in the twinkling of an eye, the trumpet shall sound.

Ismene turns to Kallisto and throws the daisy chain about her neck.

80 Shall a virgin forget her adorning or a bride the ornament of her breast?

Kallisto is lifting her arms towards the tree.

The bridegroom has come, she says, white as a fall of snow. He stands above me in a great ring of fire.

Antigone looks at me now.

Let's cover the bird up, she says. Your father will punish us all for making a disturbance.

85 He has on his garment, Kallisto says, and on his thigh is written King of Kings.

I look at the tree. If I could see with Kallisto's eyes I wouldn't be afraid of death, or punishment, or the penitentiary guards. I wouldn't be afraid of my father's belt or his honing strap or his bedroom slipper. I wouldn't be afraid of falling into the river through a knot-hole in the bridge.

But, as I look, I see the buds falling like burning lamps and I hear the sparrow twittering in its box: Woe, woe, woe because of the three trumpets which are yet to sound.

Kallisto is on her knees. She is growling like a bear. She lumbers over to the sandwiches and mauls them with her paw.

Ismene stands alone for Pan the gardener has gone.

90   Antigone is fitting a turf in place above the coffin. I go over and press
the edge of the turf with my feet. Ismene has caught me by the hand.

Go away, Antigone says.

I see my father coming down the path. He has an attendant with him.
In front of them walks Pan holding the sprinkler hook like a spear.

What are you doing here? my father asks.

Burying a bird, Antigone says.

95   Here? my father asks again.

Where else could I bury it? Antigone says.

My father looks at her.

This ground is public property, he says. No single person has any right
to an inch of it.

I've taken six inches, Antigone says. Will you dig up the bird again?

100   Some of his subjects my father restrained since they were moved to
throw themselves from high places or to tear one another to bits from jealousy or rage. Others who disturbed the public peace he taught to walk in the
airing courts or to work in the kitchen or in the garden.

If men live at all, my father said, it is because discipline saves their life
for them.

From Antigone he simply turned away.

Reading and Reacting

1. Who is the original Antigone? Why is it important to know the
   meaning of the allusion to her and to the other literary figures in
   the story?
2. Does the information that Sheila Watson grew up on the grounds
   of a mental institution because her father was the chief doctor
   have any bearing on your reaction to the story?
3. Who is telling the story? Why is this point of view chosen rather
   than Antigone's?
4. What possible commentary could the story be making on myth
   and madness?
5. Why is Antigone so determined to bury the bird? What is the significance of the "six inches" of dirt that she has used?
6. How is a mental institution like a kingdom?
7. Explain the description of Ismene's ordering of her life: "In her
   own head she made diagrams to live by, cut and fashioned after
   the eternal patterns spied out by Plato as he rummaged about in
   the sewing basket of the gods" (33). Does Watson's image of the
   sewing basket make Plato's ideas accessible?
8. **Journal Entry** Imagine that you are in a mental institution,
   either as a patient or a worker. How can you adequately explain to
   an outsider which group claims you as a member?
9. **Critical Perspective** The editors of *An Anthology of Canadian
   Literature in English* say of Watson's stories: "Delicate, fascinating
   fables, they resemble contemporary short stories of manners and

nuance except for one striking feature—their principal characters have names drawn from Greek mythology. The effect of this technique is to overlay the personal experiences at the core of these stories with the qualities of a mythic cycle." Do you agree? Can you think of other reasons why Watson may have chosen this feature in her stories?

Related Works: "A Rose for Emily" (p. 90), "Araby" (p. 267), "Death by Landscape" (p. 335)

◆ WRITING SUGGESTIONS: STYLE, TONE, AND LANGUAGE

1. "Soldier's Home" does not have a conventional plot in which characters grow and change and conflicts are resolved. For this reason, it might be argued that in this story language takes on more of a central role than it plays in other stories. Write an essay in which you examine this idea as it applies to "Soldier's Home" and to any other story in this text.

2. All of the stories in this chapter present characters who are outsiders or misfits in their social milieus. Choose two or three characters, and explain why each is estranged from others and what efforts, if any, each makes to reconcile with society. Be sure to show how language helps to convey each character's alienation.

3. In each of the chapter's four stories, the title communicates a good deal of information in a very few words. Write an essay in which you explain what each title communicates about the story's theme. In your thesis, try to draw a conclusion about the function of a title in a fictional work.

4. Imagine The Misfit in a prison cell, relating the violent incident at the end of "A Good Man Is Hard to Find" to another prisoner—or to a member of the clergy. Would his tone be boastful? Regretful? Apologetic? Defiant? Would he use the elaborate poetic style he sometimes uses in the story or more straightforward language? Tell his version of the incident in his own words.

5. Try to write "Antigone" using an omniscient narrator. Or try to write the story as if you can only see and hear the characters, not look into their minds.

6. Choose two stories and change the names of the main characters to mythological names. Explain the reasons for your choices.

CHAPTER 9

Symbol and Allegory

◇   ◆   ◇

Symbols and metaphors share several qualities, but they are far from being synonymous. Both are figurative expressions that transcend literal language. Both rely heavily on implication and suggestion. Both present the abstract in concrete terms, and both can be interpreted with varying degrees of openness or specificity. They differ, however, in important ways. A symbol expands language by substitution, a metaphor by comparison and interaction. A symbol does not ask a reader to merge two concepts but rather to let one thing suggest another. A symbol derives its meaning through development and consensus, a metaphor through invention and originality. A symbol is strengthened by repetition, but a metaphor is destroyed by it.

ROLAND BARTEL, *Metaphors and Symbols*

I think one of the worst things any writer can do is impose symbols. That's a dreadful thing, to nail them on. It should be like driftwood. You don't nail the knots on. The water washes and erodes and what's left are these hard knobs. That is the way symbols should be. They should rise out of the material naturally.

W. D. VALGARDSON, *Strong Voices*

The truth is, I do indeed include images in my work, but I don't think of them as symbols, ... To me, symbols are stand-in's for abstract ideas. They belong to the High School of Hidden Meanings: vases symbolize female orifices, broken vases symbolize a loss of virginity and innocence. Heavy stuff. I prefer using images. My writing tends toward the Elementary School of Word Pictures: the accidental shattering of a vase in an empty room changes the emotions of a scene from sanity to uneasiness, perhaps even to dread. The point is, if there are symbols in my work they exist largely by accident or through someone else's interpretive design.

AMY TAN, *The Threepenny Review*

◇   ◆   ◇

A **symbol** is a person, object, action, place, or event that, in addition to its literal meaning, suggests a more complex meaning or range of meanings. **Universal** or **archetypal symbols,** such as the Old Man, the Mother, or the Grim Reaper, are so much a part of human experience that they suggest much the same thing to most people. **Conventional symbols** are also likely to suggest the same thing to most people, provided the people have common cultural and social assumptions (a rose suggests love, a skull and crossbones denotes poison). Such symbols are often used as a kind of short-hand in films, popular literature, and advertising, where they encourage automatic responses.

Conventional symbols such as the British Union Jack, the Canadian Maple Leaf, and the American Stars and Stripes can evoke powerful feelings of pride and patriotism in a group of people who share the same orientation to the symbol. Symbols used in works of literature can function in much the same way, enabling writers to convey particular emotions or messages with a high degree of predictability. Thus, spring can be expected to suggest rebirth and promise; autumn, declining years and powers; summer, youth and beauty. Because a writer expects a dark forest to evoke fear, or a rainbow to communicate hope, he or she can be quite confident in using such an image to convey a particular idea or mood (provided the audience shares the writer's frame or reference).

Many symbols, however, suggest different things to different people. (For one thing, different cultures may react differently to the same symbols. In Canada, for example, an owl suggests wisdom; in India it suggests just the opposite.) Thus, symbols enrich meaning, expanding the possibilities for interpretation and for reader interaction with the text. Because they are so potentially rich, symbols have the power to open up a work of literature.

LITERARY SYMBOLS

◆ ◆ ◆

Both universal and conventional symbols can function as **literary symbols** that take on additional meanings in a particular work. For instance, a watch or clock denotes time; as a symbol, it might suggest the passing of time; as a literary symbol in a particular work, it might also convey anything from a character's inability to recapture the past to the idea of time running out—or, it might suggest more than one of these ideas.

Considering an object's possible symbolic significance can suggest a variety of ways to interpret a text. For instance, William Faulkner focuses attention on an unseen watch in a pivotal scene in "A Rose for Emily" (p. 90). Readers' first view of Emily Grierson reveals her as "a small, fat woman in black, with a thin gold chain descending to her waist and van-ishing into her belt." Several sentences later the narrator returns to the watch, noting that Emily's visitors "could hear the invisible watch ticking at the end of the gold chain." Like these visitors, readers are drawn to the unseen watch as it ticks away. Because Emily is portrayed as a woman living in the past, readers can assume that the watch is intended to reinforce the impression that she cannot see that time (the watch) has moved on. The vivid picture of the pale, plump woman in the musty room with the watch invisibly ticking does indeed suggest both that she has been left back in time and that she remains unaware of the progress around her. Thus, the symbol enriches both the depiction of character and the story's theme.

In "Barn Burning" (p. 234), another Faulkner story, the clock is a more complex symbol. The itinerant Snopes family is without financial security and apparently without a future. The clock the mother carries from shack to shack—"The clock inlaid with mother-of-pearl, which would not run, stopped at some fourteen minutes past two o'clock of a dead and forgotten day and time, which had been [Sarty's] mother's dowry"—is their only possession of value. The fact that the clock no longer works seems at first to suggest that time has run out for the family. On another level, the clock stands in pathetic contrast to Major de Spain's grand home, with its gold and glitter and Oriental rugs. Knowing that the clock was part of the mother's dowry, and that a dowry suggests a promise, readers may decide that the broken clock symbolizes lost hope; the fact that the mother still clings to the clock, however, could suggest her refusal to give up hope.

As you read, you should not try to find the one exact equivalent for each symbol; in fact, this kind of search is very limiting and not very productive. Instead, consider the different meanings a symbol might suggest. Then, consider how these various interpretations enrich other elements of the story and the work as a whole.

Recognizing Symbols

When is a clock just a clock, and when is it also a symbol with a meaning or meanings beyond its literal significance? If a character waiting for a friend glances once at his or her watch to verify the time, there is probably nothing symbolic about the watch or about the act of looking at it. If, however, the watch keeps appearing again and again in the story, at key moments; if the narrator devotes a good deal of time to describing it; if it is placed in a conspicuous physical location; if characters keep noticing it and commenting on its presence; if it is lost (or found) at a critical moment; if its function in some way parallels the development of plot or character (for instance, if it stops as a relationship ends or as a character dies); if the story's opening or closing paragraph focuses on the timepiece; or if the story is called "The Watch"—then the watch most likely has symbolic significance. In other words, considering how an image is used, how often it is used, and when it appears will help you to determine whether or not it functions as a symbol.

The Purpose of Symbols

Symbols expand the possible meanings of a story, thereby heightening interest and actively involving readers in the text. In "The Lottery" (p. 319), for example, the mysterious black box has symbolic significance. It is mentioned repeatedly, and it plays a pivotal role in the story's action. Of course, the black box is important on a purely literal level: it functions as a key component of the lottery. But the box has other associations as well, and it is these associations that suggest what its symbolic significance might be.

The black wooden box is very old, a relic of many past lotteries; the narrator observes that it represents tradition. It is also closed and closely guarded, suggesting mystery and uncertainty. It is shabby, "splintered badly along one side . . . and in places faded or stained." This state of disrepair could suggest that the ritual it is part of has also deteriorated or that tradition itself has deteriorated. The box is also simple in construction and design, suggesting the primitive (and therefore perhaps outdated) nature of the ritual. This symbol encourages readers to probe the story for values and ideas, to consider and weigh the suitability of a variety of interpretations. It serves as a "hot spot" that invites questions. The answers to these questions reinforce and enrich the story's theme.

ALLEGORY
◊ ◊ ◊

An **allegory** communicates a doctrine, message, or moral principle by making it into a narrative in which the characters personify ideas, concepts, qualities, or other abstractions. Thus, an allegory is a story with two parallel and consistent levels of meaning—one literal and one figurative. The figurative level, which offers some moral or political lesson, is the story's main concern. The allegorical figures are significant only because they represent something beyond their literal meaning in a fixed system.

Whereas a symbol has multiple symbolic associations as well as a literal meaning, an **allegorical figure**—a character, object, place, or event in the allegory—has just one meaning within an **allegorical framework,** the set of ideas that conveys the allegory's message. (At the simplest level, for instance, one character can stand for good and another can stand for evil.) For this reason, allegorical figures do not open up a text to various interpretations by readers the way symbols do. Because the purpose of allegory is to communicate a particular lesson, readers are not encouraged to speculate about the allegory's possible meanings; each element has only one equivalent, which readers must discover if they are to make sense of the story.

Naturally, the better a reader understands the political, religious, and literary assumptions of a writer, the easier it will be to recognize the allegorical significance of his or her work. John Bunyan's *The Pilgrim's Progress,* for example, is a famous seventeenth-century allegory based on the Christian doctrine of salvation. In order to appreciate the complexity of Bunyan's work, you would have to familiarize yourself with this doctrine—possibly by consulting an encyclopedia or a reference work such as *The Oxford Companion to English Literature.*

One type of allegory, called a **beast fable,** is a short tale, usually including a moral, in which animals assume human characteristics. Aesop's fables are the best-known examples of beast fables. More recently, contemporary writers have used beast fables to satirize the political and social conditions of our time. George Orwell's *Animal Farm* satirizes the power-mongering in twentieth-century societies through the use of animals who have human counterparts.

Some works contain both symbolic elements *and* allegorical elements, as Nathaniel Hawthorne's "Young Goodman Brown" (p. 307) does. The names of the story's two main characters, "Goodman" and "Faith," suggest that they fit within an allegorical system of some sort: Young Goodman Brown represents a good person who, despite his best efforts, strays from the path of righteousness; his wife, Faith, represents the quality he must hold on to in order to avoid temptation. As characters, they have no significance outside of their allegorical functions. Other elements of the story, however, are not so clear-cut. The older man whom Young Goodman Brown meets in the woods carries a staff that has carved on it "the likeness of a great black snake, so curiously wrought, that it might almost be seen to twist and wriggle itself like a living serpent." This staff, carried by a Satanic figure who represents evil and temptation, suggests the snake in the Garden of Eden, an association that neatly fits into the allegorical context of the story. Alternately, however, the staff could suggest the "slippery," ever-changing nature of sin, the difficulty people have in perceiving sin, or sexuality (which may explain Young Goodman Brown's susceptibility to temptation). This range of possible meanings suggests that the staff functions as a symbol that enriches Hawthorne's allegory.

Other stories work entirely on a symbolic level and contain no allegorical figures. "The Lottery," despite its moral overtones, is not an allegory because its characters, events, and objects are not arranged to serve one rigid, didactic purpose. In fact, many different interpretations have been suggested for this story. When it was first published in June 1948 in *The New Yorker,* some readers believed it to be a story about an actual custom or ritual. As Shirley Jackson reports in her essay "Biography of a Story," even those who recognized it as fiction speculated about its meaning, seeing it as (among other things) an attack on prejudice, a criticism of society's need for a scapegoat, or a treatise on witchcraft, Christian martyrdom, or village gossip. Various critics have argued that "The Lottery" is a story about the evils of violence, mob psychology, or Nazi Germany. The fact is that no single allegorical interpretation will account for every major character, object, and event in the story.

✓ CHECKLIST: WRITING ABOUT SYMBOL AND ALLEGORY

✓ Are any universal symbols used in the work? Any conventional symbols? What is their function?

✓ Is any character, place, action, event, or object given unusual prominence or emphasis in the story? If so, does this element seem to have symbolic as well as literal value?

✓ What possible meanings does each symbol suggest?

✓ How do symbols help to depict the story's characters?

✓ How do symbols help to characterize the story's setting?

✓ How do symbols help to advance the story's plot?

✓ Are any of the symbols related? Taken together, do they seem to support a common theme?

✓ Does the story have a moral or didactic purpose? What is the message, idea, or moral principle the story seeks to convey?

✓ What equivalent may be assigned to each allegorical figure in the story?

✓ Does the story combine allegorical figures and symbols? How do they work together in the story?

◈ **NATHANIEL HAWTHORNE** (1804–1864) was born in Salem, Massachusetts, the great-great-grandson of a judge who presided over the infamous Salem witch trials. After his sea captain father was killed on a voyage when Hawthorne was four years old, his childhood was one of genteel poverty. An uncle paid for his education at Bowdoin College in Maine, where Hawthorne's friends included a future president of the United States, Franklin Pierce, who in 1853 would appoint him U.S. consul in Liverpool, England. Hawthorne published four novels—*The Scarlet Letter* (1850), *The House of the Seven Gables* (1851), *The Blithedale Romance* (1852), and *The Marble Faun* (1860)—and more than one hundred short stories and sketches.

Hawthorne referred to his own work as *romance.* He used this term to mean not an escape from reality, but rather a method of confronting "the depths of our common nature" and "the truth of the heart." His stories probe the dark side of human nature and frequently paint a world that is virtuous on the surface but (as Young Goodman Brown comes to believe) "one stain of guilt, one mighty blood spot" beneath. Hawthorne's stories often emphasize the ambiguity of human experience. For example, the reader is left to wonder whether Goodman Brown actually saw a witches' coven or dreamed a dream. For Hawthorne, what is important is Brown's recognition that evil may be found everywhere. "Young Goodman Brown," as Hawthorne's neighbour and friend Herman Melville once said, is a tale "as deep as Dante."

NATHANIEL HAWTHORNE

Young Goodman Brown
(1835)

Young Goodman Brown came forth at sunset, into the street of Salem village, but put his head back, after crossing the threshold, to exchange a parting kiss with his young wife. And Faith, as the wife was aptly named, thrust her own pretty head into the street, letting the wind play with the pink ribbons of her cap, while she called to Goodman Brown.

"Dearest heart," whispered she, softly and rather sadly, when her lips were close to his ear, "prithee, put off your journey until sunrise, and sleep in your own bed to-night. A lone woman is troubled with such dreams and such thoughts, that she's afeard of herself, sometimes. Pray, tarry with me this night, dear husband, of all nights in the year!"

"My love and my Faith," replied young Goodman Brown, "of all nights in the year, this one night must I tarry away from thee. My journey, as thou callest it, forth and back again, must needs be done 'twixt now and sunrise. What, my sweet, pretty wife, dost thou doubt me already, and we but three months married!"

"Then God bless you!" said Faith with the pink ribbons, "and may you find all well, when you come back."

5   "Amen!" cried Goodman Brown. "Say thy prayers, dear Faith, and go to bed at dusk, and no harm will come to thee."

So they parted; and the young man pursued his way, until, being about to turn the corner by the meeting-house, he looked back and saw the head of Faith still peeping after him, with a melancholy air, in spite of her pink ribbons.

"Poor little Faith!" thought he, for his heart smote him. "What a wretch am I, to leave her on such an errand! She talks of dreams, too. Methought, as she spoke, there was trouble in her face, as if a dream had warned her what work is to be done to-night. But no, no! 't would kill her to think it. Well; she's a blessed angel on earth; and after this one night, I'll cling to her skirts and follow her to Heaven."

With this excellent resolve for the future, Goodman Brown felt himself justified in making more haste on his present evil purpose. He had taken a dreary road, darkened by all the gloomiest trees of the forest, which barely stood aside to let the narrow path creep through, and closed immediately behind. It was as lonely as could be; and there is this peculiarity in such a solitude, that the traveller knows not who may be concealed by the innumerable trunks and the thick boughs overhead; so that, with lonely footsteps, he may yet be passing through an unseen multitude.

"There may be a devilish Indian behind every tree," said Goodman Brown to himself; and he glanced fearfully behind him, as he added, "What if the devil himself should be at my very elbow!"

10   His head being turned back, he passed a crook of the road, and looking forward again, beheld the figure of a man, in grave and decent attire, seated at the foot of an old tree. He arose at Goodman Brown's approach, and walked onward, side by side with him.

"You are late, Goodman Brown," said he. "The clock of the Old South[1] was striking, as I came through Boston; and that is full fifteen minutes agone."

---

[1] Old South Church, Boston, renowned meeting place for American patriots during the Revolution.

"Faith kept me back awhile," replied the young man, with a tremor in his voice, caused by the sudden appearance of his companion, though not wholly unexpected.

It was now deep dusk in the forest, and deepest in that part of it where these two were journeying. As nearly as could be discerned, the second traveller was about fifty years old, apparently in the same rank of life as Goodman Brown, and bearing a considerable resemblance to him, though perhaps more in expression than features. Still, they might have been taken for father and son. And yet, though the elder person was as simply clad as the younger, and as simple in manner too, he had an indescribable air of one who knew the world, and would not have felt abashed at the governor's dinner-table, or in King William's court,[2] were it possible that his affairs should call him thither. But the only thing about him that could be fixed upon as remarkable, was his staff, which bore the likeness of a great black snake, so curiously wrought, that it might almost be seen to twist and wriggle itself like a living serpent. This, of course, must have been an ocular deception, assisted by the uncertain light.

"Come, Goodman Brown!" cried his fellow-traveller, "this is a dull pace for the beginning of a journey. Take my staff, if you are so soon weary."

15 "Friend," said the other, exchanging his slow pace for a full stop, "having kept covenant by meeting thee here, it is my purpose now to return whence I came. I have scruples, touching the matter thou wot'st of."

"Sayest thou so?" replied he of the serpent, smiling apart. "Let us walk on, nevertheless, reasoning as we go, and if I convince thee not, thou shalt turn back. We are but a little way in the forest, yet."

"Too far, too far!" exclaimed the goodman, unconsciously resuming his walk. "My father never went into the woods on such an errand, nor his father before him. We have been a race of honest men and good Christians, since the days of the martyrs. And shall I be the first of the name of Brown that ever took this path and kept—"

"Such company, thou wouldst say," observed the elder person, interrupting his pause. "Well said, Goodman Brown! I have been as well acquainted with your family as with ever a one among the Puritans; and that's no trifle to say. I helped your grandfather, the constable, when he lashed the Quaker woman so smartly through the streets of Salem. And it was I that brought your father a pitch-pine knot, kindled at my own hearth, to set fire to an Indian village, in King Philip's war.[3] They were my good friends, both; and many a pleasant walk have we had along this path, and returned merrily after midnight. I would fain be friends with you, for their sake."

"If it be as thou sayest," replied Goodman Brown, "I marvel they never spoke of these matters. Or, verily, I marvel not, seeing that the least rumor

---

[2] William III, king of England from 1689 to 1702.

[3] A war of Indian resistance, led by King Philip, or Metacomet, of the Wampanoags. The war, intended to halt expansion of English settlers in Massachusetts, collapsed after King Philip's death in August 1676.

of the sort would have driven them from New England. We are a people of prayer, and good works to boot, and abide no such wickedness."

20   "Wickedness or not," said the traveller with the twisted staff, "I have a very general acquaintance here in New England. The deacons of many a church have drunk the communion wine with me; the selectmen, of divers towns, make me their chairman; and a majority of the Great and General Court are firm supporters of my interest. The governor and I, too—but these are state secrets."

"Can this be so!" cried Goodman Brown, with a stare of amazement at his undisturbed companion. "Howbeit, I have nothing to do with the governor and council; they have their own ways, and are no rule for a simple husbandman like me. But, were I to go on with thee, how should I meet the eye of that good old man, our minister, at Salem village? Oh, his voice would make me tremble, both Sabbath-day and lecture-day!"[4]

Thus far, the elder traveller had listened with due gravity, but now burst into a fit of irrepressible mirth, shaking himself so violently, that his snake-like staff actually seemed to wriggle in sympathy.

"Ha, ha, ha!" shouted he, again and again; then composing himself, "Well, go on, Goodman Brown, go on; but, prithee, don't kill me with laughing!"

"Well, then, to end the matter at once," said Goodman Brown, considerably nettled, "there is my wife, Faith. It would break her dear little heart; and I'd rather break my own!"

25   "Nay, if that be the case," answered the other, "e'en go thy ways, Goodman Brown. I would not, for twenty old women like the one hobbling before us, that Faith should come to any harm."

As he spoke, he pointed his staff at a female figure on the path, in whom Goodman Brown recognized a very pious and exemplary dame, who had taught him his catechism in youth, and was still his moral and spiritual adviser, jointly with the minister and Deacon Gookin.

"A marvel, truly, that Goody[5] Cloyse should be so far in the wilderness, at nightfall!" said he. "But, with your leave, friend, I shall take a cut through the woods, until we have left this Christian woman behind. Being a stranger to you, she might ask whom I was consorting with, and whither I was going."

"Be it so," said his fellow-traveller. "Betake you to the woods, and let me keep the path."

Accordingly, the young man turned aside, but took care to watch his companion, who advanced softly along the road, until he had come within a staff's length of the old dame. She, meanwhile, was making the best of her way, with singular speed for so aged a woman, and mumbling some indis-

---

[4] The day of the midweek sermon, usually Thursday.

[5] A contraction of "Goodwife," a term of politeness used in addressing a woman of humble station. Goody Cloyse, like Goody Cory and Martha Carrier, who appear later in the story, was one of the Salem "witches" sentenced in 1692.

tinct words, a prayer, doubtless, as she went. The traveller put forth his staff, and touched her withered neck with what seemed the serpent's tail.

30 "The devil!" screamed the pious old lady.

"Then Goody Cloyse knows her old friend?" observed the traveller, confronting her, and leaning on his writhing stick.

"Ah, forsooth, and is it your worship, indeed?" cried the good dame. "Yea, truly is it, and in the very image of my old gossip, Goodman Brown, the grandfather of the silly fellow that now is. But, would your worship believe it? my broomstick hath strangely disappeared, stolen, as I suspect, by that unhanged witch, Goody Cory, and that, too, when I was all anointed with the juice of smallage and cinque-foil and wolf's bane—"[6]

"Mingled with fine wheat and the fat of a new-born babe," said the shape of old Goodman Brown.

"Ah, your worship knows the recipe," cried the old lady, cackling aloud. "So, as I was saying, being all ready for the meeting, and no horse to ride on, I made up my mind to foot it; for they tell me there is a nice young man to be taken into communion to-night. But now your good worship will lend me your arm, and we shall be there in a twinkling."

35 "That can hardly be," answered her friend. "I may not spare you my arm, Goody Cloyse, but here is my staff, if you will."

So saying, he threw it down at her feet, where, perhaps, it assumed life, being one of the rods which its owner had formerly lent to the Egyptian Magi. Of this fact, however, Goodman Brown could not take cognizance. He had cast his eyes in astonishment, and looking down again, beheld neither Goody Cloyse nor the serpentine staff, but his fellow-traveller alone, who waited for him as calmly as if nothing had happened.

"That old woman taught me my catechism!" said the young man; and there was a world of meaning in this simple comment.

They continued to walk onward, while the elder traveller exhorted his companion to make good speed and persevere in the path, discoursing so aptly, that his arguments seemed rather to spring up in the bosom of his auditor, than to be suggested by himself. As they went he plucked a branch of maple, to serve for a walking-stick, and began to strip it of the twigs and little boughs, which were wet with evening dew. The moment his fingers touched them, they became strangely withered and dried up, as with a week's sunshine. Thus the pair proceeded, at a good free pace, until suddenly, in a gloomy hollow of the road, Goodman Brown sat himself down on the stump of a tree, and refused to go any farther.

"Friend," said he, stubbornly, "my mind is made up. Not another step will I budge on this errand. What if a wretched old woman do choose to go to the devil, when I thought she was going to Heaven! Is that any reason why I should quit my dear Faith, and go after her?"

---

[6] All plants believed to have magical powers. "Smallage" is wild celery.

40   "You will think better of this by and by," said his acquaintance, composedly. "Sit here and rest yourself awhile; and when you feel like moving again, there is my staff to help you along."

Without more words, he threw his companion the maple stick, and was as speedily out of sight as if he had vanished into the deepening gloom. The young man sat a few moments by the roadside, applauding himself greatly, and thinking with how clear a conscience he should meet the minister, in his morning walk, nor shrink from the eye of good old Deacon Gookin. And what calm sleep would be his, that very night, which was to have been spent so wickedly, but purely and sweetly now, in the arms of Faith! Amidst these pleasant and praiseworthy meditations, Goodman Brown heard the tramp of horses along the road, and deemed it advisable to conceal himself within the verge of the forest, conscious of the guilty purpose that had brought him thither, though now so happily turned from it.

On came the hoof-tramps and the voices of the riders, two grave old voices, conversing soberly as they drew near. These mingled sounds appeared to pass along the road, within a few yards of the young man's hiding-place; but owing, doubtless, to the depth of the gloom, at that particular spot, neither the travellers nor their steeds were visible. Though their figures brushed the small boughs by the wayside, it could not be seen that they intercepted, even for a moment, the faint gleam from the strip of bright sky, athwart which they must have passed. Goodman Brown alternately crouched and stood on tiptoe, pulling aside the branches, and thrusting forth his head as far as he durst, without discerning so much as a shadow. It vexed him the more, because he could have sworn, were such a thing possible, that he recognized the voices of the minister and Deacon Gookin, jogging along quietly, as they were wont to do, when bound to some ordination or ecclesiastical council. While yet within hearing, one of the riders stopped to pluck a switch.

"Of the two, reverend Sir," said the voice like the deacon's, "I had rather miss an ordination dinner than to-night's meeting. They tell me that some of our community are to be here from Falmouth and beyond, and others from Connecticut and Rhode Island; besides several of the Indian powwows, who, after their fashion, know almost as much deviltry as the best of us. Moreover, there is a goodly young woman to be taken into communion."

"Mighty well, Deacon Gookin!" replied the solemn old tones of the minister. "Spur up, or we shall be late. Nothing can be done, you know, until I get on the ground."

45   The hoofs clattered again, and the voices, talking so strangely in the empty air, passed on through the forest, where no church had ever been gathered, nor solitary Christian prayed. Whither, then, could these holy men be journeying, so deep into the heathen wilderness? Young Goodman Brown caught hold of a tree, for support, being ready to sink down on the ground, faint and over-burthened with the heavy sickness of his heart. He looked up to the sky, doubting whether there really was a Heaven above him. Yet, there was the blue arch, and the stars brightening in it.

"With Heaven above, and Faith below, I will yet stand firm against the devil!" cried Goodman Brown.

While he still gazed upward, into the deep arch of the firmament, and had lifted his hands to pray, a cloud, though no wind was stirring, hurried across the zenith, and hid the brightening stars. The blue sky was still visible, except directly overhead, where this black mass of cloud was sweeping swiftly northward. Aloft in the air, as if from the depths of the cloud, came a confused and doubtful sound of voices. Once, the listener fancied that he could distinguish the accents of townspeople of his own, men and women, both pious and ungodly, many of whom he had met at the communion-table, and had seen others rioting at the tavern. The next moment, so indistinct were the sounds, he doubted whether he had heard aught but the murmur of the old forest, whispering without a wind. Then came a stronger swell of those familiar tones, heard daily in the sunshine, at Salem village, but never, until now, from a cloud at night. There was one voice, of a young woman, uttering lamentations, yet with an uncertain sorrow, and entreating for some favor, which, perhaps, it would grieve her to obtain. And all the unseen multitude, both saints and sinners, seemed to encourage her onward.

"Faith!" shouted Goodman Brown, in a voice of agony and desperation; and the echoes of the forest mocked him, crying—"Faith! Faith!" as if bewildered wretches were seeking her, all through the wilderness.

The cry of grief, rage, and terror was yet piercing the night, when the unhappy husband held his breath for a response. There was a scream, drowned immediately in a louder murmur of voices fading into far-off laughter, as the dark cloud swept away, leaving the clear and silent sky above Goodman Brown. But something fluttered lightly down through the air, and caught on the branch of a tree. The young man seized it and beheld a pink ribbon.

50   "My Faith is gone!" cried he, after one stupefied moment. "There is no good on earth, and sin is but a name. Come, devil! for to thee is this world given."

And maddened with despair, so that he laughed loud and long, did Goodman Brown grasp his staff and set forth again, at such a rate, that he seemed to fly along the forest path, rather than to walk or run. The road grew wilder and drearier, and more faintly traced, and vanished at length, leaving him in the heart of the dark wilderness, still rushing onward, with the instinct that guides mortal man to evil. The whole forest was peopled with frightful sounds: the creaking of the trees, the howling of wild beasts, and the yell of Indians; while, sometimes, the wind tolled like a distant church bell, and sometimes gave a broad roar around the traveller, as if all Nature was laughing him to scorn. But he was himself the chief horror of the scene, and shrank not from its other horrors.

"Ha! ha! ha!" roared Goodman Brown, when the wind laughed at him. "Let us hear which will laugh loudest! Think not to frighten me with your deviltry! Come witch, come wizard, come Indian powwow, come devil himself! and here comes Goodman Brown. You may as well fear him as he fear you!"

In truth, all through the haunted forest, there could be nothing more frightful than the figure of Goodman Brown. On he flew, among the black pines, brandishing his staff with frenzied gestures, now giving vent to an inspiration of horrid blasphemy, and now shouting forth such laughter, as set all the echoes of the forest laughing like demons around him. The fiend in his own shape is less hideous, than when he rages in the breast of man. Thus sped the demoniac on his course, until, quivering among the trees, he saw a red light before him, as when the felled trunks and branches of a clearing have been set on fire, and throw up their lurid blaze against the sky, at the hour of midnight. He paused, in a lull of the tempest that had driven him onward, and heard the swell of what seemed a hymn, rolling solemnly from a distance, with the weight of many voices. He knew the tune. It was a familiar one in the choir of the village meeting-house. The verse died heavily away, and was lengthened by a chorus, not of human voices, but of all the sounds of the benighted wilderness, pealing in awful harmony together. Goodman Brown cried out; and his cry was lost to his own ear, by its unison with the cry of the desert.

In the interval of silence, he stole forward, until the light glared full upon his eyes. At one extremity of an open space, hemmed in by the dark wall of the forest, arose a rock, bearing some rude, natural resemblance either to an altar or a pulpit, and surrounded by four blazing pines, their tops aflame, their stems untouched, like candles at an evening meeting. The mass of foliage, that had overgrown the summit of the rock, was all on fire, blazing high into the night, and fitfully illuminating the whole field. Each pendent twig and leafy festoon was in a blaze. As the red light arose and fell, a numerous congregation alternately shone forth, then disappeared in shadow, and again grew, as it were, out of the darkness, peopling the heart of the solitary woods at once.

55   "A grave and dark-clad company!" quoth Goodman Brown.

In truth, they were such. Among them, quivering to-and-fro, between gloom and splendor, appeared faces that would be seen, next day, at the council-board of the province, and others which, Sabbath after Sabbath, looked devoutly heavenward, and benignantly over the crowded pews, from the holiest pulpits in the land. Some affirm, that the lady of the governor was there. At least, there were high dames well known to her, and wives of honored husbands, and widows a great multitude, and ancient maidens, all of excellent repute, and fair young girls, who trembled lest their mothers should espy them. Either the sudden gleams of light, flashing over the obscure field, bedazzled Goodman Brown, or he recognized a score of the church members of Salem village, famous for their especial sanctity. Good old Deacon Gookin had arrived, and waited at the skirts of that venerable saint, his reverend pastor. But, irreverently consorting with these grave, reputable, and pious people, these elders of the church, these chaste dames and dewy virgins, there were men of dissolute lives and women of spotted fame, wretches given over to all mean and filthy vice, and suspected even of horrid crimes. It was strange to see, that the good shrank not from the wicked, nor were the sinners abashed by the saints. Scattered, also, among their pale-faced enemies, were the Indian priests, or powwows, who had often scared their native forest with more hideous incantations than any known to English witchcraft.

"But, where is Faith?" thought Goodman Brown; and, as hope came into his heart, he trembled.

Another verse of the hymn arose, a slow and mournful strain, such as the pious love, but joined to words which expressed all that our nature can conceive of sin, and darkly hinted at far more. Unfathomable to mere mortals is the lore of fiends. Verse after verse was sung, and still the chorus of the desert swelled between, like the deepest tone of a mighty organ. And, with the final peal of that dreadful anthem, there came a sound, as if the roaring wind, the rushing streams, the howling beasts, and every other voice of the unconverted wilderness were mingling and according with the voice of guilty man, in homage to the prince of all. The four blazing pines threw up a loftier flame, and obscurely discovered shapes and visages of horror on the smoke-wreaths, above the impious assembly. At the same moment, the fire on the rock shot redly forth, and formed a glowing arch above its base, where now appeared a figure. With reverence be it spoken, the apparition bore no slight similitude, both in garb and manner, to some grave divine of the New England churches.

"Bring forth the converts!" cried a voice, that echoed through the field and rolled into the forest.

60   At the word, Goodman Brown stepped forth from the shadow of the trees, and approached the congregation, with whom he felt a loathful brotherhood, by the sympathy of all that was wicked in his heart. He could have well-nigh sworn, that the shape of his own dead father beckoned him to advance, looking downward from a smoke-wreath, while a woman, with dim features of despair, threw out her hand to warn him back. Was it his mother? But he had no power to retreat one step, nor to resist, even in thought, when the minister and good old Deacon Gookin seized his arms, and led him to the blazing rock. Thither came also the slender form of a veiled female, led between Goody Cloyse, that pious teacher of the catechism, and Martha Carrier, who had received the devil's promise to be queen of hell. A rampant hag was she! And there stood the proselytes, beneath the canopy of fire.

"Welcome, my children," said the dark figure, "to the communion of your race! Ye have found, thus young, your nature and your destiny. My children, look behind you!"

They turned; and flashing forth, as it were, in a sheet of flame, the fiend-worshippers were seen; the smile of welcome gleamed darkly on every visage.

"There," resumed the sable form, "are all whom ye have reverenced from youth. Ye deemed them holier than yourselves, and shrank from your own sin, contrasting it with their lives of righteousness and prayerful aspirations heavenward. Yet, here are they all, in my worshipping assembly! This night it shall be granted you to know their secret deeds; how hoary-bearded elders of the church have whispered wanton words to the young maids of their households; how many a woman, eager for widow's weeds, has given her husband a drink at bedtime, and let him sleep his last sleep in her bosom; how beardless youths have made haste to inherit their father's wealth; and how fair damsels—blush not, sweet ones!—have dug little graves in the garden, and bidden me, the sole guest, to an infant's funeral. By the sympathy of your human hearts for sin, ye shall scent out all the places—whether in church, bedchamber, street, field, or forest—where crime has been committed, and shall exult to behold the whole earth one stain of guilt, one mighty blood-spot. Far more than this! It shall be yours to penetrate, in every bosom, the deep mystery of sin, the fountain of all wicked arts, and which inexhaustibly supplies more evil impulses than human power—than my power, at its utmost!—can make manifest in deeds. And now, my children, look upon each other."

They did so; and, by the blaze of the hell-kindled torches, the wretched man beheld his Faith, and the wife her husband, trembling before that unhallowed altar.

65   "Lo! there ye stand, my children," said the figure, in a deep and solemn tone, almost sad, with its despairing awfulness, as if his once angelic nature could yet mourn for our miserable race. "Depending upon one another's hearts, ye had still hoped that virtue were not all a dream! Now are ye undeceived!—Evil is the nature of mankind. Evil must be your only happiness. Welcome, again, my children, to the communion of your race!"

"Welcome!" repeated the fiend-worshippers, in one cry of despair and triumph.

And there they stood, the only pair, as it seemed, who were yet hesitating on the verge of wickedness, in this dark world. A basin was hollowed, naturally, in the rock. Did it contain water, reddened by the lurid light? or was it blood? or, perchance, a liquid flame? Herein did the Shape of Evil dip his hand, and prepare to lay the mark of baptism upon their foreheads, that they might be partakers of the mystery of sin, more conscious of the secret guilt of others, both in deed and thought, than they could now be of their own. The husband cast one look at his pale wife, and Faith at him. What polluted wretches would the next glance show them to each other, shuddering alike at what they disclosed and what they saw!

"Faith! Faith!" cried the husband. "Look up to Heaven, and resist the Wicked One!"

Whether Faith obeyed, he knew not. Hardly had he spoken, when he found himself amid calm night and solitude, listening to a roar of the wind, which died heavily away through the forest. He staggered against the rock, and felt it chill and damp, while a hanging twig, that had been all on fire, besprinkled his cheek with the coldest dew.

70   The next morning, young Goodman Brown came slowly into the street of Salem village staring around him like a bewildered man. The good old

minister was taking a walk along the grave-yard, to get an appetite for break-fast and meditate his sermon, and bestowed a blessing, as he passed, on Goodman Brown. He shrank from the venerable saint, as if to avoid an anathema. Old Deacon Gookin was at domestic worship, and the holy words of his prayer were heard through the open window. "What God doth the wizard pray to?" quoth Goodman Brown. Goody Cloyse, that excellent old Christian, stood in the early sunshine, at her own lattice, catechising a little girl, who had brought her a pint of morning's milk. Goodman Brown snatched away the child, as from the grasp of the fiend himself. Turning the corner by the meeting-house, he spied the head of Faith, with the pink rib-bons, gazing anxiously forth, and bursting into such joy at sight of him that she skipt along the street, and almost kissed her husband before the whole village. But Goodman Brown looked sternly and sadly into her face, and passed on without a greeting.

Had Goodman Brown fallen asleep in the forest, and only dreamed a wild dream of a witch-meeting?

Be it so, if you will. But, alas! it was a dream of evil omen for young Goodman Brown. A stern, a sad, a darkly meditative, a distrustful, if not a desperate man did he become, from the night of that fearful dream. On the Sabbath day, when the congregation were singing a holy psalm, he could not listen, because an anthem of sin rushed loudly upon his ear, and drowned all the blessed strain. When the minister spoke from the pulpit, with power and fervid eloquence, and with his hand on the open Bible, of the sacred truths of our religion, and of saint-like lives and triumphant deaths, and of future bliss or misery unutterable, then did Goodman Brown turn pale, dreading lest the roof should thunder down upon the gray blas-phemer and his hearers. Often, awaking suddenly at midnight, he shrank from the bosom of Faith, and at morning or eventide, when the family knelt down at prayer, he scowled, and muttered to himself, and gazed sternly at his wife, and turned away. And when he had lived long, and was borne to his grave, a hoary corpse, followed by Faith, an aged woman, and children and grand-children, a goodly procession, besides neighbors not a few, they carved no hopeful verse upon his tombstone; for his dying hour was gloom.

READING AND REACTING

1. Who is the narrator of "Young Goodman Brown"? What advantages does the narrative point of view give the author?
2. What does Young Goodman Brown mean when he says "of all nights in the year, this one must I tarry away from thee" (3)? What is important about *this* night, and why does Young Goodman Brown believe he must journey "'twixt now and sunrise"?
3. Is Young Goodman Brown surprised to encounter the second traveller on the road, or does he seem to expect him? What is the significance of their encounter? What do you make of the fact

that the stranger bears a strong resemblance to Young Goodman Brown?

4. What sins are the various characters Young Goodman Brown meets in the woods guilty of committing?

5. "Young Goodman Brown" has two distinct settings: Salem and the woods. What are the differences between these settings? What significance does each have in the story?

6. Which figures in the story are allegorical, and which are symbols? On what evidence do you base your conclusions?

7. Why do the people gather in the woods? Why do they attend the ceremony?

8. Explain the change that takes place in Young Goodman Brown at the end of the story. Why can he not listen to the singing of holy psalms or to the minister's sermons? What causes him to turn away from Faith and die in gloom?

9. **JOURNAL ENTRY** At the end of the story the narrator suggests that Goodman Brown might have fallen asleep and imagined his encounter with the witches. Do you think the events are all a dream?

10. **CRITICAL PERSPECTIVE** In *The Power of Blackness*, his classic study of nineteenth-century American writers, Harry Levin observes that Hawthorne had doubts about conventional religion. This, Levin believes, is why all efforts to read an enlightening theological message into Hawthorne's works are "doomed to failure."

What comment do you think Hawthorne is making in "Young Goodman Brown" about religious faith?

Related Works: "Town and Country Lovers" (p. 80), "The Lottery" (p. 319), "La Belle Dame sans Merci: A Ballad" (p. 850).

◊ **SHIRLEY JACKSON** (1916–1965) is best known for her restrained tales of horror and the supernatural, most notably her novel *The Haunting of Hill House* (1959) and the short story "The Lottery" (1948). Among her other works are two novels dealing with divided personalities—*The Bird's Nest* (1954) and *We Have Always Lived in the Castle* (1962)—and two collections of comic tales about her children and family life, *Life among the Savages* (1953) and *Raising Demons* (1957). A posthumous collection of stories, *Just an Ordinary Day* (1997), resulted from the discovery of a box of some of Jackson's unpublished papers in a Vermont barn and her heirs' subsequent search for other uncollected works.

Jackson was an intense, self-destructive, contradictory personality: a witty hostess to crowds of literary friends; a self-described witch, clairvoyant, and student of magic; a cookie-baking "Mom" who wrote chilling tales between loads of laundry. With her husband, literary critic Stanley Edgar Hyman, she settled in the small town of Bennington, Vermont, but was never accepted by the townspeople. "The Lottery" is set in much the same kind of small, hidebound town. The story's publication in *The New Yorker* magazine provoked a torrent of letters from enraged and horrified readers. Americans of the post–World War II era saw themselves as "good guys" defending the world against foreign evils. Jackson's story, written scarcely three years after the liberation of Auschwitz, told Americans something they did not want to hear—that the face of human evil could look just like their next-door neighbour. Horror master Stephen King dedicated his book *Firestarter* "to Shirley Jackson, who never had to raise her voice."

◊ ◊ ◊

SHIRLEY JACKSON

The Lottery
(1948)

The morning of June 27th was clear and sunny, with the fresh warmth of a full-summer day; the flowers were blossoming profusely and the grass was richly green. The people of the village began to gather in the square, between the post office and the bank, around ten o'clock; in some towns there were so many people that the lottery took two days and had to be started on June 26th, but in this village, where there were only about three hundred people, the whole lottery took less than two hours, so it could begin at ten o'clock in the morning and still be through in time to allow the villagers to get home for noon dinner.

The children assembled first, of course. School was recently over for the summer, and the feeling of liberty sat uneasily on most of them; they tended to gather together quietly for a while before they broke into boisterous play, and their talk was still of the classroom and the teacher, of books and reprimands. Bobby Martin had already stuffed his pockets full of stones, and the other boys soon followed his example, selecting the smoothest and roundest stones; Bobby and Harry Jones and Dickie Delacroix—the villagers pronounced this name "Dellacroy"—eventually made a great pile of stones in one corner of the square and guarded it against the raids of the other boys. The girls stood aside, talking among themselves, looking over their shoulders at the boys, and the very small children rolled in the dust or clung to the hands of their older brothers or sisters.

Soon the men began to gather, surveying their own children, speaking of planting and rain, tractors and taxes. They stood together, away from the pile of stones in the corner, and their jokes were quiet and they smiled rather than laughed. The women, wearing faded house dresses and sweaters, came shortly after their menfolk. They greeted one another and exchanged bits of gossip as they went to join their husbands. Soon the women, standing by their husbands, began to call to their children, and the children came reluctantly, having to be called four or five times. Bobby Martin ducked under his mother's grasping hand and ran, laughing, back to the pile of stones. His father spoke up sharply, and Bobby came quickly and took his place between his father and his oldest brother.

The lottery was conducted—as were the square dances, the teen-age club, the Halloween program—by Mr. Summers, who had time and energy to devote to civic activities. He was a round-faced, jovial man and he ran the coal business, and people were sorry for him, because he had no children and his wife was a scold. When he arrived in the square, carrying the black wooden box, there was a murmur of conversation among the villagers, and he waved and called, "Little late today, folks." The postmaster, Mr. Graves, followed him, carrying a three-legged stool, and the stool was put in the center of the square and Mr. Summers set the black box down on it. The villagers kept their distance, leaving a space between themselves and the stool, and when Mr. Summers said, "Some of you fellows want to give me a hand?" there was a hesitation before two men, Mr. Martin and his oldest son, Baxter, came forward to hold the box steady on the stool while Mr. Summers stirred up the papers inside it.

5   The original paraphernalia for the lottery had been lost long ago, and the black box now resting on the stool had been put into use even before Old Man Warner, the oldest man in town, was born. Mr. Summers spoke frequently to the villagers about making a new box, but no one liked to upset even as much tradition as was represented by the black box. There was a story that the present box had been made with some pieces of the box that had preceded it, the one that had been constructed when the first people settled down to make a village here. Every year, after the lottery, Mr. Summers began talking again about a new box, but every year the subject was allowed to fade off without anything's being done. The black box grew shabbier each year; by now it was no longer completely black but splintered badly along one side to show the original wood color, and in some places faded or stained.

Mr. Martin and his oldest son, Baxter, held the black box securely on the stool until Mr. Summers had stirred the papers thoroughly with his hand. Because so much of the ritual had been forgotten or discarded, Mr. Summers had been successful in having slips of paper substituted for the chips of wood that had been used for generations. Chips of wood, Mr. Summers had argued, had been all very well when the village was tiny, but now that the population was more than three hundred and likely to keep on growing, it was necessary to use something that would fit more easily into the black box. The night before the lottery, Mr. Summers and Mr. Graves made up the slips of paper and put them in the box, and it was then taken to the safe of Mr. Summers's coal company and locked up until Mr. Summers was ready to take it to the square next morning. The rest of the year, the box was put away, sometimes one place, sometimes another; it had spent one year in Mr. Graves's barn and another year underfoot in the post office, and sometimes it was set on a shelf in the Martin grocery and left there.

There was a great deal of fussing to be done before Mr. Summers declared the lottery open. There were the lists to make up—of heads of families, heads of households in each family, members of each household in each family. There was the proper swearing-in of Mr. Summers by the postmaster, as the official of the lottery; at one time, some people remembered, there had been a recital of some sort, performed by the official of the lottery, a perfunctory, tuneless chant that had been rattled off duly each year; some people believed that the official of the lottery used to stand just so when he said or sang it, others believed that he was supposed to walk among the people, but years and years ago this part of the ritual had been allowed to lapse. There had been, also, a ritual salute, which the official of the lottery had had to use in addressing each person who came up to draw from the box, but this also had changed with time, until now it was felt necessary only for the official to speak to each person approaching. Mr. Summers was very good at all this; in his clean white shirt and blue jeans, with one hand resting carelessly on the black box, he seemed very proper and important as he talked interminably to Mr. Graves and the Martins.

Just as Mr. Summers finally left off talking and turned to the assembled villagers, Mrs. Hutchinson came hurriedly along the path to the square, her sweater thrown over her shoulders, and slid into place in the back of the crowd. "Clean forgot what day it was," she said to Mrs. Delacroix, who stood next to her, and they both laughed softly. "Thought my old man was out back stacking wood," Mrs. Hutchinson went on, "and then I looked out the window and the kids was gone, and then I remembered it was the twenty-seventh and came a-running." She dried her hands on her apron, and Mrs. Delacroix said, "You're in time, though. They're still talking away up there."

Mrs. Hutchinson craned her neck to see through the crowd and found her husband and children standing near the front. She tapped Mrs. Delacroix on the arm as a farewell and began to make her way through the crowd. The people separated good-humoredly to let her through; two or three people said, in voices just loud enough to be heard across the crowd, "Here comes your Missus, Hutchinson," and "Bill, she made it after all." Mrs. Hutchinson reached her husband, and Mr. Summers, who had been waiting, said cheerfully, "Thought we were going to have to get on without you, Tessie." Mrs. Hutchinson said, grinning, "Wouldn't have me leave m'dishes in the sink, now, would you, Joe?," and soft laughter ran through the crowd as the people stirred back into position after Mrs. Hutchinson's arrival.

10 "Well, now," Mr. Summers said soberly, "guess we better get started, get this over with, so's we can go back to work. Anybody ain't here?"

"Dunbar," several people said. "Dunbar, Dunbar."

Mr. Summers consulted his list. "Clyde Dunbar," he said. "That's right. He's broke his leg, hasn't he? Who's drawing for him?"

"Me, I guess," a woman said, and Mr. Summers turned to look at her. "Wife draws for her husband," Mr. Summers said. "Don't you have a grown boy to do it for you, Janey?" Although Mr. Summers and everyone else in the village knew the answer perfectly well, it was the business of the official of the lottery to ask such questions formally. Mr. Summers waited with an expression of polite interest while Mrs. Dunbar answered.

"Horace's not but sixteen yet," Mrs. Dunbar said regretfully. "Guess I gotta fill in for the old man this year."

15   "Right," Mr. Summers said. He made a note on the list he was holding. Then he asked, "Watson boy drawing this year?"

A tall boy in the crowd raised his hand. "Here," he said. "I'm drawing for m'mother and me." He blinked his eyes nervously and ducked his head as several voices in the crowd said things like "Good fellow, Jack," and "Glad to see your mother's got a man to do it."

"Well," Mr. Summers said, "guess that's everyone. Old Man Warner make it?"

"Here," a voice said, and Mr. Summers nodded.

A sudden hush fell on the crowd as Mr. Summers cleared his throat and looked at the list. "All ready?" he called. "Now, I'll read the names—heads of families first—and the men come up and take a paper out of the box. Keep the paper folded in your hand without looking at it until everyone has had a turn. Everything clear?"

20   The people had done it so many times that they only half listened to the directions; most of them were quiet, wetting their lips, not looking around. Then Mr. Summers raised one hand high and said, "Adams." A man disengaged himself from the crowd and came forward. "Hi, Steve," Mr. Summers said, and Mr. Adams said, "Hi, Joe." They grinned at one another humorlessly and nervously. Then Mr. Adams reached into the black box and took out a folded paper. He held it firmly by one corner as he turned and went hastily back to his place in the crowd, where he stood a little apart from his family, not looking down at his hand.

"Allen," Mr. Summers said. "Anderson. . . . Bentham."

"Seems like there's no time at all between lotteries any more," Mrs. Delacroix said to Mrs. Graves in the back row. "Seems like we got through with the last one only last week."

"Time sure goes fast," Mrs. Graves said.

"Clark. . . . Delacroix."

25   "There goes my old man," Mrs. Delacroix said. She held her breath while her husband went forward.

"Dunbar," Mr. Summers said, and Mrs. Dunbar went steadily to the box while one of the women said, "Go on, Janey," and another said, "There she goes."

"We're next," Mrs. Graves said. She watched while Mr. Graves came around from the side of the box, greeted Mr. Summers gravely, and selected a slip of paper from the box. By now, all through the crowd there were men holding the small folded papers in their large hands, turning them over and over nervously. Mrs. Dunbar and her two sons stood together, Mrs. Dunbar holding the slip of paper.

"Harburt. . . . Hutchinson."

"Get up there, Bill," Mrs. Hutchinson said, and the people near her laughed.

30   "Jones."

"They do say," Mr. Adams said to Old Man Warner, who stood next to him, "that over in the north village they're talking of giving up the lottery."

Old Man Warner snorted. "Pack of crazy fools," he said. "Listening to the young folks, nothing's good enough for *them*. Next thing you know, they'll be wanting to go back to living in caves, nobody work any more, live *that* way for a while. Used to be a saying about 'Lottery in June, corn be heavy soon.' First thing you know, we'd all be eating stewed chickweed and acorns. There's *always* been a lottery," he added petulantly. "Bad enough to see young Joe Summers up there joking with everybody."

"Some places have already quit lotteries," Mrs. Adams said.

"Nothing but trouble in *that*," Old Man Warner said stoutly. "Pack of young fools."

35   "Martin." And Bobby Martin watched his father go forward. "Overdyke. . . . Percy."

"I wish they'd hurry," Mrs. Dunbar said to her older son. "I wish they'd hurry."

"They're almost through," her son said.

"You get ready to run tell Dad," Mrs. Dunbar said.

Mr. Summers called his own name and then stepped forward precisely and selected a slip from the box. Then he called, "Warner."

40   "Seventy-seventh year I been in the lottery," Old Man Warner said as he went through the crowd. "Seventy-seventh time."

"Watson." The tall boy came awkwardly through the crowd. Someone said, "Don't be nervous, Jack," and Mr. Summers said, "Take your time, son."

"Zanini."

● ● ●

After that, there was a long pause, a breathless pause, until Mr. Summers, holding his slip of paper in the air, said, "All right, fellows." For a minute, no one moved, and then all the slips of paper were opened. Suddenly, all the women began to speak at once, saying, "Who is it?," "Who's got it?," "Is it the Dunbars?," "Is it the Watsons?" Then the voices began to say, "It's Hutchinson. It's Bill," "Bill Hutchinson's got it."

"Go tell your father," Mrs. Dunbar said to her older son.

45   People began to look around to see the Hutchinsons. Bill Hutchinson was standing quiet, staring down at the paper in his hand. Suddenly, Tessie Hutchinson shouted to Mr. Summers, "You didn't give him time enough to take any paper he wanted. I saw you. It wasn't fair!"

"Be a good sport, Tessie," Mrs. Delacroix called, and Mrs. Graves said, "All of us took the same chance."

"Shut up, Tessie," Bill Hutchinson said.

"Well, everyone," Mr. Summers said, "that was done pretty fast, and now we've got to be hurrying a little more to get done in time." He consulted his next list. "Bill," he said, "you draw for the Hutchinson family. You got any other households in the Hutchinsons?"

"There's Don and Eva," Mrs. Hutchinson yelled, "Make *them* take their chance!"

50 "Daughters draw with their husbands' families, Tessie," Mr. Summers said gently. "You know that as well as anyone else."

"It wasn't *fair*," Tessie said.

"I guess not, Joe," Bill Hutchinson said regretfully. "My daughter draws with her husband's family, that's only fair. And I've got no other family except the kids."

"Then, as far as drawing for families is concerned, it's you," Mr. Summers said in explanation, "and as far as drawing for households is concerned, that's you, too. Right?"

"Right," Bill Hutchinson said.

55 "How many kids, Bill?" Mr. Summers asked formally.

"Three," Bill Hutchinson said. "There's Bill, Jr., and Nancy, and little Dave. And Tessie and me."

"All right, then," Mr. Summers said. "Harry, you got their tickets back?"

Mr. Graves nodded and held up the slips of paper. "Put them in the box, then," Mr. Summers directed. "Take Bill's and put it in."

"I think we ought to start over," Mrs. Hutchinson said, as quietly as she could. "I tell you it wasn't *fair*. You didn't give him time enough to choose. *Every*body saw that."

60 Mr. Graves had selected the five slips and put them in the box, and he dropped all the papers but those onto the ground, where the breeze caught them and lifted them off.

"Listen, everybody," Mrs. Hutchinson was saying to the people around her.

"Ready, Bill?" Mr. Summers asked, and Bill Hutchinson, with one quick glance around at his wife and children, nodded.

"Remember," Mr. Summers said, "take the slips and keep them folded until each person has taken one. Harry, you help little Dave." Mr. Graves took the hand of the little boy, who came willingly with him up to the box. "Take a paper out of the box, Davy," Mr. Summers said. Davy put his hand into the box and laughed. "Take just *one* paper," Mr. Summers said. "Harry, you hold it for him." Mr. Graves took the child's hand and removed the folded paper from the tight fist and held it while little Dave stood next to him and looked at him wonderingly.

"Nancy next," Mr. Summers said. Nancy was twelve, and her school friends breathed heavily as she went forward, switching her skirt, and took a slip daintily from the box. "Bill, Jr.," Mr. Summers said, and Billy, his face red and his feet overlarge, nearly knocked the box over as he got a paper out. "Tessie," Mr. Summers said. She hesitated for a minute, looking around defiantly, and then set her lips and went up to the box. She snatched a paper out and held it behind her.

65 "Bill," Mr. Summers said, and Bill Hutchinson reached into the box and felt around, bringing his hand out at last with the slip of paper in it.

The crowd was quiet. A girl whispered, "I hope it's not Nancy," and the sound of the whisper reached the edges of the crowd.

"It's not the way it used to be," Old Man Warner said clearly. "People ain't the way they used to be."

"All right," Mr. Summers said. "Open the papers. Harry, you open little Dave's."

Mr. Graves opened the slip of paper and there was a general sigh through the crowd as he held it up and everyone could see that it was blank. Nancy and Bill, Jr., opened theirs at the same time, and both beamed and laughed, turning around to the crowd and holding their slips of paper above their heads.

70   "Tessie," Mr. Summers said. There was a pause, and then Mr. Summers looked at Bill Hutchinson, and Bill unfolded his paper and showed it. It was blank.

"It's Tessie," Mr. Summers said, and his voice was hushed. "Show us her paper, Bill."

Bill Hutchinson went over to his wife and forced the slip of paper out of her hand. It had a black spot on it, the black spot Mr. Summers had made the night before with the heavy pencil in the coal-company office. Bill Hutchinson held it up, and there was a stir in the crowd.

"All right, folks," Mr. Summers said. "Let's finish quickly."

Although the villagers had forgotten the ritual and lost the original black box, they still remembered to use stones. The pile of stones the boys had made earlier was ready; there were stones on the ground with the blowing scraps of paper that had come out of the box. Mrs. Delacroix selected a stone so large she had to pick it up with both hands and turned to Mrs. Dunbar. "Come on," she said. "Hurry up."

75   Mrs. Dunbar had small stones in both hands, and she said, gasping for breath, "I can't run at all. You'll have to go ahead and I'll catch up with you."

The children had stones already, and someone gave little Davy Hutchinson a few pebbles.

Tessie Hutchinson was in the center of a cleared space by now, and she held her hands out desperately as the villagers moved in on her. "It isn't fair," she said. A stone hit her on the side of the head.

Old Man Warner was saying, "Come on, come on, everyone." Steve Adams was in the front of the crowd of villagers, with Mrs. Graves beside him.

"It isn't fair, it isn't right," Mrs. Hutchinson screamed, and then they were upon her.

READING AND REACTING

1. What possible significance, beyond their literal meaning, might each of these items have: the village square, Mrs. Hutchinson's apron, Old Man Warner, the slips of paper, the black spot?

2. "The Lottery" takes place in summer, a conventional symbol that has a positive connotation. What does this setting contribute to the story's plot? To its atmosphere?

3. What, if anything, might the names *Graves, Adams, Summers,* and *Delacroix* signify in the context of this story? Do you think these names are intended to have any special significance? Why or why not?

4. What role do the children play in the ritual? How can you explain their presence in the story? Do they have any symbolic role in the story?

5. What symbolic significance might be found in the way the characters are dressed? In their conversation?

6. In what sense is the story's title ironic?

7. Throughout the story there is a general atmosphere of excitement. What indication is there of nervousness or apprehension?

8. Early in the story, the boys stuff their pockets with stones, foreshadowing the attack in the story's conclusion. What other examples of foreshadowing can you identify?

9. **JOURNAL ENTRY** How can a ritual like the lottery continue to be held year after year? Why does no one move to end it? Can you think of a modern-day counterpart of this lottery—a situation in which people continue to act in ways they know to be wrong rather than challenge the status quo? How can you account for such behaviour?

10. **CRITICAL PERSPECTIVE** When "The Lottery" was published in the June 26, 1948, issue of *The New Yorker,* its effect was immediate. The story, as the critic Judy Oppenheimer notes in her book *Private Demons: The Life of Shirley Jackson,* "provoked an unprecedented outpouring of fury, horror, rage, disgust, and intense fascination." As a result, Jackson received hundreds of letters, which contained (among others) the following interpretations of the story:

    ◇ The story is an attack on small-town America.

    ◇ The story is a parable about the perversion of democracy.

    ◇ The story is a criticism of prejudice, particularly anti-Semitism.

    ◇ The story has no point at all.

    How plausible do you think each of these interpretations is? Which comes closest to your interpretation of the story? Why?

Related Works: "Patterns" (p. 634), "The Colonel" (p. 783), *Les Belles Soeurs* (p. 1196)

◈ **ALICE WALKER** (1944–   ) is an accomplished writer of poetry, fiction, and criticism. Her characters are mainly rural African-Americans, often living in her native Georgia, who struggle to survive in hostile environments. Her writing displays a particular sensitivity to the emotions of people who suffer physical or psychological harm in their efforts to assert their own identities.

Walker was the youngest of five boys and three girls born to Willie Lee and Minnie Tallulah Grant Walker, sharecroppers who raised cotton. She left the rural South to attend Atlanta's Spelman College (1961–1963) and Sarah Lawrence College in Bronxville, New York (1963–1965).

In 1967, Walker moved to Mississippi, where she was supported in the writing of her first novel, *The Third Life of Grange Copeland* (1970), by a National Endowment for the Arts grant. Her short story "Everyday Use" was included in *Best American Short Stories 1973*. Other novels and short story collections followed, including *In Love and Trouble: Stories of Black Women* (1973), *Meridian* (1976), *You Can't Keep a Good Woman Down* (short stories, 1981), *The Temple of My Familiar* (1989), *Possessing the Secret of Joy* (1993), *The Complete Stories* (short stories, 1994), and *By the Light of My Father's Smile* (1998). Walker's third novel, *The Color Purple* (1982), won the American Book Award and a Pulitzer Prize.

In the third year of her marriage, Walker took back her maiden name because she wanted to honour her great-great-great-grandmother who walked, carrying her two children, from Virginia to Georgia. Walker's renaming is consistent with one of her goals in writing, which is to further the process of reconnecting people to their ancestors. She has said that "it is fatal to see yourself as separate" and that if people can reaffirm the past, they can "make a different future."

◆ ◆ ◆

ALICE WALKER

Everyday Use
(1973)

for your grandma

I will wait for her in the yard that Maggie and I made so clean and wavy yesterday afternoon. A yard like this is more comfortable than most people know. It is not just a yard. It is like an extended living room. When the hard clay is swept clean as a floor and the fine sand around the edges lined with tiny, irregular grooves, anyone can come and sit and look up into the elm tree and wait for the breezes that never come inside the house.

Maggie will be nervous until after her sister goes: she will stand hopelessly in corners, homely and ashamed of the burn scars down her arms and legs, eying her sister with a mixture of envy and awe. She thinks her sister has held life always in the palm of one hand, that "no" is a word the world never learned to say to her.

You've no doubt seen those TV shows where the child who has "made it" is confronted, as a surprise, by her own mother and father, tottering in weakly from backstage. (A pleasant surprise, of course: What would they do if parent and child came on the show only to curse out and insult each other?) On TV mother and child embrace and smile into each other's faces. Sometimes the mother and father weep, the child wraps them in her arms and leans across the table to tell how she would not have made it without their help. I have seen these programs.

Sometimes I dream a dream in which Dee and I are suddenly brought together on a TV program of this sort. Out of a dark and soft-seated limousine I am ushered into a bright room filled with many people. There I meet a smiling, gray, sporty man like Johnny Carson who shakes my hand and tells me what a fine girl I have. Then we are on the stage and Dee is embracing me with tears in her eyes. She pins on my dress a large orchid, even though she has told me once that she thinks orchids are tacky flowers.

5   In real life I am a large, big-boned woman with rough, man-working hands. In the winter I wear flannel nightgowns to bed and overalls during the day. I can kill and clean a hog as mercilessly as a man. My fat keeps me hot in zero weather. I can work outside all day, breaking ice to get water for washing; I can eat pork liver cooked over the open fire minutes after it comes steaming from the hog. One winter I knocked a bull calf straight in the brain between the eyes with a sledge hammer and had the meat hung up to chill before nightfall. But of course all this does not show on television. I am the way my daughter would want me to be: a hundred pounds lighter, my skin like an uncooked barley pancake. My hair glistens in the hot bright lights. Johnny Carson has much to do to keep up with my quick and witty tongue.

But that is a mistake. I know even before I wake up. Who ever knew a Johnson with a quick tongue? Who can even imagine me looking a strange white man in the eye? It seems to me I have talked to them always with one foot raised in flight, with my head turned in whichever way is farthest from them. Dee, though. She would always look anyone in the eye. Hesitation was no part of her nature.

"How do I look, Mama?" Maggie says, showing just enough of her thin body enveloped in pink skirt and red blouse for me to know she's there, almost hidden by the door.

"Come out into the yard," I say.

Have you ever seen a lame animal, perhaps a dog run over by some careless person rich enough to own a car, sidle up to someone who is ignorant enough to be kind to him? That is the way my Maggie walks. She has been like this, chin on chest, eyes on ground, feet in shuffle, ever since the fire that burned the other house to the ground.

10   Dee is lighter than Maggie, with nicer hair and a fuller figure. She's a woman now, though sometimes I forget. How long ago was it that the other house burned? Ten, twelve years? Sometimes I can still hear the flames and

feel Maggie's arms sticking to me, her hair smoking and her dress falling off her in little black papery flakes. Her eyes seemed stretched open, blazed open by the flames reflected in them. And Dee. I see her standing off under the sweet gum tree she used to dig gum out of; a look of concentration on her face as she watched the last dingy gray board of the house fall in toward the red-hot brick chimney. Why don't you do a dance around the ashes? I'd wanted to ask her. She had hated the house that much.

I used to think she hated Maggie, too. But that was before we raised the money, the church and me, to send her to Augusta to school. She used to read to us without pity; forcing words, lies, other folks' habits, whole lives upon us two, sitting trapped and ignorant underneath her voice. She washed us in a river of make-believe, burned us with a lot of knowledge we didn't necessarily need to know. Pressed us to her with the serious way she read, to shove us away at just the moment, like dimwits, we seemed about to understand.

Dee wanted nice things. A yellow organdy dress to wear to her graduation from high school; black pumps to match a green suit she'd made from an old suit somebody gave me. She was determined to stare down any disaster in her efforts. Her eyelids would not flicker for minutes at a time. Often I fought off the temptation to shake her. At sixteen she had a style of her own, and knew what style was.

•••

I never had an education myself. After second grade the school was closed down. Don't ask me why: in 1927 colored asked fewer questions than they do now. Sometimes Maggie reads to me. She stumbles along good-naturedly but can't see well. She knows she is not bright. Like good looks and money, quickness passed her by. She will marry John Thomas (who has mossy teeth in an earnest face) and then I'll be free to sit here and I guess just sing church songs to myself. Although I never was a good singer. Never could carry a tune. I was always better at a man's job. I used to love to milk till I was hooked in the side in '49. Cows are soothing and slow and don't bother you, unless you try to milk them the wrong way.

I have deliberately turned my back on the house. It is three rooms, just like the one that burned, except the roof is tin; they don't make shingle roofs any more. There are no real windows, just some holes cut in the sides, like the portholes in a ship, but not round and not square, with rawhide holding the shutters up on the outside. This house is in a pasture, too, like the other one. No doubt when Dee sees it she will want to tear it down. She wrote me once that no matter where we "choose" to live, she will manage to come see us. But she will never bring her friends. Maggie and I thought about this and Maggie asked me, "Mama, when did Dee ever *have* any friends?"

15   She had a few. Furtive boys in pink shirts hanging about on washday after school. Nervous girls who never laughed. Impressed with her they

worshiped the well-turned phrase, the cute shape, the scalding humor that erupted like bubbles in lye. She read to them.

When she was courting Jimmy T she didn't have much time to pay to us, but turned all her faultfinding power on him. He *flew* to marry a cheap city girl from a family of ignorant flashy people. She hardly had time to recompose herself.

When she comes I will meet—but there they are!

Maggie attempts to make a dash for the house, in her shuffling way, but I stay her with my hand. "Come back here," I say. And she stops and tries to dig a well in the sand with her toe.

It is hard to see them clearly through the strong sun. But even the first glimpse of leg out of the car tells me it is Dee. Her feet were always neat-looking, as if God himself had shaped them with a certain style. From the other side of the car comes a short, stocky man. Hair is all over his head a foot long and hanging from his chin like a kinky mule tail. I hear Maggie suck in her breath. "Uhnnnh," is what it sounds like. Like when you see the wriggling end of a snake just in front of your foot on the road. "Uhnnnh."

20   Dee next. A dress down to the ground, in this hot weather. A dress so loud it hurts my eyes. There are yellows and oranges enough to throw back the light of the sun. I feel my whole face warming from the heat waves it throws out. Earrings gold, too, and hanging down to her shoulders. Bracelets dangling and making noises when she moves her arm up to shake the folds of the dress out of her armpits. The dress is loose and flows, and as she walks closer, I like it. I hear Maggie go "Uhnnnh" again. It is her sister's hair. It stands straight up like the wool on a sheep. It is black as night and around the edges are two long pigtails that rope about like small lizards disappearing behind her ears.

"Wa-su-zo-Tean-o!"[1] she says, coming on in that gliding way the dress makes her move. The short stocky fellow with the hair to his navel is all grinning and he follows up with "Asalamalakim,[2] my mother and sister!" He moves to hug Maggie but she falls back, right up against the back of my chair. I feel her trembling there and when I look up I see the perspiration falling off her chin.

"Don't get up," says Dee. Since I am stout it takes something of a push. You can see me trying to move a second or two before I make it. She turns, showing white heels through her sandals, and goes back to the car. Out she peeks next with a Polaroid. She stoops down quickly and lines up picture after picture of me sitting there in front of the house with Maggie cowering behind me. She never takes a shot without making sure the house is included. When a cow comes nibbling around the edge of the yard she snaps it and me and Maggie *and* the house. Then she puts the Polaroid in the back seat of the car, and comes up and kisses me on the forehead.

---

[1] Greeting in Swahili; Dee sounds it out one syllable at a time.

[2] Greeting in Arabic: "Peace be upon you."

Meanwhile Asalamalakim is going through motions with Maggie's hand. Maggie's hand is as limp as a fish, and probably as cold, despite the sweat, and she keeps trying to pull it back. It looks like Asalamalakim wants to shake hands but wants to do it fancy. Or maybe he don't know how people shake hands. Anyhow, he soon gives up on Maggie.

"Well," I say. "Dee."

25   "No, Mama," she says. "Not 'Dee,' Wangero Leewanika Kemanjo!"

"What happened to 'Dee'?" I wanted to know.

"She's dead," Wangero said. "I couldn't bear it any longer, being named after the people who oppress me."

"You know as well as me you was named after your aunt Dicie," I said. Dicie is my sister. She named Dee. We called her "Big Dee" after Dee was born.

"But who was *she* named after?" asked Wangero.

30   "I guess after Grandma Dee," I said.

"And who was she named after?" asked Wangero.

"Her mother," I said, and saw Wangero was getting tired. "That's about as far back as I can trace it," I said. Though, in fact, I probably could have carried it back beyond the Civil War through the branches.

"Well," said Asalamalakim, "there you are."

"Uhnnnh," I heard Maggie say.

35   "There I was not," I said, "before 'Dicie' cropped up in our family, so why should I try to trace it that far back?"

He just stood there grinning, looking down on me like somebody inspecting a Model A car. Every once in a while he and Wangero sent eye signals over my head.

"How do you pronounce this name?" I asked.

"You don't have to call me by it if you don't want to," said Wangero.

"Why shouldn't I?" I asked. "If that's what you want us to call you, we'll call you."

40   "I know it might sound awkward at first," said Wangero.

"I'll get used to it," I said. "Ream it out again."

Well, soon we got the name out of the way. Asalamalakim had a name twice as long and three times as hard. After I tripped over it two or three times he told me to just call him Hakim-a-barber. I wanted to ask him was he a barber, but I didn't really think he was, so I didn't ask.

"You must belong to those beef-cattle peoples down the road," I said. They said "Asalamalakim" when they met you, too, but they didn't shake hands. Always too busy: feeding the cattle, fixing the fences, putting up salt-lick shelters, throwing down hay. When the white folks poisoned some of the herd the men stayed up all night with rifles in their hands. I walked a mile and a half just to see the sight.

Hakim-a-barber said, "I accept some of their doctrines, but farming and raising cattle is not my style." (They didn't tell me, and I didn't ask, whether Wangero [Dee] had really gone and married him.)

45   We sat down to eat and right away he said he didn't eat collards and pork was unclean. Wangero, though, went on through the chitlins and corn bread, the greens and everything else. She talked a blue streak over the sweet potatoes. Everything delighted her. Even the fact that we still used the benches her daddy made for the table when we couldn't afford to buy chairs.

"Oh, Mama!" she cried. Then turned to Hakim-a-barber. "I never knew how lovely these benches are. You can feel the rump prints," she said, running her hands underneath her and along the bench. Then she gave a sigh and her hand closed over Grandma Dee's butter dish. "That's it!" she said. "I knew there was something I wanted to ask you if I could have." She jumped up from the table and went over in the corner where the churn stood, the milk in it clabber by now. She looked at the churn and looked at it.

"This churn top is what I need," she said. "Didn't Uncle Buddy whittle it out of a tree you all used to have?"

"Yes," I said.

"Uh huh," she said happily. "And I want the dasher, too."

50   "Uncle Buddy whittle that, too?" asked the barber.

Dee (Wangero) looked up at me.

"Aunt Dee's first husband whittled the dash," said Maggie so low you almost couldn't hear her. "His name was Henry, but they called him Stash."

"Maggie's brain is like an elephant's," Wangero said, laughing. "I can use the churn top as a centerpiece for the alcove table," she said, sliding a plate over the churn, "and I'll think of something artistic to do with the dasher."

When she finished wrapping the dasher the handle stuck out. I took it for a moment in my hands. You didn't even have to look close to see where hands pushing the dasher up and down to make butter had left a kind of sink in the wood. In fact, there were a lot of small sinks; you could see where thumb and fingers had sunk into the wood. It was beautiful light yellow wood, from a tree that grew in the yard where Big Dee and Stash had lived.

55   After dinner Dee (Wangero) went to the trunk at the foot of my bed and started rifling through it. Maggie hung back in the kitchen over the dishpan. Out came Wangero with two quilts. They had been pieced by Grandma Dee and then Big Dee and me had hung them on the quilt frames on the front porch and quilted them. One was in the Lone Star pattern. The other was Walk Around the Mountain. In both of them were scraps of dresses Grandma Dee had worn fifty and more years ago. Bits and pieces of Grandpa Jarrell's Paisley shirts. And one teeny faded blue piece, about the size of a penny matchbox, that was from Great Grandpa Ezra's uniform that he wore in the Civil War.

"Mama," Wangero said sweet as a bird. "Can I have these old quilts?"

I heard something fall in the kitchen, and a minute later the kitchen door slammed.

"Why don't you take one or two of the others?" I asked. "These old things was just done by me and Big Dee from some tops your grandma pieced before she died."

"No," said Wangero. "I don't want those. They are stitched around the borders by machine."

60   "That'll make them last better," I said.

"That's not the point," said Wangero. "These are all pieces of dresses Grandma used to wear. She did all this stitching by hand. Imagine!" She held the quilts securely in her arms, stroking them.

"Some of the pieces, like those lavender ones, come from old clothes her mother handed down to her," I said, moving up to touch the quilts. Dee (Wangero) moved back just enough so that I couldn't reach the quilts. They already belonged to her.

"Imagine!" she breathed again, clutching them closely to her bosom.

"The truth is," I said, "I promised to give them quilts to Maggie, for when she marries John Thomas."

65   She gasped like a bee had stung her. "Maggie can't appreciate these quilts!" she said. "She'd probably be backward enough to put them to everyday use."

"I reckon she would," I said. "God knows I been saving 'em for long enough with nobody using 'em. I hope she will!" I didn't want to bring up how I had offered Dee (Wangero) a quilt when she went away to college. Then she had told me they were old-fashioned, out of style.

"But, they're *priceless!*" she was saying now, furiously; for she has a temper. "Maggie would put them on the bed and in five years they'd be in rags. Less than that!"

"She can always make some more," I said. "Maggie knows how to quilt."

Dee (Wangero) looked at me with hatred. "You just will not understand. The point is these quilts, *these* quilts!"

70   "Well," I said, stumped. "What would *you* do with them?"

"Hang them," she said. As if that was the only thing you *could* do with quilts.

Maggie by now was standing in the door. I could almost hear the sound her feet made as they scraped over each other.

"She can have them, Mama," she said, like somebody used to never winning anything, or having anything reserved for her. "I can 'member Grandma Dee without the quilts."

I looked at her hard. She had filled her bottom lip with checkerberry snuff and it gave her face a kind of dopey, hangdog look. It was Grandma Dee and Big Dee who taught her how to quilt herself. She stood there with her scarred hands hidden in the folds of her skirt. She looked at her sister with something like fear but she wasn't mad at her. This was Maggie's portion. This was the way she knew God to work.

75   When I looked at her like that something hit me in the top of my head and ran down to the soles of my feet. Just like when I'm in church and the spirit of God touches me and I get happy and shout. I did something I never had done before: hugged Maggie to me, then dragged her on into the room, snatched the quilts out of Miss Wangero's hands and

dumped them into Maggie's lap. Maggie just sat there on my bed with her mouth open.

"Take one or two of the others," I said to Dee.

But she turned without a word and went out to Hakim-a-barber.

"You just don't understand," she said, as Maggie and I came out to the car.

"What don't I understand?" I wanted to know.

80   "Your heritage," she said. And then she turned to Maggie, kissed her, and said, "You ought to try to make something of yourself, too, Maggie. It's really a new day for us. But from the way you and Mama still live you'd never know it."

She put on some sunglasses that hid everything above the tip of her nose and her chin.

Maggie smiled; maybe at the sunglasses. But a real smile, not scared. After we watched the car dust settle I asked Maggie to bring me a dip of snuff. And then the two of us sat there just enjoying, until it was time to go in the house and go to bed.

READING AND REACTING

1. What is the conventional symbolic significance of a patchwork quilt?

2. What is the *literal* meaning of the two quilts to Maggie and her mother? To Dee? Beyond this literal meaning, what symbolic meaning, if any, do they have to Maggie and her mother? Do the quilts have any symbolic meaning to Dee?

3. How does the contrast between the two sisters' appearances, personalities, lifestyles, and feelings about the quilts help to convey the story's theme?

4. What does the name *Wangero* signify to Dee? To her mother and sister? Could the name be considered a symbol? Why or why not?

5. Why do you think Maggie relinquishes the quilts to her sister?

6. What is Dee's opinion of her mother and sister? Do you agree with her assessment?

7. What does the story's title suggest to you? Is it ironic? What other titles would be effective?

8. What possible meanings, aside from their literal meanings, might each of the following suggest: the family's yard, Maggie's burn scars, the trunk in which the quilts are kept, Dee's Polaroid camera? What symbolic functions, if any, do these items serve in the story?

9. **JOURNAL ENTRY** What objects have the kind of symbolic value to you that the quilts have to Maggie? What gives these objects this value?

10. **CRITICAL PERSPECTIVE** In her article "The Black Woman Artist as Wayward," critic Barbara Christian characterizes "Everyday Use" as a story in which Alice Walker examines the "creative legacy" of

ordinary African-American women. According to Christian, the story "is about the use and misuse of the concept of heritage. The mother of two daughters, one selfish and stylish, the other scarred and caring, passes on to us its true definition."

What definition of heritage does the mother attempt to pass on to her children? In what ways is this definition like or unlike Dee's definition?

Related Works: "Town and Country Lovers" (p. 80), "Digging" (p. 574), "Aunt Jennifer's Tigers" (p. 739), *Trifles* (p. 948)

◊ **MARGARET ATWOOD** (1939–   ) has published collections of poetry and fiction, novels, and works of criticism. Throughout her career, Atwood's interest has been in exploring the cultural and personal myths of her characters and the conventions that govern their lives. Atwood has explained that, for her, the novel is a "social vehicle" that reflects society. Atwood is also a major voice in the feminist movement, depicting in her work the relationship between men and women as one that is governed by power politics. Her best known earlier works include *The Edible Woman* (1969), *Surfacing* (1972), and *Lady Oracle* (1976). In *The Handmaid's Tale* (1985) Atwood draws a futuristic portrait of an American society dominated by a fundamentalist regime in which women are forced to produce offspring for the government elite. *Alias Grace* (1996) is a historical novel based on a sensational murder case that took place in Canada in the 1840s. Her novel *The Blind Assassin* (2000) won her the prestigious Booker Prize. Recent works include *Oryx and Crake: A Novel* (2003), a terrifying excursion into the future; *The Penelopiad*, a reworking of *The Odyssey* from Penelope's perspective; and *The Tent* (2006), a collection of short fiction.

◊ ◊ ◊

MARGARET ATWOOD

Death by Landscape
(1991)

Now that the boys are grown up and Rob is dead, Lois has moved to a condominium apartment in one of the newer waterfront developments. She is relieved not to have to worry about the lawn, or about the ivy pushing its muscular little suckers into the brickwork, or the squirrels gnawing their way into the attic and eating the insulation off the wiring, or about strange noises. This building has a security system, and the only plant life is in pots in the solarium.

Lois is glad she's been able to find an apartment big enough for her pictures. They are more crowded together than they were in the house, but this arrangement gives the walls a European look: blocks of pictures, above and beside one another, rather than one over the chesterfield, one over the fireplace, one in the front hall, in the old acceptable manner of sprinkling art around so it does not get too intrusive. This way has more of an impact. You know it's not supposed to be furniture.

None of the pictures is very large, which doesn't mean they aren't valuable. They are paintings, or sketches and drawings, by artists who were not nearly as well known when Lois began to buy them as they are now. Their work later turned up on stamps, or as silk-screen reproductions hung in the principals' offices of high schools, or as jigsaw puzzles, or on beautifully printed calendars sent out by corporations as Christmas gifts, to their less important clients. These artists painted mostly in the twenties and thirties and forties; they painted landscapes. Lois has two Tom Thomsons, three A. Y. Jacksons, a Lawren Harris. She has an Arthur Lismer, she has a J. E. H. MacDonald. She has a David Milne. They are pictures of convoluted tree trunks on an island of pink wave-smoothed stone, with more islands behind; of a lake with rough, bright, sparsely wooded cliffs; of a vivid river shore with a tangle of bush and two beached canoes, one red, one grey; of a yellow autumn woods with the ice-blue gleam of a pond half-seen through the interlaced branches.

It was Lois who'd chosen them. Rob had no interest in art, although he could see the necessity of having something on the walls. He left all the decorating decisions to her, while providing the money, of course. Because of this collection of hers, Lois's friends—especially the men—have given her the reputation of having a good nose for art investments.

5 But this is not why she bought the pictures, way back then. She bought them because she wanted them. She wanted something that was in them, although she could not have said at the time what it was. It was not peace: she does not find them peaceful in the least. Looking at them fills her with a wordless unease. Despite the fact that there are no people in them or even animals, it's as if there is something, or someone, looking back out.

When she was thirteen, Lois went on a canoe trip. She'd only been on overnights before. This was to be a long one, into the trackless wilderness, as Cappie put it. It was Lois's first canoe trip, and her last.

Cappie was the head of the summer camp to which Lois had been sent ever since she was nine. Camp Manitou, it was called; it was one of the better ones, for girls, though not the best. Girls of her age whose parents could afford it were routinely packed off to such camps, which bore a generic resemblance to one another. They favoured Indian names and had hearty, energetic leaders, who were called Cappie or Skip or Scottie. At these camps you learned to swim well and sail, and paddle a canoe, and perhaps ride a horse or play tennis. When you weren't doing these things you could do Arts and Crafts and turn out dingy, lumpish clay ashtrays for your mother—mothers smoked more, then—or bracelets made of coloured braided string.

Cheerfulness was required at all times, even at breakfast. Loud shouting and the banging of spoons on the tables were allowed, and even encouraged, at ritual intervals. Chocolate bars were rationed, to control tooth decay and pimples. At night, after supper, in the dining hall or outside around a mosquito-infested campfire ring for special treats, there were singsongs. Lois can still remember all the words to "My Darling Clementine," and to "My Bonnie Lies Over the Ocean," with acting-out gestures: a rippling of the hands for "the ocean," two hands together under the cheek for "lies." She will never be able to forget them, which is a sad thought.

Lois thinks she can recognize women who went to these camps, and were good at it. They have a hardness to their handshakes, even now; a way of standing, legs planted firmly and farther apart than usual; a way of sizing you up, to see if you'd be any good in a canoe—the front, not the back. They themselves would be in the back. They would call it the stern.

10   She knows that such camps still exist, although Camp Manitou does not. They are one of the few things that haven't changed much. They now offer copper enamelling, and functionless pieces of stained glass baked in electric ovens, though judging from the productions of her friends' grandchildren the artistic standards have not improved.

To Lois, encountering it in the first year after the war, Camp Manitou seemed ancient. Its log-sided buildings with the white cement in between the half-logs, its flagpole ringed with whitewashed stones, its weathered grey dock jutting out into Lake Prospect, with its woven rope bumpers and its rusty rings for tying up, its prim round flowerbed of petunias near the office door, must surely have been there always. In truth it dated only from the first decade of the century; it had been founded by Cappie's parents, who'd thought of camping as bracing to the character, like cold showers, and had been passed along to her as an inheritance, and an obligation.

Lois realized, later, that it must have been a struggle for Cappie to keep Camp Manitou going, during the Depression and then the war, when money did not flow freely. If it had been a camp for the very rich, instead of the merely well off, there would have been fewer problems. But there must have been enough Old Girls, ones with daughters, to keep the thing in operation, though not entirely shipshape: furniture was battered, painted trim was peeling, roofs leaked. There were dim photographs of these Old Girls dotted around the dining hall, wearing ample woollen bathing suits and showing their fat, dimpled legs, or standing, arms twined, in odd tennis outfits with baggy skirts.

In the dining hall, over the stone fireplace that was never used, there was a huge moulting stuffed moose head, which looked somehow carnivorous. It was a sort of mascot; its name was Monty Manitou. The older campers spread the story that it was haunted, and came to life in the dark, when the feeble and undependable lights had been turned off or, due to yet another generator failure, had gone out. Lois was afraid of it at first, but not after she got used to it.

Cappie was the same: you had to get used to her. Possibly she was forty, or thirty-five, or fifty. She had fawn-coloured hair that looked as if it was cut with a bowl. Her head jutted forward, jigging like a chicken's as she strode around the camp, clutching notebooks and checking things off in them. She was like their minister in church: both of them smiled a lot and were anxious because they wanted things to go well; they both had the same overwashed skins and stringy necks. But all this disappeared when Cappie was leading a singsong, or otherwise leading. Then she was happy, sure of herself, her plain face almost luminous. She wanted to cause joy. At these times she was loved, at others merely trusted.

15   There were many things Lois didn't like about Camp Manitou, at first. She hated the noisy chaos and spoon-banging of the dining hall, the rowdy singsongs at which you were expected to yell in order to show that you were enjoying yourself. Hers was not a household that encouraged yelling. She hated the necessity of having to write dutiful letters to her parents claiming she was having fun. She could not complain, because camp cost so much money.

She didn't much like having to undress in a roomful of other girls, even in the dim light, although nobody paid any attention, or sleeping in a cabin with seven others girls, some of whom snored because they had adenoids or colds, some of whom had nightmares, or wet their beds and cried about it. Bottom bunks made her feel closed in, and she was afraid of falling out of top ones; she was afraid of heights. She got homesick, and suspected her parents of having a better time when she wasn't there than when she was, although her mother wrote to her every week saying how much they missed her. All this was when she was nine. By the time she was thirteen she liked it. She was an old hand by then.

Lucy was her best friend at camp. Lois had other friends in winter, when there was school and itchy woollen clothing and darkness in the afternoons, but Lucy was her summer friend.

She turned up the second year, when Lois was ten, and a Bluejay. (Chickadees, Bluejays, Ravens, and Kingfishers—these were the names Camp Manitou assigned to the different age groups, a sort of totemic clan system. In those days, thinks Lois, it was birds for girls, animals for boys: wolves, and so forth. Though some animals and birds were suitable and some were not. Never vultures, for instance; never skunks, or rats.) Lois helped Lucy to unpack her tin trunk and place the folded clothes on the wooden shelves, and to make up her bed. She put her in the top bunk right above her, where she could keep an eye on her. Already she knew that Lucy was an exception, to a good many rules; already she felt proprietorial.

20   Lucy was from the United States, where the comic books came from, and the movies. She wasn't from New York or Hollywood or Buffalo, the only American cities Lois knew the names of, but from Chicago. Her house was on the lakeshore and had gates to it, and grounds. They had a maid; all of the time. Lois's family only had a cleaning lady twice a week.

The only reason Lucy was being sent to *this* camp (she cast a look of minor scorn around the cabin, diminishing it and also offending Lois, while at the same time daunting her) was that her mother had been a camper here.

Her mother had been a Canadian once, but had married her father, who had a patch over one eye, like a pirate. She showed Lois the picture of him in her wallet. He got the patch in the war. "Shrapnel," said Lucy. Lois, who was unsure about shrapnel, was so impressed she could only grunt. Her own two-eyed, unwounded father was tame by comparison.

"My father plays golf," she ventured at last.

"*Everyone* plays golf," said Lucy. "My *mother* plays golf."

Lois's mother did not. Lois took Lucy to see the outhouses and the swimming dock and the dining hall with Monty Manitou's baleful head, knowing in advance they would not measure up.

25   This was a bad beginning; but Lucy was good-natured, and accepted Camp Manitou with the same casual shrug with which she seemed to accept everything. She would make the best of it, without letting Lois forget that this was what she was doing.

However, there were things Lois knew that Lucy did not. Lucy scratched the tops off all her mosquito bites and had to be taken to the infirmary to be daubed with Ozonol. She took her T-shirt off while sailing, and although the counsellor spotted her after a while and made her put it back on, she burnt spectacularly, bright red, with the X of her bathing-suit straps standing out in alarming white; she let Lois peel the sheets of whispery-thin burned skin off her shoulders. When they sang "Alouette" around the campfire, she did not know any of the French words. The difference was that Lucy did not care about the things she didn't know, whereas Lois did.

During the next winter, and subsequent winters, Lucy and Lois wrote to each other. They were both only children, at a time when this was thought to be a disadvantage, so in their letters they pretended to be sisters, or even twins. Lois had to strain a little over this, because Lucy was so blond, with translucent skin and large blue eyes like a doll's, and Lois was nothing out of the ordinary—just a tallish, thinnish, brownish person with freckles. They signed their letters LL, with the L's entwined together like the monograms on a towel. (Lois and Lucy, thinks Lois. How our names date us: Lois Lane, Superman's girlfriend, enterprising female reporter; "I Love Lucy." Now we are obsolete, and it's little Jennifers, little Emilys, little Alexandras and Carolines and Tiffanys.)

They were more effusive in their letters than they ever were in person. They bordered their pages with X's and O's, but when they met again in the summers it was always a shock. They had changed so much, or Lucy had. It was like watching someone grow up in jolts. At first it would be hard to think up things to say.

But Lucy always had a surprise or two, something to show, some marvel to reveal. The first year she had a picture of herself in a tutu, her hair in a ballerina's knot on the top of her head; she pirouetted around the swimming dock, to show Lois how it was done, and almost fell off. The next year she had given that up and was taking horseback riding. (Camp Manitou did not have horses.) The next year her mother and father had been divorced, and she had a new stepfather, one with both eyes, and a new house, although the maid was the same. The next year, when they had graduated from Bluejays and entered Ravens, she got her period, right in the first week of camp. The two of them snitched some matches from their counsellor, who smoked illegally, and made a small fire out behind the farthest outhouse, at dusk, using their flashlights. They could set all kinds of fires by now; they had learned how in Campcraft. On this fire they burned one of Lucy's used sanitary napkins. Lois is not sure why they did this, or whose idea it was. But she can remember the feeling of deep satisfaction it gave her as the white fluff singed and the blood sizzled, as if some wordless ritual had been fulfilled.

30   They did not get caught, but then they rarely got caught at any of their camp transgressions. Lucy had such large eyes, and was such an accomplished liar.

This year Lucy is different again: slower, more languorous. She is no longer interested in sneaking around after dark, purloining cigarettes from the counsellor, dealing in black-market candy bars. She is pensive, and hard to wake in the mornings. She doesn't like her stepfather, but she doesn't want to live with her real father either, who has a new wife. She thinks her mother may be having a love affair with a doctor; she doesn't know for sure, but she's seen them smooching in his car, out on the driveway, when her stepfather wasn't there. It serves him right. She hates her private school. She has a boyfriend, who is sixteen and works as a gardener's assistant. This is how she met him: in the garden. She describes to Lois what it is like when he kisses her—rubbery at first, but then your knees go limp. She has been forbidden to see him, and threatened with boarding school. She wants to run away from home.

Lois has little to offer in return. Her own life is placid and satisfactory, but there is nothing much that can be said about happiness. "You're so lucky," Lucy tells her, a little smugly. She might as well say *boring* because this is how it makes Lois feel.

Lucy is apathetic about the canoe trip, so Lois has to disguise her own excitement. The evening before they are to leave, she slouches into the campfire ring as if coerced, and sits down with a sigh of endurance, just as Lucy does.

Every canoe trip that went out of camp was given a special send-off by Cappie and the section leader and counsellors, with the whole section in attendance. Cappie painted three streaks of red across each of her cheeks with a lipstick. They looked like three-fingered claw marks. She put a blue circle on her forehead with fountain-pen ink, and tied a twisted bandanna around her head and stuck a row of frazzle-ended feathers around it, and wrapped herself in a red-and-black Hudson's Bay blanket. The counsellors, also in blankets but with only two streaks of red, beat on tom-toms made of round wooden cheese boxes with leather stretched over the top and nailed in place. Cappie was Chief Cappeosota. They all had to say "How!" when she walked into the circle and stood there with one hand raised.

35   Looking back on this, Lois finds it disquieting. She knows too much about Indians: this is why. She knows, for instance, that they should not even be called Indians, and that they have enough worries without other people taking their names and dressing up as them. It has all been a form of stealing.

But she remembers too, that she was once ignorant of this. Once she loved the campfire, the flickering of light on the ring of faces, the sound of the fake tom-toms, heavy and fast like a scared heartbeat; she loved Cappie in a red blanket and feathers, solemn, as a chief should be, raising her hand and saying, "Greetings, my Ravens." It was not funny, it was not making fun. She wanted to be an Indian. She wanted to be adventurous and pure, and aboriginal.

"You go on big water," says Cappie. This is her idea—all their ideas—of how Indians talk. "You go where no man has ever trod. You go many moons." This is not true. They are only going for a week, not many moons. The canoe route is clearly marked, they have gone over it on a map, and there are pre-pared campsites with names which are used year after year. But when Cappie says this—and despite the way Lucy rolls up her eyes—Lois can feel the water stretching out, with the shores twisting away on either side, immense and a little frightening.

"You bring back much wampum," says Cappie. "Do good in war, my braves, and capture many scalps." This is another of her pretences: that they are boys, and bloodthirsty. But such a game cannot be played by substituting the word "squaw." It would not work at all.

Each of them has to stand up and step forward and have a red line drawn across her cheeks by Cappie. She tells them they must follow in the paths of their ancestors (who most certainly, thinks Lois, looking out the window of her apartment and remembering the family stash of daguerreo-types and sepia-coloured portraits on her mother's dressing table, the stiff-shirted, black-coated, grim-faced men and the beflounced women with their severe hair and their corseted respectability, would never have considered heading off onto an open lake, in a canoe, just for fun).

40   At the end of the ceremony they all stood and held hands around the circle, and sang taps. This did not sound very Indian, thinks Lois. It sounded like a bugle call at a military post, in a movie. But Cappie was never one to be much concerned with consistency, or with archaeology.

After breakfast the next morning they set out from the main dock, in four canoes, three in each. The lipstick stripes have not come off completely, and still show faintly pink, like healing burns. They wear their white denim sailing hats, because of the sun, and thin-striped T-shirts, and pale baggy shorts with the cuffs rolled up. The middle one kneels, propping her rear end against the rolled sleeping bags. The counsellors going with them are Pat and Kip. Kip is no-nonsense; Pat is easier to wheedle, or fool.

There are puffy clouds and a small breeze. Glints come from the little waves. Lois is in the bow of Kip's canoe. She still can't do a J-stroke very well, and she will have to be in the bow or the middle for the whole trip. Lucy is behind her; her own J-stroke is even worse. She splashes Lois with her paddle, quite a big splash.

"I'll get you back," says Lois.

"There was a stable fly on your shoulder," Lucy says.

45   Lois turns to look at her, to see if she's grinning. They're in the habit of splashing each other. Back there, the camp has vanished behind the first long point of rock and rough trees. Lois feels as if an invisible rope has broken. They're floating free, on their own, cut loose. Beneath the canoe the lake goes down, deeper and colder than it was a minute before.

"No horsing around in the canoe," says Kip. She's rolled her T-shirt sleeves up to the shoulder; her arms are brown and sinewy, her jaw determined, her stroke perfect. She looks as if she knows exactly what she is doing.

The four canoes keep close together. They sing, raucously and with defiance; they sing "The Quartermaster's Store," and "Clementine," and "Alouette." It is more like bellowing than singing.

After that the wind grows stronger, blowing slantwise against the bows, and they have to put all their energy into shoving themselves through the water.

Was there anything important, anything that would provide some sort of reason or clue to what happened next? Lois can remember everything, every detail; but it does her no good.

50   They stopped at noon for a swim and lunch, and went on in the afternoon. At last they reached Little Birch, which was the first campsite for overnight. Lois and Lucy made the fire, while the others pitched the heavy canvas tents. The fireplace was already there, flat stones piled unto a U. A burned tin can and a beer bottle had been left in it. Their fire went out, and they had to restart it. "Hustle your bustle," said Kip. "We're starving."

The sun went down, and in the pink sunset light they brushed their teeth and spat the toothpaste froth into the lake. Kip and Pat put all the food that wasn't in cans into a packsack and slung it into a tree, in case of bears.

Lois and Lucy weren't sleeping in a tent. They'd begged to be allowed to sleep out; that way they could talk without the others hearing. If it rained, they told Kip, they promised not to crawl dripping into the tent over everyone's legs: they would get under the canoes. So they were out on the point.

Lois tried to get comfortable inside her sleeping bag, which smelled of musty storage and of earlier campers, a stale salty sweetness. She curled herself up, with her sweater rolled up under her head for a pillow and her flashlight inside her sleeping bag so it wouldn't roll away. The muscles of her sore arms were making small pings, like rubber bands breaking.

Beside her Lucy was rustling around. Lois could see the glimmering oval of her white face.

55   "I've got a rock poking into my back," said Lucy.

"So do I," said Lois. "You want to go into the tent?" She herself didn't, but it was right to ask.

"No," said Lucy. She subsided into her sleeping bag. After a moment she said, "It would be nice not to go back."

"To camp?" said Lois.

"To Chicago," said Lucy. "I hate it there."

60   "What about your boyfriend?" said Lois. Lucy didn't answer. She was either asleep or pretending to be.

There was a moon, and a movement of the trees. In the sky there were stars, layers of stars that went down and down. Kip said that when the stars were bright like that instead of hazy it meant bad weather later on. Out on the lake there were two loons, calling to each other in their insane, mournful voices. At the time it did not sound like grief. It was just background.

The lake in the morning was flat calm. They skimmed along over the glassy surface, leaving V-shaped trails behind them; it felt like flying. As the sun rose higher it got hot, almost too hot. There were stable flies in the canoes, landing on a bare arm or leg for a quick sting. Lois hoped for wind.

They stopped for lunch at the next of the named campsites, Lookout Point. It was called this because, although the site itself was down near the water on a flat shelf of rock, there was a sheer cliff nearby and a trail that led up to the top. The top was the lookout, although what you were supposed to see from there was not clear. Kip said it was just a view.

Lois and Lucy decided to make the climb anyway. They didn't want to hang around waiting for lunch. It wasn't their turn to cook, though they hadn't avoided much by not doing it, because cooking lunch was no big deal, it was just unwrapping the cheese and getting out the bread and peanut butter, but Pat and Kip always had to do their woodsy act and boil up a billy tin for their own tea.

65   They told Kip where they were going. You had to tell Kip where you were going, even if it was only a little way into the woods to get dry twigs for kindling. You could never go anywhere without a buddy.

"Sure," said Kip, who was crouching over the fire, feeding driftwood into it. "Fifteen minutes to lunch."

"Where are they off to?" said Pat. She was bringing their billy tin of water from the lake.

"Lookout," said Kip.

"Be careful," said Pat. She said it as an afterthought, because it was what she always said.

70   "They're old hands," Kip said.

Lois looks at her watch: it's ten to twelve. She is the watch-minder; Lucy is careless of time. They walk up the path, which is dry earth and rocks, big rounded pinky-grey boulders or split-open ones with jagged edges. Spindly balsam and spruce trees grow to either side, the lake is blue fragments to the left. The sun is right overhead; there are no shadows anywhere. The heat comes up at them as well as down. The forest is dry and crackly.

It isn't far, but it's a steep climb and they're sweating when they reach the top. They wipe their faces with their bare arms, sit gingerly down on a scorching-hot rock, five feet from the edge but too close for Lois. It's a lookout all right, a sheer drop to the lake and a long view over the water, back the way they've come. It's amazing to Lois that they've travelled so far, over all that water, with nothing to propel them but their own arms. It makes her feel strong. There are all kinds of things she is capable of doing.

"It would be quite a dive off here," says Lucy.

"You'd have to be nuts," says Lois.

75 "Why?" says Lucy. "It's really deep. It goes straight down." She stands up and takes a step nearer the edge. Lois gets a stab in her midriff, the kind she gets when a car goes too fast over a bump. "Don't," she says.

"Don't what?" says Lucy, glancing around at her mischievously. She knows how Lois feels about heights. But she turns back. "I really have to pee," she says.

"You have toilet paper?" says Lois, who is never without it. She digs in her shorts pocket.

"Thanks," says Lucy.

They are both adept at peeing in the woods: doing it fast so the mosquitoes don't get you, the underwear pulled up between the knees, the squat with the feet apart so you don't wet your legs, facing downhill. The exposed feeling of your bum, as if someone is looking at you from behind. The etiquette when you're with someone else is not to look. Lois stands up and starts to walk back down the path, to be out of sight.

80 "Wait for me?" says Lucy.

Lois climbed down, over and around the boulders, until she could not see Lucy; she waited. She could hear the voices of the others, talking and laughing, down near the shore. One voice was yelling, "Ants! Ants!" Someone must have sat on an ant hill. Off to the side, in the woods, a raven was croaking, a hoarse single note.

She looked at her watch: it was noon. This is when she heard the shout.

She has gone over and over it in her mind since, so many times that the first, real shout has been obliterated, like a footprint trampled by other footprints. But she is sure (she is almost positive, she is nearly certain) that it was not a shout of fear. Not a scream. More like a cry of surprise, cut off too soon. Short, like a dog's bark.

"Lucy?" Lois said. Then she called "Lucy!" By now she was clambering back up, over the stones of the path. Lucy was not up there. Or she was not in sight.

85 "Stop fooling around," Lois said. "It's lunchtime." But Lucy did not rise from behind a rock or step out, smiling, from behind a tree. The sunlight was all around; the rocks looked white. "This isn't funny!" Lois said, and it wasn't, panic was rising in her, the panic of a small child who does not know where the bigger ones are hidden. She could hear her own heart. She looked quickly around; she lay down on the ground and looked over the edge of the cliff. It made her feel cold. There was nothing.

She went back down the path, stumbling; she was breathing too quickly; she was too frightened to cry. She felt terrible—guilty and dismayed, as if she had done something very bad, by mistake. Something that could never be repaired. "Lucy's gone," she told Kip.

Kip looked up from her fire, annoyed. The water in the billy can was boiling. "What do you mean, gone?" she said. "Where did she go?"

"I don't know," said Lois. "She's just gone."

No one had heard the shout, but then no one had heard Lois calling, either. They had been talking among themselves, by the water.

90 Kip and Pat went up to the lookout and searched and called, and blew their whistles. Nothing answered.

Then they came back down, and Lois had to tell exactly what had happened. The other girls all sat in a circle and listened to her. Nobody said anything. They all looked frightened, especially Pat and Kip. They were the leaders. You did not just lose a camper like this, for no reason at all.

"Why did you leave her alone?" said Kip.

"I was just down the path," said Lois. "I told you. She had to go to the bathroom." She did not say pee in front of people older than herself.

Kip looked disgusted.

95 "Maybe she just walked off into the woods and got turned around," said one of the girls.

"Maybe she's doing it on purpose," said another.

Nobody believed either of these theories.

They took the canoes and searched around the base of the cliff, and peered down into the water. But there had been no sound of falling rock; there had been no splash. There was no clue, nothing at all. Lucy had simply vanished.

That was the end of the canoe trip. It took them the same two days to go back that it had taken coming in, even though they were short a paddler. They did not sing.

100 After that, the police went in a motorboat, with dogs; they were the Mounties and the dogs were German shepherds, trained to follow trails in the woods. But it had rained since, and they could find nothing.

Lois is sitting in Cappie's office. Her face is bloated with crying, she's seen that in the mirror. By now she feels numbed; she feels as if she has drowned. She can't stay here. It has been too much of a shock. Tomorrow her parents are coming to take her away. Several of the other girls who were on the canoe trip are also being collected. The others will have to stay, because their parents are in Europe, or cannot be reached.

Cappie is grim. They've tried to hush it up, but of course everyone in camp knows. Soon the papers will know too. You can't keep it quiet, but what can be said? What can be said that makes any sense? "Girl vanishes in broad daylight, without a trace." It can't be believed. Other things, worse things, will be suspected. Negligence, at the very least. But they have always taken such care. Bad luck will gather around Camp Manitou like a fog; parents will avoid it, in favour of other, luckier places. Lois can see Cappie thinking all this, even through her numbness. It's what anyone would think.

Lois sits on the hard wooden chair in Cappie's office, beside the old wooden desk, over which hangs the thumbtacked bulletin board of normal camp routine, and gazes at Cappie through her puffy eyelids. Cappie is now smiling what is supposed to be a reassuring smile. Her manner is too casual: she's after something. Lois has seen this look on Cappie's face when she's been sniffing out contraband chocolate bars, hunting down those rumoured to have snuck out of their cabins at night.

"Tell me again," says Cappie, "from the beginning."

105   Lois has told her story so many times by now, to Pat and Kip, to Cappie, to the police, that she knows it word for word. She knows it, but she no longer believes it. It has become a story. "I told you," she said. "She wanted to go to the bathroom. I gave her my toilet paper. I went down the path, I waited for her. I heard this kind of shout . . . ."

"Yes," says Cappie, smiling confidingly, "but before that. What did you say to one another?"

Lois thinks. Nobody has asked her this before. "She said you could dive off there. She said it went straight down."

"And what did you say?"

"I said you'd have to be nuts."

110   "Were you mad at Lucy?" says Cappie, in an encouraging voice.

"No," says Lois. "Why would I be mad at Lucy? I wasn't ever mad at Lucy." She feels like crying again. The times when she has in fact been mad at Lucy have been erased already. Lucy was always perfect.

"Sometimes we're angry when we don't know we're angry," says Cappie, as if to herself. "Sometimes we get really mad and we don't even know it. Sometimes we might do a thing without meaning to, or without knowing what will happen. We lose our tempers."

Lois is only thirteen, but it doesn't take her long to figure out that Cappie is not including herself in any of this. By we she means Lois. She is accusing Lois of pushing Lucy off the cliff. The unfairness of this hits her like a slap. "I didn't!" she says.

"Didn't what?" says Cappie softly. "Didn't what, Lois?"

115   Lois does the worst thing, she begins to cry. Cappie gives her a look like a pounce. She's got what she wanted.

Later, when she was grown up, Lois was able to understand what this interview had been about. She could see Cappie's desperation, her need for a story, a real story with a reason in it; anything but the senseless vacancy Lucy had left for her to deal with. Cappie wanted Lois to supply the reason, to be the reason. It wasn't even for the newspapers or the parents, because she could never make such an accusation without proof. It was for herself: something to explain the loss of Camp Manitou and of all she had worked for, the years of entertaining spoiled children and buttering up parents and making a fool of herself with feathers stuck in her hair. Camp Manitou was in fact lost. It did not survive.

Lois worked all this out, twenty years later. But it was far too late. It was too late even ten minutes afterwards, when she'd left Cappie's office and was walking slowly back to her cabin to pack. Lucy's clothes were still there, folded on the shelves, as if waiting. She felt the other girls in the cabin watching her with speculation in their eyes. *Could she have done it? She must have done it.* For the rest of her life, she has caught people watching her in this way.

Maybe they weren't thinking this. Maybe they were merely sorry for her. But she felt she had been tried and sentenced, and this is what has stayed with her: the knowledge that she had been singled out, condemned for something that was not her fault.

Lois sits in the living room of her apartment, drinking a cup of tea. Through the knee-to-ceiling window she has a wide view of Lake Ontario, with its skin of wrinkled blue-grey light, and of the willows of Centre Island shaken by a wind, which is silent at this distance, and on this side of the glass. When there isn't too much pollution she can see the far shore, the foreign shore; though today it is obscured.

120   Possibly she could go out, go downstairs, do some shopping; there isn't much in the refrigerator. The boys say she doesn't get out enough. But she isn't hungry, and moving, stirring from this space, is increasingly an effort.

She can hardly remember, now, having her two boys in the hospital, nursing them as babies; she can hardly remember getting married, or what Rob looked like. Even at the time she never felt she was paying full attention. She was tired a lot, as if she was living not one life but two: her own, and another, shadowy life that hovered around her and would not let itself be realized—the life of what would have happened if Lucy had not stepped sideways, and disappeared from time.

She would never go up north, to Rob's family cottage or to any place with wild lakes and wild trees and the calls of loons. She would never go anywhere near. Still, it was as if she was always listening for another voice, the voice of a person who should have been there but was not. An echo.

While Rob was alive, while the boys were growing up, she could pretend she didn't hear it, this empty space in sound. But now there is nothing much left to distract her.

She turns away from the window and looks at her pictures. There is the pinkish island, in the lake, with the intertwisted trees. It's the same landscape they paddled through, that distant summer. She's seen travelogues of this country, aerial photographs; it looks different from above, bigger, more hopeless: lake after lake, random blue puddles in dark green bush, the trees like bristles.

125   How could you ever find anything there, once it was lost? Maybe if they cut it all down, drained it all away, they might find Lucy's bones, some time, wherever they are hidden. A few bones, some buttons, the buckle from her shorts.

    But a dead person is a body; a body occupies space, it exists somewhere. You can see it; you put it in a box and bury it in the ground, and then it's in a box in the ground. But Lucy is not in a box, or in the ground. Because she is nowhere definite, she could be anywhere.

    And these paintings are not landscape paintings. Because there aren't any landscapes up there, not in the old, tidy European sense, with a gentle hill, a curving river, a cottage, a mountain in the background, a golden evening sky. Instead there's a tangle, a receding maze, in which you can become lost almost as soon as you step off the path. There are no backgrounds in any of these paintings, no vistas; only a great deal of foreground that goes back and back, endlessly, involving you in its twists and turns of tree and branch and rock. No matter how far back in you go, there will be more. And the trees themselves are hardly trees; they are currents of energy, charged with violent colour.

    Who knows how many trees there were on the cliff just before Lucy disappeared? Who counted? Maybe there was one more, afterwards.

    Lois sits in her chair and does not move. Her hand with the cup is raised halfway to her mouth. She hears something, almost hears it: a shout of recognition, or of joy.

130   She looks at the paintings, she looks into them. Every one of them is a picture of Lucy. You can't see her exactly, but she's there, in behind the pink stone island or the one behind that. In the picture of the cliff she is hidden by the clutch of fallen rocks towards the bottom, in the one of the river shore she is crouching beneath the overturned canoe. In the yellow autumn woods she's behind the tree that cannot be seen because of other trees, over beside the blue sliver of pond; but if you walked into the picture and found the tree, it would be the wrong one, because the right one would be farther on.

    Everyone has to be somewhere, and this is where Lucy is. She is in Lois's apartment, in the holes that open inwards on the wall, not like windows but like doors. She is here. She is entirely alive.

READING AND REACTING

1. Cappie uses language that she believes is "how Indians talk." What significance does this language have?
2. What does the wilderness signify, and how has it shaped Lois's life from the time of her summer camp experience?

3. Lois has several pictures by important Canadian artists. Describe the paintings and consider why Lois has collected them.
4. What happens to Lucy? Why?
5. The story is written in the third person, but the narrative is focused on what Lois thinks. Why are Lucy's thoughts not included?
6. What is the significance of the title?
7. **JOURNAL ENTRY** Imagine you are Lucy and write a final letter to your friend Lois.

Related Works: "The Yellow Wall-Paper" (p. 189), "Tamarindus Indica" (p. 383), "The Love Song of J. Alfred Prufrock" (p. 833)

◈ WRITING SUGGESTIONS: SYMBOL AND ALLEGORY

1. Select a story from anywhere in this text, and discuss its use of symbols.
2. Birds figure prominently in "A Very Old Man with Enormous Wings" (p. 432) and "The Loons" (p. 249). Write an essay in which you discuss the possible symbolic significance of birds in each story.
3. Write an essay in which you discuss the conflicts present in "Young Goodman Brown," showing how the allegorical elements in the story reflect and reinforce these conflicts.
4. If Shirley Jackson had wished to write "The Lottery" as an allegory whose purpose was to expose the evils of Nazi Germany, what revisions would she have had to make to convey the dangers of blind obedience to authority? Consider the story's symbols, the characters (and their names), and the setting.
5. In a number of works in this anthology, prized possessions function as symbols—for example, the quilt in "Everyday Use," the clock and de Spain's rug in "Barn Burning," and the stamps in *Les Belles Soeurs*. Write an essay in which you discuss the symbolic significance of a prized possession in any two works in this text.

CHAPTER 10

Theme

❖ ❖ ❖

I think a writer's job is to provoke questions. I like to think that if someone's read a book of mine, they've had—I don't know—the literary equivalent of a shower. Something that would start them thinking in a slightly different way perhaps. That's what I think writers are for.

DORIS LESSING, *Writers at Work,* 9th ed.

A work of art encountered as a work of art is an experience, not a statement or an answer to a question. Art is not only about something; it is something. A work of art is a thing in the world, not just a text or commentary on the world.

SUSAN SONTAG, "On Style" in *Against Interpretation*

One of the most difficult things is the first paragraph. I have spent many months on a first paragraph, and once I get it, the rest just comes out very easily. In the first paragraph you solve most of the problems with your book. The theme is defined, the style, the tone. At least in my case, the first paragraph is a kind of sample of what the rest of the book is going to be. That's why writing a book of short stories is much more difficult than writing a novel. Every time you write a short story, you have to begin all over again.

GABRIEL GARCÍA MÁRQUEZ, *Writers at Work,* 6th ed.

With me it has something to do with the fight against death, the feeling that we lose everything everyday, and writing is a way of convincing yourself perhaps that you're doing something about this. . . . There's that feeling about the—I was talking about the external world, the sights and sounds and smells—I can't stand to let go without some effort at this, at capturing them in words, and of course I don't see why one has to do that. You can experience things directly without feeling that, but I suppose I just experience things finally when I do get them into words.

ALICE MUNRO, *Eleven Canadian Novelists*

◇ ◇ ◇

The **theme** of a work of literature is its central or dominant idea. *Theme* is not the same as *plot* or *subject,* two terms with which it is sometimes confused. A simple *plot summary* of Tadeusz Borowski's "Silence," a story about survivors of the Holocaust, could be "Prisoners are liberated from a concentration camp, and despite the warnings of the American officer, they kill a captured German guard." The statement "'Silence' is about freed prisoners and a guard" could define the *subject* of the story. A statement of the *theme* of "Silence," however, would have to do more than summarize its plot or identify its subject; it would have to convey the values and ideas expressed by the story. Many effective stories are complex, expressing more than one theme, and "Silence" is no exception. You could say, for example, that "Silence" suggests that human beings have a need for vengeance. You could also say the story demonstrates that silence is sometimes the only response possible when one is confronting unspeakable horrors. Although both these themes—and others—are expressed in the story, one theme seems to dominate—the idea that under extreme conditions the oppressed can become as morally bankrupt as their oppressors.

When writing about theme, you need to do more than tell what happens in the story. The theme you identify should be a general truth that extends beyond the story and applies to the world outside fiction. Compare these two statements about Alice Munro's "Boys and Girls" (p. 504):

> Munro's "Boys and Girls" is a "coming of age story" about a girl who lives on a farm.

> Munro's "Boys and Girls" shows the negative impact gender roles and stereotypes have on women.

The first statement merely tells what the story is about; the second statement identifies the story's theme, a general observation about humanity.

Some short works (fairy tales or fables, for example) have themes that can be summed up as *clichés*—overused phrases or expressions—or as *morals*—lessons dramatized by the work. The fairy tale "Cinderella," for example, expresses the clichéd theme that a virtuous girl who endures misfortune will eventually achieve her just reward; the fable "The Tortoise and the Hare" illustrates the moral "Slow and steady wins the race." Like "Boys and Girls," however, the stories in this anthology have themes that are more complex than clichés or morals.

INTERPRETING THEMES
◊ ◊ ◊

Contemporary critical theory holds that the theme of a work of fiction is as much the creation of readers as of the writer. The readers' backgrounds, knowledge, values, and beliefs all play a part in determining the theme or themes they will identify in a work. Most readers, for example, will realize that James Joyce's story "Araby" (p. 267)—in which the main character fails in his first romantic effort—expresses a conventional **initiation theme,** revealing growing up to be a disillusioning and painful process. Still, different readers bring different perspectives to the story and, in some cases, see different themes.

Different readers may see different themes in a story, but your interpretation of a theme must make sense in light of what is actually in the story. Evidence from the work, not just your own feelings or assumptions, must support your interpretation, and a single symbol or one statement by a character is not enough in itself to reveal a story's theme. Therefore, you must identify a cross section of examples from the text to support your interpretation of the story's theme. If you say that the theme of Joyce's "Araby" is that an innocent idealist is inevitably doomed to disillusionment, you have to find examples from the text to support your statement. You could begin with the title, concluding that the word *Araby* suggests dreams of exotic beauty that the boy tries to find when he goes to the bazaar. You could reinforce your idea about the elusiveness of beauty by pointing out that Mangan's unattainable sister is a symbol of this beauty that the boy wants so desperately to find. Finally, you could show how idealism is ultimately crushed by society: at the end of the story, the boy stands alone in the darkness and realizes that his dreams of beauty are childish fantasies. Although other readers may have different responses to "Araby," they should find your interpretation reasonable if you support it with enough examples.

IDENTIFYING THEMES

◇ ◇ ◇

Every element of a story can shed light on its themes. As you analyze a short story, look for features that reveal and reinforce what you perceive to be the story's most important ideas.

The *title* of a story can often provide insight into the theme or themes of a story. The title of Timothy Findley's "Stones" (p. 135) emphasizes a major idea in the story—that Ben "would have loved a stone" and that stones mark the ending of his father's loving disposition and his heart's turning to stone.

Sometimes a *narrator's or character's statement* can reveal a theme. For example, at the end of Alice Munro's "Boys and Girls" the narrator thinks "maybe it was true" when she is dismissed for being "only a girl." The whole question of how boys and girls are socialized and how gender is created is highlighted by the narrator's words.

The *arrangement of events* in a story can suggest a story's theme, as it does in William Faulkner's story "A Rose for Emily" (p. 90), which begins with Emily's death and then goes back in time to reveal the steps that bring Emily to her desperate action—an action that is not revealed until the end of the story. Thus, Faulkner builds sympathy for Emily before revealing her grotesque actions.

A story's *conflict* can offer clues to its theme. In "Araby" the young boy believes that his society neglects art and beauty and glorifies the mundane. This conflict between the boy's idealism and his world can help readers understand why the boy isolates himself in his room reading books and why he retreats into dreams of idealized love. A major theme of the story—that growing up leads to the loss of youthful idealism—is revealed by this central conflict.

Similarly, in Charlotte Perkins Gilman's "The Yellow Wall-Paper" (p. 189) the main character, a woman who has recently had a baby, is in conflict with the larger nineteenth-century society in which she lives. She is suffering from "temporary nervous depression," what doctors today recognize as postpartum depression. Following the practice of the time, her physician has ordered complete bed rest and has instructed her husband to deprive her of all mental and physical stimulation. This harsh treatment leads the narrator to lose her grasp on reality; eventually, she begins to hallucinate. The central conflict of the story is clearly between the woman and her society, controlled by men. This conflict communicates the theme: that in nineteenth-century North America, women are dominated not just by their husbands and the male medical establishment, but also by society as a whole.

The *point of view* of a story can also help shed light on theme. For instance, a writer's use of an unreliable first-person narrator can help to communicate the theme of a story. Thus, Montresor's self-serving first-person account of his crime in Edgar Allan Poe's "The Cask of Amontillado" (p. 227) and his convincing attempts to justify his actions enable readers to understand the dangers of irrational anger and misplaced ideas about honour. The voice of a third-person narrator can also help to convey a story's theme. For example, the detachment of the narrator in Shirley Jackson's "The Lottery" (p. 319) serves to heighten the horror of the events. The dispassionate voice of the narrator is at odds with the destruction occurring in the story.

Quite often a story will give names, places, and objects symbolic significance. These *symbols* can not only enrich the story, but also help to convey a central theme. For example, the rocking horse in D. H. Lawrence's "The Rocking-Horse Winner" (p. 370) can be seen as a symbol of the boy's desperate desire to remain a child. Interpreted in this way, it reinforces the theme that innocence cannot survive when it confronts greed and selfishness. Similarly, Nathaniel Hawthorne's "Young Goodman Brown" (p. 307) uses symbols such as the walking stick, the woods, sunset and night, and the vague shadows to develop one of its central themes: that if a person strays from the path of faith, evil is everywhere.

Finally, *changes in a character* can shed light on the theme or themes of the story. The changes in the main character in Hélène Rioux's "Opening Night" (p. 542), for example, show the lengths to which the character tries to satisfy her date while being unable to enjoy the food he has prepared.

CHECKLIST: WRITING ABOUT THEME

✓ What is the central theme of the story?

✓ What other themes can you identify?

✓ Does the title of the story suggest a theme?

✓ Does the narrator, or any character, make statements that express or imply a theme?

✓ In what way does the arrangement of events in the story suggest a theme?

✓ In what way does the central conflict of the story suggest a theme?

✓ How does the point of view shed light on the story's central theme?

✓ Do any symbols suggest a theme?

✓ Do any characters in the story change in any significant way? Do their changes convey a particular theme?

✓ Have you clearly identified the story's central theme, rather than just summarized the plot or stated the subject?

✓ Does your statement of the story's central theme make a general observation that has an application beyond the story itself?

◊ **STEVEN HEIGHTON** (1961–   ) was born in Toronto and has lived in Northern Ontario, Western Canada, and Japan. While attending Queen's University in Kingston, Heighton gained inspiration from a creative writing course he took. His stories capture the intimate inner reflections of his characters and frequently take place in international settings. In his first collection of short stories, *Flight Paths of the Emperor* (1992), he looks at the crossing of Japanese and Western cultures. *The Shadow Boxer* (2000), his first novel, is set in Northern Ontario, Toronto, and Cairo. He also wrote an extended essay titled *The Admen Move on Lhasa: Writing and Culture in a Virtual World* (1997) in which he criticizes corporate culture, mass tourism, and the ubiquity of advertising. Heighton's second novel, *Afterlands* (2005), focuses on a failed Arctic mission and its survivors.

◊ ◊ ◊

STEVEN HEIGHTON

Flight Paths of the Emperor
(1992)

I: That autumn the Emperor's death seemed imminent, but he surprised the whole nation with a last-minute rally. By November the daily reports from Tōkyō were encouraging: Hirohito-sama was in stable condition, eating regularly, rising after meals to take light exercise and each day enjoying the televised *sumo* he had always loved. Still, Ōsaka's dirty air seemed to hum with an electric tension. The old man's time was coming, that much was clear, and his death might set in motion a series of complex and precarious changes. Even in a time of fabulous prosperity, the advent of a new era was cause for concern.

In mid-December, snow appeared in the last range of hills you cross travelling north towards Ōsaka. Sandra and Nick were returning to the city by train after spending the day on a mountain dotted with temples and old tombs.

"You're cold," Sandra said to him, testing the silence, wrapping a warm, thickset arm round his shoulder. The train entered a tunnel and harsh lights snapped on above their heads. Nick looked away.

"I'll be fine," he said. "I'm not really cold."

5   "You're shaking. I can feel it."

"I'm not cold."

"Anyway we're almost home. Are you hungry? You must be hungry by now."

The train came out of the long tunnel and he turned back to her. Snow-covered hills framed her tired face.

"I said you must be hungry."

10   "We should have left at two," he said, turning from her and glaring into the aisle. A few rows ahead an old woman slumped sidelong out of her seat, half blocking the aisle, white head and tiny shoulders trembling to the rhythm of the train. She tried briefly to rouse and straighten herself, then yielded to the embrace of gravity. Her mouth lolled open as if frozen in mid-phrase. For a moment Nick hated the slack mouth, its snoring.

"I thought you wanted to see the place," Sandra said.

"We saw it this morning in two hours. It was nice. We didn't need to stay all day." He shivered. The mountain's chill had settled into his limbs and bones.

She pulled her arm away and looked out the window.

"You know we couldn't leave at two, Nick. We promised my boss. . . ."

15   "You promised," he said. "I'm the one who found the grave."

"You mean the tomb."

"You know what I mean."

"Come on Nick, we were going up anyway, it's customary for friends. . . ."

"Not on their day off it isn't. Christ. You do more than enough for him as it is." He shook his head and saw her pale knuckles tighten on the arm-rest.

20   Dusk was falling behind the mountains. To the north the glow of the city's lights crept upward, gathering strength.

"Nick, please, I've apologized. All right? I really didn't think it would take so long to find."

"Like trying to find a friendly face," he said softly, "in an Ōsaka crowd."

She stiffened. Her eyes were a soft, aquatic green, but in anger they would freeze up with a biting, brittle glint, like marbles or the glass eyes of a doll. "Oh I'm sure you'd have no trouble doing that," she whispered, "if you liked. Maybe you've already found a friendly face or two. Maybe I have myself."

"I don't believe you."

25 Her head sagged. "Don't, then. Why should you? You know by now what I'm like. . . . And I know you."

Looking numbly into his lap he saw the dull, delicate ellipse of his wedding ring, the chilled hands open, palms upward, as if showing they had nothing to hide. "I told you I was through with that when we left Canada."

"But now we're going back."

"You say it as if it's my fault."

"You mean it's mine," she said, and he saw that he had, he had meant that exactly, it was her fault, or at least her mother's—they were going back on her account.

30 "Look—not yours. I'm sorry. I'm glad we're going back."

"I know you're not."

"I am. I am, really. Sandra? Look, I'm glad we're going back."

The news hadn't been so much of a surprise. Dorothy's illness had almost kept them from leaving home in the first place. Of course she had urged them to go but under her bright brisk entreaties was a plaintive, despairing strain, another voice with its own sharp message: *Go, hurry up and go, why stay and watch a fat old lady fall apart when you can tour the Orient? You're still young, you have your health, I know you want to leave me. . . .*

Promises. A promise to sprinkle water on the tomb of the Takamuras. A promise to return if Dorothy's condition should worsen. A promise to love, honour and cherish, and so on.

35 His father-in-law's letter was curt and pointed. Dorothy might be gone by Christmas—

Sandra's body was turned from him now. Her heavy shoulders quivered. Softly she blew her nose. He checked the surrounding seats and made sure most of their neighbours were asleep; the middle-aged women across the aisle reading fashion magazines had kindly granted them the status of ghosts. In Japan it is rude to blow one's nose in public, and ruder still for a couple to fight.

"Sandra?"

She spun round. Her face was strange to him, twisted by opposing urges, her sudden hatred and the wish to be reconciled. Now she would collaborate, conniving at the cheapest, most slapdash dénouement, forced by the broadcast warning that Namba Station was just minutes away into more and more tawdry, outrageous devices; anything, anything. That was how it would be. The overhead lights came on again, adding years to her face and startling him with the knowledge he had the power to make her ugly.

II: The next day at the school is taken up with farewells. His students are disappointed to see him go, but not especially surprised, since foreign teachers seldom stay long and always leave unexpectedly. His principal is frankly suspicious about "the illness of his wife's mother"; too many teachers, she probably feels, have killed off friends and relatives in order to escape their obligations in Japan.

40   "To judge from the teachers I have employed in the last ten years," she says, "you North Americans are a uniquely unhealthy race. Never have I seen so many friends and parents and uncles and cousins die suddenly. Oh, it is a terrible thing! So many of them struck down in the prime of life. And so often the day after I distribute pay cheques or generous advances."

    No doubt her suspicions are heightened by her never having met Sandra, whose existence she is too polite to call into question. She wants to know if he will return to the school when things are taken care of at home.

    "But Yamaguchi-san," he petitions her, "my contract expires on the first of March anyway. Surely it would be more reasonable—"

    "It would be more reasonable for you to honour your contract."

    "Of course. I realize that. But I'm afraid under the circumstances. . . ."

45   "Yes, yes, I know. You foreigners are always pleading circumstances. As if a contract is conditional upon ideal unchanging circumstances. But life is not like that, Mr Asher. Perhaps the Japanese ability to face and endure adversity in lieu of shying away from it is the main factor behind our current economic success. And our social stability. Why, look at the divorce rate in America these days. . . ." And she removes her glasses to indicate the interview is at an end.

    He bows slightly, then excuses himself and hurries into the classroom for his last lesson. As he enters the room he overhears his students discussing him in Japanese, and for a disconcerting instant learns that he is about to die. Then realizes his mistake: in Japanese *to go away* and *to pass away* sound almost the same.

    At the end of the class he hands out goodwill gifts his stepmother made for him before his departure—seven felt pencil-cases embroidered with scarlet maple leaves—and the students instantly retaliate with baskets of persimmons, Japanese tea-cakes, a summer kimono, fountain pens, notebooks, and from Teruyo, his best student, a miniature brush painting of butterflies in a temple garden. She seems to find her young teacher's fondness for the old culture quaint and charming.

    On his way out he trudges up the half-lit, flickering hallway to Yamaguchi-san's office. Her door is open. He stands in the doorway ready to announce his departure, but she is stiff in her chair, unaware of him, her enlarged eyes unfocused as she listens to a news report from a hidden radio. The Emperor, he thinks. Gone. He can make out only a few words. . . . Ah, the Emperor is still alive. But fallen into a profound sleep. His doctors are extremely worried. . . .

    Yamaguchi-san sees him and asks him what he wants. She adjusts her glasses and behind them her weak eyes blink repeatedly, as if finding it hard to bring his face into focus. She frowns. In her mind he already belongs to the past, not the future that is now bearing down on her, and his present apparition does not demand the usual courtesies.

50   "Well? You're on your way?"
"Yes. I'm sorry about what happened. . . ."
"These things cannot be helped. There are other teachers."

There are other schools, he has a cruel urge to say—but does not. He knows her school is in trouble. And it is clear to him as he watches her how quickly she is aging. The dusty fluorescent lights guttering above her head give her figure a dim, flickering cast, like a dead actress in an early film; he reminds himself she is of the generation that local youths—students not much younger than he—refer to as "already ancient."

On the train from Kōbe to Ōsaka he savours for the last time the felicitous imprecision of Japanese English. Even now the earnest blunderings of subway billboarders coax a smile from his exhaustion. Across the aisle an ad for some kind of hair tonic leaps out over the slumped shoulders of two dozing salarymen: NOT ONLY DRESS UP LIKE FOP BUT TO PERFORM HIMSELF MAN MAKES UP OWN HAIR SYLE. THERE'S SOMETHING THAT MAKES MAN LOOK SHINY.

55   He covers his smile with a hand, in the Japanese way. But as the emptying train emerges from the underworld and crosses a high trestle he sees among the office towers and neon billboards a great red crab pulsing above a famous restaurant. His mind makes the necessary connections. *Cancer* is the word no one uses when talking of Dorothy and her treasonous bowels; a word that sounds today more and more like a knell, an irreversible sentence, as Black Death must have sounded to medieval ears. And if Yamaguchi-san was right about the alarming rate at which Western marriages were dissolving she would have to admit also that cancer was now the scourge of the industrially poisoned home islands. In the last year several of his students had lost parents to the epidemic. Side-effects of the new era. Perhaps Yamaguchi-san was becoming ill herself. . . .

He gets out at Nagai and heads toward the apartment for the last time. From now on, everything he does will be transformed by this sense of finality. He wonders if there is an inkling here of how it feels having only weeks to live—when at last the fabulous is seen in the banal, in the faded sheen off antique faucets, late sunlight creeping over warped linoleum and the lovely, squalid muddle of shoes by the door. . . . He notices tonight that the Love Hotels he always passes are turning a brisk trade. The coffee-shops are closing up, and a drunk man reeling out of the American Dream smiles and asks him for a light. In the glow of the flame the man's round face is a rich amber, like an old moon on the rise, or a paper lantern at New Year's. There's something, he thinks, that makes man look shiny.

III: But illness wasn't just a reason for return; it was illness that caused your departure. Your parents divorced years ago and at home you watched your father and stepmother, who lived not far from your apartment, infect each other with their ennui and spite. It was open war. Your stepmother waged a more audacious campaign and you could not help foreseeing her eventual triumph—but on some points the two of them were still allied. For example, the two of them could not conceal (from you or themselves) their view that you might have done a bit better than Sandra. When you visited for Sunday dinner your stepmother would charge from the kitchen with a great basted bird, the raised legs tipped with crowns of frilled paper so it resembled a disgraced, murdered monarch—then present Sandra with a few eviscerate scraps that seemed to settle and wilt to nothing in the time it took father to mumble grace. She would never offer Sandra dessert, she would suggest a long walk after dinner, she would find other, more subtle ways to accuse her of obesity and ugliness. "A teacher!" she'd cried on first meeting Sandra, and at the time you believed she had said it with pleasure.

Your career was devouring itself too. You were not cut out for office work. The idleness, the cramped spaces oppressed you. You thought marriage would admit you to a secure and roomy structure promising freedom and maturity and creature comforts along with its duties and responsibilities—but its unexpected confines brought out the ogre in you, the wayward, wilful child. On your desk for several years you kept a picture of your wife on your wedding day and insisted to yourself with pious regularity that this was the Sandra you'd married; and every evening when she came home (exactly twenty minutes after you) she looked less and less like the woman you spent your coffee breaks recreating. To fortify your image of the old, authentic Sandra and buttress her memory against the onslaught of this pudgy impostor, you erected along the edges of your desk a breastwork of wedding and pre-wedding pictures. And still the two of you could laugh together when recalling an incident from an office party: Gareth loudly presenting his girlfriend, a secretary from accounting who dressed plainly and used no cosmetics but had arrived made-up like an auditioning stripper— "This," he roared several times in the course of the evening, his pink face puffy with bourbon and pride, "is the *real* Barbara."

Your work suffered. Your boss dropped hints, then began to make warnings. *You'd better shape up, Asher. You call in sick too often.* And you felt his sceptical eyes upon you at the Christmas party.

60   You started an affair, as Gareth had long predicted you would.

"Listen, Nick, a guy can't hold out forever. Times are changing, join the club." Gareth always sounded like the Dictionary of Phrases you later used in classes in Japan. "It's the way of the world. You're only young once—better make hay while the sun shines." He leered and licked a silver fleck of beerfoam off the edge of his moustache. "At least that's my personal opinion."

Randi was a celluloid goddess, a high-profile big-city model with an anorexic mind. Years of indiscriminate praise and the scheming deference of suitors had atrophied her brain like a cancer. When you made love to her she behaved as if your eyes were the attentive lenses of two Hollywood cameras. It was not till two years later in Japan that you found in subway ads and T-shirt inscriptions an analogue of her crippled speech.

You could laugh at her, and you could laugh at Gareth. You could even laugh at yourself. But you could not stop what you were doing.

Sandra knew all about it. You returned one afternoon from a taxing rendezvous and her look told you everything. She was sitting on the sofa under the window, her face grey in the pale light seeping through those cheap gauze curtains she'd insisted on. During your affair she had steadily put on weight— as if billowing with pent-up shame, indignation. Dorothy sat beside her discussing laxatives. Jim, as usual, had appropriated your Lay-Z-Boy chair and was drinking your last Export, while visibly fending off sleep. In their tired faces you saw Sandra's face shadowed as if in a crude, distorting mirror, a mirror marred by hairline cracks that map out an appalling future in wrinkles.

65   Terrible thoughts you were having. You felt them crawling inside you, multiplying, probing icy tentacles into your outermost parts. Clearly you were now a monster. But monsters are not immune to fear; and so, night after night, while dawn's official duties spun towards you out of the dark, you lay awake in the arms of premonitions: you and Sandra at seventy, chastened and respectable, leaving the ballet for streets where angels in designer blue-jeans scamper by just out of grasp. You are ugly and weak, indistinguishable from your own shadow; Sandra is grey, matronly, the deep scores round her mouth puckered in a chronic reproach.

At night you thought of Dorothy's symptoms. They had become too grim for her to invent. And Randi, beautiful Randi, solace of rent-by-the-hour afternoons, whose aerobic physique agreed in every particular with the latest aesthetic norms—Randi was accusing you of letting things at home get in the way. And she was right.

So that when Gareth mentioned to the boys at the office that he was going to Japan where there were countless jobs and good money and nice Japanese girls and chances to travel (and no parents-in-law) you asked him for more information.

He was always happy to help out a friend.

Japan! The Land of the Rising Sun! A new start! An exotic eastern fief that still had an emperor, for Christ's sake! A country enjoying untold prosperity! Not to mention the longest life expectancy in the world.

70 IV: Tōkyō in mid-December. Amplified Christmas carols in garbled English, flashing ornaments and parcel-laden crowds swarming through the Ginza. You find a traditional inn tucked between two giant banks on a street behind Ueno Station. Make several trips to the headquarters of Japan Air Lines where you confirm reservations and where, if you are not very much mistaken, a bowing kimono-clad doorman exclaims in fervent English, "We hope you have enjoyed our hostility."

Silence in the East Garden. Over one of these granite walls, behind some ornate, immemorial door in the heart of the Imperial Palace, the Mikado is dying. This morning's *Japan Times* informs you that he is in critical but stable condition—a contradiction in terms you have never understood. You learn that Hirohito-sama's problems are not particular but generalized and systemic. The old man is dying of his age. He ascended the throne, you recall, in 1925. Over sixty years as "Heaven's Emperor." The miracle is that he survived the crushing defeat his kingdom endured at the end of the Second World War. It was the death of an era, an empire, and a god. A middle-aged mortal, short and slight of build, stripped of power and god-hood, lived on.

Silence in the East Garden. You and Sandra walk together in the bitter air through a light, untimely fall of snow. Not even a breath of wind. The carefully tended maples, hedges and barren flower plots maintain a breathless repose. The crooked pines under the Palace walls are static, stiffly poised, like the moment itself—frozen. Things are about to be explained. Sandra takes your hand in hers and after a moment's hesitation you grip her stubby fingers. But your hand is cold and will not thaw and she soon withdraws her own hand for the relative warmth of a pocket.

Silence in the East Garden. You see an old man, shrunk and gnarled as an antique *bonsai*, hobbling away up a crossing path. It is Hirohito, the humbled Emperor, meditating perhaps on the nature of dreams and the vanity of human wishes.

"Don't be ridiculous, Nick. You know it's not him."

75 When you tell her it would be easy to mistake him—the old folks of that generation are all small and stooped—she explains it's because of an excess of salt in the diet which eats away the bones from inside. Sandra had been obsessed with pathology since her mother became ill.

In a nearby museum you admire a painting called "Moon Through a Spider's Web."

That evening on television there are more reports on the Emperor, who once again has defied all expectations and rallied. Your shaggy translation of the commentary yields this rough gem: "And so, once more, the epoch is preserved. . . ." There is weather, of course—snow expected to continue into tomorrow—and *sumo* highlights. It seems Chiyonofuji, the Emperor's favourite wrestler, will have to settle this year for second place; the winner is a 200 kilogram import from Hawaii.

Some time after midnight, grieving, choked with desire, you wake from a dream you cannot remember and reach out. With shivering fingers you touch her exposed nape but she sleeps on, her face to the wall, her broad shoulder shrugged above you like a stone slab or the cliffs of an island. For the briefest span the mark of your fingers remains in her flesh. How deep the snow must be now in the East Garden.

V: No beating around the bush. Japan was a healthy break in an otherwise run-down marriage. In Japan there were centripetal pressures that drove us together, threw us back on mutual resources, taught us to love, honour, cherish and revere. Or words to that effect. Now we were being called back, as I knew we would be, to a painfully familiar place, by the centrifugal powers of duty and disease.

80 In the dark flickering hull of the 747, hemmed in by strangers as in our narrow eight-*tatami* flat, issued a mediocre meal and with only stale soporific films for diversion, there was nothing left to do but turn and face each other and try to talk. This might be the last time we could give each other such attention.

"You don't want to see the film," I predicted, waving toward the screen where a khaki-clad adventurer faced a doddering chieftain. My voice boomed in the silent fuselage.

"I've seen it," she said. "It's old. I saw it before I knew you."

At least eight years. "Who with?"

"I can't remember. No wait—it must have been Marco."

85   Marco. "You should have married him," I said lightly, taking a gulp of Kirin. "He would have treated you better. He wanted to marry you, didn't he?"

On the screen two grimacing tribesmen grabbed the adventurer and menaced him with spears. I finished my Kirin.

"His family wanted him to. They were crazy about me."

Light from the screen flashed cinematically across her face.

"Like mine, eh?"

90   The adventurer shook himself free and yanked a huge handgun from his trousers. Cowardly tribesmen scattered into the jungle. The adventurer managed to shoot two or three. In the seats around us, earphoned spectators were laughing robustly—perhaps at some amusing remark on the soundtrack.

"Let's not talk about it," she whispered. "They won't be at the airport, will they?"

"I doubt it."

She gnawed at a stale bun. "Tell your stepmother I lost ten pounds in Japan. Maybe now she'll be able to love me."

"I don't know. . . . Maybe if you'd flunked Teacher's College the way she did. . . ."

95   "She'd hate me more."

"She doesn't hate you."

"God, Nick, it was forty years ago she failed! Why can't she forget?"

"She doesn't hate you. It's just that—I don't think she ever learned how to love. You or anyone else."

"Sometimes I thing the same thing about your father."

100   I choked down a forkful of rice. In a close-up, the dashing, unshaven adventurer poked the barrel of his revolver into the chieftain's slack throat. The old man rolled his eyes like a minstrel in black face.

"You don't understand my father. Don't say things like that about him."

Something we couldn't hear made the adventurer spin round. Cut to a close-up of a native armed with bow-and-arrow cowering at the edge of the jungle.

"You could have had other women. Your parents would have been happier. Hey, are you listening to me?"

The native, smirking like a sinister cupid, drew his bow and shot an arrow, then slumped back with a bullet hole between the eyes.

105   "You could have had other men," I said.

Cut to the chieftain, crumpled now against a palm tree with his own man's arrow sticking out of his gut. Clearly the nimble adventurer had leapt aside in the nick of time. He stood now, proud, monumental, a smoking revolver in his sinewy fist. Leering smugly he made some remark the surrounding audience enjoyed. It struck me that at this very moment we might be plummeting out of control to the sea.

"You were it," she said.

"For better or worse."

The adventurer blew a fume of smoke from the tip of his revolver.

110 "I do love you," I said.

VI: At the Seattle airport we have a few hours to kill before boarding our connecting flight to Toronto. After reduced-scale Ōsaka we find ourselves dwarfed by hordes of *sumo*-sized specimens gobbling hamburgers and potato chips and foot-long dogs. Sandra is sitting by the windows, her manner unnaturally stiff, eyes furtive, as if waking just now to the presence of her body. She watches jetplanes with exotic insignia taxi in from the runway. I buy a copy of the *Seattle Post* and enclose myself in the aloof, comforting shell of far-off disaster.

A small story on the second page mentions that Hirohito is failing again and is not expected to see the New Year. But we know by now that the Emperor, like the old epoch, is more resilient than anyone would think.

In the back pages I find another, smaller story:

HIROHITO STIRS BRIEFLY FROM PROLONGED SLEEP

TOKYO (Reuter)—Japan's Emperor Hirohito, who collapsed in mid-September, awoke briefly from his long sleep yesterday and looked around his bedroom, a palace official said. "I don't think His Majesty wanted anything but he opened up his eyes and looked around the room," the official said. The 87-year-old emperor, whose condition is described as being close to a coma, lost a small amount of blood overnight.

I close the paper. Sandra is still staring off toward the runway.

115 Through terminal windows the huge white cone of Mt Rainier looms like Fujiyama.

VII: Jim is waiting for you on the far side of customs. Without Dorothy beside him he is insubstantial, an extra on a vast set teeming with rangy, vivacious actors. He embraces his daughter as if you are a stranger, or a ghost he can exorcise only by ignoring. His felt cap is too large for him, his beige eyes anonymous, glassy, and when he turns to give your hand a perfunctory shake there is nothing to say. You smell beer, and something stronger. On the way home those lonely bar-room odours fill the car.

The burden of strength now squarely upon her, Sandra swells with solicitude, kindness, her eyes lit up with a desperate optimism. Like a new mother, all her fears have been transformed into a brisk, efficient energy. And after all the news is not so bad.

On the way home Jim leaks the truth gently, gradually, almost with reluctance, as if unwilling to forfeit the status of victim. He seems confused by the turn of events. Perhaps he doesn't know what to feel. Dorothy, it turns out, had made great progress. The doctors are puzzled but impressed and judge that if watched and encouraged this respite could last for years. *Remission,* that is the word they are using—an echo from made-for-TV movies about cancer victims and their unstinting families. An echo from the liturgy you recited in childhood—something about the remission of sins.

You embrace Dorothy. She looks the same as before the trip, a touch thinner perhaps, but shimmering with her recovery, the pride of it, an old woman who has made a brazen unforeseen leap from the crumbling lip of her grave onto solid ground. She has put on a light floral dress, as if for an August supper on the patio. Anecdotes seethe behind her eyes. She apologizes for not coming to the airport and assures you she feels fine and could have made it if the doctors hadn't been so fussy, insisting she stay in till after New Year's. . . .

120 She has been granted a reprieve. You suggest a drink to celebrate, and ask Jim for a double. He pours two. Well, cheers, he says, his voice an anaemic, squeaky whisper. Because of a simple diagnostic error you have been summoned back into the glittering web, and trapped. Your marriage, you understand, will be slowly exterminated. You can't be sure by whom. The old cling to life and link you with the dead. There will be no brave new era.

VIII: A few days into the New Year we visit my father's parents in Buckingham, Québec. My father tells me how excited they are about our coming; our visits have been an annual rite but this year they've expected us to be off in Japan, and perhaps have sensed (I've hinted at it enough in my letters) that we'll renew our contracts and stay another year, then another year after that. . . .

The night before driving up we have dinner at my father's house.

"They can't wait to see you," my father says, nodding sharply so that his glasses slip down his nose and he can peer at me over the rims. This is meant to prepare me for a serious remark. "It's a good thing you came back."

"In some ways," my stepmother corrects him. "After all, they had to break their contracts. And don't forget the reason. Illness is hardly a good thing. Care for some more potatoes, dear?"

125 Before she can reply, my stepmother ladles a steaming cairn of mashed potatoes onto Sandra's plate; out of deference to Dorothy's reduced condition, it seems, she has relaxed her campaign to save Sandra's figure, or remind her of it, or both.

"We're so glad to hear how she's improved," she says, reddening as she struggles with a piece of chicken. "We've been calling every couple of days."

"Unfortunately your grandfather has not improved," says my father. "Physically he's still fine, but I'm afraid his mind"—he taps a forefinger against his temple—"well, he hardly knows who I am any more. He spends most of his time sleeping, or staring at the TV."

"And think of the stations they get up there!" my stepmother cries, sitting back and fingering the scarab brooch on her cardigan. "Almost all of them French! He must be miserable."

"It comes to us all," my father reflects.

130   "I don't think he knew me the last time we went up," I say. "He seemed to think Sandra was a French barmaid he'd known during the First World War."

"*Ma chère Danielle, ma chère Danielle,*" chants Sandra—and with a brisk manual motion my father replaces his glasses, chuckling politely. The evil stepmother casts Sandra a baleful glance, perhaps feeling that mirth—especially in bilingual form—is unseemly in the awkward and the ugly, who should be more penitent in their misfortune. But tonight I ignore her. I feel generous, expansive, I accept second helpings and recklessly propose a bottle of wine. Naturally there is no wine in the house, but tonight my motion is not even condemned, and since it's allowed to stand—to breathe, as it were—it seems intoxicating of itself. Tomorrow, after all, we are going on a trip, and even if the destination is near and our hosts not exactly foreign it is a kind of adventure, a kind of escape.

With arthritic fingers my stepmother smooths the skin round her carefully designed lips. She is what fashion and film magazines dub "well-preserved." But now her opaque, ash-coloured eyes seem punctured, drained by our laughter, deflated; not an evil stepmother, I think, at all.

"You be careful tomorrow in the car," she says. "You don't know how your father worries about you when you're off on your travels. It gives him grey hair and lines above the eyes."

"We'll be careful," we promise.

135   "Especially once you cross over into Quebec," she goes on, relentless in her concern, "you know how they drive up there. And the roads! It's just terrible. When I was a student about your age I lived for a year in Montreal and"—she breaks off, having received some private signal from my father, who is peering again over the rim of his glasses. Tonight her mood is delicate, frangible as fine china; usually he cannot stop her so easily. He begins to speak. "I read in the papers today that they expect Emperor Hirohito to die by tomorrow morning." And gives his napkin an urbane twirl, as if to congratulate himself on this subtle gambit. No doubt he thinks he has changed the topic to something new.

IX: There had been a thaw in the night, and when Sandra took the wheel near Prescott he was free to sit back and study the passing landscape. A midwinter thaw is a kind of remission; this far north it never lasts for long. Nick looked out over a country of dark fields, deserted farms and trailer parks, gas stations, old churchyards under a marble sky.

Outside Hull the highway began to disintegrate, but the murderous drivers his stepmother had promised them were nowhere to be seen. It was Sunday, midafternoon, a time for digesting sermons or heavy dinners and peering out through frosted window-panes, not for trying to get anywhere.

Sandra and Nick hardly spoke from Kingston to Buckingham. In a small car on a midwinter's day, he thought, the centripetal forces that fused them in Japan should be active, irresistible. And they said nothing. Sandra's free hand lay by the gearshift, twitching now and then. Her eyes glared straight ahead up the empty road. On New Year's Eve they had made love with a tentative, awakening ardour, like shy lovers giving themselves for the first time; and feeling the generous warmth of her breasts and large body around him he had been sure he could never love another woman. But the next morning she was silent, sullen, their ecstatic communion a victim of poor sleep, anxious dreams or some abrupt recognition. Now that Dorothy was flagrantly well, the energy Sandra had conjured to support her seemed to vanish. The sheen passed from her eyes, the bloom from her cheeks. She moved heavily within her skin, her body had a sad, abandoned look, as if she herself had left and caught a flight to a far-off country. Again Nick felt a nagging urge to escape her, a desire for the youthful, conspicuous good looks that asked so little effort and promised eternal life. There were times Nick thought he knew the future, and times he thought he understood the past. He always turned out to be wrong. On the train to Ōsaka, faced with the prospect of an early return, resurrecting old grievances and finding them undecayed, he'd foreseen with absolute clarity the death of his marriage. On the flight home and on New Year's Eve—and even the night before at dinner, teamed with Sandra against a flagging stepmother—he'd been equally sure they would survive. How many times he had flown between the two extremes, a trapped commuter who never seemed to touch down. And he knew, if he knew anything at all, that he never would touch down.

They reached Buckingham at three. The streets were deserted. Already lamps glowed in most of the windows.

140   Ed was sleeping when they entered the peeling clapboard house he and Emily had owned since the war. Seeing their car in the driveway Emily had tried to rouse him but he'd barked at her to leave him alone, let him rest. "I told him it was Danielle," she beamed, her gentle face a shrivelled browless version of his father's. Her wandering left eye, he saw, was now completely free of her will. Her apron and house dress sported badly faded but plucky floral designs. "Danielle from Paris, I told him, but he didn't understand. He thought I meant there was somebody French at the door." She winked. "You know how he feels about them."

Nick knew. His grandparents were of Loyalist blood and solemnly stuck to principles of remote but hallowed lineage. For forty years they had resisted the French language with such determined gallantry that Gran could now claim with good conscience she hadn't learned a single word. *Picked up* was the way she liked to put it; *I haven't picked up a thing,* she would say, as if talking of trash from a gutter or a contagious, possibly fatal disease. But times were changing—that much she would allow. She and Ed were the last of a dying breed. At one time they'd had a lot of English friends here.

Grandmother's devoted bigotry was an old joke in his family, so he was startled when she asked them over tea and buttered scones about their experiences in Japan—then listened closely to their answers. She wanted to know how the older Japanese felt about the Emperor's illness, which she had been following in the papers. Then she recalled reading about his coronation in 1925. At that time she had been just thirty. Thirty years old!

She shook her head, as if at the farfetched remark of a guest only she could see. The lamplight crossing her pale hairnet made it shimmer like a web.

"Nicholas, if you'd only come here before your tour instead of leaving in such a hurry I might have taught you some Japanese."

145   Nick asked her, politely, what she was talking about. He reminded himself that Edward's Alzheimer's was not infectious.

"Not more than a few words, mind you. Just a phrase I learned as a girl."

He put down his teacup.

"I was only ten. I'm not sure I can remember. . . ." She broke off and stared at the untouched plate of scones. "You're not eating, Nicky."

"I'll have one in a minute, Gran, I promise—but how—"

150   "I spent half the morning baking them. Please. You loved them as a boy. Now . . . when *I* was ten . . . when *I* was ten my parents worked as missionaries in Churchill. Churchill is a small town in northern Manitoba."

He nodded. He knew. She had spoken of it many times before.

"One of their friends—another missionary—returned to Churchill from Japan. It was after a war, some war they'd just fought. . . . Sandra dear, please, you'll waste away—"

"The Russo-Japanese war," he said. "1904–05." Sandra and he exchanged looks and he could see she was feeling the same wonder, the miracle of dead figures and dry bones revived by an old woman's breath.

"Yes, that war. I forget the man's name. Now I remember—Sandberg, Reverend Sandberg. A big man, bald. He brought gifts for my sister and me. I can't remember what Vicky got but he gave me a doll. *Ningyo,* he said. That means doll."

155   Nick leaned over the table. "Yes. Yes it does."

Her fingers, gnarled like the roots of a tiny, ancient tree, carved rectangular shapes from the air.

"It came in one of those wooden boxes—Sandra, dear, you must know them—the crates they put mandarin oranges in—and it was in a bed of crumpled paper. A little boy, a little warrior in a kimono with a silk belt and a small wooden sword. And when he gave it to me Reverend Sandberg taught me to say what it was in Japanese. *"Honto,"* she said, squinting, focusing cloudy eyes on the scones. *"Honto no—ko—kotaishi."*

"That means 'a real prince.'"

"Yes, yes," she said, impatient with herself, seizing her teacup and glaring into it, a fortune-teller reading tea-leaves. "But he taught me to say a full sentence."

160   Her right eye fixed on his face while the other seemed to study another guest, invisible beside him. He saw her struggling to exhume the final honorific. As a teacher he'd learned never to intervene.

"*Honto no kotaishi*"—she paused, squinting—"*de gozaimasu*. A real prince, it is."

Nick beamed and nodded. "Old Japanese," he said, "extremely polite. And you still remember this?"

She looked at him with playful disdain. "My mind's not gone yet," she said. "You'd be surprised at the things I remember." She turned her trembling head towards Sandra. "I could tell you some things about your husband here, as a little boy. . . ."

"*Honto no kotaishi de gozaimasu,*" he interrupted, shaking his head. The words were simple and familiar enough but on the tongue of a woman he'd known since birth and who'd long since lost the power to surprise him they had a fabulous, exotic sound. She had heard them half a century before his birth, then harboured the echoes all those years like a family secret. They loomed up in his mind, immense as a continent; they took on trappings like a spell or a mantra. Nothing could ever pass away.

165   "Do you still have the doll?" Sandra asked.

"The doll?" she snapped. "Oh, well, I've really no idea at all what became of it. When we left Winnipeg after the war it must have been lost in the move. Or else when I was married and left home. But I still remember the doll's face: very proud, a noble little warrior, a *samurai.*"

Emily shuddered, as if trying to shake herself from a dream. She stood up and reached with fluttering fingers for the teapot. She was still a businesslike woman, hurried and brusque, lavishly energetic like someone half her age; she never let conversations linger on her own affairs.

Sandra and Nick rose together to offer their help but she brushed them away and had them know she wasn't ready for a nursing home yet.

There was a groan from the bedroom.

170   "It's him," Emily said, glancing at the tiny wristwatch she had worn for as long as Nick could remember. "He'll be needing me now. No, please, I told you, leave the tea things alone. Make yourselves comfortable for a few minutes while I go and see him. In a little while I'll bring him out for a visit. We won't be long."

Nick poured Sandra some tea and then, in the Japanese manner, let her replenish his own cup. The sound of the trickling fluid filled the small kitchen. The windows were clouding over with steam so that patterns a dreaming finger had traced appeared and spread outward over the panes: transparent paths, cursive and meandering, illegible as a line of characters. A fit of coughing erupted from the bedroom and then, like a lullaby, soothing sounds. Over steaming cups Nick and Sandra watched each other with a new patience that was close to love.

READING AND REACTING

1. Why do Nick and Sandra plan to return to Canada?
2. How do they feel about leaving Japan?
3. What reaction does Nick get from his principal when Nick tells her about the return to Canada? What does the principal's reaction suggest about intercultural relations?
4. Marriage is an important subject in the story. What is suggested by the examples of marriage that are given?
5. In sections three and seven the narration shifts to second person. What is the effect? Why do other parts of the story have a different narrative point of view?
6. Would the story work as well if Nick and Sandra had been in a different country?
7. **JOURNAL ENTRY** What are the limits (if any) of family obligation? How are various obligations placed into an order?

Related Works: "A Rose for Emily" (p. 90), "The Loons" (p. 249), *Les Belles Soeurs* (p. 1196)

◊ **DAVID HERBERT LAWRENCE** (1885–1930) was born in Nottinghamshire, England, the son of a coal miner and a schoolteacher. Determined to escape the devastation of the mines, Lawrence taught for several years after graduating from high school. However, he soon began writing fiction and established himself in London literary circles. He married a German aristocrat, Frieda von Richthofen, in 1912.

During World War I, Lawrence and his wife were suspected of treason because of his pacifism and her connection to German aristocracy. Because Lawrence suffered from tuberculosis, he and his wife left England after the armistice in search of a healthier climate. They travelled in Australia, France, Italy, Mexico, and the United States throughout their lives.

Lawrence is recognized for his impassioned portrayal of our unconscious and instinctive natures. In his novel *Lady Chatterley's Lover* (1928), he attempted to restore explicit sexuality to English fiction, and the book was banned for years in Britain and North America. His other novels include *Sons and Lovers* (1913), *The Rainbow* (1915), *Women in Love* (1921), and *The Plumed Serpent* (1926). Lawrence was also a gifted poet, essayist, travel writer, and short story writer, and his work and personal magnetism had a strong influence on other writers.

Lawrence's fascination with the struggle between the unconscious and the intellect is revealed in his short story "The Rocking-Horse Winner" (1920). Lawrence sets his story in a house full of secrets and weaves symbolism with elements of the fairy tale and the gothic to produce a tale that is often the subject of literary debate.

◦ ◦ ◦

D. H. LAWRENCE

The Rocking-Horse Winner
(1920)

There was a woman who was beautiful, who started with all the advantages, yet she had no luck. She married for love, and the love turned to dust. She had bonny children, yet she felt they had been thrust upon her, and she could not love them. They looked at her coldly, as if they were finding fault with her. And hurriedly she felt she must cover up some fault in herself. Yet what it was that she must cover up she never knew. Nevertheless, when her children were present, she always felt the centre of her heart go hard. This troubled her, and in her manner she was all the more gentle and anxious for her children, as if she loved them very much. Only she herself knew that at the centre of her heart was a hard little place that could not feel love, no, not for anybody. Everybody else said of her: "She is such a good mother. She adores her children." Only she herself, and her children themselves, knew it was not so. They read it in each other's eyes.

There were a boy and two little girls. They lived in a pleasant house, with a garden, and they had discreet servants, and felt themselves superior to anyone in the neighbourhood.

Although they lived in style, they felt always an anxiety in the house. There was never enough money. The mother had a small income, and the father had a small income, but not nearly enough for the social position which they had to keep up. The father went into town to some office. But though he had good prospects, these prospects never materialised. There was always the grinding sense of the shortage of money, though the style was always kept up.

At last the mother said: "I will see if *I* can't make something." But she did not know where to begin. She racked her brains, and tried this thing and the other, but could not find anything successful. The failure made deep lines come into her face. Her children were growing up, they would have to go to school. There must be more money, there must be more money. The father, who was always very handsome and expensive in his tastes, seemed as if he never *would* be able to do anything worth doing. And the mother, who had a great belief in herself, did not succeed any better, and her tastes were just as expensive.

5   And so the house came to be haunted by the unspoken phrase: *There must be more money! There must be more money!* The children could hear it all the time, though nobody said it aloud. They heard it at Christmas, when the expensive and splendid toys filled the nursery. Behind the shining modern rocking-horse, behind the smart doll's house, a voice would start whispering: "There *must* be more money! There *must* be more money!" And the children would stop playing, to listen for a moment. They would look

into each other's eyes, to see if they had all heard. And each one saw in the eyes of the other two that they too had heard. "There *must* be more money! There *must* be more money!"

It came whispering from the springs of the still-swaying rocking-horse, and even the horse, bending his wooden, champing head, heard it. The big doll, sitting so pink and smirking in her new pram, could hear it quite plainly, and seemed to be smirking all the more self-consciously because of it. The foolish puppy, too, that took the place of the teddybear, he was looking so extraordinarily foolish for no other reason but that he heard the secret whisper all over the house: "There *must* be more money!"

Yet nobody ever said it aloud. The whisper was everywhere, and therefore no one spoke it. Just as no one ever says: "We are breathing!" in spite of the fact that breath is coming and going all the time.

"Mother," said the boy Paul one day, "why don't we keep a car of our own? Why do we always use uncle's, or else a taxi?"

"Because we're the poor members of the family," said the mother.

10   "But why *are* we, mother?"

"Well—I suppose," she said slowly and bitterly, "it's because your father has no luck."

The boy was silent for some time.

"Is luck money, mother?" he asked, rather timidly.

"No, Paul. Not quite. It's what causes you to have money."

15   "Oh!" said Paul vaguely. "I thought when Uncle Oscar said *filthy lucker,* it meant money."

"*Filthy lucre* does mean money," said the mother. "But it's lucre, not luck."

"Oh!" said the boy. "Then what *is* luck, mother?"

"It's what causes you to have money. If you're lucky you have money. That's why it's better to be born lucky than rich. If you're rich, you may lose your money. But if you're lucky, you will always get more money."

"Oh! Will you? And is father not lucky?"

20   "Very unlucky, I should say," she said bitterly.

The boy watched her with unsure eyes.

"Why?" he asked.

"I don't know. Nobody ever knows why one person is lucky and another unlucky."

"Don't they? Nobody at all? Does *nobody* know?"

25   "Perhaps God. But He never tells."

"He ought to, then. And aren't you lucky either, mother?"

"I can't be, if I married an unlucky husband."

"But by yourself, aren't you?"

"I used to think I was, before I married. Now I think I am very unlucky indeed."

30   "Why?"

"Well—never mind! Perhaps I'm not really," she said.

The child looked at her to see if she meant it. But he saw, by the lines of her mouth, that she was only trying to hide something from him.

"Well, anyhow," he said stoutly, "I'm a lucky person."

"Why?" said his mother, with a sudden laugh.

35 He stared at her. He didn't even know why he had said it.

"God told me," he asserted, brazening it out.

"I hope He did, dear!" she said, again with a laugh, but rather bitter.

"He did, mother!"

"Excellent!" said the mother, using one of her husband's exclamations.

40 The boy saw she did not believe him; or rather, that she paid no attention to his assertion. This angered him somewhat, and made him want to compel her attention.

He went off by himself, vaguely, in a childish way, seeking for the clue to "luck." Absorbed, taking no heed of other people, he went about with a sort of stealth, seeking inwardly for luck. He wanted luck, he wanted it, he wanted it. When the two girls were playing dolls in the nursery, he would sit on his big rocking-horse, charging madly into space, with a frenzy that made the little girls peer at him uneasily. Wildly the horse careered, the waving dark hair of the boy tossed, his eyes had a strange glare in them. The little girls dared not speak to him.

When he had ridden to the end of his mad little journey, he climbed down and stood in front of his rocking-horse, staring fixedly into its lowered face. Its red mouth was slightly open, its big eye was wide and glassy-bright.

"Now!" he would silently command the snorting steed. "Now, take me to where there is luck! Now take me!"

And he would slash the horse on the neck with the little whip he had asked Uncle Oscar for. He *knew* the horse could take him to where there was luck, if only he forced it. So he would mount again and start on his furious ride, hoping at last to get there. He knew he could get there.

45 "You'll break your horse, Paul!" said the nurse.

"He's always riding like that! I wish he'd leave off!" said his elder sister Joan.

But he only glared down on them in silence. Nurse gave him up. She could make nothing of him. Anyhow, he was growing beyond her.

One day his mother and his Uncle Oscar came in when he was on one of his furious rides. He did not speak to them.

"Hallo, you young jockey! Riding a winner?" said his uncle.

50 "Aren't you growing too big for a rocking-horse? You're not a very little boy any longer, you know," said his mother.

But Paul only gave a blue glare from his big, rather close-set eyes. He would speak to nobody when he was in full tilt. His mother watched him with an anxious expression on her face.

At last he suddenly stopped forcing his horse into the mechanical gallop and slid down.

"Well, I got there!" he announced fiercely, his blue eyes still flaring, and his sturdy long legs straddling apart.

"Where did you get to?" asked his mother.

55 "Where I wanted to go," he flared back at her.

"That's right, son!" said Uncle Oscar. "Don't you stop till you get there. What's the horse's name?"

"He doesn't have a name," said the boy.

"Gets on without all right?" asked the uncle.

"Well, he has different names. He was called Sansovino last week."

60 "Sansovino, eh? Won the Ascot.[1] How did you know this name?"

"He always talks about horse-races with Bassett," said Joan.

The uncle was delighted to find that his small nephew was posted with all the racing news. Bassett, the young gardener, who had been wounded in the left foot in the war and had got his present job through Oscar Cresswell, whose batman he had been, was a perfect blade of the "turf." He lived in the racing events, and the small boy lived with him.

Oscar Cresswell got it all from Bassett.

"Master Paul comes and asks me, so I can't do more than tell him, sir," said Bassett, his face terribly serious, as if he were speaking of religious matters.

65 "And does he ever put anything on a horse he fancies?"

"Well—I don't want to give him away—he's a young sport, a fine sport, sir. Would you mind asking him himself? He sort of takes a pleasure in it, and perhaps he'd feel I was giving him away, sir, if you don't mind."

Bassett was serious as a church.

The uncle went back to his nephew and took him off for a ride in the car.

"Say, Paul, old man, do you ever put anything on a horse?" the uncle asked.

70 The boy watched the handsome man closely.

"Why, do you think I oughtn't to?" he parried.

"Not a bit of it! I thought perhaps you might give me a tip for the Lincoln."[2]

The car sped on into the country, going down to Uncle Oscar's place in Hampshire.

"Honour bright?" said the nephew.

75 "Honour bright, son!" said the uncle.

"Well, then, Daffodil."

"Daffodil! I doubt it, sonny. What about Mirza?"

"I only know the winner," said the boy. "That's Daffodil."

"Daffodil, eh?"

80 There was a pause. Daffodil was an obscure horse comparatively.

"Uncle!"

"Yes, son?"

"You won't let it go any further, will you? I promised Bassett."

"Bassett be damned, old man! What's he got to do with it?"

---

[1] The annual horse race at Ascot Heath in England.

[2] The Lincolnshire Handicap.

85 "We're partners. We've been partners from the first. Uncle, he lent me my first five shillings, which I lost. I promised him, honour bright, it was only between me and him; only you gave me that ten-shilling note I started winning with, so I thought you were lucky. You won't let it go any further, will you?"

The boy gazed at his uncle from those big, hot, blue eyes, set rather close together. The uncle stirred and laughed uneasily.

"Right you are, son! I'll keep your tip private. Daffodil, eh? How much are you putting on him?"

"All except twenty pounds," said the boy. "I keep that in reserve."

The uncle thought it a good joke.

90 "You keep twenty pounds in reserve, do you, you young romancer? What are you betting, then?"

"I'm betting three hundred," said the boy gravely. "But it's between you and me, Uncle Oscar! Honour bright?"

The uncle burst into a roar of laughter.

"It's between you and me all right, you young Nat Gould,"[3] he said, laughing. "But where's your three hundred?"

"Bassett keeps it for me. We're partners."

95 "You are, are you! And what is Bassett putting on Daffodil?"

"He won't go quite as high as I do, I expect. Perhaps he'll go a hundred and fifty."

"What, pennies?" laughed the uncle.

"Pounds," said the child, with a surprised look at his uncle. "Bassett keeps a bigger reserve than I do."

Between wonder and amusement Uncle Oscar was silent. He pursued the matter no further, but he determined to take his nephew with him to the Lincoln races.

100 "Now, son," he said, "I'm putting twenty on Mirza, and I'll put five on for you on any horse you fancy. What's your pick?"

"Daffodil, uncle."

"No, not the fiver on Daffodil!"

"I should if it was my own fiver," said the child.

"Good! Good! Right you are! A fiver for me and a fiver for you on Daffodil."

105 The child had never been to a race-meeting before, and his eyes were blue fire. He pursed his mouth tight and watched. A Frenchman just in front had put his money on Lancelot. Wild with excitement, he flayed his arms up and down, yelling *Lancelot! Lancelot!* in his French accent.

Daffodil came in first, Lancelot second, Mirza third. The child, flushed and with eyes blazing, was curiously serene. His uncle brought him four five-pound notes, four to one.

---

[3] Nathaniel Gould (1857–1919), British journalist and writer known for his stories about horse racing.

"What am I to do with these?" he cried, waving them before the boy's eyes.

"I suppose we'll talk to Bassett," said the boy. "I expect I have fifteen hundred now; and twenty in reserve; and this twenty."

His uncle studied him for some moments.

110 "Look here, son!" he said. "You're not serious about Bassett and that fifteen hundred, are you?"

"Yes, I am. But it's between you and me, uncle. Honour bright?"

"Honour bright all right, son! But I must talk to Bassett."

"If you'd like to be a partner, uncle, with Bassett and me, we could all be partners. Only, you'd have to promise, honour bright, uncle, not to let it go beyond us three. Bassett and I are lucky, and you must be lucky, because it was your ten shillings I started winning with. . . . "

Uncle Oscar took both Bassett and Paul into Richmond Park for an afternoon, and there they talked.

115 "It's like this, you see, sir," Bassett said. "Master Paul would get me talking about racing events, spinning yarns, you know, sir. And he was always keen on knowing if I'd made or if I'd lost. It's about a year since, now, that I put five shillings on Blush of Dawn for him: and we lost. Then the luck turned, with that ten shillings he had from you: that we put on Singhalese. And since that time, it's been pretty steady, all things considering. What do you say, Master Paul?"

"We're all right when we're sure," said Paul. "It's when we're not quite sure that we go down."

"Oh, but we're careful then," said Bassett.

"But when are you *sure?*" smiled Uncle Oscar.

"It's Master Paul, sir," said Bassett in a secret, religious voice. "It's as if he had it from heaven. Like Daffodil, now, for the Lincoln. That was as sure as eggs."

120 "Did you put anything on Daffodil?" asked Oscar Cresswell.

"Yes, sir. I made my bit."

"And my nephew?"

Bassett was obstinately silent, looking at Paul.

"I made twelve hundred, didn't I, Bassett? I told uncle I was putting three hundred on Daffodil."

125 "That's right," said Bassett, nodding.

"But where's the money?" asked the uncle.

"I keep it safe locked up, sir. Master Paul can have it any minute he likes to ask for it."

"What, fifteen hundred pounds?"

"And twenty! And *forty,* that is, with the twenty he made on the course."

130 "It's amazing!" said the uncle.

"If Master Paul offers you to be partners, sir, I would, if I were you: if you'll excuse me," said Bassett.

Oscar Cresswell thought about it.

"I'll see the money," he said.

They drove home again, and, sure enough, Bassett came round to the garden-house with fifteen hundred pounds in notes. The twenty pounds reserve was left with Joe Glee, in the Turf Commission deposit.

135   "You see, it's all right, uncle, when I'm *sure!* Then we go strong, for all we're worth. Don't we, Bassett?"

"We do that, Master Paul."

"And when are you sure?" said the uncle, laughing.

"Oh, well, sometimes I'm *absolutely* sure, like about Daffodil," said the boy; "and sometimes I have an idea; and sometimes I haven't even an idea, have I, Bassett? Then we're careful, because we mostly go down."

"You do, do you! And when you're sure, like about Daffodil, what makes you sure, sonny?"

140   "Oh, well, I don't know," said the boy uneasily. "I'm sure, you know, uncle; that's all."

"It's as if he had it from heaven, sir," Bassett reiterated.

"I should say so!" said the uncle.

But he became a partner. And when the Leger[4] was coming on Paul was "sure" about Lively Spark, which was a quite inconsiderable horse. The boy insisted on putting a thousand on the horse, Bassett went for five hundred, and Oscar Cresswell two hundred. Lively Spark came in first, and the betting had been ten to one against him. Paul had made ten thousand.

"You see," he said, "I was absolutely sure of him."

145   Even Oscar Cresswell had cleared two thousand.

"Look here, son," he said, "this sort of thing makes me nervous."

"It needn't, uncle! Perhaps I shan't be sure again for a long time."

"But what are you going to do with your money?" asked the uncle.

"Of course," said the boy, "I started it for mother. She said she had no luck, because father is unlucky, so I thought if *I* was lucky, it might stop whispering."

150   "What might stop whispering?"

"Our house. I *hate* our house for whispering."

"What does it whisper?"

"Why—why"—the boy fidgeted—"why, I don't know. But it's always short of money, you know, uncle."

"I know it, son, I know it."

155   "You know people send mother writs,[5] don't you, uncle?"

"I'm afraid I do," said the uncle.

"And then the house whispers, like people laughing at you behind your back. It's awful, that is! I thought if I was lucky . . . "

"You might stop it," added the uncle.

The boy watched him with big blue eyes, that had an uncanny cold fire in them, and he said never a word.

---

[4] The St. Leger Stakes.

[5] Letters from creditors requesting payment.

160   "Well, then!" said the uncle. "What are we doing?"

"I shouldn't like mother to know I was lucky," said the boy.

"Why not, son?"

"She'd stop me."

"I don't think she would."

165   "Oh!"—and the boy writhed in an odd way—"I *don't* want her to know, uncle."

"All right, son! We'll manage it without her knowing."

They managed it very easily. Paul, at the other's suggestion, handed over five thousand pounds to his uncle, who deposited it with the family lawyer, who was then to inform Paul's mother that a relative had put five thousand pounds into his hands, which sum was to be paid out a thousand pounds at a time, on the mother's birthday, for the next five years.

"So she'll have a birthday present of a thousand pounds for five successive years," said Uncle Oscar. "I hope it won't make it all the harder for her later."

Paul's mother had her birthday in November. The house had been "whispering" worse than ever lately, and, even in spite of his luck, Paul could not bear up against it. He was very anxious to see the effect of the birthday letter, telling his mother about the thousand pounds.

170   When there were no visitors, Paul now took his meals with his parents, as he was beyond the nursery control. His mother went into town nearly every day. She had discovered that she had an odd knack of sketching furs and dress materials, so she worked secretly in the studio of a friend who was the chief "artist" for the leading drapers. She drew the figures of ladies in furs and ladies in silk and sequins for the newspaper advertisements. This young woman artist earned several thousand pounds a year, but Paul's mother only made several hundreds, and she was again dissatisfied. She so wanted to be first in something, and she did not succeed, even in making sketches for drapery advertisements.

She was down to breakfast on the morning of her birthday. Paul watched her face as she read her letters. He knew the lawyer's letter. As his mother read it, her face hardened and became more expressionless. Then a cold, determined look came on her mouth. She hid the letter under the pile of others, and said not a word about it.

"Didn't you have anything nice in the post for your birthday, mother?" said Paul.

"Quite moderately nice," she said, her voice cold and absent.

She went away to town without saying more.

175   But in the afternoon Uncle Oscar appeared. He said Paul's mother had had a long interview with the lawyer, asking if the whole five thousand could not be advanced at once, as she was in debt.

"What do you think, uncle?" asked the boy.

"I leave it to you, son."

"Oh, let her have it, then! We can get some more with the other," said the boy.

"A bird in the hand is worth two in the bush, laddie!" said Uncle Oscar.

180 "But I'm sure to *know* for the Grand National; or the Lincolnshire; or else the Derby.[6] I'm sure to know for *one* of them," said Paul.

So Uncle Oscar signed the agreement, and Paul's mother touched the whole five thousand. Then something very curious happened. The voices in the house suddenly went mad, like a chorus of frogs on a spring evening. There was certain new furnishings, and Paul had a tutor. He was *really* going to Eton, his father's school, in the following autumn. There were flowers in the winter, and a blossoming of the luxury Paul's mother had been used to. And yet the voices in the house, behind the sprays of mimosa and almond-blossom, and from under the piles of iridescent cushions, simply trilled and screamed in a sort of ecstasy: "There *must* be more money! Oh-h-h; there *must* be more money. Oh, now, now-w! Now-w-w—there *must* be more money!—more than ever! More than ever!"

It frightened Paul terribly. He studied away at his Latin and Greek with his tutor. But his intense hours were spent with Bassett. The Grand National had gone by: he had not "known," and had lost a hundred pounds. Summer was at hand. He was in agony for the Lincoln. But even for the Lincoln he didn't "know," and he lost fifty pounds. He became wild-eyed and strange, as if something were going to explode in him.

"Let it alone, son! Don't you bother about it!" urged Uncle Oscar. But it was as if the boy couldn't really hear what his uncle was saying.

"I've got to know for the Derby! I've got to know for the Derby!" the child reiterated, his big blue eyes blazing with a sort of madness.

185 His mother noticed how overwrought he was.

"You'd better go to the seaside. Wouldn't you like to go now to the seaside, instead of waiting? I think you'd better," she said, looking down at him anxiously, her heart curiously heavy because of him.

But the child lifted his uncanny blue eyes.

"I couldn't possibly go before the Derby, mother!" he said. "I couldn't possibly!"

"Why not?" she said, her voice becoming heavy when she was opposed. "Why not? You can still go from the seaside to see the Derby with your Uncle Oscar, if that's what you wish. No need for you to wait here. Besides, I think you care too much about these races. It's a bad sign. My family has been a gambling family, and you won't know till you grow up how much damage it has done. But it has done damage. I shall have to send Bassett away, and ask Uncle Oscar not to talk racing to you, unless you promise to be reasonable about it: go away to the seaside and forget it. You're all nerves!"

190 "I'll do what you like, mother, so long as you don't send me away till after the Derby," the boy said.

---

[6] Famous British horse races. The Grand National is run at Aintree, the Derby at Epsom Downs.

"Send you away from where? Just from this house?"

"Yes," he said, gazing at her.

"Why, you curious child, what makes you care about this house so much, suddenly? I never knew you loved it."

He gazed at her without speaking. He had a secret within a secret, something he had not divulged, even to Bassett or to his Uncle Oscar.

195 But his mother, after standing undecided and a little bit sullen for some moments, said:

"Very well, then! Don't go to the seaside till after the Derby, if you don't wish it. But promise me you won't let your nerves go to pieces. Promise you won't think so much about horse-racing and *events,* as you call them!"

"Oh no," said the boy casually. "I won't think much about them, mother. You needn't worry. I wouldn't worry, mother, if I were you."

"If you were me and I were you," said his mother, "I wonder what we *should* do!"

"But you know you needn't worry, mother, don't you?" the boy repeated.

200 "I should be awfully glad to know it," she said wearily.

"Oh, well, you *can,* you know. I mean, you *ought* to know you needn't worry," he insisted.

"Ought I? Then I'll see about it," she said.

Paul's secret of secrets was his wooden horse, that which had no name. Since he was emancipated from a nurse and a nursery-governess, he had had his rocking-horse removed to his own bedroom at the top of the house.

"Surely you're too big for a rocking-horse!" his mother had remonstrated.

205 "Well, you see, mother, till I can have a *real* horse, I like to have *some* sort of animal about," had been his quaint answer.

"Do you feel he keeps you company?" she laughed.

"Oh yes! He's very good, he always keeps me company, when I'm there," said Paul.

So the horse, rather shabby, stood in an arrested prance in the boy's bedroom.

The Derby was drawing near, and the boy grew more and more tense. He hardly heard what was spoken to him, he was very frail, and his eyes were really uncanny. His mother had sudden strange seizures of uneasiness about him. Sometimes, for half an hour, she would feel a sudden anxiety about him that was almost anguish. She wanted to rush to him at once, and know he was safe.

210 Two nights before the Derby, she was at a big party in town, when one of her rushes of anxiety about her boy, her firstborn, gripped her heart till she could hardly speak. She fought with the feeling, might and main, for she believed in common sense. But it was too strong. She had to leave the dance and go downstairs to telephone to the country. The children's nursery-governess was terribly surprised and startled at being rung up in the night.

"Are the children all right, Miss Wilmot?"

"Oh yes, they are quite all right."

"Master Paul? Is he all right?"

"He went to bed as right as a trivet. Shall I run up and look at him?"

215   "No," said Paul's mother reluctantly. "No! Don't trouble. It's all right. Don't sit up. We shall be home fairly soon." She did not want her son's privacy intruded upon.

"Very good," said the governess.

It was about one o'clock when Paul's mother and father drove up to their house. All was still. Paul's mother went to her room and slipped off her white fur cloak. She had told her maid not to wait up for her. She heard her husband downstairs, mixing a whisky and soda.

And then, because of the strange anxiety at her heart, she stole upstairs to her son's room. Noiselessly she went along the upper corridor. Was there a faint noise? What was it?

She stood, with arrested muscles, outside his door, listening. There was a strange, heavy, and yet not loud noise. Her heart stood still. It was a soundless noise, yet rushing and powerful. Something huge, in violent, hushed motion. What was it? What in God's name was it? She ought to know. She felt that she knew the noise. She knew what it was.

220   Yet she could not place it. She couldn't say what it was. And on and on it went, like a madness.

Softly, frozen with anxiety and fear, she turned the door-handle.

The room was dark. Yet in the space near the window, she heard and saw something plunging to and fro. She gazed in fear and amazement.

Then suddenly she switched on the light, and saw her son, in his green pyjamas, madly surging on the rocking-horse. The blaze of light suddenly lit him up, as he urged the wooden horse, and lit her up, as she stood, blonde, in her dress of pale green and crystal, in the doorway.

"Paul!" she cried. "Whatever are you doing?"

225   "It's Malabar!" he screamed in a powerful, strange voice. "It's Malabar!"

His eyes blazed at her for one strange and senseless second, as he ceased urging his wooden horse. Then he fell with a crash to the ground, and she, all her tormented motherhood flooding upon her, rushed to gather him up.

But he was unconscious, and unconscious he remained, with some brain-fever. He talked and tossed, and his mother sat stonily by his side.

"Malabar! It's Malabar! Bassett, Bassett, I *know*! It's Malabar!"

So the child cried, trying to get up and urge the rocking-horse that gave him his inspiration.

230   "What does he mean by Malabar?" asked the heart-frozen mother.

"I don't know," said the father stonily.

"What does he mean by Malabar?" she asked her brother Oscar.

"It's one of the horses running for the Derby," was the answer.

And, in spite of himself, Oscar Cresswell spoke to Bassett, and himself put a thousand on Malabar: at fourteen to one.

235   The third day of the illness was critical: they were waiting for a change. The boy, with his rather long, curly hair, was tossing ceaselessly on the pillow. He neither slept nor regained consciousness, and his eyes were like blue stones. His mother sat, feeling her heart had gone, turned actually into a stone.

In the evening, Oscar Cresswell did not come, but Bassett sent a message, saying could he come up for one moment, just one moment? Paul's mother was very angry at the intrusion, but on second thought she agreed. The boy was the same. Perhaps Bassett might bring him to consciousness.

The gardener, a shortish fellow with a little brown moustache and sharp little brown eyes, tiptoed into the room, touched his imaginary cap to Paul's mother, and stole to the bedside, staring with glittering, smallish eyes at the tossing, dying child.

"Master Paul!" he whispered. "Master Paul! Malabar came in first all right, a clean win. I did as you told me. You've made over seventy thousand pounds, you have; you've got over eighty thousand. Malabar came in all right, Master Paul."

"Malabar! Malabar! Did I say Malabar, mother? Did I say Malabar? Do you think I'm lucky, mother? I knew Malabar, didn't I? Over eighty thousand pounds! I call that lucky, don't you, mother? Over eighty thousand pounds! I knew, didn't I know I knew? Malabar came in all right. If I ride my horse till I'm sure, then I tell you, Bassett, you can go as high as you like. Did you go for all you were worth, Bassett?"

240   "I went a thousand on it, Master Paul."

"I never told you, mother, that if I can ride my horse, and *get there*, then I'm absolutely sure—oh, absolutely! Mother, did I ever tell you? I *am* lucky!"

"No, you never did," said his mother.

But the boy died in the night.

And even as he lay dead, his mother heard her brother's voice saying to her: "My God, Hester, you're eighty-odd thousand to the good, and a poor devil of a son to the bad. But, poor devil, poor devil, he's best gone out of a life where he rides his rocking-horse to find a winner."

READING AND REACTING

1. From what point of view is "The Rocking-Horse Winner" told? How does this point of view help to communicate the story's theme?

2. In what respects is "The Rocking-Horse Winner" like a fairy tale? How is it different?

3. Many fairy tales involve a hero who goes on a journey to search for something of great value. What journey does Paul go on? What does he search for? Is he successful?

4. In paragraph 5, the narrator says that the house is "haunted by the unspoken phrase: *There must be more money!*" In what way does the phrase "haunt" the house?

5. How would you characterize Paul's parents? His uncle? Bassett? Are they weak? Evil? What motivates them?

6. Beginning with paragraph 10, Paul's mother attempts to define the word *luck*. According to her definition, does she consider Paul lucky? Do you agree?

7. In what ways does Paul behave like other children? In what ways is he different? How do you account for these differences? How old do you think Paul is? Why is his age significant?

8. The rocking horse is an important literary symbol in the story. What possible meanings might the rocking horse suggest? In what ways does this symbol reinforce the story's theme?

9. What secrets do the various characters keep from one another? Why do they keep them? How do these secrets relate to the story's theme?

10. How does Paul know who the winners will be? Does the rocking horse really tell him? Does he get his information "from heaven" as Bassett suggests? Or, does he just guess?

11. **JOURNAL ENTRY** In your opinion, who or what is responsible for Paul's death?

12. **CRITICAL PERSPECTIVE** In a letter dated January 17, 1913, Lawrence wrote:

> My great religion is a belief in the blood, the flesh, as being wiser than the intellect. We can go wrong in our minds. But what our blood feels and believes and says, is always true. The intellect is only a bit and a bridle. What do I care about knowledge. All I want is to answer to my blood, direct, without fribbling intervention of mind, or moral, or what-not.

How does Lawrence's portrayal of Paul in "The Rocking-Horse Winner" support his belief in "the blood . . . being wiser than the intellect"? How does Lawrence remain true in this story to his metaphor of the intellect as bit and bridle?

Related Works: "The Ice Wagon Going Down the Street" (p. 98), "Gretel in Darkness" (p. 620), "Suicide Note" (p. 630), "Richard Cory" (p. 877), *A Doll House* (p. 1013)

◇ **DIONNE BRAND** (1953–   ) is a poet, novelist, filmmaker, and essayist. She has been nominated for many literary awards, including the Governor General's Award and the Trillium Award. Her poetry publications include *Chronicles of the Hostile Sun* (1984), *No Language is Neutral* (1990), and *Land to Light On*, for which she won the Governor General's Literary Prize for Poetry in 1997. At the age of seventeen, Brand moved to Canada from Trinidad. Early on in her career she was heavily involved in Black Power movements, and she was a member of the Communist Party. Now, much of her activism is reflected by her writing. Indeed, her writing is political: many recurring themes in her work deal with issues of oppression, particularly as they relate to race and sexuality. For Brand, poetry is dependent on politics. As she states, poetry must be "relevant, charged, politically conscious, memorable." Her recent book, *A Map to the Door of No Return* (2001), explores the importance and nature of identity and belonging in a culturally varied and rapidly changing world. Her most recent novel, *What We All Long For* (2005), develops these theories in fiction.

◆ ◆ ◆

DIONNE BRAND

Tamarindus Indica
(1999)

Tamarindus indica. He sat under this tree every day. A tree perhaps brought here from Africa in the seventeenth century. Probably brought here by his great-great-grandmother, as a seed in the pocket of her coarse dress. Probably held in her mouth as a comfort. Perhaps then germinating in her bowels. How the tree came to stand in his path he really did not know. And if it had been his great-great-grandmother, she would have brought a silk cotton tree, its high wing-like buttresses webbing out in embraces. His great-great-grandmother, however, had not passed down into memory but he had heard that silk cotton blew all the way here from Africa and that is how he thought of any ancestry before Marie Ursule, who was his great-grandmother.

This tree grew daily in purpose. It was brought; set down in his path. Or perhaps he was fooling himself again, fooling himself that any piece of the world could be arranged with him in mind; fooling himself that he had a specific heading or that he was in the middle of all actions, important.

He sat on the ground under the tree's shade each day. He had counted leaves made of fifteen pairs of leaflets, rarely more, sometimes less, fifteen pairs of leaflets as small as the nail on his baby finger. Smaller. He was noticing minute things. A sliver of blue glass between his bare callused toes, a piece of gazette paper gone black, which he used to insert in his shoes. The flower of *Tamarindus indica,* smaller still and pale yellow, not enough for a show; all the show was later in the pods he mashed open, which looked like some brown jam but was sour.

He sat there each day after his walk in the burning sun, when the sun was heavy on his back as a sack he carried, the sun a burden and a relief in the wood he had grown of his life. *Tamarindus indica*—finally shading him from the stout relentless sun which always proved too much for him in the end.

5   And so the next day his walk would have to start all over again. And then he would have to sit there under the feathers of *Tamarindus indica* and count how many leaflets on this leaf, how many leaves on this branch, his face in a stroke-like sweat and his penance unpaid. He wished the tree did not stand there, as much as, returning from his walk, he longed for its shade.

Because if, when he saw it, he felt relief, then that meant he had not done with what he owed, and if it were not there, it meant he would not have the relief to fall under it and recover to do his penance over again.

It was a fitting tree to hear his confession and take his penance since such a tree must have come in his grandfather's cheek or in his broken toes. More native to India, such a tree would have travelled this way. Yes. Such a tree, which had seen to it that it did not wash itself away in water or tears, but waited until it was spat out from his grandfather's mouth, or passed from between his legs, its seed an indigestible stone. This was the tree, *Tamarindus indica*, from which he had to beg a forgiveness to which he had no right.

Misconduct! he mumbled to himself, sweat and the sun ironing what was left of his black suit to a shine. Misconduct. The man tell me to clean his knife, get his water, clean his clothes, dig the pits. Misconduct! So *is* not me and he climb the hill on Damieh together? Is not his foot in mud just like mine, why he tell me to shine his boots, clean his knife? I not tired too? Force-march back to Jericho, one whole day and the fever fighting me in the desert and I must get his boot when we both sit down. I must dig shit pits. Who more misconduct? The man have no mind! I poorly with the fever coming and he need his clothes clean.

"Misconduct, my ass," he mumbles each day to the *Tamarindus indica* since no one else will hear him. No one wants to listen again to the story and anyway all who knew it have passed away and those who remain think that he is off his head.

It is dry and hot the morning they rout the Turks on Damieh Hill. The unexpected cold at night chills him, his leg wrappings seem meagre and the paper in his boots rank. He has been cold ever since he boarded the ship and left home. He hasn't known whether to take his boots off and rub his toes or leave them hurting in his boots. But all turned to unimportance when they received the order and the knowledge that the Turks were trapped between their lines and the assault was to ensue. The Second West India Regiment, posted in Palestine for the past five months doing labour services, advanced up the hill at Damieh like real soldiers.

10   He had come all the way here to serve the mother country, Great Britain. After all the official entreaties by the governor of the island, whose impassioned letters to the Colonial Office assured it of men, though of colour, willing to fight for Great Britain, the Second West India Regiment had received condescending assent. Men who were young and strong and of intelligence no matter their skin. And he was one of them, marching and doing their aimless drills across the parade grounds in case they were needed. And he was not feeble like the Indians all sent back not fit. He was in his physical prime, boarding the ship first to Great Britain then to Palestine. Him. Private Samuel Gordon Sones of the Second West India Regiment. The name of his grandfather, Rabindranath Ragoonanan, was buried under illegitimacy of some kind or another, and any Indian traces in him were sun-sweated to tightly curled hair. The name and the physical

signs lay dormant and unattended, unremembered, as those traces were both unimportant and a liability.

Rabindranath Ragoonanan had arrived a man-boy on the *Fatel Rozack* from India almost at the same time that Bola saw Culebra Bay turn into tin shacks and flame trees. No sooner had he found his legs to stand up, after 113 days at sea, than he was bundled off to the vast plains of the Caroni to work the cane fields. The expanse of cane overwhelmed him. The whistling and rough soughing of the stalks and leaves took over his hearing, big as the waves he had just departed. The flat unending plains, waving green turning to blue with cane, made him know that he was here to stay. His gaze never surpassed them, he could never look far enough.

Many years after, he wandered into Culebra blind, heard Bola's shell-blowing and headed for the sound. Blind, because fire had taken out his eyes, caught in a razing cane field, a flaming stalk had lashed him across his face, running for his life. It was the way he carried his head that Bola loved. He was waiting for sound because he could not see. All his direction was sound, all his life was sound because he could count on nothing else, except perhaps the feel of something on his face, so much is bound up by seeing. He ended up at Culebra because it was where some sound took him. On his road there he took all paths away from the glutted noise of coming big towns; he listened for air with space in it and he listened too for the sea, which had first brought him to the island. Though he was a man of interiors; of the heavy rains and long floods of Gorakpur where he was born, which had driven him to the port of Calcutta. As if swept down by a monsoon among the other debris and the things monsoons turn into other unrecognizable things, covered in mud and useless, Ragoonanan had been pushed and rolled and dragged to the depot at Calcutta to be sent indentured overseas.

He and 224 others, most in destitution, some in ambition, boarded the boat under the immigration scheme to feed the cocoa and cane estates of Trinidad abandoned by Black labour after slavery. He was a bit of rag by the time the *Fatel Rozack* set out and he was probably only thrown in by the inspectors at the last minute in anticipation of the casualties along the way, perhaps as a goat for the jharay to rest bad luck on instead of on the more robust. One hundred and thirteen days on the sea and he had arrived thinner than he began and scarcely able to walk. And later then the fire had scorched his eyes and he had brought his lashless stare to Culebra Bay.

Another generation had erased Ragoonanan from the face of Private Samuel Gordon Sones of the Second West India Regiment. Not deliberately but by sheer force of the tin shacks, the flame trees and Rabindranath himself; as if, not seeing, he did not see himself. Settled into the outskirts he learned another language and another race, and in his own mouth he cursed his own beginnings because if not for that he wouldn't be here. Rain put him in the foulest mood. He felt like a muddied rag sitting at the mouth of his damp shack. He remembered the monsoons, he begrudged not loving them, which, had his circumstances been different, he might have done; but were it not for them he would still have been in Gorakpur. So it did not matter if his daughter Augusta, by Bola, a woman twelve years older than he, obliterated the rest of him in a man who came round with an instrument for pulling teeth. A black man, with grainy hair, whose name was Sones, and whose name Augusta took, preferring it to Ragoonanan, or Mon Chagrin which was all Bola could offer of anything like a last name.

15   When the Second West India Regiment first disembarked at Liverpool, Augusta's son had kissed the ground, taking a handful and putting it in his pocket. He felt the wet remains of it hit his thigh as he moved up the hill with his regiment at Damieh.

War! he roars under the *Tamarindus indica*. War. I went to war for them. Misconduct, my ass. But most days he just does his penance without a word because the sun is so hot it doesn't take a word. Breath has to be rationed, and besides it is nobody's business what his penance is for. It is between him and the *Tamarindus indica* and the furnace of a sun that makes his skin weep.

When he returned in disgrace, he looked at himself in the mirror and said to his own face, "You is a English man? Take that in your arse then." He put on his black English suit with its vest and his white shirt with its stiff starched collar, his black English shoes and white socks; he tightened his tie to his neck and set out to walk the length and breadth of Culebra Bay, beginning at precisely eleven-fifty and ending at one-thirty back at the tree. He chose the time when the sun is most fierce; only this could burn away his shame and loathing.

He showed himself no mercy. His collar ate into his neck and he did not carry a handkerchief to sop his brow. Now the suit is frayed. For the first few years he had bought a new one every year but thinking after a while that this vanity was why his sin was not expiated, why each year he felt more and more criminal, he'd worn the same one now for nine years, patching it where decency required and leaving the sun to iron the sweat and dirt into the seams. He had grown thicker, more dense than the young man who had climbed with hands and feet up the hill at Damieh, slower than the young man who had shot into a fleeing Turk and, pausing in shock, was swept up by shouts and the running frightened inhuman screams of the Second West India Regiment, under the terrified command of Captain Michael De Freitas.

It was not that he hadn't noticed little by little or that he did not know his place, and yes he would be humble in that place. *Yes sir* was not a hardship. Yes sir, no sir. That was the result of his birth. But a man could rise. A man could strive. And he had been let into the Second West India Regiment, proving that men of colour were improving their situation and would be repaid for their duty. It was the public contingents that he was let into and they were just for Blacks and Indians, but no matter, his mother had said, a man could rise above all this. His mother had encouraged him to think himself a man above what Black men thought they could be in those days.

20   His mother, Augusta, was above what a woman could be. She managed his birth and the world and managed to make a son who would rise above himself. Augusta Sones built a parlour up on the roadside, selling fried fish and sweets, doing washing in the back of her shack and so, little by little,

built up her son and put shoes on his feet and sent him to school. Whenever Sones, his father, came to pull teeth with his pliers she took a few shillings from him and tied it in a knot and put it in her bosom, then lifted her dress and bent over her washtub so that Sones would give her some pleasure for herself until the next time he passed through.

And his grandfather, Rabindranath Ragoonanan, had not been less a man, given all that had been done to him. He asked for nothing, wandered off following this or that sound and returned to sit in the doorway of his shack, singing prayers and ghazals and welcoming various Hindu gods and goddesses or cursing them out of his house as the case might be. He was far away from them anyway, they could not hold him or exercise any power over him and he was far away from the pandit who was still in touch with them. He was a poor labourer who could not labour any more, but the fact that there was life at all in him made him worthy. And in his shack even Shiva and Kali and Lakshmi were lodging there only by his beneficence. Where were they when the monsoon deluged him toward the lice-stricken depot in Calcutta, where were they on the vomiting ship? He'd cried when they delivered him on land 113 days later, but his faith was stingier, smaller, and the burning cane that took out his eyes took the rest of his devotion. So when he sang prayers it was for the sound, not for any faith.

In her ninety-sixth year Bola had laughed loud in her delirium when she heard that her grandson Samuel was going off to war. Rocking on the veranda, her eyes blind, her body as robust as when young, her face collapsed around her gums and her hair patchy and balding, she laughed big and rippling as if she had heard something fantastic and absurd.

He had been afraid of her ever since he was a boy, because when he came home she would always grab him and go through his pockets like a bullying child, looking for candy. And she would slap him if he didn't have any, and if he did she would steal it and tell him not to tell. Then she would go back to her rocking, rocking, endless rocking, and all alone talking to herself, then every now and then she seemed to catch up precisely with whatever conversation was going on around her. He felt that she could read his mind when he was a boy.

Her chair was in the yard near the clothesline and she would rock there after sweeping the dirt clean leaving lines from the broom crossing themselves and making arrows and swirls, and he would play around her drawings, destroying her lines and brushing her feet with his stick. He did not know what to make of her. Senseless his mother said, senseless, she had lost her senses and he was not to interfere with her. And so, like someone who had his senses, he provoked her, happy that there was an adult whom he could mistreat, until she reached for him and grabbed him to her and rode the rocking chair on his toes and looked him square in the eyes, her own eyes emerging from their glaucomaed grey, and said when he screamed, "Don't cry. When you're wicked you can't cry. Who will hear you?"

25   He left her alone after that, playing far away and glancing toward her every now and again to see if she was about to attack or if she was still there,

sitting in her chair, rocking in the middle of nowhere, the dust swept clean around her, her occasional pointing at the sea, her internal conversations lifting her arms in delight, and mumbling, her sometimes singing, "Pain c'est viande beque, vin c'est sang beque. . . ."

So when he heard her laugh as he was going off to war dressed in his khaki breeches and leggings, he spun around, forgetting that she was still alive, his face contorting in worry. He felt an urge to pick up a stone and fling it at her but her old warning that if you hit your mother in life your hands will remain in the air in death and you would not fit into your coffin, that old warning stopped him. "Old Ma, shut up!" he screamed instead.

Rocking and chuckling to herself, Bola, the grandmother who had lived in two centuries, was living somewhere else already, though every once in a while she would catch the voices from where her body was and laugh. So they could not know that she had not heard a word as to substance but had heard a voice to help her trace her way back to where she had left her body.

When she heard it she was down by the water many years ago. The man-o'-war birds were coming in to signal to her that a ship was coming, or a whale, and far away she saw the spray, so picking up her dress tail with one hand and grabbing her shell she ran, hitting the sea in a splash, she swam to her rock and stood there blowing and blowing to tell the whales, to hitch a ride, to warn them of their coming death, to talk to them with her own air through the shell, calculating that they knew the sound of air, they understood the language of water which she needed to know.

"Don't worry with her." Samuel Sones's mother pulled his eyes back to her own. "She old and gone." But he suspected his grandmother's laugh and remembered it now, sitting in the relief of the tree.

30   Old and gone, dropping all her pieces of conversations and laughter. She lived now in the best of places, where everything happened at the same time. Her days were full of all her living, everything she had done and seen and heard, all her children and her childhood and Kamena and the red birds and the blind man and the golden man and the man whose scent was too sweet and her mother, Marie Ursule. All happening at the same time. In all of it the present was small and just a part. She saw her daughter Augusta and took her for Marie Ursule; her grandson Samuel she took for the son who flew off in the hurricane of 1875, saying to him, "I thought you gone, boy." Sometimes she thought that she had the path to the present cleared up, when Augusta and Samuel spoke long enough or high enough for her to hear them. But if it was dew light she mistook them for Marie Ursule and Kamena. Sones heard her singing sometimes. Marie Ursule. Just these two words were her whole song. But only sometimes could she leave the water and the nuns and the trumpet fish and all her living to hear something heaving like a coming whale.

He was twenty when he went away to England in the year 1917. His mother, Augusta, insisted that he be baptized the Sunday before he left. They went to the water, his grandmother trailing them, with a small crowd for his baptism. All the people were in black and the preacher broke off strips of water, blessing Sones. His mother wore a blue robe and held an umbrella. She had finished Sones' white camisole the night before and he looked regal. He clasped his hands and swallowed chunks of sky and cupfuls of land as the preacher dipped his body back into the water. His grandmother Bola sucked her teeth when he came back up from the water, her face sour like a lemon, saying, "Foolishness, that don't save nobody."

Sones was twenty-one when he returned in disgrace. Sent back for misconduct. He had spent another two years in the military jail at St. Joseph, suffocating in the hot dome half-buried in the fort's hill. They let him out as if they had forgotten him. He heard a steward wondering aloud at who he was and what he was doing there. He had been so quiet, stewing in his own flesh the whole time, the steward had not noticed him. When he was released he lingered outside the jail for many hours not knowing his direction, then walked home to Culebra, where his grandmother still sat in her centuries and his mother already dead of consumption.

"Waiting for you, boy. Your mother gone." Bola precise when she was lucid.

"Gone where?" he asked, refusing her meaning.

35   "Gone where people does go, where else?" she said as if he was stupid. Then she went back to her rocking and he to the small shack and the roadside stand to weep. Late that evening he noticed her stillness in the chair still rocking and went to give her food. Her shell was in the firm grip of her hands and her body was stiff, her face strangely had only now really fallen into its age and Samuel Sones for all he cared was alone in the world. If he had not shouldered Bola's own coffin onto a bullock cart and made his lone procession through Culebra Bay, past the flame trees, halting at the tamarind tree in recognition, and taken her coffin out to sea himself, he would have believed his eyes when he returned and found her rocking in the swept dirt.

"Waiting for you," she said again when he arrived home after her funeral. "Your mother gone, *oui*. She not strong. She catch cold easy."

He ignored her ghost, he did not trust her confidences and went about his business and she continued her rocking and her searching for the breath of whales. She lived her life as she'd always lived it, swimming and loving and birthing children, sending some off in the ocean and off in the world and keeping some. She continued her skipping from the hovering man-o'-war nuns, she continued her waiting for Kamena's return and she honed her shell-blowing, warning whales off the coast.

"Englishman," they began to call him in Culebra Bay, out of admiration that he had been abroad and in the Great War, and behind their hands in derision as he had been sent back for misconduct. He explained nothing, and some malevolence visible in him told them not to ask or laugh when he was present. But as if asking them to be cruel he began wearing his English suit everywhere. To market, to garden, to drink, to the river, to stand in the roadside stall reduced to a few dried-out provisions from Augusta's usual plenty. He stood there in his suit, offering weevil-eaten flour and ants-liquefied sweets left there since his mother. Once or twice he tried to sell a fish that he caught, but he had become so belligerent no one came to buy. As if inviting their scorn he didn't speak to anyone personably. He was abrupt, formal and dismissive. A man inviting ridicule and determined not to have any comfort.

This tree, which was hard and brown, whose fronds he remembered for stinging childhood beatings he received from Augusta, he hated and loved because it gave shade, because it forgave him and punished him for being an Englishman.

40   He had had it in mind to disappear into the English countryside with a milk-white woman. To stand like a man who was on the edge of a book page, overlooking a field and a milk-white woman. She was in a small book he had borrowed from Captain Michael De Freitas when they were both small boys and De Freitas lived in the village of Abyssinia down the road from Culebra Bay in a big house with his mother and father, and De Freitas shoved a school book through his iron fence for Samuel Sones to notice him. Sones left off rolling a tin can to snatch the book like a jewel. She would have a blue ribbon in her hair and wisps of hair across her face—he had seen her in that *Reader*, a milk-white woman going a-milking in the English country-side. Or he had it in mind to find someone called Mary. "Oh, Mary, go and call the cattle home, and call the cattle home across the sands of Dee." Yes, twice, call the cattle home and call the cattle home.

But he had seen no milk-white woman when he finally arrived in Great Britain, and no countryside. He had heard only men barking in another lan-guage and all he was aware of were his ears trying to understand. His only sense, it seemed, was his hearing, because he did not want to make a mis-take and his other senses were already overwhelmed. His eyes overwhelmed by smallness where he had expected greatness, his mouth overwhelmed by rations, and his nose overwhelmed by the stench of other men sweating their fear.

The events of it, the actual events and what things looked like he could not remember. The moment they were loaded again onto the ship at Liverpool headed for Palestine, he became senseless. He was just part of a senseless mass of physicalness. He lifted his body like others, he ate like others and he dressed like others and he wanted to do that because if he thought for a moment about himself alone he became weak, his chest and arms would sweat and his mouth turn dry and stink.

Washing linen and cleaning latrines, digging trenches and refilling them, and running to the beck and call of anyone with less colour than them, the Second West India Regiment was sent to Palestine and Sinai for labour services along with other Black soldiers from the other islands. Anyone with less colour than they could spit and they would have to clean it up. Their encampment smelled of night soil and disappointment.

One night he wrote home to his mother, "We are treated neither as Christians nor as British citizens but as West Indian 'niggers' without any-body to be interested in us or look after us." The letter arrived but his mother never opened it, nor could she read it if she had, but she kept it nailed to her stall, pointing to it and telling everyone of her son, the soldier, in the Great War.

45 The others in his battalion wanted to fight. They quarrelled each night about the back-breaking work they were doing, although they were not allowed to do combat against European soldiers because of their colour. He grew smaller and smaller inside. He wanted to go home. He wanted to get through the days.

When they were called up to fight the Turkish troops on the other side, he sank on his bunk, sweating, and thanked God that it would not depend on his own will to move but the surging upswell of the regiment, the sheer energy of these men wanting to be a credit and to prove the British Empire wrong.

He could never remember what really happened then. They routed the Turks on Damieh Hill and even that he was told. His body was so liquid events fell through him. The only thing that he remembered was the stunned Turk whom he had shot by mistake, and felt wicked after. All he could remember was a body trying to give in and the steep climb and the mud or dust, he could not say what. Whatever it was he was burdened in it and his boots were wet and hot and his toes itchy. He did not think of himself as a person any more, and his plans to return with stories of his heroism were taken over by his fear.

After the battle they marched for days toward Jericho and a fever made his remembrances more blurry. His nose was running and his eyes felt like blisters and he wanted to sit down. Sit down in his yard where his mother combed his hair and his crazy grandmother sat rocking in another world. And someone kept pulling him up every time he tried to sit down. Someone kept barking at him and by now his hearing was gone too and his head wrapped in his shirt as they used to do it when he was a child and got an attack of fever and delirium. They would soak him in bay rum to sweat his fever and wrap him in cloth and put him to lie in a warm corner of the room, and he would hear rain and he would hear night and he would hear the wind, as if they were breathing. He would see the flame tree dappling on the curtain as the sun was falling. And he wanted to cry into his mother's lap but they kept pulling him up and making him walk.

Once he lay down hearing feet pass him by, stumbling over him, and he turned his face to the ground and licked the dirt of the road and realized that he wasn't home but on the road to somewhere where something should be waiting for him and he hurried to his feet and kept going. Feeling thin in his clothes but suddenly invigorated he pushed forward, jostling other men in many stages of pain.

50 *Tamarindus indica.* The tree under which the remainder of the world passed him by. He did not see the arrival of his cousin Cordelia Rojas by small boat from Venezuela. He didn't see her, with her small grip and her hair pulled back severely, walk up the beach to begin her new life, going toward the shop that had now taken over all of his mother's business. He would not have known her anyway. Her grandfather, Esteban, was only a

rambling song in his grandmother's mouth. It came out in inconsequential verses about a man who loved gold things and who wanted her blowing shell. A man with a grip of coarse and fine cloth who had a silver compass. At first Cordelia Rojas came toward him wanting directions, not suspecting it was her cousin, but noticing his delirious walk to the tamarind tree she hesitated and went another way. She could not see her grandmother Bola then, rocking in her chair in the swept dirt as always and forever.

Four years later, in 1929, when they sank the oil well "Magdalena" five miles away in Abyssinia, and the spout of oil could be seen and felt in Culebra Bay, Sones did not look up; when the warm black spray rained on Culebra for two days, and fear that the uncapped well would explode spread, Sones sucked his teeth in derision. The transformation of cocoa pickers to oilfield workers made no impression on him, not even the emptying out of Culebra Bay to Abyssinia in search of money and modern houses. In the years to follow, the deaths by fire and mishaps in the oilfield and the growing dissatisfaction of the workers did not concern him. The strike of 1937 passed him by. When the policeman was killed and the army marched on Abyssinia and Culebra Bay to quell the rioting workers he found himself in the middle with a bloodied head among bloodier ones, only because he was walking to his tree. Even the lashes he received from the soldiers, their bullwhips whipping left, right and centre, didn't disturb him. He waded through them to his tree, his suit dripping blood. "War," he said, "war."

Small years and then decades passed him. The whole march of villages to Port-of-Spain and San Fernando looking for work. He did not notice that he was now alone. And the importation of workers from Grenada and the small islands, and the migrations to the Panama Canal and all who did not return from there. He sat impassively as boats ran aground on Culebra coral. In the deluges of water he saw fishermen disappear, he saw storms and four hurricanes between 1939 and 1952. Through all of it he made his way to the tree, which had also withstood what was immaterial.

Him. Private Samuel Gordon Sones. Next to his name in the war registry was, "Sent back for Misconduct." Not "Unfit," "Unfit," "Unfit," as was written against the names of Indians, but "Sent back for Misconduct."

De Freitas. De Freitas was a minister in the government now, a minister of water. And Samuel Sones had thought of killing him many times in the years since. But in the end of every plot he made, he ended up with himself to blame. He ended up with that stinging moment of recognition of his colour and his dreams. ". . . because who send me to them people' place? Who send me to be in their business?"

55   He had trusted De Freitas, ever since he had first seen him. A lonely boy, just like him. A lonely boy behind an iron gate, whose loneliness Sones took for friendship, but which was really envy. Envy that Sones could walk about on the road in his bare feet rolling a discarded can if he wanted and Sones could kick a rag with other boys and Sones could take a stick and whack puddles of rain water collected in ditches after rain fell. And though Sones envied De Freitas his iron gates and his orderly flower garden and his crisp clothes and shoes even when it was not Sunday, De Freitas loved and envied

the way Sones could turn away from the gate to some other child calling him and break into a gurgle of a laugh, forgetting De Freitas standing there.

But Sones trusted De Freitas if only because De Freitas had shown him his book and therefore another life, and had given him a round orange marble to play with. If only because he spent as many curious hours sitting against the fence peering in at De Freitas's world of silence as De Freitas spent looking out at his. There at the fence he grew to know the real value of things. Those reflections coupled with his mother Augusta's dissertations guided him. "I didn't lift up my skirt for you to be a old 'rab. I didn't suck salt for you to come out like the rest. I e'nt come out of the gutter for you to put me back here. I e'nt stand up on the street whole day selling nuts for you to sell nuts too. I e'nt buy you good clothes for you to jump in canal with them. I e'nt make you for you to dead on the street on me. I e'nt make you for no knife fight. I e'nt make you to get kill. I e'nt make no ragamuffin. I e'nt make no criminal. I stand up over scrubbing board for you to make bad? I stand up over hot stove? I take the meat from my mouth, I deny myself, I walk barefoot."

In the endless stream of Augusta's tongue which always began in "I" as if she were God, Sones saw more and more what he wanted to be. And what he wanted to be was De Freitas, who had a father who owned a cocoa estate and leased land to the foreign oil company and a mother who always smiled, a mother who spoke harshly only when she called him from the fence away from Sones, a mother who, when Sones observed her, unaware of him hovering at the edges of the road, played with De Freitas and laughed with him and gently held him, a mother who could afford tenderness and who was not washing, ironing, selling; a mother under whom he, Sones, could be a boy without anxieties, a boy who did not have to amount to much but who could simply, with the effects of his shade, glide into manhood as if it were his skin and his island.

When Augusta noticed her son's friendship with the De Freitas boy she encouraged it, sending Samuel with a cloth-covered dish of mangoes or pomme cytheres or pomeracs for the boy. Hoping the De Freitases would throw a little kindness to her son. She made Sones dress up to go talk with De Freitas, she asked him constantly what they spoke about and if the De Freitases had invited him in behind the fence yet. Sones became uncomfortable and didn't always go to meet De Freitas but sometimes shared the mangoes with his other friends running past De Freitas's house, only waving at him. He showed De Freitas how to pitch marbles, he digging three holes on his side of the fence and De Freitas doing the same on his; they sucked mango seeds white and sometimes De Freitas would sneak out a pretty tin of wafers, which Sones ate not wanting to eat because it would spoil the prettiness of the tin. They often stooped together against the fence in a friendship sweetened by green plums, sweet candy, salty tamarind balls, joints of sugar cane, pulpy cocoa seeds or velvety chenettes, rocking on their heels enjoying the tastes on their tongues like an unspoken world.

De Freitas went away to big school in Port-of-Spain and Sones saw only glimpses of him when he came home, taller and leaner every July, and more and more reserved. The last time they talked through the fence they were fifteen and there was not much to talk about. Sones knew that De Freitas was expected home, given that it was the end of the school year, so he lingered along the street with De Freitas's house until he saw him and De Freitas yelled, "Aye, boy!" out of habit, before realizing that perhaps he had nothing to say. Sones hurried over to the fence smiling and they both stood there awkwardly for some moments. Then Sones said, "Well, anyway, boy, I gone," and took off in a brief confused sweat.

60   Sones finished the elementary school in Abyssinia, walking the five or six miles each morning and afternoon. When he was done with that there was nowhere to go except helping the teacher to clean the blackboard and standing in front of the class taking out the talkers and those who moved their fingers from their lips when the one teacher was absent from the classroom. Augusta didn't want him helping at the roadside shop; he, she said, was not made for that. Only on Saturdays she made him stand there counting people's change out loud so that she could show people what a bright son she had, and when the roadside stall was crowded and he was warming to the numbers she would tell him loudly and chuckling, "Rest your head, child, rest your head now. Go and lie down. All your book-studying and you still want to help your poor mother out. All you see what a good child I have?"

When Sones saw De Freitas in his uniform in 1916, he adored him. He wanted a uniform just like it. He read slyly to his mother from the gazette paper that men were being mobilized for the war, hoping that she would let him join up. "But people does dead in war!" Augusta told him and cut the talk short. Sones pined away to go to the war and sat sprawled in front of the roadside stall looking like a 'rab who was going to turn into a no-account, until Augusta relented.

He'd seen De Freitas's face when they were flying into the flanks of the Turkish troops. It was as frightened as his. He was certain that he would not recognize his own face, nor would he know what feeling was passing over it. He had tried to convey some sympathy and he was sure that De Freitas acknowledged him, remembered him as the boy who used to pass by and play with him. But the next day and the following, on the march to Jericho, De Freitas was as cool as any other officer. De Freitas had received his commission, joining up in the merchant and planter contingents, the whites. It was a shock to see Sones and that same look of sympathy as if he was still behind his iron fencing and Sones on the outside, free. He avoided Sones until they arrived at Jericho.

Sones was among his group, their dehydrated bodies struggling for one more foot of ground; De Freitas himself, officer or not, was weak with exhaustion. He went over to the group, they tried to stand up straight. Pointing to Sones he said, "Soldier, fill these!" handing Sones a string of officers' water canteens. "When you're done come back and get the boots."

Any soldier in the regiment would have understood the orders and those beside Sones understood, any soldier would have moved quickly to comply but Sones stood there drooping and dumbfounded. The others became uneasy when Sones did not move and one of them made an effort to rouse him. Sones brought his eyes to De Freitas's, lunged at him, knocked him down with a ragged bruised fist then fell on De Freitas in exhaustion.

65   Lovers passed him. *Tamarindus indica.* Some who liked his fine suit, some who wanted to strip him naked, some who only wanted his baby because, dour and disagreeable as he was, he used to be handsome. Some thought that he had money when he used to change his suits each year and even after he stayed in the same one they took this as the eccentricity of people with money under their mattresses. Lovers lingered, walking slowly past him at his stall or calculating the time that he made his walks, waiting at the bench under the tree, dressed in yellow or pink, in red polka dots or white cambric, and smelling of violet water. These passed him long before he came to resemble something filthy under a tamarind tree. His cuffs frayed and gluey from mopping up every liquid that came out of him. And even after that some thought that maybe they could fix him up like a house or a water tap, brush him down like a horse, because they knew that he would be faithful. Some thought that they could fix up his roadside stall and make a go of it. Some even thought that they could get used to his ghost of a grandmother rocking in her chair. But they all failed. He was filled with so much self-loathing every time he remembered the Second West India Regiment, he tried to root out that small place inside him that had led him to it. Root out that small pain that never grew any bigger but that was like a tablet of poison. He had knocked De Freitas down. It wasn't an insult that he could just pass off. Yes, he had knocked him down and had wanted to kill him right there and then. Yet killing him would not have been sufficient because the man had insulted him and he understood that the insult would stay with him no matter if he knocked De Freitas down or killed him. And he understood that it was his fault. All of it. He deserved it for pushing himself up and thinking that he was more than he was.

He sat there through another world war and he crowed for the enemy. In August 1940, when the Germans tried to cross the English Channel and the Luftwaffe bombed London nightly, Sones was gleeful. *Tamarindus indica.* He walked back and forth to this tree through the sweep of nationalist ideas and speeches toward independence from Britain, the lowering of the Union Jack and the lifting of the blood and the earth. He sat through small children stiffly starched and sweating in the hot sun, waving the Union Jack to the motorcade of the vanishing Queen. None of that could soothe him. He had already disappointed himself too much, nothing could repair him. He laughed at the speech-making, he knew that in the end it was not grand plans that ruled the world but some petty need of some individual, some small harassment that made things go bad.

He could have picked a flame tree, cooler and at least colourful, an orange one or a red one; he could have picked a poui, again indescribably coloured, and soft, when the petals fell; he could have picked a mango tree, the rose or Julie, sweet at least, the fruit and the smell would have calmed him, but no, he had chosen *Tamarindus indica* with its sour fruit and spindly dry branches, its unnoticeable flower and its dusty bark. He didn't move from the tree now, because some days he just couldn't make the walk or some days he thought that he had already done it. Some days he in fact did the walk many times.

He grew flabby and thin at the same time, like an old man does. Fidgety and narcoleptic at the same time. Dropping off to sleep and jumping up, remembering his way again. From where he sat he could clearly hear his grandmother laughing in another century. Her hand fluttered on a shell in her lap. And he wished that he could go back before that laugh—that laugh that had filled him with uncertainty and nervousness and opened a dread in him. And he wished that he could return to the time before that laugh, just before he came home with the news that they were going to the war, because before that he was a young man in his stiff starched khaki pants and shirt; a young man who could have stayed home and married a girl and made many children, he could have become . . . And yes, he remembered . . . Well, he recalled. . . . He recalled nothing. Nothing but the hope of going to Great Britain, going home to the mother country. He recalled nothing but the plans he had made right away when he touched De Freitas's reading book, when he kept it and thumbed the pages smudgy. That was his departure, and the laugh of his senseless grandmother.

READING AND REACTING

1. Why does Samuel join the Second West India Regiment? Is he successful in his ambition?
2. Why does Samuel resume wearing his English suit?
3. How are the soldiers separated into different groups with different responsibilities?
4. De Freitas is a role model for the young Samuel. Why? When does Samuel change his mind about De Freitas?
5. In addition to being the tree under which Samuel sits, what does the *Tamarindus indica* symbolize?
6. Samuel spends the rest of his life after the war believing that he deserved his treatment. Do you agree?
7. **JOURNAL ENTRY** What does the story suggest about the requirements for friendship?

Related Works: "Stones" (p. 135), "Blackman Dead" (p. 621), *The Ecstasy of Rita Joe* (p. 1376)

⏹ **EUDORA WELTY** (1909–2001) was born and raised in Jackson, Mississippi, where she lived in her family's home until her death. After attending the Mississippi College for Women, the University of Wisconsin, and Columbia University (where she studied advertising), she returned to Jackson to pursue her long career as a writer, beginning as a journalist. In

1936, she wrote the first of her many short stories, which are gathered in *Collected Stories* (1980). Welty also authored several novels, including *Delta Wedding* (1946), *Losing Battles* (1970), and the Pulitzer Prize–winning *The Optimist's Daughter* (1972). Her volume of memoirs, *One Writer's Beginnings* (1984), was a best-seller.

Considered one of the most accomplished writers in the United States, Welty focused much of her fiction on life in Southern towns and villages peopled with dreamers, eccentrics, and close-knit families. Her sharply observed characters are sometimes presented with great humour, sometimes with poignant lyricism, but always with clarity and sympathy. "Of course any writer is in part all of his characters," she has written. "How otherwise would they be known to him, occur to him, become what they are?" In "A Worn Path," Welty creates a particularly memorable character in the tenacious Phoenix Jackson and explores a theme that transcends race and region.

◇ ◇ ◇

E U D O R A   W E L T Y

A Worn Path
(1940)

It was December—a bright frozen day in the early morning. Far out in the country there was an old Negro woman with her head tied in a red rag, coming along a path through the pinewoods. Her name was Phoenix Jackson. She was very old and small and she walked slowly in the dark pine shadows, moving a little from side to side in her steps, with the balanced heaviness and lightness of a pendulum in a grandfather clock. She carried a thin, small cane made from an umbrella, and with this she kept tapping the frozen earth in front of her. This made a grave and persistent noise in the still air, that seemed meditative like the chirping of a solitary little bird.

She wore a dark striped dress reaching down to her shoe tops, and an equally long apron of bleached sugar sacks, with a full pocket: all neat and tidy, but every time she took a step she might have fallen over her shoelaces, which dragged from her unlaced shoes. She looked straight ahead. Her eyes were blue with age. Her skin had a pattern all its own of numberless branching wrinkles and as though a whole little tree stood in the middle of her forehead, but a golden color ran underneath, and the two knobs of her cheeks were illumined by a yellow burning under the dark. Under the red rag her hair came down on her neck in the frailest of ringlets, still black, and with an odor like copper.

Now and then there was a quivering in the thicket. Old Phoenix said, "Out of my way, all you foxes, owls, beetles, jack rabbits, coons and wild animals! . . . Keep out from under these feet, little bob-whites. . . . Keep the big wild hogs out of my path. Don't let none of those come running my direction. I got a long way." Under her small black-freckled hand her cane, limber as a buggy whip, would switch at the brush as if to rouse up any hiding things.

On she went. The woods were deep and still. The sun made the pine needles almost too bright to look at, up where the wind rocked. The cones dropped as light as feathers. Down in the hollow was the mourning dove— it was not too late for him.

5   The path ran up a hill. "Seem like there is chains about my feet, time I get this far," she said, in the voice of argument old people keep to use with themselves. "Something always take a hold of me on this hill—pleads I should stay."

After she got to the top she turned and gave a full, severe look behind her where she had come. "Up through pines," she said at length. "Now down through oaks."

Her eyes opened their widest, and she started down gently. But before she got to the bottom of the hill a bush caught her dress.

Her fingers were busy and intent, but her skirts were full and long, so that before she could pull them free in one place they were caught in another. It was not possible to allow the dress to tear. "I in the thorny bush," she said. "Thorns, you doing your appointed work. Never want to let folks pass, no sir. Old eyes thought you was a pretty little *green* bush."

Finally, trembling all over, she stood free, and after a moment dared to stoop for her cane.

10   "Sun so high!" she cried, leaning back and looking, while the thick tears went over her eyes. "The time getting all gone here."

At the foot of this hill was a place where a log was laid across the creek.

"Now comes the trial," said Phoenix.

Putting her right foot out, she mounted the log and shut her eyes. Lifting her skirt, leveling her cane fiercely before her, like a festival figure in some parade, she began to march across. Then she opened her eyes and she was safe on the other side.

"I wasn't as old as I thought," she said.

15   But she sat down to rest. She spread her skirts on the bank around her and folded her hands over her knees. Up above her was a tree in a pearly cloud of mistletoe. She did not dare to close her eyes, and when a little boy brought her a plate with a slice of marble-cake on it she spoke to him. "That would be acceptable," she said. But when she went to take it there was just her own hand in the air.

So she left that tree, and had to go through a barbed-wire fence. There she had to creep and crawl, spreading her knees and stretching her fingers like a baby trying to climb the steps. But she talked loudly to herself: she could not let her dress be torn now, so late in the day, and she could not pay for having her arm or her leg sawed off if she got caught fast where she was.

At last she was safe through the fence and risen up out in the clearing. Big dead trees, like black men with one arm, were standing in the purple stalks of the withered cotton field. There sat a buzzard.

"Who you watching?"

In the furrow she made her way along.

20   "Glad this not the season for bulls," she said, looking sideways, "and the good Lord made his snakes to curl up and sleep in the winter. A pleasure I don't see no two-headed snake coming around that tree, where it come once. It took a while to get by him, back in the summer."

She passed through the old cotton and went into a field of dead corn. It whispered and shook and was taller than her head. "Through the maze now," she said, for there was no path.

Then there was something tall, black, and skinny there, moving before her.

At first she took it for a man. It could have been a man dancing in the field. But she stood still and listened, and it did not make a sound. It was as silent as a ghost.

"Ghost," she said sharply, "who be you the ghost of? For I have heard of nary death close by."

25   But there was no answer—only the ragged dancing in the wind.

She shut her eyes, reached out her hand, and touched a sleeve. She found a coat and inside that an emptiness, cold as ice.

"You scarecrow," she said. Her face lighted. "I ought to be shut up for good," she said with laughter. "My senses is gone. I too old. I the oldest people I ever know. Dance, old scarecrow," she said, "while I dancing with you."

She kicked her foot over the furrow, and with mouth drawn down, shook her head once or twice in a little strutting way. Some husks blew down and whirled in streamers about her skirts.

Then she went on, parting her way from side to side with the cane, through the whispering field. At last she came to the end, to a wagon track where the silver grass blew between the red ruts. The quail were walking around like pullets, seeming all dainty and unseen.

30   "Walk pretty," she said. "This is the easy place. This the easy going."

She followed the track, swaying through the quiet bare fields, through the little strings of trees silver in their dead leaves, past cabins silver from weather, with the doors and windows boarded shut, all like old women under a spell sitting there. "I walking in their sleep," she said, nodding her head vigorously.

In a ravine she went where a spring was silently flowing through a hollow log. Old Phoenix bent and drank. "Sweet-gum makes the water sweet," she said, and drank more. "Nobody know who made this well, for it was here when I was born."

The track crossed a swampy part where the moss hung as white as lace from every limb. "Sleep on, alligators, and blow your bubbles." Then the track went into the road.

Deep, deep the road went down between the high green-colored banks. Overhead the live-oaks met, and it was as dark as a cave.

35   A black dog with a lolling tongue came up out of the weeds by the ditch. She was meditating, and not ready, and when he came at her she only hit

him a little with her cane. Over she went in the ditch, like a little puff of milkweed.

Down there, her senses drifted away. A dream visited her, and she reached her hand up, but nothing reached down and gave her a pull. So she lay there and presently went to talking. "Old woman," she said to herself, "that black dog come up out of the weeds to stall you off, and now there he sitting on his fine tail, smiling at you."

A white man finally came along and found her—a hunter, a young man, with his dog on a chain.

"Well, Granny!" he laughed. "What are you doing there?"

"Lying on my back like a June-bug waiting to be turned over, mister," she said, reaching up her hand.

40   He lifted her up, gave her a swing in the air, and set her down. "Anything broken, Granny?"

"No sir, them old dead weeds is springy enough," said Phoenix, when she had got her breath. "I thank you for your trouble."

"Where do you live, Granny?" he asked, while the two dogs were growling at each other.

"Away back yonder, sir, behind the ridge. You can't even see it from here."

"On your way home?"

45   "No sir, I going to town."

"Why, that's too far! That's as far as I walk when I come out myself, and I get something for my trouble." He patted the stuffed bag he carried, and there hung down a little closed claw. It was one of the bob-whites, with its beak hooked bitterly to show it was dead. "Now you go on home, Granny!"

"I bound to go to town, mister," said Phoenix. "The time come around."

He gave another laugh, filling the whole landscape. "I know you old colored people! Wouldn't miss going to town to see Santa Claus!"

But something held old Phoenix very still. The deep lines in her face went into a fierce and different radiation. Without warning, she had seen with her own eyes a flashing nickel fall out of the man's pocket onto the ground.

50   "How old are you, Granny?" he was saying.

"There is no telling, mister," she said, "no telling."

Then she gave a little cry and clapped her hands and said, "Git on away from here, dog! Look! Look at that dog!" She laughed as if in admiration. "He ain't scared of nobody. He a big black dog." She whispered, "Sic him!"

"Watch me get rid of that cur," said the man. "Sic him, Pete! Sic him!"

Phoenix heard the dogs fighting, and heard the man running and throwing sticks. She even heard a gunshot. But she was slowly bending forward by that time, further and further forward, the lid stretched down over her eyes, as if she were doing this in her sleep. Her chin was lowered almost to her knees. The yellow palm of her hand came out from the fold of her apron. Her fingers slid down and along the ground under the piece of money with the grace and care they would have in lifting an egg from under a setting hen. Then she slowly straightened up, she stood erect, and the nickel was in her apron pocket. A bird flew by. Her lips moved. "God watching me the whole time. I come to stealing."

55   The man came back, and his own dog panted about them. "Well, I scared him off that time," he said, and then he laughed and lifted his gun and pointed it at Phoenix.

She stood straight and faced him.

"Doesn't the gun scare you?" he said, still pointing it.

"No, sir, I seen plenty go off closer by, in my day, and for less than what I done," she said, holding utterly still.

He smiled, and shouldered the gun. "Well, Granny," he said, "you must be a hundred years old, and scared of nothing. I'd give you a dime if I had any money with me. But you take my advice and stay home, and nothing will happen to you."

60   "I bound to go on my way, mister," said Phoenix. She inclined her head in the red rag. Then they went in different directions, but she could hear the gun shooting again and again over the hill.

She walked on. The shadows hung from the oak trees to the road like curtains. Then she smelled wood-smoke, and smelled the river, and she saw a steeple and the cabins on their steep steps. Dozens of little black children whirled around her. There ahead was Natchez shining. Bells were ringing. She walked on.

In the paved city it was Christmas time. There were red and green electric lights strung and crisscrossed everywhere, and all turned on in the daytime. Old Phoenix would have been lost if she had not distrusted her eyesight and depended on her feet to know where to take her.

She paused quietly on the sidewalk where people were passing by. A lady came along in the crowd, carrying an armful of red-, green- and silver-wrapped presents; she gave off perfume like the red roses in hot summer, and Phoenix stopped her.

"Please, missy, will you lace up my shoe?" She held up her foot.

65   "What do you want, Grandma?"

"See my shoe," said Phoenix. "Do all right for out in the country, but wouldn't look right to go in a big building."

"Stand still then, Grandma," said the lady. She put her packages down on the sidewalk beside her and laced and tied both shoes tightly.

"Can't lace 'em with a cane," said Phoenix. "Thank you, missy. I doesn't mind asking a nice lady to tie up my shoe, when I gets out on the street."

Moving slowly and from side to side, she went into the big building, and into a tower of steps, where she walked up and around and around until her feet knew to stop.

70   She entered a door, and there she saw nailed up on the wall the document that had been stamped with the gold seal and framed in the gold frame, which matched the dream that was hung up in her head.

"Here I be," she said. There was a fixed and ceremonial stiffness over her body.

"A charity case, I suppose," said an attendant who sat at the desk before her.

But Phoenix only looked above her head. There was sweat on her face, the wrinkles in her face shone like a bright net.

"Speak up, Grandma," the woman said. "What's your name? We must have your history, you know. Have you been here before? What seems to be the trouble with you?"

75   Old Phoenix only gave a twitch to her face as if a fly were bothering her.

"Are you deaf?" cried the attendant.

But then the nurse came in.

"Oh, that's just old Aunt Phoenix," she said. "She doesn't come for herself—she has a little grandson. She makes these trips just as regular as clockwork. She lives away back off the Old Natchez Trace." She bent down. "Well, Aunt Phoenix, why don't you just take a seat? We won't keep you standing after your long trip." She pointed.

The old woman sat down, bolt upright in the chair.

80   "Now, how is the boy?" asked the nurse.

Old Phoenix did not speak.

"I said, how is the boy?"

But Phoenix only waited and stared straight ahead, her face very solemn and withdrawn into rigidity.

"Is his throat any better?" asked the nurse. "Aunt Phoenix, don't you hear me? Is your grandson's throat any better since the last time you came for the medicine?"

85   With her hands on her knees, the old woman waited, silent, erect and motionless, just as if she were in armor.

"You mustn't take up our time this way, Aunt Phoenix," the nurse said. "Tell us quickly about your grandson, and get it over. He isn't dead, is he?"

At last there came a flicker and then a flame of comprehension across her face, and she spoke.

"My grandson. It was my memory had left me. There I sat and forgot why I made my long trip."

"Forgot?" The nurse frowned. "After you came so far?"

90   Then Phoenix was like an old woman begging a dignified forgiveness for waking up frightened in the night. "I never did go to school, I was too old at the Surrender,"[1] she said in a soft voice. "I'm an old woman without an education. It was my memory fail me. My little grandson, he is just the same, and I forgot it in the coming."

"Throat never heals, does it?" said the nurse, speaking in a loud, sure voice to old Phoenix. By now she had a card with something written on it, a little list. "Yes. Swallowed lye. When was it?—January—two–three years ago—"

Phoenix spoke unasked now. "No, missy, he not dead, he just the same. Every little while his throat begin to close up again, and he not able to

---

[1] Of General Robert E. Lee to General Ulysses S. Grant at the end of the American Civil War, April 9, 1865.

swallow. He not get his breath. He not able to help himself. So the time come around, and I go on another trip for the soothing medicine."

"All right. The doctor said as long as you came to get it, you could have it," said the nurse. "But it's an obstinate case."

"My little grandson, he sit up there in the house all wrapped up, waiting by himself," Phoenix went on. "We is the only two left in the world. He suffer and it don't seem to put him back at all. He got a sweet look. He going to last. He wear a little patch quilt and peep out holding his mouth open like a little bird. I remembers so plain now. I not going to forget him again, no, the whole enduring time. I could tell him from all the others in creation."

95   "All right." The nurse was trying to hush her now. She brought her a bottle of medicine. "Charity," she said, making a check mark in a book.

Old Phoenix held the bottle close to her eyes, and then carefully put it into her pocket.

"I thank you," she said.

"It's Christmas time, Grandma," said the attendant. "Could I give you a few pennies out of my purse?"

"Five pennies is a nickel," said Phoenix stiffly.

100   "Here's a nickel," said the attendant.

Phoenix rose carefully and held out her hand. She received the nickel and then fished the other nickel out of her pocket and laid it beside the new one. She stared at her palm closely, with her head on one side.

Then she gave a tap with her cane on the floor.

"This is what come to me to do," she said. "I going to the store and buy my child a little windmill they sells, made out of paper. He going to find it hard to believe there such a thing in the world. I'll march myself back where he waiting, holding it straight up in this hand."

She lifted her free hand, gave a little nod, turned around, and walked out of the doctor's office. Then her slow step began on the stairs, going down.

READING AND REACTING

1. How does the first paragraph set the scene for the story? How does it foreshadow the events that will take place later on?
2. Traditionally, a quest is a journey in which a knight overcomes a series of obstacles in order to perform a prescribed feat. In what way is Phoenix's journey like a quest? What obstacles does she face? What feat must she perform?
3. Because Phoenix is so old, she has trouble seeing. What things does she have difficulty seeing? How do her mistakes shed light on her character? How do they contribute to the impact of the story?
4. What is the major theme of this story? What other themes are expressed?

5. A phoenix is a mythical bird that would live for five hundred years, be consumed by fire, and then rise from its own ashes. In what way is this name appropriate for the main character of this story?

6. Phoenix is not intimidated by the man with the gun and has no difficulty asking a white woman to tie her shoe. In spite of this nobility of character, however, Phoenix has no qualms about stealing a nickel or taking charity from the doctor. How do you account for this apparent contradiction?

7. How do the various people Phoenix encounters react to her? Do they treat her with respect? With disdain? Why do you think they react the way they do?

8. In paragraph 90, Phoenix says that she is an old woman without an education. Does she nevertheless seem to have any knowledge that the other characters lack?

9. **JOURNAL ENTRY** Could "A Worn Path" be an **allegory?** If so, what could each of the characters represent?

10. **CRITICAL PERSPECTIVE** Writing about "A Worn Path," Eudora Welty said that the question she was asked most frequently by both students and teachers was whether Phoenix Jackson's grandson was actually dead. Here she attempts to answer that question:

> I had not meant to mystify readers by withholding any fact; it is not a writer's business to tease. The story is told through Phoenix's mind and she undertakes her errand. As the author at one with the character as I tell it, I must assume that the boy is alive. As the reader, you are free to think as you like, of course; the story invites you to believe that no matter what happens, Phoenix for as long as she is able to walk and can hold to her purpose will make her journey.

Do you think Phoenix's grandson is alive or dead?

Related Works: "Her First Ball" (p. 129), "Araby" (p. 267), "Young Goodman Brown" (p. 307)

◈ WRITING SUGGESTIONS: THEME

1. In "Tamarindus Indica" and "Flight Paths of the Emperor" characters make a long journey that has an effect on their lives. Write an essay in which you compare the outcomes of the journeys and what the characters learn from their experience.

2. Both "A Worn Path" and "Tamarindus Indica" are about elderly people who exhibit a form of stubbornness or persistence. Compare these two characters.

3. "The Rocking-Horse Winner" and "A Worn Path" also deal with characters who make journeys. What is the significance of each journey? How do the protagonists of these two stories overcome the obstacles they encounter?

FICTION

FOR FURTHER READING

CHINUA ACHEBE
(1930–   )

Dead Man's Path
(1953) (1972)

Michael Obi's hopes were fulfilled much earlier than he had expected. He was appointed headmaster of Ndume Central School in January 1949. It had always been an unprogressive school, so the Mission authorities decided to send a young and energetic man to run it. Obi accepted this responsibility with enthusiasm. He had many wonderful ideas and this was an opportunity to put them into practice. He had had sound secondary school education which designated him a "pivotal teacher" in the official records and set him apart from the other headmasters in the mission field. He was outspoken in his condemnation of the narrow views of these older and often less-educated ones.

"We shall make a good job of it, shan't we?" he asked his young wife when they first heard the joyful news of his promotion.

"We shall do our best," she replied. "We shall have such beautiful gardens and everything will be just *modern* and delightful . . ." In their two years of married life she had become completely infected by his passion for "modern methods" and his denigration of "these old and superannuated people in the teaching field who would be better employed as traders in the Onitsha market." She began to see herself already as the admired wife of the young headmaster, the queen of the school.

The wives of the other teachers would envy her position. She would set the fashion in everything . . . Then, suddenly, it occurred to her that there might not be other wives. Wavering between hope and fear, she asked her husband, looking anxiously at him.

5   "All our colleagues are young and unmarried," he said with enthusiasm which for once she did not share. "Which is a good thing," he continued.

"Why?"

"Why? They will give all their time and energy to the school."

Nancy was downcast. For a few minutes she became skeptical about the new school; but it was only for a few minutes. Her little personal misfortune could not blind her to her husband's happy prospects. She looked at him as he sat folded up in a chair. He was stoop-shouldered and looked frail. But he sometimes surprised people with sudden bursts of physical energy. In his present posture, however, all his bodily strength seemed to have retired behind his deep-set eyes, giving them an extraordinary power of penetration. He was only twenty-six, but looked thirty or more. On the whole, he was not unhandsome.

"A penny for your thoughts, Mike," said Nancy after a while, imitating the woman's magazine she read.

10   "I was thinking what a grand opportunity we've got at last to show these people how a school should be run."

Ndume School was backward in every sense of the word. Mr. Obi put his whole life into the work, and his wife hers too. He had two aims. A high standard of teaching was insisted upon, and the school compound was to be turned into a place of beauty. Nancy's dream-gardens came to life with the coming of the rains, and blossomed. Beautiful hibiscus and allamanda hedges in brilliant red and yellow marked out the carefully tended school compound from the rank neighborhood bushes.

One evening as Obi was admiring his work he was scandalized to see an old woman from the village hobble right across the compound, through a marigold flower-bed and the hedges. On going up there he found faint signs of an almost disused path from the village across the school compound to the bush on the other side.

"It amazes me," said Obi to one of his teachers who had been three years in the school, "that you people allowed the villagers to make use of this foot-path. It is simply incredible." He shook his head.

"The path," said the teacher apologetically, "appears to be very important to them. Although it is hardly used, it connects the village shrine with their place of burial."

15   "And what has that got to do with the school?" asked the headmaster.

"Well, I don't know," replied the other with a shrug of the shoulders. "But I remember there was a big row some time ago when we attempted to close it."

"That was some time ago. But it will not be used now," said Obi as he walked away. "What will the Government Education Officer think of this when he comes to inspect the school next week? The villagers might, for all I know, decide to use the schoolroom for pagan ritual during the inspection."

Heavy sticks were planted closely across the path at the two places where it entered and left the school premises. These were further strengthened with barbed wire.

Three days later the village priest of Ani called on the headmaster. He was an old man and walked with a slight stoop. He carried a stout walking-stick which he usually tapped on the floor, by way of emphasis, each time he made a new point in his argument.

20   "I have heard," he said after the usual exchange of cordialities, "that our ancestral footpath has recently been closed . . ."

"Yes," replied Mr. Obi. "We cannot allow people to make a highway of our school compound."

"Look here, my son," said the priest bringing down his walking-stick, "this path was here before you were born and before your father was born. The whole life of this village depends on it. Our dead relatives depart by it and our ancestors visit us by it. But most important, it is the path of children coming in to be born . . ."

Mr. Obi listened with a satisfied smile on his face.

"The whole purpose of our school," he said finally, "is to eradicate just such beliefs as that. Dead men do not require footpaths. The whole idea is just fantastic. Our duty is to teach your children to laugh at such ideas."

25   "What you say may be true," replied the priest, "but we follow the practices of our fathers. If you reopen the path we shall have nothing to quarrel about. What I always say is let the hawk perch and let the eagle perch." He rose to go.

"I am sorry," said the young headmaster. "But the school compound cannot be a thoroughfare. It is against our regulations. I would suggest your constructing another path, skirting our premises. We can even get our boys to help in building it. I don't suppose the ancestors will find the little detour too burdensome."

"I have no more words to say," said the old priest, already outside.

Two days later a young woman in the village died in childbed. A diviner was immediately consulted and he prescribed heavy sacrifices to propitiate ancestors insulted by the fence.

Obi woke up next morning among the ruins of his work. The beautiful hedges were torn up not just near the path but right round the school, the flowers trampled to death and one of the school buildings pulled down . . . That day, the white Supervisor came to inspect the school and wrote a nasty report on the state of the premises but more seriously about the "tribal-war situation developing between the school and the village, arising in part from the misguided zeal of the new headmaster."

RAYMOND CARVER
(1938–1988)

Cathedral
(1983)

This blind man, an old friend of my wife's, he was on his way to spend the night. His wife had died. So he was visiting the dead wife's relatives in Connecticut. He called my wife from his in-laws'. Arrangements were made. He would come by train, a five-hour trip, and my wife would meet him at the station. She hadn't seen him since she worked for him one summer in Seattle ten years ago. But she and the blind man had kept in touch. They made tapes and mailed them back and forth. I wasn't enthusiastic about his visit. He was no one I knew. And his being blind bothered me. My idea of blindness came from the movies. In the movies, the blind moved slowly and never laughed. Sometimes they were led by seeing-eye dogs. A blind man in my house was not something I looked forward to.

That summer in Seattle she had needed a job. She didn't have any money. The man she was going to marry at the end of the summer was in officers' training school. He didn't have any money, either. But she was in love with the guy, and he was in love with her, etc. She'd seen something in the paper: HELP WANTED—*Reading to Blind Man,* and a telephone number. She phoned and went over, was hired on the spot. She'd worked with this blind man all summer. She read stuff to him, case studies, reports, that sort of thing. She helped him organize his little office in the county social-service department. They'd become good friends, my wife and the blind man. How do I know these things? She told me. And she told me something else. On her last day in the office, the blind man asked if he could touch her face. She agreed to this. She told me he touched his fingers to every part of her face, her nose—even her neck! She never forgot it. She even tried to write a poem about it. She was always trying to write a poem. She wrote a poem or two every year, usually after something really important had happened to her.

When we first started going out together, she showed me the poem. In the poem, she recalled his fingers and the way they had moved around over her face. In the poem, she talked about what she had felt at the time, about what went through her mind when the blind man touched her nose and lips. I can remember I didn't think much of the poem. Of course, I didn't tell her that. Maybe I just don't understand poetry. I admit it's not the first thing I reach for when I pick up something to read.

Anyway, this man who'd first enjoyed her favors, the officer-to-be, he'd been her childhood sweetheart. So okay. I'm saying that at the end of the summer she let the blind man run his hands over her face, said goodbye to him, married her childhood etc., who was now a commissioned officer, and she moved away from Seattle. But they'd kept in touch, she and the blind man. She made the first contact after a year or so. She called him up one night from an Air Force base in Alabama. She wanted to talk. They talked.

He asked her to send a tape and tell him about her life. She did this. She sent the tape. On the tape, she told the blind man about her husband and about their life together in the military. She told the blind man she loved her husband but she didn't like it where they lived and she didn't like it that he was part of the military-industrial thing. She told the blind man she'd written a poem and he was in it. She told him that she was writing a poem about what it was like to be an Air Force officer's wife. The poem wasn't finished yet. She was still writing it. The blind man made a tape. He sent her the tape. She made a tape. This went on for years. My wife's officer was posted to one base and then another. She sent tapes from Moody AFB, McGuire, McConnell, and finally Travis,[1] near Sacramento, where one night she got to feeling lonely and cut off from people she kept losing in that moving-around life. She got to feeling she couldn't go it another step. She went in and swallowed all the pills and capsules in the medicine chest and washed them down with a bottle of gin. Then she got into a hot bath and passed out.

5　　But instead of dying, she got sick. She threw up. Her officer—why should he have a name? he was the childhood sweetheart, and what more does he want?—came home from somewhere, found her, and called the ambulance. In time, she put it all on a tape and sent the tape to the blind man. Over the years, she put all kinds of stuff on tapes and sent the tapes off lickety-split. Next to writing a poem every year, I think it was her chief means of recreation. On one tape, she told the blind man she'd decided to live away from her officer for a time. On another tape, she told him about her divorce. She and I began going out, and of course she told her blind man about it. She told him everything, or so it seemed to me. Once she asked me if I'd like to hear the latest tape from the blind man. This was a year ago. I was on the tape, she said. So I said okay, I'd listen to it. I got us drinks and we settled down in the living room. We made ready to listen. First she inserted the tape into the player and adjusted a couple of dials. Then she pushed a lever. The tape squeaked and someone began to talk in this loud voice. She lowered the volume. After a few minutes of harmless chitchat, I heard my own name in the mouth of this stranger, this blind man I didn't even know! And then this: "From all you've said about him, I can only conclude—" But we were interrupted, a knock at the door, something, and we didn't ever get back to the tape. Maybe it was just as well. I'd heard all I wanted to.

Now this same blind man was coming to sleep in my house.

"Maybe I could take him bowling," I said to my wife. She was at the draining board doing scalloped potatoes. She put down the knife she was using and turned around.

"If you love me," she said, "you can do this for me. If you don't love me, okay. But if you had a friend, any friend, and the friend came to visit, I'd make him feel comfortable." She wiped her hands with the dish towel.

"I don't have any blind friends," I said.

---

[1] Moody . . . Travis: United States Air Force bases.

10   "You don't have *any* friends," she said. "Period. Besides," she said, "goddamn it, his wife's just died! Don't you understand that? The man's lost his
wife!"

I didn't answer. She'd told me a little about the blind man's wife. Her
name was Beulah. Beulah! That's a name for a colored woman.

"Was his wife a Negro?" I asked.

"Are you crazy?" my wife said. "Have you just flipped or something?"
She picked up a potato. I saw it hit the floor, then roll under the stove.
"What's wrong with you?" she said. "Are you drunk?"

"I'm just asking," I said.

15   Right then my wife filled me in with more detail than I cared to know.
I made a drink and sat at the kitchen table to listen. Pieces of the story began
to fall into place.

Beulah had gone to work for the blind man the summer after my wife
had stopped working for him. Pretty soon Beulah and the blind man had
themselves a church wedding. It was a little wedding—who'd want to go to
such a wedding in the first place?—just the two of them, plus the minister
and the minister's wife. But it was a church wedding just the same. It was
what Beulah had wanted, he'd said. But even then Beulah must have been
carrying the cancer in her glands. After they had been inseparable for eight
years—my wife's word, inseparable—Beulah's health went into a rapid
decline. She died in a Seattle hospital room, the blind man sitting beside the
bed and holding on to her hand. They'd married, lived and worked together,
slept together—had sex, sure—and then the blind man had to bury her. All
this without his having ever seen what the goddamned woman looked like.
It was beyond my understanding. Hearing this, I felt sorry for the blind man
for a little bit. And then I found myself thinking what a pitiful life this
woman must have led. Imagine a woman who could never see herself as she
was seen in the eyes of her loved one. A woman who could go on day after
day and never receive the smallest compliment from her beloved. A woman
whose husband could never read the expression on her face, be it misery or
something better. Someone who could wear makeup or not—what difference to him? She could, if she wanted, wear green eye-shadow around one
eye, a straight pin in her nostril, yellow slacks, and purple shoes, no matter.
And then to slip off into death, the blind man's hand on her hand, his blind
eyes streaming tears—I'm imagining now—her last thought maybe this: that
he never even knew what she looked like, and she on an express to the
grave. Robert was left with a small insurance policy and a half of a twenty-
peso Mexican coin. The other half of the coin went into the box with her.
Pathetic.

So when the time rolled around, my wife went to the depot to pick him
up. With nothing to do but wait—sure, I blamed him for that—I was having
a drink and watching the TV when I heard the car pull into the drive. I got
up from the sofa with my drink and went to the window to have a look.

I saw my wife laughing as she parked the car. I saw her get out of the car
and shut the door. She was still wearing a smile. Just amazing. She went
around to the other side of the car to where the blind man was already

starting to get out. This blind man, feature this, he was wearing a full beard! A beard on a blind man! Too much, I say. The blind man reached into the backseat and dragged out a suitcase. My wife took his arm, shut the car door, and, talking all the way, moved him down the drive and then up the steps to the front porch. I turned off the TV. I finished my drink, rinsed the glass, dried my hands. Then I went to the door.

My wife said, "I want you to meet Robert. Robert, this is my husband. I've told you all about him." She was beaming. She had this blind man by his coat sleeve.

20   The blind man let go of his suitcase and up came his hand.

I took it. He squeezed hard, held my hand, and then he let it go.

"I feel like we've already met," he boomed.

"Likewise," I said. I didn't know what else to say. Then I said, "Welcome. I've heard a lot about you." We began to move then, a little group, from the porch into the living room, my wife guiding him by the arm. The blind man was carrying his suitcase in his other hand. My wife said things like, "To your left here, Robert. That's right. Now watch it, there's a chair. That's it. Sit down right here. This is the sofa. We just bought this sofa two weeks ago."

I started to say something about the old sofa. I'd liked that old sofa. But I didn't say anything. Then I wanted to say something else, small-talk, about the scenic ride along the Hudson.[2] How going to New York, you should sit on the right-hand side of the train, and coming *from* New York, the left-hand side.

25   "Did you have a good train ride?" I said. "Which side of the train did you sit on, by the way?"

"What a question, which side!" my wife said. "What's it matter which side?" she said.

"I just asked," I said.

"Right side," the blind man said. "I hadn't been on a train in nearly forty years. Not since I was a kid. With my folks. That's been a long time. I'd nearly forgotten the sensation. I have winter in my beard now," he said. "So I've been told, anyway. Do I look distinguished, my dear?" the blind man said to my wife.

"You look distinguished, Robert," she said. "Robert," she said. "Robert, it's just so good to see you."

30   My wife finally took her eyes off the blind man and looked at me. I had the feeling she didn't like what she saw. I shrugged.

I've never met, or personally known, anyone who was blind. This blind man was late forties, a heavy-set, balding man with stooped shoulders, as if he carried a great weight there. He wore brown slacks, brown shoes, a light-brown shirt, a tie, a sports coat. Spiffy. He also had this full beard. But he didn't use a cane and he didn't wear dark glasses. I'd always thought dark glasses were a must for the blind. Fact was, I wished he had a pair. At first glance, his eyes looked like anyone else's eyes. But if you looked close, there was something different about them. Too much white in the iris, for one

---

[2] Hudson: A river in New York State.

thing, and the pupils seemed to move around in the sockets without his knowing it or being able to stop it. Creepy. As I stared at his face, I saw the left pupil turn in toward his nose while the other made an effort to keep in one place. But it was only an effort, for that eye was on the roam without his knowing it or wanting it to be.

I said, "Let me get you a drink. What's your pleasure? We have a little of everything. It's one of our pastimes."

"Bub, I'm a Scotch man myself," he said fast enough in this big voice.

"Right," I said. Bub! "Sure you are. I knew it."

35 He let his fingers touch his suitcase, which was sitting alongside the sofa. He was taking his bearings. I didn't blame him for that.

"I'll move that up to your room," my wife said.

"No, that's fine," the blind man said loudly. "It can go up when I go up."

"A little water with the Scotch?" I said.

"Very little," he said.

40 "I knew it," I said.

He said, "Just a tad. The Irish actor, Barry Fitzgerald? I'm like that fellow. When I drink water, Fitzgerald said, I drink water. When I drink whiskey, I drink whiskey." My wife laughed. The blind man brought his hand up under his beard. He lifted his beard slowly and let it drop.

I did the drinks, three big glasses of Scotch with a splash of water in each. Then we made ourselves comfortable and talked about Robert's travels. First the long flight from the West Coast to Connecticut, we covered that. Then from Connecticut up here by train. We had another drink concerning that leg of the trip.

I remembered having read somewhere that the blind didn't smoke because, as speculation had it, they couldn't see the smoke they exhaled. I thought I knew that much and that much only about blind people. But this blind man smoked his cigarette down to the nubbin and then lit another one. This blind man filled his ashtray and my wife emptied it.

When we sat down at the table for dinner, we had another drink. My wife heaped Robert's plate with cube steak, scalloped potatoes, green beans. I buttered him up two slices of bread. I said, "Here's bread and butter for you." I swallowed some of my drink. "Now let us pray," I said, and the blind man lowered his head. My wife looked at me, her mouth agape. "Pray the phone won't ring and the food doesn't get cold," I said.

45 We dug in. We ate everything there was to eat on the table. We ate like there was no tomorrow. We didn't talk. We ate. We scarfed. We grazed that table. We were into serious eating. The blind man had right away located his foods, he knew just where everything was on his plate. I watched with admiration as he used his knife and fork on the meat. He'd cut two pieces of meat, fork the meat into his mouth, and then go all out for the scalloped potatoes, the beans next, and then he'd tear off a hunk of buttered bread and eat that. He'd follow this up with a big drink of milk. It didn't seem to bother him to use his fingers once in a while, either.

We finished everything, including half a strawberry pie. For a few moments, we sat as if stunned. Sweat beaded on our faces. Finally, we got up from the table and left the dirty plates. We didn't look back. We took ourselves into the living room and sank into our places again. Robert and my wife sat on the sofa. I took the big chair. We had us two or three more drinks while they talked about the major things that had come to pass for them in the past ten years. For the most part, I just listened. Now and then I joined in. I didn't want him to think I'd left the room, and I didn't want her to think I was feeling left out. They talked of things that had happened to them—to them!—these past ten years. I waited in vain to hear my name on my wife's sweet lips: "And then my dear husband came into my life"—something like that. But I heard nothing of the sort. More talk of Robert. Robert had done a little of everything, it seemed, a regular blind jack-of-all-trades. But most recently he and his wife had had an Amway distributorship, from which, I gathered, they'd earned their living, such as it was. The blind man was also a ham radio operator.[3] He talked in his loud voice about conversations he'd had with fellow operators in Guam, in the Philippines, in Alaska, and even in Tahiti. He said he'd have a lot of friends there if he ever wanted to go visit those places. From time to time, he'd turn his blind face toward me, put his hand under his beard, ask me something. How long had I been in my present position? (Three years.) Did I like my work? (I didn't.) Was I going to stay with it? (What were the options?) Finally, when I thought he was beginning to run down, I got up and turned on the TV.

My wife looked at me with irritation. She was heading toward a boil. Then she looked at the blind man and said, "Robert, do you have a TV?"

The blind man said, "My dear, I have two TVs. I have a color set and a black-and-white thing, an old relic. It's funny, but if I turn the TV on, and I'm always turning it on, I turn on the color set. It's funny, don't you think?"

I didn't know what to say to that. I had absolutely nothing to say to that. No opinion. So I watched the news program and tried to listen to what the announcer was saying.

50 "This is a color TV," the blind man said. "Don't ask me how, but I can tell."

"We traded up a while ago," I said.

The blind man had another taste of his drink. He lifted his beard, sniffed it, and let it fall. He leaned forward on the sofa. He positioned his ashtray on the coffee table, then put the lighter to his cigarette. He leaned back on the sofa and crossed his legs at the ankles.

My wife covered her mouth, and then she yawned. She stretched. She said, "I think I'll go upstairs and put on my robe. I think I'll change into something else. Robert, you make yourself comfortable," she said.

"I'm comfortable," the blind man said.

---

[3] Ham radio operator: A licensed amateur radio operator.

55 "I want you to feel comfortable in this house," she said.

"I am comfortable," the blind man said.

After she'd left the room, he and I listened to the weather report and then to the sports roundup. By that time, she'd been gone so long I didn't know if she was going to come back. I thought she might have gone to bed. I wished she'd come back downstairs. I didn't want to be left alone with a blind man. I asked him if he wanted another drink, and he said sure. Then I asked if he wanted to smoke some dope with me. I said I'd just rolled a number. I hadn't, but I planned to do so in about two shakes.

"I'll try some with you," he said.

"Damn right," I said. "That's the stuff."

60 I got our drinks and sat down on the sofa with him. Then I rolled us two fat numbers. I lit one and passed it. I brought it to his fingers. He took it and inhaled.

"Hold it as long as you can," I said. I could tell he didn't know the first thing.

My wife came back downstairs wearing her pink robe and her pink slippers.

"What do I smell?" she said.

"We thought we'd have us some cannabis," I said.

65 My wife gave me a savage look. Then she looked at the blind man and said, "Robert, I didn't know you smoked."

He said, "I do now, my dear. There's a first time for everything. But I don't feel anything yet."

"This stuff is pretty mellow," I said. "This stuff is mild. It's dope you can reason with," I said. "It doesn't mess you up."

"Not much it doesn't, bub," he said, and laughed.

My wife sat on the sofa between the blind man and me. I passed her the number. She took it and toked[4] and then passed it back to me. "Which way is this going?" she said. Then she said, "I shouldn't be smoking this. I can hardly keep my eyes open as it is. That dinner did me in. I shouldn't have eaten so much."

70 "It was the strawberry pie," the blind man said. "That's what did it," he said, and he laughed his big laugh. Then he shook his head.

"There's more strawberry pie," I said.

"Do you want some more, Robert?" my wife said.

"Maybe in a little while," he said.

We gave our attention to the TV. My wife yawned again. She said, "Your bed is made up when you feel like going to bed, Robert. I know you must have had a long day. When you're ready to go to bed, say so." She pulled his arm. "Robert?"

75 He came to and said, "I've had a real nice time. This beats tapes, doesn't it?"

---

[4] Toked: Inhaled.

I said, "Coming at you," and I put the number between his fingers. He inhaled, held the smoke, and then let it go. It was like he'd been doing it since he was nine years old.

"Thanks, bub," he said. "But I think this is all for me. I think I'm beginning to feel it," he said. He held the burning roach out for my wife.

"Same here," she said. "Ditto. Me, too." She took the roach and passed it to me. "I may just sit here for a while between you two guys with my eyes closed. But don't let me bother you, okay? Either one of you. If it bothers you, say so. Otherwise, I may just sit here with my eyes closed until you're ready to go to bed," she said. "Your bed's made up, Robert, when you're ready. It's right next to our room at the top of the stairs. We'll show you up when you're ready. You wake me up now, you guys, if I fall asleep." She said that and then she closed her eyes and went to sleep.

The news program ended. I got up and changed the channel. I sat back down on the sofa. I wished my wife hadn't pooped out. Her head lay across the back of the sofa, her mouth open. She'd turned so that her robe slipped away from her legs, exposing a juicy thigh. I reached to draw her robe back over her, and it was then that I glanced at the blind man. What the hell! I flipped the robe open again.

80 "You say when you want some strawberry pie," I said.

"I will," he said.

I said, "Are you tired? Do you want me to take you up to your bed? Are you ready to hit the hay?"

"Not yet," he said. "No, I'll stay up with you, bub. If that's all right. I'll stay up until you're ready to turn in. We haven't had a chance to talk. Know what I mean? I feel like me and her monopolized the evening." He lifted his beard and he let it fall. He picked up his cigarettes and his lighter.

"That's all right," I said. Then I said, "I'm glad for the company."

85 And I guess I was. Every night I smoked dope and stayed up as long as I could before I fell asleep. My wife and I hardly ever went to bed at the same time. When I did go to sleep, I had these dreams. Sometimes I'd wake up from one of them, my heart going crazy.

Something about the church and the Middle Ages was on the TV. Not your run-of-the-mill TV fare. I wanted to watch something else. I turned to the other channels. But there was nothing on them, either. So I turned back to the first channel and apologized.

"Bub, it's all right," the blind man said. "It's fine with me. Whatever you want to watch is okay. I'm always learning something. Learning never ends. It won't hurt me to learn something tonight. I got ears," he said.

We didn't say anything for a time. He was leaning forward with his head turned at me, his right ear aimed in the direction of the set. Very disconcerting. Now and then his eyelids drooped and then they snapped open again. Now and then he put his fingers into his beard and tugged, like he was thinking about something he was hearing on the television.

On the screen, a group of men wearing cowls was being set upon and tormented by men dressed in skeleton costumes and men dressed as devils.

The men dressed as devils wore devil masks, horns, and long tails. This pageant was part of a procession. The Englishman who was narrating the thing said it took place in Spain once a year. I tried to explain to the blind man what was happening.

90   "Skeletons," he said. "I know about skeletons," he said, and nodded.

The TV showed this one cathedral. Then there was a long, slow look at another one. Finally, the picture switched to the famous one in Paris, with its flying buttresses and its spires reaching up to the clouds. The camera pulled away to show the whole of the cathedral rising above the skyline.

There were times when the Englishman who was telling the thing would shut up, would simply let the camera move around the cathedrals. Or else the camera would tour the countryside, men in fields walking behind oxen. I waited as long as I could. Then I felt I had to say something. I said, "They're showing the outside of this cathedral now. Gargoyles. Little statues carved to look like monsters. Now I guess they're in Italy. Yeah, they're in Italy. There's paintings on the walls of this one church."

"Are those fresco[5] paintings, bub?" he asked, and he sipped from his drink.

I reached for my glass. But it was empty. I tried to remember what I could remember. "You're asking me are those frescoes?" I said. "That's a good question. I don't know."

95   The camera moved to a cathedral outside Lisbon.[6] The differences in the Portuguese cathedral compared with the French and Italian were not that great. But they were there. Mostly the interior stuff. Then something occurred to me, and I said, "Something has occurred to me. Do you have any idea what a cathedral is? What they look like, that is? Do you follow me? If somebody says cathedral to you, do you have any notion what they're talking about? Do you know the difference between that and a Baptist church, say?"

He let the smoke dribble from his mouth. "I know they took hundreds of workers fifty or a hundred years to build," he said. "I just heard the man say that, of course. I know generations of the same families worked on a cathedral. I heard him say that, too. The men who began their life's work on them, they never lived to see the completion of their work. In that wise, bub, they're no different from the rest of us, right?" He laughed. Then his eyelids drooped again. His head nodded. He seemed to be snoozing. Maybe he was imagining himself in Portugal. The TV was showing another cathedral now. This one was in Germany. The Englishman's voice droned on. "Cathedrals," the blind man said. He sat up and rolled his head back and forth. "If you want the truth, bub, that's about all I know. What I just said. What I heard him say. But maybe you could describe one to me? I wish you'd do it. I'd like that. If you want to know, I really don't have a good idea."

---

[5] Fresco: Painted plaster.

[6] Lisbon: The capital of Portugal.

I stared hard at the shot of the cathedral on the TV. How could I even begin to describe it? But say my life depended on it. Say my life was being threatened by an insane guy who said I had to do it or else.

I stared some more at the cathedral before the picture flipped off into the countryside. There was no use. I turned to the blind man and said, "To begin with, they're very tall." I was looking around the room for clues. "They reach way up. Up and up. Toward the sky. They're so big, some of them, they have to have these supports. To help hold them up, so to speak. These supports are called buttresses. They remind me of viaducts,[7] for some reason. But maybe you don't know viaducts, either? Sometimes the cathedrals have devils and such carved into the front. Sometimes lords and ladies. Don't ask me why this is," I said.

He was nodding. The whole upper part of his body seemed to be moving back and forth.

100   "I'm not doing so good, am I?" I said.

He stopped nodding and leaned forward on the edge of the sofa. As he listened to me, he was running his fingers through his beard. I wasn't getting through to him, I could see that. But he waited for me to go on just the same. He nodded, like he was trying to encourage me. I tried to think what else to say. "They're really big," I said. "They're massive. They're built of stone. Marble, too, sometimes. In those olden days, when they built cathedrals, men wanted to be close to God. In those olden days, God was an important part of everyone's life. You could tell this from their cathedral-building. I'm sorry," I said, "but it looks like that's the best I can do for you. I'm just no good at it."

"That's all right, bub," the blind man said. "Hey, listen. I hope you don't mind my asking you. Can I ask you something? Let me ask you a simple question, yes or no. I'm just curious and there's no offense. You're my host. But let me ask if you are in any way religious? You don't mind my asking?"

I shook my head. He couldn't see that, though. A wink is the same as a nod to a blind man. "I guess I don't believe in it. In anything. Sometimes it's hard. You know what I'm saying?"

"Sure, I do," he said.

105   "Right," I said.

The Englishman was still holding forth. My wife sighed in her sleep. She drew a long breath and went on with her sleeping.

"You'll have to forgive me," I said. "But I can't tell you what a cathedral looks like. It just isn't in me to do it. I can't do any more than I've done."

The blind man sat very still, his head down, as he listened to me.

I said, "The truth is, cathedrals don't mean anything special to me. Nothing. Cathedrals. They're something to look at on late-night TV. That's all they are."

110   It was then that the blind man cleared his throat. He brought something up. He took a handkerchief from his back pocket. Then he said, "I get it, bub. It's okay. It happens. Don't worry about it," he said. "Hey, listen to me. Will

---

[7] Viaducts: Long, elevated roadways.

you do me a favor? I got an idea. Why don't you find us some heavy paper? And a pen. We'll do something. We'll draw one together. Get us a pen and some heavy paper. Go on, bub, get the stuff," he said.

So I went upstairs. My legs felt like they didn't have any strength in them. They felt like they did after I'd done some running. In my wife's room, I looked around. I found some ballpoints in a little basket on her table. And then I tried to think where to look for the kind of paper he was talking about.

Downstairs, in the kitchen, I found a shopping bag with onion skins in the bottom of the bag. I emptied the bag and shook it. I brought it into the living room and sat down with it near his legs. I moved some things, smoothed the wrinkles from the bag, spread it out on the coffee table.

The blind man got down from the sofa and sat next to me on the carpet.

He ran his fingers over the paper. He went up and down the sides of the paper. The edges, even the edges. He fingered the corners.

115 "All right," he said. "All right, let's do her."

He found my hand, the hand with the pen. He closed his hand over my hand. "Go ahead, bub, draw," he said. "Draw. You'll see. I'll follow along with you. It'll be okay. Just begin now like I'm telling you. You'll see. Draw," the blind man said.

So I began. First I drew a box that looked like a house. It could have been the house I lived in. Then I put a roof on it. At either end of the roof, I drew spires. Crazy.

"Swell," he said. "Terrific. You're doing fine," he said. "Never thought anything like this could happen in your lifetime, did you, bub? Well, it's a strange life, we all know that. Go on now. Keep it up."

I put in windows with arches. I drew flying buttresses. I hung great doors. I couldn't stop. The TV station went off the air. I put down the pen and closed and opened my fingers. The blind man felt around over the paper. He moved the tips of his fingers over the paper, all over what I had drawn, and he nodded.

120 "Doing fine," the blind man said.

I took up the pen again, and he found my hand. I kept at it. I'm no artist. But I kept drawing just the same.

My wife opened up her eyes and gazed at us. She sat up on the sofa, her robe hanging open. She said, "What are you doing? Tell me, I want to know."

I didn't answer her.

The blind man said, "We're drawing a cathedral. Me and him are working on it. Press hard," he said to me. "That's right. That's good," he said. "Sure. You got it, bub, I can tell. You didn't think you could. But you can, can't you? You're cooking with gas now. You know what I'm saying? We're going to really have us something here in a minute. How's the old arm?" he said. "Put some people in there now. What's a cathedral without people?"

125 My wife said, "What's going on? Robert, what are you doing? What's going on?"

"It's all right," he said to her. "Close your eyes now," the blind man said to me.

I did it. I closed them just like he said.

"Are they closed?" he said. "Don't fudge."

"They're closed," I said.

130   "Keep them that way," he said. He said, "Don't stop now. Draw."

So we kept on with it. His fingers rode my fingers as my hand went over the paper. It was like nothing else in my life up to now.

Then he said, "I think that's it. I think you got it," he said. "Take a look. What do you think?"

But I had my eyes closed. I thought I'd keep them that way for a little longer. I thought it was something I ought to do.

"Well?" he said. "Are you looking?"

135   My eyes were still closed. I was in my house. I knew that. But I didn't feel like I was inside anything.

"It's really something," I said.

SHELDON CURRIE

(1934–   )

The Glace Bay Miner's Museum

(1979)

The first time I ever saw the bugger, I thought to myself, him as big as he is, me as small as I am, if he was astraddle on the road, naked, I could walk under him without a hair touching. That's the thought I had; he was coming down the aisle of the White Rose Café, looking to the right and looking to the left at the people in the booths. The size of him would kill you, so everybody was looking at him. I was looking at him too because I knew all the booths were full except mine. I was sitting in the last one, my back to the kitchen, so I could see everybody coming and going. He had a box in his hand, looked like a tool box, and I was wondering if he'd sit with me and show me what was in his box. I made a dollar keeping house for MacDonalds and came to the Bay to spend it on tea and chips and sit in the restaurant and watch the goings on. The goings on was the same old thing: girls sitting with boys and boys sitting with girls, trying to pair off to suit themselves, and making a cup of tea and chips last as long as they could so they wouldn't have to leave. It was hard to find somebody on the street. You could go to the show and sit in the dark and hope somebody would sit next to you and hold your hand, but that cost money too and hardly ever worked. It worked once for me, this fella sat beside me, and I knew it was a chance because the theatre was almost empty. I figured he saw my hair before the lights went out. I had this lovely long hair. I was lucky enough, I bought a nut bar on the way in and I gave him a piece. He took my hand.

He had a huge hand. Pan shovel hands we used to call people with hands like that. We used to think you got them from loading coal with a pan shovel. My hand disappeared in his in the dark. He put his big hand on top of my knees which I was keeping together. It felt like he had taken my hand off at the wrist and moved it up to my knee. I couldn't see it and for a minute I couldn't feel it and I was sitting there looking at his big mitt and wondering if my hand was still in it. Then it started to sweat and I could feel it again. We stayed like that through two shows. We never said a word. When we came out we walked down to Senator's Corner and down Commercial Street to Eaton's where the buses stopped. We never said a word. We stood next to each other and I stared at the Medical Hall and he stared at Thompson and Sutherland. Then the bus came for No. 11 and he got on. He didn't even look out the window at me.

I was sitting alone in the White Rose because none of the boys would sit with me and none of the girls would because the boys wouldn't. For one thing I had a runny nose. They called me names and if a boy went with me they called him names. George McNeill walked home with me from school one day—it was on the way to his house anyway—and I heard in the cloakroom next day—they had a vent between the boys' cloakroom and the girls'—I heard somebody from another class say to him—"I see you're taking out snot-face these days. Don't forget to kiss her on the back of her head."

For another thing I screwed a couple of boys when I was a little girl. I didn't know you weren't supposed to, but I didn't want to anyway, and I wouldn't but this fella offered me a nickel and I never had a nickel. Then he asked if I'd do it with his cousin and I said no. But then he came to me himself, the cousin, and told me he went to the washhouse every Saturday his father was on day shift for five times and waited for him to come up and waited for him to shower and followed him to pay office and asked him for a dime, and had to promise to cut enough sticks for the week. I found out later he sold two quarts of blueberries he stole, but he wanted to tell me a nice long story. Anyway I felt sorry for him, and he had fifty cents. So he told me to meet him up in the woods by the Scotchtown road between the bootleg pits and Rabbit Town. I didn't know then that he didn't want to walk up there with me. Anyway, I didn't really screw either one of them because they didn't know how to do it and it was too late before I could tell them, although, God knows, I knew little enough myself of the little there is to know. They didn't walk home with me either, neither one. But they told everybody I was a whore. So I was not only a whore but a snot-nosed whore. You could hardly blame the boys and girls for not sitting with me.

So I was sitting alone in the last booth at the White Rose Café when this giant of a man with a box in his hand came bearing down the aisle looking left and right, and he kept on coming until he got to my booth and saw there was nobody there but me. I remember it seemed like it got darker when he stood in front of me, he blacked out so much light with the size of him. He had on a big lumberjack shirt. I thought, when he stood there holding his box, before he said anything, I said to myself, I wish he'd pick me up and put me in his shirt pocket.

5   "Can I put this here on your table?" he said; he pointed his chin at his box.

"Suit yourself," I said to him awful loud. He was so big, I thought I had to yell for him to hear me.

"Can I sit down then?" he said.

"Suit yourself again," I said. So he put his box on the table and sat down opposite me, and I could feel his knees about an inch from mine. I could feel the heat coming from his knees. I could have exploded I was so happy. But I kept my lips tight.

The waitress pounced on us right away. "Hi, snooker," she said. She was dying to find out who this fella was. So was everybody in the restaurant. I could see the ones facing me. I could feel the ones not facing me wishing they had sat on the other side of the booth. Nobody knew who he was. I just wanted to know what he had in the box.

10   "Something?" Kitten said, and looked at me and looked at him.

"I had something," I said.

"Would you have something else?" the man said. "I'd like to buy you a bite to eat if you don't mind." I near died. That was the first polite thing anybody ever said to me since my father got killed.

"I don't mind if I do," I said.

"Well, what is it then?" Kitten said. "What do you want?"

15   "I'll have a cup of tea and an order of chips," I said.

"Will you now?" Kitten said.

"Yes," I said. "I will."

"I'll have the same," the man with the box said.

"Thank you," Kitten said, and wrote it down, saying very slowly to herself like she was talking to a baby: *Two orders of chips and two orders of tea.* "That will be fine," she said, looking at me and looking at him. "I'll go see if we got any."

20   She went away and I looked at my little hands and I could feel my knees getting warmer and warmer. I couldn't think of anything to say. My back was cold and I thought I might start to shake if I didn't talk, but I couldn't think of anything. I looked up at him and he was looking at his hands. He had a lot to look at. Nobody said a word till Kitten came back. "Here you are," she said, "two teas and two chips. Medium rare."

We ate a few chips and took the bags out of our teas and put them in the ashtray. Then he said, "Well, what do you think?"

"I think you're the biggest son of a bitch I ever saw," I said.

He looked at me then when I said that as if I just came in, and the look of him made me feel as if I just came in. I felt my back get warm, and I leaned back against the back of the booth. He started to laugh. He must of laughed for two minutes but it seemed to me two days, and it sounded like somebody playing some kind of instrument I never heard before. When he stopped, he said, "Know what I think?"

"What?" I said.

25   "I think you're the smallest son of a bitch I ever saw."

Then we both of us laughed for two minutes. Then we talked about the weather as if nothing happened, but I could feel the heat on my knees. After a while he said, "Well now. What's your name?"

"Margaret MacNeil."

"Well now, Miss MacNeil. It's been a pleasure meeting you. Do you come here often?"

"Every week at this same exact time," I said.

30   "Very well then," he said. "Perhaps we'll meet again. What do you think?"

"Suit yourself," I said.

"Okay," he said, "I will. My name is Neil Currie." Then he got up and opened the box.

When he got the box open it was full of brown sticks and a plaid bag. Bagpipes! I never seen bagpipes before. Never knew there was any. Never heard them before. God only knows I heard them enough since. He pulled it all out of the box and started putting sticks on sticks till it was together; then he pumped it up. It snarled a couple of times, then when he had it between his arm and his ribs he came down on it with his elbow and it started to squeal, and everybody in the café either leaned out or stood up to look at the God-awful racket.

Then his fingers started jumping and it started playing something I don't know what it was. To me it sounded like a cut cat jumping from table to table screaming like a tiger. Before you knew it the Chinaman came from the front. He didn't stop, he just slowed down to squeeze by the man and the pipes. When he got through he walked backwards a minute toward the kitchen and yelled, "Get that goddam fiddle out of here." Then two big Chinamen came out of the kitchen; I always thought Chinamen were small until I saw them two. They each had a hand of cards like they were playing cards and kept their hands so nobody could peek at them while they were out. They were just as big as Neil was, maybe bigger, and you never saw how fast two men can put one man and an armload of bagpipes out of a restaurant and into the street.

35   I went out after them. I took him out his box. I passed the Chinamen coming back in. They didn't do nothing to him, just fired him to the street and went back with their cards. He was sitting on the street. I helped him stuff his bagpipes in his box. Then he stood up and took the box in his hand. He looked down at me and he said, "One thing I thought a Chinaman would never have the nerve to do is criticize another man's music. If I wasn't drunk, I'd give you my pipes to hold and I'd go back in there and get the shit kicked out of me."

"Where do you live?" I said.

"I have a room down on Brookside."

"Want me to walk down?"

"Where do you live?"

40   "I live in Reserve."

"Let's get the bus, then. I'll see you home. Sober me up. Perhaps you could make us a cup of tea."

"Okay," I said.

"You live with your father and mother?"

"I live with my mother and grandfather. My father got killed in the pit. Come on. It's starting to rain. My brother too."

45   The rain banged on the roof of the bus all the way to Reserve and when we got off it was pouring and muddy all the way up to the shack where we lived. My father built it himself because, he said, he never would live in a company house. He had to work in the goddam company mine, but he didn't have to live in the goddam company house, with god only knows who in the next half. My mother said he was too mean to pay rent, but only when he wasn't around did she say it. She only said it once to his face. But he got killed. They had a coffin they wouldn't even open it.

It was dark even though it was only after seven. It was October. We had to take off our shoes and wring out our socks from walking in puddles up the lane. We didn't have a real road in. Just a track where they came with groceries and coal. We hung them down the side of the scuttle and our jackets on the oven door. "I'll get you an old pair of daddy's pants soon's mama gets out of the bedroom. You're the first one I ever saw could fit."

"You're right on time, Marg," Mama said. "I think I'll run up the Hall. Who you got here?"

"You'll get soaked."

"I know, but I better go. I might win the thousand."

50   "This is Neil Currie."

"Where'd you find him?"

"In the Bay."

"Are you from the Bay?"

"No. I just came."

55   "Where from?"

"St. Andrew's Channel."

"Never heard of that. You working in the pit?"

"I was. I started but I got fired."

"You look like you could shovel. Why'd they fire you?"

60   "I wouldn't talk English to the foreman."

"You an Eyetalian?"

"No."

"Well, I have to run or I'll be late. Don't forget your grandfather, Margie. I hit him about an hour ago so he's about ready."

"Okay Mom. Hope you win it."

65   "Me too."

That was my mother's joke, about hitting my grandfather. Anytime a stranger was in she said it. He had something wrong with his lungs. Every hour or two he couldn't breathe and we'd have to pound him on the chest.

So somebody had to be in the house every minute. When Mama left I got Neil the pants. "You might as well keep them," I said. "They won't fit nobody else ever comes around here." Then I went in to change my dress.

I expected to be a while because I wanted to fix myself up on my mother's makeup. It was her room, though I had to sleep in it and she had a lot of stuff for makeup. My brother slept in the other room with my grandfather. We just had the three. Where you come in was the kitchen and that's where you were if you weren't in the bedroom or in the cellar getting potatoes. But I didn't stay to fix up because I just got my dress half on when he started wailing on his bag and pipes.

I stuck my head out the door. "Are you out of your brain?" I yelled but he couldn't hear with the noise. So I got my dress all on and went out and put my hands over two of the holes the noise came out. They have three holes. He stopped. "My grandfather," I said, "you'll wake him up." I no sooner said it when the knock came. "There he is now," I said. "I'm sorry," he said. "I forgot your grandfather."

"It's okay," I said, "I think it must be time of his hit now anyway." I went in and I got the surprise of my life.

70   He could talk, my grandfather, but he didn't. It hurt him to talk after he came back from the hospital once with his lungs and he quit. I don't know if it got better or not because he never tried again; same as he quit walking after he got out of breath once from it. He took to writing notes. He had a scribbler and a pencil by him and he wrote what he wanted. thump me chest; dinner; beer; water; piss pot; did she win; did you pay the lite bill, then put on the lites; piece of bread; ask the priest to come; time to go now father; I have to get me thump; no Ian'll do it. See, that's just one page. He had a whole stack of scribblers after a while. They're all here. We have them numbered.

So I went in, and I was after sitting him up in place to do his thump; you had to put him in a certain way. And he started to bang his long finger on the scribbler he had in his hand.

"Tell him to play."

"Well, Christ in harness," I said, which is what my grandfather used to say when he talked and now I always said it to tease him. "Watch your tong," he wrote me one day. "Somebody got to say it now you're dumb," I said. "If I don't it won't get said."

"Do you want your thump?" I said, and he wrote in his scribbler, "No, tell him to play." So I told Neil to play. "Isn't that lovely?" Neil said and laughed. And he played. It sounded to me like two happy hens fighting over a bean, and when he stopped and asked me if I knew what tune it was I told him what it sounded like to me and he laughed and laughed.

75   "Do you like the tune?"

"It's not too bad."

"Would you see if your grandfather liked it?" So I went. And he was sound asleep with his scribbler on his hands on his belly. He wrote on it:

"When he comes back ask him if he can play these." And he had a list I couldn't read. Here it is here in the scribbler:

Guma slan to na ferriv chy harish achune

Va me nday Ben Doran

Bodichin a Virun

Falte go ferrin ar balech in eysgich

I took the scribbler out and showed it to Neil and he said he would. "I'll have to practice a little."

"Play some more now," I asked him. "Play that one again."

80   "What one?"

"The one you put him to sleep with."

"Mairi's wedding."

"Yes."

"About the bean and the chickens."

85   "Yes."

So he played. I was getting interested in it. My foot started tapping and my knees which I had been holding together all night fell apart. As soon as he saw that, I was sitting on a chair against the wall, he came over and came down to kiss me. I put my two feet on his chest and pushed. I was hoping to fire him across the room but nothing happened. It kept him off, but he just stayed there with his chest on my feet looking up my leg and me with a hole in my underwear.

"What's the matter with you?" he said.

I said, "Just because you play that thing don't mean you can jump me." He ran his hand down my leg and nearly drove me nuts.

"Fuck off," I said. I thought that would shock him back but he just stayed there leaning against my sneakers. He tried to take my hand but I just put the two of them behind the chair.

90   "I won't jump you till we're married," he said.

"Married?" I said. "Who'd marry you? You're nothing but a goddam Currie." Then he started laughing and moved back.

"And why wouldn't you marry a goddam Currie?" he said.

"Because they just come to your house, play a few snarls on their pipes, and they think you'll marry them for that."

"Well, well, well," he said. "I'll tell you what. I'll play for you every night till you're ready. And I'll make you a song of your own."

95   "What kind of song?"

"I don't know, we'll wait and see what I can make."

"Well, well, well," I said. "I want a song a person can sing so I'll be sure what it's saying."

"Okay, I'll make you two. One to sing and one to guess at."

"Good," I said. "If I like them. Well who knows what may happen."

100   "What would you like for the singing one?"

"I don't know."

"Well, what's the happiest thing in your life or the saddest?"

"They're both the same," I said. "My brother. Not the one living here now but my older brother, Charlie. We called him Charlie Dave, though Dave was my father's name. That was to tell him from the other Charlie MacNeils. There's quite a few around here. Charlie Pig and Charlie Spider. And a lot more. Charlie Big Dan. I really liked Charlie Dave."

"What happened to him?"

105 "He got killed in the pit with my father."

"How old was he?"

"He was just sixteen. He used to fight for me. Wouldn't let anybody call me names."

"He mustn't have been in the pit very long?"

"Not even a year. He started working with my grandfather just before he had to quit for his lungs. Then he started with my father. Then he was killed. They were both killed. He was good in school too, but he got married so he had to work. They didn't even have a chance to have their baby."

110 "What happened to his wife?"

"Oh, she's still around. She's nice. She had her baby. A sweet baby. They live up in the Rows. In a company house. With her mother and her sister." I started to cry then so I made a cup of tea.

So after that he came back every night and it was nothing but noise. My mother took to going out every night. When I told her he asked me to get married, she said: "That man will never live in a company house. You'll be moving out of one shack and into another."

"I can stand it," I said.

"You can stand it," she said. "You can stand it. And is he going to work?"

115 "He's going to look up at No. 10."

"Good," she said. "He can work with Ian. They can die together. And you can stand it. And you can live in your shack alone. Stand it, then."

The first night, after he played one of the songs my grandfather asked him, he played one he said he made for me. I loved it. It made me grin, so I kept my head down and I held my knees together with my arms.

"What's the name of it?" I asked.

"The name of it is *Two Happy Beans Fighting Over A Chicken.*"

120 "Go whan," I said.

"Do you like it?"

"Not bad. What's the real name?"

"*Margaret's Wedding,*" he said.

"Christ in harness." I almost let go my knees.

125 The next night he played it again and he played another one for my grandfather. Then we went up the Haulage Road to No. 10 to get Ian. I always went to walk home with him because when he started he was scared when he was night shift to come home alone in the dark. I kept on ever since. Sometimes he had a girl friend would go. I never asked him if he

stopped being scared. He never often had to try it alone. He didn't come home that night, he decided to work a double shift. So we walked back alone that night, but we took to going up together for Ian when he was night shift till Neil got the job there too and they were buddies in the pit so they worked the same shifts and came home together till we got married and moved to the Bay.

They fought like two mongrels. Miners said they never saw two men enjoy their work so much because it kept them close enough so they could fight every minute. Then on Sunday afternoon they came to our home and they sat in the kitchen and drank rum and played forty-five and fought and fought and fought.

What they fought about was politics and religion, or so they said. Ian would tell Neil that the only hope for the miner was to vote CCF and get a labour government.

"How are you going to manage that?"

"By voting. Organizing."

130 "When is that going to happen?"

"We have to work for it."

"The future?"

"Yes, the future."

"There's no future," Neil would say.

135 "There has to be a future."

"See in the bedroom, Ian. See your grandfather. That's the future."

"Well, he's there. The future is there."

"He's there all right. He can't breathe, he can't talk, he can't walk. You know the only thing he's got? Some old songs in his head, that he can hardly remember, that your father hardly ever knew and you don't know at all. Came here and lost their tongues, their music, their songs. Everything but their shovels."

"Too bad you wouldn't lose yours. Have a drink and shut up."

140 "I will not shut up. However, I will have a drink."

He seemed so drunk to me I thought it'd spill out of his mouth if he took more; but he took it. "Nothing left," he said. "Nothing. Only thing you can do different from a pit pony is drink rum and play forty-five."

Ian pointed to the cat curled up on the wood box. "Look, it's almost seven o'clock," he said. "Why don't you take that tomcat and go to Benediction since you like to sing so much. Then you can sing with him tonight. Out in the bushes. He goes out same time as you leave."

"What are you talking about?"

"You're buddies. You and the cat. You can sing near as good as he can. He's near fond of religion as you are."

145 "All I can say," Neil said, "is pit ponies can't go to church."

"Is that all you can say?" Ian said. "Well, all I can say is, if a pit pony went to church, that would do him some lot of good."

"Ian, you do not understand what I am talking about."

"That is the God's truth for you, Neil. Now why don't you go on the couch and have a lay down."

And that's the way Sunday afternoon and evening went. We could've been out for a walk, just as easy, and more fun.

150   But that second night that he came we walked down the Haulage Road, pitch black, and he sang me the song I asked him for about my brother. I sang it over and over till I knew it by heart. He sang it to me. "That's lovely," I told him.

I took him by the arm behind his elbow and slowed him down till he stopped and turned. I was crying but I told him anyway. "I'm going to get married to you." We kissed each other. Salt water was all over our lips. I think he must have been crying too. I wrote the song down in one of my grandfather's scribblers when we got back. Here it is here in this one here.

> My brother was a miner
> His name was Charlie David
> He spent his young life laughing
> And digging out his grave.
>
> Charlie Dave was big
> Charlie Dave was strong
> Charlie Dave was two feet wide
> And almost six feet long.
>
> When Charlie David was sixteen
> He learned to chew and spit
> And went one day with Grandpa
> To work down in the pit.
>
> (chorus)
>
> When Charlie David was sixteen
> He met his Maggie June
> On day shift week they met at eight
> On back shift week at noon
>
> (chorus)
>
> When Charlie David was sixteen
> He said to June, "Let's wed"
> Maggie June was so surprised
> She fell right out of bed.
>
> (chorus)

When Charlie David was sixteen
They had a little boy
Maggie June was not surprised
Charlie danced for joy

(chorus)

When Charlie David was sixteen
The roof fell on his head
His laughing mouth is full of coal
Charlie Dave is dead.

The next night when he came I told him I had to pay him back for his songs. I'd tell him a story.

"Okay," he said. "Tell me a story."

"This is a true story."

155   "That's the kind I like," he said.

"Okay. There was this fella worked in the pit, his name was George Stepenak, he was a Pole, they eat all kinds of stuff, took garlic in his can, used to stink. His can would stink and his breath would stink. The men used to tease him all the time, which made him cross. One day my father said, "George, what in the name of Jesus have you got in your can?"

"Shit," George said to my father.

"I know that," my father said. "But what you put on it to make it smell so bad?"

When my grandfather found out I told him a story to pay him back for the song, he wanted to tell him one. He wrote it out for him in a scribbler. Here it is here. Well he didn't write it all out, he just wrote it out for me to tell it.

160   "Tell about Jonny and Angie loading in '24, the roof so low they hadda take pancakes in their cans."

That's the way it went from then. Every night he'd come and play and sing. Me and my grandfather would tell or write stories. My brother even would sing when he was on day shift or back shift. But he worked a lot of night shift. That's the way it went till Neil got work. When he got work we got married as soon as he built this house. Soon as he got the job he said, "I got some land on North Street. I'll build a house before we get married. It's right on the ocean. You can hear the waves." And he did. He did. And you can see, it's no shack. He must have been a carpenter. Soon as the house was finished we got married and moved in. Him and my brother Ian were buddies by then, working the same shifts. They both got killed the same minute. I was up to Reserve keeping house for my mother when I heard the whistle. I heard the dogs howling for two nights before so soon's I heard the whistle

I took off for the pit. They both just were taken up when I got there. They had them in a half-ton truck with blankets over them.

"Take them to Mama's," I said.

"We got to take them to hospital."

"You take them to Mama's, Art. I'll wash them and I'll get them to the hospital."

165 "Listen, snooker, the doctor's got to see them."

"I'll call the doctor."

"I can't."

"Listen, you bastard. Whose are they, yours or mine? You haven't even got an ambulance. I'll wash them, and wherever they go, they'll go clean and in a regular ambulance, not your goddam half-broken-down truck."

So he took them down to Mama's and they carried them in and put one on Mama's bed and one on the couch in the kitchen. I knew what to get. I saw Charlie Dave keep a dead frog for two years when he was going to school. I went to the Medical Hall and got two gallons. Cost me a lot. I got back as fast as I could. I locked the house before I left so's nobody could get in. Mama was visiting her sister in Bras d'Or and I didn't know when she'd be back.

170 When I got back, there was a bunch around the door. They started to murmur.

"Fuck off," I said. "I'm busy."

To make matters worse, my grandfather was left alone all that time. He died. Choked. I took his lungs. It wasn't so much the lungs themselves, though I think they were a good thing to take, though they don't keep too well, especially the condition he was in, as just something to remind me of the doctor who told him he couldn't get compensation because he was fit to work. Then I took Neil's lungs because I thought of them connected to his pipes and they show, compared to grandfather's, what lungs should look like. I was surprised to find people have two lungs. I didn't know that before. Like Neil used to say, look and ye shall see. I took Neil's tongue since he always said he was the only one around still had one. I took his fingers too because he played his pipes with them. I didn't know what to take from Ian, so I took his dick, since he always said to Neil that was his substitute for religion to keep him from being a pit pony when he wasn't drinking rum or playing forty-five.

Then my mother came in. She went hysterical and out the door. I had each thing in its own pickle jar. I put them all in the tin suitcase with the scribblers and deck of cards wrapped in wax paper and the half empty quart of black death they left after last Sunday's drinking and arguing. I got on the bus and came home to the Bay and put in the pipes and Neil's missal and whatever pictures were around. Then I took the trunk to Marie, my friend, next door and asked her to put it in her attic till I asked for it. Don't tell anybody about it. Don't open it. Forget about it. Then I came back here and sat down and I thought of something my grandmother used to sing, "There's bread in the cupboard and meat on the shelf, and if you don't eat it, I'll eat it myself." I was hungry.

I knew they'd come and haul me off. So I packed my own suitcase, Neil's really but mine now. They came with a police car and I didn't give them a chance to even get out of the car. I jumped right into the back seat like it was a taxi I was waiting for. I just sat right in and said, "Sydney River, please." Sydney River, if you're not from around here, is the cookie jar where they put rotten tomatoes so they won't spoil in the barrel. So they put me in till they forgot about me; then when they remembered me they forgot what they put me in for. So they let me go.

175   My mother lived in the house all the time I was away. I told her to, to keep it for me and give her a better place to live. When I got back I told her, "You can stay here and live with me, mother, if you like."

"Thanks anyway," she said. "But I'm not feeling too good. I think I'll go back to Reserve."

"So stay. I'll look after you."

"Yes, you'll look after me. You'll look after me. And what if I drop dead during the night?"

"If you drop dead during the night, you're dead. Dead in Glace Bay is the same as dead in Reserve."

180   "Yes. And you'll look after me dead too, I imagine. You'll look after me. What'll you do? Cut off my tits and put them in bottles?"

I said to her, "Mother, your tits don't mean a thing to me."

By then she had her suitcase packed and she left walking. "Have you got everything?" I yelled.

"If I left anything," she yelled back, "pickle it."

"Okay," I said. She walked. Then she turned and yelled, "Keep it for a souvenir."

185   "Okay," I yelled.

I was sorry after that I said what I said. I wouldn't mind having one of her tits. After all, if it wasn't for them, we'd all die of thirst before we had our chance to get killed.

Marie came over then with the suitcase and we had a cup of tea and she helped me set things up. We had to make shelves for the jars. Everything else can go on tables and chairs or hang on the wall or from the ceiling as you can see. Marie is very artistic, she knows how to put things around. I'm the cook. We give tea and scones free to anyone who comes. You're the first. I guess not too many people know about it yet. A lot of things are not keeping as well as we would like, but it's better than nothing. Perhaps you could give us a copy of your tape when you get it done. That might make a nice item. It's hard to get real good things and you hate to fill up with junk just to have something.

GABRIEL GARCÍA MÁRQUEZ
(1928–   )

A Very Old Man with Enormous Wings

A TALE FOR CHILDREN
(1968)

Translated from the Spanish by Gregory Rabassa

On the third day of rain they had killed so many crabs inside the house that Pelayo had to cross his drenched courtyard and throw them into the sea, because the newborn child had a temperature all night and they thought it was due to the stench. The world had been sad since Tuesday. Sea and sky were a single ash-gray thing and the sands of the beach, which on March nights glimmered like powdered light, had become a stew of mud and rotten shellfish. The light was so weak at noon that when Pelayo was coming back to the house after throwing away the crabs, it was hard for him to see what it was that was moving and groaning in the rear of the courtyard. He had to go very close to see that it was an old man, a very old man, lying face down in the mud, who, in spite of his tremendous efforts, couldn't get up, impeded by his enormous wings.

Frightened by that nightmare, Pelayo ran to get Elisenda, his wife, who was putting compresses on the sick child, and he took her to the rear of the courtyard. They both looked at the fallen body with mute stupor. He was dressed like a ragpicker.[1] There were only a few faded hairs left on his bald skull and very few teeth in his mouth, and his pitiful condition of a drenched great-grandfather had taken away any sense of grandeur he might have had. His huge buzzard wings, dirty and half-plucked, were forever entangled in the mud. They looked at him so long and so closely that Pelayo and Elisenda very soon overcame their surprise and in the end found him familiar. Then they dared speak to him, and he answered in an incomprehensible dialect with a strong sailor's voice. That was how they skipped over the inconvenience of the wings and quite intelligently concluded that he was a lonely castaway from some foreign ship wrecked by the storm. And yet, they called in a neighbor woman who knew everything about life and death to see him, and all she needed was one look to show them their mistake.

"He's an angel," she told them. "He must have been coming for the child, but the poor fellow is so old that the rain knocked him down."

On the following day everyone knew that a flesh-and-blood angel was held captive in Pelayo's house. Against the judgment of the wise neighbor

---

[1] Someone who makes a living collecting rags and other refuse.

woman, for whom angels in those times were the fugitive survivors of a celestial conspiracy, they did not have the heart to club him to death. Pelayo watched over him all afternoon from the kitchen, armed with his bailiff's club, and before going to bed he dragged him out of the mud and locked him up with the hens in the wire chicken coop. In the middle of the night, when the rain stopped, Pelayo and Elisenda were still killing crabs. A short time afterward the child woke up without a fever and with a desire to eat. Then they felt magnanimous and decided to put the angel on a raft with fresh water and provisions for three days and leave him to his fate on the high seas. But when they went out into the courtyard with the first light of dawn, they found the whole neighborhood in front of the chicken coop having fun with the angel, without the slightest reverence, tossing him things to eat through the openings in the wire as if he weren't a supernatural creature but a circus animal.

5   Father Gonzaga arrived before seven o'clock, alarmed by the strange news. By that time onlookers less frivolous than those at dawn had already arrived and they were making all kinds of conjectures concerning the captive's future. The simplest among them thought that he should be named mayor of the world. Others of sterner mind felt that he should be promoted to the rank of five-star general in order to win all wars. Some visionaries hoped that he could be put to stud in order to implant on earth a race of winged wise men who could take charge of the universe. But Father Gonzaga, before becoming a priest, had been a robust woodcutter. Standing by the wire, he reviewed his catechism[2] in an instant and asked them to open the door so that he could take a close look at that pitiful man who looked more like a huge decrepit hen among the fascinated chickens. He was lying in a corner drying his open wings in the sunlight among the fruit peels and breakfast leftovers that the early risers had thrown him. Alien to the impertinences of the world, he only lifted his antiquarian[3] eyes and murmured something in his dialect when Father Gonzaga went into the chicken coop and said good morning to him in Latin. The parish priest had his first suspicion of an imposter when he saw that he did not understand the language of God or know how to greet His ministers. Then he noticed that seen close up he was much too human; he had an unbearable smell of the outdoors, the back side of his wings was strewn with parasites and his main feathers had been mistreated by terrestrial winds, and nothing about him measured up to the proud dignity of angels. Then he came out of the chicken coop and in a brief sermon warned the curious against the risks of being ingenuous. He reminded them that the devil had the bad habit of making use of carnival tricks in order to confuse the unwary. He argued that if wings were not the essential element in determining the difference

---

[2] A book that summarizes the doctrines of Roman Catholicism in question-and-answer form.

[3] Refers to someone who studies antiquities, particularly old books.

between a hawk and an airplane, they were even less so in the recognition of angels. Nevertheless, he promised to write a letter to his bishop so that the latter would write to his primate so that the latter would write to the Supreme Pontiff[4] in order to get the final verdict from the highest courts.

His prudence fell on sterile hearts. The news of the captive angel spread with such rapidity that after a few hours the courtyard had the bustle of a marketplace and they had to call in troops with fixed bayonets to disperse the mob that was about to knock the house down. Elisenda, her spine all twisted from sweeping up so much marketplace trash, then got the idea of fencing in the yard and charging five cents admission to see the angel.

The curious came from far away. A traveling carnival arrived with a flying acrobat who buzzed over the crowd several times, but no one paid any attention to him because his wings were not those of an angel but, rather, those of a sidereal[5] bat. The most unfortunate invalids on earth came in search of health: a poor woman who since childhood had been counting her heartbeats and had run out of numbers; a Portuguese man who couldn't sleep because the noise of the stars disturbed him; a sleepwalker who got up at night to undo the things he had done while awake; and many others with less serious ailments. In the midst of that shipwreck disorder that made the earth tremble, Pelayo and Elisenda were happy with fatigue, for in less than a week they had crammed their rooms with money and the line of pilgrims waiting their turn to enter still reached beyond the horizon.

The angel was the only one who took no part in his own act. He spent his time trying to get comfortable in his borrowed nest, befuddled by the hellish heat of the oil lamps and sacramental candles that had been placed along the wire. At first they tried to make him eat some mothballs, which, according to the wisdom of the wise neighbor woman, were the food prescribed for angels. But he turned them down, just as he turned down the papal lunches that the penitents brought him, and they never found out whether it was because he was an angel or because he was an old man that in the end he ate nothing but eggplant mush. His only supernatural virtue seemed to be patience. Especially during the first days, when the hens pecked at him, searching for the stellar parasites that proliferated in his wings, and the cripples pulled out feathers to touch their defective parts with, and even the most merciful threw stones at him, trying to get him to rise so they could see him standing. The only time they succeeded in arousing him was when they burned his side with an iron for branding steers, for he had been motionless for so many hours that they thought he was dead. He awoke with a start, ranting in his hermetic[6] language and with tears in his eyes, and he flapped his wings a couple of times, which brought on a whirlwind of chicken dung and lunar dust and a gale of panic that did not seem to be of this world. Although many thought that his reaction had

---

[4] The Pope.

[5] Relating to the stars.

[6] Occult, magical.

been one not of rage but of pain, from then on they were careful not to annoy him, because the majority understood that his passivity was not that of a hero taking his ease but that of a cataclysm in repose.

Father Gonzaga held back the crowd's frivolity with formulas of maid-servant inspiration while awaiting the arrival of a final judgment on the nature of the captive. But the mail from Rome showed no sense of urgency. They spent their time finding out if the prisoner had a navel, if his dialect had any connection with Aramaic,[7] how many times he could fit on the head of a pin, or whether he wasn't just a Norwegian with wings. Those meager letters might have come and gone until the end of time if a provi-dential event had not put an end to the priest's tribulations.

10   It so happened that during those days, among so many other carnival attractions, there arrived in town the traveling show of the woman who had been changed into a spider for having disobeyed her parents. The admission to see her was not only less than the admission to see the angel, but people were permitted to ask her all manner of questions about her absurd state and to examine her up and down so that no one would ever doubt the truth of her horror. She was a frightful tarantula the size of a ram and with the head of a sad maiden. What was most heart-rending, however, was not her out-landish shape but the sincere affliction with which she recounted the details of her misfortune. While still practically a child she had sneaked out of her parents' house to go to a dance, and while she was coming back through the woods after having danced all night without permission, a fearful thunder-clap rent the sky in two and through the crack came the lightning bolt of brimstone that changed her into a spider. Her only nourishment came from the meatballs that charitable souls chose to toss into her mouth. A spectacle like that, full of so much human truth and with such a fearful lesson, was bound to defeat without even trying that of a haughty angel who scarcely deigned to look at mortals. Besides, the few miracles attributed to the angel showed a certain mental disorder, like the blind man who didn't recover his sight but grew three new teeth, or the paralytic who didn't get to walk but almost won the lottery, and the leper whose sores sprouted sunflowers. Those consolation miracles, which were more like mocking fun, had already ruined the angel's reputation when the woman who had been changed into a spider finally crushed him completely. That was how Father Gonzaga was cured forever of his insomnia and Pelayo's courtyard went back to being as empty as during the time it had rained for three days and crabs walked through the bedrooms.

The owners of the house had no reason to lament. With the money they saved they built a two-story mansion with balconies and gardens and high netting so that crabs wouldn't get in during the winter, and with iron bars on the windows so that angels wouldn't get in. Pelayo also set up a rabbit warren close to town and gave up his job as bailiff for good, and Elisenda

---

[7] An ancient Middle Eastern language, believed to have been the language spoken by Jesus.

bought some satin pumps with high heels and many dresses of iridescent silk, the kind worn on Sunday by the most desirable women in those times. The chicken coop was the only thing that didn't receive any attention. If they washed it down with creolin[8] and burned tears of myrrh[9] inside it every so often, it was not in homage to the angel but to drive away the dungheap stench that still hung everywhere like a ghost and was turning the new house into an old one. At first, when the child learned to walk, they were careful that he not get too close to the chicken coop. But then they began to lose their fears and got used to the smell, and before the child got his second teeth he'd gone inside the chicken coop to play, where the wires were falling apart. The angel was no less standoffish with him than with other mortals, but he tolerated the most ingenious infamies with the patience of a dog who had no illusions. They both came down with chicken pox at the same time. The doctor who took care of the child couldn't resist the temptation to listen to the angel's heart, and he found so much whistling in the heart and so many sounds in his kidneys that it seemed impossible for him to be alive. What surprised him most, however, was the logic of his wings. They seemed so natural on that completely human organism that he couldn't understand why other men didn't have them too.

When the child began school it had been some time since the sun and rain had caused the collapse of the chicken coop. The angel went dragging himself about here and there like a stray dying man. They would drive him out of the bedroom with a broom and a moment later find him in the kitchen. He seemed to be in so many places at the same time that they grew to think that he'd been duplicated, that he was reproducing himself all through the house, and the exasperated and unhinged Elisenda shouted that it was awful living in that hell full of angels. He could scarcely eat and his antiquarian eyes had also become so foggy that he went about bumping into posts. All he had left were the bare cannulae[10] of his last feathers. Pelayo threw a blanket over him and extended him the charity of letting him sleep in the shed, and only then did they notice that he had a temperature at night, and was delirious with the tongue twisters of an old Norwegian. That was one of the few times they became alarmed, for they thought he was going to die and not even the wise neighbor woman had been able to tell them what to do with dead angels.

And yet he not only survived his worst winter, but seemed improved with the first sunny days. He remained motionless for several days in the farthest corner of the courtyard, where no one would see him, and at the beginning of December some large, stiff feathers began to grow on his wings, the feathers of a scarecrow, which looked more like another misfortune of decrepitude. But he must have known the reason for those changes, for he was quite careful that no one should notice them, that no one should hear the sea chanteys that he sometimes sang under the stars. One morning

---

[8] A disinfectant.

[9] A type of incense.

[10] Tubes at the base of feathers.

Elisenda was cutting some bunches of onions for lunch when a wind that seemed to come from the high seas blew into the kitchen. Then she went to the window and caught the angel in his first attempt at flight. They were so clumsy that his fingernails opened a furrow in the vegetable patch and he was on the point of knocking the shed down with the ungainly flapping that slipped on the light and couldn't get a grip on the air. But he did manage to gain altitude. Elisenda let out a sigh of relief, for herself and for him, when she saw him pass over the last houses, holding himself up in some way with the risky flapping of a senile vulture. She kept watching him even when she was through cutting the onions and she kept on watching until it was no longer possible for her to see him, because then he was no longer an annoyance in her life but an imaginary dot on the horizon of the sea.

JAMES JOYCE
(1884–1941)

Eveline
(1914)

She sat at the window watching the evening invade the avenue. Her head was leaned against the window curtains and in her nostrils was the odor of dusty cretonne.[1] She was tired.

Few people passed. The man out of the last house passed on his way home; she heard his footsteps clacking along the concrete pavement and afterwards crunching on the cinder path before the new red houses. One time there used to be a field there in which they used to play every evening with other people's children. Then a man from Belfast[2] bought the field and built houses in it—not like their little brown houses but bright brick houses with shining roofs. The children of the avenue used to play together in that field—the Devines, the Waters, the Dunns, little Keogh the cripple, she and her brothers and sisters. Ernest, however, never played: he was too grown up. Her father used often to hunt them in out of the field with his blackthorn stick; but usually little Keogh used to keep *nix*[3] and call out when he saw her father coming. Still they seemed to have been rather happy then. Her father was not so bad then; and besides, her mother was alive. That was a long time ago; she and her brothers and sisters were all grown up; her mother was dead. Tizzie Dunn was dead, too, and the Waters had gone back to England. Everything changes. Now she was going to go away like the others, to leave her home.

Home! She looked around the room, reviewing all its familiar objects which she had dusted once a week for so many years, wondering where on

---

[1] Heavy cloth used for curtains and upholstery.

[2] Capital of present-day Northern Ireland. This story refers to a time before the Partition of Ireland.

[3] Keep watch (slang).

earth all the dust came from. Perhaps she would never see again those familiar objects from which she had never dreamed of being divided. And yet during all those years she had never found out the name of the priest whose yellowing photograph hung on the wall above the broken harmonium beside the colored print of the promises made to Blessed Margaret Mary Alacoque. He had been a school friend of her father. Whenever he showed the photograph to a visitor her father used to pass it with a casual word:

"He is in Melbourne now."

5   She had consented to go away, to leave her home. Was that wise? She tried to weigh each side of the question. In her home anyway she had shelter and food; she had those whom she had known all her life about her. Of course she had to work hard both in the house and at business. What would they say of her in the Stores when they found out that she had run away with a fellow? Say she was a fool, perhaps; and her place would be filled up by advertisement. Miss Gavan would be glad. She had always had an edge on her, especially whenever there were people listening.

"Miss Hill, don't you see these ladies are waiting?"

"Look lively, Miss Hill, please."

She would not cry many tears at leaving the Stores.

But in her new home, in a distant unknown country, it would not be like that. Then she would be married—she, Eveline. People would treat her with respect then. She would not be treated as her mother had been. Even now, though she was over nineteen, she sometimes felt herself in danger of her father's violence. She knew it was that that had given her the palpitations. When they were growing up he had never gone for her, like he used to go for Harry and Ernest, because she was a girl; but latterly he had begun to threaten her and say what he would do to her only for her dead mother's sake. And now she had nobody to protect her. Ernest was dead and Harry, who was in the church decorating business, was nearly always down somewhere in the country. Besides, the invariable squabble for money on Saturday nights had begun to weary her unspeakably. She always gave her entire wages—seven shillings—and Harry always sent up what he could but the trouble was to get any money from her father. He said she used to squander the money, that she had no head, that he wasn't going to give her his hard-earned money to throw about the streets, and much more, for he was usually fairly bad of a Saturday night. In the end he would give her the money and ask her had she any intention of buying Sunday dinner. Then she had to rush out as quickly as she could and do her marketing, holding her black leather purse tightly in her hand as she elbowed her way through the crowds and returning home late under her load of provisions. She had hard work to keep the house together and to see that the two young children, who had been left to her charge went to school regularly and got their meals regularly. It was hard work—a hard life—but now that she was about to leave it she did not find it a wholly undesirable life.

10 She was about to explore another life with Frank. Frank was very kind, manly, open-hearted. She was to go away with him by the night-boat to be his wife and to live with him in Buenos Aires where he had a home waiting for her. How well she remembered the first time she had seen him; he was lodging in a house on the main road where she used to visit. It seemed a few weeks ago. He was standing at the gate, his peaked cap pushed back on his head and his hair tumbled forward over a face of bronze. Then they had come to know each other. He used to meet her outside the Stores every evening and see her home. He took her to see *The Bohemian Girl* and she felt elated as she sat in an unaccustomed part of the theater with him. He was awfully fond of music and sang a little. People knew that they were courting and, when he sang about the lass that loves a sailor, she always felt pleasantly confused. He used to call her Poppens out of fun. First of all it had been an excitement for her to have a fellow and then she had begun to like him. He had tales of distant countries. He had started as a deck boy at a pound a month on a ship of the Allan Line going out to Canada. He told her the names of the ships he had been on and the names of the different services. He had sailed through the Straits of Magellan[4] and he told her stories of the terrible Patagonians.[5] He had fallen on his feet in Buenos Aires, he said, and had come over to the old country just for a holiday. Of course, her father had found out the affair and had forbidden her to have anything to say to him.

"I know these sailor chaps," he said.

One day he had quarreled with Frank and after that she had to meet her lover secretly.

The evening deepened in the avenue. The white of two letters in her lap grew indistinct. One was to Harry; the other was to her father. Ernest had been her favorite but she liked Harry too. Her father was becoming old lately, she noticed; he would miss her. Sometimes he could be very nice. Not long before, when she had been laid up for a day, he had read her out a ghost story and made toast for her at the fire. Another day, when their mother was alive, they had all gone for a picnic to the Hill of Howth. She remembered her father putting on her mother's bonnet to make the children laugh.

Her time was running out but she continued to sit by the window, leaning her head against the window curtain, inhaling the odor of dusty cretonne. Down far in the avenue she could hear a street organ playing. She knew the air. Strange that it should come that very night to remind her of the promise to her mother, her promise to keep the home together as long as she could. She remembered the last night of her mother's illness; she was again in the close dark room at the other side of the hall and outside she heard a melancholy air of Italy. The organ player had been ordered to go away and given sixpence. She remembered her father strutting back into the sickroom saying:

---

[4] Sea channel at the southern tip of South America.

[5] People from Patagonia, a tableland region in southern Argentina and Chile.

15   "Damned Italians! coming over here!"

    As she mused the pitiful vision of her mother's life laid its spell on the very quick of her being—that life of commonplace sacrifices closing in final craziness. She trembled as she heard again her mother's voice saying constantly with foolish insistence:

    "Derevaun Seraun! Derevaun Seraun!"[6]

    She stood up in a sudden impulse of terror. Escape! She must escape! Frank would save her. He would give her life, perhaps love, too. But she wanted to live. Why should she be unhappy? She had a right to happiness. Frank would take her in his arms, fold her in his arms. He would save her.

    She stood among the swaying crowd in the station at the North Wall. He held her hand and she knew that he was speaking to her, saying something about the passage over and over again. The station was full of soldiers with brown baggages. Through the wide doors of the sheds she caught a glimpse of the black mass of the boat, lying in beside the quay[7] wall, with illumined portholes. She answered nothing. She felt her cheek pale and cold and, out of a maze of distress, she prayed to God to direct her, to show her what was her duty. The boat blew a long mournful whistle into the mist. If she went, tomorrow she would be on the sea with Frank, steaming toward Buenos Aires. Their passage had been booked. Could she still draw back after all he had done for her? Her distress awoke a nausea in her body and she kept moving her lips in silent, fervent prayer.

20   A bell clanged upon her heart. She felt him seize her hand:

    "Come!"

    All the seas of the world tumbled about her heart. He was drawing her into them: he would drown her. She gripped with both hands at the iron railing.

    "Come!"

    No! No! No! It was impossible. Her hands clutched the iron in frenzy. Amid the seas she sent a cry of anguish!

25   "Eveline! Evvy!"

    He rushed beyond the barrier and called to her to follow. He was shouted at to go on but he still called to her. She set her white face to him, passive, like a helpless animal. Her eyes gave him no sign of love or farewell or recognition.

---

[6] "The end of pleasure is pain!" (Irish).

[7] A paved stretch of shoreline facing navigable water, used for loading and unloading ships.

JAMAICA KINCAID
(1949–   )

Girl
(1984)

Wash the white clothes on Monday and put them on the stone heap; wash the color clothes on Tuesday and put them on the clothesline to dry; don't walk barehead in the hot sun; cook pumpkin fritters in very hot sweet oil; soak your little clothes right after you take them off; when buying cotton to make yourself a nice blouse, be sure that it doesn't have gum on it, because that way it won't hold up well after a wash; soak salt fish overnight before you cook it; is it true that you sing benna[1] in Sunday School?; always eat your food in such a way that it won't turn someone else's stomach; on Sundays try to walk like a lady and not like the slut you are so bent on becoming; don't sing benna in Sunday School; you mustn't speak to wharf-rat boys, not even to give directions; don't eat fruits on the street—flies will follow you; *but I don't sing benna on Sundays at all and never in Sunday school;* this is how to sew on a button; this is how to make a buttonhole for the button you have just sewed on; this is how to hem a dress when you see the hem coming down and so to prevent yourself from looking like the slut I know you are so bent on becoming; this is how you iron your father's khaki shirt so that it doesn't have a crease; this is how you iron your father's khaki pants so that they don't have a crease; this is how you grow okra—far from the house, because okra tree harbors red ants; when you are growing dasheen, make sure it gets plenty of water or else it makes your throat itch when you are eating it; this is how you sweep a corner; this is how you sweep a whole house; this is how you sweep a yard; this is how you smile to someone you don't like too much; this is how you smile to someone you don't like at all; this is how you smile to someone you like completely; this is how you set a table for tea; this is how you set a table for dinner; this is how you set a table for dinner with an important guest; this is how you set a table for lunch; this is how you set a table for breakfast; this is how to behave in the presence of men who don't know you very well, and this way they won't recognize immediately the slut I have warned you against becoming; be sure to wash every day, even if it is with your own spit; don't squat down to play marbles—you are not a boy, you know; don't pick people's flowers—you might catch something; don't throw stones at black-birds, because it might not be a blackbird at all; this is how to make a bread

---

[1] Calypso music.

pudding; this is how to make doukona;[2] this is how to make pepper pot; this is how to make a good medicine for a cold; this is how to make a good medicine to throw away a child before it even becomes a child; this is how to catch a fish; this is how to throw back a fish you don't like, and that way something bad won't fall on you; this is how to bully a man; this is how a man bullies you; this is how to love a man, and if this doesn't work there are other ways, and if they don't work don't feel too bad about giving up; this is how to spit up in the air if you feel like it, and this is how to move quick so that it doesn't fall on you; this is how to make ends meet; always squeeze bread to make sure it's fresh; *but what if the baker won't let me feel the bread?;* you mean to say that after all you are really going to be the kind of woman who the baker won't let near the bread?

◈ ◈ ◈

URSULA K. LE GUIN
(1929–)

The Ones Who Walk Away from Omelas
(1973)

With a clamor of bells that set the swallows soaring, the Festival of Summer came to the city. Omelas, bright-towered by the sea. The rigging of the boats in harbor sparkled with flags. In the streets between houses with red roofs and painted walls, between old moss-grown gardens and under avenues of trees, past great parks and public buildings, processions moved. Some were decorous: old people in long stiff robes of mauve and grey, grave master workmen, quiet, merry women carrying their babies and chatting as they walked. In other streets the music beat faster, a shimmering of gong and tambourine, and the people went dancing, the procession was a dance. Children dodged in and out, their high calls rising like the swallows' crossing flights over the music and the singing. All the processions wound towards the north side of the city, where on the great water-meadow called the Green Fields boys and girls, naked in the bright air, with mud-stained feet and ankles and long, lithe arms, exercised their restive horses before the race. The horses wore no gear at all but a halter without bit. Their manes were braided with streamers of silver, gold, and green. They flared their nostrils and pranced and boasted to one another; they were vastly excited, the horse being the only animal who has adopted our ceremonies as his own. Far off to the north and west the mountains stood up half encircling Omelas on her bay. The air of morning was so clear that the snow still crowning the Eighteen Peaks burned with white-gold fire across the miles of sunlit air, under the dark blue of the sky. There was just enough wind to make the banners that marked the racecourse snap and flutter now and then. In the silence of the broad green meadows one could hear the music winding

---

[2] Spicy plantain pudding.

through the city streets, farther and nearer and ever approaching, a cheerful faint sweetness of the air that from time to time trembled and gathered together and broke out into the great joyous clanging of the bells.

Joyous! How is one to tell about joy? How describe the citizens of Omelas?

They were not simple folk, you see, though they were happy. But we do not say the words of cheer much any more. All smiles have become archaic. Given a description such as this one tends to make certain assumptions. Given a description such as this one tends to look next for the King, mounted on a splendid stallion and surrounded by his noble knights, or perhaps in a golden litter borne by great-muscled slaves. But there was no king. They did not use swords, or keep slaves. They were not barbarians. I do not know the rules and laws of their society, but I suspect that they were singularly few. As they did without monarchy and slavery, so they also got on without the stock exchange, the advertisement, the secret police, and the bomb. Yet I repeat that these were not simple folk, not dulcet shepherds, noble savages, bland utopians. They were not less complex than us. The trouble is that we have a bad habit, encouraged by pedants and sophisticates, of considering happiness as something rather stupid. Only pain is intellectual, only evil interesting. This is the treason of the artist: a refusal to admit the banality of evil and the terrible boredom of pain. If you can't lick 'em, join 'em. If it hurts, repeat it. But to praise despair is to condemn delight, to embrace violence is to lose hold of everything else. We have almost lost hold; we can no longer describe a happy man, nor make any celebration of joy. How can I tell you about the people of Omelas? They were not naive and happy children—though their children were, in fact, happy. They were mature, intelligent, passionate adults whose lives were not wretched. O miracle! but I wish I could describe it better. I wish I could convince you. Omelas sounds in my words like a city in a fairy tale, long ago and far away, once upon a time. Perhaps it would be best if you imagined it as your own fancy bids, assuming it will rise to the occasion, for certainly I cannot suit you all. For instance, how about technology? I think that there would be no cars or helicopters in and above the streets; this follows from the fact that the people of Omelas are happy people. Happiness is based on a just discrimination of what is necessary, what is neither necessary nor destructive, and what is destructive. In the middle category, however—that of the unnecessary but undestructive, that of comfort, luxury, exuberance, etc.—they could perfectly well have central heating, subway trains, washing machines, and all kinds of marvelous devices not yet invented here, floating light-sources, fuelless power, a cure for the common cold. Or they could have none of that; it doesn't matter. As you like it. I incline to think that people from towns up and down the coast have been coming in to Omelas during the last days before the Festival on very fast little trains and double-decked trams, and that the train station of Omelas is actually the handsomest building in town, though plainer than the magnificent Farmers' Market. But even granted trains, I fear that Omelas so far strikes some of you as goody-goody. Smiles, bells, parades, horses, bleh. If so, please add an orgy.

If an orgy would help, don't hesitate. Let us not, however, have temples from which issue beautiful nude priests and priestesses already half in ecstasy and ready to copulate with any man or woman, lover or stranger, who desires union with the deep godhead of the blood, although that was my first idea. But really it would be better not to have any temples in Omelas—at least, not manned temples. Religion yes, clergy no. Surely the beautiful nudes can just wander about, offering themselves like divine soufflés to the hunger of the needy and the rapture of the flesh. Let them join the processions. Let tambourines be struck above the copulations, and the glory of desire be proclaimed upon the gongs, and (a not unimportant point) let the offspring of these delightful rituals be beloved and looked after by all. One thing I know there is none of in Omelas is guilt. But what else should there be? I thought at first there were not drugs, but that is puritanical. For those who like it, the faint insistent sweetness of *drooz* may perfume the ways of the city, drooz which first brings a great lightness and brilliance to the mind and limbs, and then after some hours a dreamy languor, and wonderful visions at last of the very arcana and inmost secrets of the Universe, as well as exciting the pleasure of sex beyond belief; and it is not habit-forming. For more modest tastes I think there ought to be beer. What else, what else belongs in the joyous city? The sense of victory, surely, the celebration of courage. But as we did without clergy, let us do without soldiers. The joy built upon successful slaughter is not the right kind of joy; it will not do; it is fearful and it is trivial. A boundless and generous contentment, a magnanimous triumph felt not against some outer enemy but in communion with the finest and fairest in the souls of all men everywhere and the splendor of the world's summer: this is what swells the hearts of the people of Omelas, and the victory they celebrate is that of life. I really don't think many of them need to take *drooz*.

Most of the procession have reached the Green Fields by now. A marvelous smell of cooking goes forth from the red and blue tents of the provisioners. The faces of small children are amiably sticky; in the benign grey beard of a man a couple of crumbs of rich pastry are entangled. The youths and girls have mounted their horses and are beginning to group around the starting line of the course. An old women, small, fat, and laughing, is passing out flowers from a basket, and tall young men wear her flowers in their shining hair. A child of nine or ten sits at the edge of the crowd, alone, playing on a wooden flute. People pause to listen, and they smile, but they do not speak to him, for he never ceases playing and never sees them, his dark eyes wholly rapt in the sweet, thin magic of the tune.

5   He finishes, and slowly lowers his hands holding the wooden flute.

As if that little private silence were the signal, all at once a trumpet sounds from the pavilion near the starting line: imperious, melancholy, piercing. The horses rear on their slender legs, and some of them neigh in answer. Sober-faced, the young riders stroke the horses' necks and soothe them, whispering, "Quiet, quiet, there my beauty, my hope. . . ." They begin to form in rank along the starting line. The crowds along the racecourse are like a field of grass and flowers in the wind. The Festival of Summer has begun.

Do you believe? Do you accept the festival, the city, the joy? No? Then let me describe one more thing.

In a basement under one of the beautiful public buildings of Omelas, or perhaps in the cellar of one of its spacious private homes, there is a room. It has one locked door, and no window. A little light seeps in dustily between cracks in the boards, secondhand from a cobwebbed window somewhere across the cellar. In one corner of the little room a couple of mops, with stiff, clotted, foul-smelling heads stand near a rusty bucket. The floor is dirt, a little damp to the touch, as cellar dirt usually is. The room is about three paces long and two wide: a mere broom closet or disused tool room. In the room a child is sitting. It could be a boy or a girl. It looks about six, but actually is nearly ten. It is feeble-minded. Perhaps it was born defective, or perhaps it has become imbecile through fear, malnutrition, and neglect. It picks its nose and occasionally fumbles vaguely with its toes or genitals, as it sits hunched in the corner farthest from the bucket and the two mops. It is afraid of the mops. It finds them horrible. It shuts its eyes, but it knows the mops are still standing there; and the door is locked; and nobody will come. The door is always locked; and nobody ever comes, except that sometimes— the child has no understanding of time or interval—sometimes the door rattles terribly and opens, and a person, or several people, are there. One of them may come in and kick the child to make it stand up. The others never come close, but peer in at it with frightened, disgusted eyes. The food bowl and the water jug are hastily filled, the door is locked, the eyes disappear. The people at the door never say anything, but the child, who has not always lived in the tool room, and can remember sunlight and its mother's voice, sometimes speaks. "I will be good," it says. "Please let me out. I will be good!" They never answer. The child used to scream for help at night, and cry a good deal, but now it only makes a kind of whining, "eh-haa, eh-haa," and it speaks less and less often. It is so thin there are no calves to its legs; its belly protrudes; it lives on a half-bowl of corn meal and grease a day. It is naked. Its buttocks and thighs are a mass of festered sores, as it sits in its own excrement continually.

They all know it is there, all the people of Omelas. Some of them have come to see it, others are content merely to know it is there. They all know that it has to be there. Some of them understand why, and some do not, but they all understand that their happiness, the beauty of their city, the tenderness of their friendships, the health of their children, the wisdom of their scholars, the skill of their makers, even the abundance of their harvest and the kindly weathers of their skies, depend wholly on this child's abominable misery.

10   This is usually explained to children when they are between eight and twelve, whenever they seem capable of understanding; and most of those who come to see the child are young people, though often enough an adult comes, or comes back, to see the child. No matter how well the matter has

been explained to them, these young spectators are always shocked and sickened at the sight. They feel disgust, which they had thought themselves superior to. They feel anger, outrage, impotence, despite all the explanations. They would like to do something for the child. But there is nothing they can do. If the child were brought up into the sunlight out of that vile place, if it were cleaned and fed and comforted, that would be a good thing indeed; but if it were done, in that day and hour all the prosperity and beauty and delight of Omelas would wither and be destroyed. Those are the terms. To exchange all the goodness and grace of every life in Omelas for that single, small improvement: to throw away the happiness of thousands for the chance of the happiness of one: that would be to let guilt within the walls indeed.

The terms are strict and absolute; there may not even be a kind word spoken to the child.

Often the young people go home in tears, or in a tearless rage, when they have seen the child and faced this terrible paradox. They may brood over it for weeks or years. But as time goes on they begin to realize that even if the child could be released, it would not get much good of its freedom: a little vague pleasure of warmth and food, no doubt, but little more. It is too degraded and imbecile to know any real joy. It has been afraid too long ever to be free of fear. Its habits are too uncouth for it to respond to humane treatment. Indeed, after so long it would probably be wretched without walls about it to protect it, and darkness for its eyes, and its own excrement to sit in. Their tears at the bitter injustice dry when they begin to perceive the terrible justice of reality, and to accept it. Yet it is their tears and anger, the trying of their generosity and the acceptance of their helplessness, which are perhaps the true source of the splendor of their lives. Theirs is no vapid, irresponsible happiness. They know that they, like the child, are not free. They know compassion. It is the existence of the child, and their knowledge of its existence, that makes possible the nobility of their architecture, the poignancy of their music, the profundity of their science. It is because of the child that they are so gentle with children. They know that if the wretched one were not there sniveling in the dark, the other one, the flute-player, could make no joyful music as the young riders line up in their beauty for the race in the sunlight of the first morning of summer.

Now do you believe in them? Are they not more credible? But there is one more thing to tell, and this is quite incredible.

At times one of the adolescent girls or boys who go to see the child does not go home to weep or rage, does not, in fact, go home at all. Sometimes also a man or woman much older falls silent for a day or two, and then leaves home. These people go out into the street, and walk down the street alone. They keep walking, and walk straight out of the city of Omelas, through the beautiful gates. They keep walking across the farmlands of Omelas. Each one goes alone, youth or girl, man or woman. Night falls; the traveler must pass down village streets, between the houses with yellow-lit windows, and on out into the darkness of the fields. Each alone, they go west or north, towards the mountains. They go on. They leave Omelas, they walk ahead into the darkness, and they do not come back. The place they go towards is a place even less imaginable to most of us than the city of happiness. I cannot describe it at all. It is possible that it does not exist. But they seem to know where they are going, the ones who walk away from Omelas.

✢ ❋ ✢

ALISTAIR MACLEOD
(1936–   )

The Boat

(1976)

There are times even now, when I awake at four o'clock in the morning with the terrible fear that I have overslept, when I imagine that my father is waiting for me in the room below the darkened stairs or that the shore-bound men are tossing pebbles against my window while blowing their hands and stomping their feet impatiently on the frozen steadfast earth. There are times when I am half out of bed and fumbling for socks and mumbling for words before I realize that I am foolishly alone, that no one waits at the base of the stairs and no boat rides restlessly in the waters by the pier.

At such times only the grey corpses on the overflowing ashtray beside my bed bear witness to the extinction of the latest spark and silently await the crushing out of the most recent of their fellows. And then because I am afraid to be alone with death, I dress rapidly, make a great to do about clearing my throat, turn on both faucets in the sink and proceed to make loud splashing intellectual noises. Later I go out and walk the mile to the all night restaurant.

In the winter it is a very cold walk and there are often tears in my eyes when I arrive. The waitress usually gives a sympathetic little shiver and says, "Boy, it must be really cold out there, you got tears in your eyes."

"Yes," I say, "it sure is; it really is."

5   And then the three or four of us who are always in such places at such times make uninteresting little protective chit chat until the dawn reluctantly arrives. Then I swallow the coffee which is always bitter and leave with a great busy rush because by that time I have to worry about being late and whether I have a clean shirt and whether my car will start and about all the other countless things one must worry about when he teaches at a great Midwestern university. And I know then that that day will go by as have all the days of the past ten years, for the call and the voices and the shapes and the boat were not really there in the early morning's darkness and I have all kinds of comforting reality to prove it. They are only shadows and echoes,

the animals a child's hands make on the wall by lamplight, and the voices from the rain barrel; the cuttings from an old movie made in the black and white of long ago.

I first became conscious of the boat in the same way and at almost the same time that I became aware of the people it supported. My earliest recollection of my father is a view from the floor of gigantic rubber boots and then of being suddenly elevated and having my face pressed against the stubble of his cheek, and of how it tasted of salt and of how he smelled of salt from his red-soled rubber boots to the shaggy whiteness of his hair.

When I was very small, he took me for my first ride in the boat. I rode the half-mile from our house to the wharf on his shoulders and I remember the sound of his rubber boots galumphing along the gravel beach, the tune of the indecent little song he used to sing, and the odour of the salt.

The floor of the boat was permeated with the same odour and in its constancy I was not aware of change. In the harbour we made our little circle and returned. He tied the boat by its painter, fastened the stern to its permanent anchor and lifted me high over his head to the solidity of the wharf. Then he climbed up the little iron ladder that led to the wharf's cap, placed me once more upon his shoulders and galumphed off again.

When we returned to the house everyone made a great fuss over my precocious excursion and asked, "How did you like the boat?" "Were you afraid in the boat?" "Did you cry in the boat?" They repeated "the boat" at the end of all their questions and I knew it must be very important to everyone.

10   My earliest recollection of my mother is of being alone with her in the mornings while my father was away in the boat. She seemed to be always repairing clothes that were "torn in the boat," preparing food "to be eaten in the boat" or looking for "the boat" through our kitchen window which faced upon the sea. When my father returned about noon, she would ask, "Well, how did things go in the boat today?" It was the first question I remember asking: "Well, how did things go in the boat today?" "Well, how did things go in the boat today?"

The boat in our lives was registered at Port Hawkesbury. She was what Nova Scotians called a Cape Island boat and was designed for the small inshore fishermen who sought the lobsters of the spring and the mackerel of summer and later the cod and haddock and hake. She was thirty-two feet long and nine wide, and was powered by an engine from a Chevrolet truck. She had a marine clutch and a high speed reverse gear and was painted light green with the name *Jenny Lynn* stencilled in black letters on her bow and painted on an oblong plate across her stern. Jenny Lynn had been my mother's maiden name and the boat was called after her as another link in the chain of tradition. Most of the boats that berthed at the wharf bore the names of some female member of their owner's household.

I say this now as if I knew it all then. All at once, all about boat dimensions and engines, and as if on the day of my first childish voyage I noticed the difference between a stencilled name and a painted name. But of course it was not that way at all, for I learned it all very slowly and there was not time enough.

I learned first about our house which was one of about fifty which marched around the horseshoe of our harbour and the wharf which was its heart. Some of them were so close to the water that during a storm the sea spray splashed against their windows while others were built farther along the beach as was the case with ours. The houses and their people, like those of the neighbouring towns and villages, were the result of Ireland's discontent and Scotland's Highland Clearances and America's War of Independence. Impulsive emotional Catholic Celts who could not bear to live with England and shrewd determined Protestant Puritans who, in the years after 1776, could not bear to live without.

The most important room in our house was one of those oblong old-fashioned kitchens headed by a wood- and coal-burning stove. Behind the stove was a box of kindlings and beside it a coal scuttle. A heavy wooden table with leaves that expanded or reduced its dimensions stood in the middle of the floor. There were five wooden home-made chairs which had been chipped and hacked by a variety of knives. Against the east wall, opposite the stove, there was a couch which sagged in the middle and had a cushion for a pillow, and above it a shelf which contained matches, tobacco, pencils, odd fish-hooks, bits of twine, and a tin can filled with bills and receipts. The south wall was dominated by a window which faced the sea and on the north there was a five foot board which bore a variety of clothes hooks and the burdens of each. Beneath the board there was a jumble of odd footwear, mostly of rubber. There was also, on this wall, a barometer, a map of the marine area and a shelf which held a tiny radio. The kitchen was shared by all of us and was a buffer zone between the immaculate order of ten other rooms and the disruptive chaos of the single room that was my father's.

15   My mother ran her house as her brothers ran their boats. Everything was clean and spotless and in order. She was tall and dark and powerfully energetic. In later years she reminded me of the women of Thomas Hardy, particularly Eustacia Vye,[1] in a physical way. She fed and clothed a family of seven children, making all of the meals and most of the clothes. She grew miraculous gardens and magnificent flowers and raised broods of hens and ducks. She would walk miles on berry picking expeditions and hoist her skirts to dig for clams when the tide was low. She was fourteen years younger than my father, whom she had married when she was twenty-six and had been a local beauty for a period of ten years. My mother was of the sea as were all of her people, and her horizons were the very literal ones she scanned with her dark and fearless eyes.

Between the kitchen clothes rack and barometer, a door opened into my father's bedroom. It was a room of disorder and disarray. It was as if the wind which so often clamoured about the house succeeded in entering this single room and after whipping it into turmoil stole quietly away to renew its knowing laughter from without.

---

[1] A strong female character in Thomas Hardy's *The Return of the Native*.

My father's bed was against the south wall. It always looked rumpled and unmade because he lay on top of it more than he slept within any folds it might have had. Beside it, there was a little brown table. An archaic goose-necked reading light, a battered table radio, a mound of wooden matches, one or two packages of tobacco, a deck of cigarette papers and an overflowing ashtray cluttered its surface. The brown larvae of tobacco shreds and the grey flecks of ash covered both the table and the floor beneath it. The once-varnished surface of the table was disfigured by numerous black scars and gashes inflicted by the neglected burning cigarettes of many years. They had tumbled from the ashtray unnoticed and branded their statements permanently and quietly into the wood until the odour of their burning caused the snuffing out of their lives. At the bed's foot there was a single window which looked upon the sea.

Against the adjacent wall there was a battered bureau and beside it there was a closet which held his single ill-fitting serge suit, the two or three white shirts that strangled him and the square black shoes that pinched. When he took off his more friendly clothes, the heavy woollen sweaters, mitts and socks which my mother knitted for him and the woollen and doeskin shirts, he dumped them unceremoniously on a single chair. If a visitor entered the room while he was lying on the bed, he would be told to throw the clothes on the floor and take their place upon the chair.

Magazines and books covered the bureau and competed with the clothes for domination of the chair. They further overburdened the heroic little table and lay on top of the radio. They filled a baffling and unknowable cave beneath the bed, and in the corner of the bureau they spilled from the walls and grew up from the floor.

20   The magazines were the most conventional: *Time, Newsweek, Life, Maclean's, Family Herald, Reader's Digest.* They were the result of various cut-rate subscriptions or the gift subscriptions associated with Christmas, "the two whole years for only $3.50."

The books were more varied. There were a few hard-cover magnificents and bygone Book-of-the-Month wonders and some were Christmas or birthday gifts. The majority of them, however, were used paperbacks which came from those second-hand book stores which advertise in the backs of magazines: "Miscellaneous Used Paperbacks 10¢ Each." At first he sent for them himself, although my mother resented the expense, but in later years they came more and more often from my sisters who had moved to the cities. Especially at first they were very weird and varied. Mickey Spillane and Ernest Haycox vied with Dostoyevsky and Faulkner, and the Penguin Poets edition of Gerard Manley Hopkins arrived in the same box as a little book on sex technique called *Getting the Most Out of Love.* The former had been assiduously annotated by a very fine hand using a very blue-inked fountain pen while the latter had been studied by someone with very large thumbs, the prints of which were still visible in the margins. At the slightest provocation it would open almost automatically to particularly graphic and well-smudged pages.

When he was not in the boat, my father spent most of his time lying on the bed in his socks, the top two buttons of his trousers undone, his discarded shirt on the ever-ready chair and the sleeves of the woollen Stanfield underwear, which he wore both summer and winter, drawn half way up to his elbows. The pillows propped up the whiteness of his head and the goose-necked lamp illuminated the pages in his hands. The cigarettes smoked and smouldered on the ashtray and on the table and the radio played constantly, sometimes low and sometimes loud. At midnight and at one, two, three and four, one could sometimes hear the radio, his occasional cough, the rustling thud of a completed book being tossed to the corner heap, or the movement necessitated by his sitting on the edge of the bed to roll the thousandth cigarette. He seemed never to sleep, only to doze, and the light shone constantly from his window to the sea.

My mother despised the room and all it stood for and she had stopped sleeping in it after I was born. She despised disorder in rooms and in houses and in hours and in lives, and she had not read a book since high school. There she had read *Ivanhoe* and considered it a colossal waste of time. Still the room remained, like a solid rock of opposition in the sparkling waters of a clear deep harbour, opening off the kitchen where we really lived our lives, with its door always open and its contents visible to all.

The daughters of the room and of the house were very beautiful. They were tall and willowy like my mother and had her fine facial features set off by the reddish copper-coloured hair that had apparently once been my father's before it turned to white. All of them were very clever in school and helped my mother a great deal about the house. When they were young they sang and were very happy and very nice to me because I was the youngest and the family's only boy.

25   My father never approved of their playing about the wharf like the other children, and they went there only when my mother sent them on an errand. At such times they almost always overstayed, playing screaming games of tag or hide-and-seek in and about the fishing shanties. They piled traps and tubs of trawl, shouting down to the perch that swam languidly about the wharf's algae-covered piles, or jumping in and out of the boats that tugged gently at their lines. My mother was never uneasy about them at such times and when her husband criticized her she would say, "Nothing will happen to them there," or "They could be doing worse things in worse places."

By about the ninth or tenth grade my sisters one by one discovered my father's bedroom and then the change would begin. Each would go into the room one morning when he was out. She would go with the ideal hope of imposing order or with the more practical objective of emptying the ashtray, and later she would be found spellbound by the volume in her hand. My mother's reaction was always abrupt, bordering on the angry. "Take your nose out of that trash and come and do your work," she would say, and once I saw her slap my youngest sister so hard that the print of her hand was scarletly emblazoned upon her daughter's cheek while the broken-spined paperback fluttered uselessly to the floor.

Thereafter my mother would launch a campaign against what she had discovered but could not understand. At times although she was not overly religious she would bring in God to bolster her arguments, saying, "In the next world God will see to those who waste their lives reading useless books when they should be about their work." Or without theological aid, "I would like to know how books help anyone to live a life." If my father were in, she would repeat the remarks louder than necessary, and her voice would carry into this room where he lay upon his bed. His usual reaction was to turn up the volume of the radio, although that action in itself betrayed the success of the initial thrust.

Shortly after my sisters began to read the books, they grew restless and lost interest in darning socks and baking bread, and all of them eventually went to work as summer waitresses in the Sea Food Restaurant. The restaurant was run by a big American concern from Boston and catered to the tourists that flooded the area during July and August. My mother despised the whole operation. She said the restaurant was not run by "our people," and "our people" did not eat there, and that it was run by outsiders for outsiders.

"Who are these people anyway?" she would ask, tossing back her dark hair, "and what do they, though they go about with their cameras for a hundred years, know about the way it is here, and what do they care about me and mine, and why should I care about them?"

30   She was angry that my sisters should even conceive of working in such a place and more angry when my father made no move to prevent it, and she was worried about herself and about her family and about her life. Sometimes she would say softly to her sisters, "I don't know what's the matter with my girls. It seems none of them are interested in any of the right things." And sometimes there would be bitter savage arguments. One afternoon I was coming in with three mackerel I'd been given at the wharf when I heard her say, "Well I hope you'll be satisfied when they come home knocked up and you'll have had your way."

It was the most savage thing I'd ever heard my mother say. Not just the words but the way she said them, and I stood there in the porch afraid to breathe for what seemed like the years from ten to fifteen, feeling the damp moist mackerel with their silver glassy eyes growing clammy against my leg.

Through the angle in the screen door I saw my father who had been walking into his room wheel around on one of his rubber-booted heels and look at her with his blue eyes flashing like clearest ice beneath the snow that was his hair. His usually ruddy face was drawn and grey, reflecting the exhaustion of a man of sixty-five who had been working in those rubber boots for eleven hours on an August day, and for a fleeting moment I wondered what I would do if he killed my mother while I stood there in the porch with those three foolish mackerel in my hand. Then he turned and went into his room and the radio blared forth the next day's weather forecast and I retreated under the noise and returned again, stamping my feet and slamming the door too loudly to signal my approach. My mother was busy at the stove when I came in, and did not raise her head when I threw the mackerel in a pan. As I looked into my father's room, I said, "Well, how did things go in the boat today?" and he replied, "Oh not too badly, all things considered." He was lying on his back and lighting the first cigarette and the radio was talking about the Virginia coast.

All of my sisters made good money on tips. They bought my father an electric razor which he tried to use for a while and they took out even more magazine subscriptions. They bought my mother a great many clothes of the type she was very fond of, the wide-brimmed hats and the brocaded dresses, but she locked them all in trunks and refused to wear any of them.

On one August day my sisters prevailed upon my father to take some of their restaurant customers for an afternoon ride in the boat. The tourists with their expensive clothes and cameras and sun glasses awkwardly backed down the iron ladder at the wharf's side to where my father waited below, holding the rocking *Jenny Lynn* in snug against the wharf with one hand on the iron ladder and steadying his descending passengers with the other. They tried to look both prim and wind-blown like the girls in the Pepsi-Cola ads and did the best they could, sitting on the thwarts where the newspapers were spread to cover the splattered blood and fish entrails, crowding to one side so that they were in danger of capsizing the boat, taking the inevitable pictures or merely trailing their fingers through the water of their dreams.

35   All of them liked my father very much and, after he brought them back from their circles in the harbour, they invited him to their rented cabins which were located high on a hill overlooking the village to which they were so alien. He proceeded to get very drunk up there with the beautiful view and the strange company and the abundant liquor, and late in the afternoon he began to sing.

I was just approaching the wharf to deliver my mother's summons when he began, and the familiar yet unfamiliar voice that rolled down from the cabins made me feel as I had never felt before in my young life or perhaps as I had always felt without really knowing it, and I was ashamed yet proud, young yet old and saved yet forever lost, and there was nothing I could do to control my legs which trembled nor my eyes which wept for what they could not tell.

The tourists were equipped with tape recorders and my father sang for more than three hours. His voice boomed down the hill and bounced off the surface of the harbour, which was an unearthly blue on that hot August day, and was then reflected to the wharf and the fishing shanties where it was absorbed amidst the men who were baiting their lines for the next day's haul.

He sang all the old sea chanties which had come across from the old world and by which men like him had pulled ropes for generations, and he sang the East Coast sea songs which celebrated the sealing vessels of Northumberland Strait and the long liners of the Grand Banks and of Anticosti, Sable Island, Grand Manan, Boston Harbor, Nantucket and Block

Island. Gradually he shifted to the seemingly unending Gaelic drinking songs with their twenty or more verses and inevitable refrains, and the men in the shanties smiled at the coarseness of some of the verses and at the thought that the singer's immediate audience did not know what they were applauding nor recording to take back to staid old Boston. Later as the sun was setting he switched to the laments and the wild and haunting Gaelic war songs of those spattered Highland ancestors he had never seen, and when his voice ceased, the savage melancholy of three hundred years seemed to hang over the peaceful harbour and the quiet boats and the men leaning in the doorways of their shanties with their cigarettes glowing in the dusk and the women looking to the sea from their open windows with their children in their arms.

When he came home he threw the money he had earned on the kitchen table as he did with all his earnings but my mother refused to touch it and the next day he went with the rest of the men to bait his trawl in the shanties. The tourists came to the door that evening and my mother met them there and told them that her husband was not in although he was lying on the bed only a few feet away with the radio playing and the cigarette upon his lips. She stood in the doorway until they reluctantly went away.

40   In the winter they sent him a picture which had been taken on the day of the singing. On the back it said, "To Our Ernest Hemingway" and the "Our" was underlined. There was also an accompanying letter telling how much they had enjoyed themselves, how popular the tape was proving and explaining who Ernest Hemingway was. In a way it almost did look like one of those unshaven, taken-in-Cuba pictures of Hemingway. He looked both massive and incongruous in the setting. His bulky fisherman's clothes were too big for the green and white lawn chair in which he sat, and his rubber boots seemed to take up all of the well-clipped grass square. The beach umbrella jarred with his sunburned face and because he had already been singing for some time, his lips which chapped in the winds of spring and burned in the water glare of summer had already cracked in several places, producing tiny flecks of blood at their corners and on the whiteness of his teeth. The bracelets of brass chain which he wore to protect his wrists from chafing seemed abnormally large and his broad leather belt had been slackened and his heavy shirt and underwear were open at the throat revealing an uncultivated wilderness of white chest hair bordering on the semi-controlled stubble of his neck and chin. His blue eyes had looked directly into the camera and his hair was whiter than the two tiny clouds which hung over his left shoulder. The sea was behind him and its immense blue flatness stretched out to touch the arching blueness of the sky. It seemed very far away from him or else he was so much in the foreground that he seemed too big for it.

Each year another of my sisters would read the books and work in the restaurant. Sometimes they would stay out quite late on the hot summer nights and when they came up the stairs my mother would ask them many long and involved questions which they resented and tried to avoid. Before ascending the stairs they would go into my father's room and those of us who waited above could hear them throwing his clothes off the chair before sitting on it or the squeak of the bed as they sat on its edge. Sometimes they would talk to him a long time, the murmur of their voices blending with the music of the radio into a mysterious vapour-like sound which floated softly up the stairs.

I say this again as if it all happened at once and as if all of my sisters were of identical ages and like so many lemmings going into another sea and, again, it was of course not that way at all. Yet go they did, to Boston, to Montreal, to New York with the young men they met during the summers and later married in those far-away cities. The young men were very articulate and handsome and wore fine clothes and drove expensive cars and my sisters, as I said, were very tall and beautiful with their copper-coloured hair and were tired of darning socks and baking bread.

One by one they went. My mother had each of her daughters for fifteen years, then lost them for two and finally forever. None married a fisherman. My mother never accepted any of the young men, for in her eyes they seemed always a combination of the lazy, the effeminate, the dishonest and the unknown. They never seemed to do any physical work and she could not comprehend their luxurious vacations and she did not know whence they came nor who they were. And in the end she did not really care, for they were not of her people and they were not of her sea.

I say this now with a sense of wonder at my own stupidity in thinking I was somehow free and would go on doing well in school and playing and helping in the boat and passing into my early teens while streaks of grey began to appear in my mother's dark hair and my father's rubber boots dragged sometimes on the pebbles of the beach as he trudged home from the wharf. And there were but three of us in the house that had at one time been so loud.

45   Then during the winter that I was fifteen he seemed to grow old and ill at once. Most of January he lay upon the bed, smoking and reading and listening to the radio while the wind howled about the house and the needle-like snow blistered off the ice-covered harbour and the doors flew out of people's hands if they did not cling to them like death.

In February when the men began overhauling their lobster traps he still did not move, and my mother and I began to knit lobster trap headings in the evenings. The twine was as always very sharp and harsh, and blisters formed upon our thumbs and little paths of blood soaked quietly down between our fingers while the seals that had drifted down from distant Labrador wept and moaned like human children on the ice-floes of the Gulf.

In the daytime my mother's brother who had been my father's partner as long as I could remember also came to work upon the gear. He was a year older than my mother and was tall and dark and the father of twelve children.

By March we were very far behind and although I began to work very hard in the evenings I knew it was not hard enough and that there were but eight weeks left before the opening of the season on May first. And I knew that my mother worried and my uncle was uneasy and that all of our very lives depended on the boat being ready with her gear and two men, by the date of May the first. And I knew then that *David Copperfield* and *The Tempest* and all those friends I had dearly come to love must really go forever. So I bade them all good-bye.

The night after my first full day at home and after my mother had gone upstairs he called me into his room where I sat upon the chair beside his bed. "You will go back tomorrow," he said simply.

50   I refused then, saying I had made my decision and was satisfied.

"That is no way to make a decision," he said, "and if you are satisfied I am not. It is best that you go back." I was almost angry then and told him as all children do that I wished he would leave me alone and stop telling me what to do.

He looked at me a long time then, lying there on the same bed on which he had fathered me those sixteen years before, fathered me his only son, out of who knew what emotions when he was already fifty-six and his hair had turned to snow. Then he swung his legs over the edge of the squeaking bed and sat facing me and looked into my own dark eyes with his of crystal blue and placed his hand upon my knee. "I am not telling you to do anything," he said softly, "only asking you."

The next morning I returned to school. As I left, my mother followed me to the porch and said, "I never thought a son of mine would choose useless books over the parents that gave him life."

In the weeks that followed he got up rather miraculously and the gear was ready and the *Jenny Lynn* was freshly painted by the last two weeks of April when the ice began to break up and the lonely screaming gulls returned to haunt the silver herring as they flashed within the sea.

55   On the first day of May the boats raced out as they had always done, laden down almost to the gunwales with their heavy cargoes of traps. They were almost like living things as they plunged through the waters of the spring and manoeuvred between the still floating icebergs of crystal white and emerald green on their way to the traditional grounds that they sought out every May. And those of us who sat that day in the high school on the hill, discussing the water imagery of Tennyson, watched them as they passed back and forth beneath us until by afternoon the piles of traps which had been stacked upon the wharf were no longer visible but were spread about the bottom of the sea. And the *Jenny Lynn* went too, all day, with my uncle tall and dark, like a latter-day Tashtego[2] standing at the tiller with his legs wide apart and guiding her deftly between the floating pans of ice and my father in the stern standing in the same way with his hands upon the ropes that lashed the cargo to the deck. And at night my mother asked, "Well, how did things go in the boat today?"

---

[2] A character in Herman Melville's *Moby Dick*.

And the spring wore on and the summer came and school ended in the third week of June and the lobster season on July first and I wished that the two things I loved so dearly did not exclude each other in a manner that was so blunt and too clear.

At the conclusion of the lobster season my uncle said he had been offered a berth on a deep sea dragger and had decided to accept. We all knew that he was leaving the *Jenny Lynn* forever and that before the next lobster season he would buy a boat of his own. He was expecting another child and would be supporting fifteen people by the next spring and could not chance my father against the family that he loved.

I joined my father then for the trawling season, and he made no protest and my mother was quite happy. Through the summer we baited the tubs of trawl in the afternoon and set them at sunset and revisited them in the darkness of the early morning. The men would come tramping by our house at four A.M. and we would join them and walk with them to the wharf and be on our way before the sun rose out of the ocean where it seemed to spend the night. If I was not up they would toss pebbles to my window and I would be very embarrassed and tumble downstairs to where my father lay fully clothed atop his bed, reading his book and listening to his radio and smoking his cigarette. When I appeared he would swing off his bed and put on his boots and be instantly ready and then we would take the lunches my mother had prepared the night before and walk off toward the sea. He would make no attempt to wake me himself.

It was in many ways a good summer. There were few storms and we were out almost every day and we lost a minimum of gear and seemed to land a maximum of fish and I tanned dark and brown after the manner of my uncles.

60   My father did not tan—he never tanned—because of his reddish complexion, and the salt water irritated his skin as it had for sixty years. He burned and reburned over and over again and his lips still cracked so that they bled when he smiled, and his arms, especially the left, still broke out into the oozing saltwater boils as they had ever since as a child I had first watched him soaking and bathing them in a variety of ineffectual solutions. The chafe-preventing bracelets of brass linked chain that all the men wore about their wrists in early spring were his the full season and he shaved but painfully and only once a week.

And I saw then, that summer, many things that I had seen all my life as if for the first time and I thought that perhaps my father had never been intended for a fisherman either physically or mentally. At least not in the manner of my uncles; he had never really loved it. And I remembered that, one evening in his room when we were talking about *David Copperfield*, he had said that he had always wanted to go to the university and I had dismissed it then in the way one dismisses his father's saying he would like to be a tight-rope walker, and we had gone on to talk about the Peggottys and how they loved the sea.

And I thought then to myself that there were many things wrong with all of us and all our lives and I wondered why my father, who was himself an only son, had not married before he was forty and then I wondered why he had. I even thought that perhaps he had had to marry my mother and checked the dates on the flyleaf of the Bible where I learned that my oldest sister had been born a prosaic eleven months after the marriage, and I felt myself then very dirty and debased for my lack of faith and for what I had thought and done.

And then there came into my heart a very great love for my father and I thought it was very much braver to spend a life doing what you really do not want rather than selfishly following forever your own dreams and inclinations. And I knew then that I could never leave him alone to suffer the iron-tipped harpoons which my mother would forever hurl into his soul because he was a failure as a husband and a father who had retained none of his own. And I felt that I had been very small in a little secret place within me and that even the completion of high school was for me a silly shallow selfish dream.

So I told him one night very resolutely and very powerfully that I would remain with him as long as he lived and we would fish the sea together. And he made no protest but only smiled through the cigarette smoke that wreathed his bed and replied, "I hope you will remember what you've said."

65   The room was now so filled with books as to be almost Dickensian, but he would not allow my mother to move or change them and he continued to read them, sometimes two or three a night. They came with great regularity now, and there were more hard covers, sent by my sisters who had gone so long ago and now seemed so distant and so prosperous, and sent also pictures of small red-haired grandchildren with baseball bats and dolls which he placed upon his bureau and which my mother gazed at wistfully when she thought no one would see. Red-haired grandchildren with baseball bats and dolls who would never know the sea in hatred or in love.

And so we fished through the heat of August and into the cooler days of September when the water was so clear we could almost see the bottom and the white mists rose like delicate ghosts in the early morning dawn. And one day my mother said to me, "You have given added years to his life."

And we fished on into October when it began to roughen and we could no longer risk night sets but took our gear out each morning and returned at the first sight of the squalls; and on into November when we lost three tubs of trawl and the clear blue water turned to a sullen grey and the trochoidal waves rolled rough and high and washed across our bows and decks as we ran within their troughs. We wore heavy sweaters now and the awkward rubber slickers and the heavy woollen mitts which soaked and froze into masses of ice that hung from our wrists like the limbs of gigantic monsters until we thawed them against the exhaust pipe's heat. And almost every day we would leave for home before noon, driven by the blasts of the northwest wind, coating our eyebrows with ice and freezing our eyelids closed as we leaned into a visibility that was hardly there, charting our course from the compass and the sea, running with the waves and between them but never confronting their towering might.

And I stood at the tiller now, on these homeward lunges, stood in the place and in the manner of my uncle, turning to look at my father and to shout over the roar of the engine and the slop of the sea to where he stood in the stern, drenched and dripping with the snow and the salt and the spray and his bushy eyebrows caked in ice. But on November twenty-first, when it seemed we might be making the final run of the season, I turned and he was not there and I knew even in that instant that he would never be again.

On November twenty-first the waves of the grey Atlantic are very high and the waters are very cold and there are no signposts on the surface of the sea. You cannot tell where you have been five minutes before and in the squalls of snow you cannot see. And it takes longer than you would believe to check a boat that has been running before a gale and turn her ever so carefully in a wide and stupid circle, with timbers creaking and straining, back in the face of the storm. And you know it is useless and that your voice does not carry the length of the boat and that even if you knew the original spot, the relentless waves would carry such a burden perhaps a mile or so by the time you could return. And you know also, the final irony, that your father like your uncles and all the men that form your past, cannot swim a stroke.

70   The lobster beds off the Cape Breton coast are still very rich and now, from May to July, their offerings are packed in crates of ice, and thundered by the gigantic transport trucks, day and night, through New Glasgow, Amherst, Saint John and Bangor and Portland and into Boston where they are tossed still living into boiling pots of water, their final home.

And though the prices are higher and the competition tighter, the grounds to which the *Jenny Lynn* once went remain untouched and unfished as they have for the last ten years. For if there are no signposts on the sea in storm there are certain ones in calm and the lobster bottoms were distributed in calm before any of us can remember and the grounds my father fished were those his father fished before him and there were others before and before and before. Twice the big boats have come from forty and fifty miles, lured by the promise of the grounds, and strewn the bottom with their traps and twice they have returned to find their buoys cut adrift and their gear lost and destroyed. Twice the Fisheries Officer and the Mounted Police have come and asked many long and involved questions and twice they have received no answers from the men leaning in the doors of their shanties and the women standing at their windows with their children in their arms. Twice they have gone away saying, "There are no legal boundaries in the Marine area"; "No one can own the sea"; "Those grounds don't wait for anyone."

But the men and the women, with my mother dark among them, do not care for what they say, for to them the grounds are sacred and they think they wait for me.

It is not an easy thing to know that your mother lives alone on an inadequate insurance policy and that she is too proud to accept any other aid. And that she looks through her lonely window onto the ice of winter and the hot flat calm of summer and the rolling waves of fall. And that she lies awake in the early morning's darkness when the rubber boots of the men scrunch upon the gravel as they pass beside her house on their way down to the wharf. And she knows that the footsteps never stop, because no man goes from her house, and she alone of all the Lynns has neither son or son-in-law that walks toward the boat that will take him to the sea. And it is not an easy thing to know that your mother looks upon the sea with love and on you with bitterness because the one has been so constant and the other so untrue.

But neither is it easy to know that your father was found on November twenty-eighth, ten miles to the north and wedged between two boulders at the base of the rock-strewn cliffs where he had been hurled and slammed so many many times. His hands were shredded ribbons as were his feet which had lost their boots to the suction of the sea, and his shoulders came apart in our hands when we tried to move him from the rocks. And the fish had eaten his testicles and the gulls had pecked out his eyes and the white-green stubble of his whiskers had continued to grow in death, like the grass on graves, upon the purple, bloated mass that was his face. There was not much left of my father, physically, as he lay there with the brass chains on his wrists and the seaweed in his hair.

✦   ✦   ✦

HERMAN MELVILLE
(1819–1891)

Bartleby the Scrivener

A STORY OF WALL-STREET
(1853)

I am a rather elderly man. The nature of my avocations for the last thirty years has brought me into more than ordinary contact with what would seem an interesting and somewhat singular set of men, of whom as yet nothing that I know of has ever been written:—I mean the law-copyists or scriveners. I have known very many of them, professionally and privately, and if I pleased, could relate divers histories, at which good-natured gentlemen might smile, and sentimental souls might weep. But I waive the biographies of all other scriveners for a few passages in the life of Bartleby, who was a scrivener the strangest I ever saw or heard of. While of other law-copyists I might write the complete life, of Bartleby nothing of that sort can be done. I believe that no materials exist for a full and satisfactory biography of this man. It is an irreparable loss to literature. Bartleby was one of those beings of whom nothing is ascertainable, except from the original sources, and in his case those are very small. What my own astonished eyes saw of

Bartleby, *that* is all I know of him, except, indeed, one vague report which will appear in the sequel.

Ere introducing the scrivener, as he first appeared to me, it is fit I make some mention of myself, my *employés,* my business, my chambers, and general surroundings; because some such description is indispensable to an adequate understanding of the chief character about to be presented.

Imprimis: I am a man who, from his youth upwards, has been filled with a profound conviction that the easiest way of life is the best. Hence, though I belong to a profession proverbially energetic and nervous, even to turbulence, at times, yet nothing of that sort have I ever suffered to invade my peace. I am one of those unambitious lawyers who never addresses a jury, or in any way draws down public applause; but in the cool tranquillity of a snug retreat, do a snug business among rich men's bonds and mortgages and title-deeds. All who know me, consider me an eminently *safe* man. The late John Jacob Astor,[1] a personage little given to poetic enthusiasm, had no hesitation in pronouncing my first grand point to be prudence; my next, method. I do not speak it in vanity, but simply record the fact, that I was not unemployed in my profession by the late John Jacob Astor; a name which, I admit, I love to repeat, for it hath a rounded and orbicular sound to it, and rings like unto bullion. I will freely add, that I was not insensible to the late John Jacob Astor's good opinion.

Some time prior to the period at which this little history begins, my avocations had been largely increased. The good old office, now extinct in the State of New-York, of a Master in Chancery,[2] had been conferred upon me. It was not a very arduous office, but very pleasantly remunerative. I seldom lose my temper; much more seldom indulge in dangerous indignation at wrongs and outrages; but I must be permitted to be rash here and declare, that I consider the sudden and violent abrogation of the office of Master in Chancery, by the new Constitution, as a—premature act; inasmuch as I had counted upon a life-lease of the profits, whereas I only received those of a few short years. But this is by the way.

5   My chambers were up stairs at No.— Wall-street.[3] At one end they looked upon the white wall of the interior of a spacious sky-light shaft, penetrating the building from top to bottom. This view might have been considered rather tame than otherwise, deficient in what landscape painters call "life." But if so, the view from the other end of my chambers offered, at least, a contrast, if nothing more. In that direction my windows commanded an unobstructed view of a lofty brick wall, black by age and everlasting shade; which wall required no spy-glass to bring out its lurking beauties, but for the benefit of all near-sighted spectators, was pushed up to within ten feet of my window panes. Owing to the great height of the surrounding buildings, and

---

[1] At the time of his death in 1848, Astor was the richest man in the United States.

[2] Officer of the court whose duties included taking testimonies, administering oaths, and acknowledging deeds.

[3] Located in New York City, the financial centre of the United States.

my chambers being on the second floor, the interval between this wall and mine not a little resembled a huge square cistern.

At the period just preceding the advent of Bartleby, I had two persons as copyists in my employment, and a promising lad as an office-boy. First, Turkey; second, Nippers; third, Ginger Nut. These may seem names, the like of which are not usually found in the Directory. In truth they were nicknames, mutually conferred upon each other by my three clerks, and were deemed expressive of their respective persons or characters. Turkey was a short, pursy Englishman of about my own age, that is, somewhere not far from sixty. In the morning, one might say, his face was of a fine florid hue, but after twelve o'clock, meridian—his dinner hour—it blazed like a grate full of Christmas coals; and continued blazing—but, as it were, with a gradual wane—till 6 o'clock, P.M. or thereabouts, after which I saw no more of the proprietor of the face, which gaining its meridian with the sun, seemed to set with it, to rise, culminate, and decline the following day, with the like regularity and undiminished glory. There are many singular coincidences I have known in the course of my life, not the least among which was the fact, that exactly when Turkey displayed his fullest beams from his red and radiant countenance, just then, too, at that critical moment, began the daily period when I considered his business capacities as seriously disturbed for the remainder of the twenty-four hours. Not that he was absolutely idle, or averse to business then; far from it. The difficulty was, he was apt to be altogether too energetic. There was a strange, inflamed, flurried, flighty recklessness of activity about him. He would be incautious in dipping his pen into his inkstand. All his blots upon my documents, were dropped there after twelve o'clock, meridian. Indeed, not only would he be reckless and sadly given to making blots in the afternoon, but some days he went further, and was rather noisy. At such times, too, his face flamed with augmented blazonry, as if cannel coal had been heaped on anthracite. He made an unpleasant racket with his chair; spilled his sandbox; in mending his pens, impatiently split them all to pieces, and threw them on the floor in a sudden passion; stood up and leaned over his table, boxing his papers about in a most indecorous manner, very sad to behold in an elderly man like him. Nevertheless, as he was in many ways a most valuable person to me, and all the time before twelve o'clock, meridian, was the quickest, steadiest creature too, accomplishing a great deal of work in a style not easy to be matched—for these reasons, I was willing to overlook his eccentricities, though indeed, occasionally, I remonstrated with him. I did this very gently, however, because, though the civilest, nay, the blandest and most reverential of men in the morning, yet in the afternoon he was disposed, upon provocation, to be slightly rash with his tongue, in fact, insolent. Now, valuing his morning services as I did, and resolved not to lose them; yet, at the same time made uncomfortable by his inflamed ways after twelve o'clock; and being a man of peace, unwilling by my admonitions to call forth unseemly retorts from him; I took upon me, one Saturday noon (he was always worse on Saturdays), to hint to him, very kindly, that perhaps now that he was growing old, it might be well to abridge his labors; in short, he need not come to my chambers after twelve o'clock, but, dinner over, had best go home to his lodgings and rest himself till tea-time. But no; he insisted upon his afternoon devotions. His countenance became intolerably fervid, as he oratorically assured me—gesticulating with a long ruler at the other end of the room—that if his services in the morning were useful, how indispensable, then, in the afternoon?

"With submission, sir," said Turkey on this occasion, "I consider myself your right-hand man. In the morning I but marshal and deploy my columns; but in the afternoon I put myself at their head, and gallantly charge the foe, thus!"—and he made a violent thrust with the ruler.

"But the blots, Turkey," intimated I.

"True,—but, with submission, sir, behold these hairs! I am getting old. Surely, sir, a blot or two of a warm afternoon is not to be severely urged against gray hairs. Old age—even if it blot the page—is honorable. With submission, sir, we *both* are getting old."

10   This appeal to my fellow-feeling was hardly to be resisted. At all events, I saw that go he would not. So I made up my mind to let him stay, resolving, nevertheless, to see to it, that during the afternoon he had to do with my less important papers.

Nippers, the second on my list, was a whiskered, sallow, and, upon the whole, rather piratical-looking young man of about five and twenty. I always deemed him the victim of two evil powers—ambition and indigestion. The ambition was evinced by a certain impatience of the duties of a mere copyist, an unwarrantable usurpation of strictly professional affairs, such as the original drawing up of legal documents. The indigestion seemed betokened in an occasional nervous testiness and grinning irritability, causing the teeth to audibly grind together over mistakes committed in copying; unnecessary maledictions, hissed, rather than spoken, in the heat of business; and especially by a continual discontent with the height of the table where he worked. Though of a very ingenious mechanical turn, Nippers could never get this table to suit him. He put chips under it, blocks of various sorts, bits of pasteboard, and at last went so far as to attempt an exquisite adjustment by final pieces of folded blotting-paper. But no invention would answer. If, for the sake of easing his back, he brought the table lid at a sharp angle well up towards his chin, and wrote there like a man using the steep roof of a Dutch house for his desk:—then he declared that it stopped the circulation in his arms. If now he lowered the table to his waistbands, and stooped over it in writing, then there was a sore aching in his back. In short, the truth of the matter was, Nippers knew not what he wanted. Or, if he wanted any thing, it was to be rid of a scrivener's table altogether. Among the manifestations of his diseased ambition was a fondness he had for receiving visits from certain ambiguous-looking fellows in seedy coats, whom he called his clients. Indeed I was aware that not only was he, at times, considerable of a ward-politician,[4] but he occasionally did a little business at the Justices' courts, and was not unknown on the steps of the

---

[4] Similar to an alderman or town councillor.

Tombs.[5] I have good reason to believe, however, that one individual who called upon him at my chambers, and who, with a grand air, he insisted was his client, was no other than a dun, and the alleged title-deed, a bill. But with all his failings, and the annoyances he caused me, Nippers, like his compatriot Turkey, was a very useful man to me; wrote a neat, swift hand; and, when he chose, was not deficient in a gentlemanly sort of deportment. Added to this, he always dressed in a gentlemanly sort of way; and so, incidentally, reflected credit upon my chambers. Whereas with respect to Turkey, I had much ado to keep him from being a reproach to me. His clothes were apt to look oily and smell of eating-houses. He wore his pantaloons very loose and baggy in summer. His coats were execrable; his hat not to be handled. But while the hat was a thing of indifference to me, inasmuch as his natural civility and deference, as a dependent Englishman, always led him to doff it the moment he entered the room, yet his coat was another matter. Concerning his coats, I reasoned with him; but with no effect. The truth was, I suppose, that a man with so small an income, could not afford to sport such a lustrous face and a lustrous coat at one and the same time. As Nippers once observed, Turkey's money went chiefly for red ink. One winter day I presented Turkey with a highly-respectable looking coat of my own, a padded gray coat, of a most comfortable warmth, and which buttoned straight up from the knee to the neck. I thought Turkey would appreciate the favor, and abate his rashness and obstreperousness of afternoons. But no. I verily believe that buttoning himself up in so downy and blanket-like a coat had a pernicious effect upon him; upon the same principle that too much oats are bad for horses. In fact, precisely as a rash, restive horse is said to feel his oats, so Turkey felt his coat. It made him insolent. He was a man whom prosperity harmed.

Though concerning the self-indulgent habits of Turkey I had my own private surmises, yet touching Nippers I was well persuaded that whatever might be his faults in other respects, he was, at least, a temperate young man. But indeed, nature herself seemed to have been his vintner, and at his birth charged him so thoroughly with an irritable, brandy-like disposition, that all subsequent potations were needless. When I consider how, amid the stillness of my chambers, Nippers would sometimes impatiently rise from his seat, and stooping over his table, spread his arms wide apart, seize the whole desk, and move it, and jerk it, with a grim, grinding motion on the floor, as if the table were a perverse voluntary agent, intent on thwarting and vexing him; I plainly perceive that for Nippers, brandy and water were altogether superfluous.

It was fortunate for me that, owing to its peculiar cause—indigestion— the irritability and consequent nervousness of Nippers, were mainly observable in the morning, while in the afternoon he was comparatively mild. So that Turkey's paroxysms only coming on about twelve o'clock, I never had to do with their eccentricities at one time. Their fits relieved each other like

---

[5] New York City prison.

guards. When Nippers's was on, Turkey's was off; and *vice versa*. This was a good natural arrangement under the circumstances.

Ginger Nut, the third on my list, was a lad some twelve years old. His father was a carman,[6] ambitious of seeing his son on the bench instead of a cart, before he died. So he sent him to my office as student at law, errand boy, and cleaner and sweeper, at the rate of one dollar a week. He had a little desk to himself, but he did not use it much. Upon inspection, the drawer exhibited a great array of the shells of various sorts of nuts. Indeed, to this quick-witted youth the whole noble science of the law was contained in a nut-shell. Not the least among the employments of Ginger Nut, as well as one which he discharged with the most alacrity, was his duty as cake and apple purveyor for Turkey and Nippers. Copying law papers being prover-bially a dry, husky sort of business, my two scriveners were fain to moisten their mouths very often with Spitzenbergs[7] to be had at the numerous stalls nigh the Custom House and Post Office. Also, they sent Ginger Nut very fre-quently for that peculiar cake—small, flat, round, and very spicy—after which he had been named by them. Of a cold morning when business was but dull, Turkey would gobble up scores of these cakes, as if they were mere wafers—indeed they sell them at the rate of six or eight for a penny—the scrape of his pen blending with the crunching of the crisp particles in his mouth. Of all the fiery afternoon blunders and flurried rashnesses of Turkey, was his once moistening a ginger-cake between his lips, and clapping it on to a mortgage for a seal. I came within an ace of dismissing him then. But he mollified me by making an oriental bow, and saying—"With submission, sir, it was generous of me to find you in stationery on my own account."

15   Now my original business—that of a conveyancer[8] and title hunter, and drawer-up of recondite documents of all sorts—was considerably increased by receiving the master's office. There was now great work for scriveners. Not only must I push the clerks already with me, but I must have additional help. In answer to my advertisement, a motionless young man one morning, stood upon my office threshold, the door being open, for it was summer. I can see that figure now—pallidly neat, pitiably respectable, incur-ably forlorn! It was Bartleby.

After a few words touching his qualifications, I engaged him, glad to have among my corps of copyists a man of so singularly sedate an aspect, which I thought might operate beneficially upon the flighty temper of Turkey, and the fiery one of Nippers.

    I should have stated before that ground glass folding-doors divided my premises into two parts, one of which was occupied by my scriveners, the other by myself. According to my humor I threw open these doors, or closed them. I resolved to assign Bartleby a corner by the folding-doors, but on my side of them, so as to have this quiet man within easy call, in case any

---

[6] Driver of a cart.

[7] Variety of apple.

[8] Person who prepares documents for property transfers.

trifling thing was to be done. I placed his desk close up to a small side-window in that part of the room, a window which originally had afforded a lateral view of certain grimy back-yards and bricks, but which, owing to subsequent erections, commanded at present no view at all, though it gave some light. Within three feet of the panes was a wall, and the light came down from far above, between two lofty buildings, as from a very small opening in a dome. Still further to a satisfactory arrangement, I procured a high green folding screen, which might entirely isolate Bartleby from my sight, though not remove him from my voice. And thus, in a manner, privacy and society were conjoined.

At first Bartleby did an extraordinary quantity of writing. As if long famishing for something to copy, he seemed to gorge himself on my documents. There was no pause for digestion. He ran a day and night line, copying by sun-light and by candle-light. I should have been quite delighted with his application, had he been cheerfully industrious. But he wrote on silently, palely, mechanically.

It is, of course, an indispensable part of a scrivener's business to verify the accuracy of his copy, word by word. Where there are two or more scriveners in an office, they assist each other in this examination, one reading from the copy, the other holding the original. It is a very dull, wearisome, and lethargic affair. I can readily imagine that to some sanguine temperaments it would be altogether intolerable. For example, I cannot credit that the mettlesome poet Byron[9] would have contentedly sat down with Bartleby to examine a law document of, say five hundred pages, closely written in a crimpy hand.

20   Now and then, in the haste of business, it had been my habit to assist in comparing some brief document myself, calling Turkey or Nippers for this purpose. One object I had in placing Bartleby so handy to me behind the screen, was to avail myself of his services on such trivial occasions. It was on the third day, I think, of his being with me, and before any necessity had arisen for having his own writing examined, that, being much hurried to complete a small affair I had in hand, I abruptly called to Bartleby. In my haste and natural expectancy of instant compliance, I sat with my head bent over the original on my desk, and my right hand sideways, and somewhat nervously extended with the copy, so that immediately upon emerging from his retreat, Bartleby might snatch it and proceed to business without the least delay.

In this very attitude did I sit when I called to him, rapidly stating what it was I wanted him to do—namely, to examine a small paper with me. Imagine my surprise, nay, my consternation, when without moving from his privacy, Bartleby in a singularly mild, firm voice, replied, "I would prefer not to."

---

[9] An English poet of the early nineteenth century, Byron was known for his flamboyant temperament.

I sat awhile in perfect silence, rallying my stunned faculties. Immediately it occurred to me that my ears had deceived me, or Bartleby had entirely misunderstood my meaning. I repeated my request in the clearest tone I could assume. But in quite as clear a one came the previous reply, "I would prefer not to."

"Prefer not to," echoed I, rising in high excitement, and crossing the room with a stride. "What do you mean? Are you moon-struck? I want you to help me compare this sheet here—take it," and I thrust it towards him.

"I would prefer not to," said he.

25   I looked at him steadfastly. His face was leanly composed; his gray eye dimly calm. Not a wrinkle of agitation rippled him. Had there been the least uneasiness, anger, impatience or impertinence in his manner; in other words, had there been any thing ordinarily human about him, doubtless I should have violently dismissed him from the premises. But as it was, I should have as soon thought of turning my pale plaster-of-paris bust of Cicero out of doors. I stood gazing at him awhile, as he went on with his own writing, and then reseated myself at my desk. This is very strange, thought I. What had one best do? But my business hurried me. I concluded to forget the matter for the present, reserving it for my future leisure. So calling Nippers from the other room, the paper was speedily examined.

A few days after this, Bartleby concluded four lengthy documents, being quadruplicates of a week's testimony taken before me in my High Court of Chancery. It became necessary to examine them. It was an important suit, and great accuracy was imperative. Having all things arranged I called Turkey, Nippers and Ginger Nut from the next room, meaning to place the four copies in the hands of my four clerks, while I should read from the original. Accordingly Turkey, Nippers and Ginger Nut had taken their seats in a row, each with his document in hand, when I called to Bartleby to join this interesting group.

"Bartleby! quick, I am waiting."

I heard a slow scrape of his chair legs on the uncarpeted floor, and soon he appeared standing at the entrance of his hermitage.

"What is wanted?" said he mildly.

30   "The copies, the copies," said I hurriedly. "We are going to examine them. There"—and I held towards him the fourth quadruplicate.

"I would prefer not to," he said, and gently disappeared behind the screen.

For a few moments I was turned into a pillar of salt,[10] standing at the head of my seated column of clerks. Recovering myself, I advanced towards the screen, and demanded the reason for such extraordinary conduct.

"*Why* do you refuse?"

"I would prefer not to."

---

[10] In Genesis 19, Lot's wife was turned into a pillar of salt for disobeying God's orders not to look at the evil city of Sodom, which He was destroying.

35   With any other man I should have flown outright into a dreadful passion, scorned all further words, and thrust him ignominiously from my presence. But there was something about Bartleby that not only strangely disarmed me, but in a wonderful manner touched and disconcerted me. I began to reason with him.

"These are your own copies we are about to examine. It is labor saving to you, because one examination will answer for your four papers. It is common usage. Every copyist is bound to help examine his copy. Is it not so? Will you not speak? Answer!"

"I prefer not to," he replied in a flute-like tone. It seemed to me that while I had been addressing him, he carefully revolved every statement that I made; fully comprehended the meaning; could not gainsay the irresistible conclusion; but, at the same time, some paramount consideration prevailed with him to reply as he did.

"You are decided, then, not to comply with my request—a request made according to common usage and common sense?"

He briefly gave me to understand that on that point my judgment was sound. Yes: his decision was irreversible.

40   It is not seldom the case that when a man is browbeaten in some unprecedented and violently unreasonable way, he begins to stagger in his own plainest faith. He begins, as it were, vaguely to surmise that, wonderful as it may be, all the justice and all the reason is on the other side. Accordingly, if any distinterested persons are present, he turns to them for some reinforcement for his own faltering mind.

"Turkey," said I, "what do you think of this? Am I not right?"

"With submission, sir," said Turkey, with his blandest tone, "I think that you are."

"Nippers," said I, "what do *you* think of it?"

"I think I should kick him out of the office."

45   (The reader of nice perceptions will here perceive that, it being morning, Turkey's answer is couched in polite and tranquil terms, but Nippers replies in ill-tempered ones. Or, to repeat a previous sentence, Nippers's ugly mood was on duty, and Turkey's off.)

"Ginger Nut," said I, willing to enlist the smallest suffrage in my behalf, "what do *you* think of it?"

"I think, sir, he's a little *luny*," replied Ginger Nut, with a grin.

"You hear what they say," said I, turning towards the screen, "come forth and do your duty."

But he vouchsafed no reply. I pondered a moment in sore perplexity. But once more business hurried me. I determined again to postpone the consideration of this dilemma to my future leisure. With a little trouble we made out to examine the papers without Bartleby, though at every page or two, Turkey deferentially dropped his opinion that this proceeding was quite out of the common; while Nippers, twitching in his chair with a dyspeptic nervousness, ground out between his set teeth occasional hissing maledictions against the stubborn oaf behind the screen. And for his (Nippers's) part, this was the first and the last time he would do another man's business without pay.

50   Meanwhile Bartleby sat in his hermitage, oblivious to every thing but his own peculiar business there.

Some days passed, the scrivener being employed upon another lengthy work. His late remarkable conduct led me to regard his ways narrowly. I observed that he never went to dinner; indeed that he never went any where. As yet I had never of my personal knowledge known him to be outside of my office. He was a perpetual sentry in the corner. At about eleven o'clock though, in the morning, I noticed that Ginger Nut would advance toward the opening in Bartleby's screen, as if silently beckoned thither by a gesture invisible to me where I sat. The boy would then leave the office jingling a few pence, and reappear with a handful of ginger-nuts which he delivered in the hermitage, receiving two of the cakes for his trouble.

He lives, then, on ginger-nuts, thought I; never eats a dinner, properly speaking; he must be a vegetarian then; but no; he never eats even vegetables, he eats nothing but ginger-nuts. My mind then ran on in reveries concerning the probable effects upon the human constitution of living entirely on ginger-nuts. Ginger-nuts are so called because they contain ginger as one of their peculiar constituents, and the final flavoring one. Now what was ginger? A hot, spicy thing. Was Bartleby hot and spicy? Not at all. Ginger, then, had no effect upon Bartleby. Probably he preferred it should have none.

Nothing so aggravates an earnest person as a passive resistance. If the individual so resisted be of a not inhumane temper, and the resisting one perfectly harmless in his passivity; then, in the better moods of the former, he will endeavor charitably to construe to his imagination what proves impossible to be solved by his judgment. Even so, for the most part, I regarded Bartleby and his ways. Poor fellow! thought I, he means no mischief; it is plain he intends no insolence; his aspect sufficiently evinces that his eccentricities are involuntary. He is useful to me. I can get along with him. If I turn him away, the chances are he will fall in with some less indulgent employer, and then he will be rudely treated, and perhaps driven forth miserably to starve. Yes. Here I can cheaply purchase a delicious self-approval. To befriend Bartleby; to humor him in his strange wilfulness, will cost me little or nothing, while I lay up in my soul what will eventually prove a sweet morsel for my conscience. But this mood was not invariable with me. The passiveness of Bartleby sometimes irritated me. I felt strangely goaded on to encounter him in new opposition, to elicit some angry spark from him answerable to my own. But indeed I might as well have essayed to strike fire with my knuckles against a bit of Windsor soap.[11] But one afternoon the evil impulse in me mastered me, and the following little scene ensued:

---

[11] Brown-coloured, scented soap.

"Bartleby," said I, "when those papers are all copied, I will compare them with you."

55   "I would prefer not to."

"How? Surely you do not mean to persist in that mulish vagary?"

No answer.

I threw open the folding-doors near by, and turning upon Turkey and Nippers, exclaimed:

"Bartleby a second time says, he won't examine his papers. What do you think of it, Turkey?"

60   It was afternoon, be it remembered. Turkey sat glowing like a brass boiler, his bald head steaming, his hands reeling among his blotted papers.

"Think of it?" roared Turkey; "I think I'll just step behind his screen, and black his eyes for him!"

So saying, Turkey rose to his feet and threw his arms into a pugilistic position. He was hurrying away to make good his promise, when I detained him, alarmed at the effect of incautiously rousing Turkey's combativeness after dinner.

"Sit down, Turkey," said I, "and hear what Nippers has to say. What do you think of it, Nippers? Would I not be justified in immediately dismissing Bartleby?"

"Excuse me, that is for you to decide, sir. I think his conduct quite unusual, and indeed unjust, as regards Turkey and myself. But it may only be a passing whim."

65   "Ah," exclaimed I, "you have strangely changed your mind then—you speak very gently of him now."

"All beer," cried Turkey; "gentleness is effects of beer—Nippers and I dined together to-day. You see how gentle *I* am, sir. Shall I go and black his eyes?"

"You refer to Bartleby, I suppose. No, not to-day, Turkey," I replied; "pray, put up your fists."

I closed the doors, and again advanced towards Bartleby. I felt additional incentives tempting me to my fate. I burned to be rebelled against again. I remembered that Bartleby never left the office.

"Bartleby," said I, "Ginger Nut is away; just step round to the Post Office, won't you? (it was but a three minutes' walk,) and see if there is any thing for me."

70   "I would prefer not to."

"You *will* not?"

"I *prefer* not."

I staggered to my desk, and sat there in a deep study. My blind invet-eracy returned. Was there any other thing in which I could procure myself to be ignominiously repulsed by this lean, penniless wight?—my hired clerk? What added thing is there, perfectly reasonable, that he will be sure to refuse to do?

"Bartleby!"

75   No answer.

"Bartleby," in a louder tone.

No answer.

"Bartleby," I roared.

Like a very ghost, agreeably to the laws of magical invocation, at the third summons, he appeared at the entrance of his hermitage.

80   "Go to the next room, and tell Nippers to come to me."

"I prefer not to," he respectfully and slowly said, and mildly disappeared.

"Very good, Bartleby," said I, in a quiet sort of serenely severe self-possessed tone, intimating the unalterable purpose of some terrible retribution very close at hand. At the moment I half intended something of the kind. But upon the whole, as it was drawing towards my dinner-hour, I thought it best to put on my hat and walk home for the day, suffering much from perplexity and distress of mind.

Shall I acknowledge it? The conclusion of this whole business was, that it soon became a fixed fact of my chambers, that a pale young scrivener, by the name of Bartleby, had a desk there; that he copied for me at the usual rate of four cents a folio (one hundred words); but he was permanently exempt from examining the work done by him, that duty being transferred to Turkey and Nippers, out of compliment doubtless to their superior acuteness; moreover, said Bartleby was never on any account to be dispatched on the most trivial errand of any sort; and that even if entreated to take upon him such a matter, it was generally understood that he would prefer not to— in other words, that he would refuse point-blank.

As days passed on, I became considerably reconciled to Bartleby. His steadiness, his freedom from all dissipation, his incessant industry (except when he chose to throw himself into a standing revery behind his screen), his great stillness, his unalterableness of demeanor under all circumstances, made him a valuable acquisition. One prime thing was this,—*he was always there;*—first in the morning, continually through the day, and the last at night. I had a singular confidence in his honesty. I felt my most precious papers perfectly safe in his hands. Sometimes to be sure I could not, for the very soul of me, avoid falling into sudden spasmodic passions with him. For it was exceeding difficult to bear in mind all the time those strange peculiarities, privileges, and unheard of exemptions, forming the tacit stipulations on Bartleby's part under which he remained in my office. Now and then, in the eagerness of dispatching pressing business, I would inadvertently summon Bartleby, in a short, rapid tone, to put his finger, say, on the incipient tie of a bit of red tape with which I was about compressing some papers. Of course, from behind the screen the usual answer, "I prefer not to," was sure to come; and then, how could a human creature with the common infirmities of our nature, refrain from bitterly exclaiming upon such perverseness—such unreasonableness. However, every added repulse of this sort which I received only tended to lessen the probability of my repeating the inadvertence.

85   Here it must be said, that according to the custom of most legal gentlemen occupying chambers in densely populated law buildings, there were

several keys to my door. One was kept by a woman residing in the attic, which person weekly scrubbed and daily swept and dusted my apartments. Another was kept by Turkey for convenience sake. The third I sometimes carried in my own pocket. The fourth I knew not who had.

Now, one Sunday morning I happened to go to Trinity Church, to hear a celebrated preacher, and finding myself rather early on the ground, I thought I would walk round to my chambers for a while. Luckily I had my key with me; but upon applying it to the lock, I found it resisted by something inserted from the inside. Quite surprised, I called out; when to my consternation a key was turned from within; and thrusting his lean visage at me, and holding the door ajar, the apparition of Bartleby appeared, in his shirt sleeves, and otherwise in a strangely tattered dishabille, saying quietly that he was sorry, but he was deeply engaged just then, and—preferred not admitting me at present. In a brief word or two, he moreover added, that perhaps I had better walk round the block two or three times, and by that time he would probably have concluded his affairs.

Now, the utterly unsurmised appearance of Bartleby, tenanting my law-chambers of a Sunday morning, with his cadaverously gentlemanly nonchalance, yet withal firm and self-possessed, had such a strange effect upon me, that incontinently I slunk away from my own door, and did as desired. But not without sundry twinges of impotent rebellion against the mild effrontery of this unaccountable scrivener. Indeed, it was his wonderful mildness chiefly, which not only disarmed me, but unmanned me, as it were. For I consider that one, for the time, is a sort of unmanned when he tranquilly permits his hired clerk to dictate to him, and order him away from his own premises. Furthermore, I was full of uneasiness as to what Bartleby could possibly be doing in my office in his shirt sleeves, and in an otherwise dismantled condition of a Sunday morning. Was any thing amiss going on? Nay, that was out of the question. It was not to be thought of for a moment that Bartleby was an immoral person. But what could he be doing there?—copying? Nay again, whatever might be his eccentricities, Bartleby was an eminently decorous person. He would be the last man to sit down to his desk in any state approaching to nudity. Besides, it was Sunday; and there was something about Bartleby that forbade the supposition that he would by any secular occupation violate the proprieties of the day.

Nevertheless, my mind was not pacified; and full of a restless curiosity, at last I returned to the door. Without hindrance I inserted my key, opened it, and entered. Bartleby was not to be seen. I looked round anxiously, peeped behind his screen; but it was very plain that he was gone. Upon more closely examining the place, I surmised that for an indefinite period Bartleby must have ate, dressed, and slept in my office, and that too without plate, mirror, or bed. The cushioned seat of a ricketty old sofa in one corner bore the faint impress of a lean, reclining form. Rolled away under his desk, I found a blanket; under the empty grate, a blacking box and brush; on a chair, a tin basin, with soap and a ragged towel; in a newspaper a few crumbs of ginger-nuts and a morsel of cheese. Yes, thought I, it is evident enough that Bartleby has been making his home here, keeping bachelor's hall all by himself. Immediately then the thought came sweeping across me, What miserable friendlessness and loneliness are here revealed! His poverty is great; but his solitude, how horrible! Think of it. Of a Sunday, Wall-street is deserted as Petra;[12] and every night of every day it is an emptiness. This building too, which of week-days hums with industry and life, at nightfall echoes with sheer vacancy, and all through Sunday is forlorn. And here Bartleby makes his home; sole spectator of a solitude which he has seen all populous—a sort of innocent and transformed Marius[13] brooding among the ruins of Carthage![14]

For the first time in my life a feeling of overpowering stinging melancholy seized me. Before, I had never experienced aught but a not-unpleasing sadness. The bond of a common humanity now drew me irresistibly to gloom. A fraternal melancholy! For both I and Bartleby were sons of Adam. I remembered the bright silks and sparkling faces I had seen that day, in gala trim, swan-like sailing down the Mississippi of Broadway; and I contrasted them with the pallid copyist, and thought to myself, Ah, happiness courts the light, so we deem the world is gay; but misery hides aloof, so we deem that misery there is none. These sad fancyings—chimeras, doubtless, of a sick and silly brain—led on to other and more special thoughts, concerning the eccentricities of Bartleby. Presentiments of strange discoveries hovered round me. The scrivener's pale form appeared to me laid out, among uncaring strangers, in its shivering winding sheet.

90   Suddenly I was attracted by Bartleby's closed desk, the key in open sight left in the lock.

I mean no mischief, seek the gratification of no heartless curiosity, thought I; besides, the desk is mine, and its contents too, so I will make bold to look within. Every thing was methodically arranged, the papers smoothly placed. The pigeon holes were deep, and removing the files of documents, I groped into their recesses. Presently I felt something there, and dragged it out. It was an old bandanna handkerchief, heavy and knotted. I opened it, and saw it was a savings' bank.

I now recalled all the quiet mysteries which I had noted in the man. I remembered that he never spoke but to answer; that though at intervals he had considerable time to himself, yet I had never seen him reading—no, not even a newspaper; that for long periods he would stand looking out, at his pale window behind the screen, upon the dead brick wall; I was quite sure he never visited any refectory or eating house; while his pale face clearly indicated that he never drank beer like Turkey, or tea and coffee even, like other men; that he never went any where in particular that I could learn; never went out for a walk, unless indeed that was the case at present; that he had declined telling who he was, or whence he came, or whether he had

---

[12] Destroyed and abandoned city in North Africa.

[13] Roman military commander who fled to Africa in the first century B.C.

[14] North African city destroyed by the Romans in the second century B.C.

any relatives in the world; that though so thin and pale, he never complained of ill health. And more than all, I remembered a certain unconscious air of pallid—how shall I call it?—of pallid haughtiness, say, or rather an austere reserve about him, which had positively awed me into my tame compliance with his eccentricities, when I had feared to ask him to do the slightest incidental thing for me, even though I might know, from his long-continued motionlessness, that behind his screen he must be standing in one of those dead-wall reveries of his.

Revolving all these things, and coupling them with the recently discovered fact that he made my office his constant abiding place and home, and not forgetful of his morbid moodiness; revolving all these things, a prudential feeling began to steal over me. My first emotions had been those of pure melancholy and sincerest pity; but just in proportion as the forlornness of Bartleby grew and grew to my imagination, did that same melancholy merge into fear, that pity into repulsion. So true it is, and so terrible too, that up to a certain point the thought or sight of misery enlists our best affections; but, in certain special cases, beyond that point it does not. They err who would assert that invariably this is owing to the inherent selfishness of the human heart. It rather proceeds from a certain hopelessness of remedying excessive and organic ill. To a sensitive being, pity is not seldom pain. And when at last it is perceived that such pity cannot lead to effectual succor, common sense bids the soul be rid of it. What I saw that morning persuaded me that the scrivener was the victim of innate and incurable disorder. I might give alms to his body; but his body did not pain him; it was his soul that suffered, and his soul I could not reach.

I did not accomplish the purpose of going to Trinity Church that morning. Somehow, the things I had seen disqualified me for the time from church-going. I walked homeward, thinking what I would do with Bartleby. Finally, I resolved upon this:—I would put certain calm questions to him the next morning, touching his history, &c., and if he declined to answer them openly and unreservedly (and I supposed he would prefer not), then to give him a twenty dollar bill over and above whatever I might owe him, and tell him his services were no longer required; but that if in any other way I could assist him, I would be happy to do so, especially if he desired to return to his native place, wherever that might be, I would willingly help to defray the expenses. Moreover, if, after reaching home, he found himself at any time in want of aid, a letter from him would be sure of a reply.

95 The next morning came.

"Bartleby," said I, gently calling to him behind his screen.

No reply.

"Bartleby," said I, in a still gentler tone, "come here; I am not going to ask you to do any thing you would prefer not to do—I simply wish to speak to you."

Upon this he noiselessly slid into view.

100 "Will you tell me, Bartleby, where you were born?"

"I would prefer not to."

"Will you tell me *any thing* about yourself?"

"I would prefer not to."

"But what reasonable objection can you have to speak to me? I feel friendly towards you."

105   He did not look at me while I spoke, but kept his glance fixed upon my bust of Cicero,[15] which as I then sat, was directly behind me, some six inches above my head.

"What is your answer, Bartleby?" said I, after waiting a considerable time for a reply, during which his countenance remained immovable, only there was the faintest conceivable tremor of the white attenuated mouth.

"At present I prefer to give no answer," he said, and retired into his hermitage.

It was rather weak in me I confess, but his manner on this occasion nettled me. Not only did there seem to lurk in it a certain calm disdain, but his perverseness seemed ungrateful, considering the undeniable good usage and indulgence he had received from me.

Again I sat ruminating what I should do. Mortified as I was at his behavior, and resolved as I had been to dismiss him when I entered my office, nevertheless I strangely felt something superstitious knocking at my heart, and forbidding me to carry out my purpose, and denouncing me for a villain if I dared to breathe one bitter word against this forlornest of mankind. At last, familiarly drawing my chair behind his screen, I sat down and said: "Bartleby, never mind then about revealing your history; but let me entreat you as a friend, to comply as far as may be with the usages of this office. Say now you will help to examine papers to-morrow or next day: in short, say now that in a day or two you will begin to be a little reasonable:— say so, Bartleby."

110   "At present I would prefer not to be a little reasonable," was his mildly cadaverous reply.

Just then the folding-doors opened, and Nippers approached. He seemed suffering from an unusually bad night's rest, induced by severer indigestion than common. He overheard those final words of Bartleby.

"*Prefer not,* eh?" gritted Nippers—"I'd *prefer* him, if I were you, sir," addressing me—"I'd *prefer* him; I'd give him preferences, the stubborn mule! What is it, sir, pray, that he *prefers* not to do now?"

Bartleby moved not a limb.

"Mr. Nippers," said I, "I'd prefer that you would withdraw for the present."

115   Somehow, of late I had got into the way of involuntarily using this word "prefer" upon all sorts of not exactly suitable occasions. And I trembled to think that my contact with the scrivener had already and seriously affected me in a mental way. And what further and deeper aberration might it not

---

[15] Renowned Roman orator of the first century B.C.

yet produce? This apprehension had not been without efficacy in deter-mining me to summary measures.

As Nippers, looking very sour and sulky, was departing, Turkey blandly and deferentially approached.

"With submission, sir," said he, "yesterday I was thinking about Bartleby here, and I think that if he would but prefer to take a quart of good ale every day, it would do much towards mending him, and enabling him to assist in examining his papers."

"So you have got the word too," said I, slightly excited.

"With submission, what word, sir?" asked Turkey, respectfully crowding himself into the contracted space behind the screen, and by so doing, making me jostle the scrivener. "What word, sir?"

120   "I would prefer to be left alone here," said Bartleby, as if offended at being mobbed in his privacy.

"*That's* the word, Turkey," said I—"*that's* it."

"Oh, *prefer?* oh yes—queer word. I never use it myself. But, sir, as I was saying, if he would but prefer—"

"Turkey," interrupted I, "you will please withdraw."

"Oh certainly, sir, if you prefer that I should."

125   As he opened the folding-doors to retire, Nippers at his desk caught a glimpse of me, and asked whether I would prefer to have a certain paper copied on blue paper or white. He did not in the least roguishly accent the word prefer. It was plain that it involuntarily rolled from his tongue. I thought to myself, surely I must get rid of a demented man, who already has in some degree turned the tongues, if not the heads of myself and clerks. But I thought it prudent not to break the dismission at once.

The next day I noticed that Bartleby did nothing but stand at his window in his dead-wall revery. Upon asking him why he did not write, he said that he had decided upon doing no more writing.

"Why, how now? what next?" exclaimed I, "do no more writing?"

"No more."

"And what is the reason?"

130   "Do you not see the reason for yourself?" he indifferently replied.

I looked steadfastly at him, and perceived that his eyes looked dull and glazed. Instantly it occurred to me, that his unexampled diligence in copying by his dim window for the first few weeks of his stay with me might have temporarily impaired his vision.

I was touched. I said something in condolence with him. I hinted that of course he did wisely in abstaining from writing for a while; and urged him to embrace that opportunity of taking wholesome exercise in the open air. This, however, he did not do. A few days after this, my other clerks being absent, and being in a great hurry to dispatch certain letters by the mail, I thought that, having nothing else earthly to do, Bartleby would surely be less inflexible than usual, and carry these letters to the post-office. But he blankly declined. So, much to my inconvenience, I went myself.

Still added days went by. Whether Bartleby's eyes improved or not, I could not say. To all appearance, I thought they did. But when I asked him if they did, he vouchsafed no answer. At all events, he would do no copying. At last, in reply to my urgings, he informed me that he had permanently given up copying.

"What!" exclaimed I; "suppose your eyes should get entirely well—better than ever before—would you not copy then?"

135　　"I have given up copying," he answered, and slid aside.

He remained as ever, a fixture in my chamber. Nay—if that were possible—he became still more of a fixture than before. What was to be done? He would do nothing in the office: why should he stay there? In plain fact, he had now become a millstone to me, not only useless as a necklace, but afflictive to bear. Yet I was sorry for him. I speak less than truth when I say that, on his own account, he occasioned me uneasiness. If he would but have named a single relative or friend, I would instantly have written, and urged their taking the poor fellow away to some convenient retreat. But he seemed alone, absolutely alone in the universe. A bit of wreck in the mid Atlantic. At length, necessities connected with my business tyrannized over all other considerations. Decently as I could, I told Bartleby that in six days' time he must unconditionally leave the office. I warned him to take measures, in the interval, for procuring some other abode. I offered to assist him in this endeavor, if he himself would but take the first step towards a removal. "And when you finally quit me, Bartleby," added I, "I shall see that you go not away entirely unprovided. Six days from this hour, remember."

At the expiration of that period, I peeped behind the screen, and lo! Bartleby was there.

I buttoned up my coat, balanced myself; advanced slowly towards him, touched his shoulder, and said, "The time has come; you must quit this place; I am sorry for you; here is money, but you must go."

"I would prefer not," he replied, with his back still towards me.

140　　"You *must*."

He remained silent.

Now I had an unbounded confidence in this man's common honesty. He had frequently restored to me sixpences and shillings carelessly dropped upon the floor, for I am apt to be very reckless in such shirt-button affairs. The proceeding then which followed will not be deemed extraordinary.

"Bartleby," said I, "I owe you twelve dollars on account; here are thirty-two; the odd twenty are yours.—Will you take it?" and I handed the bills towards him.

But he made no motion.

145　　"I will leave them here then," putting them under a weight on the table. Then taking my hat and cane and going to the door I tranquilly turned and added—"After you have removed your things from these offices, Bartleby, you will of course lock the door—since every one is now gone for the day but you—and if you please, slip your key underneath the mat, so that I may have it in the morning. I shall not see you again; so good-bye to you. If hereafter in your new place of abode I can be of any service to you, do not fail to advise me by letter. Good-bye, Bartleby, and fare you well."

But he answered not a word; like the last column of some ruined temple, he remained standing mute and solitary in the middle of the otherwise deserted room.

As I walked home in a pensive mood, my vanity got the better of my pity. I could not but highly plume myself on my masterly management in getting rid of Bartleby. Masterly I call it, and such it must appear to any dispassionate thinker. The beauty of my procedure seemed to consist in its perfect quietness. There was no vulgar bullying, no bravado of any sort, no choleric hectoring, and striding to and fro across the apartment, jerking out vehement commands for Bartleby to bundle himself off with his beggarly traps. Nothing of the kind. Without loudly bidding Bartleby depart—as an inferior genius might have done—I *assumed* the ground that depart he must; and upon that assumption built all I had to say. The more I thought over my procedure, the more I was charmed with it. Nevertheless, next morning, upon awakening, I had my doubts,—I had somehow slept off the fumes of vanity. One of the coolest and wisest hours a man has, is just after he wakes in the morning. My procedure seemed as sagacious as ever,—but only in theory. How it would prove in practice—there was the rub. It was truly a beautiful thought to have assumed Bartleby's departure; but, after all, that assumption was simply my own, and none of Bartleby's. The great point was, not whether I had assumed that he would quit me, but whether he would prefer so to do. He was more a man of preferences than assumptions.

After breakfast, I walked down town, arguing the probabilities *pro* and *con.* One moment I thought it would prove a miserable failure, and Bartleby would be found all alive at my office as usual; the next moment it seemed certain that I should find his chair empty. And so I kept veering about. At the corner of Broadway and Canal-street, I saw quite an excited group of people standing in earnest conversation.

"I'll take odds he doesn't," said a voice as I passed.

150   "Doesn't go?—done!" said I, "put up your money."

I was instinctively putting my hand in my pocket to produce my own, when I remembered that this was an election day. The words I had overheard bore no reference to Bartleby, but to the success or non-success of some candidate for the mayoralty. In my intent frame of mind, I had, as it were, imagined that all Broadway shared in my excitement, and were debating the same question with me. I passed on, very thankful that the uproar of the street screened my momentary absent-mindedness.

As I had intended, I was earlier than usual at my office door. I stood listening for a moment. All was still. He must be gone. I tried the knob. The door was locked. Yes, my procedure had worked to a charm; he indeed must be vanished. Yet a certain melancholy mixed with this: I was almost sorry for my brilliant success. I was fumbling under the door mat for the key, which Bartleby was to have left there for me, when accidentally my knee knocked against a panel, producing a summoning sound, and in response a voice came to me from within—"Not yet; I am occupied."

It was Bartleby.

I was thunderstruck. For an instant I stood like the man who, pipe in mouth, was killed one cloudless afternoon long ago in Virginia, by summer lightning; at his own warm open window he was killed, and remained leaning out there upon the dreamy afternoon, till some one touched him, when he fell.

155 "Not gone!" I murmured at last. But again obeying that wondrous ascendancy which the inscrutable scrivener had over me, and from which ascendancy, for all my chafing, I could not completely escape, I slowly went down stairs and out into the street, and while walking round the block, considered what I should next do in this unheard-of perplexity. Turn the man out by an actual thrusting I could not; to drive him away by calling him hard names would not do; calling in the police was an unpleasant idea; and yet, permit him to enjoy his cadaverous triumph over me,—this too I could not think of. What was to be done? or, if nothing could be done, was there any thing further that I could *assume* in the matter? Yes, as before I had prospectively assumed that Bartleby would depart, so now I might retrospectively assume that departed he was. In the legitimate carrying out of this assumption, I might enter my office in a great hurry, and pretending not to see Bartleby at all, walk straight against him as if he were air. Such a proceeding would in a singular degree have the appearance of a home-thrust. It was hardly possible that Bartleby could withstand such an application of the doctrine of assumptions. But upon second thoughts the success of the plan seemed rather dubious. I resolved to argue the matter over with him again.

"Bartleby," said I, entering the office, with a quietly severe expression, "I am seriously displeased. I am pained, Bartleby. I had thought better of you. I had imagined you of such a gentlemanly organization, that in any delicate dilemma a slight hint would suffice—in short, an assumption. But it appears I am deceived. Why," I added, unaffectedly starting, "you have not even touched that money yet," pointing to it, just where I had left it the evening previous.

He answered nothing.

"Will you, or will you not, quit me?" I now demanded in a sudden passion, advancing close to him.

"I would prefer *not* to quit you," he replied, gently emphasizing the not.

160 "What earthly right have you to stay here? Do you pay any rent? Do you pay my taxes? Or is this property yours?"

He answered nothing.

"Are you ready to go on and write now? Are your eyes recovered? Could you copy a small paper for me this morning? or help examine a few lines? or step round to the post-office? In a word, will you do any thing at all, to give a coloring to your refusal to depart the premises?"

He silently retired into his hermitage.

I was now in such a state of nervous resentment that I thought it but prudent to check myself at present from further demonstrations. Bartleby and I were alone. I remembered the tragedy of the unfortunate Adams and the still more unfortunate Colt[16] in the solitary office of the latter; and how poor Colt, being dreadfully incensed by Adams, and imprudently permitting himself to get wildly excited, was at unawares hurried into his fatal act—an act which certainly no man could possibly deplore more than the actor himself. Often it had occurred to me in my ponderings upon the subject, that had that altercation taken place in the public street, or at a private residence, it would not have terminated as it did. It was the circumstance of being alone in a solitary office, up stairs, of a building entirely unhallowed by humanizing domestic associations—an uncarpeted office, doubtless, of a dusty, haggard sort of appearance;—this it must have been, which greatly helped to enhance the irritable desperation of the hapless Colt.

165   But when this old Adam[17] of resentment rose in me and tempted me concerning Bartleby, I grappled him and threw him. How? Why, simply by recalling the divine injunction: "A new commandment give I unto you, that ye love one another." Yes, this it was that saved me. Aside from higher considerations, charity often operates as a vastly wise and prudent principle—a great safeguard to its possessor. Men have committed murder for jealousy's sake, and anger's sake, and hatred's sake, and selfishness' sake, and spiritual pride's sake; but no man that ever I heard of, ever committed a diabolical murder for sweet charity's sake. Mere self-interest, then, if no better motive can be enlisted, should, especially with high-tempered men, prompt all beings to charity and philanthropy. At any rate, upon the occasion in question, I strove to drown my exasperated feelings towards the scrivener by benevolently construing his conduct. Poor fellow, poor fellow! thought I, he don't mean any thing; and besides, he has seen hard times, and ought to be indulged.

I endeavored also immediately to occupy myself, and at the same time to comfort my despondency. I tried to fancy that in the course of the morning, at such time as might prove agreeable to him, Bartleby, of his own free accord, would emerge from his hermitage, and take up some decided line of march in the direction of the door. But no. Half-past twelve o'clock came; Turkey began to glow in the face, overturn his inkstand, and become generally obstreperous; Nippers abated down into quietude and courtesy; Ginger Nut munched his noon apple; and Bartleby remained standing at his window in one of his profoundest dead-wall reveries. Will it be credited? Ought I to acknowledge it? That afternoon I left the office without saying one further word to him.

---

[16] Samuel Adams was killed in 1841 in a fight with John Colt, a brother of the manufacturer of guns.

[17] Reference to the biblical first man, whose temperament was believed to have been passed on to all the human race.

Some days now passed, during which, at leisure intervals I looked a little into "Edwards on the Will,"[18] and "Priestley on Necessity."[19] Under the circumstances, those books induced a salutary feeling. Gradually I slid into the persuasion that these troubles of mine touching the scrivener, had been all predestinated from eternity, and Bartleby was billeted upon me for some mysterious purpose of an all-wise Providence, which it was not for a mere mortal like me to fathom. Yes, Bartleby, stay there behind your screen, thought I; I shall persecute you no more; you are harmless and noiseless as any of these old chairs; in short, I never feel so private as when I know you are here. At last I see it, I feel it; I penetrate to the predestinated purpose of my life. I am content. Others may have loftier parts to enact; but my mission in this world, Bartleby, is to furnish you with office-room for such period as you may see fit to remain.

I believe that this wise and blessed frame of mind would have continued with me, had it not been for the unsolicited and uncharitable remarks obtruded upon me by my professional friends who visited the rooms. But thus it often is, that the constant friction of illiberal minds wears out at last the best resolves of the more generous. Though to be sure, when I reflected upon it, it was not strange that people entering my office should be struck by the peculiar aspect of the unaccountable Bartleby, and so be tempted to throw out some sinister observations concerning him. Sometimes an attorney having business with me, and calling at my office, and finding no one but the scrivener there, would undertake to obtain some sort of precise information from him touching my whereabouts; but without heeding his idle talk, Bartleby would remain standing immovable in the middle of the room. So after contemplating him in that position for a time, the attorney would depart, no wiser than he came.

Also, when a Reference[20] was going on, and the room full of lawyers and witnesses and business was driving fast; some deeply occupied legal gentleman present, seeing Bartleby wholly unemployed, would request him to run round to his (the legal gentleman's) office and fetch some papers for him. Thereupon, Bartleby would tranquilly decline, and yet remain idle as before. Then the lawyer would give a great stare, and turn to me. And what could I say? At last I was made aware that all through the circle of my professional acquaintance, a whisper of wonder was running round, having reference to the strange creature I kept at my office. This worried me very much. And as the idea came upon me of his possibly turning out a long-lived man, and keep occupying my chambers, and denying my authority; and perplexing my visitors; and scandalizing my professional reputation; and casting a general gloom over the premises; keeping soul and body

---

[18] Eighteenth-century American philosopher who believed that human beings' will was controlled by God.

[19] Eighteenth-century English philosopher who believed that, to prevent revolution, rulers should act in the interests of those they govern.

[20] Legal hearing in which two parties submit their differences to an arbitrator.

together to the last upon his savings (for doubtless he spent but half a dime a day), and in the end perhaps outlive me, and claim possession of my office by right of his perpetual occupancy: as all these dark anticipations crowded upon me more and more, and my friends continually intruded their relentless remarks upon the apparition in my room, a great change was wrought in me. I resolved to gather all my faculties together, and for ever rid me of this intolerable incubus.

170   Ere revolving any complicated project, however, adapted to this end, I first simply suggested to Bartleby the propriety of his permanent departure. In a calm and serious tone, I commended the idea to his careful and mature consideration. But having taken three days to meditate upon it, he apprised me that his original determination remained the same; in short, that he still preferred to abide with me.

What shall I do? I now said to myself, buttoning up my coat to the last button. What shall I do? what ought I to do? what does conscience say I *should* do with this man, or rather ghost? Rid myself of him, I must; go, he shall. But how? You will not thrust him, the poor, pale, passive mortal,—you will not thrust such a helpless creature out of your door? you will not dishonor yourself by such cruelty? No, I will not, I cannot do that. Rather would I let him live and die here, and then mason up his remains in the wall. What then will you do? For all your coaxing, he will not budge. Bribes he leaves under your own paper-weight on your table; in short, it is quite plain that he prefers to cling to you.

Then something severe, something unusual must be done. What! surely you will not have him collared by a constable, and commit his innocent pallor to the common jail? And upon what ground could you procure such a thing to be done?—a vagrant, is he? What! he a vagrant, a wanderer, who refuses to budge? It is because he will *not* be a vagrant, then, that you seek to count him *as* a vagrant. That is too absurd. No visible means of support: there I have him. Wrong again: for undubitably he *does* support himself, and that is the only unanswerable proof that any man can show of his possessing the means so to do. No more then. Since he will not quit me, I must quit him. I will change my offices; I will move elsewhere; and give him fair notice, that if I find him on my new premises I will then proceed against him as a common trespasser.

Acting accordingly, next day I thus addressed him: "I find these chambers too far from the City Hall; the air is unwholesome. In a word, I propose to remove my offices next week, and shall no longer require your services. I tell you this now, in order that you may seek another place."

He made no reply, and nothing more was said.

175   On the appointed day I engaged carts and men, proceeded to my chambers, and having but little furniture, every thing was removed in a few hours. Throughout, the scrivener remained standing behind the screen, which I directed to be removed the last thing. It was withdrawn; and being folded up like a huge folio, left him the motionless occupant of a naked

room. I stood in the entry watching him a moment, while something from within me upbraided me.

I re-entered, with my hand in my pocket—and—and my heart in my mouth.

"Good-bye, Bartleby; I am going—good-bye, and God some way bless you; and take that," slipping something in his hand. But it dropped upon the floor, and then,—strange to say—I tore myself from him whom I had so longed to be rid of.

Established in my new quarters, for a day or two I kept the door locked, and started at every footfall in the passages. When I returned to my rooms after any little absence, I would pause at the threshold for an instant, and attentively listen, ere applying my key. But these fears were needless. Bartleby never came nigh me.

I thought all was going well, when a perturbed looking stranger visited me, inquiring whether I was the person who had recently occupied rooms at No.— Wall-street.

180   Full of forebodings, I replied that I was.

"Then sir," said the stranger, who proved a lawyer, "you are responsible for the man you left there. He refuses to do any copying; he refuses to do any thing; he says he prefers not to; and he refuses to quit the premises."

"I am very sorry, sir" said I, with assumed tranquillity, but an inward tremor, "but, really, the man you allude to is nothing to me—he is no relation or apprentice of mine, that you should hold me responsible for him."

"In mercy's name, who is he?"

"I certainly cannot inform you. I know nothing about him. Formerly I employed him as a copyist; but he has done nothing for me now for some time past."

185   "I shall settle him then,—good morning, sir."

Several days passed, and I heard nothing more; and though I often felt a charitable prompting to call at the place and see poor Bartleby, yet a certain squeamishness of I know not what withheld me.

All is over with him, by this time, thought I at last, when through another week no further intelligence reached me. But coming to my room the day after, I found several persons waiting at my door in a high state of nervous excitement.

"That's the man—here he comes," cried the foremost one, whom I recognized as the lawyer who had previously called upon me alone.

"You must take him away, sir, at once," cried a portly person among them, advancing upon me, and whom I knew to be the landlord of No.— Wall-street. "These gentlemen, my tenants, cannot stand it any longer; Mr. B——," pointing to the lawyer, "has turned him out of his room, and he now persists in haunting the building generally, sitting upon the banisters of the stairs by day, and sleeping in the entry by night. Every body is concerned; clients are leaving the offices; some fears are entertained of a mob; something you must do, and that without delay."

190 Aghast at this torrent, I fell back before it, and would fain have locked myself in my new quarters. In vain I persisted that Bartleby was nothing to me—no more than to any one else. In vain:—I was the last person known to have any thing to do with him, and they held me to the terrible account. Fearful then of being exposed in the papers (as one person present obscurely threatened) I considered the matter, and at length said, that if the lawyer would give me a confidential interview with the scrivener, in his (the lawyer's) own room, I would that afternoon strive my best to rid them of the nuisance they complained of.

Going up stairs to my old haunt, there was Bartleby silently sitting upon the banister at the landing.

"What are you doing here, Bartleby?" said I.

"Sitting upon the banister," he mildly replied.

I motioned him into the lawyer's room, who then left us.

195 "Bartleby," said I, "are you aware that you are the cause of great tribulation to me, by persisting in occupying the entry after being dismissed from the office?"

No answer.

"Now one of two things must take place. Either you must do something, or something must be done to you. Now what sort of business would you like to engage in? Would you like to re-engage in copying for some one?"

"No; I would prefer not to make any change."

"Would you like a clerkship in a dry-goods store?"

200 "There is too much confinement about that. No, I would not like a clerkship; but I am not particular."

"Too much confinement," I cried, "why you keep yourself confined all the time!"

"I would prefer not to take a clerkship," he rejoined, as if to settle that little item at once.

"How would a bar-tender's business suit you? There is no trying of the eyesight in that."

"I would not like it at all; though, as I said before, I am not particular."

205 His unwonted wordiness inspirited me. I returned to the charge.

"Well then, would you like to travel through the country collecting bills for the merchants? That would improve your health."

"No, I would prefer to be something else."

"How then would going as a companion to Europe, to entertain some young gentleman with your conversation,—how would that suit you?"

"Not at all. It does not strike me that there is any thing definite about that. I like to be stationary. But I am not particular."

210 "Stationary you shall be then," I cried, now losing all patience, and for the first time in all my exasperating connection with him fairly flying into a passion. "If you do not go away from these premises before night, I shall feel bound—indeed I *am* bound—to—to—to quit the premises myself!" I rather absurdly concluded, knowing not with what possible threat to try to frighten his immobility into compliance. Despairing of all further efforts, I

was precipitately leaving him, when a final thought occurred to me—one which had not been wholly unindulged before.

"Bartleby," said I, in the kindest tone I could assume under such exciting circumstances, "will you go home with me now—not to my office, but my dwelling—and remain there till we can conclude upon some convenient arrangement for you at our leisure? Come, let us start now, right away."

"No: at present I would prefer not to make any change at all."

I answered nothing; but effectually dodging every one by the suddenness and rapidity of my flight, rushed from the building, ran up Wall-street towards Broadway, and jumping into the first omnibus was soon removed from pursuit. As soon as tranquillity returned I distinctly perceived that I had now done all that I possibly could, both in respect to the demands of the landlord and his tenants, and with regard to my own desire and sense of duty, to benefit Bartleby, and shield him from rude persecution. I now strove to be entirely care-free and quiescent; and my conscience justified me in the attempt; though indeed it was not so successful as I could have wished. So fearful was I of being again hunted out by the incensed landlord and his exasperated tenants, that, surrendering my business to Nippers, for a few days I drove about the upper part of the town and through the suburbs, in my rockaway;[21] crossed over to Jersey City and Hoboken, and paid fugitive visits to Manhattanville and Astoria. In fact I almost lived in my rockaway for the time.

When again I entered my office, lo, a note from the landlord lay upon the desk. I opened it with trembling hands. It informed me that the writer had sent to the police, and had Bartleby removed to the Tombs as a vagrant. Moreover, since I knew more about him than any one else, he wished me to appear at that place, and make a suitable statement of the facts. These tidings had a conflicting effect upon me. At first I was indignant; but at last almost approved. The landlord's energetic, summary disposition, had led him to adopt a procedure which I do not think I would have decided upon myself; and yet as a last resort, under such peculiar circumstances, it seemed the only plan.

215   As I afterwards learned, the poor scrivener, when told that he must be conducted to the Tombs, offered not the slightest obstacle, but in his pale unmoving way, silently acquiesced.

Some of the compassionate and curious bystanders joined the party; and headed by one of the constables arm in arm with Bartleby, the silent procession filed its way through all the noise, and heat, and joy of the roaring thoroughfares at noon.

The same day I received the note I went to the Tombs, or to speak more properly, the Halls of Justice. Seeking the right officer, I stated the purpose of my call, and was informed that the individual I described was indeed within. I then assured the functionary that Bartleby was a perfectly honest man, and greatly to be compassionated, however unaccountably eccentric. I

---

[21] Luxury carriage.

narrated all I knew, and closed by suggesting the idea of letting him remain in as indulgent confinement as possible till something less harsh might be done—though indeed I hardly knew what. At all events, if nothing else could be decided upon, the alms-house must receive him. I then begged to have an interview.

Being under no disgraceful charge, and quite serene and harmless in all his ways, they had permitted him freely to wander about the prison, and especially in the inclosed grass-platted yards thereof. And so I found him there, standing all alone in the quietest of the yards, his face towards a high wall, while all around, from the narrow slits of the jail windows, I thought I saw peering out upon him the eyes of murderers and thieves.

"Bartleby!"

220   "I know you," he said, without looking round,—"and I want nothing to say to you."

"It was not I that brought you here, Bartleby," said I, keenly pained at his implied suspicion. "And to you, this should not be so vile a place. Nothing reproachful attaches to you by being here. And see, it is not so sad a place as one might think. Look, there is the sky, and here is the grass."

"I know where I am," he replied, but would say nothing more, and so I left him.

As I entered the corridor again, a broad meat-like man, in an apron, accosted me, and jerking his thumb over his shoulder said—"Is that your friend?"

"Yes."

225   "Does he want to starve? If he does, let him live on the prison fare, that's all."

"Who are you?" asked I, not knowing what to make of such an unofficially speaking person in such a place.

"I am the grub-man. Such gentlemen as have friends here, hire me to provide them with something good to eat."

"Is this so?" said I, turning to the turnkey.

He said it was.

230   "Well then," said I, slipping some silver into the grub-man's hands (for so they called him), "I want you to give particular attention to my friend there; let him have the best dinner you can get. And you must be as polite to him as possible."

"Introduce me, will you?" said the grub-man, looking at me with an expression which seemed to say he was all impatience for an opportunity to give a specimen of his breeding.

Thinking it would prove of benefit to the scrivener, I acquiesced; and asking the grub-man his name, went up with him to Bartleby.

"Bartleby, this is Mr. Cutlets; you will find him very useful to you."

"Your sarvant, sir, your sarvant," said the grub-man, making a low salutation behind his apron. "Hope you find it pleasant here, sir; nice grounds— cool apartments, sir—hope you'll stay with us some time—try to make it agreeable. May Mrs. Cutlets and I have the pleasure of your company to dinner, sir, in Mrs. Cutlets' private room?"

235 "I prefer not to dine to-day," said Bartleby, turning away. "It would disagree with me; I am unused to dinners." So saying he slowly moved to the other side of the inclosure, and took up a position fronting the dead-wall.

"How's this?" said the grub-man, addressing me with a stare of astonishment. "He's odd, aint he?"

"I think he is a little deranged," said I, sadly.

"Deranged? deranged is it? Well now, upon my word, I thought that friend of yourn was a gentleman forger; they are always pale and genteel-like, them forgers. I can't help pity 'em—can't help it, sir. Did you know Monroe Edwards?" he added touchingly, and paused. Then, laying his hand pityingly on my shoulder, sighed, "he died of consumption at Sing-Sing.[22] So you weren't acquainted with Monroe?"

"No, I was never socially acquainted with any forgers. But I cannot stop longer. Look to my friend yonder. You will not lose by it. I will see you again."

240 Some few days after this, I again obtained admission to the Tombs, and went through the corridors in quest of Bartleby; but without finding him.

"I saw him coming from his cell not long ago," said a turnkey, "may be he's gone to loiter in the yards."

So I went in that direction.

"Are you looking for the silent man?" said another turnkey passing me. "Yonder he lies—sleeping in the yard there. 'Tis not twenty minutes since I saw him lie down."

The yard was entirely quiet. It was not accessible to the common prisoners. The surrounding walls, of amazing thickness, kept off all sounds behind them. The Egyptian character of the masonry weighed upon me with its gloom. But a soft imprisoned turf grew under foot. The heart of the eternal pyramids, it seemed, wherein, by some strange magic, through the clefts, grass-seed, dropped by birds, had sprung.

245 Strangely huddled at the base of the wall, his knees drawn up, and lying on his side, his head touching the cold stones, I saw the wasted Bartleby. But nothing stirred. I paused; then went close up to him; stooped over, and saw that his dim eyes were open; otherwise he seemed profoundly sleeping. Something prompted me to touch him. I felt his hand, when a tingling shiver ran up my arm and down my spine to my feet.

The round face of the grub-man peered upon me now. "His dinner is ready. Won't he dine to-day, either? Or does he live without dining?"

"Lives without dining," said I, and closed the eyes.

"Eh!—He's asleep, aint he?"

"With kings and counsellors,"[23] murmured I.

---

[22] State prison north of New York City.

[23] See Job 3:14. A reference to death as a condition of tranquillity.

* * *

250   There would seem little need for proceeding further in this history. Imagination will readily supply the meagre recital of poor Bartleby's interment. But ere parting with the reader, let me say, that if this little narrative has sufficiently interested him, to awaken curiosity as to who Bartleby was, and what manner of life he led prior to the present narrator's making his acquaintance, I can only reply, that in such curiosity I fully share, but am wholly unable to gratify it. Yet here I hardly know whether I should divulge one little item of rumor, which came to my ear a few months after the scrivener's decease. Upon what basis it rested, I could never ascertain; and hence, how true it is I cannot now tell. But inasmuch as this vague report has not been without a certain strange suggestive interest to me, however sad, it may prove the same with some others; and so I will briefly mention it. The report was this: that Bartleby had been a subordinate clerk in the Dead Letter Office at Washington, from which he had been suddenly removed by a change in the administration. When I think over this rumor, hardly can I express the emotions which seize me. Dead letters! does it not sound like dead men? Conceive a man by nature and misfortune prone to a pallid hopelessness, can any business seem more fitted to heighten it than that of continually handling these dead letters, and assorting them for the flames? For by the cart-load they are annually burned. Sometimes from out the folded paper the pale clerk takes a ring:—the finger it was meant for, perhaps, moulders in the grave; a bank-note sent in swiftest charity:—he whom it would relieve, nor eats nor hungers any more; pardon for those who died despairing; hope for those who died unhoping; good tidings for those who died stifled by unrelieved calamities. On errands of life, these letters speed to death.

Ah Bartleby! Ah humanity!

◇ ◇ ◇

ROHINTON MISTRY
(1952–   )

Swimming Lessons
(1987)

The old man's wheelchair is audible today as he creaks by in the hallway: on some days it's just a smooth whirr. Maybe the way he slumps in it, or the way his weight rests has something to do with it. Down to the lobby he goes, and sits there most of the time, talking to people on their way out or in. That's where he first spoke to me a few days ago. I was waiting for the elevator, back from Eaton's with my new pair of swimming-trunks.

"Hullo," he said. I nodded, smiled.

"Beautiful summer day we've got."

"Yes," I said, "it's lovely outside."

5 He shifted the wheelchair to face me squarely. "How old do you think I am?"

I looked at him blankly, and he said, "Go on, take a guess."

I understood the game; he seemed about seventy-five although the hair was still black, so I said, "Sixty-five?" He made a sound between a chuckle and a wheeze: "I'll be seventy-seven next month." Close enough.

I've heard him ask that question several times since, and everyone plays by the rules. Their faked guesses range from sixty to seventy. They pick a lower number when he's more depressed than usual. He reminds me of Grandpa as he sits on the sofa in the lobby, staring vacantly at the parking lot. Only difference is, he sits with the stillness of stroke victims, while Grandpa's Parkinson's disease would bounce his thighs and legs and arms all over the place. When he could no longer hold the *Bombay Samachar* steady enough to read, Grandpa took to sitting on the veranda and staring emptily at the traffic passing outside Firozsha Baag. Or waving to anyone who went by in the compound: Rustomji, Nariman Hansotia in his 1932 Mercedes-Benz, the fat ayah Jaakaylee with her shopping-bag, the *kuchrawalli* with her basket and long bamboo broom.

The Portuguese woman across the hall has told me a little about the old man. She is the communicator for the apartment building. To gather and disseminate information, she takes the liberty of unabashedly throwing open her door when newsworthy events transpire. Not for Portuguese Woman the furtive peerings from thin cracks or spyholes. She reminds me of a character in a movie, *Barefoot In The Park* I think it was, who left empty beer cans by the landing for anyone passing to stumble and give her the signal. The PW does not need beer cans. The gutang-khutang of the elevator opening and closing is enough.

10 The old man's daughter looks after him. He was living alone till his stroke, which coincided with his youngest daughter's divorce in Vancouver. She returned to him and they moved into this low-rise in Don Mills. PW says the daughter talks to no one in the building but takes good care of her father.

Mummy used to take good care of Grandpa, too, till things became complicated and he was moved to the Parsi General Hospital. Parkinsonism and osteoporosis laid him low. The doctor explained that Grandpa's hip did not break because he fell, but he fell because the hip, gradually growing brittle, snapped on that fatal day. That's what osteoporosis does, hollows out the bones and turns effect into cause. It has an unusually high incidence in the Parsi community, he said, but did not say why. Just one of those mysterious things. We are the chosen people where osteoporosis is concerned. And divorce. The Parsi community has the highest divorce rate in India. It also claims to be the most westernized community in India. Which is the result of the other? Confusion again, of cause and effect.

The hip was put in traction. Single-handed, Mummy struggled valiantly with bedpans and dressings for bedsores which soon appeared like grim spectres on his back. *Mamaiji*, bent double with her weak back, could give no assistance. My help would be enlisted to roll him over on his side while Mummy changed the dressing. But after three months, the doctor pronounced a patch upon Grandpa's lungs, and the male ward of Parsi General swallowed him up. There was no money for a private nursing home. I went to see him once, at Mummy's insistence. She used to say that the blessings of an old person were the most valuable and potent of all, they would last my whole life long. The ward had rows and rows of beds; the din was enormous, the smells nauseating, and it was just as well that Grandpa passed most of his time in a less than conscious state.

But I should have gone to see him more often. Whenever Grandpa went out, while he still could in the days before parkinsonism, he would bring back pink and white sugar-coated almonds for Percy and me. Every time I remember Grandpa, I remember that; and then I think: I should have gone to see him more often. That's what I also thought when our telephone-owning neighbour, esteemed by all for that reason, sent his son to tell us the hospital had phoned that Grandpa died an hour ago.

The postman rang the doorbell the way he always did, long and continuous; Mother went to open it, wanting to give him a piece of her mind but thought better of it, she did not want to risk the vengeance of postmen, it was so easy for them to destroy letters; workers nowadays thought no end of themselves, strutting around like peacocks, ever since all this Shiv Sena agitation about Maharashtra for Maharashtrians, threatening strikes and Bombay bundh all the time, with no respect for the public; bus drivers and conductors were the worst, behaving as if they owned the buses and were doing favours to commuters, pulling the bell before you were in the bus, the driver purposely braking and moving with big jerks to make the standees lose their balance, the conductor so rude if you did not have the right change.

15   *But when she saw the airmail envelope with a Canadian stamp her face lit up, she said wait to the postman, and went in for a fifty paisa piece, a little baksheesh for you, she told him, then shut the door and kissed the envelope, went in running, saying my son has written, my son has sent a letter, and Father looked up from the newspaper and said, don't get too excited, first read it, you know what kind of letters he writes, a few lines of empty words, I'm fine, hope you are all right, your loving son — that kind of writing I don't call letter-writing.*

Then Mother opened the envelope and took out one small page and began to read silently, and the joy brought to her face by the letter's arrival began to ebb; Father saw it happening and knew he was right, he said read aloud, let me also hear what our son is writing this time, so Mother read: My dear Mummy and Daddy, Last winter was terrible, we had record-breaking low temperatures all through February and March, and the first official day of spring was colder than the first official day of winter had been, but it's getting warmer now. Looks like it will be a nice warm summer. You asked about my new apartment. It's small, but not bad at all. This is just a quick note to let you know I'm fine, so you won't worry about me. Hope everything is okay at home.

After Mother put it back in the envelope, Father said everything about his life is locked in silence and secrecy, I still don't understand why he bothered to visit us last year if he had nothing to say; every letter of his has been a quick note so we won't worry — what does he think we worry about, his health, in that country everyone eats well whether they work or not, he should be worrying about us with all the black market and rationing, has he forgotten already how he used to go to the ration-shop and wait in line every week; and what kind of apartment description is that, not bad at all; and if it is a Canadian weather report I need from him, I can go with Nariman Hansotia from A Block to the Cawasji Framji Memorial Library and read all about it, there they get newspapers from all over the world.

The sun is hot today. Two women are sunbathing on the stretch of patchy lawn at the periphery of the parking lot. I can see them clearly from my kitchen. They're wearing bikinis and I'd love to take a closer look. But I have no binoculars. Nor do I have a car to saunter out to and pretend to look under the hood. They're both luscious and gleaming. From time to time they smear lotion over their skin, on the bellies, on the inside of the thighs, on the shoulders. Then one of them gets the other to undo the string of her top and spread some there. She lies on her stomach with the straps undone. I wait. I pray that the heat and haze make her forget, when it's time to turn over, that the straps are undone.

But the sun is not hot enough to work this magic for me. When it's time to come in, she flips over, deftly holding up the cups, and reties the top. They arise, pick up towels, lotions and magazines, and return to the building.

20   This is my chance to see them closer. I race down the stairs to the lobby. The old man says hullo. "Down again?"

"My mailbox," I mumble.

"It's Saturday," he chortles. For some reason he finds it extremely funny. My eye is on the door leading in from the parking lot.

Through the glass panel I see them approaching. I hurry to the elevator and wait. In the dimly lit lobby I can see their eyes are having trouble adjusting after the bright sun. They don't seem as attractive as they did from the kitchen window. The elevator arrives and I hold it open, inviting them in with what I think is a gallant flourish. Under the fluorescent glare in the elevator I see their wrinkled skin, aging hands, sagging bottoms, varicose veins. The lustrous trick of sun and lotion and distance has ended.

I step out and they continue to the third floor. I have Monday night to look forward to, my first swimming lesson. The high school behind the apartment building is offering, among its usual assortment of macramé and ceramics and pottery classes, a class for non-swimming adults.

25   The woman at the registration desk is quite friendly. She even gives me the opening to satisfy the compulsion I have about explaining my non-swimming status.

"Are you from India?" she asks. I nod. "I hope you don't mind my asking, but I was curious because an Indian couple, husband and wife, also registered a few minutes ago. Is swimming not encouraged in India?"

"On the contrary," I say. "Most Indians swim like fish. I'm an exception to the rule. My house was five minutes walking distance from Chaupatty beach in Bombay. It's one of the most beautiful beaches in Bombay, or was, before the filth took over. Anyway, even though we lived so close to it, I never learned to swim. It's just one of those things."

"Well," says the woman, "that happens sometimes. Take me, for instance. I never learned to ride a bicycle. It was the mounting that used to scare me, I was afraid of falling." People have lined up behind me. "It's been very nice talking to you," she says, "hope you enjoy the course."

The art of swimming had been trapped between the devil and the deep blue sea. The devil was money, always scarce, and kept the private swimming clubs out of reach; the deep blue sea of Chaupatty beach was grey and murky with garbage, too filthy to swim in. Every so often we would muster our courage and Mummy would take me there to try and teach me. But a few minutes of paddling was all we could endure. Sooner or later something would float up against our legs or thighs or waist, depending on how deep we'd gone in, and we'd be revulsed and stride out to the sand.

30   Water imagery in my life is recurring. Chaupatty beach, now the high-school swimming pool. The universal symbol of life and regeneration did nothing but frustrate me. Perhaps the swimming pool will overturn that failure.

When images and symbols abound in this manner, sprawling or rolling across the page without guile or artifice, one is prone to say, how obvious, how skilless; symbols, after all, should be still and gentle as dewdrops, tiny, yet shining with a world of meaning. But what happens when, on the page of life itself, one encounters the ever-moving, all-engirdling sprawl of the filthy sea? Dewdrops and oceans both have their rightful places; Nariman Hansotia certainly knew that when he told his stories to the boys of Firozsha Baag.

The sea of Chaupatty was fated to ensure the finales of life's everyday functions. It seemed that the dirtier it became, the more crowds it attracted: street urchins and beggars and beachcombers, looking through the junk that washed up. (Or was it the crowds that made it dirtier? — another instance of cause and effect blurring and evading identification.)

Too many religious festivals also used the sea as repository for their finales. Its use should have been rationed, like rice and kerosene. On Ganesh Chaturthi, clay idols of the god Ganesh, adorned with garlands and all manner of finery, were carried in processions to the accompaniment of drums and a variety of wind instruments. The music got more frenzied the closer the procession got to Chaupatty and to the moment of immersion.

Then there was Coconut Day, which was never as popular as Ganesh Chaturthi. From a bystander's viewpoint, coconuts chucked into the sea do not provide as much of a spectacle. We used the sea, too, to deposit the left-overs from Parsi religious ceremonies, things such as flowers, or the ashes of the sacred sandalwood fire, which just could not be dumped with the regular garbage but had to be entrusted to the care of Avan Yazad, the guardian of the sea. And things which were of no use but which no one had the heart to destroy were also given to Avan Yazad. Such as old photographs.

35   After Grandpa died, some of his things were flung out to sea. It was high tide; we always checked the newspaper when going to perform these disposals; an ebb would mean a long walk in squelchy sand before finding water. Most of the things were probably washed up on shore. But we tried to throw them as far out as possible, then waited a few minutes; if they did not float back right away we would pretend they were in the permanent safe-keeping of Avan Yazad, which was a comforting thought. I can't remember everything we sent out to sea, but his brush and comb were in the parcel, his *kusti*, and some Kemadrin pills, which he used to take to keep the parkinsonism under control.

Our paddling sessions stopped for lack of enthusiasm on my part. Mummy wasn't too keen either, because of the filth. But my main concern was the little guttersnipes, like naked fish with little buoyant penises, taunting me with their skills, swimming underwater and emerging unexpectedly all around me, or pretending to masturbate — I think they were too young to achieve ejaculation. It was embarrassing. When I look back, I'm surprised that Mummy and I kept going as long as we did.

I examine the swimming-trunks I bought last week. Surf King, says the label, Made in Canada-Fabriqué Au Canada. I've been learning bits and pieces of French from bilingual labels at the supermarket too. These trunks are extremely sleek and streamlined hipsters, the distance from waistband to pouch tip the barest minimum. I wonder how everything will stay in place, not that I'm boastful about my endowments. I try them on, and feel that the tip of my member lingers perilously close to the exit. Too close, in fact, to conceal the exigencies of my swimming lesson fantasy: a gorgeous woman in the class for non-swimmers, at whose sight I will be instantly aroused, and she, spying the shape of my desire, will look me straight in the eye with her intentions; she will come home with me, to taste the pleasure of my delectable Asian brown body whose strangeness has intrigued her and unleashed uncontrollable surges of passion inside her throughout the duration of the swimming lesson.

I drop the Eaton's bag and wrapper in the garbage can. The swimming-trunks cost fifteen dollars, same as the fee for the ten weekly lessons. The garbage bag is almost full. I tie it up and take it outside. There is a medicinal smell in the hallway; the old man must have just returned to his apartment.

PW opens her door and says, "Two ladies from the third floor were lying in the sun this morning. In bikinis."

40   "That's nice," I say, and walk to the incinerator chute. She reminds me of Najamai in Firozsha Baag, except that Najamai employed a bit more subtlety while going about her life's chosen work.

PW withdraws and shuts her door.

Mother had to reply because Father said he did not want to write to his son till his son had something sensible to write to him, his questions had been ignored long enough, and if he wanted to keep his life a secret, fine, he would get no letters from his father.

But after Mother started the letter he went and looked over her shoulder, telling her what to ask him, because if they kept on writing the same questions, maybe he would understand how interested they were in knowing about things over there; Father said go on, ask him what his work is at the insurance company, tell him to take some courses at night school, that's how everyone moves ahead over there, tell him not to be discouraged if his job is just clerical right now, hard work will get him ahead, remind him he is a Zoroastrian: manashni, gavashni, kunashni, better write the translation also: good thoughts, good words, good deed — he must have forgotten what it means, and tell him to say prayers and do kusti at least twice a day.

Writing it all down sadly, Mother did not believe he wore his sudra and kusti anymore, she would be very surprised if he remembered any of the prayers; when she had asked him if he needed new sudras he said not to take any trouble because the Zoroastrian Society of Ontario imported them from Bombay for their members, and this sounded like a story he was making up, but she was leaving it in the hands of God, ten thousand miles away there was nothing she could do but write a letter and hope for the best.

45   *Then she sealed it, and Father wrote the address on it as usual because his writing was much neater than hers, handwriting was important in the address and she did not want the postman in Canada to make any mistake; she took it to the post office herself, it was impossible to trust anyone to mail it ever since the postage rates went up because people just tore off the stamps for their own use and threw away the letter, the only safe way was to hand it over the counter and make the clerk cancel the stamps before your own eyes.*

Berthe, the building superintendent, is yelling at her son in the parking lot. He tinkers away with his van. This happens every fine-weathered Sunday. It must be the van that Berthe dislikes because I've seen mother and son together in other quite amicable situations.

Berthe is a big Yugoslavian with high cheekbones. Her nationality was disclosed to me by PW. Berthe speaks a very rough-hewn English, I've over-heard her in the lobby scolding tenants for late rents and leaving dirty lint screens in the dryers. It's exciting to listen to her, her words fall like rocks and boulders, and one can never tell where or how the next few will drop. But her Slavic yells at her son are a different matter, the words fly swift and true, well-aimed missiles that never miss. Finally, the son slams down the hood in disgust, wipes his hands on a rag, accompanies mother Berthe inside.

Berthe's husband has a job in a factory. But he loses several days of work every month when he succumbs to the booze, a word Berthe uses often in her Slavic tirades on those days, the only one I can understand, as it clunks down heavily out of the tight-flying formation of Yugoslavian sentences. He lolls around in the lobby, submitting passively to his wife's tongue-lashings.

The bags under his bloodshot eyes, his stringy moustache, stubbled chin, dirty hair are so vulnerable to the poison-laden barbs (poison works the same way in any language) emanating from deep within the powerful watermelon bosom. No one's presence can embarrass or dignify her into silence.

No one except the old man who arrives now. "Good morning," he says, and Berthe turns, stops yelling, and smiles. Her husband rises, positions the wheelchair at the favourite angle. The lobby will be peaceful as long as the old man is there.

50 It was hopeless. My first swimming lesson. The water terrified me. When did that happen, I wonder, I used to love splashing at Chaupatty, carried about by the waves. And this was only a swimming pool. Where did all that terror come from? I'm trying to remember.

Armed with my Surf King I enter the high school and go to the pool area. A sheet with instructions for the new class is pinned to the bulletin board. All students must shower and then assemble at eight by the shallow end. As I enter the showers three young boys, probably from a previous class, emerge. One of them holds his nose. The second begins to hum, under his breath: Paki Paki, smell like curry. The third says to the first two: pretty soon all the water's going to taste of curry. They leave.

It's a mixed class, but the gorgeous woman of my fantasy is missing. I have to settle for another, in a pink one-piece suit, with brown hair and a bit of a stomach. She must be about thirty-five. Plain-looking.

The instructor is called Ron. He gives us a pep talk, sensing some nervousness in the group. We're finally all in the water, in the shallow end. He demonstrates floating on the back, then asks for a volunteer. The pink one-piece suit wades forward. He supports her, telling her to lean back and let her head drop in the water.

She does very well. And as we all regard her floating body, I see what was not visible outside the pool: her bush, curly bits of it, straying out at the pink Spandex V. Tongues of water lapping against her delta, as if caressing it teasingly, make the brown hair come alive in a most tantalizing manner. The crests and troughs of little waves, set off by the movement of our bodies in a circle around her, dutifully irrigate her; the curls alternately wave free inside the crest, then adhere to her wet thighs, beached by the inevitable trough. I could watch this forever, and I wish the floating demonstration would never end.

55 Next we are shown how to grasp the rail and paddle, face down in the water. Between practising floating and paddling, the hour is almost gone. I have been trying to observe the pink one-piece suit, getting glimpses of her straying pubic hair from various angles. Finally, Ron wants a volunteer for the last demonstration, and I go forward. To my horror he leads the class to the deep end. Fifteen feet of water. It is so blue, and I can see the bottom. He picks up a metal hoop attached to a long wooden stick. He wants me to grasp the hoop, jump in the water, and paddle, while he guides me by the stick. Perfectly safe, he tells me. A demonstration of how paddling propels the body.

It's too late to back out; besides, I'm so terrified I couldn't find the words to do so even if I wanted to. Everything he says I do as if in a trance. I don't remember the moment of jumping. The next thing I know is, I'm swallowing water and floundering, hanging on to the hoop for dear life. Ron draws me to the rails and helps me out. The class applauds.

We disperse and one thought is on my mind: what if I'd lost my grip? Fifteen feet of water under me. I shudder and take deep breaths. This is it. I'm not coming next week. This instructor is an irresponsible person. Or he does not value the lives of non-white immigrants. I remember the three teenagers. Maybe the swimming pool is a hangout of some racist group, bent on eliminating all non-white swimmers, to keep their waters pure and their white sisters unogled.

The elevator takes me upstairs. Then gutang-khutang. PW opens her door as I turn the corridor of medicinal smells. "Berthe was screaming loudly at her husband tonight," she tells me.

"Good for her," I say, and she frowns indignantly at me.

60 The old man is in the lobby. He's wearing thick wool gloves. He wants to know how the swimming was, must have seen me leaving with my towel yesterday. Not bad, I say.

"I used to swim a lot. Very good for the circulation." He wheezes. "My feet are cold all the time. Cold as ice. Hands too."

Summer is winding down, so I say stupidly, "Yes, it's not so warm any more."

The thought of the next swimming lesson sickens me. But as I comb through the memories of that terrifying Monday, I come upon the straying curls of brown pubic hair. Inexorably drawn by them, I decide to go.

It's a mistake, of course. This time I'm scared even to venture in the shallow end. When everyone has entered the water and I'm the only one outside, I feel a little foolish and slide in.

65 Instructor Ron says we should start by reviewing the floating technique. I'm in no hurry. I watch the pink one-piece pull the swim-suit down around her cheeks and flip back to achieve perfect flotation. And then reap disappointment. The pink Spandex triangle is perfectly streamlined today, nothing strays, not a trace of fuzz, not one filament, not even a sign of post-depilation irritation. Like the airbrushed parts of glamour magazine models. The barrenness of her impeccably packaged apex is a betrayal. Now she is shorn like the other women in the class. Why did she have to do it?

The weight of this disappointment makes the water less manageable, more lung-penetrating. With trepidation, I float and paddle my way through the remainder of the hour, jerking my head out every two seconds and breathing deeply, to continually shore up a supply of precious, precious air without, at the same time, seeming too anxious and losing my dignity.

I don't attend the remaining classes. After I've missed three, Ron the instructor telephones. I tell him I've had the flu and am still feeling poorly, but I'll try to be there the following week.

He does not call again. My Surf King is relegated to an unused drawer. Total losses: one fantasy plus thirty dollars. And no watery rebirth. The swimming pool, like Chaupatty beach, has produced a stillbirth. But there is a difference. Water means regeneration only if it is pure and cleansing. Chaupatty was filthy, the pool was not. Failure to swim through filth must mean something other than failure of rebirth — failure of symbolic death? Does that equal success of symbolic life? death of a symbolic failure? death of a symbol? What is the equation?

The postman did not bring a letter but a parcel, he was smiling because he knew that every time something came from Canada his baksheesh was guaranteed, and this time because it was a parcel Mother gave him a whole rupee, she was quite excited, there were so many stickers on it besides the stamps, one for Small Parcel, another Printed Papers, a red sticker saying Insured; she showed it to Father, and opened it, then put both hands on her cheeks, not able to speak because the surprise and happiness was so great, tears came to her eyes and she could not stop smiling, till Father became impatient to know and finally got up and came to the table.

70   *When he saw it he was surprised and happy too, he began to grin, then hugged Mother saying our son is a writer, and we didn't even know it, he never told us a thing, here we are thinking he is still clerking away at the insurance company, and he has written a book full of stories, all these years in school and college he kept his talent hidden, making us think he was just like one of the boys in the Baag, shouting and playing the fool in the compound, and now what a surprise; then Father opened the book and began reading it, heading back to the easy chair, and Mother so excited, still holding his arm, walked with him, saying it was not fair him reading it first, she wanted to read it too, and they agreed that he would read the first story, then give it to her so she could also read it, and they would take turns in that manner.*

Mother removed the staples from the padded envelope in which he had mailed the book, and threw them away, then straightened the folded edges of the envelope and put it away safely with the other envelopes and letters she had collected since he left.

The leaves are beginning to fall. The only ones I can identify are maple. The days are dwindling like the leaves. I've started a habit of taking long walks every evening. The old man is in the lobby when I leave, he waves as I go by. By the time I'm back, the lobby is usually empty.

Today I was woken up by a grating sound outside that made my flesh crawl. I went to the window and saw Berthe raking the leaves in the parking lot. Not the expanse of patchy lawn on the periphery, but in the parking lot proper. She was raking the black tarred surface. I went back to bed and dragged a pillow over my head, not releasing it till noon.

When I return from my walk in the evening, PW, summoned by the elevator's gutang-khutang, says, "Berthe filled six big black garbage bags with leaves today."

75　　　"Six bags!" I say. "Wow!"

Since the weather turned cold, Berthe's son does not tinker with his van on Sundays under my window. I'm able to sleep late.

Around eleven, there's a commotion outside. I reach out and switch on the clock radio. It's a sunny day, the window curtains are bright. I get up, curious, and see a black Olds Ninety-Eight in the parking lot, by the entrance to the building. The old man is in his wheelchair, bundled up, with a scarf wound several times round his neck as though to immobilize it, like a surgical collar. His daughter and another man, the car-owner, are helping him from the wheelchair into the front seat, encouraging him with words like: that's it, easy does it, attaboy. From the open door of the lobby, Berthe is shouting encouragement too, but hers is confined to one word: yah, repeated at different levels of pitch and volume, with variations on vowel-length. The stranger could be the old man's son, he has the same jet black hair and piercing eyes.

Maybe the old man is not well, it's an emergency. But I quickly scrap that thought — this isn't Bombay, an ambulance would have arrived. They're probably taking him out for a ride. If he is his son, where has he been all this time, I wonder.

The old man finally settles in the front seat, the wheelchair goes in the trunk, and they're off. The one I think is the son looks up and catches me at the window before I can move away, so I wave, and he waves back.

80　　　In the afternoon I take down a load of clothes to the laundry room. Both machines have completed their cycles, the clothes inside are waiting to be transferred to dryers. Should I remove them and place them on top of a dryer, or wait? I decide to wait. After a few minutes, two women arrive, they are in bathrobes, and smoking. It takes me a while to realize that these are the two disappointments who were sunbathing in bikinis last summer.

"You didn't have to wait, you could have removed the clothes and carried on, dear," says one. She has a Scottish accent. It's one of the few I've learned to identify. Like maple leaves.

"Well," I say, "some people might not like strangers touching their clothes."

"You're not a stranger, dear," she says, "you live in this building, we've seen you before."

"Besides, your hands are clean," the other one pipes in. "You can touch my things any time you like."

85　　　Horny old cow. I wonder what they've got on under their bathrobes. Not much, I find, as they bend over to place their clothes in the dryer.

"See you soon," they say, and exit, leaving me behind in an erotic wake of smoke and perfume and deep images of cleavages. I start the washers and depart, and when I come back later, the dryers are empty.

PW tells me, "The old man's son took him out for a drive today. He has a big beautiful black car."

I see my chance, and shoot back: "Olds Ninety-Eight."

"What?"

90   "The car," I explain, "it's an Oldsmobile Ninety-Eight."

She does not like this at all, my giving her information. She is visibly nettled, and retreats with a sour face.

Mother and Father read the first five stories, and she was very sad after reading some of them, she said he must be so unhappy there, all his stories are about Bombay, he remembers every little thing about his childhood, he is thinking about it all the time even though he is ten thousand miles away, my poor son, I think he misses his home and us and everything he left behind, because if he likes it over there why would he not write stories about that, there must be so many new ideas that his new life could give him.

But Father did not agree with this, he said it did not mean that he was unhappy, all writers worked the same way, they used their memories and experiences and made stories out of them, changing some things, adding some, imagining some, all writers were very good at remembering details of their lives.

Mother said, how can you be sure that he is remembering because he is a writer, or whether he started to write because he is unhappy and thinks of his past, and wants to save it all by making stories of it; and Father said that it is not a sensible question, anyway, it is now my turn to read the next story.

95   The first snow has fallen, and the air is crisp. It's not very deep, about two inches, just right to go for a walk in. I've been told that immigrants from hot countries always enjoy the snow the first year, maybe for a couple of years more, then inevitably the dread sets in, and the approach of winter gets them fretting and moping. On the other hand, if it hadn't been for my conversation with the woman at the swimming registration desk, they might now be saying that India is a nation of non-swimmers.

Berthe is outside, shovelling the snow off the walkway in the parking lot. She has a heavy, wide pusher which she wields expertly.

The old radiators in the apartment alarm me incessantly. They continue to broadcast a series of variations on death throes, and go from hot to cold and cold to hot at will, there's no controlling their temperature. I speak to Berthe about it in the lobby. The old man is there too, his chin seems to have sunk deeper into his chest, and his face is a yellowish grey.

"Nothing, not to worry about anything," says Berthe, dropping rough-hewn chunks of language around me. "Radiator no work, you tell me. You feel cold, you come to me, I keep you warm," and she opens her arms wide, laughing. I step back, and she advances, her breasts preceding her like the gallant prows of two ice-breakers. She looks at the old man to see if he is appreciating the act: "You no feel scared, I keep you safe and warm."

But the old man is staring outside, at the flakes of falling snow. What thoughts is he thinking as he watches them? Of childhood days, perhaps, and snowmen with hats and pipes, and snowball fights, and white Christmases, and Christmas trees? What will I think of, old in this country, when I sit and watch the snow come down? For me, it is already too late for

snowmen and snowball fights, and all I will have is thoughts about childhood thoughts and dreams, built around snowscapes and winter-wonder-
lands on the Christmas cards so popular in Bombay; my snowmen and
snowball fights and Christmas trees are in the pages of Enid Blyton's books,
dispersed amidst the adventures of the Famous Five, and the Five Find-
Outers, and the Secret Seven. My snowflakes are even less forgettable than
the old man's, for they never melt.

100 It finally happened. The heat went. Not the usual intermittent coming and
going, but out completely. Stone cold. The radiators are like ice. And so is everything else. There's no hot water. Naturally. It's the hot water that goes through
the rads and heats them. Or is it the other way around? Is there no hot water
because the rads have stopped circulating it? I don't care, I'm too cold to sort
out the cause and effect relationship. Maybe there is no connection at all.

I dress quickly, put on my winter jacket, and go down to the lobby. The
elevator is not working because the power is out, so I take the stairs. Several
people are gathered, and Berthe has announced that she has telephoned the
office, they are sending a man. I go back up the stairs. It's only one floor, the
elevator is just a bad habit. Back in Firozsha Baag they were broken most of
the time. The stairway enters the corridor outside the old man's apartment,
and I think of his cold feet and hands. Poor man, it must be horrible for him
without heat.

As I walk down the long hallway, I feel there's something different but I
can't pin it down. I look at the carpet, the ceiling, the wallpaper: it all seems
the same. Maybe it's the freezing cold that imparts a feeling of difference.

PW opens her door: "The old man had another stroke yesterday. They
took him to the hospital."

The medicinal smell. That's it. It's not in the hallway any more.

105 *In the stories that he'd read so far Father said that all the Parsi families were poor
or middle-class, but that was okay; nor did he mind that the seeds for the stories
were picked from the sufferings of their own lives; but there should also have been
something positive about Parsis, there was so much to be proud of: the great Tatas
and their contribution to the steel industry, or Sir Dinshaw Petit in the textile
industry who made Bombay the Manchester of the East, or Dadabhai Naoroji in the
freedom movement, where he was the first to use the word* swaraj, *and the first to
be elected to the British Parliament where he carried on his campaign; he should
have found some way to bring some of these wonderful facts into his stories, what
would people reading these stories think, those who did not know about Parsis —
that the whole community was full of cranky, bigoted people; and in reality it was
the richest, most advanced and philanthropic community in India, and he did not
need to tell his own son that Parsis had a reputation for being generous and family-
oriented. And he could have written something also about the historic background,
how Parsis came to India from Persia because of Islamic persecution in the seventh
century, and were the descendants of Cyrus the Great and the magnificent Persian
Empire. He could have made a story of all this, couldn't he?*

Mother said what she liked best was his remembering everything so well, how beautifully he wrote about it all, even the sad things, and though he changed some of it, and used his imagination, there was truth in it.

My hope is, Father said, that there will be some story based on his Canadian experience, that way we will know something about our son's life there, if not through his letters then in his stories; so far they are all about Parsis and Bombay, and the one with a little bit about Toronto, where a man perches on top of the toilet, is shameful and disgusting, although it is funny at times and did make me laugh, I have to admit, but where does he get such an imagination from, what is the point of such a fantasy; and Mother said that she would also enjoy some stories about Toronto and the people there; it puzzles me, she said, why he writes nothing about it, especially since you say that writers use their own experience to make stories out of.

Then Father said this is true, but he is probably not using his Toronto experience because it is too early; what do you mean, too early, asked Mother and Father explained that it takes a writer about ten years time after an experience before he is able to use it in his writing, it takes that long to be absorbed internally and understood, thought out and thought about, over and over again, he haunts it and it haunts him if it is valuable enough, till the writer is comfortable with it to be able to use it as he wants; but this is only one theory I read somewhere, it may or may not be true.

That means, said Mother, that his childhood in Bombay and our home here is the most valuable thing in his life just now, because he is able to remember it all to write about it, and you were so bitterly saying he is forgetting where he came from; and that may be true, said Father, but that is not what the theory means, according to the theory he is writing of these things because they are far enough in the past for him to deal with objectively, he is able to achieve what critics call artistic distance, without emotions interfering; and what do you mean emotions, said Mother, you are saying he does not feel anything for his characters, how can he write so beautifully about so many sad things without any feelings in his heart?

110 *But before Father could explain more, about beauty and emotion and inspiration and imagination, Mother took the book and said it was her turn now and too much theory she did not want to listen to, it was confusing and did not make as much sense as reading the stories, she would read them her way and Father could read them his.*

My books on the windowsill have been damaged. Ice has been forming on the inside ledge, which I did not notice, and melting when the sun shines in. I spread them in a corner of the living room to dry out.

The winter drags on. Berthe wields her snow pusher as expertly as ever, but there are signs of weariness in her performance. Neither husband nor son is ever seen outside with a shovel. Or anywhere else, for that matter. It occurs to me that the son's van is missing, too.

The medicinal smell is in the hall again, I sniff happily and look forward to seeing the old man in the lobby. I go downstairs and peer into the mailbox, see the blue and magenta of an Indian aerogramme with Don Mills, Ontario, Canada in Father's flawless hand through the slot.

I pocket the letter and enter the main lobby. The old man is there, but not in his usual place. He is not looking out through the glass door. His wheelchair is facing a bare wall where the wallpaper is torn in places. As though he is not interested in the outside world any more, having finished with all that, and now it's time to see inside. What does he see inside, I wonder? I go up to him and say hullo. He says hullo without raising his sunken chin. After a few seconds his grey countenance faces me. "How old do you think I am?" His eyes are dull and glazed; he is looking even further inside than I first presumed.

115   "Well, let's see, you're probably close to sixty-four."

"I'll be seventy-eight next August." But he does not chuckle or wheeze. Instead, he continues softly, "I wish my feet did not feel so cold all the time. And my hands." He lets his chin fall again.

In the elevator I start opening the aerogramme, a tricky business because a crooked tear means lost words. Absorbed in this while emerging, I don't notice PW occupying the centre of the hallway, arms folded across her chest: "They had a big fight. Both of them have left."

I don't immediately understand her agitation. "What . . . who?"

"Berthe. Husband and son both left her. Now she is all alone."

120   Her tone and stance suggest that we should not be standing here talking but do something to bring Berthe's family back. "That's very sad," I say, and go in. I picture father and son in the van, driving away, driving across the snow-covered country, in the dead of winter, away from wife and mother; away to where? how far will they go? Not son's van nor father's booze can take them far enough. And the further they go, the more they'll remember, they can take it from me.

All the stories were read by Father and Mother, and they were sorry when the book was finished, they felt they had come to know their son better now, yet there was much more to know, they wished there were many more stories; and this is what they mean, said Father, when they say that the whole story can never be told, the whole truth can never be known; what do you mean, they say, asked Mother, who they, and Father said writers, poets, philosophers. I don't care what they say, said Mother, my son will write as much or as little as he wants to, and if I can read it I will be happy.

The last story they liked the best of all because it had the most in it about Canada, and now they felt they knew at least a little bit, even if it was a very little bit, about his day-to-day life in his apartment; and Father said if he continues to write about such things he will become popular because I am sure they are interested there in reading about life through the eyes of an immigrant, it provides a different viewpoint; the only danger is if he changes and becomes so much like them that he will write like one of them and lose the important difference.

The bathroom needs cleaning. I open a new can of Ajax and scour the tub. Sloshing with mug from bucket was standard bathing procedure in the bathrooms of Firozsha Baag, so my preference now is always for a shower. I've never used the tub as yet; besides, it would be too much like Chaupatty or the swimming pool, wallowing in my own dirt. Still, it must be cleaned.

When I've finished, I prepare for a shower. But the clean gleaming tub and the nearness of the vernal equinox give me the urge to do something different today. I find the drain plug in the bathroom cabinet, and run the bath.

125   I've spoken so often to the old man, but I don't know his name. I should have asked him the last time I saw him, when his wheelchair was facing the bare wall because he had seen all there was to see outside and it was time to see what was inside. Well, tomorrow. Or better yet, I can look it up in the directory in the lobby. Why didn't I think of that before? It will only have an initial and a last name, but then I can surprise him with: hullo Mr. Wilson, or whatever it is.

The bath is full. Water imagery is recurring in my life: Chaupatty beach, swimming pool, bathtub. I step in and immerse myself up to the neck. It feels good. The hot water loses its opacity when the chlorine, or whatever it is, has cleared. My hair is still dry. I close my eyes, hold my breath, and dunk my head. Fighting the panic, I stay under and count to thirty. I come out, clear my lungs and breathe deeply.

I do it again. This time I open my eyes under water, and stare blindly without seeing, it takes all my will to keep the lids from closing. Then I am slowly able to discern the underwater objects. The drain plug looks different, slightly distorted; there is a hair trapped between the hole and the plug, it waves and dances with the movement of the water. I come up, refresh my lungs, examine quickly the overwater world of the washroom, and go in again. I do it several times, over and over. The world outside the water I have seen a lot of, it is now time to see what is inside.

The spring session for adult non-swimmers will begin in a few days at the high school. I must not forget the registration date.

The dwindled days of winter are now all but forgotten; they have grown and attained a respectable span. I resume my evening walks, it's spring, and a vigorous thaw is on. The snowbanks are melting, the sound of water on its gushing, gurgling journey to the drains is beautiful. I plan to buy a book of trees, so I can identify more than the maple as they begin to bloom.

130   When I return to the building, I wipe my feet energetically on the mat because some people are entering behind me, and I want to set a good example. Then I go to the board with its little plastic letters and numbers. The old man's apartment is the one on the corner by the stairway, that makes it number 201. I run down the list, come to 201, but there are no little white plastic letters beside it. Just the empty black rectangle with holes where the letters would be squeezed in. That's strange. Well, I can introduce myself to him, then ask his name.

However, the lobby is empty. I take the elevator, exit at the second floor, wait for gutang-khutang. It does not come: the door closes noiselessly, smoothly. Berthe has been at work, or has made sure someone else has. PW's cue has been lubricated out of existence.

But she must have the ears of a cockroach. She is waiting for me. I whistle my way down the corridor. She fixes me with an accusing look. She waits till I stop whistling, then says: "You know the old man died last night."

I cease groping for my key. She turns to go and I take a step towards her, my hand still in my trouser pocket. "Did you know his name?" I ask, but she leaves without answering.

Then Mother said, the part I like the best in the last story is about Grandpa, where he wonders if Grandpa's spirit is really watching him and blessing him, because you know I really told him that, I told him helping an old suffering person who is near death is the most blessed thing to do, because that person will ever after watch over you from heaven, I told him this when he was disgusted with Grandpa's urine-bottle and would not touch it, would not hand it to him even when I was not at home.

135   *Are you sure, said Father, that you really told him this, or you believe you told him because you like the sound of it; you said yourself the other day that he changes and adds and alters things in the stories but he writes it all so beautifully that it seems true, so how can you be sure; this sounds like another theory, said Mother, but I don't care, he says I told him and I believe now I told him, so even if I did not tell him then it does not matter now.*

Don't you see, said Father, that you are confusing fiction with facts, fiction does not create facts, fiction can come from facts, it can grow out of facts by compounding, transposing, augmenting, diminishing, or altering them in any way; but you must not confuse cause and effect, you must not confuse what really happened with what the story says happened, you must not lose your grasp on reality, that way madness lies.

Then Mother stopped listening because, as she told Father so often, she was not very fond of theories, and she took out her writing pad and started a letter to her son; Father looked over her shoulder, telling her to say how proud they were of him and were waiting for his next book, he also said, leave a little space for me at the end, I want to write a few lines when I put the address on the envelope.

◇   ◇   ◇

ALICE MUNRO
(1931–   )

Boys and Girls
(1968)

My father was a fox farmer. That is, he raised silver foxes, in pens; and in the fall and early winter, when their fur was prime, he killed them and skinned them and sold their pelts to the Hudson's Bay Company or the Montreal Fur Traders. These companies supplied us with heroic calendars to hang, one on each side of the kitchen door. Against a background of cold blue sky and black pine forests and treacherous northern rivers, plumed adventurers planted the flags of England or of France; magnificent savages bent their backs to the portage.[1]

For several weeks before Christmas, my father worked after supper in the cellar of our house. The cellar was whitewashed, and lit by a hundred-watt bulb over the worktable. My brother Laird and I sat on the top step and watched. My father removed the pelt inside-out from the body of the fox, which looked surprisingly small, mean and rat-like, deprived of its arrogant weight of fur. The naked, slippery bodies were collected in a sack and buried at the dump. One time the hired man, Henry Bailey, had taken a swipe at me with this sack, saying, "Christmas present!" My mother thought that was not funny. In fact she disliked the whole pelting operation—that was what the killing, skinning, and preparation of the furs was called—and wished it did not have to take place in the house. There was the smell. After the pelt had been stretched inside-out on a long board my father scraped away delicately, removing the little clotted webs of blood vessels, the bubbles of fat; the smell of blood and animal fat, with the strong primitive odour of the fox itself, penetrated all parts of the house. I found it reassuringly seasonal, like the smell of oranges and pine needles.

Henry Bailey suffered from bronchial troubles. He would cough and cough until his narrow face turned scarlet, and his light blue, derisive eyes filled up with tears; then he took the lid off the stove, and, standing well back, shot out a great clot of phlegm—hsss—straight into the heart of the flames. We admired him for his performance and for his ability to make his stomach growl at will, and for his laughter, which was full of high whistlings and gurglings and involved the whole faulty machinery of his chest. It was sometimes hard to tell what he was laughing at, and always possible that it might be us.

After we had been sent to bed we could still smell fox and still hear Henry's laugh, but these things, reminders of the warm, safe, brightly lit downstairs world, seemed lost and diminished, floating on the stale cold air upstairs. We were afraid at night in the winter. We were not afraid of *outside* though this was the time of year when snowdrifts curled around our house like sleeping whales and the wind harassed us all night, coming up from the buried fields, the frozen swamp, with its old bugbear chorus of threats and misery. We were afraid of *inside,* the room where we slept. At this time the upstairs of our house was not finished. A brick chimney went up one wall. In the middle of the floor was a square hole, with a wooden railing around it; that was where the stairs came up. On the other side of the stairwell were the things that nobody had any use for any more—a soldiery roll of linoleum, standing on end, a wicker baby carriage, a fern basket, china jugs and basins with cracks in them, a picture of the Battle of Balaclava, very sad to look at. I had told Laird, as soon as he was old enough to understand such

---

[1] Carrying boats or goods overland from one body of water to another or around an obstacle such as rapids.

things, that bats and skeletons lived over there; whenever a man escaped from the county jail, twenty miles away, I imagined that he had somehow let himself in the window and was hiding behind the linoleum. But we had rules to keep us safe. When the light was on, we were safe as long as we did not step off the square of worn carpet which defined our bedroom-space; when the light was off no place was safe but the beds themselves. I had to turn out the light kneeling on the end of my bed, and stretching as far as I could to reach the cord.

5   In the dark we lay on our beds, our narrow life rafts, and fixed our eyes on the faint light coming up the stairwell, and sang songs. Laird sang "Jingle Bells," which he would sing any time, whether it was Christmas or not, and I sang "Danny Boy." I love the sound of my own voice, frail and suppli-cating, rising in the dark. We could make out the tall frosted shapes of the windows now, gloomy and white. When I came to the part, *When I am dead, as dead I well may be*—a fit of shivering caused not by the cold sheets but by pleasurable emotion almost silenced me. *You'll kneel and say, an Ave there above me*—What was an Ave? Every day I forgot to find out.

Laird went straight from singing to sleep. I could hear his long, satisfied, bubbly breaths. Now for the time that remained to me, the most perfectly private and perhaps the best time of the whole day, I arranged myself tightly under the covers and went on with one of the stories I was telling myself from night to night. These stories were about myself, when I had grown a little older; they took place in a world that was recognizably mine, yet one that presented opportunities for courage, boldness and self-sacrifice, as mine never did. I rescued people from a bombed building (it discouraged me that the real war had gone on so far away from Jubilee). I shot two rabid wolves who were menacing the schoolyard (the teachers cowered terrified at my back). I rode a fine horse spiritedly down the main street of Jubilee, acknowl-edging the towns-people's gratitude for some yet-to-be-worked-out piece of heroism (nobody ever rode a horse there, except King Billy in the Orangemen's Day parade). There was always riding and shooting in these stories, though I had only been on a horse twice—bareback because we did not own a saddle—and the second time I had slid right around and dropped under the horse's feet; it had stepped placidly over me. I really was learning to shoot, but I could not hit anything yet, not even tin cans on fence posts.

Alive, the foxes inhabited a world my father made for them. It was sur-rounded by a high guard fence, like a medieval town, with a gate that was padlocked at night. Along the streets of this town were ranged large, sturdy pens. Each of them had a real door that a man could go through, a wooden ramp along the wire, for the foxes to run up and down on, and a kennel— something like a clothes chest with airholes—where they slept and stayed in winter and had their young. There were feeding and watering dishes attached to the wire in such a way that they could be emptied and cleaned from the outside. The dishes were made of old tin cans, and the ramps and kennels of odds and ends of old lumber. Everything was tidy and ingenious;

my father was tirelessly inventive and his favourite book in the world was *Robinson Crusoe*. He had fitted a tin drum on a wheelbarrow, for bringing water down to the pens. This was my job in summer, when the foxes had to have water twice a day. Between nine and ten o'clock in the morning, and again after supper, I filled the drum at the pump and trundled it down through the barnyard to the pens, where I parked it, and filled my watering can and went along the streets. Laird came too, with his little cream and green gardening can, filled too full and knocking against his legs and slopping water on his canvas shoes. I had the real watering can, my father's, though I could only carry it three-quarters full.

The foxes all had names, which were printed on a tin plate and hung beside their doors. They were not named when they were born, but when they survived the first year's pelting and were added to the breeding stock. Those my father had named were called names like Prince, Bob, Wally and Betty. Those I had named were called Star or Turk, or Maureen or Diana. Laird named one Maud after a hired girl we had when he was little, one Harold after a boy at school, and one Mexico, he did not say why.

Naming them did not make pets out of them, or anything like it. Nobody but my father ever went into the pens, and he had twice had blood-poisoning from bites. When I was bringing them their water they prowled up and down on the paths they had made inside their pens, barking seldom—they saved that for nighttime, when they might get up a chorus of community frenzy—but always watching me, their eyes burning, clear gold, in their pointed, malevolent faces. They were beautiful for their delicate legs and heavy, aristocratic tails and the bright fur sprinkled on dark down their backs—which gave them their name—but especially for their faces, drawn exquisitely sharp in pure hostility, and their golden eyes.

10   Besides carrying water I helped my father when he cut the long grass, and the lamb's quarter and flowering money-musk, that grew between the pens. He cut with the scythe and I raked into piles. Then he took a pitchfork and threw fresh-cut grass all over the top of the pens, to keep the foxes cooler and shade their coats, which were browned by too much sun. My father did not talk to me unless it was about the job we were doing. In this he was quite different from my mother, who, if she was feeling cheerful, would tell me all sorts of things—the name of a dog she had had when she was a little girl, the names of boys she had gone out with later on when she was grown up, and what certain dresses of hers had looked like—she could not imagine now what had become of them. Whatever thoughts and stories my father had were private, and I was shy of him and would never ask him questions. Nevertheless I worked willingly under his eyes, and with a feeling of pride. One time a feed salesman came down into the pens to talk to him and my father said, "Like to have you meet my new hired man." I turned away and raked furiously, red in the face with pleasure.

"Could of fooled me," said the salesman. "I thought it was only a girl."

After the grass was cut, it seemed suddenly much later in the year. I walked on stubble in the earlier evening, aware of the reddening skies, the entering silences, of fall. When I wheeled the tank out of the gate and put the padlock on, it was almost dark. One night at this time I saw my mother and father standing talking on the little rise of ground we called the gangway, in front of the barn. My father had just come from the meathouse; he had his stiff bloody apron on, and a pail of cut-up meat in his hand.

It was an odd thing to see my mother down at the barn. She did not often come out of the house unless it was to do something—hang out the wash or dig potatoes in the garden. She looked out of place, with her bare lumpy legs, not touched by the sun, her apron still on and damp across the stomach from the supper dishes. Her hair was tied up in a kerchief, wisps of it falling out. She would tie her hair up like this in the morning, saying she did not have time to do it properly, and it would stay tied up all day. It was true, too; she really did not have time. These days our back porch was piled with baskets of peaches and grapes and pears, bought in town, and onions and tomatoes and cucumbers grown at home, all waiting to be made into jelly and jam and preserves, pickles and chili sauce. In the kitchen there was a fire in the stove all day, jars clinked in boiling water, sometimes a cheesecloth bag was strung on a pole between two chairs, straining blue-black grape pulp for jelly. I was given jobs to do and I would sit at the table peeling peaches that had been soaked in the hot water, or cutting up onions, my eyes smarting and streaming. As soon as I was done I ran out of the house, trying to get out of earshot before my mother thought of what she wanted me to do next. I hated the hot dark kitchen in summer, the green blinds and the flypapers, the same old oilcloth table and wavy mirror and bumpy linoleum. My mother was too tired and pre-occupied to talk to me, she had no heart to tell about the Normal School Graduation Dance; sweat trickled over her face and she was always counting under her breath, pointing at jars, dumping cups of sugar. It seemed to me that work in the house was endless, dreary and peculiarly depressing; work done out of doors, and in my father's service, was ritual-istically important.

I wheeled the tank up to the barn, where it was kept, and I heard my mother saying, "Wait till Laird gets a little bigger, then you'll have a real help."

15 What my father said I did not hear. I was pleased by the way he stood listening, politely as he would to a salesman or a stranger, but with an air of wanting to get on with his real work. I felt my mother had no business down here and I wanted him to feel the same way. What did she mean about Laird? He was no help to anybody. Where was he now? Swinging himself sick on the swing, going around in circles, or trying to catch caterpillars. He never once stayed with me till I was finished.

"And then I can use her more in the house," I heard my mother say. She had a dead-quiet, regretful way of talking about me that always made me uneasy. "I just get my back turned and she runs off. It's not like I had a girl in the family at all."

I went and sat on a feedbag in the corner of the barn, not wanting to appear when this conversation was going on. My mother, I felt, was not to be trusted. She was kinder than my father and more easily fooled, but you could not depend on her, and the real reasons for the things she said and did were not to be known. She loved me, and she sat up late at night making a dress of the difficult style I wanted, for me to wear when school started, but she was also my enemy. She was always plotting. She was plotting now to get me to stay in the house more, although she knew I hated it (*because* she knew I hated it) and keep me from working for my father. It seemed to me she would do this simply out of perversity, and to try her power. It did not occur to me that she could be lonely, or jealous. No grown-up could be; they were too fortunate. I sat and kicked my heels monotonously against a feedbag, raising dust, and did not come out till she was gone.

At any rate, I did not expect my father to pay any attention to what she said. Who could imagine Laird doing my work—Laird remembering the padlock and cleaning out the watering-dishes with a leaf on the end of a stick, or even wheeling the tank without it tumbling over? It showed how little my mother knew about the way things really were.

I have forgotten to say what the foxes were fed. My father's bloody apron reminded me. They were fed horsemeat. At this time most farmers still kept horses, and when a horse got too old to work, or broke a leg or got down and would not get up, as they sometimes did, the owner would call my father, and he and Henry went out to the farm in the truck. Usually they shot and butchered the horse there, paying the farmer from five to twelve dollars. If they had already too much meat on hand, they would bring the horse back alive, and keep it for a few days or weeks in our stable, until the meat was needed. After the war the farmers were buying tractors and gradually getting rid of horses altogether, so it sometimes happened that we got a good healthy horse, that there was just no use for any more. If this happened in the winter we might keep the horse in our stable till spring, for we had plenty of hay and if there was a lot of snow—and the plow did not always get our road cleared—it was convenient to be able to go to town with a horse and cutter.

20   The winter I was eleven years old we had two horses in the stable. We did not know what names they had had before, so we called them Mack and Flora. Mack was an old black workhorse, sooty and indifferent. Flora was a sorrel mare, a driver. We took them both out in the cutter. Mack was slow and easy to handle. Flora was given to fits of violent alarm, veering at cars and even at other horses, but we loved her speed and high-stepping, her general air of gallantry and abandon. On Saturdays we went down to the stable and as soon as we opened the door on its cosy, animal-smelling darkness Flora threw up her head, rolled her eyes, whinnied despairingly and pulled herself through a crisis of nerves on the spot. It was not safe to go into her stall; she would kick.

This winter also I began to hear a great deal more on the theme my mother had sounded when she had been talking in front of the barn. I no longer felt safe. It seemed that in the minds of the people around me there was a steady undercurrent of thought, not to be deflected, on this one subject. The word *girl* had formerly seemed to me innocent and unburdened, like the word *child;* now it appeared that it was no such thing. A girl was not, as I had supposed, simply what I was; it was what I had to become. It was a definition, always touched with emphasis, with reproach and disappointment. Also it was a joke on me. Once Laird and I were fighting, and for the first time ever I had to use all my strength against him; even so, he caught and pinned my arm for a moment, really hurting me. Henry saw this, and laughed, saying, "Oh, that there Laird's gonna show you, one of these days!" Laird was getting a lot bigger. But I was getting bigger too.

My grandmother came to stay with us for a few weeks and I heard other things. "Girls don't slam doors like that." "Girls keep their knees together when they sit down." And worse still, when I asked some questions, "That's none of girls' business." I continued to slam the doors and sit as awkwardly as possible, thinking that by such measures I kept myself free.

When spring came, the horses were let out in the barnyard. Mack stood against the barn wall trying to scratch his neck and haunches, but Flora trotted up and down and reared at the fences, clattering her hooves against the rails. Snow drifts dwindled quickly, revealing the hard grey and brown earth, the familiar rise and fall of the ground, plain and bare after the fantastic landscape of winter. There was a great feeling of opening-out, of release. We just wore rubbers now, over our shoes; our feet felt ridiculously light. One Saturday we went out to the stable and found all the doors open, letting in the unaccustomed sunlight and fresh air. Henry was there, just idling around looking at his collection of calendars which were tacked up behind the stalls in a part of the stable my mother had probably never seen.

"Come to say goodbye to your old friend Mack?" Henry said. "Here, you give him a taste of oats." He poured some oats into Laird's cupped hands and Laird went to feed Mack. Mack's teeth were in bad shape. He ate very slowly, patiently shifting the oats around in his mouth, trying to find a stump of a molar to grind it on. "Poor old Mack," said Henry mournfully. "When a horse's teeth's gone, he's gone. That's about the way."

25   "Are you going to shoot him today?" I said. Mack and Flora had been in the stable so long I had almost forgotten they were going to be shot.

Henry didn't answer me. Instead he started to sing in a high, trembly, mocking-sorrowful voice, *Oh, there's no more work, for poor Uncle Ned, he's gone where the good darkies go.* Mack's thick, blackish tongue worked diligently at Laird's hand. I went out before the song was ended and sat down on the gangway.

I had never seen them shoot a horse, but I knew where it was done. Last summer Laird and I had come upon a horse's entrails before they were buried. We had thought it was a big black snake, coiled up in the sun. That was around in the field that ran up beside the barn. I thought that if we went inside the barn, and found a wide crack or a knothole to look through, we would be able to see them do it. It was not something I wanted to see; just the same, if a thing really happened, it was better to see it, and know.

My father came down from the house, carrying the gun.

"What are you doing here?" he said.

30   "Nothing."

"Go on up and play around the house."

He sent Laird out of the stable. I said to Laird, "Do you want to see them shoot Mack?" and without waiting for an answer led him around to the front door of the barn, opened it carefully, and went in. "Be quiet or they'll hear us," I said. We could hear Henry and my father talking in the stable, then the heavy, shuffling steps of Mack being backed out of his stall.

In the loft it was cold and dark. Thin, crisscrossed beams of sunlight fell through the cracks. The hay was low. It was a rolling country, hills and hollows, slipping under our feet. About four feet up was a beam going around the walls. We piled hay up in one corner and I boosted Laird up and hoisted myself. The beam was not very wide; we crept along it with our hands flat on the barn walls. There were plenty of knotholes, and I found one that gave me the view I wanted—a corner of the barnyard, the gate, part of the field. Laird did not have a knothole and began to complain.

I showed him a widened crack between two boards. "Be quiet and wait. If they hear you you'll get us in trouble."

35   My father came in sight carrying the gun. Henry was leading Mack by the halter. He dropped it and took out his cigarette papers and tobacco; he rolled cigarettes for my father and himself. While this was going on Mack nosed around in the old, dead grass along the fence. Then my father opened the gate and they took Mack through. Henry led Mack away from the path to a patch of ground and they talked together, not loud enough for us to hear. Mack again began searching for a mouthful of fresh grass, which was not to be found. My father walked away in a straight line, and stopped short at a distance which seemed to suit him. Henry was walking away from Mack too, but sideways, still negligently holding on to the halter. My father raised the gun and Mack looked up as if he had noticed something and my father shot him.

Mack did not collapse at once but swayed, lurched sideways and fell, first on his side; then he rolled over on his back and, amazingly, kicked his legs for a few seconds in the air. At this Henry laughed, as if Mack had done a trick for him. Laird, who had drawn a long, groaning breath of surprise when the shot was fired, said out loud, "He's not dead." And it seemed to me it might be true. But his legs stopped, he rolled on his side again, his muscles quivered and sank. The two men walked over and looked at him in a businesslike way; they bent down and examined his forehead where the bullet had gone in, and now I saw his blood on the brown grass.

"Now they just skin him and cut him up," I said. "Let's go." My legs were a little shaky and I jumped gratefully down into the hay. "Now you've seen how they shoot a horse," I said in a congratulatory way, as if I had seen it many times before. "Let's see if any barn cat's had kittens in the hay."

Laird jumped. He seemed young and obedient again. Suddenly I remembered how, when he was little, I had brought him into the barn and told him to climb the ladder to the top beam. That was in the spring, too, when the hay was low. I had done it out of a need for excitement, a desire for something to happen so that I could tell about it. He was wearing a little bulky brown and white checked coat, made down from one of mine. He went all the way up, just as I told him, and sat down on the top beam with the hay far below him on one side, and the barn floor and some old machinery on the other. Then I ran screaming to my father, "Laird's up on the top beam!" My father came, my mother came, my father went up the ladder talking very quietly and brought Laird down under his arm, at which my mother leaned against the ladder and began to cry. They said to me, "Why weren't you watching him?" but nobody ever knew the truth. Laird did not know enough to tell. But whenever I saw the brown and white checked coat hanging in the closet, or at the bottom of the rag bag, which was where it ended up, I felt a weight in my stomach, the sadness of unexorcized guilt.

I looked at Laird who did not even remember this, and I did not like the look on his thin, winter-pale face. His expression was not frightened or upset, but remote, concentrating. "Listen," I said, in an unusually bright and friendly voice, "you aren't going to tell, are you?"

"No," he said absently.

40   "Promise."

"Promise," he said. I grabbed the hand behind his back to make sure he was not crossing his fingers. Even so, he might have a nightmare; it might come out that way. I decided I had better work hard to get all thoughts of what he had seen out of his mind—which, it seemed to me, could not hold very many things at a time. I got some money I had saved and that afternoon we went into Jubilee and saw a show, with Judy Canova, at which we both laughed a great deal. After that I thought it would be all right.

Two weeks later I knew they were going to shoot Flora. I knew from the night before, when I heard my mother ask if the hay was holding out all right, and my father said, "Well, after to-morrow there'll just be the cow, and we should be able to put her out to grass in another week." So I knew it was Flora's turn in the morning.

This time I didn't think of watching it. That was something to see just one time. I had not thought about it very often since, but sometimes when I was busy, working at school, or standing in front of the mirror combing my hair and wondering if I would be pretty when I grew up, the whole scene would flash into my mind: I would see the easy, practised way my father raised the gun, and hear Henry laughing when Mack kicked his legs in the air. I did not have any great feeling of horror and opposition, such as a city child might have had; I was too used to seeing the death of animals as a necessity by which we lived. Yet I felt a little ashamed, and there was a new wariness, a sense of holding-off, in my attitude to my father and his work.

It was a fine day, and we were going around the yard picking up tree branches that had been torn off in winter storms. This was something we had been told to do, and also we wanted to use them to make a teepee. We heard Flora whinny, and then my father's voice and Henry's shouting, and we ran down to the barnyard to see what was going on.

45   The stable door was open. Henry had just brought Flora out, and she had broken away from him. She was running free in the barnyard, from one end to the other. We climbed up on the fence. It was exciting to see her running, whinnying, going up on her hind legs, prancing and threatening like a horse in a Western movie, an unbroken ranch horse, though she was just an old driver, an old sorrel mare. My father and Henry ran after her and tried to grab the dangling halter. They tried to work her into a corner, and they had almost succeeded when she made a run between them, wild-eyed, and disappeared around the corner of the barn. We heard the rails clatter down as she got over the fence, and Henry yelled, "She's into the field now!"

That meant she was in the long L-shaped field that ran up by the house. If she got around the center, heading towards the lane, the gate was open; the truck had been driven into the field this morning. My father shouted to me, because I was on the other side of the fence, nearest the lane, "Go shut the gate!"

I could run very fast. I ran across the garden, past the tree where our swing was hung, and jumped across a ditch into the lane. There was the open gate. She had not got out, I could not see her up on the road; she must have run to the other end of the field. The gate was heavy. I lifted it out of the gravel and carried it across the roadway. I had it half-way across when she came in sight, galloping straight towards me. There was just time to get the chain on. Laird came scrambling through the ditch to help me.

Instead of shutting the gate, I opened it as wide as I could. I did not make any decision to do this, it was just what I did. Flora never slowed down; she galloped straight past me, and Laird jumped up and down, yelling, "Shut it, shut it!" even after it was too late. My father and Henry appeared in the field a moment too late to see what I had done. They only saw Flora heading for the township road. They would think I had not got there in time.

They did not waste any time asking about it. They went back to the barn and got the gun and the knives they used, and put these in the truck; then they turned the truck around and came bouncing up the field toward us. Laird called to them, "Let me go too, let me go too!" and Henry stopped the truck and they took him in. I shut the gate after they were all gone.

50   I supposed Laird would tell. I wondered what would happen to me. I had never disobeyed my father before, and I could not understand why I had done it. Flora would not really get away. They would catch up with her in the truck. Or if they did not catch her this morning somebody would see her and telephone us this afternoon or tomorrow. There was no wild country here for her to run to, only farms. What was more, my father had paid for

her, we needed the meat to feed the foxes, we needed the foxes to make our living. All I had done was make more work for my father who worked hard enough already. And when my father found out about it he was not going to trust me any more; he would know that I was not entirely on his side. I was on Flora's side, and that made me no use to anybody, not even to her. Just the same, I did not regret it; when she came running at me and I held the gate open, that was the only thing I could do.

I went back to the house, and my mother said, "What's all the commotion?" I told her that Flora had kicked down the fence and got away. "Your poor father," she said, "now he'll have to go chasing over the countryside. Well, there isn't any use planning dinner before one." She put up the ironing board. I wanted to tell her, but thought better of it and went upstairs and sat on my bed.

Lately I had been trying to make my part of the room fancy, spreading the bed with old lace curtains, and fixing myself a dressing-table with some leftovers of cretonne for a skirt. I planned to put up some kind of barricade between my bed and Laird's, to keep my section separate from his. In the sunlight, the lace curtains were just dusty rags. We did not sing at night any more. One night when I was singing Laird said, "You sound silly," and I went right on but the next night I did not start. There was not so much need to anyway, we were no longer afraid. We knew it was just old furniture over there, old jumble and confusion. We did not keep to the rules. I still stayed awake after Laird was asleep and told myself stories, but even in these stories something different was happening, mysterious alterations took place. A story might start off in the old way, with a spectacular danger, a fire or wild animals, and for a while I might rescue people; then things would change around, and instead, somebody would be rescuing me. It might be a boy from our class at school, or even Mr. Campbell, our teacher, who tickled girls under the arms. And at this point the story concerned itself at great length with what I looked like—how long my hair was, and what kind of dress I had on; by the time I had these details worked out the real excitement of the story was lost.

It was later than one o'clock when the truck came back. The tarpaulin was over the back, which meant there was meat in it. My mother had to heat dinner up all over again. Henry and my father had changed from their bloody overalls into ordinary working overalls in the barn, and they washed their arms and necks and faces at the sink, and splashed water on their hair and combed it. Laird lifted his arm to show off a streak of blood. "We shot old Flora," he said, "and cut her up in fifty pieces."

"Well, I don't want to hear about it," my mother said. "And don't come to my table like that."

55   My family made him go and wash the blood off.

We sat down and my father said grace and Henry pasted his chewing-gum on the end of his fork, the way he always did; when he took it off he would have us admire the pattern. We began to pass the bowls of steaming, overcooked vegetables. Laird looked across the table at me and said proudly, distinctly, "Anyway it was her fault Flora got away."

"What?" my father said.

"She could of shut the gate and she didn't. She just open' it up and Flora run out."

"Is that right?" my father said.

60   Everybody at the table was looking at me. I nodded, swallowing food with great difficulty. To my shame, tears flooded my eyes.

My father made a curt sound of disgust. "What did you do that for?"

I did not answer. I put down my fork and waited to be sent from the table, still not looking up.

But this did not happen. For some time nobody said anything, then Laird said matter-of-factly, "She's crying."

"Never mind," my father said. He spoke with resignation, even good humour, the words which absolved and dismissed me for good. "She's only a girl," he said.

65   I didn't protest that, even in my heart. Maybe it was true.

ALICE MUNRO
(1931–   )

How I Met My Husband
(1974)

We heard the plane come over at noon, roaring through the radio news, and we were sure it was going to hit the house, so we all ran out into the yard. We saw it come in over the tree tops, all red and silver, the first close-up plane I ever saw. Mrs. Peebles screamed.

"Crash landing," their little boy said. Joey was his name.

"It's okay," said Dr. Peebles. "He knows what he's doing." Dr. Peebles was only an animal doctor, but had a calming way of talking, like any doctor.

This was my first job—working for Dr. and Mrs. Peebles, who had bought an old house out on the Fifth Line, about five miles out of town. It was just when the trend was starting of town people buying up old farms, not to work them but to live on them.

5   We watched the plane land across the road, where the fairgrounds used to be. It did make a good landing field, nice and level for the old race track, and the barns and display sheds torn down now for scrap lumber so there was nothing in the way. Even the old grandstand boys had burned.

"All right," said Mrs. Peebles, snappy as she always was when she got over her nerves. "Let's go back in the house. Let's not stand here gawking like a set of farmers."

She didn't say that to hurt my feelings. It never occurred to her.

I was just setting the dessert down when Loretta Bird arrived, out of breath, at the screen door.

"I thought it was going to crash into the house and kill youse all!"

10 She lived on the next place and the Peebles thought she was a country-woman, they didn't know the difference. She and her husband didn't farm, he worked on the roads and had a bad name for drinking. They had seven children and couldn't get credit at the Hi-Way Grocery. The Peebles made her welcome, not knowing any better, as I say, and offered her dessert.

Dessert was never anything to write home about, at their place. A dish of Jello or sliced bananas or fruit out of a tin. "Have a house without a pie, be ashamed until you die," my mother used to say, but Mrs. Peebles operated differently.

Loretta Bird saw me getting the can of peaches.

"Oh, never mind," she said. "I haven't got the right kind of a stomach to trust what comes out of those tins, I can only eat home canning."

I could have slapped her. I bet she never put down fruit in her life.

15 "I know what he's landed here for," she said. "He's got permission to use the fairgrounds and take people up for rides. It costs a dollar. It's the same fellow who was over at Palmerston last week and was up the lakeshore before that. I wouldn't go up, if you paid me."

"I'd jump at the chance," Dr. Peebles said. "I'd like to see this neighborhood from the air."

Mrs. Peebles said she would just as soon see it from the ground. Joey said he wanted to go and Heather did, too. Joey was nine and Heather was seven.

"Would you, Edie?" Heather said.

I said I didn't know. I was scared, but I never admitted that, especially in front of children I was taking care of.

20 "People are going to be coming out here in their cars raising dust and trampling your property, if I was you I would complain," Loretta said. She hooked her legs around the chair rung and I knew we were in for a lengthy visit. After Dr. Peebles went back to his office or out on his next call and Mrs. Peebles went for her nap, she would hang around me while I was trying to do the dishes. She would pass remarks about the Peebles in their own house.

"She wouldn't find time to lay down in the middle of the day, if she had seven kids like I got."

She asked me did they fight and did they keep things in the dresser drawer not to have babies with. She said it was a sin if they did. I pretended I didn't know what she was talking about.

I was fifteen and away from home for the first time. My parents had made the effort and sent me to high school for a year, but I didn't like it. I was shy of strangers and the work was hard, they didn't make it nice for you or explain the way they do now. At the end of the year the averages were published in the paper, and mine came out at the very bottom, 37 per cent. My father said that's enough and I didn't blame him. The last thing I wanted, anyway, was to go on and end up teaching school. It happened the very day the paper came out with my disgrace in it, Dr. Peebles was staying at our place for dinner, having just helped one of our cows have twins, and he said I looked smart to him and his wife was looking for a girl to help. He said she felt tied down, with the two children, out in the country. I guess she would, my mother said, being polite, though I could tell from her face she was wondering what on earth it would be like to have only two children and no barn work, and then to be complaining.

When I went home I would describe to them the work I had to do, and it made everybody laugh. Mrs. Peebles had an automatic washer and dryer, the first I ever saw. I have had those in my own home for such a long time now it's hard to remember how much of a miracle it was to me, not having to struggle with the wringer and hang up and haul down. Let alone not having to heat water. Then there was practically no baking. Mrs. Peebles said she couldn't make pie crust, the most amazing thing I ever heard a woman admit. I could, of course, and I could make light biscuits and a white cake and a dark cake, but they didn't want it, she said they watched their figures. The only thing I didn't like about working there, in fact, was feeling half hungry a lot of the time. I used to bring back a box of doughnuts made out at home, and hide them under my bed. The children found out, and I didn't mind sharing, but I thought I better bind them to secrecy.

25   The day after the plane landed Mrs. Peebles put both children in the car and drove over to Chesley, to get their hair cut. There was a good woman then at Chesley for doing hair. She got hers done at the same place, Mrs. Peebles did, and that meant they would be gone a good while. She had to pick a day Dr. Peebles wasn't going out into the country, she didn't have her own car. Cars were still in short supply then, after the war.

I loved being left in the house alone, to do my work at leisure. The kitchen was all white and bright yellow, with fluorescent lights. That was before they ever thought of making the appliances all different colors and doing the cupboards like dark old wood and hiding the lighting. I loved light. I loved the double sink. So would anybody new-come from washing dishes in a dishpan with a rag-plugged hole on an oilcloth-covered table by light of a coal-oil lamp. I kept everything shining.

The bathroom too. I had a bath in there once a week. They wouldn't have minded if I took one oftener, but to me it seemed like asking too much, or maybe risking making it less wonderful. The basin and the tub and the toilet were all pink, and there were glass doors with flamingoes painted on them, to shut off the tub. The light had a rosy cast and the mat sank under your feet like snow, except that it was warm. The mirror was three-way. With the mirror all steamed up and the air like a perfume cloud, from things I was allowed to use, I stood up on the side of the tub and admired myself naked, from three directions. Sometimes I thought about the way we lived out at home and the way we lived here and how one way was so hard to imagine when you were living the other way. But I thought it was still a lot easier, living the way we lived at home, to picture something like this, the painted flamingoes and the warmth and the soft mat, than it was for anybody knowing only things like this to picture how it was the other way. And why was that?

I was through my jobs in no time, and had the vegetables peeled for supper and sitting in cold water besides. Then I went into Mrs. Peebles' bedroom. I had been in there plenty of times, cleaning, and I always took a good look in her closet, at the clothes she had hanging there. I wouldn't have looked in her drawers, but a closet is open to anybody. That's a lie. I would have looked in drawers, but I would have felt worse doing it and been more scared she could tell.

Some clothes in her closet she wore all the time, I was quite familiar with them. Others she never put on, they were pushed to the back. I was disappointed to see no wedding dress. But there was one long dress I could just see the skirt of, and I was hungering to see the rest. Now I took note of where it hung and lifted it out. It was satin, a lovely weight on my arm, light bluish-green in color, almost silvery. It had a fitted, pointed waist and a full skirt and an off-the-shoulder fold hiding the little sleeves.

30   Next thing was easy. I got out of my own things and slipped it on. I was slimmer at fifteen than anybody would believe who knows me now and the fit was beautiful. I didn't, of course, have a strapless bra on, which was what it needed, I just had to slide my straps down my arms under the material. Then I tried pinning up my hair, to get the effect. One thing led to another. I put on rouge and lipstick and eyebrow pencil from her dresser. The heat of the day and the weight of the satin and all the excitement made me thirsty, and I went out to the kitchen, got-up as I was, to get a glass of ginger ale with ice cubes from the refrigerator. The Peebles drank ginger ale, or fruit drinks, all day, like water, and I was getting so I did too. Also there was no limit on ice cubes, which I was so fond of I would even put them in a glass of milk.

I turned from putting the ice tray back and saw a man watching me through the screen. It was the luckiest thing in the world I didn't spill the ginger ale down the front of me then and there.

"I never meant to scare you. I knocked but you were getting the ice out, you didn't hear me."

I couldn't see what he looked like, he was dark the way somebody is pressed up against a screen door with the bright daylight behind them. I only knew he wasn't from around here.

"I'm from the plane over there. My name is Chris Watters and what I was wondering was if I could use that pump."

35   There was a pump in the yard. That was the way the people used to get their water. Now I noticed he was carrying a pail.

"You're welcome," I said. "I can get it from the tap and save you pumping." I guess I wanted him to know we had piped water, didn't pump ourselves.

"I don't mind the exercise." He didn't move, though, and finally he said, "Were you going to a dance?"

Seeing a stranger there had made me entirely forget how I was dressed.

"Or is that the way ladies around here generally get dressed up in the afternoon?"

40   I didn't know how to joke back then. I was too embarrassed.

"You live here? Are you the lady of the house?"

"I'm the hired girl."

Some people change when they find that out, their whole way of looking at you and speaking to you changes, but his didn't.

"Well, I just wanted to tell you you look very nice. I was so surprised when I looked in the door and saw you. Just because you looked so nice and beautiful."

45   I wasn't even old enough then to realize how out of the common it is, for a man to say something like that to a woman, or somebody he is treating like a woman. For a man to say a word like *beautiful*. I wasn't old enough to realize or to say anything back, or in fact to do anything but wish he would go away. Not that I didn't like him, but just that it upset me so, having him look at me, and me trying to think of something to say.

He must have understood. He said good-bye, and thanked me, and went and started filling his pail from the pump. I stood behind the Venetian blinds in the dining room, watching him. When he had gone, I went into the bedroom and took the dress off and put it back in the same place. I dressed in my own clothes and took my hair down and washed my face, wiping it on Kleenex, which I threw in the wastebasket.

The Peebles asked me what kind of man he was. Young, middle-aged, short, tall? I couldn't say.

"Good-looking?" Dr. Peebles teased me.

I couldn't think a thing but that he would be coming to get his water again, he would be talking to Dr. or Mrs. Peebles, making friends with them, and he would mention seeing me that first afternoon, dressed up. Why not mention it? He would think it was funny. And no idea of the trouble it would get me into.

50   After supper the Peebles drove into town to go to a movie. She wanted to go somewhere with her hair fresh done. I sat in my bright kitchen wondering what to do, knowing I would never sleep. Mrs. Peebles might not fire me, when she found out, but it would give her a different feeling about me altogether. This was the first place I ever worked but I already had picked up things about the way people feel when you are working for them. They like to think you aren't curious. Not just that you aren't dishonest, that isn't enough. They like to feel you don't notice things, that you don't think or wonder about anything but what they liked to eat and how they like things ironed, and so on. I don't mean they weren't kind to me, because they were. They had me eat my meals with them (to tell the truth I expected to, I didn't know there were families who don't) and sometimes they took me along in the car. But all the same.

I went up and checked on the children being asleep and then I went out. I had to do it. I crossed the road and went in the old fairgrounds gate. The plane looked unnatural sitting there, and shining with the moon. Off at the far side of the fairgrounds, where the bush was taking over, I saw his tent.

He was sitting outside it smoking a cigarette. He saw me coming.

"Hello, were you looking for a plane ride? I don't start taking people up till tomorrow." Then he looked again and said, "Oh, it's you. I didn't know you without your long dress on."

My heart was knocking away, my tongue was dried up. I had to say something. But I couldn't. My throat was closed and I was like a deaf-and-dumb.

55 "Did you want a ride? Sit down. Have a cigarette."

I couldn't even shake my head to say no, so he gave me one.

"Put it in your mouth or I can't light it. It's a good thing I'm used to shy ladies."

I did. It wasn't the first time I had smoked a cigarette, actually. My girl friend out home, Muriel Lower, used to steal them from her brother.

"Look at your hand shaking. Did you just want to have a chat, or what?"

60 In one burst I said, "I wisht you wouldn't say anything about that dress."

"What dress? Oh, the long dress."

"It's Mrs. Peebles'."

"Whose? Oh, the lady you work for? Is that it? She wasn't home so you got dressed up in her dress, eh? You got dressed up and played queen. I don't blame you. You're not smoking that cigarette right. Don't just puff. Draw it in. Did nobody ever show you how to inhale? Are you scared I'll tell on you? Is that it?"

I was so ashamed at having to ask him to connive this way I couldn't nod. I just looked at him and he saw *yes*.

65 "Well I won't. I won't in the slightest way mention it or embarrass you. I give you my word of honor."

Then he changed the subject, to help me out, seeing I couldn't even thank him.

"What do you think of this sign?"

It was a board sign lying practically at my feet.

SEE THE WORLD FROM THE SKY. ADULTS $1.00, CHILDREN 50¢. QUALIFIED PILOT.

70 "My old sign was getting pretty beat up, I thought I'd make a new one. That's what I've been doing with my time today."

The lettering wasn't all that handsome, I thought. I could have done a better one in half an hour.

"I'm not an expert at sign making."

"It's very good," I said.

"I don't need it for publicity, word of mouth is usually enough. I turned away two carloads tonight. I felt like taking it easy. I didn't tell them ladies were dropping in to visit me."

75 Now I remembered the children and I was scared again, in case one of them had waked up and called me and I wasn't there.

"Do you have to go so soon?"

I remembered some manners. "Thank you for the cigarette."

"Don't forget. You have my word of honor."

I tore off across the fairgrounds, scared I'd see the car heading home from town. My sense of time was mixed up, I didn't know how long I'd been out of the house. But it was all right, it wasn't late, the children were asleep. I got in bed myself and lay thinking what a lucky end to the day, after all, and among things to be grateful for I could be grateful Loretta Bird hadn't been the one who caught me.

80   The yard and borders didn't get trampled, it wasn't as bad as that. All the same it seemed very public, around the house. The sign was on the fairgrounds gate. People came mostly after supper but a good many in the afternoon, too. The Bird children all came without fifty cents between them and hung on the gate. We got used to the excitement of the plane coming in and taking off, it wasn't excitement any more. I never went over, after that one time, but would see him when he came to get his water. I would be out on the steps doing sitting-down work, like preparing vegetables, if I could.

"Why don't you come over? I'll take you up in my plane."

"I'm saving my money," I said, because I couldn't think of anything else.

"For what? For getting married?"

I shook my head.

85   "I'll take you up for free if you come sometime when it's slack. I thought you would come, and have another cigarette."

I made a face to hush him, because you never could tell when the children would be sneaking around the porch, or Mrs. Peebles herself listening in the house. Sometimes she came out and had a conversation with him. He told her things he hadn't bothered to tell me. But then I hadn't thought to ask. He told her he had been in the War, that was where he learned to fly a plane, and now he couldn't settle down to ordinary life, this was what he liked. She said she couldn't imagine anybody liking such a thing. Though sometimes, she said, she was almost bored enough to try anything herself, she wasn't brought up to living in the country. It's all my husband's idea, she said. This was news to me.

"Maybe you ought to give flying lessons," she said.

"Would you take them?"

She just laughed.

90   Sunday was a busy flying day in spite of it being preached against from two pulpits. We were all sitting out watching. Joey and Heather were over on the fence with the Bird kids. Their father had said they could go, after their mother saying all week they couldn't.

A car came down the road past the parked cars and pulled up right in the drive. It was Loretta Bird who got out, all importance, and on the driver's side another woman got out, more sedately. She was wearing sunglasses.

"This is a lady looking for the man that flies the plane," Loretta Bird said. "I heard her inquire in the hotel coffee shop where I was having a Coke and I brought her out."

"I'm sorry to bother you," the lady said. "I'm Alice Kelling, Mr. Watters' fiancée."

This Alice Kelling had on a pair of brown and white checked slacks and a yellow top. Her bust looked to me rather low and bumpy. She had a worried face. Her hair had had a permanent, but had grown out, and she wore a yellow band to keep it off her face. Nothing in the least pretty or even young-looking about her. But you could tell from how she talked she was from the city, or educated, or both.

95   Dr. Peebles stood up and introduced himself and his wife and me and asked her to be seated.

"He's up in the air right now, but you're welcome to sit and wait. He gets his water here and he hasn't been yet. He'll probably take his break about five."

"That is him, then?" said Alice Kelling, wrinkling and straining at the sky.

"He's not in the habit of running out on you, taking a different name?" Dr. Peebles laughed. He was the one, not his wife, to offer iced tea. Then she sent me into the kitchen to fix it. She smiled. She was wearing sunglasses too.

"He never mentioned his fiancée," she said.

100   I loved fixing iced tea with lots of ice and slices of lemon in tall glasses. I ought to have mentioned before, Dr. Peebles was an abstainer, at least around the house, or I wouldn't have been allowed to take the place. I had to fix a glass for Loretta Bird too, though it galled me, and when I went out she had settled in my lawn chair, leaving me the steps.

"I knew you was a nurse when I first heard you in that coffee shop."

"How would you know a thing like that?"

"I get my hunches about people. Was that how you met him, nursing?"

"Chris? Well yes. Yes, it was."

105   "Oh, were you overseas?" said Mrs. Peebles.

"No, it was before he went overseas. I nursed him when he was stationed at Centralia and had a ruptured appendix. We got engaged and then he went overseas. My, this is refreshing, after a long drive."

"He'll be glad to see you," Dr. Peebles said. "It's a rackety kind of life, isn't it, not staying one place long enough to really make friends."

"Youse've had a long engagement," Loretta Bird said.

Alice Kelling passed that over. "I was going to get a room at the hotel, but when I was offered directions I came on out. Do you think I could phone them?"

110   "No need," Dr. Peebles said. "You're five miles away from him if you stay at the hotel. Here, you're right across the road. Stay with us. We've got rooms on rooms, look at this big house."

Asking people to stay, just like that, is certainly a country thing, and maybe seemed natural to him now, but not to Mrs. Peebles, from the way she said, oh yes, we have plenty of room. Or to Alice Kelling, who kept protesting, but let herself be worn down. I got the feeling it was a temptation to her, to be that close. I was trying for a look at her ring. Her nails were painted red, her fingers were freckled and wrinkled. It was a tiny stone. Muriel Lowe's cousin had one twice as big.

Chris came to get his water, late in the afternoon just as Dr. Peebles had predicted. He must have recognized the car from a way off. He came smiling.

"Here I am chasing after you to see what you're up to," called Alice Kelling. She got up and went to meet him and they kissed, just touched, in front of us.

"You're going to spend a lot on gas that way," Chris said.

115   Dr. Peebles invited Chris to stay for supper, since he had already put up the sign that said: NO MORE RIDES TILL 7 P.M. Mrs. Peebles wanted it served in the yard, in spite of bugs. One thing strange to anybody from the country is this eating outside. I had made a potato salad earlier and she had made a jellied salad, that was one thing she could do, so it was just a matter of getting those out, and some sliced meat and cucumbers and fresh leaf lettuce. Loretta Bird hung around for some time saying, "Oh, well, I guess I better get home to those yappers," and, "It's so nice just sitting here, I sure hate to get up," but nobody invited her, I was relieved to see, and finally she had to go.

That night after rides were finished Alice Kelling and Chris went off somewhere in her car. I lay awake till they got back. When I saw the car lights sweep my ceiling I got up to look down on them through the slats of my blind. I don't know what I thought I was going to see. Muriel Lowe and I used to sleep on her front veranda and watch her sister and her sister's boy friend saying good night. Afterwards we couldn't get to sleep, for longing for somebody to kiss us and rub up against us and we would talk about suppose you were out in a boat with a boy and he wouldn't bring you in to shore unless you did it, or what if somebody got you trapped in a barn, you would have to, wouldn't you, it wouldn't be your fault. Muriel said her two girl cousins used to try with a toilet paper roll that one of them was the boy. We wouldn't do anything like that; just lay and wondered.

All that happened was that Chris got out of the car on one side and she got out on the other and they walked off separately—him towards the fairgrounds and her towards the house. I got back in bed and imagined about me coming home with him, not like that.

Next morning Alice Kelling got up late and I fixed a grapefruit for her the way I had learned and Mrs. Peebles sat down with her to visit and have another cup of coffee. Mrs. Peebles seemed pleased enough now, having company: Alice Kelling said she guessed she better get used to putting in a day just watching Chris take off and come down, and Mrs. Peebles said she didn't know if she should suggest it because Alice Kelling was the one with the car, but the lake was only twenty-five miles away and what a good day for a picnic.

Alice Kelling took her up on the idea and by eleven o'clock they were in the car, with Joey and Heather and a sandwich lunch I had made. The only thing was that Chris hadn't come down, and she wanted to tell him where they were going.

120   "Edie'll go over and tell him," Mrs. Peebles said. "There's no problem."

Alice Kelling wrinkled her face and agreed.

"Be sure and tell him we'll be back by five!"

I didn't see that he would be concerned about knowing this right away, and I thought of him eating whatever he ate over there, alone, cooking on his camp stove, so I got to work and mixed up a crumb cake and baked it, in between the other work I had to do; then, when it was a bit cooled, wrapped it in a tea towel. I didn't do anything to myself but take off my apron and comb my hair. I would like to have put some make-up on, but I was too afraid it would remind him of the way he first saw me, and that would humiliate me all over again.

He had come and put another sign on the gate: NO RIDES THIS P.M. APOLOGIES. I worried that he wasn't feeling well. No sign of him outside and the tent flap was down. I knocked on the pole.

125   "Come in," he said, in a voice that would just as soon have said *Stay out.* I lifted the flap.

"Oh, it's you. I'm sorry. I didn't know it was you."

He had been just sitting on the side of the bed, smoking. Why not at least sit and smoke in the fresh air?

"I brought a cake and hope you're not sick," I said.

130   "Why would I be sick? Oh—that sign. That's all right. I'm just tired of talking to people. I don't mean you. Have a seat." He pinned back the tent flap. "Get some fresh air in here."

I sat on the edge of the bed, there was no place else. It was one of those fold-up cots, really: I remembered and gave him his fiancée's message.

He ate some of the cake. "Good."

"Put the rest away for when you're hungry later."

"I'll tell you a secret. I won't be around here much longer."

135   "Are you getting married?"

"Ha ha. What time did you say they'd be back?"

"Five o'clock."

"Well, by that time this place will have seen the last of me. A plane can get farther than a car." He unwrapped the cake and ate another piece of it, absent-mindedly.

"Now you'll be thirsty."

140   "There's some water in the pail."

"It won't be very cold. I could bring some fresh. I could bring some ice from the refrigerator."

"No," he said. "I don't want you to go. I want a nice long time of saying good-bye to you."

He put the cake away carefully and sat beside me and started those little kisses, so soft, I can't ever let myself think about them, such kindness in his face and lovely kisses, all over my eyelids and neck and ears, all over, then me kissing back as well as I could (I had only kissed a boy on a dare before, and kissed my own arms for practice) and we lay back on the cot and pressed together, just gently, and he did some other things, not bad things or not in a bad way. It was lovely in the tent, that smell of grass and hot tent cloth with the sun beating down on it, and he said, "I wouldn't do you any harm for the world." Once, when he had rolled on top of me and we were sort of rocking together on the cot, he said softly, "Oh, no," and freed himself and jumped up and got the water pail. He splashed some of it on his neck and face, and the little bit left, on me lying there.

"That's to cool us off, Miss."

145   When we said good-bye I wasn't at all sad, because he held my face and said, "I'm going to write you a letter. I'll tell you where I am and maybe you can come and see me. Would you like that? Okay then. You wait." I was really glad I think to get away from him, it was like he was piling presents on me I couldn't get the pleasure of till I considered them alone.

No consternation at first about the plane being gone. They thought he had taken somebody up, and I didn't enlighten them. Dr. Peebles had phoned he had to go to the country, so there was just us having supper, and then Loretta Bird thrusting her head in the door and saying, "I see he's took off."

"What?" said Alice Kelling, and pushed back her chair.

"The kids come and told me this afternoon he was taking down his tent. Did he think he'd run through all the business there was around here? He didn't take off without letting you know, did he?"

"He'll send me word," Alice Kelling said. "He'll probably phone tonight. He's terribly restless, since the War."

150   "Edie, he didn't mention to you, did he?" Mrs. Peebles said. "When you took over the message?"

"Yes," I said. So far so true.

"Well why didn't you say?" All of them were looking at me. "Did he say where he was going?"

"He said he might try Bayfield," I said. What made me tell such a lie? I didn't intend it.

"Bayfield, how far is that?" said Alice Kelling.

155   Mrs. Peebles said, "Thirty, thirty-five miles."

"That's not far. Oh, well, that's really not far at all. It's on the lake, isn't it?"

You'd think I'd be ashamed of myself, setting her on the wrong track. I did it to give him more time, whatever time he needed. I lied for him, and also, I have to admit, for me. Women should stick together and not do things like that. I see that now, but didn't then. I never thought of myself as being in any way like her, or coming to the same troubles, ever.

She hadn't taken her eyes off me. I thought she suspected my lie.

"When did he mention this to you?"

160   "Earlier."

"When you were over at the plane?"

"Yes."

"You must've stayed and had a chat." She smiled at me, not a nice smile. "You must've stayed and had a little visit with him."

"I took a cake," I said, thinking that telling some truth would spare me telling the rest.

165   "We didn't have a cake," said Mrs. Peebles rather sharply.

"I baked one."

Alice Kelling said, "That was very friendly of you."

"Did you get permission?" said Loretta Bird. "You never know what these girls'll do next," she said. "It's not they mean harm so much, as they're ignorant."

"The cake is neither here nor there," Mrs. Peebles broke in. "Edie, I wasn't aware you knew Chris that well."

170   I didn't know what to say.

"I'm not surprised," Alice Kelling said in a high voice. "I knew by the look of her as soon as I saw her. We get them at the hospital all the time." She looked hard at me with her stretched smile. "Having their babies. We have to put them in a special ward because of their diseases. Little country tramps. Fourteen and fifteen years old. You should see the babies they have, too."

"There was a bad woman here in town had a baby that pus was running out of its eyes," Loretta Bird put in.

"Wait a minute," said Mrs. Peebles. "What is this talk? Edie. What about you and Mr. Watters? Were you intimate with him?"

"Yes," I said. I was thinking of us lying on the cot and kissing, wasn't that intimate? And I would never deny it.

175   They were all one minute quiet, even Loretta Bird.

"Well," said Mrs. Peebles. "I am surprised. I think I need a cigarette. This is the first of any such tendencies I've seen in her," she said, speaking to Alice Kelling, but Alice Kelling was looking at me.

"Loose little bitch." Tears ran down her face. "Loose little bitch, aren't you? I knew as soon as I saw you. Men despise girls like you. He just made use of you and went off, you know that, don't you? Girls like you are just nothing, they're just public conveniences, just filthy little rags!"

"Oh, now," said Mrs. Peebles.

"Filthy," Alice Kelling sobbed. "Filthy little rag!"

180   "Don't get yourself upset," Loretta Bird said. She was swollen up with pleasure at being in on this scene. "Men are all the same."

"Edie, I'm very surprised," Mrs. Peebles said. "I thought your parents were so strict. You don't want to have a baby, do you?"

I'm still ashamed of what happened next. I lost control, just like a six-year-old, I started howling. "You don't get a baby from just doing that!"

"You see. Some of them are that ignorant," Loretta Bird said.

But Mrs. Peebles jumped up and caught my arms and shook me.

185   "Calm down. Don't get hysterical. Calm down. Stop crying. Listen to me. Listen. I'm wondering, if you know what being intimate means. Now tell me. What did you think it meant?"

"Kissing," I howled.

She let go. "Oh, Edie. Stop it. Don't be silly. It's all right. It's all a misunderstanding. Being intimate means a lot more than that. Oh, I *wondered*."

"She's trying to cover up, now," said Alice Kelling. "Yes. She's not so stupid. She sees she got herself in trouble."

"I believe her," Mrs. Peebles said. "This is an awful scene."

190 "Well there is one way to find out," said Alice Kelling, getting up. "After all, I am a nurse."

Mrs. Peebles drew a breath and said, "No. No. Go to your room, Edie. And stop that noise. That is too disgusting."

I heard the car start in a little while. I tried to stop crying, pulling back each wave as it started over me. Finally I succeeded, and lay heaving on the bed.

Mrs. Peebles came and stood in the doorway.

"She's gone," she said. "That Bird woman too. Of course, you know you should never have gone near that man and that is the cause of all this trouble. I have a headache. As soon as you can, go and wash your face in cold water and get at the dishes and we will not say any more about this."

195 Nor we didn't. I didn't figure out till years later the extent of what I had been saved from. Mrs. Peebles was not very friendly to me afterwards, but she was fair. Not very friendly is the wrong way of describing what she was. She never had been very friendly. It was just that now she had to see me all the time and it got on her nerves, a little.

As for me, I put it all out of my mind like a bad dream and concentrated on waiting for my letter. The mail came every day except Sunday, between one-thirty and two in the afternoon, a good time for me because Mrs. Peebles was always having her nap. I would get the kitchen all cleaned and then go up to the mailbox and sit in the grass, waiting. I was perfectly happy, waiting, I forgot all about Alice Kelling and her misery and awful talk and Mrs. Peebles and her chilliness and the embarrassment of whether she had told Dr. Peebles and the face of Loretta Bird, getting her fill of other people's troubles. I was always smiling when the mailman got there, and continued smiling even after he gave me the mail and I saw today wasn't the day. The mailman was a Carmichael. I knew by his face because there are a lot of Carmichaels living out by us and so many of them have a sort of sticking-out top lip. So I asked his name (he was a young man, shy, but good humored, anybody could ask him anything) and then I said, "I knew by your face!" He was pleased by that and always glad to see me and got a little less shy. "You've got the smile I've been waiting on all day!" he used to holler out the car window.

It never crossed my mind for a long time a letter might not come. I believed in it coming just like I believed the sun would rise in the morning. I just put off my hope from day to day, and there was the goldenrod out around the mailbox and the children gone back to school, and the leaves turning, and I was wearing a sweater when I went to wait. One day walking back with the hydro bill stuck in my hand, that was all, looking across at the fairgrounds with the full-blown milkweed and dark teasels, so much like fall, it just struck me: *No letter was ever going to come.* It was an impossible idea to get used to. No, not impossible. If I thought about Chris's face when he said he was going to write to me, it was impossible, but if I forgot that and thought about the actual tin mailbox, empty, it was plain and true. I kept on going to meet the mail, but my heart was heavy now like a lump of lead. I only smiled because I thought of the mailman counting on it, and he didn't have an easy life, with the winter driving ahead.

Till it came to me one day there were women doing this with their lives, all over. There were women just waiting and waiting by mailboxes for one letter or another. I imagined me making this journey day after day and year after year, and my hair starting to go gray, and I thought, I was never made to go on like that. So I stopped meeting the mail. If there were women all through life waiting, and women busy and not waiting, I knew which I had to be. Even though there might be things the second kind of women have to pass up and never know about, it still is better.

I was surprised when the mailman phoned the Peebles' place in the evening and asked for me. He said he missed me. He asked if I would like to go to Goderich where some well-known movie was on, I forget now what. So I said yes, and I went out with him for two years and he asked me to marry him, and we were engaged a year more while I got my things together, and then we did marry. He always tells the children the story of how I went after him by sitting by the mailbox every day, and naturally I laugh and let him, because I like for people to think what pleases them and makes them happy.

◇ ◇ ◇

TIM O'BRIEN
(1946–   )

The Things They Carried
(1986)

First Lieutenant Jimmy Cross carried letters from a girl named Martha, a junior at Mount Sebastian College in New Jersey. They were not love letters, but Lieutenant Cross was hoping, so he kept them folded in plastic at the bottom of his rucksack. In the late afternoon, after a day's march, he would dig his foxhole, wash his hands under a canteen, unwrap the letters, hold them with the tips of his fingers, and spend the last hour of light pretending. He would imagine romantic camping trips into the White Mountains in New Hampshire. He would sometimes taste the envelope flaps, knowing her tongue had been there. More than anything, he wanted Martha to love him as he loved her, but the letters were mostly chatty, elusive on the matter of love. She was a virgin, he was almost sure. She was an English major at Mount Sebastian, and she wrote beautifully about her professors and room-mates and midterm exams, about her respect for Chaucer and her great affection for Virginia Woolf. She often quoted lines of poetry; she never mentioned the war, except to say, Jimmy, take care of yourself. The letters weighed ten ounces. They were signed "Love, Martha," but Lieutenant Cross understood that "Love" was only a way of signing and did not mean what he sometimes pretended it meant. At dusk, he would carefully return the let-ters to his rucksack. Slowly, a bit distracted, he would get up and move among his men, checking the perimeter, then at full dark he would return to his hole and watch the night and wonder if Martha was a virgin.

The things they carried were largely determined by necessity. Among the necessities or near necessities were P-38 can openers, pocket knives, heat tabs, wrist watches, dog tags, mosquito repellent, chewing gum, candy, cig-arettes, salt tablets, packets of Kool-Aid, lighters, matches, sewing kits, Military Payment Certificates, C rations, and two or three canteens of water. Together, these items weighed between fifteen and twenty pounds, depending upon a man's habits or rate of metabolism. Henry Dobbins, who was a big man, carried extra rations; he was especially fond of canned peaches in heavy syrup over pound cake. Dave Jensen, who practiced field hygiene, carried a toothbrush, dental floss, and several hotel-size bars of soap he'd stolen on R&R in Sydney, Australia. Ted Lavender, who was scared, carried tranquilizers until he was shot in the head outside the village of Than Khe in mid-April. By necessity, and because it was SOP, they all carried steel helmets that weighed five pounds including the liner and camouflage cover. They carried the standard fatigue jackets and trousers. Very few car-ried underwear. On their feet they carried jungle boots—2.1 pounds—and Dave Jensen carried three pairs of socks and a can of Dr. Scholl's foot powder as a precaution against trench foot. Until he was shot, Ted Lavender carried six or seven ounces of premium dope, which for him was a necessity. Mitchell Sanders, the RTO, carried condoms. Norman Bowker carried a diary. Rat Kiley carried comic books. Kiowa, a devout Baptist, carried an illus-trated New Testament that had been presented to him by his father, who taught Sunday school in Oklahoma City, Oklahoma. As a hedge against bad times, however, Kiowa also carried his grandmother's distrust of the white man, his grandfather's old hunting hatchet. Necessity dictated. Because the land was mined and booby-trapped, it was SOP for each man to carry a steel-centered, nylon-covered flak jacket, which weighed 6.7 pounds, but which on hot days seemed much heavier. Because you could die so quickly, each man carried at least one large compress bandage, usually in the helmet band for easy access. Because the nights were cold, and because the monsoons were wet, each carried a green plastic poncho that could be used as a rain-coat or ground sheet or makeshift tent. With its quilted liner, the poncho weighed almost two pounds, but it was worth every ounce. In April, for instance, when Ted Lavender was shot, they used his poncho to wrap him up, then to carry him across the paddy, then to lift him into the chopper that took him away.

They were called legs or grunts.

To carry something was to "hump" it, as when Lieutenant Jimmy Cross humped his love for Martha up the hills and through the swamps. In its intransitive form, "to hump" meant "to walk," or "to march," but it implied burdens far beyond the intransitive.

5   Almost everyone humped photographs. In his wallet, Lieutenant Cross carried two photographs of Martha. The first was a Kodachrome snapshot signed "Love," though he knew better. She stood against a brick wall. Her eyes were gray and neutral, her lips slightly open as she stared straight-on at the camera. At night, sometimes, Lieutenant Cross wondered who had taken the picture, because he knew she had boyfriends, because he loved her so much, and because he could see the shadow of the picture taker spreading out against the brick wall. The second photograph had been clipped from the 1968 Mount Sebastian yearbook. It was an action shot—women's volleyball—and Martha was bent horizontal to the floor, reaching, the palms of her hands in sharp focus, the tongue taut, the expression frank and competitive. There was no visible sweat. She wore white gym shorts. Her legs, he thought, were almost certainly the legs of a virgin, dry and without hair, the left knee cocked and carrying her entire weight, which was just over one hundred pounds. Lieutenant Cross remembered touching that left knee. A dark theater, he remembered, and the movie was *Bonnie and Clyde,* and Martha wore a tweed skirt, and during the final scene, when he touched her knee, she turned and looked at him in a sad, sober way that made him pull his hand back, but he would always remember the feel of the tweed skirt and the knee beneath it and the sound of the gunfire that killed Bonnie and Clyde, how embarrassing it was, how slow and oppressive. He remembered kissing her good night at the dorm door. Right then, he thought, he should've done something brave. He should've carried her up the stairs to her room and tied her to the bed and touched that left knee all night long. He should've risked it. Whenever he looked at the photographs, he thought of new things he should've done.

What they carried was partly a function of rank, partly of field specialty.

As a first lieutenant and platoon leader, Jimmy Cross carried a compass, maps, code books, binoculars, and a .45-caliber pistol that weighed 2.9 pounds fully loaded. He carried a strobe light and the responsibility for the lives of his men.

As an RTO, Mitchell Sanders carried the PRC-25 radio, a killer, twenty-six pounds with its battery.

As a medic, Rat Kiley carried a canvas satchel filled with morphine and plasma and malaria tablets and surgical tape and comic books and all the things a medic must carry, including M&M's for especially bad wounds, for a total weight of nearly twenty pounds.

10   As a big man, therefore a machine gunner, Henry Dobbins carried the M-60, which weighed twenty-three pounds unloaded, but which was almost always loaded. In addition, Dobbins carried between ten and fifteen pounds of ammunition draped in belts across his chest and shoulders.

As PFCs or Spec 4s, most of them were common grunts and carried the standard M-16 gas-operated assault rifle. The weapon weighed 7.5 pounds unloaded, 8.2 pounds with its full twenty-round magazine. Depending on numerous factors, such as topography and psychology, the riflemen carried anywhere from twelve to twenty magazines, usually in cloth bandoliers, adding on another 8.4 pounds at minimum, fourteen pounds at maximum. When it was available, they also carried M-16 maintenance gear—rods and steel brushes and swabs and tubes of LSA oil—all of which weighed about a pound. Among the grunts, some carried the M-79 grenade launcher, 5.9 pounds unloaded, a reasonably light weapon except for the ammunition, which was heavy. A single round weighed ten ounces. The typical load was twenty-five rounds. But Ted Lavender, who was scared, carried thirty-four rounds when he was shot and killed outside Than Khe, and he went down under an exceptional burden, more than twenty pounds of ammunition, plus the flak jacket and helmet and rations and water and toilet paper and tranquilizers and all the rest, plus the unweighed fear. He was dead weight. There was no twitching or flopping. Kiowa, who saw it happen, said it was like watching a rock fall, or a big sandbag or something—just boom, then down—not like the movies where the dead guy rolls around and does fancy spins and goes ass over teakettle—not like that, Kiowa said, the poor bastard just flat-fuck fell. Boom. Down. Nothing else. It was a bright morning in mid-April. Lieutenant Cross felt the pain. He blamed himself. They stripped off Lavender's canteens and ammo, all the heavy things, and Rat Kiley said the obvious, the guy's dead, and Mitchell Sanders used his radio to report one U.S. KIA and to request a chopper. Then they wrapped Lavender in his poncho. They carried him out to a dry paddy, established security, and sat smoking the dead man's dope until the chopper came. Lieutenant Cross kept to himself. He pictured Martha's smooth young face, thinking he loved her more than anything, more than his men, and now Ted Lavender was dead because he loved her so much and could not stop thinking about her. When the dust-off arrived, they carried Lavender aboard. Afterward they burned Than Khe. They marched until dusk, then dug their holes, and that night Kiowa kept explaining how you had to be there, how fast it was, how the poor guy just dropped like so much concrete. Boom-down, he said. Like cement.

*   *   *

In addition to the three standard weapons—the M-60, M-16, and M-79—they carried whatever presented itself, or whatever seemed appropriate as a means of killing or staying alive. They carried catch-as-catch-can. At various times, in various situations, they carried M-14s and CAR-15s and Swedish Ks and grease guns and captured AK-47s and Chi-Coms and RPGs and Simonov carbines and black-market Uzis and .38-caliber Smith & Wesson handguns and 66 mm LAWs and shotguns and silencers and black-jacks and bayonets and C-4 plastic explosives. Lee Strunk carried a slingshot; a weapon of last resort, he called it. Mitchell Sanders carried brass knuckles. Kiowa carried his grandfather's feathered hatchet. Every third or fourth man carried a Claymore antipersonnel mine—3.5 pounds with its firing device. They all carried fragmentation grenades—fourteen ounces each. They all carried at least one M-18 colored smoke grenade—twenty-four ounces. Some carried CS or tear-gas grenades. Some carried white-phosphorus grenades. They carried all they could bear, and then some, including a silent awe for the terrible power of the things they carried.

In the first week of April, before Lavender died, Lieutenant Jimmy Cross received a good-luck charm from Martha. It was a simple pebble, an ounce at most. Smooth to the touch, it was a milky-white color with flecks of orange and violet, oval-shaped, like a miniature egg. In the accompanying letter, Martha wrote that she had found the pebble on the Jersey shoreline, precisely where the land touched water at high tide, where things came together but also separated. It was this separate-but-together quality, she wrote, that had inspired her to pick up the pebble and to carry it in her breast pocket for several days, where it seemed weightless, and then to send it through the mail, by air, as a token of her truest feelings for him. Lieutenant Cross found this romantic. But he wondered what her truest feelings were, exactly, and what she meant by separate-but-together. He wondered how the tides and waves had come into play on that afternoon along the Jersey shoreline when Martha saw the pebble and bent down to rescue it from geology. He imagined bare feet. Martha was a poet, with the poet's sensibilities, and her feet would be brown and bare, the toenails unpainted, the eyes chilly and somber like the ocean in March, and though it was painful, he wondered who had been with her that afternoon. He imagined a pair of shadows moving along the strip of sand where things came together but also separated. It was phantom jealousy, he knew, but he couldn't help himself. He loved her so much. On the march, through the hot days of early April, he carried the pebble in his mouth, turning it with his tongue, tasting sea salts and moisture. His mind wandered. He had difficulty keeping his attention on the war. On occasion he would yell at his men to spread out the column, to keep their eyes open, but then he would slip away into daydreams, just pretending, walking barefoot along the Jersey shore, with Martha, carrying nothing. He would feel himself rising. Sun and waves and gentle winds, all love and lightness.

What they carried varied by mission.

15   When a mission took them to the mountains, they carried mosquito netting, machetes, canvas tarps, and extra bug juice.

If a mission seemed especially hazardous, or if it involved a place they knew to be bad, they carried everything they could. In certain heavily mined

AOs, where the land was dense with Toe Poppers and Bouncing Betties, they took turns humping a twenty-eight-pound mine detector. With its headphones and big sensing plate, the equipment was a stress on the lower back and shoulders, awkward to handle, often useless because of the shrapnel in the earth, but they carried it anyway, partly for safety, partly for the illusion of safety.

On ambush, or other night missions, they carried peculiar little odds and ends. Kiowa always took along his New Testament and a pair of moccasins for silence. Dave Jensen carried night-sight vitamins high in carotin. Lee Strunk carried his slingshot; ammo, he claimed, would never be a problem. Rat Kiley carried brandy and M&M's. Until he was shot, Ted Lavender carried the starlight scope, which weighed 6.3 pounds with its aluminum carrying case. Henry Dobbins carried his girlfriend's panty-hose wrapped around his neck as a comforter. They all carried ghosts. When dark came, they would move out single file across the meadows and paddies to their ambush coordinates, where they would quietly set up the Claymores and lie down and spend the night waiting.

Other missions were more complicated and required special equipment. In mid-April, it was their mission to search out and destroy the elaborate tunnel complexes in the Than Khe area south of Chu Lai. To blow the tunnels, they carried one-pound blocks of pentrite high explosives, four blocks to a man, sixty-eight pounds in all. They carried wiring, detonators, and battery-powered clackers. Dave Jensen carried earplugs. Most often, before blowing the tunnels, they were ordered by higher command to search them, which was considered bad news, but by and large they just shrugged and carried out orders. Because he was a big man, Henry Dobbins was excused from tunnel duty. The others would draw numbers. Before Lavender died there were seventeen men in the platoon, and whoever drew the number seventeen would strip off his gear and crawl in head first with a flashlight and Lieutenant Cross's .45-caliber pistol. The rest of them would fan out as security. They would sit down or kneel, not facing the hole, listening to the ground beneath them, imagining cobwebs and ghosts, whatever was down there—the tunnel walls squeezing in—how the flashlight seemed impossibly heavy in the hand and how it was tunnel vision in the very strictest sense, compression in all ways, even time, and how you had to wiggle in—ass and elbows—a swallowed-up feeling—and how you found yourself worrying about odd things—will your flashlight go dead? Do rats carry rabies? If you screamed, how far would the sound carry? Would your buddies hear it? Would they have the courage to drag you out? In some respects, though not many, the waiting was worse than the tunnel itself. Imagination was a killer.

On April 16, when Lee Strunk drew the number seventeen, he laughed and muttered something and went down quickly. The morning was hot and very still. Not good, Kiowa said. He looked at the tunnel opening, then out across a dry paddy toward the village of Than Khe. Nothing moved. No clouds or birds or people. As they waited, the men smoked and drank Kool-Aid, not talking much, feeling sympathy for Lee Strunk but also feeling the luck of the draw. You win some, you lose some, said Mitchell Sanders, and sometimes you settle for a rain check. It was a tired line and no one laughed.

20   Henry Dobbins ate a tropical chocolate bar. Ted Lavender popped a tranquilizer and went off to pee.

After five minutes, Lieutenant Jimmy Cross moved to the tunnel, leaned down, and examined the darkness. Trouble, he thought—a cave-in maybe. And then suddenly, without willing it, he was thinking about Martha. The stresses and fractures, the quick collapse, the two of them buried alive under all that weight. Dense, crushing love. Kneeling, watching the hole, he tried to concentrate on Lee Strunk and the war, all the dangers, but his love was too much for him, he felt paralyzed, he wanted to sleep inside her lungs and breathe her blood and be smothered. He wanted her to be a virgin and not a virgin, all at once. He wanted to know her. Intimate secrets—why poetry? Why so sad? Why that grayness in her eyes? Why so alone? Not lonely, just alone—riding her bike across campus or sitting off by herself in the cafeteria. Even dancing, she danced alone—and it was the aloneness that filled him with love. He remembered telling her that one evening. How she nodded and looked away. And how, later, when he kissed her, she received the kiss without returning it, her eyes wide open, not afraid, not a virgin's eyes, just flat and uninvolved.

Lieutenant Cross gazed at the tunnel. But he was not there. He was buried with Martha under the white sand at the Jersey shore. They were pressed together, and the pebble in his mouth was her tongue. He was smiling. Vaguely, he was aware of how quiet the day was, the sullen paddies, yet he could not bring himself to worry about matters of security. He was beyond that. He was just a kid at war, in love. He was twenty-two years old. He couldn't help it.

A few moments later Lee Strunk crawled out of the tunnel. He came up grinning, filthy but alive. Lieutenant Cross nodded and closed his eyes while the others clapped Strunk on the back and made jokes about rising from the dead.

Worms, Rat Kiley said. Right out of the grave. Fuckin' zombie.

25   The men laughed. They all felt great relief.

Spook City, said Mitchell Sanders.

Lee Strunk made a funny ghost sound, a kind of moaning, yet very happy, and right then, when Strunk made that high happy moaning sound, when he went *Ahhooooo*, right then Ted Lavender was shot in the head on his way back from peeing. He lay with his mouth open. The teeth were broken. There was a swollen black bruise under his left eye. The cheekbone was gone. Oh shit, Rat Kiley said, the guy's dead. The guy's dead, he kept saying, which seemed profound—the guy's dead. I mean really.

The things they carried were determined to some extent by superstition. Lieutenant Cross carried his good-luck pebble. Dave Jensen carried a rabbit's foot. Norman Bowker, otherwise a very gentle person, carried a thumb that had been presented to him as a gift by Mitchell Sanders. The thumb was dark brown, rubbery to the touch, and weighed four ounces at most. It had been cut from a VC corpse, a boy of fifteen or sixteen. They'd found him at the bottom of an irrigation ditch, badly burned, flies in his mouth and eyes. The boy wore black shorts and sandals. At the time of his death he had been carrying a pouch of rice, a rifle, and three magazines of ammunition.

You want my opinion, Mitchell Sanders said, there's a definite moral here.

30   He put his hand on the dead boy's wrist. He was quiet for a time, as if counting a pulse, then he patted the stomach, almost affectionately, and used Kiowa's hunting hatchet to remove the thumb.

Henry Dobbins asked what the moral was.

Moral?

You know. *Moral.*

Sanders wrapped the thumb in toilet paper and handed it across to Norman Bowker. There was no blood. Smiling, he kicked the boy's head, watched the flies scatter, and said, It's like with that old TV show—Paladin. Have gun, will travel.

35   Henry Dobbins thought about it.

Yeah, well, he finally said. I don't see no moral.

There it is, man.

Fuck off.

They carried USO stationery and pencils and pens. They carried Sterno, safety pins, trip flares, signal flares, spools of wire, razor blades, chewing tobacco, liberated joss sticks and statuettes of the smiling Buddha, candles, grease pencils, The *Stars and Stripes,* fingernail clippers, Psy Ops leaflets, bush hats, bolos, and much more. Twice a week, when the resupply choppers came in, they carried hot chow in green Mermite cans and large canvas bags filled with iced beer and soda pop. They carried plastic water containers, each with a two-gallon capacity. Mitchell Sanders carried a set of starched tiger fatigues for special occasions. Henry Dobbins carried Black Flag insecticide. Dave Jensen carried empty sandbags that could be filled at night for added protection. Lee Strunk carried tanning lotion. Some things they carried in common. Taking turns, they carried the big PRC-77 scrambler radio, which weighed thirty pounds with its battery. They shared the weight of memory. They took up what others could no longer bear. Often, they carried each other, the wounded or weak. They carried infections. They carried chess sets, basketballs, Vietnamese-English dictionaries, insignia of rank, Bronze Stars and Purple Hearts, plastic cards imprinted with the Code of Conduct. They carried diseases, among them malaria and dysentery. They carried lice and ringworm and leeches and paddy algae and various rots and molds. They carried the land itself—Vietnam, the place, the soil—a powdery orange-red dust that covered their boots and fatigues and faces. They carried the sky. The whole atmosphere, they carried it, the humidity, the monsoons, the stink of fungus and decay, all of it, they carried gravity. They moved like mules. By daylight they took sniper fire, at night they were mortared, but it was not battle, it was just the endless march, village to village, without purpose, nothing won or lost. They marched for the sake of the march. They plodded along slowly, dumbly, leaning forward against the heat, unthinking, all blood and bone, simple grunts, soldiering with their legs, toiling up the hills and down into the paddies and across the rivers and up again and down, just humping, one step and then the next and then another, but no volition, no will, because it was automatic, it was anatomy, and the war was entirely a matter of posture and carriage, the hump was everything, a kind of inertia, a kind of emptiness, a dullness of desire and intellect and conscience and hope and human sensibility. Their principles were in their feet. Their calculations were biological. They had no sense of strategy or mission. They searched the villages without knowing what to look for, not caring, kicking over jars of rice, frisking children and old men, blowing tunnels, sometimes setting fires and sometimes not, then forming up and moving on to the next village, then other villages, where it would always be the same. They carried their own lives. The pressures were enormous. In the heat of early afternoon, they would remove their helmets and flak jackets, walking bare, which was dangerous but which helped ease the strain. They would often discard things along the route of march. Purely for comfort, they would throw away rations, blow their Claymores and grenades, no matter, because by nightfall the resupply choppers would arrive with more of the same, then a day or two later still more, fresh watermelons and crates of ammunition and sunglasses and woolen sweaters—the resources were stunning—sparklers for the Fourth of July, colored eggs for Easter. It was the great American war chest—the fruits of science, the smokestacks, the canneries, the arsenals at Hartford, the Minnesota forests, the machine shops, the vast fields of corn and wheat—they carried like freight trains; they carried it on their backs and shoulders—and for all the ambiguities of Vietnam, all the mysteries and unknowns, there was at least the single abiding certainty that they would never be at a loss for things to carry.

*   *   *

40   After the chopper took Lavender away, Lieutenant Jimmy Cross led his men into the village of Than Khe. They burned everything. They shot chickens and dogs, they trashed the village well, they called in artillery and watched the wreckage, then they marched for several hours through the hot afternoon, and then at dusk, while Kiowa explained how Lavender died, Lieutenant Cross found himself trembling.

He tried not to cry. With his entrenching tool, which weighed five pounds, he began digging a hole in the earth.

He felt shame. He hated himself. He had loved Martha more than his men, and as a consequence Lavender was now dead, and this was something he would have to carry like a stone in his stomach for the rest of the war.

All he could do was dig. He used his entrenching tool like an ax, slashing, feeling both love and hate, and then later, when it was full dark, he sat at the bottom of his foxhole and wept. It went on for a long while. In part, he was grieving for Ted Lavender, but mostly it was for Martha, and for himself, because she belonged to another world, which was not quite real, and because she was a junior at Mount Sebastian College in New Jersey, a poet and a virgin and uninvolved, and because he realized she did not love him and never would.

Like cement, Kiowa whispered in the dark. I swear to God—boom-down. Not a word.

45   I've heard this, said Norman Bowker.

A pisser, you know? Still zipping himself up. Zapped while zipping.

All right, fine. That's enough.

Yeah, but you had to see it, the guy just—

I *heard,* man. Cement. So why not shut the fuck *up?*

50   Kiowa shook his head sadly and glanced over at the hole where Lieutenant Jimmy Cross sat watching the night. The air was thick and wet. A warm, dense fog had settled over the paddies and there was the stillness that precedes rain.

After a time Kiowa sighed.

One thing for sure, he said. The Lieutenant's in some deep hurt. I mean that crying jag—the way he was carrying on—it wasn't fake or anything, it was real heavy-duty hurt. The man cares.

Sure, Norman Bowker said.

Say what you want, the man does care.

55   We all got problems.

Not Lavender.

No, I guess not, Bowker said. Do me a favor, though.

Shut up?

That's a smart Indian. Shut up.

60   Shrugging, Kiowa pulled off his boots. He wanted to say more, just to lighten up his sleep, but instead he opened his New Testament and arranged it beneath his head as a pillow. The fog made things seem hollow and unattached. He tried not to think about Ted Lavender, but then he was thinking how fast it was, no drama, down and dead, and how it was hard to feel anything except surprise. It seemed un-Christian. He wished he could find some great sadness, or even anger, but the emotion wasn't there and he couldn't make it happen. Mostly he felt pleased to be alive. He liked the smell of the New Testament under his cheek, the leather and ink and paper and glue, whatever the chemicals were. He liked hearing the sounds of night. Even his fatigue, it felt fine, the stiff muscles and the prickly awareness of his own body, a floating feeling. He enjoyed not being dead. Lying there, Kiowa admired Lieutenant Jimmy Cross's capacity for grief. He wanted to share the man's pain, he wanted to care as Jimmy Cross cared. And yet when he closed his eyes, all he could think was Boom-down, and all he could feel was the pleasure of having his boots off and the fog curling in around him and the damp soil and the Bible smells and the plush comfort of night.

After a moment Norman Bowker sat up in the dark.

What the hell, he said. You want to talk, talk. Tell it to me.

Forget it.

No, man, go on. One thing I hate, it's a silent Indian.

65   For the most part they carried themselves with poise, a kind of dignity. Now and then, however, there were times of panic, when they squealed or wanted to squeal but couldn't, when they twitched and made moaning sounds and covered their heads and said Dear Jesus and flopped around on the earth and fired their weapons blindly and cringed and sobbed and begged for the noise to stop and went wild and made stupid promises to themselves and to God and to their mothers and fathers, hoping not to die. In different ways, it happened to all of them. Afterward, when the firing ended, they would blink and peek up. They would touch their bodies, feeling shame, then quickly hiding it. They would force themselves to stand. As if in slow motion, frame by frame, the world would take on the old logic—absolute silence, then the wind, then sunlight, then voices. It was the burden of being alive. Awkwardly, the men would reassemble themselves, first in private, then in groups, becoming soldiers again. They would repair the leaks in their eyes. They would check for casualties, call in dust-offs, light cigarettes, try to smile, clear their throats and spit and begin cleaning their weapons. After a time someone would shake his head and say, No lie, I almost shit my pants, and someone else would laugh, which meant it was bad, yes, but the guy had obviously not shit his pants, it wasn't that bad, and in any case nobody would ever do such a thing and then go ahead and talk about it. They would squint into the dense, oppressive sunlight. For a few moments, perhaps, they would fall silent, lighting a joint and tracking its passage from man to man, inhaling, holding in the humiliation. Scary stuff, one of them might say. But then someone else would grin or flick his eyebrows and say, Roger-dodger, almost cut me a new asshole, *almost.*

There were numerous such poses. Some carried themselves with a sort of wistful resignation, others with pride or stiff soldierly discipline or good humor or macho zeal. They were afraid of dying but they were even more afraid to show it.

They found jokes to tell.

They used a hard vocabulary to contain the terrible softness. *Greased,* they'd say. *Offed, lit up,*[1] *zapped while zipping.*[2] It wasn't cruelty, just stage presence. They were actors and the war came at them in 3-D. When someone died, it wasn't quite dying, because in a curious way it seemed scripted, and because they had their lines mostly memorized, irony mixed with tragedy, and because they called it by other names, as if to encyst and destroy the reality of death itself. They kicked corpses. They cut off thumbs. They talked grunt lingo. They told stories about Ted Lavender's supply of

---

[1] Offed, lit up: Killed.

[2] Zapped while zipping: Killed while urinating.

tranquilizers, how the poor guy didn't feel a thing, how incredibly tranquil he was.

There's a moral here, said Mitchell Sanders.

70   They were waiting for Lavender's chopper, smoking the dead man's dope.

The moral's pretty obvious, Sanders said, and winked. Stay away from drugs. No joke, they'll ruin your day every time.

Cute, said Henry Dobbins.

Mind-blower, *get* it? Talk about wiggy—nothing left, just blood and brains.

They made themselves laugh.

75   There it is, they'd say, over and over, as if the repetition itself were an act of poise, a balance between crazy and almost crazy, knowing without going. There it is, which meant be cool, let it ride, because oh yeah, man, you can't change what can't be changed, there it is, there it absolutely and positively and fucking well is.

They were tough.

They carried all the emotional baggage of men who might die. Grief, terror, love, longing—these were intangibles, but the intangibles had their own mass and specific gravity, they had tangible weight. They carried shameful memories. They carried the common secret of cowardice barely restrained, the instinct to run or freeze or hide, and in many respects this was the heaviest burden of all, for it could never be put down, it required perfect balance and perfect posture. They carried their reputations. They carried the soldier's greatest fear, which was the fear of blushing. Men killed, and died, because they were embarrassed not to. It was what had brought them to the war in the first place, nothing positive, no dreams of glory or honor, just to avoid the blush of dishonor. They died so as not to die of embarrassment. They crawled into tunnels and walked point and advanced under fire. Each morning, despite the unknowns, they made their legs move. They endured. They kept humping. They did not submit to the obvious alternative, which was simply to close the eyes and fall. So easy, really. Go limp and tumble to the ground and let the muscles unwind and not speak and not budge until your buddies picked you up and lifted you into the chopper that would roar and dip its nose and carry you off to the world. A mere matter of falling, yet no one ever fell. It was not courage, exactly; the object was not valor. Rather, they were too frightened to be cowards.

By and large they carried these things inside, maintaining the masks of composure. They sneered at sick call. They spoke bitterly about guys who had found release by shooting off their own toes or fingers. Pussies, they'd say. Candyasses. It was fierce, mocking talk, with only a trace of envy or awe, but even so, the image played itself out behind their eyes.

They imagined the muzzle against flesh. They imagined the quick, sweet pain, then the evacuation to Japan, then a hospital with warm beds and cute geisha nurses.

80   They dreamed of freedom birds.

At night, on guard, staring into the dark, they were carried away by jumbo jets. They felt the rush of takeoff. *Gone!* they yelled. And then velocity, wings and engines, a smiling stewardess—but it was more than a plane, it was a real bird, a big sleek silver bird with feathers and talons and high screeching. They were flying. The weights fell off, there was nothing to bear. They laughed and held on tight, feeling the cold slap of wind and altitude, soaring, thinking *It's over, I'm gone!*—they were naked, they were light and free—it was all lightness, bright and fast and buoyant, light as light, a helium buzz in the brain, a giddy bubbling in the lungs as they were taken up over the clouds and the war, beyond duty, beyond gravity and mortification and global entanglements—*Sin loi!* they yelled, *I'm sorry, motherfuckers, but I'm out of it, I'm goofed, I'm on a space cruise, I'm gone!*—and it was a restful, disencumbered sensation, just riding the light waves, sailing that big silver freedom bird over the mountains and oceans, over America, over the farms and great sleeping cities and cemeteries and highways and the golden arches of McDonald's. It was flight, a kind of fleeing, a kind of falling, falling higher and higher, spinning off the edge of the earth and beyond the sun and through the vast, silent vacuum where there were no burdens and where everything weighed exactly nothing. *Gone!* they screamed, *I'm sorry but I'm gone!* And so at night, not quite dreaming, they gave themselves over to lightness, they were carried, they were purely borne.

On the morning after Ted Lavender died, First Lieutenant Jimmy Cross crouched at the bottom of his foxhole and burned Martha's letters. Then he burned the two photographs. There was a steady rain falling, which made it difficult, but he used heat tabs and Sterno to build a small fire, screening it with his body, holding the photographs over the tight blue flame with the tips of his fingers.

He realized it was only a gesture. Stupid, he thought. Sentimental, too, but mostly just stupid.

Lavender was dead. You couldn't burn the blame.

85   Besides, the letters were in his head. And even now, without photographs, Lieutenant Cross could see Martha playing volleyball in her white gym shorts and yellow T-shirt. He could see her moving in the rain.

When the fire died out, Lieutenant Cross pulled his poncho over his shoulders and ate breakfast from a can.

There was no great mystery, he decided.

In those burned letters Martha had never mentioned the war, except to say, Jimmy, take care of yourself. She wasn't involved. She signed the letters "Love," but it wasn't love, and all the fine lines and technicalities did not matter.

The morning came up wet and blurry. Everything seemed part of everything else, the fog and Martha and the deepening rain.

90   It was a war, after all.

Half smiling, Lieutenant Jimmy Cross took out his maps. He shook his head hard, as if to clear it, then bent forward and began planning the day's march. In ten minutes, or maybe twenty, he would rouse the men and they would pack up and head west, where the maps showed the country to be green and inviting. They would do what they had always done. The rain might add some weight, but otherwise it would be one more day layered upon all the other days.

He was realistic about it. There was that new hardness in his stomach.

No more fantasies, he told himself.

Henceforth, when he thought about Martha, it would be only to think that she belonged elsewhere. He would shut down the daydreams. This was not Mount Sebastian, it was another world, where there were no pretty poems or midterm exams, a place where men died because of carelessness and gross stupidity. Kiowa was right. Boom-down, and you were dead, never partly dead.

95   Briefly, in the rain, Lieutenant Cross saw Martha's gray eyes gazing back at him.

He understood.

It was very sad, he thought. The things men carried inside. The things men did or felt they had to do.

He almost nodded at her, but didn't.

Instead he went back to his maps. He was now determined to perform his duties firmly and without negligence. It wouldn't help Lavender, he knew that, but from this point on he would comport himself as a soldier. He would dispose of his good-luck pebble. Swallow it, maybe, or use Lee Strunk's slingshot, or just drop it along the trail. On the march he would impose strict field discipline. He would be careful to send out flank security, to prevent straggling or bunching up, to keep his troops moving at the proper pace and at the proper interval. He would insist on clean weapons. He would confiscate the remainder of Lavender's dope. Later in the day, perhaps, he would call the men together and speak to them plainly. He would accept the blame for what had happened to Ted Lavender. He would be a man about it. He would look them in the eyes, keeping his chin level, and he would issue the new SOPs in a calm, impersonal tone of voice, an officer's voice, leaving no room for argument or discussion. Commencing immediately, he'd tell them, they would no longer abandon equipment along the route of march. They would police up their acts. They would get their shit together, and keep it together, and maintain it neatly and in good working order.

100   He would not tolerate laxity. He would show strength, distancing himself.

Among the men there would be grumbling, of course, and maybe worse, because their days would seem longer and their loads heavier, but Lieutenant Cross reminded himself that his obligation was not to be loved but to lead. He would dispense with love; it was not now a factor. And if anyone quarreled or complained, he would simply tighten his lips and arrange his shoulders in the correct command posture. He might give a curt little nod. Or he might not. He might just shrug and say Carry on, then they would saddle up and form into a column and move out toward the villages west of Than Khe.

HÉLÈNE RIOUX
(1949–   )

Opening Night
(1993)

Translated by Diane Schoemperlen

One day in July the opera lover with whom I was almost having an affair invited me for supper. I remember the heat of the day, forty in the shade. The opera lover had just moved into a lovely air-conditioned apartment on the twenty-fourth floor of a high-rise. He said to me: "We are going to have a housewarming party together." But what he meant was, "Just the two of us, a little romantic meal. You will see what you will see." He loved to cook.

When I arrived, I was confused by the different smells. I sniffed without distinguishing them. He said, "Don't ask what we're having, it's a surprise." Then, "Make yourself at home, I'll bring you a drink." I sat down on the leather couch. He offered me a Tequila Sunrise decorated with a carcinogenic maraschino cherry; it was in a long-stemmed glass of Bohemian crystal. In an identical glass he served himself a Perrier water on the rocks with a slice of lemon gorged with vitamin C. "I don't drink," he said, "but I'll have a little wine when we eat, just to keep you company." On the lacquered table, he set out a plate of sturgeon caviar on toast and bite-size pastries stuffed with asparagus. "Are you pleased?" he asked. "Is it good?" His eyes were shining. He had been cooking all day when he could have been swimming in the pool or suntanning on the balcony. He must have liked me. Or at least he was very determined to win me over.

He went to the kitchen to check on the food, to stir the sauces, add a dash of salt, a sprig of rosemary, a few drops of spice oils. "It's ready. Are you hungry?" I was hungry. But the meal was a disaster. It began with quail stuffed with green grapes and flambéed with port. I had to look away. "Poor little sparrows." He flamed them at the table, a fate medieval and spectacular, the little birds held in the hollow of his hand, the flame licking the carcasses curled up there so tenderly, plump and round, the little innocent bodies. He was proud of himself. I made excuses, saying, "Sparrows, really, I couldn't." I tried a grape, which although still a grape, having been cooked with quails, no longer tasted the same. Disappointed expression on his face . . .

He took the plates away, he didn't dare swallow a mouthful in front of me. "It doesn't matter, I'll bring the next course." The next course was frogs' legs in basilic butter. "Taste it at least, it's delicious, I promise; it is more tender than chicken. The sauce is a masterpiece, with fresh basil, butter, reduced with white burgundy . . . All right, I understand. And do you also dislike cheese?" I'd lost my appetite but all the same I murmured, "Cheese, that's fine. As long as it's not Roquefort." It was Roquefort.

5   For the rest of the evening he was sullen. I was also unhappy but I was determined to drag a smile out of him. I felt guilty, I had spoiled the party.

Trying to get him to smile I suggested, "Next time, you can make me tofu, a cucumber sandwich"—oh no, his smiles, he would not waste them—"And poutine, a millet pie." He remained cold.

To cheer him up I told him of the time when this character, you know, he'd just come back from India, I've already told you about that, we went to school together, and he came to my house late one afternoon with a white plastic bag full of food dangling at the end of his skinny arms, you know, he was always dressed in orange, a linen tunic, rope sandals, he'd gone to a guru in India where he was given a name meaning "sun" or something like that, I forget the Hindu word, on this occasion he had decreed that he would make the supper, my eating habits were horrible, it was shameful. He was busy in the kitchen for three hours before finally serving an entrée of raw corn on the cob, and in order to eat it, he took out his dentures. Then came a murky gruel which he called oats and turnips au gratin. He assured me it was very good for one's health, the minerals, the proteins, very balanced, very zen.

I was finally successful in extracting a smile. It was a slight one, fleeting, forced. He said I was making fun of him, going over his head, and I replied that his head was well above my means.

He cleared the table, the dishes and the glasses clinking in the kitchen. I was exhausted, ravenous and nauseous at the same time. Not a breath of air came through the open French windows. The air conditioning was clearly defective. It is always this way. Always a cold spell when the furnace breaks down. Always rain for a holiday week. The toast only falls on the buttered side. It's Murphy's Law.

Total immobility, very heavy. Covered with sweat, we listened to *La Bohème*, then *Aida* and *Madame Butterfly*. He still did not have a compact disc player but a very sophisticated stereo system to regulate the flats and sharps, it's a long story, he wanted the pure sound, the perfect balance, he had a fine ear, the most imperceptible distortion caused a grimace of grief to bloom across his face. Then he suggested a game of chess and I lost. I don't have the head for it, I'm hopeless at chess. Besides I had such a horror of losing that I intentionally speeded up my defeat and this triumph without glory humiliated him even more.

10   I had finished the bottle of Alsatian wine, I felt sick, I ran to the bathroom. He followed me, he knocked on the door, "My flower, you don't feel good? Come here and stretch out." He placed a wet washcloth wrapped around ice cubes on my forehead, he made me drink some mouthfuls of an infusion, held my hand, spoke those soothing words one whispers to the dying or to children who cry. "It's all right, you didn't do it, it's all my fault, I should have asked you before making all this . . . but I wanted to surprise you, serves me right . . . here, drink a little more verbena . . ." And the verbena would not go down. He was holding a cut-glass salad bowl, he was really in love with me, nothing was too good for me, he wouldn't want me to vomit into a plastic bucket or a saucepan, he held the salad bowl in front of me while I unloaded everything inside me: the tequila and the cherry, the

green grape, the bread crusts and the fish eggs in a suspension of white wine. He patted me gently on the back while repeating with a contrite air that he should have known better, that he had seen how in a restaurant I always ordered salads, fish, a steak if need be, and between two hiccups I tried to drag forth one of his precious smiles. "It looks rather like oats with turnips, you know," I commented, casting an eye into the salad bowl.

With an uncertain air, he asked, "You made up that story, didn't you?"

"Dear friend, don't you know that truth is stranger than fiction? . . . I would never have enough imagination to make that up."

"I hate it when you call me 'dear friend.'"

"Dear friend . . . quickly . . . the salad bowl."

15 He held out the salad bowl. He went to rinse it and returned with cold compresses for my forehead. Meanwhile I had vomit in my hair but he said, "It's nothing serious, I'm going to run you a bath." I was so limp that he had to take off my clothes. I was so limp he had to lead me to the bathroom. "Do you want me to help you?" I stammered yes, otherwise I would certainly drown myself. The water was lukewarm. I was shivering. I demanded, "More hot, please . . . dear friend." He poured the shampoo on my hair, he massaged my head which was rattling, my head was so heavy, my head was so sick, then with one hand he held it, while with the other he ran a stream from the shower. "More cold now . . . very cold . . . hot now . . ."

"Is it a hot and cold shower that you want?"

"I want my spirits to return . . . they are returning . . . I feel them returning . . ."

And after three or four of these brutal transitions from boiling to freezing, they had returned very well. I was still staggering a little coming out of the bath, but only a little, and it was from weakness. He gave me a very effective pill for my headache, and a toothbrush, of which he kept some in reserve. I chose the yellow with hard bristles, I brushed vigorously and gargled with mouthwash. My haggard features peered out at me from the mirror. He dried me with a big Turkish towel, a chaste kiss on my belly, my knees, my feet. "And what would you like now? Would you like to lie down?"

He carried me as far as his bed. I was a little drowsy, nearly swaying. I sensed him at regular intervals entering the room, approaching me, leaning over me with solicitude. At one point I turned on the bedside lamp. He came at once and said, "You must be starving, my poor flower."

20 "I am ravenous."

"If you would like to go out . . ."

"I have nothing to wear."

"True . . . And if I ordered Chinese, would that bother you?"

"Go for Chinese."

25 "Egg noodles."

"Go for the noodles."

"With vegetables only."

"Go for the vegetables."

"We'll eat on the balcony."

30   We ate on the balcony by the glimmer of two candles under the crescent moon and a garden of stars. It looked like a hanging garden, an upside-down garden. We tilted our heads, hoping to see a shooting star, a meteorite streaking through space. He asked, "Now how's it going? Things are improving?" "Yes, yes." "The bouillon is light, isn't it?" "Very light." We drank weak green tea. He had loaned me one of his t-shirts. The blue night streaked to burgundy or vice versa. I put my feet beside his thigh on his cushioned chair. He caressed them absentmindedly, then with more eagerness. He said, "The feet, what a neglected part of the body, unappreciated, sometimes even despised." He said, "Me, feet, they turn me on. They look solid but they are vulnerable. Full of hollows and bumps, like valleys, a foot, it is like a landscape." I raised the stakes, saying, "And then, it is sympathetic. Without pretension." He passed his finger between my toes, saying, "Here, between the toes, it is secret, sensitive, it is fluttering." Under the influence of this light caress, I felt myself becoming euphoric little by little. He massaged the sole of my foot. He remarked, "You have soft soles. Sometimes the sole is rough."

"In winter it is rough."

"Yes, the heating."

"Nylon stockings, boots."

"It stirs me up when it's rough, it stirs me up when it's soft. You have a silky sole."

35   He put my feet on his knees. He took them one by one in his hands as if they were birds, quivering quails. He approached them with his lips. He said, "By the way, this character . . ."

"What character?"

"The comical person you were talking about a few minutes ago . . ."

"Oats with turnips?"

"Yes."

40   He kissed my toes one at a time, holding my heel in the palm of his hand, he caressed my arch with his thumb, I began to feel suggestive tickles all the length of my legs, rising up the inner sides, microscopic ants climbing single file up a mountain path.

"What puzzles you?"

"Well, I don't know . . . who he was, how you became friends with him. It's so very strange to imagine you with that kind of man."

"We met in school, we were in grade twelve. Then he had a brush cut, heavy black-rimmed glasses, the kind with Coke bottle bottoms, he wore a steel grey suit, his father's ties. The laughing stock of the class, I'll tell you. He was always like that. The butt of their jokes, the scapegoat."

"The whipping boy."

45   "The bogeyman."

"First in the class?"

"No, not so. Below average. No good in math, no good in physical education, strong in history. Crazy about overly elaborate philosophy, deadly boring. His speech was slow and hesitant . . . I like that, your tongue under my toes . . ."

"They remind me of little pillows . . . In short, you took pity on him, right?"

"No, at that time I never said a word to him. I was content to laugh at him, like everybody else. It was only some years later, I frequently visited a man, you know, I told you about him, who was into transcendental meditation."

50 "You never told me about that."

"It's not important . . . anyway, him, he knew him. He had returned from India. Oats with turnips, I'll say."

"You're easy to follow."

"A cult, over there, he'd been renamed. At first I didn't recognize him. He held immersion sessions."

"Immersion?"

55 "Yes, in a bath. You had to be completely under the water, a tube in the mouth, you know, like a periscope."

"A snorkel, you mean."

"All right, a snorkel, if you wish, but me, it reminded me of a periscope, a contraption which rose out of the water to spy all around . . . Apparently it was like a return to the mother's womb. A very beneficial technique. The Rebirth."

"Yes, I've heard something about that. So, did you take the plunge?"

"You're kidding me . . . No, the mother's womb, it didn't really inspire me. And besides, I couldn't bring myself to be naked in the bath with him all around holding the periscope. I should say the snorkel. His monastic air literally froze me. But he did calculate my biorhythm and my astrological chart."

60 "And then?"

"According to these calculations we were meant for each other. Our physiological clocks marked the same hour, our planets coincided very strangely. Venus in Taurus for both of us. The harmony of our libidos was supposed to be complete."

"You verified this?"

"Alas, he was not my type. When I explained this to him, he couldn't believe his ears. I had to handle it with three pairs of white gloves. It is difficult to tell a man he is unattractive. They cannot conceive that we are rejecting them because they are unattractive. A certain kind of unattractiveness, I should say. Because another kind, on the contrary, can be irresistible."

"You mean a virile unattractiveness?"

65 "Like yours. But he was, you could say . . . too macrobiotic . . . . And then, I don't know, but his false teeth, his pimples."

(Just thinking of it, I nearly vomited again.)

"And then, he had to redo his calculations?"

"Calculus."

"What did you say?"

70   "I was joking. No, he didn't redo his calculations, he was infallible, the pope of the arcane. But he stared at me for several seconds, then declared, with grand condescension, that my aura was completely blurred."

"Me, I find your aura delicious."

I was feeling beautiful, these touches to my feet made me give in to a state of subtle enjoyment, as if the centre of sensation had been transported there, concentrated between my toes and my ankles. I leaned my head against the back of the garden chair, I contemplated the moon smiling with self-satisfaction, I dreamed of the constellations constellating and the galaxies turning. Like the stars turning around their sun, his thumb was delicately turning around my anklebone. Then I closed my eyes and I kept moaning very slowly. My breathing speeded up, I could hear a soft moaning coming from my mouth, I felt my lips forming the sound "yes" at closer and closer intervals, I had my head thrown back, my feet abandoned to his hands. When he began to suck my toes, tiny bubbles burst under my skin, my mouth went dry while elsewhere another part of my body was liquefied (is this the principle of body language?). Images filed through my head: precise, vague, vague, precise, colours, black, colours, sprays of colours, geysers which splashed through the black in my head, I never wanted to open my eyes again, never wanted to move again, I would stay there spellbound in this no-man's time, clutching the fleeting beauty of this instant which was escaping me, all of my strength holding out against its ending and refusing at the same time the idea of attaining it, holding off till infinity the culmination, the final act, one more minute, my tormentor, isn't it so, the little death is so slow in coming, then all at once a long shudder shook me, I arched under the manifold eye of the night, these wonderful stars, and I cried out, I think.

CAROL SHIELDS
(1935–2003)

Scenes
(1990)

In 1974 Frances was asked to give a lecture in Edmonton, and on the way there her plane was forced to make an emergency landing in a barley field. The man sitting next to her—they had not spoken—turned and asked if he might put his arms around her. She assented. They clung together, her size 12 dress and his wool suit. Later, he gave her his business card.

She kept the card for several weeks poked in the edge of her bedroom mirror. It is a beautiful mirror, a graceful rectangle in a pine frame, and very,

very old. Once it was attached to the back of a bureau belonging to Frances's grandmother. Leaves, vines, flowers and fruit are shallowly carved in the soft wood of the frame. The carving might be described as primitive—and this is exactly why Frances loves it, being drawn to those things that are incomplete or in some way flawed. Furthermore, the mirror is the first thing she remembers seeing, *really* seeing, as a child. Visiting her grandmother, she noticed the stiff waves of light and shadow on the frame, the way square pansies interlocked with rigid grapes, and she remembers creeping out of her grandmother's bed where she had been put for an afternoon nap and climbing on a chair so she could touch the worked surface with the flat of her hand.

Her grandmother died. It was discovered by the aunts and uncles that on the back of the mirror was stuck a piece of adhesive tape and on the tape was written: "For my vain little granddaughter Frances." Frances's mother was affronted, but put it down to hardening of the arteries. Frances, who was only seven, felt uniquely, mysteriously honoured.

She did not attend the funeral; it was thought she was too young, and so instead she was taken one evening to the funeral home to bid goodbye to her grandmother's body. The room where the old lady lay was large, quiet, and hung all around with swags of velvet. Frances's father lifted her up so she could see her grandmother, who was wearing a black dress with a white crêpe jabot, her powdered face pulled tight as though with a drawstring into a sort of grimace. A lovely blanket with satin edging covered her trunky legs and torso. Laid out, calm and silent as a boat, she looked almost generous.

5   For some reason Frances was left alone with the casket for a few minutes, and she took this chance—she had to pull herself up on tiptoe—to reach out and touch her grandmother's lips with the middle finger of her right hand. It was like pressing in the side of a rubber ball. The lips did not turn to dust—which did not surprise Frances at all, but rather confirmed what she had known all along. Later, she would look at her finger and say to herself, "This finger has touched dead lips." Then she would feel herself grow rich with disgust. The touch, she knew, had not been an act of love at all, but only a kind of test.

With the same middle finger she later touched the gelatinous top of a goldfish swimming in a little glass bowl at school. She touched the raised mole on the back of her father's white neck. Shuddering, she touched horse turds in the back lane, and she touched her own urine springing on to the grass as she squatted behind the snowball bush by the fence. When she looked into her grandmother's mirror, now mounted on her own bedroom wall, she could hardly believe that she, Frances, had contravened so many natural laws.

The glass itself was bevelled all the way around, and she can remember that she took pleasure in lining up her round face so that the bevelled edge split it precisely in two. When she was fourteen she wrote in her diary, "Life is like looking into a bevelled mirror." The next day she crossed it out and, peering into the mirror, stuck out her tongue and made a face. All her life she'd had this weakness for preciosity, but mainly she'd managed to keep it in check.

She is a lithe and toothy woman with strong, thick, dark-brown hair, now starting to grey. She can be charming. "Frances can charm the bees out of the hive," said a friend of hers, a man she briefly thought she loved. Next year she'll be forty-five—terrible!—but at least she's kept her figure. A western sway to her voice is what people chiefly remember about her, just as they remember other people for their chins or noses. This voice sometimes makes her appear inquisitive, but, in fact, she generally hangs back and leaves it to others to begin a conversation.

Once, a woman got into an elevator with her and said, "Will you forgive me if I speak my mind. This morning I came within an inch of taking my life. There was no real reason, only everything had got suddenly so dull. But I'm all right now. In fact, I'm going straight to a restaurant and treat myself to a plate of french fries. Just fries, not even a sandwich to go with them. I was never allowed to have french fries when I was a little girl, but the time comes when a person should do what she wants to do."

10 The subject of childhood interests Frances, especially its prohibitions, so illogical and various, and its random doors and windows which appear solidly shut, but can, in fact, be opened easily with a touch or a password or a minute of devout resolution. It helps to be sly, also to be quick. There was a time when she worried that fate had pencilled her in as "debilitated by guilt," but mostly she takes guilt for what it is, a kind of lover who can be shrugged off or greeted at the gate. She looks at her two daughters and wonders if they'll look back resentfully, recalling only easy freedoms and an absence of terror—in other words, meagreness—and envy her for her own stern beginnings. It turned out to have been money in the bank, all the various shames and sweats of growing up. It was instructive; it kept things interesting; she still shivers, remembering how exquisitely sad she was as a child.

"It's only natural for children to be sad," says her husband, Theo, who, if he has a fault, is given to reductive statements. "Children are unhappy because they are inarticulate and hence lonely."

Frances can't remember being lonely, but telling this to Theo is like blowing into a hurricane. She was spoiled—a lovely word, she thinks—and adored by her parents, her plump, white-faced father and her skinny, sweet-tempered mother. Their love was immense and enveloping like a fall of snow. In the evenings, winter evenings, she sat between the two of them on a blue nubby sofa, listening to the varnished radio and taking sips from their cups of tea from time to time or sucking on a spoonful of sugar. The three of them sat enthralled through "Henry Aldrich" and "Fibber Magee and Molly," and when Frances laughed they looked at her and laughed too. Frances has no doubt that those spoonfuls of sugar and the roar of Fibber Magee's closet and her parents' soft looks were taken in and preserved so that she, years later, boiling an egg or making love or digging the garden, is sometimes struck by a blow of sweetness that seems to come out of nowhere.

The little brown house where she grew up sat in the middle of a block crowded with other such houses. In front of each lay a tiny lawn and a flower bed edged with stones. Rows of civic trees failed to flourish, but did not die either. True, there was terror in the back lane where the big boys played with sticks and jackknives, but the street was occupied mainly by quiet, hard-working families, and in the summertime hopscotch could be played in the street, there was so little traffic.

Frances's father spent his days "at the office." Her mother stayed at home, wore bib aprons, made jam and pickles and baked custard, and every morning before school brushed and braided Frances's hair. Frances can remember, or thinks she can remember, that one morning her mother walked as far as the corner with her and said, "I don't know why, but I'm so full of happiness today I can hardly bear it." The sun came fretting through the branches of a scrubby elm at that minute and splashed across her mother's face, making her look like someone in a painting or like one of the mothers in her school reader.

15   Learning to read was like falling into a mystery deeper than the mystery of airwaves or the halo around the head of the baby Jesus. Deliberately she made herself stumble and falter over the words in her first books, trying to hold back the rush of revelation. She saw other children being matter-of-fact and methodical, puzzling over vowels and consonants and sounding out words as though they were dimes and nickels that had to be extracted from the slot of a bank. She felt suffused with light and often skipped or hopped or ran wildly to keep herself from flying apart.

Her delirium, her failure to ingest books calmly, made her suspect there was something wrong with her or else with the world, yet she deeply distrusted the school librarian who insisted that a book could be a person's best friend. (Those subject to preciosity instantly spot others with the same affliction.) This librarian, Miss Mayes, visited all the classes. She was tall and soldierly with a high, light voice. "Boys and girls," she cried, bringing large red hands together, "a good book will never let you down." She went on; books could take you on magic journeys; books could teach you where the rain came from or how things used to be in the olden days. A person who truly loved books need never feel alone.

But, she continued, holding up a finger, there are people who do shameful things to books. They pull them from the shelves by their spines. They turn down the corners of pages; they leave them on screened porches where the rain and other elements can warp their covers; and they use curious and inappropriate objects as bookmarks.

From a petit-point bag she drew a list of objects that had been wrongly, criminally inserted between fresh clean pages: a blue-jay feather, an oak leaf, a matchbook cover, a piece of coloured chalk and, on one occasion—"on one occasion, boys and girls"—*a strip of bacon.*

A strip of bacon. In Frances's mind the strip of bacon was uncooked, cold and fatty with a pathetic streaking of lean. Its oil would press into the paper, a porky abomination, and its ends would flop out obscenely. The thought was thrilling: someone, someone who lived in the same school district, had had the audacity, the imagination, to mark the pages of a book with a strip of bacon. The existence of this person and his outrageous act penetrated the fever that had come over her since she'd learned to read, and she began to look around again and see what the world had to offer.

20 Next door lived Mr and Mrs Shaw, and upstairs, fast asleep, lived Louise Shaw, aged eighteen. She had been asleep for ten years. A boy across the street named Jackie McConnell told Frances that it was the sleeping sickness, that Louise Shaw had been bitten by the sleeping sickness bug, but Frances's mother said no, it was the coma. One day Mrs Shaw, smelling of chlorine bleach and wearing a flower-strewn housedress, stopped Frances on the sidewalk, held the back of her hand to the side of Frances's face and said, "Louise was just your age when we lost her. She was forever running or skipping rope or throwing a ball up against the side of the garage. I used to say to her, don't make such a ruckus, you'll drive me crazy. I used to yell all the time at her, she was so full of beans and such a chatterbox." After that Frances felt herself under an obligation to Mrs Shaw, and whenever she saw her she made her body speed up and whirl on the grass or do cartwheels.

A little later she learned to negotiate the back lane. There, between board fences, garbage cans, garage doors and stands of tough weeds, she became newly nimble and strong. She learned to swear—damn, hell and dirty bastard—and played piggy-move-up and spud and got herself roughly kissed a number of times, and then something else happened: one of the neighbours put up a basketball hoop. For a year, maybe two—Frances doesn't trust her memory when it comes to time—she was obsessed with doing free throws. She became known as the queen of free throws; she acquired status, even with the big boys, able to sink ten out of ten baskets, but never, to her sorrow, twenty out of twenty. She threw free throws in the morning before school, at lunchtime, and in the evening until it got dark. Nothing made her happier than when the ball dropped silently through the ring without touching it or banking on the board. At night she dreamed of these silky baskets, the rush of air and the sinuous movement of the net, then the ball striking the pavement and returning to her hands. ("Sounds a bit Freudian to me," her husband, Theo, said when she tried to describe for him her time of free-throw madness, proving once again how far apart the two of them were in some things.) One morning she was up especially early. There was no one about. The milkman hadn't come yet, and there was dew shining on the tarry joints of the pavement. Holding the ball in her hands was like holding on to a face, it was so dearly familiar with its smell of leather and its seams and laces. That morning she threw twenty-seven perfect free throws before missing. Each time the ball went through the hoop she felt an additional oval of surprise grow round her body. She had springs inside her, in her arms and in the insteps of her feet. What stopped her finally was her mother calling her name, demanding to know what she was doing outside so early. "Nothing," Frances said, and knew for the first time the incalculable reward of self-possession.

There was a girl in her sewing class named Pat Leonard. She was older than the other girls, had a rough pitted face and a brain pocked with grotes-queries. "Imagine," she said to Frances, "sliding down a banister and suddenly it turns into a razor blade." When she trimmed the seams of the skirt she was making and accidentally cut through the fabric, she laughed out loud. To amuse the other girls she sewed the skin of her fingers together. She told a joke, a long story about a pickle factory that was really about eating excrement. In her purse was a packet of cigarettes. She had a boyfriend who went to the technical school, and several times she'd reached inside his pants and squeezed his thing until it went off like a squirt gun. She'd flunked math twice. She could hardly read. One day she wasn't there, and the sewing teacher said she'd been expelled. Frances felt as though she'd lost her best friend, even though she wouldn't have been seen dead walking down the hall with Pat Leonard. Melodramatic tears swam into her eyes, and then real tears that wouldn't stop until the teacher brought her a glass of water and offered to phone her mother.

Another time, she was walking home from a friend's in the early evening. She passed by a little house not far from her own. The windows were open and, floating on the summer air, came the sound of people speaking in a foreign language. There seemed to be a great number of them, and the conversation was very rapid and excited. They might have been quarrelling or telling old stories; Frances had no idea which. It could have been French or Russian or Portuguese they spoke. The words ran together and made queer little dashes and runs and choking sounds. Frances imagined immense, wide-branching grammars and steep, stone streets rising out of other centuries. She felt as though she'd been struck by a bolt of good fortune, and all because the world was bigger than she'd been led to believe.

At university, where she studied languages, she earned pocket money by working in the library. She and a girl named Ursula were entrusted with the key, and it was their job to open the library on Saturday mornings. During the minute or two before anyone else came, the two of them galloped at top speed through the reference room, the periodical room, the reading room, up and down the rows of stacks, filling that stilled air with what could only be called primal screams. Why this should have given Frances such exquisite pleasure she couldn't have said, since she was in rebellion against nothing she knew of. By the time the first students arrived, she and Ursula would be standing behind the main desk, date stamp in hand, sweet as dimity.

25   One Saturday, the first person who came was a bushy-headed, serious-minded zoology student named Theodore, called Theo by his friends. He gave Frances a funny look, then in a cracked, raspy voice asked her to come with him later and have a cup of coffee. A year later he asked her to marry

him. He had a mind unblown by self-regard and lived, it seemed to Frances, in a nursery world of goodness and badness with not much room to move in between.

It's been mainly a happy marriage. Between the two of them, they've invented hundreds of complex ways of enslaving each other, some of them amazingly tender. Like other married people, they've learned to read each other's minds. Once Theo said to Frances as they drove around and around, utterly lost in a vast treeless suburb, "In every one of these houses there's been a declaration of love," and this was exactly the thought Frances had been thinking.

She has been faithful. To her surprise, to everyone's surprise, she turned out to have an aptitude for monogamy. Nevertheless, many of the scenes that have come into her life have involved men. Once she was walking down a very ordinary French street on a hot day. A man, bare-chested, drinking Perrier at a café table, sang out, *"Bonjour."* Not *"bonjour, Madame"* or *"bonjour, Mademoiselle"* just *"bonjour."* Cheeky. She was wearing white pants, a red blouse, a straw hat and sunglasses. *"Bonjour,"* she sang back and gave a sassy little kick, which became the start of a kind of dance. The man at the table clapped his hands over his head to keep time as she went dancing by.

Once she went to the British Museum to finish a piece of research. There was a bomb alert just as she entered, and everyone's shopping bags and briefcases were confiscated and searched. It happened that Frances had just bought a teddy bear for the child of a friend she was going to visit later in the day. The guard took it, shook it till its eyes rolled, and then carried it away to be X-rayed. Later he brought it to Frances, who was sitting at a table examining a beautiful old manuscript. As he handed her the bear, he kissed the air above its fuzzy head, and Frances felt her mouth go into the shape of a kiss, too, a kiss she intended to be an expression of her innocence, only that. He winked. She winked back. He leaned over and whispered into her ear a suggestion that was hideously, comically, obscene. She pretended not to hear, and a few minutes later she left, hurrying down the street full of cheerful shame, her work unfinished.

These are just some of the scenes in Frances's life. She thinks of them as scenes because they're much too fragmentary to be stories and far too immediate to be memories. They seem to bloom out of nothing, out of the thin, uncoloured air of defeats and pleasures. A curtain opens, a light appears, there are voices or music or sometimes a wide transparent stream of silence. Only rarely do they point to anything but themselves. They're difficult to talk about. They're useless, attached to nothing, can't be traded in or shaped into instruments to prise open the meaning of the universe.

30   There are people who think such scenes are ornaments suspended from lives that are otherwise busy and useful. Frances knows perfectly well that they are what a life is made of, one fitting against the next like English paving stones.

Or sometimes she thinks of them as little keys on a chain, keys that open nothing, but simply exist for the beauty of their toothed edges and the way they chime in her pocket.

Other times she is reminded of the Easter eggs her mother used to bring out every year. These were real hens' eggs with a hole poked in the top and bottom and the contents blown out. The day before Easter, Frances and her mother always sat down at the kitchen table with paint brushes, a glass of water and a box of watercolours. They would decorate half-a-dozen eggs, maybe more, but only the best were saved from year to year. These were taken from a cupboard just before Easter, removed from their shoebox, and carefully arranged, always on the same little pewter cake stand. The eggs had to be handled gently, especially the older ones.

Frances, when she was young, liked to pick up each one in turn and examine it minutely. She had a way of concentrating her thoughts and shutting everything else out, thinking only of this one little thing, this little egg that was round like the world, beautiful in colour and satin to the touch, and that fit into the hollow of her hand as though it were made for that very purpose.

POETRY

CHAPTER 11

Understanding Poetry

> ◆ ◇

NIKKI GIOVANNI
(1945–   )

Poetry
(1975)

poetry is motion graceful
as a fawn
gentle as a teardrop
strong like the eye
5 finding peace in a crowded room
we poets tend to think
our words are golden
though emotion speaks too
loudly to be defined
10 by silence

sometimes after midnight or just before
the dawn
we sit typewriter in hand
pulling loneliness around us
15 forgetting our lovers or children
who are sleeping
ignoring the weary wariness
of our own logic
to compose a poem

20 no one understands it
it never says "love me" for poets are
beyond love
it never says "accept me" for poems seek not

acceptance but controversy
25 it only says "i am" and therefore
i concede that you are too
a poem is pure energy
horizontally contained
between the mind
30 of the poet and the ear of the reader
if it does not sing discard the ear
for poetry is song
if it does not delight discard
the heart for poetry is joy
35 if it does not inform then close
off the brain for it is dead
if it cannot heed the insistent message
that life is precious

which is all we poets
40 wrapped in our loneliness
are trying to say

◊ ◊ ◊

ARCHIBALD MACLEISH
(1892–1982)

Ars Poetica[1]
(1926)

A poem should be palpable and mute
As a globed fruit,

Dumb
As old medallions to the thumb,

5 Silent as the sleeve-worn stone
Of casement ledges where the moss has grown—

A poem should be wordless
As the flight of birds.

A poem should be motionless in time
10 As the moon climbs,

---

[1] Art of Poetry.

Leaving, as the moon releases
Twig by twig the night-entangled trees,

Leaving, as the moon behind the winter leaves,
Memory by memory the mind—

15 A poem should be motionless in time
As the moon climbs.

A poem should be equal to:
Not true.

For all the history of grief
20 An empty doorway and a maple leaf.

For love
The leaning grasses and two lights above the sea—

A poem should not mean
But be.

◊ ◊ ◊

IRVING LAYTON
(1912–2006)

Whatever Else Poetry Is Freedom
(1958)

Whatever else poetry is freedom.
Forget the rhetoric, the trick of lying
All poets pick up sooner or later. From the river,
Rising like the thin voice of grey castratos—the mist;
5 Poplars and pines grow straight but oaks are gnarled;
Old codgers must speak of death, boys break windows;
Women lie honestly by their men at last.

And I who gave my Kate a blackened eye
Did to its vivid changing colours
10 Make up an incredible musical scale;
And now I balance on wooden stilts and dance
And thereby sing to the loftiest casements.
See how with polish I bow from the waist.
Space for these stilts! More space or I fail!

15 And a crown I say for my buffoon's head.
Yet no more fool am I than King Canute,
Lord of our tribe, who scanned and scorned;
Who half-deceived, believed; and, poet, missed

The first white waves come nuzzling at his feet;
20 Then damned the courtiers and the foolish trial
With a most bewildering and unkingly jest.

It was the mist. It lies inside one like a destiny.
A real Jonah it lies rotting like a lung.
And I know myself undone who am a clown
25 And wear a wreath of mist for a crown;
Mist with the scent of dead apples,
Mist swirling from black oily waters at evening,
Mist from the fraternal graves of cemeteries.

It shall drive me to beg my food and at last
30 Hurl me broken I know and prostrate on the road;
Like a huge toad I saw, entire but dead,
That Time mordantly had blacked; O pressed
To the moist earth it pled for entry.
I shall be I say that stiff toad for sick with mist
35 And crazed I smell the odour of mortality.

And Time flames like a paraffin stove
And what it burns are the minutes I live.
At certain middays I have watched the cars
Bring me from afar their windshield suns;
40 What lay to my hand were blue fenders,
The suns extinguished, the drivers wearing sunglasses.
And it made me think I had touched a hearse.

So whatever else poetry is freedom. Let
Far off the impatient cadences reveal
45 A padding for my breathless stilts. Swivel,
O hero, in the fleshy groves, skin and glycerine,
And sing of lust, the sun's accompanying shadow
Like a vampire's wing, the stillness in dead feet—
Your stave brings resurrection, O aggrievèd king.

DEFINING POETRY
◇ ◇ ◇

Throughout history and across various national and cultural boundaries, poetry has held an important place. In ancient China and Japan, for example, poetry was prized above all else. One story tells of a samurai warrior who, when defeated, asked for a pen and paper. Thinking that he wanted to write a will before being executed, his captor granted his wish.

Instead of writing a will, however, the warrior wrote a farewell poem that so moved his captor that he immediately released him.

To the ancient Greeks and Romans, poetry was the medium of spiritual and philosophical expression. Epics such as the *Iliad* and the *Aeneid* are written in verse, and so are dramas such as *Oedipus the King* (p. 1293). Passages of the Bible, the Koran, and the Hindu holy books are also written in poetry. Today, throughout the world, poetry continues to delight and to inspire. For many people, in many places, poetry is the language of the emotions, the medium of expression they use when they speak from the heart.

Despite the longstanding place of poetry in our lives, however, many people—including poets themselves—have difficulty deciding just what poetry is. Is a poem "pure energy / horizontally contained / between the mind / of the poet and the ear of the reader," as Nikki Giovanni describes it? Or is a poem, as Archibald MacLeish says, "Dumb," "Silent," "wordless," and "motionless in time"? Or is it "freedom," as Irving Layton says?

One way of defining poetry is to say that it uses language to condense experience into an intensely concentrated package, with each sound, each word, each image, and each line carrying great weight. But beyond this, it is difficult to pin down what makes a particular arrangement of words or lines a poem. Part of the problem is that poetry has many guises: a poem may be short or long, accessible or obscure; it may express a mood or tell a story; it may conform to a familiar poetic form—a sonnet, a couplet, a haiku—or follow no conventional pattern; it may or may not have a regular, identifiable metre or a rhyme scheme; it may depend heavily on elaborate imagery, figures of speech, irony, complex allusions or symbols, or repeated sounds—or it may include none of these features conventionally associated with poetry.

To further complicate the issue, different readers, different poets, different generations of readers and poets, and different cultures may have different expectations about poetry. As a result, they have different assumptions about poetry, and these different assumptions raise questions. Must poetry be written to delight or inspire, or can a poem have a political or social message? And must this message be conveyed subtly, embellished with imaginatively chosen sounds and words, or can it be explicit and straightforward? These questions, which have been debated by literary critics as well as by poets for many years, have no easy answers—and perhaps no answers at all. A haiku—short, rich in imagery, adhering to a rigid formal structure—is certainly poetry, and so is a political poem like Wole Soyinka's "Telephone Conversation" (p. 8). To some Western readers, however, a haiku might seem too plain and understated to be poetic, and Soyinka's poem might seem to be a political tract masquerading as poetry. Still, most of these readers would agree that the following lines qualify as poetry.

WILLIAM SHAKESPEARE
(1564–1616)

That Time of Year Thou Mayst in Me Behold
(1609)

That time of year thou mayst in me behold
When yellow leaves, or none, or few, do hang
Upon those boughs which shake against the cold,
Bare ruined choirs, where late the sweet birds sang.
5 In me thou see'st the twilight of such day
As after sunset fadeth in the west,
Which by and by black night doth take away,
Death's second self that seals up all in rest.
In me thou see'st the glowing of such fire,
10 That on the ashes of his youth doth lie,
As the deathbed whereon it must expire,
Consumed with that which it was nourished by.
   This thou perceiv'st, which makes thy love more strong,
   To love that well which thou must leave ere long.

This poem possesses many of the characteristics that Western readers have come to associate with poetry. For instance, its lines have a regular pattern of rhyme and metre that identifies it as a sonnet. The poem also includes a complex network of related imagery and figurative language that compares the lost youth of the aging speaker to the sunset and to autumn. Finally, the pair of rhyming lines at the end of the poem states a familiar poetic theme: the lovers' knowledge that they must eventually die makes their love stronger.

Even though the next poem is quite different from the preceding sonnet, most readers would probably agree that it too is a poem.

LORNA CROZIER
(1948–   )

Poem about Nothing
(1985)

Zero is the one we didn't understand
at school. Multiplied by anything
it remains nothing.

When I ask my friend
5 the mathematician who studies rhetoric
if zero is a number, he says yes
and I feel great relief.

If it were a landscape
it would be a desert.
10 If it had anything to do
with anatomy, it would be
a mouth, a missing limb,
a lost organ.

Ø

15 Zero worms its way
             between one and one
and changes everything.

It is the vowel on a mute tongue,
the pupil in a blind man's eye,
20 the image
       of the face
he holds on his fingertips.

Ø

When you look up
25 from the bottom of a dry well
zero is what you see,
the terrible blue of it.

It is the rope
you knot around your throat
30 when your heels itch for wings.

Icarus[1] understood zero
as he caught the smell
of burning feathers
and fell into the sea.

35   Ø

---

[1] According to Greek myth, Icarus and his father, Daedalus, escaped the labyrinth of Knossos by using wings fashioned out of feathers and wax. Icarus ignored his father's advice and flew too close to the sun. As a result, his wax wings melted, and he fell into the sea and drowned.

If you roll zero down a hill
it will grow,
swallow the towns, the farms,
the people at their tables
40 playing tic-tac-toe.

Ø

When the Cree chiefs
signed the treaties on the plains
they wrote X
45 beside their names.

In English, X equals zero.

Ø

I ask my friend
the rhetorician who studies mathematics
50 *What does zero mean and keep it simple.*

He says *Zip.*

Ø

Zero is the pornographer's number.
He orders it through the mail
55 under a false name. It is the number
of the last man on death row,
the number of the girl who jumps
three stories to abort.

Zero starts and ends
60 at the same place. Some compare it
to driving across the Prairies all day
and feeling you've gone nowhere.

Ø Ø Ø

In the beginning God made zero.

Unlike Shakespeare's sonnet, Crozier's poem does not have a regular metrical pattern or rhyme scheme. Its diction is more conversational than poetic, and one of its images—"a missing limb"—stands in stark contrast to the other, more conventionally "poetic" images. Nevertheless, the subject is a traditional one. Finally, the poem's division into stanzas and its use of figurative language ("It is the vowel on a mute tongue") are unmistakably poetic.

Although the two preceding works can easily be classified as poems, readers might have trouble with the following lines.

E. E. CUMMINGS
(1894–1962)

1(a

(1923)

l(a

le
af
fa

5 ll

s)
one
l

iness

Unlike the preceding two poems, "l(a" does not seem to have any of the characteristics normally associated with poetry. It has no metre, rhyme, or imagery. It has no repeated sounds, no figures of speech, no symbols. It cannot even be read aloud because its "lines" are fragments of words. In spite of its odd appearance, however, "l(a" does present an idea that is poetic. Reconstructed, the words Cummings broke apart—"l (a leaf falls) one l iness"—express a conventional poetic theme: the loneliness and isolation of the individual, as reflected in nature. At the same time, by breaking words into bits and pieces, Cummings suggests the flexibility of language and conveys the need to break out of customary ways of using words to define experience.

As the preceding discussion illustrates, defining what a poem is (and is not) is almost impossible. It is true that most poems, particularly those divided into stanzas, look like poems, and it is also true that poems tend to use compressed language. Beyond this, however, what makes a poem a poem is more a matter of degree than a question of whether or not it conforms to a strict set of rules. A poem is likely to use *more* imagery, figurative language, rhyme, and so on than a prose piece—but, then again, it may not.

READING POETRY

◊ ◊ ◊

Some readers say they do not like poetry because they find it obscure or intimidating. One reason some people have difficulty reading poetry is that it tends to present information in subtle (and therefore potentially confusing) ways; it does not immediately "get to the point" as journalistic articles or business letters do. One could certainly argue that by concentrating experience, poetry actually "gets to the point" in ways—and to degrees—that other kinds of writing do not. Even so, some readers see poetry as an alien form. They have the misconception that poetry is always filled with obscure allusions, complex metrical schemes, and flowery diction. Others, feeling excluded from what they see as its secret language and mysterious structure, approach poetry as something that must be deciphered. Certainly, reading poetry often requires hard work and concentration. Because it is compressed, poetry often omits exposition and explanation; consequently, readers must be willing to take the time to read closely—to interpret ideas and supply missing connections. Many readers are simply not motivated to dig deeply for what they perceive to be uncertain rewards. But not all poems are difficult, and even those that are difficult are often well worth the effort. (For specific suggestions about how to read poetry, see Chapter 12.)

RECOGNIZING KINDS OF POETRY
◊ ◊ ◊

Most poems are either *narrative* poems, which recount a story, or *lyric* poems, which communicate a speaker's mood, feelings, or state of mind.

NARRATIVE POETRY

Although any brief poem that tells a story, such as Edwin Arlington Robinson's "Richard Cory" (p. 877), may be considered a narrative poem, the two most familiar forms of narrative poetry are the *epic* and the *ballad.*

Epic poems recount the accomplishments of heroic figures, typically including expansive settings, superhuman feats, and gods and supernatural beings. The language of epic poems tends to be formal, even elevated, and often quite elaborate. Epics span many cultures—from the *Odyssey* (Greek) to *Beowulf* (Anglo-Saxon) to *The Epic of Gilgamesh* (Babylonian). In ancient times, epics were handed down orally; more recently, poets have written literary epics, such as John Milton's 1667 *Paradise Lost* and Nobel Prize–winning poet Derek Walcott's 1990 *Omeros,* which follow many of the same conventions.

The **ballad** is another type of narrative poetry with roots in an oral tradition. Originally intended to be sung, a ballad uses repeated words and phrases, including a refrain, to advance its story. Some—but not all—ballads use the **ballad stanza.** For examples of traditional ballads in this text, see "Bonny Barbara Allen" (p. 818) and "Western Wind" (p. 819).

LYRIC POETRY

Like narrative poems, lyric poems take various forms.

An **elegy** is a poem in which a poet mourns the death of a specific person, as in A. E. Housman's "To an Athlete Dying Young" (p. 677). Another example of an elegy is Marlene Nourbese Philip's "Blackman Dead" (p. 621).

An **ode** is a long lyric poem, formal and serious in style, tone, and subject matter. An ode typically has a fairly complex stanzaic pattern, such as the **terza rima** used by Percy Bysshe Shelley in "Ode to the West Wind" (p. 881). Another ode in this text is "Ode on a Grecian Urn" (p. 852).

An **aubade** is a poem about morning, usually celebrating the coming of dawn. An example is Philip Larkin's "Aubade" (p. 858).

An **occasional poem** is written to celebrate a particular event or occasion. An example is George Herbert's "Easter Wings" (p. 787).

A **meditation** is a lyric poem that focuses on a physical object, using this object as a vehicle for considering larger issues. Edmund Waller's "Go, Lovely Rose" (p. 891) is a meditation.

A **pastoral**—for example, Christopher Marlowe's "The Passionate Shepherd to His Love" (p. 578)—is a lyric poem that celebrates the simple, idyllic pleasures of country life.

Finally, a **dramatic monologue** is a poem whose speaker addresses one or more silent listeners, often revealing much more than he or she intends. Robert Browning's "My Last Duchess" (p. 624) and "Porphyria's Lover" (p. 640) and Alfred, Lord Tennyson's "Ulysses" (p. 886) are three dramatic monologues that appear in this text.

DISCOVERING THEMES IN POETRY

◊ ◊ ◊ ◊ ◊

A poem can be about anything, from the mysteries of the universe to poetry itself. Although no subject is really inappropriate for poetic treatment, certain conventional subjects recur frequently. For example, poets often write about love, war, nature, death, family, the folly of human desires, and the inevitability of growing old.

A poem's **theme,** however, is more than its general subject matter. It denotes the ideas the poet explores, the concerns the poem examines. More specifically, a poem's theme is its main point or idea. Poems "about nature," for instance, may praise the beauty of nature, assert the superiority of its simplest creatures over humans, consider its evanescence, or mourn its destruction. Similarly, poems "about death" may examine the difficulty of facing one's own mortality, eulogize a friend, assert the need for the acceptance of life's cycles, cry out against death's inevitability, or explore the **carpe diem** theme ("life is brief, so let us seize the day").

In order to discover the theme of a poem, readers look at its form, its voice, its language, its images, its allusions, its sound—all of its individual elements.

Together, these elements convey the ideas that are important in the poem. (Of course, a poem may not communicate the same meaning to every reader. Different readers bring different backgrounds, attitudes, and experiences to a poem and therefore see different things and give weight to different ideas.)

The following poem is rich enough in language and content to suggest a variety of different interpretations.

◊ ◊ ◊

ADRIENNE RICH
(1929–   )

A Woman Mourned by Daughters
(1984)

Now, not a tear begun,
we sit here in your kitchen,
spent, you see, already.
You are swollen till you strain
5 this house and the whole sky.
You, whom we so often
succeeded in ignoring!
You are puffed up in death
like a corpse pulled from the sea;
10 we groan beneath your weight.
And yet you were a leaf,
a straw blown on the bed,
you had long since become
crisp as a dead insect.
15 What is it, if not you,
that settles on us now
like satin you pulled down
over our bridal heads?
What rises in our throats
20 like food you prodded in?
Nothing could be enough.
You breathe upon us now
through solid assertions
of yourself: teaspoons, goblets,
25 seas of carpet, a forest
of old plants to be watered,
an old man in an adjoining
room to be touched and fed.
And all this universe
30 dares us to lay a finger
anywhere, save exactly
as you would wish it done.

In general terms, "A Woman Mourned by Daughters" is, of course, about the speaker's mother. More specifically, this poem explores a number of different ideas: the passing of time; the relationships between mother and daughters, father and daughters, husband and wife; the power of memory. Its central theme, however, may be expressed as a **paradox:** "In death, a person may be a stronger presence than she was when she was alive."

Many different elements in the poem suggest this interpretation. The poem's speaker directly addresses her mother. Her voice is searching, questioning, and the poem's unpoetic diction ("You, whom we so often / succeeded in ignoring") and metrical irregularities give it a halting, uncertain quality. The words, images, and figurative language work together to establish the central idea: alive, the mother was light as a leaf or a straw or a dead insect; dead, she seems "swollen" and "puffed up," and the daughters feel crushed by her weight. The concrete details of her life—"teaspoons, goblets, / seas of carpet . . ."—weigh on her survivors and keep them under her spell. In her kitchen, her memory is alive; in death, she has tremendous power over her daughters.

Like most complex poems, this one supports several alternate readings. Some readers will focus on the negative language used to describe the mother; others might emphasize the images of domesticity; still others might concentrate on the role of the sisters and the almost-absent father. Any of these focuses can lead to a redefinition of the poem's theme.

The following poem is also about a parent who inspires ambivalent feelings in a child.

> ◆ ◆ ◆

RAYMOND CARVER
(1938–1988)

Photograph of My Father in His Twenty-Second Year
(1983)

October. Here in this dank, unfamiliar kitchen
I study my father's embarrassed young man's face.
Sheepish grin, he holds in one hand a string
of spiny yellow perch, in the other
5 a bottle of Carlsbad beer.

In jeans and denim shirt, he leans
against the front fender of a 1934 Ford.
He would like to pose bluff and hearty for his posterity,
wear his old hat cocked over his ear.
10 All his life my father wanted to be bold.

But the eyes give him away, and the hands
that limply offer the string of dead perch

and the bottle of beer. Father, I love you,
   yet how can I say thank you, I who can't hold my liquor either,
15 and don't even know the places to fish?

Like Rich's speaker, Carver's is in a kitchen. Studying a photograph, this speaker sees through his father's façade. Instead of seeing the "bold," "bluff and hearty" young man his father wanted to be, he sees him as he was: "embarrassed" and "sheepish," with limp hands. In the last three lines of the poem, the speaker addresses his father directly, comparing his father's shortcomings and his own. This frank acknowledgment of his own vulnerability and the explicit link between father and son suggest that the poem has more to do with the speaker than with his father. Still, it is clear that the poem has something universal to say about parents and children—specifically, about the ambivalent feelings that children have for parents who pass on to them their own faults and failings.

   The following poem also looks back on a parent.

◇ ◇ ◇

PATRICK LANE
(1939–   )

Fathers and Sons
(1991)

I will walk across the long slow grass
where the desert sun waits among the stones
and reach down into the heavy earth
and lift your body back into the day.
5 My hands will swim down through the clay
like white fish who wander in the pools
of underground caves and they will find you
where you lie in the century of your sleep.

My arms will be as huge as the roots of trees,
10 my shoulders leaves, my hands as delicate
as the wings of fish in white water.
When I find you I will lift you out
into the sun and hold you
the way a son must who is now
15 as old as you were when you died.
I will lift you in my arms and bear you back.

My breath will blow away the earth
from your eyes and my lips will touch
your lips. They will say the years have been
20 long. They will speak into your flesh
the word *love* over and over,
as if it was the first word of the whole

earth. I will dance with you and you
will be as a small child asleep in my arms
25 as I say to the sun, bless this man who died.

I will hold you then, your hurt mouth curled
into my chest, and take your lost flesh
into me, make of you myself, and when you are
bone of my bone, and blood of my blood,
30 I will walk you into the hills and sit
alone with you and neither of us
will be ashamed. My hand and your hand.

I will take those two hands and hold them
together, palm against palm, and lift them
35 and say, this is praise, this is the holding
that is father and son. This I promise you
as I wanted to have promised in the days
of our silence, the nights of our sleeping.

Wait for me. I am coming across the grass
40 and through the stones. The eyes
of the animals and birds are upon me.
I am walking with my strength.
See, I am almost there.
If you listen you can hear me.
45 My mouth is open and I am singing.

As an adult the speaker is trying to connect with his dead father. The speaker is as old as the father was when he died, and the sense of mortality pervades the poem. In addition, the feeling of love of the son for his father is palpable: "[My lips] will speak into your flesh / the word *love* over and over . . ." (20–21). The son wishes he and his father had been able to express their love for one another when the father was alive.

◆ POEMS FOR FURTHER READING: POEMS ABOUT PARENTS

THEODORE ROETHKE
(1908–1963)

My Papa's Waltz
(1948)

The whiskey on your breath
Could make a small boy dizzy;
But I hung on like death:
Such waltzing was not easy.

5   We romped until the pans
     Slid from the kitchen shelf;
     My mother's countenance
     Could not unfrown itself.

     The hand that held my wrist
10 Was battered on one knuckle;
     At every step you missed
     My right ear scraped a buckle.

     You beat time on my head
     With a palm caked hard by dirt,
15 Then waltzed me off to bed
     Still clinging to your shirt.

◇ ◇ ◇

DYLAN THOMAS
(1914–1953)

Do Not Go Gentle into
That Good Night[1]
(1952)

Do not go gentle into that good night,
Old age should burn and rave at close of day;
Rage, rage against the dying of the light.

Though wise men at their end know dark is right,
5   Because their words had forked no lightning they
Do not go gentle into that good night.

Good men, the last wave by, crying how bright
Their frail deeds might have danced in a green bay,
Rage, rage against the dying of the light.

10 Wild men who caught and sang the sun in flight,
And learn, too late, they grieved it on its way,
Do not go gentle into that good night.

Grave men, near death, who see with blinding sight
Blind eyes could blaze like meteors and be gay,
15 Rage, rage against the dying of the light.

And you, my father, there on the sad height,
Curse, bless, me now with your fierce tears, I pray,
Do not go gentle into that good night.
Rage, rage against the dying of the light.

---

[1] This poem was written during the last illness of the poet's father, D. J. Thomas.

DIONNE BRAND
(1953–   )

Blues Spiritual for Mammy Prater
(1990)

On looking at "the photograph of Mammy Prater an ex-slave,
115 years old when her photograph was taken"

she waited for her century to turn
she waited until she was one hundred and fifteen
years old to take a photograph
to take a photograph and to put those eyes in it
5 she waited until the technique of photography was
suitably developed
to make sure the picture would be clear
to make sure no crude daguerreotype[1] would lose
her image
10 would lose her lines and most of all her eyes
and her hands
she knew the patience of one hundred and fifteen years
she knew that if she had the patience,
to avoid killing a white man
15 that I would see this photograph
she waited until it suited her
to take this photograph and to put those eyes in it.

in the hundred and fifteen years which it took her to
wait for this photograph she perfected this pose
20 she sculpted it over a shoulder of pain,
a thing like despair which she never called
this name for she would not have lasted
the fields, the ones she ploughed
on the days that she was a mule, left
25 their etching on the gait of her legs
deliberately and unintentionally
she waited, not always silently, not always patiently,
for this self portrait
by the time she sat in her black dress, white collar,
30 white handkerchief, her feet had turned to marble,
her heart burnished red,
and her eyes.

---

[1] Picture produced by a method invented in 1839 by Louis Daguerre (1789–1851); the
image was taken upon a silver-coated copper plate sensitized by iodine and was developed by being treated with vapour of mercury.

she waited one hundred and fifteen years
until the science of photography passed tin and
35 talbotype[2] for a surface sensitive enough
to hold her eyes
she took care not to lose the signs
to write in those eyes what her fingers could not script
a pact of blood across a century, a decade and more
40 she knew then that it would be me who would find
her will, her meticulous account, her eyes,
her days when waiting for this photograph
was all that kept her sane
she planned it down to the day,
45 the light,
the superfluous photographer
her breasts,
her hands
this moment of
50 my turning the leaves of a book,
noticing, her eyes.

✦ ✦ ✦

ROBERT HAYDEN
(1913–1980)

Those Winter Sundays
(1962)

Sundays too my father got up early
and put his clothes on in the blueblack cold,
then with cracked hands that ached
from labor in the weekday weather made
5 banked fires blaze. No one ever thanked him.

I'd wake and hear the cold splintering, breaking.
When the rooms were warm, he'd call,
and slowly I would rise and dress,
fearing the chronic angers of that house,

10 Speaking indifferently to him,
who had driven out the cold
and polished my good shoes as well.
What did I know, what did I know
of love's austere and lonely offices?

---

[2] A tintype, also known as a ferrotype, is a photograph taken as a positive image on a sheet of coated tin or iron; the talbotype (originally called the callotype) was named after its inventor, William Henry Fox Talbot (1800–77), who, in 1841, patented a process for producing photographic images on paper sensitized with iodide of silver.

SEAMUS HEANEY[1]
(1939–   )

Digging
(1966)

Between my finger and my thumb
The squat pen rests; snug as a gun.

Under my window, a clean rasping sound
When the spade sinks into gravelly ground:
5 My father, digging. I look down

Till his straining rump among the flowerbeds
Bends low, comes up twenty years away
Stooping in rhythm through potato drills
Where he was digging.

10 The coarse boot nestled on the lug, the shaft
Against the inside knee was levered firmly.
He rooted out tall tops, buried the bright edge deep
To scatter new potatoes that we picked
Loving their cool hardness in our hands.

15 By God, the old man could handle a spade.
Just like his old man.

My grandfather cut more turf in a day
Than any other man on Toner's bog.
Once I carried him milk in a bottle
20 Corked sloppily with paper. He straightened up
To drink it, then fell to right away

Nicking and slicing neatly, heaving sods
Over his shoulder, going down and down
For the good turf. Digging.

25 The cold smell of potato mould, the squelch and slap
Of soggy peat, the curt cuts of an edge
Through living roots awaken in my head.
But I've no spade to follow men like them.

Between my finger and my thumb
30 The squat pen rests.
I'll dig with it.

---

[1] Winner of the 1995 Nobel Prize in Literature.

IRVING LAYTON
(1912–2006)

Keine Lazarovitch 1870–1959
(1961)

When I saw my mother's head on the cold pillow,
Her white waterfalling hair in the cheeks' hollows,
I thought, quietly circling my grief, of how
She had loved God but cursed extravagantly his creatures.

5 For her final mouth was not water but a curse,
A small black hole, a black rent in the universe,
Which damned the green earth, stars and trees in its stillness
And the inescapable lousiness of growing old.

And I record she was comfortless, vituperative,
10 Ignorant, glad, and much else besides; I believe
She endlessly praised her black eyebrows, their thick weave,
Till plagiarizing Death leaned down and took them for his mould.

And spoiled a dignity I shall not again find,
And the fury of her stubborn limited mind;
15 Now none will shake her amber beads and call God blind,
Or wear them upon a breast so radiantly.

O fierce she was, mean and unaccommodating;
But I think now of the toss of her gold earrings,
Their proud carnal assertion, and her youngest sings
20 While all the rivers of her red veins move into the sea.

MICHAEL ONDAATJE
(1943–   )

Letters & Other Worlds
(1973)
"for there was no more darkness for him and, no doubt
like Adam before the fall, he could see in the dark"[1]

My father's body was a globe of fear
His body was a town we never knew

---

[1] From *"Descendit ad infernos"* (He Descends to the Underworld), a chapter for Alfred
Jarry's *La dragonne* (1943), quoted in Roger Shattuck's *The Banquet Years: The Arts in
France, 1885–1918* (1955). The clause immediately preceding the section Ondaatje
quotes is "But soon he could drink no more."

He hid that he had been where we were going
His letters were a room he seldom lived in
5 In them the logic of his love could grow

My father's body was a town of fear
He was the only witness to its fear dance
He hid where he had been that we might lose him
His letters were a room his body scared

10 He came to death with his mind drowning.
On the last day he enclosed himself
in a room with two bottles of gin, later
fell the length of his body
so that brain blood moved
15 to new compartments
that never knew the wash of fluid
and he died in minutes of a new equilibrium.

His early life was a terrifying comedy
and my mother divorced him again and again.
20 He would rush into tunnels magnetized
by the white eye of trains
and once, gaining instant fame,
managed to stop a Perahara[2] in Ceylon
—the whole procession of elephants dancers
25 local dignitaries—by falling
dead drunk onto the street.

As a semi-official, and semi-white at that,
the act was seen as a crucial
turning point in the Home Rule Movement
30 and led to Ceylon's independence in 1948.

(My mother had done her share too—
her driving so bad
she was stoned by villagers
whenever her car was recognized)

35 For 14 years of marriage
each of them claimed he or she
was the injured party.
Once on the Colombo docks
saying goodbye to a recently married couple
40 my father, jealous

---

[2] Sinhalese for procession; a *perahara* was most frequently associated with a religious celebration or marriage.

at my mother's articulate emotion,
dove into the waters of the harbour
and swam after the ship waving farewell.
My mother pretending no affiliation
45 mingled with the crowd back to the hotel.

Once again he made the papers
though this time my mother
with a note to the editor
corrected the report—saying he was drunk
50 rather than broken hearted at the parting of friends.
The married couple received both editions
of *The Ceylon Times* when their ship reached Aden.[3]

And then in his last years
he was the silent drinker,
55 the man who once a week
disappeared into his room with bottles
and stayed there until he was drunk
and until he was sober.

There speeches, head dreams, apologies,
60 the gentle letters, were composed.
With the clarity of architects
he would write of the row of blue flowers
his new wife had planted,
the plans for electricity in the house,
65 how my half-sister fell near a snake
and it had awakened and not touched her.
Letters in a clear hand of the most complete empathy
his heart widening and widening and widening
to all manner of change in his children and friends
70 while he himself edged
into the terrible acute hatred
of his own privacy
till he balanced and fell
the length of his body
75 the blood screaming in
the empty reservoir of bones
the blood searching in his head without metaphor

---

[3] The capital of the British colony of Aden and later the capital of the People's
Democratic Republic of Yemen; port of call on voyages through the Suez Canal.

READING AND REACTING: POEMS ABOUT PARENTS

1. What is each speaker's attitude toward his or her parent?
2. Which words and images suggest positive associations? Which help to create a negative impression?
3. How would you characterize each poem's tone? For example, is the poem sentimental, humorous, angry, resentful, or regretful?
4. What ideas about parent-child relationships are explored in each poem? What do you think is the poem's central theme?
5. What does each poem say about the parent? What does it reveal about the speaker?

Related Works: "Stones" (p. 135), "Borders" (p. 218), "The Rocking-Horse Winner" (p. 370), "Daddy" (p. 712), *Hamlet* (p. 1093)

❖ POEMS FOR FURTHER READING: POEMS ABOUT LOVE

◊ ◊ ◊

CHRISTOPHER MARLOWE
(1564–1593)

The Passionate Shepherd
to His Love
(1600)

Come live with me and be my love,
And we will all the pleasures prove
That valleys, groves, hills, and fields,
Woods, or steepy mountain yields.

5 And we will sit upon the rocks,
Seeing the shepherds feed their flocks
By shallow rivers, to whose falls
Melodious birds sing madrigals.

And I will make thee beds of roses
10 And a thousand fragrant posies,
A cap of flowers and a kirtle[1]
Embroidered all with leaves of myrtle;

A gown made of the finest wool
Which from our pretty lambs we pull;
15 Fair-linèd slippers for the cold,
With buckles of the purest gold;

A belt of straw and ivy buds,
With coral clasps and amber studs.

---
[1] Skirt.

And if these pleasures may thee move,
20 Come live with me and be my love.

The shepherds' swains shall dance and sing
For thy delight each May morning.
If these delights thy mind may move,
Then live with me and be my love.

⋄ ⋄ ⋄

SIR WALTER RALEIGH
(1552?–1618)

The Nymph's Reply
to the Shepherd
(1600)

If all the world and love were young,
And truth in every shepherd's tongue,
These pretty pleasures might me move
To live with thee and be thy love.

5 Time drives the flocks from field to fold,
When rivers rage and rocks grow cold;
And Philomel[1] becometh dumb;
The rest complains of cares to come.

The flowers do fade, and wanton fields
10 To wayward winter reckoning yields:
A honey tongue, a heart of gall,
Is fancy's spring, but sorrow's fall.

Thy gowns, thy shoes, thy beds of roses,
Thy cap, thy kirtle, and thy posies
15 Soon break, soon wither, soon forgotten,
In folly ripe, in reason rotten.

Thy belt of straw and ivy buds,
Thy coral clasps and amber studs.
All these in me no means can move
20 To come to thee and be thy love.

But could youth last, and love still breed,
Had joys no date, nor age no need,
Then these delights my mind might move
To live with thee and be thy love.

---

[1] The nightingale.

◊ ◊ ◊

THOMAS CAMPION
(1567–1620)

There Is a Garden in Her Face
(1617)

There is a garden in her face
Where roses and white lilies grow;
A heav'nly paradise is that place
Wherein all pleasant fruits do flow.
5   There cherries grow which none may buy
Till "Cherry-ripe" themselves do cry.

Those cherries fairly do enclose
Of orient pearl a double row,
Which when her lovely laughter shows,
10 They look like rose-buds filled with snow;
Yet them nor peer nor prince can buy,
Till "Cherry-ripe" themselves do cry.

Her eyes like angels watch them still;
Her brows like bended bows do stand,
15   Threat'ning with piercing frowns to kill
All that attempt, with eye or hand
Those sacred cherries to come nigh
Till "Cherry-ripe" themselves do cry.

◊ ◊ ◊

WILLIAM SHAKESPEARE
(1564–1616)

My Mistress' Eyes Are
Nothing like the Sun
(1609)

My mistress' eyes are nothing like the sun;
Coral is far more red than her lips' red;
If snow be white, why then her breasts are dun;
If hairs be wires, black wires grow on her head.
5 I have seen roses damasked red and white,
But no such roses see I in her cheeks;
And in some perfumes is there more delight
Than in the breath that from my mistress reeks.
I love to hear her speak, yet well I know
10 That music hath a far more pleasing sound;
I grant I never saw a goddess go:

My mistress, when she walks, treads on the ground.
    And yet, by heaven, I think my love as rare
    As any she, belied with false compare.

◆ ◆ ◆

ELIZABETH BARRETT BROWNING
(1806–1861)

How Do I Love Thee?[1]
(1850)

How do I love thee? Let me count the ways.
I love thee to the depth and breadth and height
My soul can reach, when feeling out of sight
For the ends of being and ideal grace.
5 I love thee to the level of every day's
Most quiet need, by sun and candle-light.
I love thee freely, as men strive for right.
I love thee purely, as they turn from praise.
I love thee with the passion put to use
10 In my old griefs, and with my childhood's faith.
I love thee with a love I seemed to lose
With my lost saints. I love thee with the breath,
Smiles, tears, of all my life; and, if God choose,
I shall but love thee better after death.

◆ ◆ ◆

MARGARET ATWOOD
(1939–   )

Variations on the Word *Love*
(1981)

This is a word we use to plug
holes with. It's the right size for those warm
blanks in speech, for those red heart-
shaped vacancies on the page that look nothing
5 like real hearts. Add lace
and you can sell
it. We insert it also in the one empty
space on the printed form
that comes with no instructions. There are whole
10 magazines with not much in them

---

[1] Elizabeth Barrett Browning's "Sonnets from the Portuguese" was originally published in 1850 in a two volume publication titled *Poems*. "How Do I Love Thee?" is sonnet number XLIII from that work.

but the word *love*, you can
rub it all over your body and you
can cook with it too. How do we know
it isn't what goes on at the cool
15 debaucheries of slugs under damp
pieces of cardboard? As for the weed-
seedlings nosing their tough snouts up
among the lettuces, they shout it.
Love! Love! sing the soldiers, raising
20 their glittering knives in salute.

Then there's the two
of us. This word
is far too short for us, it has only
four letters, too sparse
25 to fill those deep bare
vacuums between the stars
that press on us with their deafness.
It's not love we don't wish
to fall into, but that fear.
30 This word is not enough but it will
have to do. It's a single
vowel in this metallic
silence, a mouth that says
O again and again in wonder
35 and pain, a breath, a finger-
grip on a cliffside. You can
hold on or let go.

◊ ◊ ◊

W. H. AUDEN
(1907–1973)

Stop All the Clocks,
Cut Off the Telephone[1]
(1936)

Stop all the clocks, cut off the telephone,
Prevent the dog from barking with a juicy bone,
Silence the pianos and with muffled drum
Bring out the coffin, let the mourners come.

---

[1] This poem was featured in the 1994 movie *Four Weddings and a Funeral*. The poem was originally titled "Funeral Blues," and Auden wrote it for the London production of his play *The Ascent of F6*. In his poem, Auden laments the death of love in whatever form. "Funeral Blues" reappeared substantially changed in *Another Time*, a 1940 Random House collection of Auden's poems.

5 Let aeroplanes circle moaning overhead
Scribbling on the sky the message He Is Dead,
Put the crepe bows round the white necks of the public doves,
Let the traffic policemen wear black cotton gloves.

He was my North, my South, my East and West,
10 My working week and my Sunday rest,
My noon, my midnight, my talk, my song;
I thought that love would last for ever. I was wrong.

The stars are not wanted now: put out every one;
Pack up the moon and dismantle the sun;
15 Pour away the ocean and sweep up the wood.
For nothing now can ever come to any good.

◇ ◇ ◇

DOROTHY PARKER
(1893–1967)

General Review of
the Sex Situation
(1933)

Woman wants monogamy;
Man delights in novelty.
Love is woman's moon and sun;
Man has other forms of fun.
5 Woman lives but in her lord;
Count to ten, and man is bored.
With this the gist and sum of it,
What earthly good can come of it?

◇ ◇ ◇

SYLVIA PLATH
(1932–1963)

Wreath for a Bridal
(1956)

What though green leaves only witness
Such pact as is made once only; what matter
That owl voice sole 'yes', while cows utter
Low moos of approve; let sun surpliced in brightness
5 Stand stock still to laud these mated ones
Whose stark act all coming double luck joins.

Couched daylong in cloisters of stinging nettle
They lie, cut-grass assaulting each separate sense
With savor; coupled so, pure paragons of constance,

10 This pair seek single state from that dual battle.
Now speak some sacrament to parry scruple
For wedlock wrought within love's proper chapel.

Call here with flying colors all watchful birds
To people the twigged aisles; lead babel tongues
15 Of animals to choir: 'Look what thresh of wings
Wields guard of honor over these!' Starred with words
Let night bless that luck-rotted mead of clover
Where, bedded like angels, two burn one in fever.

From this holy day on, all pollen blown
20 Shall strew broadcast so rare a seed on wind
That every breath, thus teeming, set the land
Sprouting fruit, flowers, children most fair in legion
To slay spawn of dragon's teeth: speaking this promise,
Let flesh be knit, and each step hence go famous.

◊ ◊ ◊

TED HUGHES
(1930–1998)

A Pink Wool Knitted Dress
(1996)

In your pink wool knitted dress
Before anything had smudged anything
You stood at the altar. Bloomsday.
Rain—so that a just-bought umbrella
5 Was the only furnishing about me
Newer than three years inured.
My tie—sole, drab, veteran RAF black—
Was the used-up symbol of a tie.
My cord jacket—thrice-dyed black, exhausted,
10 Just hanging on to itself.

I was a post-war, utility son-in-law!
Not quite the Frog-Prince. Maybe the Swineherd
Stealing this daughter's pedigree dreams
From under her watchtowered searchlit future.

15 No ceremony could conscript me
Out of my uniform. I wore my whole wardrobe—
Except for the odd, spare, identical item.
My wedding, like Nature, wanted to hide.
However—if we were going to be married
20 It had better be Westminster Abbey. Why not?

The Dean told us why not. That is how
I learned that I had a Parish Church.
St George of the Chimney Sweeps.
So we squeezed into marriage finally.
25 Your mother, brave even in this
US Foreign Affairs gamble,
Acted all bridesmaids and all guests,
Even—magnanimity—represented
My family
30 Who had heard nothing about it.
I had invited only their ancestors.
I had not even confided my theft of you
To a closest friend. For Best Man—my squire
To hold the meanwhile rings—
35 We requisitioned the sexton. Twist of the outrage:
He was packing children into a bus,
Taking them to the Zoo—in that downpour!
All the prison animals had to be patient
While we married.
40   You were transfigured.
So slender and new and naked,
A nodding spray of wet lilac.
You shook, you sobbed with joy, you were ocean depth
Brimming with God.
45 You said you saw the heavens open
And how riches, ready to drop upon us.
Levitated beside you, I stood subjected
To a strange tense: the spellbound future.

In that echo-gaunt, weekday chancel
50 I see you
Wrestling to contain your flames
In your pink wool knitted dress
And in your eye-pupils—great cut jewels
Jostling their tear-flames, truly like big jewels
55 Shaken in a dice-cup and held up to me.

◊ ◊ ◊

TOM WAYMAN
(1945–   )

Wayman in Love
(1973)

At last Wayman gets the girl into bed.
He is locked in one of those embraces

so passionate his left arm is asleep
when suddenly he is bumped in the back.
5 "Excuse me," a voice mutters, thick with German.
Wayman and the girl sit up astounded
as a furry gentleman in boots and a frock coat
climbs in under the covers.

"My name is Doktor Marx," the intruder announces
10 settling his neck comfortably on the pillow.
"I am here to consider for you the cost of a kiss."
He pulls out a notepad. "Let's see now,
we have the price of the mattress, this room must be rented,
your time off work, groceries for two,
15 medical fees in case of accidents. . . ."

"Look," Wayman says,
"couldn't we do this later?"
The philosopher sighs, and continues: "You are affected too, Miss.
If you are not working, you are going to resent
20 your dependent position. This will influence
I assure you, your most intimate moments. . . ."

"Doctor, please," Wayman says. "All we want
is to be left alone."
But another beard, more nattily dressed,
25 is also getting into the bed.
There is a shifting and heaving of bodies
as everyone wriggles out room for themselves.
"I want you to meet a friend from Vienna,"
Marx says. "This is Doktor Freud."

30 The newcomer straightens his glasses,
peers at Wayman and the girl.
"I can see," he begins,
"that you two have problems. . . ."

READING AND REACTING: POEMS ABOUT LOVE

1. What conventional images does each speaker use to express love?
2. Does the speaker use any images that are unexpected or shocking?
3. What ideas about love are expressed by each poem?
4. What is the tone of each poem? Is it happy? Sad? Celebratory? Regretful?
5. What does each poem reveal about the speaker? About the person to whom the poem is addressed?

Related Works: "Living in Sin" (p. 662), "I Knew a Woman" (p. 665), "The Faithful Wife" (p. 671), "A Valediction: Forbidding Mourning" (p. 710), "To My Dear and Loving Husband" (p. 718), "You Fit into Me" (p. 723), *The Brute* (p. 1081)

❖ POEMS FOR FURTHER READING: POEMS ABOUT WAR

◊ ◊ ◊

RUPERT BROOKE
(1887–1915)

The Soldier[1]
(1915)

If I should die, think only this of me;
    That there's some corner of a foreign field
That is for ever England. There shall be
    In that rich earth a richer dust concealed;
5 A dust whom England bore, shaped, made aware,
    Gave, once, her flowers to love, her ways to roam,
A body of England's breathing English air,
    Washed by the rivers, blest by suns of home.

And think, this heart, all evil shed away,
10   A pulse in the eternal mind, no less
        Gives somewhere back the thoughts by England given;
Her sights and sounds; dreams happy as her day;
    And laughter, learnt of friends; and gentleness,
        In hearts at peace, under an English heaven.

◊ ◊ ◊

WILFRED OWEN
(1893–1918)

Anthem for Doomed Youth
(1917?)

What passing-bells for these who die as cattle?
    Only the monstrous anger of the guns.
Only the stuttering rifles' rapid rattle
Can patter out their hasty orisons.
5 No mockeries now for them; no prayers nor bells,
    Nor any voice of mourning save the choirs,—
The shrill, demented choirs of wailing shells;
    And bugles calling for them from sad shires.

---

[1] Brooke's poem "The Soldier" appeared in 1915 in a posthumously published collection of his work titled *1914 and Other Poems.*

What candles may be held to speed them all?
10   Not in the hands of boys, but in their eyes
        Shall shine the holy glimmers of good-byes.
The pallor of girls' brows shall be their pall;
Their flowers the tenderness of patient minds,
And each slow dusk a drawing-down of blinds.

⟩ ⟩ ⟩

WILLIAM BUTLER YEATS
(1865–1939)

An Irish Airman
Foresees His Death
(1919)

I know that I shall meet my fate
Somewhere among the clouds above;
Those that I fight I do not hate,
Those that I guard I do not love;
5 My country is Kiltartan Cross
My countrymen Kiltartan's poor,
No likely end could bring them loss
Or leave them happier than before.
Nor law, nor duty bade me fight,
10 Nor public men, nor cheering crowds,
A lonely impulse of delight
Drove to this tumult in the clouds;
I balanced all, brought all to mind,
The years to come seemed waste of breath,
15 A waste of breath the years behind
In balance with this life, this death.

⟩ ⟩ ⟩

W. H. AUDEN
(1907–1973)

The Shield of Achilles[1]
(1955)

She looked over his shoulder
    For vines and olive trees,
Marble well-governed cities,
    And ships upon untamed seas,

---

[1] In Greek mythology, Achilles was a fierce warrior who was the epitome of great
warriors and was noted for his pride and honour. In Homer's *The Iliad,* the pictures on
the shield of Achilles represent the city at war and the city at peace. The city at peace
depicts prosperity and life in perfect balance while the city at war depicts death,
destruction, and chaos.

5 But there on the shining metal
  His hands had put instead
  An artificial wilderness
  And a sky like lead.

A plain without a feature, bare and brown,
10 No blade of grass, no sign of neighborhood,
Nothing to eat and nowhere to sit down,
  Yet, congregated on its blankness, stood
  An unintelligible multitude.
A million eyes, a million boots in line,
15 Without expression, waiting for a sign.

Out of the air a voice without a face
  Proved by statistics that some cause was just
In tones as dry and level as the place:
  No one was cheered and nothing was discussed;
20 Column by column in a cloud of dust
They marched away enduring a belief
Whose logic brought them, somewhere else, to grief.

◇ ◇ ◇

ROBERT LOWELL
(1917–1977)

For the Union Dead
(1959)

"Relinquunt omnia servare rem publicam."[1]

The old South Boston Aquarium stands
in a Sahara of snow now. Its broken windows are boarded.
The bronze weathervane cod has lost half its scales.
The airy tanks are dry.

5 Once my nose crawled like a snail on the glass;
my hand tingled
to burst the bubbles
drifting from the noses of the cowed, compliant fish.

My hand draws back. I often sigh still
10 for the dark downward and vegetating kingdom
of the fish and reptile. One morning last March,
I pressed against the new barbed and galvanized

---

[1] "They gave up everything to preserve the Republic." A monument in Boston Common
bears a similar form of this quotation. Designed by Augustus Saint-Gaudens, the monument is dedicated to Colonel Robert Gould Shaw and the African-American troops he
commanded during a Civil War battle at Fort Wagner, South Carolina, on July 18,
1863.

fence on the Boston Common. Behind their cage,
yellow dinosaur steamshovels were grunting
15 as they cropped up tons of mush and grass
to gouge their underworld garage.

Parking spaces luxuriate like civic
sandpiles in the heart of Boston.
A girdle of orange, Puritan-pumpkin colored girders
20 braces the tingling Statehouse,

shaking over the excavations, as it faces Colonel Shaw
and his bell-cheeked Negro infantry
on St. Gauden's shaking Civil War relief,
propped by a plant splint against the garage's earthquake.

25 Two months after marching through Boston,
half the regiment was dead;
at the dedication,
William James[2] could almost hear the bronze Negroes breathe.

Their monument sticks like a fishbone
30 in the city's throat.
Its Colonel is as lean
as a compass-needle.

He has an angry wrenlike vigilance,
a greyhound's gentle tautness;
35 he seems to wince at pleasure,
and suffocate for privacy.

He is out of bounds now. He rejoices in man's lovely,
peculiar power to choose life and death—
when he leads his black soldiers to death,
40 he cannot bend his back.

On a thousand small town New England greens,
the old white churches hold their air
of sparse, sincere rebellion; frayed flags
quilt the graveyards of the Grand Army of the Republic.

45 The stone statues of the abstract Union Soldier
grow slimmer and younger each year—
wasp-waisted, they doze over muskets
and muse through their sideburns . . .

Shaw's father wanted no monument
50 except the ditch,
where his son's body was thrown
and lost with his "niggers."

---

[2] Harvard psychologist and philosopher (1842–1910).

The ditch is nearer.
There are no statues for the last war here;
55 on Boylston Street, a commercial photograph
shows Hiroshima boiling

over a Mosler Safe,[3] the "Rock of Ages"
that survived the blast. Space is nearer.
When I crouch to my television set,
60 the drained faces of Negro school-children rise like balloons.

Colonel Shaw
is riding on his bubble,
he waits
for the blessed break.

65 The Aquarium is gone. Everywhere,
giant finned cars nose forward like fish;
a savage servility
slides by on grease.

· · ·

DENISE LEVERTOV
(1923–1997)

What Were They Like?
(1966)

1) Did the people of Viet Nam
use lanterns of stone?
2) Did they hold ceremonies
to reverence the opening of buds?
5 3) Were they inclined to rippling laughter?
4) Did they use bone and ivory,
jade and silver, for ornament?
5) Had they an epic poem?
6) Did they distinguish between speech and singing?

10 1) Sir, their light hearts turned to stone.
It is not remembered whether in gardens
stone lanterns illumined pleasant ways.
2) Perhaps they gathered once to delight in blossom,
but after the children were killed
15 there were no more buds.

---

[3] A brand of safe known for being especially strong.

3) Sir, laughter is bitter to the burned mouth.

4) A dream ago, perhaps. Ornament is for joy.
   All the bones were charred.

5) It is not remembered. Remember,
20   most were peasants; their life
   was in rice and bamboo.
   When peaceful clouds were reflected in the paddies
   and the water buffalo stepped surely along terraces,
   maybe fathers told their sons old tales.
25 When bombs smashed the mirrors
   there was time only to scream.

6) There is an echo yet, it is said,
   of their speech which was like a song.
   It is reported their singing resembled
30 the flight of moths in moonlight.
   Who can say? It is silent now.

♦ ♦ ♦

VIKRAM SETH
(1952–   )

Work and Freedom
(1990)

Even small events that others might not notice,
I found hard to forget. In Auschwitz truly
I had no reason to complain of boredom.
If an incident affected me too deeply
5 I could not go straight home to my wife and children.
I would ride my horse till the terrible picture faded.
Often at night I would wander through the stables
And seek relief among my beloved horses.
At home my thoughts, often and with no warning,
10 Turned to such things. When I saw my children playing
Or observed my wife's delight over our youngest,
I would walk out and stand beside the transports,
The firepits, crematoriums, or gas chambers.
My wife ascribed my gloom to some annoyance
15 Connected with my work—but I was thinking,
"How long will our happiness last?" I was not happy
Once the mass exterminations had started.

My work, such unease aside, was never-ending,
My colleagues untrustworthy, those above me
20 Reluctant to understand or even to listen—

Yet everyone thought the commandant's life was heaven.
My wife and children, true, were well looked after.
Her garden was a paradise of flowers.
The prisoners, trying no doubt to attract attention,
25 Never once failed in little acts of kindness.
Not one of them, in our house, was badly treated:
My wife would have loved to give the prisoners presents—
And as for the children, they begged for cigarettes for them,
Especially for those who worked in the garden and brought
    them
30 Tortoises, martens, lizards, cats. Each Sunday
We'd walk to the stable, never omitting the kennels
Where the dogs were kept. My children loved all creatures
But most of all our foal and our two horses.
In summer they splashed in the wading pool, but their
    greatest
35 Joy was to bathe together with Daddy—who had
Limited hours, alas, for these childish pleasures.
My wife said, "Think of us, not only the service."
How could she know what lay so heavily on me?
(It made life hard, this excessive sense of duty.)

40 When Auschwitz was divided, Pohl in a kindly
And quite exceptional gesture gave me the option
—Perhaps as recompense for this last assignment—
To head DK or to run Sachsenhausen.
I had one day to decide. At first the thought of
45 Uprooting myself from Auschwitz made me unhappy,
So involved had I grown in its tasks and troubles.
But in the end I was glad to gain my freedom.

⬧ ⬧ ⬧

ANDREW SUKNASKI
(1942–   )

The Bitter Word
(1976)

from fort walsh
colonel irvine brings the bitter word
to sitting bull at wood mountain
makes clear the government welcomes the teton—
5 yet they must not expect provisions
or food from canada

sitting bull proudly replies:
when did i ever ask you for provisions?
before I beg
10 *i will cut willows for my young men to use*
while killing mice to survive

in the spring of 1881
sitting bull gathers his remaining 1200 sioux
and treks to fort qu'appelle to make
15 the final request for a reservation—
inspector sam steele tells them
the great white mother wishes them to return
to their own country
(a rather curious view of a people
20 whose meaning of country changes with
the migrations of tatanka)[1]
steele politely refuses the request
and supplies enough provisions for the return
to wood mountain
25 death by summer is certain
while irvine makes sure
provisions and seed never arrive
seeing the migrating game
sitting bull knew the tatanka
30 would never return
though his people dreamed of white tatanka rising
from the subterranean meadows others fled to
(hideous shrieks of red river carts grating in
their ears)
35 he must have sensed the hunger to follow
which was exactly what the authorities hoped for
on both sides of the border

◇ ◇ ◈

BORIS SLUTSKY[1]

How Did They Kill
My Grandmother?

Translated by Elaine Feinstein

How did they kill my grandmother?
I'll tell you how they killed her.

---

[1] A Lakota-Nakota (Sioux) word meaning "god-animal" and referring to the buffalo.

---

[1] Birth date of author and publication date of poem are not available.

One morning a tank rolled up to
a building where
5 the hundred and fifty Jews of our town who,
weightless
          from a year's starvation,
and white
          with the knowledge of death,
10 were gathered holding their bundles.
And the German polizei[2] were
herding the old people briskly;
and their tin mugs clanked as
the young men led them away
15   far away.

But my small grandmother
my seventy-year-old grandmother
began to curse and
scream at the Germans;
20 shouting that I was a soldier.
She yelled at them: My grandson
is off at the front fighting!
Don't you dare
touch me!
25 Listen, you
          can hear our guns!

Even as she went off, my grandmother
cried abuse,
          starting all over again
30 with her curses.
From every window then
Ivanovnas and Andreyevnas
Sidorovnas and Petrovnas
sobbed: You tell them, Polina
35 Matveyevna, keep it up!
They all yelled together:
          "What can we do against
this enemy, the Hun?"
Which was why the Germans chose
40 to kill her inside the town.

A bullet struck her hair
and kicked her grey plait down.
My grandmother fell to the ground.
That is how she died there.

---

[2] Police.

MIRIAM WADDINGTON
(1917–2004)

How I Spent the Year Listening to the Ten O'Clock News
(1986)

Last year
there were executions
in Chile
bribes in
5 America no
transit for Jews
in Austria
and lies
lies everywhere.

10 The children
of Ireland are
also in the news,
they have become
hardened street
15 fighters some of
them murderers,
I ask myself
where will it
all end?

20 Of course
the interests of
Canadian citizens
(read corporations)
must be protected
25 at any cost no
matter how many
good men are
shot like dogs
in the streets
30 of Chile or
how many poets
die of a broken
heart.

They claim
35 the world is

changing getting
better they have
the moon walk
and moon walkers
40 to prove it,
but my brain
is bursting my
guts are twisted
I have too much
45 to say thank
God I am too old
to bear children.

✦   ✦   ✦

ROBERT BRINGHURST
(1946–   )

For the Bones of Josef Mengele, Disinterred June 1985
(1995)

Master of Auschwitz, angel of death,
murderer, deep in Brazil they are breaking
your bones—or somebody's bones: my
bones, your bones, his bones, whose
5 bones does not matter. Deep in Brazil they are breaking
bones like loaves of old bread. The angel
of death is not drowning but eating.

Speak! they are saying. *Speak! Speak!*
If you don't speak we will open and read you!
10 Something you too might have said in your time.
Are these bones guilty? they say. And the bones
are already talking. The bones, with guns
to their heads, are already saying, *Yes!*
Yes! It is true, we are guilty!

15 Butcher, baker, lampshade and candlestick
maker: yes, it is true. But the bones? The bones,
earth, metals, teeth, the body?
These are not guilty. The minds of the dead
are not to be found in the bones of the dead.
20 The minds of the dead are not anywhere to be found,
outside the minds of the living.

Reading and Reacting: Poems about War

1. What is each speaker's attitude toward war?
2. What conventional images does each poem use to express its ideas about war?
3. Do any of the poems use unusual, unexpected, or shocking images?
4. How would you describe each poem's tone? Angry? Cynical? Sad? Disillusioned? Resigned?
5. What does each poem reveal about the speaker?
6. What is the central theme of each poem?

Related Works: "The Man He Killed" (p. 633), "Patterns" (p. 634), "The Death of the Ball Turret Gunner" (p. 708), "Naming of Parts" (p. 876)

CHAPTER 12

Reading and Writing
about Poetry

READING POETRY

◇ ◇ ◇

Sometimes readers approach poetry purely for pleasure. At other times, reading a poem is the first step toward writing about it. The following guidelines, which focus on issues discussed elsewhere in this section of the text, may help direct your reading.

◇ Rephrase the poem in your own words. What does your paraphrase reveal about the poem's subject and central concerns? What is lost or gained in your paraphrase of the poem?

◇ Consider the poem's **voice.** Who is the poem's persona or speaker? How would you characterize the poem's tone? Is the poem ironic? (See Chapter 13.)

◇ Study the poem's **diction** and look up unfamiliar words in a dictionary. How does word choice affect your reaction to the poem? What do the connotations of words reveal about the poem? What level of diction is used? Is dialect used? Is word order unusual or unexpected? How does the arrangement of words contribute to your understanding of the poem? (See Chapter 14.)

◇ Examine the poem's **imagery.** What kind of imagery predominates? What specific images are used? Is a pattern of imagery present? How does imagery enrich the poem? (See Chapter 15.)

◊ Identify the poem's **figures of speech.** Does the poet use metaphor? Simile? Personification? Hyperbole? Understatement? Metonymy or synecdoche? Apostrophe? How do figures of speech affect your reading of the poem? (See Chapter 16.)

◊ Listen to the **sound** of the poem. Are rhythm and metre regular or irregular? How do rhythm and metre reinforce the poem's central concerns? Does the poem use alliteration? Assonance? Rhyme? How do these elements enhance the poem? (See Chapter 17.)

◊ Look at the poem's **form.** Is the poem written in closed or open form? Is the poem constructed as a sonnet? A sestina? A villanelle? An epigram? A haiku? Is the poem an example of concrete poetry? How does the poem's form reinforce its ideas? (See Chapter 18.)

◊ Consider the poem's use of **symbol, allegory, allusion,** or **myth.** Does the poem make use of symbols? Allusions? How do symbols or allusions support its theme? Is the poem an allegory? Does the poem retell or interpret a myth? (See Chapter 19.)

◊ Identify the poem's **theme.** What central theme or themes does the poem explore? How are the themes expressed? (See Chapter 11.)

ACTIVE READING

When you approach a poem that you plan to write about, you engage in the same active reading strategies you use when you read a short story or a play. When you finish recording your reactions to the poem, you focus on a topic, develop ideas about that topic, decide on a thesis, prepare an outline, and draft and revise your essay.

Catherine Whittaker, a student in an introduction to literature course, was asked to write a three- to five-page essay comparing any *two* of the seven poems about parents that appear in the exercise in Chapter 11 (pp. 570–78). Her instructor told the class that the essay should reflect students' own reactions to the poems, not the opinions of literary critics. As Catherine planned and wrote her paper, she was guided by the process described in Chapter 2, "Reading and Writing about Literature."

Previewing

Catherine began her work by previewing the poems, eliminating those she considered obscure or difficult and those whose portrait of the speaker's parent did not seem sympathetic.

This process helped Catherine to narrow down her choices. As she looked through "Those Winter Sundays," she was struck by words in the opening lines ("Sundays too . . ."; "blueblack cold"). She had the same reaction to "The squat pen rests; snug as a gun" in line 2 of "Digging." In each case, the words made Catherine want to examine the poem further. She noticed too that both poems were divided into stanzas of varying lengths and that both focused on fathers. Keeping these features in mind, Catherine began a close reading of each poem.

Highlighting and Annotating

As Catherine read and reread "Those Winter Sundays" and "Digging," she recorded her comments and questions. The highlighted and annotated poems follow.

⬥ ⬥ ⬥

ROBERT HAYDEN
(1913–1980)

Those Winter Sundays
(1962)

Were there many Sundays like these? ←

Sundays [too] my father got up early — *Like all other days of the week?*

and put his clothes on in the blueblack cold, *Why did he get up before dawn?*

then with cracked hands that ached *What kind of job did the father have?*

from labor in the weekday weather made

5 banked fires blaze. No one ever thanked him. *Was there a large family?*

I'd wake and hear the cold splintering, breaking.

When the rooms were warm, he'd call,

and slowly I would rise and dress,

fearing the chronic angers of that house, *Were there problems in the family?*

10 Speaking indifferently to him,

who had driven out the cold

and polished my good shoes as well. *Was there a mother around?*

What did I know, what did I know

of love's austere and lonely offices? → *Offices = duties or functions assigned to someone*

Austere = without adornment or ornamentation, simple, bare — simple without luxury, harsh

SEAMUS HEANEY
(1939–   )

Digging
(1966)

Between my finger and my thumb
The squat pen rests; snug as a gun.

[handwritten: gun = snug?]
[handwritten: Why a "squat" pen?]

Under my window, a clean rasping sound
When the spade sinks into gravelly ground:
5 My father, digging. I look down

Till his straining rump among the flowerbeds
Bends low, comes up twenty years away
Stooping in rhythm through potato drills
Where he was digging.

[handwritten: Is he thinking about the past?]

[handwritten: Like the poet's pen?]

10 The coarse boot nestled on the lug, the shaft
Against the inside knee was levered firmly.
He rooted out tall tops, buried the bright edge deep
To scatter new potatoes that we picked
Loving their cool hardness in our hands.

[handwritten: Was this a family task?]

15 By God, the old man could handle a spade.
Just like his old man.

[handwritten: Two generations could "handle a spade." Can the poet dig?]

My grandfather cut more turf in a day
Than any other man on Toner's bog.
Once I carried him milk in a bottle
20 Corked sloppily with paper. He straightened up
To drink it, then fell to right away

[handwritten: The grandfather was a hard worker.]

Nicking and slicing neatly, heaving sods

Almost like an art of digging?

Over his shoulder, going down and down

For the good turf. Digging.

25 The cold smell of potato mould, the squelch and slap

Of soggy peat, the curt cuts of an edge

→ What does it make him remember?

Through living roots awaken in my head.

But I've no spade to follow men like them.

→ What are "men like them" like?

Between my finger and my thumb

Same as first 2 lines {

30 The squat pen rests.

→ Why is this repeated?

I'll dig with it.

↳ Dig for what?

Catherine found the language of both poems appealing, and she believed her highlighting and annotating had given her some valuable insights. For example, she noticed some parallels between the two poems: both focus on the past, both portray fathers as hard workers, and neither mentions a mother.

Writing about Poetry

◇ ◇ ◇

Planning an Essay

Even though Catherine still had to find a specific topic for her paper, her preliminary work suggested some interesting possibilities. She was especially intrigued by the way both poems depict fathers as actively engaged in physical tasks.

Choosing a Topic

One idea Catherine thought she might want to write about was the significance of the sons' attitudes toward their fathers: although both see their fathers as hard workers, the son in "Those Winter Sundays" seems to have mixed feelings about his father's devotion to his family, whereas the son in "Digging" is more appreciative. Catherine explored this idea in the two journal entries that follow:

"Those Winter Sundays"

Why did the father get up early every morning? One
could imagine that he had a large family and little
money. There is no mention of a mother. Images are
created of the utter coldness and "chronic angers" of the
house. The father not only made fires to warm the house
but also polished his child's (or children's) shoes--
maybe for church. And yet, the child seems not to care
about or appreciate the father's efforts. Is he too young
to say thank you, or are there other problems in the
house for which the child blames the father?

"Digging"

In the poem, the poet seems to be contemplating the
subject about which to write when the sounds of digging
capture his attention. He remembers the steady, artful
rhythm of his father's digging of the potatoes and how
they (probably the poet and his brothers and sisters)
picked out the cool potatoes. His memories appear to be
entirely appreciative of his father's and grandfather's
hard work and skill. He does, however, feel regret that
he is not like these dedicated men. Even though he cannot
use a shovel, he hopes to use his pen in order to make
his own contributions as a writer.

When Catherine reread her journal entries, she thought she was close to
a specific topic for her paper. The more she reviewed the two poems, the
more confident she felt exploring their similar views of the fathers' roles
and their contrasting attitudes toward these fathers. (In fact, she had so
many ideas that she did not feel she had to brainstorm to generate more
material.) Before she could write a draft of her paper, however, Catherine
needed to identify specific similarities and differences between the two
poems.

Seeing Connections

Listing Catherine returned to the highlighted and annotated poems in
order to compile the following lists:

Differences

"Those Winter Sundays"	"Digging"

--memories of family
  problems
	--only happy memories
	  are involved

```
--the child acts                --the child admires his
  ambivalently toward his         father
  father
--atmosphere of tension         --atmosphere of happiness
                                  and togetherness


               Similarities
--the fathers are hard workers
--the fathers appear to love their children
--similar time--impression that the events happened years
  ago
--children, now grown, appreciate their fathers'
  dedication
--children, now grown, are inspired by their fathers'
  determination
```

At this point, Catherine reviewed her notes carefully. As connections between the two poems came into focus, she was able to decide on a tentative thesis and on a possible order for her ideas.

Deciding on a Thesis

The more Catherine thought about the two poems, the more she focused on their similarities. She expressed a possible main idea for her paper in the following tentative thesis statement:

```
Although their family backgrounds are different, both now-
grown poets realize the determination and dedication of
their fathers and are consequently impassioned in their
writing.
```

Preparing an Outline

Catherine reviewed her notes to identify the specific ideas she wanted to address in her first draft. Then she arranged those ideas in a logical order in a scratch outline:

```
"Those Winter Sundays"
     Poet reflects back on childhood
          --father's hard work
          --his misunderstanding and lack of appreciation
            for everything his father did
```

Family setting in childhood
    --tension in the house
    --no mother mentioned in the poem
Poet's realization of father's love and dedication

"Digging"

Poet reminisces
    --father's skill and hard work
    --grandfather's steady heaving of sods
    --children's participation and acceptance
Happiness of the family
The desire for the poet to continue the tradition

Drafting an Essay

With a thesis statement and scratch outline to guide her, Catherine wrote the following first draft of her essay. Her instructor's comments appear in the margins and at the end of the paper.

(first draft)

A Comparison of Two Poems about Fathers

Robert Hayden's "Those Winter Sundays" and "Digging" by Seamus Heaney are poems that were inspired by fathers and composed as tributes to fathers. Although their family backgrounds are different, both now-grown (poets) realize the determination and dedication of their fathers and are consequently impassioned in their writing.

Careful you're confusing poet and speaker.

In "Those Winter Sundays," Hayden reflects back on his childhood. He remembers the many Sundays when his father got up early to start the fires to make the house warm for his children's awakening. The poet pictures his father's hands made rough by his weekday work. These same hands not only made the fires on Sunday but also polished his son's good shoes, in preparation, no doubt, for church.

Hayden also quite clearly remembers that his father was never thanked for his work. The reader imagines that the father had many children and may have been poor. There were inner tensions in the house and, quite noticeably, there is no mention of a mother.

Good detail— but quotations would be helpful.

Looking back, the poet now realizes the love and dedication with which his father took care of the family. As a child, he never thanked his father, but now, as an adult, the poet seems to appreciate the simple kindness of his father.

In a similar sense, Seamus Heaney writes "Digging" as a tribute to his father and grandfather. He also reminisces about his father and remembers with clarity the skill with which his father dug potatoes. The grandfather too is remembered, as is his technique

Here two quotations from the poem would strengthen your discussion.

Add Line number in parentheses. →

for "heaving sods." There is an atmosphere of happiness in this poem. With the children helping the father harvest the potatoes, a sense of family togetherness is created. The reader feels that this family is a hard-working, but nevertheless happy, one.

As the poet reminisces about his childhood, he realizes that, unlike his father and grandfather, he will never be a master of digging or a person who uses physical strength to earn a living. He wishes to be like his father before him, desiring to accomplish and contribute. However, for the poet, any "digging" to be done will be by his pen, in the form of literature.

To conclude, the fathers in these poets' pasts inspire them to write. An appreciation for their fathers' dedication is achieved only after the children mature into adults. It is then that the fathers' impact on their children's lives is realized for its true importance.

Good start! When you revise, focus on the following:
- *Edit use of "poet" and "speaker" carefully. You can't assume that these poems reflect the poets' own lives or attitudes toward their fathers.*
- *Add more specific references to the poems, particularly quotations. (Don't forget to give line numbers.)*
- *Consider adding brief references to other poems about parents. (Check the text.)*
- *Consider rearranging your material into a point-by-point comparison, which will make the specific points of similarity and differences clearer.*

Let's discuss this draft in a conference.

First Draft: Commentary

After submitting her first draft, Catherine met with her instructor. Together, they reviewed not only her first draft but also her annotations, journal entries, lists of similarities and differences, and scratch outline. During the conference, her instructor explained his marginal comments and, building on Catherine's own ideas, helped her develop a plan for revision.

Catherine's instructor agreed that the poems' similarities were worth exploring in detail. He thought, however, that her references to the poems' language and ideas needed to be much more specific and that her paper's structure—discussing "Those Winter Sundays" first and then moving on to consider "Digging"—made the specific similarities between the two poems difficult to see.

Because the class had studied other poems in which speakers try to resolve their ambivalent feelings toward their parents, Catherine's instructor also suggested that she mention these poems to provide a wider context for her ideas. Finally, he explained the difference between the perspective of the poet and that of the **speaker,** a persona the poet creates, encouraging her to edit with this difference in mind.

As she reexamined her ideas in light of her discussion with her instructor, Catherine looked again at both the annotated poems and her notes about them. She then recorded her thoughts about her progress in an additional journal entry:

> After reviewing the poems again and talking to Professor Jackson, I discovered some additional points that I want to include in my next draft. The connection between the poet's pen and the shovel is evident in "Digging," and so is the link between the cold and the tensions in the house in "Those Winter Sundays." The tone of each poem should also be discussed. Specifically, I think that the poet's choice of <u>austere</u> in "Those Winter Sundays" has significance and should be included. In my next draft, I'll expand my first draft--hopefully, without reading into the poems too much. I also need to reorganize my ideas so parallels between the two poems will be clearer.

Because this journal entry suggested a new arrangement for her ideas, Catherine prepared a new scratch outline to guide her revision:

> Reflections on their fathers
>   Both poems
>   --fathers' dedication and hard work

```
    Family similarities and differences
      "Digging"
            --loving and caring
      "Those Winter Sundays"
            --family problems (tone of the poem)
    Lessons learned from father
      "Digging"
            --inspiration (images of pen and shovel)
            --realization of father's inner strength
      "Those Winter Sundays"
            --realization of father's inner strength
            --"austere" caring (images of cold)
    Brief discussion of other poems about fathers
```

REVISING AND EDITING AN ESSAY

After once again reviewing all the material she had accumulated, Catherine wrote a second draft.

(second draft)

A Comparison of Two Poems about Fathers

Robert Hayden's "Those Winter Sundays" and Seamus Heaney's "Digging" are two literary pieces that are tributes to the speakers' fathers. The inspiration and admiration the speakers feel are evident in each poem. Although the nature of the two family relationships may differ, the common thread of the love of fathers for their children weaves through each poem.

Reflections on one's childhood can bring assorted memories to light. Presumably, the speakers are now adults and reminisce on their childhood with a mature sense of enlightenment not found in childhood. Both speakers describe their fathers' hard work and dedication to their families. Hayden's speaker remembers that even after working hard all week, his father would get up early on Sunday to warm the house in preparation for his children's rising. The speaker vividly portrays his father's hands, describing "cracked hands that ached from labor in the weekday weather" (3-4). And yet, these same hands not only built the fires that drove out the cold but also polished his children's good shoes.

In a similar way, Heaney's speaker reminisces about his father's and grandfather's digging of soil and sod, elaborating on their skill and dedication to their task.

The fathers in these poems appear to be the hardest of workers, labourers who sought to support their families. Not only did they have a dedication to their work, but they also cared about and undoubtedly loved their children. Looking back, Hayden's speaker realizes that, although his childhood may not have been perfect nor his family life entirely without problems, his father loved him. Heaney's description of the potato picking makes us imagine a loving family led by a father and grandfather who worked together and included the children in both work and celebration. Heaney's speaker grows to become a man who has nothing but respect for his father and grandfather, wishing to be like them and somehow follow their greatness.

Although some similarities exist between the sons and fathers in the poems, the family life differs between the two. Perhaps it is the tone of the poems that best typifies the family atmosphere. The tone of "Digging" is wholesome, earthy, natural, and happy, emphasizing the healthy and caring nature of the poet's childhood. In reminiscing, Heaney's speaker seems to have no bad memories concerning his father or family. In contrast, the tone of Hayden's poem is very much like the coldness of the Sunday mornings. Even though the father warmed the house, the "chronic angers of that house" (9) did not leave with the cold. The speaker, as a child, seems full of resentment toward the father, no doubt blaming him for the family problems. (Curiously, it is the father and not the mother who polishes the children's good shoes. Was there no mother?) The reader senses that the father-son communication evident in Heaney's family is missing in Hayden's.

"Digging" and "Those Winter Sundays" are poems written from the inspirations of sons, admiring and appreciating their fathers. Childhood memories act not only as images of the past but also as aids for the speakers' self-realization and enlightenment. Even after childhood, the fathers' influence over their sons is evident; only now do the speakers appreciate its true importance.

Second Draft: Commentary

When she reread her second draft, Catherine thought she had accomplished some of what she had set out to do. She had, for example, tightened her thesis statement, rearranged her discussion, added specific details, and changed *poet* to *speaker* where necessary. However, she still was not satisfied with her analysis of the poems' language and tone (she had not, for example, considered the importance of the word *austere* or examined the significance of Heaney's equation of *spade* and *pen*). Finally, she planned to edit and proofread carefully as she prepared her final draft.

Whittaker 1

Catherine Whittaker

Professor Jackson

English 102

5 March 2007

Digging for Memories

Robert Hayden's "Those Winter Sundays" and Seamus Heaney's "Digging" are two literary pieces that are tributes to the speakers' fathers. Although the depiction of the families and the tones of the two poems are different, the common thread of love between fathers and children extends through the two poems, and each speaker is inspired by his father's example.

As these poems reveal, reflections on childhood can bring complex memories to light, as they do for Hayden's and Heaney's speakers. Now adults, they reminisce about their childhoods with a mature sense of enlightenment not found in childhood. Both speakers describe their fathers' hard work and dedication to their families. Hayden's speaker remembers that even after working hard all week, his father would get up early on Sunday to warm the house in preparation for his sleeping children. The speaker vividly portrays his father's hands, describing "cracked hands that ached from labor in the weekday weather" (3–4). And yet, these same hands not only built the fires that drove out the cold, but also polished his children's good shoes. In a similar way, Heaney's speaker reminisces about his father's and grandfather's digging of soil and sod, pointing out their skill and their dedication to their tasks.

The fathers in these poems appear to be hard workers, labourers who struggled to support their families. Not only were they dedicated to their work, but they also loved their children. Looking back, Hayden's

Thesis statement — marginal note pointing to thesis paragraph.

Parenthetical reference cites line numbers. — marginal note.

speaker realizes that, although his childhood may not have been perfect and his family life was not entirely without problems, his father loved him. Heaney's description of the potato picking makes us imagine a loving family led by a father and grandfather who worked together and included the children in both work and celebration. Heaney's speaker grows into a man who has nothing but respect for his father and grandfather, wishing to be like them and to somehow fill their shoes.

Although some similarities exist between the sons and fathers in the poems, the family life the two poems depict is very different. Perhaps it is the tone of the poems that best reveals the family atmosphere. The tone of "Digging" is wholesome, earthy, natural, and happy, emphasizing the healthy and caring nature of the speaker's childhood. Heaney's speaker seems to have no bad memories of his father or family. In contrast, the tone of Hayden's poem is very much like the coldness of the Sunday mornings. Even though the father warmed the house, the "chronic angers of that house" (9) did not leave with the cold. The speaker, as a child, seems to have resented his father, no doubt blaming him for the family's problems. The reader senses that the warm relationship between the father and the son in Heaney's poem is absent in Hayden's.

In spite of these differences, the reader cannot go away from either poem without the impression that both speakers learned important lessons from their fathers. Both fathers had a great amount of inner strength and dedication to their families. As the years pass, Hayden's speaker has come to realize the depth of his father's devotion to his family. He uses the image of the "blueblack cold" (2) that was splintered and broken by the fires lovingly prepared by his father to suggest the father's efforts to keep his family free from harm. The cold suggests the tensions of the family that the father is determined to force out of the house through his "austere and lonely offices" (14).

In Heaney's poem, the father and grandfather also had a profound impact on the young speaker. As the memories come pouring back, the speaker's admiration for the men who came before him forces him to reflect on his own life and work. He realizes that he will never have the ability (or the desire) to do the physical labour of his relatives: "I've no spade to follow men like them" (28). However, just as the spade was the tool of his father and grandfather, the pen will be the tool with which the speaker will work. The shovel suggests the hard work, effort, and determination of the men who came before him, and the pen is the literary equivalent of the shovel. Heaney's speaker has been inspired by his father and grandfather and hopes to accomplish with a pen in the world of literature what they accomplished with a shovel on the land.

"Digging" and "Those Winter Sundays" are poems written from the perspective of sons, admiring and appreciating their fathers. Childhood memories not only act as images of the past but also evoke the speakers' self-realization and enlightenment. Even after childhood, the fathers' influence over their sons is evident; only now, however, do the speakers appreciate its true importance.

Conclusion reinforces thesis.

Final Draft: Commentary

As she wrote her final draft, Catherine expanded her analysis, looking more closely at the language and tone of the two poems. To support and clarify her points, she added more direct quotations, taking care to reproduce words and punctuation marks accurately and to cite line numbers in parentheses after each quotation. (Because all the students in Catherine's class had to select poems from Chapter 11 of this anthology, their instructor did not require a Works Cited page.)

CHAPTER 13

Voice

◆ ◆ ◆

What makes a poem significant? What makes it memorable? Passion and thought, emotionally charged language, fresh imagery, surprising use of metaphor . . . yes. But also, I think, the very sure sense that the moment we enter the world of the poem we are participating in another episode of the myth-journey of humankind; that a voice has taken up the tale once more. The individual experience as related or presented in the poem renews our deep, implicit faith in that greater experience. A poem remains with us to the extent that it allows us to feel that we are listening to a voice at once contemporary and ancient. This makes all the difference.

JOHN HAINES, "The Hole in the Bucket"

The lyric continues to hold the attention of poets, since it represents the spirit in full song, the most highly charged dance of language and feeling. The lyric impulse continues to drive poems of all sizes. However, the lyric poem, as signature and advertisement of the self, raises questions about the role of the individual ego and its potential to interfere with the poetic quest for a deeper and, perhaps, a larger truth.

GARY GEDDES, Preface to *Fifteen Canadian Poets × 3*

◆ ◆ ◆

EMILY DICKINSON
(1830–1886)

I'm Nobody! Who Are You?
(1891)

I'm Nobody! Who are you?
Are you—Nobody—Too?
Then there's a pair of us?
Don't tell! they'd advertise—you know!

5 How dreary—to be—Somebody!
How public—like a Frog—
To tell one's name—the livelong June—
To an admiring Bog!

THE SPEAKER IN THE POEM

◇ ◇ ◇

In fiction, the author's careful choice and arrangement of words enable readers to form an impression of the narrator and to decide whether he or she is sophisticated or unsophisticated, trustworthy or untrustworthy, innocent or experienced. Like fiction, poetry depends on a **speaker** who describes events, feelings, and ideas to readers. Finding out as much as possible about this speaker can help readers to interpret the poem. For example, the speaker in Emily Dickinson's "I'm Nobody! Who Are You?" seems at once shy and playful. The first stanza of the poem suggests that the speaker is a private person, perhaps with little self-esteem. As the poem continues, however, the voice becomes almost defiant. In a sense the speaker's two voices represent two ways of relating to the world. The first voice expresses the private self—internal, isolated, and revealed through poetry; the second expresses the public self—external, self-centred, and inevitably superficial. Far from being defeated by shyness, the speaker claims to have chosen her status as "nobody."

One question readers might ask about "I'm Nobody! Who Are You?" is how close the speaker's voice is to the poet's. Readers who conclude that the poem is about the conflict between a poet's public and private responsibilities may be tempted to see the speaker and the poet as one. But this is not necessarily the case. Like the narrator of a short story, the speaker of a poem is a **persona,** or mask, that the poet assumes. Granted, in some poems little distance exists between the poet and the speaker. Without hard evidence to support a link between speaker and poet, however, readers should not assume they are one and the same.

In most cases the speaker is quite different from the poet. And even when the speaker's voice conveys the attitude of the poet, it may do so only indirectly. In "Suicide Note" (p. 630), for example, Janice Mirikitani assumes the voice of a college student who has committed suicide because of perceived pressures placed upon her by her parents and her culture. Mirikitani imagines what it would be like to be the young student and how she is driven to her final, desperate act. Clearly, the author and speaker of the poem are two different people: the author has assumed a persona to show the pain and confusion of the student and to criticize the conditions under which the student has made a terrible choice. Evidently the author sympathizes with the student and through the adoption of the persona of the student hopes to effect an understanding of reasons for the suicide and possibly a change in behaviour so that other students will not react the same way as the troubled and despairing persona.

Sometimes the poem's speaker is anonymous. In this case—as in William Carlos Williams's "The Red Wheelbarrow" (p. 686), for instance—the first-person voice is absent and the speaker remains outside the poem. At other times, the speaker has a set identity—a king, a beggar, a highwayman, a sheriff, a husband, a wife, a rich man, a student, a child, a mythical figure, an explorer, a teacher, a faithless lover, a saint, or even a flower, an animal, or a clod of earth. Whatever the case, the speaker is not the poet, but rather a creation that the poet uses to convey his or her ideas. (For this reason, poems by a single poet may have very different voices. See Robert Browning's "My Last Duchess" [p. 624] and "Porphyria's Lover" [p. 640], for example.)

In the following poem, the poet assumes the mask of a fictional character, Gretel from the fairy tale "Hansel and Gretel."

LOUISE GLÜCK
(1943–   )

Gretel in Darkness
(1971)

This is the world we wanted. All who would have seen us dead
Are dead. I hear the witch's cry
Break in the moonlight through a sheet of sugar: God rewards.
Her tongue shrivels into gas. . . .

5   Now, far from women's arms
And memory of women, in our father's hut
We sleep, are never hungry.
Why do I not forget?
My father bars the door, bars harm
10 From this house, and it is years.

No one remembers. Even you, my brother.
Summer afternoons you look at me as though you meant
To leave, as though it never happened. But I killed for you.
I see armed firs, the spires of that gleaming kiln come back, come
     back—

15 Nights I turn to you to hold me but you are not there.
Am I alone? Spies
Hiss in the stillness, Hansel we are there still, and it is real, real,
That black forest, and the fire in earnest.

The speaker in this poem comments on her life in the years after her encounter with the witch in the forest. Speaking to her brother, Gretel observes that they now live in the world they wanted: they live with their father in his hut, and the witch and the wicked stepmother are dead. Even so, the memory of the events in the forest haunt Gretel and make it impossible for her to live "happily ever after." The "armed firs," the "gleaming kiln," and "the black forest" break through the "sheet of sugar" that her life has become.

By assuming the persona of Gretel, Glück is able to convey some interesting and complex ideas. On one level, Gretel represents any person who has lived through a traumatic experience. Memories of the event keep breaking through into the present, frustrating her attempts to reestablish her belief in the goodness of the world. The voice we hear is sad, alone, and frightened: "Nights I turn to you to hold me," she says, "but you are not there." Although the murder Gretel committed for her brother was justified, it seems to haunt her. "No one remembers," laments Gretel, not even her brother. At some level, she realizes that by killing the witch she has killed a part of herself, perhaps the part of women that men fear and consequently transform into witches and wicked stepmothers. The world that is left after the killing is the father's and the brother's, not hers, and she is now alone in a dark world haunted by the memories of the black forest. In this sense, Gretel—"Now, far from women's arms / And memory of women"—may be the voice of all victimized women who, because of men, act against their own best interests—and regret it.

As "Gretel in Darkness" illustrates, a title can identify a poem's speaker, but the speaker's own words can provide much more information. For example, in the following poem, the idiom of Trinidad helps to define the poem's frame of reference and to characterize the speaker.

◊　◊　◊

MARLENE NOURBESE PHILIP
(1947–　　)

Blackman Dead
(1980)

The magnum pistol barked
its last command
broke his chest—
red words of silence erupt
5　silken ribbons of death
wreathe the sullen Sunday morning madness.

A magnum pistol broke the secret
Sunday morning pact,
red roads of silence
10　lead us
nowhere

but to bury him
bury him
in a plain pine coffin
15 and repeat after me
how bad he was because,
because he was
just another immigrant
I say repeat
20 after me
how he deserved to die
because he didn't learn our ways
the ways of death
repeat
25 after me blackman dead, blackman dead
blackman dead.

as we dress dong
in we tree piece suit
we disco dress
30 an' we fancy wheels—
dere is a magnum fe each one a we.

Listen me, listen me,
dey say every man palace is 'is 'ome
dat no man is
35 one hisland honto 'imself
dat if yuh mark one crass
pon yuh door
in blood
all we fus born is safe,

40 I say repeat
after me
how he deserved to die
because he didn't learn our ways
the ways of death
45 repeat
after me
blackman dead, blackman dead
blackman dead.

Toronto has no silk cotton trees
50 strong enough to bear
one blackman's neck
the only crosses that burn
are those upon our souls

and the lynch mobs meet
55 at Winstons[1]....

Blackman dead, blackman dead,
blood seeps beneath
the subterfuged lie
living as men
60 how can we die as niggers,
red roads of silence
lead us where
no birds sing
blackman dead
65 blackman dead
black roses for blackman dead.

In this poem, the speaker is caught between two cultures and two ways of using English. The shift from so-called "standard" English to Trinidadian English and back indicates the speaker's anger at racism and how difficult immigrants may find life in Canada because of their colour and language.

In the following poem, direct statements by the speaker also help to characterize him and define his perspective.

❧ ❧ ❧

GEORGE ELLIOTT CLARKE
(1960–   )

Blank Sonnet
(1990)

The air smells of rhubarb, occasional
Roses, or first birth of blossoms, a fresh,
Undulant hurt, so body snaps and curls
Like flower. I step through snow as thin as script,
5 Watch white stars spin dizzy as drunks, and yearn
To sleep beneath a patchwork quilt of rum.
I want the slow, sure collapse of language
Washed out by alcohol. Lovely Shelley,[1]
I have no use for measured, cadenced verse
10 If you won't read. Icarus-like,[2] I'll fall

---

[1] An upscale restaurant, now defunct.

---

[1] Shelley Clemence, a female resident of the fictional Whylah Falls, is the beloved of the narrator, known as X.

[2] In Greek mythology, Icarus, son of Daedalus, escaped from Crete on wings his father had made for him. He flew so close to the sun, however, that the wax holding together the wings melted, and he fell into the Aegean Sea.

Against this page of snow, tumble blackly
Across vision to drown in the white sea
That closes every poem—the white reverse
That cancels the blackness of each image.

Here the speaker, identifying himself as a person who "tumble[s] blackly" (11), indicates his race and his vocation as a writer. The juxtaposition of black and white is central to the speaker's position as both person and poet. In comparing himself to Icarus, the speaker may be commenting on his pride and his aspirations. Like Icarus, he would rather fail than not try to make his mark.

In each of the preceding poems, the speaker is alone. The following poem, a **dramatic monologue,** presents a more complex situation in which the poet creates a complete dramatic scene. The speaker is developed as a character whose distinctive personality is revealed through his words as he addresses a silent listener.

ROBERT BROWNING
(1812–1889)

My Last Duchess
(1842)

Ferrara

That's my last Duchess painted on the wall,
Looking as if she were alive. I call
That piece a wonder, now: Frà Pandolf's[1] hands
Worked busily a day, and there she stands.
5 Will't please you sit and look at her? I said
"Frà Pandolf" by design, for never read
Strangers like you that pictured countenance,
The depth and passion of its earnest glance,
But to myself they turned (since none puts by
10 The curtain I have drawn for you, but I)
And seemed as they would ask me, if they durst,
How such a glance came there; so, not the first
Are you to turn and ask thus. Sir, 'twas not
Her husband's presence only, called that spot
15 Of joy into the Duchess' cheek: perhaps
Frà Pandolf chanced to say "Her mantle laps

---

[1] "Brother" Pandolf, a fictive painter.

Over my lady's wrist too much," or "Paint
Must never hope to reproduce the faint
Half-flush that dies along her throat": such stuff
20 Was courtesy, she thought, and cause enough
For calling up that spot of joy. She had
A heart—how shall I say?—too soon made glad,
Too easily impressed; she liked whate'er
She looked on, and her looks went everywhere.
25 Sir, 'twas all one! My favor at her breast,
The dropping of the daylight in the West,
The bough of cherries some officious fool
Broke in the orchard for her, the white mule
She rode with round the terrace—all and each
30 Would draw from her alike the approving speech,
Or blush, at least. She thanked men—good! but thanked
Somehow—I know not how—as if she ranked
My gift of a nine-hundred-years-old name
With anybody's gift. Who'd stoop to blame
35 This sort of trifling? Even had you skill
In speech—(which I have not)—to make your will
Quite clear to such an one, and say, "Just this
Or that in you disgusts me; here you miss,
Or there exceed the mark"—and if she let
40 Herself be lessoned so, nor plainly set
Her wits to yours, forsooth, and made excuse
—E'en then would be some stooping; and I choose
Never to stoop. Oh sir, she smiled, no doubt,
Whene'er I passed her; but who passed without
45 Much the same smile? This grew; I gave commands;
Then all smiles stopped together. There she stands
As if alive. Will't please you rise? We'll meet
The company below, then. I repeat,
The Count your master's known munificence
50 Is ample warrant that no just pretense
Of mine for dowry will be disallowed;
Though his fair daughter's self, as I avowed
At starting, is my object. Nay, we'll go
Together down, sir. Notice Neptune,[2] though,
55 Taming a sea horse, thought a rarity,
Which Claus of Innsbruck[3] cast in bronze for me!

---

[2] God of the sea.

[3] An imaginary—or unidentified—sculptor. The count of Tyrol's capital was at Innsbrück, Austria.

The speaker is probably Alfonso II, duke of Ferrara, Italy, whose young wife, Lucrezia, died in 1561 after only three years of marriage. Shortly after her death, the duke began negotiations to marry again. When the poem opens, the duke is showing a portrait of his late wife to an emissary of an unnamed count who is there to arrange a marriage between the duke and the count's daughter. The duke remarks that the artist, Frà Pandolf, has caught a certain look upon the duchess's face. This look aroused the jealousy of the duke, who thought that it should have been for him alone. According to the duke, the duchess's crime was to have a heart "too soon made glad," "Too easily impressed." Eventually the duke could stand the situation no longer; he "gave commands," and "all smiles stopped together."

Much of what readers learn about the duke's state of mind comes from what is implied by his words. As he discusses the painting, the duke unintentionally reveals himself to be obsessively possessive and jealous, referring to "*my* last Duchess," "*my* favor at her breast," and "*my* gift of a nine-hundred-years-old name." He keeps the picture of his late wife well hidden behind a curtain that no one draws except him. His interest in the picture has little to do with the memory of his wife, however. In death, the duchess has become just what the duke always wanted her to be: a personal possession that reflects his good taste.

The listener plays a subtle but important role in the poem: his presence establishes the dramatic situation that allows the character of the duke to be revealed. The purpose of the story is to communicate to the emissary exactly what the duke expects from his prospective bride, and from her father. As he speaks, the duke conveys only the information that he wants the emissary to take back to his master, the count. Although he appears vain and superficial, the duke is actually extraordinarily shrewd. Throughout the poem, he turns the conversation to his own ends and gains the advantage through flattery and false modesty. Notice, for example, that he claims he has little skill in speaking when actually he is cleverly manipulating the conversation. The success of the poem lies in the poet's ability to develop the voice of this complex character, who embodies both superficial elegance and shocking cruelty.

❖ POEMS FOR FURTHER READING: THE SPEAKER IN THE POEM

◇ ◇ ◇

BILLY COLLINS
(1941–)

Victoria's Secret
(1998)

The one in the upper left-hand corner
is giving me a look
that says I know you are here

and I have nothing better to do
5 for the remainder of human time
than return your persistent but engaging stare.
She is wearing a deeply scalloped
flame-stitch halter top
with padded push-up styling
10 and easy side-zip tap pants.

The one on the facing page, however,
who looks at me over her bare shoulder,
cannot hide the shadow of annoyance in her brow.
You have interrupted me,
15 she seems to be saying,
with your coughing and your loud music.
Now please leave me alone;
let me finish whatever it was I was doing
in my organza-trimmed
20 whisperweight camisole with
keyhole closure and a point d'esprit mesh back.

I wet my thumb and flip the page.
Here, the one who happens to be reclining
in a satin and lace merry widow
25 with an inset lace-up front,
decorated underwire cups and bodice
with lace ruffles along the bottom
and hook-and-eye closure in the back,
is wearing a slightly contorted expression,
30 her head thrust back, mouth partially open,
a confusing mixture of pain and surprise
as if she had stepped on a tack
just as I was breaking down
her bedroom door with my shoulder.

35 Nor does the one directly beneath her
look particularly happy to see me.
She is arching one eyebrow slightly
as if to say, so what if I am wearing nothing
but this stretch panne velvet bodysuit
40 with a low sweetheart neckline
featuring molded cups and adjustable straps.
Do you have a problem with that?!

The one on the far right is easier to take,
her eyes half-closed
45 as if she were listening to a medley
of lullabies playing faintly on a music box.
Soon she will drop off to sleep,

her head nestled in the soft crook of her arm,
and later she will wake up in her
50 Spandex slip dress with the high side slit,
deep scoop neckline, elastic shirring,
and concealed back zip and vent.

But opposite her,
stretched out catlike on a couch
55 in the warm glow of a paneled library,
is one who wears a distinctly challenging expression,
her face tipped up, exposing
her long neck, her perfectly flared nostrils.
Go ahead, her expression tells me,
60 take off my satin charmeuse gown
with a sheer, jacquard bodice
decorated with a touch of shimmering Lurex.
Go ahead, fling it into the fireplace.
What do I care, her eyes say, we're all going to hell anyway.

65 I have other mail to open,
but I cannot help noticing her neighbor
whose eyes are downcast,
her head ever so demurely bowed to the side
as if she were the model who sat for Coreggio
70 when he painted "The Madonna of St. Jerome,"
only, it became so ungodly hot in Parma
that afternoon, she had to remove
the traditional blue robe
and pose there in his studio
75 in a beautifully shaped satin teddy
with an embossed V-front,
princess seaming to mold the bodice,
and puckered knit detail.

And occupying the whole facing page
80 is one who displays that expression
we have come to associate with photographic beauty.
Yes, she is pouting about something,
all lower lip and cheekbone.
Perhaps her ice cream has tumbled
85 out of its cone onto the parquet floor.
Perhaps she has been waiting all day
for a new sofa to be delivered,
waiting all day in a stretch lace hipster

with lattice edging, satin frog closures,
90 velvet scrollwork, cuffed ankles,
flare silhouette, and knotted shoulder straps
available in black, champagne, almond,
cinnabar, plum, bronze, mocha,
peach, ivory, caramel, blush, butter, rose, and periwinkle.
95 It is, of course, impossible to say,
impossible to know what she is thinking,
why her mouth is the shape of petulance.

But this is already too much.
Who has the time to linger on these delicate
100 lures, these once unmentionable things?
Life is rushing by like a mad, swollen river.
One minute roses are opening in the garden
and the next, snow is flying past my window.
Plus the phone is ringing.
105 The dog is whining at the door.
Rain is beating on the roof.
And as always there is a list of things I have to do
before the night descends, black and silky,
and the dark hours begin to hurtle by,
110 before the little doors of the body swing shut
and I ride to sleep, my closed eyes
still burning from all the glossy lights of day.

READING AND REACTING

1. Why is the speaker looking at a Victoria's Secret catalogue? What details of the pictures does he appear to be most interested in?
2. Does the catalogue have the desired effect of selling merchandise to the speaker?
3. **JOURNAL ENTRY** Pick one of the models described in the poem and write a response to the speaker's assessment of your picture.
4. **CRITICAL PERSPECTIVE** In an interview in *The Christian Science Monitor* (April 25, 2002), Collins said that a poem "should be taking you somewhere; you should find yourself moved, taken into some wonderful location where the rules of logic have been changed." Does "Victoria's Secret" have that effect on you? Why or why not?

Related Works: "The Ice Wagon Going Down the Street" (p. 98), "A Very Old Man with Enormous Wings" (p. 432), "My Mistress' Eyes Are Nothing like the Sun" (p. 580), *The Importance of Being Earnest* (p. 961)

JANICE MIRIKITANI
(1942–)

Suicide Note

(1987)

. . . An Asian-American college student was reported to have jumped to her death from her dormitory window. Her body was found two days later under a deep cover of snow. Her suicide note contained an apology to her parents for having received less than a perfect four point grade average. . . .

How many notes written . . .
ink smeared like birdprints in snow.

not good enough   not pretty enough   not smart enough
dear mother and father.
5   I apologize
for disappointing you.
I've worked very hard,
                    not good enough
harder, perhaps to please you.
10 If only I were a son, shoulders broad
as the sunset threading through pine,
I would see the light in my mother's
eyes, or the golden pride reflected
in my father's dream
15 of my wide, male hands worthy of work
and comfort.
I would swagger through life
muscled and bold and assured,
drawing praises to me
20 like currents in the bed of wind, virile
with confidence.
          not good enough   not strong enough   not good enough

I apologize.
Tasks do not come easily.
25 Each failure, a glacier.
Each disapproval, a bootprint.
Each disappointment,
ice above my river.
So I have worked hard.
30   not good enough
My sacrifice I will drop
bone by bone, perched

on the ledge of my womanhood,
fragile as wings.
35   not strong enough
It is snowing steadily
surely not good weather
for flying—this sparrow
sillied and dizzied by the wind
40 on the edge.
                    not smart enough
I make this ledge my altar
to offer penance.
This air will not hold me,
45 the snow burdens my crippled wings,
my tears drop like bitter cloth
softly into the gutter below.
    not good enough   not strong enough   not smart enough
                    Choices thin as shaved
50   ice. Notes shredded
                    drift like snow
on my broken body,
cover me like whispers
of sorries
55 sorries.
Perhaps when they find me
they will bury
my bird bones beneath
a sturdy pine
60 and scatter my feathers like
unspoken song
over this white and cold and silent
breast of earth.

READING AND REACTING

1. This poem presents a suicide note that is also an apology. Why does the speaker feel she must apologize?
2. What attitude does the speaker convey toward her parents?
3. **JOURNAL ENTRY** Is the college student who speaks in this poem a stranger to you? Or is her voice in any way like that of students you know?

Related Works: "All about Suicide" (p. 7), "The Rocking-Horse Winner" (p. 370), "The Boat" (p. 447)

The Tone of the Poem

◊ ◊ ◊

The **tone** of a poem conveys the speaker's attitude toward his or her subject or audience. In speech, this attitude can be conveyed easily: stressing a word in a sentence can modify or colour a statement, drastically affecting the meaning of a sentence. For example, the statement "Of course, you would want to go to that restaurant" is quite straightforward, but changing the emphasis to "Of course *you* would want to go to *that* restaurant" transforms a neutral statement into a sarcastic one. For poets, however, conveying a particular tone to readers represents a challenge because readers rarely hear their spoken voices. Instead, poets indicate tone by using techniques such as rhyme, metre, word choice, sentence structure, figures of speech, and imagery.

The range of possible tones is wide. For example, a poem's speaker may be joyful, sad, playful, serious, comic, intimate, formal, relaxed, condescending, or ironic. The detached tone of the following poem conveys the speaker's attitude toward the subject.

◊ ◊ ◊

ROBERT FROST
(1874–1963)

Fire and Ice
(1923)

Some say the world will end in fire,
Some say in ice.
From what I've tasted of desire
I hold with those who favor fire.
5 But if it had to perish twice,
I think I know enough of hate
To say that for destruction ice
Is also great
And would suffice.

Here the speaker uses word choice, rhyme, and understatement to comment on the human condition. The conciseness and the simple, regular metre and rhyme suggest an **epigram**—a short poem that makes a pointed comment in an unusually clear, and often witty, manner. This pointedness is consistent with the speaker's glib, unemotional tone, as is the last line's wry understatement that ice "would suffice." The contrast between the poem's serious message—that active hatred and indifference are equally destructive—and its informal style and offhand tone is consistent with the speaker's detached, almost smug, posture.

Sometimes shifts in tone reveal changes in the speaker's attitude. In the following poem, changes in tone reveal a shift in the speaker's attitude toward war.

◊ ◊ ◊

THOMAS HARDY
(1840–1928)

The Man He Killed
(1902)

"Had he and I but met
By some old ancient inn,
We should have sat us down to wet
Right many a nipperkin![1]

5 "But ranged as infantry,
And staring face to face,
I shot at him as he at me,
And killed him in his place.

"I shot him dead because—
10 Because he was my foe,
Just so: my foe of course he was;
That's clear enough; although

"He thought he'd 'list,[2] perhaps,
Off-hand-like—just as I—
15 Was out of work—had sold his traps—
No other reason why.

"Yes; quaint and curious war is!
You shoot a fellow down
You'd treat if met where any bar is,
20 Or help to half-a-crown."

The speaker in this poem is a soldier relating his wartime experiences. Quotation marks indicate that he is engaged in conversation—perhaps in a pub—and his dialect indicates that he is probably of the English working class. For him, at least at first, the object of war is simple: kill or be killed. To Hardy, this speaker represents all men who are thrust into a war without understanding its underlying economic or ideological causes. In this sense, the speaker and his enemy are both victims of forces beyond their comprehension or control.

---

[1] A small container of liquor.

[2] Enlist.

The tone of "The Man He Killed" changes as the speaker tells his story. As the poem unfolds, its sentence structure deteriorates, and this in turn helps to convey the speaker's changing attitude toward the war in which he has fought. In the first two stanzas of the poem, sentences are smooth and unbroken, establishing the speaker's matter-of-fact tone and reflecting his confidence that he has done what he had to do. In the third and fourth stanzas, however, broken syntax reflects the narrator's increasingly disturbed state of mind as he tells about the man he killed. The poem's singsong metre and regular rhyme scheme *(met/wet, inn/nipperkin)* suggest that the speaker is trying hard to maintain his composure; the smooth sentence structure of the last stanza and the use of a cliché in an attempt to trivialize the incident ("Yes; quaint and curious war is!") show the speaker's efforts to regain his control.

Sometimes a poem's tone can establish an ironic contrast between the speaker and his or her subject. In the next poem, the speaker's abrupt change of tone at the end of the poem establishes just such a contrast.

A M Y   L O W E L L
(1874–1925)

Patterns
(1915)

I walk down the garden-paths,
And all the daffodils
Are blowing, and the bright blue squills.
I walk down the patterned garden-paths
5 In my stiff, brocaded gown.
With my powdered hair and jewelled fan,
I too am a rare
Pattern. As I wander down
The garden-paths.

10 My dress is richly figured,
And the train
Makes a pink and silver stain
On the gravel, and the thrift
Of the borders.
15 Just a plate of current fashion
Tripping by in high-heeled, ribboned shoes.
Not a softness anywhere about me,
Only whalebone[1] and brocade.

---

[1] Used in making corsets.

And I sink on a seat in the shade
20 Of a lime tree. For my passion
Wars against the stiff brocade.
The daffodils and squills
Flutter in the breeze
As they please.
25 And I weep;
For the lime-tree is in blossom
And one small flower has dropped upon my bosom.
And the plashing of waterdrops
In the marble fountain
30 Comes down the garden-paths.
The dripping never stops.
Underneath my stiffened gown
Is the softness of a woman bathing in a marble basin,
A basin in the midst of hedges grown
35 So thick, she cannot see her lover hiding,
But she guesses he is near,
And the sliding of the water
Seems the stroking of a dear
Hand upon her.
40 What is Summer in a fine brocaded gown!
I should like to see it lying in a heap upon the ground.
All the pink and silver crumpled up on the ground.

I would be the pink and silver as I ran along the paths,
And he would stumble after,
45 Bewildered by my laughter.
I should see the sun flashing from his sword-hilt and buckles
        on his shoes.
I would choose
To lead him in a maze along the patterned paths,
A bright and laughing maze for my heavy-booted lover.
50 Till he caught me in the shade,
And the buttons of his waistcoat bruised my body as he clasped me,
Aching, melting, unafraid.
With the shadows of the leaves and the sundrops,
And the plopping of the waterdrops,
55 All about us in the open afternoon—
I am very like to swoon
        With the weight of this brocade,
        For the sun sifts through the shade.

Underneath the fallen blossom
60 In my bosom,
Is a letter I have hid.

It was brought to me this morning by a rider from the Duke.
Madam, we regret to inform you that Lord Hartwell
Died in action Thursday se'nnight.[2]
65 As I read it in the white, morning sunlight,
The letters squirmed like snakes.
"Any answer, Madam," said my footman.
"No," I told him.
"See that the messenger takes some refreshment.
70 No, no answer."
And I walked into the garden,
Up and down the patterned paths,
In my stiff, correct brocade.
The blue and yellow flowers stood up proudly in the sun,
75 Each one.
I stood upright too,
Held rigid to the pattern
By the stiffness of my gown.
Up and down I walked.
80 Up and down.

In a month he would have been my husband.
In a month, here, underneath this lime,
We would have broken the pattern;
He for me, and I for him,
85 He as Colonel, I as Lady,
On this shady seat.
He had a whim
That sunlight carried blessing.
And I answered, "It shall be as you have said."
90 Now he is dead.

In Summer and in Winter I shall walk
Up and down
The patterned garden-paths
In my stiff, brocaded gown.
95 The squills and daffodils
Will give place to pillared roses, and to asters, and to snow.
I shall go
Up and down,
In my gown.
100 Gorgeously arrayed,
Boned and stayed.
And the softness of my body will be guarded from embrace
By each button, hook, and lace.
For the man who should loose me is dead,

---

[2] "Seven night," or a week ago Thursday.

105 Fighting with the Duke in Flanders,[3]
   In a pattern called a war.
   Christ! What are patterns for?

The speaker begins by describing herself walking down garden paths. She wears a stiff brocaded gown, has powdered hair, and carries a jewelled fan. By her own admission she is "a plate of current fashion." Although her tone is controlled, she is preoccupied by sensual thoughts. Beneath her "stiffened gown" is the "softness of a woman bathing in a marble basin," and the "sliding of the water" in a fountain reminds the speaker of the stroking of her lover's hand. She imagines herself shedding her brocaded gown and running with her lover along the maze of "patterned paths." The sensuality of the speaker's thoughts stands in ironic contrast to the images of stiffness and control that dominate the poem; her passion "wars against the stiff brocade." She is also full of repressed rage. After all, she knows that her lover has been killed, and she realizes the meaninglessness of the patterns of her life, patterns to which she has conformed, just as her lover has conformed by going to war and doing what he was supposed to do. Throughout the poem, the speaker's tone reflects her barely contained anger and frustration. In the last line of the poem, when she finally lets out her rage, the poem's point about the senselessness of war becomes apparent.

❖ POEMS FOR FURTHER READING: THE TONE OF THE POEM

✦ ✦ ✦

WILLIAM WORDSWORTH
(1770–1850)

The World Is Too Much with Us
(1807)

The world is too much with us; late and soon,
Getting and spending, we lay waste our powers;
Little we see in Nature that is ours;
We have given our hearts away, a sordid boon!
5 This Sea that bares her bosom to the moon;
The winds that will be howling at all hours,
And are up-gathered now like sleeping flowers;
For this, for everything, we are out of tune;
It moves us not. Great God! I'd rather be
10 A Pagan suckled in a creed outworn;
So might I, standing on this pleasant lea,

---

[3] Region in northwestern Europe, including part of northern France and western Belgium. Flanders was the site of a historic World War I battle.

Have glimpses that would make me less forlorn;
Have sight of Proteus[1] rising from the sea;
Or hear old Triton[2] blow his wreathèd horn.

READING AND REACTING

1. What is the speaker's attitude toward the contemporary world? How is this attitude revealed through the poem's tone?

2. This poem is a **sonnet,** a highly structured traditional form. How do the rhyme scheme and the regular metre establish the poem's tone?

3. **JOURNAL ENTRY** Imagine you are a modern-day environmentalist, labour organizer, or corporate executive. Write a response to the sentiments expressed in this poem.

4. **CRITICAL PERSPECTIVE** According to M. H. Abrams in his 1972 essay "Two Roads to Wordsworth," critics have tended to follow one of two different paths to the poet, and these approaches have yielded two different versions of the poet:

   One Wordsworth is simple, elemental, forthright, the other is complex, paradoxical, problematic; one is an affirmative poet of life, love, and joy, the other is an equivocal or self-divided poet whose affirmations are implicitly qualified . . . by a pervasive sense of morality and an ever-incipient despair of life; . . . one is the Wordsworth of light, the other the Wordsworth of [shadow], or even darkness.

   Does your reading of "The World Is Too Much with Us" support one of these versions of Wordsworth over the other? Which one? Why?

   Related Works: "The Rocking-Horse Winner" (p. 370), "The City of the End of Things" (p. 855), "She Dwelt among the Untrodden Ways" (p. 897)

---

[1] Sometimes said to be Poseidon's son, this Greek sea god had the ability to change shapes at will and to tell the future.

[2] The trumpeter of the sea, this sea god is usually pictured blowing on a conch shell. Triton was the son of Poseidon, ruler of the sea.

R O B E R T   H E R R I C K
(1591–1674)

To the Virgins, to Make Much of Time
(1646)

Gather ye rosebuds while ye may,
Old Time is still a-flying;
And this same flower that smiles today,
Tomorrow will be dying.

5 The glorious lamp of heaven, the sun,
The higher he's a-getting,
The sooner will his race be run,
And nearer he's to setting.

That age is best which is the first,
10 When youth and blood are warmer;
But being spent, the worse, and worst
Times still succeed the former.

Then be not coy, but use your time,
And while ye may, go marry;
15 For having lost but once your prime,
You may forever tarry.

READING AND REACTING

1. How would you characterize the speaker? Do you think he
   expects his listeners to share his views? How might his expectations affect his tone?
2. This poem is developed almost like an argument. What is the
   speaker's main point? How does he support it?
3. What effect does the poem's use of rhyme have on its tone?
4. **JOURNAL ENTRY** Whose side are you on—the speaker's or those
   he addresses?

Related Works: "The Passionate Shepherd to His Love" (p. 578),
"Cinderella" (p. 646), *The Brute* (p. 1081)

Irony

◊ ◊ ◊

Just as in fiction and drama, **irony** in poetry occurs when a discrepancy exists between two levels of meaning or experience. Consider the tone of the following lines by Stephen Crane:

> Do not weep, maiden, for war is kind.
> Because your lover threw wild hands toward the sky
> And the afrightened steed ran on alone,
> Do not weep.
> War is kind.

How can war be "kind"? Isn't war exactly the opposite of "kind"? Surely the speaker does not intend his words to be taken literally. By making this ironic statement, the speaker actually conveys the opposite idea: war is a cruel, mindless exercise of violence.

Skillfully used, irony is a powerful way of making a pointed comment about a situation or of manipulating a reader's emotions. Implicit in irony is the writer's assumption that readers will not be misled by the literal meaning of a statement. In order for irony to work, readers must recognize the disparity between what is said and what is meant, or between what a character or speaker thinks is occurring and what readers know to be occurring.

One kind of irony that appears in poetry is **dramatic irony,** which occurs when a speaker believes one thing and readers realize something else. In the following poem, the poet uses a deranged speaker to tell a story that is filled with irony.

◊ ◊ ◊

ROBERT BROWNING
(1812–1889)

Porphyria's Lover
(1836)

> The rain set early in to-night,
>   The sullen wind was soon awake,
> It tore the elm-tops down for spite,
>   And did its worst to vex the lake:
> 5   I listened with heart fit to break.
> When glided in Porphyria; straight
>   She shut the cold out and the storm,
> And kneeled and made the cheerless grate
>   Blaze up, and all the cottage warm;
> 10   Which done, she rose, and from her form
> Withdrew the dripping cloak and shawl,
>   And laid her soiled gloves by, untied
> Her hat and let the damp hair fall,

And, last, she sat down by my side
15   And called me. When no voice replied,
She put my arm about her waist,
    And made her smooth white shoulder bare,
And all her yellow hair displaced,
    And, stooping, made my cheek lie there,
20   And spread, o'er all, her yellow hair,
Murmuring how she loved me—she
    Too weak, for all her heart's endeavour,
To set its struggling passion free
    From pride, and vainer ties dissever,
25   And give herself to me for ever.
But passion sometimes would prevail,
    Nor could to-night's gay feast restrain
A sudden thought of one so pale
    For love of her, and all in vain:
30   So, she was come through wind and rain.
Be sure I looked up at her eyes
    Happy and proud; at last I knew
Porphyria worshipped me; surprise
    Made my heart swell, and still it grew
35   While I debated what to do.
That moment she was mine, mine, fair,
    Perfectly pure and good: I found
A thing to do, and all her hair
    In one long yellow string I wound
40   Three times her little throat around,
And strangled her. No pain felt she;
    I am quite sure she felt no pain.
As a shut bud that holds a bee,
    I warily oped her lids: again
45   Laughed the blue eyes without a stain.
And I untightened next the tress
    About her neck; her cheek once more
Blushed bright beneath my burning kiss:
    I propped her head up as before,
50   Only, this time my shoulder bore
Her head, which droops upon it still:
    The smiling rosy little head,
So glad it has its utmost will,
    That all it scorned at once is fled,
55   And I, its love, am gained instead!
Porphyria's love: she guessed not how
    Her darling one wish would be heard.
And thus we sit together now,
    And all night long we have not stirred,
60   And yet God has not said a word!

Like Browning's "My Last Duchess" (p. 624) this poem is a **dramatic monologue.** The speaker recounts his story in a straightforward manner, seemingly unaware of the horror of his tale. In fact, much of the effect of this poem comes from the speaker's telling his tale of murder in a flat, unemotional tone—and from readers' gradual realization that the speaker is mad.

The irony of the poem, and of its title, becomes apparent as the monologue progresses. At first the speaker fears that Porphyria is too weak to free herself from pride and vanity to love him. As he looks in her eyes, however, he comes to believe that she worships him. To preserve the perfection of Porphyria's love, the speaker strangles her with her own hair. He assures his silent listener, "I am quite sure she felt no pain." Like many of Browning's narrators, the speaker in this poem exhibits a selfish and perverse need to possess another person totally. The moment the speaker realizes that Porphyria loves him, he feels compelled to kill her and keep her his forever. According to him, she is at this point "mine, mine, fair, / Perfectly pure and good," and he believes that by murdering her he actually fulfills "Her darling one wish"—to stay with him forever. As he attempts to justify his actions, the speaker reveals himself to be a deluded psychopathic killer.

Another kind of irony is **situational irony,** which occurs when the situation itself contradicts readers' expectations. For example, in "Porphyria's Lover" the meeting of two lovers results not in joy and passion but in murder. In the next poem too the situation creates irony.

◊ ◊ ◊

PERCY BYSSHE SHELLEY
(1792–1822)

Ozymandias
(1818)

I met a traveler from an antique land
Who said: Two vast and trunkless legs of stone
Stand in the desert. Near them, on the sand,
Half sunk, a shattered visage lies, whose frown,
5 And wrinkled lip, and sneer of cold command,
Tell that its sculptor well those passions read
Which yet survive, stamped on these lifeless things,
The hand that mocked them, and the heart that fed;
And on the pedestal these words appear:
10 "My name is Ozymandias,[1] king of kings:
Look on my works, ye Mighty, and despair!"
Nothing beside remains. Round the decay
Of that colossal wreck, boundless and bare
The lone and level sands stretch far away.

---

[1] The Greek name for Ramses II, ruler of Egypt in the thirteenth century B.C.

The speaker tells a tale about a colossal statue that lies shattered in the desert. Its head lies separated from the trunk, and the face has a wrinkled lip and a "sneer of cold command." On the pedestal of the monument are words exhorting all those who pass: "Look on my works, ye Mighty, and despair!" The situational irony of the poem has its source in the contrast between the "colossal wreck" and the boastful inscription on its base. To the speaker, Ozymandias stands for the vanity of those who mistakenly think they can withstand the ravages of time.

Perhaps the most common kind of irony found in poetry is **verbal irony,** which is created when words say one thing but mean another, often exactly the opposite. When verbal irony is particularly biting, it is called **sarcasm.** In speech, verbal irony is easy to detect through the speaker's change in tone or emphasis. In writing, when these signals are absent, verbal irony becomes more difficult to convey. Poets must depend on the context of a remark or on the contrast between a word and other images in the poem to create irony.

Consider how verbal irony is established in the following poem.

◆ ◆ ◆

A R I E L D O R F M A N
(1942–   )

Hope
(1988)

Translated by Edith Grossman with the author

My son has been
missing
since May 8
of last year.

5   They took him
just for a few hours
they said
just for some routine
questioning.

10 After the car left,
the car with no license plate,
we couldn't

    find out

anything else
15 about him.
But now things have changed.
We heard from a compañero
who just got out

that five months later
20 they were torturing him
in Villa Grimaldi,
at the end of September
they were questioning him
in the red house
25 that belonged to the Grimaldis.

They say they recognized
his voice his screams
they say.

Somebody tell me frankly
30 what times are these
what kind of world
what country?
What I'm asking is
how can it be
35 that a father's
joy
a mother's
joy
is knowing
40 that they
that they are still
torturing
their son?
Which means
45 that he was alive
five months later
and our greatest
hope
will be to find out
50 next year
that they're still torturing him
eight months later

and he may   might   could
still be alive.

Although it is not necessary to know the background of the poet to appreciate this poem, it does help to know that Ariel Dorfman is a native of Chile.
After the assassination of Salvador Allende, Chile's elected socialist president,
in September 1973, the civilian government was replaced by a military dictatorship. Civil rights were suspended, and activists, students, and members
of opposition parties were arrested and often detained indefinitely; sometimes they simply disappeared. The irony of this poem originates in the discrepancy between the way the word *hope* is used in the poem and the way it

is usually used. For most people, hope has positive connotations, but in this poem it takes on a different meaning. This irony is not lost on the speaker.

◈ POEMS FOR FURTHER READING: IRONY

◊ ◊ ◊

W. H. AUDEN
(1907–1973)

The Unknown Citizen
(1939)

(To JS/07/M/378
This Marble Monument Is Erected by the State)

He was found by the Bureau of Statistics to be
One against whom there was no official complaint,
And all the reports on his conduct agree
That, in the modern sense of an old-fashioned word, he was a saint,
5 For in everything he did he served the Greater Community.
Except for the War till the day he retired
He worked in a factory and never got fired,
But satisfied his employers, Fudge Motors Inc.
Yet he wasn't a scab or odd in his views,
10 For his Union reports that he paid his dues,
(Our report on his Union shows it was sound)
And our Social Psychology workers found
That he was popular with his mates and liked a drink.
The Press are convinced that he bought a paper every day
15 And that his reactions to advertisements were normal in every way.
Policies taken out in his name prove that he was fully insured,
And his Health-card shows he was once in hospital but left it cured.
Both Producers Research and High-Grade Living declare
He was fully sensible to the advantages of the Installment Plan
20 And had everything necessary to the Modern Man,
A phonograph, a radio, a car and a frigidaire.
Our researchers into Public Opinion are content
That he held the proper opinions for the time of year;
When there was peace, he was for peace; when there was war, he went.
25 He was married and added five children to the population,
Which our Eugenist[1] says was the right number for a parent of his
      generation,
And our teachers report that he never interfered with their education.

---

[1] One who studies the science of human improvement, especially through genetic control.

Was he free? Was he happy? The question is absurd:
Had anything been wrong, we should certainly have heard.

READING AND REACTING

1. The "unknown citizen" represents modern citizens, who, according to the poem, are programmed like machines. How does the title help to establish the tone of the poem? How does the inscription on the monument help to establish the tone?
2. Who is the speaker? What is his attitude toward the unknown citizen? How can you tell?
3. What kinds of irony are present in the poem? Identify several examples.
4. **JOURNAL ENTRY** This poem was written in 1939. Does its criticism apply to contemporary society, or does the poem seem dated?
5. **CRITICAL PERSPECTIVE** In 1939, the same year this poem was published, Auden argued in his essay "The Public vs. The Late Mr. William Butler Yeats" that poetry can never really change anything. He reiterated this point as late as 1971 in his biographical *A Certain World:*

> By all means let a poet, if he wants to, write poems . . . [that protest] against this or that political evil or social injustice. But let him remember this. The only person who will benefit from them is himself; they will enhance his literary reputation among those who feel as he does. The evil or injustice, however, will remain exactly what it would have been if he had kept his mouth shut.

Do you believe that poetry—or any kind of literature—has the power to combat "evil or injustice" in the world? Do you consider "The Unknown Citizen" a political poem? How might this poem effect positive social or political change?

Related Works: "A&P" (p. 122), "The Man He Killed" (p. 633), "You Fit into Me" (p. 723), *A Doll House* (p. 1013)

✧ ✦ ✧

A N N E   S E X T O N
(1928–1974)

Cinderella
(1970)

You always read about it:
the plumber with twelve children
who wins the Irish Sweepstakes.
From toilets to riches.
5   That story.

Or the nursemaid,
some luscious sweet from Denmark
who captures the oldest son's heart.
From diapers to Dior.[1]
10 That story.

Or a milkman who serves the wealthy,
eggs, cream, butter, yogurt, milk,
the white truck like an ambulance
who goes into real estate
15 and makes a pile.
From homogenized to martinis at lunch.

Or the charwoman
who is on the bus when it cracks up
and collects enough from the insurance.
20 From mops to Bonwit Teller.[2]
That story.

Once
the wife of a rich man was on her deathbed
and she said to her daughter Cinderella:
25 Be devout. Be good. Then I will smile
down from heaven in the seam of a cloud.
The man took another wife who had
two daughters, pretty enough
but with hearts like blackjacks.
30 Cinderella was their maid.
She slept on the sooty hearth each night
and walked around looking like Al Jolson.[3]
Her father brought presents home from town,
jewels and gowns for the other women
35 but the twig of a tree for Cinderella.
She planted that twig on her mother's grave
and it grew to a tree where a white dove sat.
Whenever she wished for anything the dove
would drop it like an egg upon the ground.
40 The bird is important, my dears, so heed him.

Next came the ball, as you all know.
It was a marriage market.
The prince was looking for a wife.
All but Cinderella were preparing
45 and gussying up for the big event.

---

[1] Fashion designer Christian Dior.

[2] Exclusive department store.

[3] Al Jolson (Asa Yoelson; 1886–1950)—American singer and songwriter, famous for his "black-face" minstrel performances.

Cinderella begged to go too.
Her stepmother threw a dish of lentils
into the cinders and said: Pick them
up in an hour and you shall go.
50 The white dove brought all his friends;
all the warm wings of the fatherland came,
and picked up the lentils in a jiffy.
No, Cinderella, said the stepmother,
you have no clothes and cannot dance.
55 That's the way with stepmothers.

Cinderella went to the tree at the grave
and cried forth like a gospel singer:
Mama! Mama! My turtledove,
send me to the prince's ball!
60 The bird dropped down a golden dress
and delicate little gold slippers.
Rather a large package for a simple bird.
So she went. Which is no surprise.
Her stepmother and sisters didn't
65 recognize her without her cinder face
and the prince took her hand on the spot
and danced with no other the whole day.

As nightfall came she thought she'd better
get home. The prince walked her home
70 and she disappeared into the pigeon house
and although the prince took an axe and broke
it open she was gone. Back to her cinders.
These events repeated themselves for three days.
However on the third day the prince
75 covered the palace steps with cobbler's wax
and Cinderella's gold shoe stuck upon it.
Now he would find whom the shoe fit
and find his strange dancing girl for keeps.
He went to their house and the two sisters
80 were delighted because they had lovely feet.
The eldest went into a room to try the slipper on
but her big toe got in the way so she simply
sliced it off and put on the slipper.
The prince rode away with her until the white dove
85 told him to look at the blood pouring forth.
That is the way with amputations.
They don't just heal up like a wish.
The other sister cut off her heel
but the blood told as blood will.
90 The prince was getting tired.

He began to feel like a shoe salesman.
But he gave it one last try.
This time Cinderella fit into the shoe
like a love letter into its envelope.

95 At the wedding ceremony
the two sisters came to curry favor
and the white dove pecked their eyes out.
Two hollow spots were left
like soup spoons.

100 Cinderella and the prince
lived, they say, happily ever after,
like two dolls in a museum case
never bothered by diapers or dust,
never arguing over the timing of an egg,
105 never telling the same story twice,
never getting a middle-aged spread,
their darling smiles pasted on for eternity
Regular Bobbsey Twins.[4]
That story.

READING AND REACTING

1. The first twenty-one lines of the poem act as a prelude. How does this prelude help to establish the speaker's ironic tone?
2. At times the speaker talks directly to readers. What effect do these statements have on you? Would the poem be stronger without them?
3. Throughout the poem, the speaker mixes contemporary collo-quial expressions with the conventional diction of a fairy tale. Find examples of these two kinds of language. How does the juxtaposition of these different kinds of diction create irony?
4. **JOURNAL ENTRY** What details of the fairy tale does Sexton change in her poem? Why do you think she makes these changes?
5. **CRITICAL PERSPECTIVE** In his 1973 book *Confessional Poets*, Robert Phillips comments on Anne Sexton's use of the Grimm Brothers' fairy tales in her book *Transformations*. According to Phillips, by transforming the Grimms' stories into symbols of our own time, Sexton "has managed to offer us understandable images of the world around us":

> ["Cinderella"] she takes to be a prototype of the old rags to riches theme ("From diapers to Dior. / That story."). Cinderella

---

[4] The two sets of twins—Nan and Bert, Flossie and Freddie—in a popular series of early twentieth-century children's books. They led an idealized, problem-free life.

is said to have slept on the sooty hearth each night and "walked around looking like Al Jolson"—a comparison indicative of the level of invention and humor in the book. At the end, when Cinderella marries the handsome prince to live happily ever after, . . . Sexton pulls a double whammy and reveals that the ending, in itself, is another fairy tale within a fairy tale, totally unreal and unlikely.

Is "Cinderella," written in 1970, still a "symbol of our own time"? In what way does it offer us "understandable images of the world around us"?

Related Works: "The Story of an Hour" (p. 77), "Boys and Girls" (p. 504), "The Faithful Wife" (p. 671), *The Importance of Being Earnest* (p. 961)

◊ ◊ ◊

MARILYN DUMONT
(1955–   )

The Devil's Language
(1996)

1. I have since reconsidered Eliot[1]
   and the Great White way of writing English
   standard that is
   the great white way
5   has measured, judged and assessed me   all my life
   by its
   lily white words
   its picket fence sentences
   and manicured paragraphs
10   one wrong sound and you're shelved in the Native Literature section
   resistance writing
   a mad Indian
   unpredictable
   on the war path
15   native ethnic protest
   the Great White way could silence us all
   if we let it
   it's had its hand over my mouth since my first day of school
   since Dick and Jane, ABC's and fingernail checks

---

[1] T. S. Eliot (1888–1965), influential American-born English poet, playwright, and critic. In the essay "Tradition and the Individual Talent" (1922), Eliot argues that individuals shape literary history, and his examples of poets are white males.

20   syntactic laws: use the wrong order or
       register and you're a dumb Indian
       dumb, drunk or violent
       my father doesn't read or write
       the King's English says he's
25   dumb but he speaks Cree
       how many of you speak Cree?
       correct Cree not correct English
       grammatically correct Cree
       is there one?

30 2. is there a Received Pronunciation of Cree, is there
       a Modern Cree Usage?
       the Chief's Cree not the King's English

       as if violating God the Father and standard English
       is like talking back(wards)

35   as if speaking the devil's language is
       talking back
       back(words)
       back to your mother's sound, your mother's tongue, your mother's language
       back to that clearing in the bush
40   in the tall black spruce

   3. near the sound of horses and wind
       where you sat on her knee in a canvas tent
       and she fed you bannock and tea
       and syllables
45   that echo in your mind now, now
       that you can't make the sound
       of that voice that rocks you and sings you to sleep
       in the devil's language.

READING AND REACTING

1. What do we know about the speaker in this poem in terms of language, ethnicity, education, and experience?
2. Which two languages are being compared, and what conclusions does the speaker come to regarding the importance of language and one's placement in society?
3. How does the three-part structure of the poem contribute to a consideration of the effects of language?
4. Is irony present in the term "the devil's language"?
5. Language can both shape and reflect reality. How does the speaker in "The Devil's Language" demonstrate this aspect?

6. **JOURNAL ENTRY** Write about an experience in which you were
not able to communicate effectively because you did not share a
common language with another person. Or write about how you
may adjust the levels of your language use depending on circumstance.

Related Works: "A&P" (p. 122), "Speak White" (p. 806), "My Ledders"
(p. 845)

 CHECKLIST: WRITING ABOUT VOICE

THE SPEAKER IN THE POEM

✓ What do we know about the speaker?

✓ Is the speaker anonymous, or does he or she have a particular
identity?

✓ How does assuming a particular persona help the poet to convey his
or her ideas?

✓ Does the title give information about the speaker's identity?

✓ In what way does word choice provide information about the
speaker?

✓ Does the speaker make any direct statements that help you to
establish his or her identity or character?

✓ Does the speaker address anyone? How can you tell? Does the
presence of a listener seem to affect the speaker?

THE TONE OF THE POEM

✓ What is the speaker's attitude toward his or her subject?

✓ How do word choice, rhyme, metre, sentence structure, figures of
speech, and imagery help to convey the attitude of the speaker?

✓ Is the tone of the poem consistent? How do shifts in tone reflect the
changing mood or attitude of the speaker?

IRONY

✓ Does any dramatic irony exist in the poem?

✓ Does the poem include situational irony?

✓ Does verbal irony appear in the poem?

◆ WRITING SUGGESTIONS: VOICE

1. Poet Robert Frost once said that he wanted to write "poetry that talked." According to Frost, "whenever I write a line it is because that line has already been spoken clearly by a voice with my mind, an audible voice." Choose some poems in this chapter (or elsewhere in the book) that you consider "talking poems." Then, write an essay about how successful they are in communicating "an audible voice."

2. Compare the women's voices in "Cinderella" (p. 646) and "Gretel in Darkness" (p. 620). In what way are their attitudes toward men similar? In what way are they different?

3. The theme of Herrick's poem "To the Virgins, to Make Much of Time" (p. 639) is known as **carpe diem** or "seize the day." Read Andrew Marvell's "To His Coy Mistress" (p. 719), which has the same theme, and compare its tone with that of "To the Virgins, to Make Much of Time."

4. Read the following poem, and compare the speaker's use of the word *hope* with the way the speaker uses the word in Ariel Dorfman's "Hope" (p. 643).

EMILY DICKINSON
(1830–1886)

"Hope" Is the Thing
with Feathers
(1861)

"Hope" is the thing with feathers—
That perches in the soul—
And sings the tune without the words—
And never stops—at all—

5   And sweetest—in the Gale—is heard—
And sore must be the storm—
That could abash the little Bird—
That kept so many warm—

I've heard it in the chillest land—
10 And on the strangest Sea—
Yet, never, in Extremity,
It asked a crumb—of Me.

5. Because the speaker and the poet are not necessarily the same, poems by the same author can have different voices. Compare the voices of several poems by Sylvia Plath, W. H. Auden, William Blake, or any poet in this anthology.

CHAPTER 14

Word Choice, Word Order

◊　◊　◊

The poet's love of language must, if language is to reward him with unlooked-for miracles, that is, with poetry, amount to a passion. The passion for the things of the world and the passion for naming them must be in him indistinguishable.

DENISE LEVERTOV, "Origins of a Poem"

Normal human vileness, philistine materialism, racial prejudice, anti-Semitism, hypocrisy and the relentless pursuit of ass in parliaments, universities, Salvation army hostels, editorial offices, court-houses, hospitals and morgues—out of this glorious fecund rubbish heap and out of occasional glimpses of beauty, goodness and mercy I have made my poems. I have dipped my broomstick into the life swirling around me and written it into the hearts and speech of men. Yahoos, sex-drained executives, pimps and poetasters, limping critics, graceless sluts and the few, the rare few, who gave me moments of insight or ecstasy: I am crazy enough to think I have given them immortality. They will, I hope, never die. Not, anyhow, for as long as style and passion are still valued; or the language which these have sometimes tinged with vitality and distinction.

IRVING LAYTON, Foreword to *The Collected Poems of Irving Layton*

I like *mountain* and *prairie* and *sky.* When I write poetry, I use such words and I also use abstract words. But it is difficult to give you a list of favorite words because words become vital—they come alive—within a certain context. A given word is extremely important and vital in one context and not very interesting in another. It depends upon what's around the word. The environment. Although some words are naturally interesting, in my opinion. Like some creatures. The fox, I think, is a creature of almost immediate interest to most people. Other words are not as immediately interesting, or are even negatively received. Like some other creatures. The lizard, for example, is a creature most people wouldn't ordinarily care about. But in its natural habitat and in its dimension of wilderness, the lizard can be seen as a beautiful thing. Its movements are very wonderful to watch. Similarly, you can take almost any word and make it interesting by the way in which you use it.

N. SCOTT MOMADAY, in *Ancestral Voices*

◊　◊　◊

◊ ◊ ◊
SIPHO SEPAMLA
(1932–   )

Words, Words, Words[1]

We don't speak of tribal wars anymore
we say simple faction fights
there are no tribes around here
only nations
5 it makes sense you see
'cause from there
one moves to multinational
it makes sense you get me
'cause from there
10 one gets one's homeland
which is a reasonable idea
'cause from there
one can dabble with independence
which deserves warm applause
15 —the bloodless revolution

we are talking of words
words tossed around as if
denied location by the wind
we mean those words some spit
20 others grab
dress them up for the occasion
fling them on the lap of an audience
we are talking of those words
that stalk our lives like policemen
25 words no dictionary can embrace
words that change sooner than seasons
we mean words
that spell out our lives
words, words, words
30 for there's a kind of poetic licence
doing the rounds in these parts

---

[1] Publication date is not available.

◇ ◇ ◇

LEONARD COHEN
(1934–   )

God Is Alive

(1966)

From Beautiful Losers

God is alive. Magic is afoot. God is alive. Magic is afoot. God is afoot. Magic is alive. Alive is afoot. Magic never died. God never sickened. Many poor men lied. Many sick men lied. Magic never weakened. Magic never hid. Magic always ruled. God is afoot. God never died. God was ruler though his
5   funeral lengthened. Though his mourners thickened Magic never fled. Though his shrouds were hoisted the naked God did live. Though his words were twisted the naked Magic thrived. Though his death was published round and round the world the heart did not believe. Many hurt men wondered. Many struck men bled. Magic never faltered. Magic always led.
10 Many stones were rolled but God would not lie down. Many wild men lied. Many fat men listened. Though they offered stones Magic still was fed. Though they locked their coffers God was always served. Magic is afoot. God rules. Alive is afoot. Alive is in command. Many weak men hungered. Many strong men thrived. Though they boasted solitude God was at their side. Nor
15 the dreamer in his cell, nor the captain on the hill. Magic is alive. Though his death was pardoned round and round the world the heart would not believe. Though laws were carved in marble they could not shelter men. Though altars built in parliaments they could not order men. Police arrested Magic and Magic went with them for Magic loves the hungry. But Magic
20 would not tarry. It moves from arm to arm. It would not stay with them. Magic is afoot. It cannot come to harm. It rests in an empty palm. It spawns in an empty mind. But Magic is no instrument. Magic is the end. Many men drove Magic but Magic stayed behind. Many strong men lied. They only passed through Magic and out the other side. Many weak men lied. They
25 came to God in secret and though they left him nourished they would not tell who healed. Though mountains danced before them they said that God was dead. Though his shrouds were hoisted the naked God did live. This I mean to whisper to my mind. This I mean to laugh with in my mind. This I mean my mind to serve till service is but Magic moving through the world,
30 and mind itself is Magic coursing through the flesh, and flesh itself is Magic dancing on a clock, and time itself the Magic Length of God.

Words identify and name, characterize and distinguish, compare and contrast. Words describe, limit, and embellish; words locate and measure. Without words, there cannot be a poem. Even though words may be elusive and uncertain and changeable, in poetry, as in love and in politics, words matter.

Beyond the quantitative—how many words, how many letters and syllables—is one much more important consideration: the *quality* of words. Which are chosen, and why? Why are certain words placed next to others? What does a word suggest in a particular context? How are the words arranged? What exactly constitutes the right word?

WORD CHOICE

◈ ◈◈◈

In poetry, even more than in fiction or drama, words tend to become the focus—sometimes even the true subject—of a work. For this reason, the choice of one word over another can be crucial. Because most poems are brief, they must compress many ideas into a few lines; poets know how much weight each individual word carries, and so they choose with great care, trying to select words that imply more than they state.

A poet may choose a word because of its sound. For instance, a word may echo another word's sound, and such repetition may place emphasis on both words; it may rhyme with another word and therefore be needed to preserve the poem's rhyme scheme; or, it may have a certain combination of stressed and unstressed syllables needed to maintain the poem's metrical pattern. Occasionally, a poet may even choose a word because of how it looks on the page. Most often, though, poets select words because they help to communicate their ideas.

At the same time, poets may choose words for their degree of concreteness or abstraction, specificity or generality. A *concrete* word refers to an item that is a perceivable, tangible entity—for example, a kiss or a flag. An *abstract* word refers to an intangible idea, condition, or quality, something that cannot be perceived by the senses—love, patriotism, and so on. *Specific* words refer to particular items; *general* words refer to entire classes or groups of items. As the following example illustrates, whether a word is specific or general is relative; its degree of specificity or generality depends on its relationship to other words:

> Poem → closed form poem → sonnet → seventeenth-century sonnet →
> Elizabethan sonnet → sonnet by Shakespeare → "My Mistress' Eyes Are
> Nothing like the Sun"

Sometimes a poet wants a precise word, one that is both specific and concrete. At other times, however, a poet might prefer general or abstract language, which may allow for more subtlety—or even for intentional ambiguity.

Finally, a word may be chosen for its **connotation**—what it suggests. Every word has one or more **denotations**—what it signifies without emotional associations, judgments, or opinions. The word *family*, for example, denotes "a group of related things or people." Connotation is a more complex matter, however, because a single word may have many different associations. In general terms, a word may have a connotation that is positive, neutral, or negative. Thus, *family* may have a positive connotation when it describes a group of loving relatives, a neutral connotation when it describes a biological category, and an ironically negative connotation when it describes an organized crime family. Beyond this distinction, *family*, like any other word, may have a variety of emotional and social associations, suggesting loyalty, warmth, home, security, or duty. In fact, many words have somewhat different meanings in different contexts. When poets choose words, then, they must consider what a particular word may suggest to readers as well as what it denotes.

In the poem that follows, the poet chooses words for their sounds, their relationships to other words, and their connotations.

⬩ ⬩ ⬩

WALT WHITMAN
(1819–1892)

When I Heard the Learn'd Astronomer

(1865)

When I heard the learn'd astronomer,
When the proofs, the figures, were ranged in columns before me,
When I was shown the charts and diagrams, to add, divide, and
    measure them,
4 When I sitting heard the astronomer where he lectured with much
    applause in the lecture-room,
How soon unaccountable I became tired and sick,
Till rising and gliding out I wander'd off by myself,
In the mystical moist night-air, and from time to time,
8 Look'd up in perfect silence at the stars.

This poem might be paraphrased as follows: "When I grew restless listening to an astronomy lecture, I went outside, where I found I learned more just by looking at the stars than I had learned inside." But the paraphrase is obviously neither as rich nor as complex as the poem. Through careful use of diction, Whitman establishes a dichotomy that supports the poem's central theme about the relative merits of two ways of learning.

The poem can be divided into two groups of four lines. The first four lines, unified by the repetition of "When," introduce the astronomer and his tools: "proofs," "figures," and "charts and diagrams" to be added, divided, and measured. In this section of the poem, the speaker is passive: he sits and listens ("I heard"; "I was shown"; "I sitting heard"). The repetition of "When" reinforces the dry monotony of the lecture. In the next four lines, the choice of words signals the change in the speaker's actions and reactions. The confined lecture hall is replaced by "the mystical moist night-air," and the dry lecture and automatic applause give way to "perfect silence"; instead of sitting passively, the speaker becomes active (he rises, glides, wanders); instead of listening, he looks. The mood of the first half of the poem is restrained: the language is concrete and physical, and the speaker is studying, receiving information from a "learn'd" authority. The rest of the poem, celebrating intuitive knowledge and feelings, is more abstract, freer. Throughout the poem, the lecture hall contrasts sharply with the natural world outside its walls.

After considering the poem as a whole, readers should not find it hard to understand why the poet selected certain words. Whitman's use of "lectured" in line 4 rather than a more neutral word like "spoke" is appropriate both because it suggests formality and distance and because it echoes "lecture-room" in the same line. The word "sick" in line 5 is striking because it connotes physical as well as emotional distress, more effectively conveying the extent of the speaker's discomfort than "bored" or "restless" would. "Rising" and "gliding" (6) are used rather than "standing" and "walking out" both because of the way their stressed vowel sounds echo each other (and echo "time to time" in the next line) and because of their connotation of dreaminess, which is consistent with "wander'd" (6) and "mystical" (7). The word "moist" (7) is chosen not only because its consonant sounds echo the *m* and *st* sounds in "mystical," but also because it establishes a contrast with the dry, airless lecture hall. Finally, line 8's "perfect silence" is a better choice than a reasonable substitute like "complete silence" or "total silence," either of which would suggest the degree of the silence but not its quality.

In the next poem, the poet also pays careful attention to word choice.

AL PURDY
(1918–2000)

The Cariboo Horses
(1965)

At 100 Mile House the cowboys ride in rolling
stagey cigarettes with one hand reining
half-tame bronco rebels on a morning grey as stone
—so much like riding dangerous women
5   with whiskey coloured eyes—
such women as once fell dead with their lovers
with fire in their heads and slippery froth on thighs
—Beaver and Carrier women maybe or
     Blackfoot squaws far past the edge of this valley
10 on the other side of those two toy mountain ranges
     from the sunfierce plains beyond—

But only horses
                    waiting in stables
            hitched at taverns
15   standing at dawn
            pastured outside the town with
            jeeps and fords and chevvys and
            busy muttering stake trucks rushing
            importantly over roads of man's devising
20   over the safe known roads of the ranchers
            families and merchants of the town—
                    On the high prairie
            are only horse and rider
                    wind in dry grass
25   clopping in silence under the toy mountains
            dropping sometimes and
                    lost in the dry grass
                    golden oranges of dung—

        Only horses
30   no stopwatch memories or palace ancestors
            not Kiangs hauling undressed stone in the Nile Valley
            and having stubborn Egyptian tantrums or
            Onagers racing thru Hither Asia and
            the last Quagga screaming in African highlands
35   lost relatives of these
                    whose hooves were thunder
            the ghosts of horses battering thru the wind
            whose names were the wind's common usage
            whose life was the sun's
40   arriving here at chilly noon
            in the gasoline smell of the
            dust and waiting 15 minutes
            at the grocer's—

A number of words in "The Cariboo Horses" are noteworthy for their exotic qualities and others for their mundaneness. This word choice sets up the contrast between the horses' roles in the past and their present unimportance. For example, Purdy uses the words "Kiangs" (31), "Onagers" (33), and "Quagga" (34) to refer to the special horses of the past and their extraordinary tasks such as helping with the building of pyramids.

The present-day horses of B.C.'s Cariboo country are "only horses" (12), and they are rapidly being displaced by "jeeps and fords and chevvys" (17), vehicles measured in horsepower, but which have little connection to the past or to the passion suggested by the similarity of riding horses and sexual activity. The Cariboo horses are demystified and displaced by the objects of contemporary society, and they must wait "in the gasoline smell of the /

dust . . . " (41–42) unlike the horses of ancient Egypt, Africa, and Asia that have achieved a mythic status.

The denotation of the Cariboo horses is clear—the horses who live in that locale. But as the poem develops, the connotation becomes more evident. These Cariboo horses are unlike their named predecessors, and they are losing importance and usefulness. Their lives are mundane, as are the words used to describe them: "waiting" (13), "hitched" (14), "standing" (15), "pastured" (16), "clopping" (25), and "dropping" (26).

The comparison of horses and women is evident in the first stanza: riding horses is "so much like riding dangerous women / with whiskey coloured eyes" (4–5). The women have "slippery froth on thighs" (7) like the sweat a horse works up when being ridden. The "dangerous women" (4) are "Beaver and Carrier women maybe or / Blackfoot" (8–9); however, this image is of the past—like the contrast with the Old World horses, these Cariboo horses are being contrasted with the horses who lived before them on the high plains. The horses of the past have turned into "ghosts" (37), and the current Cariboo horses are "only horses" (12).

With the diction, Purdy shows the changes in the practical uses of horses and in their mythological significance. The uncapitalized names of the vehicles indicate their lowered status in the speaker's mind while the proper nouns of the Old World horses show their high status. The only time the Cariboo horses are named is in the title, a specific use of the proper noun to show the diminishing role of the horses.

Among the other techniques of the poem, Purdy's word choice effectively develops a lament for the decreasing role of horses and the changes in society to more mechanization.

❖ POEMS FOR FURTHER READING: WORD CHOICE

RALPH GUSTAFSON
(1909–1995)

In the Yukon
(1960)

In Europe, you can't move without going down into history.
Here, all is a beginning. I saw a salmon jump,
Again and again, against the current,
The timbered hills a background, wooded green
5 Unpushed through; the salmon jumped, silver.
This was news, was commerce, at the end of the summer
The leap for dying. Moose came down to the water edge
To drink and the salmon turned silver arcs.
At night, the northern lights played, great over country
10 Without tapestry and coronations, kings crowned

With weights of gold. They were green,
Green hangings and great grandeur, over the north
Going to what no man can hold hard in mind,
The dredge of that gravity, being without experience.

READING AND REACTING

1. Evaluate Gustafson's decision to use each of the following words: "salmon" (2), "moose" (7), "green" (4), "silver" (5), "gold" (11), "dredge" (14). Do any of these words seem unexpected, even unsettling, in the context in which he uses them?
2. What thematic relationship, if any, do you see between "kings crowned / With weights of gold" (10–11) and "The dredge of that gravity, being without experience" (14)?
3. **JOURNAL ENTRY** What comment does this poem seem to be making about the setting of the Yukon. What does Gustafson say is the difference between Europe and Northern Canada?

Related Works: "Bushed" (p. 21), "A Field of Wheat" (p. 173), "Death of a Young Son by Drowning" (p. 702)

◊ ◊ ◊

ADRIENNE RICH
(1929–   )

Living in Sin
(1955)

She had thought the studio would keep itself,
no dust upon the furniture of love.
Half heresy, to wish the taps less vocal,
the panes relieved of grime. A plate of pears,
5 a piano with a Persian shawl, a cat
stalking the picturesque amusing mouse
had risen at his urging.
Not that at five each separate stair would writhe
under the milkman's tramp; that morning light
10 so coldly would delineate the scraps
of last night's cheese and three sepulchral bottles;
that on the kitchen shelf among the saucers
a pair of beetle-eyes would fix her own—
envoy from some village in the mouldings . . .
15 Meanwhile, he, with a yawn,
sounded a dozen notes upon the keyboard,
declared it out of tune, shrugged at the mirror,
rubbed at his beard, went out for cigarettes;
while she, jeered by the minor demons,

20 pulled back the sheets and made the bed and found
   a towel to dust the table-top,
   and let the coffee-pot boil over on the stove.
   By evening she was back in love again,
   though not so wholly but throughout the night
25 she woke sometimes to feel the daylight coming
   like a relentless milkman up the stairs.

READING AND REACTING

1. How might the poem's impact change if each of these words were deleted: "Persian" (5), "picturesque" (6), "sepulchral" (11), "minor" (19), "sometimes" (25)?
2. What words in the poem have strongly negative connotations? What do these words suggest about the relationship the poem describes? How does the image of the "relentless milkman" (26) sum up this relationship?
3. This poem, about a woman in love, uses very few words conventionally associated with love poems. Instead, many of its words denote the everyday routine of housekeeping. Give examples of such words. Why do you think they are used?
4. **JOURNAL ENTRY** What connotations does the title have? What other phrases have similar denotative meanings? How do their connotations differ? Why do you think Rich chose the title she did?
5. **CRITICAL PERSPECTIVE** In "Her Cargo: Adrienne Rich and the Common Language," a 1979 essay examining the poet's work over almost thirty years, Alicia Ostriker notes that early poems by Rich, including "Living in Sin," reflect popular male poets' "resigned sense of life as a diminished thing" and only "tremble on the brink of indignation":

   > They seem about to state explicitly . . . a connection between feminine subordination in male-dominated middle-class relationships, and emotionally lethal inarticulateness for both sexes. But the poetry . . . is minor because it is polite. It illustrates symptoms but does not probe sources. There is no disputing the ideas of the predecessors, and Adrienne Rich at this point is a cautious good poet in the sense of being a good girl, a quality noted with approval by her reviewers.

   Does your reading of "Living in Sin" support Ostriker's characterization of the poem as "resigned," "polite," and "cautious"? Do you think Rich is "being a good girl"?

Related Works: "The Story of an Hour" (p. 77), "The Faithful Wife" (p. 671), *Trifles* (p. 948)

E. E. CUMMINGS
(1894–1962)

in Just-[1]

(1923)

in Just-
spring   when the world is mud-
luscious the little
lame balloonman
5   whistles   far   and wee

and eddieandbill come
running from marbles and
piracies and it's
spring

10   when the world is puddle-wonderful
the queer
old balloonman whistles
far   and   wee
and bettyandisbel come dancing
15   from hop-scotch and jump-rope and
it's
spring
and
the
20   goat-footed

balloonMan   whistles
far
and
wee

READING AND REACTING

1. In this poem, Cummings coins a number of words that he uses to
   modify other words. Identify these coinages. What other, more
   conventional, words could be used in their place? What does
   Cummings accomplish by using the coined words instead?

---

[1] Also known as "Chansons Innocentes I."

2. What do you think Cummings means by "far and wee" in lines 5, 13, and 22–24? Why do you think he arranges the three words in a different way each time he uses them?

3. **JOURNAL ENTRY** Evaluate this poem. Do you like it? Is it memorable or moving—or just clever?

4. **CRITICAL PERSPECTIVE** In "Latter-Day Notes on E. E. Cummings' Language" (1955), Robert E. Maurer suggests that Cummings often coined new words in the same way that children do: for example, "by adding the normal *-er* or *-est (beautifuler, chiefest),* or stepping up the power of a word such as *last,* which is already superlative, and saying *lastest,*" creating words such as *givingest* and *whirlingest.* In addition to "combining two or more words to form a single new one . . . to give an effect of wholeness, of one quality" (for example, *yellowgreen*), "in the simplest of his word coinages, he merely creates a new word by analogy as a child would without adding any shade of meaning other than that inherent in the prefix or suffix he utilizes, as in the words *unstrength* and *untimid.* . . ." Many early reviewers, Maurer notes, criticized such coinages because they "convey a thrill but not a precise impression," a criticism also levelled at Cummings's poetry more broadly.

Consider the coinages in "in Just-." Do you agree that many do not add "shades of meaning" or provide a "precise impression"? Or, do you find that the coinages contribute to the whole in a meaningful way?

Related Works: "anyone lived in a pretty how town" (p. 676), "Constantly Risking Absurdity" (p. 704), "Jabberwocky" (p. 754), "the sky was can dy" (p. 777)

⋄▼⋄ ⋄

THEODORE ROETHKE
(1908–1963)

I Knew a Woman
(1958)

I knew a woman, lovely in her bones,
When small birds sighed, she would sigh back at them;
Ah, when she moved, she moved more ways than one:
The shapes a bright container can contain!
5 Of her choice virtues only gods should speak,
Or English poets who grew up on Greek
(I'd have them sing in chorus, cheek to cheek).

How well her wishes went! She stroked my chin,
She taught me Turn, and Counter-turn, and Stand;
10 She taught me Touch, that undulant white skin;

I nibbled meekly from her proffered hand;
She was the sickle; I, poor I, the rake,
Coming behind her for her pretty sake
(But what prodigious mowing we did make).

15 Love likes a gander, and adores a goose:
Her full lips pursed, the errant note to seize;
She played it quick, she played it light and loose;
My eyes, they dazzled at her flowing knees;
Her several parts could keep a pure repose,
20 Or one hip quiver with a mobile nose
(She moved in circles, and those circles moved).

Let seed be grass, and grass turn into hay:
I'm martyr to a motion not my own;
What's freedom for? To know eternity.
25 I swear she cast a shadow white as stone.
But who would count eternity in days?
These old bones live to learn her wanton ways:
(I measure time by how a body sways).

READING AND REACTING

1. Many of the words in Roethke's poem have double meanings—for example, "gander" and "goose" in line 15. Identify other words that have more than one meaning, and consider the function these multiple meanings serve.
2. The poem's language contains many surprises; often, the word we expect is not the one we get. For example, "container" in line 4 is not a conventional means of describing a woman. What other words are used in unusual ways? What does Roethke achieve by choosing such words?
3. Is there a difference between the denotation or connotation of the word "bones" in the phrases "lovely in her bones" (1) and "These old bones" (27)? Explain.
4. **JOURNAL ENTRY** How does this poem differ from your idea of what a love poem should be?

Related Works: "My Mistress' Eyes Are Nothing like the Sun" (p. 580), "Oh, My Love Is like a Red, Red Rose" (p. 706), "She Walks in Beauty" (p. 827)

LEVELS OF DICTION

❖ ❖ ❖

Like other writers, poets use various levels of diction to convey their ideas. The diction of a poem may be formal or informal or fall anywhere in between, depending on the identity of the speaker and on the speaker's attitude toward the reader and toward his or her subject. At one extreme, very formal poems can be far removed in style and vocabulary from everyday speech. At the other extreme, highly informal poems can be full of jargon, regionalisms, and slang. Many poems, of course, use language that falls somewhere between formal and informal diction.

FORMAL DICTION

Formal diction is characterized by a learned vocabulary and grammatically correct forms. In general, formal diction does not include colloquialisms, such as contractions and shortened word forms (*phone* for *telephone*). As the following poem illustrates, a speaker who uses formal diction can sound aloof and impersonal.

❖ ❖ ❖

MARGARET ATWOOD
(1939–   )

The City Planners
(1966)

Cruising these residential Sunday
streets in dry August sunlight:
what offends us is
the sanities:
5 the houses in pedantic rows, the planted
sanitary trees, assert
levelness of surface like a rebuke
to the dent in our car door.
No shouting here, or
10 shatter of glass; nothing more abrupt
than the rational whine of a power mower
cutting a straight swath in the discouraged grass.

But though the driveways neatly
sidestep hysteria
15 by being even, the roofs all display
the same slant of avoidance to the hot sky,
certain things:
the smell of spilled oil a faint

sickness lingering in the garages,
20 a splash of paint on brick surprising as a bruise,
a plastic hose poised in a vicious
coil; even the too-fixed stare of the wide windows

give momentary access to
the landscape behind or under
25 the future cracks in the plaster

when the houses, capsized, will slide
obliquely into the clay seas, gradual as glaciers
that right now nobody notices.

That is where the City Planners
30 with the insane faces of political conspirators
are scattered over unsurveyed
territories, concealed from each other,
each in his own private blizzard;

guessing directions, they sketch
35 transitory lines rigid as wooden borders
on a wall in the white vanishing air

tracing the panic of suburb
order in a bland madness of snows.

Atwood's speaker is clearly concerned about the poem's central issue, but
rather than use *I*, the poem uses the first-person plural (*us*) to maintain distance and to convey emotional detachment. Although phrases such as
"sickness lingering in the garages" and "insane faces of political conspirators" communicate the speaker's disapproval, formal words—"pedantic,"
"rebuke," "display," "poised," "obliquely," "conspirators," "transitory"—
help her to maintain her distance. Both the speaker herself and her attack
on the misguided city planners gain credibility through her balanced, measured tone and through the use of language that is as formal and "professional" as theirs, with no slang, nonstandard diction, or colloquialisms.

INFORMAL DICTION

Informal diction is the language closest to everyday conversation. It
includes colloquialisms—contractions, shortened word forms, and the
like—and may also include slang, regional expressions, and even nonstandard words.

In the poem that follows, the speaker uses informal diction to highlight
the contrast between James Baca, a law student speaking to the graduating
class of his old high school, and the graduating seniors.

JIM SAGEL
(1947–   )

Baca Grande[1]
(1982)

Una vaca se topó con un ratón y le dice:
"Tú—¿tan chiquito y con bigote?" Y le responde el ratón:
"Y tú tan grandota—¿y sin brassiere?"[2]

It was nearly a miracle
James Baca remembered anyone at all
from the old hometown gang
having been two years at Yale
5   no less
and halfway through law school
at the University of California at Irvine
They hardly recognized him either
in his three-piece grey business suit
10 and surfer-swirl haircut
with just the menacing hint
of a tightly trimmed Zapata moustache
     for cultural balance
and relevance

15 He had come to deliver the keynote address
to the graduating class of 80
at his old alma mater
and show off his well-trained lips
which laboriously parted
20   each Kennedyish "R"
and drilled the first person pronoun
through the microphone
like an oil bit
with the slick, elegantly honed phrases
25 that slid so smoothly
off his meticulously bleached
     tongue
He talked Big Bucks
with astronautish fervor and if he

---

[1] *Baca* is both a phonetic spelling of the Spanish word "vaca" (cow) and the last name of one of the poem's characters. *Grande* means "large."

[2] A cow ran into a rat and said: "You—so small and with a moustache?" The rat responded: "And you—so big and without a bra?"

30 the former bootstrapless James A. Baca
could dazzle the ass
off the universe
then even you
    yes you

35 Joey Martinez toying with your yellow
    tassle
and staring dumbly into space
could emulate Mr. Baca someday
    possibly
40 well
there was of course
such a thing
as being an outrageously successful
gas station attendant too
45   let us never forget
it doesn't really matter what you do
so long as you excel
    James said
never believing a word
50 of it
for he had already risen
    as high as they go

Wasn't nobody else
from this deprived environment
55 who'd ever jumped
    straight out of college
into the Governor's office
and maybe one day
he'd sit in that big chair
60   himself
and when he did
he'd forget this damned town
and all the petty little people
in it
65 once and for all

That much he promised himself

"Baca Grande" uses numerous colloquialisms, including contractions; conversational placeholders, such as "no less" and "well"; shortened word forms, such as "gas"; slang terms, such as "Big Bucks"; whimsical coinages ("Kennedyish," "astronautish," "bootstrapless"); nonstandard grammatical constructions, such as "Wasn't nobody else"; and even profanity. The level of language is perfectly appropriate for the students Baca addresses—suspicious, streetwise, and unimpressed by Baca's "three-piece grey business suit" and "surfer-swirl haircut." In fact, the informal diction is a key element in the poem, expressing the gap between the slick James Baca, with "his well-trained lips / which laboriously parted / each Kennedyish 'R'" and members of his audience, with their unpretentious, forthright speech. In this sense "Baca Grande" is as much a linguistic commentary as a social one.

◈ POEMS FOR FURTHER READING: LEVELS OF DICTION

◊ ◊ ◊

BARBARA L. GREENBERG
(1932–)

The Faithful Wife
(1978)

But if I *were* to have a lover, it would be someone
who could take nothing from you. I would, in conscience,
not dishonor you. He and I would eat at Howard Johnson's

which you and I do not enjoy. With him I would go
5 fishing because it is not your sport. He would wear blue
which is your worst color; he would have none of your virtues.

Not strong, not proud, not just, not provident, my lover
would blame me for his heart's distress, which you would never
think to do. He and I would drink too much and weep together

10 and I would bruise his face as I would not bruise your face
even in my dreams. Yes I would dance with him, but to a music
you and I would never choose to hear, and in a place

where you and I would never wish to be. He and I would speak
Spanish, which is not your tongue, and we would take
15 long walks in fields of burdock, to which you are allergic.

We would make love only in the morning. It would be
altogether different. I would know him with my other body,
the one that you have never asked to see.

READING AND REACTING

1. In what respect does this poem sound like everyday speech? What colloquial elements usually present in conversation are absent here?
2. The speaker seems to be addressing her husband. What words or phrases in the poem sound out of place given the identities of the participants in the conversation?

3. **Journal Entry** How do you interpret the poem's title? In what sense is it ironic? In what sense is it not?

Related Works: "The Nymph's Reply to the Shepherd" (p. 579), "You Fit into Me" (p. 723), *A Doll House* (p. 1013)

R I C H A R D   W I L B U R
(1921–   )

For the Student Strikers
(1970)

Go talk with those who are rumored to be unlike you,
And whom, it is said, you are so unlike.
Stand on the stoops of their houses and tell them why
You are out on strike.

5   It is not yet time for the rock, the bullet, the blunt
Slogan that fuddles the mind toward force.
Let the new sound in our streets be the patient sound
Of your discourse.

Doors will be shut in your faces, I do not doubt.
10 Yet here or there, it may be, there will start,
Much as the lights blink on in a block at evening,
Changes of heart.

They are your houses; the people are not unlike you;
Talk with them, then, and let it be done
15 Even for the grey wife of your nightmare sheriff
And the guardsman's son.

Reading and Reacting

1. Is this poem's diction primarily formal or informal? List the words that support your conclusion.
2. Besides its vocabulary, what elements in the poem might lead you to characterize it as formal or informal?
3. **Journal Entry** This poem is an *exhortation,* a form of discourse intended to incite or encourage listeners to take action. Given the speaker's audience and subject matter, is its level of diction appropriate? Explain.

Related Works: "First Fight. Then Fiddle" (p. 766), "Cornflowers & Saffron Robes Belittle the Effort" (p. 893)

❖ ❖ ❖
CHARLES BUKOWSKI
(1920–1994)

Dog Fight
(1984)

he draws up against my rear bumper in the fast lane,
I can see his head in the rear view mirror, his eyes
are blue and he sucks upon a dead cigar.
I pull over. he passes, then slows. I don't like
5 this.
I pull back into the fast lane, engage myself upon
his rear bumper. we are as a team passing through
Compton.
I turn the radio on and light a cigarette.
10 he ups it 5 mph, I do likewise. we are as a team
entering Inglewood.
he pulls out of the fast lane and I drive past.
then I slow. when I check the rear view he is
upon my bumper again.
15 he has almost made me miss my turnoff at Century.
I hit the blinker and fire across 3 lanes of
traffic, just make the off-ramp ...
blazing past the front of an inflammable tanker.
blue eyes comes down from behind the tanker and
20 we veer down the ramp in separate lanes to the signal
and we sit there side by side, not looking at each
other.
I am caught behind an empty school bus as he idles
behind a Mercedes.
25 the signal switches and he is gone. I cut to the
inner lane behind him, then I see that the parking
lane is open and I flash by inside of him and the
Mercedes, turn up the radio, make the green as the
Mercedes and blue eyes run the yellow into the red.
30 they make it as I power it and switch back ahead of
them in their lane in order to miss a parked vegetable
truck.
now we are running 1-2-3, not a cop in sight, we are
moving through a 1980 California July
35 we are driving with skillful nonchalance
we are moving in perfect anger
we are as a team
approaching LAX:[1]
1-2-3
40 2-3-1
3-2-1.

---

[1] Los Angeles International Airport.

READING AND REACTING

1. "Dog Fight" describes a car race from the emotionally charged perspective of a driver. Given this persona, comment on the appropriateness of the level of diction of the following words: "likewise" (10), "upon" (14), "nonchalance" (35), "perfect" (36).

2. Many of the words in the poem are **jargon**—specialized language associated with a particular trade or profession. In this case, Bukowski uses automotive terms and the action words and phrases that typically describe driving manoeuvres. Would you characterize these words as formal, informal, or neither? Explain.

3. What colloquialisms are present in the poem? Could noncolloquial expressions be substituted for any of them? How would such substitutions change the poem?

4. **JOURNAL ENTRY** Look up the phrase *dog fight* in a dictionary. What meanings are listed? Which one do you think Bukowski had in mind? Why?

5. **CRITICAL PERSPECTIVE** In a 1978 review in the *Village Voice*, critic Michael Lally defended Bukowski's poetry:

   > Despite what some criticize as prose in Bukowski's poetry, there is in much of his work a poetic sensibility that, though arrogantly smart-ass and self-protective as well as self-promotional (he's the granddaddy of "punk" sensibility for sure), is also sometimes poignant, emotionally revealing, uniquely "American." . . .

   Is "Dog Fight" prose, or do you see in it a "poetic sensibility"?

Related Works: "We Real Cool" (p. 826), "My Tragic Opera" (p. 859)

WORD ORDER

◊ ◊ ◊

The order in which words are arranged in a poem is just as important as the choice of words. Because English sentences nearly always have a subject-verb-object sequence, with adjectives preceding the nouns they modify, a departure from this order calls attention to itself. Thus, poets can use readers' expectations about word order to their advantage. Poets often manipulate word order in order to place emphasis on a word. Sometimes they achieve this emphasis by using a very unconventional sequence; sometimes they simply place the word first or last in a line or place it in a stressed position in the line. Poets may also choose a particular word order to make two related—or startlingly unrelated—words fall in adjacent or parallel position, calling attention to the similarity (or the difference) between them. In other cases, poets may manipulate syntax to preserve a poem's rhyme or metre or highlight sound correspondences that might otherwise not be noticeable. Finally, irregular syntax may be used throughout a poem to reveal a speaker's mood—for example, to give a playful quality to a poem or to suggest a speaker's disoriented state.

In the poem that follows, the placement of many words departs from conventional English syntax.

⟩ ⟩ ⟩

EDMUND SPENSER
(1552–1599)

One Day I Wrote Her Name upon the Strand
(1595)

One day I wrote her name upon the strand,[1]
But came the waves and washed it away:
Again I wrote it with a second hand,
But came the tide and made my pains his prey.
5 "Vain man," said she, "that doest in vain assay,
A mortal thing so to immortalize,
For I myself shall like to this decay,
And eek[2] my name be wiped out likewise."
"Not so," quod[3] I, "let baser things devise,
10 To die in dust, but you shall live by fame:
My verse your virtues rare shall eternize,
And in the heavens write your glorious name.
Where whenas death shall all the world subdue,
Our love shall live, and later life renew."

"One Day I Wrote Her Name upon the Strand," a sonnet, has a fixed metrical pattern and rhyme scheme. To accommodate the sonnet's rhyme and metre, Spenser makes a number of adjustments in syntax. For example, to make sure certain rhyming words fall at the ends of lines, the poet sometimes moves words out of their conventional order, as the following three comparisons illustrate.

CONVENTIONAL WORD ORDER	INVERTED SEQUENCE
"'Vain man,' she said, that doest *assay in vain*."	"'Vain man,' said she, that doest *in vain assay*." ("Assay" appears at end of line 5, to rhyme with line 7's "decay.")
"My verse shall *eternize your rare virtues*."	"My verse *your virtues rare shall eternize*." ("Eternize" appears at end of line 11 to rhyme with line 9's "devise.")

---

[1] Beach.
[2] Also, indeed.
[3] Said.

"Where whenas death shall *subdue all the world*, / Our love shall live, and *later renew life*."

"Where whenas death shall *all the world subdue*, / Our love shall live, and *later life renew*." (Rhyming words "subdue" and "renew" are placed at ends of lines.)

To make sure the metrical pattern stresses certain words, the poet occasionally moves a word out of order so it will fall on a stressed syllable. The following comparison illustrates this technique.

<u>CONVENTIONAL WORD ORDER</u>

"But *the waves came* and washed it away."

<u>INVERTED SEQUENCE</u>

"But *came the waves* and washed it away." (Stress in line 2 falls on "waves" rather than on "the.")

As the comparisons show, Spenser's adjustments in syntax are motivated at least in part by a desire to preserve the sonnet's rhyme and metre.

The following poem does more than simply invert words; it presents an intentionally disordered syntax.

◈ ◈ ◈

E. E. CUMMINGS
(1894–1962)

anyone lived in a
pretty how town
(1940)

anyone lived in a pretty how town
(with up so floating many bells down)
spring summer autumn winter
he sang his didn't he danced his did.

5 Women and men (both little and small)
cared for anyone not at all
they sowed their isn't they reaped their same
sun moon stars rain

children guessed (but only a few
10 and down they forgot as up they grew
autumn winter spring summer)
that noone loved him more by more

when by now and tree by leaf
she laughed his joy she cried his grief
15 bird by snow and stir by still
anyone's any was all to her

> someones married their everyones
> laughed their cryings and did their dance
> (sleep wake hope and then) they
> 20 said their nevers they slept their dream
>
> stars rain sun moon
> (and only the snow can begin to explain
> how children are apt to forget to remember
> with up so floating many bells down)
>
> 25 one day anyone died i guess
> (and noone stooped to kiss his face)
> busy folk buried them side by side
> little by little and was by was
>
> all by all and deep by deep
> 30 and more by more they dream their sleep
> noone and anyone earth by april
> wish by spirit and if by yes.
>
> Women and men (both dong and ding)
> ` summer autumn winter spring
> 35 reaped their sowing and went their came
> sun moon stars rain

At times Cummings, like Spenser, manipulates syntax in response to the demands of rhyme and metre—for example, in line 10. But Cummings goes much further, using unconventional syntax as part of a scheme that encompasses other unusual elements of the poem, such as its unexpected departures from the musical metrical pattern (for example, in line 3 and line 8) and from the rhyme scheme (for example, in lines 3 and 4), and its use of parts of speech in unfamiliar contexts. Together, these techniques give the poem a playful quality. The refreshing disorder of the syntax (for instance, in lines 1–2, line 10, and line 24) adds to the poem's whimsical effect.

❖ POEMS FOR FURTHER READING: WORD ORDER

A. E. HOUSMAN
(1859–1936)

To an Athlete Dying Young
(1896)

> The time you won your town the race
> We chaired you through the market-place;
> Man and boy stood cheering by,
> And home we brought you shoulder-high.

5 Today, the road all runners come,
   Shoulder-high we bring you home,
   And set you at your threshold down,
   Townsman of a stiller town.

   Smart lad, to slip betimes away
10 From fields where glory does not stay,
   And early though the laurel grows
   It withers quicker than the rose.

   Eyes the shady night has shut
   Cannot see the record cut,
15 And silence sounds no worse than cheers
   After earth has stopped the ears.

   Now you will not swell the rout
   Of lads that wore their honors out,
   Runners whom renown outran
20 And the name died before the man.

   So set, before its echoes fade,
   The fleet foot on the sill of shade,
   And hold to the low lintel up
   The still-defended challenge-cup.

25 And round that early-laureled head
   Will flock to gaze the strengthless dead,
   And find unwithered on its curls
   The garland briefer than a girl's.

READING AND REACTING

1. Where does the poem's metre or rhyme scheme require the poet to depart from conventional syntax?
2. Reword the poem using conventional word order. Do your changes improve the poem?
3. **JOURNAL ENTRY** Who do you think the speaker is? What is his relationship to the athlete?

Related Works: "Anthem for Doomed Youth" (p. 587), "Nothing Gold Can Stay" (p. 693)

EMILY DICKINSON
(1830–1886)

My Life Had Stood—
A Loaded Gun
(c. 1863)

My Life had stood—a Loaded Gun—
In Corners—till a Day
The Owner passed—identified—
And carried Me away—

5 And now We roam in Sovereign Woods—
And now We hunt the Doe—
And every time I speak for Him—
The Mountains straight reply—

And do I smile, such cordial light
10 Upon the Valley glow—
It is as a Vesuvian[1] face
Had let its pleasure through—

And when at Night—Our good Day done—
I guard My Master's Head—
15 'Tis better than the Eider-Duck's[2]
Deep Pillow—to have shared—

To foe of His—I'm deadly foe—
None stir the second time—
On whom I lay a Yellow Eye—
20 Or an emphatic Thumb—

Though I than He—may longer live
He longer must—than I—
For I have but the power to kill,
Without—the power to die—

READING AND REACTING

1. Identify lines in which word order departs from conventional
   English syntax. Can you explain in each case why the word order
   has been manipulated?

---

[1] Refers to Mount Vesuvius, a volcano that erupted in 79 A.D., destroying the city of
Pompeii.

[2] Refers to the duck that produces eiderdown, used for stuffing pillows.

2. Do any words gain added emphasis by virtue of their unexpected position? Which ones? How are these words important to the poem's meaning?

3. **JOURNAL ENTRY** Why do you think the speaker might be comparing her life to a loaded gun?

4. **CRITICAL PERSPECTIVE** Writing in the *New York Times,* Elizabeth Schmidt offers this evaluation of Dickinson's poetry:

> Her formal discipline—the economy of her language and her elaborate, idiosyncratic metrical schemes—turns out to be anything but off-putting. She chose forms that readers could learn by heart, creating one of literature's great, and most unlikely, combinations of style and content. Her poems are often conceptually difficult, and yet they are also surprisingly inviting, whether they coax you to guess a riddle or carry you along to the beat of a familiar tune.

Do you find Dickinson's poetry as inviting as Schmidt does, or do you think a poem like "My Life Had Stood—A Loaded Gun" *is* "off-putting"?

Related Works: "Because I Could Not Stop for Death" (p. 737), "I Heard a Fly Buzz—When I Died" (p. 830)

✦ ✦ ✦

SHARON THESEN
(1946–   )

Animals[1]

When I come out of the bathroom
animals are waiting in the hall
and when I settle down to read
an animal comes between me
5 and my book and when I put on
a fancy dinner, a few animals
are under the table staring at the guests,
and when I mail a letter
or go to the Safeway there's always
10 an animal tagging along
or crying left at home and when I get
home from work animals leap joyously
around my old red car so I feel like
an avatar with flowers & presents all over
15 her body, and when I dance around
the kitchen at night wild & feeling

---

[1] Publication date is not available.

lovely as Margie Gillis, the animals
try to dance too, they stagger on
back legs and open their mouths, pink
20   and black and fanged, and I take their paws
in my hands and bend toward them,
happy and full of love.

READING AND REACTING

1. To what kind of animal is the speaker referring?
2. What is the relationship between the speaker and the animals?
3. Who is Margie Gillis, and why does the speaker compare herself to this person?
4. Make sure you understand the meaning of the word "avatar," and consider the change in diction with this word.
5. **JOURNAL ENTRY** Write about how animals (perhaps your pets) make you feel.

Related Works: "The Prize Cat" (p. 794), "The Bull Moose" (p. 811)

CHECKLIST: WRITING ABOUT WORD CHOICE AND WORD ORDER

WORD CHOICE

✓ Which words are of key importance in the poem?

✓ What is the denotative meaning of each of these key words?

✓ Why is each word chosen instead of a synonym? (For example, is the word chosen for its sound? Its connotation? Its relationship to other words in the poem? Its contribution to the poem's metrical pattern?)

✓ What other words could be effectively used in place of words now in the poem?

✓ How would substitutions change the poem's meaning?

✓ Which key words have neutral connotations? Which have negative connotations? Which have positive connotations? Beyond its literal meaning, what does each word suggest?

✓ Are any words repeated? Why?

LEVELS OF DICTION

✓ How would you characterize the poem's level of diction? Why is this level of diction used? Is it effective?

✓ Does the poem mix different levels of diction? To what end?

✓ Does the poem use dialect? For what purpose?

WORD ORDER

✓ Is the poem's syntax conventional, or are words arranged in unexpected order?

✓ Which phrases represent departures from conventional syntax?

✓ What is the purpose of the unusual syntax? (For example, does it preserve the poem's metre or rhyme scheme? Does it highlight particular sound correspondences? Does it place emphasis on a particular word or phrase? Does it reflect the speaker's mood?)

✓ How would the poem's impact change if conventional syntax were used?

◊ **WRITING SUGGESTIONS: WORD CHOICE, WORD ORDER**

1. Reread the two poems by E. E. Cummings—"in Just-" (p. 664) and "anyone lived in a pretty how town" (p. 676)—in this chapter. If you like, you may also read one or two additional poems in this text by Cummings. Do you believe Cummings chose words primarily for their sound? For their appearance on the page? What other factors might have influenced his choices?

2. Reread "Animals" (p. 680) and read "My Ledders" (p. 845). Choose another poem in the text whose speaker is a woman. Compare the three speakers' level of diction and choice of words. What does their speech reveal about their lives?

3. Reread "The Cariboo Horses" (p. 659) alongside Michèle Lalonde's "Speak White" (p. 806). What does each poem's choice of words reveal about the speaker's attitude toward the subject?

4. Analyze the choice of words and the level of diction in Margaret Atwood's "The City Planners" (p. 667), Louise Bernice Halfe's "My Ledders" (p. 845), Langston Hughes's "Theme for English B" (p. 849), and Denise Levertov's "What Were They Like?" (p. 591). Pay particular attention to each poem's use of language to express social or political criticism.

CHAPTER 15

Imagery

◇ ◇ ◇

Images are probably the most important part of the poem. First of all, you want to tell a story, but images are what are going to shore it up and get to the heart of the matter. . . . If they're not coming, I'm not even writing a poem, it's pointless.

ANNE SEXTON, *Writers at Work,* 4th Ed.

The difference between a literature that includes the image, and a literature that excludes the image (such as the newspaper or the scientific Newtonian essay) is that the first helps us to bridge the gap between ourselves and nature, and the second encourages us to remain isolated, living despairingly in the gap. Many philosophers and critics urge us to remain in the gap, and let the world of nature and the world of men fall further and further apart. We can do that; or a human being can reach out with his right hand to the natural world, and with his left hand to the world of human intelligence, and touch both at the same moment. Apparently no one but human beings can do this.

ROBERT BLY, "What the Image Can Do"

Of all the art forms, poetry—rooted as it is in the inescapably concrete, both in image and in verbal usage—is the least easily translatable from place to place as well as from language to language.

MARGARET ATWOOD, Introduction to
The New Oxford Book of Canadian Verse in English

It is better to present one Image in a lifetime than to produce voluminous works.

EZRA POUND, "A Retrospect"

◇ ◇ ◇

◊ ◊ ◊

ROBERT KROETSCH
(1927–   )

Meditation on Tom Thomson
(1975)

Tom Thomson I love you   therefore I apologize
for what I must say   but I must say
damn your jack pines   they are beautiful

I love your bent trees   and I love your ice
5 in spring   candled into its green rot
and I love the way you drowned   all alone

with your canoe   and our not even knowing
the time of day   and the grave mystery
of your genius   interrupted   is *our* story

10 and art, man, art   is the essential
luxury   the imperative QUESTION(?)
the re-sounding say   of the night's loon

and holy shit mother   the muskeg snatch
of the old north   the bait that caught
15 the fishing father   into his own feast

the swimming art-man   who did not drown
in the lake   in his pictures
who drowned   for murder or grief or

the weave of the water   would not hold
20 the shoulders of the sky   were deep
the maelstrom would not spin   to spit him

free, daddy, FREE FREE FREE   (but I must say
DAMN your jack pines)   for the whorl
of the whirlpool breaks us   one by one

25 we stretch and tear   the joints
opening like curtains   on a cool
Algonquin morning   onto a red sun

or down onto the black bottom   or far
(the grammar of our days   is ill defined)
30 or rapt in the root and fire   of that wind

bent forest   (about your pine trees
this evening   one of them moved
across my wall)   daring the light

daring the bright and lover's leap   across
35   the impassible gap   the uncertain
    principle of time and space   straight down

    he dove   and he would seize unearthly
    shades   and he would seize the drowned land
    the picture from the pool   the pool's picture

40   and the gods cried   Tom, Tom, you asshole
    let go   and you had found their secret
    and would not ever   let go   they cry

Because the purpose of poetry—and, for that matter, of all literature—is to expand the perception of readers, poets try to appeal to the senses. In "Meditation on Tom Thomson," for example, Robert Kroetsch uses details, such as "bent trees" (4) and "the whorl / of the whirlpool" (23–24), to enable readers to visualize particular scenes in both Thomson's paintings and his life. As Thomson drowned under mysterious circumstances, the image of water is often inseparable from any thought of his paintings, which often feature twisted, wind-carved pine trees. Thus, "Meditation on Tom Thomson" combines an appreciation for the painter's work and a series of questions about his life. The poem is about the ability of the artist—poet or painter—to call up images in the mind of an audience. To achieve this end, a poet uses **imagery,** language that evokes a physical sensation produced by one of the five senses—sight, hearing, taste, touch, or smell.

Although the effect can be quite complex, the way images work is simple: when you see the word *red*, your memory of the various red things that you have seen determines how you picture the image. In addition, the word *red* may have emotional associations, or **connotations,** that define your response. A red sunset, for example, can have a positive connotation or a negative one depending on whether it is associated with the end of a perfect day or with air pollution. By choosing an image carefully, then, poets not only create pictures in a reader's mind, but also suggest a number of imaginative associations. These associations help poets to establish the **atmosphere** or **mood** of the poem. The description of the music of Bartok in Dorothy Livesay's "Bartok and the Geranium" (p. 792) creates a wild, excitable, intense mood.

Readers come to a poem with unique experiences, so an image in a poem does not always suggest the same thing to all readers. In "Meditation on Tom Thomson," for example, the poet presents an image of the painter being taken by the deep water. Although most readers will probably see a picture that is consistent with the one the poet sees, no two images will be identical. Readers will have their own distinct mental images of Thomson's drowning: some images may result from experience whereas others will be imaginative creations. Readers familiar with Thomson's paintings of trees and water in what is now Algonquin Park in Ontario or with the landscape itself will bring a particular perspective to the poem. (For a selection of Thomson's work, see www.canadahistory.com/sections/art/arts.htm.)

By conveying what the poet sees and experiences, images open readers' minds and enrich their reading with perceptions and associations different from—and possibly more original and complex than—their own.

One advantage of imagery is its extreme economy. Just a few words enable poets to evoke a range of emotions and reactions. In the following poem, just a few visual images are enough to create a picture.

◇ ◇ ◇

WILLIAM CARLOS WILLIAMS
(1883–1963)

The Red Wheelbarrow
(1923)

so much depends
upon

a red wheel
barrow

5 glazed with rain
water

beside the white
chickens

"The Red Wheelbarrow" asks readers to pause for a moment to consider the uniqueness and mystery of everyday objects. What is immediately apparent is the poem's verbal economy. The poet does not tell readers what the barn-yard smells like or what sounds the animals make. In fact, he does not even paint a detailed picture of the scene. How large is the wheelbarrow? In what condition is it? How many chickens are in the barnyard? In this poem, the answers to these questions are not important. Even without answering these questions, the poet is able to use simple imagery to create a scene upon which, he says, "so much depends."

The wheelbarrow establishes a momentary connection between the poet and his world. Like a still-life painting, the red wheelbarrow beside the white chickens gives order to a world that is full of seemingly unrelated objects. By asserting the importance of the objects in the poem, the poet suggests that our ability to perceive the objects of this world gives our lives meaning and that our ability to convey our perceptions to others is central to our lives as well as to art.

Images enable poets to present ideas that would be difficult to convey in any other way. Just one look at a dictionary will illustrate that concepts such as *beauty* and *mystery* are so abstract that they are difficult to define, let alone to discuss in specific terms. By choosing an image or series of images to embody these ideas, however, poets can effectively and persuasively make their feelings known, as Ezra Pound does in the brief poem that follows.

◇ ◇ ◇

EZRA POUND
(1885–1972)

In a Station of the Metro
(1916)

> The apparition of these faces in the crowd;
> Petals on a wet, black bough.

This poem is almost impossible to paraphrase because the information it communicates is less important than the feelings associated with this information. The poem's title indicates that the first line is meant to suggest a group of people gathered in a station of the Paris subway. The scene, however, is presented not as a clear picture but as an "apparition," suggesting that it is unexpected or even dreamlike. In contrast with the image of the subway platform is the image of the people's faces as flower petals on the dark branch of a tree. Thus, the subway platform—dark, cold, wet, subterranean (associated with baseness, death, and hell)—is juxtaposed with white flowers—delicate, pale, radiant, lovely (associated with the ideal, life, and heaven). These contrasting images, presented without comment, bear the entire weight of the poem.

Although images can be strikingly visual, they can also appeal to the senses of hearing, smell, taste, and touch. The following poem uses images of sound and taste as well as visual images.

◇ ◇ ◇

GARY SNYDER
(1930–   )

Some Good Things to Be
Said for the Iron Age
(1970)

> A ringing tire iron
>   dropped on the pavement
> Whang of a saw
>   brusht on limbs
> 5 the taste
>   of rust

Here Snyder presents two commonplace aural images: the ringing of a tire iron and the sound of a saw. These somewhat ordinary images gain power, however, through their visual isolation in the poem. Together they produce a harsh and jarring chord that in turn creates a sense of uneasiness in the reader. This poem does more than present sensory images, though. It also conveys the speaker's interpretations of these images. The last two lines of the poem imply not only that the time in which we live (the Iron Age) is base and mundane, but also that it is declining, decaying into an age of rust. This idea is reinforced by the repeated consonant sounds in *taste* and *rust,* which encourage readers to hold the final image of the poem on their tongues. The title of the poem makes an ironic comment, suggesting that compared to the time that is approaching, the age of iron may be "good." Thus, in the mind of the poet, ordinary events gain added significance, and images that spring from everyday experience become sources of enlightenment and insight.

In shorter poems, such as most of those discussed earlier, one or two images may serve as focal points. A longer poem may introduce a cluster of related images, creating a more complex tapestry of sensory impressions—as in the following poem, where several related images are woven together.

◇ ◇ ◇

ERIN MOURÉ
(1955–   )

It Is Only Me
(1983)

For Aline Kouhi Klemenic

Say there is a woman
in the locked-up cornfield.
She is making a desert for herself, not me.
Like the poet said: Fumbling the sky's queer wires,
5   asking for
mercy, abstract collusion, a kind of awe;
she hikes across the frozen furrows in mid-November
ready to observe nearly anything,
self-consciously, as if the turned dirt
10 would see her singing,
would answer with arguments on Kandinsky & Klee.[1]

At least she can't hear
the saxophone playing scales in the next room,
taking the colours out of the air;
15 they become discordant sounds & no longer answer.
The words stay silent on the page, their usual selves,
picking lice from under their collars,
not yet torn, or interested, or censored,
or even free.
20 There are never enough groceries, does the woman
know this in the strange field?

---

[1] Wassily Kandinsky (1866–1944), Russian expressionist painter; Paul Klee (1899–1940), Swiss abstract painter. Both taught at the Bauhaus in Germany.

Probably she has thought of it before, a few minutes,
but now the long furrows
are turning her over & over, like a leaf
25 in the wind.

Never mind the sound,
the saxophonist is in another country, its mountains
stop him from reaching her.
It is only me, with my bad language, my long distance whisky:
30 I see her far away, it is very cold, I am
calling her out of her field.

"It Is Only Me" presents related images that together evoke emptiness and isolation. It begins with the images of a "locked-up cornfield" (2) and "a desert" (3). It progresses to "frozen furrows" (7), and then the imagery opens to include aural and visual references: "singing" (10) and "Kandinsky & Klee" (11). In the second stanza the aural and visual images are combined:

At least she can't hear
the saxophone playing scales in the next room,
taking the colours out of the air[.] (12–14)

The speaker attempts to bridge the distance between speaker and subject, but the imagery focuses on the harshness of the cold and separation between the two. The care with which Mouré leaves ambiguous the gender of the speaker allows for various images to be created in the reader's mind. The resulting variety of images may challenge the reader's assumptions about gender and connection.

Much visual imagery is **static,** freezing the moment and thereby giving it the timeless quality of painting or sculpture. ("The Red Wheelbarrow" and "In a Station of the Metro" present such a tableau.) Some imagery, however, is **kinetic,** conveying a sense of motion or change.

◇ ◇ ◆

WILLIAM CARLOS WILLIAMS
(1883–1963)

The Great Figure
(1938)

Among the rain
and lights
I saw the figure 5
in gold
5 on a red
firetruck
moving
tense

　　　　　　　　　　　unheeded
　　　10　to gong clangs
　　　　　　　siren howls
　　　　　　　and wheels rumbling
　　　　　　　through the dark city.

Commenting on this poem in his autobiography, Williams explains that while walking in New York, he heard the sound of a fire engine. As he turned

◊ Charles Demuth (1883–1935). *I Saw the Figure 5 in Gold*. Oil on composition board, 36 × 29¾ in. The Metropolitan Museum of Art, the Alfred Steiglitz Collection, 1949. (49.59.1) All rights reserved, the Metropolitan Museum of Art.

the corner, he saw a golden figure 5 on a red background speed by. The impression was so forceful that he immediately jotted down a poem about it. In the poem, Williams attempts to re-create the sensation the figure 5 made as it moved into his consciousness, presenting the image as if it were a picture taken by a camera with a high-speed shutter. The poet presents images in the order in which he perceived them: first the 5 and then the red fire truck howling and clanging into the darkness. Thus, "The Great Figure" uses images of sight, sound, and movement to re-create for readers the poet's experience. The American painter Charles Demuth was fascinated by the kinetic quality of the poem. Working closely with his friend Williams, he attempted to capture the stop-action feature of the poem in the painting reproduced on page 690.

A special use of imagery, called **synesthesia,** occurs when one sense is described in a way that is more appropriate for another—for instance, when a sound is described with colour. When people say they are feeling *blue* or describe music as *hot,* they are using synesthesia. The poet John Keats uses this technique in the following lines from "Ode to a Nightingale":

> O, for a draught of vintage! that hath been
>   Cool'd a long age in the deep-delvéd earth,
> Tasting of Flora and the country green,
>   Dance and Provençal song, and sunburnt mirth!

In these lines, the speaker describes the taste of wine in terms of images that appeal to a variety of senses: flowers, a grassy field, dance, song, and sun.

❖ POEMS FOR FURTHER READING: IMAGERY

◇ ◇ ◇

MATSUO BASHO
(1644?–1694)

Four Haiku[1]

Translated by Geoffrey Bownas and Anthony Thwaite

Spring:
A hill without a name
Veiled in morning mist.

The beginning of autumn:
Sea and emerald paddy
Both the same green.

The winds of autumn
Blow: yet still green
The chestnut husks.

---

[1] Publication dates are not available.

A flash of lightning:
Into the gloom
Goes the heron's cry.

READING AND REACTING

1. A **haiku** is a three-line poem, a Japanese form that traditionally
   has seventeen syllables. Haiku are admired for their extreme
   economy and their striking images. What are the central images
   in each of Basho's haiku? To what senses do these images appeal?
2. In another poem, Basho says that art begins with "The depths of
   the country / and a rice-planting song." What do you think he
   means? In what way do the preceding poems exemplify this idea?
3. Do you think the conciseness of these poems increases or
   decreases the impact of their images?
4. **JOURNAL ENTRY** "In a Station of the Metro" (p. 687) is Ezra
   Pound's version of a haiku. How successful do you think Pound
   was? Do you think a longer poem could have conveyed the
   images more effectively?

Related Works: "the sky was can dy" (p. 777)

◊

CAROLYN KIZER
(1925–   )

After Basho
(1984)

Tentatively, you
slip onstage this evening,
pallid, famous moon.

READING AND REACTING

1. What possible meanings might the word "After" have in the title?
   What does the title tell readers about the writer's purpose?
2. What visual picture does the poem suggest? What mood does the
   poem's central image create?
3. What is the impact of "tentatively" in the first line and "famous"
   in the last line? How do the connotations of these words affect
   the image of the moon?

Related Works: "Photograph of My Father in His Twenty-Second Year"
(p. 568), "Widow's Lament" (p. 774)

RICHARD WILBUR
(1921–   )

Sleepless at Crown Point
(1973)

All night, this headland
Lunges into the rumpling
Capework of the wind.

READING AND REACTING

1. What scene is the speaker describing?
2. What is the significance of the title?
3. What are the poem's central images? How do the words "lunges"
   and "capework" help to establish these images?

Related Works: "The Story of an Hour" (p. 77), "Fog" (p. 879), "The Dance"
(p. 895)

ROBERT FROST
(1874–1963)

Nothing Gold Can Stay
(1923)

Nature's first green is gold,
Her hardest hue to hold.
Her early leaf's a flower;
But only so an hour.
5 Then leaf subsides to leaf.
So Eden sank to grief.
So dawn goes down to day.
Nothing gold can stay.

READING AND REACTING

1. What central idea does this poem express?
2. What do you think the first line of the poem means? In what
   sense is this line ironic?
3. What is the significance of the colours green and gold in this
   poem? What do these colours have to do with "Eden" and
   "dawn"?

4. **JOURNAL ENTRY** How do the various images in the poem prepare readers for the last line?
5. **CRITICAL PERSPECTIVE** In "The Figure a Poem Means," the introduction to the first edition of his *Collected Poems* (1930), Frost laid out a theory of poetry:

> It begins in delight, it inclines to the impulse, it assumes direction with the first line laid down, it runs a course of lucky events, and ends in a clarification of life—not necessarily a great clarification . . . but a momentary stay against confusion. . . . Like a piece of ice on a hot stove the poem must ride on its own melting. . . . Read it a hundred times: it will forever keep its freshness as a metal keeps its fragrance. It can never lose its sense of a meaning that once unfolded by surprise as it went.

Can you apply Frost's remarks to "Nothing Gold Can Stay"?

Related Works: "Shall I Compare Thee to a Summer's Day?" (p. 701), "God's Grandeur" (p. 848)

◇ ◇ ◇

GEORGE ELLIOTT CLARKE
(1960–   )

Casualties
(1992)
January 16, 1991

Snow annihilates all beauty
this merciless January.
A white blitzkrieg, Klan—cruel,
arsons and obliterates.

5 Piercing lies numb us to pain.
Nerves and words fail so we
can't feel agony or passion,
so we can't flinch or cry,

when we spy blurred children's
10 charred bodies protruding
from the smoking rubble
of statistics or see a man

stumbling in a blizzard
of bullets. Everything is
15 normal, absurdly normal.
We see, as if through a snow-

storm, darkly. Reporters
rat-a-tat-tat tactics,

stratagems. Missiles bristle
20 behind newspaper lines.

Our minds chill; we weather
the storm, huddle in dreams.
Exposed, though, a woman,
lashed by lightning, repents

25 of her flesh, becomes a living
X-ray, "collateral damage."
The first casualty of war
is language.

READING AND REACTING

1. The first stanza introduces two conflicting images. What are they, and how do they work together?
2. How does the poem develop the destructive image of language? How is disaster changed into something "absurdly normal" (15)?
3. What ideas are traditionally associated with the image of snow? The Klan? (You may want to consult a reference work, such as *A Dictionary of Symbols* by J. E. Cirlot.) In what way does the speaker rely on these associations to help him convey his ideas? Can you appreciate the poem without understanding these associations?

Related Works: "The Loons" (p. 249), "Dulce et Decorum Est" (p. 695)

WILFRED OWEN
(1893–1918)

Dulce et Decorum Est[1]
(1920)

Bent double, like old beggars under sacks,
Knock-kneed, coughing like hags, we cursed through sludge,
Till on the haunting flares we turned our backs
And towards our distant rest began to trudge.
5 Men marched asleep. Many had lost their boots
But limped on, blood-shod. All went lame; all blind;
Drunk with fatigue; deaf even to the hoots
Of tired, outstripped Five-Nines[2] that dropped behind.

Gas! Gas! Quick, boys!—An ecstasy of fumbling,

---

[1] The title and last lines are from Horace, *Odes* 3.2: "Sweet and fitting it is to die for one's country."

[2] Artillery shells that explode on impact.

10 Fitting the clumsy helmets just in time;
But someone still was yelling out and stumbling
And flound'ring like a man in fire or lime . . .
Dim, through the misty panes and thick green light,
As under a green sea, I saw him drowning.

15 In all my dreams, before my helpless sight,
He plunges at me, guttering, choking, drowning.

If in some smothering dreams you too could pace
Behind the wagon that we flung him in,
And watch the white eyes writhing in his face,
20 His hanging face, like a devil's sick of sin;
If you could hear, at every jolt, the blood
Come gargling from the froth-corrupted lungs,
Obscene as cancer, bitter as the cud
Of vile, incurable sores on innocent tongues,—
25 My friend, you would not tell with such high zest
To children ardent for some desperate glory,
The old Lie: Dulce et decorum est
Pro patria mori.

READING AND REACTING

1. Who is the speaker in this poem? What is his attitude toward his subject?

2. What images are traditionally associated with soldiers? How do the images in this poem depart from convention? Why do you think Owen selected such images?

3. To what senses (other than sight) does the poem appeal? Is any of the imagery kinetic?

4. **JOURNAL ENTRY** Does the knowledge that Owen died in World War I change your reaction to the poem, or are the poem's images compelling enough to eliminate the need for biographical background?

5. **CRITICAL PERSPECTIVE** Like many other British poets who experienced fighting in the European trenches during World War I, Owen struggled to find a new poetic idiom to describe the horrors of this new kind of war. In his 1986 biography *Owen the Poet*, Dominic Hibberd praises the "controlled and powerful anger in 'Dulce et Decorum Est' which for some readers will be the poem's most valuable quality" and goes on to note that the "organization and clarity of the first half is replaced [beginning at line 15] by confused, choking syntax and a vocabulary of sickness and disgust, matching the nightmare which is in progress."

    Give some examples to support Hibberd's statements. How does the movement from control to confusion convey the poem's message to readers?

TED HUGHES
(1930–1998)

Dehorning
(1979)

Bad-tempered bullying bunch, the horned cows
Among the unhorned. Feared, spoilt.
Cantankerous at the hay, at assemblies, at crowded
Yard operations. Knowing their horntips' position
5 To a fraction, every other cow knowing it too,
Like their own tenderness. Horning of bellies, hair-tufting
Of horntips. Handy levers. But
Off with the horns.
So there they all are in the yard—
10 The pick of the bullies, churning each other
Like thick fish in a bucket, churning their mud.
One by one, into the cage of the crush: the needle,
A roar not like a cow—more like a tiger,
Blast of air down a cavern, and long, long,
15 Beginning in pain and ending in terror—then the next.
The needle between the horn and the eye, so deep
Your gut squirms for the eyeball twisting
In its pink-white fastenings of tissue. This side and that.
Then the first one anesthetized, back in the crush.
20 The bulldog pincers in the septum, stretched full strength,
The horn levered right over, the chin pulled round
With the pincers, the mouth drooling, the eye
Like a live eye caught in a pan, like the eye of a fish
Imprisoned in air. Then the cheese cutter
25 Of braided wire, and stainless-steel peg handles,
Aligned on the hair-bedded root of the horn, then leaning
Backward full weight, pull-punching backwards,
Left right left right and the blood leaks
Down over the cheekbone, the wire bites
30 And buzzes, the ammonia horn-burn smokes
And the cow groans, roars shapelessly, hurls
Its half-ton commotion in the tight cage. Our faces
Grimace like faces in the dentist's chair. The horn
Rocks from its roots, the wire pulls through
35 The last hinge of hair, the horn is heavy and free,
And a water-pistol jet of blood
Rains over the one who holds it—a needle jet
From the white-rasped and bloody skull crater. Then tweezers
Twiddle the artery nozzle, knotting it enough,

40 And purple antiseptic squirts a cuttlefish cloud over it.
   Then the other side the same. We collect
   A heap of horns. The floor of the crush
   Is a trampled puddle of scarlet. The purple-crowned cattle,
   The bullies, with suddenly no horns to fear,
45 Start ramming and wrestling. Maybe their heads
   Are still anesthetized. A new order
   Among the hornless. The bitchy high-headed
   Straight-back brindle, with her Spanish bull trot,
   And her head-shaking snorting advance and her crazy spirit,
50 Will have to get maternal. What she's lost
   In weapons, she'll have to make up for in tits.
   But they've all lost one third of their beauty.

READING AND REACTING

1. Why are the cows being dehorned? Whose purpose is being served?
2. What is the difference between the cows with horns and the cows without them?
3. What is the perspective of the speaker? How does the speaker describe the process of dehorning? What figures of speech are used?
4. Why does the speaker say the dehorned cows have lost beauty?
5. **JOURNAL ENTRY** Write about how animals are often used for the benefit of human beings and in doing so undergo painful treatment. Is dehorning a cow significantly different from docking the ears and tails of dogs, for example?

Related Works: "The Loons" (p. 249), "The Bull Moose" (p. 811)

✓ CHECKLIST: WRITING ABOUT IMAGERY

✓ Do the images in the poem appeal to the sense of sight, touch, hearing, smell, or taste?

✓ Does the poem depend on a single image or on a variety of different images?

✓ Does the poem depend on a cluster of related images?

✓ What details make the images memorable?

✓ What mood do the images create?

✓ Are the images static or kinetic? Are there any examples of synesthesia?

✓ How do the poem's images help to convey its theme?

✓ How effective are the images? In what way do the images enhance your enjoyment of the poem?

◆ WRITING SUGGESTIONS: IMAGERY

1. How are short poems such as "Some Good Things to Be Said for the Iron Age" (p. 687) and "In a Station of the Metro" (p. 687) like and unlike haiku?

2. Reread "Meditation on Tom Thomson" (p. 684) and "The Great Figure" (p. 689), and read "Musée des Beaux Arts" (p. 815). Study the paintings accompanying the poems in the text and look up a Tom Thomson painting. Then, write a paper in which you draw some conclusions about the differences between artistic and poetic images.

3. Reread "It Is Only Me" (p. 688) and the discussion that accompanies it. Then, analyze the role of imagery in the depiction of the relationships in "My Papa's Waltz" (p. 570) and "Letters & Other Worlds" (p. 575). How does each poem's imagery convey the nature of the relationship it describes?

4. Write an essay in which you discuss the colour imagery in "Nothing Gold Can Stay" (p. 693), "Casualties" (p. 694), and "The Yellow Wall-Paper" (p. 189). In what way does colour reinforce the themes of these works?

5. Sometimes imagery can be used to make a comment about the society in which a scene takes place. Choose two selections in which imagery functions in this way—"The Colonel" (p. 783), "Speak White" (p. 806), "Dehorning" (p. 697), or "Tamarindus Indica" (p. 383), for example—and discuss how the images chosen reinforce the social statement each work makes.

CHAPTER 16

Figures of Speech

The metaphor is probably the most fertile power possessed by man.

JOSÉ ORTEGA Y GASSET

The core of poetic thinking leaping from the rut. The world, my perception of it, my movement through it; the world as human civilization and natural physical reality. Thinking with eyes and ears. Thinking with my hands. A way of thinking. Earth, with intimations.

PATRICK FRIESEN, *Event*, Spring 2002

I suppose we shall never be able to distinguish absolutely and with a hard edge the image from the metaphor, any more than anyone has so distinguished prose from poetry. . . . We shall very often be able to tell, just as we can very often tell the difference between snow and rain; but there are some weathers which are either-neither, and so here there is an area where our differences will mingle. If the poet says, simply, "The red bird," we shall probably take that as an image. But as soon as we read the rest of the line—"The red bird flies across the golden floor"—there arise obscure thoughts of relationships that lead in the direction of parable: the line alone is not, strictly, a metaphor, but its resonances take it prospectively beyond a pure perception. . . . Metaphor stands somewhat as a mediating term squarely between a thing and a thought, which may be why it is so likely to compose itself about a word of sense and a word of thought, as in this example of a common Shakespearean formula: "Even to the teeth and forehead of my fault."

HOWARD NEMEROV, "On Metaphor"

Metaphor is not to be considered, . . . as the alternative of the poet, which he may elect to use or not, since he may state the matter directly and straightforwardly if he chooses. It is frequently the only means available if he is to write at all. . . .

CLEANTH BROOKS, "Metaphor and the Tradition"

◇   ◇   ◇

WILLIAM SHAKESPEARE
(1564–1616)

Shall I Compare Thee to a Summer's Day?
(1609)

Shall I compare thee to a summer's day?
Thou art more lovely and more temperate.
Rough winds do shake the darling buds of May,
And summer's lease hath all too short a date.
5 Sometime too hot the eye of heaven shines,
And often is his gold complexion dimmed;
And every fair from fair sometimes declines,
By chance, or nature's changing course, untrimmed.
But thy eternal summer shall not fade,
10 Nor lose possession of that fair thou ow'st;[1]
Nor shall death brag thou wand'rest in his shade,
When in eternal lines to time thou grow'st.
    So long as men can breathe or eyes can see,
    So long lives this, and this gives life to thee.

Although figurative language is used in all kinds of writing, poets in particular recognize the power of a figure of speech to take readers beyond the literal meaning of a word. For this reason, **figures of speech**—expressions that describe one thing in terms of something else—are more prominent in poetry than in other kinds of writing. For example, the preceding sonnet by Shakespeare compares a loved one to a summer's day in order to make the point that, unlike the fleeting summer, the loved one will—within the poem—remain forever young. But this sonnet goes beyond the obvious equation (loved one = summer's day); the speaker's assertion that his loved one will live forever in his poem actually says more about his confidence in his own talent and reputation (and about the power of figurative language) than about the loved one's beauty.

SIMILE, METAPHOR, AND PERSONIFICATION
◇ ◇◆◇ ◇

When William Wordsworth opens a poem with "I wandered lonely as a cloud" (p. 897), he conveys a good deal more than he would if he simply said "I wandered, lonely." By comparing himself in his loneliness to a cloud, he

---

[1] Beauty you possess.

suggests that like the cloud he is a part of nature and that he too is drifting, passive, blown by winds, and lacking will or substance. Thus, by using a figure of speech, the poet can suggest a wide variety of feelings and associations in very few words. The phrase "I wandered lonely as a cloud" is a **simile,** a comparison between two unlike items that includes *like* or *as.* When an imaginative comparison between two unlike items does not include *like* or *as*—that is, when it says "a is b" rather than "a is like b"—it is a **metaphor.**

Accordingly, when the speaker in Adrienne Rich's "Living in Sin" (p. 662) speaks of "daylight coming / like a relentless milkman up the stairs," she is using a strikingly original simile to suggest that daylight brings not the conventional associations of promise and awakening, but rather a stale, never-ending routine that is greeted without enthusiasm. This idea is consistent with the rest of the poem, an account of an unhappy relationship. However, when the speaker in Audre Lorde's poem says "Rooming houses are old women" (p. 705), she uses a metaphor, equating two elements to stress their common associations with emptiness, transience, and hopelessness. In addition, by identifying rooming houses as old women, Lorde is using **personification,** a special kind of comparison, closely related to metaphor, that gives life or human characteristics to inanimate objects or abstract ideas.

Sometimes, as in Wordsworth's "I wandered lonely as a cloud," a single brief simile or metaphor can be appreciated for what it communicates on its own. At other times, however, a simile or metaphor may be one of several related figures of speech that work together to communicate a poem's meaning. The following poem, for example, presents a series of related similes and metaphors. Together, they suggest the depth of the problem the poem explores in a manner that each individual simile or metaphor could not do alone.

M A R G A R E T   A T W O O D
(1939–   )

Death of a Young Son by Drowning
(1970)

> He, who navigated with success
> the dangerous river of his own birth
> once more set forth
>
> on a voyage of discovery
> 5 into the land I floated on
> but could not touch to claim.
>
> His feet slid on the bank,
> the currents took him;
> he swirled with ice and trees in the swollen water

10 and plunged into distant regions,
his head a bathysphere;
through his eyes' thin glass bubbles

he looked out, reckless adventurer
on a landscape stranger than Uranus
15 we have all been to and some remember.

There was an accident; the air locked,
he was hung in the river like a heart;
they retrieved the swamped body,

cairn of my plans and future charts,
20 with poles and hooks
from among the nudging logs.

It was spring, the sun kept shining, the new grass
lept to solidity;
my hands glistened with details.

25 After the long trip I was tired of waves.
My foot hit rock. The dreamed sails
collapsed, ragged.

I planted him in this country
like a flag.

Margaret Atwood uses several similes and metaphors to express the reaction of her speaker to the death of a son. Overall the poem uses the image of a voyage to depict the child's movement from life to death. A "dangerous river" (2) is a metaphor for the birth canal, which the child successfully navigates, but once out in the world, the child enters into a "voyage of discovery" (4) that will culminate in his death in a literal river. His head is a "bathysphere" (11) in his voyage to death, a voyage through a "landscape stranger than Uranus" (14). The figures of speech develop the idea of the strange journey from life to death, emphasizing death's inevitability while contrasting the river of life with the river of death. The final simile of the poem, "I planted him in this country / like a flag" (28–29), identifies the cost of becoming a part of the new country. The son's death and burial ties the parent to the land in a way that had not been considered, a way that is laden with grief. The sense of loss is heightened by the figures of speech.

Sometimes a single *extended simile* or *extended metaphor* is developed throughout a poem. The poem that follows, for example, develops an extended simile, comparing a poet to an acrobat.

LAWRENCE FERLINGHETTI
(1919–)

Constantly Risking Absurdity

(1958)

Constantly risking absurdity
　　　　　　　　　and death
　　　　　whenever he performs
　　　　　　　　above the heads
5　　　　　　　　　　　　of his audience
　　the poet like an acrobat
　　　　　　　climbs on rime
　　　　　　　to a high wire of his own making
　　and balancing on eyebeams
10　　　　　　　　above a sea of faces
　　　　　　paces his way
　　　　　　to the other side of day
　　　performing entrechats
　　　　　　　and sleight-of-foot tricks
15　and other high theatrics
　　　　　　　and all without mistaking
　　　　　any thing
　　　　　　for what it may not be

　　　For he's the super realist
20　　　　　　　　who must perforce perceive
　　　　taut truth
　　　　　　before the taking of each stance or step
　　in his supposed advance
　　　　　　　toward that still higher perch
25　where Beauty stands and waits
　　　　　　　with gravity
　　　　　　　　to start her death-defying leap

　　And he
　　　　a little charleychaplin man
30　　　　　　who may or may not catch
　　her fair eternal form
　　　　　　spreadeagled in the empty air
　　of existence

In his extended comparison between a poet and an acrobat, Ferlinghetti
characterizes the poet as a kind of all-purpose circus performer, at once
swinging recklessly on a trapeze and balancing carefully on a tightrope.

What the poem suggests is that the poet, like an acrobat, works hard at his craft but manages to make it all look easy. Something of an exhibitionist, the poet is innovative and creative, taking impossible chances yet also building on traditional skills in his quest for truth and beauty. Moreover, like an acrobat, the poet is balanced "on eyebeams / above a sea of faces," for he too depends on audience reaction to help him keep his performance focused. The poet may be "the super realist," but he also has plenty of playful tricks up his sleeve: "entrechats / and sleight-of-foot tricks / and other high theatrics," including puns ("above the heads / of his audience"), unexpected rhyme ("climbs on rime"), alliteration ("taut truth"), coinages ("a little charleychaplin man"), and all the other linguistic acrobatics available to poets. (Even the arrangement of the poem's lines on the page suggests the acrobatics it describes.) Like these tricks, the poem's central simile is a whimsical one, perhaps suggesting that Ferlinghetti is poking fun at poets who take their craft too seriously. In any case, the simile helps him to illustrate the acrobatic possibilities of language in a fresh and original manner.

The following poem develops an extended metaphor, personifying rooming houses as old women.

❖ ❖ ❖

AUDRE LORDE
(1934–1992)

Rooming Houses Are Old Women
(1968)

Rooming houses are old women
rocking dark windows into their whens
waiting incomplete circles
rocking
5 rent office to stoop to
community bathrooms to gas rings and
under-bed boxes of once useful garbage
city issued with a twice monthly check
and the young men next door
10 with their loud midnight parties
and fishy rings left in the bathtub
no longer arouse them
from midnight to mealtime no stops inbetween
light breaking to pass through jumbled up windows
15 and who was it who married the widow that Buzzie's son messed with?

To Welfare and insult form the slow shuffle
from dayswork to shopping bags
heavy with leftovers

Rooming houses
20 are old women waiting
   searching
   through darkening windows
   the end or beginning of agony
   old women seen through half-ajar doors
25 hoping
   they are not waiting
   but being
   the entrance to somewhere
   unknown and desired
30 but not new.

So closely does Lorde equate rooming houses and women in this poem that at times it is difficult to tell which of the two is actually the poem's subject. Despite the poem's assertion, rooming houses are *not* old women; however, they are *comparable to* the old women who live there, because their walls enclose a lifetime of disappointments as well as the physical detritus of life. Like the old women, rooming houses are in decline, rocking away their remaining years. Like the houses they inhabit, these women's boundaries are fixed—"rent office to stoop to / community bathrooms to gas rings"—and their hopes and expectations are few. They are surrounded by other people's loud parties, but their own lives have been reduced to a "slow shuffle" to nowhere, a hopeless, frightened—and perhaps pointless—"waiting / searching." Over time, the women and the places in which they live have become one. By using an unexpected comparison between two seemingly unrelated entities, the poem illuminates both the essence of the rooming houses and the essence of their elderly occupants.

❖ Poems for Further Reading: Simile, Metaphor, and Personification

ROBERT BURNS
(1759–1796)

Oh, My Love Is like a Red, Red Rose
(1796)

Oh, my love is like a red, red rose
   That's newly sprung in June;
My love is like the melody
   That's sweetly played in tune.

5 So fair art thou, my bonny lass,
    So deep in love am I;
And I will love thee still, my dear,
    Till a' the seas gang[1] dry.

Till a' the seas gang dry, my dear,
10   And the rocks melt wi' the sun;
And I will love thee still, my dear,
    While the sands o' life shall run.

And fare thee weel, my only love!
    And fare thee weel awhile!
15 And I will come again, my love
    Though it were ten thousand mile.

READING AND REACTING

1. Why does the speaker compare his love to a rose? What other simile is used in the poem? For what purpose is it used?
2. Why do you suppose Burns begins his poem with similes? Would moving them to the end change the poem's impact?
3. Where does the speaker seem to exaggerate the extent of his love? Why does he exaggerate? Do you think this exaggeration weakens the effectiveness of the poem? Explain.

Related Works: "Araby" (p. 267), "My Mistress' Eyes Are Nothing like the Sun" (p. 580), "To His Coy Mistress" (p. 719)

⟩ ◇ ⟩

PAT LOWTHER
(1935–1975)

Wanting
(1974)

Wanting
to be broken
utterly
split apart with a mighty tearing
5 like an apple broken
to unfold
the delicate open veined petal pattern
inside the fruit

I am arrogant
10 knowing
what I can do
for a man

---

[1] Go.

I am arrogant
for fear
15 I may be broken
utterly open
and he not see
the flower shape of me

READING AND REACTING

1. Explain the use of simile in the first stanza and metaphor in the last. What two elements make up each figure of speech? How are the two elements in each pair alike?
2. What is the effect of the repetition of the line "I am arrogant"? How does that thought fit with the speaker's desire "to be broken"? What figure of speech is used when the speaker says she is "[w]anting / to be broken"?
3. **JOURNAL ENTRY** What do you think about the sexual implications of the speaker's desire? Why is the speaker fearful that the man will "not see / the flower shape of [her]"?

Related Works: "A Rose for Emily" (p. 90), "General Review of the Sex Situation" (p. 583), "Bartok and the Geranium" (p. 792)

◈ ◈ ◈

RANDALL JARRELL
(1914–1965)

The Death of the Ball Turret Gunner
(1945)

From my mother's sleep I fell into the State
And I hunched in its belly till my wet fur froze.
Six miles from earth, loosed from its dream of life,
I woke to black flak and the nightmare fighters.
5 When I died they washed me out of the turret with a hose.

READING AND REACTING

1. Who is the speaker? To what does he compare himself in the poem's first two lines? What words establish this comparison?
2. Contrast the speaker's actual identity with the one he creates for himself in lines 1–2. What elements of his actual situation do you think lead him to characterize himself as he does in these lines?
3. **JOURNAL ENTRY** Both this poem and "Dulce et Decorum Est" (p. 695) use figurative language to describe the horrors of war. Which poem has a greater impact on you? How does the poem's figurative language contribute to this impact?

4. **CRITICAL PERSPECTIVE** In a 1974 article, Frances Ferguson criticizes "The Death of the Ball Turret Gunner," arguing that the poem "thoroughly manifests the lack of a middle between the gunner's birth and his death. . . . Because the poem presents a man who seems to have lived in order to die, we forget the fiction that he must have lived." However, in a 1978 explication, Patrick J. Horner writes that the "manipulation of time reveals the stunning brevity of the gunner's waking life and the State's total disregard for that phenomenon. . . . Because of the telescoping of time, . . . [the poem] resonates with powerful feeling."

With which critic do you agree? That is, do you see the "lack of a middle" as a positive or negative quality of this poem?

Related Works: "An Irish Airman Foresees His Death" (p. 588), "How I Spent the Year Listening to the Ten O'Clock News" (p. 596), "Dulce et Decorum Est" (p. 695)

◊ ◊ ◊

MARGE PIERCY
(1936–   )

The Secretary Chant
(1973)

My hips are a desk.
From my ears hang
chains of paper clips.
Rubber bands form my hair.
5 My breasts are wells of mimeograph ink.
My feet bear casters.
Buzz. Click.
My head is a badly organized file.
My head is a switchboard
10 where crossed lines crackle.
Press my fingers
and in my eyes appear
credit and debit.
Zing. Tinkle.
15 My navel is a reject button.
From my mouth issue canceled reams.
Swollen, heavy, rectangular
I am about to be delivered
of a baby
20 Xerox machine.
File me under W
because I wonce
was
a woman.

READING AND REACTING

1. Examine each of the poem's figures of speech. Do they all make reasonable comparisons, or are some far-fetched or hard to visualize? Explain the relationship between the secretary and each item with which she is compared.

2. **JOURNAL ENTRY** Using as many metaphors and similes as you can, write a "chant" about a job you have held.

3. **CRITICAL PERSPECTIVE** In a review of a recent collection of Piercy's poetry, feminist critic Sandra Gilbert notes instances of "a kind of bombast" (pompous language) and remarks, "As most poets realize, political verse is almost the hardest kind to write."

   In what sense can "The Secretary Chant" be seen as "political verse"? Do you think Piercy successfully achieves her political purpose, or does she undercut it with "bombast"?

Related Works: "The Story of an Hour" (p. 77), "A Garden of Her Own" (p. 202), "Women" (p. 786), "The Stenographers" (p. 795)

◊ ◊ ◊

JOHN DONNE
(1572–1631)

A Valediction:
Forbidding Mourning
(1611)

As virtuous men pass mildly away,
    And whisper to their souls to go,
Whilst some of their sad friends do say
    The breath goes now, and some say no:

5 So let us melt, and make no noise,
    No tear-floods, nor sigh-tempests move;
'Twere profanation of our joys
    To tell the laity[1] our love.

Moving of th' earth brings harms and fears;
10   Men reckon what it did and meant;
But trepidation of the spheres,
    Though greater far, is innocent.

Dull sublunary lovers' love
    (Whose soul is sense) cannot admit
15 Absence, because it doth remove
    Those things which elemented it.

---

[1] Here, "common people."

But we, by a love so much refined
     That ourselves know not what it is,
Inter-assurèd of the mind,
20   Care less, eyes, lips, and hands to miss.

Our two souls, therefore, which are one,
     Though I must go, endure not yet
A breach, but an expansion,
     Like gold to airy thinness beat.

25 If they be two, they are two so
     As stiff twin compasses[2] are two:
Thy soul, the fixed foot, makes no show
     To move, but doth, if th' other do.

And though it in the center sit,
30   Yet when the other far doth roam,
It leans and harkens after it,
     And grows erect as that comes home.

Such wilt thou be to me, who must,
     Like th' other foot, obliquely run;
35 Thy firmness makes my circle just,[3]
     And makes me end where I begun.

READING AND REACTING

1. Beginning with line 25, the poem develops an extended
    metaphor, called a **conceit,** which compares the speaker and his
    loved one to "twin compasses" (26), attached and yet separate.
    Why is the compass an especially apt metaphor? What qualities
    of the compass does the poet emphasize?

2. The poem uses other figures of speech to characterize both the
    lovers' union and their separation. To what other events does the
    speaker compare his separation from his loved one? To what
    other elements does he compare their attachment? Do you think
    these comparisons are effective?

3. **JOURNAL ENTRY** To what other object could Donne have com-
    pared his loved one and himself? Explain the logic of the
    extended metaphor you suggest.

4. **CRITICAL PERSPECTIVE** In *John Donne and the Metaphysical
    Poets* (1970), Judah Stampfer writes of this poem's "thin, dry tex-
    ture, its stanzas of pinched music," noting that its form "has too
    clipped a brevity to qualify as a song" and that its "music wobbles
    on a dry, measured beat." Yet, he argues, "the poem comes

---

[2] The reference here is to the V-shaped instrument used to draw circles, not to the device
used to determine direction.
[3] Perfect.

choked with emotional power" because "the speaker reads as a naturally reticent man, leaving his beloved in uncertainty and deep trouble." Stampfer concludes, "Easy self-expression here would be self-indulgent, if not reprehensible. . . . For all his careful dignity, we feel a heart is breaking here."

Do you find such emotional power in this highly intellectual poem?

Related Works: "How Do I Love Thee?" (p. 581), "To My Dear and Loving Husband" (p. 718), "The Cinnamon Peeler" (p. 868), *A Doll House* (p. 1013)

HYPERBOLE AND UNDERSTATEMENT
◊ ◊ ◊

Two additional kinds of figurative language, *hyperbole* and *understatement*, also give poets opportunities to suggest meaning beyond the literal level of language.

Hyperbole is intentional exaggeration—saying more than is actually meant. In the poem "Oh, My Love Is like a Red, Red Rose" (p. 706), when the speaker says that he will love his lady until all the seas go dry, he is using hyperbole. **Understatement** is just the opposite—saying less than is meant. When the speaker in the poem "Fire and Ice" (p. 632), weighing two equally grim alternatives for the end of the world, says that "for destruction ice / Is also great / And would suffice," he is using understatement. In both cases, poets rely on their readers to understand that their words are not to be taken literally.

By using hyperbole and understatement, poets attract readers' attention. For example, poets can use hyperbole to convey exaggerated anger or graphic images of horror—and to ridicule and satirize as well as to inflame and shock. With understatement, poets can convey the same kind of powerful emotions subtly, without artifice or embellishment, thereby leading readers to look more closely than they would otherwise do.

The emotionally charged poem that follows uses hyperbole to attract attention, conveying anger and bitterness that seem almost beyond the power of words.

◊ ◊ ◊

SYLVIA PLATH
(1932–1963)

Daddy
(1965)

You do not do, you do not do
Any more, black shoe
In which I have lived like a foot

For thirty years, poor and white,
5 Barely daring to breathe or Achoo.

Daddy, I have had to kill you.
You died before I had time—
Marble-heavy, a bag full of God,
Ghastly statue with one grey toe
10 Big as a Frisco seal

And a head in the freakish Atlantic
Where it pours bean green over blue
In the waters off beautiful Nauset.
I used to pray to recover you.
15 Ach, du.[1]

In the German tongue, in the Polish town[2]
Scraped flat by the roller
Of wars, wars, wars.
But the name of the town is common.
20 My Polack friend

Says there are a dozen or two.
So I never could tell where you
Put your foot, your root,
I never could talk to you.
25 The tongue stuck in my jaw.

It stuck in a barb wire snare.
Ich, ich, ich, ich,[3]
I could hardly speak.
I thought every German was you.
30 And the language obscene

An engine, an engine
Chuffing me off like a Jew.
A Jew to Dachau, Auschwitz, Belsen.[4]
I began to talk like a Jew.
35 I think I may well be a Jew.

The snows of the Tyrol, the clear beer of Vienna
Are not very pure or true.
With my gypsy ancestress and my weird luck
And my Taroc pack and my Taroc pack
40 I may be a bit of a Jew.

---

[1] Ah, you. (German)

[2] Grabôw, where Plath's father was born.

[3] I. (German)

[4] Nazi concentration camps.

I have always been scared of *you*,
With your Luftwaffe,[5] your gobbledygoo.
And your neat moustache
And your Aryan eye, bright blue.
45 Panzer[6]-man, panzer-man, O You—

Not God but a swastika
So black no sky could squeak through.
Every woman adores a Fascist,
The boot in the face, the brute
50 Brute heart of a brute like you.

You stand at the blackboard, daddy,
In the picture I have of you,
A cleft in your chin instead of your foot
But no less a devil for that, no not
55 Any less the black man who

Bit my pretty red heart in two.
I was ten when they buried you.
At twenty I tried to die
And get back, back, back to you.
60 I thought even the bones would do.

But they pulled me out of the sack,
And they stuck me together with glue.
And then I knew what to do.
I made a model of you,
65 A man in black with a Meinkampf[7] look

And a love of the rack and the screw.
And I said I do, I do.
So daddy, I'm finally through.
The black telephone's off at the root,
70 The voices just can't worm through.

If I've killed one man, I've killed two—
The vampire who said he was you
And drank my blood for a year,
Seven years, if you want to know.
75 Daddy, you can lie back now.

There's a stake in your fat black heart
And the villagers never liked you.
They are dancing and stamping on you.
They always *knew* it was you.
80 Daddy, daddy, you bastard, I'm through.

---

[5] The German air force.
[6] Protected by armour. The Panzer division was the German armoured division.
[7] *Mein Kampf* (My Struggle) is Adolf Hitler's autobiography.

In her anger and frustration, the speaker sees herself as a helpless victim—a foot entrapped in a shoe, a Jew in a concentration camp—of her father's (and, later, her husband's) absolute tyranny. Thus, her hated father is characterized as a "black shoe," "a bag full of God," a "ghastly statue," and, eventually, a Nazi, a torturer, the devil, a vampire. The poem "Daddy" is widely accepted by scholars as autobiographical, and the fact that Plath's own father was actually neither a Nazi nor a sadist (nor, obviously, the devil or a vampire) makes it clear that the figurative comparisons in the poem are wildly exaggerated. Even so, they may convey the poet's true feelings toward her father—and, perhaps, toward the patriarchal society in which she lived.

Plath uses hyperbole as the medium through which to communicate these emotions to readers who she knows cannot possibly feel the way she does. Her purpose, therefore, is not just to shock but also to enlighten, to persuade, and perhaps even to empower her readers. Throughout the poem, the inflammatory language is set in ironic opposition to the childish, affectionate term "Daddy"—most strikingly in the last line's choked out "Daddy, daddy, you bastard, I'm through." The result of the exaggerated rhetoric is a poem that is vivid and shocking. And, although some might believe that Plath's almost wild exaggeration undermines the poem's impact, others would argue that the powerful figurative language is necessary to convey the extent of the speaker's rage.

Like "Daddy," the next poem presents a situation whose emotional impact is strong. In this case, however, the poet does not use emotional language; instead, he uses understatement, presenting the events without embellishment.

◆ ◆ ◆

AL PURDY
(1918–2000)

Lament for the Dorsets
(1968)
(Eskimos extinct in the 14th century A.D.)[1]

Animal bones and some mossy tent rings
scrapers and spearheads   carved ivory swans
all that remains of the Dorset giants
who drove the Vikings back to their long ships
5 talked to spirits of earth and water
—a picture of terrifying old men
so large they broke the backs of bears

---

[1] In about A.D. 1000, the Dorset people were displaced from most of the Arctic regions by Thule Inuit from Alaska, but they continued to live in northern Quebec and Labrador until about 1500, when they disappeared.

so small they lurk behind bone rafters
in the brain of modern hunters
10 among good thoughts and warm things
and come out at night
to spit on the stars

The big men with clever fingers
who had no dogs and hauled their sleds
15 over the frozen northern oceans
awkward giants
                    killers of seal
they couldn't compete with little men
who came from the west with dogs
20 Or else in a warm climatic cycle
the seals went back to cold waters
and the puzzled Dorsets scratched their heads
with hairy thumbs around 1350 A.D.
—couldn't figure it out
25 went around saying to each other
plaintively
          "What's wrong? What happened?
          Where are the seals gone?"
And died

30 Twentieth-century people
apartment dwellers
executives of neon death
warmakers with things that explode
— they have never imagined us in their future
35 how could we imagine them in the past
squatting among the moving glaciers
six hundred years ago
with glowing lamps?
As remote or nearly
40 as the trilobites and swamps
when coal became
or the last great reptile hissed
at a mammal the size of a mouse
that squeaked and fled

45 Did they ever realize at all
what was happening to them?
Some old hunter with one lame leg
a bear had chewed
sitting in a caribou-skin tent
50 — the last Dorset?

Let's say his name was Kudluk
and watch him sitting there
carving 2-inch ivory swans
for a dead grand-daughter
55 taking them out of his mind
the places in his mind
where pictures are
He selects a sharp stone tool
to gouge a parallel pattern of lines
60 on both sides of the swan
holding it with his left hand
bearing down and transmitting
his body's weight
from brain to arm and right hand
65 and one of his thoughts
turns to ivory
The carving is laid aside
in beginning darkness
at the end of hunger
70 and after a while wind
blows down the tent and snow
begins to cover him

After 600 years
the ivory thought
75 is still warm

Although "Lament for the Dorsets" relates a tragic event—the loss of an entire race of people—the tone of the poem is inquisitive and curious more than sad. The speaker could have used inflated language and hyperbole to criticize the death of the Dorsets and the subsequent effect on future generations. The reason for the destruction of the Dorsets is unclear. Maybe the men "who came from the west" were better hunters, or maybe the Dorsets were caught in a climatic change they could not cope with. As the seals disappeared, so did the Dorsets. Perhaps that is what happened. Purdy's speaker never gives a definitive reason. Instead, the speaker plays on the idea of the people of the past never imagining what life would be like in the future, just as we cannot really know what life was like for the Dorsets.

Throughout the poem, events are expressed with a sense of wonder and mystery. The speaker imagines the last Dorset alone in his tent "carving 2-inch ivory swans / for a dead grand-daughter" (53–54). With this single image, the poem bridges the gap of centuries and shows a man making something—out of love—for his granddaughter. Initially the poem focuses on the difference between the Dorsets and us; by the end, the poem focuses on the similarity of human connection and love. And the poem shows the lasting value of a work of art: "After 600 years / the ivory thought / is still warm"; evidently the love of the last Dorset transcends his life, and Purdy shows this magnificence in a quiet, controlled way. A dead granddaughter's toy joins human beings across the ages. The intensity of the feeling is made greater by the simplicity with which it is presented.

❖ POEMS FOR FURTHER READING: HYPERBOLE AND UNDERSTATEMENT

ANNE BRADSTREET
(1612?–1672)

To My Dear and Loving Husband
(1678)

If ever two were one, then surely we.
If ever man were lov'd by wife, then thee;
If ever wife was happy in a man,
Compare with me ye women if you can.
5 I prize thy love more than whole Mines of gold,
Or all the riches that the East doth hold.
My love is such that Rivers cannot quench,
Nor ought but love from thee, give recompense.
Thy love is such I can no way repay,
10 The heavens reward thee manifold I pray.
Then while we live, in love let's so persever,
That when we live no more, we may live ever.

READING AND REACTING

1. Review the claims the poem's speaker makes about her husband in lines 5–8. Are such exaggerated declarations of love necessary, or would the rest of the poem be sufficient to convey the extent of her devotion to her husband?

2. **JOURNAL ENTRY** Compare this poem's declarations of love to those of John Donne's speaker in "A Valediction: Forbidding Mourning" (p. 710). Which speaker do you believe is more convincing? Why?

   Related Works: "A Rose for Emily" (p. 90), "Stop All the Clocks, Cut Off the Telephone" (p. 582), "To His Coy Mistress" (p. 719)

ANDREW MARVELL
(1621–1678)

To His Coy Mistress
(1681)

Had we but world enough and time,
This coyness, lady, were no crime.
We would sit down and think which way
To walk, and pass our long love's day.
5 Thou by the Indian Ganges' side
Should'st rubies find; I by the tide
Of Humber[1] would complain. I would
Love you ten years before the Flood,
And you should, if you please, refuse
10 Till the conversion of the Jews.
My vegetable love should grow
Vaster than empires, and more slow.
An hundred years should go to praise
Thine eyes, and on thy forehead gaze,
15 Two hundred to adore each breast,
But thirty thousand to the rest.
An age at least to every part,
And the last age should show your heart.
For, lady, you deserve this state,
20 Nor would I love at lower rate.
　　But at my back I always hear
Time's wingèd chariot hurrying near,
And yonder all before us lie
Deserts of vast eternity.
25 Thy beauty shall no more be found,
Nor in thy marble vault shall sound
My echoing song; then worms shall try
That long preserved virginity,
And your quaint honor turn to dust,
30 And into ashes all my lust.
The grave's a fine and private place,
But none, I think, do there embrace.
　　Now therefore, while the youthful hue
Sits on thy skin like morning glew[2]
35 And while thy willing soul transpires

---

[1] An estuary in the east coast of England.
[2] Dew.

> At every pore with instant fires,
> Now let us sport us while we may;
> And now, like amorous birds of prey,
> Rather at once our time devour
> 40 Than languish in his slow-chapped[3] power.
> Let us roll all our strength and all
> Our sweetness up into one ball
> And tear our pleasures with rough strife
> Thorough the iron gates of life.
> 45 Thus, though we cannot make our sun
> Stand still, yet we will make him run.

READING AND REACTING

1. In this poem, Marvell's speaker sets out to convince a reluctant woman to become his lover. In order to make his case more convincing, he uses hyperbole, exaggerating time periods, sizes, spaces, and the possible fate of the woman, should she refuse him. Identify as many examples of hyperbole as you can.

2. The tone of "To His Coy Mistress" is more whimsical than serious. Given this tone, what do you see as the purpose of Marvell's use of hyperbole?

3. **JOURNAL ENTRY** Using contemporary prose, paraphrase the first four lines of the poem. Then, beginning with the word *But,* write a few additional sentences, continuing the argument Marvell's speaker makes.

4. **CRITICAL PERSPECTIVE** In his poem "The Definition of Love," Marvell laments love that is kept apart by fate. He writes:

   > For Fate with jealous eye does see
   > Two perfect loves, nor lets them close;
   > Their union would her ruin be,
   > And her tyrannic pow'r depose.

   How does Marvell propose to compensate for Fate's determination to keep true love apart in "To His Coy Mistress"?

Related Works: "The Passionate Shepherd to His Love" (p. 578), "To the Virgins, to Make Much of Time" (p. 639), "Wanting" (p. 707), *The Brute* (p. 1081)

---

[3] Slowly crushing.

ROBERT FROST
(1874–1963)

"Out, Out—"
(1916)

The buzz saw snarled and rattled in the yard
And made dust and dropped stove-length sticks of wood,
Sweet-scented stuff when the breeze drew across it.
And from there those that lifted eyes could count
5 Five mountain ranges one behind the other
Under the sunset far into Vermont.
And the saw snarled and rattled, snarled and rattled,
As it ran light, or had to bear a load.
And nothing happened: day was all but done.
10 Call it a day, I wish they might have said
To please the boy by giving him the half hour
That a boy counts so much when saved from work.
His sister stood beside them in her apron
To tell them "Supper." At the word, the saw,
15 As if to prove saws knew what supper meant,
Leaped out at the boy's hand, or seemed to leap—
He must have given the hand. However it was,
Neither refused the meeting. But the hand!
The boy's first outcry was a rueful laugh,
20 As he swung toward them holding up the hand
Half in appeal, but half as if to keep
The life from spilling. Then the boy saw all—
Since he was old enough to know, big boy
Doing a man's work, though a child at heart—
25 He saw all spoiled. "Don't let him cut my hand off—
The doctor, when he comes. Don't let him, sister!"
So. But the hand was gone already.
The doctor put him in the dark of ether.
He lay and puffed his lips out with his breath.
30 And then—the watcher at his pulse took fright.
No one believed. They listened at his heart.
Little—less—nothing!—and that ended it.
No more to build on there. And they, since they
Were not the one dead, turned to their affairs.

READING AND REACTING

1. The poem's title is an **allusion** to a passage in Shakespeare's
   Macbeth (5.5.23–28) that attacks the brevity and meaninglessness
   of life in very emotional terms:

> "Out, out brief candle!
> Life's but a walking shadow, a poor player,
> That struts and frets his hour upon the stage
> And then is heard no more. It is a tale
> Told by an idiot, full of sound and fury,
> Signifying nothing."

What idea do you think Frost wants to convey through the title "Out, Out—"?

2. Explain why each of the following qualifies as understatement:

    "Neither refused the meeting." (18)

    "He saw all spoiled." (25)

    ". . . that ended it." (32)

    "No more to build on there." (33)

    Can you identify any other examples of understatement in the poem?

3. **Journal Entry** Do you think the poem's impact is strengthened or weakened by its understated tone? Why?

4. **Critical Perspective** In an essay on Frost in his 1985 book *Affirming Limits*, Robert Pack focuses on the single word "So" in line 27 of "Out, Out—":

    > For a moment, his narration is reduced to the impotent word "So," and in that minimal word all his restrained grief is held. . . . That "So" is the narrator's cry of bearing witness to a story that must be what it is in a scene he cannot enter. He cannot rescue or protect the boy. . . . In the poem's sense of human helplessness in an indifferent universe, we are all "watchers," and what we see is death without redemption, "signifying nothing." So. So? So! How shall we read that enigmatic word?

    How do you read this "enigmatic word" in the poem?

Related Works: "The Lottery" (p. 319), "What Were They Like?" (p. 591), "Hope" (p. 643), "The Death of the Ball Turret Gunner" (p. 708)

◊ ◊ ◊

DONALD HALL
(1928–   )

My Son, My Executioner
(1955)

> My son, my executioner,
> I take you in my arms,
> Quiet and small and just astir,
> And whom my body warms.

5 Sweet death, small son, our instrument
Of immortality,
Your cries and hungers document
Our bodily decay.

We twenty-five and twenty-two,
10   Who seemed to live forever,
Observe enduring life in you
And start to die together.

READING AND REACTING

1. Because the speaker is a young man holding his newborn son in his arms, the equation in line 1 comes as a shock. What is Hall's purpose in opening with such a startling statement?
2. In what sense is the comparison between baby and executioner a valid one? Could you argue that, given the underlying similarities between the two, Hall is *not* using hyperbole? Explain.

Related Works: "That Time of Year Thou Mayst in Me Behold" (p. 561), "Cornflowers & Saffron Robes Belittle the Effort" (p. 893), "Sailing to Byzantium" (p. 899)

MARGARET ATWOOD
(1939–   )

You Fit into Me
(1971)

you fit into me
like a hook into an eye

a fish hook
an open eye

READING AND REACTING

1. What connotations does Atwood expect readers to associate with the phrase "you fit into me"? What does the speaker seem at first to mean by "like a hook into an eye" in line 2?
2. The speaker's shift to the brutal suggestions of lines 3 and 4 is calculated to shock readers. Does the use of hyperbole here have another purpose in the context of the poem? Explain.

Related Works: "A Rose for Emily" (p. 90), "Daddy" (p. 712), *A Doll House* (p. 1013)

METONYMY AND SYNECDOCHE

◇ ◇ ◇

Metonymy and synecdoche are two related figures of speech. **Metonymy** is the substitution of the name of one thing for the name of another thing that most readers associate with the first—for example, using *hired gun* to mean "paid assassin" or *suits* to mean "business executives." A specific kind of metonymy, called **synecdoche,** is the substitution of a part for the whole (for example, using *bread*—as in "Give us this day our daily bread"—to mean "food") or the whole for a part (for example, saying "You can take the boy out of Saskatchewan, but you can't take Saskatchewan [meaning its distinctive traits] out of the boy"). With metonymy and synecdoche, instead of describing something by saying it is like something else (as in simile) or by equating it with something else (as in metaphor), writers can characterize an object or concept by using a term that evokes it. The following poem illustrates the use of synecdoche.

◇ ◇ ◇

RICHARD LOVELACE
(1618–1658)

To Lucasta Going to the Wars
(1649)

Tell me not, Sweet, I am unkind
    That from the nunnery
Of thy chaste breast and quiet mind,
    To war and arms I fly.

5 True, a new mistress now I chase,
    The first foe in the field;
And with a stronger faith embrace
    A sword, a horse, a shield.

Yet this inconstancy is such
10   As you too shall adore;
I could not love thee, Dear, so much,
    Loved I not Honor more.

Here, Lovelace's use of synecdoche allows him to condense a number of complex ideas into a very few words. In line 3, when the speaker says that he is flying from his loved one's "chaste breast and quiet mind," he is using "breast" and "mind" to stand for all his loved one's physical and intellectual attributes. In line 8, when he says that he is embracing "A sword, a horse, a shield," he is using these three items to represent all the trappings of war—and, thus, to represent war itself.

❖ POEM FOR FURTHER READING: METONYMY AND SYNECDOCHE

ALICE WALKER
(1944–   )

Women
(1970)

They were women then
My mama's generation
Husky of voice—Stout of
Step
5 With fists as well as
Hands
How they battered down
Doors
And ironed
10 Starched white
Shirts
How they led
Armies
Headragged Generals
15 Across mined
Fields
Booby-trapped
Ditches
To discover books
20 Desks
A place for us
How they knew what we
Must know
Without knowing a page
25 Of it
Themselves.

APOSTROPHE
◊ ◊ ◊

With **apostrophe,** a poem's speaker addresses an absent person or thing—
for example, a historical or literary figure or even an inanimate object or an
abstract concept.

In the following poem, the speaker addresses a lover.

LEONARD COHEN
(1934–   )

Coming Back to You
(1984)

Maybe I'm still hurting,
I can't turn the other cheek.
But you know that I still love you;
it's just that I can't speak.
5 I looked for you in everyone
and they called me on that too;
I lived alone but I was only
coming back to you

They're shutting down the factory now
10 just when all the bills are due;
and the fields they're under lock and key
though the rain and the sun come through.
And springtime starts but then it stops
in the name of something new;
15 and all my senses rise against this
coming back to you

They're handing down my sentence now,
and I know what I must do:
another mile of silence while I'm
20 *coming back to you*

There are many in your life
and many still to be.
Since you are a shining light,
there's many that you'll see.
25 But I have to deal with envy
when you choose the precious few
who've left their pride on the other side of
coming back to you

Even in your arms I know
30 I'll never get it right;
even when you bend
to give me comfort in the night.
I've got to have your word on this
or none of it is true,
35 and all I've said was just instead of
coming back to you

Cohen's speaker verbalizes his love even though he is unable to say the words directly to his lover. The words eventually replace the action "*coming back to you*," and the pain of the speaker is eloquently expressed even as he denies his ability to articulate his love.

❖ POEM FOR FURTHER READING: APOSTROPHE

❖ ❖ ❖

ALLEN GINSBERG
(1926–1997)

A Supermarket in California
(1956)

What thoughts I have of you tonight, Walt Whitman,[1] for I
walked down the sidestreets under the trees with a headache
self-conscious looking at the full moon.
    In my hungry fatigue, and shopping for images, I went
5   into the neon fruit supermarket, dreaming of your
enumerations!
    What peaches and what penumbras! Whole families
shopping at night! Aisles full of husbands! Wives in the
avocados, babies in the tomatoes!—and you, Garcia Lorca,[2]
10   what were you doing down by the watermelons?

    I saw you, Walt Whitman, childless, lonely old grubber,
poking among the meats in the refrigerator and eyeing the
grocery boys.[3]
    I heard you asking questions of each: Who killed the pork
15   chops? What price bananas? Are you my Angel?
    I wandered in and out of the brilliant stacks of cans
following you, and followed in my imagination by the store
detective.
    We strode down the open corridors together in our
20   solitary fancy tasting artichokes, possessing every frozen
delicacy, and never passing the cashier.

---

[1] *Walt Whitman:* American poet (1819–92) whose poems frequently praise the common-place and often contain lengthy "enumerations."

[2] *Federico García Lorca:* Spanish poet and dramatist (1899–1936).

[3] *eyeing the grocery boys:* Whitman's sexual orientation is the subject of much debate. Ginsberg is suggesting here that Whitman was homosexual.

Where are we going, Walt Whitman? The doors close in an
hour. Which way does your beard point tonight?
(I touch your book[4] and dream of our odyssey in the
25 supermarket and feel absurd.)
Will we walk all night through solitary streets? The trees add
shade to shade, lights out in the houses, we'll both be lonely.
Will we stroll dreaming of the lost America of love past
blue automobiles in driveways, home to our silent cottage?
30 Ah, dear father, graybeard, lonely old courage-teacher,
what America did you have when Charon[5] quit poling his ferry
and you got out on a smoking bank and stood watching the
boat disappear on the black waters of Lethe?[6]

Reading and Reacting

1. In this poem, Ginsberg's speaker wanders through the aisles of a
   supermarket, speaking to the nineteenth-century poet Walt
   Whitman and asking Whitman a series of questions. Why do you
   think the speaker addresses Whitman? What kinds of answers do
   you think he is looking for?
2. In paragraph 2, the speaker says he is "shopping for images."
   What does he mean? Why does he look for these images in a
   supermarket? Does he find them?
3. Is this poem about supermarkets? About Walt Whitman? About
   poetry? About love? About America? What do you see as its primary theme? Why?
4. **Journal Entry** Does the incongruous image of the respected poet
   "poking among the meats" (paragraph 4) in the supermarket
   strengthen the poem's impact, or does it undercut any serious
   "message" the poem might have? Explain.
5. **Critical Perspective** The critic Leslie Fiedler discusses some of
   the ways in which Ginsberg's style resembles that of Walt
   Whitman:

   > Everything about Ginsberg's style resembles that of Walt
   > Whitman: his meter is resolutely anti-iambic, his line groupings
   > stubbornly anti-stanzaic, his diction aggressively colloquial and
   > American, his voice public.

   Can you identify ways in which the poem is "American" and
   "public"?

---

[4] *your book: Leaves of Grass.*

[5] *Charon:* In Greek mythology, the ferryman who transported the dead over the river Styx
to Hades.

[6] *Lethe:* In Greek mythology, the river of forgetfulness (one of five rivers in Hades).

✓ CHECKLIST: WRITING ABOUT FIGURES OF SPEECH

✓ Are any figures of speech present in the poem? Identify each example of simile, metaphor, personification, hyperbole, understatement, metonymy, synecdoche, and apostrophe.

✓ What two elements are being compared in each use of simile, metaphor, and personification? Is the comparison logical? What characteristics are shared by the two items being compared?

✓ How do figures of speech contribute to the impact of the poem as a whole?

✓ Does the poet use hyperbole? Why? For example, is it used to move or to shock readers, or is its use intended to produce a humorous or satirical effect?

✓ Does the poet use understatement? For what purpose? Would more straightforward language be more effective?

✓ In metonymy and synecdoche, what item is being substituted for another? What purpose does the substitution serve?

✓ If the poem includes apostrophe, whom or what does the speaker address? What is accomplished through the use of apostrophe?

◈ WRITING SUGGESTIONS: FIGURES OF SPEECH

1. Various figures of speech are often used to portray characters in a poem. Choose two or three poems that focus on a single character—for example, "My Ledders" (p. 845), "Meditation on Tom Thomson" (p. 684), or "Richard Cory" (p. 877)—and explain how figures of speech are used to characterize each poem's central figure.

2. Write an essay in which you discuss the different ways poets use figures of speech to examine the nature of poetry itself. What kinds of figures of speech do poets use to describe their craft? (You might begin by reading the three poems about poetry that open Chapter 11.)

3. Write a letter replying to the speaker in a poem by Marvell, Bradstreet, Donne, or Burns that appears in this chapter. Use figurative language to express the depth of your love and the extent of your devotion.

4. Choose two or three poems that have a common subject—for example, love, nature, war, art, or mortality—and write a paper in which you draw some general conclusions about the relative effectiveness of the poems' use of figurative language to examine that subject.

5. Select a poem and a short story that treat the same subject matter, and write a paper in which you compare their use of figures of speech.

CHAPTER 17

Sound

◇ ◇ ◇

A primary pleasure in poetry is . . . the pleasure of saying something over for its own sweet sake and because it sounds just right. For myself, . . . the thing said over will not necessarily be A Great Thought, though great thoughts are not necessarily excluded either; it may be as near as not to meaningless, especially if one says it without much attention to its context. For instance, a riddling song has the refrain: Sing ninety-nine and ninety. I can remember being charmed enough with that to say it over and over to myself for days, without ever having a single thought about its meaning except for a certain bemused wonder about how different it was from singing a hundred and eighty-nine.

HOWARD NEMEROV, "Poetry and Meaning"

I've never taught a poetry writing class that has not suffered my reiteration of Duke Ellington's line: "It don't mean a thing if it ain't got that swing." How can you describe the feeling of reading a Roethke poem, . . . when the rhythm is so palpable it is as if the poem could be cupped in your hands? Those poems move great distances in meaning between sentences and yet they hold together, largely because of the sound. The same thing is operating in a song that makes you want to get up and dance.

MICHAEL RYAN, "On the Nature of Poetry"

The most obvious function of the line-break is rhythmic: it can record the slight (but meaningful) hesitations between word and word that are characteristic of the mind's dance among perceptions but which are not noted by grammatical punctuation. Regular punctuation is a part of regular sentence structure, that is, of the expression of completed thoughts; and this expression is typical of prose, even though prose is not at all times bound by its logic. But in poems one has the opportunity not only, as in expressive prose, to depart from the syntactic norm, but . . . to present the dynamics of perception *along with* its arrival at full expression. The line-break is a form of punctuation *additional* to the punctuation that forms part of the logic of completed thoughts.

DENISE LEVERTOV, "On the Function of Line"

◇ ◇ ◇

730

WALT WHITMAN
(1819–1892)

Had I the Choice[1]

Had I the choice to tally greatest bards,
To limn[2] their portraits, stately, beautiful, and emulate at will,
Homer with all his wars and warriors—Hector, Achilles, Ajax,
Or Shakespeare's woe-entangled Hamlet, Lear, Othello—Tennyson's
    fair ladies,
5 Meter or wit the best, or choice conceit to wield in perfect rhyme,
    delight of singers;
These, these, O sea, all these I'd gladly barter,
Would you the undulation of one wave, its trick to me transfer,
Or breathe one breath of yours upon my verse,
And leave its odor there.

RHYTHM

◊ ◊ ◊

Rhythm—the regular recurrence of sounds—is at the heart of all natural
phenomena: the beating of a heart, the lapping of waves against the shore,
the croaking of frogs on a summer's night, the whispering of wheat swaying
in the wind. In fact, even mechanical phenomena, such as the movement
of rush-hour traffic through a city's streets, have a kind of rhythm. Poetry,
which explores these phenomena, often tries to reflect the same rhythms.
Walt Whitman makes this point in "Had I the Choice" when he says that
he would gladly trade the "perfect rhyme" of Shakespeare for the ability to
reproduce "the undulation of one wave" in his verse.

    Effective public speakers frequently repeat key words and phrases to
create rhythm. For example, in his famous speech to Quebeckers during the
1980 Quebec referendum on sovereignty-association, the prime minister at
the time, Pierre Elliott Trudeau, repeats the phrase "Canada . . . our home
and native land," a line from our anthem, to illustrate the collective nature
of our belonging to Canada:

    Well, we won't let [Canada] die. Our answer is No to those who would
    kill it.
        We won't let this country die, this Canada, our home and native
    land, this Canada which really is, as our national anthem says, our

---

[1] Publication date is not available.
[2] To describe, depict.

home and native land. We are going to say to those who want us to stop being Canadians, we are going to say a resounding, an over-whelming No.

Poets too create rhythm by using repeated words and phrases, as Gwendolyn Brooks does in the poem that follows.

⟩ ⟩ ⟩

GWENDOLYN BROOKS
(1917–2000)

Sadie and Maud
(1945)

Maud went to college.
Sadie stayed at home.
Sadie scraped life
With a fine-tooth comb.

5 She didn't leave a tangle in.
Her comb found every strand.
Sadie was one of the livingest chits
In all the land.

Sadie bore two babies
10 Under her maiden name.
Maud and Ma and Papa
Nearly died of shame.

When Sadie said her last so-long
Her girls struck out from home.
15 (Sadie had left as heritage
Her fine-tooth comb.)

Maud, who went to college,
Is a thin brown mouse.
She is living all alone
20 In this old house.

Much of the force of this poem comes from its balanced structure and reg-ular rhyme and metre, underscored by the repeated words "Sadie" and "Maud," which shift the focus from one subject to the other and back again ("Maud went to college / Sadie stayed home"). The poem's singsong rhythm recalls the rhymes children recite when jumping rope. This evocation of carefree childhood ironically contrasts with the adult realities that both Sadie and Maud face as they grow up: Sadie stays at home and has two children out of wedlock; Maud goes to college and ends up "a thin brown mouse." The speaker implies that the alternatives Sadie and Maud represent are both undesirable. Although Sadie "scraped life / with a fine-tooth comb," she dies young and leaves nothing to her girls but her desire to experience life. Maud, who graduated from college, shuts out life and cuts herself off from her roots.

Just as the repetition of words and phrases can create rhythm, so can the distribution of words among the lines of a poem—and even the appearance of words on a printed page. How a poem looks is especially important in **open form** poetry (see p. 775), which dispenses with traditional patterns of versification. In the following excerpt from a poem by E. E. Cummings, for example, an unusual arrangement of words forces readers to slow down and then to speed up, creating a rhythm that emphasizes a key phrase—"The / lily":

> the moon is hiding
> in her hair.
> The
> lily
> of heaven
> full of all dreams,
> draws down.

Poetic rhythm—the repetition of stresses and pauses—is an essential element in poetry. Rhythm helps to establish a poem's mood, and, in combination with other poetic elements, it conveys the poet's emphasis and helps communicate the poem's meaning. Although rhythm can be affected by the regular repetition of words and phrases or by the arrangement of words into lines, poetic rhythm is largely created by **metre,** the recurrence of regular units of stressed and unstressed syllables.

METRE

◇ ◇ ◇

A **stress** (or accent) occurs when one syllable is emphasized more than another, unstressed, syllable: *fór • ceps, bá • sic, il • lú • sion, ma • lár • i • a.* In a poem, even one-syllable words can be stressed to create a particular effect. For example, in Elizabeth Barrett Browning's line "How do I love thee? Let me count the ways," the metrical pattern that places stress on "love" creates one meaning; stressing "I" would create another.

Scansion is the process of analyzing patterns of stressed and unstressed syllables within a line. The most common method of poetic notation involves indicating stressed syllables with a ˈ and unstressed syllables with a ˘. Although scanning its lines gives readers the "beat" of the poem, scansion only approximates the sound of spoken language, which contains an infinite variety of stresses. By providing a graphic representation of the stressed and unstressed syllables of a poem, scansion aids understanding, but it is no substitute for reading the poem aloud and experimenting with various patterns of emphasis.

The basic unit of metre is a **foot**—a group of syllables with a fixed pattern of stressed and unstressed syllables. The following chart illustrates the most common types of metrical feet in English-language verse.

FOOT	STRESS PATTERN	EXAMPLE
Iamb	⌣ |	To strive | to seek | to find | and not to yield (Alfred, Lord Tennyson)
Trochee	| ⌣	Thou, when | thou re|turn'st, wilt | tell me. (John Donne)
Anapest	⌣ ⌣ |	With a hey, | and a ho, | and a hey | nonino (William Shakespeare)
Dactyl	| ⌣ ⌣	Constantly | risking ab|surdity (Lawrence Ferlinghetti)

Iambic and *anapestic* metres are called *rising metres* because they progress from unstressed to stressed syllables. *Trochaic* and *dactylic* metres are called *falling metres* because they progress from stressed to unstressed syllables.

The following types of metrical feet, less common than those listed above, are used to emphasize or to provide variety rather than to create the dominant metre of a poem.

Spondee	| |	Pomp, pride | and circumstance of glorious war! (William Shakespeare)

Pyrrhic ◡ ◡   Ă hórse! ă hórse!

                                               Mý king|dŏm fŏr |

                                               ă hórse! (William

                                               Shakespeare)

A metric line of poetry is measured by the number of feet it contains.

monometer one foot   **pentameter** five feet

dimeter two feet   **hexameter** six feet

trimeter three feet   **heptameter** seven feet

tetrameter four feet   **octameter** eight feet

The name for a metrical pattern of a line of verse identifies the name of the foot used and the number of feet the line contains. For example, the most common foot in English poetry is the **iamb,** most often occurring in lines of three or five feet.

Eight hun|dred of | the brave   Iambic trimeter

(William Cowper)

O, how | much more | doth   Iambic pentameter

beau|ty beau|teous seem

(William Shakespeare)

Because **iambic pentameter** is so well suited to the rhythms of English speech, writers frequently use it in plays and poems. Shakespeare's plays, for example, are written in unrhymed lines of iambic pentameter called **blank verse** (see p. 761).

Many other material combinations are also possible; a few are illustrated here:

Like a | high-born | maiden   Trochaic trimeter

(Percy Bysshe Shelley)

The As sy|rian came down | Anapestic tetrameter

like the wolf | on the fold

(Lord Byron)

Maid en most | beau ti ful | Dactylic hexameter

mother most | boun ti ful, | la

dy of | lands, (A. C. Swinburne)

The yel|low fog | that rubs | its   Iambic heptameter

back | upon | the win |

dow-panes (T. S. Eliot)

Scansion can be an extremely technical process, and when readers become bogged down with anapests and dactyls, they can easily forget that poetic metre is not an end in itself. Metre should be appropriate for the ideas expressed by the poem, and it should help to create a suitable tone. A light, skipping rhythm, for example, would be inappropriate for an **elegy,** and a slow, heavy rhythm would surely be out of place in an **epigram** or a limerick. The following lines of a poem by Samuel Taylor Coleridge illustrate the different types of metrical feet:

Trochee trips from long to short;

From long to long in solemn sort

Slow Spondee stalks; strong foot! yet ill able

Ever to come up with Dactyl trisyllable.

Iambics march from short to long—

With a leap and a bound the swift Anapests throng;

One syllable long, with one short at each side,

Amphibrachys hastes with a stately stride—

First and last being long, middle short, Amphimacer

Strikes his thundering hoofs like a proud high-bred Racer.

A poet may use one kind of metre—iambic metre, for example— throughout a poem. Even so, the poet may vary line length to relieve monotony or to accommodate the demands of meaning or emphasis. In the following poem, the poet uses iambic lines of different lengths.

EMILY DICKINSON
(1830–1886)

Because I Could Not
Stop for Death
(1863)

Because I could not stop for Death—
He kindly stopped for me—
The Carriage held but just Ourselves—
And Immortality.

5 We slowly drove—He knew no haste
And I had put away
My labor and my leisure too,
For His Civility—

We passed the School, where Children strove
10 At Recess—in the Ring—
We passed the Fields of Gazing Grain—
We passed the Setting Sun—

Or rather—He passed Us—
The Dews drew quivering and chill—
15 For only Gossamer, my Gown—
My Tippet[1]—only Tulle—

We paused before a House that seemed
A Swelling of the Ground—
The Roof was scarcely visible—
20 The Cornice—in the Ground—

Since then—'tis Centuries—and yet
Feels shorter than the Day
I first surmised the Horses' Heads
Were toward Eternity—

This poem is two sentences. The first sentence comprises the first stanza. The rest of the poem is one long thought with various interruptions. Iambic lines of varying lengths actually suggest the movements of the carriage. Lines of iambic tetrameter, such as the first, give readers a sense of steady, rhythmic movement, and shorter lines ("And I had put away") suggest the carriage's varied, but rhythmic motion. The alternation of longer and shorter lines emulates the gait of the horses. The poem starts with iambic tetrameter and then shifts back and forth between that metre and iambic trimeter. The interplay of long and short lines contributes to the poem's argument about time and the speaker's attitude toward it.

---

[1] Cape.

A poet can also use more than one type of metrical foot. Any variation in a metrical pattern—the substitution of a trochee for an iamb, for instance—immediately calls attention to itself. Poets are aware of this fact and use it to their advantage. For example, in the following segment from "The Rime of the Ancient Mariner," Samuel Taylor Coleridge departs from his poem's dominant metre:

> The ship | was cheered, | the har|bor cleared,
> Merri|ly did | we drop
> Below | the kirk, | below | the hill,
> Below | the light|house top.

Although these lines are arranged in iambic tetrameter, the poet uses a trochee in the second line, breaking the metre in order to accommodate the natural pronunciation of "merrily" as well as to place stress on the word.

Another way of varying the metre is to introduce a pause in the rhythm known as a **caesura**—a Latin word meaning "a cutting"—within a line. When scanning a poem, you indicate a caesura with two parallel lines: ‖. Unless a line of poetry is extremely short, it probably will contain a caesura.

A caesura occurs after a punctuation mark or at a natural break in phrasing:

> How do I love thee? ‖ Let me count the ways.
> **ELIZABETH BARRETT BROWNING**

> Two loves I have ‖ of comfort and despair.
> **WILLIAM SHAKESPEARE**

> High on a throne of royal state, ‖ which far
> Outshone the wealth of Ormus ‖ and of Ind
> **JOHN MILTON**

Sometimes, more than one caesura occurs in a single line:

> 'Tis good. ‖ Go to the gate. ‖ Somebody knocks.
> **WILLIAM SHAKESPEARE**

Although the end of a line may mark the end of a metrical unit, it does not always coincide with the end of a sentence. Poets may choose to indicate a pause at this point, or they may continue, without a break, to the next line. Lines that have distinct pauses at the end—usually signalled by punctuation—are called **end-stopped lines.** Lines that do not end with strong pauses are called **run-on lines.** (Sometimes the term **enjambment** is used to describe this type of line.) End-stopped lines can seem formal, or even forced, because their length is rigidly dictated by the poem's metre, rhythm, and rhyme scheme. In the following excerpt from

John Keats's "La Belle Dame sans Merci" (p. 850), for example, rhythm, metre, and rhyme dictate the pauses that occur at the ends of the lines:

> O, what can ail thee, knight-at-arms,
>   Alone and palely loitering?
> The sedge has withered from the lake,
>   And no birds sing.

In contrast to end-stopped lines, run-on lines seem more natural. Because their ending points are determined by the rhythms of speech and by the meaning and emphasis the poet wishes to convey rather than by metre and rhyme, run-on lines are suited to the open form of much modern poetry. In the following lines from the 1967 poem "We Have Come Home," by the poet Lenrie Peters, run-on lines give readers the sense of spoken language:

> We have come home
> From the bloodless war
> With sunken hearts
> Our boots full of pride—
> From the true massacre of the soul
> When we have asked
> 'What does it cost
> To be loved and left alone?'

Rather than relying exclusively on end-stopped or run-on lines, poets often use a combination of the two to produce the effects they want. In the following lines from "Blackman Dead" by Marlene Nourbese Philip, for example, the juxtaposition of end-stopped and run-on lines controls the rhythm:

> The magnum pistol barked
> its last command
> broke his chest—
> red words of silence erupt
> silken ribbons of death
> wreathe the sullen Sunday morning madness.

❖ **POEMS FOR FURTHER READING: RHYTHM AND METRE**

◇ ◈ ◇

A D R I E N N E   R I C H
(1929–   )

Aunt Jennifer's Tigers
(1951)

Aunt Jennifer's tigers prance across a screen,
Bright topaz denizens of a world of green.

They do not fear the men beneath the tree;
They pace in sleek chivalric certainty.

5 Aunt Jennifer's fingers fluttering through her wool
Find even the ivory needle hard to pull.
The massive weight of Uncle's wedding band
Sits heavily upon Aunt Jennifer's hand.

When Aunt is dead, her terrified hands will lie
10 Still ringed with ordeals she was mastered by.
The tigers in the panel that she made
Will go on prancing, proud and unafraid.

READING AND REACTING

1. What is the dominant metrical pattern of the poem? In what way does the metre enhance the contrast the poem develops?
2. The lines in the first stanza are end-stopped, and those in the second and third stanzas combine end-stopped and run-on lines. What does the poet achieve by varying the rhythm?
3. What ideas do the caesuras in the first and fourth lines of the last stanza emphasize?
4. **JOURNAL ENTRY** What is the speaker's opinion of Aunt Jennifer's marriage? Do you think she is commenting on this particular marriage or on marriage in general?
5. **CRITICAL PERSPECTIVE** In her 1986 study of Rich's work, *The Aesthetics of Power*, Claire Keyes writes of this poem that although it is formally beautiful, almost perfect, its voice creates problems:

> [T]he tone seldom approaches intimacy, the speaker seeming fairly detached from the fate of Aunt Jennifer. . . . The dominant voice of the poem asserts the traditional theme that art outlives the person who produces it. . . . The speaker is almost callous in her disregard for Aunt's death. . . . Who cares that Aunt Jennifer dies? The speaker does not seem to; she gets caught up in those gorgeous tigers. . . . Here lies the dominant voice: Aunt is not compelling; her creation is.

Do you agree with Keyes's reading of the poem?

Related Works: "A Rose for Emily" (p. 90), "Rooming Houses Are Old Women" (p. 705), "The Stenographers" (p. 795)

❖   ❖   ❖

ETHERIDGE KNIGHT
(1931–1991)

For Malcolm,[1] a Year After
(1986)

    Compose for Red[2] a proper verse;
    Adhere to foot and strict iamb;
    Control the burst of angry words
    Or they might boil and break the dam.
5 Or they might boil and overflow
    And drench me, drown me, drive me mad.
    So swear no oath, so shed no tear,
    And sing no song blue Baptist sad.
    Evoke no image, stir no flame,
10 And spin no yarn across the air.
    Make empty anglo tea lace words—
    Make them dead white and dry bone bare.

    Compose a verse for Malcolm man,
    And make it rime and make it prim.
15 The verse will die—as all men do—
    But not the memory of him!
    Death might come singing sweet like C,
    Or knocking like the old folk say,
    The moon and stars may pass away,
20 But not the anger of that day.

READING AND REACTING

1. Why do you think Knight chooses to write a "proper verse" in "strict iamb"? Do you think this metre is an appropriate choice for his subject?
2. What sounds and words are repeated in this poem? How does this repetition enhance the poem's rhythm?
3. Where in the poem does Knight use caesuras? Why does he use this device in each instance?
4. **JOURNAL ENTRY** How would you describe the mood of the speaker? Is the poem's metre consistent with his mood or in conflict with it? Explain.

Related Works: "Meditation on Tom Thomson" (p. 684), "In Memory of Donald A. Stauffer" (p. 771)

---

[1] Malcolm X.

[2] Malcolm X's nickname when he was a young man.

♪ ♪ ♪

TIM LILBURN
(1950–   )

Pumpkins[1]

Oompah Oompah Oompah, fattening
on the stem, tuba girthed, puffing like perorating parliamentarians,
Boompa Boompah Booompah,
earth hogs slurping swill from the sun,
5 jowels burp fat with photons, bigger, bigger, garden elephants,
mirthed like St Francis, dancing (thud), dancing (thud,
brümpht, thud, brümpht) with the Buddha-bellied sun,
dolphin sweet, theatrical as suburban
children, yahooing a yellow
10 which whallops air. Pure. They are Socratically
ugly, God's jokes. O jongleurs, O belly laughs
quaking the matted patch, O my blimpish Prussian
generals, O garden sausages, golden zeppelins. How do? How do? How do?

Doo dee doo dee doooo.
15 What a rabble, some explode,
or sing, in the panic of September
sun, idiot praise for the sun that burns like a grand hotel,
for the sun, monstrous pulp in a groaning rind, flame seeded.
Popeyes, my dears, muscular fruit,
20 apoplexies of grunted energy flexed from the forearm vine,
self-hefted on the hill and shot
putted in the half-acre.

Carro-caroo.   Are you well,
my sweets, pleasure things, my baubles, my Poohs,
25 well?
I, weeding farmer, I, Caruso
them at dawn crow in the sun
cymballing mornings
and they Brunhilde back, foghorns, bloated alto notes
30 baroquely happy.
Not hoe teeth, not Rhotenone, but love,
bruited, busied, blessed these being-ward, barn-big,
bibulous on light, rampantly stolid
as Plato's Ideas, Easter Island
35 flesh lumps of meaning, rolling heads
in my 6-year-old nightmares,

---

[1] Date of publication is unavailable.

vegetables on a ball and chain, sun anvils
booming with blows of temperature.

Come, phenomena, gourds of light, teach
40 your joy esperanto, your intense Archimedean aha
of yellow to me, dung-booted serf, whose unhoed brain,
the garden's brightest fruit, ones
communion with the cowfaced cauliflowers,
cucumbers twinkling like toes, and you,
45 clown prince,
sun dauphin of the rioting plot.

ALLITERATION AND ASSONANCE

◊ ◊ ◊

Just as poetry depends on rhythm, it also depends on the sounds of individual
words. An effect pleasing to the ear, such as "Did he who made the Lamb
make thee?" from William Blake's "The Tyger" (p. 823), is called **euphony.** A
jarring or discordant effect, such as "The vorpal blade went snicker-snack!"
from Lewis Carroll's "Jabberwocky" (p. 754), is called **cacophony.**

One of the earliest, and perhaps the most primitive, methods of
enhancing sound is **onomatopoeia,** which occurs when the sound of a
word echoes its meaning, as it does in common words such as *bang, crash,*
and *hiss.* Poets make broad application of this technique by using combinations of words that suggest a correspondence between sound and
meaning, as Edgar Allan Poe does in the following lines from his poem "The
Bells":

Yet the ear, it fully knows,
  By the twanging
  And the clanging,
How the danger ebbs and flows;
Yet the ear distinctly tells,
  In the jangling
  And the wrangling
How the danger sinks and swells
By the sinking or the swelling in the anger of the bells—
  Of the bells,—
  Of the bells, bells, bells, bells. . . .

Poe's primary objective in this poem is to re-create the sound of ringing
bells. Although he succeeds, the poem (113 lines long in its entirety) is

extremely tedious. A more subtle use of onomatopoetic words appears in the following passage from *An Essay on Criticism* by Alexander Pope:

> Soft is the strain when Zephyr gently blows,
> And the smooth stream in smoother numbers flows;
> But when the loud surges lash the sounding shore,
> The hoarse, rough verse should like the torrent roar:
> When Ajax strives some rock's vast weight to throw,
> The line too Labors, and the words move slow.

After earlier admonishing readers that sound must echo sense, Pope uses onomatopoetic words such as *lash* and *roar* to convey the fury of the sea, and he uses repeated consonants to echo the sounds these words suggest. Notice, for example, how the *s* and *m* sounds suggest the gently blowing Zephyr and the flowing of the smooth stream and how the series of *r* sounds echoes the torrent's roar.

Alliteration—the repetition of consonant sounds in consecutive or neighbouring words, usually at the beginning of words—is another device used to enhance sound in a poem. Both Poe ("<u>s</u>inks and <u>s</u>wells") and Pope ("<u>s</u>mooth <u>s</u>tream") make use of alliteration in the preceding excerpts, and so does Alfred, Lord Tennyson in the following poem.

◆ ◆ ◆

ALFRED, LORD TENNYSON
(1809–1892)

The Eagle
(1851)

> He clasps the crag with crooked hands;
> Close to the sun in lonely lands,
> Ringed with the azure world, he stands.
>
> The wrinkled sea beneath him crawls:
> 5 He watches from his mountain walls,
> And like a thunderbolt he falls.

Throughout the poem, *c*, *l*, and *w* sounds occur repeatedly. The poem is drawn together by the recurrence of these sounds, and as a result it flows smoothly from beginning to end.

The following poem also uses alliteration to create special aural effects.

N. SCOTT MOMADAY
(1934–   )

Comparatives
(1976)

Sunlit sea,
the drift of fronds,
and banners
of bobbing boats—
5   the seaside
upon the planks,
the coil and
crescent of flesh
extending
10   just into death.

Even so,
in the distant,
inland sea,
a shadow runs,
15   radiant,
rude in the rock:
fossil fish,
fissure of bone
forever.
20   It is perhaps
the same thing,
an agony
twice perceived.

It is most like
25   wind on waves—
mere commotion,
mute and mean,
perceptible—
that is all.

Throughout the poem, Momaday uses alliteration to create a pleasing effect
and to link certain words and ideas. Each stanza of the poem has its own
alliterative pattern: the first stanza contains repeated *s* and *b* sounds, the

second stanza contains repeated *r* and *f* sounds, and the third stanza contains repeated *w* and *m* sounds. Not only does this use of alliteration create a pleasing effect, but also it reinforces the development of the poem's theme from stanza to stanza.

Assonance—the repetition of the same or similar vowel sounds, especially in stressed syllables—can also enrich a poem. When used solely to produce aural effects, assonance can be distracting. Consider, for example, the clumsiness of the repeated vowel sounds in Tennyson's "Many a morning on the moorland did we hear the copses ring. . . . " When used more subtly, however, assonance can enhance a poem's effectiveness.

Assonance can also unify an entire poem. In the following poem, assonance emphasizes the thematic connections among words and thus unifies the poem's ideas.

ROBERT HERRICK
(1591–1674)

Delight in Disorder
(1648)

A sweet disorder in the dress
Kindles in clothes a wantonness.
A lawn[1] about the shoulders thrown
Into a fine distractión;
5 An erring lace, which here and there
Enthralls the crimson stomacher;[2]
A cuff neglectful, and thereby
Ribbons to flow confusedly;
A winning wave, deserving note,
10 In the tempestuous petticoat;
A careless shoestring, in whose tie
I see a wild civility;
Do more bewitch me than when art
Is too precise in every part.

Repeated vowel sounds extend throughout this poem—for instance, "shoulders" and "thrown" in line 3; and "tie," "wild," and "precise" in lines 11, 12, and 14. Using alliteration as well as assonance, Herrick subtly links certain words—"tempestuous petticoat," for example. By connecting these words, he calls attention to the pattern of imagery that helps to convey the poem's theme.

---

[1] A shawl made of fine fabric.
[2] A heavily embroidered garment worn by females over the chest and stomach.

RHYME

❖ ❖ ❖

In addition to alliteration and assonance, poets create sound patterns with **rhyme**—the use of matching sounds in two or more words: "tight" and "might"; "born" and "horn"; "sleep" and "deep." For a rhyme to be **perfect**, final vowel and consonant sounds must be the same, as they are in each of the preceding examples. **Imperfect rhyme** (also called *near rhyme, slant rhyme, approximate rhyme,* or *consonance*) occurs when the final consonant sounds in two words are the same but vowel sounds are different— "learn/barn" or "pads/lids," for example. William Stafford uses imperfect rhyme in "Traveling through the Dark" (p. 884) when he rhymes "road" with "dead." Finally, **eye rhyme** occurs when two words look as if they should rhyme but do not—for example, "watch" and "catch."

Rhyme can also be classified according to the position of the rhyming syllables in a line of verse. The most common type of rhyme is **end rhyme**, which occurs at the end of a line:

> Tyger! Tyger! burning <u>bright</u>
> In the forests of the <u>night</u>
> <small>**WILLIAM BLAKE**, "The Tyger"</small>

Internal rhyme occurs within a line:

> The Sun came up upon the left,
> Out of the <u>sea</u> came <u>he</u>!
> And he shone <u>bright</u> and on the <u>right</u>
> Went down into the sea.
> <small>**SAMUEL TAYLOR COLERIDGE**, "The Rime of the Ancient Mariner"</small>

Beginning rhyme occurs at the beginning of a line:

> <u>For</u> what the world admires, I'll wish no more,
> <u>Nor</u> court that airy nothing of a name:
> Such flitting shadows let the proud adore,
> Let them be suppliants for an empty fame.
> <small>**LADY MARY CHUDLEIGH**, "The Resolve"</small>

Rhyme can also be classified according to the number of corresponding syllables. **Masculine rhyme** (also called **rising rhyme**) occurs when single syllables correspond ("can"/"ran"; "descend"/"contend"). **Feminine rhyme** (also called **double rhyme** or **falling rhyme**) occurs when two syllables, a stressed one followed by an unstressed one, correspond ("ocean"/"motion"; "leaping"/"sleeping"). Finally, **triple rhyme** occurs when three syllables correspond. Less common than the other two, triple rhyme is often used for humorous or satiric purposes, as in the following lines from the long poem *Don Juan* by Lord Byron:

> Sagest of women, even of widows, she
>> Resolved that Juan should be quite a <u>paragon</u>,
> And worthy of the noblest pedigree:
>> (His sire of Castile, his dam from <u>Aragon</u>).

In some cases—for example, when it is overused or used in unexpected places—rhyme can create unusual and even comic effects. In the following poem, humour is created by the incongruous connections established by rhymes such as "priest"/"beast" and "pajama"/"lllama."

OGDEN NASH
(1902–1971)

The Lama
(1931)

> The one-l lama
> He's a priest.
> The two-l llama,
> He's a beast.
> 5 And I will bet
> A silk pajama
> There isn't any
> Three-l lllama.

The conventional way to describe a poem's rhyme scheme is to chart rhyming sounds that appear at the ends of lines. The sound that ends the first line is designated *a*, and all subsequent lines that end in that sound are also labelled *a*. The next sound to appear at the end of a line is designated *b*, and all other lines whose last sounds rhyme with it are also designated *b*— and so on through the alphabet. The lines of the poem that follows have been labelled in this manner.

RICHARD WILBUR
(1921–   )

A Sketch
(1975)

> Into the lower right   *a*
> Square of the window frame   *b*
> There came   *b*
>> with scalloped flight   *a*

5 A goldfinch, lit upon   *c*
    The dead branch of a pine,   *d*
    Shining,   *d*
            and then was gone,   *c*

    Tossed in a double arc   *e*
10 Upward into the thatched   *f*
    And cross-hatched   *f*
            pine-needle dark.   *e*

    Briefly, as fresh drafts stirred   *g*
    The tree, he dulled and gleamed   *h*
15 And seemed   *h*
            more coal than bird,   *g*

    Then, dodging down, returned   *i*
    In a new light, his perch   *j*
    A birch—   *j*
20   twig, where he burned   *i*

    In the sun's broadside ray,   *k*
    Some seed pinched in his bill.   *l*
    Yet still   *l*
            he did not stay,   *k*

25 But into a leaf-choken pane,   *m*
    Changeful as even in heaven,   *n*
    Even   *n*
          in Saturn's reign,   *m*

    Tunneled away and hid.   *o*
30 And then? But I cannot well   *p*
    Tell   *p*
          you all that he did.   *o*

    It was like glancing at rough   *q*
    Sketches tacked on a wall,   *r*
35 And all   *r*
            so less than enough   *q*

    Of gold on beaten wing,   *s*
    I could not choose that one   *t*
    Be done   *t*
40   as the finished thing.   *s*

Although the rhyme scheme of this poem (*abba, cddc,* and so on) is regular, it is hardly noticeable until it is charted. Despite its subtlety, however, the rhyme scheme is not unimportant. In fact, it reinforces the poem's meaning and binds lines into structural units, connecting the first and fourth as well as the second and third lines of each stanza. In stanza 1, "right" and "flight" draw lines 1 and 4 of the stanza together, enclosing "frame" and "came" in lines 2 and 3. The pattern begins again with the next stanza and continues through the rest of the poem. Like the elusive goldfinch the poet describes, the rhymes are difficult to follow with the eye. In this sense, the rhyme reflects the central theme of the poem: the difficulty of capturing in words a reality that, like the goldfinch, is forever shifting.

Naturally, rhyme does not have to be subtle to enrich a poem. An obvious rhyme scheme can communicate meaning by connecting ideas that are not normally linked. Notice how Alexander Pope uses this technique in the following excerpt from *An Essay on Man:*

> Honour and shame from no condition rise;
> Act well your part, there all the honour lies.
> Fortune in men has some small diff'rence made,
> One flaunts in rags, one flutters in brocade;
> The cobbler aproned, and the parson gowned,
> The friar hooded, and the monarch crowned.
> "What differ more (you cry) than crown and cowl?"
> I'll tell you, friend; a wise man and a fool.
>
> You'll find, if once the monarch acts the monk,
> Or, cobbler-like, the parson will be drunk,
> Worth makes the man, and want of it, the fellow;
> The rest is all but leather or prunella.[1]
> Stuck o'er with titles and hung round with strings,
> That thou mayest be by kings, or whores of kings.
> Boast the pure blood of an illustrious race,
> In quiet flow from Lucrece[2] to Lucrece;
> But by your fathers' worth if yours you rate,
> Count me those only who were good and great.

The lines of this poem are written in **heroic couplets,** with a rhyme scheme of *aa, bb, cc, dd,* and so on. In heroic couplets, greater stress falls on the second line of each pair, usually on the last word of the line. Coming at the end of the line, this word receives double emphasis: it is strengthened both because of its position in the line and because it is rhymed with the last word of the couplet's first line. In some cases, rhyme joins opposing ideas, thereby reinforcing a theme that runs through the passage: the contrast between the high and the low, the virtuous and the immoral. For example, "gowned" and "crowned" in lines 5 and 6 convey the opposite conditions of the parson and the monarch and exemplify the idea expressed in lines 3 and 4 that fortune, not virtue, determines one's station.

---

[1] Heavy cloth the colour of prunes.
[2] In Roman legend, she stabbed herself after being defiled by Sextus Tarquinius.

▨ POEMS FOR FURTHER READING: ALLITERATION,
ASSONANCE, AND RHYME

GERARD MANLEY HOPKINS
(1844–1889)

Pied Beauty
(1918)

Glory be to God for dappled things—
    For skies of couple-color as a brinded[1] cow;
        For rose-moles all in stipple upon trout that swim;
Fresh-firecoal chestnut-falls; finches' wings;
5   Landscape plotted and pieced—fold, fallow, and plow;
        And áll trádes, their gear and tackle and trim.[2]

All things counter, original, spare, strange;
    Whatever is fickle, freckled (who knows how?)
        With swift, slow; sweet, sour; adazzle, dim;
10 He fathers-forth whose beauty is past change:
        Praise him.

READING AND REACTING

1. Identify examples of onomatopoeia, alliteration, assonance, imperfect rhyme, and perfect rhyme. Do you think all these techniques are essential to the poem? Are any of them annoying or distracting?
2. What is the central idea of this poem? In what way do the sounds of the poem help to communicate this idea?
3. Identify examples of masculine and feminine rhyme.
4. **JOURNAL ENTRY** Hopkins uses both pleasing and discordant sounds in his poem. Identify uses of euphony and cacophony, and explain how these techniques affect your reactions to the poem.

Related Works: "Women" (p. 786), "Britain Street" (p. 866)

---

[1] Brindled (streaked).
[2] Equipment.

◇ ◇ ◇

W. H. AUDEN
(1907–1973)

As I Walked Out One Evening
(1940)

As I walked out one evening,
    Walking down Bristol Street,
The crowds upon the pavement
    Were fields of harvest wheat.

5 And down by the brimming river
    I heard a lover sing
Under an arch of the railway:
    "Love has no ending.

"I'll love you, dear, I'll love you
10   Till China and Africa meet,
And the river jumps over the mountain
    And the salmon sing in the street,

"I'll love you till the ocean
    Is folded and hung up to dry,
15 And the seven stars go squawking
    Like geese about the sky.

"The years shall run like rabbits,
    For in my arms I hold
The Flower of the Ages,
20   And the first love of the world."

But all the clocks in the city
    Began to whirr and chime:
"O let not Time deceive you,
    You cannot conquer Time.

25 "In the burrows of the Nightmare
    Where Justice naked is,
Time watches from the shadow
    And coughs when you would kiss.

"In headaches and in worry
30   Vaguely life leaks away,
And Time will have his fancy
    Tomorrow or today.

"Into many a green valley
    Drifts the appalling snow;
35 Time breaks the threaded dances
    And the diver's brilliant bow.

"O plunge your hands in water,
    Plunge them in up to the wrist;
Stare, stare in the basin
40   And wonder what you've missed.

"The glacier knocks in the cupboard,
    The desert sighs in the bed,
And the crack in the teacup opens
    A lane to the land of the dead.

45 "Where the beggars raffle the banknotes
    And the Giant is enchanting to Jack,
And the Lily-white Boy is a Roarer,
    And Jill goes down on her back.

"O look, look in the mirror,
50   O look in your distress;
Life remains a blessing
    Although you cannot bless.

"O stand, stand at the window
    As the tears scald and start;
55 You shall love your crooked neighbor
    With your crooked heart."

It was late, late in the evening,
    The lovers they were gone;
The clocks had ceased their chiming,
60   And the deep river ran on.

READING AND REACTING

1. In lines 2 and 4 of almost every stanza, Auden uses perfect end rhyme. In stanzas 5 and 7, however, he uses imperfect rhyme. Should he have been more consistent in his use of rhyme? Would the poetic effect have been better had he consistently used perfect rhyme?
2. Chart the poem's rhyme scheme. Does Auden use internal rhyme? Where does he use alliteration and assonance? In what other ways does he use sound?
3. Does Auden's use of sound reinforce the poem's content or undercut it? Explain.
4. **JOURNAL ENTRY** Could this poem be considered a love poem? How are its sentiments about love different from those conventionally expressed in poems about love?
5. **CRITICAL PERSPECTIVE** In a 1940 British review of Auden's work, T. C. Worlsey made the following comments about this poem:

There is no technical reason why such a poem as [this] should not be popular; the metre and the rhythm are easy and helpful, and the symbols have reference to a world of experience common to every inhabitant of these islands. Here . . . the poet has gone as far as he can along the road to creating a popular poetry.

Does Auden's poem strike you as a model for "popular" poetry—that is, poetry for people who don't usually read poetry?

Related Works: "Araby" (p. 267), "Oh, My Love Is like a Red, Red Rose" (p. 706), "To His Coy Mistress" (p. 719), "Not Marble, nor the Gilded Monuments" (p. 881)

◇ ◇ ◇

LEWIS CARROLL
(1832–1898)

Jabberwocky
(1871)

'Twas brillig, and the slithy toves
    Did gyre and gimble in the wabe:
All mimsy were the borogoves,
    And the mome raths outgrabe.

5 "Beware the Jabberwock, my son!
    The jaws that bite, the claws that catch!
Beware the Jubjub bird, and shun
    The frumious Bandersnatch!"

He took his vorpal sword in hand;
10   Long time the manxome foe he sought—
So rested he by the Tumtum tree
    And stood awhile in thought.

And, as in uffish thought he stood,
    The Jabberwock, with eyes of flame,
15 Came whiffling through the tulgey wood,
    And burbled as it came!

One, two! One, two! And through and through
   The vorpal blade went snicker-snack!
He left it dead, and with its head
20   He went galumphing back.

"And hast thou slain the Jabberwock?
   Come to my arms, my beamish boy!
O frabjous day! Callooh, Callay!"
   He chortled in his joy.

25 'Twas brillig, and the slithy toves
   Did gyre and gimble in the wabe:
All mimsy were the borogoves,
   And the mome raths outgrabe.

READING AND REACTING

1. Many words in this poem may be unfamiliar to you. Are they actual words? Use a dictionary to check before you dismiss any. Do some words seem to have meaning in the context of the poem regardless of whether or not they appear in the dictionary? Explain.

2. This poem contains many examples of onomatopoeia. What ideas do the various words' sounds suggest?

3. **JOURNAL ENTRY** Summarize the story the poem tells. In what sense is this poem a story of a young man's initiation into adulthood?

4. **CRITICAL PERSPECTIVE** According to Humpty Dumpty in Carroll's *Alice in Wonderland*, the nonsense words in the poem are *portmanteau words* (that is, words whose form and meaning are derived from two other distinct words—as *smog* is a portmanteau of *smoke* and *fog*). Critic Elizabeth Sewell, however, rejects this explanation: "*[F]rumious*, for instance, is not a word, and does not have two meanings packed up in it; it is a group of letters without any meaning at all. . . . [I]t looks like other words, and almost certainly more than two."

   Which nonsense words in the poem seem to you to be portmanteau words, and which do not? Can you suggest possible sources for those words that are not portmanteau words?

Related Works: "A&P" (p. 122), "Rite of Passage" (p. 867)

CHECKLIST: WRITING ABOUT SOUND

RHYTHM AND METRE

✓ Does the poem contain repeated words and phrases? If so, how do they help to create rhythm?

✓ Does the poem have one kind of metre, or does the metre vary from line to line?

✓ How does the metre contribute to the overall effect of the poem?

✓ Which lines of the poem contain caesuras? What effect do they have?

✓ Are the lines of the poem end-stopped, run-on, or a combination of the two? What effects are produced by the presence or absence of pauses at the ends of lines?

ALLITERATION, ASSONANCE, AND RHYME

✓ Does the poem contain any examples of onomatopoeia?

✓ Are there any examples of alliteration or assonance?

✓ Does the poem have a regular rhyme scheme?

✓ Does the poem use internal rhyme? Beginning rhyme?

✓ Does the poem include examples of masculine, feminine, or triple rhyme?

✓ In what ways does rhyme unify the poem?

✓ How does rhyme reinforce the poem's ideas?

◆ WRITING SUGGESTIONS: SOUND

1. William Blake's "The Tyger" appeared in a collection entitled *Songs of Experience*. Compare this poem (p. 823) to "The Lamb" (p. 822), which appeared in a collection called *Songs of Innocence*. In what way are the speakers in these two poems relatively "innocent" or "experienced"? How does sound help to convey the voice of the speakers in these two poems?

2. "Sadie and Maud" (p. 732), like "The Faithful Wife" (p. 671), "Fathers and Sons" (p. 569), "My Papa's Waltz" (p. 570), and "Daddy" (p. 712), communicates attitudes toward home and family. How does the presence or absence of rhyme in these poems help to reinforce their themes?

3. Robert Frost once said that writing poems that have no fixed metrical pattern is like playing tennis without a net. What do you think he meant? Do you agree? After reading "'Out, Out—'" (p. 721) and "The Road Not Taken" (p. 837), write an essay in

which you discuss Frost's use of metre, or consider his comments regarding metre in two poems by another poet.

4. Select two or three contemporary poems that have no end rhyme. Write an essay in which you discuss what these poets gain and lose by not using rhyme.

5. Prose writers as well as poets use techniques such as assonance and alliteration. Choose a passage of prose—from "Araby" (p. 267), "Barn Burning" (p. 234), "The Loons" (p. 249), or "The Boat" (p. 447), for example—and discuss its use of assonance and alliteration. Where do assonance and alliteration occur? How do these techniques help the writer make his or her point?

CHAPTER 18

Form

◇ ◇ ◇

Dryden chose the couplet because he thought it the plainest mode available, the verse "nearest prose," and he chose it in conscious reaction against the artificial stanzaic modes that had dominated English poetry during most of the sixteenth and seventeenth centuries. In short, he and his followers thought they were liberating poetry, just as Coleridge and Wordsworth liberated it a hundred years later, or Pound and Williams a hundred years after that. The history of poetry is a continual fixing and freeing of conventions.

HAYDEN CARRUTH, "The Question of Poetic Form"

Yeats said that the finished poem made a sound like the click of the lid on a perfectly made box. One-hundred-and-forty syllables, organized into a sonnet, do not necessarily make a click; the same number of syllables, dispersed in asymmetric lines of free verse, will click like a lid if the poem is good. In the sonnet and in the free verse poem, the poet improvises toward that click, and achieves his resolution in unpredictable ways. The rhymes and line lengths of the sonnet are too gross to contribute greatly to that sense of resolution. The click is our sense of lyric *form*.

DONALD HALL, "Goatfoot, Milktongue, Twinbird"

No verse can be free; it must be governed by some measure, but not by the old measure.

WILLIAM CARLOS WILLIAMS, "On Measure"

J O H N   K E A T S
(1795–1821)

On the Sonnet
(1819)

If by dull rhymes our English must be chained,
And like Andromeda,[1] the sonnet sweet
Fettered, in spite of painéd loveliness,
Let us find, if we must be constrained,
5 Sandals more interwoven and complete
To fit the naked foot of Poesy:
Let us inspect the lyre, and weigh the stress
Of every chord, and see what may be gained
By ear industrious, and attention meet;
10 Misers of sound and syllable, no less
Than Midas[2] of his coinage, let us be
Jealous of dead leaves in the bay-wreath crown;
So, if we may not let the Muse be free,
She will be bound with garlands of her own.

The **form** of a literary work is its structure or shape, the way its parts fit together to form a whole; **poetic form** is the design of a poem described in terms of rhyme, metre, and stanzaic pattern.

Until the twentieth century, most poetry was written in **closed form** (sometimes called **fixed form**), characterized by regular patterns of metre, rhyme, line length, and stanzaic divisions. Early poems that were passed down orally—epics and ballads, for example—relied on regular form to facilitate memorization. Even after poems began to be written down, poets tended to favour regular patterns. In fact, until relatively recently, regular form was what distinguished poetry from prose. Of course, strict adherence to regular patterns sometimes produced poems that were, in John Keats's words, "chained" by "dull rhymes" and "fettered" by the rules governing a particular form. But rather than feeling "constrained" by form, many poets experimented with imagery, figures of speech, allusion, and other techniques—stretching closed form to its limits.

As they sought new ways in which to express themselves, poets also used forms from other cultures, adapting them to the demands of their own languages. English and North American poets, for example, adopted (and still use) early French forms, such as the villanelle and the sestina, and early Italian forms, such as the Petrarchan sonnet and terza rima. More recently, the nineteenth-century American poet Henry Wadsworth Longfellow

---

[1] In Greek mythology, Andromeda was chained to a rock to appease a sea monster.
[2] King Midas was granted his wish that all he touched would turn to gold.

studied Icelandic epics; the twentieth-century poet Ezra Pound studied the works of French troubadours; and Pound and other twentieth-century poets were inspired by Japanese haiku.

As time went on, more and more poets moved away from closed form to experiment with **open form** poetry (sometimes called **free verse** or *vers libre*), varying line length within a poem, dispensing with stanzaic divisions, breaking lines in unexpected places, and even abandoning any semblance of formal structure. In English, nineteenth-century poets—such as William Blake and Matthew Arnold—experimented with lines of irregular metre and length, and Walt Whitman wrote **prose poems,** open form poems whose long lines made them look like prose. (Well before this time, Asian poetry and some biblical passages had used a type of free verse.) In nineteenth-century France, Symbolist poets such as Baudelaire, Rimbaud, Verlaine, and Mallarmé also used free verse. Later, in the early twentieth century, a group of poets including Ezra Pound, Richard Aldington, HD (Hilda Doolittle), William Carlos Williams, and Amy Lowell, who were associated with a movement known as **imagism,** wrote poetry that dispensed with traditional principles of English versification, creating new rhythms and metres.

Although much contemporary poetry in English is composed in open form, many poets also write in closed form—even in very traditional, highly structured patterns. Still, new forms, and new variations of old forms, are being created all the time. And, because contemporary poets do not necessarily feel bound by rules or restrictions about what constitutes "acceptable" poetic form, they experiment freely, trying to discover the form that best suits the poem's purpose, subject, language, and theme.

CLOSED FORM

◇ ◇ ◇

A **closed form** (or *fixed form*) poem looks symmetrical; it has an identifiable, repeated pattern, with lines of similar length arranged in groups of two, three, four, or more. Such poems also tend to rely on regular metrical patterns and rhyme schemes.

Despite what its name suggests, closed form poetry does not have to be confining or conservative. In fact, sometimes contemporary poets experiment by using characteristics of open form poetry (such as lines of varying length) within a closed form, or by moving back and forth within a single poem from open to closed to open form. Sometimes they (like their eighteenth-century counterparts) experiment with closed form by combining different stanzaic forms (stanzas of two and three lines, for example) within a single poem.

Even when poets work within a traditional closed form, such as a *sonnet, sestina,* or *villanelle,* they can break new ground. For example, they can create a sonnet with an unexpected metre or rhyme scheme, add an extra line or even extra stanzas to a traditional sonnet form, combine two different traditional sonnet forms in a single poem, or write an abbreviated version of a sestina or villanelle. (See the sections on traditional closed forms in this chapter for examples of such experiments.) In other words, poets can use traditional forms as building blocks, combining them in innovative ways to create new patterns and new forms.

Sometimes a pattern (such as *blank verse*) simply determines the metre of a poem's individual lines. At other times, the pattern extends to the level of the *stanza*, with lines arranged into groups (*couplets, quatrains,* and so on). At still other times, as in the case of traditional closed forms like sonnets, a poetic pattern gives shape to an entire poem.

BLANK VERSE

Blank verse is unrhymed poetry with each line written in a set pattern of five stressed and five unstressed syllables called **iambic pentameter** (see p. 735). Many passages from Shakespeare's plays, such as the following lines from *Hamlet,* are written in blank verse:

> To sleep, perchance to dream, ay there's the rub,
> For in that sleep of death what dreams may come
> When we have shuffled off this mortal coil
> Must give us pause—there's the respect
> That makes calamity of so long life . . .

STANZA

A **stanza** is a group of two or more lines with the same metrical pattern— and often with a regular rhyme scheme as well—separated by blank space from other such groups of lines. The stanza in poetry is like the paragraph in prose: it groups related thoughts into units.

A two-line stanza with rhyming lines of similar length and metre is called a **couplet.** The **heroic couplet,** first used by Chaucer and especially popular throughout the eighteenth century, consists of two rhymed lines of iambic pentameter, with a weak pause after the first line and a strong pause after the second. The following example, from Alexander Pope's *An Essay on Criticism,* is a heroic couplet:

> True ease in writing comes from art, not chance,
> As those move easiest who have learned to dance.

A three-line stanza with lines of similar length and a set rhyme scheme is called a **tercet.** Percy Bysshe Shelley's "Ode to the West Wind" (p. 881) is built largely of tercets:

> O wild West Wind, thou breath of Autumn's being,
> Thou, from whose unseen presence the leaves dead
> Are driven, like ghosts from an enchanter fleeing,
>
> Yellow, and black, and pale, and hectic red,
> Pestilence-stricken multitudes: O Thou,
> Who chariotest to their dark wintry bed

Although in many tercets all three lines rhyme, "Ode to the West Wind" uses a special rhyme scheme, also used by Dante, called **terza rima.** This rhyme scheme (*aba, bcb, cdc, ded,* and so on) creates an interlocking series of stanzas. Line 2's *dead* looks ahead to the rhyming words *red* and *bed,* which close lines 4 and 6, and the pattern continues throughout the poem.

A four-line stanza with lines of similar length and a set rhyme scheme is called a **quatrain.** The quatrain, the most widely used and versatile unit in English poetry, is used by William Wordsworth in the following excerpt from "She Dwelt among the Untrodden Ways" (p. 897):

> A violet by a mossy stone
>   Half hidden from the eye!
> Fair as a star, when only one
>   Is shining in the sky.

Quatrains are frequently used by contemporary poets as well—for instance, in Theodore Roethke's "My Papa's Waltz" (p. 570), Adrienne Rich's "Aunt Jennifer's Tigers" (p. 739), and William Stafford's "Traveling through the Dark" (p. 884).

One special kind of quatrain, called the **ballad stanza,** alternates lines of eight and six syllables; typically, only the second and fourth lines rhyme. The following lines from the traditional Scottish ballad "Sir Patrick Spence" illustrate the ballad stanza:

> The king sits in Dumferling toune,
>   Drinking the blude-reid wine:
> "O whar will I get guid sailor
>   To sail this schip of mine?"

Common measure, a four-line stanzaic pattern closely related to the ballad stanza, is used in hymns as well as in poetry. It differs from the ballad stanza in that its rhyme scheme is *abab* rather than *abcb.* This pattern appears in Donald Hall's 1955 poem "My Son, My Executioner" (p. 722).

Other stanzaic forms include **rhyme royal,** a seven-line stanza (*ababbcc*) set in iambic pentameter, used in Sir Thomas Wyatt's sixteenth-century poem "They Flee from Me That Sometimes Did Me Seke" as well as in Theodore Roethke's twentieth-century "I Knew a Woman" (p. 665); **ottava rima,** an eight-line stanza (*abababcc*) set in iambic pentameter; and the Spenserian stanza, a nine-line form (*ababbcbcc*) whose first eight lines are set in iambic pentameter and whose last line is in iambic hexameter. The Romantic poets John Keats and Percy Bysshe Shelley were among those who used this form. (See Chapter 17 for definitions and examples of various metrical patterns.)

THE SONNET

Perhaps the most familiar kind of traditional closed form poem written in English is the **sonnet,** a fourteen-line poem with a distinctive rhyme scheme and metrical pattern. The English or **Shakespearean sonnet,** which consists of fourteen lines divided into three quatrains and a concluding couplet, is written in iambic pentameter and follows the rhyme scheme *abab cdcd efef gg.* The **Petrarchan sonnet,** popularized in the fourteenth century by the Italian poet Francesco Petrarch, also consists of fourteen lines of iambic pentameter, but these lines are divided into an eight-line unit called an **octave** and a six-line unit (composed of two tercets) called a **sestet.** The rhyme scheme of the octave is *abba abba;* the rhyme scheme of the sestet is *cde cde.*

The conventional structures of these sonnet forms reflect the arrangement of ideas within a poem. In the Shakespearean sonnet, the poet typically presents three "paragraphs" of related thoughts, introducing an idea in the first quatrain, developing it in the two remaining quatrains, and summing up in a succinct closing couplet. In the Petrarchan sonnet, the octave introduces a problem that is resolved in the sestet. (Many Shakespearean sonnets also have a problem-solution structure.) Some poets vary the traditional patterns somewhat to suit the poem's language or ideas. For example, they may depart from the pattern to sidestep a forced rhyme or unnatural stress on a syllable, or they may not place the problem-solution break between octave and sestet.

The following poem follows the form of a traditional English sonnet.

WILLIAM SHAKESPEARE
(1564–1616)

When, in Disgrace with Fortune and Men's Eyes
(1609)

When, in disgrace with Fortune and men's eyes,
I all alone beweep my outcast state,
And trouble deaf heaven with my bootless[1] cries,
And look upon myself and curse my fate,
5 Wishing me like to one more rich in hope,
Featured like him, like him with friends possessed,
Desiring this man's art, and that man's scope,
With what I most enjoy contented least,
Yet in these thoughts myself almost despising,
10 Haply[2] I think on thee, and then my state,
Like to the lark at break of day arising
From sullen earth, sings hymns at heaven's gate;
   For thy sweet love rememb'red such wealth brings
   That then I scorn to change my state with kings.

This sonnet is written in iambic pentameter and has a conventional rhyme scheme: *abab* (eyes-state-cries-fate), *cdcd* (hope-possessed-scope-least), *efef*

---

[1] Futile.
[2] Luckily.

(despising-state-arising-gate), *gg* (brings-kings). In this poem, in which the speaker explains how thoughts of his loved one can rescue him from despair, each quatrain is unified by rhyme as well as by subject. In the first quatrain, the speaker presents his problem: he is down on his luck and out of favour with his peers, isolated in self-pity and cursing his fate. In the second quatrain, he develops this idea further: he is envious of others and dissatisfied with things that usually please him. In the third quatrain, the focus shifts. Although the first two quatrains develop a dependent clause ("When. . . . ") that introduces a problem, line 9 begins to present the resolution. In the third quatrain the speaker explains how, in the midst of his despair and self-hatred, he thinks of his loved one, and his spirits soar. The closing couplet sums up the mood transformation the poem describes and explains its significance: when the speaker realizes the emotional riches his loved one gives him, he is no longer envious of others.

❖ POEMS FOR FURTHER READING: THE SONNET

▸ ◇ ◇

SIR CHARLES G. D. ROBERTS
(1860–1943)

The Winter Fields
(1890)

Winds here, and sleet, and frost that bites like steel.
   The low bleak hill rounds under the low sky.
   Naked of flock and fold the fallows lie,
Thin streaked with meagre drift. The gusts reveal
5 By fits the dim grey snakes of fence, that steal
   Through the white dusk. The hill-foot poplars sigh,
   While storm and death with winter trample by,
And the iron fields ring sharp, and blind lights reel.
Yet in the lonely ridges, wrenched with pain
10   Harsh solitary hillocks, bound and dumb,
Grave glebes[1] close-lipped beneath the scourge and chain,
   Lurks hid the germ of ecstasy—the sum
Of life that waits on summer, till the rain
   Whisper in April and the crocus come.

READING AND REACTING

1. What is the speaker's mood?
2. How does the speaker present the winter scene?
3. What change in attitude is made between the octave and the sestet?

---

[1] Fields.

4. **JOURNAL ENTRY** What is the "germ of ecstasy," and is the idea applicable across Canada or around the world?

Related Works: "The Way the Weather Chose to Be Born" (p. 838), "Green Rain" (p. 860), "Fog" (p. 879)

✧   ✧

JOHN KEATS
(1795–1821)

On First Looking into Chapman's Homer[1]
(1816)

Much have I traveled in the realms of gold,
    And many goodly states and kingdoms seen;
    Round many western islands have I been
Which bards in fealty to Apollo[2] hold.
5 Oft of one wide expanse had I been told
    That deep-browed Homer ruled as his demesne,[3]
    Yet did I never breathe its pure serene[4]
Till I heard Chapman speak out loud and bold.
Then felt I like some watcher of the skies
10   When a new planet swims into his ken;
Or like stout Cortez[5] when with eagle eyes
    He stared at the Pacific—and all his men
Looked at each other with a wild surmise—
    Silent, upon a peak in Darien.[6]

READING AND REACTING

1. Is this a Petrarchan or a Shakespearean sonnet? Explain your conclusion.

2. **JOURNAL ENTRY** The sestet's change of focus is introduced with the word "Then" in line 9. How does the mood of the sestet differ from the mood of the octave? How does the language differ?

3. **CRITICAL PERSPECTIVE** Biographer Aileen Ward offers an interesting explanation to suggest the reason for the excitement Keats felt "On First Looking into Chapman's Homer." Homer's epic tales of gods and heroes were known to most readers of Keats's day only in a very formal eighteenth-century translation

---

[1] The translation of Homer by Elizabethan poet George Chapman.

[2] Greek god of light, truth, reason, male beauty; associated with music and poetry.

[3] Realm, domain.

[4] Air, atmosphere.

[5] It was Vasco de Balboa (not Hernando Cortez as Keats suggests) who first saw the Pacific Ocean, from "a peak in Darien."

[6] Former name of the Isthmus of Panama.

by Alexander Pope. For instance, this is Pope's description of Ulysses escaping from a shipwreck:

> his knees no more
> Perform'd their office, or his weight upheld:
> His swoln heart heav'd, his bloated body swell'd:
> From mouth to nose the briny torrent ran,
> And lost in lassitude lay all the man,
> Deprived of voice, of motion, and of breath,
> The soul scarce waking in the arms of death . . .

In a rare 1616 edition of Chapman's translation, Keats discovered a very different poem:

> both knees falt'ring, both
> His strong hands hanging down, and all with froth
> His cheeks and nostrils flowing, voice and breath
> Spent to all use, and down he sank to death.
> The sea had soak'd his heart through. . . .

This, as Ward notes, was "poetry of a kind that had not been written in England for two hundred years."

Can you understand why Keats was so moved by Chapman's translation? Do you think Keats's own poem seems closer in its form and language to Pope or to Chapman?

Related Works: "Araby" (p. 267), "When I Heard the Learn'd Astronomer" (p. 658)

◇ ◇ ◇

G W E N D O L Y N B R O O K S
(1917–2000)

First Fight. Then Fiddle
(1949)

> First fight. Then fiddle. Ply the slipping string
> With feathery sorcery; muzzle the note
> With hurting love; the music that they wrote
> Bewitch, bewilder. Qualify to sing
> 5 Threadwise. Devise no salt, no hempen thing
> For the dear instrument to bear. Devote
> The bow to silks and honey. Be remote
> A while from malice and from murdering.
> But first to arms, to armor. Carry hate
> 10 In front of you and harmony behind.
> Be deaf to music and to beauty blind.
> Win war. Rise bloody, maybe not too late
> For having first to civilize a space
> Wherein to play your violin with grace.

Reading and Reacting

1. What is the subject of Brooks's poem? What do you think she means by "fight" and "fiddle"?
2. What is the poem's rhyme scheme? Is it an essential element of the poem? Would the poem be equally effective if it did not include end rhyme? Explain your position.
3. Study the poem's use of capitalization and punctuation carefully. Why do you think Brooks chooses to end many of her sentences in midline? How do her choices determine how you read the poem?

Related Works: "The Soldier" (p. 587), "Dulce et Decorum Est" (p. 695)

The Sestina

The **sestina,** introduced in thirteenth-century France, is composed of six six-line stanzas and a three-line conclusion called an **envoi.** Although the sestina does not require end rhyme, it does require that each line end with one of six key words, which are repeated throughout the poem in a fixed order. The alternation of these six words in different positions—but always at the ends of lines—in each of the poem's six stanzas creates a rhythmic verbal pattern that unifies the poem, as the key words do in the poem that follows.

ALBERTO ALVARO RÍOS
(1952–   )

Nani
(1982)

Sitting at her table, she serves
the sopa de arroz[1] to me
instinctively, and I watch her,
the absolute mamá, and eat words
5   I might have had to say more
out of embarrassment. To speak,
now-foreign words I used to speak,
too, dribble down her mouth as she serves
me albóndigas.[2] No more
10   than a third are easy to me.
By the stove she does something with words
and looks at me only with her
back. I am full. I tell her
I taste the mint, and watch her speak

---

[1] Rice soup.
[2] Meatballs.

15 smiles at the stove. All my words
make her smile. Nani never serves
herself, she only watches me
with her skin, her hair. I ask for more.

I watch the mamá warming more
20 tortillas for me. I watch her
fingers in the flame for me.
Near her mouth, I see a wrinkle speak
of a man whose body serves
the ants like she serves me, then more words
25 from more wrinkles about children, words
about this and that, flowing more
easily from these other mouths. Each serves
as a tremendous string around her,
holding her together. They speak
30 nani was this and that to me
and I wonder just how much of me
will die with her, what were the words
I could have been, was. Her insides speak
through a hundred wrinkles, now, more
35 than she can bear, steel around her,
shouting, then, What is this thing she serves?
She asks me if I want more.
I own no words to stop her.
Even before I speak, she serves.

In many respects Ríos's poem closely follows the form of the traditional sestina. For instance, it interweaves six key words—"serves," "me," "her," "words," "more," and "speak"—through six groups of six lines each, rearranging the order in which the words appear so that the first line of each group of six lines ends with the key word that closed the preceding group of lines. The poem repeats the key words in exactly the order prescribed: *abcdef*, *faebdc, cfdabe,* and so on. In addition, the sestina closes with a three-line envoi that includes all six of the poem's key words, three at the ends of lines and three within the lines. However, Ríos departs from the sestina form by grouping his six sets of six lines not into six separate stanzas but rather into two eighteen-line stanzas.

The sestina form suits Ríos's subject matter. The focus of the poem, on the verbal and nonverbal interaction between the poem's "me" and "her," is reinforced by each of the related words. "Nani" is a poem about communication, and the key words return to probe this theme again and again. Throughout the poem these repeated words help to create a fluid, melodic, and tightly woven work.

❖ POEM FOR FURTHER READING: THE SESTINA

◇ ◇ ◇

ELIZABETH BISHOP
(1911–1979)

Sestina
(1965)

September rain falls on the house.
In the failing light, the old grandmother
sits in the kitchen with the child
beside the Little Marvel Stove,
5 reading the jokes from the almanac,
laughing and talking to hide her tears.

She thinks that her equinoctial tears
and the rain that beats on the roof of the house
were both foretold by the almanac,
10 but only known to a grandmother.
The iron kettle sings on the stove.
She cuts some bread and says to the child,

It's time for tea now; but the child
is watching the teakettle's small hard tears
15 dance like mad on the hot black stove,
the way the rain must dance on the house.
Tidying up, the old grandmother
hangs up the clever almanac

on its string. Birdlike, the almanac
20 hovers half open above the child,
hovers above the old grandmother
and her teacup full of dark brown tears.
She shivers and says she thinks the house
feels chilly, and puts more wood in the stove.

25 *It was to be,* says the Marvel Stove.
I know what I know, says the almanac.
With crayons the child draws a rigid house
and a winding pathway. Then the child
puts in a man with buttons like tears
30 and shows it proudly to the grandmother.

But secretly, while the grandmother
busies herself about the stove,
the little moons fall down like tears
from between the pages of the almanac
35 into the flower bed the child
has carefully placed in the front of the house.

Time to plant tears, says the almanac.
The grandmother sings to the marvellous stove
and the child draws another inscrutable house.

READING AND REACTING

1. Does the poet's adherence to a traditional form create any problems? For example, do you think the syntax is strained at any point? Explain.
2. How does this sestina use sound—metre, rhyme, alliteration, assonance, and so on? Could sound have been used more effectively? How?
3. **JOURNAL ENTRY** How are the six key words related to the poem's theme?

Related Works: "My Papa's Waltz" (p. 570), "Nani" (p. 767)

THE VILLANELLE

The **villanelle,** first introduced in France in the Middle Ages, is a nineteen-line poem composed of five tercets and a concluding quatrain; its rhyme scheme is *aba aba aba aba aba abaa.* Two different lines are systematically repeated in the poem: line 1 appears again in lines 6, 12, and 18, and line 3 reappears as lines 9, 15, and 19. Thus, each tercet concludes with an exact (or close) duplication of either line 1 or line 3, and the final quatrain concludes by repeating both line 1 and line 3.

THEODORE ROETHKE
(1908–1963)

The Waking
(1953)

I wake to sleep, and take my waking slow.
I feel my fate in what I cannot fear.
I learn by going where I have to go.

We think by feeling. What is there to know?
5 I hear my being dance from ear to ear.
I wake to sleep, and take my waking slow.

Of those so close beside me, which are you?
God bless the Ground! I shall walk softly there,
And learn by going where I have to go.

10 Light takes the Tree; but who can tell us how?
The lowly worm climbs up a winding stair;
I wake to sleep, and take my waking slow.

Great Nature has another thing to do
To you and me; so take the lively air,
15 And, lovely, learn by going where to go.

This shaking keeps me steady. I should know.
What falls away is always. And is near.
I wake to sleep, and take my waking slow.
I learn by going where I have to go.

"The Waking," like all villanelles, closely intertwines threads of sounds and words. The repeated lines and the very regular rhyme and metre give the poem a monotonous, almost hypnotic, rhythm. This poem uses end rhyme and repeats entire lines. It also makes extensive use of alliteration (I feel my fate in what I cannot fear") and internal rhyme ("I hear my being dance from ear to ear"; "I wake to sleep and take my waking slow"). The result is a tightly constructed poem of overlapping sounds and images. (For another well-known example of a villanelle, see Dylan Thomas's "Do Not Go Gentle into That Good Night," p. 571.)

◈ POEM FOR FURTHER READING: THE VILLANELLE

WILLIAM MEREDITH
(1919–   )

In Memory of Donald A. Stauffer
(1987)

Armed with an indiscriminate delight
His ghost left Oxford five summers ago,
Still on the sweet, obvious side of right.

How many friends and students talked all night
5 With this remarkable teacher? How many go
Still armed with his indiscriminate delight?

He liked, but often could not reach, the bright:
Young people sometimes prefer not to know
About the sweet or obvious sides of right.

10 But how all arrogance involves a slight
To knowledge, his humility would show
Them, and his indiscriminate delight

In what was true. This was why he could write
Commonplace books: his patience lingered so
15 Fondly on the sweet, obvious side of right.

What rare anthology of ghosts sits till first light
In the understanding air where he talks now,
Armed with his indiscriminate delight
There on the sweet and obvious side of right?

READING AND REACTING

1. Review the definition of *villanelle,* and explain how Meredith's poem expands the possibilities of the traditional villanelle.
2. Try to make the changes you believe are necessary to make Meredith's poem absolutely consistent with the traditional villanelle form. How does your editing change the poem?
3. **JOURNAL ENTRY** What kinds of subjects do you think would be most appropriate for villanelles? Why? What subjects, if any, do you think would not be appropriate? Explain.

Related Works: "Do Not Go Gentle into That Good Night" (p. 571), "The Waking" (p. 770)

THE EPIGRAM

Originally, an epigram was an inscription carved in stone on a monument or statue. As a literary form, an **epigram** is a very brief poem that makes a pointed, often sarcastic, comment in a surprising twist at the end. In a sense, it is a poem with a punch line. Although some epigrams rhyme, others do not. Many are only two lines long, but others are somewhat longer. What they have in common is their economy of language and their tone. One of the briefest of epigrams, written by Ogden Nash, appeared in *The New Yorker* magazine in 1931:

The Bronx?
No thonx.

In just four words, Nash manages to convey the unexpected, using rhyme and creative spelling to convey his assessment of a borough of New York City. The poem's two lines are perfectly balanced, making the contrast between the noncommittal tone of the first and the negative tone of the second quite striking.

■ POEMS FOR FURTHER READING: THE EPIGRAM

› › ›

SAMUEL TAYLOR COLERIDGE
(1772–1834)

What Is an Epigram?
(1802)

What is an epigram? a dwarfish whole,
Its body brevity, and wit its soul.

› ◇ ◇

WILLIAM BLAKE
(1757–1827)

Her Whole Life Is an Epigram
(c. 1793–1811)

Her whole life is an epigram: smack, smooth & neatly penned,
Platted[1] quite neat to catch applause, with a sliding noose at the end.

READING AND REACTING

1. Read the two preceding epigrams, and explain the point each one makes.
2. Evaluate each poem. What qualities do you conclude make an epigram effective?

   Related Works: "General Review of the Sex Situation" (p. 583), "Fire and Ice" (p. 632), "You Fit into Me" (p. 723)

HAIKU

Like an epigram, a haiku compresses words into a very small package. Unlike an epigram, however, a haiku focuses on an image, not an idea. A traditional Japanese form, the **haiku** is a brief unrhymed poem that presents the essence of some aspect of nature, concentrating a vivid image in just three lines. Although in the strictest sense a haiku consists of seventeen syllables divided into lines of five, seven, and five syllables, respectively, not all poets conform to this rigid form.

---

[1] Braided.

The following poem is a translation of a classic Japanese haiku by Matsuo Basho:

> Silent and still: then
> Even sinking into the rocks,
> The cicada's screech.

Notice that this poem conforms to the haiku's three-line structure and traditional subject matter, vividly depicting a natural scene without comment or analysis.

As the next poem illustrates, haiku in English is not always consistent with the traditional haiku in form or subject matter.

RICHARD BRAUTIGAN
(1935–1984)

Widow's Lament[1]

> It's not quite cold enough
> to go borrow some firewood
> from the neighbors.

Brautigan's haiku adheres to the traditional pattern's number of lines and syllables, and its central idea is expressed in very concentrated terms. The poem's focus, however, is not the natural world but human psychology. Moreover, without the title, the poem would be so ambiguous as to be meaningless. In this sense, the poet "cheats" the form, depending on the title's four syllables as well as on the seventeen of the poem itself to convey his ideas.

READING AND REACTING

1. **JOURNAL ENTRY** Referring to the additional haiku poems in Chapter 15 as well as to those in this chapter, write a broad definition of *haiku* that applies to all of them.

Related Works: "Fog" (p. 879), "I Wandered Lonely as a Cloud" (p. 897)

---

[1] Publication date is not available.

OPEN FORM
◊ ◊ ◊

An **open form** poem (sometimes called **free verse** or *vers libre*) makes occasional use of rhyme and metre, but it has no easily identifiable pattern or design—that is, it has no conventional stanzaic divisions, no consistent metrical pattern, and no repeated rhyme scheme. Still, although open form poetry has no distinguishable pattern of metre, rhyme, or line length, it is not necessarily shapeless, untidy, or randomly ordered. All poems have form, and the form of a poem may be determined by factors such as the appearance of words on the printed page or pauses in natural speech as well as by conventional metrical patterns or rhyme schemes.

Open form poetry invites readers to participate in the creative process, to discover the relationship between form and meaning. Some modern poets believe that only open form offers them freedom to express their ideas or that the subject matter or mood of their poetry demands a relaxed, experimental approach to form. For example, when Lawrence Ferlinghetti portrays the poet as an acrobat who "climbs on rime" (p. 704), he constructs his poem in a way that is consistent with the poet/acrobat's willingness to take risks. Thus, the poem's idiosyncratic form supports its ideas about the possibilities of poetry and the poet as experimenter.

Without a predetermined pattern, however, poets must create forms that suit their needs, and they must continue to shape and reshape the look of the poem on the page as they revise its words. Thus, open form represents a challenge, a way to experiment with fresh arrangements of words and new juxtapositions of ideas.

For some poets, such as Tim Bowling, open form provides an opportunity to create **prose poems.**

◊ ◊ ◊

TIM BOWLING
(1964–   )

Hamlet
(2001)

A matinee, late winter, in a theatre converted from the city's old
bus-barns. An audience of perhaps twelve, fewer than the cast.
Three seats over, a critic, wolf-lean and melancholy as the Dane,
scoffingly responds to my wife's question of "Business or
5 pleasure?" with "Shakespeare? Oh, business, business." So begins
the twenty-first century.

The pigeon-grey light of a snow-holding sky sifts in through
narrow windows high over the char-black stage. The language
clips, barks, coddles, sighs. "Seems, I know not seems," Hamlet

10 scowls, and I am out of the play a moment. In my pocket, a letter
from my mother. In the letter, a photocopy of a telegram from
1916, informing my grandmother that my grandfather had been
seriously wounded at a battle in France. Reality more than thrice-
removed, the Chinese box-in-box of facts. It only seems we
15 understand the lives we're from, the lives we love. Now Hamlet is
mad at his mother, or is his antic disposition on? I'm back in the
slurry of syllables, the jaw-clench of consonants, older than the
wars of any living memory.

When Hamlet jounces the skull of Yorick, I wonder whose skull it
20 is. How long in the company? Borrowed from a medical
classroom, a legacy from some dead Hamlet's will, the director
gone mad with gravedigging? The skull of X as the skull of Yorick,
a creation out of the skull of Shakespeare (who might not be who
we think he is) held by four centuries of players memorizing in
25 four centuries of skulls the words that flow around the borrowed
hoisted skull. Box-in-box-in-box. My mother's letter white as a
skull, the snow about to fall, a breaking skull. And on my neck, my
own, in which my thoughts, the play, the past converge.

The players have settled in their black snow to the stage. They
30 have died and yet they rise and bow. After the crow's caw of
applause, I rub the blank letters of my palms, as if to find their
real colour, but that's another play, another business, another
death of pleasure. The lights come up. Twelve skulls enter the
cool air. The snow falls, its faint sound English and old, fanned by
35 the wings of drifting cygnets. All the way home, in the chill,
regnant down of mortality, the fading light whispers "seems."

"Hamlet" uses capitalization and punctuation conventionally, but the format
of the poem looks more like prose than poetry (perhaps acknowledging that
the difference is not absolute). The poem is divided into four stanzas/para-
graphs, and the arrangement of the words on the page seems to follow the
form of prose—the writing that goes all the way over to the right-hand side of
the page. But Bowling plays with the idea of appearance and reality—in the
form of his piece and in its content—and to emphasize the discrepancy
between appearance and reality, he alludes to *Hamlet*, a play that is built on
false appearances. Hamlet, himself, says, "I know not 'seems'" when criticized
by his mother for what appears to be excessive grief at the death of his father.
Bowling's speaker is watching a production of *Hamlet* and contemplating a
photocopy of a 1916 telegram announcing that his grandfather had been
wounded in the war. The copy is in a letter from his mother, and the speaker's
attention flickers between the letter and its contents and the play. The blocks
of type indicate the density of the subjects: relationships between mother and
son; convergence of living and dead, dramatic and poetic; and the overriding

aspect of appearance. When the speaker ends with the word "'seems,'" he pays homage to Hamlet and to the reality of death.

Bowling's format reminds the readers of Shakespeare's poetry in the play, along with its enduring concerns. While a poet could certainly use other forms, Bowling has effectively generated imagery and consideration of theme through a prose poem.

Open form poetry need not look like Bowling's poem. The following poem experiments with a different kind of open form.

◊   ◊   ◊

E. E. CUMMINGS
(1894–1962)

the sky was can dy
(1925)

<pre>
        the
            sky
                was
        can   dy lu
 5   minous
                edible
        spry
                pinks shy
        lemons
10   greens   coo   l choc
        olate
        s.

            un   der,
            a lo
15   co
        mo
            tive   s pout
                        ing
                            vi
20   o
                        lets
</pre>

Like many of Cummings's poems, this one seems ready to skip off the page. Its irregular line length and its unconventional capitalization, punctuation, and word divisions immediately draw readers' attention to its form. Despite these oddities, and despite the absence of orderly rhyme and metre, the poem does have its conventional elements. A closer examination reveals that the poem's theme—the beauty of the sky—is quite conventional; that the poem is divided, although somewhat crudely, into two sections; and that the poet does use some rhyme—"spry" and "shy," for example. However, Cummings's sky is described not in traditional terms, but rather as something "edible," not only in terms of colour but of flavour as well. The breaks within words ("can dy lu / minous"; "coo l choc / olate / s") seem to expand each word's possibilities, visually stretching them to the limit, extending their taste and visual image over several lines and, in the case of the last two words, visually reinforcing the picture the words describe. In addition, the isolation of syllables exposes hidden rhyme, as in "lo / co / mo" and "lu" / "coo." By using open form, Cummings makes a clear statement about the capacity of a poem to move beyond the traditional boundaries set by words and lines.

❖ POEMS FOR FURTHER READING: OPEN FORM

LORNA CROZIER
(1948–   )

Inventing the Hawk
(1992)

She didn't believe the words
when she first heard them, that blue
bodiless sound entering her ear.
But now something was in the air,
5   a sense of waiting as if
the hawk itself were there
just beyond the light, blinded
by a fine-stitched leather hood
she must take apart with her fingers.
10   Already she had its voice,
the scream that rose from her belly
echoed in the dark inverted
canyon of her skull.

She built its wings, feather by feather,
15   the russet smoothness of its head,
the bead-bright eyes,
in that moment between sleep and waking.

Was she the only one
who could remember them,
20   who knew their shape and colours, the way

they could tilt the world with a list of wings?
Perhaps it was her reason for living
so long in this hard place
of wind and sky, the stunted trees
25 reciting their litany of loss
outside her window.

Elsewhere surely someone was drawing
gophers and mice out of the air.
Maybe that was also her job,
30 so clearly she could see them.
She'd have to lie here forever,
dreaming hair after hair,
summoning the paws (her own heart
turning timid, her nostrils twitching).

35 Then she would cause the seeds
in their endless variety—the ones
floating light as breath,
the ones with burrs and spears
that caught in her socks
40 when she was a child,
the radiant, uninvented blades of grass.

READING AND REACTING

1. The poem has open form, but it is strictly arranged into five stanzas. What is the purpose of the division?
2. What does the hawk represent other than itself?
3. Why choose a hawk as opposed to a different bird or animal?
4. How are the sentences arranged into lines? What is the organizing principle?
5. Hawks, mice, and gophers are all mentioned in the poem. What setting do these creatures suggest?
6. The final stanza focuses on the image of seeds and the power of the imagination to bring the seeds to fruition. What is the poet suggesting about poetry?
7. **JOURNAL ENTRY** How does the spirit of place infuse the poem with emotion?

Related Works: "The Yellow Wall-Paper" (p. 189), "Whatever Else Poetry Is Freedom" (p. 558), "Pumpkins" (p. 742)

BILLIE LIVINGSTON
(1965–   )

Letter from Lucy
(2001)

I'm riding in the back of some guy's car tonight
high, feeling Jamaican wind play my cheeks
with a million   separate   breaths
that sidle
5   down, puff my shirt like a sail
and patter cotton lush against my breasts
knowing back home it's December for real.

I'm ready to swoon
when my mind starts
10 rummaging through pockets for guilt.
There's a letter there—Lucy's—my father's ex,
the one who fawned on me,
envied my mother's luck having a girl,
who told her off for saying I had the uglies at six.

15 I can see her like I saw her at seven,
making peanut butter sandwiches,
backhanding bleach-blonde from her eyes
cussing in the heat, talking sex
with my mother like I'd never understand, flirting
20 with cops who'd come to complain about me.

I read her letter on the plane over here, then stuffed
it in a pocket where I wouldn't be reminded
on my vacation. My mind is just now cracking
the page like fresh newspaper, reading
25 snatches out like headlines:

ONE OF THOSE ANIMALS
WHO LIKES TO BE ALONE WHEN THEY'RE SICK

Wish this guy driving would pick up speed—punch
the wind a little harder, whip
30 the page out my ears through the open window
to the sugar cane fields we're passing.

WEEK OF RADIATION—

Step on the gas you bastard.

THEY SAY THEY WOULDN'T WASTE THE MONEY
35 IF IT DIDN'T HELP

He's stopping at a red light, leaning
out the window, shooting
the breeze with a pal.

CANCER ON LUNG, LIVER,
40 I FEEL LIKE SHIT.

I sit tight, try to breathe the fat, hanging air
but there's peanut butter in my throat
and they're about to arrest me for stealing candy.

READING AND REACTING

1. Examine the line lengths in Livingston's poem. What control is
   exerted over the syntax of the sentences?
2. Why is the placement of words in the first stanza less regular than
   in other stanzas? How does the form mirror the emotional state
   of the speaker?
3. How does the memory of childhood events contribute to the
   effect of the poem?
4. Capitalization is used for what purpose?
5. Why is the speaker desperate for the driver to go more quickly?
6. **JOURNAL ENTRY** How do the thoughts of the speaker reveal her
   character?

Related Works: "Flight Paths of the Emperor" (p. 354), "Not Waving but
Drowning" (p. 884), *Hamlet* (p. 1093)

◆ ◆ ◆

WILLIAM CARLOS WILLIAMS
(1883–1963)

Spring and All
(1923)

By the road to the contagious hospital
under the surge of the blue
mottled clouds driven from the
northeast—a cold wind. Beyond, the

5 waste of broad, muddy fields
brown with dried weeds, standing and fallen

patches of standing water
the scattering of tall trees

All along the road the reddish
10 purplish, forked, upstanding, twiggy
stuff of bushes and small trees
with dead, brown leaves under them
leafless vines—

Lifeless in appearance, sluggish
15 dazed spring approaches—

They enter the new world naked,
cold, uncertain of all
save that they enter. All about them
the cold, familiar wind—

20 Now the grass, tomorrow
the stiff curl of wildcarrot leaf
One by one objects are defined—
It quickens: clarity, outline of leaf

But now the stark dignity of
25 entrance—Still, the profound change
has come upon them: rooted, they
grip down and begin to awaken

READING AND REACTING

1. What elements of traditional closed form poems are present in "Spring and All"? What elements are absent?
2. What does Williams accomplish by isolating two sets of two lines each (7–8; 14–15)?
3. "Spring and All" uses assonance, alliteration, and repetition. Give several examples of each technique, and explain what each adds to the poem.
4. **JOURNAL ENTRY** "Spring and All" includes only two periods. Elsewhere, where readers might expect to find end punctuation, the poet uses colons, dashes, or no punctuation at all. Why do you think the poet made these decisions about the use of punctuation?
5. **CRITICAL PERSPECTIVE** In the book *Spring and All,* in which this poem appeared, Williams claimed to be staking out a "new world" of poetry addressed "to the imagination." However, in *Lives of the Modern Poets* (1980), William H. Pritchard challenges this claim:

[T]o believe that Williams's talk about the Imagination, the "new world," points to some radical way in which this poem is in advance of more traditional versifiers seems to me mistaken. Consider the last five lines of a poem [Robert] Frost had written, in conventional meters, a few years before:

> How Love burns through the Putting in the Seed
> On through the watching for that early birth
> When, just as the soil tarnishes with weed,
> The sturdy seedling with arched body comes
> Shouldering its way and shedding the earth crumbs.

This birth is every bit as imaginative, every bit as much of a new world, as anything in ["Spring and All"].

What do you think of Pritchard's evaluation of Williams's poem?

Related Works: "Comparatives" (p. 745), "Pied Beauty" (p. 751)

◊ ◊ ◊

CAROLYN FORCHÉ
(1950–   )

The Colonel
(1978)

What you have heard is true. I was in his house. His wife carried a tray of coffee and sugar. His daughter filed her nails, his son went out for the night. There were daily papers, pet dogs, a pistol on the cushion beside him. The moon swung bare on its black cord over
5 the house. On the television was a cop show. It was in English. Broken bottles were embedded in the walls around the house to scoop the kneecaps from a man's legs or cut his hands to lace. On the windows there were gratings like those in liquor stores. We had dinner, rack of lamb, good wine, a gold bell was on the table for
10 calling the maid. The maid brought green mangoes, salt, a type of bread. I was asked how I enjoyed the country. There was a brief commercial in Spanish. His wife took everything away. There was some talk then of how difficult it had become to govern. The parrot said hello on the terrace. The colonel told it to shut up, and pushed
15 himself from the table. My friend said to me with his eyes: say nothing. The colonel returned with a sack used to bring groceries home. He spilled many human ears on the table. They were like dried peach halves. There is no other way to say this. He took one of them in his hands, shook it in our faces, dropped it into a water
20 glass. It came alive there. I am tired of fooling around he said. As for the rights of anyone, tell your people they can go fuck themselves. He swept the ears to the floor with his arm and held the last of his wine in the air. Something for your poetry, no? he said. Some

of the ears on the floor caught this scrap of his voice. Some of the
25 ears on the floor were pressed to the ground.

READING AND REACTING

1. Treating Forché's prose poem as prose rather than poetry, try
   dividing it into paragraphs. What determines where you make
   your divisions?
2. If you were to reshape "The Colonel" into a more conventional-
   looking poem, what options might you have? Rewrite the poem
   so it "looks like poetry," and compare your revision to the original. Which version do you find more effective? Why?
3. What is the main point of "The Colonel"? How does the form
   help Forché to communicate this point?
4. **JOURNAL ENTRY** Do you think "The Colonel" is poetry or
   prose? Consider its subject matter and language as well as its form.
5. **CRITICAL PERSPECTIVE** Writing in the *New York Times Book
   Review,* critic Katha Pollitt focuses on "poetic clichés," which, she
   says, are "attempts to energize the poem by annexing a subject
   that is guaranteed to produce a knee-jerk response in the reader.
   This saves a lot of bother all around, and enables poet and reader
   to drowse together in a warm bath of mutual admiration for each
   other's capacity for deep feeling and right thinking." Among these
   poetic clichés is something she calls "the CNN poem, which
   retells in overheated free verse a prominent news story involving
   war, famine, torture, child abuse or murder."

   Do you think "The Colonel" is a "CNN poem," or do you see it
   as something more than just a "poetic cliché"?

Related Works: "All about Suicide" (p. 7), "Hope" (p. 643)

⋄ ⋄ ⋄

CZESLAW MILOSZ
(1911–2004)

Christopher Robin[1]
(1998)

I must think suddenly of matters too difficult for a bear of little
brain. I have never asked myself what lies beyond the place
where we live, I and Rabbit, Piglet and Eeyore, with our friend
Christopher Robin. That is, we continued to live here, and

---

[1] In April of 1996 the international press carried the news of the death, at age seventy-five,
of Christopher Robin Milne, immortalized in a book by his father, A. A. Milne, *Winnie-
the-Pooh,* as Christopher Robin.

5 nothing changed, and I just ate my little something. Only
Christopher Robin left for a moment.

Owl says that immediately beyond our garden Time begins,
and that it is an awfully deep well. If you fall in it, you go
down and down, very quickly, and no one knows what
10 happens to you next. I was a bit worried about Christopher
Robin falling in, but he came back and then I asked him about
the well. "Old bear," he answered. "I was in it and I was falling
and I was changing as I fell. My legs became long, I was a big
person, I wore trousers down to the ground, I had a gray
15 beard, then I grew old, hunched, and I walked with a cane,
and then I died. It was probably just a dream, it was quite
unreal. The only real thing was you, old bear, and our shared
fun. Now I won't go anywhere, even if I'm called for an
afternoon snack."

READING AND REACTING

1. Who is the poem's speaker? How do you know? How would you
   characterize the speaker's voice?
2. For what purpose was this poem written? Considering this purpose, is the speaker the logical one to tell the poem's story? Who
   else could tell this story?
3. Does this **prose poem** include any conventional poetic elements? Could you argue that it is not in fact a poem? Explain.
4. **JOURNAL ENTRY** As the footnote to the poem points out, the real
   Christopher Robin Milne died in 1996. What has happened to the
   fictional Christopher Robin? How do you know?
5. **CRITICAL PERSPECTIVE** In a critical review of *Road-side Dog*, the
   volume of poems that includes "Christopher Robin," David S.
   Gross discusses the way in which Milosz wrestles with funda-
   mental issues in his work:

   > This process of trying to arrive at an honest, dynamic sense of
   > self as the basis for then making sense of the world has been
   > for Milosz a lifelong vocation. *Road-side Dog* is the fruit of the
   > ninth decade of his life, the tenth decade of this century, still
   > trying to understand what it means to be human, what it has
   > meant to be human in this century, clearly still seeking, and
   > fashioning his meanings provisionally, on the basis of where
   > he is at this latest point in his search for self-definition.

   In what sense does "Christopher Robin" deal with the issue of
   "what it means to be human"?

Related Works: "Antigone" (p. 293), "Musée des Beaux Arts" (p. 815), *The
Shape of a Girl* (p. 1348)

CONCRETE POETRY

◆ ◆ ◆

With roots in the ancient Greek *pattern poems* and the sixteenth- and seventeenth-century *emblem poems,* contemporary **concrete poetry** uses words—and, sometimes, different fonts and type sizes—to shape a picture on the page. The form of a concrete poem is not something that emerges from the poem's words and images, but rather something predetermined by the visual image the poet has decided to create. Although some concrete poems are little more than novelties, others—like the poem that follows— can be original and enlightening.

◆ ◆ ◆

MAY SWENSON
(1913–1989)

Women
(1970)

Women	Or they
should be	should be
pedestals	little horses
moving	those wooden
5 pedestals	sweet
moving	oldfashioned
to the	painted
motions	rocking
of men	horses
10 the gladdest things in the toyroom	
The	feelingly
pegs	and then
of their	unfeelingly
ears	To be
15 so familiar	joyfully
and dear	ridden
to the trusting	rockingly
fists	ridden until
To be chafed	the restored
20 egos dismount and the legs stride away	
Immobile	willing
sweetlipped	to be set
sturdy	into motion
and smiling	Women
25 women	should be
should always	pedestals
be waiting	to men

The curved shape of the poem immediately reinforces its title, and the arrangement of words on the page suggests a variety of visual directions readers might follow. The two columns seem at first to suggest two alternatives: "Women should be. . . ." / "Or they should be. . . ." A closer look, however, reveals that the poem's central figures of speech, such as woman as rocking horse and woman as pedestal, move back and forth between the two columns of images. This exchange of positions might suggest that the two possibilities are really just two ways of looking at one limited role. Thus, the experimental form of the poem visually challenges the apparent complacency of its words, suggesting that women, like words, need not fall into traditional roles or satisfy conventional expectations.

❖ POEMS FOR FURTHER READING: CONCRETE POETRY

◊ ◊ ◊

GEORGE HERBERT
(1593–1633)

Easter Wings
(1633)

Lord, who createdst man in wealth and store,
Though foolishly he lost the same,
Decaying more and more
Till he became
Most poor,
With thee
Oh, let me rise
As larks, harmoniously,
And sing this day thy victories; 5
Then shall the fall further the flight in me.

My tender age in sorrow did begin; 10
And still with sicknesses and shame
Thou didst so punish sin,
That I became
Most thin.
With thee 15
Let me combine,
And feel this day thy victory;
For if I imp my wing on thine,
Affliction shall advance the flight in me. 20

READING AND REACTING

1. In this example of an **emblem poem,** lines are arranged so that shape and language reinforce each other. Explain how this is

accomplished. (For example, how does line length support the poem's images and ideas?)

2. This poem has a definite rhyme scheme. How would you describe it? What relationship do you see between the rhyme scheme and the poem's visual divisions?

Related Works: "l(a" (p. 564), "A Valediction: Forbidding Mourning" (p. 710), "Because I Could Not Stop for Death" (p. 737)

◇ ◇ ◇

BP NICHOL
(1944–1988)

Blues
(1970)

READING AND REACTING

1. "Blues" cannot be read as a linear poem can be, but must be looked at as a picture. How does the arrangement of letters and words help to convey an attitude about love?

2. Although "Blues" can be seen as a playful poem, does it have a serious component?

Related Works: "l(a" (p. 564), "Variations on the Word *Love*" (p. 581), "Bartok and the Geranium" (p. 792)

 # CHECKLIST: WRITING ABOUT FORM

✓ Is the poem written in open or closed form? On what characteristics do you base your conclusion?

✓ Why did the poet choose open or closed form? For example, is the poem's form consistent with its subject matter, tone, or theme? Is it determined by the conventions of the historical period in which it was written?

✓ If the poem is arranged in closed form, does the pattern apply to single lines, to groups of lines, or to the entire poem? What factors determine the breaks between groups of lines?

✓ Is the poem a sonnet? A sestina? A villanelle? An epigram? A haiku? How do the traditional form's conventions suit the poet's language and theme? Is the poem consistent with the requirements of the form at all times, or does it break any new ground?

✓ If the poem is arranged in open form, what determines the breaks at the ends of lines?

✓ Are certain words or phrases isolated on lines? Why?

✓ How do elements such as assonance, alliteration, rhyme, and repetition of words give the poem form?

✓ What use does the poet make of punctuation and capitalization? Of white space on the page?

✓ Is the poem a prose poem? How does this form support the poem's subject matter?

✓ Is the poem a concrete poem? How does the poet use the visual shape of the poem to convey meaning?

◆ WRITING SUGGESTIONS: FORM

1. Reread the definitions of *closed form* and *open form* in this chapter. Do you consider concrete poetry "open" or "closed"? Explain your position in a short essay, supporting your conclusion with specific references to the three concrete poems in this chapter.

2. Some poets—for example, Emily Dickinson and Robert Frost— write both open and closed form poems. Choose one open and one closed form poem by a single poet, and explain the poet's

possible reasons for choosing each type of form. In your analysis of the two poems, defend the poet's choices if you can.

3. Do you see complex forms, such as the villanelle and the sestina, as just exercises, or even merely opportunities for poets to show off their skills, or do you believe the special demands of the forms add something valuable to the poem? To help you answer this question, read "Do Not Go Gentle into That Good Night" (p. 571), and analyze Dylan Thomas's use of the villanelle's structure to enhance his poem's theme. Or, study Elizabeth Bishop's "Sestina" (p. 769), and consider how her use of the sestina's form helps her to convey her ideas.

4. The following open form poem is an alternate version of May Swenson's "Women" (p. 786). Read the two versions carefully, and write an essay in which you compare them. What differences do you notice? Which do you think was written first? Why? Do the two poems make the same point? Which makes the point with less ambiguity? Which is more effective? Why?

Women

Women should be pedestals
moving pedestals
moving to the motions of men
Or they should be little horses
5 those wooden sweet oldfashioned painted rocking horses
the gladdest things in the toyroom
The pegs of their ears so familiar and dear
to the trusting fists
To be chafed feelingly
10 and then unfeelingly
To be joyfully ridden
until the restored egos dismount and the legs stride away
Immobile sweetlipped sturdy and smiling
women should always be waiting
15 willing to be set into motion
Women should be pedestals to men

5. Look through the "Poetry for Further Reading" section that follows Chapter 19 of this text, and identify one or two prose poems. Write an essay in which you consider why the form seems suitable for the poem or poems you have chosen. Is there a particular kind of subject matter that seems especially appropriate for a prose poem?

CHAPTER 19

Symbol, Allegory, Allusion, Myth

◆ ◆ ◆

What the reader gets from a symbol depends not only upon what the author has put into it but upon the reader's sensitivity and his consequent apprehension of what is there. The feeling of profundity that accompanies it comes from a gradual but never final penetration of the form.

WILLIAM YORK TINDALL, "Excellent Dumb Discourse"

Myth is an arrangement of the past, whether real or imagined, in patterns that resonate with a culture's deepest values and aspirations. Myths create and reinforce archetypes so taken for granted, so seemingly axiomatic, that they go unchallenged. Myths are so fraught with meaning that we live and die by them. They are the maps by which cultures navigate through time.

RONALD WRIGHT, *Stolen Continents: The "New World" through Indian Eyes*

A myth is not "a large controlling image." The future of mythical poetry does not depend upon reconciling poetry with an image. It depends rather upon making of poetry something it is always striving against human bias and superficiality to become. The poetical imagination when it attains any consistent fire and efficacy is always displacing the texture of the mind into the external world so that it becomes a theater of preternatural forces. A certain control and direction given the poetical emotions, and poetry, as it always has, becomes mythical.

RICHARD CHASE, "Notes on the Study of Myth"

◆ ◆ ◆

◊ ◊ ◊

WILLIAM BLAKE
(1757–1827)

The Sick Rose
(1794)

O Rose thou art sick.
The invisible worm
That flies in the night,
In the howling storm:

5 Has found out thy bed
Of crimson joy:
And his dark secret love
Does thy life destroy.

SYMBOL
◊ ◊ ◊

As in fiction and drama, symbols in poetry function as a kind of shorthand, as a subtle way of introducing a significant idea or attitude. A **symbol** is an idea or image that suggests something else—but not in the simple way that a dollar sign stands for money or a flag represents a country. A symbol is an image that transcends its literal, or denotative, meaning in a complex way. For instance, if someone gives a rose to a loved one, it could simply be a sign of love. But in the poem "The Sick Rose," the rose has a range of contradictory and complementary meanings. For what does the rose stand? Beauty? Perfection? Passion? Something else? As this poem illustrates, the distinctive trait of a symbol is that its meaning cannot easily be pinned down or defined.

Such ambiguity can be frustrating, but it is precisely this characteristic of a symbol that enables it to enrich a work and to give it additional layers of meaning.

◊ ◊ ◊

DOROTHY LIVESAY
(1909–1996)

Bartok[1] and the Geranium
(1955)

She lifts her green umbrellas
Towards the pane
Seeking her fill of sunlight

---

[1] Béla Bartók (1881–1945), Hungarian pianist and composer.

Or of rain;
5 Whatever falls
She has no commentary
Accepts, extends,
Blows out her furbelows,
Her bustling boughs;

10 And all the while he whirls
Explodes in space,
Never content with this small room;
Not even can he be
Confined to sky
15 But must speed high
From galaxy to galaxy,
Wrench from the stars their momentary calm,
Stir music on the moon.

She's daylight;
20 He is dark,
She's heaven's held breath;
He storms and crackles
Spits with hell's own spark.

Yet in this room, this moment now
25 These together breathe and be:
She, essence of serenity,
He in a mad intensity
Soars beyond sight
Then hurls, lost Lucifer,[2]
30 From heaven's height.
And when he's done, he's out:

She lays a lip against the glass
And preens herself in light.

The central symbols in this poem are the geranium and the music of Bartok. A possible interpretation of the symbols is that the geranium represents females, even female sexuality, and the music represents males and male sexuality. The female symbol is contained and content, but the male symbol must move powerfully and resists enclosure.

Symbols that appear in works of fiction, poetry, or drama can be *conventional*, *universal*, or *private*. **Conventional symbols** are those recognized by people who share certain cultural and social assumptions. National flags, for example, evoke a general and agreed-upon response in most

---

[2] Satan.

people of a particular country and, for better or for worse, Canadians have for years perceived hockey and beer as symbolizing Canada. **Universal symbols** are those likely to be recognized by people regardless of their culture. In 1890, the noted Scottish anthropologist Sir James George Frazer wrote the first version of his work *The Golden Bough,* in which he showed parallels between the rites and beliefs of early cultures and those of Christianity. Fascinated by Frazer's work, the psychologist Carl Jung sought to explain these parallels by formulating a theory of **archetypes,** which held that certain images or ideas reside in the subconscious of all people. According to Jung, archetypal, or universal, symbols include water, symbolizing rebirth; spring, symbolizing growth; and winter, symbolizing death.

Sometimes symbols can be obscure or highly idiosyncratic **private symbols.** The works of William Blake and W. B. Yeats, for example, combine symbols from different cultural, theological, and philosophical sources to form complex networks of symbolic associations. To Blake, for example, the scientist Isaac Newton represents the tendency of scientists to quantify experience while ignoring the beauty and mystery of nature. Readers cannot begin to understand Blake's use of Newton as a symbol until they have read a number of his more difficult poems.

Most often, however, symbols in poems are not this challenging. In the following poem, for instance, the poet introduces a house cat—a symbol of domesticity—and makes his own use of it.

E. J. PRATT

(1882–1964)

The Prize Cat

(1937)

Pure blood domestic, guaranteed,
Soft-mannered, musical in purr,
The ribbon had declared the breed,
Gentility was in the fur.

5 Such feline culture in the gads[1]
No anger ever arched her back—
What distance since those velvet pads
Departed from the leopard's track!

And when I mused how Time had thinned
10 The jungle strains within the cells,
How human hands had disciplined
Those prowling optic parallels;

I saw the generations pass
Along the reflex of a spring,

---

[1] Claws.

15 A bird had rustled in the grass,
The tab had caught it on the wing:

Behind the leap so furtive-wild
Was such ignition in the gleam,
I thought an Abyssinian child
20 Had cried out in the whitethroat's[2] scream.

The symbolism in E. J. Pratt's "The Prize Cat" is not immediately obvious, but that opportunity for interpretation opens the poem to a variety of possibilities. One view is that the cat, which initially appears to be domesticated and gentle, symbolizes human beings with their thin veneer of civilized behaviour. Once the cat attacks the bird—an action common to cats—the veneer of gentility is peeled back to reveal the killer instinct beneath. By mentioning "an Abyssinian child," the speaker draws our attention to the atrocities that took place in Abyssinia (Ethiopia) in the early part of the last century. Pratt often used historical events for his poems: *Towards the Last Spike* is about the building of the CPR and its role in Canadian Confederation, and *The Titanic* is about the famous disaster at sea.

The symbolism in "The Prize Cat" is consistent in that the bird the cat catches is a "whitethroat" and therefore symbolizes the innocence of the children killed in Abyssinia. And the speed with which the cat moves toward its prey and the surprise of the human observer underline the narrow division between civilization and violence. Cats are bred to kill. Are human beings?

It is not enough simply to identify a series of symbols. Your decision that a particular item has some symbolic significance must be supported by the details of the poem and make sense within the context of the ideas developed within the poem. Moreover, the symbol must support the poem's ideas.

◊   ◊   ◊

P. K. PAGE
(1916–   )

The Stenographers
(1946)

After the brief bivouac of Sunday,
their eyes, in the forced march of Monday to Saturday,
hoist the white flag, flutter in the snow-storm of paper,
haul it down and crack in the mid-sun of temper.

5 In the pause between the first draft and the carbon
they glimpse the smooth hours when they were children—
the ride in the ice-cart, the ice-man's name,
the end of the route and the long walk home;

---

[2] Sparrow.

remember the sea where floats at high tide
10 were sea marrows growing on the scatter-green vine
or spools of grey toffee, or wasps' nests on water;
remember the sand and the leaves of the country.

Bell rings and they go and the voice draws their pencil
like a sled across snow; when its runners are frozen
15 rope snaps and the voice then is pulling no burden
but runs like a dog on the winter of paper.

Their climates are winter and summer—no wind
for the kites of their hearts—no wind for a flight;
a breeze at the most, to tumble them over
20 and leave them like rubbish—the boy-friends of blood.

In the inch of the noon as they move they are stagnant.
The terrible calm of the noon is their anguish;
the lip of the counter, the shapes of the straws
like icicles breaking their tongues, are invaders.

25 Their beds are their oceans—salt water of weeping
the waves that they know—the tide before sleep;
and fighting to drown they assemble their sheep
in columns and watch them leap desks for their fences
and stare at them with their own mirror-worn faces.

30 In the felt of the morning the calico-minded,
sufficiently starched, insert papers, hit keys,
efficient and sure as their adding machines;
yet they weep in the vault, they are taut as net curtains
stretched upon frames. In their eyes I have seen
35 the pin men of madness in marathon trim
race round the track of the stadium pupil.

P. K. Page's "The Stenographers" uses symbols effectively to show the unhappiness of the women trapped in their jobs as office workers. The language of the first stanza, for example, creates a military image: "bivouac," "forced march," and "white flag." Comparing being a stenographer to being a soldier in war—and defeat—symbolizes with sadness the plight of the stenographers, who see no end to their battle, their suffering. The poem is filled with symbols of oppression and despair. "Beds" are "oceans," and waves of tears that they shed reveal their personal collective loss. The lives of these women who are condemned to repetitive, unfulfilling tasks, tasks in which they are much like the machines with which they work, are hopeless and will lead, the speaker says, to "madness." Page's use of symbolism makes the imagery of the poem come alive and reinforces the argument that such work is soul-destroying.

❖ POEMS FOR FURTHER READING: SYMBOL

◊ ◊ ◊

LANGSTON HUGHES
(1902–1967)

Island
(1951)

Wave of sorrow,
Do not drown me now:

I see the island
Still ahead somehow.

5 I see the island
And its sands are fair:

Wave of sorrow,
Take me there.

READING AND REACTING

1. What makes you suspect that the island has symbolic significance in this poem? Is it a universal, conventional, or private symbol? Explain your answer.
2. Is the "wave of sorrow" also a symbol?
3. **JOURNAL ENTRY** Beyond its literal meaning, what might the island in this poem suggest? Consider several possibilities.
4. **CRITICAL PERSPECTIVE** In *Langston Hughes,* a 1973 study of the poet's work, Onwuchekwa Jemie writes that "the black writer's problem is . . . how to actualize the oral tradition in written form":

   The black writer . . . has no long written tradition of his own to emulate; and for him to abandon the effort to translate into written form that oral medium which is the full reservoir of his culture would be to annihilate his identity and become a zombie, a programmed vehicle for "the message of another people."

   Do you think "Island" successfully "actualizes the oral tradition in written form"? What elements help it to qualify as "oral" poetry?

Related Works: "A Worn Path" (p. 397), "Sea Grapes" (p. 813)

THEODORE ROETHKE
(1908–1963)

Night Crow
(1944)

When I saw that clumsy crow
Flap from a wasted tree,
Over the gulfs of dream
Flew a tremendous bird
5   Further and further away
Into a moonless black,
Deep in the brain, far back.

READING AND REACTING

1. What does the title suggest? How does it help you to interpret the symbolic significance of the crow?
2. How is the "clumsy crow" different from the crow "Deep in the brain"? What visual image does each suggest?
3. **JOURNAL ENTRY** It has been suggested that "Night Crow" is a commentary on the difference between reality and imagination. Does the poem's use of symbol support such an interpretation? Explain.

Related Works: "The Cask of Amontillado" (p. 227), "Inventing the Hawk" (p. 778), "The Tyger" (p. 823)

ALLEGORY
◊ ◊ ◊

Allegory is a form of narrative that conveys a message or doctrine by using people, places, or things to stand for abstract ideas. **Allegorical figures,** each with a strict equivalent, form an **allegorical framework,** a set of ideas that conveys the allegory's message or lesson. Thus, the allegory takes place on two levels: a literal level that tells a story and a figurative level where the allegorical figures in the story stand for ideas, concepts, and other qualities. Like symbols, allegory uses things to suggest other things. But unlike symbols, which have a range of possible meanings, allegorical figures can always be assigned specific meanings. (Because writers use allegory to instruct, they gain nothing by hiding its significance.) Thus, symbols open up possibilities for interpretation, whereas allegories tend to restrict possibilities.

   Quite often an allegory involves a journey or an adventure, as in the case of Dante's *Divine Comedy,* which traces a journey through Hell, Purgatory, and Heaven. Within an allegory, everything can have meaning: the road upon which the characters walk, the people they encounter, or a phrase that one of them repeats throughout the journey. Once you understand the allegorical framework, your main task is to see how the various elements fit within this system. Some poems can be relatively straightforward, but others can be so complicated that it takes a great deal of time and effort to unlock their meaning. In the following poem, a journey is central to the allegory.

◊ ◊ ◊

CHRISTINA ROSSETTI
(1830–1894)

Uphill
(1861)

Does the road wind uphill all the way?
  Yes, to the very end.
Will the day's journey take the whole long day?
  From morn to night, my friend.

5 But is there for the night a resting-place?
  A roof for when the slow dark hours begin.
May not the darkness hide it from my face?
  You cannot miss that inn.

Shall I meet other wayfarers at night?
10 Those who have gone before.
Then must I knock, or call when just in sight?
  They will not keep you standing at that door.

Shall I find comfort, travel-sore and weak?
  Of labor you shall find the sum.
15 Will there be beds for me and all who seek?
  Yea, beds for all who come.

"Uphill" uses a question-and-answer structure to describe a journey along an uphill road. Like the journey described in John Bunyan's seventeenth-century allegory *The Pilgrim's Progress,* this is a spiritual one that suggests a person's uphill journey through life. The day-and-night duration of the journey stands for life and death, and the inn at the end of the road stands for the grave, the final resting place.

◈ POEM FOR FURTHER READING: ALLEGORY

◈ ◈ ◈

ADRIENNE RICH
(1929–   )

Diving into the Wreck
(1973)

First having read the book of myths,
and loaded the camera,
and checked the edge of the knife-blade,
I put on
5 the body-armor of black rubber
the absurd flippers
the grave and awkward mask.
I am having to do this
not like Cousteau with his
10 assiduous team
aboard the sun-flooded schooner
but here alone.

There is a ladder.
The ladder is always there
15 hanging innocently
close to the side of the schooner.
We know what it is for,
we who have used it.
Otherwise
20 it's a piece of maritime floss
some sundry equipment.

I go down.
Rung after rung and still
the oxygen immerses me
25 the blue light
the clear atoms
of our human air.
I go down.
My flippers cripple me,
30 I crawl like an insect down the ladder
and there is no one
to tell me when the ocean
will begin.

First the air is blue and then
35 it is bluer and then green and then
black I am blacking out and yet

my mask is powerful
it pumps my blood with power
the sea is another story
40 the sea is not a question of power
I have to learn alone
to turn my body without force
in the deep element.

And now: it is easy to forget
45 what I came for
among so many who have always
lived here
swaying their crenellated fans
between the reefs
50 and besides
you breathe differently down here.

I came to explore the wreck.
The words are purposes.
The words are maps.
55 I came to see the damage that was done
and the treasures that prevail.
I stroke the beam of my lamp
slowly along the flank
of something more permanent
60 than fish or weed

the thing I came for:
the wreck and not the story of the wreck
the thing itself and not the myth
the drowned face always staring
65 toward the sun
the evidence of damage
worn by salt and sway into this threadbare beauty
the ribs of the disaster
curving their assertion
70 among the tentative haunters.

This is the place.
And I am here, the mermaid whose dark hair
streams black, the merman in his armored body
We circle silently
75 about the wreck
we dive into the hold.
I am she: I am he

whose drowned face sleeps with open eyes
whose breasts still bear the stress

80 whose silver, copper, vermeil cargo lies
obscurely inside barrels
half-wedged and left to rot
we are the half-destroyed instruments
that once held to a course
85 the water-eaten log
the fouled compass

We are, I am, you are
by cowardice or courage
the one who find our way
90 back to this scene
carrying a knife, a camera
a book of myths
in which
our names do not appear.

READING AND REACTING

1. On one level this poem is about a deep-sea diver's exploration of a wrecked ship. What details suggest that the poet wants you to see something more?
2. Explain the allegorical figures presented in the poem. What, for example, might the diver and the wreck represent?
3. Does the poem contain any symbols? How can you tell they are symbols and not allegorical figures?
4. **JOURNAL ENTRY** In lines 62–63, the speaker says that she came for "the wreck and not the story of the wreck / the thing itself and not the myth." What do you think the speaker is really looking for?
5. **CRITICAL PERSPECTIVE** A number of critics have seen "Diving into the Wreck" as an attempt by Rich to reimagine or reinvent the myths of Western culture. Rachel Blau DuPlessis makes this observation:

   In this poem of journey and transformation Rich is tapping the energies and plots of myth, while re-envisioning the content. While there is a hero, a quest, and a buried treasure, the hero is a woman; the quest is a critique of old myths; the treasure is knowledge. . . .

   Why do you suppose Rich decided to "reinvent" myth?

Related Works: "Young Goodman Brown" (p. 307), "The Love Song of J. Alfred Prufrock" (p. 833), "The Way the Weather Chose to Be Born" (p. 838)

ALLUSION

◊   ◊   ◊

An **allusion** is a brief reference to a person, place, or event, fictional or actual, that readers are expected to recognize. Like symbols and allegories, allusions enrich a work by introducing associations and attitudes from another context.

When poets use allusions, they assume that they and their readers have a common body of knowledge. If, when reading a poem, you come across a reference with which you are not familiar, take the time to look it up in a dictionary or an encyclopedia. As you have probably realized by now, your understanding of the meaning of a poem may depend on your ability to interpret an unfamiliar reference.

Although most poets expect readers to recognize their references, some use allusions to exclude readers from their work. In his 1922 poem "The Waste Land," for example, T. S. Eliot makes allusions to historical events, ancient languages, and obscure literary works. He even includes a set of notes to accompany his poem, but they do little more than complicate an already difficult text. (As you might expect, critical response to this poem was mixed, with some critics saying that it was a work of genius and others saying that it was pretentious.)

Allusions can come from any source: history, the arts, other works of literature, the Bible, current events, or even the personal life of the poet. In the following poem, the Nigerian poet and playwright Wole Soyinka alludes to several contemporary political figures.

◊   ◊   ◊

WOLE SOYINKA
(1934–   )

Future Plans
(1972)

The meeting is called
To odium: Forgers, framers
Fabricators Inter-
national. Chairman,
5   A dark horse, a circus nag turned blinkered sprinter
Mach Three
We rate him—one for the Knife
Two for 'iavelli, Three—
Breaking speed
10   Of the truth barrier by a swooping detention decree

Projects in view:
Mao Tse Tung in league
With Chiang Kai. Nkrumah
Makes a secret
15 Pact with Verwood, sworn by Hastings Banda.

Proven: Arafat
In flagrante cum
Golda Meir. Castro drunk
With Richard Nixon
20 Contraceptives stacked beneath the papal bunk . . .
. . . and more to come

This poem is structured like an agenda for a meeting. From the moment it announces that a meeting has been called "To odium" (a pun on "to *order*"), it is clear that the poem will be a bitter political satire. Those in attendance are "Forgers, framers / Fabricators." The second stanza contains three allusions that shed light on the character of the chairman. The first is to Mack the Knife, a petty criminal in Bertolt Brecht and Kurt Weill's 1933 *Threepenny Opera*. The second is to Niccolò Machiavelli, whose 1532 book *The Prince* advocates the use of unscrupulous means to strengthen the State. The last is to the term *mach,* which denotes the speed of an airplane in relation to the speed of sound—mach one, two, three, and so on. Through these allusions the poem implies that the meeting's chairman has been chosen for his ability to engage in violence, to be ruthless, and to break the "truth barrier"—that is, to lie.

The rest of the poem alludes to individuals involved in global politics—specifically, the politics of developing nations. According to the speaker, instead of fighting for the rights of the oppressed, these people consolidate their own political power by collaborating with those who oppose their positions. Thus, Mao Tse-tung, the former communist leader of China, is "in league with" Chiang Kai-shek, his old Nationalist Chinese enemy; Yassir Arafat, the leader of the Palestine Liberation Organization, is linked with Golda Meir, the former prime minister of Israel; Kwame Nkrumah, the first president of Ghana, conspires with Hendrick Verwoerd, the former prime minister of South Africa, assassinated in 1966; and former President Richard Nixon gets drunk with Cuba's communist leader, Fidel Castro. These allusions suggest the self-serving nature of political alliances and the extreme disorder of world politics. The ideological juxtapositions show the underlying sameness and interchangeability of various political philosophies, none of which has the answer to the world's problems. Whether the poem is satirizing the United Nations and its idealistic agenda, criticizing the tendency of politics to make strange bedfellows, or showing how corrupt all politicians are, its allusions enable the poet to broaden his frame of reference and thus make the poem more meaningful to readers.

The following poem uses allusions to writers, as well as to a myth, to develop its theme.

WILLIAM MEREDITH
(1919–   )

Dreams of Suicide
(1980)

(in sorrowful memory of Ernest Hemingway, Sylvia Plath, and John Berryman)

I

I reach for the awkward shotgun not to disarm
you, but to feel the metal horn,
furred with the downy membrane of dream.
More surely than the unicorn,
5 you are the mythical beast.

II

Or I am sniffing an oven. On all fours
I am imitating a totemic animal
but she is not my totem or the totem
of my people, this is not my magic oven.

III

10 If I hold you tight by the ankles,
still you fly upward from the iron railing.
Your father made these wings,
after he made his own, and now from beyond
he tells you *fly down,* in the voice
15 my own father might say *walk, boy.*

This poem is dedicated to the memory of three writers who committed suicide. In each stanza, the speaker envisions in a dream the death of one of
the writers. In the first stanza, he dreams of Ernest Hemingway, who killed
himself with a shotgun. The speaker grasps the "metal horn" of
Hemingway's shotgun and transforms him into a mythical beast who, like
a unicorn, represents the rare, unique talent of the artist. In the second
stanza, the speaker dreams of Sylvia Plath, who asphyxiated herself in a gas
oven. He sees himself, like Plath, on his knees imitating an animal sniffing
an oven. Finally, in the third stanza, the speaker dreams of John Berryman,
who leaped to his death. Berryman is characterized as Icarus, a mythological figure who, along with his father Daedalus, fled Crete by building wings
made of feathers and wax. Together they flew away, but, ignoring his
father's warning, Icarus flew too close to the sun and, when the wax melted,
fell to his death in the sea. Like Icarus, Berryman ignores the warning of his
father and, like Daedalus, the speaker tries to stop Berryman. In this poem,
then, the speaker uses allusions to make a point about the difficult lives of
writers—and, perhaps, to convey his own empathy for those who could not
survive the struggle to reconcile art and life.

❖ POEM FOR FURTHER READING: ALLUSION

◊ ◊ ◊

MICHÈLE LALONDE
(1937–)

Speak White
(1969)
Translated by D. G. Jones

Speak white
it is so lovely to listen to you
speaking of Paradise Lost
or the anonymous, graceful profile trembling in the sonnets of
    Shakespeare

5 We are a rude and stammering people
but we are not deaf to the genius of a language
speak with the accent of Milton and Byron and Shelley and Keats
speak white
and please excuse us if in return
10 we've only our rough ancestral songs
and the chagrin of Nelligan[1]

speak white
speak of places, this and that
speak to us of the Magna Carta
15 of the Lincoln Monument
of the cloudy charm of the Thames
or blossom-time on the Potomac
speak to us of your traditions
We are a people who are none too bright
20 but we are quick to sense
the great significance of crumpets
or the Boston Tea Party

But when you really speak white
when you get down to brass tacks
25 to speak of Better Homes and Gardens
and the high standard of living
and the Great Society
a little louder then speak white

---

[1] Émile Nelligan, a popular Quebec poet (1879–1941).

       raise your foremen's voices
30 we are a little hard of hearing
       we live too close to the machines
       and only hear our heavy breathing over the tools
       speak white and loud
       so we can hear you clearly
35 from Saint Henri to Santo Domingo
       yes, what a marvellous language
       for hiring and firing
       for giving the orders
       for fixing the hour to be worked to death
40 and that pause that refreshes
       and bucks up the dollar

       Speak white
       tell us that God is a great big shot
       and that we're paid to trust him
45 speak white
       speak to us of production, profits and percentages
       speak white
       it's a rich language
       for buying
50 but for selling oneself
       but for selling one's soul
       but for selling oneself

       Ah
       speak white
55 big deal
       but for telling about
       the eternity of a day on strike
       for telling the whole
       life-story of a nation of caretakers
60 for coming back home in the evening
       at the hour when the sun's gone bust in the alleys
       for telling you yes the sun does set yes
       every day of our lives to the east of your empires
       Nothing's as good as a language of oaths
65 our mode of expression none too clean
       dirtied with oil and with axle grease

       Speak white
       feel at home with your words
       we are a bitter people
70 but we'd never reproach a soul
       for having a monopoly
       on how to improve one's speech

In the sweet tongue of Shakespeare
with the accent of Longfellow
75 speak a French purely and atrociously white
as in Viet Nam, in the Congo
speak impeccable German
a yellow star between your teeth
speak Russian speak of the right to rule speak of repression
80 speak white
it's a universal language
we were born to understand it
with its tear-gas phrases
with its billy-club words

85 Speak white
tell us again about freedom and democracy
We know that liberty is a Black word
as misery is Black
as blood is muddied with the dust of Algiers² or of Little Rock³

90 Speak white
from Westminster to Washington take turns
speak white as on Wall Street
white as in Watts
Be civilized
95 and understand our conventional answer
when you ask us politely
how do you do
and we mean to reply
we're doing all right
100 we're doing fine
we
are not alone

We know now
that we are not alone.

READING AND REACTING

1. To what does the poem's title refer? Why does Lalonde use allusions to English writers?
2. Look up the FLQ (Front de libération du Québec). Note that Pierre Vallières, one of the members of the FLQ, wrote a book called

---

² Capital city of Algeria, which achieved independence from France in 1962, following seven years of war.

³ The United States Supreme Court's decision to desegregate schools in Little Rock, Arkansas, provoked demonstrations in 1958.

Nègres blancs d'Amérique (English translation: *White Niggers of America*). How necessary is knowledge of Quebec history to understand this poem?

3. Research the War Measures Act, which was invoked in the fall of 1970 (the October Crisis). Do these events fit the image Canadians often have of their country?

4. The poem broadens its focus from Quebec to other places around the world. What do they have in common?

5. **JOURNAL ENTRY** Consider the importance of language in the formation of individual and group identity. How can language work against self-identification?

Related Works: "The Loons" (p. 249), "The Devil's Language" (p. 650), "My Ledders" (p. 845), *The Shape of a Girl* (p. 1348)

MYTH

◊ ◊ ◊

A **myth** is a narrative that embodies—and in some cases helps to explain—the religious, philosophical, moral, and political values of a culture. Using gods and supernatural beings, myths try to make sense of occurrences in the natural world. (The term *myth* can also refer to a private belief system invented by an individual poet as well as to any fully realized fictitious setting in which a literary work takes place, such as the myths of William Faulkner's Yoknapatawpha County or Lawrence Durrell's Alexandria.) Contrary to popular usage, *myth* is not the same as *falsehood*. In the broadest sense, myths are stories—usually whole groups of stories—that can be true or partly true as well as false; regardless of their degree of accuracy, however, myths frequently express the deepest beliefs of a culture. According to this definition, then, the *Iliad* and the *Odyssey*, the Koran, and the Old and New Testaments can all be regarded as myths.

According to the mythologist Joseph Campbell, myths contain truths that link people together, whether they live today or lived 2,500 years ago. Myths do, after all, attempt to explain phenomena that human beings care about regardless of when and where they live. It is not surprising, then, that myths frequently contain archetypal images that cut across cultural and racial boundaries and touch us on a very deep level. Many Greek myths illustrate this power. For example, when Orpheus descends into Hades to rescue his wife, Eurydice, he acts out the human desire to transcend death; and when Telemachus sets out in search of his father, Odysseus, he reminds readers that we all are lost children searching for parents. When Icarus ignores his father and flies too near the sun and when Pandora cannot resist looking into a box that she has been told not to open, we are reminded of the human weaknesses we all share.

When poets use myths, they are actually making allusions. They expect readers to bring to the poem the cultural, emotional, and ethical context of the myths to which they are alluding. At one time, when all educated individuals studied the Greek and Latin classics as well as the Bible, poets could be reasonably sure that readers would recognize the mythological allusions they made. Many contemporary readers, however, are unable to understand the full significance of an allusion or its application within the poem. Although many of the poems in this anthology are accompanied by notes, these notes may not provide all the information you will need to understand each mythological allusion and determine its significance within a poem. Occasionally you may have to look for answers beyond this text, in dictionaries, encyclopedias, or collections of myths, such as the *New Larousse Encyclopedia of Mythology* or *Bulfinch's Mythology,* for example.

Sometimes a poet will allude to a myth in a title; sometimes references to various myths will appear throughout a poem; at other times, an entire poem will focus on a single myth. In each case, as in the following poem, the use of myth can help to communicate the poem's theme.

? ? ?

COUNTEE CULLEN
(1903–1946)

Yet Do I Marvel
(1925)

I doubt not God is good, well-meaning, kind,
And did He stoop to quibble could tell why
The little buried mole continues blind,
Why flesh that mirrors Him must some day die,
5 Make plain the reason tortured Tantalus
Is baited by the fickle fruit, declare
If merely brute caprice dooms Sisyphus
To struggle up a never-ending stair.
Inscrutable His ways are, and immune
10 To catechism by a mind too strewn
With petty cares to slightly understand
What awful brain compels His awful hand.
Yet do I marvel at this curious thing:
To make a poet black, and bid him sing!

The speaker in this poem begins by affirming his belief in the benevolence of God, but he then goes on to question why God engages in what appear to be capricious acts. As part of his catalogue of questions, the speaker mentions Tantalus and Sisyphus, two figures from Greek mythology. Tantalus was a king who was admitted to the society of the gods. Because he behaved so badly, he was condemned to Hades and forced to stand up to his chin in a pool of water over which hung a branch laden with fruit. When he got thirsty and tried to drink, the level of the water would drop, and when he got hungry and reached for fruit, it would move just out of his grasp. Thus, Tantalus was doomed to be near what he most desired, but forever unable to obtain it. Like Tantalus, Sisyphus was also condemned to Hades. For his disrespect to Zeus, he was sentenced to endless toil. Every day, Sisyphus would push a gigantic boulder up a steep hill. As he neared the top, the boulder would slip down the hill, and he would have to begin again. Like Tantalus, the speaker cannot have what he wants; like Sisyphus, he is forced to toil in vain. He wonders why a well-meaning God would "make a poet black, and bid him sing" in a racist society that does not listen to his voice. Thus, the poet's two allusions to Greek mythology enrich the poem by connecting the suffering of the speaker to a universal drama that has been acted out again and again.

❖ POEMS FOR FURTHER READING: MYTH

ALDEN NOWLAN
(1933–1983)

The Bull Moose
(1962)

Down from the purple mist of trees on the mountain,
lurching through forests of white spruce and cedar,
stumbling through tamarack swamps,
came the bull moose
5 to be stopped at last by a pole-fenced pasture.

Too tired to turn or, perhaps, aware
there was no place left to go, he stood with the cattle.
They, scenting the musk of death, seeing his great head
like the ritual mask of a blood god, moved to the other end
10 of the field, and waited.

The neighbours heard of it, and by afternoon
cars lined the road. The children teased him
with alder switches and he gazed at them
like an old, tolerant collie. The women asked
15 if he could have escaped from a Fair.

The oldest man in the parish remembered seeing
a gelded moose yoked with an ox for plowing.
The young men snickered and tried to pour beer
down his throat, while their girlfriends took their pictures.

20 And the bull moose let them stroke his tick-ravaged flanks,
let them pry open his jaws with bottles, let a giggling girl
plant a little purple cap
of thistles on his head.

When the wardens came, everyone agreed it was a shame
25 to shoot anything so shaggy and cuddlesome.
He looked like the kind of pet
women put to bed with their sons.

So they held their fire. But just as the sun dropped in the river
the bull moose gathered his strength
30 like a scaffolded king, straightened and lifted his horns
so that even the wardens backed away as they raised their rifles.
When he roared, people ran to their cars. All the young men
leaned on their automobile horns as he toppled.

READING AND REACTING

1. The treatment of the bull moose parallels the treatment of a religious figure: Jesus Christ. The moose is depicted as a martyr to the encroachment of human civilization. He comes "down from the purple mist." Purple can signify royalty. What other phrases connect the moose to Christ?
2. Are allusions to Christianity readily understood, or must they be explained? Why or why not?
3. What do the reactions of the various people suggest? Are the reactions stereotypical?
4. The altercation between man and nature in this poem results in the death of the moose. What does that ending suggest about human beings and their treatment of the earth?
5. **JOURNAL ENTRY** Is the death of the moose inevitable? Could it have been avoided, and if so, how?

Related Works: "Bushed" (p. 21), "The Loons" (p. 249), "The Cariboo Horses" (p. 659)

WILLIAM BUTLER YEATS
(1865–1939)

Leda and the Swan
(1924)

A sudden blow: the great wings beating still
Above the staggering girl, her thighs caressed
By the dark webs, her nape caught in his bill,
He holds her helpless breast upon his breast.

5 How can those terrified vague fingers push
The feathered glory from her loosening thighs?
And how can body, laid in that white rush,
But feel the strange heart beating where it lies?

A shudder in the loins engenders there
10 The broken wall, the burning roof and tower

And Agamemnon dead.

Being so caught up,
So mastered by the brute blood of the air,
Did she put on his knowledge with his power
15 Before the indifferent beak could let her drop?

READING AND REACTING

1. Look up the myth of Leda in an encyclopedia. What event is described in this poem? What is the mythological significance of the event?

2. How is Leda portrayed? Why is the swan described as a "feathered glory" (6)? Why in the poem's last line is Leda dropped by his "indifferent beak"?

3. The third stanza refers to the Trojan War, which was indirectly caused by the event described in the poem. How does the allusion to the Trojan War develop the theme of the poem?

4. **JOURNAL ENTRY** Does the poem answer the question asked in its last two lines? Explain.

5. **CRITICAL PERSPECTIVE** According to Richard Ellmann this poem deals with "transcendence of opposites." The bird's rape of the human, the coupling of god and woman, the moment at which one epoch ended and another began . . . : "in the act which included all these Yeats had the violent symbol for the transcendence of opposites which he needed."

   What opposite or contrary forces exist in the myth of Leda and the swan? Do you think the poem implies that these forces can be reconciled?

Related Works: "Antigone" (p. 293), "The Way the Weather Chose to Be Born" (p. 838), "The Second Coming" (p. 900)

DEREK WALCOTT[1]
(1930–   )

Sea Grapes[2]
(1971)

That sail which leans on light,
tired of islands,
a schooner beating up the Caribbean

for home, could be Odysseus,
5 home-bound on the Aegean;
that father and husband's

---

[1] Winner of the 1992 Nobel Prize in literature.
[2] Small trees found on tropical sandy beaches.

longing, under gnarled sour grapes, is
like the adulterer hearing Nausicaa's[3] name
in every gull's outcry.

10 This brings nobody peace. The ancient war
between obsession and responsibility
will never finish and has been the same

for the sea-wanderer or the one on shore
now wriggling on his sandals to walk home,
15 since Troy sighed its last flame,

and the blind giant's boulder heaved the trough
from whose ground-swell the great hexameters come
to the conclusions of exhausted surf.

The classics can console. But not enough.

READING AND REACTING

1. Read a plot summary of the *Odyssey* in an encyclopedia. In the context of the myth of Odysseus, what is the "ancient war / between obsession and responsibility" (10–11) to which the speaker refers? Does this conflict have a wider application in the context of the poem? Explain.

2. Consider the following lines from the poem: "and the blind giant's boulder heaved the trough / from whose ground-swell the great hexameters come / to the conclusions of exhausted surf" (16–18). In what sense does the blind giant's boulder create the "great hexameters"? In what way does the trough end up as "exhausted surf"?

3. **JOURNAL ENTRY** This poem includes many references to Homer's *Odyssey*. Could you have appreciated it if you had not read a plot summary of the *Odyssey*?

4. **CRITICAL PERSPECTIVE** Asked in an interview about the final line of "Sea Grapes," Derek Walcott made the following comments:

   All of us have been to the point where, in extreme agony and distress, you turn to a book, and look for parallels, and you look for a greater grief than maybe your own. . . . But the truth of human agony is that a book does not assuage a toothache. It isn't that things don't pass and heal. Perhaps the only privilege that a poet has is that, in that agony, whatever chafes and hurts, if the person survives, [he] produces something that is hopefully lasting and moral from the experience.

   How do Walcott's remarks help to explain the poem's last line?

Related Works: "Musée des Beaux Arts" (p. 815), "Dover Beach" (p. 819), "Ulysses" (p. 886)

---

[3] A young woman who befriended Odysseus.

› ♪ ◇

W. H. AUDEN
(1907–1973)

Musée des Beaux Arts
(1940)

About suffering they were never wrong,
The Old Masters: how well they understood
Its human position; how it takes place
While someone else is eating or opening a window or just walking
    dully along;
5 How, when the aged are reverently, passionately waiting
For the miraculous birth, there always must be
Children who did not specially want it to happen, skating
On a pond at the edge of the wood:
They never forgot
10 That even the dreadful martyrdom must run its course
Anyhow in a corner, some untidy spot
Where the dogs go on with their doggy life and the torturer's horse
Scratches its innocent behind on a tree.
In Brueghel's *Icarus*, for instance: how everything turns away
15 Quite leisurely from the disaster; the ploughman may
Have heard the splash, the forsaken cry,
But for him it was not an important failure; the sun shone
As it had to on the white legs disappearing into the green
Water; and the expensive delicate ship that must have seen
20 Something amazing, a boy falling out of the sky,
Had somewhere to get to and sailed calmly on.

READING AND REACTING

1. Reread the summary of the myth of Icarus on page 805. Is Auden's allusion to the myth essential to the poem?
2. What point does the poet make by referring to the "Old Masters" (2)?
3. **JOURNAL ENTRY** Look at the painting on the following page. How does looking at Brueghel's *Landscape with the Fall of Icarus* help you to understand the poem? To what specific details in the painting does the poet refer?

Related Works: "One Day I Wrote Her Name upon the Strand" (p. 675), "Shall I Compare Thee to a Summer's Day?" (p. 701), "Death of a Young Son by Drowning" (p. 702), "Ethics" (p. 871), "Not Waving but Drowning" (p. 884)

⟩ Brueghel, Pieter the Elder (c. 1525–1569). *Landscape with the Fall of Icarus.* Musée d'Art Ancien, Musées Royaux des Beaux-Arts, Brussels, Belgium. Scala/Art Resource, NY.

CHECKLIST: WRITING ABOUT SYMBOL, ALLEGORY, ALLUSION, MYTH

SYMBOL

✓ Are there any symbols in the poem? What leads you to believe they are symbols?

✓ Are these symbols conventional?

✓ Are they universal or archetypal?

✓ Does the poem contain any private symbols?

✓ What is the literal meaning of each symbol in the context of the poem?

✓ Beyond its literal meaning, what else could each symbol suggest?

✓ How does your interpretation of each symbol enhance your understanding of the poem?

ALLEGORY

✓ Is the poem an allegory?

✓ Are there any allegorical figures within the poem? How can you tell?

✓ What do the allegorical figures signify on a literal level?

✓ What lesson does the allegory illustrate?

ALLUSION

✓ Are there any allusions in the poem?

✓ Do you recognize the names, places, historical events, or literary works to which the poet alludes?

✓ What does each allusion add to the poem? In what way does each deepen the poem's meaning? Does any allusion interfere with your understanding or enjoyment of the poem?

✓ Would the poem be more effective without a particular allusion?

MYTH

✓ What myths or mythological figures are alluded to?

✓ How does the poem use myth to convey its meaning?

✓ How faithful is the poem to the myth? Does the poet add material to the myth? Are any details from the original myth omitted? Is any information distorted? Why?

◆ WRITING SUGGESTIONS: SYMBOL, ALLEGORY, ALLUSION, MYTH

1. Read "Aunt Jennifer's Tigers" (p. 739) and "Diving into the Wreck" (p. 800) by Adrienne Rich. Then, write an essay in which you discuss similarities and differences in Rich's use of symbols in the two poems.
2. Many popular songs make use of allusion. Choose one or two popular songs and analyze their use of allusion, paying particular attention to whether the allusions expand the impact and meaning of the song or create barriers to your understanding.
3. Read the Emily Dickinson poem "Because I Could Not Stop for Death" (p. 737), and then write an interpretation of the poem, identifying the allegorical figures in the poem.
4. What applications do the lessons of myth have for life in the twentieth-first century? Choose two or three poems from the section on myth, and consider how you can use myth to make generalizations about your own life.
5. The "discovery" myth is prominent in Western culture. Choose one poem or two poems that deal with the meeting of European and Native North American cultures, and discuss how a prevailing myth can change perceptions.

POETRY

> > > >

ANONYMOUS

Bonny Barbara Allan

(traditional Scottish ballad)

It was in and about the Martinmas[1] time,
    When the green leaves were afalling,
That Sir John Graeme, in the West Country,
    Fell in love with Barbara Allan.

5 He sent his men down through the town,
    To the place where she was dwelling;
"O haste and come to my master dear,
    Gin[2] ye be Barbara Allan."

O hooly,[3] hooly rose she up,
10   To the place where he was lying,
And when she drew the curtain by:
    "Young man, I think you're dying."

"O it's I'm sick, and very, very sick,
    And 'tis a' for Barbara Allan."—
15 "O the better for me ye's never be,
    Tho your heart's blood were aspilling.

"O dinna ye mind,[4] young man," said she,
    "When ye was in the tavern adrinking,
That ye made the health gae round and round,
20   And slighted Barbara Allan?"

---

[1] Saint Martin's Day, November 11.
[2] If.
[3] Slowly.
[4] Don't you remember.

818

He turned his face unto the wall,
    And death was with him dealing:
"Adieu, adieu, my dear friends all,
    And be kind to Barbara Allan."

25 And slowly, slowly raise she up,
    And slowly, slowly left him,
And sighing said she could not stay,
    Since death of life had reft him.

She had not gane a mile but twa,[5]
30   When she heard the dead-bell ringing,
And every jow[6] that the dead-bell geid,
    It cried, "Woe to Barbara Allan!"

"O mother, mother, make my bed!
    O make it saft and narrow!
35 Since my love died for me today,
    I'll die for him tomorrow."

Western Wind

(English lyric)

Western wind, when wilt thou blow,
The[1] small rain down can rain?
Christ, if my love were in my arms,
And I in my bed again!

⬦ ⬦ ⬦

MATTHEW ARNOLD
(1822–1888)

Dover Beach
(1867)

The sea is calm tonight.
The tide is full, the moon lies fair
Upon the straits;—on the French coast the light
Gleams and is gone; the cliffs of England stand,
5 Glimmering and vast, out in the tranquil bay.
Come to the window, sweet is the night-air!
Only, from the long line of spray

---

[5] Two.

[6] Stroke.

---

[1] [So that] the.

Where the sea meets the moon-blanched[1] land,
Listen! you hear the grating roar
10 Of pebbles which the waves draw back, and fling,
At their return, up the high strand,[2]
Begin, and cease, and then again begin,
With tremulous cadence slow, and bring
The eternal note of sadness in.

15 Sophocles[3] long ago
Heard it on the Aegean,[4] and it brought
Into his mind the turbid ebb and flow
Of human misery; we
Find also in the sound a thought,
20 Hearing it by this distant northern sea.

The Sea of Faith
Was once, too, at the full, and round earth's shore
Lay like the folds of a bright girdle furled.
But now I only hear
25 Its melancholy, long, withdrawing roar,
Retreating, to the breath
Of the night-wind, down the vast edges drear
And naked shingles[5] of the world.

Ah, love, let us be true
30 To one another! for the world, which seems
To lie before us like a land of dreams,
So various, so beautiful, so new,
Hath really neither joy, nor love, nor light,
Nor certitude, nor peace, nor help for pain;
35 And we are here as on a darkling[6] plain
Swept with confused alarms of struggle and flight,
Where ignorant armies clash by night.

---

[1] Whitened by the moon.
[2] Beach.
[3] Greek playwright (496–406 B.C.), author of tragedies including *Oedipus Rex* and *Antigone*.
[4] Sea between Greece and Turkey.
[5] Gravel beaches.
[6] Darkening.

◊ ◊ ◊
MARGARET ATWOOD
(1939–   )

The Animals in That Country
(1968)

In that country the animals
have the faces of people:

the ceremonial
cats possessing the streets

5 the fox run
politely to earth, the huntsmen
standing around him, fixed
in their tapestry of manners

the bull, embroidered
10 with blood and given
an elegant death, trumpets, his name
stamped on him, heraldic brand
because

(when he rolled
15 on the sand, sword in his heart, the teeth
in his blue mouth were human)
he is really a man

even the wolves, holding resonant
conversations in their
20 forests thickened with legend.

       In this country the animals
       have the faces of
       animals.

       Their eyes
25   flash once in car headlights
       and are gone.

       Their deaths are not elegant.

       They have the faces of
       no-one.

◦ ◦ ◦

MARGARET AVISON
(1918–   )

The Swimmer's Moment
(1962)

For everyone
The swimmer's moment at the whirlpool comes,
But many at that moment will not say
"This is the whirlpool, then."
5 By their refusal they are saved
From the black pit, and also from contesting
The deadly rapids, and emerging in
The mysterious, and more ample, further waters.
And so their bland-blank faces turn and turn
10 Pale and forever on the rim of suction
They will not recognize.
Of those who dare the knowledge
Many are whirled into the ominous centre
That, gaping vertical, seals up
15 For them an eternal boon of privacy,
So that we turn away from their defeat
With a despair, not for their deaths, but for
Ourselves, who cannot penetrate their secret
Nor even guess at the anonymous breadth
20 Where one or two have won:
(The silver reaches of the estuary).

◦ ◦ ◦

WILLIAM BLAKE
(1757–1827)

The Lamb
(1789)

Little Lamb, who made thee?
Dost thou know who made thee?
Gave thee life & bid thee feed,
By the stream & o'er the mead;
5 Gave thee clothing of delight,
Softest clothing wooly bright;
Gave thee such a tender voice,
Making all the vales rejoice!

Little Lamb who made thee?
10   Dost thou know who made thee?

Little Lamb I'll tell thee,
Little Lamb I'll tell thee!
He is callèd by thy name,
For he calls himself a Lamb:
15 He is meek & he is mild,
He became a little child:
I a child & thou a lamb,
We are callèd by his name.
Little Lamb God bless thee.
20   Little Lamb God bless thee.

London
(1794)

I wander through each chartered street,
Near where the chartered Thames does flow,
And mark in every face I meet
Marks of weakness, marks of woe.

5 In every cry of every man,
In every infant's cry of fear,
In every voice, in every ban,
The mind-forged manacles I hear.

How the chimney-sweeper's cry
10 Every black'ning church appalls;
And the hapless soldier's sigh
Runs in blood down palace walls.

But most through midnight streets I hear
How the youthful harlot's curse
15 Blasts the new born infant's tear,
And blights with plagues the marriage hearse.

The Tyger
(1794)

Tyger! Tyger! burning bright
In the forests of the night,
What immortal hand or eye
Could frame thy fearful symmetry?

5 In what distant deeps or skies
Burnt the fire of thine eyes?
On what wings dare he aspire?
What the hand dare seize the fire?

And what shoulder, and what art,
10 Could twist the sinews of thy heart?
And when thy heart began to beat,
What dread hand? and what dread feet?

What the hammer? what the chain?
In what furnace was thy brain?
15 What the anvil? what dread grasp
Dare its deadly terrors clasp?

When the stars threw down their spears,
And watered heaven with their tears,
Did he smile his work to see?
20 Did he who made the Lamb make thee?

Tyger! Tyger! burning bright
In the forests of the night,
What immortal hand or eye
Dare frame thy fearful symmetry?

ROO BORSON
(1952–   )

After a Death
(1989)

Seeing that there's no other way,
I turn his absence into a chair.
I can sit in it,
gaze out through the window.
5 I can do what I do best
and then go out into the world.
And I can return then with my useless love,
to rest,
because the chair is there.

❧ ❧ ◇

ANNE BRADSTREET
(1612?–1672)

The Author to Her Book[1]
(1678)

Thou ill-formed offspring of my feeble brain,
Who after birth did'st by my side remain,
Till snatched from thence by friends, less wise than true,
Who thee abroad exposed to public view;
5 Made thee in rags, halting, to the press to trudge,
Where errors were not lessened, all may judge.
At thy return my blushing was not small,
My rambling brat (in print) should mother call;
I cast thee by as one unfit for light,
10 Thy visage was so irksome in my sight;
Yet being mine own, at length affection would
Thy blemishes amend, if so I could:
I washed thy face, but more defects I saw,
And rubbing off a spot, still made a flaw.
15 I stretched thy joints to make thee even feet,[2]
Yet still thou run'st more hobbling than is meet;[3]
In better dress to trim thee was my mind,
But nought save homespun cloth in the house I find.
In this array, 'mongst vulgars[4] may'st thou roam;
20 In critics' hands beware thou dost not come;
And take thy way where yet thou are not known.
If for thy Father asked, say thou had'st none;
And for thy Mother, she alas is poor,
Which caused her thus to send thee out of door.

---

[1] Bradstreet addresses *The Tenth Muse*, a collection of her poetry, which was published without her consent in 1650.
[2] Metrical feet.
[3] Appropriate or decorous.
[4] Common people.

✦ ◇ ◇

GWENDOLYN BROOKS
(1917–2000)

We Real Cool
(1960)

The Pool Players.
Seven at the Golden Shovel.

We real cool. We
Left School. We

Lurk late. We
Strike straight. We

5　Sing sin. We
Thin gin. We

Jazz June. We
Die soon.

ROBERT BURNS
(1759–1796)

John Anderson My Jo, John
(1790)

John Anderson my jo,[1] John,
　　When we were first acquent,[2]
Your locks were like the raven,
　　Your bonny brow was brent;[3]
5　But now your brow is beld,[4] John,
　　Your locks are like the snaw;
But blessings on your frosty pow,[5]
　　John Anderson my jo.

John Anderson my jo, John,
10　　We clamb the hill thegither;

---

[1] Dear.
[2] Acquainted.
[3] Unwrinkled.
[4] Bald.
[5] Head.

And mony a canty[6] day, John,
   We've had wi' ane anither:
Now we maun[7] totter down, John,
   And hand in hand we'll go,
15 And sleep thegither at the foot,
   John Anderson my jo.

GEORGE GORDON, LORD BYRON
(1788–1824)

She Walks in Beauty
(1815)

1

She walks in beauty, like the night
   Of cloudless climes and starry skies;
And all that's best of dark and bright
   Meet in her aspect and her eyes:
5 Thus mellowed to that tender light
   Which heaven to gaudy day denies.

2

One shade the more, one ray the less,
   Had half impaired the nameless grace
Which waves in every raven tress,
10   Or softly lightens o'er her face;
Where thoughts serenely sweet express
   How pure, how dear their dwelling place.

3

And on that cheek, and o'er that brow,
   So soft, so calm, yet eloquent,
15 The smiles that win, the tints that glow,
   But tell of days in goodness spent,
A mind at peace with all below,
   A heart whose love is innocent!

---

[6] Happy.
[7] Must.

SAMUEL TAYLOR COLERIDGE
(1772–1834)

Kubla Khan[1]
(1797, 1798)

Or, a Vision in a Dream. A Fragment.

In Xanadu did Kubla Khan
A stately pleasure-dome decree:
Where Alph,[2] the sacred river, ran
Through caverns measureless to man
5   Down to a sunless sea.
So twice five miles of fertile ground
With walls and towers were girdled round;
And there were gardens bright with sinuous rills,
Where blossomed many an incense-bearing tree;
10 And here were forests ancient as the hills,
Enfolding sunny spots of greenery.

But oh! that deep romantic chasm which slanted
Down the green hill athwart a cedarn cover!
A savage place! as holy and enchanted
15 As e'er beneath a waning moon was haunted
By woman wailing for her demon-lover!
And from this chasm, with ceaseless turmoil seething,
As if this earth in fast thick pants were breathing,
A mighty fountain momently was forced:
20 Amid whose swift half-intermitted burst
Huge fragments vaulted like rebounding hail,
Or chaffy grain beneath the thresher's flail:
And 'mid these dancing rocks at once and ever
It flung up momently the sacred river.
25 Five miles meandering with a mazy motion
Through wood and dale the sacred river ran,
Then reached the caverns measureless to man,
And sank in tumult to a lifeless ocean:
And 'mid this tumult Kubla heard from far
30 Ancestral voices prophesying war!

    The shadow of the dome of pleasure
    Floated midway on the waves;

---

[1] Coleridge mythologizes the actual Kublai Khan, a thirteenth-century Mongol emperor, as well as the Chinese city of Xanadu.

[2] Probably derived from the Greek river Alpheus, whose waters, according to legend, rose from the Ionian Sea in Sicily as the fountain of Arethusa.

Where was heard the mingled measure
From the fountain and the caves.
35 It was a miracle of rare device,
A sunny pleasure-dome with caves of ice!

A damsel with a dulcimer
In a vision once I saw:
It was an Abyssinian maid,
40   And on her dulcimer she played,
Singing of Mount Abora.[3]
Could I revive within me
Her symphony and song,
To such a deep delight 'twould win me,
45 That with music loud and long,
I would build that dome in air,
That sunny dome! those caves of ice!
And all who heard should see them there,
And all should cry, Beware! Beware!
50 His flashing eyes, his floating hair!
Weave a circle round him thrice,[4]
And close your eyes with holy dread,
For he on honey-dew hath fed,
And drunk the milk of Paradise.

◊ ◊ ◊

E. E. CUMMINGS
(1894–1962)

Buffalo Bill's
(1923)

Buffalo Bill's
defunct
          who used to
          ride a watersmooth-silver
5   stallion
and break onetwothreefourfive pigeonsjustlikethat
                                        Jesus
he was a handsome man
                      and what i want to know is
10 how do you like your blueeyed boy
Mister Death

---

[3] Some scholars see a reminiscence here of John Milton's *Paradise Lost 4.* 280–82: "where Abassin kings their issue guard / Mount Amara, though this by some supposed / True Paradise under the Ethiop Line."

[4] A magic ritual, to keep away intruding spirits.

EMILY DICKINSON
(1830–1886)

I Heard a Fly Buzz–When I Died
(c. 1862)

I heard a Fly buzz—when I died—
The Stillness in the Room
Was like the Stillness in the Air—
Between the Heaves of Storm—

5   The Eyes around—had wrung them dry—
And Breaths were gathering firm
For that last Onset—when the King
Be witnessed—in the Room—

I willed my Keepsakes—Signed away
10 What portion of me be
Assignable—and then it was
There interposed a Fly—

With Blue—uncertain stumbling Buzz—
Between the light—and me—
15 And then the Windows failed—and then
I could not see to see—

JOHN DONNE
(1572–1631)

Death Be Not Proud
(c. 1610)

Death be not proud, though some have callèd thee
Mighty and dreadful, for thou art not so;
For those whom thou think'st thou dost overthrow
Die not, poor Death, nor yet canst thou kill me.
5   From rest and sleep, which but thy pictures be,
Much pleasure, then from thee much more must flow,
And soonest our best men with thee do go,
Rest of their bones, and soul's delivery.
Thou art slave to fate, chance, kings, and desperate men,
10 And dost with poison, war, and sickness dwell,
And poppy, or charms can make us sleep as well,
And better than thy stroke; why swell'st thou then?
One short sleep past, we wake eternally,
And death shall be no more; Death, thou shalt die.

RITA DOVE
(1952–   )

The Satisfaction Coal Company
(1986)

1

What to do with a day.
Leaf through *Jet.* Watch T.V.
Freezing on the porch
but he goes anyhow, snow too high
5 for a walk, the ice treacherous.
Inside, the gas heater takes care of itself;
he doesn't even notice being warm.

Everyone says he looks great.
Across the street a drunk stands smiling
10 at something carved in a tree.
The new neighbor with the floating hips
scoots out to get the mail
and waves once, brightly,
storm door clipping her heel on the way in.

2

15 Twice a week he had taken the bus down Glendale hill
to the corner of Market. Slipped through
the alley by the canal and let himself in.
Started to sweep
with terrible care, like a woman
20 brushing shine into her hair,
same motion, same lullaby.
No curtains—the cop on the beat
stopped outside once in the hour
to swing his billy club and glare.

25 It was better on Saturdays
when the children came along:
he mopped while they emptied
ashtrays, clang of glass on metal
then a dry scutter. Next they counted
30 nailheads studding the leather cushions.
Thirty-four! they shouted,
that was the year and
they found it mighty amusing.

But during the week he noticed more—
35 lights when they gushed or dimmed
at the Portage Hotel, the 10:32

picking up speed past the B & O switchyard,
floorboards trembling and the explosive
kachook kachook kachook kachook
40 and the oiled rails ticking underneath.

3

They were poor then but everyone had been poor.
He hadn't minded the sweeping,
just the thought of it—like now
when people ask him what he's thinking
45 and he says *I'm listening.*

Those nights walking home alone,
the bucket of coal scraps banging his knee,
he'd hear a roaring furnace
with its dry, familiar heat. Now the nights
50 take care of themselves—as for the days,
there is the canary's sweet curdled song,
the wino smiling through his dribble.
Past the hill, past the gorge
choked with wild sumac in summer,
55 the corner has been upgraded.
Still, he'd like to go down there someday
to stand for a while, and get warm.

PAUL LAURENCE DUNBAR
(1872–1906)

We Wear the Mask
(1913)

We wear the mask that grins and lies,
It hides our cheeks and shades our eyes—
This debt we pay to human guile;
With torn and bleeding hearts we smile,
5 And mouth with myriad subtleties.

Why should the world be over-wise,
In counting all our tears and sighs?
Nay, let them only see us, while
    We wear the mask.

10 We smile, but, O great Christ, our cries
To thee from tortured souls arise.
We sing, but oh the clay is vile
Beneath our feet, and long the mile;
But let the world dream otherwise,
15   We wear the mask!

T. S. ELIOT
(1888–1965)

The Love Song of
J. Alfred Prufrock
(1917)

S'io credessi che mia risposta fosse
A persona che mai tornasse al mondo,
Questa fiamma staria senza piu scosse.
Ma perciocche giammai di questo fondo
Non torno vivo alcun, s'i'odo il vero,
Senza tema d'infamia ti rispondo.[1]

Let us go then, you and I,
When the evening is spread out against the sky
Like a patient etherized upon a table;
Let us go, through certain half-deserted streets,
5 The muttering retreats
Of restless nights in one-night cheap hotels
And sawdust restaurants with oyster-shells:
Streets that follow like a tedious argument
Of insidious intent
10 To lead you to an overwhelming question . . .
Oh, do not ask, "What is it?"
Let us go and make our visit.

In the room the women come and go
Talking of Michelangelo.

15 The yellow fog that rubs its back upon the window-panes,
The yellow smoke that rubs its muzzle on the window-panes
Licked its tongue into the corners of the evening,
Lingered upon the pools that stand in drains,
Let fall upon its back the soot that falls from chimneys,
20 Slipped by the terrace, made a sudden leap,
And seeing that it was a soft October night,
Curled once about the house, and fell asleep.

And indeed there will be time
For the yellow smoke that slides along the street,
25 Rubbing its back upon the window-panes;

---

[1] The epigraph is from Dante's *Inferno*, Canto 27. In response to the poet's question about his identity, Guido da Montefelto, who for his sin of fraud must spend eternity wrapped in flames, replies: "If I thought that I was speaking to someone who could go back to the world, this flame would shake me no more. But since from this place nobody ever returns alive, if what I hear is true, I answer you without fear of infamy."

There will be time, there will be time
To prepare a face to meet the faces that you meet;
There will be time to murder and create,
And time for all the works and days[2] of hands
30 That lift and drop a question on your plate;
Time for you and time for me,
And time yet for a hundred indecisions,
And for a hundred visions and revisions,
Before the taking of a toast and tea.

35 In the room the women come and go
Talking of Michelangelo.

And indeed there will be time
To wonder, "Do I dare?" and, "Do I dare?"
Time to turn back and descend the stair,
40 With a bald spot in the middle of my hair—
(They will say: "How his hair is growing thin!")
My morning coat, my collar mounting firmly to the chin,
My necktie rich and modest, but asserted by a simple pin—
(They will say: "But how his arms and legs are thin!")
45 Do I dare
Disturb the universe?
In a minute there is time
For decisions and revisions which a minute will reverse.

For I have known them all already, known them all—
50 Have known the evenings, mornings, afternoons,
I have measured out my life with coffee spoons;
I know the voices dying with a dying fall[3]
Beneath the music from a farther room.
　　So how should I presume?

55 And I have known the eyes already, known them all—
The eyes that fix you in a formulated phrase,
And when I am formulated, sprawling on a pin,
When I am pinned and wriggling on the wall,
Then how should I begin
60 To spit out all the butt-ends of my days and ways?
　　And how should I presume?

And I have known the arms already, known them all—
Arms that are braceleted and white and bare
(But in the lamplight, downed with light brown hair!)
65 Is it perfume from a dress
That makes me so digress?
Arms that lie along a table, or wrap about a shawl.

---

[2] "Works and Days" is the title of a work by the eighth-century B.C. Greek Hesiod, whose poem celebrates farmwork.
[3] Allusion to Orsino's speech in *Twelfth Night* (1.1), "That strain again! It had a dying fall."

And should I then presume?
And how should I begin?

* * *

70 Shall I say, I have gone at dusk through narrow streets
And watched the smoke that rises from the pipes
Of lonely men in shirt-sleeves, leaning out of windows? . . .

I should have been a pair of ragged claws
Scuttling across the floors of silent seas.

* * *

75 And the afternoon, the evening, sleeps so peacefully!
Smoothed by long fingers,
Asleep . . . tired . . . or it malingers,
Stretched on the floor, here beside you and me.
Should I, after tea and cakes and ices,
80 Have the strength to force the moment to its crisis?
But though I have wept and fasted, wept and prayed,
Though I have seen my head (grown slightly bald) brought in upon
   a platter,[4]
I am no prophet—and here's no great matter;
I have seen the moment of my greatness flicker,
85 And I have seen the eternal Footman[5] hold my coat, and snicker,
And in short, I was afraid.

And would it have been worth it, after all,
After the cups, the marmalade, the tea,
Among the porcelain, among some talk of you and me,
90 Would it have been worth while,
To have bitten off the matter with a smile,
To have squeezed the universe into a ball
To roll it toward some overwhelming question,
To say: "I am Lazarus,[6] come from the dead,
95 Come back to tell you all, I shall tell you all"—
If one, settling a pillow by her head,
   Should say: "That is not what I meant at all.
   That is not it, at all."

And would it have worth it, after all,
100 Would it have been worth while,
After the sunsets and the dooryards and the sprinkled streets,
After the novels, after the teacups, after the skirts that trail along the
   floor—
And this, and so much more?—
It is impossible to say just what I mean!

---

[4] Like John the Baptist, who was beheaded by King Herod (see Matthew 14:3–11).
[5] Perhaps death, or fate.
[6] Lazarus was raised from the dead by Christ (see John 11:1–44).

105 But as if a magic lantern threw the nerves in patterns on a screen:
Would it have been worth while
If one, settling a pillow or throwing off a shawl,
And turning toward the window, should say:
  "That is not it at all,
110 That is not what I meant, at all."

* * *

No! I am not Prince Hamlet, nor was meant to be;
Am an attendant lord, one that will do
To swell a progress,[7] start a scene or two,
Advise the prince; no doubt, an easy tool,
115 Deferential, glad to be of use,
Politic, cautious, and meticulous;
Full of high sentence,[8] but a bit obtuse;
At times, indeed, almost ridiculous—
Almost, at times, the Fool.

120 I grow old . . . I grow old . . .
I shall wear the bottoms of my trousers rolled.

Shall I part my hair behind? Do I dare to eat a peach?
I shall wear white flannel trousers, and walk upon the beach.
I have heard the mermaids singing, each to each.

125 I do not think that they will sing to me.

I have seen them riding seaward on the waves
Combing the white hair of the waves blown back
When the wind blows the water white and black.

We have lingered in the chambers of the sea
130 By sea-girls wreathed with seaweed red and brown
Till human voices wake us, and we drown.

◈ ◈ ◈

ROBERT FROST
(1874–1963)

Mending Wall
(1914)

Something there is that doesn't love a wall,
That sends the frozen-ground-swell under it,
And spills the upper boulders in the sun;
And makes gaps even two can pass abreast.
5 The work of hunters is another thing:

---

[7] Here, in the Elizabethan sense of a royal journey.
[8] Opinions.

I have come after them and made repair
Where they have left not one stone on a stone,
But they would have the rabbit out of hiding,
To please the yelping dogs. The gaps I mean,
10 No one has seen them made or heard them made,
But at spring mending-time we find them there.
I let my neighbor know beyond the hill;
And on a day we meet to walk the line
And set the wall between us once again.
15 We keep the wall between us as we go.
To each the boulders that have fallen to each.
And some are loaves and some so nearly balls
We have to use a spell to make them balance:
"Stay where you are until our backs are turned!"
20 We wear our fingers rough with handling them.
Oh, just another kind of outdoor game,
One on a side. It comes to little more:
There where it is we do not need the wall:
He is all pine and I am apple orchard.
25 My apple trees will never get across
And eat the cones under his pines, I tell him.
He only says, "Good fences make good neighbors."
Spring is the mischief in me, and I wonder
If I could put a notion in his head:
30 "*Why* do they make good neighbors? Isn't it
Where there are cows? But here there are no cows.
Before I built a wall I'd ask to know
What I was walling in or walling out,
And to whom I was like to give offense.
35 Something there is that doesn't love a wall,
That wants it down." I could say "Elves" to him,
But it's not elves exactly, and I'd rather
He said it for himself. I see him there
Bringing a stone grasped firmly by the top
40 In each hand, like an old-stone savage armed.
He moves in darkness as it seems to me,
Not of woods only and the shade of trees.
He will not go behind his father's saying,
And he likes having thought of it so well
45 He says again, "Good fences make good neighbors."

The Road Not Taken
(1915)

Two roads diverged in a yellow wood,
And sorry I could not travel both
And be one traveler, long I stood

And looked down one as far as I could
5 To where it bent in the undergrowth;

Then took the other, as just as fair,
And having perhaps the better claim,
Because it was grassy and wanted wear;
Though as for that the passing there
10 Had worn them really about the same,

And both that morning equally lay
In leaves no step had trodden black.
Oh, I kept the first for another day!
Yet knowing how way leads on to way,
15 I doubted if I should ever come back.

I shall be telling this with a sigh
Somewhere ages and ages hence:
Two roads diverged in a wood, and I—
I took the one less traveled by,
20 And that has made all the difference.

⟩ ⟩ ⟩

GHANDL
(c. 1851–c. 1920)

The Way the Weather Chose to Be Born
(c. 1900)

Translated by Robert Bringhurst, 2000

There was a child of good family, they say,
at Swiftcurrent Creek.
And her father had one of his slaves
    constantly watching her.
She said to the slave,
5 "Tell that one I want to make love to him."

The day after that,
    when she went out of doors with the slave,
she asked if he'd said
what she told him to say.

And the slave said to the young woman,
10 "He says he's afraid of your father."
But the slave had spoken to no one.
The slave was in love with her, they say.

When she had decided on somebody else,
she gave the slave the same instructions.
15 He failed again to deliver the message.

He told her again
that the man was afraid of her father.

After sending the message to each of her father's ten nephews,
the one of good family make love with the slave, they say.
20 And her father found out it had happened.

So they all moved away from her, they say.
And no one but her youngest uncle's wife
    left food for her, they say.

She went digging for shellfish, they say.
After a while, she dug up a cockleshell.
25 The cry of a child came from inside it.

She looked at it closely.
The embryo of a child was living inside it.
She carried it into the house.
She put birds' down around it.

30 Then, though she gave it no milk,
it grew very quickly.
Soon it started crawling
Soon after that it was walking.

One day the child said,
35 "Mother, like this."
He was gesturing with his hands.
When he did it again,
she knew what he wanted.

She hammered a copper bracelet into a bow.
40 She hammered another one into an arrow.
After she finished a second arrow,
she gave him the weapons.
Then he was happy.

And then he went hunting for birds.
45 He came back with a cormorant for his mother.
She ate it.

The next day again he went hunting for birds,
and he brought in a goose for his mother, they say.
She ate it.

50 The next day again he went hunting for birds.
He brought in a wren.
He skinned it himself,
and he dried the skin.
He cherished it.

55 Next day, he brought in a song sparrow.
This too he skinned by himself,
and he dried the skin.

The next day he brought in a Steller's jay,
and he skinned it
60 and dried it.

The day after that, he brought in a redheaded sapsucker.
He skinned it as well,
and he dried it.

Then in the night something spoke to his mother.
65 Just at that moment, the house started creaking.
Next morning he woke in a well-finished building.
The carvings on the houseposts winked their eyes.
Master Carver had adopted him, they say.

He got up.
70 And his father said to him,
"Well, my young lord, let me paint you."

He went to his father.
His father put level streaks of cloud on his face.
"Now, my young lord, sit facing the sea."
75 And the moment he did so, the weather was fine.

Then one day he asked his father
    to come with him on a fishing trip, they say.
"We're going to catch the fish-catching octopus."
And he fished for it and caught it.

They drifted with the current over House Banks.
80 He told his father to sit in the bow.
He looked at the rising sun for a while.

Then he said, "Father, say this:
The Largest One of Them All is thinking of biting."
His father said these very words.

85 "Father, say this:
The One Who Travels All around the Islands
    is thinking of biting."
And he spoke these very words.

"Father, say *Sir, shadows are falling on Steep Rock Mountain.*
Make up your mind."
90 And he spoke these very words.

"Father, say this:
The Big One Who Comes to Swiftcurrent Creek
   is thinking of biting."
And he said those very words.

"Father, say this:
95 *The Big One Slurping Up Pebbles is thinking of biting."*
He said it.

And then, "Father, say this:
The One with White Stone Eyes has looked it over."

"Father, say this:
100 *The Big One Who Feeds Wherever He Pleases*
   is thinking of biting."
He said these very words.

As soon as he had said these things,
it took the bait, they say.
And then it towed them right around the Islands.

105 He slapped the canoe on the gunwales, they say.
And he said to it,
"Master Carver made you.
Swim with your head up."
Then it towed them round the Islands once again.

110 When they came to rest,
he hauled in the line.
And he brought to the surface the face
   of something amazing.

A forest of broad-bladed kelp surrounded its mouth.
There were halibut nesting all over it.
115 Then, they say, he started to bring them aboard.

He filled his canoe.
Then he stretched it out larger.
He kept on hauling them aboard,
and he again filled his canoe.
120 Then they released it.

They paddled back to town in their canoe.
Master Carver brought the halibut up to his wife.
She cut it and dried it.

Then he called his son once more, they say.
125 And after he had painted him, he said,

"My son, your uncles are living in that direction.
Go there and see."
And he went there, they say.

At the edge of the town, he sat down.
130 When he had sat there awhile, they saw him.
They crowded around him.

They knew him at once, they say.
And then they moved back where his mother was living.

When all of them had lived there for a while,
135 he went out of the house
    dressed in his wren skin, they say.
"Come look at me, mother," he said.
And his mother followed him outside.
She saw him poised above the sea as a cumulus cloud.

Then they came in,
140 and he said to his mother,
"Did I look handsome?"
"Yes, my young lord, you looked fine."

Next, they say, he went out in the skin of the Steller's jay.
And he said to his mother,
145 "Come look at me."
She followed him outside.
Above the sea, her son was spread out wide and blue.

Then they came in,
and he said, "Did I look handsome, mother?"
150 "Yes, my young lord, you looked fine."

Then he went out in his sapsucker skin.
And he said, "Come look at me, mother."
His mother followed him outside.
He was bright red high above the sea.

155 She smiled at her son.
When they came back in, he said,
"Did I look handsome, mother?"
"Yes, my young lord.
The gods will never grow tired of seeing your face."

160 "This is the last I will see of you, mother," he said.
"I am going away.
Whenever I sit where the Tallgrass River reaches the sea,
no wind will blow from any direction,
The sky will be mine.

165 "Whenever my face is the same as my father painted it,
no wind will blow from any direction.
Humans will feed themselves through me."

"Very well, my young lord.
Whenever you sit there,
170 I will scatter feathers in your honor."

Then he left his mother, they say.
And his father got ready to leave her as well.

"I also am going away," he said.
"Make your home at the headwaters.
175 I will be watching for you there,
and I will also be watching for my son."
Then he left her there, they say.

As the day was ending,
she called her youngest uncle aside.
180 "Tomorrow," she said,
    "when you and your brothers go fishing,
wear a new hat
and take a new paddle."

And early next day, they all went out fishing.
She sat at the end of the town
185 and stretched out her legs.
When she pulled up her skirt,
the wind blew out of the inlet.

The higher she raised it, the fiercer the wind.
When her skirt came up over her knees,
190 a gale was blowing.

And she clung to the thread
of the one who wore a new hat.
She saved him, they say, and him only,
because of his wife, who had left her some food.
195 She is Fairweather Woman, they say.

Then she went inland, they say,
taking her mats and all her belongings.
She walked up the bed of the creek,
and she settled there.

200 Later a trail was cut over top of her.
The traffic disturbed her, she said,
and she moved farther inland.

She sank to her buttocks, they say.
There, they say, she is one with the ground.

205 When her son takes his place,
she scatters flakes of snow for him.
Those are the feathers.

That is the end.

NIKKI GIOVANNI
(1943–   )

Nikki-Rosa
(1968)

childhood remembrances are always a drag
if you're Black
you always remember things like living in Woodlawn[1]
with no inside toilet
5 and if you become famous or something
they never talk about how happy you were to have your mother
all to yourself and
how good the water felt when you got your bath from one of those
big tubs that folk in chicago barbecue in
10 and somehow when you talk about home
it never gets across how much you
understood their feelings
as the whole family attended meetings about Hollydale
and even though you remember
15 your biographers never understand
your father's pain as he sells his stock
and another dream goes
and though you're poor it isn't poverty that
concerns you
20 and though they fought a lot
it isn't your father's drinking that makes any difference
but only that everybody is together and you
and your sister have happy birthdays and very good christmasses
and I really hope no white person ever has cause to write about me
25 because they never understand Black love is Black wealth and they'll
probably talk about my hard childhood and never understand that
all the while I was quite happy

---

[1] A predominantly black suburb of Cincinnati, Ohio.

LOUISE BERNICE HALFE
(1953–   )

My Ledders
(1994)

dear pope
i no, i no, you tired of my ledders
i couldn't let dis one go
i dought you could do somedin 'bout it.
5 years ago you stopped *nō khom* and *nimosō m*[1]
from prayin in da sweatlodge and sundance,
drummin, singin and dancin.
you even stopped dem from Indian speakin
and storydellin.
10 well you must have some kind of bower
cuz da govment sure listen.

well, pope
last night on DV
i watched some whitemen
15 sweat in da lodge, and at
dinner dime on da radio
i heard dat man dell us
dat some darafist was havin a retreat
and to register.
20 what dat mean, i not sure
anyway he is buildin' a sweatlodge.
i never hear anybody before on da radio
dell da whole world dat.
i sure surprise and kinda made me mad.

25 i wonder if you could dell da govment
to make dem laws dat stop dat
whiteman from dakin our *isistāwina*[2]
cuz i dell you pope
i don't dink you like it
30 if i dook you
gold cup and wine
pass it 'round our circles

---

[1] My grandmother and my grandfather.
[2] A word that can have deep, sacred implications, but essentially meaning customs, rites, or beliefs.

cuz i don't have you drainin
from doze schools.
35　i haven't married you jeesuz
and i don't kneel to him,
cuz he ain't my god.

dese men, pope, don't know what
tobacco mean, what suffer mean,
40　alls dey no is you jeesuz die for dem
dey don't no what fastin' mean
dey jist dake and gobble our *mātotsān*[3]
as if dey own it.
dey don't no what it mean to dake
45　from da earth and give somedin' back
i so dired of all dis *kimoti*,[4] pope
deach your children.
eat your jeesuz body.
drink his blood.
50　dell dem to go back to dere own deachings,
pope.

⋄ ⋄ ⋄

THOMAS HARDY
(1840–1928)

The Convergence of the Twain
(1912)

(Lines on the loss of the 'Titanic')

I

In a solitude of the sea
Deep from human vanity,
And the Pride of Life that planned her, stilly couches she.

II

Steel chambers, late the pyres[1]
5　　Of her salamandrine fires,[2]
Cold currents thrid,[3] and turn to rhythmic tidal lyres.

---

[3] Sweat lodges.
[4] Theft.

---

[1] Funeral pyres; piles of wood on which corpses were burned in ancient rites.
[2] Refers to the old belief that salamanders could live in fire.
[3] Thread (archaic verb form).

III

Over the mirrors meant
To glass the opulent
The sea-worm crawls—grotesque, slimed, dumb, indifferent.

IV

10   Jewels in joy designed
To ravish the sensuous mind
Lie lightless, all their sparkles bleared and black and blind.

V

Dim moon-eyed fishes near
Gaze at the gilded gear
15 And query: "What does this vaingloriousness down here?" . . .

VI

Well: while was fashioning
This creature of cleaving wing,
The Immanent[4] Will that stirs and urges everything

VII

Prepared a sinister mate
20   For her—so gaily great—
A Shape of Ice, for the time far and dissociate.

VIII

And as the smart ship grew
In stature, grace, and hue,
In shadowy silent distance grew the Iceberg too.

IX

25   Alien they seemed to be:
No mortal eye could see
The intimate welding of their later history,

X

Or sign that they were bent
By paths coincident
30 On being anon[5] twin halves of one august[6] event,

XI

Till the Spinner of the Years
Said "Now!" And each one hears,
And consummation comes, and jars two hemispheres.

---

[4] Inherent, dwelling within.
[5] Soon.
[6] Awe-inspiring, majestic.

NEL

◊ ◊ ◊

SEAMUS HEANEY
(1939–   )

Lightenings viii
(1995)

The annals[1] say: when the monks of Clonmacnoise[2]
Were all at prayers inside the oratory
A ship appeared above them in the air.

The anchor dragged along behind so deep
5 It hooked itself into the altar rails
And then, as the big hull[3] rocked to a standstill,

A crewman shinned and grappled down a rope
And struggled to release it. But in vain.
"This man can't bear our life here and will drown,"

10 The abbot[4] said, "Unless we help him." So
They did, the freed ship sailed and the man climbed back
Out of the marvelous as he had known it.

◊ ◊ ◊

GERARD MANLEY HOPKINS
(1844–1889)

God's Grandeur
(1877)

The world is charged with the grandeur of God.
    It will flame out, like shining from shook foil;
    It gathers to a greatness, like the ooze of oil
Crushed. Why do men then now not reck his rod?
5 Generations have trod, have trod, have trod;
    And all is seared with trade; bleared, smeared with toil;
    And wears man's smudge and shares man's smell: the soil
Is bare now, nor can foot feel, being shod.
And for all this, nature is never spent;
10   There lives the dearest freshness deep down things;
And though the last lights off the black West went
    Oh, morning, at the brown brink eastward, springs—
Because the Holy Ghost over the bent
    World broods with warm breast and with ah! bright wings.

---

[1] Journals containing yearly records.
[2] An Irish abbey founded in 541, destroyed by the English in 1552.
[3] The frame or body of a ship.
[4] The monk in authority over a community of monks.

LANGSTON HUGHES
(1902–1967)

Theme for English B
(1951)

The instructor said,

Go home and write
a page tonight.
And let that page come out of you—
5 *Then, it will be true.*

I wonder if it's that simple?

I am twenty-two, colored, born in Winston-Salem.
I went to school there, then Durham, then here
to this college on the hill above Harlem.
10 I am the only colored student in my class.
The steps from the hill lead down into Harlem,
through a park, then I cross St. Nicholas,
Eighth Avenue, Seventh, and I come to the Y,
the Harlem Branch Y, where I take the elevator
15 up to my room, sit down, and write this page:

It's not easy to know what is true for you or me
at twenty-two, my age. But I guess I'm what
I feel and see and hear. Harlem, I hear you:
hear you, hear me—we two—you, me, talk on this page.
20 (I hear New York, too.) Me—who?

Well, I like to eat, sleep, drink, and be in love.
I like to work, read, learn, and understand life.
I like a pipe for a Christmas present,
or records—Bessie,[1] bop, or Bach.
25 I guess being colored doesn't make me *not* like
the same things other folks like who are other races.

So will my page be colored that I write?
Being me, it will not be white.
But it will be
30 a part of you, instructor.
You are white—
yet a part of me, as I am a part of you.
That's American.

---

[1] Bessie Smith (1898?–1937), a popular blues singer.

Sometimes perhaps you don't want to be a part of me.
35 Nor do I often want to be a part of you.
But we are, that's true!
As I learn from you,
I guess you learn from me—
although you're older—and white—
40 and somewhat more free.

This is my page for English B.

◊   ◊   ◊

JOHN KEATS
(1795–1821)

La Belle Dame sans Merci: A Ballad[1]
(1819, 1820)

1

O what can ail thee, knight at arms,
    Alone and palely loitering?
The sedge has wither'd from the lake,
    And no birds sing.

2

5 O what can ail thee, knight at arms,
    So haggard and so woe-begone?
The squirrel's granary is full,
    And the harvest's done.

3

I see a lily on thy brow
10   With anguish moist and fever dew,
And on thy cheeks a fading rose
    Fast withereth too.

4

I met a lady in the meads,
    Full beautiful, a fairy's child;
15 Her hair was long, her foot was light,
    And her eyes were wild.

---

[1] The title, which means "The Lovely Lady without Pity," was taken from a medieval poem by Alain Chartier.

5

I made a garland for her head,
 And bracelets too, and fragrant zone;[2]
She look'd at me as she did love,
20   And made sweet moan.

6

I set her on my pacing steed,
 And nothing else saw all day long,
For sidelong would she bend, and sing
      A fairy's song.

7

25 She found me roots of relish sweet,
 And honey wild, and manna dew,
And sure in language strange she said—
      I love thee true.

8

She took me to her elfin grot,[3]
30   And there she wept, and sigh'd full sore,
And there I shut her wild wild eyes
      With kisses four.

9

And there she lullèd me asleep,
 And there I dream'd—Ah! woe betide!
35 The latest[4] dream I ever dream'd
      On the cold hill's side.

10

I saw pale kings, and princes too,
 Pale warriors, death pale were they all;
They cried—"La belle dame sans merci
40   Hath thee in thrall!"

11

I saw their starv'd lips in the gloam[5]
 With horrid warning gapèd wide,
And I awoke and found me here
      On the cold hill's side.

---

[2] Belt.
[3] Grotto.
[4] Last.
[5] Twilight.

12

45 And this is why I sojourn here,
   Alone and palely loitering,
   Though the sedge is wither'd from the lake,
   And no birds sing.

Ode on a Grecian Urn[1]
(1819)

1

Thou still unravish'd bride of quietness,
   Thou foster-child of silence and slow time,
Sylvan[2] historian, who canst thus express
A flowery tale more sweetly than our rhyme:
5 What leaf-fring'd legend haunts about thy shape
   Of deities or mortals, or of both,
      In Tempe[3] or the dales of Arcady?[4]
   What men or gods are these? What maidens loth?
What mad pursuit? What struggle to escape?
10   What pipes and timbrels? What wild ecstasy?

2

Heard melodies are sweet, but those unheard
   Are sweeter; therefore, ye soft pipes, play on;
Not to the sensual ear, but, more endear'd,
   Pipe to the spirit ditties of no tone:
15 Fair youth, beneath the trees, thou canst not leave
   Thy song, nor ever can those trees be bare;
      Bold lover, never, never canst thou kiss,
   Though winning near the goal—yet, do not grieve;
      She cannot fade, though thou hast not thy bliss,
20   For ever wilt thou love, and she be fair!

3

Ah, happy, happy boughs! that cannot shed
   Your leaves, nor ever bid the spring adieu;
And, happy melodist, unwearied,
   For ever piping songs for ever new;
25 More happy love! more happy, happy love!

---

[1] Though many urns similar to the one Keats describes actually exist, the subject of the poem is purely imaginary.

[2] Pertaining to woods or forests.

[3] A beautiful valley in Greece.

[4] The valleys of Arcadia, a mountainous region on the Greek peninsula. Like Tempe, they represent a rustic pastoral ideal.

For ever warm and still to be enjoy'd,
    For ever panting, and for ever young;
All breathing human passion far above,
    That leaves a heart high-sorrowful and cloy'd,
30   A burning forehead, and a parching tongue.

4

Who are these coming to the sacrifice?
    To what green altar, O mysterious priest,
Lead'st thou that heifer lowing at the skies,
    And all her silken flanks with garlands drest?
35 What little town by river or sea shore,
    Or mountain-built with peaceful citadel,
        Is emptied of this folk, this pious morn?
And, little town, thy streets for evermore
    Will silent be; and not a soul to tell
40   Why thou art desolate, can e'er return.

5

O Attic[5] shape! Fair attitude! with brede[6]
    Of marble men and maidens overwrought,[7]
With forest branches and the trodden weed;
    Thou, silent form, dost tease us out of thought
45 As doth eternity: Cold Pastoral!
    When old age shall this generation waste,
        Thou shalt remain, in midst of other woe
Than ours, a friend to man, to whom thou say'st,
    "Beauty is truth, truth beauty,"—that is all
50   Ye know on earth, and all ye need to know.

When I Have Fears

(1818)

When I have fears that I may cease to be
    Before my pen has gleaned my teeming brain,
Before high-piléd books, in charact'ry,[1]
    Hold like rich garners the full-ripened grain;
5 When I behold, upon the night's starred face,
    Huge cloudy symbols of a high romance,
And think that I may never live to trace

---

[5] Characteristic of Athens or Athenians.
[6] Braid.
[7] Elaborately ornamented.

---

[1] Print.

Their shadows, with the magic hand of chance;
And when I feel, fair creature of an hour,
10   That I shall never look upon thee more,
Never have relish in the faery power
    Of unreflecting love!—then on the shore
Of the wide world I stand alone, and think
Till Love and Fame to nothingness do sink.

To Autumn
(1820)

1

Season of mists and mellow fruitfulness,
    Close bosom-friend of the maturing sun;
Conspiring with him how to load and bless
    With fruit the vines that round the thatch-eves run;
5 To bend with apples the moss'd cottage-trees,
    And fill all fruit with ripeness to the core;
        To swell the gourd, and plump the hazel shells
With a sweet kernel; to set budding more,
    And still more, later flowers for the bees,
10   Until they think warm days will never cease,
        For Summer has o'er-brimm'd their clammy cells.

2

Who hath not seen thee oft amid thy store?
    Sometimes whoever seeks abroad may find
Thee sitting careless on a granary floor,
15   Thy hair soft-lifted by the winnowing wind;
Or on a half-reap'd furrow sound asleep,
    Drows'd with the fume of poppies, while thy hook
        Spares the next swath and all its twined flowers:
And sometimes like a gleaner thou dost keep
20   Steady thy laden head across a brook;
    Or by a cyder-press, with patient look,
        Thou watchest the last oozings hours by hours.

3

Where are the songs of Spring? Ay, where are they?
    Think not of them, thou hast thy music too,—
25 While barred clouds bloom the soft-dying day,
    And touch the stubble-plains with rosy hue;
Then in a wailful choir the small gnats mourn
    Among the river sallows, borne aloft
        Or sinking as the light wind lives or dies;

30 And full-grown lambs loud bleat from hilly bourn;
    Hedge-crickets sing; and now with treble soft
    The red-breast whistles from a garden-croft;
    And gathering swallows twitter in the skies.

ARCHIBALD LAMPMAN
(1861–1899)

The City of the End of Things
(1895)

Beside the pounding cataracts
Of midnight streams unknown to us
'Tis builded in the leafless tracts
And valleys huge of Tartarus.[1]
5 Lurid and lofty and vast it seems;
It hath no rounded name that rings,
But I have heard it called in dreams
The City of the End of Things.

Its roofs and iron towers have grown
10 None knoweth how high within the night,
But in its murky streets far down
A flaming terrible and bright
Shakes all the stalking shadows there,
Across the walls, across the floors,
15 And shifts upon the upper air
From out a thousand furnace doors;
And all the while an awful sound
Keeps roaring on continually,
And crashes in the ceaseless round
20 Of a gigantic harmony.
Through its grim depths re-echoing
And all its weary height of walls,
With measured roar and iron ring,
The inhuman music lifts and falls.
25 Where no thing rests and no man is,
And only fire and night hold sway;
The beat, the thunder and the hiss

---

[1] The lowest, gloomiest region of Hades, into which Zeus hurled the Titans and Giants; hell.

Cease not, and change not, night nor day.
And moving at unheard commands,
30 The abysses and vast fires between,
Flit figures that with clanking hands
Obey a hideous routine;
They are not flesh, they are not bone,
They see not with the human eye,
35 And from their iron lips is blown
A dreadful and monotonous cry;
And whoso of our mortal race
Should find that city unaware,
Lean Death would smite him face to face,
40 And blanch him with its venomed air:
Or caught by the terrific spell,
Each thread of memory snapt and cut,
His soul would shrivel and its shell
Go rattling like an empty nut.

45 It was not always so, but once,
In days that no man thinks upon,
Fair voices echoed from its stones,
The light above it leaped and shone:
Once there were multitudes of men,
50 That built that city in their pride,
Until its might was made, and then
They withered age by age and died.
But now of that prodigious race,
Three only in an iron tower,
55 Set like carved idols face to face,
Remain the masters of its power;
And at the city gate a fourth,
Gigantic and with dreadful eyes,
Sits looking toward the lightless north,
60 Beyond the reach of memories;
Fast rooted to the lurid floor,
A bulk that never moves a jot,
In his pale body dwells no more,
Or mind or soul,—an idiot!
65 But sometime in the end those three
Shall perish and their hands be still,
And with the master's touch shall flee
Their incommunicable skill.
A stillness absolute as death
70 Along the slacking wheels shall lie,
And, flagging at a single breath,
The fires that moulder out and die.
The roar shall vanish at its height,

And over that tremendous town
75 The silence of eternal night
Shall gather close and settle down.
All its grim grandeur, tower and hall,
Shall be abandoned utterly,
And into rust and dust shall fall
80 From century to century;
Nor ever living thing shall grow,
Nor trunk of tree, nor blade of grass;
No drop shall fall, no wind shall blow,
Nor sound of any foot shall pass:
85 Alone of its accursèd state,
One thing the hand of Time shall spare,
For the grim Idiot at the gate
Is deathless and eternal there.

PATRICK LANE
(1939–)

Albino Pheasants
(1977)

At the bottom of the field
where thistles throw their seeds
and poplars grow from cotton into trees
in a single season I stand among the weeds.
5 Fenceposts hold each other up with sagging wire.
Here no man walks except in wasted time.
Men circle me with cattle, cars and wheat.
Machines rot on my margins.
They say the land is wasted when it's wild
10 and offer plows and apple trees to tame
but in the fall when I have driven them away
with their guns and dogs and dreams
I walk alone. While those who'd kill
lie sleeping in soft beds
15 huddled against the bodies of their wives
I go with speargrass and hooked burrs
and wait upon the ice alone.

Delicate across the mesh of snow
I watch the pale birds come
20 with beaks the colour of discarded flesh.
White, their feathers are white,

as if they had been born in caves
and only now have risen to the earth
to watch with pink and darting eyes
25 the slowly moving shadows of the moon.
There is no way to tell men what to do . . .
the dance they make in sleep
withholds its meaning from their dreams.
That which has been nursed in bone
30 rests easy upon frozen stone
and what is wild is lost behind closed eyes:
albino birds, pale sisters, succubi.

PHILIP LARKIN
(1922–1985)

Aubade
(1977)

I work all day, and get half-drunk at night.
Waking at four to soundless dark, I stare.
In time the curtain-edges will grow light.
Till then I see what's really always there:
5 Unresting death, a whole day nearer now,
Making all thought impossible but how
And where and when I shall myself die.
Arid interrogation: yet the dread
Of dying, and being dead,
10 Flashes afresh to hold and horrify.

The mind blanks at the glare. Not in remorse
—The good not done, the love not given, time
Torn off unused—nor wretchedly because
An only life can take so long to climb
15 Clear of its wrong beginnings, and may never;
But at the total emptiness for ever,
The sure extinction that we travel to
And shall be lost in always. Not to be here,
Not to be anywhere,
20 And soon; nothing more terrible, nothing more true.

This is a special way of being afraid
No trick dispels. Religion used to try,
That vast moth-eaten musical brocade
Created to pretend we never die,
25 And specious stuff that says *No rational being
Can fear a thing it will not feel,* not seeing
That this is what we fear—no sight, no sound,

No touch or taste or smell, nothing to think with,
Nothing to love or link with,
30 The anaesthetic from which none come round.

And so it stays just on the edge of vision,
A small unfocused blur, a standing chill
That slows each impulse down to indecision.
Most things may never happen: this one will,
35 And realization of it rages out
In furnace-fear when we are caught without
People or drink. Courage is no good:
It means not scaring others. Being brave
Lets no one off the grave.
40 Death is no different whined at than withstood.

Slowly light strengthens, and the room takes shape.
It stands plain as a wardrobe, what we know,
Have always known, know that we can't escape,
Yet can't accept. One side will have to go.
45 Meanwhile telephones crouch, getting ready to ring
In locked-up offices, and all the uncaring
Intricate rented world begins to rouse.
The sky is white as clay, with no sun.
Work has to be done.
50 Postmen like doctors go from house to house.

EVELYN LAU
(1971–   )

My Tragic Opera
(1994)

Your home is the house with the leaded windows
gleaming gothic as flames toss in the fireplace.
Your bed is white as the whites of your eyes,
white as egg-whites, in the tomato-walled room
5 of the kitchen where you stand,
the neck of a bottle of Chivas[1] in your hand.
The eerie blue light of your eyes wavers in the dark
as I make my way towards you holding my ice-laden glass.

Across the street, a line of empty houses on the block,
10 hooded in the snow that hides flaws in the foundations
and the painted structures. Yet sales remain slow.
Your real estate signs stay stabbed in the ground

---

[1] Brand of Scotch whisky.

like stakes or crosses, as you take me out
onto your newly-built porch, as my thinly-clad feet
15 sink deep into the punishment of snow.

But to fuck you in your nuptial bed while your wife
and children toss in hammocks in the tropics!
Upstairs, evidence of your daughters everywhere
in Doc Martens,[2] denim and Beverly Hills 90210[3] pinups.
20 The eldest has starved herself beyond menstruation,
the middle one is the compulsive liar,
only the youngest remains a virgin in her white party dress.

Watercolours framed from first efforts in kindergarten,
drugstore alarm clocks, rows of pencils with erasers
25 that smell of peaches or passionfruit—
Don't tell me these things don't belong to me!
I will become bulimic and purge into your daughter's toilet,
sing my tragic opera in the shower with the reflective tiles,
lower my wifely bountiful body into the bath . . .

30 Along the Oregon coast an 18-year-old prostitute
lurches out of a bar, aims her thumb in the direction
she wants the road to take her, is raped then stabbed
as many times as the years she was old. In extreme cold,
a plastic object will shatter at a single touch.
35 Tonight the city is crippled by ice, cars mumble
through the side streets, their movements precarious
as those perfect high notes in the opera at the coliseum.
Laughing, I test all your daughters' beds for comfort,
steal their lunch money, destroy their teenage trinkets.

◆ ◆ ◆

DOROTHY LIVESAY
(1909–1996)

Green Rain
(1932)

I remember long veils of green rain
Feathered like the shawl of my grandmother—
Green from the half-green of the spring trees
Waving in the valley.

---

[2] Popular brand of shoes and boots.
[3] Television series popular with teenagers.

5　I remember the road
Like the one which leads to my grandmother's house,
A warm house, with green carpets,
Geraniums, a trilling canary
And shining horse-hair chairs;
10　And the silence, full of the rain's falling
Was like my grandmother's parlour
Alive with herself and her voice, rising and falling—
Rain and wind intermingled.

I remember on that day
15　I was thinking only of my love
And of my love's house.
But now I remember the day
As I remember my grandmother.
I remember the rain as the feathery fringe of her shawl.

The Three Emilys [1]
(1953)

These women crying in my head
Walk alone, uncomforted:
The Emilys, these three
Cry to be set free—
5　And others whom I will not name
Each different, each the same.

Yet they had liberty!
Their kingdom was the sky:
They batted clouds with easy hand,
10　Found a mountain for their stand;
From wandering lonely they could catch
The inner magic of a heath—
A lake their palette, any tree
Their brush could be.

15　And still they cry to me
As in reproach—
I, born to hear their inner storm
Of separate man in woman's form,

---

[1] A note identifying the three as Emily Brontë, Emily Dickinson, and Emily Carr
appeared with first publication of this poem in *The Canadian Forum* (September 1953).
Emily Brontë (1818–48) was a British poet and author of the novel *Wuthering Heights*
(1848); Emily Dickinson (1830–86) was an American poet; Emily Carr (1871–1945) was
a Canadian painter and author.

I yet possess another kingdom, barred
20 To them, these three, this Emily.[2]
I move as mother in a frame,
My arteries
Flow the immemorial way
Towards the child, the man;
25 And only for brief span
Am I an Emily on mountain snows
And one of these.

And so the whole that I possess
Is still much less—
30 They move triumphant through my head:
I am the one
Uncomforted.

◦ ◦ ◦

GWENDOLYN MACEWEN
(1941–1987)

A Breakfast for Barbarians
(1966)

my friends, my sweet barbarians,
there is that hunger which is not for food—
but an eye at the navel turns the appetite
round
5 with visions of some fabulous sandwich,
the brain's golden breakfast
                    eaten with beasts
                    with books on plates

let us make an anthology of recipes,
10 let us edit for breakfast
our most unspeakable appetites—
let us pool spoons, knives
and all cutlery in a cosmic cuisine,
let us answer hunger
15 with boiled chimera[1]
and apocalyptic tea,
an arcane salad of spiced bibles,

---

[2] None of the three Emilys married or gave birth, whereas Livesay married and raised two children.

---

[1] In Greek mythology, a fire-breathing monster with a lion's head, a goat's body, and a serpent's tail; also used figuratively to indicate an absurdly fanciful or impossible idea.

tossed dictionaries—

(O my barbarians
20   we will consume our mysteries)

and can we, can we slake the gaping eye of our desires?
we will sit around our hewn wood table
until our hair is long and our eyes are feeble,
eating, my people, O my insatiates,
25 eating until we are no more able
to jack up the jaws any longer—

to no more complain of the soul's vulgar cavities,
to gaze at each other over the rust-heap of cutlery,
drinking a coffee that takes an eternity—
30 till, bursting, bleary,
we laugh, barbarians, and rock the universe—
and exclaim to each other over the table
over the table of bones and scrap metal
over the gigantic junk-heaped table:

35 by God that was a meal

◇ ◇ ◇

JOHN MILTON
(1608–1674)

When I Consider How
My Light Is Spent[1]
(1655?)

When I consider how my light is spent,
    Ere half my days in this dark world and wide,
    And that one talent[2] which is death to hide
Lodged with me useless, though my soul more bent
5 To serve therewith my Maker, and present
    My true account, lest He returning chide;
    "Doth God exact day-labor, light denied?"
I fondly[3] ask. But Patience, to prevent
That murmur, soon replies, "God doth not need
10   Either man's work or His own gifts. Who best
    Bear His mild yoke, they serve Him best. His state
Is kingly: thousands at His bidding speed,
    And post o'er land and ocean without rest;
    They also serve who only stand and wait."

---

[1] A meditation on his blindness.
[2] See Jesus' parable of the talents in Matthew 25:14–30.
[3] Foolishly.

› › ›

PABLO NERUDA
(1904–1973)

The United Fruit Co.[1]
(1950)

Translated by Robert Bly

When the trumpet sounded, it was
all prepared on the earth,
and Jehovah parceled out the earth
to Coca-Cola, Inc., Anaconda,
5 Ford Motors, and other entities:
The Fruit Company, Inc.
reserved for itself the most succulent,
the central coast of my own land,
the delicate waist of America.
10 It rechristened its territories
as the "Banana Republics"
and over the sleeping dead,
over the restless heroes
who brought about the greatness,
15 the liberty and the flags,
it established the comic opera:
abolished the independencies,
presented crowns of Caesar,
unsheathed envy, attracted
20 the dictatorship of the flies,
Trujillo flies, Tacho flies,
Carias flies, Martinez flies,
Ubico flies,[2] damp flies
of modest blood and marmalade,
25 drunken flies who zoom
over the ordinary graves,
circus flies, wise flies
well trained in tyranny.

---

[1] Incorporated in New Jersey in 1899 by Andrew Preston and Minor C. Keith, United Fruit became the major force in growing, transporting, and merchandising Latin American produce, especially bananas. The company is also notorious for its involvement in politics and is a symbol for many people of "Yankee" imperialism and oppression.

[2] Trujillo, Tacho, Carias, Martinez, and Ubico are all political dictators.

Among the bloodthirsty flies
30 the Fruit Company lands its ships,
taking off the coffee and the fruit;
the treasure of our submerged
territories flows as though
on plates into the ships.

35 Meanwhile Indians are falling
into the sugared chasms
of the harbors, wrapped
for burial in the mist of the dawn:
a body rolls, a thing
40 that has no name, a fallen cipher,
a cluster of dead fruit
thrown down on the dump.

◊ ◊ ◊

BP NICHOL
(1944–1988)

from "The Captain Poetry Poems"
(1971)

dear Captain Poetry,
your poetry is trite.
you cannot write a sonnet
tho you've tried to every night
5 since i've known you.
we're thru !!
Madame X

dear Madame X

Look how the sun leaps now upon our faces
10 Stomps & boots our eyes into our skulls
Drives all thot to weird & foreign places
Till the world reels & the kicked mind dulls,
Drags our hands up across our eyes
Sends all white hurling into black
15 Makes the inner cranium our skies
And turns all looks sent forward burning back.
And you, my lady, who should be gentler, kind,
Have yet the fiery aspect of the sun
Sending words to burn into my mind
20 Destroying all my feelings one by one;
You who should have tiptoed thru my halls
Have slammed my doors & smashed me into walls.

love
Cap Poetry

ALDEN NOWLAN
(1933–1983)

Britain Street
(1967)

Saint John, New Brunswick

This is a street at war.
The smallest children
battle with clubs
till the blood comes,
5 shout "fuck you!"
like a rallying cry—

while mothers shriek
from doorsteps and windows
as though the very names
10 of their young were curses:

"Brian! Marlene!
Damn you! God damn you!"

or waddle into the street
to beat their own with switches:
15 "I'll teach you, Brian!
I'll teach you, God damn you!"

On this street
even the dogs
would rather fight
20 than eat.

I have lived here nine months
and in all that time
have never once heard
a gentle word spoken.

25 I like to tell myself
that is only because
gentle words are whispered
and harsh words shouted.

◆ ◆ ◆

SHARON OLDS
(1942–   )

Rite of Passage
(1983)

As the guests arrive at my son's party
they gather in the living room—
short men, men in first grade
with smooth jaws and chins.
5 Hands in pockets, they stand around
jostling, jockeying for place, small fights
breaking out and calming. One says to another
How old are you? Six. I'm seven. So?
They eye each other, seeing themselves
10 tiny in the other's pupils. They clear their
throats a lot, a room of small bankers,
they fold their arms and frown. *I could beat you
up,* a seven says to a six,
the dark cake, round and heavy as a
15 turret, behind them on the table. My son,
freckles like specks of nutmeg on his cheeks,
chest narrow as the balsa[1] keel[2] of a
model boat, long hands
cool and thin as the day they guided him
20 out of me, speaks up as a host
for the sake of the group.
We could easily kill a two-year-old,
he says in his clear voice. The other
men agree, they clear their throats
25 like Generals, they relax and get down to
playing war, celebrating my son's life.

---

[1] A lightweight wood.
[2] The piece of wood that runs lengthwise along the centre of a ship's bottom.

◇ ◆ ◇

MICHAEL ONDAATJE
(1943–   )

The Cinnamon Peeler
(1981)

If I were a cinnamon peeler
I would ride your bed
and leave the yellow bark dust
on your pillow.

5 Your breasts and shoulders would reek
you could never walk through markets
without the profession of my fingers
floating over you. The blind would
stumble certain of whom they approached
10 though you might bathe
under rain gutters, monsoon.

Here on the upper thigh
at this smooth pasture
neighbour to your hair
15 or the crease
that cuts your back. This ankle.
You will be known among strangers
as the cinnamon peeler's wife.

I could hardly glance at you
20 before marriage
never touch you
—your keen nosed mother, your rough brothers.
I buried my hands
in saffron, disguised them
25 over smoking tar,
helped the honey gatherers . . .

*

When we swam once
I touched you in water
and our bodies remained free,
30 you could hold me and be blind of smell.
You climbed the bank and said

this is how you touch other women
the grass cutter's wife, the lime burner's daughter.

And you searched your arms
35 for the missing perfume
                and knew

                  what good is it
to be the lime burner's daughter
left with no trace
40 as if not spoken to in the act of love
as if wounded without the pleasure of a scar.

You touched
your belly to my hands
in the dry air and said
45 I am the cinnamon
peeler's wife. Smell me.

Dates[1]

It becomes apparent that I miss great occasions.
My birth was heralded by nothing
but the anniversary of Winston Churchill's marriage.
No monuments bled, no instruments
5 agreed on a specific weather.
It was a seasonal insignificance.

I console myself with my mother's eighth month.
While she sweated out her pregnancy in Ceylon[2]
a servant ambling over the lawn
10 with a tray of iced drinks,
a few friends visiting her
to placate her shape, and I
drinking the life lines,
Wallace Stevens sat down in Connecticut
15 a glass of orange juice at his table
so hot he wore only shorts
and on the back of a letter
began to write "The Well Dressed Man with a Beard."

That night while my mother slept
20 her significant belly cooled
by the bedroom fan
Stevens put words together

---

[1] Publication date is not available.
[2] Now known as Sri Lanka.

that grew to sentences
and shaved them clean and
25 shaped them, the page suddenly
becoming thought where nothing had been,
his head making his hand
move where he wanted
and he saw his hand was saying
30 the mind is never finished, no, never
and I in my mother's stomach was growing
as were the flowers outside the Connecticut windows.

P. K. PAGE
(1916–)

After Reading *Albino Pheasants*
(1978)

For Pat Lane

Pale beak . . . pale eye . . . the dark imagination
flares like magnesium. Add but pale flesh
and I am lifted to a weightless world
watered cerulean, chrome-yellow (light)
5 and green, veronese—if I remember—a soft wash
recalls a summer evening sky.

At Barro de Navidad we watched the sky
fade softly like a bruise. Was it imagination
that showed us Venus phosphorescent in a wash
10 of air and ozone?—a phosphorescence flesh
wears like a mantle in bright moonlight,
a natural skin-tone in that other world.

Why should I wish to escape this world?
Why should three phrases alter the colour of the sky
15 the clarity, texture even, of the light?
What is there about the irrepressible imagination
that the adjective *pale* modifying *beak, eye* and *flesh*
can set my sensibilities awash?

If with my thickest brush I were to lay a wash
20 of thinnest watercolour I could make a world
as unlike my own dense flesh
as the high-noon midsummer sky;
but it would not catch at my imagination
or change the waves or particles of light

25 yet *pale* can tip the scales, make light
 this heavy planet. If I were to wash
 everything I own in mercury, would imagination
 run rampant in that suddenly silver world—
 free me from gravity, set me floating sky-
30 ward—thistledown—permanently disburdened of my flesh?

Like cygnets hatched by ducks, our minds and flesh
 are imprinted early—what to me is light
 may be dark to one born under a sunny sky.
 And however cool the water my truth won't wash
35 without shrinking except in its own world
 which is one part matter, nine parts imagination.

I fear flesh which blocks imagination,
 the light of reason which constricts the world.
 Pale beak . . . pale eye . . . pale flesh . . . My sky's awash.

◇ ◇ ◇

LINDA PASTAN
(1932–   )

Ethics
(1980)

In ethics class so many years ago
 our teacher asked this question every fall:
 if there were a fire in a museum
 which would you save, a Rembrandt painting
5 or an old woman who hadn't many
 years left anyhow? Restless on hard chairs
 caring little for pictures or old age
 we'd opt one year for life, the next for art
 and always half-heartedly. Sometimes
10 the woman borrowed my grandmother's face
 leaving her usual kitchen to wander
 some drafty, half imagined museum.
 One year, feeling clever, I replied
 why not let the woman decide herself?
15 Linda, the teacher would report, eschews
 the burdens of responsibility.
 This fall in a real museum I stand
 before a real Rembrandt, old woman,
 or nearly so, myself. The colors
20 within this frame are darker than autumn,
 darker even than winter—the browns of earth,
 though earth's most radiant elements burn

through the canvas. I know now that woman
and painting and season are almost one
25 and all beyond saving by children.

◈ ◈ ◈

MARGE PIERCY
(1936–   )

Barbie Doll
(1973)

This girlchild was born as usual
and presented dolls that did pee-pee
and miniature GE stoves and irons
and wee lipsticks the color of cherry candy.
5 Then in the magic of puberty, a classmate said:
You have a great big nose and fat legs.

She was healthy, tested intelligent,
possessed strong arms and back,
abundant sexual drive and manual dexterity.
10 She went to and fro apologizing.
Everyone saw a fat nose on thick legs.

She was advised to play coy,
exhorted to come on hearty,
exercise, diet, smile and wheedle.
15 Her good nature wore out
like a fan belt.
So she cut off her nose and her legs
and offered them up.
In the casket displayed on satin she lay
20 with the undertaker's cosmetics painted on,
a turned-up putty nose,
dressed in a pink and white nightie.
Doesn't she look pretty? everyone said.
Consummation at last.
25 To every woman a happy ending.

◇ ◈ ◈

EZRA POUND
(1885–1972)

The River-Merchant's
Wife: A Letter[1]
(1515)

While my hair was still cut straight across my forehead
I played about the front gate, pulling flowers.
You came by on bamboo stilts, playing horse,
You walked about my seat, playing with blue plums.
5 And we went on living in the village of Chokan:[2]
Two small people, without dislike or suspicion.
At fourteen I married My Lord you.
I never laughed, being bashful.
Lowering my head, I looked at the wall.
10 Called to, a thousand times, I never looked back.

At fifteen I stopped scowling,
I desired my dust to be mingled with yours
Forever and forever and forever.
Why should I climb the lookout?
15 At sixteen you departed,
You went into far Ku-to-yen,[3] by the river of swirling eddies,
And you have been gone five months.
The monkeys make sorrowful noise overhead.

You dragged your feet when you went out.
20 By the gate now, the moss is grown, the different mosses,
Too deep to clear them away!
The leaves fall early this autumn, in wind.
The paired butterflies are already yellow with August
Over the grass in the West garden;
25 They hurt me. I grow older.
If you are coming down through the narrows of the river Kiang,[4]
Please let me know beforehand,
And I will come out to meet you
    As far as Cho-fu-sa.[5]

---

[1] This is one of many translations Pound made of Chinese poems. The poem is a free translation of Li Po's (701–762) "Two Letters from Chang-Kan."

[2] Chang-Kan.

[3] An island in the river Ch'ū-t'ang.

[4] The Japanese name for the river Ch'ū-t'ang (see note 3). Pound's translations are based on commentaries derived from Japanese scholars; therefore, he usually uses Japanese instead of Chinese names.

[5] A beach several hundred miles upstream of Nanking.

◊ ◊ ◊

AL PURDY
(1918–2000)

The Country North of Belleville
(1965)

Bush land scrub land—
    Cashel Township and Wollaston
Elzevir McClure and Dungannon
green lands of Weslemkoon Lake
5 where a man might have some
    opinion of what beauty
is and none deny him
          for miles—

Yet this is the country of defeat
10 where Sisyphus[1] rolls a big stone
year after year up the ancient hills
picnicking glaciers have left strewn
with centuries' rubble
         backbreaking days
15   in the sun and rain
when realization seeps slow in the mind
without grandeur or self deception in
        noble struggle
of being a fool—

20 A country of quiescence and still distance
lean land
      not like the fat south
with inches of black soil on
      earth's round belly—
25 And where the farms are
      it's as if a man stuck
both thumbs in the stony earth and pulled

        it apart
        to make room
30 enough between the trees
for a wife
      and maybe some cows and
      room for some

---

[1] King of Corinth whose punishment in Hades was to roll a heavy stone up a hill, only to have it roll down again when it neared the top.

of the more easily kept illusions—
35 And where the farms have gone back
to forest
         are only soft outlines
         shadowy differences—

Old fences drift vaguely among the trees
40   a pile of moss-covered stones
gathered for some ghost purpose
has lost meaning under the meaningless sky
         —they are like cities under water
and the undulating green waves of time
45   are laid on them—

This is the country of our defeat
         and yet
during the fall plowing a man
might stop and stand in a brown valley of the furrows
50   and shade his eyes to watch for the same
         red patch mixed with gold
         that appears on the same
         spot in the hills
         year after year
55   and grow old
plowing and plowing a ten-acre field until
the convolutions run parallel with his own brain—

And this is a country where the young
         leave quickly
60 unwilling to know what their fathers know
or think the words their mothers do not say—

Herschel Monteagle and Faraday
lakeland rockland and hill country
a little adjacent to where the world is
65 a little north of where the cities are and
sometime
we may go back there
         to the country of our defeat
Wollaston Elzevir and Dungannon
70 and Weslemkoon lake land
where the high townships of Cashel
         McClure and Marmora once were—
But it's been a long time since
and we must enquire the way
75   of strangers—

HENRY REED
(1914–1986)

Naming of Parts
(1946)

Today we have naming of parts. Yesterday,
We had daily cleaning. And tomorrow morning,
We shall have what to do after firing. But today,
Today we have naming of parts. Japonica[1]
5 Glistens like coral in all of the neighboring gardens,
    And today we have naming of parts.

This is the lower sling swivel. And this
Is the upper sling swivel, whose use you will see,
When you are given your slings. And this is the piling swivel,
10 Which in your case you have not got. The branches
Hold in the gardens their silent, eloquent gestures,
    Which in our case we have not got.

This is the safety-catch, which is always released
With an easy flick of the thumb. And please do not let me
15 See anyone using his finger. You can do it quite easy
If you have any strength in your thumb. The blossoms
Are fragile and motionless, never letting anyone see
    Any of them using their finger.

And this you can see is the bolt. The purpose of this
20 Is to open the breech, as you see. We can slide it
Rapidly backwards and forwards: we call this
Easing the spring. And rapidly backwards and forwards
The early bees are assaulting and fumbling the flowers:
    They call it easing the Spring.

25 They call it easing the Spring: it is perfectly easy
If you have any strength in your thumb: like the bolt,
And the breech, and the cocking-piece, and the point of balance,
Which in our case we have not got; and the almond-blossom
Silent in all of the gardens and the bees going backwards and
    forwards,
30   For today we have the naming of parts.

---

[1] A shrub having waxy flowers in a variety of colours.

EDWIN ARLINGTON ROBINSON
(1869–1935)

Richard Cory
(1897)

Whenever Richard Cory went down town,
We people on the pavement looked at him:
He was a gentleman from sole to crown,
Clean favored, and imperially slim.

5 And he was always quietly arrayed,
And he was always human when he talked;
But still he fluttered pulses when he said,
"Good-morning," and he glittered when he walked.

And he was rich—yes, richer than a king—
10 And admirably schooled in every grace:
In fine, we thought that he was everything
To make us wish that we were in his place.

So on we worked, and waited for the light,
And went without the meat, and cursed the bread;
15 And Richard Cory, one calm summer night,
Went home and put a bullet through his head.

ARMAND GARNET RUFFO
(1955–)

Creating a Country
(1994)

They came to North America in search of a new life,
clinging to their few possessions, hungry for prosperity.
They'd had enough poverty and suffering to last a lifetime.
And so they believed with all their hearts
5 that if they laboured they would all become barons
in a classless society. Patriots were thus born
on both sides of the border. But the process of creating
a country took much longer than most ever imagined.
For there were a myriad of unforeseen obstacles
10 in this formidable new land. Like mosquitoes and Indians.
Undaunted, the pioneering spirit persisted.

In Canada, Susanna Moodie[1] arrived to take notes.
After writing, anti-slavery tracts in England,

---

[1] Nineteenth-century writer who wrote about emigrating from Britain and life in Canada
in *Roughing It in the Bush*.

she thought it only natural to document the burden
15 of roughing it in the bush. Susanna shied away
from both mosquitoes and Indians. One day, however,
quite by accident, she met a young Mohawk
whom she thought handsome and for a period flirted
with the notion of what it would be like to be swept away
20 by him. But she soon tired of such thoughts and nothing ever
became of it. Later she would say neither Indians nor mosquitoes
make good company. She did make it perfectly clear
that she bore no grudge. She believed everything has a place.

Just as she believed her place was across the ocean,
25 but she too had heard stories of golden opportunities.
Lies! She could be heard screaming. Nothing but lies!
Susanna also believed she was turning life into art
and creating the first semblance of culture
in a godforsaken land.
30 It was her only compensation.
When she spoke about her life her eyes rolled in her head
like a ship leaving port. She never gave up the dream
of returning home. Dreamed so hard
that even on her death bed she never stopped
35 talking to herself.

South of the border, Lt. Col. George Armstrong Custer
never once worried about mosquitoes.
It's said that he too was interested in culture
and for this reason carried a gun.
40 He was a soldier, not an artist, and made no pretence
about it. Custer rarely wrote and never spoke
unless formally addressed. Yet, he was a passionate man
who dreamed the same dream every night.
He fancied that he had discovered the final solution.
45 Each night he rounded up all the buffalo
in what is now Montana and shot every last one of them.

As a son of European peasantry, he had heard stories
about what it was like to go hungry.
He also knew Indians could starve
50 just like white people. As a patriot,
he believed his solution was perfectly reasonable.
He also believed American politicians
would see to it that both the buffalo and the Indian
would find a new home
55 on the American nickel.

Susanna Moodie never met General Golden Hair (as Custer
was affectionately called), she never liked Americans anyway.
She was an old lady of 73 when he died young on the plains
of Little Bighorn trying to live out his dream.
60 They say that Custer was singing,
'The Girl I Left Behind Me' the day he headed west.
We know he wasn't singing to Susanna Moodie.
We also know that after hearing what the U.S. Cavalry
was doing south of the border, Susanna thought
65 about the anti-slavery tracts she had written years before
and, for a brief moment, about what had ever become
of her young Mohawk,
if he fared any better.

◈ ◈ ◈

CARL SANDBURG
(1878–1967)

Fog
(1916)

The fog comes
on little cat feet.
It sits looking
over harbor and city
5 on silent haunches
and then moves on.

◈ ◈ ◈

F. R. SCOTT
(1899–1985)

Laurentian Shield
(1954)

Hidden in wonder and snow, or sudden with summer,
This land stares at the sun in a huge silence
Endlessly repeating something we cannot hear.
Inarticulate, arctic,
5 Not written on by history, empty as paper,
It leans away from the world with songs in its lakes
Older than love, and lost in the miles.

This waiting is wanting.
It will choose its language
10 When it has chosen its technic,
A tongue to shape the vowels of its productivity.
A language of flesh and of roses.[1]

Now there are pre-words,
Cabin syllables,
15 Nouns of settlement
Slowly forming, with steel syntax,
The long sentence of its exploitation.

The first cry was the hunter, hungry for fur,
And the digger for gold, nomad, no-man, a particle;
20 Then the bold commands of monopoly, big with machines,
Carving its kingdoms out of the public wealth;
And now the drone of the plane, scouting the ice,
Fills all the emptiness with neighbourhood
And links our future over the vanished pole.

25 But a deeper note is sounding, heard in the mines,
The scattered camps and the mills, a language of life,
And what will be written in the full culture of occupation
Will come, presently, tomorrow,
From millions whose hands can turn this rock into children.

◊ ◊ ◊

WILLIAM SHAKESPEARE
(1564–1616)

Let Me Not to the
Marriage of True Minds
(1609)

Let me not to the marriage of true minds
Admit impediments.[1] Love is not love
Which alters when it alteration finds,
Or bends with the remover to remove:
5 Oh, no! it is an ever-fixéd mark,
That looks on tempests and is never shaken;

---

[1] Line from Stephen Spender's "The Making of a Poem," an essay in which Spender discusses the landscape of an English mining region as a kind of language expressing human thoughts and wishes; Spender argues that humans aspire to "a language of flesh and roses."

---

[1] A reference to "The Order of Solemnization of Matrimony" in the Anglican *Book of Common Prayer:* "I require that if either of you know any impediments why ye may not be lawfully joined together in Matrimony, ye do now confess it."

It is the star to every wandering bark,
Whose worth's unknown, although his height[2] be taken.
Love's not Time's fool,[3] though rosy lips and cheeks
10 Within his bending sickle's compass come;
Love alters not with his brief hours and weeks,
But bears it out even to the edge of doom.[4]
　　If this be error and upon me proved,
　　I never writ, nor no man ever loved.

Not Marble, nor the Gilded Monuments
(1609)

Not marble, nor the gilded monuments
Of princes, shall outlive this powerful rhyme;
But you shall shine more bright in these contents
Than unswept stone, besmeared with sluttish time.
5 When wasteful war shall statues overturn,
And broils root out the work of masonry,
Nor Mars[1] his sword nor war's quick fire shall burn
The living record of your memory.
'Gainst death and all-oblivious enmity
10 Shall you pace forth; your praise shall still find room
Even in the eyes of all posterity
That wear this world out to the ending doom.
　　So, till the judgment that yourself arise,
　　You live in this, and dwell in lovers' eyes.

◇ ◇ ◇

PERCY BYSSHE SHELLEY
(1792–1822)

Ode to the West Wind
(1820)

I

O wild West Wind, thou breath of Autumn's being,
Thou, from whose unseen presence the leaves dead
Are driven, like ghosts from an enchanter fleeing,

---

[2] Although the altitude of a star may be measured, its worth is unknowable.
[3] That is, mocked by Time.
[4] Doomsday.

---

[1] God of War.

Yellow, and black, and pale, and hectic[1] red,
5 Pestilence-stricken multitudes: O Thou,
Who chariotest to their dark wintry bed

The winged seeds, where they lie cold and low,
Each like a corpse within its grave, until
Thine azure sister of the Spring[2] shall blow

10 Her clarion o'er the dreaming earth, and fill
(Driving sweet buds like flocks to feed in air)
With living hues and odours plain and hill:

Wild Spirit, which art moving everywhere;
Destroyer and Preserver; hear, O hear!

II

15 Thou on whose stream, mid the steep sky's commotion,
Loose clouds like Earth's decaying leaves are shed,
Shook from the tangled boughs of Heaven and Ocean,

Angels of rain and lightning: there are spread
On the blue surface of thine aery surge,
20 Like the bright hair uplifted from the head

Of some fierce Maenad,[3] even from the dim verge
Of the horizon to the zenith's height,
The locks of the approaching storm. Thou Dirge

Of the dying year, to which this closing night
25 Will be the dome of a vast sepulchre,
Vaulted with all thy congregated might

Of vapours, from whose solid atmosphere
Black rain and fire and hail will burst: O hear!

III

Thou who didst waken from his summer dreams
30 The blue Mediterranean, where he lay,
Lulled by the coil of his crystalline streams,

Beside a pumice isle in Baiae's bay,[4]
And saw in sleep old palaces and towers
Quivering within the wave's intenser day,

---

[1] Reference to a tubercular fever that produces flushed cheeks.
[2] The west wind of the spring.
[3] A female votary who danced wildly in ceremonies for Dionysus (or Bacchus), Greek god of wine and vegetation, who according to legend died in the fall and was reborn in the spring.
[4] A bay in the Mediterranean Sea, west of Naples. It was known for the opulent villas built by Roman emperors along its shores.

35 All overgrown with azure moss and flowers
So sweet, the sense faints picturing them! Thou
For whose path the Atlantic's level powers

Cleave themselves into chasms, while far below
The sea-blooms and the oozy woods which wear
40 The sapless foliage of the ocean, know

Thy voice, and suddenly grow grey with fear,
And tremble and despoil themselves: O hear!

IV

If I were a dead leaf thou mightest bear;
If I were a swift cloud to fly with thee;
45 A wave to pant beneath thy power, and share

The impulse of thy strength, only less free
Than thou, O Uncontrollable! If even
I were as in my boyhood, and could be

The comrade of thy wanderings over Heaven,
50 As then, when to outstrip thy skiey speed
Scarce seemed a vision; I would ne'er have striven

As thus with thee in prayer in my sore need,
Oh! lift me as a wave, a leaf, a cloud!
I fall upon the thorns of life! I bleed!

55 A heavy weight of hours has chained and bowed
One too like thee: tameless, and swift, and proud.

V

Make me thy lyre,[5] even as the forest is:
What if my leaves are falling like its own!
The tumult of thy mighty harmonies

60 Will take from both a deep, autumnal tone,
Sweet though in sadness. Be thou, Spirit fierce,
My spirit! Be thou me, impetuous one!

Drive my dead thoughts over the universe
Like withered leaves to quicken a new birth!
65 And, by the incantation of this verse,

Scatter, as from an unextinguished hearth
Ashes and sparks, my words among mankind!
Be through my lips to unawakened Earth

The trumpet of a prophecy! O Wind,
70 If Winter comes, can Spring be far behind?

---

[5] An Aeolian harp, a stringed instrument that produces musical sounds when exposed to the wind.

STEVIE SMITH
(1902–1971)

Not Waving but Drowning
(1957)

Nobody heard him, the dead man,
But still he lay moaning:
I was much further out than you thought
And not waving but drowning.

5 Poor chap, he always loved larking
And now he's dead
It must have been too cold for him his heart gave way,
They said.

Oh, no no no, it was too cold always
10 (Still the dead one lay moaning)
I was much too far out all my life
And not waving but drowning.

◊ ◊ ◊

WILLIAM STAFFORD
(1914–1993)

Traveling through the Dark
(1962)

Traveling through the dark I found a deer
dead on the edge of the Wilson River road.
It is usually best to roll them into the canyon:
that road is narrow; to swerve might make more dead.

5 By glow of the tail-light I stumbled back of the car
and stood by the heap, a doe, a recent killing;
she had stiffened already, almost cold.
I dragged her off; she was large in the belly.

My fingers touching her side brought me the reason—
10 her side was warm; her fawn lay there waiting,
alive, still, never to be born.
Beside that mountain road I hesitated.

The car aimed ahead its lowered parking lights;
under the hood purred the steady engine.
15 I stood in the glare of the warm exhaust turning red;
around our group I could hear the wilderness listen.

I thought hard for us all—my only swerving—
then pushed her over the edge into the river.

◇ ◇ ◇
WALLACE STEVENS
(1879–1955)

Anecdote of the Jar
(1923)

I placed a jar in Tennessee,
And round it was, upon a hill.
It made the slovenly wilderness
Surround that hill.

5 The wilderness rose up to it,
And sprawled around, no longer wild.
The jar was round upon the ground
And tall and of a port in air.

It took dominion everywhere.
10 The jar was gray and bare.
It did not give of bird or bush,
Like nothing else in Tennessee.

The Emperor of Ice-Cream
(1923)

Call the roller of big cigars,
The muscular one, and bid him whip
In kitchen cups concupiscent curds.
Let the wenches dawdle in such dress
5 As they are used to wear, and let the boys
Bring flowers in last month's newspapers.
Let be be finale of seem.
The only emperor is the emperor of ice-cream.

Take from the dresser of deal,[1]
10 Lacking the three glass knobs, that sheet
On which she embroidered fantails[2] once
And spread it so as to cover her face.
If her horny feet protrude, they come
To show how cold she is, and dumb.
15 Let the lamp affix its beam.
The only emperor is the emperor of ice-cream.

---

[1] Fir or pine wood.
[2] According to Stevens, "the word fantails does not mean fans, but fantail pigeons."

◈ ▶ ◈

ALFRED, LORD TENNYSON
(1809–1892)

Ulysses[1]
(1833)

It little profits that an idle king,
By this still hearth, among these barren crags,
Matched with an agèd wife, I mete and dole
Unequal laws unto a savage race
5 That hoard, and sleep, and feed, and know not me.
I cannot rest from travel; I will drink
Life to the lees. All times I have enjoyed
Greatly, have suffered greatly, both with those
That loved me, and alone; on shore, and when
10 Through scudding drifts the rainy Hyades[2]
Vexed the dim sea. I am become a name;
For always roaming with a hungry heart
Much have I seen and known—cities of men
And manners, climates, councils, governments,
15 Myself not least, but honored of them all—
And drunk delight of battle with my peers,
Far on the ringing plains of windy Troy.[3]
I am a part of all that I have met;
Yet all experience is an arch wherethrough
20 Gleams that untraveled world whose margin fades
Forever and forever when I move.
How dull it is to pause, to make an end,
To rust unburnished, not to shine in use!
As though to breathe were life! Life piled on life
25 Were all too little, and of one to me
Little remains; but every hour is saved
From that eternal silence, something more,
A bringer of new things; and vile it were
For some three suns to store and hoard myself,

---

[1] A legendary Greek king of Ithaca and hero of Homer's *Odyssey*, Ulysses (or Odysseus) is noted for his daring and cunning. After his many adventures—including encounters with the Cyclops, the cannibalistic Laestrygones, and the enchantress Circe—Ulysses returned home to his faithful wife, Penelope. Tennyson portrays an older Ulysses pondering his situation.

[2] A group of stars whose rising was supposedly followed by rain, and hence stormy seas.

[3] An ancient city in Asia Minor. According to legend, Paris, King of Troy, abducted Helen, initiating the famed Trojan War, in which numerous Greek heroes, including Ulysses, fought.

30 And this grey spirit yearning in desire
To follow knowledge like a sinking star,
Beyond the utmost bound of human thought.
    This is my son, mine own Telemachus,
To whom I leave the scepter and the isle—
35 Well-loved of me, discerning to fulfill
This labor, by slow prudence to make mild
A rugged people, and through soft degrees
Subdue them to the useful and the good.
Most blameless is he, centered in the sphere
40 Of common duties, decent not to fail
In offices of tenderness, and pay
Meet adoration to my household gods,
When I am gone. He works his work, I mine.
    There lies the port; the vessel puffs her sail;
45 There gloom the dark, broad seas. My mariners,
Souls that have toiled, and wrought, and thought with me—
That ever with a frolic welcome took
The thunder and the sunshine, and opposed
Free hearts, free foreheads—you and I are old;
50 Old age hath yet his honor and his toil.
Death closes all; but something ere the end,
Some work of noble note, may yet be done,
Not unbecoming men that strove with Gods.
The lights begin to twinkle from the rocks;
55 The long day wanes; the low moon climbs; the deep
Moans round with many voices. Come, my friends,
'Tis not too late to seek a newer world.
Push off, and sitting well in order smite
The sounding furrows; for my purpose holds
60 To sail beyond the sunset, and the baths
Of all the western stars, until I die.
It may be that the gulfs will wash us down;
It may be we shall touch the Happy Isles,[4]
And see the great Achilles,[5] whom we knew.
65 Though much is taken, much abides; and though
We are not now that strength which in old days
Moved earth and heaven, that which we are, we are—
One equal temper of heroic hearts,
Made weak by time and fate, but strong in will
70 To strive, to seek, to find, and not to yield.

---

[4] Elysium, or Paradise, believed to be in the far western ocean.
[5] Famed Greek hero of the Trojan War.

◇ ◇ ◇ ◇ ◇

DYLAN THOMAS
(1914–1953)

Fern Hill
(1946)

Now as I was young and easy under the apple boughs
About the lilting house and happy as the grass was green,
   The night above the dingle[1] starry,
     Time let me hail and climb
5   Golden in the heydays of his eyes,
And honored among wagons I was prince of the apple towns
And once below a time I lordly had the trees and leaves
     Trail with daisies and barley
   Down the rivers of the windfall light.

10 And as I was green and carefree, famous among the barns
About the happy yard and singing as the farm was home,
    In the sun that is young once only,
     Time let me play and be
   Golden in the mercy of his means,
15 And green and golden I was huntsman and herdsman, the calves
Sang to my horn, the foxes on the hills barked clear and cold,
    And the sabbath rang slowly
    In the pebbles of the holy streams.

All the sun long it was running, it was lovely, the hay
20 Fields high as the house, the tunes from the chimneys, it was air
    And playing, lovely and watery
     And fire green as grass.
    And nightly under the simple stars
As I rode to sleep the owls were bearing the farm away,
25 All the moon long I heard, blessed among stables, the nightjars
    Flying with the ricks, and the horses
    Flashing into the dark.

And then to awake, and the farm, like a wanderer white
With the dew, come back, the cock on his shoulder: it was all
30   Shining, it was Adam and maiden,
     The sky gathered again
    And the sun grew round that very day.
So it must have been after the birth of the simple light
In the first, spinning place, the spellbound horses walking warm
35   Out of the whinnying green stable
     On to the fields of praise.

---

[1] Wooded valley.

And honored among foxes and pheasants by the gay house
Under the new made clouds and happy as the heart was long,
   In the sun born over and over,
40   I ran my heedless ways,
   My wishes raced through the house high hay
And nothing I cared, at my sky blue trades, that time allows
In all his tuneful turning so few and such morning songs
   Before the children green and golden
45   Follow him out of grace,

Nothing I cared, in the lamb white days, that time would take me
Up to the swallow thronged loft by the shadow of my hand,
   In the moon that is always rising,
      Nor that riding to sleep
50   I should hear him fly with the high fields
And wake to the farm forever fled from the childless land.
Oh as I was young and easy in the mercy of his means,
   Time held me green and dying
   Though I sang in my chains like the sea.

◊   ◊   ◊

BRONWEN WALLACE
(1945–1989)

A Simple Poem for Virginia Woolf
(1983)

This started out as a simple poem
for Virginia Woolf   you know the kind
we women writers write these days
in our own rooms
5 on our own time
a salute   a gesture of friendship
a psychological debt
paid off
I wanted it simple
10 and perfectly round
hard as an
egg   I thought
only once I'd said egg
I thought of the smell
15 of bacon grease and dirty frying-pans
and whether there were enough for breakfast
I couldn't help it
I wanted the poem to be carefree and easy

like children playing in the snow
20 I didn't mean to mention
the price of snowsuits or
how even on the most expensive ones
the zippers always snag
just when you're late for work
25 and trying to get the children
off to school on time
a straightforward poem
for Virginia Woolf   that's all
I wanted really
30 not something tangled in
domestic life the way
Jane Austen's novels tangled
with her knitting her embroidery
whatever it was she hid them under
35 I didn't mean to go into all that
didn't intend to get confessional
and tell you how
every time I read a good poem
by a woman writer I'm always peeking
40 behind it trying to see
if she's still married
or has a lover at least
wanted to know what she did
with her kids while she wrote it
45 or whether she had any
and if she didn't if she'd chosen
not to or if she did did she
choose and why   I didn't mean
to bother with that
50 and I certainly wasn't going
to tell you about the time
my best friend was sick in intensive care
and I went down to see her
but they wouldn't let me in
55 because I wasn't her husband
or her father   her mother
I wasn't family
I was just her friend
and the friendship of women
60 wasn't mentioned
in hospital policy
or how I went out and kicked
a dent in the fender of my car
and sat there crying because
65 if she died I wouldn't be able

to tell her how much I loved her
(though she didn't and we laugh
about it now) but that's what got me
started I suppose   wanting to write
70 a gesture of friendship
for a woman for a woman writer
for Virginia Woolf
and thinking I could do it
easily   separating the words
75 from the lives they come from
that's what a good poem should do
after all and I wasn't going to make excuses
for being a woman   blaming years of silence
for leaving us
80 so much to say

This started out as a simple poem
for Virginia Woolf
it wasn't going to mention history
or choices or women's lives
85 the complexities of women's friendships
or the countless gritty details
of an ordinary woman's life
that never appear in poems at all
yet even as I write these words
90 those ordinary details intervene
between the poem I meant to write
and this one   where the delicate faces
of my children   faces of friends
of women I have never even seen
95 glow on the blank pages
and deeper than any silence
press around me
waiting their turn

◆ ◆ ◆

EDMUND WALLER
(1606–1687)

Go, Lovely Rose
(1645)

Go, lovely rose,
Tell her that wastes her time and me
That now she knows,
When I resemble her to thee,
5 How sweet and fair she seems to be.

Tell her that's young
And shuns to have her graces spied,
That hadst thou sprung
In deserts where no men abide,
10 Thou must have uncommended died.

Small is the worth
Of beauty from the light retired:
Bid her come forth,
Suffer herself to be desired,
15 And not blush so to be admired.

Then die, that she
The common fate of all things rare
May read in thee,
How small a part of time they share
20 That are so wondrous sweet and fair.

◊ ◊ ◊

TOM WAYMAN
(1945–   )

Did I Miss Anything?
(1991)

Question frequently asked by
students after missing a class

Nothing. When we realized you weren't here
we sat with our hands folded on our desks
in silence, for the full two hours

Everything. I gave an exam worth
5   40 per cent of the grade for this term
and assigned some reading due today
on which I'm about to hand out a quiz
worth 50 per cent.

Nothing. None of the content of this course
10 has value or meaning
Take as many days off as you like:
any activities we undertake as a class
I assure you will not matter either to you or me
and are without purpose

15   Everything. A few minutes after we began last time
a shaft of light descended and an angel

or other heavenly being appeared
and revealed to us what each woman or man must do
to attain divine wisdom in this life and
20   the hereafter
This is the last time the class will meet
before we disperse to bring this good news to all people on earth

Nothing. When you are not present
how could something significant occur?

25   Everything. Contained in this classroom
is a microcosm of human existence
assembled for you to query and examine and ponder
This is not the only place such an opportunity has been
gathered

30   but it was one place

And you weren't here

PHYLLIS WEBB
(1927–   )

Cornflowers & Saffron Robes Belittle the Effort
(1982)

Ssh, sigh, silence is coming, the night time blues. Hark.
Ahem. Sir? I lift my arm, the wind chimes through my
holy raiment. Mesmeric bells reduce the flies to slum-
ber. Pajama party. The end of the Raj.

◇   ◇   ◇

WALT WHITMAN
(1819–1892)

from "Song of Myself"
(1855)

1

I celebrate myself, and sing myself,
And what I assume you shall assume,
For every atom belonging to me as good belongs to you.

I loafe and invite my soul,
5 I lean and loafe at my ease observing a spear of summer grass.

My tongue, every atom of my blood, form'd from this soil, this air,
Born here of parents born here from parents the same, and their
     parents the same,
I, now thirty-seven years old in perfect health begin,
Hoping to cease not till death.

10 Creeds and schools in abeyance,
Retiring back a while suffic'd at what they are, but never forgotten,
I harbor for good or bad, I permit to speak at every hazard,
Nature without check with original energy.

2

Houses and rooms are full of perfumes, the shelves are crowded with
     perfumes,
15 I breathe the fragrance myself and know it and like it,
The distillation would intoxicate me also, but I shall not let it.

The atmosphere is not a perfume, it has no taste of the distillation,
     it is odorless,
It is for my mouth forever, I am in love with it,
I will go to the bank by the wood and become undisguised and naked,
20 I am mad for it to be in contact with me.

The smoke of my own breath,
Echoes, ripples, buzz'd whispers, love-root, silk-thread, crotch and vine,
My respiration and inspiration, the beating of my heart, the passing
     of blood and air through my lungs,
The sniff of green leaves and dry leaves, and of the shore and dark-
     color'd sea-rocks, and of hay in the barn,
25 The sound of the belch'd words of my voice loos'd to the eddies of
     the wind,
A few light kisses, a few embraces, a reaching around of arms,
The play of shine and shade on the trees as the supple boughs wag,
The delight alone or in the rush of the streets, or along the fields and
     hill-sides,
The feeling of health, the full-noon trill, the song of me rising from bed
     and meeting the sun.

30 Have you reckon'd a thousand acres much? have you reckon'd the
     earth much?
Have you practis'd so long to learn to read?
Have you felt so proud to get at the meaning of poems?

Stop this day and night with me and you shall possess the origin of
     all poems,

You shall possess the good of the earth and sun, (there are millions
    of suns left,)
35 You shall no longer take things at second or third hand, nor look
    through the eyes of the dead, nor feed on the spectres in books,
You shall not look through my eyes either, nor take things from me,
You shall listen to all sides and filter them from your self.

WILLIAM CARLOS WILLIAMS
(1883–1963)

The Dance
(1944)

In Breughel's[1] great picture, The Kermess,[2]
the dancers go round, they go round and
around, the squeal and the blare and the
tweedle of bagpipes, a bugle and fiddles
5 tipping their bellies (round as the thick-
sided glasses whose wash they impound)
their hips and their bellies off balance
to turn them. Kicking and rolling about
the Fair Grounds, swinging their butts, those
10 shanks must be sound to bear up under such
rollicking measures, prance as the dance
in Breughel's great picture, The Kermess.

JIM WONG-CHU
(1949–   )

old chinese cemetery
kamloops july 1977
(1977)

like a child lost
wandering about
touching   feeling
tattered grounds
5 touching   seeing
wooden boards

---

[1] Refers to the Flemish painter Peter Breughel (1525–1569).

[2] The Church Mass; Breughel's painting (1567) of peasants dancing at a church
festival.

etched in ink
etched in weather
etched in fading memories
10 etched
faded
forgotten

I walk
on earth
15 above the bones
of a multitude
of golden mountain men
searching for scraps
of memory

20 like a child unloved
his face pressed hard
against the wet window

peering in
for a desperate moment
25 I touch my past

◊   ◊   ◊

WILLIAM WORDSWORTH
(1770–1850)

Composed upon Westminster Bridge, September 3, 1802
(1807)

Earth has not anything to show more fair:
Dull would he be of soul who could pass by
A sight so touching in its majesty:
This City now doth, like a garment, wear
5 The beauty of the morning; silent, bare,
Ships, towers, domes, theatres, and temples lie
Open unto the fields, and to the sky;
All bright and glittering in the smokeless air.
Never did sun more beautifully steep
10 In his first splendor, valley, rock, or hill;
Ne'er saw I, never felt, a calm so deep!
The river glideth at his own sweet will:
Dear God! the very houses seem asleep;
And all that mighty heart is lying still!

I Wandered Lonely as a Cloud
(1807)

I wandered lonely as a cloud
    That floats on high o'er vales and hills,
When all at once I saw a crowd,
    A host, of golden daffodils,
5 Beside the lake, beneath the trees,
Fluttering and dancing in the breeze.

Continuous as the stars that shine
    And twinkle on the milky way,
They stretched in never-ending line
10   Along the margin of a bay:
Ten thousand saw I at a glance,
Tossing their heads in sprightly dance.

The waves beside them danced; but they
    Out-did the sparkling waves in glee;
15 A poet could not but be gay,
    In such a jocund company;
I gazed—and gazed—but little thought
What wealth the show to me had brought:

For oft, when on my couch I lie
20   In vacant or in pensive mood,
They flash upon that inward eye
    Which is the bliss of solitude;
And then my heart with pleasure fills,
And dances with the daffodils.

She Dwelt among the
Untrodden Ways
(1800)

She dwelt among the untrodden ways
    Beside the springs of Dove,[1]
A Maid whom there were none to praise
    And very few to love:
5 A violet by a mossy stone
    Half hidden from the eye!
—Fair as a star, when only one
    Is shining in the sky.

---

[1] River in the Lake District of England.

The Solitary Reaper[1]
(1807)

Behold her, single in the field,
Yon solitary Highland lass!
Reaping and singing by herself;
Stop here, or gently pass!
5   Alone she cuts and binds the grain,
And sings a melancholy strain;
O listen! for the vale profound
Is overflowing with the sound.

No nightingale did ever chaunt
10 More welcome notes to weary bands
Of travelers in some shady haunt
Among Arabian sands.
A voice so thrilling ne'er was heard
In springtime from the cuckoo-bird,
15 Breaking the silence of the seas
Among the farthest Hebrides.[2]

Will no one tell me what she sings?—
Perhaps the plaintive numbers flow
For old, unhappy, far-off things,
20 And battles long ago.
Or is it some more humble lay,
Familiar matter of today?
Some natural sorrow, loss, or pain,
That has been, and may be again?

25 Whate'er the theme, the maiden sang
As if her song could have no ending;
I saw her singing at her work,
And o'er the sickle[3] bending—
I listened, motionless and still;
30 And, as I mounted up the hill,
The music in my heart I bore
Long after it was heard no more.

---

[1] A person who harvests grain.
[2] A group of islands off the west coast of Scotland.
[3] A curved blade used for harvesting grain or cutting grass.

WILLIAM BUTLER YEATS
(1865–1939)

Crazy Jane Talks with the Bishop
(1933)

I met the Bishop on the road
And much said he and I.
"Those breasts are flat and fallen now,
Those veins must soon be dry;
5 Live in a heavenly mansion,
Not in some foul sty."

"Fair and foul are near of kin,
And fair needs foul," I cried.
"My friends are gone, but that's a truth
10 Nor grave nor bed denied,
Learned in bodily lowliness
And in the heart's pride.

"A woman can be proud and stiff
When on love intent;
15 But Love has pitched his mansion in
The place of excrement;
For nothing can be sole or whole
That has not been rent."

Sailing to Byzantium
(1927)

That is no country for old men. The young
In one another's arms, birds in the trees
—Those dying generations—at their song,
The salmon-falls, the mackerel-crowded seas,
5 Fish, flesh, or fowl, commend all summer long
Whatever is begotten, born, and dies.
Caught in that sensual music all neglect
Monuments of unaging intellect.

An aged man is but a paltry thing,
10 A tattered coat upon a stick, unless
Soul clap its hands and sing, and louder sing
For every tatter in its mortal dress,
Nor is there singing school but studying
Monuments of its own magnificence;

15 And therefore I have sailed the seas and come
To the holy city of Byzantium.

O sages standing in God's holy fire
As in the gold mosaic of a wall,
Come from the holy fire, perne in a gyre,
20 And be the singing-masters of my soul.
Consume my heart away; sick with desire
And fastened to a dying animal
It knows not what it is; and gather me
Into the artifice of eternity.

25 Once out of nature I shall never take
My bodily form from any natural thing,
But such a form as Grecian goldsmiths make
Of hammered gold and gold enameling
To keep a drowsy Emperor awake;
30 Or set upon a golden bough to sing
To lords and ladies of Byzantium
Of what is past, or passing, or to come.

The Second Coming[1]
(1921)

Turning and turning in the widening gyre[2]
The falcon cannot hear the falconer;
Things fall apart; the center cannot hold;
Mere anarchy is loosed upon the world,
5 The blood-dimmed tide is loosed, and everywhere
The ceremony of innocence is drowned;
The best lack all conviction, while the worst
Are full of passionate intensity.[3]

Surely some revelation is at hand;
10 Surely the Second Coming is at hand;
The Second Coming! Hardly are those words out
When a vast image out of *Spiritus Mundi*[4]
Troubles my sight: somewhere in sands of the desert
A shape with lion body and the head of a man,

---

[1] The Second Coming usually refers to the return of Christ. Yeats theorized cycles of history, much like the turning of a wheel. Here he offers a poetic comment on his view of the dissolution of civilization at the end of one such cycle.

[2] Spiral.

[3] Lines 4–8 refer to the Russian Revolution (1917).

[4] The Spirit of the World. Yeats believed all souls to be connected by a "Great Memory."

15 A gaze blank and pitiless as the sun,
Is moving its slow thighs, while all about it
Reel shadows of the indignant desert birds.
The darkness drops again; but now I know
That twenty centuries[5] of stony sleep
20 Were vexed to nightmare by a rocking cradle,
And what rough beast, its hour come round at last,
Slouches towards Bethlehem to be born?

◊   ◊   ◊

JAN ZWICKY
(1955–   )

Border Station

(1998)

There had been flooding all that summer, I recall,
acres of grey-brown footage from the Midwest—
but with reports confined to property, and human interest,
the reasons for the land's incontinence suppressed, those images
5 had skimmed past, seeming, as usual, not quite real.
The day had been hot, clear,
we'd eaten supper on the porch, and
later, quite late, had turned the radio on upstairs—
some thought of midnight news, perhaps—
10 I don't remember now.
The signal we pulled in—strongly,
because we weren't far from the border then—
was the last half-hour of a Brewers-Red Sox game.
It was coming from Milwaukee,
15 top of the ninth, two out, the Brewers leading,
and we hadn't been listening long when the announcer,
between a line out and Hatcher's
coming to the plate, commented on the weather:
there'd been a rain delay, it had been raining heavily before,
20 but now was easing up, just a light shower falling,
though a lot of lightning was still visible to the east and south.
Raised on the prairies, I
could see it clearly, suddenly
could see the whole scene clearly:
25 the crowd dwindling, several
umbrellas, the glittering aluminum of vacated seats,
the misted loaf of arc-lit light, the night,

---

[5] The centuries since the birth of Christ.

deeper by contrast, thick and wet and brown
around it, flickering.
30 And at the same time I was struck, too—like
looking out across a huge relief map—by the hundreds of miles
between our bedroom and Milwaukee, by that continental
distance, and was overtaken inexplicably
by sorrow.
35   It was as though
in that moment of deep focus
I had tasted the idea of America.
As though it really might have had
something to do with baseball, and radio, and the beauty
40 of the storms that can form in the vast light above the plains—or,
no, extremity of some kind—clarity, or tenderness—
as though, that close to the end, levels
already rising on the leveed banks again,
the mistakes might have been human:
45 not justifiable, but as though
some sort of story might be told, simply,
from defeat, without apology, the way you might describe
the fatal accident—not to make sense of it,
but just to say, too late but still to say,
50 something had happened:
there was blood, blood everywhere, we hadn't realized,
by the time we noticed, rivers of it,
nothing could be done.

DRAMA

CHAPTER 20

Understanding Drama

DRAMATIC LITERATURE

❖ ❖ ❖

The distinctive appearance of a script, with its stage directions, character parts, and divisions into acts and scenes, identifies **drama** as a unique form of literature. A play is written to be performed in front of an audience by actors who take on the roles of the characters and who present the story through dialogue and action. (An exception is **closet drama,** which is meant to be read, not performed.) Indeed, the term *theatre* comes from the Greek word *theasthai,* which means "to view" or "to see." Thus, drama is different from novels and short stories, which are meant to be read.

Dramatic works differ from other prose works in a number of other ways as well. Unlike novels and short stories, plays do not usually have narrators to tell the audience what a character is thinking or what happened in the past; the audience knows only what the characters reveal. Drama develops primarily by means of **dialogue,** the lines spoken by the characters. The plot and the action of drama unfold on the stage as the characters interact. Playwrights employ various techniques to compensate for the absence of a narrator. For example, playwrights use **monologues**—extended speeches by one character. (A monologue in which a character expresses private thoughts while alone on the stage is called a **soliloquy.**) Playwrights can also use **asides**—brief comments by an actor who addresses the audience but is not heard by the other characters—to reveal the thoughts of the speaker. Like the observations of a narrator, these dramatic techniques give the audience insight into a character's motives and attitudes. In addition, makeup, costumes, scenery, and lighting enhance a dramatic performance, as do actors' and directors' interpretations of dialogue and stage directions.

THE ORIGINS OF THE MODERN THEATRE
◇ ◇ ◇

THE ANCIENT GREEK THEATRE

The dramatic presentations of ancient Greece developed out of religious rites performed to honour gods or to mark the coming of spring. Playwrights such as Aeschylus (525–456 B.C.), Sophocles (496–406 B.C.), and Euripides (480?–406 B.C.) composed plays to be performed and judged at competitions held during the yearly Dionysian festivals. Works were chosen by a selection board and evaluated by a panel of judges. To compete in the contest, authors had to submit three tragedies, which could be either based on a common theme or unrelated, and one comedy. Unfortunately, relatively few of these ancient Greek plays survive today.

The open-air semicircular ancient Greek theatre, built into the side of a hill, looked much like a primitive version of a modern sports stadium. Some Greek theatres, such as the Athenian theatre, could seat almost seventeen thousand spectators. Sitting in tiered seats, the audience would look down on the *orchestra*, or "dancing place," occupied by the **chorus**—originally a group of men (led by an individual called the *choragos*) who danced and

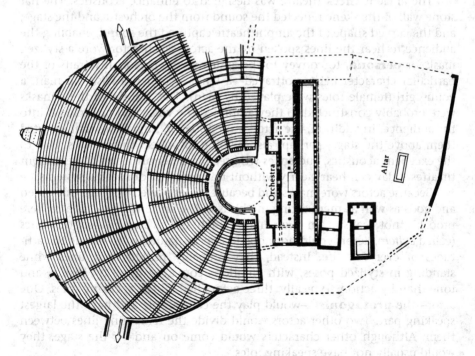

◇ **The Theatre of Dionysus at Athens.** Redrawn from a drawing by R. C. Flickinger, *The Greek Theater and Its Drama* (Chicago: U of Chicago P, 1918).

chanted and later a group of onlookers who commented on the drama. Raised a few steps above the orchestra was a platform on which the actors performed, behind which was a *skene,* or building, that originally served as a resting place or dressing room. (The modern term *scene* is derived from the Greek *skene.*) Behind the skene was a line of pillars called a *colonnade,* which was covered by a roof. Actors used the skene for entrances and exits; beginning with the plays of Sophocles, painted backdrops were hung there. These backdrops, however, were most likely more decorative than realistic. Historians believe that realistic props and scenery were probably absent from the ancient Greek theatre. Instead, the setting was suggested by the play's dialogue, and the audience had to imagine the specific physical details of a scene.

Two mechanical devices were used. One, a rolling cart or platform, was sometimes employed to introduce action that had occurred offstage. For example, actors frozen in position could be rolled onto the roof of the skene to illustrate an event such as the killing of Oedipus's father, which occurred before the play began. Another mechanical device, a small crane, was used to show gods ascending to or descending from heaven. Such devices enabled playwrights to dramatize many of the myths that were celebrated at the Dionysian festivals.

The ancient Greek theatre was designed to enhance acoustics. The flat stone wall of the skene reflected the sound from the orchestra and the stage, and the curved shape of the amphitheatre captured the sound, enabling the audience to hear the lines spoken by the actors. Each actor wore a stylized mask, or **persona,** to convey to the audience the personality traits of the particular character being portrayed—a king, a soldier, a wise old man, a young girl (female roles were played by men). The mouths of these masks were probably constructed so they amplified the voice and projected it into the audience. In addition, the actors wore *kothorni,* high shoes that elevated them above the stage, perhaps also helping to project their voices. Due to the excellent acoustics, audiences who see plays performed in these ancient theatres today can hear clearly without microphones or speaker systems.

Because actors wore masks and because males played the parts of women and gods as well as men, acting methods in the ancient Greek theatre were probably not realistic. In their masks, high shoes, and full-length tunics (called *chiton*), actors could not hope to appear natural or to mimic the attitudes of everyday life. Instead, they probably recited their lines while standing in stylized poses, with emotions conveyed more by gesture and tone than by action. Typically, three actors had all the speaking roles. One actor—the **protagonist**—would play the central role and have the largest speaking part. Two other actors would divide the remaining lines between them. Although other characters would come on and off the stage, they would usually not have speaking roles.

Ancient Greek tragedies were typically divided into five parts. First came the *prologos* or prologue, in which an actor gave the background or explanations that the audience needed to follow the rest of the drama. Then came the *párodos,* in which the chorus entered and commented on the events presented in the prologue. Following this were several *episodia,* or episodes, in which characters spoke to one another on the stage and developed the central conflict of the play. Alternating with episodes were *stasimon* (choral odes), in which the chorus commented on the exchanges that had taken place during the preceding episode. Frequently the choral odes were divided into *strophes,* or stanzas, that were recited or sung as the chorus moved across the orchestra in one direction, and *antistrophes* that were recited as it moved in the opposite direction. (Interestingly, the chorus stood between the audience and the actors, often functioning as an additional audience, expressing the political, social, and moral views of the community.) Finally came the *exodos,* the last scene of the play, during which the conflict was resolved and the actors left the stage.

Using music, dance, and verse—as well as a variety of architectural and technical innovations—the ancient Greek theatre was able to convey traditional themes of tragedy. Thus, the theatre powerfully expressed ideas that were central to the religious festivals in which they first appeared: the reverence for the cycles of life and death, the unavoidable dictates of the gods, and the inscrutable workings of fate.

THE ELIZABETHAN THEATRE

The Elizabethan theatre, influenced by the classical traditions of Roman and Greek dramatists, traces its roots back to local religious pageants performed at medieval festivals during the twelfth and thirteenth centuries. Town guilds, organizations of craftsmen who worked in the same profession, reenacted Old and New Testament stories: the fall of man, Noah and the flood, David and Goliath, and the crucifixion of Christ, for example. Church fathers encouraged these plays because they brought the Bible to a largely illiterate audience. Sometimes these spectacles, called **mystery plays,** were presented in the market square or on the church steps, and at other times actors appeared on movable stages or wagons called *pageants,* which could be wheeled to a given location. (Some of these wagons were quite elaborate, with trapdoors and pulleys and an upper tier that simulated heaven.) As mystery plays became more popular, they were performed in series over several days, presenting an entire cycle of a holiday—the death and resurrection of Christ during Easter, for example.

Related to mystery plays are **morality plays,** which developed in the fourteenth and fifteenth centuries. Unlike mystery plays, which depict scenes from the Bible, morality plays allegorize the Christian way of life. Typically, characters representing various virtues and vices struggle or debate over the soul of man. *Everyman* (1500), the best known of these plays, dramatizes the good and bad qualities of Everyman and shows his struggle to determine what is of value to him as he journeys toward death.

By the middle of the sixteenth century, mystery and morality plays had lost ground to a new secular drama. One reason for this decline was that mystery and morality plays were associated with Catholicism and consequently discouraged by the Protestant clergy. In addition, newly discovered plays of ancient Greece and Rome introduced a dramatic tradition that supplanted the traditions of religious drama. English plays that followed the classic model were sensational and bombastic, often dealing with murder, revenge, and blood retribution. Appealing to privileged classes and commoners alike, these plays were extremely popular. (One source estimates that between 20,000 and 25,000 people attended the London theatres each week.) Companies of professional actors performed works such as Christopher Marlowe's *Tamburlaine* and Thomas Kyd's *The Spanish Tragedy* in tavern courtyards and then eventually in theatres. According to scholars, the structure of the Elizabethan theatre evolved from these tavern courtyards.

The Globe Theatre (a corner of which was unearthed in 1989), where Shakespeare's plays were performed, consisted of a large main stage that extended out into the open-air *yard* where the *groundlings,* or common people, stood. Spectators who paid more sat on small stools in two or three levels of galleries that extended in front of and around the stage. (The theatre could probably seat almost two thousand people at a performance.) Most of the play's action occurred on the stage, which had no curtain and could be seen from three sides. Beneath the stage was a space called the *hell,* which could be reached when the floorboards were removed. This space enabled actors to "disappear" or descend into a hole or grave when the play called for such action. Above the stage was a roof called the *heavens,* which protected the actors from the weather and contained ropes and pulleys used to lower props or to create special effects.

At the rear of the stage was a narrow alcove covered by a curtain that could be open or closed. This curtain, often painted, functioned as a decorative rather than a realistic backdrop. The main function of this alcove was to enable actors to hide when the script called for them to do so. Some Elizabethan theatres contained a rear stage instead of an alcove. Because the rear stage was concealed by a curtain, props could be arranged on it ahead of time. When the action on the rear stage was finished, the curtain would be drawn and the action would continue on the front stage.

On either side of the rear stage was a door through which the actors could enter and exit the front stage. Above the rear stage was an upper, curtained stage called the *chamber,* which functioned as a balcony or as any other setting located above the action taking place on the stage below. On either side of the chamber were casement windows, which actors could use when a play called for a conversation with someone leaning out a window or standing on a balcony. Above the chamber was the *music gallery,* a balcony that housed the musicians who provided musical interludes throughout the play (and that doubled as a stage if the play required it). The *huts,* windows located above the music gallery, could be used by characters playing lookouts or sentries. Because of the many acting sites, more than one action could take place simultaneously. For example, lookouts could

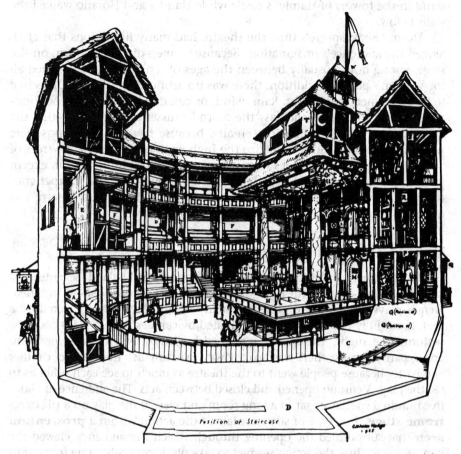

Position of Staircase

The Globe Playhouse,

1599-1613

A CONJECTURAL

RECONSTRUCTION

KEY

AA Main entrance
B The Yard
CC Entrances to lowest gallery
D Entrances to staircase and upper galleries
E Corridor serving the different sections of the middle gallery
F Middle gallery ('Twopenny Rooms')
G 'Gentlemen's Rooms' or 'Lords' Rooms'
H The stage

J The hanging being put up round the stage
K The 'Hell' under the stage
L The stage trap, leading down to the Hell
MM Stage doors
N Curtained 'place behind the stage'
O Gallery above the stage, used as required sometimes by musicians, sometimes by spectators, and often as part of the play
P Back-stage area (the tiring-house)
Q Tiring-house door
R Dressing-rooms
S Wardrobe and storage
T The hut housing the machine for lowering enthroned gods, etc., to the stage
U The 'Heavens'
W Hoisting the playhouse flag

◈ **The Globe Playhouse.** 1599–1613; a conjectural reconstruction. From C. Walter Hodges, *The Globe Restored: A Study of the Elizabethan Theatre.*

stand in the towers of Hamlet's castle while Hamlet and Horatio walked the walls below.

During Shakespeare's time the theatre had many limitations that challenged the audience's imagination. Because women did not perform on the stage, young boys—usually between the ages of ten and twelve—played all the women's parts. In addition, there was no artificial lighting, so plays had to be performed in daylight. Rain, wind, or clouds could disrupt a performance or ruin an image—such as "the morn in russet mantle clad"—that the audience was asked to imagine. Finally, because few sets and props were used, the audience had to visualize the high walls of a castle or the trees of a forest. The plays themselves were performed without intermission, except for musical interludes that occurred at various points. Thus, the experience of seeing one of Shakespeare's plays staged in the Elizabethan theatre was different from seeing it staged today in a modern theatre.

THE MODERN THEATRE

Unlike the theatres of ancient Greece and Elizabethan England, seventeenth- and eighteenth-century theatres—such as the Palais Royal, where the great French playwright Molière presented many of his plays—were covered by a roof, beautifully decorated, and illuminated by candles so that plays could be performed at night. The theatre remained brightly lit even during performances, partly because there was no easy way to extinguish hundreds of candles and partly because people went to the theatre as much to see each other as to see the play. A curtain opened and closed between acts. The audience of about five hundred spectators sat in a long room and viewed the play on a **picture-frame stage.** This type of stage contained the action within a **proscenium arch** that surrounded the opening through which the audience viewed the performance. Thus, the action seemed to take place in an adjoining room with one of its walls cut away. Painted scenery (some of it quite elaborate), intricately detailed costumes, and stage makeup were commonplace, and for the first time women performed female roles. Because the theatres were small, audiences were relatively close to the stage, so actors could use subtle movements and facial expressions to enhance their performances.

Many of the first innovations in the theatre were quite basic. For example, the first stage lighting was produced by candles lining the front of the stage. This method of lighting was not only ineffective—actors were lit from below and had to step forward to be fully illuminated—but also dangerous. Costumes and even entire theatres could and did accidentally catch fire. Later, covered lanterns with reflectors provided more light. In the nineteenth century a device that used an oxyhydrogen flame directed on a cylinder of lime created extremely bright illumination that could, with the aid of a lens, be concentrated into a spotlight. (It is from this method of stage lighting that we get the expression *to be in the limelight*.) Eventually, in the twentieth century, electric lights provided a dependable and safe way of lighting the stage. Electric spotlights, footlights, and ceiling light bars made the actors clearly visible and enabled playwrights to create special effects.

Along with electric lighting came other innovations, such as electronic amplification. Microphones made it possible for actors to speak conversationally and to avoid using unnaturally loud "stage diction" to project their voices to the rear of the theatre. Microphones placed at various points around the stage enabled actors and actresses to interact naturally and to deliver their lines audibly even without facing the audience. More recently, small wireless microphones eliminated the unwieldy wires and the "dead spaces" left between upright or hanging microphones, allowing characters to move freely around the stage.

The true revolutions in staging came with the advent of **realism** in the middle of the nineteenth century. Until this time, scenery was painted on canvas backdrops that trembled visibly, especially when they were intersected by doors through which actors and actresses entered. With realism came settings that were accurate down to the smallest detail. (Improved lighting, which revealed the inadequacies of painted backdrops, made such realistic stage settings necessary.) Backdrops were replaced by the **box set,** three flat panels arranged to form connected walls, with the fourth wall removed so the audience had the illusion of looking into a room. The room itself was decorated with real furniture, plants, and pictures on the walls; the door of one room might connect to another completely furnished room, or a window might open to a garden filled with realistic foliage. In addition, new methods of changing scenery were employed. Elevator stages, hydraulic lifts, and moving platforms enabled directors to make complicated changes in scenery out of the audience's view.

During the late nineteenth and early twentieth centuries, however, some playwrights reacted against what they saw as the excesses of realism. They introduced **surrealistic** stage settings, in which colour and scenery mirrored the uncontrolled images of dreams, and **expressionistic** stage settings, in which costumes and scenery were exaggerated and distorted to reflect the workings of a troubled, even unbalanced mind. In addition, playwrights used lighting to create areas of light, shadow, and colour that reinforced the themes of the play or reflected the emotions of the protagonist.

Sets in contemporary plays run the gamut from realistic to fantastic, from a detailed re-creation of a room in a production of Susan Glaspell's *Trifles* (p. 948) to the dreamlike sets in George Ryga's *The Ecstasy of Rita Joe* (p. 1376). Motorized devices, such as revolving turntables, and *wagons*— scenery mounted on wheels—make possible rapid changes of scenery. The Broadway musical *Les Misérables*, for example, requires scores of elaborate sets—Parisian slums, barricades, walled gardens—to be shifted as the audience watches. A gigantic barricade constructed on stage at one point in the play is later rotated to show the carnage that has taken place on both sides of a battle. Light, sound, and smoke are used to heighten the impact of the scene.

Today, as dramatists attempt to break down the barriers that separate audiences from the action they are viewing, plays are not limited to the picture-frame stage; in fact, they are performed on many different kinds of stages. Some plays, for example, take place on a **thrust stage,** which has an area that projects out into the audience. Others are performed on an **arena stage,** with the audience surrounding the actors. This kind of performance is often called **theatre in the round.** In addition, experiments have been done with *environmental staging,* in which the stage surrounds the audience or several stages are situated at various locations throughout the audience. Plays may also be performed outdoors, in settings ranging from parks to city streets. Some playwrights even try to blur the line that divides the audience from the stage by having actors move through or sit in the audience—or even by eliminating the stage entirely. Today, no single architectural form defines the theatre. The modern stage is a flexible space suited to the many varieties of contemporary theatrical production.

THE CANADIAN THEATRE (ENGLISH)

While theatre was a part of life in Canada from the time of settlement by Europeans, its focus tended to entertainment and was largely foreign in origin. Drama in Canada came into its own in the twentieth century, and it

◆ **Thrust-Stage Theatre.** With seats on three sides of the stage area, the thrust stage and its background can assume many forms other than the conventional living-room interior in the illustration. Entrances can be made from the aisles, from the sides, through the stage floor, and from the back.

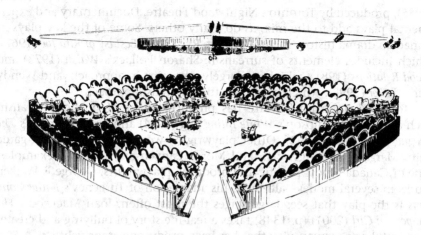

◆ **Arena Theatre.** The audience surrounds the stage area, which may or may not be raised. Use of scenery is limited—perhaps to a single piece of scenery standing alone in the middle of the stage.

developed in different ways. Because of the growing cost of touring groups, Canadians had to rely more on homegrown talent. Two noted playwrights of the early twentieth century include Elsie Park Gowan and Mazo de la Roche. Marjorie Pickthall's *The Woodcarver's Wife* (1920) deals with the shadow of imperialism falling over both women and Natives (the distinction itself says something about the content). Gwen Pharis Ringwood's *Still Stands the House* (1939) is a fine example of prairie realism, and as with Canadian literature in general, setting proves to be an important aspect of Canadian drama.

During World War II, much drama was in support of the war effort, but after the war, several companies, both professional and amateur, sprang up. For example, Dora Mavor Moore's New Play Society produced more than forty plays between 1946 and 1956. The Dora Mavor Moore Award is now a prestigious award for drama.

Regional theatres sprang up in the 1960s, providing a necessary location for play production. Among these are the Vancouver Playhouse (1962); the Neptune Theatre, Halifax (1963); the Citadel Theatre, Edmonton (1965); the National Arts Centre, Ottawa (1969); and Theatre Calgary (1968).

The growth of the genre in Canada was aided by a number of theatre companies working with a clear vision to create new plays in a collective fashion. Collective theatre often drew on political and social issues. Examples include James Reaney's *The Donnellys* (1974–77), produced by the Toronto Workshop Productions; *The Farm Show,* an episodic work produced by Toronto's Théâtre Passe Muraille; John Gray's *Billy Bishop Goes to War* (1978), also produced by Théâtre Passe Muraille; and *This Is for You, Anna*

(1985), produced by Toronto's Nightwood Theatre. Documentary and experimental plays add to the mix, as do many others. Some of the key plays in Canadian drama history include George Ryga's *The Ecstasy of Rita Joe* (1967), which includes elements of surrealism; Sharon Pollack's *Walsh* (1973) and *Blood Relations* (1981), which are largely naturalist in approach; and Wendy Lill's *Corker* (1998), which continues the naturalist approach.

Toronto's Tarragon Theatre has produced plays of poetic naturalism such as Judith Thompson's *White Biting Dog* (1984) and Jason Herman's *The League of Nathans* (1992). Other playwrights work in a more avant-garde vein: Margaret Hollingsworth and Morris Panych are only two examples. One of Canada's most prolific and produced playwrights, George F. Walker, works in several modes—although his adaptation of Turgenev's *Fathers and Sons* is the play that sees large stages the most often. Joan MacLeod's *The Shape of a Girl* (2001) (p. 1348) takes a real-life story of bullying and creates a powerful one-woman play that has been produced extensively.

Clowning and mime have their place in Canadian theatre, and various marginalized groups are finding their way to the stage. Gay playwrights such as Brad Fraser, who goes for the sensational in *Unidentified Human Remains and the True Nature of Love* (1990), and Daniel McIvor, who creates powerful one-man shows, give a sense of the range of drama being created. And Michel Tremblay is as well known in English as in French.

As cultural concerns become more evident, and Canadians move to embrace, or at least grapple with, the cultural diversity of the country, drama about difference and difficulty has flourished. One of the richest areas in drama and culture has been the explosion of First Nations plays. Tomson Highway uses both comedy and tragedy to show the destruction of the European occupation of the country. Daniel David Moses, in *Almighty Voice and His Wife* (1991), reclaims material used by previous and non-Native writers.

Canadian playwrights, including Cree and Ojibway and many others, have created a distinctive drama. They have used the possibilities afforded by all forms of drama and have taken human issues of all kinds to fashion a vibrant and thought-provoking body of work. Considering that the main developments in Canadian drama have happened in the last forty years, it is evident that much talent and persistence reside on or near the stage in Canada.

KINDS OF DRAMA
◊ ◊ ◊

TRAGEDY

In his *Poetics*, Aristotle (384–322 B.C.) sums up ancient Greek thinking about drama when he writes that a **tragedy** is a drama treating a serious subject and involving persons of significance. According to Aristotle, when the members of an audience see a tragedy, they should feel both pity (and thus closeness to the protagonist) and fear (and thus revulsion) because they recognize in themselves the potential for similar reactions. The purging of these emotions that the audience experiences as they see the dramatic action unfold is called **catharsis.** For this catharsis to occur, the protagonist of a tragedy must be worthy of the audience's attention and sympathy. Because of his or her exalted position, the fall of a tragic protagonist is greater than that of an average person; therefore, it arouses more pity and fear in the audience. Often the entire society suffers as a result of the actions of the protagonist. Before the action of Sophocles' *Oedipus the King* (p. 1293), for example, Oedipus has freed Thebes from the deadly grasp of the Sphinx by answering her riddle, and as a result he has been welcomed as king. But because of his sins, Oedipus is an affront to the gods and brings famine and pestilence to the city. When his fall finally comes, it is sudden and absolute.

According to Aristotle, the protagonist of a tragedy is neither all good nor all evil, but a mixture of the two. He is like the rest of us—only more exalted—and may possess some weakness or flaw. Aristotle used the word *hamartia*, which has been translated as "tragic flaw" but which has also been translated as "tragic error." The tragic error (possibly *hubris* or overwhelming pride) is typically the element that creates the conditions for tragedy. Shakespeare's Romeo and Juliet, for example, are so much in love they think they can ignore the blood feud that rages between their two families. However, their naive efforts to sustain their love despite the feud lead them to their tragic deaths. Similarly, Richard III's blind ambition to gain the throne causes him to murder all those who stand in his way. His unscrupulousness sets into motion the forces that eventually cause his death.

Irony is central to tragedy. **Dramatic irony** (also called **tragic irony**) emerges from a situation in which the audience knows more about the dramatic situation than a character does. As a result, the character's words and actions may be consistent with what he or she expects but at odds with what the audience knows will happen. Thus, a character may say or do something that causes the audience to infer a meaning beyond what the character intends or realizes. The dramatic irony is clear, for example, when Oedipus announces that whoever has disobeyed the dictates of the gods will be exiled. The audience knows, although Oedipus does not, that he has just condemned himself. **Cosmic irony,** also called **irony of fate,** occurs when God, fate, or some larger, uncontrollable force seems to be intentionally deceiving characters into believing they can escape their fate. Too late, they realize that trying to avoid their destiny is futile. Years before Oedipus was born, for example, the oracle of Apollo foretold that Oedipus would kill his parents. Naturally, his parents attempted to thwart the prophecy, but ironically, their actions ensured that the prophecy would be fulfilled.

At some point in a tragedy—usually after the climax—the protagonist recognizes the reasons for his or her downfall. It is this recognition (and the accompanying acceptance) that elevates tragic protagonists to grandeur and gives their suffering meaning. Without this recognition there would be no tragedy, just **pathos**—suffering that exists simply to satisfy the sentimental or morbid sensibilities of the audience. In spite of the death of the protagonist, then, tragedy enables the audience to see the nobility of the character and thus to experience a sense of elation. In Shakespeare's *King Lear,* for example, a king at the height of his powers decides to divide his kingdom among his three daughters. Too late, he realizes that without his power, he is just a bothersome old man to his ambitious children. Only after going mad does he understand the vanity of his former existence; he dies a humbled but enlightened man.

According to Aristotle, a tragedy achieves the illusion of reality only when it has *unity of action*—that is, when the play contains only those actions that lead to its tragic outcome. Later critics interpreted this to mean that including subplots or mixing tragic and comic elements would destroy this unity. To the concept of unity of action, these later critics added two other requirements: *unity of place*—the requirement that the play have a single setting—and *unity of time*—the requirement that the events depicted by the play take no longer than the actual duration of the play (or, at most, a single day).

The three unities have had a long and rather uneven history. In some of his plays—*The Tempest* and *The Comedy of Errors,* for example—Shakespeare observed the unities. Shakespeare, however, had no compunctions about writing plays with subplots and frequent changes of location. He also wrote **tragicomedies,** such as *The Merchant of Venice,* that have a serious theme appropriate for tragedy but end happily, usually because of a sudden turn of events. During the eighteenth century, with its emphasis on classic form, the unities were adhered to quite strictly, but in the late eighteenth and early nineteenth centuries, with the onset of romanticism and its emphasis on the natural, interest in the unities of place and time waned. Even though some modern dramatists occasionally observe the unities, few adhere to them strictly.

Ideas about appropriate subjects for tragedy have also changed. For Aristotle, the protagonist of a tragedy had to be exceptional—a king, for example. The protagonists of Greek tragedies were usually historical or mythical figures. Shakespeare often used kings and princes as protagonists—Richard II and Hamlet, for example—but he also used people of lesser rank, as in *Romeo and Juliet.* In our times, interest in the lives of monarchs has been overshadowed by involvement in the lives of ordinary people. Modern tragedies are more likely to focus on a travelling salesman than on a king.

With the rise of the middle class in the nineteenth century, ideas about the nature of tragedy changed. Responding to the age's desire for sentimentality, playwrights produced **melodramas,** sensational plays that appealed mainly to the emotions. Melodramas contain many of the elements of tragedy but end happily and often rely on conventional plots and stock characters. Because the protagonists in melodramas—often totally virtuous heroines suffering at the hands of impossibly wicked villains—helplessly endure their tribulations without ever gaining insight or enlightenment, they never achieve tragic status. As a result, they remain cardboard cutouts who exist only to exploit the emotions of the audience. Melodrama survives today in many films and in television soap operas.

Realism, which arose in the late nineteenth century as a response to the artificiality of melodrama, presented serious (and sometimes tragic) themes and believable characters in the context of everyday contemporary life. Writers of realistic drama used their plays to educate their audiences about the problems of the society in which they lived. For this reason, realistic drama focuses on the commonplace and eliminates the unlikely coincidences and excessive sentimentality of melodrama. Dramatists like Henrik Ibsen scrutinize the lives of ordinary people, not larger-than-life characters. After great suffering, these characters rise above the limitations of their mediocre lives and exhibit courage or emotional strength. The insight they gain often focuses attention on a social problem—the restrictive social conventions that define the behaviour of women in nineteenth-century marriages, for example. Realistic drama also features settings and props similar to those used in people's daily lives and includes dialogue that reflects the way people actually speak.

Developing alongside realism was another literary movement called **naturalism.** Like realism, naturalism rejected the unrealistic plots and sentimentality of melodrama, but unlike realism, naturalism sought to explore the depths of the human condition. Influenced by Charles Darwin's ideas about evolution and natural selection and Karl Marx's ideas about economic forces that shape people's lives, naturalism is a pessimistic philosophy that presents a world which at worst is hostile and at best is indifferent to human concerns. It pictures human beings as higher-order animals who are driven by basic instincts—especially hunger, fear, and sexuality—and who are subject to economic, social, and biological forces beyond their understanding or control. It is, therefore, well suited to tragic themes.

The nineteenth-century French writer Émile Zola did much to develop the theory of naturalism. Naturalism also finds its way into the work of contemporary dramatists. Unlike other tragic protagonists, the protagonists of naturalist works are crushed not by the gods or by fate, but by poverty, animal drives, or social class. The characters in *The Ecstasy of Rita Joe*, for example, are subject to racism in a society that has not come to terms with its multiculturalism.

COMEDY

A **comedy** is a dramatic work that treats themes and characters with humour and typically has a happy ending. Whereas tragedy focuses on the hidden dimensions of the tragic hero's character, comedy focuses on the public persona, the protagonist as a social being. Tragic figures are typically seen in isolation, questioning the meaning of their lives and trying to comprehend their suffering. Hamlet—draped in black, longing for death, and self-consciously contemplating his duty—epitomizes the isolation of the tragic hero.

Unlike tragic heroes, comic figures are seen in the public arena, where people intentionally assume the masks of pretension and self-importance. The purpose of comedy is to strip away these masks and expose human beings for what they are. Tragedy reveals the nobility of the human condition, while comedy reveals its inherent folly, portraying human beings as selfish, hypocritical, vain, weak, irrational, and capable of self-delusion. Thus, the basic function of comedy is critical—to tell people that things are not what they seem and that appearances are not necessarily reality. In the comic world nothing is solid or predictable, and accidents and coincidences are more important to the plot than reason. Many of Shakespeare's comedies, for example, depend on exchanged or confused identities. The wordplay and verbal nonsense of comedy add to this general confusion.

Comedies typically rely on certain familiar plot devices. Many comedies begin with a startling or unusual situation that attracts the audience's attention. In Shakespeare's *A Midsummer Night's Dream*, for example, Theseus, the duke of Athens, rules that Hermia will either marry the man her father has chosen for her or be put to death. Such an event could lead to tragedy if comedy did not intervene to save the day.

Comedy often depends on obstacles and hindrances to further its plot: the more difficult the problems the lovers face, the more satisfying their eventual triumph will be. For this reason, the plot of a comedy is usually more complex than the plot of a tragedy. Compare the rather straightforward plot of *Hamlet* (p. 1093)—a prince ordered to avenge his murdered father's death is driven mad with indecision and, after finally acting decisively, is killed himself—with the mix-ups, mistaken identities, and general confusion of *The Importance of Being Earnest* (p. 961).

Finally, comedies have happy endings. Whereas tragedy ends with death, comedy ends with an affirmation of life. Eventually the confusion and misunderstandings reach a point where some resolution must be achieved: the difficulties of the lovers are overcome, the villains are banished, and the lovers marry—or at least express their intention to do so. In this way the lovers establish their connection with the rest of society, and its values are affirmed.

The first comedies, written in Greece in the fifth century B.C., heavily satirized the religious and social issues of the day. In the fourth and third centuries B.C., this **Old Comedy** gave way to **New Comedy,** a comedy of romance with stock characters—lovers and untrustworthy servants, for example—and conventional settings. Lacking the bitter satire and bawdiness of Old Comedy, New Comedy depends on outrageous plots, mistaken identities, young lovers, interfering parents, and conniving servants. Ultimately the young lovers outwit all those who stand between them and in so doing affirm the primacy of youth and love over old age and death.

Old and New Comedy represent two distinct lines of humour that extend to modern times. Old Comedy depends on **satire**—bitter humour that diminishes a person, idea, or institution by ridiculing it or holding it up to scorn. Unlike comedy, which exists simply to make people laugh, satire is social criticism, deriding hypocrisy, pretension, and vanity or condemning vice. At its best, satire appeals to the intellect, has a serious purpose, and arouses thoughtful laughter. New Comedy may also be satiric, but it frequently contains elements of **farce,** comedy in which stereotypical characters engage in boisterous horseplay and slapstick humour, all the while making jokes and sexual innuendoes—as they do in Anton Chekhov's *The Brute* (p. 1081).

English comedy got its start in the sixth century A.D. in the form of farcical episodes that appeared in morality plays. During the Renaissance, comedy developed rapidly, beginning in 1533 with Nicholas Udall's *Ralph Roister Doister* and eventually evolving into Shakespeare's **romantic comedy**—such as *A Midsummer Night's Dream,* in which love is the main subject and idealized heroines and lovers endure great difficulties until the inevitable happy ending is reached.

Also during the Renaissance, particularly in the latter part of the sixteenth century, writers like Ben Jonson experimented with a different type of comedy—the **comedy of humours,** which focused on characters whose behaviour was controlled by a characteristic trait, or *humour.* During the Renaissance a person's temperament was thought to be determined by the mix of fluids, or humours, in the body. When one humour dominated, a certain type of disposition resulted. Playwrights capitalized on this belief, writing comedies in which characters are motivated by stereotypical behaviours that result from the imbalance of the humours. In comedies such as Jonson's *Volpone* and *The Alchemist,* characters such as the suspicious husband and the miser can be manipulated by others because of their predictable dispositions.

Closely related to the comedy of humours is the satiric **comedy of manners,** which developed during the sixteenth century and achieved great popularity in the nineteenth century. This form focuses on the manners and customs of society and directs its satire against characters who violate social conventions and rules of behaviour. These plays tend to be memorable more for their witty dialogue than for their development of characters or setting. Oliver Goldsmith's *She Stoops to Conquer,* George Bernard Shaw's *Pygmalion,* and even some television sitcoms are examples of this type of comedy.

In the eighteenth century, a reaction against the perceived immorality of the comedy of manners led to **sentimental comedy,** which eventually achieved great popularity. This kind of comedy relies on sentimental emotion rather than on wit or humour to move an audience. It also dwells on the virtues rather than on the vices of life. The heroes of sentimental comedy are unimpeachably noble, moral, and honourable; the pure, virtuous, middle-class heroines suffer trials and tribulations calculated to move the audience to tears rather than laughter. Eventually, the distress of the hero and heroine is resolved in a sometimes contrived (but always happy) ending.

In his 1877 essay *The Idea of Comedy,* novelist and critic George Meredith suggests that comedy that appeals to the intellect should be called **high comedy.** Shakespeare's *As You Like It* and Shaw's *Pygmalion* can be characterized in this way. When comedy has little or no intellectual appeal, according to Meredith, it is **low comedy.** Low comedy appears in parts of Shakespeare's *The Taming of the Shrew* and as comic relief in *Macbeth.*

The twentieth century has developed its own characteristic comic forms. Most reflect the uncertainty and pessimism of a century that has seen two world wars, the Holocaust, and nuclear destruction, as well as threats posed by environmental pollution and ethnic and racial conflict. Combining laughter and hints of tragedy, these modern tragicomedies feature **antiheroes,** characters who, instead of manifesting dignity and power, are ineffectual or petty. Their plight frequently elicits laughter, not pity and fear, from the audience. **Black** or **dark comedies,** for example, rely for their comedy on the morbid and the absurd. These works are usually so satiric and bitter that they threaten to slip over the edge into tragedy. The screenplay of Joseph Heller's novel *Catch-22,* which ends with a character dropping bombs on his own men, is a classic example of such comedy. **Theatre of the absurd,** which includes comedies such as Samuel Beckett's *Krapp's Last Tape* (p. 1368), begins with the assumption that the human condition is irrational. Typically, this type of drama does not have a discernible plot; instead, it presents a series of apparently unrelated images and illogical exchanges of dialogue meant to reinforce the idea that human beings live in a remote, confusing, and often incomprehensible universe. Absurdist dramas seem to go in circles, never progressing to a climax or achieving a resolution, reinforcing the theme of the endless and meaningless repetition that characterizes modern life.

A NOTE ON TRANSLATIONS
◈ ◈ ◈

Many dramatic works that we read or see are translations. For example, Ibsen wrote in Norwegian, Sophocles in Greek, Molière in French, and Chekhov in Russian. Before English-speaking viewers or readers can evaluate the language of a translated play, they must understand that the language they hear or read is the translator's interpretation of what the playwright intended to communicate. Translation is interpretation, not just a search for literal equivalents; as a result, a translation is always different from the original. Moreover, different translations are different from one another. During the course of Henrik Ibsen's 1879 play *A Doll House* (p. 1013), for instance, Nora, the main character, refers several times to a symbolic gesture of support she expects from her husband Torvald. In the translation in this text, that gesture is translated as "the miracle"; in another translation, it is translated as "the wonderful." Not only is *miracle* more consistent with idiomatic

English usage, but also it is a more absolute, and therefore a more forceful, term.

The choices translators make can be very different. Compare these two versions of an exchange of dialogue from two different translations of the same Chekhov play, called *The Brute* in the translation that begins on page 1081 and *The Bear* in the alternate version.

—From *The Brute*:

> **SMIRNOV:** You'd like me to come simpering to you in French, I suppose. *"Enchanté, madame! Merci beaucoup* for not paying zee money, *madame! Pardonnez-moi* if I 'ave disturbed you, *madame!* How *charmante* you look in mourning, *madame!"*
>
> **MRS. POPOV:** Now you're being silly, Mr. Smirnov.
>
> **SMIRNOV:** *(mimicking)* "Now you're being silly, Mr. Smirnov." "You don't know how to talk to a lady, Mr. Smirnov." Look here, Mrs. Popov. I've known more women than you've known pussy cats. I've fought three duels on their account. I've jilted twelve, and been jilted by nine others. Oh, yes, Mrs. Popov, I've played the fool in my time, whispered sweet nothings, bowed and scraped and endeavored to please. Don't tell me I don't know what it is to love, to pine away with longing, to have the blues, to melt like butter, to be weak as water. I was full of tender emotion. I was carried away with passion. I squandered half my fortune on the sex. I chattered about women's emancipation. But there's an end to everything, dear madam.

—From *The Bear*:

> **SMIRNOV:** Ach, it's astonishing! How would you like me to talk to you? In French, perhaps? *(Lisps in anger.) Madame, je vous prie.... how happy I am that you're not paying me the money.... Ah, pardon, I've made you uneasy! Such lovely weather we're having today! And you look so becoming in your mourning dress. (Bows and scrapes.)*
>
> **MRS. POPOV:** That's rude and not very clever!
>
> **SMIRNOV:** *(teasing)* Rude and not very clever! I don't know how to behave in the company of ladies. Madam, in my time I've seen far more women than you've seen sparrows. Three times I've fought duels over women; I've jilted twelve women, nine have jilted me! Yes! There was a time when I played the fool; I became sentimental over women, used honeyed words, fawned on them, bowed and scraped.... I loved, suffered, sighed at the moon; I became limp, melted, shivered... I loved passionately, madly, every which way, devil take me, I chattered away like a magpie about the emancipation of women, ran through half my fortune as a result of my tender feelings; but now, if you will excuse me, I'm on to your ways! I've had enough!

Although both translations convey Smirnov's anger and frustration, they use different words (with different connotations), different phrasing—and even different stage directions. In *The Bear*, for instance, only one French phrase is used, whereas *The Brute* uses several and specifies a French accent as well; other differences between the two translations include *The Bear*'s use of "teasing," "sparrows," and "I've had enough!" where *The Brute* uses "mimicking," "pussy cats," and "But there's an end to everything, dear madam." (Elsewhere in the play *The Bear* uses profanity while *The Brute* uses more polite language.) Many words and idiomatic expressions used in daily speech cannot be translated exactly from one language to another; as a result, the two translators made different choices.

CHAPTER 21

Reading and Writing
about Drama

READING DRAMA

◇ ◇ ◇

When you read a play, you will notice features it shares with works of fiction—for instance, its use of language and symbols, the interaction among its characters, and its development of a theme or themes. In addition, you will notice features that distinguish it from fiction—for example, the presence of stage directions and the division into acts and scenes.

The following guidelines, designed to help you explore works of dramatic literature, focus on issues that will be examined in depth in chapters to come.

◇ Trace the play's **plot.** What conflicts are present? Where does the rising action reach a climax? Where does the falling action begin? What techniques move the action along? (See Chapter 22.)

◇ Analyze the play's **characters.** Who are the central characters? What are their most distinctive traits? How do you learn about their personalities, backgrounds, appearances, and strengths and weaknesses? (See Chapter 23.)

◇ Examine the play's language. How does dialogue reveal characters' emotions, conflicts, opinions, and motivation? (See Chapter 23.)

◇ Does the play include soliloquies or asides? What do they contribute to your knowledge of the play's characters and events? (See Chapter 23.)

◇ How do the characters interact with one another? Do the characters change and grow in response to the play's events, or do they remain essentially unchanged? (See Chapter 23.)

◇ Read the play's stage directions. What do you learn from the descriptions of the characters, including their dress, gestures, and facial expressions? (See Chapter 23.) What information do you gain from studying the playwright's descriptions of the play's setting? Do the stage directions include information about lighting, props, music, or sound effects? (See Chapter 24.)

◇ Consider the play's **staging.** Where and when does the action take place? What techniques are used to convey a sense of time and place to the audience? (See Chapter 24.)

◇ Try to interpret the play's **themes.** What main idea does the play communicate? What additional themes are explored? (See Chapter 25.)

◇ Identify any symbolic elements in the play. How do such symbols enhance the play's themes? (See Chapter 25.)

ACTIVE READING

As you read a play about which you plan to write, you follow the same process that guides you when you read any work of literature: you read actively, marking the text as you proceed. Then, you go on to select a topic and generate ideas about it, decide on a thesis, prepare an outline, and write and revise several drafts.

Kimberly Allison, a student in an introduction to literature course, was given the following assignment:

> Without consulting any outside sources, write a three- to five-page essay about any play in our literature anthology. You may focus on action, character, staging, or theme, or you may consider more than one of these elements.

Previewing

Kim decided to write her paper on Susan Glaspell's play *Trifles,* which begins on page 948. She began by previewing *Trifles,* noting its brief length, its one-act structure, its list of characters, and its setting in John Wright's farm house. Kim noticed immediately that John Wright does not appear in the play, and this aroused her curiosity.

Highlighting and Annotating

As Kim read *Trifles,* she highlighted the dialogue and stage directions she thought she might want to examine closely, identified possible links among ideas and patterns of action and language, and jotted down questions and observations. She found herself especially interested in the female and male characters' different reactions to the objects discovered in the house and in the interaction between women and men.

The following highlighted and annotated passage illustrates some of her responses to the play.

The men laugh; the women looked abashed. **Why do the men and women react so differently?**

COUNTY ATTORNEY: (*Rubbing his hands over the stove*) Frank's fire didn't do much up there, did it? Well, let's go out to the barn and get that cleared up.

The men go outside.

MRS. HALE: ((*resentfully*)) I don't know as there's anything so strange, our taken' up our time with (little things) while we're waiting for them to get the evidence. (*She sits down at the big table smoothing out a block with decision.*) I don't see as it's anything to laugh about.

Why do the men go and the women stay?

MRS. PETERS: (*apologetically*) Of course they've got awful important things on their minds. **Like what? Why does she make excuses for the men?**

Pulls up a chair and joins Mrs. Hale at the table.

Most of Kim's highlighting and annotations, like the preceding notes, focused on the play's characters, suggesting some interesting possibilities for her essay.

WRITING ABOUT DRAMA

◊ ◊ ◊

PLANNING AN ESSAY

After Kim decided to write about the play's characters, she knew she had to narrow her focus. Her notes suggested that gender roles in general, and the role of the women in particular, would make an interesting topic, so she decided to explore this idea further.

Choosing a Topic

To help her decide on a direction for her paper, Kim wrote the following entry in her journal:

```
What is the role of the women in this play? Although the
women have gone with their husbands to get some items for
Mrs. Wright, they seem to be primarily interested in why
Mrs. Wright would leave her house in such disarray. They
find several objects that suggest that Mrs. Wright was
lonely and that she was dominated by her husband. But
```

these women are left on their own and seem to band
together. Their guilt about not visiting Mrs. Wright also
seems to connect them with the murder suspect. Mrs. Hale
even begins to empathize with Mrs. Wright's loss of her
bird. The women find the details, or "trifles," of Mrs.
Wright's life interesting and learn from them the facts
surrounding the murder while the men wander aimlessly
around the house and yard. The real clue to the murder
appears to be Mrs. Wright's untended house, but the men
do not seem to understand the implications of the
disorder. The women appear to have an understanding that
comes from their own experiences as women, which the men
are unable to tap into.

At this point, Kim concluded that the idea of the role of the women in *Trifles* would be the best focus for her paper. As she went on to gather ideas to write about, she also planned to examine the women characters' interaction with the men.

Finding Something to Say

Brainstorming　Kim's next step was to generate the specific ideas she would discuss in her paper. She reread the play and her annotations, brainstorming about her topic and jotting down ideas about men and women as she proceeded. Some of her brainstorming notes appear below:

Sheriff Peters says there is nothing in the kitchen
but kitchen stuff; he thinks Mrs. Wright is a typical
woman, worried about her preserves while imprisoned for
murder.

Mrs. Hale feels animosity toward the men for
laughing about the women's interest in the quilt; she
regrets not visiting Mrs. Wright; she feels sorry for Mrs.
Wright because she had no children.

Mr. Henderson eventually sides with the other two
men, claiming that women's worries are trifles.

Mr. Hale mentions Mr. Wright's cheapness; he seems
to know Mr. Wright best.

Men think women are shallow and worry only about
trifles.

Women empathize with Mrs. Wright because they
understand her treatment.

Mrs. Peters (wife of Sheriff) empathizes with Mrs. Wright's loss of bird; notes that keeping house was Mrs. Wright's duty.

Mrs. Wright restricted by husband; never leaves the house; loses control after her bird is killed.

John Wright strips wife of her identity; controls her every move; stops her from singing, which she enjoys; kills canary.

When she reread her notes, the first thing Kim noticed was that the women and men have two entirely different attitudes about women's lives and concerns: the men think their work is much more important than that of the women, which they see as trivial; the women realize they are not much different from Mrs. Wright. Now Kim saw that in order to discuss the role of women in the play, she must first define that role in relation to the role of the men. To do so, she needed to find a logical arrangement for her ideas that would enable her to clarify the differences between the men's role and the women's.

Seeing Connections

Listing At this point, Kim decided that listing ideas under the heads *Men* and *Women* could help her clarify the differences between men's and women's roles:

Men's Role	Women's Role
working outside the home	making preserves
making decisions about financial expenditures	cleaning house
	making quilts
think women should do just housework	raising children
create and enforce law	going to ladies' clubs for socializing
dictate wives' actions	must follow laws that men create and enforce
have separate identities and power	subordinate to their husbands
actions are accepted by society	must act defiantly to break boundaries set by social role

Listing enabled Kim to confirm her idea that the men's and the women's roles are portrayed very differently in *Trifles*. Both men and women seem to agree that they have different responsibilities, and both seem to understand and accept the fact that power and freedom are unevenly distributed between the two genders.

Deciding on a Thesis

Kim's listing clarified her understanding of the limited role women have in the society portrayed in *Trifles*. This in turn enabled her to develop the following tentative thesis statement, which she could use to help guide her essay's first draft:

> The central focus of <u>Trifles</u> is not on finding out who
> killed Mr. Wright, but on the limited, even subservient,
> role of women like Mrs. Wright.

Preparing an Outline

Guided by her thesis statement and the information she had collected in her notes, Kim made a scratch outline, arranging her supporting details in a logical order under appropriate headings:

> <u>Mrs. Hale and Mrs. Peters had limited roles</u>
>   --Subservient to husbands
>   --Do domestic chores
>   --Confined to kitchen
>   --Identify with Minnie Wright's loneliness
> <u>Minnie Wright had limited role</u>
>   --Did what husband told her to do
>   --Had no link with outside world
>   --Couldn't sing
>   --Had no friends
>   --Had no identity

DRAFTING AN ESSAY

Following her scratch outline, Kim wrote the following first draft of her essay. Before she began, she reviewed her highlighting to look for details that would illustrate and support her generalizations about the play.

first draft

The Women's Role in <u>Trifles</u>

Susan Glaspell's <u>Trifles</u> seems to focus on the murder of John Wright. Mr. Wright had little concern for his wife's opinions. Mr. Hale suggested that Minnie Wright was powerless against her husband, and Sheriff Henry Peters questioned whether Minnie was allowed to quilt her log cabin pattern. Perhaps, because Mr. Wright did not spend his money freely, he would have made Minnie knot the quilt because it cost less. Minnie was controlled by her husband. He forced her to perform repetitive domestic chores. The central focus of <u>Trifles</u> is not on who killed Mr. Wright, but on the limited, even subservient role of women like Mrs. Wright.

Mrs. Peters and Mrs. Hale were similar to Minnie. Mrs. Peters and Mrs. Hale also performed domestic chores and had to do what their husbands wanted them to do, and they too were confined to Mrs. Wright's kitchen. The kitchen was the focal point of the play. Mrs. Peters and Mrs. Hale remained confined to the kitchen while their husbands exercised their freedom to enter and exit the house at will. This mirrored Minnie's life because she stayed home while her husband went to work and into town. The two women discussed Minnie's isolation. Beginning to identify with Minnie's loneliness, Mrs. Peters and Mrs. Hale recognized that while they were busy in their own homes, they had, in fact, participated in isolating and confining Minnie.

Eventually, the women found that the kitchen held the clues to Mrs. Wright's loneliness and to the details of the murder. The two women discovered that Minnie's only connection to the outside world was her bird. Minnie too was a caged bird because she was kept from singing and communicating with others by her husband. And piecing together the evidence, the women came to believe that John Wright had broken the bird's neck.

At the same time, Mrs. Peters and Mrs. Hale discovered the connection between the dead canary and Minnie's situation, and they began to recognize that they had to band together in order to exert their strength against the men. They realized that Minnie's independence and identity were crushed by her husband and that their own husbands believed women's lives were trivial and unimportant. The revelation that Mrs. Peters and Mrs. Hale experienced urged them to commit an act as rebellious as the one that got Minnie in trouble: they concealed their discovery from their husbands and from the law.

Because Mrs. Hale and Mrs. Peters empathized with Minnie's condition, they suppressed the evidence they found and endured the men's insults rather than confronting their husbands. And through this, the women attempted to break through the boundaries of their social roles, just as Minnie had done before them.

First Draft: Commentary

Kim's peer review group suggested that she develop her paper, especially paragraph 3, further. They also agreed that her paper's sentences seemed choppy—many needed to be linked with transitional words and phrases— and that her introduction was unfocused.

When Kim reread her first draft, she realized that she had gone beyond the scope of her tentative thesis statement and scratch outline. She had considered not just the women's subservient role but also the actions they take to break free of this role. She decided to revise her thesis statement to reflect this new emphasis—and, then, to expand her paper to develop this aspect of her thesis more fully.

When she met with her instructor to discuss her new ideas, he encouraged her to expand her paper's focus and to use quotations and specific examples to support her ideas. He also reminded her to use the present tense in her paper—not "Mrs. Peters and Mrs. Hale *were* similar to Minnie" but "Mrs. Peters and Mrs. Hale *are* similar to Minnie." (He explained that only events that occurred *before* the time in which the play takes place—for example, the murder itself or Minnie's girlhood experiences—should be described in past tense.)

After her meeting with her instructor, Kim made a new scratch outline to guide her as she continued to revise:

Subservient role of women
    --Minnie's husband didn't respect her opinion
    --Didn't let her sing
    --Could perform only domestic chores
Confinement of women in home
    --Mrs. Hale and Mrs. Peters are confined to kitchen
    --Minnie didn't belong to Ladies Aid
    --Minnie was lonely at home because she had no
      children
    --Minnie was a caged bird
Women's defiance
    --Mrs. Hale and Mrs. Peters solve "mystery"
    --Realize they must band together
    --Take action
    --Defy men's law

REVISING AND EDITING AN ESSAY

Before she wrote her next draft, Kim reviewed the suggestions she had recorded in meetings with classmates and with her instructor. Then she incorporated this material, along with her own new ideas, into her second draft, which appears on pages 932–35.

second draft

Confinement and Rebellion in Trifles

Susan Glaspell's play <u>Trifles</u> involves the solving of a murder. Two women, Mrs. Peters and Mrs. Hale, discover that Mrs. Wright, who remains in jail throughout the play, has indeed murdered her husband. Interestingly, the women make this discovery through the examination of evidence in Mrs. Wright's kitchen, which their husbands, Sheriff Henry Peters and farmer Lewis Hale, along with the county attorney, Mr. Henderson, dismiss as women's "trifles." The focus of <u>Trifles</u>, however, is not on the murder of John Wright but on the subservient role of women, the confinement of the wife in the home, and the desperate measures women had to take to achieve autonomy.

The role of Minnie Foster (Mrs. Wright) becomes evident in the first few minutes of the play, when Mr. Hale declares, "I didn't know as what his wife wanted made much difference to John--" (949). Minnie's powerlessness is revealed further when the women discuss how Mr. Wright forced Minnie to give up the thing she loved--singing. Both of these observations suggest that Minnie's every action was controlled and stifled by her husband. She was not allowed to make decisions or be an individual; instead, she was permitted to perform only domestic chores.

Doing domestic chores was the only part of life that Minnie was allowed to exert some power over, a condition that is shared by Mrs. Peters and Mrs. Hale, especially because these two women can be assumed to work only in the home and because their behaviour as wives is also determined by their husbands.

The men are free to walk throughout the house and outside of it while the women are, not surprisingly, confined to the kitchen, just as Minnie had been confined to the house. Early in the play, Mrs. Hale refers to Minnie's isolation, saying she "kept so much to herself. She didn't even belong to the Ladies Aid" (953). Mrs. Hale goes on to mention Minnie's lack of nice clothing, which further suggests her confinement in the home: if she never left her home, she wouldn't need to look nice, and why would she want to leave home if she had no nice clothes? Minnie's isolation is further revealed when Mrs. Hale contemplates Minnie's lack of children: "Not having children makes less work--but it makes a quiet house, and Wright out to work all day, and no company when he did come in" (956). As a result, Minnie's only connection to the outside world was her bird, which becomes the symbol of Minnie's confinement, because Minnie herself was a caged bird. In a sense, Mr. Wright strangled her, as he did the bird, by preventing her from talking to other people in the community. Unlike the men, Mrs. Peters and Mrs. Hale realize the connection between the dead canary and Minnie's situation as "<u>Their eyes meet</u>" and they share "<u>A look of growing comprehension, of horror</u>" (957).

The comprehension that Mrs. Peters and Mrs. Hale experience urges them to rebel by concealing their discovery from their husbands and from the law. Mrs. Peters does concede that "the law is the law," but she also understands that because Mr. Wright treated his wife badly, treating her as a domestic slave and isolating her from the world, Minnie is justified in killing him. And even if Minnie had been able to communicate the abuse she suffered, the law would not take the abuse into account because the men on the jury would not be sympathetic to a woman's complaints about how her husband treated her.

The dialogue in <u>Trifles</u> reveals a huge difference in how women and men view their experiences. From the opening of the play, the gulf between the men and women emerges, and as the play progresses, the polarization of the male and female characters becomes clearer. Once the men leave the kitchen to find what they consider to be significant criminal evidence, the men and women are divided physically as well as emotionally. The men create their own community, as do the women, leading them to separate according to gender. With the women alone in the kitchen, the focus of the dialogue is on the female experience. The women discuss the preserves, the quilt, and the disarray in the kitchen, emphasizing that Mrs. Wright would not leave her home in disorder unless she was distracted by some more pressing situation.

Women accept servitude voluntarily, making the work in the home their main interest, and this role keeps them subservient. But the men further trivialize Mrs. Wright's and other women's significance when they criticize her role as homemaker. The county attorney condemns Minnie, sarcastically observing, "I shouldn't say she had the homemaking instinct" (952). Minnie has attempted to keep her home clean and do her chores, but the lack of heat has exploded her preserves, and her husband has dirtied the towels. What has caused Minnie to neglect her chores is something of great importance: her desire for independence and freedom from the servitude she once accepted voluntarily.

What makes this play most interesting is that the women come to realize that they too have volunteered to be subservient to their husbands. They even accept the fact that their husbands will trivialize their discovery about the murder, as the men earlier trivialized their discussions of Minnie's daily tasks. Therefore, the women band together and conceal the information, breaking through their subservient roles as wives. And in the end, they find their own independence and significance in society.

Second Draft: Commentary

When she read her second draft, Kim had mixed feelings. She thought it was an improvement over her first draft, primarily because she had expanded the focus of her thesis and added specific details and quotations to support her points. She also believed her essay was now clearer, with smoother transitions.

Even though she knew what she wanted to say, however, Kim thought her paper's logic was somewhat difficult to follow, and she thought clearer topic sentences might correct this problem by guiding readers more smoothly through her essay. She also thought her organization, which did not follow her revised scratch outline, was somewhat confusing. (For example, she discussed the women's subservient role in two different parts of her essay—paragraphs 2 and 7.) In addition, Kim thought her third paragraph could be developed further, and she still believed her essay could use additional supporting details and quotations throughout. After rereading her notes, she wrote her final draft, which appears on the following pages.

Allison 1

Kimberly Allison

English 1013

Professor Johnson

1 March 2007

Desperate Measures: Acts of

Defiance in <u>Trifles</u>

Susan Glaspell wrote her best-known play, <u>Trifles</u>, in 1916, at a time when women were beginning to challenge their socially defined roles, realizing that their identities as wives and domestics kept them in a subordinate position in society. Because women were demanding more autonomy, traditional institutions such as marriage, which confined women to the home and made them mere extensions of their husbands, were beginning to be reexamined.

As a married woman, Glaspell was evidently touched by these concerns, perhaps because when she wrote <u>Trifles</u> she was at the mercy of her husband's wishes and encountered barriers in pursuing her career as a writer because she was a woman. But for whatever reason, Glaspell chose as the play's protagonist a married woman, Minnie Foster (Mrs. Wright), who has challenged society's expectations in a very extreme way: by murdering her husband. Minnie's defiant act has occurred before the action begins, and as the play unfolds two women, Mrs. Peters and Mrs. Hale, who accompany their husbands on an investigation of the murder scene, piece together the details of the situation surrounding the murder. As the events unfold, however, it becomes clear that the focus of <u>Trifles</u> is not on

Double-space.

Opening sentence identifies author and work.

Introduction places play in historical context.

Allison 2

Thesis statement

who killed John Wright, but on the themes of the subordinate role of women, the confinement of the wife in the home, and the experiences all women share; through these themes, Glaspell shows her audience the desperate measures women had to take to achieve autonomy.

Topic sentence identifies first point paper will discuss: women's subordinate role.

The subordinate role of women, particularly Minnie's role in her marriage, becomes evident in the first few minutes of the play when Mr. Hale observes that the victim, John Wright, had little concern for his wife's opinions: "I didn't know as what his wife wanted made much difference to John" (949). Here Mr. Hale suggests that Minnie was powerless against the wishes of her husband. Indeed, as these characters imply, Minnie's every act and thought were controlled by her husband, who tried to break her spirit by forcing her to perform repetitive domestic chores alone in the home. Minnie's only power in the household remained her kitchen work, a situation that Mrs. Peters and Mrs. Hale understand because each of these women's behaviour is determined by her husband. Therefore, when Sheriff Peters makes fun of Minnie's concern about her preserves, saying, "Well, can you beat the women! Held for murder and worryin' about her preserves" (951), he is, in a sense, criticizing all three of the women for worrying about domestic matters rather than about the murder that has been committed. Indeed, the sheriff's comment suggests that he assumes women's lives are trivial, an assumption that influences the thoughts and speech of all three men.

Allison 3

Topic
sentence
introduces
second point
paper will
discuss:
women's
confinement.

Mrs. Peters and Mrs. Hale are similar to Minnie
in another way as well: throughout the play, they are
confined to the kitchen of the Wrights' house. As a
result, the kitchen becomes the focal point of the
play. The women find that the kitchen holds the clues
to Mrs. Wright's loneliness and to the details of the
murder. Mrs. Peters and Mrs. Hale remain confined to
the kitchen while their husbands enter and exit the
house at will. This scenario mirrors Minnie's daily
life, as she remained in the home while her husband
went to work and into town. The two women discuss Minnie's isolation in being housebound: "Not having children makes less work--but it makes a quiet house, and
Wright out to work all day, and no company when he did
come in" (956). Beginning to identify with Minnie's
loneliness, Mrs. Peters and Mrs. Hale recognize that,
busy in their own homes, they have, in fact, participated in isolating and confining Minnie. Mrs. Hale declares, "I _wish_ I'd come over here once in a while!
That was a crime! That was a crime! Who's going to
punish that? . . . I might have known she needed
help!" (958)

Transitional
paragraph
discusses
women's
observations
and
conclusions.

Soon the two women discover that Minnie's only
connection to the outside world was her bird, the symbol of her confinement; Minnie was a caged bird who
was kept from singing and communicating with others
because of her restrictive husband. And piecing together the evidence--the disorderly kitchen, the mis-
stitched quilt pieces, and the dead canary--the women
come to believe that John Wright broke the bird's neck
just as he had broken Minnie's spirit. At this point,

Allison 4

Mrs. Peters and Mrs. Hale figure out the connection between the dead canary and Minnie's situation. The stage directions describe the moment when the women become aware of the truth behind the murder: "<u>Their eyes meet</u>," and the women share "<u>A look of growing comprehension, of horror</u>" (957).

Through their observations and discussions in Mrs. Wright's kitchen, Mrs. Hale and Mrs. Peters come to understand the commonality of women's experiences. Mrs. Hale speaks for both of them when she says, "I know how things can be--for women. . . . We all go through the same things--it's all just a different kind of the same thing" (958). And, once the two women realize the experiences they share, they begin to recognize that they must join together in order to challenge a male-oriented society; although their experiences may seem trivial to the men, the "trifles" of their lives are significant to them. They realize that Minnie's independence and identity were crushed by her husband and that their own husbands have asserted that women's lives are trivial and unimportant as well. This realization leads them to commit an act as defiant as the one that has gotten Minnie into trouble: they conceal their discovery from their husbands and from the law.

Significantly, Mrs. Peters does acknowledge that "the law is the law," yet she understands that because Mr. Wright treated his wife badly, Minnie is justified in killing him. They also realize, however, that for men the law is black and white and that an all-male jury will not take into account the extenuating circumstances

Topic sentence introduces third point paper will discuss: commonality of women's experiences.

Allison 5

that prompted Minnie to kill her husband. And even if
Minnie were allowed to communicate to the all-male
court the psychological abuse she has suffered, the
law would undoubtedly view her experience as trivial
because a woman who complained about how her husband
treated her would be seen as ungrateful.

Nevertheless, because Mrs. Hale and Mrs. Peters
empathize with Minnie's condition, they suppress the
evidence they find, enduring their husbands' condescension rather than standing up to them. And, through
this desperate action, the women break through the
boundaries of their social role, just as Minnie has
done. Although Minnie is imprisoned for her crime, she
has freed herself; and, although Mrs. Peters and Mrs.
Hale conceal their knowledge, fearing the men will
laugh at them, these women are really challenging society and freeing themselves as well.

Conclusion
places play in
historical
context.

In Trifles, Susan Glaspell addresses many of the
problems shared by early twentieth-century women, including their subordinate status and their confinement
in the home. In order to emphasize the pervasiveness
of these problems and the desperate measures women had to
take to break out of restrictive social roles, Glaspell
does more than focus on the plight of a woman who has
ended her isolation and loneliness by committing a
heinous crime against society. By presenting three male
and two female characters who demonstrate the vast differences between male and female experience, she illustrates how men define the roles of women and how women
can challenge these roles in search of their own significance in society and their eventual independence.

Final Draft: Commentary

Kim made many changes in her final draft. Although her focus is much the same as it was in her previous draft, she has expanded her paper considerably. Most important, she added a discussion of the commonality of women's experience in paragraph 6 and elsewhere, and this material helps to explain what motivates Mrs. Hale and Mrs. Peters to conceal evidence from their husbands.

As she expanded her essay, Kim added illustrative explanations, details, and quotations, taking care to provide accurate page numbers in parentheses after each quotation. (Because students were required to use only a play from this anthology, and no outside sources, Kim's instructor did not require a Works Cited page.) She also worked hard to make her topic sentences clearer, and she used information from her class notes to help her write a new introduction and conclusion that discussed the status of women at the time in which *Trifles* was written. Finally, she added a new title and revised her thesis statement to emphasize the focus of her essay on the "desperate measures" all three women are driven to in response to their subjugation and confinement.

CHAPTER 22

Plot

◇ ◇ ◇

We assume that, for the finest form of tragedy, the plot must be not simple but complex; and further, that it must imitate actions arousing fear and pity, since that is the distinctive function of this kind of imitation. It follows, therefore, that there are three forms of plot to be avoided. (1) A good man must not be seen passing from happiness to misery, or (2) a bad man from misery to happiness. The first situation is not fear-inspiring or piteous, but simply odious to us. The second is the most untragic that can be; it has not one of the requisites of tragedy; it does not appeal either to the human feeling in us, or to our pity, or to our fears. Nor, on the other hand, should (3) an extremely bad man be seen falling from happiness into misery. Such a story may arouse the human feeling in us, but it will not move us to either pity or fear; pity is occasioned by undeserved misfortune, and fear by that of one like ourselves; so that there will be nothing either piteous or fear-inspiring in the situation. . . .

ARISTOTLE, *Poetics*, trans. Ingram Bywater

Great character creation is a fine thing in a drama, but the sum of all its characters is the story that they enact. Aristotle puts the plot at the head of the dramatic elements; of all these he thinks plot the most difficult and the most expressive. And he is right.

STARK YOUNG, *The Theatre*

If, as T. S. Eliot said, "Bad poets borrow, good poets steal," Shakespeare was the prince of thieves. Casting his eye over world literature, from epics of the Greeks to contemporary prose romances, he liberally helped himself to whatever he liked and made use of it in fashioning his plots. . . . Shakespeare had a keen eye for a good story and knew what would work.

NORRIE EPSTEIN, *The Friendly Shakespeare*

◇ ◇ ◇

Plot denotes the way events are arranged in a work of literature. Although the accepted conventions of drama require that the plot of a play be presented somewhat differently from the plot of a short story, the same components of plot are present in both. Plot in a dramatic work, like plot in a short story, presents conflicts that are revealed, intensified, and resolved during the course of the play through the characters' actions. (See Chapter 4 for a discussion of **conflict.**)

PLOT STRUCTURE
◆   ◆   ◆

In 1863, the German critic Gustav Freytag devised a pyramid to represent a prototype for the plot of a dramatic work. According to Freytag, a play typically begins with **exposition,** which presents characters and setting and introduces the basic situation in which the characters are involved. Then, during the **rising action,** complications develop, conflicts emerge, suspense builds, and crises occur. The rising action culminates in a **climax,** at which point the plot's tension peaks. Finally, during the **falling action,** the intensity subsides, eventually winding down to a **resolution,** or **denouement,** in which all loose ends are tied up.

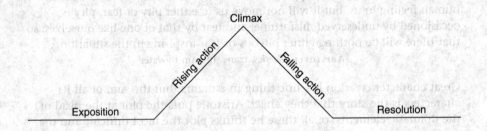

The familiar plot of a detective story follows Freytag's concept of plot: the exposition section includes the introduction of the detective and the explanation of the crime; the rising action develops as the investigation of the crime proceeds, with suspense increasing as the solution approaches; the high point of the action, the climax, comes with the revelation of the crime's solution; and the falling action presents the explanation of the solution. The story concludes with a resolution typically characterized by the capture of the criminal and the restoration of order.

The action of Susan Glaspell's one-act play *Trifles* (p. 948), which in many ways resembles a detective story, might be diagrammed as follows:

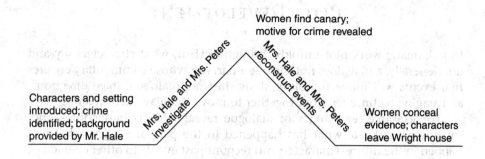

Women find canary; motive for crime revealed

Mrs. Hale and Mrs. Peters reconstruct events

Mrs. Hale and Mrs. Peters investigate

Characters and setting introduced; crime identified; background provided by Mr. Hale

Women conceal evidence; characters leave Wright house

Of course, the plot of a complex dramatic work rarely conforms to the neat pattern represented by Freytag's pyramid. In fact, a play can lack exposition or resolution entirely, and the climax can occur at the beginning. Because long stretches of exposition can be dull, a playwright may arouse audience interest by moving directly into conflict. *Oedipus the King* (p. 1293), for example, begins with the conflict. Similarly, because audiences tend to lose interest after the play's climax is reached, a playwright may choose to dispense with extended falling action. Thus, after Hamlet's death, the play ends abruptly.

PLOT AND SUBPLOT

While the main plot is developing, another, parallel plot, called a **subplot,** may be developing alongside it. This structural device is common in the works of Shakespeare and in many other plays as well.

The subplot's function may not immediately be clear, so at first it may seem to draw attention away from the main plot. Eventually, however, the subplot reinforces elements of the primary plot. In Henrik Ibsen's *A Doll House* (p. 1013), for example, the threat of Dr. Rank's impending death parallels the threat of Nora's approaching exposure; for both of them, time is running out. In Shakespeare's *King Lear,* a more elaborate subplot involves the earl of Gloucester who, like Lear, misjudges his children, favouring a deceitful son who does not deserve his support and overlooking a more deserving one. Both families suffer greatly as a result of the fathers' misplaced loyalties. Thus, the parallel plot places additional emphasis on Lear's poor judgment and magnifies the consequences of his misguided acts: both fathers, and all but one of the five children, are dead by the play's end. A subplot can also set up a contrast—as it does in *Hamlet,* where Fortinbras acts decisively to avenge his father, an action that emphasizes Hamlet's inability to act decisively because of the secrecy involving King Hamlet's murder. Hamlet's revenge for the death of his father is much more complicated than Fortinbras's revenge.

PLOT DEVELOPMENT

◊ ◊ ◊

In a dramatic work plot unfolds through **action,** what characters say and do. Generally, a play does not include a narrator whose commentary ensures that events will move smoothly along. Instead, dialogue, stage directions, and staging techniques work together to move the play's action along.

For example, exchanges of dialogue reveal what is happening—and, sometimes, indicate what has happened in the past or suggest what will happen in the future. Characters can recount past events to other characters, announce an intention to take some action in the future, or summarize events that are occurring offstage. In such cases, dialogue takes the place of formal narrative. On the printed page, stage directions efficiently move readers from one location and time period to another by specifying entrances and exits and identifying the play's structural divisions—acts and scenes—and their accompanying changes of setting.

Staging techniques can also advance a play's action. A change in lighting, for instance, can shift the focus to another part of the stage—and thus to another place and time. Similarly, an adjustment of **scenery** or **props**—for instance, a breakfast table, complete with morning paper, replacing a bedtime setting—can indicate that the action has moved forward in time, as can a change of costumes. Music can also move a play's action along, predicting excitement or doom or a romantic interlude—or a particular character's entrance. Less often, a narrator advances the action. In Thornton Wilder's 1938 play *Our Town,* for example, a character known as the Stage Manager functions as a narrator, not only describing the play's setting and introducing the characters to the audience, but also soliciting questions from characters scattered around the audience, prompting characters, and interrupting dialogue.

FLASHBACKS

Many plays include **flashbacks,** which depict events that occurred before the play's main action. In addition, dialogue can overcome the limitations set by the chronological action on stage by recounting events that occurred earlier. Thus, Mr. Hale in *Trifles* tells the other characters how he discovered John Wright's murder, and Nora in *A Doll House* confides her secret past to her friend Kristine. As characters on stage are brought up to date, the audience is also given necessary information—facts that are essential to an understanding of the characters' motivation. Naturally, characters must have plausible reasons for explaining past events. In *Trifles,* Mr. Hale is the only character who has witnessed the events he describes, and in *A Doll House,* Kristine, formerly Nora's friend and confidante, has not seen her in years. Thus, a character's need for information provides playwrights with a convenient excuse for supplying readers with necessary background. In less realistic dramas, however, no such excuse is necessary: characters can interrupt the action to deliver long monologues or soliloquies that fill in background details—or even address the audience directly.

FORESHADOWING

In addition to revealing past events, dialogue can **foreshadow,** or look ahead to, future action. In many cases, seemingly unimportant comments have significance that becomes clear as the play develops. For example, in act 3 of *A Doll House* Torvald Helmer says to Kristine, "An exit should always be effective, Mrs. Linde, but that's what I can't get Nora to grasp." At the end of the play, Nora's exit is not only effective, but also memorable.

Elements of staging can also suggest events to come. Various bits of **stage business**—gestures or movements designed to attract the audience's attention—may also foreshadow future events. In *A Doll House,* for instance, Nora's sneaking forbidden macaroons seems at first to suggest her fear of her husband, but her actions actually foreshadow her eventual defiance of his authority.

 ## CHECKLIST: WRITING ABOUT PLOT

- ✓ Summarize the play's events.
- ✓ What is the play's central conflict? How is it resolved? What other conflicts are present?
- ✓ What section of the play constitutes its rising action?
- ✓ Where does the play's climax occur?
- ✓ What crises can you identify?
- ✓ How is suspense created?
- ✓ What section of the play constitutes its falling action?
- ✓ Does the play contain a subplot? What is its purpose? How is it related to the main plot?
- ✓ Does the play have flashbacks? Does the play's dialogue contain summaries of past events or references to events in the future? How does the use of flashbacks or foreshadowing advance the play's plot?
- ✓ Does the play include a narrator?
- ✓ How does the dialogue advance the play's plot?
- ✓ How do characters' actions advance the play's plot?
- ✓ How do stage directions advance the play's plot?
- ✓ How does staging advance the play's plot?
- ✓ Does the play use any other devices to advance the plot?

◆ **SUSAN GLASPELL** (1882–1948) was born in Davenport, Iowa, and graduated from Drake University in 1899. First a reporter and then a freelance writer, she lived in Chicago (where she was part of the Chicago Renaissance that included poet Carl Sandburg and novelist Theodore Dreiser) and later in Greenwich Village. Her works include two plays in addition to *Trifles, The Verge* (1921) and *Alison's House* (1930), and several novels, including *Fidelity* (1915) and *The Morning Is Near Us* (1939). With her husband, George Cram Cook, she founded the Provincetown Players, which became the staging ground for innovative plays by Eugene O'Neill, among others.

Glaspell herself wrote plays for the Provincetown Players, beginning with *Trifles*, which she created for the 1916 season although she had never previously written a drama. The play opened on August 8, 1916, with Glaspell and her husband in the cast. Glaspell said she wrote *Trifles* in one afternoon, sitting in the empty theatre and looking at the bare stage: "After a time, the stage became a kitchen—a kitchen there all by itself." She remembered a murder trial she had covered in Iowa in her days as a reporter, and the story began to play itself out on the stage as she gazed. Throughout her revisions, she said, she returned to look at the stage to see whether the events she was recording came to life on it. Although Glaspell later rewrote *Trifles* in the form of a short story called "A Jury of Her Peers," the play remains her most successful and memorable work.

◇ ◇ ◇

S U S A N   G L A S P E L L

Trifles
(1916)

CHARACTERS

GEORGE HENDERSON, *county attorney*
HENRY PETERS, *sheriff*
LEWIS HALE, *a neighbouring farmer*
MRS. PETERS
MRS. HALE

SCENE

The kitchen in the now abandoned farmhouse of John Wright, a gloomy kitchen, and left without having been put in order—unwashed pans under the sink, a loaf of bread outside the breadbox, a dish towel on the table—other signs of incompleted work. At the rear the outer door opens and the Sheriff comes in followed by the County Attorney and Hale. The Sheriff and Hale are men in middle life, the County Attorney is a young man; all are much bundled up and go at once to the stove. They are followed by two women—the Sheriff's wife first; she is a slight wiry woman, a thin nervous face. Mrs. Hale is larger and would ordinarily be called more comfortable looking, but she is disturbed now and looks fearfully about as she enters. The women have come in slowly, and stand close together near the door.

COUNTY ATTORNEY: *(rubbing his hands)* This feels good. Come up to the fire, ladies.

MRS. PETERS: *(after taking a step forward)* I'm not—cold.

SHERIFF: *(unbuttoning his overcoat and stepping away from the stove as if to mark the beginning of official business)* Now, Mr. Hale, before we move things about, you explain to Mr. Henderson just what you saw when you came here yesterday morning.

COUNTY ATTORNEY: By the way, has anything been moved? Are things just as you left them yesterday?

5 SHERIFF: *(looking about)* It's just the same. When it dropped below zero last night I thought I'd better send Frank out this morning to make a fire for us—no use getting pneumonia with a big case on, but I told him not to touch anything except the stove—and you know Frank.

COUNTY ATTORNEY: Somebody should have been left here yesterday.

SHERIFF: Oh—yesterday. When I had to send Frank to Morris Center for that man who went crazy—I want you to know I had my hands full yesterday. I knew you could get back from Omaha by today and as long as I went over everything here myself—

COUNTY ATTORNEY: Well, Mr. Hale, tell just what happened when you came here yesterday morning.

HALE: Harry and I had started to town with a load of potatoes. We came along the road from my place and as I got here I said, "I'm going to see if I can't get John Wright to go in with me on a party telephone." I spoke to Wright about it once before and he put me off, saying folks talked too much anyway, and all he asked was peace and quiet—I guess you know about how much he talked himself; but I thought maybe if I went to the house and talked about it before his wife, though I said to Harry that I didn't know as what his wife wanted made much difference to John—

10 COUNTY ATTORNEY: Let's talk about that later, Mr. Hale. I do want to talk about that, but tell now just what happened when you got to the house.

HALE: I didn't hear or see anything; I knocked at the door, and still it was all quiet inside. I knew they must be up, it was past eight o'clock. So I knocked again, and I thought I heard somebody say, "Come in." I wasn't sure, I'm not sure yet, but I opened the door—this door *(indicating the door by which the two women are still standing)* and there in that rocker—*(pointing to it)* sat Mrs. Wright.

They all look at the rocker.

COUNTY ATTORNEY: What—was she doing?

HALE: She was rockin' back and forth. She had her apron in her hand and was kind of—pleating it.

COUNTY ATTORNEY: And how did she—look?

15 HALE: Well, she looked queer.

COUNTY ATTORNEY: How do you mean—queer?

HALE: Well, as if she didn't know what she was going to do next. And kind of done up.

COUNTY ATTORNEY: How did she seem to feel about your coming?

HALE: Why, I don't think she minded—one way or other. She didn't pay much attention. I said, "How do, Mrs. Wright, it's cold, ain't it?" And she said, "Is it?"—and went on kind of pleating at her apron. Well, I was surprised; she didn't ask me to come up to the stove, or to set down, but just sat there, not even looking at me, so I said, "I want to see John." And then she—laughed. I guess you would call it a laugh. I thought of Harry and the team outside, so I said a little sharp: "Can't I see John?" "No," she says, kind o' dull like. "Ain't he home?" says I. "Yes," says she, "he's home." "Then why can't I see him?" I asked her, out of patience. "'Cause he's dead," says she. *"Dead?"* says I. She just nodded her head, not getting a bit excited, but rockin' back and forth. "Why—where is he?" says I, not knowing what to say. She just pointed upstairs—like that. *(Himself pointing to the room above.)* I got up, with the idea of going up there. I walked from there to here—then I says, "Why, what did he die of?" "He died of a rope round his neck," says she, and just went on pleatin' at her apron. Well, I went out and called Harry. I thought I might—need help. We went upstairs and there he was lyin'—

20   COUNTY ATTORNEY: I think I'd rather have you go into that upstairs, where you can point it all out. Just go on now with the rest of the story.

HALE: Well, my first thought was to get that rope off. It looked . . . *(stops, his face twitches)* . . . but Harry, he went up to him, and he said, "No, he's dead all right, and we'd better not touch anything." So we went back down stairs. She was still sitting that same way. "Has anybody been notified?" I asked. "No," says she, unconcerned. "Who did this, Mrs. Wright?" said Harry. He said it businesslike—and she stopped pleatin' of her apron. "I don't know," she says. "You don't *know?*" says Harry. "No," says she. "Weren't you sleepin' in the bed with him?" says Harry. "Yes," says she, "but I was on the inside." "Somebody slipped a rope round his neck and strangled him and you didn't wake up?" says Harry. "I didn't wake up," she said after him. We must 'a looked as if we didn't see how that could be, for after a minute she said, "I sleep sound." Harry was going to ask her more questions but I said maybe we ought to let her tell her story first to the coroner, or the sheriff, so Harry went fast as he could to Rivers' place, where there's a telephone.

COUNTY ATTORNEY: And what did Mrs. Wright do when she knew that you had gone for the coroner?

HALE: She moved from that chair to this one over here *(pointing to a small chair in the corner)* and just sat there with her hands held together and looking down. I got a feeling that I ought to make some conversation, so I said I had come in to see if John wanted to put in a telephone, and at that she started to laugh, and then she stopped and looked at me—scared. *(The County Attorney, who has had his notebook out, makes a note.)* I dunno, maybe it wasn't scared. I wouldn't like to say it was.

Soon Harry got back, and then Dr. Lloyd came, and you, Mr. Peters,
and so I guess that's all I know that you don't.

COUNTY ATTORNEY: *(looking around)* I guess we'll go upstairs first—and then
out to the barn and around there. *(To the Sheriff.)* You're convinced
that there was nothing important here—nothing that would point to
any motive.

25 SHERIFF: Nothing here but kitchen things.

*The County Attorney, after again looking around the kitchen, opens the door of a
cupboard closet. He gets up on a chair and looks on a shelf. Pulls his hand away,
sticky.*

COUNTY ATTORNEY: Here's a nice mess.

The women draw nearer.

MRS. PETERS: *(to the other woman)* Oh, her fruit; it did freeze. *(To the County
Attorney.)* She worried about that when it turned so cold. She said the
fire'd go out and her jars would break.

SHERIFF: Well, can you beat the women! Held for murder and worryin'
about her preserves.

COUNTY ATTORNEY: I guess before we're through she may have something
more serious than preserves to worry about.

30 HALE: Well, women are used to worrying over trifles.

The two women move a little closer together.

COUNTY ATTORNEY: *(with the gallantry of a young politician)* And yet, for all
their worries, what would we do without the ladies? *(The women do not
unbend. He goes to the sink, takes a dipperful of water from the pail and
pouring it into a basin, washes his hands. Starts to wipe them on the roller
towel, turns it for a cleaner place.)* Dirty towels! *(Kicks his foot against the
pans under the sink.)* Not much of a housekeeper, would you say, ladies?

MRS. HALE: *(stiffly)* There's a great deal of work to be done on a farm.

COUNTY ATTORNEY: To be sure. And yet *(with a little bow to her)* I know there
are some Dickson county farmhouses which do not have such roller
towels.

He gives it a pull to expose its full length again.

MRS. HALE: Those towels get dirty awful quick. Men's hands aren't always
as clean as they might be.

35 COUNTY ATTORNEY: Ah, loyal to your sex, I see. But you and Mrs. Wright
were neighbors. I suppose you were friends, too.

MRS. HALE: *(shaking her head)* I've not seen much of her of late years. I've
not been in this house—it's more than a year.

COUNTY ATTORNEY: And why was that? You didn't like her?

MRS. HALE: I liked her all well enough. Farmers' wives have their hands
full, Mr. Henderson. And then—

COUNTY ATTORNEY: Yes—?

40 MRS. HALE: *(looking about)* It never seemed a very cheerful place.

COUNTY ATTORNEY: No—it's not cheerful. I shouldn't say she had the homemaking instinct.

MRS. HALE: Well, I don't know as Wright had, either.

COUNTY ATTORNEY: You mean that they didn't get on very well?

MRS. HALE: No, I don't mean anything. But I don't think a place'd be any cheerfuller for John Wright's being in it.

45 COUNTY ATTORNEY: I'd like to talk more of that a little later. I want to get the lay of things upstairs now.

He goes to the left, where three steps lead to a stair door.

SHERIFF: I suppose anything Mrs. Peters does'll be all right. She was to take in some clothes for her, you know, and a few little things. We left in such a hurry yesterday.

COUNTY ATTORNEY: Yes, but I would like to see what you take, Mrs. Peters, and keep an eye out for anything that might be of use to us.

MRS. PETERS: Yes, Mr. Henderson.

The women listen to the men's steps on the stairs, then look about the kitchen.

MRS. HALE: I'd hate to have men coming into my kitchen, snooping around and criticizing.

She arranges the pans under sink which the County Attorney had shoved out of place.

50 MRS. PETERS: Of course it's no more than their duty.

MRS. HALE: Duty's all right, but I guess that deputy sheriff that came out to make the fire might have got a little of this on. *(Gives the roller towel a pull.)* Wish I'd thought of that sooner. Seems mean to talk about her for not having things slicked up when she had to come away in such a hurry.

MRS. PETERS: *(who has gone to a small table in the left rear corner of the room, and lifted one end of a towel that covers a pan)* She had bread set.

Stands still.

MRS. HALE: *(eyes fixed on a loaf of bread beside the breadbox, which is on a low shelf at the other side of the room. Moves slowly toward it.)* She was going to put this in there. *(Picks up loaf, then abruptly drops it. In a manner of returning to familiar things.)* It's a shame about her fruit. I wonder if it's all gone. *(Gets up on the chair and looks.)* I think there's some here that's all right, Mrs. Peters. Yes—here; *(holding it toward the window)* this is cherries, too. *(Looking again.)* I declare I believe that's the only one. *(Gets down, bottle in her hand. Goes to the sink and wipes it off on the outside.)* She'll feel awful bad after all her hard work in the hot weather. I remember the afternoon I put up my cherries last summer.

She puts the bottle on the big kitchen table, center of the room. With a sigh, is about to sit down in the rocking-chair. Before she is seated realizes what chair it is;

with a slow look at it, steps back. The chair which she has touched rocks back and forth.

MRS. PETERS: Well, I must get those things from the front room closet. *(She goes to the door at the right, but after looking into the other room, steps back.)* You coming with me, Mrs. Hale? You could help me carry them.

They go in the other room; reappear, Mrs. Peters carrying a dress and skirt, Mrs. Hale following with a pair of shoes.

55 MRS. PETERS: My, it's cold in there.

She puts the clothes on the big table, and hurries to the stove.

MRS. HALE: *(examining her skirt)* Wright was close. I think maybe that's why she kept so much to herself. She didn't even belong to the Ladies Aid. I suppose she felt she couldn't do her part, and then you don't enjoy things when you feel shabby. She used to wear pretty clothes and be lively, when she was Minnie Foster, one of the town girls singing in the choir. But that—oh, that was thirty years ago. This all you was to take in?

MRS. PETERS: She said she wanted an apron. Funny thing to want, for there isn't much to get you dirty in jail, goodness knows. But I suppose just to make her feel more natural. She said they was in the top drawer in this cupboard. Yes, here. And then her little shawl that always hung behind the door. *(Opens stair door and looks.)* Yes, here it is.

Quickly shuts door leading upstairs.

MRS. HALE: *(abruptly moving toward her)* Mrs. Peters?

MRS. PETERS: Yes, Mrs. Hale?

60 MRS. HALE: Do you think she did it?

MRS. PETERS: *(in a frightened voice)* Oh, I don't know.

MRS. HALE: Well, I don't think she did. Asking for an apron and her little shawl. Worrying about her fruit.

MRS. PETERS: *(starts to speak, glances up, where footsteps are heard in the room above. In a low voice.)* Mr. Peters says it looks bad for her. Mr. Henderson is awful sarcastic in a speech and he'll make fun of her sayin' she didn't wake up.

MRS. HALE: Well, I guess John Wright didn't wake when they was slipping that rope under his neck.

65 MRS. PETERS: No, it's strange. It must have been done awful crafty and still. They say it was such a—funny way to kill a man, rigging it all up like that.

MRS. HALE: That's just what Mr. Hale said. There was a gun in the house. He says that's what he can't understand.

MRS. PETERS: Mr. Henderson said coming out that what was needed for the case was a motive; something to show anger, or—sudden feeling.

MRS. HALE: *(who is standing by the table)* Well, I don't see any signs of anger around here. (*She puts her hand on the dish towel which lies on the table, stands looking down at table, one half of which is clean, the other half messy.)* It's wiped to here. *(Makes a move as if to finish work, then turns and looks at loaf of bread outside the breadbox. Drops towel. In that voice of coming back to familiar things.)* Wonder how they are finding things upstairs. I hope she had it a little more red-up[1] up there. You know, it seems kind of *sneaking.* Locking her up in town and then coming out here and trying to get her own house to turn against her!

MRS. PETERS: But Mrs. Hale, the law is the law.

70   MRS. HALE: I s'pose 'tis. *(Unbuttoning her coat.)* Better loosen up your things, Mrs. Peters. You won't feel them when you go out.

Mrs. Peters takes off her fur tippet, goes to hang it on hook at back of room, stands looking at the under part of the small corner table.

MRS. PETERS: She was piecing a quilt.

She brings the large sewing basket and they look at the bright pieces.

MRS. HALE: It's log cabin pattern. Pretty, isn't it? I wonder if she was goin' to quilt it or just knot it?

Footsteps have been heard coming down the stairs. The Sheriff enters followed by Hale and the County Attorney.

SHERIFF: They wonder if she was going to quilt it or just knot it!

The men laugh; the women look abashed.

COUNTY ATTORNEY: *(rubbing his hands over the stove)* Frank's fire didn't do much up there, did it? Well, let's go out to the barn and get that cleared up.

The men go outside.

75   MRS. HALE: *(resentfully)* I don't know as there's anything so strange, our takin' up our time with little things while we're waiting for them to get the evidence. *(She sits down at the big table smoothing out a block with decision.)* I don't see as it's anything to laugh about.

MRS. PETERS: *(apologetically)* Of course they've got awful important things on their minds.

Pulls up a chair and joins Mrs. Hale at the table.

MRS. HALE: *(examining another block)* Mrs. Peters, look at this one. Here, this is the one she was working on, and look at the sewing! All the rest of it has been so nice and even. And look at this! It's all over the place! Why, it looks as if she didn't know what she was about!

After she has said this they look at each other, then start to glance back at the door. After an instant Mrs. Hale has pulled at a knot and ripped the sewing.

---

[1] Spruced up. (slang)

MRS. PETERS: Oh, what are you doing, Mrs. Hale?

MRS. HALE: *(mildly)* Just pulling out a stitch or two that's not sewed very good. *(Threading a needle.)* Bad sewing always made me fidgety.

80   MRS. PETERS: *(nervously)* I don't think we ought to touch things.

MRS. HALE: I'll just finish up this end. *(Suddenly stopping and leaning forward.)* Mrs. Peters?

MRS. PETERS: Yes, Mrs. Hale?

MRS. HALE: What do you suppose she was so nervous about?

MRS. PETERS: Oh—I don't know. I don't know as she was nervous. I sometimes sew awful queer when I'm just tired. *(Mrs. Hale starts to say something, looks at Mrs. Peters, then goes on sewing.)* Well, I must get these things wrapped up. They may be through sooner than we think. *(Putting apron and other things together.)* I wonder where I can find a piece of paper, and string.

85   MRS. HALE: In that cupboard, maybe.

MRS. PETERS: *(looking in cupboard)* Why, here's a birdcage. *(Holds it up.)* Did she have a bird, Mrs. Hale?

MRS. HALE: Why, I don't know whether she did or not—I've not been here for so long. There was a man around last year selling canaries cheap, but I don't know as she took one; maybe she did. She used to sing real pretty herself.

MRS. PETERS: *(glancing around)* Seems funny to think of a bird here. But she must have had one, or why would she have a cage? I wonder what happened to it.

MRS. HALE: I s'pose maybe the cat got it.

90   MRS. PETERS: No, she didn't have a cat. She's got that feeling some people have about cats—being afraid of them. My cat got in her room and she was real upset and asked me to take it out.

MRS. HALE: My sister Bessie was like that. Queer, ain't it?

MRS. PETERS: *(examining the cage)* Why, look at this door. It's broke. One hinge is pulled apart.

MRS. HALE: *(looking too)* Looks as if someone must have been rough with it.

MRS. PETERS: Why, yes.

She brings the cage forward and puts it on the table.

95   MRS. HALE: I wish if they're going to find any evidence they'd be about it. I don't like this place.

MRS. PETERS: But I'm awful glad you came with me, Mrs. Hale. It would be lonesome for me sitting here alone.

MRS. HALE: It would, wouldn't it? *(Dropping her sewing.)* But I tell you what I do wish, Mrs. Peters. I wish I had come over sometimes when *she* was here. I—*(looking around the room)*—wish I had.

MRS. PETERS: But of course you were awful busy, Mrs. Hale—your house and your children.

MRS. HALE: I could've come. I stayed away because it weren't cheerful—and that's why I ought to have come. I—I've never liked this place. Maybe because it's down in a hollow and you don't see the road. I dunno what it is but it's a lonesome place and always was. I wish I had come over to see Minnie Foster sometimes. I can see now—

Shakes her head.

100 MRS. PETERS: Well, you mustn't reproach yourself, Mrs. Hale. Somehow we just don't see how it is with other folks until—something comes up.

MRS. HALE: Not having children makes less work—but it makes a quiet house, and Wright out to work all day, and no company when he did come in. Did you know John Wright, Mrs. Peters?

MRS. PETERS: Not to know him; I've seen him in town. They say he was a good man.

MRS. HALE: Yes—good; he didn't drink, and kept his word as well as most, I guess, and paid his debts. But he was a hard man, Mrs. Peters. Just to pass the time of day with him—*(Shivers.)* Like a raw wind that gets to the bone. *(Pauses, her eye falling on the cage.)* I should think she would 'a wanted a bird. But what do you suppose went with it?

MRS. PETERS: I don't know, unless it got sick and died.

She reaches over and swings the broken door, swings it again. Both women watch it.

105 MRS. HALE: You weren't raised round here, were you? *(Mrs. Peters shakes her head.)* You didn't know—her?

MRS. PETERS: Not till they brought her yesterday.

MRS. HALE: She—come to think of it, she was kind of like a bird herself— real sweet and pretty, but kind of timid and—fluttery. How—she— did—change. *(Silence; then as if struck by a happy thought and relieved to get back to everyday things.)* Tell you what, Mrs. Peters, why don't you take the quilt in with you? It might take up her mind.

MRS. PETERS: Why, I think that's a real nice idea, Mrs. Hale. There couldn't possibly be any objection to it, could there? Now, just what would I take? I wonder if her patches are in here—and her things.

They look in the sewing basket.

MRS. HALE: Here's some red. I expect this has got sewing things in it. *(Brings out a fancy box.)* What a pretty box. Looks like something somebody would give you. Maybe her scissors are in here. *(Opens box. Suddenly puts her hand to her nose.)* Why—*(Mrs. Peters bends nearer, then turns her face away.)* There's something wrapped up in this piece of silk.

110 MRS. PETERS: Why, this isn't her scissors.

MRS. HALE: *(lifting the silk)* Oh, Mrs. Peters—it's—

Mrs. Peters bends closer.

MRS. PETERS: It's the bird.

MRS. HALE: *(jumping up)* But, Mrs. Peters—look at it! Its neck! Look at its neck! It's all—other side *to*.

MRS. PETERS: Somebody—wrung—its—neck.

Their eyes meet. A look of growing comprehension, of horror. Steps are heard outside. Mrs. Hale slips box under quilt pieces, and sinks into her chair. Enter Sheriff and County Attorney. Mrs. Peters rises.

115 COUNTY ATTORNEY: *(as one turning from serious things to little pleasantries)* Well, ladies, have you decided whether she was going to quilt it or knot it?

MRS. PETERS: We think she was going to—knot it.

COUNTY ATTORNEY: Well, that's interesting, I'm sure. *(Seeing the birdcage.)* Has the bird flown?

MRS. HALE: *(putting more quilt pieces over the box)* We think the—cat got it.

COUNTY ATTORNEY: *(preoccupied)* Is there a cat?

Mrs. Hale glances in a quick covert way at Mrs. Peters.

120 MRS. PETERS: Well, not *now*. They're superstitious, you know. They leave.

COUNTY ATTORNEY: *(to Sheriff Peters, continuing an interrupted conversation)* No sign at all of anyone having come from the outside. Their own rope. Now let's go up again and go over it piece by piece. *(They start upstairs.)* It would have to have been someone who knew just the—

Mrs. Peters sits down. The two women sit there not looking at one another, but as if peering into something and at the same time holding back. When they talk now it is in the manner of feeling their way over strange ground, as if afraid of what they are saying, but as if they cannot help saying it.

MRS. HALE: She liked the bird. She was going to bury it in that pretty box.

MRS. PETERS: *(in a whisper)* When I was a girl—my kitten—there was a boy took a hatchet, and before my eyes—and before I could get there—*(Covers her face an instant.)* If they hadn't held me back I would have—*(catches herself, looks upstairs where steps are heard, falters weakly)*—hurt him.

MRS. HALE: *(with a slow look around her)* I wonder how it would seem never to have had any children around. *(Pause.)* No, Wright wouldn't like the bird—a thing that sang. She used to sing. He killed that, too.

125 MRS. PETERS: *(moving uneasily)* We don't know who killed the bird.

MRS. HALE: I knew John Wright.

MRS. PETERS: It was an awful thing was done in this house that night, Mrs. Hale. Killing a man while he slept, slipping a rope around his neck that choked the life out of him.

MRS. HALE: His neck. Choked the life out of him.

Her hand goes out and rests on the birdcage.

MRS. PETERS: *(with rising voice)* We don't know who killed him. We don't know.

130 MRS. HALE: *(her own feeling not interrupted)* If there'd been years and years of nothing, then a bird to sing to you, it would be awful—still, after the bird was still.

MRS. PETERS: *(something within her speaking)* I know what stillness is. When we homesteaded in Dakota, and my first baby died—after he was two years old, and me with no other then—

MRS. HALE: *(moving)* How soon do you suppose they'll be through, looking for the evidence?

MRS. PETERS: I know what stillness is. *(Pulling herself back.)* The law has got to punish crime, Mrs. Hale.

MRS. HALE: *(not as if answering that)* I wish you'd seen Minnie Foster when she wore a white dress with blue ribbons and stood up there in the choir and sang. *(A look around the room.)* Oh, I *wish* I'd come over here once in a while! That was a crime! That was a crime! Who's going to punish that?

135 MRS. PETERS: *(looking upstairs)* We mustn't—take on.

MRS. HALE: I might have known she needed help! I know how things can be—for women. I tell you, it's queer, Mrs. Peters. We live close together and we live far apart. We all go through the same things—it's all just a different kind of the same thing. *(Brushes her eyes; noticing the bottle of fruit, reaches out for it.)* If I was you I wouldn't tell her her fruit was gone. Tell her it *ain't.* Tell her it's all right. Take this in to prove it to her. She—she may never know whether it was broke or not.

MRS. PETERS: *(takes the bottle, looks about for something to wrap it in; takes petticoat from the clothes brought from the other room, very nervously begins winding this around the bottle. In a false voice)* My, it's a good thing the men couldn't hear us. Wouldn't they just laugh! Getting all stirred up over a little thing like a—dead canary. As if that could have anything to do with—with—wouldn't they *laugh!*

The men are heard coming down stairs.

MRS. HALE: *(under her breath)* Maybe they would—maybe they wouldn't.

COUNTY ATTORNEY: No, Peters, it's all perfectly clear except a reason for doing it. But you know juries when it comes to women. If there was some definite thing. Something to show—something to make a story about—a thing that would connect up with this strange way of doing it—

The women's eyes meet for an instant. Enter Hale from outer door.

140 HALE: Well, I've got the team around. Pretty cold out there.

COUNTY ATTORNEY: I'm going to stay here a while by myself. *(To the Sheriff.)* You can send Frank out for me, can't you? I want to go over everything. I'm not satisfied that we can't do better.

SHERIFF: Do you want to see what Mrs. Peters is going to take in?

The County Attorney goes to the table, picks up the apron, laughs.

COUNTY ATTORNEY: Oh, I guess they're not very dangerous things the ladies have picked out. (*Moves a few things about, disturbing the quilt pieces which cover the box. Steps back.*) No, Mrs. Peters doesn't need supervising. For that matter, a sheriff's wife is married to the law. Ever think of it that way, Mrs. Peters?

MRS. PETERS: Not—just that way.

145   SHERIFF: (*chuckling*) Married to the law. (*Moves toward the other room.*) I just want you to come in here a minute, George. We ought to take a look at these windows.

COUNTY ATTORNEY: (*scoffingly*) Oh, windows!

SHERIFF: We'll be right out, Mr. Hale.

Hale goes outside. The Sheriff follows the County Attorney into the other room. Then Mrs. Hale rises, hands tight together, looking intensely at Mrs. Peters, whose eyes make a slow turn, finally meeting Mrs. Hale's. A moment Mrs. Hale holds her, then her own eyes point the way to where the box is concealed. Suddenly Mrs. Peters throws back quilt pieces and tries to put the box in the bag she is wearing. It is too big. She opens box, starts to take bird out, cannot touch it, goes to pieces, stands there helpless. Sound of a knob turning in the other room. Mrs. Hale snatches the box and puts it in the pocket of her big coat. Enter County Attorney and Sheriff.

COUNTY ATTORNEY: (*facetiously*) Well, Henry, at least we found out that she was not going to quilt it. She was going to—what is it you call it, ladies?

MRS. HALE: (*her hand against her pocket*) We call it—knot it, Mr. Henderson.

READING AND REACTING

1. What key events have occurred before the play begins? Why do you suppose these events are not presented in the play itself?

2. What are the "trifles" to which the title refers? How do these "trifles" advance the play's plot?

3. Glaspell's short story version of *Trifles* is called "A Jury of Her Peers." Who are Mrs. Wright's peers? What do you suppose the verdict would be if she were tried for her crime in 1916, when only men were permitted to serve on juries? If the trial were held today, do you think the jury might reach a different verdict?

4. *Trifles* is a one-act play, and all its action occurs in the Wrights' kitchen. Does this static setting slow down the flow of the plot? Are there any advantages to this setting? Explain.

5. All background information about Mrs. Wright is provided by Mrs. Hale. Do you consider her to be a reliable source of information? Why or why not?

6. Mr. Hale's summary of his conversation with Mrs. Wright is the reader's only chance to hear her version of events. How would Mrs. Wright's presence change the play?

7. *Trifles* is a relatively slow-moving, "talky" play, with very little physical action. Is this a weakness of the play, or is the slow development consistent with the effect Glaspell is trying to achieve? Explain.

8. How does each of the following events advance the play's action: the men's departure from the kitchen, the discovery of the quilt pieces, the discovery of the dead bird?

9. How do the county attorney's sarcastic comments and his patronizing attitude toward Mrs. Hale and Mrs. Peters advance the play's action?

10. How do Mrs. Peters's memories of her own life advance the action?

11. What assumptions about women do the male characters make? In what ways do the female characters conform to or depart from these assumptions?

12. In what sense is the process of making a quilt an appropriate metaphor for the plot of *Trifles*?

13. **JOURNAL ENTRY** Do you think Mrs. Hale and Mrs. Peters do the right thing by concealing evidence?

14. **CRITICAL PERSPECTIVE** Gary A. Richardson writes in *American Drama from the Colonial Period through World War I* that in *Trifles*, Glaspell "developed a new structure for her action. . . .":

> While action in the traditional sense is minimal, Glaspell is nevertheless able to rivet attention on the two women, wed the audience to their perspective, and make a compelling case for the fairness of their actions. Existing on the margins of their society, Mrs. Peters and Mrs. Hale become emotional surrogates for the jailed Minnie Wright, effectively exonerating her action as "justifiable homicide."
>
> *Trifles* is carefully crafted to match Glaspell's subject matter—the action meanders, without a clearly delineated beginning, middle, or end. . . .

Exactly how does Glaspell "rivet attention on" Mrs. Hale and Mrs. Peters? Do you agree that the play's action "meanders, without a clearly delineated beginning, middle, or end"? If so, do you too see this "meandering" as appropriate for Glaspell's subject matter?

Related Works: "I Stand Here Ironing" (p. 181), "A Garden of Her Own" (p. 202), "The Cask of Amontillado" (p. 227), "Everyday Use" (p. 327)

◆ **OSCAR WILDE** (1854–1900) was born in Dublin, the son of a surgeon and writer. He attended Trinity College, Dublin, where he won the Berkeley Gold Medal for Greek, and Magdalen College, Oxford, where he won the Newdigate Prize for his poem "Ravenna." He graduated from Oxford with first-class honours and went to London, where he published poetry, plays, essays, and his famous novel *The Picture of Dorian Gray*, in whose preface he announced: "There is no such thing as a moral or an immoral book. Books are well written or badly written. That is all." Wilde's belief in aestheticism (art for art's sake) and his personal flamboyant style tended to attract negative attention. But he was a successful writer, even going on reading tours in Canada and the United States. He married in 1884, and he published a volume of fairy tales in 1888 for his sons. His social comedies, such as *Lady Windermere's Fan* (1892), *A Woman of No Importance* (1893), and *An Ideal Husband* (1895), mocked the morality and pretensions of late Victorian society, and they were huge successes, culminating in *The Importance of Being Earnest* (1895), a splendid farce that surpasses his other plays for witty satire.

Wilde's life took a tragic turn when he was imprisoned for homosexuality in 1895. Upon his release in 1897 he went to Paris, where he died, bankrupt and bitter.

❖ ❖ ❖

OSCAR WILDE

The Importance of Being Earnest
(1895)

THE PERSONS OF THE PLAY

JOHN WORTHING, J.P.
ALGERNON MONCRIEFF
REV. CANON CHASUBLE, D.D.
MERRIMAN, *butler*
LANE, *manservant*

LADY BRACKNELL
HON. GWENDOLEN FAIRFAX
CECILY CARDEW
MISS PRISM, *governess*

THE SCENES OF THE PLAY

ACT I

Algernon Moncrieff's flat in Half-Moon Street, W.

ACT II

The garden at the Manor House, Woolton

ACT III

Drawing-room at the Manor House, Woolton

TIME
The Present

FIRST ACT

SCENE *Morning-room in Algernon's flat in Half-Moon Street.*[1] *The room is luxuriously and artistically furnished. The sound of a piano is heard in the adjoining room.*

(*Lane is arranging afternoon tea on the table and, after the music has ceased, Algernon enters.*)

ALGERNON: Did you hear what I was playing, Lane?

LANE: I didn't think it polite to listen, sir.

ALGERNON: I'm sorry for that, for your sake. I don't play accurately— anyone can play accurately—but I play with wonderful expression. As far as the piano is concerned, sentiment is my forte. I keep science for Life.

LANE: Yes, sir.

5 ALGERNON: And, speaking of the science of Life, have you got the cucumber sandwiches cut for Lady Bracknell?

LANE: Yes, sir. (*Hands them on a salver.*)

ALGERNON: (*Inspects them, takes two, and sits down on the sofa*) Oh! . . . by the way, Lane, I see from your book that on Thursday night, when Lord Shoreman and Mr Worthing were dining with me, eight bottles of champagne are entered as having been consumed.

LANE: Yes, sir; eight bottles and a pint.

ALGERNON: Why is it that at a bachelor's establishment the servants invariably drink the champagne? I ask merely for information.

10 LANE: I attribute it to the superior quality of the wine, sir. I have often observed that in married households the champagne is rarely of a first-rate brand.

ALGERNON: Good heavens! Is marriage so demoralising as that?

LANE: I believe it *is* a very pleasant state, sir. I have had very little experience of it myself up to the present. I have only been married once. That was in consequence of a misunderstanding between myself and a young person.

ALGERNON: (*languidly*) I don't know that I am much interested in your family life, Lane.

LANE: No, sir; it is not a very interesting subject. I never think of it myself.

15 ALGERNON: Very natural, I am sure. That will do, Lane, thank you.

LANE: Thank you, sir.

(*Lane goes out.*)

ALGERNON: Lane's views on marriage seem somewhat lax. Really, if the lower orders don't set us a good example, what on earth is the use of them? They seem, as a class, to have absolutely no sense of moral responsibility.

---

[1] Street in London's fashionable West End just off Piccadilly near Green Park.

(Enter Lane.)

LANE: Mr Ernest Worthing.

(Enter Jack. Lane goes out.)

ALGERNON: How are you, my dear Ernest? What brings you up to town?

20 JACK: Oh, pleasure, pleasure! What else should bring one anywhere? Eating
as usual, I see, Algy!

ALGERNON: *(stiffly)* I believe it is customary in good society to take some
slight refreshment at five o'clock. Where have you been since
last Thursday?

JACK: *(sitting down on the sofa)* In the country.

ALGERNON: What on earth do you do there?

JACK: *(pulling off his gloves)* When one is in town one amuses oneself.
When one is in the country one amuses other people. It is
excessively boring.

25 ALGERNON: And who are the people you amuse?

JACK: *(airily)* Oh, neighbours, neighbours.

ALGERNON: Got nice neighbours in your part of Shropshire?[2]

JACK: Perfectly horrid! Never speak to one of them.

ALGERNON: How immensely you must amuse them! *(Goes over and takes
sandwich.)* By the way, Shropshire is your county, is it not?

30 JACK: Eh? Shropshire? Yes, of course. Hallo! Why all these cups? Why
cucumber sandwiches? Why such reckless extravagance in one
so young? Who is coming to tea?

ALGERNON: Oh! merely Aunt Augusta and Gwendolen.

JACK: How perfectly delightful!

ALGERNON: Yes, that is all very well; but I am afraid Aunt Augusta won't
quite approve of your being here.

JACK: May I ask why?

35 ALGERNON: My dear fellow, the way you flirt with Gwendolen is perfectly
disgraceful. It is almost as bad as the way Gwendolen flirts with
you.

JACK: I am in love with Gwendolen. I have come up to town expressly to
propose to her.

ALGERNON: I thought you had come up for pleasure? . . . I call that business.

JACK: How utterly unromantic you are!

ALGERNON: I really don't see anything romantic in proposing. It is very
romantic to be in love. But there is nothing romantic about a
definite proposal. Why, one may be accepted. One usually is, I
believe. Then the excitement is all over. The very essence of
romance is uncertainty. If ever I get married, I'll certainly try to
forget the fact.

---

[2] Jack's country place is in Hertfordshire north of London, but he attempts to deceive
Algernon by insisting on this false location. Shropshire is far to the west on the Welsh
border.

40 JACK: I have no doubt about that, dear Algy. The Divorce Court was specially invented for people whose memories are so curiously constituted.

ALGERNON: Oh! there is no use speculating on that subject. Divorces are made in Heaven—*(Jack puts out his hand to take a sandwich. Algernon at once interferes.)* Please don't touch the cucumber sandwiches. They are ordered specially for Aunt Augusta. *(Takes one and eats it.)*

JACK: Well, you have been eating them all the time.

ALGERNON: That is quite a different matter. She is my aunt. *(Takes plate from below.)* Have some bread and butter. The bread and butter is for Gwendolen. Gwendolen is devoted to bread and butter.

JACK: *(advancing to table and helping himself)* And very good bread and butter it is too.

45 ALGERNON: Well, my dear fellow, you need not eat as if you were going to eat it all. You behave as if you were married to her already. You are not married to her already, and I don't think you ever will be.

JACK: Why on earth do you say that?

ALGERNON: Well, in the first place, girls never marry the men they flirt with. Girls don't think it right.

JACK: Oh, that is nonsense!

ALGERNON: It isn't. It is a great truth. It accounts for the extraordinary number of bachelors that one sees all over the place. In the second place, I don't give my consent.

50 JACK: Your consent!

ALGERNON: My dear fellow, Gwendolen is my first cousin. And before I allow you to marry her, you will have to clear up the whole question of Cecily. *(Rings bell.)*

JACK: Cecily! What on earth do you mean? What do you mean, Algy, by Cecily! I don't know any one of the name of Cecily.

(Enter Lane.)

ALGERNON: Bring me that cigarette case Mr Worthing left in the smoking-room the last time he dined here.

LANE: Yes, sir.

(Lane goes out.)

55 JACK: Do you mean to say you have had my cigarette case all this time? I wish to goodness you had let me know. I have been writing frantic letters to Scotland Yard about it. I was very nearly offering a large reward.

ALGERNON: Well, I wish you would offer one. I happen to be more than usually hard up.

JACK: There is no good offering a large reward now that the thing is found.

(Enter Lane with the cigarette case on a salver. Algernon takes it at once. Lane goes out.)

ALGERNON: I think that is rather mean of you, Ernest, I must say. *(Opens case and examines it.)* However, it makes no matter, for, now that I look at the inscription inside, I find that the thing isn't yours after all.

JACK: Of course it's mine. *(Moving to him.)* You have seen me with it a hundred times, and you have no right whatsoever to read what is written inside. It is a very ungentlemanly thing to read a private cigarette case.

60 ALGERNON: Oh! it is absurd to have a hard and fast rule about what one should read and what one shouldn't. More than half of modern culture depends on what one shouldn't read.

JACK: I am quite aware of the fact, and I don't propose to discuss modern culture. It isn't the sort of thing one should talk of in private. I simply want my cigarette case back.

ALGERNON: Yes; but this isn't your cigarette case. This cigarette case is a present from someone of the name of Cecily, and you said you didn't know anyone of that name.

JACK: Well, if you want to know, Cecily happens to be my aunt.

ALGERNON: Your aunt!

65 JACK: Yes. Charming old lady she is, too. Lives at Tunbridge Wells. Just give it back to me, Algy.

ALGERNON: *(retreating to back of sofa)* But why does she call herself little Cecily if she is your aunt and lives at Tunbridge Wells? *(Reading.)* "From little Cecily with her fondest love."

JACK: *(moving to sofa and kneeling upon it)* My dear fellow, what on earth is there in that? Some aunts are tall, some aunts are not tall. That is a matter that surely an aunt may be allowed to decide for herself. You seem to think that every aunt should be exactly like your aunt! That is absurd! For Heaven's sake give me back my cigarette case. *(Follows Algernon round the room.)*

ALGERNON: Yes. But why does your aunt call you her uncle? "From little Cecily, with her fondest love to her dear Uncle Jack." There is no objection, I admit, to an aunt being a small aunt, but why an aunt, no matter what her size may be, should call her own nephew her uncle, I can't quite make out. Besides, your name isn't Jack at all; it is Ernest.

JACK: It isn't Ernest; it's Jack.

70 ALGERNON: You have always told me it was Ernest. I have introduced you to everyone as Ernest. You answer to the name of Ernest. You look as if your name was Ernest. You are the most earnest-looking person I ever saw in my life. It is perfectly absurd your saying that your name isn't Ernest. It's on your cards. Here is one of

them. *(Taking it from case.)* "Mr Ernest Worthing, B.4, The Albany." I'll keep this as a proof that your name is Ernest if ever you attempt to deny it to me, or to Gwendolen, or to anyone else. *(Puts the card in his pocket.)*

JACK: Well, my name is Ernest in town and Jack in the country, and the cigarette case was given to me in the country.

ALGERNON: Yes, but that does not account for the fact that your small Aunt Cecily, who lives at Tunbridge Wells, calls you her dear uncle. Come, old boy, you had much better have the thing out at once.

JACK: My dear Algy, you talk exactly as if you were a dentist. It is very vulgar to talk like a dentist when one isn't a dentist. It produces a false impression.

ALGERNON: Well, that is exactly what dentists always do. Now, go on! Tell me the whole thing. I may mention that I have always suspected you of being a confirmed and secret Bunburyist; and I am quite sure of it now.

75 JACK: Bunburyist? What on earth do you mean by a Bunburyist?

ALGERNON: I'll reveal to you the meaning of that incomparable expression as soon as you are kind enough to inform me why you are Ernest in town and Jack in the country.

JACK: Well, produce my cigarette case first.

ALGERNON: Here it is. *(Hands cigarette case.)* Now produce your explanation, and pray make it improbable. *(Sits on sofa.)*

JACK: My dear fellow, there is nothing improbable about my explanation at all. In fact it's perfectly ordinary. Old Mr Thomas Cardew, who adopted me when I was a little boy, made me in his will guardian to his grand-daughter, Miss Cecily Cardew. Cecily, who addresses me as her uncle from motives of respect that you could not possibly appreciate, lives at my place in the country under the charge of her admirable governess, Miss Prism.

80 ALGERNON: Where is that place in the country, by the way?

JACK: That is nothing to you, dear boy. You are not going to be invited. . . . I may tell you candidly that the place is not in Shropshire.

ALGERNON: I suspected that, my dear fellow! I have Bunburyed all over Shropshire on two separate occasions. Now, go on. Why are you Ernest in town and Jack in the country?

JACK: My dear Algy, I don't know whether you will be able to understand my real motives. You are hardly serious enough. When one is placed in the position of guardian, one has to adopt a very high moral tone on all subjects. It's one's duty to do so. And as a high moral tone can hardly be said to conduce very much to either one's health or one's happiness, in order to get up to town I have always pretended to have a younger brother of the name of Ernest, who lives in the Albany, and gets into the most dreadful scrapes. That, my dear Algy, is the whole truth pure and simple.

ALGERNON: The truth is rarely pure and never simple. Modern life would be very tedious if it were either, and modern literature a complete impossibility!

85 JACK: That wouldn't be at all a bad thing.

ALGERNON: Literary criticism is not your forte, my dear fellow. Don't try it. You should leave that to people who haven't been at a University. They do it so well in the daily papers. What you really are is a Bunburyist. I was quite right in saying you were a Bunburyist. You are one of the most advanced Bunburyists I know.

JACK: What on earth do you mean?

ALGERNON: You have invented a very useful younger brother called Ernest, in order that you may be able to come up to town as often as you like. I have invented an invaluable permanent invalid called Bunbury, in order that I may be able to go down into the country whenever I choose. Bunbury is perfectly invaluable. If it wasn't for Bunbury's extraordinary bad health, for instance, I wouldn't be able to dine with you at Willis's[3] tonight, for I have been really engaged to Aunt Augusta for more than a week.

JACK: I haven't asked you to dine with me anywhere tonight.

90 ALGERNON: I know. You are absurdly careless about sending out invitations. It is very foolish of you. Nothing annoys people so much as not receiving invitations.

JACK: You had much better dine with your Aunt Augusta.

ALGERNON: I haven't the smallest intention of doing anything of the kind. To begin with, I dined there on Monday, and once a week is quite enough to dine with one's own relations. In the second place, whenever I do dine there I am always treated as a member of the family, and sent down[4] with either no woman at all, or two. In the third place, I know perfectly well whom she will place me next to, tonight. She will place me next Mary Farquhar, who always flirts with her own husband across the dinner-table. That is not very pleasant. Indeed, it is not even decent . . . and that sort of thing is enormously on the increase. The amount of women in London who flirt with their own husbands is perfectly scandalous. It looks so bad. It is simply washing one's clean linen in public. Besides, now that I know you to be a confirmed Bunburyist I naturally want to talk to you about Bunburying. I want to tell you the rules.

JACK: I'm not a Bunburyist at all. If Gwendolen accepts me, I am going to kill my brother, indeed I think I'll kill him in any case. Cecily is a little too much interested in him. It is rather a bore. So I am

---

[3] Fashionable restaurant in King St. near St. James's Theatre.

[4] At formal Victorian dinners, guests congregated in a drawing room upstairs before being "sent down" to the dining room with their partners.

going to get rid of Ernest. And I strongly advise you to do the same with Mr . . . with your invalid friend who has the absurd name.

ALGERNON: Nothing will induce me to part with Bunbury, and if you ever get married, which seems to me extremely problematic, you will be very glad to know Bunbury. A man who marries without knowing Bunbury has a very tedious time of it.

95 JACK: That is nonsense. If I marry a charming girl like Gwendolen, and she is the only girl I ever saw in my life that I would marry, I certainly won't want to know Bunbury.

ALGERNON: Then your wife will. You don't seem to realize, that in married life three is company and two is none.

JACK: *(sententiously)* That, my dear young friend, is the theory[5] that the corrupt French Drama has been propounding for the last fifty years.

ALGERNON: Yes; and that the happy English home has proved in half the time.

JACK: For heaven's sake, don't try to be cynical. It's perfectly easy to be cynical.

100 ALGERNON: My dear fellow, it isn't easy to be anything nowadays. There's such a lot of beastly competition about. *(The sound of an electric bell is heard.)* Ah! that must be Aunt Augusta. Only relatives, or creditors, ever ring in that Wagnerian manner.[6] Now, if I get her out of the way for ten minutes, so that you can have an opportunity for proposing to Gwendolen, may I dine with you tonight at Willis's?

JACK: I suppose so, if you want to.

ALGERNON: Yes, but you must be serious about it. I hate people who are not serious about meals. It is so shallow of them.

(Enter Lane.)

LANE: Lady Bracknell and Miss Fairfax.

(Algernon goes forward to meet them. Enter Lady Bracknell and Gwendolen.)

LADY BRACKNELL: Good afternoon, dear Algernon, I hope you are behaving very well.

105 ALGERNON: I'm feeling very well, Aunt Augusta.

LADY BRACKNELL: That's not quite the same thing. In fact the two things rarely go together. *(Sees Jack and bows to him with icy coldness.)*

ALGERNON: *(to Gwendolen)* Dear me, you are smart![7]

GWENDOLEN: I am always smart! Am I not, Mr Worthing?

JACK: You're quite perfect, Miss Fairfax.

---

[5] This refers to the recurrent theme of marital infidelity.

[6] The loud music of the operas of Richard Wagner.

[7] Well-dressed.

110 GWENDOLEN: Oh! I hope I am not that. It would leave no room for developments, and I intend to develop in many directions.

(Gwendolen and Jack sit down together in the corner.)

LADY BRACKNELL: I'm sorry if we are a little late, Algernon, but I was obliged to call on dear Lady Harbury. I hadn't been there since her poor husband's death. I never saw a woman so altered; she looks quite twenty years younger. And now I'll have a cup of tea, and one of those nice cucumber sandwiches you promised me.

ALGERNON: Certainly, Aunt Augusta. *(Goes over to tea-table.)*

LADY BRACKNELL: Won't you come and sit here, Gwendolen?

GWENDOLEN: Thanks, mamma, I'm quite comfortable where I am.

115 ALGERNON: *(picking up empty plate in horror)* Good heavens! Lane! Why are there no cucumber sandwiches? I ordered them specially.

LANE: *(gravely)* There were no cucumbers in the market this morning, sir. I went down twice.

ALGERNON: No cucumbers!

LANE: No, sir. Not even for ready money.

ALGERNON: That will do, Lane, thank you.

120 LANE: Thank you, sir. *(Goes out.)*

ALGERNON: I am greatly distressed, Aunt Augusta, about there being no cucumbers, not even for ready money.

LADY BRACKNELL: It really makes no matter, Algernon. I had some crumpets[8] with Lady Harbury, who seems to me to be living entirely for pleasure now.

ALGERNON: I hear her hair has turned quite gold from grief.

LADY BRACKNELL: It certainly has changed its colour. From what cause I, of course, cannot say. *(Algernon crosses and hands tea.)* Thank you, I've quite a treat for you tonight, Algernon. I am going to send you down with Mary Farquhar. She is such a nice woman, and so attentive to her husband. It's delightful to watch them.

125 ALGERNON: I am afraid, Aunt Augusta, I shall have to give up the pleasure of dining with you tonight after all.

LADY BRACKNELL: *(frowning)* I hope not, Algernon. It would put my table completely out. Your uncle would have to dine upstairs. Fortunately he is accustomed to that.

ALGERNON: It is a great bore, and, I need hardly say, a terrible disappointment to me, but the fact is I have just had a telegram to say that my poor friend Bunbury is very ill again. *(Exchanges glances with Jack.)* They seem to think I should be with him.

LADY BRACKNELL: It is very strange. This Mr Bunbury seems to suffer from curiously bad health.

ALGERNON: Yes; poor Bunbury is a dreadful invalid.

---

8 Soft cake like a waffle, usually toasted.

130 LADY BRACKNELL: Well, I must say, Algernon, that I think it is high time
that Mr Bunbury made up his mind whether he was going to
live or to die. This shilly-shallying with the question is absurd.
Nor do I in any way approve of the modern sympathy with
invalids. I consider it morbid. Illness of any kind is hardly a
thing to be encouraged in others. Health is the primary duty of
life. I am always telling that to your poor uncle, but he never
seems to take much notice . . . as far as any improvement in his
ailments goes. I should be much obliged if you would ask Mr
Bunbury, from me, to be kind enough not to have a relapse on
Saturday, for I rely on you to arrange my music for me. It is my
last reception, and one wants something that will encourage
conversation, particularly at the end of the season when
everyone has practically said whatever they had to say, which,
in most cases, was probably not much.

ALGERNON: I'll speak to Bunbury, Aunt Augusta, if he is still conscious, and
I think I can promise you he'll be all right by Saturday. Of
course the music is a great difficulty. You see, if one plays good
music, people don't listen, and if one plays bad music people
don't talk. But I'll run over the programme I've drawn out, if
you will kindly come into the next room for a moment.

LADY BRACKNELL: Thank you, Algernon. It is very thoughtful of you. *(Rising,
and following Algernon.)* I'm sure the programme will be
delightful, after a few expurgations. French songs I cannot
possibly allow. People always seem to think that they are
improper, and either look shocked, which is vulgar, or laugh,
which is worse. But German sounds a thoroughly respectable
language, and indeed, I believe is so. Gwendolen, you will
accompany me.

GWENDOLEN: Certainly, mamma.

(Lady Bracknell and Algernon go into the music-room, Gwendolen remains behind.)

JACK: Charming day it has been, Miss Fairfax.

135 GWENDOLEN: Pray don't talk to me about the weather, Mr Worthing.
Whenever people talk to me about the weather, I always feel
quite certain that they mean something else. And that makes
me so nervous.

JACK: I do mean something else.

GWENDOLEN: I thought so. In fact, I am never wrong.

JACK: And I would like to be allowed to take advantage of Lady Bracknell's
temporary absence . . .

GWENDOLEN: I would certainly advise you to do so. Mamma has a way of
coming back suddenly into a room that I have often had to
speak to her about.

140 JACK: *(nervously)* Miss Fairfax, ever since I met you I have admired you
more than any girl . . . I have ever met since . . . I met you.

GWENDOLEN: Yes, I am quite well aware of the fact. And I often wish that in public, at any rate, you had been more demonstrative. For me you have always had an irresistible fascination. Even before I met you I was far from indifferent to you. *(Jack looks at her in amazement.)* We live, as I hope you know, Mr Worthing, in an age of ideals. The fact is constantly mentioned in the more expensive monthly magazines, and has reached the provincial pulpits, I am told; and my ideal has always been to love someone of the name of Ernest. There is something in that name that inspires absolute confidence. The moment Algernon first mentioned to me that he had a friend called Ernest, I knew I was destined to love you.

JACK: You really love me, Gwendolen?

GWENDOLEN: Passionately!

JACK: Darling! You don't know how happy you've made me.

145 GWENDOLEN: My own Ernest!

JACK: But you don't really mean to say that you couldn't love me if my name wasn't Ernest?

GWENDOLEN: But your name is Ernest.

JACK: Yes, I know it is. But supposing it was something else? Do you mean to say you couldn't love me then?

GWENDOLEN: *(glibly)* Ah! that is clearly a metaphysical speculation, and like most metaphysical speculations has very little reference at all to the actual facts of real life, as we know them.

150 JACK: Personally, darling, to speak quite candidly, I don't much care about the name of Ernest. . . . I don't think the name suits me at all.

GWENDOLEN: It suits you perfectly. It is a divine name. It has music of its own. It produces vibrations.

JACK: Well, really, Gwendolen, I must say that I think there are lots of other much nicer names. I think Jack, for instance, a charming name.

GWENDOLEN: Jack? . . . No, there is very little music in the name Jack, if any at all, indeed. It does not thrill. It produces absolutely no vibrations. . . . I have known several Jacks, and they all, without exception, were more than usually plain. Besides, Jack is a notorious domesticity for John! And I pity any woman who is married to a man called John. She would probably never be allowed to know the entrancing pleasure of a single moment's solitude. The only really safe name is Ernest.

JACK: Gwendolen, I must get christened at once—I mean we must get married at once. There is no time to be lost.

155 GWENDOLEN: Married, Mr Worthing?

JACK: *(astounded)* Well . . . surely. You know that I love you, and you led me to believe, Miss Fairfax, that you were not absolutely indifferent to me.

GWENDOLEN: I adore you. But you haven't proposed to me yet. Nothing has been said at all about marriage. The subject has not even been touched on.

JACK: Well . . . may I propose to you now?

GWENDOLEN: I think it would be an admirable opportunity. And to spare you any possible disappointment, Mr Worthing, I think it only fair to tell you quite frankly beforehand that I am fully determined to accept you.

160 JACK: Gwendolen!

GWENDOLEN: Yes, Mr Worthing, what have you got to say to me?

JACK: You know what I have got to say to you.

GWENDOLEN: Yes, but you don't say it.

JACK: Gwendolen, will you marry me? *(Goes on his knees.)*

165 GWENDOLEN: Of course I will, darling. How long you have been about it! I am afraid you have had very little experience in how to propose.

JACK: My own one, I have never loved anyone in the world but you.

GWENDOLEN: Yes, but men often propose for practice. I know my brother Gerald does. All my girl-friends tell me so. What wonderfully blue eyes you have, Ernest! They are quite, quite blue. I hope you will always look at me just like that, especially when there are other people present.

(Enter Lady Bracknell.)

LADY BRACKNELL: Mr Worthing! Rise, sir, from this semi-recumbent posture. It is most indecorous.

GWENDOLEN: Mamma! *(He tries to rise; she restrains him.)* I must beg you to retire. This is no place for you. Besides, Mr Worthing has not quite finished yet.

170 LADY BRACKNELL: Finished what, may I ask?

GWENDOLEN: I am engaged to Mr Worthing, mamma. *(They rise together.)*

LADY BRACKNELL: Pardon me, you are not engaged to anyone. When you do become engaged to some one, I, or your father, should his health permit him, will inform you of the fact. An engagement should come on a young girl as a surprise, pleasant or unpleasant, as the case may be. It is hardly a matter that she could be allowed to arrange for herself. . . . And now I have a few questions to put to you, Mr Worthing. While I am making these inquiries, you, Gwendolen, will wait for me below in the carriage.

GWENDOLEN: *(reproachfully)* Mamma!

LADY BRACKNELL: In the carriage, Gwendolen! *(Gwendolen goes to the door. She and Jack blow kisses to each other behind Lady Bracknell's back. Lady Bracknell looks vaguely about as if she could not understand what the noise was. Finally turns round.)* Gwendolen, the carriage!

175 GWENDOLEN: Yes, mamma. *(Goes out, looking back at Jack.)*

LADY BRACKNELL: *(sitting down)* You can take a seat, Mr Worthing.

(Looks in her pocket for note-book and pencil.)

JACK: Thank you, Lady Bracknell, I prefer standing.

LADY BRACKNELL: *(pencil and note-book in hand)* I feel bound to tell you that
you are not down on my list of eligible young men, although I
have the same list as the dear Duchess of Bolton has. We work
together, in fact. However, I am quite ready to enter your name,
should your answers be what a really affectionate mother
requires. Do you smoke?

JACK: Well, yes, I must admit I smoke.

180 LADY BRACKNELL: I am glad to hear it. A man should always have an
occupation of some kind. There are far too many idle men in
London as it is. How old are you?

JACK: Twenty-nine.

LADY BRACKNELL: A very good age to be married at. I have always been of
opinion that a man who desires to get married should know
either everything or nothing. Which do you know?

JACK: *(after some hesitation)* I know nothing, Lady Bracknell.

LADY BRACKNELL: I am pleased to hear it. I do not approve of anything that
tampers with natural ignorance. Ignorance is like a delicate
exotic fruit; touch it and the bloom is gone. The whole theory
of modern education is radically unsound. Fortunately in
England, at any rate, education produces no effect whatsoever.
If it did, it would prove a serious danger to the upper classes,
and probably lead to acts of violence in Grosvenor Square.[9]
What is your income?

185 JACK: Between seven and eight thousand a year.

LADY BRACKNELL: *(makes a note in her book)* In land, or in investments?

JACK: In investments, chiefly.

LADY BRACKNELL: That is satisfactory. What between the duties expected of
one during one's lifetime, and the duties[10] exacted from one
after one's death, land has ceased to be either a profit or a
pleasure. It gives one position, and prevents one from keeping it
up. That's all that can be said about land.

JACK: I have a country house with some land, of course, attached to it,
about fifteen hundred acres, I believe; but I don't depend on
that for my real income. In fact, as far as I can make out, the
poachers are the only people who make anything out of it.

190 LADY BRACKNELL: A country house! How many bedrooms? Well, that point
can be cleared up afterwards. You have a town house, I hope? A
girl with a simple, unspoiled nature, like Gwendolen, could
hardly be expected to reside in the country.

JACK: Well, I own a house in Belgrave Square, but it is let by the year to
Lady Bloxham. Of course, I can get it back whenever I like, at
six months' notice.

LADY BRACKNELL: Lady Bloxham? I don't know her.

---

[9] Fashionable area in London's Mayfair district.

[10] Taxes.

JACK: Oh, she goes about very little. She is a lady considerably advanced in years.

LADY BRACKNELL: Ah, nowadays that is no guarantee of respectability of character. What number in Belgrave Square?

195 JACK: 149.

LADY BRACKNELL: *(shaking her head)* The unfashionable side. I thought there was something. However, that could easily be altered.

JACK: Do you mean the fashion, or the side?

LADY BRACKNELL: *(sternly)* Both, if necessary, I presume. What are your politics?

JACK: Well, I am afraid I really have none. I am a Liberal Unionist.

200 LADY BRACKNELL: Oh, they count as Tories. They dine with us. Or come in the evening, at any rate. Now to minor matters. Are your parents living?

JACK: I have lost both my parents.

LADY BRACKNELL: To lose one parent, Mr Worthing, may be regarded as a misfortune; to lose both looks like carelessness. Who was your father? He was evidently a man of some wealth. Was he born in what the Radical papers call the purple of commerce,[11] or did he rise from the ranks of the aristocracy?

JACK: I am afraid I really don't know. The fact is, Lady Bracknell, I said I had lost my parents. It would be nearer the truth to say that my parents seem to have lost me. . . . I don't actually know who I am by birth. I was . . . well, I was found.

LADY BRACKNELL: Found!

205 JACK: The late Mr Thomas Cardew, an old gentleman of a very charitable and kindly disposition, found me, and gave me the name of Worthing, because he happened to have a first-class ticket for Worthing in his pocket at the time. Worthing is a place in Sussex. It is a seaside resort.

LADY BRACKNELL: Where did the charitable gentleman who had a first-class ticket for this seaside resort find you?

JACK: *(gravely)* In a hand-bag.

LADY BRACKNELL: A hand-bag?

JACK: *(very seriously)* Yes, Lady Bracknell. I was in a hand-bag—a somewhat large, black leather hand-bag, with handles to it—an ordinary hand-bag in fact.

210 LADY BRACKNELL: In what locality did this Mr James, or Thomas, Cardew come across this ordinary hand-bag?

JACK: In the cloak-room at Victoria Station. It was given to him in mistake for his own.

LADY BRACKNELL: The cloak-room at Victoria Station?

JACK: Yes. The Brighton line.

---

[11] "Born in the purple": of aristocratic birth.

LADY BRACKNELL: The line is immaterial. Mr Worthing, I confess I feel
somewhat bewildered by what you have just told me. To be
born, or at any rate bred, in a hand-bag, whether it had handles
or not, seems to me to display a contempt for the ordinary
decencies of family life that reminds one of the worst excesses
of the French Revolution. And I presume you know what that
unfortunate movement led to? As for the particular locality in
which the hand-bag was found, a cloak-room at a railway
station might serve to conceal a social indiscretion—has
probably, indeed, been used for that purpose before now—but it
could hardly be regarded as an assured basis for a recognised
position in good society.

215 JACK: May I ask you then what you would advise me to do? I need hardly
say I would do anything in the world to ensure Gwendolen's
happiness.

LADY BRACKNELL: I would strongly advise you, Mr Worthing, to try and
acquire some relations as soon as possible, and to make a
definite effort to produce at any rate one parent, of either sex,
before the season is quite over.

JACK: Well, I don't see how I could possibly manage to do that. I can
produce the hand-bag at any moment. It is in my dressing-room
at home. I really think that should satisfy you, Lady Bracknell.

LADY BRACKNELL: Me, sir! What has it to do with me? You can hardly
imagine that I and Lord Bracknell would dream of allowing our
only daughter—a girl brought up with the utmost care—to
marry into a cloak-room, and form an alliance with a parcel?
Good morning, Mr Worthing!

(Lady Bracknell sweeps out in majestic indignation.)

JACK: Good morning! *(Algernon, from the other room, strikes up the Wedding
March. Jack looks perfectly furious, and goes to the door.)* For
goodness' sake don't play that ghastly tune, Algy! How idiotic
you are!

(The music stops and Algernon enters cheerily.)

220 ALGERNON: Didn't it go off all right, old boy? You don't mean to say
Gwendolen refused you? I know it is a way she has. She is
always refusing people. I think it is most ill-natured of her.

JACK: Oh, Gwendolen is as right as a trivet.[12] As far as she is concerned, we
are engaged. Her mother is perfectly unbearable. Never met
such a Gorgon. . . . I don't really know what a Gorgon is like,
but I am quite sure that Lady Bracknell is one. In any case, she
is a monster, without being a myth, which is rather unfair. . . . I

---

[12] Three- or four-legged stand for a hot pot or a teapot. The allusion is that it must be level
and standing firmly on its legs ("right").

beg your pardon, Algy, I suppose I shouldn't talk about your own aunt in that way before you.

ALGERNON: My dear boy, I love hearing my relations abused. It is the only thing that makes me put up with them at all. Relations are simply a tedious pack of people, who haven't got the remotest knowledge of how to live, nor the smallest instinct about when to die.

JACK: Oh, that is nonsense!

ALGERNON: It isn't!

225 JACK: Well, I won't argue about the matter. You always want to argue about things.

ALGERNON: That is exactly what things were originally made for.

JACK: Upon my word, if I thought that, I'd shoot myself. . . . (A pause.) You don't think there is any chance of Gwendolen becoming like her mother in about a hundred and fifty years, do you, Algy?

ALGERNON: All women become like their mothers. That is their tragedy. No man does. That's his.

JACK: Is that clever?

230 ALGERNON: It is perfectly phrased! and quite as true as any observation in civilised life should be.

JACK: I am sick to death of cleverness. Everybody is clever nowadays. You can't go anywhere without meeting clever people. The thing has become an absolute public nuisance. I wish to goodness we had a few fools left.

ALGERNON: We have.

JACK: I should extremely like to meet them. What do they talk about?

ALGERNON: The fools? Oh! about the clever people, of course.

235 JACK: What fools!

ALGERNON: By the way, did you tell Gwendolen the truth about your being Ernest in town, and Jack in the country?

JACK: (in a very patronizing manner) My dear fellow, the truth isn't quite the sort of thing one tells to a nice, sweet, refined girl. What extraordinary ideas you have about the way to behave to a woman!

ALGERNON: The only way to behave to a woman is to make love to her, if she is pretty, and to someone else, if she is plain.

JACK: Oh, that is nonsense.

240 ALGERNON: What about your brother? What about the profligate Ernest?

JACK: Oh, before the end of the week I shall have got rid of him. I'll say he died in Paris of apoplexy. Lots of people die of apoplexy, quite suddenly, don't they?

ALGERNON: Yes, but it's hereditary, my dear fellow. It's a sort of thing that runs in families. You had much better say a severe chill.

JACK: You are sure a severe chill isn't hereditary, or anything of that kind?

ALGERNON: Of course it isn't!

245 JACK: Very well, then. My poor brother Ernest is carried off suddenly, in
        Paris, by a severe chill. That gets rid of him.

ALGERNON: But I thought you said that . . . Miss Cardew was a little too
        much interested in your poor brother Ernest? Won't she feel his
        loss a good deal?

JACK: Oh, that is all right. Cecily is not a silly romantic girl, I am glad to
        say. She has got a capital appetite, goes on long walks, and pays
        no attention at all to her lessons.

ALGERNON: I would rather like to see Cecily.

JACK: I will take very good care you never do. She is excessively pretty, and
        she is only just eighteen.

250 ALGERNON: Have you told Gwendolen yet that you have an excessively
        pretty ward who is only just eighteen?

JACK: Oh! one doesn't blurt these things out to people. Cecily and
        Gwendolen are perfectly certain to be extremely great friends.
        I'll bet you anything you like that half an hour after they have
        met, they will be calling each other sister.

ALGERNON: Women only do that when they have called each other a lot of
        other things first. Now, my dear boy, if we want to get a good
        table at Willis's, we really must go and dress. Do you know it is
        nearly seven?

JACK: *(irritably)* Oh! it always is nearly seven.

ALGERNON: Well, I'm hungry.

255 JACK: I never knew you when you weren't. . . .

ALGERNON: What shall we do after dinner? Go to a theatre?

JACK: Oh no! I loathe listening.

ALGERNON: Well, let us go to the Club?

JACK: Oh, no! I hate talking.

260 ALGERNON: Well, we might trot round to the Empire[13] at ten?

JACK: Oh, no! I can't bear looking at things. It is so silly.

ALGERNON: Well, what shall we do?

JACK: Nothing!

ALGERNON: It is awfully hard work doing nothing. However, I don't mind
        hard work where there is no definite object of any kind.

(Enter Lane.)

265 LANE: Miss Fairfax.

(Enter Gwendolen. Lane goes out.)

ALGERNON: Gwendolen, upon my word!

GWENDOLEN: Algy, kindly turn your back. I have something very particular
        to say to Mr Worthing.

---

[13] A music hall in Leicester Square, London, featuring acrobatics and burlesque ballet.

Algernon: Really, Gwendolen, I don't think I can allow this at all.

Gwendolen: Algy, you always adopt a strictly immoral attitude towards life. You are not quite old enough to do that. *(Algernon retires to the fireplace.)*

270 Jack: My own darling!

Gwendolen: Ernest, we may never be married. From the expression on mamma's face I fear we never shall. Few parents nowadays pay any regard to what their children say to them. The old-fashioned respect for the young is fast dying out. Whatever influence I ever had over mamma, I lost at the age of three. But although she may prevent us from becoming man and wife, and I may marry someone else, and marry often, nothing that she can possibly do can alter my eternal devotion to you.

Jack: Dear Gwendolen!

Gwendolen: The story of your romantic origin, as related to me by mamma, with unpleasing comments, has naturally stirred the deeper fibres of my nature. Your Christian name has an irresistible fascination. The simplicity of your character makes you exquisitely incomprehensible to me. Your town address at the Albany I have. What is your address in the country?

Jack: The Manor House, Woolton, Hertfordshire.

(Algernon, who has been carefully listening, smiles to himself, and writes the address on his shirt-cuff. Then picks up the Railway Guide.)

275 Gwendolen: There is a good postal service, I suppose? It may be necessary to do something desperate. That of course will require serious consideration. I will communicate with you daily.

Jack: My own one!

Gwendolen: How long do you remain in town?

Jack: Till Monday.

Gwendolen: Good! Algy, you may turn round now.

280 Algernon: Thanks, I've turned round already.

Gwendolen: You may also ring the bell.

Jack: You will let me see you to your carriage, my own darling?

Gwendolen: Certainly.

Jack: *(to Lane, who now enters)* I will see Miss Fairfax out.

285 Lane: Yes, sir. *(Jack and Gwendolen go off.)*

(Lane presents several letters on a salver, to Algernon. It is to be surmised that they are bills, as Algernon, after looking at the envelopes, tears them up.)

Algernon: A glass of sherry, Lane.

Lane: Yes, sir.

Algernon: Tomorrow, Lane, I'm going Bunburying.

Lane: Yes, sir.

290 Algernon: I shall probably not be back till Monday. You can put up my dress clothes, my smoking jacket, and all the Bunbury suits . . .

Lane: Yes, sir. *(Handing sherry.)*

ALGERNON: I hope tomorrow will be a fine day, Lane.

LANE: It never is, sir.

ALGERNON: Lane, you're a perfect pessimist.

295 LANE: I do my best to give satisfaction, sir.

(Enter Jack. Lane goes off.)

JACK: There's a sensible, intellectual girl! the only girl I ever cared for in my
life. *(Algernon is laughing immoderately.)* What on earth are you
so amused at?

ALGERNON: Oh, I'm a little anxious about poor Bunbury, that is all.

JACK: If you don't take care, your friend Bunbury will get you into a serious
scrape some day.

ALGERNON: I love scrapes. They are the only things that are never serious.

300 JACK: Oh, that's nonsense, Algy. You never talk anything but nonsense.

ALGERNON: Nobody ever does.

*(Jack looks indignantly at him, and leaves the room. Algernon lights a cigarette,
reads his shirt-cuff, and smiles.)*

Act Drop

SECOND ACT

SCENE *Garden at the Manor House. A flight of grey stone steps leads up to
the house. The garden, an old-fashioned one, full of roses. Time of year,
July. Basket chairs, and a table covered with books, are set under a large
yew-tree.*

(Miss Prism discovered seated at the table. Cecily is at the back watering flowers.)

MISS PRISM: *(calling)* Cecily, Cecily! Surely such a utilitarian occupation as
the watering of flowers is rather Moulton's duty than yours?
Especially at a moment when intellectual pleasures await you.
Your German grammar is on the table. Pray open it at page
fifteen. We will repeat yesterday's lesson.

CECILY: *(coming over very slowly)* But I don't like German. It isn't at all a
becoming language. I know perfectly well that I look quite plain
after my German lesson.

MISS PRISM: Child, you know how anxious your guardian is that you
should improve yourself in every way. He laid particular stress
on your German, as he was leaving for town yesterday. Indeed,
he always lays stress on your German when he is leaving for
town.

CECILY: Dear Uncle Jack is so very serious! Sometimes he is so serious that I
think he cannot be quite well.

5 MISS PRISM: *(drawing herself up)* Your guardian enjoys the best of health,
and his gravity of demeanour is especially to be commended in
one so comparatively young as he is. I know no one who has a
higher sense of duty and responsibility.

CECILY: I suppose that is why he often looks a little bored when we three are together.

MISS PRISM: Cecily! I am surprised at you. Mr Worthing has many troubles in his life. Idle merriment and triviality would be out of place in his conversation. You must remember his constant anxiety about that unfortunate young man his brother.

CECILY: I wish Uncle Jack would allow that unfortunate young man, his brother, to come down here sometimes. We might have a good influence over him, Miss Prism. I am sure you certainly would. You know German, and geology, and things of that kind influence a man very much. *(Cecily begins to write in her diary.)*

MISS PRISM: *(shaking her head)* I do not think that even I could produce any effect on a character that according to his own brother's admission is irretrievably weak and vacillating. Indeed I am not sure that I would desire to reclaim him. I am not in favour of this modern mania for turning bad people into good people at a moment's notice. As a man sows so let him reap. You must put away your diary, Cecily. I really don't see why you should keep a diary at all.

10 CECILY: I keep a diary in order to enter the wonderful secrets of my life. If I didn't write them down, I should probably forget all about them.

MISS PRISM: Memory, my dear Cecily, is the diary that we all carry about with us.

CECILY: Yes, but it usually chronicles the things that have never happened, and couldn't possibly have happened. I believe that Memory is responsible for nearly all the three-volume novels that Mudie[1] sends us.

MISS PRISM: Do not speak slightingly of the three-volume novel, Cecily. I wrote one myself in earlier days.

CECILY: Did you really, Miss Prism? How wonderfully clever you are! I hope it did not end happily? I don't like novels that end happily. They depress me so much.

15 MISS PRISM: The good ended happily, and the bad unhappily. That is what Fiction means.

CECILY: I suppose so. But it seems very unfair. And was your novel ever published?

MISS PRISM: Alas! no. The manuscript unfortunately was abandoned. *(Cecily starts.)* I use the word in the sense of lost or mislaid. To your work, child, these speculations are profitless.

CECILY: *(smiling)* But I see dear Dr Chasuble coming up through the garden.

MISS PRISM: *(rising and advancing)* Dr Chasuble! This is indeed a pleasure.

(Enter Canon Chasuble.)

---

[1] Well-known circulating library and bookstore.

20 CHASUBLE: And how are we this morning? Miss Prism, you are, I trust, well?

CECILY: Miss Prism has just been complaining of a slight headache. I think it would do her so much good to have a short stroll with you in the Park, Dr Chasuble.

MISS PRISM: Cecily, I have not mentioned anything about a headache.

CECILY: No, dear Miss Prism, I know that, but I felt instinctively that you had a headache. Indeed I was thinking about that, and not about my German lesson, when the Rector came in.

CHASUBLE: I hope, Cecily, you are not inattentive.

25 CECILY: Oh, I am afraid I am.

CHASUBLE: That is strange. Were I fortunate enough to be Miss Prism's pupil, I would hang upon her lips. *(Miss Prism glares.)* I spoke metaphorically.—My metaphor was drawn from bees. Ahem! Mr Worthing, I suppose, has not returned from town yet?

MISS PRISM: We do not expect him till Monday afternoon.

CHASUBLE: Ah yes, he usually likes to spend his Sunday in London. He is not one of those whose sole aim is enjoyment, as, by all accounts, that unfortunate young man his brother seems to be. But I must not disturb Egeria[2] and her pupil any longer.

MISS PRISM: Egeria? My name is Laetitia, Doctor.

30 CHASUBLE: *(bowing)* A classical allusion merely, drawn from the Pagan authors. I shall see you both no doubt at Evensong?

MISS PRISM: I think, dear Doctor, I will have a stroll with you. I find I have a headache after all, and a walk might do it good.

CHASUBLE: With pleasure, Miss Prism, with pleasure. We might go as far as the schools and back.

MISS PRISM: That would be delightful. Cecily, you will read your Political Economy in my absence. The chapter on the Fall of the Rupee[3] you may omit. It is somewhat too sensational. Even these metallic problems have their melodramatic side.

(Goes down the garden with Dr Chasuble.)

CECILY: *(picks up books and throws them back on table)* Horrid Political Economy! Horrid Geography! Horrid, horrid German!

(Enter Merriman with a card on a salver.)

35 MERRIMAN: Mr Ernest Worthing has just driven over from the station. He has brought his luggage with him.

CECILY: *(takes the card and reads it)* "Mr Ernest Worthing, B.4, The Albany, W." Uncle Jack's brother! Did you tell him Mr Worthing was in town?

---

[2] In Roman mythology, a nymph who was the wife and instructor of a Roman king and who was transformed into a fountain at his death.

[3] The basic unit of money in India and Pakistan, part of the British Empire in Wilde's time.

MERRIMAN: Yes, Miss. He seemed very much disappointed. I mentioned that you and Miss Prism were in the garden. He said he was anxious to speak to you privately for a moment.

CECILY: Ask Mr Ernest Worthing to come here. I suppose you had better talk to the housekeeper about a room for him.

MERRIMAN: Yes, Miss. *(Merriman goes off.)*

40   CECILY: I have never met any really wicked person before. I feel rather frightened. I am so afraid he will look just like every one else.

(Enter Algernon, very gay and debonair.)

He does!

ALGERNON: *(raising his hat)* You are my little cousin Cecily, I'm sure.

CECILY: You are under some strange mistake. I am not little. In fact, I believe I am more than usually tall for my age. *(Algernon is rather taken aback.)* But I am your cousin Cecily. You, I see from your card, are Uncle Jack's brother, my cousin Ernest, my wicked cousin Ernest.

ALGERNON: Oh! I am not really wicked at all, Cousin Cecily. You mustn't think that I am wicked.

CECILY: If you are not, then you have certainly been deceiving us all in a very inexcusable manner. I hope you have not been leading a double life, pretending to be wicked and being really good all the time. That would be hypocrisy.

45   ALGERNON: *(looks at her in amazement)* Oh! Of course I have been rather reckless.

CECILY: I am glad to hear it.

ALGERNON: In fact, now you mention the subject, I have been very bad in my own small way.

CECILY: I don't think you should be so proud of that, though I am sure it must have been very pleasant.

ALGERNON: It is much pleasanter being here with you.

50   CECILY: I can't understand how you are here at all. Uncle Jack won't be back till Monday afternoon.

ALGERNON: That is a great disappointment. I am obliged to go up by the first train on Monday morning. I have a business appointment that I am anxious . . . to miss!

CECILY: Couldn't you miss it anywhere but in London?

ALGERNON: No: the appointment is in London.

CECILY: Well, I know, of course, how important it is not to keep a business engagement, if one wants to retain any sense of the beauty of life, but still I think you had better wait till Uncle Jack arrives. I know he wants to speak to you about your emigrating.

55   ALGERNON: About my what?

CECILY: Your emigrating. He has gone up to buy your outfit.

ALGERNON: I certainly wouldn't let Jack buy my outfit. He has no taste in neckties at all.

CECILY: I don't think you will require neckties. Uncle Jack is sending you to
 Australia.

ALGERNON: Australia! I'd sooner die.

60 CECILY: Well, he said at dinner on Wednesday night, that you would have
 to choose between this world, the next world, and Australia.

ALGERNON: Oh, well! The accounts I have received of Australia and the next
 world are not particularly encouraging. This world is good
 enough for me, Cousin Cecily.

CECILY: Yes, but are you good enough for it?

ALGERNON: I'm afraid I'm not that. That is why I want you to reform me.
 You might make that your mission, if you don't mind, Cousin
 Cecily.

CECILY: I'm afraid I've no time, this afternoon.

65 ALGERNON: Well, would you mind my reforming myself this afternoon?

CECILY: It is rather Quixotic of you. But I think you should try.

ALGERNON: I will. I feel better already.

CECILY: You are looking a little worse.

ALGERNON: That is because I am hungry.

70 CECILY: How thoughtless of me. I should have remembered that when one
 is going to lead an entirely new life, one requires regular and
 wholesome meals. Won't you come in?

ALGERNON: Thank you. Might I have a buttonhole[4] first? I never have any
 appetite unless I have a buttonhole first.

CECILY: A Maréchal Niel?[5] *(Picks up scissors.)*

ALGERNON: No, I'd sooner have a pink rose.

CECILY: Why? *(Cuts a flower.)*

75 ALGERNON: Because you are like a pink rose, Cousin Cecily.

CECILY: I don't think it can be right for you to talk to me like that. Miss
 Prism never says such things to me.

ALGERNON: Then Miss Prism is a short-sighted old lady. *(Cecily puts the rose
 in his buttonhole.)* You are the prettiest girl I ever saw.

CECILY: Miss Prism says that all good looks are a snare.

ALGERNON: They are a snare that every sensible man would like to be
 caught in.

80 CECILY: Oh, I don't think I would care to catch a sensible man. I shouldn't
 know what to talk to him about.

(They pass into the house. Miss Prism and Dr Chasuble return.)

MISS PRISM: You are too much alone, dear Dr Chasuble. You should get
 married. A misanthrope I can understand—a woman-thrope,
 never!

---

[4] Flower worn on a jacket lapel.

[5] Exotic breed of yellow rose.

CHASUBLE: *(with a scholar's shudder)* Believe me, I do not deserve so neologistic a phrase. The precept as well as the practice of the Primitive Church was distinctly against matrimony.

MISS PRISM: *(sententiously)* That is obviously the reason why the Primitive Church has not lasted up to the present day. And you do not seem to realize, dear Doctor, that by persistently remaining single, a man converts himself into a permanent public temptation. Men should be more careful; this very celibacy leads weaker vessels astray.

CHASUBLE: But is a man not equally attractive when married?

85 MISS PRISM: No married man is ever attractive except to his wife.

CHASUBLE: And often, I've been told, not even to her.

MISS PRISM: That depends on the intellectual sympathies of the woman. Maturity can always be depended on. Ripeness can be trusted. Young women are green. *(Dr Chasuble starts.)* I spoke horticulturally. My metaphor was drawn from fruits. But where is Cecily?

CHASUBLE: Perhaps she followed us to the schools.

(Enter Jack slowly from the back of the garden. He is dressed in the deepest mourning, with crape hatband and black gloves.)

MISS PRISM: Mr Worthing!

90 DR CHASUBLE: Mr Worthing?

MISS PRISM: This is indeed a surprise. We did not look for you till Monday afternoon.

JACK: *(shakes Miss Prism's hand in a tragic manner)* I have returned sooner than I expected. Dr Chasuble, I hope you are well?

CHASUBLE: Dear Mr Worthing, I trust this garb of woe does not betoken some terrible calamity?

JACK: My brother.

95 MISS PRISM: More shameful debts and extravagance?

CHASUBLE: Still leading his life of pleasure?

JACK: *(shaking his head)* Dead!

CHASUBLE: Your brother Ernest dead?

JACK: Quite dead.

100 MISS PRISM: What a lesson for him! I trust he will profit by it.

CHASUBLE: Mr Worthing, I offer you my sincere condolence. You have at least the consolation of knowing that you were always the most generous and forgiving of brothers.

JACK: Poor Ernest! He had many faults, but it is a sad, sad blow.

CHASUBLE: Very sad indeed. Were you with him at the end?

JACK: No. He died abroad; in Paris, in fact. I had a telegram last night from the manager of the Grand Hotel.

105 CHASUBLE: Was the cause of death mentioned?

JACK: A severe chill, it seems.

MISS PRISM: As a man sows, so shall he reap.

CHASUBLE: *(raising his hand)* Charity, dear Miss Prism, charity! None of us are perfect. I myself am peculiarly susceptible to draughts. Will the interment take place here?

JACK: No. He seems to have expressed a desire to be buried in Paris.

110 CHASUBLE: In Paris! *(Shakes his head.)* I fear that hardly points to any very serious state of mind at the last. You would no doubt wish me to make some slight allusion to this tragic domestic affliction next Sunday. *(Jack presses his hand convulsively.)* My sermon on the meaning of the manna in the wilderness can be adapted to almost any occasion, joyful, or, as in the present case, distressing. *(All sigh.)* I have preached it at harvest celebrations, christenings, confirmations, on days of humiliation and festal days. The last time I delivered it was in the Cathedral, as a charity sermon on behalf of the Society for the Prevention of Discontent among the Upper Orders. The Bishop, who was present, was much struck by some of the analogies I drew.

JACK: Ah! that reminds me, you mentioned christenings I think, Dr Chasuble? I suppose you know how to christen all right? *(Dr Chasuble looks astounded.)* I mean, of course, you are continually christening, aren't you?

MISS PRISM: It is, I regret to say, one of the Rector's most constant duties in this parish. I have often spoken to the poorer classes on the subject. But they don't seem to know what thrift is.

CHASUBLE: But is there any particular infant in whom you are interested, Mr Worthing? Your brother was, I believe, unmarried, was he not?

JACK: Oh, yes.

115 MISS PRISM: *(bitterly)* People who live entirely for pleasure usually are.

JACK: But it is not for any child, dear Doctor. I am very fond of children. No! the fact is, I would like to be christened myself, this afternoon, if you have nothing better to do.

CHASUBLE: But surely, Mr Worthing, you have been christened already?

JACK: I don't remember anything about it.

CHASUBLE: But have you any grave doubts on the subject?

120 JACK: I certainly intend to have. Of course I don't know if the thing would bother you in any way, or if you think I am a little too old now.

CHASUBLE: Not at all. The sprinkling, and, indeed, the immersion of adults is a perfectly canonical practice.

JACK: Immersion!

CHASUBLE: You need have no apprehensions. Sprinkling is all that is necessary, or indeed I think advisable. Our weather is so changeable. At what hour would you wish the ceremony performed?

JACK: Oh, I might trot round about five if that would suit you.

125 CHASUBLE: Perfectly, perfectly! In fact I have two similar ceremonies to perform at that time. A case of twins that occurred recently in

> one of the outlying cottages on your own estate. Poor Jenkins the carter, a most hard-working man.

JACK: Oh! I don't see much fun in being christened along with other babies. It would be childish. Would half-past five do?

CHASUBLE: Admirably! Admirably! *(Takes out watch.)* And now, dear Mr Worthing, I will not intrude any longer into a house of sorrow. I would merely beg you not to be too much bowed down by grief. What seem to us bitter trials are often blessings in disguise.

MISS PRISM: This seems to me a blessing of an extremely obvious kind.

(Enter Cecily from the house.)

CECILY: Uncle Jack! Oh, I am pleased to see you back. But what horrid clothes you have got on! Do go and change them.

130 MISS PRISM: Cecily!

CHASUBLE: My child! my child! *(Cecily goes towards Jack; he kisses her brow in a melancholy manner.)*

CECILY: What is the matter, Uncle Jack? Do look happy! You look as if you had toothache, and I have got such a surprise for you. Who do you think is in the dining-room? Your brother!

JACK: Who?

CECILY: Your brother Ernest. He arrived about half an hour ago.

135 JACK: What nonsense! I haven't got a brother.

CECILY: Oh, don't say that. However badly he may have behaved to you in the past he is still your brother. You couldn't be so heartless as to disown him. I'll tell him to come out. And you will shake hands with him, won't you, Uncle Jack? *(Runs back into the house.)*

CHASUBLE: These are very joyful tidings.

MISS PRISM: After we had all been resigned to his loss, his sudden return seems to me peculiarly distressing.

JACK: My brother is in the dining-room? I don't know what it all means. I think it is perfectly absurd.

(Enter Algernon and Cecily hand in hand. They come slowly up to Jack.)

140 JACK: Good heavens! *(Motions Algernon away.)*

ALGERNON: Brother John, I have come down from town to tell you that I am very sorry for all the trouble I have given you, and that I intend to lead a better life in the future. *(Jack glares at him and does not take his hand.)*

CECILY: Uncle Jack, you are not going to refuse your own brother's hand?

JACK: Nothing will induce me to take his hand. I think his coming down here disgraceful. He knows perfectly well why.

CECILY: Uncle Jack, do be nice. There is some good in everyone. Ernest has just been telling me about his poor invalid friend Mr Bunbury whom he goes to visit so often. And surely there must be much

good in one who is kind to an invalid, and leaves the pleasures
of London to sit by a bed of pain.

145 JACK: Oh! he has been talking about Bunbury, has he?

CECILY: Yes, he has told me all about poor Mr Bunbury, and his terrible
state of health.

JACK: Bunbury! Well, I won't have him talk to you about Bunbury or about
anything else. It is enough to drive one perfectly frantic.

ALGERNON: Of course I admit that the faults were all on my side. But I must
say that I think that Brother John's coldness to me is peculiarly
painful. I expected a more enthusiastic welcome, especially
considering it is the first time I have come here.

CECILY: Uncle Jack, if you don't shake hands with Ernest I will never
forgive you.

150 JACK: Never forgive me?

CECILY: Never, never, never!

JACK: Well, this is the last time I shall ever do it. *(Shakes hands with
Algernon and glares.)*

CHASUBLE: It's pleasant, is it not, to see so perfect a reconciliation? I think
we might leave the two brothers together.

MISS PRISM: Cecily, you will come with us.

155 CECILY: Certainly, Miss Prism. My little task of reconciliation is over.

CHASUBLE: You have done a beautiful action today, dear child.

MISS PRISM: We must not be premature in our judgments.

CECILY: I feel very happy. *(They all go off except Jack and Algernon.)*

JACK: You young scoundrel, Algy, you must get out of this place as soon as
possible. I don't allow any Bunburying here.

(Enter Merriman.)

160 MERRIMAN: I have put Mr Ernest's things in the room next to yours, sir. I
suppose that is all right?

JACK: What?

MERRIMAN: Mr Ernest's luggage, sir. I have unpacked it and put it in the
room next to your own.

JACK: His luggage?

MERRIMAN: Yes, sir. Three portmanteaus, a dressing-case, two hat-boxes,
and a large luncheon-basket.

165 ALGERNON: I am afraid I can't stay more than a week this time.

JACK: Merriman, order the dog-cart[6] at once. Mr Ernest has been suddenly
called back to town.

MERRIMAN: Yes, sir. *(Goes back into the house.)*

ALGERNON: What a fearful liar you are, Jack. I have not been called back to
town at all.

JACK: Yes, you have.

---

[6] Small two-wheeled cart with two seats, often including a box for transporting hunting
dogs.

170   ALGERNON: I haven't heard anyone call me.

JACK: Your duty as a gentleman calls you back.

ALGERNON: My duty as a gentleman has never interfered with my pleasures
in the smallest degree.

JACK: I can quite understand that.

ALGERNON: Well, Cecily is a darling.

175   JACK: You are not to talk of Miss Cardew like that. I don't like it.

ALGERNON: Well, I don't like your clothes. You look perfectly ridiculous in
them. Why on earth don't you go up and change? It is perfectly
childish to be in deep mourning for a man who is actually
staying for a whole week with you in your house as a guest. I
call it grotesque.

JACK: You are certainly not staying with me for a whole week as a guest or
anything else. You have got to leave . . . by the four-five train.

ALGERNON: I certainly won't leave you so long as you are in mourning. It
would be most unfriendly. If I were in mourning you would stay
with me, I suppose. I should think it very unkind if you didn't.

JACK: Well, will you go if I change my clothes?

180   ALGERNON: Yes, if you are not too long. I never saw anybody take so long
to dress, and with such little result.

JACK: Well, at any rate, that is better than being always over-dressed as you
are.

ALGERNON: If I am occasionally a little over-dressed, I make up for it by
being always immensely over-educated.

JACK: Your vanity is ridiculous, your conduct an outrage, and your presence
in my garden utterly absurd. However, you have got to catch
the four-five, and I hope you will have a pleasant journey back
to town. This Bunburying, as you call it, has not been a great
success for you.

(Goes into the house.)

ALGERNON: I think it has been a great success. I'm in love with Cecily, and
that is everything.

*(Enter Cecily at the back of the garden. She picks up the can and begins to water
the flowers.)*

But I must see her before I go, and make arrangements for
another Bunbury. Ah, there she is.

185   CECILY: Oh, I merely came back to water the roses. I thought you were
with Uncle Jack.

ALGERNON: He's gone to order the dog-cart for me.

CECILY: Oh, is he going to take you for a nice drive?

ALGERNON: He's going to send me away.

CECILY: Then have we got to part?

190   ALGERNON: I am afraid so. It's a very painful parting.

CECILY: It is always painful to part from people whom one has known for a very brief space of time. The absence of old friends one can endure with equanimity. But even a momentary separation from any one to whom one has just been introduced is almost unbearable.

ALGERNON: Thank you.

(Enter Merriman.)

MERRIMAN: The dog-cart is at the door, sir.

(Algernon looks appealingly at Cecily.)

CECILY: It can wait, Merriman . . . for . . . five minutes.

195 MERRIMAN: Yes, Miss.

(Exit Merriman.)

ALGERNON: I hope, Cecily, I shall not offend you if I state quite frankly and openly that you seem to me to be in every way the visible personification of absolute perfection.

CECILY: I think your frankness does you great credit, Ernest. If you will allow me, I will copy your remarks into my diary. *(Goes over to table and begins writing in diary.)*

ALGERNON: Do you really keep a diary? I'd give anything to look at it. May I?

CECILY: Oh no. *(Puts her hand over it.)* You see, it is simply a very young girl's record of her own thoughts and impressions, and consequently meant for publication. When it appears in volume form I hope you will order a copy. But pray, Ernest, don't stop. I delight in taking down from dictation. I have reached "absolute perfection." You can go on. I am quite ready for more.

200 ALGERNON: *(somewhat taken aback)* Ahem! Ahem!

CECILY: Oh, don't cough, Ernest. When one is dictating one should speak fluently and not cough. Besides, I don't know how to spell a cough. *(Writes as Algernon speaks.)*

ALGERNON: *(speaking very rapidly)* Cecily, ever since I first looked upon your wonderful and incomparable beauty, I have dared to love you wildly, passionately, devotedly, hopelessly.

CECILY: I don't think that you should tell me that you love me wildly, passionately, devotedly, hopelessly. Hopelessly doesn't seem to make much sense, does it?

ALGERNON: Cecily!

(Enter Merriman.)

205 MERRIMAN: The dog-cart is waiting, sir.

ALGERNON: Tell it to come round next week, at the same hour.

MERRIMAN: *(looks at Cecily, who makes no sign)* Yes, sir.

(Merriman retires.)

CECILY: Uncle Jack would be very much annoyed if he knew you were staying on till next week, at the same hour.

ALGERNON: Oh, I don't care about Jack. I don't care for anybody in the whole world but you. I love you, Cecily. You will marry me, won't you?

210 CECILY: You silly boy! Of course. Why, we have been engaged for the last three months.

ALGERNON: For the last three months?

CECILY: Yes, it will be exactly three months on Thursday.

ALGERNON: But how did we become engaged?

CECILY: Well, ever since dear Uncle Jack first confessed to us that he had a younger brother who was very wicked and bad, you of course have formed the chief topic of conversation between myself and Miss Prism. And of course a man who is much talked about is always very attractive. One feels there must be something in him, after all. I daresay it was foolish of me, but I fell in love with you, Ernest.

215 ALGERNON: Darling! And when was the engagement actually settled?

CECILY: On the 14th of February last. Worn out by your entire ignorance of my existence, I determined to end the matter one way or the other, and after a long struggle with myself I accepted you under this dear old tree here. The next day I bought this little ring in your name, and this is the little bangle with the true lover's knot I promised you always to wear.

ALGERNON: Did I give you this? It's very pretty, isn't it?

CECILY: Yes, you've wonderfully good taste, Ernest. It's the excuse I've always given for your leading such a bad life. And this is the box in which I keep all your dear letters. *(Kneels at table, opens box, and produces letters tied up with blue ribbon.)*

ALGERNON: My letters! But, my own sweet Cecily, I have never written you any letters.

220 CECILY: You need hardly remind me of that, Ernest. I remember only too well that I was forced to write your letters for you. I wrote always three times a week, and sometimes oftener.

ALGERNON: Oh, do let me read them, Cecily?

CECILY: Oh, I couldn't possibly. They would make you far too conceited. *(Replaces box.)* The three you wrote me after I had broken off the engagement are so beautiful, and so badly spelled, that even now I can hardly read them without crying a little.

ALGERNON: But was our engagement ever broken off?

CECILY: Of course it was. On the 22nd of last March. You can see the entry if you like. *(Shows diary.)* "Today I broke off my engagement with Ernest. I feel it is better to do so. The weather still continues charming."

225 ALGERNON: But why on earth did you break it off? What had I done? I had
     done nothing at all. Cecily, I am very much hurt indeed to hear
     you broke it off. Particularly when the weather was so
     charming.

CECILY: It would hardly have been a really serious engagement if it hadn't
     been broken off at least once. But I forgave you before the week
     was out.

ALGERNON: *(crossing to her, and kneeling)* What a perfect angel you are,
     Cecily.

CECILY: You dear romantic boy. *(He kisses her, she puts her fingers through his
     hair.)* I hope your hair curls naturally, does it?

ALGERNON: Yes, darling, with a little help from others.

230 CECILY: I am so glad.

ALGERNON: You'll never break off our engagement again, Cecily?

CECILY: I don't think I could break it off now that I have actually met you.
     Besides, of course, there is the question of your name.

ALGERNON: Yes, of course. *(Nervously.)*

CECILY: You must not laugh at me, darling, but it had always been a girlish
     dream of mine to love some one whose name was Ernest.
     (Algernon rises, Cecily also.) There is something in that name that
     seems to inspire absolute confidence. I pity any poor married
     woman whose husband is not called Ernest.

235 ALGERNON: But, my dear child, do you mean to say you could not love me
     if I had some other name?

CECILY: But what name?

ALGERNON: Oh, any name you like—Algernon—for instance . . .

CECILY: But I don't like the name of Algernon.

ALGERNON: Well, my own dear, sweet, loving little darling, I really can't see
     why you should object to the name of Algernon. It is not at all
     a bad name. In fact, it is rather an aristocratic name. Half of the
     chaps who get into the Bankruptcy Court are called Algernon.
     But seriously, Cecily . . . *(moving to her)* . . . if my name was
     Algy, couldn't you love me?

240 CECILY: *(rising)* I might respect you, Ernest, I might admire your character,
     but I fear that I should not be able to give you my undivided
     attention.

ALGERNON: Ahem! Cecily! *(Picking up hat.)* Your Rector here is, I suppose,
     thoroughly experienced in the practice of all the rites and
     ceremonials of the Church?

CECILY: Oh, yes, Dr Chasuble is a most learned man. He has never written
     a single book, so you can imagine how much he knows.

ALGERNON: I must see him at once on a most important christening—I
     mean on most important business.

CECILY: Oh!

245 ALGERNON: I shan't be away more than half an hour.

CECILY: Considering that we have been engaged since February the 14th, and that I only met you today for the first time, I think it is rather hard that you should leave me for so long a period as half an hour. Couldn't you make it twenty minutes?

ALGERNON: I'll be back in no time. (*Kisses her and rushes down the garden.*)

CECILY: What an impetuous boy he is! I like his hair so much. I must enter his proposal in my diary.

(*Enter Merriman.*)

MERRIMAN: A Miss Fairfax has just called to see Mr Worthing. On very important business, Miss Fairfax states.

250 CECILY: Isn't Mr Worthing in his library?

MERRIMAN: Mr Worthing went over in the direction of the Rectory some time ago.

CECILY: Pray ask the lady to come out here; Mr Worthing is sure to be back soon. And you can bring tea.

MERRIMAN: Yes, Miss.

(*Goes out.*)

CECILY: Miss Fairfax! I suppose one of the many good elderly women who are associated with Uncle Jack in some of his philanthropic work in London. I don't quite like women who are interested in philanthropic work. I think it is so forward of them.

(*Enter Merriman.*)

255 MERRIMAN: Miss Fairfax.

(*Enter Gwendolen. Exit Merriman.*)

CECILY: (*advancing to meet her*) Pray let me introduce myself to you. My name is Cecily Cardew.

GWENDOLEN: Cecily Cardew? (*Moving to her and shaking hands.*) What a very sweet name! Something tells me that we are going to be great friends. I like you already more than I can say. My first impressions of people are never wrong.

CECILY: How nice of you to like me so much after we have known each other such a comparatively short time. Pray sit down.

GWENDOLEN: (*still standing up*) I may call you Cecily, may I not?

260 CECILY: With pleasure!

GWENDOLEN: And you will always call me Gwendolen, won't you?

CECILY: If you wish.

GWENDOLEN: Then that is all quite settled, is it not?

CECILY: I hope so. (*A pause. They both sit down together.*)

265 GWENDOLEN: Perhaps this might be a favourable opportunity for my mentioning who I am. My father is Lord Bracknell. You have never heard of papa, I suppose?

CECILY: I don't think so.

GWENDOLEN: Outside the family circle, papa, I am glad to say, is entirely
    unknown. I think that is quite as it should be. The home seems
    to me to be the proper sphere for the man. And certainly once a
    man begins to neglect his domestic duties he becomes painfully
    effeminate, does he not? And I don't like that. It makes men so
    very attractive. Cecily, mamma, whose views on education are
    remarkably strict, has brought me up to be extremely short-
    sighted; it is part of her system; so do you mind my looking at
    you through my glasses?
CECILY: Oh! not at all, Gwendolen. I am very fond of being looked at.
GWENDOLEN: *(after examining Cecily carefully through a lorgnette)* You are here
    on a short visit, I suppose.
270 CECILY: Oh no! I live here.
GWENDOLEN: *(severely)* Really? Your mother, no doubt, or some female
    relative of advanced years, resides here also?
CECILY: Oh no! I have no mother, nor, in fact, any relations.
GWENDOLEN: Indeed?
CECILY: My dear guardian, with the assistance of Miss Prism, has the
    arduous task of looking after me.
275 GWENDOLEN: Your guardian?
CECILY: Yes, I am Mr Worthing's ward.
GWENDOLEN: Oh! It is strange he never mentioned to me that he had a
    ward. How secretive of him! He grows more interesting hourly. I
    am not sure, however, that the news inspires me with feelings
    of unmixed delight. *(Rising and going to her.)* I am very fond of
    you, Cecily; I have liked you ever since I met you! But I am
    bound to state that now that I know that you are Mr Worthing's
    ward, I cannot help expressing a wish you were—well, just a
    little older than you seem to be—and not quite so very alluring
    in appearance. In fact, if I may speak candidly—
CECILY: Pray do! I think that whenever one has anything unpleasant to say,
    one should always be quite candid.
GWENDOLEN: Well, to speak with perfect candour, Cecily, I wish that you
    were fully forty-two, and more than usually plain for your age.
    Ernest has a strong upright nature. He is the very soul of truth
    and honour. Disloyalty would be as impossible to him as
    deception. But even men of the noblest possible moral character
    are extremely susceptible to the influence of the physical
    charms of others. Modern, no less than Ancient History,
    supplies us with many most painful examples of what I refer to.
    If it were not so, indeed, History would be quite unreadable.
280 CECILY: I beg your pardon, Gwendolen, did you say Ernest?
GWENDOLEN: Yes.
CECILY: Oh, but it is not Mr Ernest Worthing who is my guardian. It is his
    brother—his elder brother.
GWENDOLEN: *(sitting down again)* Ernest never mentioned to me that he had
    a brother.

Cecily: I am sorry to say they have not been on good terms for a long
time.

285 Gwendolen: Ah! that accounts for it. And now that I think of it I have
never heard any man mention his brother. The subject seems
distasteful to most men. Cecily, you have lifted a load from my
mind. I was growing almost anxious. It would have been
terrible if any cloud had come across a friendship like ours,
would it not? Of course you are quite, quite sure that it is not
Mr Ernest Worthing who is your guardian?

Cecily: Quite sure. *(A pause.)* In fact, I am going to be his.

Gwendolen: *(inquiringly)* I beg your pardon?

Cecily: *(rather shy and confidingly)* Dearest Gwendolen, there is no reason
why I should make a secret of it to you. Our little county
newspaper is sure to chronicle the fact next week. Mr Ernest
Worthing and I are engaged to be married.

Gwendolen: *(quite politely, rising)* My darling Cecily, I think there must be
some slight error. Mr Ernest Worthing is engaged to me. The
announcement will appear in the *Morning Post* on Saturday at
the latest.

290 Cecily: *(very politely, rising)* I am afraid you must be under some
misconception. Ernest proposed to me exactly ten minutes ago.
(Shows diary.)

Gwendolen: *(examines diary through her lorgnette carefully)* It is very curious,
for he asked me to be his wife yesterday afternoon at 5:30. If
you would care to verify the incident, pray do so. *(Produces diary
of her own.)* I never travel without my diary. One should always
have something sensational to read in the train. I am so sorry,
dear Cecily, if it is any disappointment to you, but I am afraid I
have the prior claim.

Cecily: It would distress me more than I can tell you, dear Gwendolen, if it
caused you any mental or physical anguish, but I feel bound to
point out that since Ernest proposed to you he clearly has
changed his mind.

Gwendolen: *(meditatively)* If the poor fellow has been entrapped into any
foolish promise I shall consider it my duty to rescue him at
once, and with a firm hand.

Cecily: *(thoughtfully and sadly)* Whatever unfortunate entanglement my
dear boy may have got into, I will never reproach him with it
after we are married.

295 Gwendolen: Do you allude to me, Miss Cardew, as an entanglement? You
are presumptuous. On an occasion of this kind it becomes more
than a moral duty to speak one's mind. It becomes a pleasure.

Cecily: Do you suggest, Miss Fairfax, that I entrapped Ernest into an
engagement? How dare you? This is no time for wearing the
shallow mask of manners. When I see a spade I call it a spade.

Gwendolen: *(satirically)* I am glad to say that I have never seen a spade. It
is obvious that our social spheres have been widely different.

(Enter Merriman, followed by the footman. He carries a salver, table cloth, and plate stand. Cecily is about to retort. The presence of the servants exercises a restraining influence, under which both girls chafe.)

MERRIMAN: Shall I lay tea here as usual, Miss?

CECILY: *(sternly, in a calm voice)* Yes, as usual. *(Merriman begins to clear table and lay cloth. A long pause. Cecily and Gwendolen glare at each other.)*

300 GWENDOLEN: Are there many interesting walks in the vicinity, Miss Cardew?

CECILY: Oh! yes! a great many. From the top of one of the hills quite close one can see five counties.

GWENDOLEN: Five counties! I don't think I should like that; I hate crowds.

CECILY: *(sweetly)* I suppose that is why you live in town? *(Gwendolen bites her lip, and beats her foot nervously with her parasol.)*

GWENDOLEN: *(looking around)* Quite a well-kept garden this is, Miss Cardew.

305 CECILY: So glad you like it, Miss Fairfax.

GWENDOLEN: I had no idea there were any flowers in the country.

CECILY: Oh, flowers are as common here, Miss Fairfax, as people are in London.

GWENDOLEN: Personally I cannot understand how anybody manages to exist in the country, if anybody who is anybody does. The country always bores me to death.

CECILY: Ah! This is what the newspapers call agricultural depression, is it not? I believe the aristocracy are suffering very much from it just at present. It is almost an epidemic amongst them, I have been told. May I offer you some tea, Miss Fairfax?

310 GWENDOLEN: *(with elaborate politeness)* Thank you. *(Aside.)* Detestable girl! But I require tea!

CECILY: *(sweetly)* Sugar?

GWENDOLEN: *(superciliously)* No, thank you. Sugar is not fashionable any more. *(Cecily looks angrily at her, takes up the tongs and puts four lumps of sugar into the cup.)*

CECILY: *(severely)* Cake or bread and butter?

GWENDOLEN: *(in a bored manner)* Bread and butter, please. Cake is rarely seen at the best houses nowadays.

315 CECILY: *(cuts a very large slice of cake and puts it on the tray)* Hand that to Miss Fairfax.

(Merriman does so, and goes out with footman. Gwendolen drinks the tea and makes a grimace. Puts down cup at once, reaches out her hand to the bread and butter, looks at it, and finds it is cake. Rises in indignation.)

GWENDOLEN: You have filled my tea with lumps of sugar, and though I asked most distinctly for bread and butter, you have given me cake. I am known for the gentleness of my disposition, and the extraordinary sweetness of my nature, but I warn you, Miss Cardew, you may go too far.

CECILY: *(rising)* To save my poor, innocent, trusting boy from the machinations of any other girl there are no lengths to which I would not go.

GWENDOLEN: From the moment I saw you I distrusted you. I felt that you were false and deceitful. I am never deceived in such matters. My first impressions of people are invariably right.

CECILY: It seems to me, Miss Fairfax, that I am trespassing on your valuable time. No doubt you have many other calls of a similar character to make in the neighbourhood.

(Enter Jack.)

320   GWENDOLEN: *(catching sight of him)* Ernest! My own Ernest!

JACK: Gwendolen! Darling! *(Offers to kiss her.)*

GWENDOLEN: *(drawing back)* A moment! May I ask if you are engaged to be married to this young lady? *(Points to Cecily.)*

JACK: *(laughing)* To dear little Cecily! Of course not! What could have put such an idea into your pretty little head?

GWENDOLEN: Thank you. You may! *(Offers her cheek.)*

325   CECILY: *(very sweetly)* I knew there must be some misunderstanding, Miss Fairfax. The gentleman whose arm is at present round your waist is my guardian, Mr John Worthing.

GWENDOLEN: I beg your pardon?

CECILY: This is Uncle Jack.

GWENDOLEN: *(receding)* Jack! Oh!

(Enter Algernon.)

CECILY: Here is Ernest.

330   ALGERNON: *(goes straight over to Cecily without noticing anyone else)* My own love! *(Offers to kiss her.)*

CECILY: *(drawing back)* A moment, Ernest! May I ask you—are you engaged to be married to this young lady?

ALGERNON: *(looking round)* To what young lady? Good heavens! Gwendolen!

CECILY: Yes! to good heavens, Gwendolen, I mean to Gwendolen.

ALGERNON: *(laughing)* Of course not! What could have put such an idea into your pretty little head?

335   CECILY: Thank you. *(Presenting her cheek to be kissed.)* You may. *(Algernon kisses her.)*

GWENDOLEN: I felt there was some slight error, Miss Cardew. The gentleman who is now embracing you is my cousin, Mr Algernon Moncrieff.

CECILY: *(breaking away from Algernon)* Algernon Moncrieff! Oh! *(The two girls move towards each other and put their arms round each other's waists as if for protection.)*

CECILY: Are you called Algernon?

ALGERNON: I cannot deny it.

340   CECILY: Oh!

GWENDOLEN: Is your name really John?

JACK: *(standing rather proudly)* I could deny it if I liked. I could deny
  anything if I liked. But my name certainly is John. It has been
  John for years.

CECILY: *(to Gwendolen)* A gross deception has been practised on both of us.

GWENDOLEN: My poor wounded Cecily!

345   CECILY: My sweet wronged Gwendolen!

GWENDOLEN: *(slowly and seriously)* You will call me sister, will you not?
  (They embrace. Jack and Algernon groan and walk up and down.)

CECILY: *(rather brightly)* There is just one question I would like to be
  allowed to ask my guardian.

GWENDOLEN: An admirable idea! Mr Worthing, there is just one question I
  would like to be permitted to put to you. Where is your brother
  Ernest? We are both engaged to be married to your brother
  Ernest, so it is a matter of some importance to us to know
  where your brother Ernest is at present.

JACK: *(slowly and hesitatingly)* Gwendolen—Cecily—it is very painful for me
  to be forced to speak the truth. It is the first time in my life that
  I have ever been reduced to such a painful position, and I am
  really quite inexperienced in doing anything of the kind.
  However, I will tell you quite frankly that I have no brother
  Ernest. I have no brother at all. I never had a brother in my life,
  and I certainly have not the smallest intention of ever having
  one in the future.

350   CECILY: *(surprised)* No brother at all?

JACK: *(cheerily)* None!

GWENDOLEN: *(severely)* Had you never a brother of any kind?

JACK: *(pleasantly)* Never. Not even of any kind.

GWENDOLEN: I am afraid it is quite clear, Cecily, that neither of us is
  engaged to be married to anyone.

355   CECILY: It is not a very pleasant position for a young girl suddenly to find
  herself in. Is it?

GWENDOLEN: Let us go into the house. They will hardly venture to come
  after us there.

CECILY: No, men are so cowardly, aren't they?

(They retire into the house with scornful looks.)

JACK: This ghastly state of things is what you call Bunburying, I suppose?

ALGERNON: Yes, and a perfectly wonderful Bunbury it is. The most
  wonderful Bunbury I have ever had in my life.

360   JACK: Well, you've no right whatsoever to Bunbury here.

ALGERNON: That is absurd. One has a right to Bunbury anywhere one
  chooses. Every serious Bunburyist knows that.

JACK: Serious Bunburyist? Good heavens!

ALGERNON: Well, one must be serious about something, if one wants to
  have any amusement in life. I happen to be serious about

Bunburying. What on earth you are serious about I haven't got the remotest idea. About everything, I should fancy. You have such an absolutely trivial nature.

JACK: Well, the only small satisfaction I have in the whole of this wretched business is that your friend Bunbury is quite exploded. You won't be able to run down to the country quite so often as you used to do, dear Algy. And a very good thing too.

365 ALGERNON: Your brother is a little off colour, isn't he, dear Jack? You won't be able to disappear to London quite so frequently as your wicked custom was. And not a bad thing either.

JACK: As for your conduct towards Miss Cardew, I must say that your taking in a sweet, simple, innocent girl like that is quite inexcusable. To say nothing of the fact that she is my ward.

ALGERNON: I can see no possible defence at all for your deceiving a brilliant, clever, thoroughly experienced young lady like Miss Fairfax. To say nothing of the fact that she is my cousin.

JACK: I wanted to be engaged to Gwendolen, that is all. I love her.

ALGERNON: Well, I simply wanted to be engaged to Cecily. I adore her.

370 JACK: There is certainly no chance of your marrying Miss Cardew.

ALGERNON: I don't think there is much likelihood, Jack, of you and Miss Fairfax being united.

JACK: Well, that is no business of yours.

ALGERNON: If it was my business, I wouldn't talk about it. *(Begins to eat muffins.)* It is very vulgar to talk about one's business. Only people like stockbrokers do that, and then merely at dinner parties.

JACK: How can you sit there, calmly eating muffins when we are in this horrible trouble, I can't make out. You seem to me to be perfectly heartless.

375 ALGERNON: Well, I can't eat muffins in an agitated manner. The butter would probably get on my cuffs. One should always eat muffins quite calmly. It is the only way to eat them.

JACK: I say it's perfectly heartless your eating muffins at all, under the circumstances.

ALGERNON: When I am in trouble, eating is the only thing that consoles me. Indeed, when I am in really great trouble, as any one who knows me intimately will tell you, I refuse everything except food and drink. At the present moment I am eating muffins because I am unhappy. Besides, I am particularly fond of muffins. *(Rising.)*

JACK: *(rising)* Well, that is no reason why you should eat them all in that greedy way. *(Takes muffins from Algernon.)*

ALGERNON: *(offering tea-cake)* I wish you would have tea-cake instead. I don't like tea-cake.

380 JACK: Good heavens! I suppose a man may eat his own muffins in his own garden.

ALGERNON: But you have just said it was perfectly heartless to eat muffins.

JACK: I said it was perfectly heartless of you, under the circumstances. That is a very different thing.

ALGERNON: That may be. But the muffins are the same. *(He seizes the muffin-dish from Jack.)*

JACK: Algy, I wish to goodness you would go.

385 ALGERNON: You can't possibly ask me to go without having some dinner. It's absurd. I never go without my dinner. No one ever does, except vegetarians and people like that. Besides I have just made arrangements with Dr Chasuble to be christened at a quarter to six under the name of Ernest.

JACK: My dear fellow, the sooner you give up that nonsense the better. I made arrangements this morning with Dr Chasuble to be christened myself at 5.30, and I naturally will take the name of Ernest. Gwendolen would wish it. We cannot both be christened Ernest. It's absurd. Besides, I have a perfect right to be christened if I like. There is no evidence at all that I ever have been christened by anybody. I should think it extremely probable I never was, and so does Dr Chasuble. It is entirely different in your case. You have been christened already.

ALGERNON: Yes, but I have not been christened for years.

JACK: Yes, but you have been christened. That is the important thing.

ALGERNON: Quite so. So I know my constitution can stand it. If you are not quite sure about your ever having been christened, I must say I think it rather dangerous your venturing on it now. It might make you very unwell. You can hardly have forgotten that someone very closely connected with you was very nearly carried off this week in Paris by a severe chill.

390 JACK: Yes, but you said yourself that a severe chill was not hereditary.

ALGERNON: It usen't to be, I know—but I daresay it is now. Science is always making wonderful improvements in things.

JACK: *(picking up the muffin-dish)* Oh, that is nonsense; you are always talking nonsense.

ALGERNON: Jack, you are at the muffins again! I wish you wouldn't. There are only two left. *(Takes them.)* I told you I was particularly fond of muffins.

JACK: But I hate tea-cake.

395 ALGERNON: Why on earth then do you allow tea-cake to be served up for your guests? What ideas you have of hospitality!

JACK: Algernon! I have already told you to go. I don't want you here. Why don't you go!

ALGERNON: I haven't quite finished my tea yet! and there is still one muffin left. *(Jack groans, and sinks into a chair. Algernon continues eating.)*

Act Drop

THIRD ACT

SCENE *Drawing-room at the Manor House*

(Gwendolen and Cecily are at the window, looking out into the garden.)

GWENDOLEN: The fact that they did not follow us at once into the house, as anyone else would have done, seems to me to show that they have some sense of shame left.

CECILY: They have been eating muffins. That looks like repentance.

GWENDOLEN: *(after a pause)* They don't seem to notice us at all. Couldn't you cough?

CECILY: But I haven't got a cough.

5 GWENDOLEN: They're looking at us. What effrontery!

CECILY: They're approaching. That's very forward of them.

GWENDOLEN: Let us preserve a dignified silence.

CECILY: Certainly. It's the only thing to do now.

(Enter Jack followed by Algernon. They whistle some dreadful popular air from a British Opera.)

GWENDOLEN: This dignified silence seems to produce an unpleasant effect.

10 CECILY: A most distasteful one.

GWENDOLEN: But we will not be the first to speak.

CECILY: Certainly not.

GWENDOLEN: Mr Worthing, I have something very particular to ask you. Much depends on your reply.

CECILY: Gwendolen, your common sense is invaluable. Mr Moncrieff, kindly answer me the following question. Why did you pretend to be my guardian's brother?

15 ALGERNON: In order that I might have an opportunity of meeting you.

CECILY: *(to Gwendolen)* That certainly seems a satisfactory explanation, does it not?

GWENDOLEN: Yes, dear, if you can believe him.

CECILY: I don't. But that does not affect the wonderful beauty of his answer.

GWENDOLEN: True. In matters of grave importance, style, not sincerity, is the vital thing. Mr Worthing, what explanation can you offer to me for pretending to have a brother? Was it in order that you might have an opportunity of coming up to town to see me as often as possible?

20 JACK: Can you doubt it, Miss Fairfax?

GWENDOLEN: I have the gravest doubts upon the subject. But I intend to crush them. This is not the moment for German scepticism.[1] *(Moving to Cecily.)* Their explanations appear to be quite

---

[1] Scepticism holds that no knowledge is absolute and that doubt is necessary to achieve an approximation of certainty. German theological writings at this time were considered especially sceptical in the English popular mind.

satisfactory, especially Mr Worthing's. That seems to me to have
the stamp of truth upon it.

CECILY: I am more than content with what Mr Moncrieff said. His voice
alone inspires one with absolute credulity.

GWENDOLEN: Then you think we should forgive them?

CECILY: Yes. I mean no.

25 GWENDOLEN: True! I had forgotten. There are principles at stake that one
cannot surrender. Which of us should tell them? The task is not
a pleasant one.

CECILY: Could we not both speak at the same time?

GWENDOLEN: An excellent idea! I nearly always speak at the same time as
other people. Will you take the time from me?

CECILY: Certainly. *(Gwendolen beats time with uplifted finger.)*

GWENDOLEN and CECILY: *(speaking together)* Your Christian names are still an
insuperable barrier. That is all!

30 JACK and ALGERNON: *(speaking together)* Our Christian names! Is that all? But
we are going to be christened this afternoon.

GWENDOLEN: *(to Jack)* For my sake you are prepared to do this terrible
thing?

JACK: I am.

CECILY: *(to Algernon)* To please me you are ready to face this fearful ordeal?

ALGERNON: I am!

35 GWENDOLEN: How absurd to talk about the equality of the sexes! Where
questions of self-sacrifice are concerned, men are infinitely
beyond us.

JACK: We are. *(Clasps hands with Algernon.)*

CECILY: They have moments of physical courage of which we women know
absolutely nothing.

GWENDOLEN: *(to Jack)* Darling!

ALGERNON: *(to Cecily)* Darling! *(They fall into each other's arms.)*

(Enter Merriman. When he enters he coughs loudly, seeing the situation.)

40 MERRIMAN: Ahem! Ahem! Lady Bracknell!

JACK: Good heavens!

(Enter Lady Bracknell. The couples separate in alarm. Exit Merriman.)

LADY BRACKNELL: Gwendolen! What does this mean?

GWENDOLEN: Merely that I am engaged to be married to Mr Worthing,
mamma.

LADY BRACKNELL: Come here. Sit down. Sit down immediately. Hesitation
of any kind is a sign of mental decay in the young, of physical
weakness in the old. *(Turns to Jack.)* Apprised, sir, of my
daughter's sudden flight by her trusty maid, whose confidence I
purchased by means of a small coin, I followed her at once by a
luggage train. Her unhappy father is, I am glad to say, under the
impression that she is attending a more than usually lengthy
lecture by the University Extension Scheme on the Influence of

a permanent income on Thought. I do not propose to undeceive him. Indeed I have never undeceived him on any question. I would consider it wrong. But of course, you will clearly understand that all communication between yourself and my daughter must cease immediately from this moment. On this point, as indeed on all points, I am firm.

45   JACK: I am engaged to be married to Gwendolen, Lady Bracknell!

LADY BRACKNELL: You are nothing of the kind, sir. And now as regards Algernon! . . . Algernon!

ALGERNON: Yes, Aunt Augusta.

LADY BRACKNELL: May I ask if it is in this house that your invalid friend Mr Bunbury resides?

ALGERNON: *(stammering)* Oh! No! Bunbury doesn't live here. Bunbury is somewhere else at present. In fact, Bunbury is dead.

50   LADY BRACKNELL: Dead! When did Mr Bunbury die? His death must have been extremely sudden.

ALGERNON: *(airily)* Oh! I killed Bunbury this afternoon. I mean poor Bunbury died this afternoon.

LADY BRACKNELL: What did he die of?

ALGERNON: Bunbury? Oh, he was quite exploded.

LADY BRACKNELL: Exploded! Was he the victim of a revolutionary outrage? I was not aware that Mr Bunbury was interested in social legislation. If so, he is well punished for his morbidity.

55   ALGERNON: My dear Aunt Augusta, I mean he was found out! The doctors found out that Bunbury could not live, that is what I mean—so Bunbury died.

LADY BRACKNELL: He seems to have had great confidence in the opinion of his physicians. I am glad, however, that he made up his mind at the last to some definite course of action, and acted under proper medical advice. And now that we have finally got rid of this Mr Bunbury, may I ask, Mr Worthing, who is that young person whose hand my nephew Algernon is now holding in what seems to me a peculiarly unnecessary manner?

JACK: That lady is Miss Cecily Cardew, my ward. *(Lady Bracknell bows coldly to Cecily.)*

ALGERNON: I am engaged to be married to Cecily, Aunt Augusta.

LADY BRACKNELL: I beg your pardon?

60   CECILY: Mr Moncrieff and I are engaged to be married, Lady Bracknell.

LADY BRACKNELL: *(with a shiver, crossing to the sofa and sitting down)* I do not know whether there is anything peculiarly exciting in the air of this particular part of Hertfordshire, but the number of engagements that go on seems to me considerably above the proper average that statistics have laid down for our guidance. I think some preliminary inquiry on my part would not be out of place. Mr Worthing, is Miss Cardew at all connected with any of the larger railway stations in London? I merely desire information. Until yesterday I had no idea that there were any families or persons whose origin was a Terminus. *(Jack looks perfectly furious, but restrains himself.)*

JACK: *(in a cold, clear voice)* Miss Cardew is the grand-daughter of the late Mr Thomas Cardew of 149 Belgrave Square, S.W.; Gervase Park, Dorking, Surrey; and the Sporran, Fifeshire, N.B.[2]

LADY BRACKNELL: That sounds not unsatisfactory. Three addresses always inspire confidence, even in tradesmen. But what proof have I of their authenticity?

JACK: I have carefully preserved the Court Guides[3] of the period. They are open to your inspection, Lady Bracknell.

65 LADY BRACKNELL: *(grimly)* I have known strange errors in that publication.

JACK: Miss Cardew's family solicitors are Messrs Markby, Markby, and Markby.

LADY BRACKNELL: Markby, Markby, and Markby? A firm of the very highest position in their profession. Indeed I am told that one of the Mr Markby's is occasionally to be seen at dinner parties. So far I am satisfied.

JACK: *(very irritably)* How extremely kind of you, Lady Bracknell! I have also in my possession, you will be pleased to hear, certificates of Miss Cardew's birth, baptism, whooping cough, registration, vaccination, confirmation, and the measles; both the German and the English variety.

LADY BRACKNELL: Ah! A life crowded with incident, I see; though perhaps somewhat too exciting for a young girl. I am not myself in favour of premature experiences. *(Rises, looks at her watch.)* Gwendolen! the time approaches for our departure. We have not a moment to lose. As a matter of form, Mr Worthing, I had better ask you if Miss Cardew has any little fortune?

70 JACK: Oh! about a hundred and thirty thousand pounds in the Funds.[4] That is all. Good-bye, Lady Bracknell. So pleased to have seen you. → *Jack leaves*

LADY BRACKNELL: *(sitting down again)* A moment, Mr Worthing. A hundred and thirty thousand pounds! And in the Funds! Miss Cardew seems to me a most attractive young lady, now that I look at her. Few girls of the present day have any really solid qualities, any of the qualities that last, and improve with time. We live, I regret to say, in an age of surfaces. *(To Cecily.)* Come over here, dear. *(Cecily goes across.)* Pretty child! your dress is sadly simple, and your hair seems almost as Nature might have left it. But we can soon alter all that. A thoroughly experienced French maid produces a really marvellous result in a very brief space of time.

---

[2] North Britain (used commonly in Wilde's day for postal addresses north of the Scottish border).

[3] A directory of addresses of the English gentry and nobility.

[4] Government bonds.

I remember recommending one to young Lady Lancing, and after three months her own husband did not know her.

JACK: And after six months nobody knew her.

LADY BRACKNELL: *(glares at Jack for a few moments. Then bends, with a practised smile, to Cecily)* Kindly turn round, sweet child. *(Cecily turns completely round.)* No, the side view is what I want. *(Cecily presents her profile.)* Yes, quite as I expected. There are distinct social possibilities in your profile. The two weak points in our age are its want of principle and its want of profile. The chin a little higher, dear. Style largely depends on the way the chin is worn. They are worn very high, just at present. Algernon!

ALGERNON: Yes, Aunt Augusta!

75 LADY BRACKNELL: There are distinct social possibilities in Miss Cardew's profile.

ALGERNON: Cecily is the sweetest, dearest, prettiest girl in the whole world. And I don't care twopence about social possibilities.

LADY BRACKNELL: Never speak disrespectfully of Society, Algernon. Only people who can't get into it do that. *(To Cecily.)* Dear child, of course you know that Algernon has nothing but his debts to depend upon. But I do not approve of mercenary marriages. When I married Lord Bracknell I had no fortune of any kind. But I never dreamed for a moment of allowing that to stand in my way. Well, I suppose I must give my consent.

ALGERNON: Thank you, Aunt Augusta.

LADY BRACKNELL: Cecily, you may kiss me!

80 CECILY: *(kisses her)* Thank you, Lady Bracknell.

LADY BRACKNELL: You may also address me as Aunt Augusta for the future.

CECILY: Thank you, Aunt Augusta.

LADY BRACKNELL: The marriage, I think, had better take place quite soon.

ALGERNON: Thank you, Aunt Augusta.

85 CECILY: Thank you, Aunt Augusta.

LADY BRACKNELL: To speak frankly, I am not in favour of long engagements. They give people the opportunity of finding out each other's character before marriage, which I think is never advisable.

JACK: I beg your pardon for interrupting you, Lady Bracknell, but this engagement is quite out of the question. I am Miss Cardew's guardian, and she cannot marry without my consent until she comes of age. That consent I absolutely decline to give.

LADY BRACKNELL: Upon what grounds, may I ask? Algernon is an extremely, I may almost say ostentatiously, eligible young man. He has nothing, but he looks everything. What more can one desire?

JACK: It pains me very much to have to speak frankly to you, Lady Bracknell, about your nephew, but the fact is that I do not approve at all of his moral character. I suspect him of being untruthful. *(Algernon and Cecily look at him in indignant amazement.)*

90 LADY BRACKNELL: Untruthful! My nephew Algernon? Impossible! He is an
Oxonian.[5]

JACK: I fear there can be no possible doubt about the matter. This
afternoon during my temporary absence in London on an
important question of romance, he obtained admission to my
house by means of the false pretence of being my brother.
Under an assumed name he drank, I've just been informed by
my butler, an entire pint bottle of my Perrier-Jouet, Brut, '89;
wine I was specially reserving for myself. Continuing his
disgraceful deception, he succeeded in the course of the
afternoon in alienating the affections of my only ward. He
subsequently stayed to tea, and devoured every single muffin.
And what makes his conduct all the more heartless is, that he
was perfectly well aware from the first that I have no brother,
that I never had a brother, and that I don't intend to have a
brother, not even of any kind. I distinctly told him so myself
yesterday afternoon.

LADY BRACKNELL: Ahem! Mr Worthing, after careful consideration I have
decided entirely to overlook my nephew's conduct to you.

JACK: That is very generous of you, Lady Bracknell. My own decision,
however, is unalterable. I decline to give my consent.

LADY BRACKNELL: *(to Cecily)* Come here, sweet child. *(Cecily goes over.)* How
old are you, dear?

95 CECILY: Well, I am really only eighteen, but I always admit to twenty when
I go to evening parties.

LADY BRACKNELL: You are perfectly right in making some slight alteration.
Indeed, no woman should ever be quite accurate about her age.
It looks so calculating. . . . *(In a meditative manner.)* Eighteen, but
admitting to twenty at evening parties. Well, it will not be very
long before you are of age and free from the restraints of
tutelage. So I don't think your guardian's consent is, after all, a
matter of any importance.

JACK: Pray excuse me, Lady Bracknell, for interrupting you again, but it is
only fair to tell you that according to the terms of her
grandfather's will Miss Cardew does not come legally of age till
she is thirty-five.

LADY BRACKNELL: That does not seem to me to be a grave objection. Thirty-
five is a very attractive age. London society is full of women of
the very highest birth who have, of their own free choice,
remained thirty-five for years. Lady Dumbleton is an instance in
point. To my own knowledge she has been thirty-five ever since
she arrived at the age of forty, which was many years ago now. I
see no reason why our dear Cecily should not be even still more

---

[5] Graduate of Oxford University.

attractive at the age you mention than she is at present. There
will be a large accumulation of property.

CECILY: Algy, could you wait for me till I was thirty-five?

100 ALGERNON: Of course I could, Cecily. You know I could.

CECILY: Yes, I felt it instinctively, but I couldn't wait all that time. I hate
waiting even five minutes for anybody. It always makes me
rather cross. I am not punctual myself, I know, but I do like
punctuality in others, and waiting, even to be married, is quite
out of the question.

ALGERNON: Then what is to be done, Cecily?

CECILY: I don't know, Mr Moncrieff.

LADY BRACKNELL: My dear Mr Worthing, as Miss Cardew states positively
that she cannot wait till she is thirty-five—a remark which I am
bound to say seems to me to show a somewhat impatient
nature—I would beg of you to reconsider your decision.

105 JACK: But my dear Lady Bracknell, the matter is entirely in your own
hands. The moment you consent to my marriage with
Gwendolen, I will most gladly allow your nephew to form an
alliance with my ward.

LADY BRACKNELL: *(rising and drawing herself up)* You must be quite aware
that what you propose is out of the question.

JACK: Then a passionate celibacy is all that any of us can look forward to.

LADY BRACKNELL: That is not the destiny I propose for Gwendolen.
Algernon, of course, can choose for himself. *(Pulls out her
watch.)* Come, dear *(Gwendolen rises)*, we have already missed
five, if not six, trains. To miss any more might expose us to
comment on the platform.

(Enter Dr Chasuble.)

CHASUBLE: Everything is quite ready for the christenings.

110 LADY BRACKNELL: The christenings, sir! Is not that somewhat premature?

CHASUBLE: *(looking rather puzzled, and pointing to Jack and Algernon)* Both
these gentlemen have expressed a desire for immediate baptism.

LADY BRACKNELL: At their age? The idea is grotesque and irreligious!
Algernon, I forbid you to be baptized. I will not hear of such
excesses. Lord Bracknell would be highly displeased if he
learned that that was the way in which you wasted your time
and money.

CHASUBLE: Am I to understand then that there are to be no christenings at
all this afternoon?

JACK: I don't think that, as things are now, it would be of much practical
value to either of us, Dr Chasuble.

115 CHASUBLE: I am grieved to hear such sentiments from you, Mr Worthing.
They savour of the heretical views of the Anabaptists,[6] views

---

[6] Protestant sect that opposed infant baptism and required a second or adult baptism.

that I have completely refuted in four of my unpublished sermons. However, as your present mood seems to be one peculiarly secular, I will return to the church at once. Indeed, I have just been informed by the pew-opener[7] that for the last hour and a half Miss Prism has been waiting for me in the vestry.

LADY BRACKNELL: *(starting)* Miss Prism! Did I hear you mention a Miss Prism?

CHASUBLE: Yes, Lady Bracknell. I am on my way to join her.

LADY BRACKNELL: Pray allow me to detain you for a moment. This matter may prove to be one of vital importance to Lord Bracknell and myself. Is this Miss Prism a female of repellent aspect, remotely connected with education?

CHASUBLE: *(somewhat indignantly)* She is the most cultivated of ladies, and the very picture of respectability.

120 LADY BRACKNELL: It is obviously the same person. May I ask what position she holds in your household?

CHASUBLE: *(severely)* I am a celibate, madam.

JACK: *(interposing)* Miss Prism, Lady Bracknell, has been for the last three years Miss Cardew's esteemed governess and valued companion.

LADY BRACKNELL: In spite of what I hear of her, I must see her at once. Let her be sent for.

CHASUBLE: *(looking off)* She approaches; she is nigh.

(Enter Miss Prism hurriedly.)

125 MISS PRISM: I was told you expected me in the vestry, dear Canon. I have been waiting for you there for an hour and three-quarters. *(Catches sight of Lady Bracknell, who has fixed her with a stony glare. Miss Prism grows pale and quails. She looks anxiously round as if desirous to escape.)*

LADY BRACKNELL: *(in a severe, judicial voice)* Prism! *(Miss Prism bows her head in shame.)* Come here, Prism! *(Miss Prism approaches in a humble manner.)* Prism! Where is that baby? *(General consternation. The canon starts back in horror. Algernon and Jack pretend to be anxious to shield Cecily and Gwendolen from hearing the details of a terrible public scandal.)* Twenty-eight years ago, Prism, you left Lord Bracknell's house, Number 104, Upper Grosvenor Street, in charge of a perambulator that contained a baby of the male sex. You never returned. A few weeks later, through the elaborate investigations of the Metropolitan police, the perambulator was discovered at midnight standing by itself in a remote corner of Bayswater. It contained the manuscript of a three-volume novel of more than usually revolting sentimentality. *(Miss Prism starts*

---

[7] An usher; pews in older churches were enclosed boxes of seats that were reserved for particular families.

in involuntary indignation.) But the baby was not there! *(Everyone looks at Miss Prism.)* Prism! Where is that baby? *(A pause.)*

Miss Prism: Lady Bracknell, I admit with shame that I do not know. I only wish I did. The plain facts of the case are these. On the morning of the day you mention, a day that is for ever branded on my memory, I prepared as usual to take the baby out in its perambulator. I had also with me a somewhat old, but capacious hand-bag in which I intended to place the manuscript of a work of fiction that I had written during my few unoccupied hours. In a moment of mental abstraction, for which I never can forgive myself, I deposited the manuscript in the bassinette, and placed the baby in the hand-bag.

Jack: *(who has been listening attentively)* But where did you deposit the hand-bag?

Miss Prism: Do not ask me, Mr Worthing.

130 Jack: Miss Prism, this is a matter of no small importance to me. I insist on knowing where you deposited the hand-bag that contained that infant.

Miss Prism: I left it in the cloak-room of one of the larger railway stations in London.

Jack: What railway station?

Miss Prism: *(quite crushed)* Victoria. The Brighton line. *(Sinks into a chair.)*

Jack: I must retire to my room for a moment. Gwendolen, wait here for me.

135 Gwendolen: If you are not too long, I will wait here for you all my life.

(Exit Jack in great excitement.)

Chasuble: What do you think this means, Lady Bracknell?

Lady Bracknell: I dare not even suspect, Dr Chasuble. I need hardly tell you that in families of high position strange coincidences are not supposed to occur. They are hardly considered the thing.

(Noises heard overhead as if someone was throwing trunks about. Everyone looks up.)

Cecily: Uncle Jack seems strangely agitated.

Chasuble: Your guardian has a very emotional nature.

140 Lady Bracknell: This noise is extremely unpleasant. It sounds as if he was having an argument. I dislike arguments of any kind. They are always vulgar, and often convincing.

Chasuble: *(looking up)* It has stopped now. *(The noise is redoubled.)*

Lady Bracknell: I wish he would arrive at some conclusion.

Gwendolen: This suspense is terrible. I hope it will last.

(Enter Jack with a hand-bag of black leather in his hand.)

Jack: *(rushing over to Miss Prism)* Is this the hand-bag, Miss Prism? Examine it carefully before you speak. The happiness of more than one life depends on your answer.

145 MISS PRISM: *(calmly)* It seems to be mine. Yes, here is the injury it received through the upsetting of a Gower Street omnibus in younger and happier days. Here is the stain on the lining caused by the explosion of a temperance beverage, an incident that occurred at Leamington. And here, on the lock, are my initials. I had forgotten that in an extravagant mood I had had them placed there. The bag is undoubtedly mine. I am delighted to have it so unexpectedly restored to me. It has been a great inconvenience being without it all these years.

JACK: *(in a pathetic voice)* Miss Prism, more is restored to you than this hand-bag. I was the baby you placed in it.

MISS PRISM: *(amazed)* You?

JACK: *(embracing her)* Yes . . . mother!

MISS PRISM: *(recoiling in indignant astonishment)* Mr Worthing! I am unmarried!

150 JACK: Unmarried! I do not deny that is a serious blow. But after all, who has the right to cast a stone against one who has suffered? Cannot repentance wipe out an act of folly? Why should there be one law for men, and another for women? Mother, I forgive you. *(Tries to embrace her again.)*

MISS PRISM: *(still more indignant)* Mr Worthing, there is some error. *(Pointing to Lady Bracknell.)* There is the lady who can tell you who you really are.

JACK: *(after a pause)* Lady Bracknell, I hate to seem inquisitive, but would you kindly inform me who I am?

LADY BRACKNELL: I am afraid that the news I have to give you will not altogether please you. You are the son of my poor sister, Mrs Moncrieff, and consequently Algernon's elder brother.

JACK: Algy's elder brother! Then I have a brother after all. I knew I had a brother! I always said I had a brother! Cecily—how could you have ever doubted that I had a brother? *(Seizes hold of Algernon.)* Dr Chasuble, my unfortunate brother. Miss Prism, my unfortunate brother. Gwendolen, my unfortunate brother. Algy, you young scoundrel, you will have to treat me with more respect in the future. You have never behaved to me like a brother in all your life.

155 ALGERNON: Well, not till today, old boy, I admit. I did my best, however, though I was out of practice.

(Shakes hands.)

GWENDOLEN: *(to Jack)* My own! But what own are you? What is your Christian name, now that you have become someone else?

JACK: Good heavens! . . . I had quite forgotten that point. Your decision on the subject of my name is irrevocable, I suppose?

GWENDOLEN: I never change, except in my affections.

CECILY: What a noble nature you have, Gwendolen!

160 JACK: Then the question had better be cleared up at once. Aunt Augusta, a
      moment. At the time when Miss Prism left me in the hand-bag,
      had I been christened already?

LADY BRACKNELL: Every luxury that money could buy, including
      christening, had been lavished on you by your fond and doting
      parents.

JACK: Then I was christened! That is settled. Now, what name was I given?
      Let me know the worst.

LADY BRACKNELL: Being the eldest son you were naturally christened after
      your father.

JACK: *(irritably)* Yes, but what was my father's Christian name?

165 LADY BRACKNELL: *(meditatively)* I cannot at the present moment recall what
      the General's Christian name was. But I have no doubt he had
      one. He was eccentric, I admit. But only in later years. And that
      was the result of the Indian climate, and marriage, and
      indigestion, and other things of that kind.

JACK: Algy! Can't you recollect what our father's Christian name was?

ALGERNON: My dear boy, we were never even on speaking terms. He died
      before I was a year old.

JACK: His name would appear in the Army Lists of the period, I suppose,
      Aunt Augusta?

LADY BRACKNELL: The General was essentially a man of peace, except in his
      domestic life. But I have no doubt his name would appear in
      any military directory.

170 JACK: The Army Lists of the last forty years are here. These delightful
      records should have been my constant study. *(Rushes to bookcase
      and tears the books out.)* M. Generals . . . Mallam, Maxbohm,
      Magley—what ghastly names they have—Markby, Migsby,
      Mobbs, Moncrieff! Lieutenant 1840, Captain, Lieutenant-
      Colonel, Colonel, General 1869, Christian names, Ernest John.
      (Puts book very quietly down and speaks quite calmly.) I always told
      you, Gwendolen, my name was Ernest, didn't I? Well, it is
      Ernest after all. I mean it naturally is Ernest.

LADY BRACKNELL: Yes, I remember now that the General was called Ernest. I
      knew I had some particular reason for disliking the name.

GWENDOLEN: Ernest! My own Ernest! I felt from the first that you could
      have no other name!

JACK: Gwendolen, it is a terrible thing for a man to find out suddenly that
      all his life he has been speaking nothing but the truth. Can you
      forgive me?

GWENDOLEN: I can. For I feel that you are sure to change.

175 JACK: My own one!

CHASUBLE: *(to Miss Prism)* Laetitia! *(Embraces her.)*

MISS PRISM: *(enthusiastically)* Frederick! At last!

ALGERNON: Cecily! *(Embraces her.)* At last!

JACK: Gwendolen! *(Embraces her.)* At last!

180 LADY BRACKNELL: My nephew, you seem to be displaying signs of triviality.

JACK: On the contrary, Aunt Augusta, I've now realised for the first time in my life the vital Importance of Being Earnest.

Tableau

Curtain

READING AND REACTING

1. What elements of satire can you identify in the play? What are the main aspects of society that the play makes fun of—for the purpose of improvement?
2. What elements of farce can you identify in the play?
3. *The Importance of Being Earnest* can be seen as a comedy of manners; that is, the comedy is often generated by wit although the characters tend to be stock figures. Are Wilde's characters merely stock characters?
4. "Bunburying" is an essential part of the plot. Explain what is meant, and consider whether characters other than Algernon have similar techniques for negotiating society.
5. What is the significance of the title?
6. How important is the written word in the play? What examples of writing are crucial to the plot?
7. Analyze the prospect of setting the play within another time and place. What aspects could be changed? What aspects would need to be retained?
8. Gwendolen and Cecily both want to marry a man named Ernest. Why? What point is Wilde making about their apparent idealism?
9. What is Lady Bracknell's role in the plot of the play and in the theme(s)? Is it necessary to have someone like her—the voice of authority—in a play that mocks authority?
10. Three characters are not paired up at the end of the play. Identify them and provide reasons for their solitary state.
11. Find examples of each of the following techniques: non sequitur, unexpected word, parallelism, and pun.
12. What's the purpose of food in the play?
13. **JOURNAL ENTRY** Which character are you most like? Which character would you prefer to be like?
14. **CRITICAL PERSPECTIVE** In *Oscar Wilde*, Katherine Worth describes *The Importance of Being Earnest* as existential farce and goes on to say:

> Wilde does . . . show the world as tending to cruelty and heartlessness, life as an absurd performance, personality as a fluid thing, endlessly forming and reforming itself with the aid of masks . . . But Wilde's optimistic, benevolent nature required a

more harmonious ending for his farce than anything . . . any modern existentialist would be likely to envisage. *The Importance of Being Earnest* ends with all the dissonances resolved and harmony achieved. It can happen only in Utopia which means "nowhere"—but as Wilde said, "A map of the world that does not include Utopia is not worth even glancing at, for it leaves out the one country at which Humanity is always landing."

Discuss this view of the play.

Related Works: "A Rose for Emily" (p. 90), "A&P" (p. 122), *The Brute* (p. 1081), *Hamlet* (p. 1093)

◊ **HENRIK IBSEN** (1828–1906) is Norway's foremost dramatist. He was born in Skien, Norway, into a prosperous family, but his father lost his fortune when Ibsen was six; when Ibsen was fifteen, he was apprenticed to an apothecary away from home and was permanently estranged from his family. He studied to enter the university and wrote plays during his apprenticeship; though he did not pass the university entrance exam, his second play, *The Warrior's Barrow*, was produced by the Christiania Theatre in 1850. He began a life in the theatre, writing plays and serving as artistic director of a theatrical company. Disillusioned by the public's lack of interest in theatre, he left Norway, living in Italy and Germany with his wife and son between 1864 and 1891. By the time he returned to Norway, he was famous and revered. Ibsen's most notable plays include *Brand* (1865), *Peer Gynt* (1867), *A Doll House* (1879), *Ghosts* (1881), *An Enemy of the People* (1882), *The Wild Duck* (1884), *Hedda Gabler* (1890), and *When We Dead Awaken* (1899).

A Doll House marks the beginning of Ibsen's successful realist period, during which he explored the ordinary lives of small-town people—in this case, what he called "a modern tragedy." Ibsen based the play on a true story, which closely paralleled the main events of the play: a wife borrows money to finance a trip for an ailing husband, repayment is demanded, she forges a cheque and is discovered. (In the real-life story, however, the husband demanded a divorce, and the wife had a nervous breakdown and was committed to a mental institution.) The issue in *A Doll House*, he said, is that there are "two kinds of moral law, . . . one in man and a completely different one in woman. They do not understand each other. . . . " Nora and Helmer destroy their marriage because they cannot comprehend or accept their differences. Though the play begins conventionally, it does not fulfill its audience's expectations for a tidy resolution; as a result, the play was not very successful when first performed. Nevertheless, the publication of *A Doll House* made Ibsen internationally famous.

◊ ◊ ◊

HENRIK IBSEN

A Doll House
(1879)

Translated by Rolf Fjelde

CHARACTERS

TORVALD HELMER, *a lawyer*
NORA, *his wife*
DR. RANK
MRS. LINDE
A DELIVERY BOY

NILS KROGSTAD, *a bank clerk*
THE HELMERS' THREE SMALL
   CHILDREN
ANNE-MARIE, *their nurse*
HELENE, *a maid*

The action takes place in Helmer's residence.

ACT I

A comfortable room, tastefully but not expensively furnished. A door to the right in the back wall leads to the entryway; another to the left leads to Helmer's study. Between these doors, a piano. Midway in the left-hand wall a door, and further back a window. Near the window a round table with an armchair and a small sofa. In the right-hand wall, toward the rear, a door, and nearer the foreground a porcelain stove with two armchairs and a rocking chair beside it. Between the stove and the side door, a small table. Engravings on the walls. An étagère with china figures and other small art objects; a small bookcase with richly bound books; the floor carpeted; a fire burning in the stove. It is a winter day.

   A bell rings in the entryway; shortly after we hear the door being unlocked. Nora comes into the room, humming happily to herself; she is wearing street clothes and carries an armload of packages, which she puts down on the table to the right. She has left the hall door open; and through it a Delivery Boy is seen, holding a Christmas tree and a basket, which he gives to the Maid who let them in.

NORA: Hide the tree well, Helene. The children mustn't get a glimpse of it till this evening, after it's trimmed. *(To the Delivery Boy, taking out her purse.)* How much?
DELIVERY BOY: Fifty, ma'am.
NORA: There's a crown. No, keep the change. *(The Boy thanks her and leaves. Nora shuts the door. She laughs softly to herself while taking off her street things. Drawing a bag of macaroons from her pocket, she eats a couple, then steals over and listens at her husband's study door.)* Yes, he's home. *(Hums again as she moves to the table right.)*
HELMER: *(from the study)* Is that my little lark twittering out there?
5 NORA: *(busy opening some packages)* Yes, it is.
HELMER: Is that my squirrel rummaging around?

NORA: Yes!

HELMER: When did my squirrel get in?

NORA: Just now. *(Putting the macaroon bag in her pocket and wiping her mouth.)* Do come in, Torvald, and see what I've bought.

10 HELMER: Can't be disturbed. *(After a moment he opens the door and peers in, pen in hand.)* Bought, you say? All that there? Has the little spendthrift been out throwing money around again?

NORA: Oh, but Torvald, this year we really should let ourselves go a bit. It's the first Christmas we haven't had to economize.

HELMER: But you know we can't go squandering.

NORA: Oh yes, Torvald, we can squander a little now. Can't we? Just a tiny, wee bit. Now that you've got a big salary and are going to make piles and piles of money.

HELMER: Yes—starting New Year's. But then it's a full three months till the raise comes through.

15 NORA: Pooh! We can borrow that long.

HELMER: Nora! *(Goes over and playfully takes her by the ear.)* Are your scatterbrains off again? What if today I borrowed a thousand crowns, and you squandered them over Christmas week, and then on New Year's Eve a roof tile fell on my head, and I lay there—

NORA: *(putting her hand on his mouth)* Oh! Don't say such things!

HELMER: Yes, but what if it happened—then what?

NORA: If anything so awful happened, then it just wouldn't matter if I had debts or not.

20 HELMER: Well, but the people I'd borrowed from?

NORA: Them? Who cares about them! They're strangers.

HELMER: Nora, Nora, how like a woman! No, but seriously, Nora, you know what I think about that. No debts! Never borrow! Something of freedom's lost—and something of beauty, too—from a home that's founded on borrowing and debt. We've made a brave stand up to now, the two of us; and we'll go right on like that the little while we have to.

NORA: *(going toward the stove)* Yes, whatever you say, Torvald.

HELMER: *(following her)* Now, now, the little lark's wings mustn't droop. Come on, don't be a sulky squirrel. *(Taking out his wallet.)* Nora, guess what I have here.

25 NORA: *(turning quickly)* Money!

HELMER: There, see. *(Hands her some notes.)* Good grief, I know how costs go up in a house at Christmastime.

NORA: Ten—twenty—thirty—forty. Oh, thank you, Torvald; I can manage no end on this.

HELMER: You really will have to.

NORA: Oh yes, I promise I will! But come here so I can show you everything I bought. And so cheap! Look, new clothes for Ivar here—and a sword. Here a horse and a trumpet for Bob. And a doll and a doll's bed here for Emmy; they're nothing much, but she'll tear them to bits in no time anyway. And here I have dress material and handkerchiefs for the maids. Old Anne-Marie really deserves something more.

30 HELMER: And what's in that package there?

NORA: *(with a cry)* Torvald, no! You can't see that till tonight!

HELMER: I see. But tell me now, you little prodigal, what have you thought of for yourself?

NORA: For myself? Oh, I don't want anything at all.

HELMER: Of course you do. Tell me just what—within reason—you'd most like to have.

35 NORA: I honestly don't know. Oh, listen, Torvald—

HELMER: Well?

NORA: *(fumbling at his coat buttons, without looking at him)* If you want to give me something, then maybe you could—you could—

HELMER: Come on, out with it.

NORA: *(hurriedly)* You could give me money, Torvald. No more than you think you can spare; then one of these days I'll buy something with it.

40 HELMER: But Nora—

NORA: Oh, please, Torvald darling, do that! I beg you, please. Then I could hang the bills in pretty gilt paper on the Christmas tree. Wouldn't that be fun?

HELMER: What are those little birds called that always fly through their fortunes?

NORA: Oh yes, spendthrifts; I know all that. But let's do as I say, Torvald; then I'll have time to decide what I really need most. That's very sensible, isn't it?

HELMER: *(smiling)* Yes, very—that is, if you actually hung onto the money I give you, and you actually used it to buy yourself something. But it goes for the house and for all sorts of foolish things, and then I only have to lay out some more.

45 NORA: Oh, but Torvald—

HELMER: Don't deny it, my dear little Nora. *(Putting his arm around her waist.)* Spendthrifts are sweet, but they use up a frightful amount of money. It's incredible what it costs a man to feed such birds.

NORA: Oh, how can you say that! Really, I save everything I can.

HELMER: *(laughing)* Yes, that's the truth. Everything you can. But that's nothing at all.

NORA: *(humming, with a smile of quiet satisfaction)* Hm, if you only knew what expenses we larks and squirrels have, Torvald.

50 HELMER: You're an odd little one. Exactly the way your father was. You're never at a loss for scaring up money; but the moment you have it, it runs right out through your fingers; you never know what you've done with it. Well, one takes you as you are. It's deep in your blood. Yes, these things are hereditary, Nora.

NORA: Ah, I could wish I'd inherited many of Papa's qualities.

HELMER: And I couldn't wish you anything but just what you are, my sweet little lark. But wait; it seems to me you have a very—what should I call it?—a very suspicious look today—

NORA: I do?

Helmer: You certainly do. Look me straight in the eye.

55 Nora: *(looking at him)* Well?

Helmer: *(shaking an admonitory finger)* Surely my sweet tooth hasn't been running riot in town today, has she?

Nora: No. Why do you imagine that?

Helmer: My sweet tooth really didn't make a little detour through the confectioner's?

Nora: No, I assure you, Torvald—

60 Helmer: Hasn't nibbled some pastry?

Nora: No, not at all.

Helmer: Nor even munched a macaroon or two?

Nora: No, Torvald, I assure you, really—

Helmer: There, there now. Of course I'm only joking.

65 Nora: *(going to the table, right)* You know I could never think of going against you.

Helmer: No, I understand that; and you *have* given me your word. *(Going over to her.)* Well, you keep your little Christmas secrets to yourself, Nora darling. I expect they'll come to light this evening, when the tree is lit.

Nora: Did you remember to ask Dr. Rank?

Helmer: No. But there's no need for that; it's assumed he'll be dining with us. All the same, I'll ask him when he stops by here this morning. I've ordered some fine wine. Nora, you can't imagine how I'm looking forward to this evening.

Nora: So am I. And what fun for the children, Torvald!

70 Helmer: Ah, it's so gratifying to know that one's gotten a safe, secure job, and with a comfortable salary. It's a great satisfaction, isn't it?

Nora: Oh, it's wonderful!

Helmer: Remember last Christmas? Three whole weeks before, you shut yourself in every evening till long after midnight, making flowers for the Christmas tree, and all the other decorations to surprise us. Ugh, that was the dullest time I've ever lived through.

Nora: It wasn't at all dull for me.

Helmer: *(smiling)* But the outcome *was* pretty sorry, Nora.

75 Nora: Oh, don't tease me with that again. How could I help it that the cat came in and tore everything to shreds.

Helmer: No, poor thing, you certainly couldn't. You wanted so much to please us all, and that's what counts. But it's just as well that the hard times are past.

Nora: Yes, it's really wonderful.

Helmer: Now I don't have to sit here alone, boring myself, and you don't have to tire your precious eyes and your fair little delicate hands—

Nora: *(clapping her hands)* No, is it really true, Torvald, I don't have to? Oh, how wonderfully lovely to hear! *(Taking his arm.)* Now I'll tell you just how I've thought we should plan things. Right after Christmas—*(The*

doorbell rings.) Oh, the bell. (Straightening the room up a bit.) Somebody
would have to come. What a bore!

80 HELMER: I'm not at home to visitors, don't forget.

MAID: (from the hall doorway) Ma'am, a lady to see you—

NORA: All right, let her come in.

MAID: (to Helmer) And the doctor's just come too.

HELMER: Did he go right to my study?

85 MAID: Yes, he did.

*Helmer goes into his room. The Maid shows in Mrs. Linde, dressed in traveling
clothes, and shuts the door after her.*

MRS. LINDE: (in a dispirited and somewhat hesitant voice) Hello, Nora.

NORA: (uncertain) Hello—

MRS. LINDE: You don't recognize me.

NORA: No, I don't know—but wait, I think—(Exclaiming.) What! Kristine! Is
it really you?

90 MRS. LINDE: Yes, it's me.

NORA: *Kristine!* To think I didn't recognize you. But then, how could I?
(More quietly.) How you've changed, Kristine!

MRS. LINDE: Yes, no doubt I have. In nine—ten long years.

NORA: Is it so long since we met! Yes, it's all of that. Oh, these last eight
years have been a happy time, believe me. And so now you've come
in to town, too. Made the long trip in the winter. That took courage.

MRS. LINDE: I just got here by ship this morning.

95 NORA: To enjoy yourself over Christmas, of course. Oh, how lovely! Yes,
enjoy ourselves, we'll do that. But take your coat off. You're not still
cold? (Helping her.) There now, let's get cozy here by the stove. No, the
easy chair there! I'll take the rocker here. (Seizing her hands.) Yes, now
you have your old look again; it was only in that first moment. You're
a bit more pale, Kristine—and maybe a bit thinner.

MRS. LINDE: And much, much older, Nora.

NORA: Yes, perhaps a bit older; a tiny, tiny bit; not much at all. (Stopping
short; suddenly serious.) Oh, but thoughtless me, to sit here, chattering
away. Sweet, good Kristine, can you forgive me?

MRS. LINDE: What do you mean, Nora?

NORA: (softly) Poor Kristine, you've become a widow.

100 MRS. LINDE: Yes, three years ago.

NORA: Oh, I knew it, of course: I read it in the papers. Oh, Kristine, you
must believe me; I often thought of writing you then, but I kept
postponing it, and something always interfered.

MRS. LINDE: Nora dear, I understand completely.

NORA: No, it was awful of me, Kristine. You poor thing, how much you
must have gone through. And he left you nothing?

MRS. LINDE: No.

105 NORA: And no children?

MRS. LINDE: No.

NORA: Nothing at all, then?

MRS. LINDE: Not even a sense of loss to feed on.

NORA: *(looking incredulously at her)* But Kristine, how could that be?

110 MRS. LINDE: *(smiling wearily and smoothing her hair)* Oh, sometimes it
happens, Nora.

NORA: So completely alone. How terribly hard that must be for you. I have
three lovely children. You can't see them now; they're out with the
maid. But now you must tell me everything—

MRS. LINDE: No, no, no, tell me about yourself.

NORA: No, you begin. Today I don't want to be selfish. I want to think only
of you today. But there *is* something I must tell you. Did you hear of
the wonderful luck we had recently?

MRS. LINDE: No, what's that?

115 NORA: My husband's been made manager in the bank, just think!

MRS. LINDE: Your husband? How marvelous!

NORA: Isn't it? Being a lawyer is such an uncertain living, you know,
especially if one won't touch any cases that aren't clean and decent.
And of course Torvald would never do that, and I'm with him
completely there. Oh, we're simply delighted, believe me! He'll join
the bank right after New Year's and start getting a huge salary and lots
of commissions. From now on we can live quite differently—just as we
want. Oh, Kristine, I feel so light and happy! Won't it be lovely to
have stacks of money and not a care in the world?

MRS. LINDE: Well, anyway, it would be lovely to have enough for
necessities.

NORA: No, not just for necessities, but stacks and stacks of money!

120 MRS. LINDE: *(smiling)* Nora, Nora, aren't you sensible yet? Back in school
you were such a free spender.

NORA: *(with a quiet laugh)* Yes, that's what Torvald still says. *(Shaking her
finger.)* But "Nora, Nora" isn't as silly as you all think. Really, we've
been in no position for me to go squandering. We've had to work,
both of us.

MRS. LINDE: You too?

NORA: Yes, at odd jobs—needlework, crocheting, embroidery, and such—
(casually) and other things too. You remember that Torvald left the
department when we were married? There was no chance of
promotion in his office, and of course he needed to earn more money.
But that first year he drove himself terribly. He took on all kinds of
extra work that kept him going morning and night. It wore him down,
and then he fell deathly ill. The doctors said it was essential for him to
travel south.

MRS. LINDE: Yes, didn't you spend a whole year in Italy?

125 NORA: That's right. It wasn't easy to get away, you know. Ivar had just been
born. But of course we had to go. Oh, that was a beautiful trip, and it
saved Torvald's life. But it cost a frightful sum, Kristine.

MRS. LINDE: I can well imagine.

NORA: Four thousand, eight hundred crowns it cost. That's really a lot of money.

MRS. LINDE: But it's lucky you had it when you needed it.

NORA: Well, as it was, we got it from Papa.

130 MRS. LINDE: I see. It was just about the time your father died.

NORA: Yes, just about then. And, you know, I couldn't make that trip out to nurse him. I had to stay here, expecting Ivar any moment, and with my poor sick Torvald to care for. Dearest Papa, I never saw him again, Kristine. Oh, that was the worst time I've known in all my marriage.

MRS. LINDE: I know how you loved him. And then you went off to Italy?

NORA: Yes. We had the means now, and the doctors urged us. So we left a month after.

MRS. LINDE: And your husband came back completely cured?

135 NORA: Sound as a drum!

MRS. LINDE: But—the doctor?

NORA: Who?

MRS. LINDE: I thought the maid said he was a doctor, the man who came in with me.

NORA: Yes, that was Dr. Rank—but he's not making a sick call. He's our closest friend, and he stops by at least once a day. No, Torvald hasn't had a sick moment since, and the children are fit and strong, and I am, too. *(Jumping up and clapping her hands.)* Oh, dear God, Kristine, what a lovely thing to live and be happy! But how disgusting of me— I'm talking of nothing but my own affairs. *(Sits on a stool close by Kristine, arms resting across her knees.)* Oh, don't be angry with me! Tell me, is it really true that you weren't in love with your husband? Why did you marry him, then?

140 MRS. LINDE: My mother was still alive, but bedridden and helpless—and I had my two younger brothers to look after. In all conscience, I didn't think I could turn him down.

NORA: No, you were right there. But was he rich at the time?

MRS. LINDE: He was very well off, I'd say. But the business was shaky, Nora. When he died, it all fell apart, and nothing was left.

NORA: And then—?

MRS. LINDE: Yes, so I had to scrape up a living with a little shop and a little teaching and whatever else I could find. The last three years have been like one endless workday without a rest for me. Now it's over, Nora. My poor mother doesn't need me, for she's passed on. Nor the boys, either; they're working now and can take care of themselves.

145 NORA: How free you must feel—

MRS. LINDE: No—only unspeakably empty. Nothing to live for now. *(Standing up anxiously.)* That's why I couldn't take it any longer out in that desolate hole. Maybe here it'll be easier to find something to do and keep my mind occupied. If I could only be lucky enough to get a steady job, some office work—

NORA: Oh, but Kristine, that's so dreadfully tiring, and you already look so tired. It would be much better for you if you could go off to a bathing resort.

MRS. LINDE: *(going toward the window)* I have no father to give me travel money, Nora.

NORA: *(rising)* Oh, don't be angry with me.

150 MRS. LINDE: *(going to her)* Nora dear, don't you be angry with me. The worst of my kind of situation is all the bitterness that's stored away. No one to work for, and yet you're always having to snap up your opportunities. You have to live; and so you grow selfish. When you told me the happy change in your lot, do you know I was delighted less for your sakes than for mine?

NORA: How so? Oh, I see. You think Torvald could do something for you.

MRS. LINDE: Yes, that's what I thought.

NORA: And he will, Kristine! Just leave it to me; I'll bring it up so delicately—find something attractive to humor him with. Oh, I'm so eager to help you.

MRS. LINDE: How very kind of you, Nora, to be so concerned over me—doubly kind, considering you really know so little of life's burdens yourself.

155 NORA: I—? I know so little—?

MRS. LINDE: *(smiling)* Well my heavens—a little needlework and such— Nora, you're just a child.

NORA: *(tossing her head and pacing the floor)* You don't have to act so superior.

MRS. LINDE: Oh?

NORA: You're just like the others. You all think I'm incapable of anything serious—

160 MRS. LINDE: Come now—

NORA: That I've never had to face the raw world.

MRS. LINDE: Nora dear, you've just been telling me all your troubles.

NORA: Hm! Trivial! *(Quietly.)* I haven't told you the big thing.

MRS. LINDE: Big thing? What do you mean?

165 NORA: You look down on me so, Kristine, but you shouldn't. You're proud that you worked so long and hard for your mother.

MRS. LINDE: I don't look down on a soul. But it *is* true: I'm proud—and happy, too—to think it was given to me to make my mother's last days almost free of care.

NORA: And you're also proud thinking of what you've done for your brothers.

MRS. LINDE: I feel I've a right to be.

NORA: I agree. But listen to this, Kristine—I've also got something to be proud and happy for.

170 MRS. LINDE: I don't doubt it. But whatever do you mean?

NORA: Not so loud. What if Torvald heard! He mustn't, not for anything in the world. Nobody must know, Kristine. No one but you.

MRS. LINDE: But what is it, then?

NORA: Come here. *(Drawing her down beside her on the sofa.)* It's true—I've also got something to be proud and happy for. I'm the one who saved Torvald's life.

MRS. LINDE: Saved—? Saved how?

175 NORA: I told you about the trip to Italy. Torvald never would have lived if he hadn't gone south—

MRS. LINDE: Of course; your father gave you the means—

NORA: *(smiling)* That's what Torvald and all the rest think, but—

MRS. LINDE: But—?

NORA: Papa didn't give us a pin. I was the one who raised the money.

180 MRS. LINDE: You? That whole amount?

NORA: Four thousand, eight hundred crowns. What do you say to that?

MRS. LINDE: But Nora, how was it possible? Did you win the lottery?

NORA: *(disdainfully)* The lottery? Pooh! No art to that.

MRS. LINDE: But where did you get it from then?

185 NORA: *(humming, with a mysterious smile)* Hmm, tra-la-la-la.

MRS. LINDE: Because you couldn't have borrowed it.

NORA: No? Why not?

MRS. LINDE: A wife can't borrow without her husband's consent.

NORA: *(tossing her head)* Oh, but a wife with a little business sense, a wife who knows how to manage—

190 MRS. LINDE: Nora, I simply don't understand—

NORA: You don't have to. Whoever said I *borrowed* the money? I could have gotten it other ways. *(Throwing herself back on the sofa.)* I could have gotten it from some admirer or other. After all, a girl with my ravishing appeal—

MRS. LINDE: You lunatic.

NORA: I'll bet you're eaten up with curiosity, Kristine.

MRS. LINDE: Now listen here, Nora—you haven't done something indiscreet?

195 NORA: *(sitting up again)* Is it indiscreet to save your husband's life?

MRS. LINDE: I think it's indiscreet that without his knowledge you—

NORA: But that's the point: he mustn't know! My Lord, can't you understand? He mustn't ever know the close call he had. It was to *me* the doctors came to say his life was in danger—that nothing could save him but a stay in the south. Didn't I try strategy then! I began talking about how lovely it would be for me to travel abroad like other young wives; I begged and I cried; I told him please to remember my condition, to be kind and indulge me; and then I dropped a hint that he could easily take out a loan. But at that, Kristine, he nearly exploded. He said I was frivolous, and it was his duty as man of the house not to indulge me in whims and fancies—as I think he called them. Aha, I thought, now you'll just have to be saved—and that's when I saw my chance.

MRS. LINDE: And your father never told Torvald the money wasn't from him?

NORA: No, never. Papa died right about then. I'd considered bringing him into my secret and begging him never to tell. But he was too sick at the time—and then, sadly, it didn't matter.

200 MRS. LINDE: And you've never confided in your husband since?

NORA: For heaven's sake, no! Are you serious? He's so strict on that subject. Besides—Torvald, with all his masculine pride—how painfully humiliating for him if he ever found out he was in debt to me. That would just ruin our relationship. Our beautiful, happy home would never be the same.

MRS. LINDE: Won't you ever tell him?

NORA: *(thoughtfully, half smiling)* Yes—maybe sometime, years from now, when I'm no longer so attractive. Don't laugh! I only mean when Torvald loves me less than now, when he stops enjoying my dancing and dressing up and reciting for him. Then it might be wise to have something in reserve—*(Breaking off.)* How ridiculous! That'll never happen—Well, Kristine, what do you think of my big secret? I'm capable of something too, hm? You can imagine, of course, how this thing hangs over me. It really hasn't been easy meeting the payments on time. In the business world there's what they call quarterly interest and what they call amortization, and these are always so terribly hard to manage. I've had to skimp a little here and there, wherever I could, you know. I could hardly spare anything from my house allowance, because Torvald has to live well. I couldn't let the children go poorly dressed; whatever I got for them, I felt I had to use up completely—the darlings!

MRS. LINDE: Poor Nora, so it had to come out of your own budget, then?

205 NORA: Yes, of course. But I was the one most responsible, too. Every time Torvald gave me money for new clothes and such, I never used more than half; always bought the simplest, cheapest outfits. It was a godsend that everything looks so well on me that Torvald never noticed. But it did weigh me down at times, Kristine. It *is* such a joy to wear fine things. You understand.

MRS. LINDE: Oh, of course.

NORA: And then I found other ways of making money. Last winter I was lucky enough to get a lot of copying to do. I locked myself in and sat writing every evening till late in the night. Ah, I was tired so often, dead tired. But still it was wonderful fun, sitting and working like that, earning money. It was almost like being a man.

MRS. LINDE: But how much have you paid off this way so far?

NORA: That's hard to say, exactly. These accounts, you know, aren't easy to figure. I only know that I've paid out all I could scrape together. Time and again I haven't known where to turn. *(Smiling.)* Then I'd sit here dreaming of a rich old gentleman who had fallen in love with me—

210 MRS. LINDE: What! Who is he?

NORA: Oh, really! And that he'd died, and when his will was opened, there in big letters it said, "All my fortune shall be paid over in cash, immediately, to that enchanting Mrs. Nora Helmer."

MRS. LINDE: But Nora dear—who *was* this gentleman?

NORA: Good grief, can't you understand? The old man never existed; that was only something I'd dream up time and again whenever I was at my wits' end for money. But it makes no difference now; the old fossil can go where he pleases for all I care; I don't need him or his will—because now I'm free. *(Jumping up.)* Oh, how lovely to think of that, Kristine! Carefree! To know you're carefree, utterly carefree; to be able to romp and play with the children, and to keep up a beautiful, charming home—everything just the way Torvald likes it! And think, spring is coming, with big blue skies. Maybe we can travel a little then. Maybe I'll see the ocean again. Oh yes, it *is* so marvelous to live and be happy!

The front doorbell rings.

MRS. LINDE: *(rising)* There's the bell. It's probably best that I go.

215 NORA: No, stay. No one's expected. It must be for Torvald.

MAID: *(from the hall doorway)* Excuse me, ma'am—there's a gentleman here to see Mr. Helmer, but I didn't know—since the doctor's with him—

NORA: Who is the gentleman?

KROGSTAD: *(from the doorway)* It's me, Mrs. Helmer.

Mrs. Linde starts and turns away toward the window.

NORA: *(stepping toward him, tense, her voice a whisper)* You? What is it? Why do you want to speak to my husband?

220 KROGSTAD: Bank business—after a fashion. I have a small job in the investment bank, and I hear now your husband is going to be our chief—

NORA: In other words, it's—

KROGSTAD: Just dry business, Mrs. Helmer. Nothing but that.

NORA: Yes, then please be good enough to step into the study. *(She nods indifferently as she sees him out by the hall door, then returns and begins stirring up the stove.)*

MRS. LINDE: Nora—who was that man?

225 NORA: That was a Mr. Krogstad—a lawyer.

MRS. LINDE: Then it really was him.

NORA: Do you know that person?

MRS. LINDE: I did once—many years ago. For a time he was a law clerk in our town.

NORA: Yes, he's been that.

230 MRS. LINDE: How he's changed.

NORA: I understand he had a very unhappy marriage.

MRS. LINDE: He's a widower now.

NORA: With a number of children. There now, it's burning. *(She closes the stove door and moves the rocker a bit to one side.)*

MRS. LINDE: They say he has a hand in all kinds of business.

235 NORA: Oh? That may be true: I wouldn't know. But let's not think about business. It's so dull.

Dr. Rank enters from Helmer's study.

RANK: *(still in the doorway)* No, no, really—I don't want to intrude, I'd just as soon talk a little while with your wife. *(Shuts the door, then notices Mrs. Linde.)* Oh, beg pardon. I'm intruding here too.

NORA: No, not at all. *(Introducing him.)* Dr. Rank, Mrs. Linde.

RANK: Well now, that's a name much heard in this house. I believe I passed the lady on the stairs as I came.

MRS. LINDE: Yes, I take the stairs very slowly. They're rather hard on me.

240 RANK: Uh-hm, some touch of internal weakness?

MRS. LINDE: More overexertion, I'd say.

RANK: Nothing else? Then you're probably here in town to rest up in a round of parties?

MRS. LINDE: I'm here to look for work.

RANK: Is that the best cure for overexertion?

245 MRS. LINDE: One has to live, Doctor.

RANK: Yes, there's a common prejudice to that effect.

NORA: Oh, come on, Dr. Rank—you really do want to live yourself.

RANK: Yes, I really do. Wretched as I am, I'll gladly prolong my torment indefinitely. All my patients feel like that. And it's quite the same, too, with the morally sick. Right at this moment there's one of those moral invalids in there with Helmer—

MRS. LINDE: *(softly)* Ah!

250 NORA: Who do you mean?

RANK: Oh, it's a lawyer, Krogstad, a type you wouldn't know. His character is rotten to the root—but even he began chattering all-importantly about how he had to *live.*

NORA: Oh? What did he want to talk to Torvald about?

RANK: I really don't know. I only heard something about the bank.

NORA: I didn't know that Krog—that this man Krogstad had anything to do with the bank.

255 RANK: Yes, he's gotten some kind of berth down there. *(To Mrs. Linde.)* I don't know if you also have, in your neck of the woods, a type of person who scuttles about breathlessly, sniffing out hints of moral corruption, and then maneuvers his victim into some sort of key position where he can keep an eye on him. It's the healthy these days that are out in the cold.

MRS. LINDE: All the same, it's the sick who most need to be taken in.

RANK: *(with a shrug)* Yes, there we have it. That's the concept that's turning society into a sanatorium.

Nora, lost in her thoughts, breaks out into quiet laughter and claps her hands.

RANK: Why do you laugh at that? Do you have any real idea of what society is?

NORA: What do I care about dreary old society? I was laughing at something quite different—something terribly funny. Tell me, Doctor—is everyone who works in the bank dependent now on Torvald?

260 RANK: Is that what you find so terribly funny?

NORA: *(smiling and humming)* Never mind, never mind! *(Pacing the floor.)* Yes, that's really immensely amusing: that we—that Torvald has so much power now over all those people. *(Taking the bag out of her pocket.)* Dr. Rank, a little macaroon on that?

RANK: See here, macaroons! I thought they were contraband here.

NORA: Yes, but these are some that Kristine gave me.

MRS. LINDE: What? I—?

265 NORA: Now, now, don't be afraid. You couldn't possibly know that Torvald had forbidden them. You see, he's worried they'll ruin my teeth. But hmp! Just this once! Isn't that so, Dr. Rank? Help yourself! *(Puts a macaroon in his mouth.)* And you too, Kristine. And I'll also have one, only a little one—or two, at the most. *(Walking about again.)* Now I'm really tremendously happy. Now there's just one last thing in the world that I have an enormous desire to do.

RANK: Well! And what's that?

NORA: It's something I have such a consuming desire to say so Torvald could hear.

RANK: And why can't you say it?

NORA: I don't dare. It's quite shocking.

270 MRS. LINDE: Shocking?

RANK: Well, then it isn't advisable. But in front of us you certainly can. What do you have such a desire to say so Torvald could hear?

NORA: I have such a huge desire to say—to hell and be damned!

RANK: Are you crazy?

MRS. LINDE: My goodness, Nora!

275 RANK: Go on, say it. Here he is.

NORA: *(hiding the macaroon bag)* Shh, shh, shh!

Helmer comes in from his study, hat in hand, overcoat over his arm.

NORA: *(going toward him)* Well, Torvald dear, are you through with him?

HELMER: Yes, he just left.

NORA: Let me introduce you—this is Kristine, who's arrived here in town.

280 HELMER: Kristine—? I'm sorry, but I don't know—

NORA: Mrs. Linde, Torvald dear. Mrs. Kristine Linde.

HELMER: Of course. A childhood friend of my wife's, no doubt?

MRS. LINDE: Yes, we knew each other in those days.

NORA: And just think, she made the long trip down here in order to talk with you.

285 HELMER: What's this?

MRS. LINDE: Well, not exactly—

Nora: You see, Kristine is remarkably clever in office work, and so she's
terribly eager to come under a capable man's supervision and add
more to what she already knows—

Helmer: Very wise, Mrs. Linde.

Nora: And then when she heard that you'd become a bank manager—the
story was wired out to the papers—then she came in as fast as she
could and—Really, Torvald, for my sake you can do a little something
for Kristine, can't you?

290 Helmer: Yes, it's not at all impossible. Mrs. Linde, I suppose you're a
widow?

Mrs. Linde: Yes.

Helmer: Any experience in office work?

Mrs. Linde: Yes, a good deal.

Helmer: Well, it's quite likely that I can make an opening for you—

295 Nora: (clapping her hands) You see, you see!

Helmer: You've come at a lucky moment, Mrs. Linde.

Mrs. Linde: Oh, how can I thank you?

Helmer: Not necessary. (Putting his overcoat on.) But today you'll have to
excuse me—

Rank: Wait, I'll go with you. (He fetches his coat from the hall and warms it at
the stove.)

300 Nora: Don't stay out long, dear.

Helmer: An hour; no more.

Nora: Are you going too, Kristine?

Mrs. Linde: (putting on her winter garments) Yes, I have to see about a room
now.

Helmer: Then perhaps we can all walk together.

305 Nora: (helping her) What a shame we're so cramped here, but it's quite
impossible for us to—

Mrs. Linde: Oh, don't even think of it! Good-bye, Nora dear, and thanks
for everything.

Nora: Good-bye for now. Of course you'll be back this evening. And you
too, Dr. Rank. What? If you're well enough? Oh, you've got to be!
Wrap up tight now.

*In a ripple of small talk the company moves out into the hall; children's voices are
heard outside on the steps.*

Nora: There they are! There they are! (She runs to open the door. The children
come in with their nurse, Anne-Marie.) Come in, come in! (Bends down
and kisses them.) Oh, you darlings—! Look at them, Kristine. Aren't
they lovely!

Rank: No loitering in the draft here.

310 Helmer: Come, Mrs. Linde—this place is unbearable now for anyone but
mothers.

*Dr. Rank, Helmer, and Mrs. Linde go down the stairs. Anne-Marie goes into the
living room with the children. Nora follows, after closing the hall door.*

NORA: How fresh and strong you look. Oh, such red cheeks you have! Like apples and roses. *(The children interrupt her throughout the following.)* And it was so much fun? That's wonderful. Really? You pulled both Emmy and Bob on the sled? Imagine, all together! Yes, you're a clever boy, Ivar. Oh, let me hold her a bit, Anne-Marie. My sweet little doll baby! *(Takes the smallest from the nurse and dances with her.)* Yes, yes, Mama will dance with Bob as well. What? Did you throw snowballs? Oh, if I'd only been there! No, don't bother, Anne-Marie—I'll undress them myself. Oh yes, let me. It's such fun. Go in and rest; you look half frozen. There's hot coffee waiting for you on the stove. *(The nurse goes into the room to the left. Nora takes the children's winter things off, throwing them about, while the children talk to her all at once.)* Is that so? A big dog chased you? But it didn't bite? No, dogs never bite little, lovely doll babies. Don't peek in the packages, Ivar! What is it? Yes, wouldn't you like to know. No, no, it's an ugly something. Well? Shall we play? What shall we play? Hide-and-seek? Yes, let's play hide-and-seek. Bob must hide first. I must? Yes, let me hide first. *(Laughing and shouting, she and the children play in and out of the living room and the adjoining room to the right. At last Nora hides under the table. The children come storming in, search, but cannot find her, then hear her muffled laughter, dash over to the table, lift the cloth up and find her. Wild shouting. She creeps forward as if to scare them. More shouts. Meanwhile, a knock at the hall door; no one has noticed it. Now the door half opens, and Krogstad appears. He waits a moment; the game goes on.)*

KROGSTAD: Beg pardon, Mrs. Helmer—

NORA: *(with a strangled cry, turning and scrambling to her knees)* Oh! What do you want?

KROGSTAD: Excuse me. The outer door was ajar; it must be someone forgot to shut it—

315 NORA: *(rising)* My husband isn't home, Mr. Krogstad.

KROGSTAD: I know that.

NORA: Yes—then what do you want here?

KROGSTAD: A word with you.

NORA: With—? *(To the children, quietly.)* Go in to Anne-Marie. What? No, the strange man won't hurt Mama. When he's gone, we'll play some more. *(She leads the children into the room to the left and shuts the door after them. Then, tense and nervous.)* You want to speak to me?

320 KROGSTAD: Yes, I want to.

NORA: Today? But it's not yet the first of the month—

KROGSTAD: No, it's Christmas Eve. It's going to be up to you how merry a Christmas you have.

NORA: What is it you want? Today I absolutely can't—

KROGSTAD: We won't talk about that till later. This is something else. You do have a moment to spare, I suppose?

325 NORA: Oh yes, of course—I do, except—

KROGSTAD: Good. I was sitting over at Olsen's Restaurant when I saw your husband go down the street—

Nora: Yes?

Krogstad: With a lady.

Nora: Yes. So?

330 Krogstad: If you'll pardon my asking: wasn't that lady a Mrs. Linde?

Nora: Yes.

Krogstad: Just now come into town?

Nora: Yes, today.

Krogstad: She's a good friend of yours?

335 Nora: Yes, she is. But I don't see—

Krogstad: I also knew her once.

Nora: I'm aware of that.

Krogstad: Oh? You know all about it. I thought so. Well, then let me ask you short and sweet: is Mrs. Linde getting a job in the bank?

Nora: What makes you think you can cross-examine me, Mr. Krogstad— you, one of my husband's employees? But since you ask, you might as well know—yes, Mrs. Linde's going to be taken on at the bank. And I'm the one who spoke for her, Mr. Krogstad. Now you know.

340 Krogstad: So I guessed right.

Nora: (pacing up and down) Oh, one does have a tiny bit of influence, I should hope. Just because I am a woman, don't think it means that— When one has a subordinate position, Mr. Krogstad, one really ought to be careful about pushing somebody who—hm—

Krogstad: Who has influence?

Nora: That's right.

Krogstad: (in a different tone) Mrs. Helmer, would you be good enough to use your influence on my behalf?

345 Nora: What? What do you mean?

Krogstad: Would you please make sure that I keep my subordinate position in the bank?

Nora: What does that mean? Who's thinking of taking away your position?

Krogstad: Oh, don't play the innocent with me. I'm quite aware that your friend would hardly relish the chance of running into me again; and I'm also aware now whom I can thank for being turned out.

Nora: But I promise you—

350 Krogstad: Yes, yes, yes, to the point: there's still time, and I'm advising you to use your influence to prevent it.

Nora: But Mr. Krogstad, I have absolutely no influence.

Krogstad: You haven't? I thought you were just saying—

Nora: You shouldn't take me so literally. I! How can you believe that I have any such influence over my husband?

Krogstad: Oh, I've known your husband from our student days. I don't think the great bank manager's more steadfast than any other married man.

355 Nora: You speak insolently about my husband, and I'll show you the door.

Krogstad: The lady has spirit.

NORA: I'm not afraid of you any longer. After New Year's, I'll soon be done
with the whole business.

KROGSTAD: *(restraining himself)* Now listen to me, Mrs. Helmer. If necessary,
I'll fight for my little job in the bank as if it were life itself.

NORA: Yes, so it seems.

360 KROGSTAD: It's not just a matter of income; that's the least of it. It's
something else—All right, out with it! Look, this is the thing. You
know, just like all the others, of course, that once, a good many years
ago, I did something rather rash.

NORA: I've heard rumors to that effect.

KROGSTAD: The case never got into court; but all the same, every door was
closed in my face from then on. So I took up those various activities
you know about. I had to grab hold somewhere; and I dare say I
haven't been among the worst. But now I want to drop all that. My
boys are growing up. For their sakes, I'll have to win back as much
respect as possible here in town. That job in the bank was like the first
rung in my ladder. And now your husband wants to kick me right
back down in the mud again.

NORA: But for heaven's sake, Mr. Krogstad, it's simply not in my power to
help you.

KROGSTAD: That's because you haven't the will to—but I have the means to
make you.

365 NORA: You certainly won't tell my husband that I owe you money?

KROGSTAD: Hm—what if I told him that?

NORA: That would be shameful of you. *(Nearly in tears.)* This secret—my joy
and my pride—that he should learn it in such a crude and disgusting
way—learn it from you. You'd expose me to the most horrible
unpleasantness—

KROGSTAD: Only unpleasantness?

NORA: *(vehemently)* But go on and try. It'll turn out the worse for you,
because then my husband will really see what a crook you are, and
then you'll *never* be able to hold your job.

370 KROGSTAD: I asked if it was just domestic unpleasantness you were afraid of.

NORA: If my husband finds out, then of course he'll pay what I owe at
once, and then we'd be through with you for good.

KROGSTAD: *(a step closer)* Listen, Mrs. Helmer—you've either got a very bad
memory, or else no head at all for business. I'd better put you a little
more in touch with the facts.

NORA: What do you mean?

KROGSTAD: When your husband was sick, you came to me for a loan of four
thousand, eight hundred crowns.

375 NORA: Where else could I go?

KROGSTAD: I promised to get you that sum—

NORA: And you got it.

KROGSTAD: I promised to get you that sum, on certain conditions. You were
so involved in your husband's illness, and so eager to finance your

trip, that I guess you didn't think out all the details. It might just be a good idea to remind you. I promised you the money on the strength of a note I drew up.

NORA: Yes, and that I signed.

380 KROGSTAD: Right. But at the bottom I added some lines for your father to guarantee the loan. He was supposed to sign down there.

NORA: Supposed to? He did sign.

KROGSTAD: I left the date blank. In other words, your father would have dated his signature himself. Do you remember that?

NORA: Yes, I think—

KROGSTAD: Then I gave you the note for you to mail to your father. Isn't that so?

385 NORA: Yes.

KROGSTAD: And naturally you sent it at once—because only some five, six days later you brought me the note, properly signed. And with that, the money was yours.

NORA: Well, then; I've made my payments regularly, haven't I?

KROGSTAD: More or less. But—getting back to the point—those were hard times for you then, Mrs. Helmer.

NORA: Yes, they were.

390 KROGSTAD: Your father was very ill, I believe.

NORA: He was near the end.

KROGSTAD: He died soon after?

NORA: Yes.

KROGSTAD: Tell me, Mrs. Helmer, do you happen to recall the date of your father's death? The day of the month, I mean.

395 NORA: Papa died the twenty-ninth of September.

KROGSTAD: That's quite correct; I've already looked into that. And now we come to a curious thing—*(taking out a paper)* which I simply cannot comprehend.

NORA: Curious thing? I don't know—

KROGSTAD: This is the curious thing: that your father co-signed the note for your loan three days after his death.

NORA: How—? I don't understand.

400 KROGSTAD: Your father died the twenty-ninth of September. But look. Here your father dated his signature October second. Isn't that curious, Mrs. Helmer? *(Nora is silent.)* Can you explain it to me? *(Nora remains silent.)* It's also remarkable that the words "October second" and the year aren't written in your father's hand, but rather in one that I think I know. Well, it's easy to understand. Your father forgot perhaps to date his signature, and then someone or other added it, a bit sloppily, before anyone knew of his death. There's nothing wrong in that. It all comes down to the signature. And there's no question about *that*, Mrs. Helmer. It really *was* your father who signed his own name here, wasn't it?

NORA: *(after a short silence, throwing her head back and looking squarely at him)* No, it wasn't. *I* signed Papa's name.

KROGSTAD: Wait, now—are you fully aware that this is a dangerous confession?

NORA: Why? You'll soon get your money.

KROGSTAD: Let me ask you a question—why didn't you send the paper to your father?

405 NORA: That was impossible. Papa was so sick. If I'd asked him for his signature, I also would have had to tell him what the money was for. But I couldn't tell him, sick as he was, that my husband's life was in danger. That was just impossible.

KROGSTAD: Then it would have been better if you'd given up the trip abroad.

NORA: I couldn't possibly. The trip was to save my husband's life. I couldn't give that up.

KROGSTAD: But didn't you ever consider that this was a fraud against me?

NORA: I couldn't let myself be bothered by that. You weren't any concern of mine. I couldn't stand you, with all those cold complications you made, even though you knew how badly off my husband was.

410 KROGSTAD: Mrs. Helmer, obviously you haven't the vaguest idea of what you've involved yourself in. But I can tell you this: it was nothing more and nothing worse than I once did—and it wrecked my whole reputation.

NORA: You? Do you expect me to believe that you ever acted bravely to save your wife's life?

KROGSTAD: Laws don't inquire into motives.

NORA: Then they must be very poor laws.

KROGSTAD: Poor or not—if I introduce this paper in court, you'll be judged according to law.

415 NORA: This I refuse to believe. A daughter hasn't a right to protect her dying father from anxiety and care? A wife hasn't a right to save her husband's life? I don't know much about laws, but I'm sure that somewhere in the books these things are allowed. And you don't know anything about it—you who practice the law? You must be an awful lawyer, Mr. Krogstad.

KROGSTAD: Could be. But business—the kind of business we two mixed up in—don't you think I know about that? All right. Do what you want now. But I'm telling you *this:* if I get shoved down a second time, you're going to keep me company. *(He bows and goes out through the hall.)*

NORA: *(pensive for a moment, then tossing her head)* Oh, really! Trying to frighten me! I'm not so silly as all that. *(Begins gathering up the children's clothes, but soon stops.)* But—? No, but that's impossible! I did it out of love.

THE CHILDREN: *(in the doorway, left)* Mama, that strange man's gone out the door.

Nora: Yes, yes, I know it. But don't tell anyone about the strange man. Do you hear? Not even Papa!

420 The Children: No, Mama. But now will you play again?

Nora: No, not now.

The Children: Oh, but Mama, you promised.

Nora: Yes, but I can't now. Go inside; I have too much to do. Go in, go in, my sweet darlings. *(She herds them gently back in the room and shuts the door after them. Settling on the sofa, she takes up a piece of embroidery and makes some stitches, but soon stops abruptly.)* No! *(Throws the work aside, rises, goes to the hall door and calls out.)* Helene! Let me have the tree in here. *(Goes to the table, left, opens the table drawer, and stops again.)* No, but that's utterly impossible!

Maid: *(with the Christmas tree)* Where should I put it, ma'am?

425 Nora: There. The middle of the floor.

Maid: Should I bring anything else?

Nora: No, thanks. I have what I need.

The Maid, who has set the tree down, goes out.

Nora: *(absorbed in trimming the tree)* Candles here—and flowers here. That terrible creature! Talk, talk, talk! There's nothing to it at all. The tree's going to be lovely. I'll do anything to please you, Torvald. I'll sing for you, dance for you—

Helmer comes in from the hall, with a sheaf of papers under his arm.

Nora: Oh! You're back so soon?

430 Helmer: Yes. Has anyone been here?

Nora: Here? No.

Helmer: That's odd. I saw Krogstad leaving the front door.

Nora: So? Oh yes, that's true. Krogstad was here a moment.

Helmer: Nora, I can see by your face that he's been here, begging you to put in a good word for him.

435 Nora: Yes.

Helmer: And it was supposed to seem like your own idea? You were to hide it from me that he'd been here. He asked you that, too, didn't he?

Nora: Yes, Torvald, but—

Helmer: Nora, Nora, and you could fall for that? Talk with that sort of person and promise him anything? And then in the bargain, tell me an untruth.

Nora: An untruth—?

440 Helmer: Didn't you say that no one had been here? *(Wagging his finger.)* My little songbird must never do that again. A songbird needs a clean beak to warble with. No false notes. *(Putting his arm about her waist.)* That's the way it should be, isn't it? Yes, I'm sure of it. *(Releasing her.)* And so, enough of that. *(Sitting by the stove.)* Ah, how snug and cozy it is here. *(Leafing among his papers.)*

Nora: *(busy with the tree, after a short pause)* Torvald!

HELMER: Yes.

NORA: I'm so much looking forward to the Stenborgs' costume party, day
   after tomorrow.

HELMER: And I can't wait to see what you'll surprise me with.

445 NORA: Oh, that stupid business!

HELMER: What?

NORA: I can't find anything that's right. Everything seems so ridiculous, so
   inane.

HELMER: So my little Nora's come to *that* recognition?

NORA: *(going behind his chair, her arms resting on its back)* Are you very busy,
   Torvald?

450 HELMER: Oh—

NORA: What papers are those?

HELMER: Bank matters.

NORA: Already?

HELMER: I've gotten full authority from the retiring management to make
   all necessary changes in personnel and procedure. I'll need Christmas
   week for that. I want to have everything in order by New Year's.

455 NORA: So that was the reason this poor Krogstad—

HELMER: Hm.

NORA: *(still leaning on the chair and slowly stroking the nape of his neck)* If you
   weren't so very busy, I would have asked you an enormous favor,
   Torvald.

HELMER: Let's hear. What is it?

NORA: You know, there isn't anyone who has your good taste—and I want
   so much to look well at the costume party. Torvald, couldn't you take
   over and decide what I should be and plan my costume?

460 HELMER: Ah, is my stubborn little creature calling for a lifeguard?

NORA: Yes, Torvald, I can't get anywhere without your help.

HELMER: All right—I'll think it over. We'll hit on something.

NORA: Oh, how sweet of you. *(Goes to the tree again. Pause.)* Aren't the red
   flowers pretty—? But tell me, was it really such a crime that this
   Krogstad committed?

HELMER: Forgery. Do you have any idea what that means?

465 NORA: Couldn't he have done it out of need?

HELMER: Yes, or thoughtlessness, like so many others. I'm not so heartless
   that I'd condemn a man categorically for just one mistake.

NORA: No, of course not, Torvald!

HELMER: Plenty of men have redeemed themselves by openly confessing
   their crimes and taking their punishment.

NORA: Punishment—?

470 HELMER: But now Krogstad didn't go that way. He got himself out by sharp
   practices, and that's the real cause of his moral breakdown.

NORA: Do you really think that would—?

HELMER: Just imagine how a man with that sort of guilt in him has to lie
   and cheat and deceive on all sides, has to wear a mask even with the

nearest and dearest he has, even with his own wife and children. And
with the children, Nora—that's where it's most horrible.

NORA: Why?

HELMER: Because that kind of atmosphere of lies infects the whole life of a
home. Every breath the children take in is filled with the germs of
something degenerate.

475 NORA: *(coming closer behind him)* Are you sure of that?

HELMER: Oh, I've seen it often enough as a lawyer. Almost everyone who
goes bad early in life has a mother who's a chronic liar.

NORA: Why just—the mother?

HELMER: It's usually the mother's influence that's dominant, but the father's
works in the same way, of course. Every lawyer is quite familiar with it.
And still this Krogstad's been going home year in, year out, poisoning
his own children with lies and pretense; that's why I call him morally
lost. *(Reaching his hands out toward her.)* So my sweet little Nora must
promise me never to plead his cause. Your hand on it. Come, come,
what's this? Give me your hand. There, now. All settled. I can tell you
it'd be impossible for me to work alongside of him. I literally feel
physically revolted when I'm anywhere near such a person.

NORA: *(withdraws her hand and goes to the other side of the Christmas tree)*
How hot it is here! And I've got so much to do.

480 HELMER: *(getting up and gathering his papers)* Yes, and I have to think about
getting some of these read through before dinner. I'll think about your
costume, too. And something to hang on the tree in gilt paper, I may
even see about that. *(Putting his hand on her head.)* Oh you, my darling
little songbird. *(He goes into his study and closes the door after him.)*

NORA: *(softly, after a silence)* Oh, really! It isn't so. It's impossible. It must be
impossible.

ANNE-MARIE: *(in the doorway, left)* The children are begging so hard to come
in to Mama.

NORA: No, no, no, don't let them in to me! You stay with them, Anne-
Marie.

ANNE-MARIE: Of course, ma'am. *(Closes the door.)*

485 NORA: *(pale with terror)* Hurt my children—! Poison my home? *(A moment's
pause; then she tosses her head.)* That's not true. Never. Never in all the
world.

ACT II

*Same room. Beside the piano the Christmas tree now stands stripped of ornaments,
burned-down candle stubs on its ragged branches. Nora's street clothes lie on the
sofa. Nora, alone in the room, moves restlessly about; at last she stops at the sofa
and picks up her coat.*

NORA: *(dropping the coat again)* Someone's coming! *(Goes toward the door,
listens.)* No—there's no one. Of course—nobody's coming today,

Christmas Day—or tomorrow, either. But maybe—*(Opens the door and looks out.)* No, nothing in the mailbox. Quite empty. *(Coming forward.)* What nonsense! He won't do anything serious. Nothing terrible could happen. It's impossible. Why, I have three small children.

Anne-Marie, with a large carton, comes in from the room to the left.

ANNE-MARIE: Well, at last I found the box with the masquerade clothes.

NORA: Thanks. Put it on the table.

ANNE-MARIE: *(does so)* But they're all pretty much of a mess.

5 NORA: Ahh! I'd love to rip them in a million pieces!

ANNE-MARIE: Oh, mercy, they can be fixed right up. Just a little patience.

NORA: Yes, I'll go get Mrs. Linde to help me.

ANNE-MARIE: Out again now? In this nasty weather? Miss Nora will catch cold—get sick.

NORA: Oh, worse things could happen—How are the children?

10 ANNE-MARIE: The poor mites are playing with their Christmas presents, but—

NORA: Do they ask for me much?

ANNE-MARIE: They're so used to having Mama around, you know.

NORA: Yes. But Anne-Marie, I *can't* be together with them as much as I was.

ANNE-MARIE: Well, small children get used to anything.

15 NORA: You think so? Do you think they'd forget their mother if she was gone for good?

ANNE-MARIE: Oh, mercy—gone for good!

NORA: Wait, tell me, Anne-Marie—I've wondered so often—how could you ever have the heart to give your child over to strangers?

ANNE-MARIE: But I had to, you know, to become little Nora's nurse.

NORA: Yes, but how could you *do* it?

20 ANNE-MARIE: When I could get such a good place? A girl who's poor and who's gotten in trouble is glad enough for that. Because that slippery fish, he didn't do a thing for me, you know.

NORA: But your daughter's surely forgotten you.

ANNE-MARIE: Oh, she certainly has not. She's written to me, both when she was confirmed and when she was married.

NORA: *(clasping her about the neck)* You old Anne-Marie, you were a good mother for me when I was little.

ANNE-MARIE: Poor little Nora, with no other mother but me.

25 NORA: And if the babies didn't have one, then I know that you'd—What silly talk! *(Opening the carton.)* Go in to them. Now I'll have to— Tomorrow you can see how lovely I'll look.

ANNE-MARIE: Oh, there won't be anyone at the party as lovely as Miss Nora. *(She goes off into the room, left.)*

NORA: *(begins unpacking the box, but soon throws it aside)* Oh, if I dared to go out. If only nobody would come. If only nothing would happen here while I'm out. What craziness—nobody's coming. Just don't think. This muff—needs a brushing. Beautiful gloves, beautiful gloves. Let it

go. Let it go! One, two, three, four, five, six—*(With a cry.)* Oh, there
they are! *(Poises to move toward the door, but remains irresolutely standing.
Mrs. Linde enters from the hall, where she has removed her street clothes.)*

NORA: Oh, it's you, Kristine. There's no one else out there? How good that
you've come.

MRS. LINDE: I hear you were up asking for me.

30 NORA: Yes, I just stopped by. There's something you really can help me
with. Let's get settled on the sofa. Look, there's going to be a costume
party tomorrow evening at the Stenborgs' right above us, and now
Torvald wants me to go as a Neapolitan peasant girl and dance the
tarantella that I learned in Capri.

MRS. LINDE: Really, are you giving a whole performance?

NORA: Torvald says yes, I should. See, here's the dress. Torvald had it made
for me down there; but now it's all so tattered that I just don't know—

MRS. LINDE: Oh, we'll fix that up in no time. It's nothing more than the
trimmings—they're a bit loose here and there. Needle and thread?
Good, now we have what we need.

NORA: Oh, how sweet of you!

35 MRS. LINDE: *(sewing)* So you'll be in disguise tomorrow, Nora. You know
what? I'll stop by then for a moment and have a look at you all
dressed up. But listen, I've absolutely forgotten to thank you for that
pleasant evening yesterday.

NORA: *(getting up and walking about)* I don't think it was as pleasant as usual
yesterday. You should have come to town a bit sooner, Kristine—Yes,
Torvald really knows how to give a home elegance and charm.

MRS. LINDE: And you do, too, if you ask me. You're not your father's
daughter for nothing. But tell me, is Dr. Rank always so down in the
mouth as yesterday?

NORA: No, that was quite an exception. But he goes around critically ill all
the time—tuberculosis of the spine, poor man. You know, his father
was a disgusting thing who kept mistresses and so on—and that's why
the son's been sickly from birth.

MRS. LINDE: *(lets her sewing fall to her lap)* But my dearest Nora, how do you
know about such things?

40 NORA: *(walking more jauntily)* Hmp! When you've had three children, then
you've had a few visits from—from women who know something of
medicine, and they tell you this and that.

MRS. LINDE: *(resumes sewing; a short pause)* Does Dr. Rank come here every
day?

NORA: Every blessed day. He's Torvald's best friend from childhood, and *my*
good friend, too. Dr. Rank almost belongs to this house.

MRS. LINDE: But tell me—is he quite sincere? I mean, doesn't he rather
enjoy flattering people?

NORA: Just the opposite. Why do you think that?

45 MRS. LINDE: When you introduced us yesterday, he was proclaiming that
he'd often heard my name in this house; but later I noticed that your

husband hadn't the slightest idea who I really was. So how could Dr. Rank—?

NORA: But it's all true, Kristine. You see, Torvald loves me beyond words, and, as he puts it, he'd like to keep me all to himself. For a long time he'd almost be jealous if I even mentioned any of my old friends back home. So of course I dropped that. But with Dr. Rank I talk a lot about such things, because he likes hearing about them.

MRS. LINDE: Now listen, Nora; in many ways you're still like a child. I'm a good deal older than you, with a little more experience. I'll tell you something: you ought to put an end to all this with Dr. Rank.

NORA: What should I put an end to?

MRS. LINDE: Both parts of it, I think. Yesterday you said something about a rich admirer who'd provide you with money—

50 NORA: Yes, one who doesn't exist—worse luck. So?

MRS. LINDE: Is Dr. Rank well off?

NORA: Yes, he is.

MRS. LINDE: With no dependents?

NORA: No, no one. But—

55 MRS. LINDE: And he's over here every day?

NORA: Yes, I told you that.

MRS. LINDE: How can a man of such refinement be so grasping?

NORA: I don't follow you at all.

MRS. LINDE: Now don't try to hide it, Nora. You think I can't guess who loaned you the forty-eight hundred crowns?

60 NORA: Are you out of your mind? How could you think such a thing! A friend of ours, who comes here every single day. What an intolerable situation that would have been!

MRS. LINDE: Then it really wasn't him.

NORA: No, absolutely not. It never even crossed my mind for a moment— And he had nothing to lend in those days; his inheritance came later.

MRS. LINDE: Well, I think that was a stroke of luck for you, Nora dear.

NORA: No, it never would have occurred to me to ask Dr. Rank—Still, I'm quite sure that if I had asked him—

65 MRS. LINDE: Which you won't, of course.

NORA: No, of course not. I can't see that I'd ever need to. But I'm quite positive that if I talked to Dr. Rank—

MRS. LINDE: Behind your husband's back?

NORA: I've got to clear up this other thing; *that's* also behind his back. I've *got* to clear it all up.

MRS. LINDE: Yes, I was saying that yesterday, but—

70 NORA: (*pacing up and down*) A man handles these problems so much better than a woman—

MRS. LINDE: One's husband does, yes.

NORA: Nonsense. (*Stopping.*) When you pay everything you owe, then you get your note back, right?

MRS. LINDE: Yes, naturally.

Nora: And can rip it into a million pieces and burn it up—that filthy scrap of paper!

75 Mrs. Linde: *(looking hard at her, laying her sewing aside, and rising slowly)* Nora, you're hiding something from me.

Nora: You can see it in my face?

Mrs. Linde: Something's happened to you since yesterday morning. Nora, what is it?

Nora: *(hurrying toward her)* Kristine! *(Listening.)* Shh! Torvald's home. Look, go in with the children a while. Torvald can't bear all this snipping and stitching. Let Anne-Marie help you.

Mrs. Linde: *(gathering up some of the things)* All right, but I'm not leaving here until we've talked this out. *(She disappears into the room, left, as Torvald enters from the hall.)*

80 Nora: Oh, how I've been waiting for you, Torvald dear.

Helmer: Was that the dressmaker?

Nora: No, that was Kristine. She's helping me fix up my costume. You know, it's going to be quite attractive.

Helmer: Yes, wasn't that a bright idea I had?

Nora: Brilliant! But then wasn't I good as well to give in to you?

85 Helmer: Good—because you give in to your husband's judgment? All right, you little goose, I know you didn't mean it like that. But I won't disturb you. You'll want to have a fitting, I suppose.

Nora: And you'll be working?

Helmer: Yes. *(Indicating a bundle of papers.)* See. I've been down to the bank. *(Starts toward his study.)*

Nora: Torvald.

Helmer: *(stops)* Yes.

90 Nora: If your little squirrel begged you, with all her heart and soul, for something—?

Helmer: What's that?

Nora: Then would you do it?

Helmer: First, naturally, I'd have to know what it was.

Nora: Your squirrel would scamper about and do tricks, if you'd only be sweet and give in.

95 Helmer: Out with it.

Nora: Your lark would be singing high and low in every room—

Helmer: Come on, she does that anyway.

Nora: I'd be a wood nymph and dance for you in the moonlight.

Helmer: Nora—don't tell me it's that same business from this morning?

100 Nora: *(coming closer)* Yes, Torvald, I beg you, please!

Helmer: And you actually have the nerve to drag that up again?

Nora: Yes, yes, you've got to give in to me; you *have* to let Krogstad keep his job in the bank.

Helmer: My dear Nora, I've slated his job for Mrs. Linde.

Nora: That's awfully kind of you. But you could just fire another clerk instead of Krogstad.

105 HELMER: This is the most incredible stubbornness! Because you go and give
 an impulsive promise to speak up for him, I'm expected to—
 NORA: That's not the reason, Torvald. It's for your own sake. That man
 does writing for the worst papers; you said it yourself. He could do you
 any amount of harm. I'm scared to death of him—
 HELMER: Ah, I understand. It's the old memories haunting you.
 NORA: What do you mean by that?
 HELMER: Of course, you're thinking about your father.
110 NORA: Yes, all right. Just remember how those nasty gossips wrote in the
 papers about Papa and slandered him so cruelly. I think they'd have
 had him dismissed if the department hadn't sent you up to
 investigate, and if you hadn't been so kind and open-minded toward
 him.
 HELMER: My dear Nora, there's a notable difference between your father
 and me. Your father's official career was hardly above reproach. But
 mine is; and I hope it'll stay that way as long as I hold my position.
 NORA: Oh, who can ever tell what vicious minds can invent? We could be
 so snug and happy now in our quiet, carefree home—you and I and
 the children, Torvald! That's why I'm pleading with you so—
 HELMER: And just by pleading for him you make it impossible for me to
 keep him on. It's already known at the bank that I'm firing Krogstad.
 What if it's rumored around now that the new bank manager was
 vetoed by his wife—
 NORA: Yes, what then—?
115 HELMER: Oh yes—as long as our little bundle of stubbornness gets her
 way—! I should go and make myself ridiculous in front of the whole
 office—give people the idea I can be swayed by all kinds of outside
 pressure. Oh, you can bet I'd feel the effects of that soon enough!
 Besides—there's something that rules Krogstad right out at the bank as
 long as I'm the manager.
 NORA: What's that?
 HELMER: His moral failings I could maybe overlook if I had to—
 NORA: Yes, Torvald, why not?
 HELMER: And I hear he's quite efficient on the job. But he was a crony of
 mine back in my teens—one of those rash friendships that crop up
 again and again to embarrass you later in life. Well, I might as well say
 it straight out: we're on a first-name basis. And that tactless fool makes
 no effort at all to hide it in front of others. Quite the contrary—he
 thinks that entitles him to take a familiar air around me, and so every
 other second he comes booming out with his "Yes, Torvald!" and "Sure
 thing, Torvald!" I tell you, it's been excruciating for me. He's out to
 make my place in the bank unbearable.
120 NORA: Torvald, you can't be serious about all this.
 HELMER: Oh no? Why not?
 NORA: Because these are such petty considerations.
 HELMER: What are you saying? Petty? You think I'm petty!

NORA: No, just the opposite, Torvald dear. That's exactly why—

125 HELMER: Never mind. You call my motives petty; then I might as well be just that. Petty! All right! We'll put a stop to this for good. *(Goes to the hall door and calls.)* Helene!

NORA: What do you want?

HELMER: *(searching among his papers)* A decision. *(The Maid comes in.)* Look here; take this letter; go out with it at once. Get hold of a messenger and have him deliver it. Quick now. It's already addressed. Wait, here's some money.

MAID: Yes, sir. *(She leaves with the letter.)*

HELMER: *(straightening his papers)* There, now, little Miss Willful.

130 NORA: *(breathlessly)* Torvald, what was that letter?

HELMER: Krogstad's notice.

NORA: Call it back, Torvald! There's still time. Oh, Torvald, call it back! Do it for my sake—for your sake, for the children's sake! Do you hear, Torvald; do it! You don't know how this can harm us.

HELMER: Too late.

NORA: Yes, too late.

135 HELMER: Nora dear, I can forgive you this panic, even though basically you're insulting me. Yes, you are! Or isn't it an insult to think that I should be afraid of a courtroom hack's revenge? But I forgive you anyway, because this shows so beautifully how much you love me. *(Takes her in his arms.)* This is the way it should be, my darling Nora. Whatever comes, you'll see: when it really counts, I have strength and courage enough as a man to take on the whole weight myself.

NORA: *(terrified)* What do you mean by that?

HELMER: The whole weight, I said.

NORA: *(resolutely)* No, never in all the world.

HELMER: Good. So we'll share it, Nora, as man and wife. That's as it should be. *(Fondling her.)* Are you happy now? There, there, there—not these frightened dove's eyes. It's nothing at all but empty fantasies—Now you should run through your tarantella and practice your tambourine. I'll go to the inner office and shut both doors, so I won't hear a thing; you can make all the noise you like. *(Turning in the doorway.)* And when Rank comes, just tell him where he can find me. *(He nods to her and goes with his papers into the study, closing the door.)*

140 NORA: *(standing as though rooted, dazed with fright, in a whisper)* He really could do it. He will do it. He'll do it in spite of everything. No, not that, never, never! Anything but that! Escape! A way out—*(The doorbell rings.)* Dr. Rank! Anything but that! *Anything*, whatever it is! *(Her hands pass over her face, smoothing it; she pulls herself together, goes over and opens the hall door. Dr. Rank stands outside, hanging his fur coat up. During the following scene, it begins getting dark.)*

NORA: Hello, Dr. Rank. I recognized your ring. But you mustn't go in to Torvald yet; I believe he's working.

RANK: And you?

NORA: For you, I always have an hour to spare—you know that. *(He has entered, and she shuts the door after him.)*

RANK: Many thanks. I'll make use of these hours while I can.

145 NORA: What do you mean by that? While you can?

RANK: Does that disturb you?

NORA: Well, it's such an odd phrase. Is anything going to happen?

RANK: What's going to happen is what I've been expecting so long—but I honestly didn't think it would come so soon.

NORA: *(gripping his arm)* What is it you've found out? Dr. Rank, you have to tell me!

150 RANK: *(sitting by the stove)* It's all over with me. There's nothing to be done about it.

NORA: *(breathing easier)* Is it you—then—?

RANK: Who else? There's no point in lying to one's self. I'm the most miserable of all my patients, Mrs. Helmer. These past few days I've been auditing my internal accounts. Bankrupt! Within a month I'll probably be laid out and rotting in the churchyard.

NORA: Oh, what a horrible thing to say.

RANK: The thing itself is horrible. But the worst of it is all the other horror before it's over. There's only one final examination left; when I'm finished with that, I'll know about when my disintegration will begin. There's something I want to say. Helmer with his sensitivity has such a sharp distaste for anything ugly. I don't want him near my sickroom.

155 NORA: Oh, but Dr. Rank—

RANK: I won't have him in there. Under no condition. I'll lock my door to him—As soon as I'm completely sure of the worst, I'll send you my calling card marked with a black cross, and you'll know then the wreck has started to come apart.

NORA: No, today you're completely unreasonable. And I wanted you so much to be in a really good humor.

RANK: With death up my sleeve? And then to suffer this way for somebody else's sins. Is there any justice in that? And in every single family, in some way or another, this inevitable retribution of nature goes on—

NORA: *(her hands pressed over her ears)* Oh, stuff! Cheer up! Please—be gay!

160 RANK: Yes, I'd just as soon laugh at it all. My poor, innocent spine, serving time for my father's gay army days.

NORA: *(by the table, left)* He was so infatuated with asparagus tips and *pâté de foie gras,* wasn't that it?

RANK: Yes—and with truffles.

NORA: Truffles, yes. And then with oysters, I suppose?

RANK: Yes, tons of oysters, naturally.

165 NORA: And then the port and champagne to go with it. It's so sad that all these delectable things have to strike at our bones.

RANK: Especially when they strike at the unhappy bones that never shared in the fun.

NORA: Ah, that's the saddest of all.

RANK: *(looks searchingly at her)* Hm.

NORA: *(after a moment)* Why did you smile?

170 RANK: No, it was you who laughed.

NORA: No, it was you who smiled, Dr. Rank!

RANK: *(getting up)* You're even a bigger tease than I'd thought.

NORA: I'm full of wild ideas today.

RANK: That's obvious.

175 NORA: *(putting both hands on his shoulders)* Dear, dear Dr. Rank, you'll never die for Torvald and me.

RANK: Oh, that loss you'll easily get over. Those who go away are soon forgotten.

NORA: *(looks fearfully at him)* You believe that?

RANK: One makes new connections, and then—

NORA: Who makes new connections?

180 RANK: Both you and Torvald will when I'm gone. I'd say you're well under way already. What was that Mrs. Linde doing here last evening?

NORA: Oh, come—you can't be jealous of poor Kristine?

RANK: Oh yes, I am. She'll be my successor here in the house. When I'm down under, that woman will probably—

NORA: Shh! Not so loud. She's right in there.

RANK: Today as well. So you see.

185 NORA: Only to sew on my dress. Good gracious, how unreasonable you are. *(Sitting on the sofa.)* Be nice now, Dr. Rank. Tomorrow you'll see how beautifully I'll dance; and you can imagine then that I'm dancing only for you—yes, and of course for Torvald, too—that's understood. *(Takes various items out of the carton.)* Dr. Rank, sit over here and I'll show you something.

RANK: *(sitting)* What's that?

NORA: Look here. Look.

RANK: Silk stockings.

NORA: Flesh-colored. Aren't they lovely? Now it's so dark here, but tomorrow—No, no, no, just look at the feet. Oh well, you might as well look at the rest.

190 RANK: Hm—

NORA: Why do you look so critical? Don't you believe they'll fit?

RANK: I've never had any chance to form an opinion on that.

NORA: *(glancing at him a moment)* Shame on you. *(Hits him lightly on the ear with the stockings.)* That's for you. *(Puts them away again.)*

RANK: And what other splendors am I going to see now?

195 NORA: Not the least bit more, because you've been naughty. *(She hums a little and rummages among her things.)*

RANK: *(after a short silence)* When I sit here together with you like this, completely easy and open, then I don't know—I simply can't imagine—whatever would have become of me if I'd never come into this house.

NORA: *(smiling)* Yes, I really think you feel completely at ease with us.

RANK: *(more quietly, staring straight ahead)* And then to have to go away
from it all—

NORA: Nonsense, you're not going away.

200 RANK: *(his voice unchanged)*—and not even be able to leave some poor show
of gratitude behind, scarcely a fleeting regret—no more than a vacant
place that anyone can fill.

NORA: And if I asked you now for—? No—

RANK: For what?

NORA: For a great proof of your friendship—

RANK: Yes, yes?

205 NORA: No, I mean—for an exceptionally big favor—

RANK: Would you really, for once, make me so happy?

NORA: Oh, you haven't the vaguest idea what it is.

RANK: All right, then tell me.

NORA: No, but I can't, Dr. Rank—it's all out of reason. It's advice and help,
too—and a favor—

210 RANK: So much the better. I can't fathom what you're hinting at. Just speak
out. Don't you trust me?

NORA: Of course. More than anyone else. You're my best and truest friend,
I'm sure. That's why I want to talk to you. All right, then, Dr. Rank:
there's something you can help me prevent. You know how deeply,
how inexpressibly dearly Torvald loves me; he'd never hesitate a
second to give up his life for me.

RANK: *(leaning close to her)* Nora—do you think he's the only one—

NORA: *(with a slight start)* Who—?

RANK: Who'd gladly give up his life for you.

215 NORA: *(heavily)* I see.

RANK: I swore to myself you should know this before I'm gone. I'll never
find a better chance. Yes, Nora, now you know. And also you know
now that you can trust me beyond anyone else.

NORA: *(rising, natural and calm)* Let me by.

RANK: *(making room for her, but still sitting)* Nora—

NORA: *(in the hall doorway)* Helene, bring the lamp in. *(Goes over to the
stove.)* Ah, dear Dr. Rank, that was really mean of you.

220 RANK: *(getting up)* That I've loved you just as deeply as somebody else? Was
that mean?

NORA: No, but that you came out and told me. That was quite
unnecessary—

RANK: What do you mean? Have you known—?

The Maid comes in with the lamp, sets it on the table, and goes out again.

RANK: Nora—Mrs. Helmer—I'm asking you: have you known about it?

NORA: Oh, how can I tell what I know or don't know? Really, I don't know
what to say—Why did you have to be so clumsy, Dr. Rank! Everything
was so good.

225 RANK: Well, in any case, you now have the knowledge that my body and
soul are at your command. So won't you speak out?

NORA: *(looking at him)* After that?

RANK: Please, just let me know what it is.

NORA: You can't know anything now.

RANK: I have to. You mustn't punish me like this. Give me the chance to
do whatever is humanly possible for you.

230 NORA: Now there's nothing you can do for me. Besides, actually, I don't
need any help. You'll see—it's only my fantasies. That's what it is. Of
course! *(Sits in the rocker, looks at him, and smiles.)* What a nice one you
are, Dr. Rank. Aren't you a little bit ashamed, now that the lamp is
here?

RANK: No, not exactly. But perhaps I'd better go—for good?

NORA: No, you certainly can't do that. You must come here just as you
always have. You know Torvald can't do without you.

RANK: Yes, but *you?*

NORA: You know how much I enjoy it when you're here.

235 RANK: That's precisely what threw me off. You're a mystery to me. So many
times I've felt you'd almost rather be with me than with Helmer.

NORA: Yes—you see, there are some people that one loves most and other
people that one would almost prefer being with.

RANK: Yes, there's something to that.

NORA: When I was back home, of course I loved Papa most. But I always
thought it was so much fun when I could sneak down to the maids'
quarters, because they never tried to improve me, and it was always so
amusing, the way they talked to each other.

RANK: Aha, so it's *their* place that I've filled.

240 NORA: *(jumping up and going to him)* Oh, dear, sweet Dr. Rank, that's not
what I mean at all. But you can understand that with Torvald it's just
the same as with Papa—

The Maid enters from the hall.

MAID: Ma'am—please! *(She whispers to Nora and hands her a calling card.)*

NORA: *(glancing at the card)* Ah! *(Slips it into her pocket.)*

RANK: Anything wrong?

NORA: No, no, not at all. It's only some—it's my new dress—

245 RANK: Really? But—there's your dress.

NORA: Oh, that. But this is another one—I ordered it—Torvald mustn't
know—

RANK: Ah, now we have the big secret.

NORA: That's right. Just go in with him—he's back in the inner study. Keep
him there as long as—

RANK: Don't worry. He won't get away. *(Goes into the study.)*

250 NORA: *(to the Maid)* And he's standing waiting in the kitchen?

MAID: Yes, he came up by the back stairs.

NORA: But didn't you tell him somebody was here?

MAID: Yes, but that didn't do any good.

NORA: He won't leave?

255 MAID: No, he won't go till he's talked with you, ma'am.

NORA: Let him come in, then—but quietly. Helene, don't breathe a word about this. It's a surprise for my husband.

MAID: Yes, yes, I understand—*(Goes out.)*

NORA: This horror—it's going to happen. No, no, no, it can't happen, it mustn't. *(She goes and bolts Helmer's door. The Maid opens the hall door for Krogstad and shuts it behind him. He is dressed for travel in a fur coat, boots, and a fur cap.)*

NORA: *(going toward him)* Talk softly. My husband's home.

260 KROGSTAD: Well, good for him.

NORA: What do you want?

KROGSTAD: Some information.

NORA: Hurry up, then. What is it?

KROGSTAD: You know, of course, that I got my notice.

265 NORA: I couldn't prevent it, Mr. Krogstad. I fought for you to the bitter end, but nothing worked.

KROGSTAD: Does your husband's love for you run so thin? He knows everything I can expose you to, and all the same he dares to—

NORA: How can you imagine he knows anything about this?

KROGSTAD: Ah, no—I can't imagine it either, now. It's not at all like my fine Torvald Helmer to have so much guts—

NORA: Mr. Krogstad, I demand respect for my husband!

270 KROGSTAD: Why, of course—all due respect. But since the lady's keeping it so carefully hidden, may I presume to ask if you're also a bit better informed than yesterday about what you've actually done?

NORA: More than you ever could teach me.

KROGSTAD: Yes, I *am* such an awful lawyer.

NORA: What is it you want from me?

KROGSTAD: Just a glimpse of how you are, Mrs. Helmer. I've been thinking about you all day long. A cashier, a night-court scribbler, a—well, a type like me also has a little of what they call a heart, you know.

275 NORA: Then show it. Think of my children.

KROGSTAD: Did you or your husband ever think of mine? But never mind. I simply wanted to tell you that you don't need to take this thing too seriously. For the present, I'm not proceeding with any action.

NORA: Oh no, really! Well—I knew that.

KROGSTAD: Everything can be settled in a friendly spirit. It doesn't have to get around town at all; it can stay just among us three.

NORA: My husband must never know anything of this.

280 KROGSTAD: How can you manage that? Perhaps you can pay me the balance?

NORA: No, not right now.

KROGSTAD: Or you know some way of raising the money in a day or two?

NORA: No way that I'm willing to use.

KROGSTAD: Well, it wouldn't have done you any good, anyway. If you stood in front of me with a fistful of bills, you still couldn't buy your signature back.

285 NORA: Then tell me what you're going to do with it.

KROGSTAD: I'll just hold onto it—keep it on file. There's no outsider who'll even get wind of it. So if you've been thinking of taking some desperate step—

NORA: I have.

KROGSTAD: Been thinking of running away from home—

NORA: I have!

290 KROGSTAD: Or even of something worse—

NORA: How could you guess that?

KROGSTAD: You can drop those thoughts.

NORA: How could you guess I was thinking of *that*?

KROGSTAD: Most of us think about *that* at first. I thought about it too, but I discovered I hadn't the courage—

295 NORA: *(lifelessly)* I don't either.

KROGSTAD: *(relieved)* That's true, you haven't the courage? You too?

NORA: I don't have it—I don't have it.

KROGSTAD: It would be terribly stupid, anyway. After that first storm at home blows out, why, then—I have here in my pocket a letter for your husband—

NORA: Telling everything?

300 KROGSTAD: As charitably as possible.

NORA: *(quickly)* He mustn't ever get that letter. Tear it up. I'll find some way to get money.

KROGSTAD: Beg pardon, Mrs. Helmer, but I think I just told you—

NORA: Oh, I don't mean the money I owe you. Let me know how much you want from my husband, and I'll manage it.

KROGSTAD: I don't want any money from your husband.

305 NORA: What do you want, then?

KROGSTAD: I'll tell you what. I want to recoup, Mrs. Helmer; I want to get on in the world—and there's where your husband can help me. For a year and a half I've kept myself clean of anything disreputable—all that time struggling with the worst conditions; but I was satisfied, working my way up step by step. Now I've been written right off, and I'm just not in the mood to come crawling back. I tell you, I want to move on. I want to get back in the bank—in a better position. Your husband can set up a job for me—

NORA: He'll never do that!

KROGSTAD: He'll do it. I know him. He won't dare breathe a word of protest. And once I'm in there together with him, you just wait and see! Inside of a year, I'll be the manager's right-hand man. It'll be Nils Krogstad, not Torvald Helmer, who runs the bank.

NORA: You'll never see the day!

310 KROGSTAD: Maybe you think you can—

NORA: I have the courage now—for *that*.

KROGSTAD: Oh, you don't scare me. A smart, spoiled lady like you—

NORA: You'll see; you'll see!

KROGSTAD: Under the ice, maybe? Down in the freezing, coal-black water? There, till you float up in the spring, ugly, unrecognizable, with your hair falling out—

315 NORA: You don't frighten me.

KROGSTAD: Nor do you frighten me. One doesn't do these things, Mrs. Helmer. Besides, what good would it be? I'd still have him safe in my pocket.

NORA: Afterwards? When I'm no longer—?

KROGSTAD: Are you forgetting that *I'll* be in control then over your final reputation? *(Nora stands speechless, staring at him.)* Good; now I've warned you. Don't do anything stupid. When Helmer's read my letter, I'll be waiting for his reply. And bear in mind that it's your husband himself who's forced me back to my old ways. I'll never forgive him for that. Good-bye, Mrs. Helmer. *(He goes out through the hall.)*

NORA: *(goes to the hall door, opens it a crack, and listens)* He's gone. Didn't leave the letter. Oh no, no, that's impossible too! *(Opening the door more and more.)* What's that? He's standing outside—not going downstairs. He's thinking it over? Maybe he'll—? *(A letter falls in the mailbox; then Krogstad's footsteps are heard, dying away down a flight of stairs. Nora gives a muffled cry and runs over toward the sofa table. A short pause.)* In the mailbox. *(Slips warily over to the hall door.)* It's lying there. Torvald, Torvald—now we're lost!

320 MRS. LINDE: *(entering with the costume from the room, left)* There now, I can't see anything else to mend. Perhaps you'd like to try—

NORA: *(in a hoarse whisper)* Kristine, come here.

MRS. LINDE: *(tossing the dress on the sofa)* What's wrong? You look upset.

NORA: Come here. See that letter? *There!* Look—through the glass in the mailbox.

MRS. LINDE: Yes, yes, I see it.

325 NORA: That letter's from Krogstad—

MRS. LINDE: Nora—it's Krogstad who loaned you the money!

NORA: Yes, and now Torvald will find out everything.

MRS. LINDE: Believe me, Nora, it's best for both of you.

NORA: There's more you don't know. I forged a name.

330 MRS. LINDE: But for heaven's sake—?

NORA: I only want to tell you that, Kristine, so that you can be my witness.

MRS. LINDE: Witness? Why should I—?

NORA: If I should go out of my mind—it could easily happen—

MRS. LINDE: Nora!

335 NORA: Or anything else occurred—so I couldn't be present here—

MRS. LINDE: Nora, Nora, you aren't yourself at all!

NORA: And someone should try to take on the whole weight, all of the guilt, you follow me—

MRS. LINDE: Yes, of course, but why do you think—?

NORA: Then you're the witness that it isn't true, Kristine. I'm very much
myself; my mind right now is perfectly clear; and I'm telling you:
nobody else has known about this; I alone did everything. Remember
that.

340 MRS. LINDE: I will. But I don't understand all this.

NORA: Oh, how could you ever understand it? It's the miracle now that's
going to take place.

MRS. LINDE: The miracle?

NORA: Yes, the miracle. But it's so awful, Kristine. It mustn't take place, not
for anything in the world.

MRS. LINDE: I'm going right over and talk with Krogstad.

345 NORA: Don't go near him; he'll do you some terrible harm!

MRS. LINDE: There was a time once when he'd gladly have done anything
for me.

NORA: He?

MRS. LINDE: Where does he live?

NORA: Oh, how do I know? Yes. *(Searches in her pocket.)* Here's his card. But
the letter, the letter—!

350 HELMER: *(from the study, knocking on the door)* Nora!

NORA: *(with a cry of fear)* Oh! What is it? What do you want?

HELMER: Now, now, don't be so frightened. We're not coming in. You
locked the door—are you trying on the dress?

NORA: Yes, I'm trying it. I'll look just beautiful, Torvald.

MRS. LINDE: *(who has read the card)* He's living right around the corner.

355 NORA: Yes, but what's the use? We're lost. The letter's in the box.

MRS. LINDE: And your husband has the key?

NORA: Yes, always.

MRS. LINDE: Krogstad can ask for his letter back unread; he can find some
excuse—

NORA: But it's just this time that Torvald usually—

360 MRS. LINDE: Stall him. Keep him in there. I'll be back as quick as I can. *(She
hurries out through the hall entrance.)*

NORA: *(goes to Helmer's door, opens it, and peers in)* Torvald!

HELMER: *(from the inner study)* Well—does one dare set foot in one's own
living room at last? Come on, Rank, now we'll get a look—*(In the
doorway.)* But what's this?

NORA: What, Torvald dear?

HELMER: Rank had me expecting some grand masquerade.

365 RANK: *(in the doorway)* That was my impression, but I must have been
wrong.

NORA: No one can admire me in my splendor—not till tomorrow.

HELMER: But Nora dear, you look so exhausted. Have you practiced too
hard?

NORA: No, I haven't practiced at all yet.

HELMER: You know, it's necessary—

370 NORA: Oh, it's absolutely necessary, Torvald. But I can't get anywhere
without your help. I've forgotten the whole thing completely.

HELMER: Ah, we'll soon take care of that.

NORA: Yes, take care of me, Torvald, please! Promise me that? Oh, I'm so
nervous. That big party—You must give up everything this evening for
me. No business—don't even touch your pen. Yes? Dear Torvald,
promise?

HELMER: It's a promise. Tonight I'm totally at your service—you little
helpless thing. Hm—but first there's one thing I want to—*(Goes toward
the hall door.)*

NORA: What are you looking for?

375 HELMER: Just to see if there's any mail.

NORA: No, no, don't do that, Torvald!

HELMER: Now what?

NORA: Torvald, please. There isn't any.

HELMER: Let me look, though. *(Starts out. Nora, at the piano, strikes the first
notes of the tarantella. Helmer, at the door, stops.)* Aha!

380 NORA: I can't dance tomorrow if I don't practice with you.

HELMER: *(going over to her)* Nora dear, are you really so frightened?

NORA: Yes, so terribly frightened. Let me practice right now; there's still
time before dinner. Oh, sit down and play for me, Torvald. Direct me.
Teach me, the way you always have.

HELMER: Gladly, if it's what you want. *(Sits at the piano.)*

NORA: *(snatches the tambourine up from the box, then a long, varicolored shawl,
which she throws around herself, whereupon she springs forward and cries
out)* Play for me now! Now I'll dance!

*Helmer plays and Nora dances. Rank stands behind Helmer at the piano and looks
on.*

385 HELMER: *(as he plays)* Slower. Slow down.

NORA: Can't change it.

HELMER: Not so violent, Nora!

NORA: Has to be just like this.

HELMER: *(stopping)* No, no, that won't do at all.

390 NORA: *(laughing and swinging her tambourine)* Isn't that what I told you?

RANK: Let me play for her.

HELMER: *(getting up)* Yes, go on. I can teach her more easily then.

*Rank sits at the piano and plays; Nora dances more and more wildly. Helmer has
stationed himself by the stove and repeatedly gives her directions; she seems not to
hear them; her hair loosens and falls over her shoulders; she does not notice, but
goes on dancing. Mrs. Linde enters.*

MRS. LINDE: *(standing dumbfounded at the door)* Ah—!

NORA: *(still dancing)* See what fun, Kristine!

395 HELMER: But Nora darling, you dance as if your life were at stake.

NORA: And it is.

HELMER: Rank, stop! This is pure madness. Stop it, I say!

Rank breaks off playing, and Nora halts abruptly.

HELMER: *(going over to her)* I never would have believed it. You've forgotten everything I taught you.

NORA: *(throwing away the tambourine)* You see for yourself.

400 HELMER: Well, there's certainly room for instruction here.

NORA: Yes, you see how important it is. You've got to teach me to the very last minute. Promise me that, Torvald?

HELMER: You can bet on it.

NORA: You mustn't, either today or tomorrow, think about anything else but me; you mustn't open any letters—or the mailbox—

HELMER: Ah, it's still the fear of that man—

405 NORA: Oh yes, yes, that too.

HELMER: Nora, it's written all over you—there's already a letter from him out there.

NORA: I don't know. I guess so. But you mustn't read such things now; there mustn't be anything ugly between us before it's all over.

RANK: *(quietly to Helmer)* You shouldn't deny her.

HELMER: *(putting his arm around her)* The child can have her way. But tomorrow night, after you've danced—

410 NORA: Then you'll be free.

MAID: *(in the doorway, right)* Ma'am, dinner is served.

NORA: We'll be wanting champagne, Helene.

MAID: Very good, ma'am. *(Goes out.)*

HELMER: So—a regular banquet, hm?

415 NORA: Yes, a banquet—champagne till daybreak! *(Calling out.)* And some macaroons, Helene. Heaps of them—just this once.

HELMER: *(taking her hands)* Now, now, now—no hysterics. Be my own little lark again.

NORA: Oh, I will soon enough. But go on in—and you, Dr. Rank. Kristine, help me put up my hair.

RANK: *(whispering, as they go)* There's nothing wrong—really wrong, is there?

HELMER: Oh, of course not. It's nothing more than this childish anxiety I was telling you about. *(They go out, right.)*

420 NORA: Well?

MRS. LINDE: Left town.

NORA: I could see by your face.

MRS. LINDE: He'll be home tomorrow evening. I wrote him a note.

NORA: You shouldn't have. Don't try to stop anything now. After all, it's a wonderful joy, this waiting here for the miracle.

425 MRS. LINDE: What is it you're waiting for?

NORA: Oh, you can't understand that. Go in to them: I'll be along in a moment.

Mrs. Linde goes into the dining room. Nora stands a short while as if composing herself; then she looks at her watch.

NORA: Five. Seven hours to midnight. Twenty-four hours to the midnight after, and then the tarantella's done. Seven and twenty-four? Thirty-one hours to live.

HELMER: *(in the doorway, right)* What's become of the little lark?

NORA: *(going toward him with open arms)* Here's your lark!

ACT III

Same scene. The table, with chairs around it, has been moved to the center of the room. A lamp on the table is lit. The hall door stands open. Dance music drifts down from the floor above. Mrs. Linde sits at the table, absently paging through a book, trying to read, but apparently unable to focus her thoughts. Once or twice she pauses, tensely listening for a sound at the outer entrance.

MRS. LINDE: *(glancing at her watch)* Not yet—and there's hardly any time left. If only he's not—(*Listening again.*) Ah, there he is. *(She goes out in the hall and cautiously opens the outer door. Quiet footsteps are heard on the stairs. She whispers:)* Come in. Nobody's here.

KROGSTAD: *(in the doorway)* I found a note from you at home. What's back of all this?

MRS. LINDE: I just *had* to talk to you.

KROGSTAD: Oh? And it just *had* to be here in this house?

5 MRS. LINDE: At my place it was impossible; my room hasn't a private entrance. Come in; we're all alone. The maid's asleep, and the Helmers are at the dance upstairs.

KROGSTAD: *(entering the room)* Well, well, the Helmers are dancing tonight? Really?

MRS. LINDE: Yes, why not?

KROGSTAD: How true—why not?

MRS. LINDE: All right, Krogstad, let's talk.

10 KROGSTAD: Do we two have anything more to talk about?

MRS. LINDE: We have a great deal to talk about.

KROGSTAD: I wouldn't have thought so.

MRS. LINDE: No, because you've never understood me, really.

KROGSTAD: Was there anything more to understand—except what's all too common in life? A calculating woman throws over a man the moment a better catch comes by.

15 MRS. LINDE: You think I'm so thoroughly calculating? You think I broke it off lightly?

KROGSTAD: Didn't you?

MRS. LINDE: Nils—is that what you really thought?

KROGSTAD: If I cared, then why did you write me the way you did?

MRS. LINDE: What else could I do? If I had to break off with you, then it was my job as well to root out everything you felt for me.

20 KROGSTAD: *(wringing his hands)* So that was it. And this—all this, simply for money!

Mrs. Linde: Don't forget I had a helpless mother and two small brothers. We couldn't wait for you, Nils; you had such a long road ahead of you then.

Krogstad: That may be; but you still hadn't the right to abandon me for somebody else's sake.

Mrs. Linde: Yes—I don't know. So many, many times I've asked myself if I did have that right.

Krogstad: *(more softly)* When I lost you, it was as if all the solid ground dissolved from under my feet. Look at me; I'm a half-drowned man now, hanging onto a wreck.

25 Mrs. Linde: Help may be near.

Krogstad: It was near—but then you came and blocked it off.

Mrs. Linde: Without my knowing it, Nils. Today for the first time I learned that it's you I'm replacing at the bank.

Krogstad: All right—I believe you. But now that you know, will you step aside?

Mrs. Linde: No, because that wouldn't benefit you in the slightest.

30 Krogstad: Not "benefit" me, hm! I'd step aside anyway.

Mrs. Linde: I've learned to be realistic. Life and hard, bitter necessity have taught me that.

Krogstad: And life's taught me never to trust fine phrases.

Mrs. Linde: Then life's taught you a very sound thing. But you do have to trust in actions, don't you?

Krogstad: What does that mean?

35 Mrs. Linde: You said you were hanging on like a half-drowned man to a wreck.

Krogstad: I've good reason to say that.

Mrs. Linde: I'm also like a half-drowned woman on a wreck. No one to suffer with; no one to care for.

Krogstad: You made your choice.

Mrs. Linde: There wasn't any choice then.

40 Krogstad: So—what of it?

Mrs. Linde: Nils, if only we two shipwrecked people could reach across to each other.

Krogstad: What are you saying?

Mrs. Linde: Two on one wreck are at least better off than each on his own.

Krogstad: Kristine!

45 Mrs. Linde: Why do you think I came into town?

Krogstad: Did you really have some thought of me?

Mrs. Linde: I have to work to go on living. All my born days, as long as I can remember, I've worked, and it's been my best and my only joy. But now I'm completely alone in the world; it frightens me to be so empty and lost. To work for yourself—there's no joy in that. Nils, give me something—someone to work for.

Krogstad: I don't believe all this. It's just some hysterical feminine urge to go out and make a noble sacrifice.

Mrs. Linde: Have you ever found me to be hysterical?

50 Krogstad: Can you honestly mean this? Tell me—do you know everything about my past?

Mrs. Linde: Yes.

Krogstad: And you know what they think I'm worth around here.

Mrs. Linde: From what you were saying before, it would seem that with me you could have been another person.

Krogstad: I'm positive of that.

55 Mrs. Linde: Couldn't it happen still?

Krogstad: Kristine—you're saying this in all seriousness? Yes, you are! I can see it in you. And do you really have the courage, then—?

Mrs. Linde: I need to have someone to care for; and your children need a mother. We both need each other. Nils, I have faith that you're good at heart—I'll risk everything together with you.

Krogstad: *(gripping her hands)* Kristine, thank you, thank you—Now I know I can win back a place in their eyes. Yes—but I forgot—

Mrs. Linde: *(listening)* Shh! The tarantella. Go now! Go on!

60 Krogstad: Why? What is it?

Mrs. Linde: Hear the dance up there? When that's over, they'll be coming down.

Krogstad: Oh, then I'll go. But—it's all pointless. Of course, you don't know the move I made against the Helmers.

Mrs. Linde: Yes, Nils, I know.

Krogstad: And all the same, you have the courage to—?

65 Mrs. Linde: I know how far despair can drive a man like you.

Krogstad: Oh, if I only could take it all back.

Mrs. Linde: You easily could—your letter's still lying in the mailbox.

Krogstad: Are you sure of that?

Mrs. Linde: Positive. But—

70 Krogstad: *(looks at her searchingly)* Is that the meaning of it, then? You'll save your friend at any price. Tell me straight out. Is that it?

Mrs. Linde: Nils—anyone who's sold herself for somebody else once isn't going to do it again.

Krogstad: I'll demand my letter back.

Mrs. Linde: No, no.

Krogstad: Yes, of course. I'll stay here till Helmer comes down; I'll tell him to give me my letter again—that it only involves my dismissal—that he shouldn't read it—

75 Mrs. Linde: No, Nils, don't call the letter back.

Krogstad: But wasn't that exactly why you wrote me to come here?

Mrs. Linde: Yes, in that first panic. But it's been a whole day and night since then, and in that time I've seen such incredible things in this house. Helmer's got to learn everything; this dreadful secret has to be aired; those two have to come to a full understanding; all these lies and evasions can't go on.

KROGSTAD: Well, then, if you want to chance it. But at least there's one thing I can do, and do right away—

MRS. LINDE: *(listening)* Go now, go, quick! The dance is over. We're not safe another second.

80 KROGSTAD: I'll wait for you downstairs.

MRS. LINDE: Yes, please do; take me home.

KROGSTAD: I can't believe it; I've never been so happy. *(He leaves by way of the outer door; the door between the room and the hall stays open.)*

MRS. LINDE: *(straightening up a bit and getting together her street clothes)* How different now! How different! Someone to work for, to live for—a home to build. Well, it is worth the try! Oh, if they'd only come! *(Listening.)* Ah, there they are. Bundle up. *(She picks up her hat and coat. Nora's and Helmer's voices can be heard outside; a key turns in the lock, and Helmer brings Nora into the hall almost by force. She is wearing the Italian costume with a large black shawl about her; he has on evening dress, with a black domino open over it.)*

NORA: *(struggling in the doorway)* No, no, no, not inside! I'm going up again. I don't want to leave so soon.

85 HELMER: But Nora dear—

NORA: Oh, I beg you, please, Torvald. From the bottom of my heart, *please*—only an hour more!

HELMER: Not a single minute, Nora darling. You know our agreement. Come on, in we go; you'll catch cold out here. *(In spite of her resistance, he gently draws her into the room.)*

MRS. LINDE: Good evening.

NORA: Kristine!

90 HELMER: Why, Mrs. Linde—are you here so late?

MRS. LINDE: Yes, I'm sorry, but I did want to see Nora in costume.

NORA: Have you been sitting here, waiting for me?

MRS. LINDE: Yes. I didn't come early enough; you were all upstairs; and then I thought I really couldn't leave without seeing you.

HELMER: *(removing Nora's shawl)* Yes, take a good look. She's worth looking at, I can tell you that, Mrs. Linde. Isn't she lovely?

95 MRS. LINDE: Yes, I should say—

HELMER: A dream of loveliness, isn't she? That's what everyone thought at the party, too. But she's horribly stubborn—this sweet little thing. What's to be done with her? Can you imagine, I almost had to use force to pry her away.

NORA: Oh, Torvald, you're going to regret you didn't indulge me, even for just a half hour more.

HELMER: There, you see. She danced her tarantella and got a tumultuous hand—which was well earned, although the performance may have been a bit too naturalistic—I mean it rather overstepped the proprieties of art. But never mind—what's important is, she made a success, an overwhelming success. You think I could let her stay on after that and spoil the effect? Oh no; I took my lovely little Capri girl—my capricious little Capri girl, I should say—took her under my arm; one quick tour of the ballroom, a curtsy to every side, and then— as they say in novels—the beautiful vision disappeared. An exit should always be effective, Mrs. Linde, but that's what I can't get Nora to grasp. Phew, it's hot in here. (*Flings the domino on a chair and opens the door to his room.*) Why's it dark in here? Oh yes, of course. Excuse me. (*He goes in and lights a couple of candles.*)

NORA: (*in a sharp, breathless whisper*) So?

100 MRS. LINDE: (*quietly*) I talked with him.

NORA: And—?

MRS. LINDE: Nora—you must tell your husband everything.

NORA: (*dully*) I knew it.

MRS. LINDE: You've got nothing to fear from Krogstad, but you have to speak out.

105 NORA: I won't tell.

MRS. LINDE: Then the letter will.

NORA: Thanks, Kristine. I know now what's to be done. Shh!

HELMER: (*reentering*) Well, then, Mrs. Linde—have you admired her?

MRS. LINDE: Yes, and now I'll say good night.

110 HELMER: Oh, come, so soon? Is this yours, this knitting?

MRS. LINDE: Yes, thanks. I nearly forgot it.

HELMER: Do you knit, then?

MRS. LINDE: Oh yes.

HELMER: You know what? You should embroider instead.

115 MRS. LINDE: Really? Why?

HELMER: Yes, because it's a lot prettier. See here, one holds the embroidery so, in the left hand, and then one guides the needle with the right— so—in an easy, sweeping curve—right?

MRS. LINDE: Yes, I guess that's—

HELMER: But, on the other hand, knitting—it can never be anything but ugly. Look, see here, the arms tucked in, the knitting needles going up and down—there's something Chinese about it. Ah, that was really a glorious champagne they served.

MRS. LINDE: Yes, good night, Nora, and don't be stubborn any more.

120 HELMER: Well put, Mrs. Linde!

MRS. LINDE: Good night, Mr. Helmer.

HELMER: (*accompanying her to the door*) Good night, good night. I hope you get home all right. I'd be very happy to—but you don't have far to go. Good night, good night. (*She leaves. He shuts the door after her and returns.*) There, now, at last we got her out the door. She's a deadly bore, that creature.

NORA: Aren't you pretty tired, Torvald?

HELMER: No, not a bit.

125 NORA: You're not sleepy?

HELMER: Not at all. On the contrary, I'm feeling quite exhilarated. But you? Yes, you really look tired and sleepy.

NORA: Yes, I'm very tired. Soon now I'll sleep.

HELMER: See! You see! I was right all along that we shouldn't stay longer.

NORA: Whatever you do is always right.

130 HELMER: *(kissing her brow)* Now my little lark talks sense. Say, did you notice what a time Rank was having tonight?

NORA: Oh, was he? I didn't get to speak with him.

HELMER: I scarcely did either, but it's a long time since I've seen him in such high spirits. *(Gazes at her a moment, then comes nearer her.)* Hm— it's marvelous, though, to be back home again—to be completely alone with you. Oh, you bewitchingly lovely young woman!

NORA: Torvald, don't look at me like that!

HELMER: Can't I look at my richest treasure? At all that beauty that's mine, mine alone—completely and utterly.

135 NORA: *(moving around to the other side of the table)* You mustn't talk to me that way tonight.

HELMER: *(following her)* The tarantella is still in your blood, I can see—and it makes you even more enticing. Listen. The guests are beginning to go. *(Dropping his voice.)* Nora—it'll soon be quiet through this whole house.

NORA: Yes, I hope so.

HELMER: You do, don't you, my love? Do you realize—when I'm out at a party like this with you—do you know why I talk to you so little, and keep such a distance away; just send you a stolen look now and then— you know why I do it? It's because I'm imagining then that you're my secret darling, my secret young bride-to-be, and that no one suspects there's anything between us.

NORA: Yes, yes; oh, yes, I know you're always thinking of me.

140 HELMER: And then when we leave and I place the shawl over those fine young rounded shoulders—over that wonderful curving neck—then I pretend that you're my young bride, that we're just coming from the wedding, that for the first time I'm bringing you into my house—that for the first time I'm alone with you—completely alone with you, your trembling young beauty! All this evening I've longed for nothing but you. When I saw you turn and sway in the tarantella—my blood was pounding till I couldn't stand it—that's why I brought you down here so early—

NORA: Go away, Torvald! Leave me alone. I don't want all this.

HELMER: What do you mean? Nora, you're teasing me. You will, won't you? Aren't I your husband—?

A knock at the outside door.

NORA: *(startled)* What's that?

HELMER: *(going toward the hall)* Who is it?

145 RANK: *(outside)* It's me. May I come in a moment?

HELMER: *(with quiet irritation)* Oh, what does he want now? *(Aloud.)* Hold on. *(Goes and opens the door.)* Oh, how nice that you didn't just pass us by!

RANK: I thought I heard your voice, and then I wanted so badly to have a look in. *(Lightly glancing about.)* Ah, me, these old familiar haunts. You have it snug and cozy in here, you two.

HELMER: You seemed to be having it pretty cozy upstairs, too.

RANK: Absolutely. Why shouldn't I? Why not take in everything in life? As much as you can, anyway, and as long as you can. The wine was superb—

150 HELMER: The champagne especially.

RANK: You noticed that too? It's amazing how much I could guzzle down.

NORA: Torvald also drank a lot of champagne this evening.

RANK: Oh?

NORA: Yes, and that always makes him so entertaining.

155 RANK: Well, why shouldn't one have a pleasant evening after a well spent day?

HELMER: Well spent? I'm afraid I can't claim that.

RANK: *(slapping him on the back)* But I can, you see!

NORA: Dr. Rank, you must have done some scientific research today.

RANK: Quite so.

160 HELMER: Come now—little Nora talking about scientific research!

NORA: And can I congratulate you on the results?

RANK: Indeed you may.

NORA: Then they were good?

RANK: The best possible for both doctor and patient—certainty.

165 NORA: *(quickly and searchingly)* Certainty?

RANK: Complete certainty. So don't I owe myself a gay evening afterwards?

NORA: Yes, you're right, Dr. Rank.

HELMER: I'm with you—just so long as you don't have to suffer for it in the morning.

RANK: Well, one never gets something for nothing in life.

170 NORA: Dr. Rank—are you very fond of masquerade parties?

RANK: Yes, if there's a good array of odd disguises—

NORA: Tell me, what should we two go as at the next masquerade?

HELMER: You little featherhead—already thinking of the next!

RANK: We two? I'll tell you what: you must go as Charmed Life—

175 HELMER: Yes, but find a costume for *that!*

RANK: Your wife can appear just as she looks every day.

HELMER: That was nicely put. But don't you know what you're going to be?

RANK: Yes, Helmer, I've made up my mind.

HELMER: Well?

180 RANK: At the next masquerade I'm going to be invisible.

HELMER: That's a funny idea.

RANK: They say there's a hat—black, huge—have you never heard of the hat that makes you invisible? You put it on, and then no one on earth can see you.

HELMER: *(suppressing a smile)* Ah, of course.

RANK: But I'm quite forgetting what I came for. Helmer, give me a cigar, one of the dark Havanas.

185 HELMER: With the greatest of pleasure. *(Holds out his case.)*

RANK: Thanks. *(Takes one and cuts off the tip.)*

NORA: *(striking a match)* Let me give you a light.

RANK: Thank you. *(She holds the match for him; he lights the cigar.)* And now good-bye.

HELMER: Good-bye, good-bye, old friend.

190 NORA: Sleep well, Doctor.

RANK: Thanks for that wish.

NORA: Wish me the same.

RANK: You? All right, if you like—Sleep well. And thanks for the light. *(He nods to them both and leaves.)*

HELMER: *(his voice subdued)* He's been drinking heavily.

195 NORA: *(absently)* Could be. *(Helmer takes his keys from his pocket and goes out in the hall.)* Torvald—what are you after?

HELMER: Got to empty the mailbox; it's nearly full. There won't be room for the morning papers.

NORA: Are you working tonight?

HELMER: You know I'm not. Why—what's this? Someone's been at the lock.

NORA: At the lock—?

200 HELMER: Yes, I'm positive. What do you suppose—? I can't imagine one of the maids—? Here's a broken hairpin. Nora, it's yours—

NORA: *(quickly)* Then it must be the children—

HELMER: You'd better break them of that. Hm, hm—well, opened it after all. *(Takes the contents out and calls into the kitchen.)* Helene! Helene, would you put out the lamp in the hall. *(He returns to the room, shutting the hall door, then displays the handful of mail.)* Look how it's piled up. *(Sorting through them.)* Now what's this?

NORA: *(at the window)* The letter! Oh, Torvald, no!

HELMER: Two calling cards—from Rank.

205 NORA: From Dr. Rank?

HELMER: *(examining them)* "Dr. Rank, Consulting Physician." They were on top. He must have dropped them in as he left.

NORA: Is there anything on them?

HELMER: There's a black cross over the name. See? That's a gruesome notion. He could almost be announcing his own death.

NORA: That's just what he's doing.

210 HELMER: What! You've heard something? Something he's told you?

NORA: Yes. That when those cards came, he'd be taking his leave of us. He'll shut himself in now and die.

HELMER: Ah, my poor friend! Of course I knew he wouldn't be here much longer. But so soon—And then to hide himself away like a wounded animal.

NORA: If it has to happen, then it's best it happens in silence—don't you think so, Torvald?

HELMER: *(pacing up and down)* He'd grown right into our lives. I simply can't imagine him gone. He with his suffering and loneliness—like a dark cloud setting off our sunlit happiness. Well, maybe it's best this way. For him, at least. *(Standing still.)* And maybe for us too, Nora. Now we're thrown back on each other, completely. *(Embracing her.)* Oh you, my darling wife, how can I hold you close enough? You know what, Nora—time and again I've wished you were in some terrible danger, just so I could stake my life and soul and everything, for your sake.

215 NORA: *(tearing herself away, her voice firm and decisive)* Now you must read your mail, Torvald.

HELMER: No, no, not tonight. I want to stay with you, dearest.

NORA: With a dying friend on your mind?

HELMER: You're right. We've both had a shock. There's ugliness between us—these thoughts of death and corruption. We'll have to get free of them first. Until then—we'll stay apart.

NORA: *(clinging about his neck)* Torvald—good night! Good night!

220 HELMER: *(kissing her on the cheek)* Good night, little songbird. Sleep well, Nora. I'll be reading my mail now. *(He takes the letters into his room and shuts the door after him.)*

NORA: *(with bewildered glances, groping about, seizing Helmer's domino, throwing it around her, and speaking in short, hoarse, broken whispers)* Never see him again. Never, never. *(Putting her shawl over her head.)* Never see the children either—them, too. Never, never. Oh, the freezing black water! The depths—down—Oh, I wish it were over—He has it now; he's reading it—now. Oh no, no, not yet. Torvald, good-bye, you and the children—*(She starts for the hall; as she does, Helmer throws open his door and stands with an open letter in his hand.)*

HELMER: Nora!

NORA: *(screams)* Oh—!

HELMER: What is this? You know what's in this letter?

225 NORA: Yes, I know. Let me go! Let me out!

HELMER: *(holding her back)* Where are you going?

NORA: *(struggling to break loose)* You can't save me, Torvald!

HELMER: *(slumping back)* True! Then it's true what he writes? How horrible! No, no, it's impossible—it can't be true.

NORA: It *is* true. I've loved you more than all this world.

230 HELMER: Ah, none of your slippery tricks.

NORA: *(taking one step toward him)* Torvald—!

HELMER: What *is* this you've blundered into!

NORA: Just let me loose. You're not going to suffer for my sake. You're not going to take on my guilt.

HELMER: No more playacting. *(Locks the hall door.)* You stay right here and give me a reckoning. You understand what you've done? Answer! You understand?

235 NORA: *(looking squarely at him, her face hardening)* Yes. I'm beginning to understand everything now.

NEL

HELMER: *(striding about)* Oh, what an awful awakening! In all these eight years—she who was my pride and joy—a hypocrite, a liar—worse, worse—a criminal! How infinitely disgusting it all is! The shame! *(Nora says nothing and goes on looking straight at him. He stops in front of her.)* I should have suspected something of the kind. I should have known. All your father's flimsy values—Be still! All your father's flimsy values have come out in you. No religion, no morals, no sense of duty—Oh, how I'm punished for letting him off! I did it for your sake, and you repay me like this.

NORA: Yes, like this.

HELMER: Now you've wrecked all my happiness—ruined my whole future. Oh, it's awful to think of. I'm in a cheap little grafter's hands; he can do anything he wants with me, ask for anything, play with me like a puppet—and I can't breathe a word. I'll be swept down miserably into the depths on account of a featherbrained woman.

NORA: When I'm gone from this world, you'll be free.

240　HELMER: Oh, quit posing. Your father had a mess of those speeches too. What good would that ever do me if you were gone from this world, as you say? Not the slightest. He can still make the whole thing known; and if he does, I could be falsely suspected as your accomplice. They might even think that I was behind it—that I put you up to it. And all that I can thank you for—you that I've coddled the whole of our marriage. Can you see now what you've done to me?

NORA: *(icily calm)* Yes.

HELMER: It's so incredible, I just can't grasp it. But we'll have to patch up whatever we can. Take off the shawl. I said, take if off! I've got to appease him somehow or other. The thing has to be hushed up at any cost. And as for you and me, it's got to seem like everything between us is just as it was—to the outside world, that is. You'll go right on living in this house, of course. But you can't be allowed to bring up the children; I don't dare trust you with them—Oh, to have to say this to someone I've loved so much! Well, that's done with. From now on happiness doesn't matter; all that matters is saving the bits and pieces, the appearance—*(The doorbell rings. Helmer starts.)* What's that? And so late. Maybe the worst—? You think he'd—? Hide, Nora! Say you're sick. *(Nora remains standing motionless. Helmer goes and opens the door.)*

MAID: *(half dressed, in the hall)* A letter for Mrs. Helmer.

HELMER: I'll take it. *(Snatches the letter and shuts the door.)* Yes, it's from him. You don't get it; I'm reading it myself.

245　NORA: Then read it.

HELMER: *(by the lamp)* I hardly dare. We may be ruined, you and I. But— I've got to know. *(Rips open the letter, skims through a few lines, glances at an enclosure, then cries out joyfully.)* Nora! *(Nora looks inquiringly at him.)* Nora! Wait—better check it again—Yes, yes, it's true. I'm saved. Nora, I'm saved!

NORA: And I?

HELMER: You too, of course. We're both saved, both of us. Look. He's sent back your note. He says he's sorry and ashamed—that a happy development in his life—oh, who cares what he says! Nora, we're saved! No one can hurt you. Oh, Nora, Nora—but first, this ugliness all has to go. Let me see—*(Takes a look at the note.)* No, I don't want to see it; I want the whole thing to fade like a dream. *(Tears the note and both letters to pieces, throws them into the stove and watches them burn.)* There—now there's nothing left—He wrote that since Christmas Eve you—Oh, they must have been three terrible days for you, Nora.

NORA: I fought a hard fight.

250 HELMER: And suffered pain and saw no escape but—No, we're not going to dwell on anything unpleasant. We'll just be grateful and keep on repeating: it's over now, it's over! You hear me, Nora? You don't seem to realize—it's over. What's it mean—that frozen look? Oh, poor little Nora, I understand. You can't believe I've forgiven you. But I have, Nora; I swear I have. I know that what you did, you did out of love for me.

NORA: That's true.

HELMER: You loved me the way a wife ought to love her husband. It's simply the means that you couldn't judge. But you think I love you any the less for not knowing how to handle your affairs? No, no—just lean on me; I'll guide you and teach you. I wouldn't be a man if this feminine helplessness didn't make you twice as attractive to me. You mustn't mind those sharp words I said—that was all in the first confusion of thinking my world had collapsed. I've forgiven you, Nora; I swear I've forgiven you.

NORA: My thanks for your forgiveness. *(She goes out through the door, right.)*

HELMER: No, wait—*(Peers in.)* What are you doing in there?

255 NORA: *(inside)* Getting out of my costume.

HELMER: *(by the open door)* Yes, do that. Try to calm yourself and collect your thoughts again, my frightened little songbird. You can rest easy now; I've got wide wings to shelter you with. *(Walking about close by the door.)* How snug and nice our home is, Nora. You're safe here; I'll keep you like a hunted dove I've rescued out of a hawk's claws. I'll bring peace to your poor, shuddering heart. Gradually it'll happen, Nora; you'll see. Tomorrow all this will look different to you; then everything will be as it was. I won't have to go on repeating I forgive you; you'll feel it for yourself. How can you imagine I'd ever conceivably want to disown you—or even blame you in any way? Ah, you don't know a man's heart, Nora. For a man there's something indescribably sweet and satisfying in knowing he's forgiven his wife—and forgiven her out of a full and open heart. It's as if she belongs to him in two ways now: in a sense he's given her fresh into the world again, and she's become his wife and his child as well. From now on that's what you'll be to me—you little, bewildered, helpless thing. Don't be afraid of anything, Nora; just open your heart to me, and I'll

be conscience and will to you both—*(Nora enters in her regular clothes.)*
What's this? Not in bed? You've changed your dress?

NORA: Yes, Torvald, I've changed my dress.

HELMER: But why now, so late?

NORA: Tonight I'm not sleeping.

260 HELMER: But Nora dear—

NORA: *(looking at her watch)* It's still not so very late. Sit down, Torvald; we
have a lot to talk over. *(She sits at one side of the table.)*

HELMER: Nora—what is this? That hard expression—

NORA: Sit down. This'll take some time. I have a lot to say.

HELMER: *(sitting at the table directly opposite her)* You worry me, Nora. And I
don't understand you.

265 NORA: No, that's exactly it. You don't understand me. And I've never
understood you either—until tonight. No, don't interrupt. You can just
listen to what I say. We're closing out accounts, Torvald.

HELMER: How do you mean that?

NORA: *(after a short pause)* Doesn't anything strike you about our sitting
here like this?

HELMER: What's that?

NORA: We've been married now eight years. Doesn't it occur to you that
this is the first time we two, you and I, man and wife, have ever talked
seriously together?

270 HELMER: What do you mean—seriously?

NORA: In eight whole years—longer even—right from our first
acquaintance, we've never exchanged a serious word on any serious
thing.

HELMER: You mean I should constantly go and involve you in problems
you couldn't possibly help me with?

NORA: I'm not talking of problems. I'm saying that we've never sat down
seriously together and tried to get to the bottom of anything.

HELMER: But dearest, what good would that ever do you?

275 NORA: That's the point right there: you've never understood me. I've been
wronged greatly, Torvald—first by Papa, and then by you.

HELMER: What! By us—the two people who've loved you more than
anyone else?

NORA: *(shaking her head)* You never loved me. You've thought it fun to be
in love with me, that's all.

HELMER: Nora, what a thing to say!

NORA: Yes, it's true now, Torvald. When I lived at home with Papa, he told
me all his opinions, so I had the same ones too; or if they were
different I hid them, since he wouldn't have cared for that. He used to
call me his doll-child, and he played with me the way I played with
my dolls. Then I came into your house—

280 HELMER: How can you speak of our marriage like that?

NORA: *(unperturbed)* I mean, then I went from Papa's hands into yours. You
arranged everything to your own taste, and so I got the same taste as

you—or I pretended to; I can't remember. I guess a little of both, first one, then the other. Now when I look back, it seems as if I'd lived here like a beggar—just from hand to mouth. I've lived by doing tricks for you, Torvald. But that's the way you wanted it. It's a great sin what you and Papa did to me. You're to blame that nothing's become of me.

HELMER: Nora, how unfair and ungrateful you are! Haven't you been happy here?

NORA: No, never. I thought so—but I never have.

HELMER: Not—not happy!

285 NORA: No, only lighthearted. And you've always been so kind to me. But our home's been nothing but a playpen. I've been your doll-wife here, just as at home I was Papa's doll-child. And in turn the children have been my dolls. I thought it was fun when you played with me, just as they thought it fun when I played with them. That's been our marriage, Torvald.

HELMER: There's some truth in what you're saying—under all the raving exaggeration. But it'll all be different after this. Playtime's over; now for the schooling.

NORA: Whose schooling—mine or the children's?

HELMER: Both yours and the children's, dearest.

NORA: Oh, Torvald, you're not the man to teach me to be a good wife to you.

290 HELMER: And you can say that?

NORA: And I—how am I equipped to bring up children?

HELMER: Nora!

NORA: Didn't you say a moment ago that that was no job to trust me with?

HELMER: In a flare of temper! Why fasten on that?

295 NORA: Yes, but you were so very right. I'm not up to the job. There's another job I have to do first. I have to try to educate myself. You can't help me with that. I've got to do it alone. And that's why I'm leaving you now.

HELMER: *(jumping up)* What's that?

NORA: I have to stand completely alone, if I'm ever going to discover myself and the world out there. So I can't go on living with you.

HELMER: Nora, Nora!

NORA: I want to leave right away. Kristine should put me up for the night—

300 HELMER: You're insane! You've no right! I forbid you!

NORA: From here on, there's no use forbidding me anything. I'll take with me whatever is mine. I don't want a thing from you, either now or later.

HELMER: What kind of madness is this!

NORA: Tomorrow I'm going home—I mean, home where I came from. It'll be easier up there to find something to do.

HELMER: Oh, you blind, incompetent child!

305 NORA: I must learn to be competent, Torvald.

HELMER: Abandon your home, your husband, your children! And you're not even thinking what people will say.

NORA: I can't be concerned about that. I only know how essential this is.

HELMER: Oh, it's outrageous. So you'll run out like this on your most sacred vows.

NORA: What do you think are my most sacred vows?

310 HELMER: And I have to tell you that! Aren't they your duties to your husband and children?

NORA: I have other duties equally sacred.

HELMER: That isn't true. What duties are they?

NORA: Duties to myself.

HELMER: Before all else, you're a wife and a mother.

315 NORA: I don't believe in that any more. I believe that, before all else, I'm a human being, no less than you—or anyway, I ought to try to become one. I know the majority thinks you're right, Torvald, and plenty of books agree with you, too. But I can't go on believing what the majority says, or what's written in books. I have to think over these things myself and try to understand them.

HELMER: Why can't you understand your place in your own home? On a point like that, isn't there one everlasting guide you can turn to? Where's your religion?

NORA: Oh, Torvald, I'm really not sure what religion is.

HELMER: What—?

NORA: I only know what the minister said when I was confirmed. He told me religion was this thing and that. When I get clear and away by myself, I'll go into that problem too. I'll see if what the minister said was right, or, in any case, if it's right for me.

320 HELMER: A young woman your age shouldn't talk like that. If religion can't move you, I can try to rouse your conscience. You do have some moral feeling? Or, tell me—has that gone too?

NORA: It's not easy to answer that, Torvald. I simply don't know. I'm all confused about these things. I just know I see them so differently from you. I find out, for one thing, that the law's not at all what I'd thought—but I can't get it through my head that the law is fair. A woman hasn't a right to protect her dying father or save her husband's life! I can't believe that.

HELMER: You talk like a child. You don't know anything of the world you live in.

NORA: No, I don't. But now I'll begin to learn for myself. I'll try to discover who's right, the world or I.

HELMER: Nora, you're sick; you've got a fever. I almost think you're out of your head.

325 NORA: I've never felt more clearheaded and sure in my life.

HELMER: And—clearheaded and sure—you're leaving your husband and children?

NORA: Yes.

HELMER: Then there's only one possible reason.

NORA: What?

330 HELMER: You no longer love me.

NORA: No. That's exactly it.

HELMER: Nora! You can't be serious!

NORA: Oh, this is so hard, Torvald—you've been so kind to me always. But I can't help it. I don't love you any more.

HELMER: *(struggling for composure)* Are you also clearheaded and sure about that?

335 NORA: Yes, completely. That's why I can't go on staying here.

HELMER: Can you tell me what I did to lose your love?

NORA: Yes, I can tell you. It was this evening when the miraculous thing didn't come—then I knew you weren't the man I'd imagined.

HELMER: Be more explicit; I don't follow you.

NORA: I've waited now so patiently eight long years—for, my Lord, I know miracles don't come every day. Then this crisis broke over me, and such a certainty filled me: *now* the miraculous event would occur. While Krogstad's letter was lying out there, I never for an instant dreamed that you could give in to his terms. I was so utterly sure you'd say to him: go on, tell your tale to the whole wide world. And when he'd done that—

340 HELMER: Yes, what then? When I'd delivered my own wife into shame and disgrace—!

NORA: When he'd done that, I was so utterly sure that you'd step forward, take the blame on yourself and say: I am the guilty one.

HELMER: Nora—!

NORA: You're thinking I'd never accept such a sacrifice from you? No, of course not. But what good would my protests be against you? That was the miracle I was waiting for, in terror and hope. And to stave that off, I would have taken my life.

HELMER: I'd gladly work for you day and night, Nora—and take on pain and deprivation. But there's no one who gives up honor for love.

345 NORA: Millions of women have done just that.

HELMER: Oh, you think and talk like a silly child.

NORA: Perhaps. But you neither think nor talk like the man I could join myself to. When your big fright was over—and it wasn't from any threat against me, only for what might damage you—when all the danger was past, for you it was just as if nothing had happened. I was exactly the same, your little lark, your doll, that you'd have to handle with double care now that I'd turned out so brittle and frail. *(Gets up.)* Torvald—in that instant it dawned on me that for eight years I've been living here with a stranger, and that I'd even conceived three children— oh, I can't stand the thought of it! I could tear myself to bits.

HELMER: *(heavily)* I see. There's a gulf that's opened between us—that's clear. Oh, but Nora, can't we bridge it somehow?

NORA: The way I am now, I'm no wife for you.

350 HELMER: I have the strength to make myself over.

NORA: Maybe—if your doll gets taken away.

HELMER: But to part! To part from you! No, Nora, no—I can't imagine it.

NORA: *(going out, right)* All the more reason why it has to be. *(She reenters with her coat and a small overnight bag, which she puts on a chair by the table.)*

HELMER: Nora, Nora, not now! Wait till tomorrow.

355 NORA: I can't spend the night in a strange man's room.

HELMER: But couldn't we live here like brother and sister—

NORA: You know very well how long that would last. *(Throws her shawl about her.)* Good-bye, Torvald. I won't look in on the children. I know they're in better hands than mine. The way I am now, I'm no use to them.

HELMER: But someday, Nora—someday—?

NORA: How can I tell? I haven't the least idea what'll become of me.

360 HELMER: But you're my wife, now and wherever you go.

NORA: Listen, Torvald—I've heard that when a wife deserts her husband's house just as I'm doing, then the law frees him from all responsibility. In any case, I'm freeing you from being responsible. Don't feel yourself bound, any more than I will. There has to be absolute freedom for us both. Here, take your ring back. Give me mine.

HELMER: That too?

NORA: That too.

HELMER: There it is.

365 NORA: Good. Well, now it's all over. I'm putting the keys here. The maids know all about keeping up the house—better than I do. Tomorrow, after I've left town, Kristine will stop by to pack up everything that's mine from home. I'd like those things shipped up to me.

HELMER: Over! All over! Nora, won't you ever think about me?

NORA: I'm sure I'll think of you often, and about the children and the house here.

HELMER: May I write you?

NORA: No—never. You're not to do that.

370 HELMER: Oh, but let me send you—

NORA: Nothing. Nothing.

HELMER: Or help you if you need it.

NORA: No. I accept nothing from strangers.

HELMER: Nora—can I never be more than a stranger to you?

375 NORA: *(picking up the overnight bag)* Ah, Torvald—it would take the greatest miracle of all—

HELMER: Tell me the greatest miracle!

NORA: You and I both would have to transform ourselves to the point that—Oh, Torvald, I've stopped believing in miracles.

HELMER: But I'll believe. Tell me! Transform ourselves to the point that—?

NORA: That our living together could be a true marriage. *(She goes out down the hall.)*

380 HELMER: *(sinks down on a chair by the door, face buried in his hands)* Nora! Nora! *(Looking about and rising.)* Empty. She's gone. *(A sudden hope leaps in him.)* The greatest miracle—?

From below, the sound of a door slamming shut.

READING AND REACTING

1. What is your attitude toward Nora at the beginning of the play? How does your attitude toward her change as the play progresses? What actions and/or lines of dialogue change your assessment of her?

2. List the key events that occur before the play begins. How do we learn of each event?

3. In act 1, how do the various references to macaroons in the stage directions reinforce plot developments?

4. Explain the role of each of the following in advancing the play's action: the Christmas tree, the locked mailbox, Dr. Rank's calling cards.

5. In act 2, Torvald says, "Whatever comes, you'll see: when it really counts, I have strength and courage enough as a man to take on the whole weight myself." How does this statement influence Nora's subsequent actions?

6. How do the upcoming costume party and Nora's dance influence the development of the play's plot? Where does the play's climax occur?

7. Explain how the following foreshadow events that will occur later in the play: Torvald's comments about Krogstad's children (act 1); Torvald's attitude toward Nora's father (act 2); Krogstad's suggestions about suicide (act 2).

8. In addition to the play's main plot—which concerns the blackmail of Nora by Krogstad and her attempts to keep her crime secret from Torvald—the play contains several subplots, some of which have developed before the play begins and some of which unfold alongside the main plot. Identify these subplots. How do they advance the themes of survival, debt, sacrifice, and duty that run through the play?

9. Is Kristine Linde essential to the play? How might the play be different without her?

10. Is Mrs. Linde as much of a "modern woman" as Nora? Is she actually *more* of a modern woman? Explain.

11. Do you think *A Doll House* is primarily about the struggle between the needs of the individual and the needs of society, or about the conflict between women's roles in the family and in the larger society? Explain.

12. **JOURNAL ENTRY** Nora makes a drastic decision at the end of the play. Do you think she overreacts? What other options does she have? What other options might she have today?

13. **CRITICAL PERSPECTIVE** Since its earliest performances, there has been much comment on the conclusion of *A Doll House*. Many viewers have found the play's ending unrealistically harsh. In fact, a famous German actress refused to play the scene as written because she insisted she would never leave her children. (Ibsen

reluctantly rewrote the ending for her; in this version, Helmer forces Nora to the doorway of the children's bedroom, and she sinks to the floor as the curtain falls.) Moreover, many critics have found it hard to accept Nora's transformation from, in Elizabeth Hardwick's words, "the girlish, charming wife to the radical, courageous heroine setting out alone" ("Ibsen's Women" in *Seduction and Betrayal*).

What is your response to the play's ending? Do you think it makes sense in light of what we have learned about Nora and her marriage? Or do you, for example, agree with Hardwick that Nora's abandonment of her children is not only implausible but also a "rather casual" gesture that "drops a stain on our admiration of Nora"?

Related Works: "The Story of an Hour" (p. 77), "Inland Passage" (p. 150), "The Rocking-Horse Winner" (p. 370), "Girl" (p. 441), "Barbie Doll" (p. 872)

◆ WRITING SUGGESTIONS: PLOT

1. Central to the plots of both *Trifles* and *A Doll House* is a woman who commits a crime. Compare and contrast the reactions of the two plays' other characters, particularly each woman's friends, to her crime.

2. Write an essay in which you compare the influence of Nora's father on the plot of *A Doll House* to the role of an absent father in another play.

3. In both *Trifles* and *A Doll House,* the plot depends to some extent on the fact that male characters misjudge—and perhaps underestimate—women. Write an essay in which you compare and contrast the attitudes the men in these plays hold toward women, the ways in which they reveal these attitudes, and the ways in which the women react.

4. All three of the plays in this chapter deal with marriage. Suppose you were a marriage counsellor and one of the couples came to you for help. What would you say to them? Write an essay in which you give the troubled couple advice for saving their relationship.

5. Compare the economic reasons for marriage in the three plays in this chapter.

CHAPTER 23

Character

◇ ◇ ◇

Character in a play is like a blank check which a dramatist accords to the actor for him to fill in—not entirely blank, for a number of indications of individuality are already there, but to a far less definite and absolute degree than in the novel.

THORNTON WILDER, "Some Thoughts on Playwriting"

A character living onstage is a union of the creative talents of the actor and the dramatist. Any argument over which of the two is more important is futile because they are completely interdependent. The actor requires the character created by the dramatist to provide the initial and vital stimulus. The dramatist requires the embodiment of the character by the actor to bring his creation to fulfillment. The result of this collaboration is the finished performance to which both the actor and the dramatist have made a unique contribution. The result can be neither Shakespeare's Macbeth nor the actor's Macbeth. It must be the actor *as* Shakespeare's Macbeth. An audience can never see a character as the dramatist conceived him. They always see whatever significance a particular actor has been able to find.

CHARLES McGRAW, *Acting Is Believing*, 2d Ed.

Shakespeare is above all writers, at least above all modern writers, the poet of nature: the poet that holds up to his readers a faithful mirror of manners and life. His characters are not modified by the customs of particular places, unpracticed by the rest of the world; by the peculiarities of studies or professions, which can operate but upon small numbers; or by the accidents of transient fashions or temporary opinions: they are the genuine progeny of common humanity, such as the world will always supply, and observation will always find. . . . In the writings of other poets a character is too often an individual; in those of Shakespeare it is commonly a species.

From the Preface to Samuel Johnson's Edition of Shakespeare

◇ ◇ ◇

Readers learn about characters from their own words and from comments by others about them, as well as from the characters' actions and from the playwright's stage directions. At a performance, the audience has the added advantage of seeing the actors' interpretations of the characters.

Characters in plays, like characters in novels and short stories, may be **round** or **flat, static** or **dynamic.** Generally speaking, major characters are likely to be round, whereas minor characters are likely to be flat. Through the language and the actions of the characters, audiences learn whether the characters are multidimensional, skimpily developed, or perhaps merely **foils,** players whose main purpose is to shed light on more important characters. Audiences also learn about the emotions, attitudes, and values that help to shape the characters—their hopes and fears, their strengths and weaknesses. In addition, by comparing characters' early words and actions with later ones, audiences learn from the play whether or not characters grow and change emotionally.

Characters' Words

◈ ◈ ◈

Characters' words reveal the most about their attitudes, feelings, beliefs, and values. Sometimes information is communicated (to other characters as well as to the audience) in a **monologue**—an extended speech by one character. This device is used with great success in Joan MacLeod's *The Shape of a Girl* (p. 1348). A **soliloquy**—a monologue revealing a character's thoughts and feelings, directed at the audience and presumed not to be heard by other characters—can also convey information about a character. For example, Hamlet's well-known soliloquy that begins "To be or not to be" eloquently communicates his distraught mental state—his resentment of his mother and uncle, his confusion about what course of action to take, his suicidal thoughts. Finally, **dialogue**—an exchange of words between two characters—can reveal misunderstanding or conflict between them, or it can show their agreement, mutual support, or similar beliefs.

In Henrik Ibsen's *A Doll House* (p. 1013), dialogue reveals a good deal about the characters. Nora Helmer, the spoiled young wife, has broken the law and kept her crime secret from her husband. Through her words, we learn about her motivation, her emotions, and her reactions to other characters and to her potentially dangerous situation. We learn, for instance, that she is flirtatious—"If your little squirrel begged you, with all her heart and soul. . . . " (act 2)—and that she is childishly unrealistic about the consequences of her actions. When her husband, Torvald, asks what she would do if he was seriously injured, leaving her in debt, she says, "If anything so awful happened, then it just wouldn't matter if I had debts or not" (act 1). When Torvald presses, "Well, but the people I'd borrowed from?" she dismisses them: "Them? Who cares about them! They're strangers." As the play progresses, Nora's lack of understanding of the power of the law becomes more and more significant as she struggles with her moral and ethical dilemma.

The inability of both Nora and Torvald to confront ugly truths is also revealed through their words. When, in act 1, Nora tells Krogstad, her black-mailer, that his revealing her secret could expose her to "the most horrible unpleasantness," he responds, "Only unpleasantness?" Yet later on, in act 3, Torvald uses the same word, fastidiously dismissing the horror with, "No, we're not going to dwell on anything unpleasant."

The ease with which Torvald is able to dismiss his dying friend Dr. Rank in act 3 ("He with his suffering and loneliness—like a dark cloud setting off our sunlit happiness. Well, maybe it's best this way.") exposes his egocen-trism and foreshadows the lack of support he will give Nora immediately thereafter. Especially revealing is his use of *I* and *my* and *me*, which convey his self-centredness:

> Now you've wrecked all my happiness—ruined my whole future. Oh, it's awful to think of. I'm in a cheap little grafter's hands; he can do any-thing he wants with me, ask for anything, play with me like a puppet— and I can't breathe a word. I'll be swept down miserably into the depths on account of a featherbrained woman.

Just as Torvald's words reveal that he has not been changed by the play's events, Nora's words show that she has changed significantly. Her dialogue near the end of act 3 shows that she has become a responsible, determined woman—one who understands her situation and her options and is no longer blithely oblivious to her duties. When she says, "I've never felt more clearheaded and sure in my life," she is calm and decisive; when she says, "Our home's been nothing but a playpen. I've been your doll-wife here, just as at home I was Papa's doll-child," she reveals her newly found self-awareness. When she confronts her husband, she displays complete hon-esty—perhaps for the first time in her relationship with Torvald.

Sometimes what other characters say to or about a character can reveal more to an audience than the character's own words. (Keep in mind, how-ever, that you should measure the accuracy of characters' comments against what you already know about them.) For instance, in act 2 of *A Doll House,* when the dying Dr. Rank says, apparently without malice, "[Torvald] Helmer with his sensitivity has such a sharp distaste for anything ugly," readers not only think ill of the man who is too "sensitive" to visit his sick friend but also question his ability to withstand situations that may be emotionally or morally "ugly" as well.

When a character is offstage for much (or even all) of the action, the audience must rely on other characters' assessments of the absent character. In Susan Glaspell's *Trifles* (p. 948) the play's focus is on an absent character, Minnie Wright, who is described solely through other characters' remarks. The evidence suggests that Mrs. Wright has killed her husband, and only Mrs. Hale's and Mrs. Peters's comments about Mrs. Wright's dreary life can delineate her character and suggest a likely motive for the murder. Although we never meet Mrs. Wright, we learn essential information from the other women: that as a young girl she liked to sing and that more recently she was so distraught about the lack of beauty in her life that even her sewing revealed her distress.

Whether they are in the form of a monologue, a soliloquy, or dialogue, and whether they reveal information about the character who is speaking or about someone else, a character's words are always revealing. Explicitly or implicitly, they convey a character's nature, attitudes, and relationships with other characters. A character may, for instance, use learned words, foreign words, elaborate figurative language, irony or sarcasm, regionalisms, slang, jargon, clichés, or profanity. Words can also be used to indicate tone—for example, to express irony. Any of these uses of language may communicate vital information to the audience about a character's background, attitudes, and motivation. And, of course, a character's language may change as a play progresses, and this change too may be revealing.

FORMAL AND INFORMAL LANGUAGE

One character in a dramatic work may be very formal and aloof, using absolutely correct grammar, a learned vocabulary, and long, complex sentences; another may be informal, using conversational speech, colloquialisms, and slang. At times, two characters with different levels of language may be set in opposition for dramatic effect, as they are in Irish playwright George Bernard Shaw's 1912 play *Pygmalion,* which updates the ancient Greek myth of a sculptor who creates (and falls in love with) a statue of a woman. In Shaw's version, a linguistics professor sets out to teach "proper" speech and manners to a lowly flower seller. Throughout the play, the contrasting language of Henry Higgins, the professor, and Eliza Doolittle, the flower seller, indicates their differing social standing:

> **LIZA:** I ain't got no mother. Her that turned me out was my sixth stepmother. But I done without them. And I'm a good girl, I am.
> **HIGGINS:** Very well, then, what on earth is all this fuss about?

A character's accent or dialect may also be significant. In comedies of manners, for instance, rustic or provincial characters, identified by their speech, were often objects of humour. In *Pygmalion* Eliza Doolittle uses cockney dialect, the dialect spoken in the East End of London. At first, her colourful, distinctive language (complete with expressions like *Nah-ow, garn,* and *ah-ah-ah-ow-ow-ow-oo*) and her nonstandard grammatical constructions make her an object of ridicule; later, the transformation of her speech parallels the dramatic changes in her character.

PLAIN AND ELABORATE STYLE

A character's speech can be simple and straightforward or complex and convoluted; it can be plain and unadorned, or it can be embellished with elaborate **figures of speech.** The relative complexity or lack of complexity of a character's speech can have different effects on the audience. For example, a character whose language is simple and unsophisticated may seem to be unintelligent, unenlightened, gullible, or naive—especially if he or she also uses slang, dialect, or colloquial expressions. Conversely, a character's plain, down-to-earth language can convey common sense or intelligence. Plain language can also be quite powerful. For example, Pelajia poignantly expresses her view on life in *The Rez Sisters* (p. 1248): "Well, sister, guess you finally hit the big jackpot. Best bingo game we've ever been to in our lives, huh? You know, life's like that, I figure. When all is said and done. Kinda' silly, innit, this business of living? But. What choice do we have? When some fool of a being goes and puts us Indians plunk down in the middle of this old earth, dishes out this lot we got right now. But. I figure we gotta make the most of it while we're here."

Like plain speech, elaborate language may have different effects in different contexts. Sometimes, use of figurative language can make a character seem to have depth and insight and analytical skills absent in other characters. In the following excerpt from a soliloquy from *Hamlet,* for example, complex language reveals Hamlet's anguish:

> **HAMLET:** O, that this too too solid flesh would melt,
> Thaw, and resolve itself into a dew!
> Or that the Everlasting had not fix'd
> His canon 'gainst self-slaughter! O God! O God!
> How weary, stale, flat, and unprofitable
> Seem to me all the uses of this world!
> Fie on't, O fie, 'tis an unweeded garden,
> That grows to seed. . . . (1.2.129–36)

In the preceding lines, Hamlet compares the world to a garden gone to seed. His use of imagery and figurative language vividly communicates his feelings about the world and his internal struggle against the temptation to commit suicide.

Sometimes, however, elaborate figurative language may make a character seem pompous or untrustworthy. In the following passages from Shakespeare's *King Lear,* for example, Goneril and Regan, the deceitful daughters, use elaborate language to conceal their true feelings from their father, King Lear. However, Cordelia—the loyal, loving daughter—uses simple, straightforward prose that suggests her sincerity and lack of artifice. Compare the three speeches:

> **GONERIL:** Sir, I love you more than words can wield the matter;
> Dearer than eyesight, space, and liberty;
> Beyond what can be valued, rich or rare;
> No less than life, with grace, health, beauty, honour;
> As much as child e'er lov'd, or father found;
> A love that makes breath poor, and speech unable.
> Beyond all manner of so much I love you. (1.1.56–62)

> **REGAN:** Sir, I am made
> Of the selfsame metal that my sister is,
> And prize me at her worth. In my true heart
> I find she names my very deed of love;

> Only she comes too short, that I profess
> Myself an enemy to all other joys
> Which the most precious square of sense possesses,
> And find I am alone felicitate
> In your dear Highness' love. (1.1.70–78)

> CORDELIA: Unhappy that I am, I cannot heave
> My heart into my mouth. I love your Majesty
> According to my bond; no more no less. (1.1.93–95)

Cordelia's unwillingness, even when she is prodded by Lear, to exaggerate her feelings or misrepresent her love through inflated language shows the audience her honesty and nobility. The contrast between her language and that of her sisters makes their very different motives clear to the audience.

TONE

Tone reveals a character's mood or attitude. Tone can be flat or hysterical, bitter or accepting, affectionate or aloof, anxious or calm. Contrasts in tone can indicate differences in outlook or emotional state between two characters; changes in tone from one point in the play to another can suggest corresponding changes within a character. At the end of *A Doll House,* for instance, Nora is resigned to what she must do, and her language is appropriately controlled. Her husband, however, is desperate to change her mind, and his language reflects this desperation. The following exchanges from act 3 of the play illustrate their contrasting emotional states:

> HELMER: But to part! To part from you! No, Nora, no—I can't imagine it.
> NORA: *(going out, right)* All the more reason why it has to be.

> HELMER: Over! All over! Nora, won't you ever think about me?
> NORA: I'm sure I'll think of you often, and about the children and the house here.

In earlier scenes between the two characters, Nora is emotional—at times, hysterical—and her husband is considerably more controlled. As the preceding dialogue indicates, both Nora and Torvald Helmer change drastically during the course of the play.

IRONY

Irony, a contradiction or discrepancy between two different levels of meaning, can reveal a great deal about character. **Verbal irony**—a contradiction between what a character says and what he or she means—is very important in drama, where the verbal interplay between characters carries the weight of the play. For example, when Nora and Dr. Rank discuss the latest news about his health in *A Doll House,* there is deep irony in his use of the phrase "complete certainty." Although the phrase usually suggests reassuring news, here it is meant to suggest death, and both Nora and Dr. Rank understand this.

Dramatic irony depends on the audience's knowing something that a character has not yet realized, or on one character's knowing something that other characters do not know. In some cases, dramatic irony is created by an audience's awareness of historical background or events of which characters are unaware. (Familiar with the story of Oedipus, for instance, the audience knows that the man who has caused all the problems in Thebes—the man Oedipus vows to find and take revenge on—is Oedipus himself.) In other cases, dramatic irony emerges when the audience learns something—something the characters do not yet know or comprehend—from a play's unfolding action. The central irony in *A Doll House,* for example, is that the family's "happy home" rests on a foundation of secrets, lies, and deception. Torvald does not know about the secrets, and Nora does not understand how they have poisoned her marriage. The audience, however, quickly becomes aware of the atmosphere of deceit—and aware of how it threatens the family's happiness.

Dramatic irony may also be conveyed through dialogue. Typically, dramatic irony is revealed when a character, in conversation, delivers lines that give the audience information that other characters, offstage at the time, do not know. In *A Doll House,* the audience knows—because Nora has explained her situation to Kristine—that Nora has spent the previous Christmas season hard at work, earning money to pay her secret debt. Torvald, however, remains unaware of her activities and believes her story that she was using the time to make holiday decorations, which the cat destroyed. This belief is consistent with his impression of her as an irresponsible child, yet the audience has quite a different impression of Nora. This discrepancy, one of many contradictions between the audience's view of Nora and Torvald's view of her, helps to create dramatic tension in the play.

Finally, **asides** can create dramatic irony by undercutting dialogue, providing ironic contrast between what the characters on stage know and what the audience knows. In Anton Chekhov's *The Brute* (p. 1081), for example, the audience knows that Mr. Smirnov is succumbing to Mrs. Popov's charms because he says, in an aside, "My god, what eyes she has! They're setting me on fire." Mrs. Popov, however, is not yet aware of his infatuation. The discrepancy between the audience's awareness and the character's adds to the play's humour.

CHARACTERS' ACTIONS

⟡ ⟡ ⟡

Through their actions, characters convey their values and attitudes to the audience. Actions also reveal aspects of a character's personality. When Nora in *A Doll House* plays hide-and-seek with her children, eats forbidden macaroons, and takes childish joy in Christmas, her immaturity is apparent.

Readers also learn about characters from what they do *not* do. Thus, Nora's failure to remain in touch with her friend Kristine, who has had a hard life, reveals her selfishness, and the failure of Mrs. Peters and Mrs. Hale in *Trifles* to communicate their evidence to the sheriff indicates their support for Mrs. Wright and their understanding of what motivated her to take such drastic action.

Audiences also learn a good deal about characters by observing how they interact with other characters. In William Shakespeare's *Othello*, Iago is the embodiment of evil, and as the play's action unfolds, we discover his true nature. He reveals the secret marriage of Othello and Desdemona to her father; he schemes to arouse Othello's jealousy, making him believe Desdemona has been unfaithful with his lieutenant, Cassio; he persuades Cassio to ask Desdemona to plead his case with Othello, knowing this act will further arouse Othello's suspicions; he encourages Othello to be suspicious of Desdemona's defence of Cassio; he plants Desdemona's handkerchief in Cassio's room; and, finally, he persuades Othello to kill Desdemona and then kills his own wife, Emilia, to prevent her from exposing his role in the intrigue. As the play progresses, then, Iago's dealings with others consistently reveal him to be evil and corrupt.

Stage Directions
❖ ❖ ❖

When we read a play, we also read the playwright's italicized **stage directions,** the notes that concern **staging**—the scenery, props, lighting, music, sound effects, costumes, and other elements that contribute to the way the play looks and sounds to an audience (Chapter 24). In addition to commenting on staging, stage directions may supply physical details about the characters, suggesting their age, appearance, movements, gestures, relative positions, and facial expressions. These details may in turn convey additional information about characters: appearance may reveal social position or economic status, expressions may reveal attitudes, and so on. Stage directions may also indicate the manner in which a line of dialogue is to be delivered—haltingly, confidently, hesitantly, or loudly, for instance. The way a line is spoken may reveal a character to be excited, upset, angry, shy, or disappointed. Finally, stage directions may indicate *changes* in characters—for instance, a character whose speech is described as timid in early scenes may deliver lines emphatically and forcefully later on in the play.

Some plays' stage directions provide a good deal of detail about character; others do little more than list characters' names. In *The Rez Sisters*, Tomson Highway uses detailed stage directions to explain action and develop character:

At the store. Annie Cook, Marie-Adele Starblanket, Veronique St. Pierre, and Zhaboonigan Peterson have arrived. Emily Dictionary makes a sudden appearance, carrying a huge bag of flour on her shoulder. She is one tough lady, wearing cowboy boots, tight blue jeans, a black leather jacket—all three items worn to the seams—and she sports one black eye.

Highway's stage directions are numerous and often lengthy.

George Bernard Shaw is notorious for the full character description in his stage directions. In these directions—seen by readers of the play but not heard by audiences—he communicates complex information about characters' attitudes and values, strengths and weaknesses, motivation and reactions, and relationships with other characters. In doing so Shaw functions as a narrator, explicitly communicating his own attitudes toward various characters. Shaw's stage directions for *Pygmalion* initially describe Eliza Doolittle as follows:

She is not at all an attractive person. She is perhaps eighteen, perhaps twenty, hardly older. She wears a little sailor hat of black straw that has long been exposed to the dust and soot of London and has seldom if ever been brushed. Her hair needs washing rather badly; its mousy color can hardly be natural. She wears a shoddy black coat that reaches nearly to her knees and is shaped to her waist. She has a brown skirt with a coarse apron. Her boots are much the worse for wear. She is no doubt as clean as she can afford to be; but compared to the ladies she is very dirty. Her features are no worse than theirs; but their condition leaves something to be desired; and she needs the services of a dentist.

Rather than providing an objective summary of the character's most notable physical attributes, Shaw injects subjective comments (*"seldom if ever brushed"; "color can hardly be natural"; "no doubt as clean as she can afford to be"*) that reveal his attitude toward Eliza. This initially supercilious attitude, which he shares with Professor Higgins, is tempered considerably by the end of the play, helping to make Eliza's transformation more obvious to readers than it would be if measured by her words and actions alone. By act 5 the tone of the stage directions characterizing Eliza has changed to admiration: *"Eliza enters, sunny, self-possessed, and giving a staggeringly convincing exhibition of ease of manner."*

Stage directions in *Hamlet* are not nearly as comprehensive. Characters are introduced with only the barest identifying tags: "Claudius, *King of Denmark*"; "Hamlet, *Son to the former, and nephew to the present King*"; "Gertrude, *Queen of Denmark, mother to Hamlet.*" Most stage directions do little more than chronicle the various characters' entrances and exits or specify particular physical actions: *"Enter Ghost"; "Spreads his arms"; "Ghost beckons Hamlet"; "He kneels"; "Sheathes his sword"; "Leaps in the grave."* Occasionally, stage directions specify a prop (*"Puts down the skull"*); a sound effect (*"A noise within"*); or a costume (*"Enter the ghost in his night-gown"*).

Such brevity is typical of Shakespeare's plays, in which characters are delineated almost solely by their words—and, not incidentally, by the way actors have interpreted the characters over the years. In fact, because Shakespeare's stage directions only suggest characters' gestures, physical reactions, movements, and facial expressions, actors have been left quite free to experiment, reading various interpretations into Shakespeare's characters.

Actors' Interpretations

◆ ◆ ◆

When we watch a play, we gain insight into a character not merely through what the character says and does or how other characters react, but also through the way an actor interprets the role. If a playwright does not specify a character's mannerisms, gestures, or movements, or does not indicate how a line is to be delivered (and sometimes even if he or she does), an actor is free to interpret the role as he or she believes it should be played. Even when a playwright *does* specify such actions, the actor has a good deal of freedom to decide which gestures or expressions will convey a certain emotion.

In "Some Thoughts on Playwriting," dramatist Thornton Wilder argues that "the theatre is an art which reposes upon the work of many collaborators" rather than on "one governing selecting will." Citing examples from Shakespeare and Ibsen, Wilder illustrates the great degree of "intervention" that may occur in dramatic productions. For instance, Wilder observes, Shakespeare's Shylock has been portrayed by two different actors as "noble, wronged and indignant" and as "a vengeful and hysterical buffoon"—and both performances were considered positive contributions to the theatre. As noted earlier, the absence of detailed stage directions in Shakespeare's plays makes possible (and perhaps even encourages) such widely diverging interpretations. However, as Wilder notes, even when playing roles created by a dramatist such as Ibsen, whose stage directions are typically quite specific, actors and directors have a good deal of leeway. Thus, Janet McTeer, who played the part of Ibsen's Nora in the 1997 London production of *A Doll House*, saw Nora and Torvald, despite their many problems, as "the perfect couple," deeply in love and involved in a passionate marriage. "You have to make that marriage sexually credible," McTeer told the *New York Times*, "to imagine they have a wonderful time in bed, so there becomes something to lose. If you play them as already past it or no longer attracted to each other, then there is no play." This interpretation is not inconsistent with the play, but it does go beyond what Ibsen actually wrote. In a sense, then, the playwright's words on the page are just the beginning of the character's lives.

Irish playwright Samuel Beckett devotes a good deal of attention to indicating actors' movements and gestures and their physical reactions to one another. In his 1952 play *Waiting for Godot,* for example, Beckett seems to choreograph every gesture, every emotion, every intention, with stage directions such as the following:

◇ *(he looks at them ostentatiously in turn to make it clear they are both meant)*

◇ *Vladimir seizes Lucky's hat. Silence of Lucky. He falls. Silence. Panting of the victors.*

◇ *Estragon hands him the boot. Vladimir inspects it, throws it down angrily.*

◇ *Estragon pulls, stumbles, falls. Long silence.*

◇ *He goes feverishly to and fro, halts finally at extreme left, broods.*

Clearly, Beckett provides full and obviously carefully thought-out stage directions and, in so doing, attempts to retain a good deal of control over his characters. Still, in a 1988 production of *Godot,* director Mike Nichols and comic actors Robin Williams and Steve Martin felt free to improvise, adding gestures and movements not specified or even hinted at—and most critics believed that this production managed to remain true to the tragi-comic spirit of Beckett's existentialist play.

 # CHECKLIST: WRITING ABOUT CHARACTER

✓ Does any character serve as a narrator? If so, what information does this narrator supply about the other characters? How reliable is the narrator?

✓ Are the major characters fully developed?

✓ Do the major characters change and grow during the course of the play, or do they remain essentially unchanged?

✓ What function does each of the minor characters serve in the play?

✓ What elements reveal changes in the characters?

✓ What is revealed about the characters through their words?

✓ Do characters use foreign words, regionalisms, slang, jargon, clichés, or profanity? What does such use of language reveal about characters? About theme?

✓ Is the language formal or informal?

✓ Do characters speak in dialect? Do they have accents?

✓ Is the language elaborate or plain?

✓ Do different characters exhibit contrasting styles or levels of language? What is the significance of these differences?

✓ In what way does language reveal characters' emotional states?

✓ Does the tone or style of any character's language change significantly as the play progresses? What does this change reveal?

✓ Does the play include verbal irony? Dramatic irony? How is irony conveyed? What purpose does irony achieve?

✓ What is revealed about the characters through what others say about them?

✓ Is the audience encouraged to react sympathetically to the character?

✓ What is revealed about the characters through their actions?

✓ What is revealed about the characters through the playwright's stage directions?

✓ How might different actors' interpretations change an audience's understanding of the characters?

◆ **ANTON CHEKHOV** (1860–1904) is the major nineteenth-century Russian playwright and short story writer. He became a doctor and, as a young adult, supported the rest of his family following his father's bankruptcy. After his early adult years in Moscow, Chekhov spent the rest of his life in the country, moving to Yalta, a resort town in Crimea, for his health (he suffered from tuberculosis). He continued to write plays, mostly for the Moscow Art Theatre, although he could not supervise their production as he would have wished. His plays include *The Seagull* (1896), *Uncle Vanya* (1898), *The Three Sisters* (1901), and *The Cherry Orchard* (1904).

The Brute, or *The Bear* (1888), is one of a number of one-act farces Chekhov wrote just before his major plays. It is based on a French farce (*Les Jurons de Cadillac* by Pierre Breton) about a man who cannot refrain from swearing. The woman he loves offers to marry him if he can avoid swearing for one hour.

ANTON CHEKHOV

The Brute

A JOKE IN ONE ACT
(1888)

English Version by Eric Bentley

CHARACTERS

MRS. POPOV, *widow and landowner,*
  small, with dimpled cheeks
MR. GRIGORY S. SMIRNOV, *gentleman*
  farmer, middle-aged
LUKA, *Mrs. Popov's footman, an old*
  man

GARDENER
COACHMAN
HIRED MEN

SCENE

The drawing room of a country house. Mrs. Popov, in deep mourning, is staring hard at a photograph. Luka is with her.

LUKA: It's not right, ma'am, you're killing yourself. The cook has gone off with the maid to pick berries. The cat's having a high old time in the yard catching birds. Every living thing is happy. But you stay moping here in the house like it was a convent, taking no pleasure in nothing. I mean it, ma'am! It must be a full year since you set foot out of doors.

MRS. POPOV: I must never set foot out of doors again, Luka. Never! I have nothing to set foot out of doors *for*. My life is done. *He* is in his grave. I have buried myself alive in this house. We are *both* in our graves.

LUKA: You're off again, ma'am. I just won't listen to you no more. Mr. Popov is dead, but what can we do about that? It's God's doing. God's will be done. You've cried over him, you've done your share of mourning, haven't you? There's a limit to everything. You can't go on weeping and wailing forever. My old lady died, for that matter, and I wept and wailed over her a whole month long. Well, that was it. I couldn't weep and wail all my life. She just wasn't worth it. *(He sighs.)* As for the neighbors, you've forgotten all about them, ma'am. You don't visit them and you don't let them visit you. You and I are like a pair of spiders—excuse the expression, ma'am—here we are in this house like a pair of spiders, we never see the light of day. And it isn't like there was no nice people around either. The whole county's swarming with 'em. There's a regiment quartered at Riblov, and the officers are so good-looking! The girls can't take their eyes off them— There's a ball at the camp every Friday—The military band plays most every day of the week—What do you say, ma'am? You're young, you're pretty, you could enjoy yourself! Ten years from now you may want to strut and show your feathers to the officers, and it'll be too late.

Mrs. Popov: *(firmly)* You must never bring this subject up again, Luka. Since Popov died, life has been an empty dream to me, you know that. *You* may think I am alive. Poor ignorant Luka! You are wrong. I am dead. I'm in my grave. Never more shall I see the light of day, never strip from my body this . . . raiment of death! Are you listening, Luka? Let his ghost learn how I love him! Yes, *I* know, and *you* know, he was often unfair to me, he was cruel to me, and he was unfaithful to me. What of it? *I* shall be faithful to *him*, that's all. I will show him how *I* can love. Hereafter, in a better world than this, he will welcome me back, the same loyal girl I always was—

5 Luka: Instead of carrying on this way, ma'am, you should go out in the garden and take a bit of a walk, ma'am. Or why not harness Toby and take a drive? Call on a couple of the neighbours, ma'am?

Mrs. Popov: *(breaking down)* Oh, Luka!

Luka: Yes, ma'am? What have I said, ma'am? Oh, dear!

Mrs. Popov: Toby! You said Toby! He adored that horse. When he drove me out to the Korchagins and the Vlasovs, it was always with Toby! He was a wonderful driver, do you remember, Luka? So graceful! So strong! I can see him now, pulling at those reins with all his might and main! Toby! Luka, tell them to give Toby an extra portion of oats today.

Luka: Yes, ma'am.

A bell rings.

10 Mrs. Popov: Who is that? Tell them I'm not at home.

Luka: Very good, ma'am. *(Exit.)*

Mrs. Popov: *(gazing again at the photograph)* You shall see, my Popov, how a wife can love and forgive. Till death do us part. Longer than that. Till death re-unite us forever! *(Suddenly a titter breaks through her tears.)* Aren't you ashamed of yourself, Popov? Here's your little wife, being good, being faithful, so faithful she's locked up here waiting for her own funeral, while you—doesn't it make you ashamed, you naughty boy? You were terrible, you know. You were unfaithful, and you made those awful scenes about it, you stormed out and left me alone for weeks—

Enter Luka.

Luka: *(upset)* There's someone asking for you, ma'am. Says he must—

Mrs. Popov: I suppose you told him that since my husband's death I see no one?

15 Luka: Yes, ma'am. I did, ma'am. But he wouldn't listen, ma'am. He says it's urgent.

Mrs. Popov: *(shrilly)* I see no one!!

Luka: He won't take no for an answer, ma'am. He just curses and swears and comes in anyway. He's a perfect monster, ma'am. He's in the dining room right now.

MRS. POPOV: In the dining room, is he? I'll give him his come-uppance. Bring him in here this minute.

Exit Luka.

(*Suddenly sad again.*) Why do they do this to me? Why? Insulting my grief, intruding on my solitude? (*She sighs.*) I'm afraid I'll have to enter a convent. I will, I *must* enter a convent!

Enter Mr. Smirnov and Luka.

SMIRNOV: (*to Luka*) Dolt! Idiot! You talk too much! (*Seeing Mrs. Popov. With dignity.*) May I have the honor of introducing myself, madam? Grigory S. Smirnov, landowner and lieutenant of artillery, retired. Forgive me, madam, if I disturb your peace and quiet, but my business is both urgent and weighty.

20 MRS. POPOV: (*declining to offer him her hand*) What is it you wish, sir?

SMIRNOV: At the time of his death, your late husband—with whom I had the honor to be acquainted, ma'am—was in my debt to the tune of twelve hundred rubles. I have two notes to prove it. Tomorrow, ma'am, I must pay the interest on a bank loan. I have therefore no alternative, ma'am, but to ask you to pay me the money today.

MRS. POPOV: Twelve hundred rubles? But what did my husband owe it to you for?

SMIRNOV: He used to buy his oats from me, madam.

MRS. POPOV: (*to Luka, with a sigh*) Remember what I said, Luka: tell them to give Toby an extra portion of oats today!

Exit Luka.

My dear Mr.—what was the name again?

25 SMIRNOV: Smirnov, ma'am.

MRS. POPOV: My dear Mr. Smirnov, if Mr. Popov owed you money, you shall be paid—to the last ruble, to the last kopeck. But today—you must excuse me, Mr.—what was it?

SMIRNOV: Smirnov, ma'am.

MRS. POPOV: Today, Mr. Smirnov, I have no ready cash in the house. (*Smirnov starts to speak.*) Tomorrow, Mr. Smirnov, no, the day after tomorrow, all will be well. My steward will be back from town. I shall see that he pays what is owing. Today, no. In any case, today is exactly seven months from Mr. Popov's death. On such a day you will understand that I am in no mood to think of money.

SMIRNOV: Madam, if you don't pay up now, you can carry me out feet foremost. They'll seize my estate.

30 MRS. POPOV: You can have your money. (*He starts to thank her.*) Tomorrow. (*He again starts to speak.*) That is: the day after tomorrow.

SMIRNOV: I don't need the money the day after tomorrow. I need it today.

MRS. POPOV: I'm sorry, Mr.—

35

SMIRNOV: *(shouting)* Smirnov!

MRS. POPOV: *(sweetly)* Yes, of course. But you can't have it today.

SMIRNOV: But I can't wait for it any longer!

MRS. POPOV: Be sensible, Mr. Smirnov. How can I pay you if I don't have it?

SMIRNOV: You don't have it?

MRS. POPOV: I don't have it.

SMIRNOV: Sure?

40 MRS. POPOV: Positive.

SMIRNOV: Very well. I'll make a note to that effect. *(Shrugging.)* And then they want me to keep cool. I meet the tax commissioner on the street, and he says, "Why are you always in such a bad humor, Smirnov?" Bad humor! How can I help it, in God's name? I need money, I need it desperately. Take yesterday: I leave home at the crack of dawn, I call on all my debtors. Not a one of them pays up. Footsore and weary, I creep at midnight into some little dive, and try to snatch a few winks of sleep on the floor by the vodka barrel. Then today, I come here, fifty miles from home, saying to myself, "At last, at last, I can be sure of something," and you're not in the mood! You give me a mood! Christ, how can I help getting all worked up?

MRS. POPOV: I thought I'd made it clear, Mr. Smirnov, that you'll get your money the minute my steward is back from town.

SMIRNOV: What the hell do I care about your steward? Pardon the expression, ma'am. But it was you I came to see.

MRS. POPOV: What language! What a tone to take to a lady! I refuse to hear another word. *(Quickly, exit.)*

45 SMIRNOV: Not in the mood, huh? "Exactly seven months since Popov's death," huh? How about me? *(Shouting after her.)* Is there this interest to pay, or isn't there? I'm asking you a question: is there this interest to pay, or isn't there? So your husband died, and you're not in the mood, and your steward's gone off some place, and so forth and so on, but what can *I* do about all that, huh? What do *you* think I should do? Take a running jump and shove my head through the wall? Take off in a balloon? You don't know my *other* debtors. I call on Gruzdeff. Not at home. I look for Yaroshevitch. He's hiding out. I find Kooritsin. He kicks up a row, and I have to throw him through the window. I work my way right down the list. Not a kopeck. Then I come to you, and God damn it to hell, if you'll pardon the expression, you're not in the mood! *(Quietly, as he realizes he's talking to air.)* I've spoiled them all, that's what, I've let them play me for a sucker. Well, I'll show them. I'll show this one. I'll stay right here till she pays up. Ugh! *(He shudders with rage.)* I'm in a rage! I'm in a positively towering rage! Every nerve in my body is trembling at forty to the dozen! I can't breathe, I feel ill, I think I'm going to faint, hey, you there!

Enter Luka.

LUKA: Yes, sir? Is there anything you wish, sir?

SMIRNOV: Water! Water! No, make it vodka.

Exit Luka.

> Consider the logic of it. A fellow creature is desperately in need of cash, so desperately in need that he has to seriously contemplate hanging himself, and this woman, this mere chit of a girl, won't pay up, and why not? Because, forsooth, she isn't in the mood! Oh, the logic of women! Come to that, I never have liked them, I could do without the whole sex. Talk to a woman? I'd rather sit on a barrel of dynamite, the very thought gives me gooseflesh. Women! Creatures of poetry and romance! Just to see one in the distance gets me mad. My legs start twitching with rage. I feel like yelling for help.

Enter Luka, handing Smirnov a glass of water.

LUKA: Mrs. Popov is indisposed, sir. She is seeing no one.

SMIRNOV: Get out.

Exit Luka.

> Indisposed, is she? Seeing no one, huh? Well, she can see me or not, but I'll be here, I'll be right here till she pays up. If you're sick for a week, I'll be here for a week. If you're sick for a year, I'll be here for a year. You won't get around me with your widow's weeds and your schoolgirl dimples. I know all about dimples. *(Shouting through the window.)* Semyon, let the horses out of those shafts, we're not leaving, we're staying, and tell them to give the horses some oats, yes, oats, you fool, what do you think? *(Walking away from the window.)* What a mess, what an unholy mess! I didn't sleep last night, the heat is terrific today, not a damn one of 'em has paid up, and here's this—this skirt in mourning that's not in the mood! My head aches, where's that—*(He drinks from the glass.)* Water, ugh! You there!

Enter Luka.

50 **LUKA:** Yes, sir. You wish for something, sir?

SMIRNOV: Where's that confounded vodka I asked for?

Exit Luka.

> *(Smirnov sits and looks himself over.)* Oof! A fine figure of a man *I* am! Unwashed, uncombed, unshaven, straw on my vest, dust all over me. The little woman must've taken me for a highwayman. *(Yawns.)* I suppose it wouldn't be considered polite to barge into a drawing room in this state, but who cares? I'm not a visitor, I'm a creditor—most unwelcome of guests, second only to Death.

Enter Luka.

LUKA: *(handing him the vodka)* If I may say so, sir, you take too many liberties, sir.

SMIRNOV: What?!

LUKA: Oh, nothing, sir, nothing.

55 SMIRNOV: Who in hell do you think you're talking to? Shut your mouth!

LUKA: *(aside)* There's an evil spirit abroad. The Devil must have sent him. Oh! *(Exit Luka.)*

SMIRNOV: What a rage I'm in! I'll grind the whole world to powder. Oh, I feel ill again. You there!

Enter Mrs. Popov.

MRS. POPOV: *(looking at the floor)* In the solitude of my rural retreat, Mr. Smirnov, I've long since grown unaccustomed to the sound of the human voice. Above all, I cannot bear shouting. I must beg you not to break the silence.

SMIRNOV: Very well. Pay me my money and I'll go.

60 MRS. POPOV: I told you before, and I tell you again, Mr. Smirnov. I have no cash, you'll have to wait till the day after tomorrow. Can I express myself more plainly?

SMIRNOV: And *I* told *you* before, and *I* tell *you* again, that I need the money today, that the day after tomorrow is too late, and that if you don't pay, and pay now, I'll have to hang myself in the morning!

MRS. POPOV: But I have no cash. This is quite a puzzle.

SMIRNOV: You won't pay, huh?

MRS. POPOV: I *can't* pay, Mr. Smirnov.

65 SMIRNOV: In that case, I'm going to sit here and wait. *(Sits down.)* You'll pay up the day after tomorrow? Very good. Till the day after tomorrow, here I sit. *(Pause. He jumps up.)* Now look, do I have to pay that interest tomorrow, or don't I? Or do you think I'm joking?

MRS. POPOV: I must ask you not to raise your voice, Mr. Smirnov. This is not a stable.

SMIRNOV: Who said it was? Do I have to pay the interest tomorrow or not?

MRS. POPOV: Mr. Smirnov, do you know how to behave in the presence of a lady?

SMIRNOV: No, madam, I do not know how to behave in the presence of a lady.

70 MRS. POPOV: Just what I thought. I look at you, and I say: ugh! I hear you talk, and I say to myself: "That man doesn't know how to talk to a lady."

SMIRNOV: You'd like me to come simpering to you in French, I suppose. "*Enchanté, madame! Merci beaucoup* for not paying zee money, *madame! Pardonnez-moi* if I 'ave disturbed you, *madame*! How *charmante* you look in mourning, *madame!*"

MRS. POPOV: Now you're being silly, Mr. Smirnov.

SMIRNOV: *(mimicking)* "Now you're being silly, Mr. Smirnov." "You don't know how to talk to a lady, Mr. Smirnov." Look here, Mrs. Popov, I've known more women than you've known pussy cats. I've fought three

duels on their account. I've jilted twelve, and been jilted by nine
others. Oh, yes, Mrs. Popov, I've played the fool in my time, whispered
sweet nothings, bowed and scraped and endeavored to please. Don't
tell me I don't know what it is to love, to pine away with longing, to
have the blues, to melt like butter, to be weak as water. I was full of
tender emotion. I was carried away with passion. I squandered half my
fortune on the sex. I chattered about women's emancipation. But
there's an end to everything, dear madam. Burning eyes, dark
eyelashes, ripe, red lips, dimpled cheeks, heaving bosoms, soft
whisperings, the moon above; the lake below—I don't give a rap for
that sort of nonsense any more, Mrs. Popov. I've found out about
women. Present company excepted, they're liars. Their behavior is
mere play acting; their conversation is sheer gossip. Yes, dear lady,
women, young or old, are false, petty, vain, cruel, malicious,
unreasonable. As for intelligence, any sparrow could give them points.
Appearances, I admit, can be deceptive. In appearance, a woman may
be all poetry and romance, goddess and angel, muslin and fluff. To
look at her exterior is to be transported to heaven. But I have looked at
her interior, Mrs. Popov, and what did I find there—in her very soul? A
crocodile. *(He has gripped the back of the chair so firmly that it snaps.)*
And, what is more revolting, a crocodile with an illusion, a crocodile
that imagines tender sentiments are its own special province, a
crocodile that thinks itself queen of the realm of love! Whereas, in
sober fact, dear madam, if a woman can love anything except a lapdog
you can hang me by the feet on that nail. For a man, love is suffering,
love is sacrifice. A woman just swishes her train around and tightens
her grip on your nose. Now, you're a woman, aren't you, Mrs. Popov?
You must be an expert on some of this. Tell me, quite frankly, did you
ever know a woman to be—faithful, for instance? Or even sincere?
Only old hags, huh? Though some women are old hags from birth.
But as for the others? You're right: a faithful woman is a freak of
nature—like a cat with horns.

MRS. POPOV: Who *is* faithful, then? Who *have* you cast for the faithful
lover? Not man?

75 SMIRNOV: Right first time, Mrs. Popov: man.

MRS. POPOV: *(going off into a peal of bitter laughter)* Man! Man is faithful!
that's a new one! *(Fiercely.)* What right do you have to say this, Mr.
Smirnov? Men faithful? Let me tell you something. Of all the men I
have ever known my late husband Popov was the best. I loved him,
and there are women who know how to love, Mr. Smirnov. I gave him
my youth, my happiness, my life, my fortune. I worshipped the
ground he trod on—and what happened? The best of men was
unfaithful to me, Mr. Smirnov. Not once in a while. All the time. After
he died, I found his desk drawer full of love letters. While he was alive,
he was always going away for the week-end. He squandered my
money. He made love to other women before my very eyes. But, in

spite of all, Mr. Smirnov, *I* was faithful. Unto death. And beyond. I am
still faithful, Mr. Smirnov! Buried alive in this house, I shall wear
mourning till the day I, too, am called to my eternal rest.

SMIRNOV: *(laughing scornfully)* Expect me to believe that? As if I couldn't see
through all this hocus-pocus. Buried alive! Till you're called to your
eternal rest! Till when? Till some little poet—or some little subaltern
with his first moustache—comes riding by and asks: "Can that be the
house of the mysterious Tamara who for love of her late husband has
buried herself alive, vowing to see no man?" Ha!

MRS. POPOV: *(flaring up)* How dare you? How dare you insinuate—?

SMIRNOV: You may have buried yourself alive, Mrs. Popov, but you haven't
forgotten to powder your nose.

80 MRS. POPOV: *(incoherent)* How dare you? How—?

SMIRNOV: Who's raising his voice now? Just because I call a spade a spade.
Because I shoot straight from the shoulder. Well, don't shout at me,
I'm not your steward.

MRS. POPOV: I'm not shouting, you're shouting! Oh, leave me alone!

SMIRNOV: Pay me the money, and I will.

MRS. POPOV: You'll get no money out of me!

85 SMIRNOV: Oh, so that's it!

MRS. POPOV: Not a ruble, not a kopeck. Get out! Leave me alone!

SMIRNOV: Not being your husband, I must ask you not to make scenes with
me. *(He sits.)* I don't like scenes.

MRS. POPOV: *(choking with rage)* You're sitting down?

SMIRNOV: Correct, I'm sitting down.

90 MRS. POPOV: I asked you to leave!

SMIRNOV: Then give me the money. *(Aside.)* Oh, what a rage I'm in, what a
rage!

MRS. POPOV: The impudence of the man! I won't talk to you a moment
longer. Get out. *(Pause.)* Are you going?

SMIRNOV: No.

MRS. POPOV: No?!

95 SMIRNOV: No.

MRS. POPOV: On your head be it. Luka!

Enter Luka.

Show the gentleman out, Luka.

LUKA: *(approaching)* I'm afraid, sir, I'll have to ask you, um, to leave, sir,
now, um—

SMIRNOV: *(jumping up)* Shut your mouth, you old idiot! Who do you think
you're talking to? I'll make mincemeat of you.

LUKA: *(clutching his heart)* Mercy on us! Holy saints above! *(He falls into an
armchair.)* I'm taken sick! I can't breathe!!

100 MRS. POPOV: Then where's Dasha? Dasha! Dasha! Come here at once! *(She
rings.)*

LUKA: They gone picking berries, ma'am, I'm alone here—Water, water, I'm
taken sick!

MRS. POPOV: *(to Smirnov)* Get out, you!

SMIRNOV: Can't you even be polite with me, Mrs. Popov?

MRS. POPOV: *(clenching her fists and stamping her feet)* With you? You're a wild animal, you were never house-broken!

105 SMIRNOV: What? What did you say?

MRS. POPOV: I said you were a wild animal, you were never house-broken.

SMIRNOV: *(advancing upon her)* And what right do you have to talk to me like that?

MRS. POPOV: Like what?

SMIRNOV: You have insulted me, madam.

110 MRS. POPOV: What of it? Do you think I'm scared of you?

SMIRNOV: So you think you can get away with it because you're a woman. A creature of poetry and romance, huh? Well, it doesn't go down with me. I hereby challenge you to a duel.

LUKA: Mercy on us! Holy saints alive! Water!

SMIRNOV: I propose we shoot it out.

MRS. POPOV: Trying to scare me again? Just because you have big fists and a voice like a bull? You're a brute.

115 SMIRNOV: No one insults Grigory S. Smirnov with impunity! And I don't care if you *are* a female.

MRS. POPOV: *(trying to outshout him)* Brute, brute, brute!

SMIRNOV: The sexes are equal, are they? Fine: then it's just prejudice to expect men alone to pay for insults. I hereby challenge—

MRS. POPOV: *(screaming)* All right! You want to shoot it out? All right! Let's shoot it out!

SMIRNOV: And let it be here and now!

120 MRS. POPOV: Here and now! All right! I'll have Popov's pistols here in one minute! *(Walks away, then turns.)* Putting one of Popov's bullets through your silly head will be a pleasure! Au revoir. *(Exit.)*

SMIRNOV: I'll bring her down like a duck, a sitting duck. I'm not one of your little poets, I'm no little subaltern with his first moustache. No, sir, there's no weaker sex where I'm concerned!

LUKA: Sir! Master! *(He goes down on his knees.)* Take pity on a poor old man, and do me a favor: go away. It was bad enough before, you nearly scared me to death. But a duel—!

SMIRNOV: *(ignoring him)* A duel! That's equality of the sexes for you! That's women's emancipation! Just as a matter of principle I'll bring her down like a duck. But what a woman! "Putting one of Popov's bullets through your silly head . . . ." Her cheeks were flushed, her eyes were gleaming! And, by God, she's accepted the challenge! I never knew a woman like this before!

LUKA: Sir! Master! Please go away! I'll always pray for you!

125 SMIRNOV: *(again ignoring him)* What a woman! Phew!! *She's* no sour puss, *she's* no cry baby. She's fire and brimstone. She's a human cannon ball. What a shame I have to kill her!

LUKA: *(weeping)* Please, kind sir, please, go away!

SMIRNOV: *(as before)* I like her, isn't that funny? With those dimples and all?

I like her. I'm even prepared to consider letting her off that debt. And where's my rage? It's gone. I never knew a woman like this before.

Enter Mrs. Popov with pistols.

MRS. POPOV: *(boldly)* Pistols, Mr. Smirnov! *(Matter of fact.)* But before we start, you'd better show me how it's done. I'm not too familiar with these things. In fact I never gave a pistol a second look.

LUKA: Lord, have mercy on us, I must go hunt up the gardener and the coachman. Why has this catastrophe fallen upon us, O Lord? *(Exit.)*

130   SMIRNOV: *(examining the pistols)* Well, it's like this. There are several makes: one is the Mortimer, with capsules, especially constructed for dueling. What you have here are Smith and Wesson triple-action revolvers, with extractor, first-rate job, worth ninety rubles at the very least. You hold it this way. *(Aside.)* My God, what eyes she has! They're setting me on fire.

MRS. POPOV: This way?

SMIRNOV: Yes, that's right. You cock the trigger, take aim like this, head up, arm out like this. Then you just press with this finger here, and it's all over. The main thing is, keep cool, take slow aim, and don't let your arm jump.

MRS. POPOV: I see. And if it's inconvenient to do the job here, we can go out in the garden.

SMIRNOV: Very good. Of course, I should warn you: I'll be firing in the air.

135   MRS. POPOV: What? This is the end. Why?

SMIRNOV: Oh, well—because—for private reasons.

MRS. POPOV: Scared, huh? *(She laughs heartily.)* Now don't you try to get out of it, Mr. Smirnov. My blood is up. I won't be happy till I've drilled a hole through that skull of yours. Follow me. What's the matter? Scared?

SMIRNOV: That's right. I'm scared.

MRS. POPOV: Oh, come on, what's the matter with you?

140   SMIRNOV: Well, um, Mrs. Popov, I, um, I like you.

MRS. POPOV: *(laughing bitterly)* Good God! He likes me, does he? The gall of the man. *(Showing him the door.)* You may leave, Mr. Smirnov.

SMIRNOV: *(Quietly puts the gun down, takes his hat, and walks to the door. Then he stops and the pair look at each other without a word. Then, approaching gingerly.)* Listen, Mrs. Popov. Are you still mad at me? I'm in the devil of a temper myself, of course. But then, you see—what I mean is—it's this way—the fact is—(Roaring.) Well, is it my fault, damn it, if I like you? *(Clutches the back of a chair. It breaks.)* Christ, what fragile furniture you have here. I like you. Know what I mean? I could fall in love with you.

MRS. POPOV: I hate you. Get out!

SMIRNOV: What a woman! I never saw anything like it. Oh, I'm lost, I'm done for, I'm a mouse in a trap.

145   MRS. POPOV: Leave this house, or I shoot!

SMIRNOV: Shoot away! What bliss to die of a shot that was fired by that little velvet hand! To die gazing into those enchanting eyes. I'm out of my mind. I know: you must decide at once. Think for one second, then decide. Because if I leave now, I'll never be back. Decide! I'm a pretty decent chap. Landed gentleman, I should say. Ten thousand a year. Good stable. Throw a kopeck up in the air, and I'll put a bullet through it. Will you marry me?

MRS. POPOV: *(indignant, brandishing the gun)* We'll shoot it out! Get going! Take your pistol!

SMIRNOV: I'm out of my mind. I don't understand anything any more. *(Shouting.)* You there! That vodka!

MRS. POPOV: No excuses! No delays! We'll shoot it out!

150 SMIRNOV: I'm out of my mind. I'm falling in love. I *have* fallen in love. *(He takes her hand vigorously; she squeals.)* I love you. *(He goes down on his knees.)* I love you as I've never loved before. I jilted twelve, and was jilted by nine others. But I didn't love a one of them as I love you. I'm full of tender emotion. I'm melting like butter. I'm weak as water. I'm on my knees like a fool, and I offer you my hand. It's a shame, it's a disgrace. I haven't been in love in five years. I took a vow against it. And now, all of a sudden, to be swept off my feet, it's a scandal. I offer you my hand, dear lady. Will you or won't you? You won't? Then don't! *(He rises and walks toward the door.)*

MRS. POPOV: I didn't say anything.

SMIRNOV: *(stopping)* What?

MRS. POPOV: Oh, nothing, you can go. Well, no, just a minute. No, you can go. Go! I detest you! But, just a moment. Oh, if you knew how furious I feel! *(Throws the gun on the table.)* My fingers have gone to sleep holding that horrid thing. *(She is tearing her handkerchief to shreds.)* And what are you standing around for? Get out of here!

SMIRNOV: Goodbye.

155 MRS. POPOV: Go, go, go! *(Shouting.)* Where are you going? Wait a minute! No, no, it's all right, just go. I'm fighting mad. Don't come near me, don't come near me!

SMIRNOV: *(who is coming near her)* I'm pretty disgusted with myself—falling in love like a kid, going down on my knees like some moongazing whippersnapper, the very thought gives me gooseflesh. *(Rudely.)* I love you. But it doesn't make sense. Tomorrow, I have to pay that interest, and we've already started mowing. *(He puts his arm about her waist.)* I shall never forgive myself for this.

MRS. POPOV: Take your hands off me, I hate you! Let's shoot it out!

A long kiss. Enter Luka with an axe, the gardener with a rake, the coachman with a pitchfork, hired men with sticks.

LUKA: *(seeing the kiss)* Mercy on us! Holy saints above!

MRS. POPOV: *(dropping her eyes)* Luka, tell them in the stable that Toby is *not* to have any oats today.

Reading and Reacting

1. Are Mr. Smirnov and Mrs. Popov round or flat characters? Are they static or dynamic?

2. Which of the two characters do you think has the upper hand in their relationship?

3. Although Mrs. Popov's husband is dead, he is, in a sense, an important character in *The Brute*. What do we know about him? How does he influence the play's two main characters?

4. Why are Mrs. Popov and Mr. Smirnov distrustful of members of the opposite sex? How is this distrust revealed to the audience?

5. Do you think this play reinforces gender stereotypes or challenges them? Explain.

6. Because *The Brute* is a **farce**, Chekhov's characters frequently exaggerate for comic effect. For instance, Smirnov tells Mrs. Popov, "I've known more women than you've known pussy cats. I've fought three duels on their account. I've jilted twelve, and been jilted by nine others." Give some additional examples of such broadly exaggerated language, and explain its function.

7. Give some examples of physical actions used to reinforce emotions or attitudes in *The Brute*.

8. Explain and illustrate how the characters' words reveal each of the following moods: Mrs. Popov's anger at Mr. Smirnov, Mrs. Popov's ambivalence toward her late husband, Mr. Smirnov's impatience with Mrs. Popov, Mr. Smirnov's stubbornness.

9. As the play progresses, Mrs. Popov's changing language communicates her changing attitude toward her husband. Give some examples that illustrate this change in attitude.

10. What can you infer about Mrs. Popov's relationship with Luka from the language she uses when she addresses him? From the language he uses with her? What function does Luka serve in the play?

11. At what point in the play does Mr. Smirnov's speech become more elaborate? What does his use of figurative language suggest?

12. Where in the play does dramatic irony occur? Is verbal irony also present?

13. Identify all the asides in the play. What is their function?

14. **Journal Entry** If you had to take a side in the dispute between Mrs. Popov and Mr. Smirnov, whose side would you be on? Why?

15. **Critical Perspective** Critic Harvey Pilcher characterizes *The Brute*, like Chekhov's other one-act "farce-vaudevilles," as a "comedy of situation":

> Although they contain an assortment of comic ingredients—parody, slapstick, misunderstandings, the absurd, the grotesque, irony, and social satire—the vaudevilles still belong to the genre of "comedy of situation." This is because . . . the emphasis for an audience is "not on mystery and surprise, but

on the working-out of a known situation . . . not so much on what will happen next as to how it will happen." In the best of the comedy of situation stories, the situation itself opens the door to comedy of characterization. There is a comic psychological inevitability about the way Smirnov . . . fails to live up to his misogynistic principles and [Mrs. Popov] abandons the role of the faithful widow. . . .

In what way is the "comedy of situation" Pilcher describes similar to today's television "situation comedies" (sitcoms)?

Related Works: "You Fit into Me" (p. 723), "Women" (p. 786), *The Importance of Being Earnest* (p. 961)

◊ **WILLIAM SHAKESPEARE** (1564–1616) was born in Stratford-on-Avon, England, and raised his family there, although he spent most of his adult life in London. Though relatively little is known of his daily life, he was deeply involved in all aspects of the theatre: he was an actor who joined the Lord Chamberlain's Men (an acting company) in 1594; a shareholder in that company; a part owner of the Globe Theatre from 1599; and, most significantly, the author of at least thirty-six plays. Most of his plays were not published during his lifetime; his friends issued the first legitimate version of his collected plays, the First Folio edition, in 1623.

It is difficult to date many of Shakespeare's plays exactly because they must be dated by records of their first performance (often hard to come by) and topical references in the text. We do know from an entry in the *Stationers' Register* that a play called the *Revenge of Hamlett Prince Denmarke* was presented around July 26, 1602, though Shakespeare's company probably first staged the play at the Globe Theatre in 1600 or 1601. Some scholars believe the play was composed as early as 1598, though no earlier, because it was not among Shakespeare's plays listed in Francis Meres's *Palladis Tamis*, published in 1598.

◊ ◊ ◊

WILLIAM SHAKESPEARE

Hamlet

PRINCE OF DENMARK*
(c. 1600)

CHARACTERS

CLAUDIUS, *King of Denmark*
HAMLET, *son to the former and*
   nephew to the present king

POLONIUS, *Lord Chamberlain*
HORATIO, *friend to Hamlet*
LAERTES, *son to Polonius*

---

* Note that individual lines are numbered in the following play. When a line is shared by two or more characters, it is counted as one line.

VOLTIMAND
CORNELIUS
ROSENCRANTZ } *courtiers*
GUILDENSTERN
OSRIC
A GENTLEMAN
A PRIEST
FRANCISCO, *a soldier*
MARCELLUS
BERNARDO } *officers*
REYNALDO, *servant to Polonius*
PLAYERS

TWO CLOWNS, *grave-diggers*
FORTINBRAS, *Prince of Norway*
A CAPTAIN
ENGLISH AMBASSADORS
GHOST OF HAMLET'S FATHER
GERTRUDE, *Queen of Denmark*
   and mother of Hamlet
OPHELIA, *daughter to Polonius*
LORDS, LADIES, OFFICERS,
SOLDIERS, SAILORS
MESSENGERS, AND OTHER
ATTENDANTS

ACT I
SCENE 1

Elsinore. A platform before the castle.

(Francisco at his post. Enter to him Bernardo.)

BERNARDO: Who's there?

FRANCISCO: Nay, answer me: stand, and unfold yourself.

BERNARDO: Long live the king!

FRANCISCO: Bernardo?

BERNARDO: He.

FRANCISCO: You come most carefully upon your hour.

5 BERNARDO: 'Tis now struck twelve; get thee to bed, Francisco.

FRANCISCO: For this relief much thanks: 'tis bitter cold,
    And I am sick at heart.

BERNARDO: Have you had quiet guard?

FRANCISCO: Not a mouse stirring.

BERNARDO: Well, good-night.

10   If you do meet Horatio and Marcellus,
    The rivals of my watch, bid them make haste.

FRANCISCO: I think I hear them.—Stand, ho! Who is there?

(Enter Horatio and Marcellus.)

HORATIO: Friends to this ground.

MARCELLUS: And liegemen to the Dane.

15 FRANCISCO: Give you good-night.

MARCELLUS: O, farewell, honest soldier:
    Who hath reliev'd you?

FRANCISCO: Bernardo has my place.
    Give you good-night.

(Exit.)

MARCELLUS: Holla! Bernardo!

BERNARDO: Say.

What, is Horatio there?

HORATIO: A piece of him.

BERNARDO: Welcome, Horatio:—welcome, good Marcellus.

20 MARCELLUS: What, has this thing appear'd again to-night?

BERNARDO: I have seen nothing.

MARCELLUS: Horatio says 'tis but our fantasy,
And will not let belief take hold of him
Touching this dreaded sight, twice seen of us:

25 Therefore I have entreated him along
With us to watch the minutes of this night;
That, if again this apparition come
He may approve our eyes and speak to it.

HORATIO: Tush, tush, 'twill not appear.

BERNARDO: Sit down awhile,

30 And let us once again assail your ears,
That are so fortified against our story,
What we two nights have seen.

HORATIO: Well, sit we down,
And let us hear Bernardo speak of this.

BERNARDO: Last night of all,

35 When yon same star that's westward from the pole
Had made his course to illume that part of heaven
Where now it burns, Marcellus and myself,
The bell then beating one,—

MARCELLUS: Peace, break thee off; look where it comes again!

(Enter Ghost, armed.)

40 BERNARDO: In the same figure, like the king that's dead.

MARCELLUS: Thou art a scholar; speak to it, Horatio.

BERNARDO: Looks it not like the king? mark it, Horatio.

HORATIO: Most like:—it harrows me with fear and wonder.

BERNARDO: It would be spoke to.

MARCELLUS: Question it, Horatio.

45 HORATIO: What art thou, that usurp'st this time of night,
Together with that fair and warlike form
In which the majesty of buried Denmark
Did sometimes march? by heaven I charge thee, speak!

MARCELLUS: It is offended.

BERNARDO: See, it stalks away!

50 HORATIO: Stay! speak, speak! I charge thee, speak!

(Exit Ghost.)

MARCELLUS: 'Tis gone, and will not answer.

BERNARDO: How now, Horatio! you tremble and look pale:
Is not this something more than fantasy?
What think you on't?

55 HORATIO: Before my God, I might not this believe
    Without the sensible and true avouch
    Of mine own eyes.

MARCELLUS: Is it not like the king?

HORATIO: As thou art to thyself:
    Such was the very armor he had on
60   When he the ambitious Norway combated;
    So frown'd he once when, in an angry parle,[1]
    He smote the sledded Polacks on the ice.
    'Tis strange.

MARCELLUS: Thus twice before, and just at this dead hour,
65   With martial stalk hath he gone by our watch.

HORATIO: In what particular thought to work I know not;
    But, in the gross and scope of my opinion,
    This bodes some strange eruption to our state.

MARCELLUS: Good now, sit down, and tell me, he that knows,
70   Why this same strict and most observant watch
    So nightly toils the subject of the land;
    And why such daily cast of brazen cannon,
    And foreign mart for implements of war;
    Why such impress of shipwrights, whose sore task
75   Does not divide the Sunday from the week;
    What might be toward, that this sweaty haste
    Doth make the night joint-laborer with the day:
    Who is't that can inform me?

HORATIO: That can I;
    At least, the whisper goes so. Our last king,
80   Whose image even but now appear'd to us,
    Was, as you know, by Fortinbras of Norway,
    Thereto prick'd on by a most emulate pride,
    Dar'd to the combat; in which our valiant Hamlet,—
    For so this side of our known world esteem'd him,—
85   Did slay this Fortinbras; who, by a seal'd compact,
    Well ratified by law and heraldry,
    Did forfeit, with his life, all those his lands.
    Which he stood seiz'd of,[2] to the conqueror:
    Against the which, a moiety competent[3]
90   Was gagéd[4] by our king; which had return'd
    To the inheritance of Fortinbras,
    Had he been vanquisher; as by the same cov'nant,
    And carriage of the article design'd,
    His fell to Hamlet. Now, sir, young Fortinbras,

---

[1] *parle:* parley, or conference.
[2] *seiz'd of:* possessed.
[3] *moiety competent:* a sufficient portion of his lands.
[4] *gagéd:* engaged or pledged.

95 Of unimproved mettle hot and full,
  Hath in the skirts of Norway, here and there,
  Shark'd up a list of landless resolutes,
  For food and diet, to some enterprise
  That hath a stomach in't: which is no other,—
100 As it doth well appear unto our state,—
  But to recover of us by strong hand,
  And terms compulsatory, those foresaid lands
  So by his father lost: and this, I take it,
  Is the main motive of our preparations,
105 The source of this our watch, and the chief head
  Of this post-haste and romage[5] in the land.
BERNARDO: I think it be no other, but e'en so:
  Well may it sort that this portentous figure
  Comes armed through our watch; so like the king
110 That was and is the question of these wars.
HORATIO: A mote it is to trouble the mind's eye.
  In the most high and palmy state of Rome,
  A little ere the mightiest Julius fell,
  The graves stood tenantless, and the sheeted dead
115 Did squeak and gibber in the Roman streets:
  As, stars with trains of fire and dews of blood,
  Disasters in the sun; and the moist star,
  Upon whose influence Neptune's empire stands,
  Was sick almost to doomsday with eclipse:
120 And even the like precurse of fierce events,—
  As harbingers preceding still the fates,
  And prologue to the omen coming on,—
  Have heaven and earth together demonstrated
  Unto our climature and countrymen.—
125 But, soft, behold! lo, where it comes again!

(Re-enter Ghost.)

  I'll cross it, though it blast me.—Stay, illusion!
  If thou hast any sound or use of voice,
  Speak to me:
  If there be any good thing to be done,
130 That may to thee do ease, and grace to me,
  Speak to me:
  If thou art privy to thy country's fate,
  Which, happily,[6] foreknowing may avoid,
  O, speak!
135 Or if thou has uphoarded in thy life

---

[5] *post-haste and romage:* general activity.
[6] *happily:* haply, or perhaps.

Extorted treasure in the womb of earth,
For which, they say, you spirits oft walk in death,

(Cock crows.)

Speak of it:—stay, and speak!—Stop it, Marcellus.
MARCELLUS: Shall I strike at it with my partisan?[7]
140 HORATIO: Do, if it will not stand.
BERNARDO: 'Tis here!
HORATIO: 'Tis here!
MARCELLUS: 'Tis gone!

(Exit Ghost.)

We do it wrong, being so majestical,
To offer it the show of violence;
For it is, as the air, invulnerable,
145 And our vain blows malicious mockery.
BERNARDO: It was about to speak when the cock crew.
HORATIO: And then it started like a guilty thing
Upon a fearful summons. I have heard,
The cock, that is the trumpet to the morn,
150 Doth with his lofty and shrill-sounding throat
Awake the god of day; and at his warning,
Whether in sea or fire, in earth or air,
The extravagant and erring spirit hies
To his confine: and of the truth herein
155 This present object made probation.[8]
MARCELLUS: It faded on the crowing of the cock.
Some say that ever 'gainst that season comes
Wherein our Saviour's birth is celebrated,
The bird of dawning singeth all night long:
160 And then, they say, no spirit can walk abroad;
The nights are wholesome; then no planets strike,
No fairy takes, nor witch hath power to charm;
So hallow'd and so gracious is the time.
HORATIO: So have I heard, and do in part believe.
165 But, look, the morn, in russet mantle clad,
Walks o'er the dew of yon high eastern hill:
Break we our watch up: and, by my advice,
Let us impart what we have seen to-night
Unto young Hamlet; for, upon my life,
170 This spirit, dumb to us, will speak to him:
Do you consent we shall acquaint him with it,
As needful in our loves, fitting our duty?

---

[7] *partisan*: pike.
[8] *probation*: proof.

MARCELLUS: Let's do't, I pray; and I this morning know
    Where we shall find him most conveniently.

(Exeunt.)

<u>SCENE 2</u>

Elsinore. A room of state in the castle.

(Enter the King, Queen, Hamlet, Polonius, Laertes, Voltimand, Cornelius, Lords, and Attendants.)

KING: Though yet of Hamlet our dear brother's death
    The memory be green; and that it us befitted
    To bear our hearts in grief, and our whole kingdom
    To be contracted in one brow of woe;
5   Yet so far hath discretion fought with nature
    That we with wisest sorrow think on him,
    Together with remembrance of ourselves.
    Therefore our sometime sister, now our queen,
    The imperial jointress of this warlike state,
10   Have we, as 'twere with defeated joy,—
    With one auspicious and one dropping eye,
    With mirth and funeral, and with dirge in marriage,
    In equal scale weighing delight and dole,—
    Taken to wife: nor have we herein barr'd
15   Your better wisdoms, which have freely gone
    With this affair along:—for all, our thanks.
    Now follows that you know, young Fortinbras,
    Holding a weak supposal of our worth,
    Or thinking by our late dear brother's death
20   Our state to be disjoint and out of frame,
    Colleagued with the dream of his advantage,
    He hath not fail'd to pester us with message,
    Importing the surrender of those lands
    Lost by his father, with all bonds of law,
25   To our most valiant brother. So much for him.—
    Now for ourself, and for this time of meeting:
    Thus much the business is:—we have here writ
    To Norway, uncle of young Fortinbras,—
    Who, impotent and bed-rid, scarcely hears
30   Of this his nephew's purpose,—to suppress
    His further gait herein; in that the levies,
    The lists, and full proportions, are all made
    Out of his subject:—and we here despatch
    You, good Cornelius, and you, Voltimand,
35   For bearers of this greeting to old Norway;
    Giving to you no further personal power

To business with the king more than the scope
Of these dilated articles allow.
Farewell; and let your haste commend your duty.

40 CORNELIUS and VOLTIMAND: In that and all things will we show our duty.
KING: We doubt it nothing: heartily farewell.

(Exeunt Voltimand and Cornelius.)

And now, Laertes, what's the news with you?
You told us of some suit; what is't, Laertes?
You cannot speak of reason to the Dane,
45 And lose your voice: what wouldst thou beg, Laertes,
That shall not be my offer, nor thy asking?
The head is not more native to the heart,
The hand more instrumental to the mouth,
Than is the throne of Denmark to thy father.
50 What wouldst thou have, Laertes?

LAERTES: Dread my lord,
Your leave and favor to return to France;
From whence though willingly I came to Denmark,
To show my duty in your coronation;
Yet now, I must confess, that duty done,
55 My thoughts and wishes bend again toward France.
And bow them to your gracious leave and pardon.

KING: Have you your father's leave? What says Polonius?
POLONIUS: He hath, my lord, wrung from me my slow leave
    By laborsome petition; and at last
60 Upon his will I seal'd my hard consent:
I do beseech you, give him leave to go.
KING: Take thy fair hour, Laertes; time be thine,
And thy best graces spend it at thy will!—
But now, my cousin Hamlet, and my son,—
65 HAMLET: *(Aside)* A little more than kin, and less than kind.
KING: How is it that the clouds still hang on you?
HAMLET: Not so, my lord; I am too much i' the sun.
QUEEN: Good Hamlet, cast thy nighted color off,
And let thine eye look like a friend on Denmark.
70 Do not for ever with thy vailed[1] lids
Seek for thy noble father in the dust:
Thou know'st 'tis common,—all that live must die,
Passing through nature to eternity.
HAMLET: Ay, madam, it is common.
QUEEN: If it be,
75 Why seems it so particular with thee?
HAMLET: Seems, madam! nay, it is; I know not seems.
'Tis not alone my inky cloak, good mother,

---

[1] *vailed:* downcast.

Nor customary suits of solemn black,
Nor windy suspiration of forc'd breath,
80 No, nor the fruitful river in the eye,
Nor the dejected 'havior of the visage,
Together with all forms, moods, shows of grief,
That can denote me truly: these, indeed, seem;
For they are actions that a man might play:
85 But I have that within which passeth show;
These but the trappings and the suits of woe.
KING: 'Tis sweet and cómmendable in your nature, Hamlet,
To give these mourning duties to your father:
But, you must know, your father lost a father;
90 That father lost, lost his; and the survivor bound,
In filial obligation, for some term
To do obsequious sorrow: but to persever[2]
In obstinate condolement is a course
Of impious stubbornness; 'tis unmanly grief:
95 It shows a will most incorrect to heaven;
A heart unfortified, a mind impatient;
An understanding simple and unschool'd:
For what we know must be, and is as common
As any the most vulgar thing to sense,[3]
100 Why should we, in our peevish opposition,
Take it to heart? Fie! 'tis a fault to heaven,
A fault against the dead, a fault to nature,
To reason most absurd; whose common theme
Is death of fathers, and who still[4] hath cried,
105 From the first corse till he that died to-day,
This must be so. We pray you, throw to earth
This unprevailing woe; and think of us
As of a father: for let the world take note
You are the most immediate to our throne;
110 And with no less nobility of love
Than that which dearest father bears his son
Do I impart toward you. For your intent
In going back to school in Wittenberg,
It is most retrograde to our desire:
115 And we beseech you bend you to remain
Here, in the cheer and comfort of our eye,
Our chiefest courtier, cousin, and our son.
QUEEN: Let not thy mother lose her prayers, Hamlet:
I pray thee, stay with us; go not to Wittenberg.

---

[2] *persever:* persevere.
[3] *any . . . sense:* anything that is very commonly seen or heard.
[4] *still:* ever, or always.

120 HAMLET: I shall in all my best obey you, madam.
    KING: Why, 'tis a loving and a fair reply:
       Be as ourself in Denmark.—Madam, come;
       This gentle and unforc'd accord of Hamlet
       Sits smiling to my heart: in grace whereof,
125   No jocund health that Denmark drinks to-day
       But the great cannon to the clouds shall tell;
       And the king's rouse[5] the heavens shall bruit[6] again,
       Re-speaking earthly thunder. Come away.

(Exeunt all but Hamlet.)

HAMLET: O, that this too too solid flesh would melt,
130   Thaw, and resolve itself into a dew!
       Or that the Everlasting had not fix'd
       His canon 'gainst self-slaughter! O God! O God!
       How weary, stale, flat, and unprofitable
       Seem to me all the uses of this world!
135   Fie on't! O fie! 'tis an unweeded garden,
       That grows to seed; things rank and gross in nature
       Possess it merely. That it should come to this!
       But two months dead!—nay, so much, not two:
       So excellent a king; that was, to this,
140   Hyperion[7] to a satyr: so loving to my mother,
       That he might not beteem the winds of heaven
       Visit her face too roughly. Heaven and earth!
       Must I remember? why, she would hang on him
       As if increase of appetite had grown
145   By what it fed on: and yet, within a month,—
       Let me not think on't,—Frailty, thy name is woman!—
       A little month; or ere those shoes were old
       With which she follow'd my poor father's body
       Like Niobe, all tears;—why she, even she,—
150   O God! a beast, that wants discourse of reason,
       Would have mourn'd longer,—married with mine uncle,
       My father's brother; but no more like my father
       Than I to Hercules: within a month;
       Ere yet the salt of most unrighteous tears
155   Had left the flushing in her galled eyes,
       She married:—O, most wicked speed, to post
       With such dexterity to incestuous sheets!
       It is not, nor it cannot come to good;
       But break, my heart,—for I must hold my tongue!

---

[5] *rouse:* drink.
[6] *bruit:* echo.
[7] *Hyperion:* the Greek sun god, the brightest and most beautiful of the gods.

(Enter Horatio, Marcellus, and Bernardo.)

160 HORATIO: Hail to your lordship!

HAMLET: I am glad to see you well:
    Horatio,—or I do forget myself.

HORATIO: The same, my lord, and your poor servant ever.

HAMLET: Sir, my good friend; I'll change that name with you:
    And what make you from Wittenberg, Horatio?—Marcellus?

165 MARCELLUS: My good lord,—

HAMLET: I am very glad to see you.—Good even, sir.—
    But what, in faith, make you from Wittenberg?

HORATIO: A truant disposition, good my lord.

HAMLET: I would not hear your enemy say so;
170   Nor shall you do mine ear that violence,
    To make it truster of your own report
    Against yourself: I know you are no truant.
    But what is your affair in Elsinore?
    We'll teach you to drink deep ere you depart.

175 HORATIO: My lord, I came to see your father's funeral.

HAMLET: I pray thee, do not mock me, fellow-student;
    I think it was to see my mother's wedding.

HORATIO: Indeed, my lord, it follow'd hard upon.

HAMLET: Thrift, thrift, Horatio! the funeral-bak'd meats
180   Did coldly furnish forth the marriage tables.
    Would I had met my dearest foe[8] in heaven
    Ere I had ever seen that day, Horatio!—
    My father,—methinks I see my father.

HORATIO: Where, my lord?

HAMLET: In my mind's eye, Horatio.

185 HORATIO: I saw him once; he was a goodly[9] king.

HAMLET: He was a man, take him for all in all,
    I shall not look upon his like again.

HORATIO: My lord, I think I saw him yester-night.

HAMLET: Saw who?

190 HORATIO: My lord, the king your father.

HAMLET: The king my father!

HORATIO: Season your admiration[10] for awhile
    With an attent ear, till I may deliver,
    Upon the witness of these gentlemen,
    This marvel to you.

HAMLET: For God's love, let me hear.

195 HORATIO: Two nights together had these gentlemen,
    Marcellus and Bernardo, in their watch,

---

[8] *dearest foe:* worst enemy.

[9] *goodly:* handsome.

[10] *admiration:* astonishment.

In the dead vast and middle of the night,
Been thus encounter'd. A figure like your father,
Arm'd at all points exactly, cap-a-pe,[11]
200   Appears before them, and with solemn march
Goes slow and stately by them: thrice he walk'd
By their oppress'd[12] and fear-surprised eyes,
Within his truncheon's length; whilst they, distill'd
Almost to jelly with the act of fear,
205   Stand dumb, and speak not to him. This to me
In dreadful secrecy impart they did;
And I with them the third night kept the watch:
Where, as they had deliver'd, both in time,
Form of the thing, each word made true and good,
210   The apparition comes: I knew your father;
These hands are not more like.

HAMLET: But where was this?

MARCELLUS: My lord, upon the platform where we watch'd.

HAMLET: Did you not speak to it?

HORATIO: My lord, I did;
But answer made it none: yet once methought
215   It lifted up its head, and did address
Itself to motion, like as it would speak:
But even then the morning cock crew loud,
And at the sound it shrunk in haste away,
And vanish'd from our sight.

HAMLET: 'Tis very strange.

220 HORATIO: As I do live, my honor'd lord, 'tis true;
And we did think it writ down in our duty
To let you know of it.

HAMLET: Indeed, indeed, sirs, but this troubles me.
Hold you the watch to-night?

225 MARCELLUS and BERNARDO: We do, my lord.

HAMLET: Arm'd, say you?

MARCELLUS and BERNARDO: Arm'd, my lord.

HAMLET: From top to toe?

MARCELLUS and BERNARDO: My lord, from head to foot.

230 HAMLET: Then saw you not his face?

HORATIO: O yes, my lord; he wore his beaver up.

HAMLET: What, look'd he frowningly?

HORATIO: A countenance more in sorrow than in anger.

HAMLET: Pale or red?

235 HORATIO: Nay, very pale.

HAMLET: And fix'd his eyes upon you?

---

[11] *cap-a-pe:* from head to toe.
[12] *oppress'd:* overwhelmed.

HORATIO: Most constantly.
HAMLET: I would I had been there.
HORATIO: It would have much amaz'd you.
HAMLET: Very like, very like. Stay'd it long?
HORATIO: While one with moderate haste might tell[13] a hundred.
240 MARCELLUS and BERNARDO: Longer, longer.
HORATIO: Not when I saw't.
HAMLET: His beard was grizzled,—no?
HORATIO: It was, as I have seen it in his life,
    A sable silver'd.
HAMLET: I will watch to-night;
    Perchance 'twill walk again.
HORATIO: I warrant it will.
245 HAMLET: If it assume my noble father's person
    I'll speak to it, though hell itself should gape
    And bid me hold my peace. I pray you all,
    If you have hitherto conceal'd this sight,
    Let it be tenable in your silence still;
250   And whatsoever else shall hap to-night,
    Give it an understanding, but no tongue:
    I will requite your loves. So, fare ye well:
    Upon the platform, 'twixt eleven and twelve,
    I'll visit you.
ALL: Our duty to your honor.
255 HAMLET: Your loves, as mine to you: farewell.

(Exeunt Horatio, Marcellus, and Bernardo.)

    My father's spirit in arms; all is not well;
    I doubt some foul play: would the night were come!
    Till then sit still, my soul: foul deeds will rise,
    Though all the earth o'erwhelm them, to men's eyes.

(Exit.)

SCENE 3

A room in Polonius' house.

(Enter Laertes and Ophelia.)

LAERTES: My necessaries are embark'd: farewell:
    And, sister, as the winds give benefit,
    And convoy[1] is assistant, do not sleep,
    But let me hear from you.
OPHELIA: Do you doubt that?

---

[13] *tell:* count.

---

[1] *convoy:* means of conveyance.

5 LAERTES: For Hamlet, and the trifling of his favor,
      Hold it a fashion and a toy in blood:
      A violet in the youth of primy nature,
      Forward, not permanent, sweet, not lasting,
      The perfume and suppliance of a minute;
10   No more.
  OPHELIA: No more but so?
  LAERTES: Think it no more:
      For nature, crescent,[2] does not grow alone
      In thews and bulk; but as this temple[3] waxes,
      The inward service of the mind and soul
      Grows wide withal. Perhaps he loves you now;
15   And now no soil nor cautel[4] doth besmirch
      The virtue of his will: but you must fear,
      His greatness weigh'd, his will is not his own;
      For he himself is subject to his birth:
      He may not, as unvalu'd persons do,
20   Carve for himself; for on his choice depends
      The safety and the health of the whole state;
      And therefore must his choice be circumscrib'd
      Unto the voice and yielding of that body
      Whereof he is the head. Then if he says he loves you,
25   It fits your wisdom so far to believe it
      As he in his particular act and place
      May give his saying deed; which is no further
      Than the main[5] voice of Denmark goes withal.
      Then weigh what loss your honor may sustain
30   If with too credent ear you list his songs,
      Or lose your heart, or your chaste treasure open
      To his unmaster'd importunity.
      Fear it, Ophelia, fear it, my dear sister;
      And keep within the rear of your affection,
35   Out of the shot and danger of desire.
      The chariest maid is prodigal enough
      If she unmask her beauty to the moon:
      Virtue itself scrapes not calumnious strokes:
      The canker galls the infants of the spring
40   Too oft before their buttons be disclos'd;
      And in the morn and liquid dew of youth
      Contagious blastments are most imminent.
      Be wary, then; best safety lies in fear:
      Youth to itself rebels, though none else near.

---

[2] *crescent:* growing.
[3] *temple:* body.
[4] *cautel:* deceit.
[5] *main:* strong, or mighty.

45 OPHELIA: I shall the effect of this good lesson keep
As watchman to my heart. But, good my brother,
Do not, as some ungracious pastors do,
Show me the steep and thorny way to heaven;
Whilst like a puff'd and reckless libertine,
50 Himself the primrose path of dalliance treads,
And recks not his own rede.[6]
LAERTES: O, fear me not.
I stay too long:—but here my father comes.

(Enter Polonius.)

A double blessing is a double grace;
Occasion smiles upon a second leave.
55 POLONIUS: Yet here, Laertes! aboard, aboard, for shame!
The wind sits in the shoulder of your sail,
And you are stay'd for. There,—my blessing with you!

(Laying his hand on Laertes' head.)

And these few precepts in thy memory
See thou character.[7] Give thy thoughts no tongue,
60 Nor any unproportion'd thought his act.
Be thou familiar, but by no means vulgar.
The friends thou hast, and their adoption tried,
Grapple them to thy soul with hoops of steel;
But do not dull thy palm with entertainment
65 Of each new-hatch'd, unfledg'd comrade. Beware
Of entrance to a quarrel; but, being in,
Bear't that the opposèd may beware of thee.
Give every man thine ear, but few thy voice:
Take each man's censure,[8] but reserve thy judgment.
70 Costly thy habit as thy purse can buy,
But not express'd in fancy; rich, not gaudy:
For the apparel oft proclaims the man;
And they in France of the best rank and station
Are most select and generous chief in that.
75 Neither a borrower nor a lender be:
For a loan oft loses both itself and friend;
And borrowing dulls the edge of husbandry.
This above all,—to thine own self be true;
And it must follow, as the night the day,
80 Thou canst not then be false to any man.
Farewell: my blessing season this in thee!
LAERTES: Most humbly do I take my leave, my lord.

---

[6] *rede:* counsel.
[7] *in . . . character:* engrave in your mind.
[8] *censure:* opinion.

POLONIUS: The time invites you; go, your servants tend.[9]

LAERTES: Farewell, Ophelia; and remember well

85   What I have said to you.

OPHELIA: 'Tis in my memory lock'd,

    And you yourself shall keep the key of it.

LAERTES: Farewell. *(Exit.)*

POLONIUS: What is't, Ophelia, he hath said to you?

OPHELIA: So please you, something touching the Lord Hamlet.

90 POLONIUS: Marry, well bethought:

    'Tis told me he hath very oft of late

    Given private time to you; and you yourself

    Have of your audience been most free and bounteous:

    If it be so,—as so 'tis put on me,

95   And that in way of caution,—I must tell you,

    You do not understand yourself so clearly

    As it behoves my daughter and your honor.

    What is between you? give me up the truth.

OPHELIA: He hath, my lord, of late made many tenders

100   Of his affection to me.

POLONIUS: Affection! pooh! you speak like a green girl,

    Unsifted in such perilous circumstance.

    Do you believe his tenders,[10] as you call them?

OPHELIA: I do not know, my lord, what I should think.

105 POLONIUS: Marry, I'll teach you: think yourself a baby;

    That you have ta'en these tenders for true pay,

    Which are not sterling. Tender yourself more dearly;

    Or,—not to crack the wind of the poor phrase,

    Wronging it thus,—you'll tender me a fool.

110 OPHELIA: My lord, he hath impórtun'd me with love

    In honorable fashion.

POLONIUS: Ay, fashion you may call it; go to, go to.

OPHELIA: And hath given countenance to his speech, my lord,

    With almost all the holy vows of heaven.

115 POLONIUS: Ay, springes to catch woodcocks. I do know,

    When the blood burns, how prodigal the soul

    Lends the tongue vows: these blazes, daughter,

    Giving more light than heat,—extinct in both,

    Even in their promise, as it is a-making,—

120   You must not take for fire. From this time

    Be somewhat scanter of your maiden presence;

    Set your entreatments at a higher rate

    Than a command to parley. For Lord Hamlet,

    Believe so much in him, that he is young;

---

[9] *tend*: wait.

[10] *tenders:* offers.

125   And with a larger tether may he walk
Than may be given you: in few, Ophelia,
Do not believe his vows; for they are brokers,[11]—
Not of that die which their investments show,
But mere implorators of unholy suits,

130   Breathing like sanctified and pious bawds,
The better to beguile. This is for all,—
I would not, in plain terms, from this time forth,
Have you so slander any moment leisure
As to give words or talk with the Lord Hamlet.

135   Look to't, I charge you; come your ways.
OPHELIA: I shall obey, my lord.

(Exeunt.)

SCENE 4

The platform.

(Enter Hamlet, Horatio, and Marcellus.)

HAMLET: The air bites shrewdly; it is very cold.
HORATIO: It is a nipping and an eager air.
HAMLET: What hour now?
HORATIO: I think it lacks of twelve.
MARCELLUS: No, it is struck.
5 HORATIO: Indeed? I heard it not: then it draws near the season
Wherein the spirit held his wont to walk.

(A flourish of trumpets, and ordnance shot off within.)

What does this mean, my lord?
HAMLET: The king doth wake to-night, and takes his rouse,
Keeps wassail, and the swaggering upspring[1] reels;
10   And, as he drains his draughts of Rhenish down,
The kettle-drum and trumpet thus bray out
The triumph of his pledge.[2]
HORATIO: Is it a custom?
HAMLET: Ay, marry, is't:
But to my mind,—though I am native here,
15   And to the manner born,—it is a custom
More honor'd in the breach than the observance.
This heavy-headed revel east and west
Makes us traduc'd and tax'd of other nations:
They clepe us drunkards, and with swinish phrase

---

[11] *brokers:* procurers.

---

[1] *upspring:* a dance.
[2] *triumph . . . pledge:* the glory of his toasts.

20 Soil our addition;³ and, indeed, it takes
 From our achievements, though perform'd at height,
 The pith and marrow of our attribute.
 So oft it chances in particular men
 That, for some vicious mole of nature in them,
25 As in their birth,—wherein they are not guilty,
 Since nature cannot choose his origin,—
 By the o'ergrowth of some complexion,
 Oft breaking down the pales and forts of reason;
 Or by some habit, that too much o'erleavens
30 The form of plausive⁴ manners;—that these men,—
 Carrying, I say, the stamp of one defect,
 Being nature's livery or fortune's star,—
 Their virtues else,—be they as pure as grace,
 As infinite as man may undergo,—
35 Shall in the general censure take corruption
 From that particular fault: the dram of evil
 Doth all the noble substance of a doubt
 To his own scandal.

HORATIO: Look, my lord, it comes!

(Enter Ghost.)

HAMLET: Angels and ministers of grace defend us!—
40 Be thou a spirit of health or goblin damn'd,
 Bring with thee airs from heaven or blasts from hell,
 Be thy intents wicked or charitable,
 Thou com'st in such a questionable shape
 That I will speak to thee: I'll call thee Hamlet,
45 King, father, royal Dane: O, answer me!
 Let me not burst in ignorance; but tell
 Why thy canóniz'd bones, hearsèd in death,
 Have burst their cerements; why the sepulchre,
 Wherein we saw thee quietly in-urn'd,
50 Hath op'd his ponderous and marble jaws
 To cast thee up again! What may this mean,
 That thou, dead corse, again in còmplete steel,
 Revisit'st thus the glimpses of the moon,
 Making night hideous and we⁵ fools of nature
55 So horridly to shake our disposition
 With thoughts beyond the reaches of our souls?
 Say, why is this? wherefore? what should we do?

(Ghost beckons Hamlet.)

---

³ *addition:* reputation.
⁴ *plausive:* pleasing.
⁵ *we:* us.

Horatio: It beckons you to go away with it,
    As if it some impartment did desire
60   To you alone.
Marcellus: Look, with what courteous action
    It waves you to a more removed ground:
    But do not go with it.
Horatio: No, by no means.
Hamlet: It will not speak; then will I follow it.
Horatio: Do not, my lord.
Hamlet: Why, what should be the fear?
65   I do not set my life at a pin's fee;
    And for my soul, what can it do to that,
    Being a thing immortal as itself?
    It waves me forth again;—I'll follow it.
Horatio: What if it tempt you toward the flood, my lord.
70   Or to the dreadful summit of the cliff
    That beetles o'er his base into the sea,
    And there assume some other horrible form,
    Which might deprive your sovereignty of reason,
    And draw you into madness? think of it:
75   The very place puts toys of desperation,
    Without more motive, into every brain
    That looks so many fathoms to the sea
    And hears it roar beneath.
Hamlet: It waves me still.—
    Go on; I'll follow thee.
80 Marcellus: You shall not go, my lord.
Hamlet: Hold off your hands.
Horatio: Be rul'd; you shall not go.
Hamlet: My fate cries out,
    And makes each petty artery in this body
    As hardy as the Némean lion's[6] nerve.—

(Ghost beckons.)

    Still am I call'd;—unhand me, gentlemen;—*(Breaking from them)*
85   By heaven, I'll make a ghost of him that lets[7] me.
    I say, away!—Go on; I'll follow thee.

(Exeunt Ghost and Hamlet.)

Horatio: He waxes desperate with imagination.
Marcellus: Let's follow; 'tis not fit thus to obey him.
Horatio: Have after.—To what issue will this come?
90 Marcellus: Something is rotten in the state of Denmark.

---

[6] *Némean lion's:* the fierce lion that Hercules was called upon to slay as one of his
    "twelve labours."
[7] *lets:* hinders.

HORATIO: Heaven will direct it.
MARCELLUS: Nay, let's follow him.

(Exeunt.)

SCENE 5

A more remote part of the platform.

(Enter Ghost and Hamlet.)

HAMLET: Where wilt thou lead me? speak, I'll go no further.
GHOST: Mark me.
HAMLET: I will.
GHOST: My hour is almost come,
    When I to sulphurous and tormenting flames
    Must render up myself.
HAMLET: Alas, poor ghost!
5 GHOST: Pity me not, but lend thy serious hearing
    To what I shall unfold.
HAMLET: Speak; I am bound to hear.
GHOST: So art thou to revenge, when thou shalt hear.
HAMLET: What?
GHOST: I am thy father's spirit;
10   Doom'd for a certain term to walk the night,
    And, for the day, confin'd to waste in fires
    Till the foul crimes[1] done in my days of nature
    Are burnt and purg'd away. But that I am forbid
    To tell the secrets of my prison-house,
15   I could a tale unfold whose lightest word
    Would harrow up thy soul; freeze thy young blood;
    Make thy two eyes, like stars, start from their spheres;
    Thy knotted and combined locks to part,
    And each particular hair to stand on end,
20   Like quills upon the fretful porcupine:
    But this eternal blazon[2] must not be
    To ears of flesh and blood.—List, list, O, list!—
    If thou didst ever thy dear father love,—
HAMLET: O God!
25 GHOST: Revenge his foul and most unnatural murder.
HAMLET: Murder!
GHOST: Murder—most foul, as in the best it is;
    But this most foul, strange, and unnatural.
HAMLET: Haste me to know't, that I, with wings as swift
30   As meditation or the thoughts of love,
    May sweep to my revenge.

---

[1] *foul crimes:* rather, sins or faults.
[2] *eternal blazon:* disclosure of information concerning the other world.

GHOST: I find thee apt;
And duller shouldst thou be than the fat weed
That rots itself in ease on Lethe[3] wharf,
Wouldst thou not stir in this. Now, Hamlet,
35 'Tis given out that, sleeping in mine orchard,
A serpent stung me; so the whole ear of Denmark
Is by a forged process of my death
Rankly abus'd: but know, thou noble youth,
The serpent that did sting thy father's life
40 Now wears his crown.

HAMLET: O my prophetic soul! mine uncle!

GHOST: Ay, that incestuous, that adulterate beast,
With witchcraft of his wit, with traitorous gifts,—
O wicked wit and gifts that have the power
So to seduce!—won to his shameful lust
45 The will of my most seeming virtuous queen:
O Hamlet, what a falling-off was there!
From me, whose love was of that dignity
That it went hand in hand even with the vow
I made to her in marriage: and to decline
50 Upon a wretch whose natural gifts were poor
To those of mine!
But virtue, as it never will be mov'd,
Though lewdness court it in a shape of heaven;
So lust, though to a radiant angel link'd,
55 Will sate itself in a celestial bed
And prey on garbage.
But, soft! methinks I scent the morning air;
Brief let me be.—Sleeping within mine orchard,
My custom always in the afternoon,
60 Upon my sécure hour thy uncle stole,
With juice of cursed hebenon[4] in a vial,
And in the porches of mine ears did pour
The leperous distilment; whose effect
Holds such an enmity with blood of man
65 That, swift as quicksilver, it courses through
The natural gates and alleys of the body;
And with a sudden vigor it doth posset[5]
And curd, like eager[6] droppings into milk,
The thin and wholesome blood: so did it mine;
70 And a most instant tetter bark'd about,
Most lazar-like,[7] with vile and loathsome crust,

---

[3] *Lethe:* the river of forgetfulness of the past, out of which the dead drink.

[4] *hebenon:* ebony.

[5] *posset:* coagulate.

[6] *eager:* acid.

[7] *lazar-like:* like a leper, whose skin is rough.

All my smooth body.
Thus was I, sleeping, by a brother's hand,
Of life, of crown, of queen, at once despatch'd:
75 Cut off even in the blossoms of my sin,
Unhousel'd, unanointed, unanel'd;
No reckoning made, but sent to my account
With all my imperfections on my head:
O, horrible! O, horrible! most horrible!
80 If thou hast nature in thee, bear it not;
Let not the royal bed of Denmark be
A couch for luxury[8] and damned incest.
But, howsoever thou pursu'st this act,
Taint not thy mind, nor let thy soul contrive
85 Against thy mother aught: leave her to heaven,
And to those thorns that in her bosom lodge,
To prick and sting her. Fare thee well at once!
The glowworm shows the matin to be near,
And 'gins to pale his uneffectual fire:
90 Adieu, adieu! Hamlet, remember me. *(Exit.)*
HAMLET: O all you host of heaven! O earth! what else?
And shall I couple hell?—O, fie!—Hold, my heart;
And you, my sinews, grow not instant old,
But bear me stiffly up.—Remember thee!
95 Ay, thou poor ghost, while memory holds a seat
In this distracted globe. Remember thee!
Yea, from the table of my memory
I'll wipe away all trivial fond[9] recórds,
All saws of books, all forms, all pressures past,
100 That youth and observation copied there;
And thy commandment all alone shall live
Within the book and volume of my brain,
Unmix'd with baser matter: yes, by heaven.—
O most pernicious woman!
105 O villain, villain, smiling, damned villain!
My tables,—meet it is I set it down,
That one may smile, and smile, and be a villain;
At least, I am sure, it may be so in Denmark:

(Writing.)

So, uncle, there you are. Now to my word;
110 It is, *Adieu, adieu! remember me:*
I have sworn't.
HORATIO: *(Within)* My lord, my lord,—

---

[8] *luxury:* lechery.
[9] *fond:* foolish.

MARCELLUS: *(Within)*   Lord Hamlet,—

HORATIO: *(Within)*   Heaven secure
    him!

MARCELLUS: *(Within)* So be it!

HORATIO: *(Within)* Illo, ho, ho, my lord!

115 HAMLET: Hillo, ho, ho, boy! come, bird, come.[10]

(Enter Horatio and Marcellus.)

MARCELLUS: How is't, my noble lord?

HORATIO: What news, my lord?

HAMLET: O, wonderful!

HORATIO: Good my lord, tell it.

HAMLET: No; you'll reveal it.

HORATIO: Not I, my lord, by heaven.

MARCELLUS: Nor I, my lord.

120 HAMLET: How say you, then; would heart of man once think it?—
    But you'll be secret?

HORATIO and MARCELLUS: Ay, by heaven, my lord.

HAMLET: There's ne'er a villain dwelling in all Denmark
    But he's an arrant knave.

125 HORATIO: There needs no ghost, my lord, come from the grave
    To tell us this.

HAMLET: Why, right; you are i' the right;
    And so, without more circumstance at all,
    I hold it fit that we shake hands and part:

130   You, as your business and desire shall point you,—
    For every man has business and desire,
    Such as it is;—and for mine own poor part,
    Look you, I'll go pray.

HORATIO: These are but wild and whirling words, my lord.

135 HAMLET: I'm sorry they offend you, heartily;
    Yes, faith, heartily.

HORATIO: There's no offence, my lord.

HAMLET: Yes, by Saint Patrick, but there is, Horatio,
    And much offence too. Touching this vision here,—
    It is an honest ghost, that let me tell you:

140   For you desire to know what is between us,
    O'ermaster't as you may. And now, good friends,
    As you are friends, scholars, and soldiers,
    Give me one poor request.

HORATIO: What is't, my lord? we will.

145 HAMLET: Never make known what you have seen to-night.

HORATIO and MARCELLUS: My lord, we will not.

HAMLET: Nay, but swear't.

---

[10] *bird:* Hamlet uses the word "bird" because this is a falconer's call.

HORATIO: In faith,
    My lord, not I.
MARCELLUS: Nor I, my lord, in faith.
HAMLET: Upon my sword.
MARCELLUS: We have sworn, my lord, already.
HAMLET: Indeed, upon my sword, indeed.
150 GHOST: *(Beneath)* Swear.
HAMLET: Ha, ha, boy! say'st thou so? art thou there, truepenny?—
    Come on,—you hear this fellow in the cellarage,—
    Consent to swear.
HORATIO: Propose the oath, my lord.
HAMLET: Never to speak of this that you have seen,
155   Swear by my sword.
GHOST: *(Beneath)* Swear.
HAMLET: *Hic et ubique?*[11] then we'll shift our ground.—
    Come hither, gentlemen,
    And lay your hands again upon my sword:
160   Never to speak of this that you have heard,
    Swear by my sword.
GHOST: *(Beneath)* Swear.
HAMLET: Well said! old mole! canst work i' the earth so fast?
    A worthy pioneer![12]—Once more remove, good friends.
165 HORATIO: O day and night, but this is wondrous strange!
HAMLET: And therefore as a stranger give it welcome.
    There are more things in heaven and earth, Horatio,
    Than are dreamt of in your philosophy.
    But come;—
170   Here, as before, never, so help you mercy,
    How strange or odd soe'er I bear myself,—
    As I, perchance, hereafter shall think meet
    To put an antic disposition on,—
    That you, at such times seeing me, never shall,
175   With arms encumber'd[13] thus, or this headshake,
    Or by pronouncing of some doubtful phrase,
    As, *Well, well, we know;*—or, *We could, an if we would;*—
    Or, *If we list to speak;*—or, *There be, an if they might;*—
    Or such ambiguous giving out, to note
180   That you know aught of me:—this not to do,
    So grace and mercy at your most need help you,
    Swear.
GHOST: *(Beneath)* Swear.
HAMLET: Rest, rest, perturbed spirit!—So, gentlemen,

---

[11] *Hic et ubique:* here and everywhere?
[12] *pioneer:* a soldier who digs trenches and undermines fortresses.
[13] *encumber'd:* folded.

185 With all my love I do commend to you:
And what so poor a man as Hamlet is
May do, to express his love and friending to you,
God willing, shall not lack. Let us go in together;
And still your fingers on your lips, I pray.
190 The time is out of joint:—O cursed spite,
That ever I was born to set it right!—
Nay, come, let's go together.

(Exeunt.)

ACT II
SCENE 1

A room in Polonius' house.

(Enter Polonius and Reynaldo.)

POLONIUS: Give him this money and these notes, Reynaldo.
REYNALDO: I will, my lord.
POLONIUS: You shall do marvelous wisely, good Reynaldo,
Before you visit him, to make inquiry
5 On his behavior.
REYNALDO: My lord, I did intend it.
POLONIUS: Marry, well said; very well said. Look you, sir,
Inquire me first what Danskers[1] are in Paris;
And how, and who, what means, and where they keep,
What company, at what expense; and finding,
10 By this encompassment and drift of question,
That they do know my son, come you more nearer
Than your particular demands will touch it:
Take you, as 'twere, some distant knowledge of him;
As thus, *I know his father and his friends,*
15 *And in part him;*—do you mark this, Reynaldo?
REYNALDO: Ay, very well, my lord.
POLONIUS: *And in part him;*—but, you may say, *not well:*
But if't be he I mean, he's very wild;
Addicted so and so; and there put on him
20 What forgeries you please; marry, none so rank
As may dishonor him; take heed of that;
But, sir, such wanton, wild, and usual slips
As are companions noted and most known
To youth and liberty.
REYNALDO: As gaming, my lord.
25 POLONIUS: Ay, or drinking, fencing, swearing, quarreling,

---

[1] *Danskers:* Danes.

Drabbing:[2]—you may go so far.

REYNALDO: My lord, that would dishonor him.

POLONIUS: Faith, no; as you may season it in the charge.
You must not put another scandal on him,

30   That he is open to incontinency;
That's not my meaning: but breathe his faults so quaintly
That they may seem the taints of liberty;
The flash and outbreak of a fiery mind;
A savageness in unreclaimed blood,

35   Of general assault.

REYNALDO: But, my good lord,—

POLONIUS: Wherefore should you do this?

REYNALDO: Ay, my lord,
I would know that.

POLONIUS: Marry, sir, here's my drift;
And I believe it is a fetch of warrant:[3]
You laying these slight sullies on my son.

40   As 'twere a thing a little soil'd i' the working,
Mark you,
Your party in converse, him you would sound,
Having ever seen in the prenominate crimes
The youth you breathe of guilty, be assur'd

45   He closes with you in this consequence;
Good sir, or so; or *friend,* or *gentleman,*—
According to the phrase or the addition[4]
Of man and country.

REYNALDO: Very good, my lord.

POLONIUS: And then, sir, does he this,—he does,—

50   What was I about to say?—By the mass, I was
About to say something:—where did I leave?

REYNALDO: At *closes in the consequence,*
At *friend or so,* and *gentleman.*

POLONIUS: At—closes in the consequence,—ay, marry;

55   He closes with you thus:—*I know the gentleman;*
I saw him yesterday, or t'other day,
Or then, or then; with such, or such; and, as you say,
There was he gaming; there o'ertook in's rouse;
There falling out at tennis: or perchance,

60   *I saw him enter such a house of sale,*—
Videlicet, a brothel,—or so forth.—
See you now;
Your bait of falsehood takes this carp of truth:

---

[2] *Drabbing:* going about with loose women.
[3] *fetch of warrant:* a good device.
[4] *addition:* form of address.

And thus do we of wisdom and of reach,
65   With windlasses, and with assays of bias,
By indirections find directions out:
So, by my former lecture and advice,
Shall you my son. You have me, have you not?
REYNALDO: My lord, I have.
POLONIUS: God b' wi' you; fare you well.
70 REYNALDO: Good my lord!
POLONIUS: Observe his inclination in yourself.
REYNALDO: I shall, my lord.
POLONIUS: And let him ply his music.
REYNALDO: Well, my lord.
POLONIUS: Farewell!

(Exit Reynaldo.)

(Enter Ophelia.)

75   How now, Ophelia! what's the matter?
OPHELIA: Alas, my lord, I have been so affrighted.
POLONIUS: With what, i' the name of God?
OPHELIA: My lord, as I was sewing in my chamber,
Lord Hamlet,—with his doublet all unbrac'd;
80   No hat upon his head; his stockings foul'd,
Ungarter'd, and down-gyved[5] to his ankle;
Pale as his shirt; his knees knocking each other;
And with a look so piteous in purport
As if he had been loosed out of hell
85   To speak of horrors,—he comes before me.
POLONIUS: Mad for thy love?
OPHELIA: My lord, I do not know;
But truly I do fear it.
POLONIUS: What said he?
OPHELIA: He took me by the wrist, and held me hard;
Then goes he to the length of all his arm;
90   And with his other hand thus o'er his brow,
He falls to such perusal of my face
As he would draw it. Long stay'd he so;
At last,—a little shaking of mine arm,
And thrice his head thus waving up and down,—
95   He rais'd a sigh so piteous and profound
That it did seem to shatter all his bulk
And end his being; that done, he lets me go:
And, with his head over his shoulder turn'd,
He seem'd to find his way without his eyes;

---

[5] *down-gyved:* dangling like chains.

100 For out o' doors he went without their help,
And to the last bended their light on me.
POLONIUS: Come, go with me: I will go seek the king.
This is the very ecstasy[6] of love;
Whose violent property fordoes itself,[7]
105 And leads the will to desperate undertakings,
As oft as any passion under heaven
That does afflict our nature. I am sorry,—
What, have you given him any hard words of late?
OPHELIA: No, my good lord; but, as you did command,
110 I did repel his letters, and denied
His access to me.
POLONIUS: That hath made him mad.
I am sorry that with better heed and judgment
I had not quoted him: I fear'd he did but trifle,
And meant to wreck thee; but, beshrew my jealousy!
115 It seems it is as proper to our age
To cast beyond ourselves in our opinions
As it is common for the younger sort
To lack discretion. Come, go we to the king:
This must be known; which, being kept close, might move
120 More grief to hide than hate to utter love.

(Exeunt.)

SCENE 2

A room in the castle.

(Enter King, Queen, Rosencrantz, Guildenstern, and Attendants.)

KING: Welcome, dear Rosencrantz and Guildenstern!
Moreover that we much did long to see you,
The need we have to use you did provoke
Our hasty sending. Something have you heard
5 Of Hamlet's transformation; so I call it,
Since nor the exterior nor the inward man
Resembles that it was. What it should be,
More than his father's death, that thus hath put him
So much from the understanding of himself,
10 I cannot dream of: I entreat you both,
That being of so young days brought up with him,
And since so neighbor'd to his youth and humor,

---

[6] *ecstasy:* madness.
[7] *fordoes itself:* destroys itself.

That you vouchsafe your rest here in our court
Some little time: so by your companies
15 To draw him on to pleasures, and to gather,
So much as from occasion you may glean,
Whether aught, to us unknown, afflicts him thus,
That, open'd, lies within our remedy.
Queen: Good gentlemen, he hath much talk'd of you;
20 And sure I am two men there are not living
To whom he more adheres. If it will please you
To show us so much gentry and good-will
As to expend your time with us awhile,
For the supply and profit of our hope,
25 Your visitation shall receive such thanks
As fits a king's remembrance.
Rosencrantz: Both your majesties
Might, by the sovereign power you have of us,
Put your dread pleasures more into command
Than to entreaty.
Guildenstern: We both obey,
30 And here give up ourselves, in the full bent,
To lay our service freely at your feet,
To be commanded.
King: Thanks, Rosencrantz and gentle Guildenstern.
Queen: Thanks, Guildenstern and gentle Rosencrantz:
35 And I beseech you instantly to visit
My too-much-changed son.—Go, some of you,
And bring these gentlemen where Hamlet is.
Guildenstern: Heavens make our presence and our practices
Pleasant and helpful to him!
Queen: Ay, amen!

(Exeunt Rosencrantz, Guildenstern, and some Attendants.)

(Enter Polonius.)

40 Polonius: The ambassadors from Norway, my good lord,
Are joyfully return'd.
King: Thou still has been the father of good news.
Polonius: Have I, my lord? Assure you, my good liege,
I hold my duty, as I hold my soul,
45 Both to my God and to my gracious king:
And I do think,—or else this brain of mine
Hunts not the trail of policy[1] so sure
As it hath us'd to do,—that I have found
The very cause of Hamlet's lunacy.

---

[1] *trail of policy:* statecraft.

50   KING: O, speak of that; that do I long to hear.
     POLONIUS: Give first admittance to the ambassadors;
        My news shall be the fruit to that great feast.
     KING: Thyself do grace to them, and bring them in.

(Exit Polonius.)

        He tells me, my sweet queen, that he hath found
55   The head and source of all your son's distemper.
     QUEEN: I doubt it is no other but the main,—
        His father's death and our o'erhasty marriage.
     KING: Well, we shall sift him.

(Re-enter Polonius, with Voltimand and Cornelius.)

                        Welcome, my good friends!
        Say, Voltimand, what from our brother Norway?
60   VOLTIMAND: Most fair return of greetings and desires.
        Upon our first, he sent out to suppress
        His nephew's levies; which to him appear'd
        To be a preparation 'gainst the Polack;
        But, better look'd into, he truly found
65   It was against your highness: whereat griev'd,—
        That so his sickness, age, and impotence
        Was falsely borne in hand,—sends out arrests
        On Fortinbras; which he, in brief, obeys;
        Receives rebuke from Norway; and, in fine,
70   Makes vows before his uncle never more
        To give the assay of arms against your majesty.
        Whereon old Norway, overcome with joy,
        Gives him three thousand crowns in annual fee;
        And his commission to employ those soldiers,
75   So levied as before, against the Polack:
        With an entreaty, herein further shown, *(gives a paper)*
        That it might please you to give quiet pass
        Through your dominions for this enterprise,
        On such regards of safety and allowance
80   As therein are set down.
     KING: It likes us well;
        And at our more consider'd time we'll read,
        Answer, and think upon this business.
        Meantime we thank you for your well-took labor:
        Go to your rest; at night we'll feast together:
85   Most welcome home!

(Exeunt Voltimand and Cornelius.)

     POLONIUS: This business is well ended.—
        My liege, and madam,—to expostulate
        What majesty should be, what duty is,

Why day is day, night night, and time is time,
Were nothing but to waste night, day, and time.
90 Therefore, since brevity is the soul of wit,
And tediousness the limbs and outward flourishes,
I will be brief:—your noble son is mad:
Mad call I it; for to define true madness,
What is't but to be nothing else but mad?
95 But let that go.
QUEEN: More matter with less art.
POLONIUS: Madam, I swear I use no art at all.
That he is mad, 'tis true 'tis pity;
And pity 'tis 'tis true: a foolish figure;
But farewell it, for I will use no art.
100 Mad let us grant him, then: and now remains
That we find out the cause of this effect;
Or rather say, the cause of this defect,
For this effect defective comes by cause:
Thus it remains, and the remainder thus.
105 Perpend.
I have a daughter,—have whilst she is mine,—
Who, in her duty and obedience, mark,
Hath given me this: now gather, and surmise

(Reads)

To the celestial, and my soul's idol, the most beautified Ophelia,—
110 That's an ill phrase, a vile phrase,—*beautified* is a vile phrase: but
you shall hear. Thus:

(Reads)

In her excellent white bosom, these, &c.
QUEEN: Came this from Hamlet to her?
POLONIUS: Good madam, stay a while; I will be faithful.

(Reads)

115 *Doubt thou the stars are fire;*
     Doubt that the sun doth move;
Doubt truth to be a liar;
     But never doubt I love.
     O dear Ophelia, I am ill at these numbers,
120 *I have not art to reckon my groans: but that I love thee best, O most*
          best, believe it. Adieu.
          Thine evermore, most dear lady, whilst this machine is to him, Hamlet

This, in obedience, hath my daughter show'd me:
And more above, hath his solicitings,
125 As they fell out by time, by means, and place,
All given to mine ear.

KING: But how hath she
  Receiv'd his love?
POLONIUS: What do you think of me?
KING: As of a man faithful and honorable.
POLONIUS: I would fain prove so. But what might you think,
130 When I had seen this hot love on the wing,—
  As I perceiv'd it, I must tell you that,
  Before my daughter told me,—what might you,
  Or my dear majesty your queen here, think,
  If I had play'd the desk or table-book;[2]
135 Or given my heart a winking, mute and dumb;
  Or look'd upon this love with idle sight;—
  What might you think? No, I went round to work,
  And my young mistress thus I did bespeak:
  Lord Hamlet is a prince out of thy sphere;
140 *This must not be:* and then I precepts gave her,
  That she should lock herself from his resort,
  Admit no messengers, receive no tokens.
  Which done, she took the fruits of my advice;
  And he, repulsed,—a short tale to make,—
145 Fell into a sadness; then into a fast;
  Thence to a watch; thence into a weakness;
  Thence to a lightness; and, by this declension,
  Into the madness wherein now he raves
  And all we wail for.
 KING: Do you think 'tis this?
150 QUEEN: It may be, very likely.
POLONIUS: Hath there been such a time,—I'd fain know that,—
  That I have positively said, *'Tis so,*
  When it prov'd otherwise?
KING: Not that I know.
POLONIUS: Take this from this, if this be otherwise: *(Pointing to his head and*
  shoulder)
155 If circumstances lead me, I will find
  Where truth is hid, though it were hid indeed
  Within the center.
KING: How may we try it further?
POLONIUS: You know, sometimes he walks for hours together
  Here in the lobby.
 QUEEN: So he does, indeed.
160 POLONIUS: At such a time I'll loose my daughter to him:
  Be you and I behind an arras[3] then;
  Mark the encounter: if he love her not,

---

[2] *table-book:* memorandum pad.
[3] *arras:* tapestry, hung some distance away from a wall.

And be not from his reason fall'n thereon,
Let me be no assistant for a state,
165   But keep a farm and carters.
KING: We will try it.
QUEEN: But look, where sadly the poor wretch comes reading.
POLONIUS: Away, I do beseech you, both away:
    I'll board[4] him presently:—O, give me leave.

(Exeunt King, Queen, and Attendants.)

(Enter Hamlet, reading.)

    How does my good Lord Hamlet?
170 HAMLET: Well, God-a-mercy.
POLONIUS: Do you know me, my lord?
HAMLET: Excellent, excellent well; you're a fishmonger.
POLONIUS: Not I, my lord.
HAMLET: Then I would you were so honest a man.
175 POLONIUS: Honest, my lord!
HAMLET: Ay, sir; to be honest, as this world goes, is to be one man
    picked out of ten thousand.
POLONIUS: That's very true, my lord.
HAMLET: For if the sun breed maggots in a dead dog, being a god
180   kissing carrion,—Have you a daughter?
POLONIUS: I have, my lord.
HAMLET: Let her not walk i' the sun: conception is a blessing; but not
    as your daughter may conceive:—friend, look to't.
POLONIUS: How say you by that?—*(Aside)* Still harping on my
185   daughter:—yet he knew me not at first; he said I was a fishmonger:
    he is far gone, far gone: and truly in my youth I suffered much
    extremity for love; very near this. I'll speak to him again.—What do
    you read, my lord?
HAMLET: Words, words, words.
190 POLONIUS: What is the matter, my lord?
HAMLET: Between who?
POLONIUS: I mean, the matter that you read, my lord.
HAMLET: Slanders, sir: for the satirical slave says here that old men
    have gray beards; that their faces are wrinkled; their eyes purging
195   thick amber and plum-tree gum; and that they have a plentiful
    lack of wit, together with most weak hams: all which, sir, though I
    most powerfully and potently believe, yet I hold it not honesty to
    have it thus set down; for you yourself, sir, should be old as I am,
    if, like a crab, you could go backward.
200 POLONIUS: *(Aside)* Though this be madness, yet there is method in't.—
    ill you walk out of the air, my lord?

---

[4] *board:* address.

HAMLET: Into my grave?

POLONIUS: Indeed, that is out o' the air.—*(Aside)* How pregnant[5]
   sometimes his replies are! a happiness that often madness hits on,
205   which reason and sanity could not so prosperously be delivered of.
   I will leave him, and suddenly contrive the means of meeting
   between him and my daughter.—More honorable lord, I will most
   humbly take my leave of you.

HAMLET: You cannot, sir, take from me anything that I will more
210   willingly part withal,—except my life, except my life, except my life.

POLONIUS: Fare you well, my lord.

HAMLET: These tedious old fools!

(Enter Rosencrantz and Guildenstern.)

POLONIUS: You go to seek the Lord Hamlet; there he is.

ROSENCRANTZ: *(To Polonius)* God save you, sir!

(Exit Polonius.)

215   GUILDENSTERN: Mine honored lord!

ROSENCRANTZ: My most dear lord!

HAMLET: My excellent good friends! How dost thou, Guildenstern?
   Ah, Rosencrantz? Good lads, how do ye both?

ROSENCRANTZ: As the indifferent children of the earth.

220   GUILDENSTERN: Happy in that we are not overhappy; on fortune's cap
   we are not the very button.

HAMLET: Nor the soles of her shoe?

ROSENCRANTZ: Neither, my lord.

HAMLET: Then you live about her waist, or in the middle of her favors?

225   GUILDENSTERN: Faith, her privates we.

HAMLET: In the secret parts of fortune? O, most true; she is a strumpet.
   What's the news?

ROSENCRANTZ: None, my lord, but that the world's grown honest.

HAMLET: Then is doomsday near: but your news is not true. Let me
230   question more in particular: what have you, my good friends,
   deserved at the hands of fortune, that she sends you to prison
   hither?

GUILDENSTERN: Prison, my lord!

HAMLET: Denmark's a prison.

235   ROSENCRANTZ: Then is the world one.

HAMLET: A goodly one; in which there are many confines, wards, and
   dungeons, Denmark being one o' the worst.

ROSENCRANTZ: We think not so, my lord.

HAMLET: Why, then, 'tis none to you; for there is nothing either good
240   or bad, but thinking makes it so: to me it is a prison.

ROSENCRANTZ: Why, then, your ambition makes it one; 'tis too
   narrow for your mind.

---

[5] *pregnant:* ready, and clever.

HAMLET: O God, I could be bounded in a nutshell, and count myself
a king of infinite space, were it not that I have bad dreams.

245 GUILDENSTERN: Which dreams, indeed, are ambition; for the very
substance of the ambitious is merely the shadow of a dream.

HAMLET: A dream itself is but a shadow.

ROSENCRANTZ: Truly, and I hold ambition of so airy and light a quality
that it is but a shadow's shadow.

250 HAMLET: Then are our beggars bodies, and our monarchs and
outstretched heroes the beggars' shadows. Shall we to the court? for,
by my fay, I cannot reason.

ROSENCRANTZ and GUILDENSTERN: We'll wait upon you.

HAMLET: No such matter: I will not sort you with the rest of my
255 servants, for, to speak to you like an honest man, I am most
dreadfully attended. But, in the beaten way of friendship, what make
you at Elsinore?

ROSENCRANTZ: To visit you, my lord; no other occasion.

HAMLET: Beggar that I am, I am even poor in thanks; but I thank you:
260 and sure, dear friends, my thanks are too dear a halfpenny. Were
you not sent for? Is it your own inclining? Is it a free visitation?
Come, deal justly with me: come, come; nay, speak.

GUILDENSTERN: What should we say, my lord?

HAMLET: Why, anything—but to the purpose. You were sent for; and
265 there is a kind of confession in your looks, which your modesties
have not craft enough to color: I know the good king and queen
have sent for you.

ROSENCRANTZ: To what end, my lord?

HAMLET: That you must teach me. But let me conjure you, by the rights
270 of our fellowship, by the consonancy of our youth, by the obligation
of our ever-preserved love, and by what more dear a better proposer
could charge you withal, be even and direct with me, whether you
were sent for or no?

ROSENCRANTZ: What say you? *(To Guildenstern)*

275 HAMLET: *(Aside)* Nay, then, I have an eye of you.—If you love me,
hold not off.

GUILDENSTERN: My lord, we were sent for.

HAMLET: I will tell you why; so shall my anticipation prevent your
discovery, and your secrecy to the king and queen moult no
280 feather. I have of late,—but wherefore I know not,—lost all my
mirth, forgone all custom of exercises; and, indeed, it goes so
heavily with my disposition that this goodly frame, the earth,
seems to me a sterile promontory; this most excellent canopy, the
air, look you, this brave o'erhanging firmament, this majestical
285 roof fretted[6] with golden fire,—why, it appears no other thing to
me than a foul and pestilent congregation of vapors. What a piece

---

[6] *roof fretted:* a roof with fretwork.

of work is man! How noble in reason! how infinite in faculties! in form and moving, how express and admirable! in action, how like an angel! in apprehension, how like a god! the beauty of the world!
290   the paragon of animals! And yet, to me, what is this quintessence of dust? man delights not me; no, nor woman neither, though by your smiling you seem to say so.

ROSENCRANTZ: My lord, there was no such stuff in my thoughts.

HAMLET: Why did you laugh, then, when I said, *Man delights not me*?

295 ROSENCRANTZ: To think, my lord, if you delight not in man, what lenten entertainment[7] the players shall receive from you: we coted[8] them on the way; and hither are they coming, to offer you service.

HAMLET: He that plays the king shall be welcome,—his majesty shall have tribute of me; the adventurous knight shall use his foil and
300   target; the lover shall not sigh gratis; the humorous[9] man shall end his part in peace; the clown shall make those laugh whose lungs are tickled o' the sere;[10] and the lady shall say her mind freely, or the blank verse shall halt[11] for't.—What players are they?

ROSENCRANTZ: Even those you were wont to take delight in,—the
305   tragedians of the city.

HAMLET: How chances it they travel? their residence, both in reputation and profit, was better both ways.

ROSENCRANTZ: I think their inhibition[12] comes by the means of the late innovation.

310 HAMLET: Do they hold the same estimation they did when I was in the city? Are they so followed?

ROSENCRANTZ: No, indeed, they are not.

HAMLET: How comes it? do they grow rusty?

ROSENCRANTZ: Nay, their endeavor keeps in the wonted pace; but there
315   is, sir, an aery[13] of children, little eyases,[14] that cry out on the top of question, and are most tyrannically clapped for't: these are now the fashion; and so berattle the common stages,—so they call them,— that many wearing rapiers are afraid of goose-quills, and dare scarce come thither.

320 HAMLET: What, are they children? who maintains 'em? how are they escoted?[15] Will they pursue the quality[16] no longer than they can sing? will they not say afterwards, if they should grow themselves

---

[7] *lenten entertainment:* poor reception.

[8] *coted:* passed.

[9] *humorous:* eccentric.

[10] *whose . . . sere:* whose lungs, for laughter, are easily tickled.

[11] *halt:* limp.

[12] *inhibition:* difficulty, preventing them from remaining in the capital.

[13] *aery:* brood of birds of prey.

[14] *little eyases:* young hawks; a reference to the boys' companies that became popular rivals of Shakespeare's company of players.

[15] *escoted:* financially supported.

[16] *quality:* profession.

to common players,—as it is most like, if their means are no better,
—their writers do them wrong, to make them exclaim against
325   their own succession?
ROSENCRANTZ: Faith, there has been much to do on both sides; and
the nation holds it no sin to tarre[17] them to controversy: there was
for awhile no money bid for argument, unless the poet and the
player went to cuffs in the question.
330   HAMLET: Is't possible?
GUILDENSTERN: O, there has been much throwing about of brains.
HAMLET: Do the boys carry it away?
ROSENCRANTZ: Ay, that they do, my lord; Hercules and his load[18] too.
HAMLET: It is not strange; for mine uncle is king of Denmark, and those
335   that would make mouths at him while my father lived, give twenty,
forty, fifty, an hundred ducats a-piece for his picture in little.
'Sblood, there is something in this more than natural, if philosophy
could find it out.

(Flourish of trumpets within.)

GUILDENSTERN: There are the players.
340   HAMLET: Gentlemen, you are welcome to Elsinore. Your hands, come:
the appurtenance of welcome is fashion and ceremony: let me comply
with you in this garb; lest my extent[19] to the players, which, I
tell you, must show fairly outward, should more appear like
entertainment[20] than yours. You are welcome: but my uncle-father
345   and aunt-mother are deceived.
GUILDENSTERN: In what, my dear lord?
HAMLET: I am but mad north-north-west: when the wind is southerly
I know a hawk from a handsaw.

(Enter Polonius.)

POLONIUS: Well be with you, gentlemen!
350   HAMLET: Hark you, Guildenstern;—and you too;—at each ear a hearer:
that great baby you see there is not yet out of his swathing-clouts.
ROSENCRANTZ: Happily he's the second time come to them; for they
say an old man is twice a child.
HAMLET: I will prophesy he comes to tell me of the players; mark it.
355   You say right, sir: o' Monday morning; 'twas so indeed.
POLONIUS: My lord, I have news to tell you.
HAMLET: My lord, I have news to tell you. When Roscius was an actor
in Rome,—
POLONIUS: The actors are come hither, my lord.
360   HAMLET: Buzz, buzz!

---

[17] *tarre*: egg them on.
[18] *load*: the globe, or the world.
[19] *extent*: show of friendliness.
[20] *entertainment*: welcome.

POLONIUS: Upon mine honor,—

HAMLET: Then came each actor on his ass,—

POLONIUS: The best actors in the world, either for tragedy, comedy, history, pastoral, pastoral-comical, historical-pastoral, tragical-
365   historical, tragical-comical-historical-pastoral, scene individable,[21] or poem unlimited:[22] Seneca cannot be too heavy nor Plautus too light. For the law of writ and the liberty,[23] these are the only men.

HAMLET: O Jephthah, judge of Israel, what a treasure hadst thou!

POLONIUS: What a treasure had he, my lord?

370 HAMLET: Why—

> One fair daughter, and no more,
> The which he loved passing well.

POLONIUS: *(Aside)* Still on my daughter.

HAMLET: Am I not i' the right, old Jephthah?

375 POLONIUS: If you call me Jephthah, my lord, I have a daughter that I love passing well.

HAMLET: Nay, that follows not.

POLONIUS: What follows, then, my lord?

HAMLET: Why—

380   > As by lot, God wot,

and then, you know,

> It came to pass, as most like it was,

the first row of the pious chanson will show you more; for look where my abridgement comes.

(Enter four or five Players.)

385   You are welcome, masters; welcome, all:—I am glad to see thee well:—welcome, good friends.—O, my old friend! Thy face is valanced since I saw thee last; comest thou to beard me in Denmark?—What, my young lady and mistress! By'r lady, your ladyship is nearer heaven than when I saw you last, by the altitude
390   of a chopine.[24] Pray God, your voice, like a piece of uncurrent gold, be not cracked within the ring.—Masters, you are all welcome. We'll e'en to't like French falconers, fly at anything we see: we'll have a speech straight: come, give us a taste of your quality; come, a passionate speech.

395 1ST PLAYER: What speech, my lord?

HAMLET: I heard thee speak me a speech once,—but it was never acted; or, if it was, not above once; for the play, I remember, pleased not the million; 'twas caviare to the general: but it was,—

---

[21] *scene individable:* a play that observes the unities of time and place.

[22] *poem unlimited:* a typical multiscened Elizabethan type of drama, not restricted by the unities; examples are *Hamlet, Macbeth, King Lear,* and virtually any other play by Shakespeare.

[23] *For . . . liberty:* for the laws of the unities and for playwriting that is not so restricted.

[24] *chopine:* a wooden stilt more than a foot high used under a woman's shoe; a Venetian fashion introduced into England.

as I received it, and others whose judgments in such matters cried
400 in the top of mine,—an excellent play, well digested in the scenes,
set down with as much modesty as cunning. I remember, one said
there were no sallets in the lines to make the matter savory, nor no
matter in the phrase that might indite the author of affectation;
but called it an honest method, as wholesome as sweet, and by
405 very much more handsome than fine. One speech in it I chiefly loved:
'twas Aeneas' tale to Dido; and thereabout of it especially
where he speaks of Priam's slaughter: if it live in your memory,
begin at this line;—let me see, let me see:—
The rugged Pyrrhus, like the Hyrcanian beast,[25]

410 —it is not so:—it begins with Pyrrhus:—

The rugged Pyrrhus,—he whose sable arms,
Black as his purpose, did the night resemble
When he lay couched in the ominous horse,—
Hath now this dread and black complexion smear'd
415 With heraldry more dismal; head to foot
Now is he total gules; horridly trick'd
With blood of fathers, mothers, daughters, sons,
Bak'd and impasted with the parching streets,
That lend a tyrannous and damned light
420 To their vile murders: roasted in wrath and fire,
And thus o'er-sized with coagulate gore,
With eyes like carbuncles, the hellish Pyrrhus
Old grandsire Priam seeks.—

So proceed you.
425 POLONIUS: 'Fore God, my lord, well spoken, with good accent and
good discretion.
1ST PLAYER: Anon he finds him
Striking too short at Greeks; his antique sword,
Rebellious to his arm, lies where it falls,
430 Repugnant to command: unequal match'd,
Pyrrhus at Priam drives; in rage strikes wide;
But with the whiff and wind of his fell sword
The unnerved father falls. Then senseless Ilium,
Seeming to feel this blow, with flaming top
435 Stoops to his base; and with a hideous crash
Takes prisoner Pyrrhus' ear: for, lo! his sword,
Which was declining on the milky head
Of reverend Priam, seem'd i' the air to stick:
So, as a painted tyrant, Pyrrhus stood;
440 And, like a neutral to his will and matter,

---

[25] *The rugged . . . :* this speech is an example of the declamatory style of drama, which
Shakespeare surely must have considered outmoded.

Did nothing.
But as we often see, against some storm,
A silence in the heavens, the rack stand still,
The blood winds speechless, and the orb below
445 As hush as death, anon the dreadful thunder
Doth rend the region; so, after Pyrrhus' pause,
A roused vengeance sets him new a-work;
And never did the Cyclops' hammers fall
On Mars his armor, forg'd for proof eterne,
450 With less remorse than Pyrrhus' bleeding sword
Now falls on Priam.—
Out, out, thou strumpet, Fortune! All you gods,
In general synod, take away her power;
Break all the spokes and fellies from her wheel,
455 And bowl the round knave down the hill of heaven,
As low as to the fiends!

POLONIUS: This is too long.

HAMLET: It shall to the barber's, with your beard.—Pr'ythee, say
on.—He's for a jig, or a tale of bawdry, or he sleeps:—say on; come
460 to Hecuba.

1ST PLAYER: But who, O, who had seen the mobled queen,—

HAMLET: *The mobled queen?*

POLONIUS: That's good; *mobled queen* is good.

1ST PLAYER: Run barefoot up and down, threatening the flames
465 With bissom rheum; a clout upon that head
Where late the diadem stood; and, for a robe,
About her lank and all o'er-teemed loins,
A blanket, in the alarm of fear caught up;—
Who this had seen, with tongue in venom steep'd,
470 'Gainst Fortune's state would treason have pronounc'd:
But if the gods themselves did see her then,
When she saw Pyrrhus make malicious sport
In mincing with his sword her husband's limbs,
The instant burst of clamor that she made,—
475 Unless things mortal move them not at all,—
Would have made milch the burning eyes of heaven,
And passion in the gods.

POLONIUS: Look, whether he has not turn'd his color, and has tears
in's eyes.—Pray you, no more.

480 HAMLET: 'Tis well; I'll have thee speak out the rest soon.—Good my
lord, will you see the players well bestowed? Do you hear, let them
be well used; for they are the abstracts and brief chronicles of the
time; after your death you were better have a bad epitaph than
their ill report while you live.

485 POLONIUS: My lord, I will use them according to their desert.

HAMLET: God's bodykins,[26] man, better: use every man after his desert, and who should 'scape whipping? Use them after your own honor and dignity: the less they deserve the more merit is in your bounty. Take them in.

490 POLONIUS: Come, sirs.

HAMLET: Follow him, friends: we'll hear a play to-morrow.

(Exit Polonius with all the Players but the First.)

Dost thou hear me, old friend; can you play the Murder of Gonzago?

1ST PLAYER: Ay, my lord.

HAMLET: We'll ha't to-morrow night. You could, for a need, study a
495 speech of some dozen or sixteen lines which I would set down and insert in't? could you not?

1ST PLAYER: Ay, my lord.

HAMLET: Very well.—Follow that lord; and look you mock him not.

(Exit First Player.)

—My good friends, *(to Rosencrantz and Guildenstern)* I'll leave you
500 till night: you are welcome to Elsinore.

ROSENCRANTZ: Good my lord!

(Exeunt Rosencrantz and Guildenstern.)

HAMLET: Ay, so God b' wi' ye!—Now I am alone.
O, what a rogue[27] and peasant slave am I!
Is it not monstrous that this player here,
505 But in a fiction, in a dream of passion,
Could force his soul so to his own conceit[28]
That from her working all his visage wan'd;
Tears in his eyes, distraction in's aspéct,
A broken voice, and his whole function suiting
510 With forms to his conceit? And all for nothing!
For Hecuba?
What's Hecuba to him or he to Hecuba,
That he should weep for her? What would he do,
Had he the motive and the cue for passion
515 That I have? He would drown the stage with tears,
And cleave the general ear with horrid speech;
Make mad the guilty, and appal the free;
Confound the ignorant, and amaze, indeed,
The very faculties of eyes and ears.
520 Yet I,

---

[26] *God's bodykins:* by God's little body.
[27] *rogue:* wretched creature.
[28] *conceit:* conception.

A dull and muddy-mettled rascal, peak,
Like John-a-dreams, unpregnant of my cause,
And can say nothing; no, not for a king
Upon whose property and most dear life
525   A damn'd defeat was made. Am I a coward?
Who calls me villain? breaks my pate across?
Plucks off my beard and blows it in my face?
Tweaks me by the nose? gives me the lie i' the throat,
As deep as to the lungs? who does me this, ha?
530   'Swounds, I should take it: for it cannot be
But I am pigeon-liver'd, and lack gall
To make oppression bitter; or ere this
I should have fatted all the region kites
With this slave's offal:—bloody, bawdy villain!
535   Remorseless, treacherous, lecherous, kindless villain!
O, vengeance!
Why, what an ass am I! This is most brave,
That I, the son of a dear father murder'd,
Prompted to my revenge by heaven and hell,
540   Must, like a whore, unpack my heart with words,
And fall a-cursing like a very drab,
A scullion!
Fie upon't! foh!—About, my brain! I have heard
That guilty creatures, sitting at a play,
545   Have by the very cunning of the scene
Been struck so to the soul that presently
They have proclaim'd their malefactions;
For murder, though it have no tongue, will speak
With most miraculous organ. I'll have these players
550   Play something like the murder of my father
Before mine uncle: I'll observe his looks;
I'll tent[29] him to the quick: if he but blench,
I know my course. The spirit that I have seen
May be the devil: and the devil hath power
555   To assume a pleasing shape; yea, and perhaps
Out of my weakness and my melancholy,—
As he is very potent with such spirits,—
Abuses me to damn me: I'll have grounds
More relative than this:—the play's the thing
560   Wherein I'll catch the conscience of the king. *(Exit.)*

---

[29] *tent*: probe.

ACT III
<u>**SCENE 1**</u>

A room in the castle.

(Enter King, Queen, Polonius, Ophelia, Rosencrantz, and Guildenstern.)

KING: And can you, by no drift of circumstance,
  Get from him why he puts on this confusion,
  Grating so harshly all his days of quiet
  With turbulent and dangerous lunacy?

5 ROSENCRANTZ: He does confess he feels himself distracted;
  But from what cause he will by no means speak.

GUILDENSTERN: Nor do we find him forward to be sounded;
  But, with a crafty madness, keeps aloof
  When we would bring him on to some confession

10   Of his true state.

QUEEN: Did he receive you well?

ROSENCRANTZ: Most like a gentleman.

GUILDENSTERN: But with much forcing of his disposition.

ROSENCRANTZ: Niggard of question; but, of our demands,
  Most free in his reply.

QUEEN: Did you assay him

15   To any pastime?

ROSENCRANTZ: Madam, it so fell out that certain players
  We o'er-raught on the way: of these we told him;
  And there did seem in him a kind of joy
  To hear of it: they are about the court;

20   And, as I think, they have already order
  This night to play before him.

POLONIUS: 'Tis most true:
  And he beseech'd me to entreat your majesties
  To hear and see the matter.

KING: With all my heart; and it doth much content me

25   To hear him so inclin'd.
  Good gentlemen, give him a further edge,
  And drive his purpose on to these delights.

ROSENCRANTZ: We shall, my lord.

(Exeunt Rosencrantz and Guildenstern.)

KING: Sweet Gertrude, leave us too;
  For we have closely sent for Hamlet hither

30   That he, as 'twere by accident, may here
  Affront Ophelia:
  Her father and myself,—lawful espials,[1]—

---

[1] *espials:* spies.

Will so bestow ourselves that, seeing, unseen,
We may of their encounter frankly judge;
35 And gather by him, as he is behav'd,
If't be the affliction of his love or no
That thus he suffers for.
QUEEN: I shall obey you:—
And for your part, Ophelia, I do wish
That your good beauties be the happy cause
40 Of Hamlet's wildness: so shall I hope your virtues
Will bring him to his wonted way again,
To both your honors.
OPHELIA: Madam, I wish it may.

(Exit Queen.)

POLONIUS: Ophelia, walk you here.—Gracious, so please you,
We will bestow ourselves.—*(To Ophelia)* Read on this book;
45 That show of such an exercise may color
Your loneliness.—We are oft to blame in this,—
'Tis too much prov'd,—that with devotion's visage
And pious action we do sugar o'er
The devil himself.
KING: *(Aside)*   O, 'tis too true!
50 How smart a lash that speech doth give my conscience!
The harlot's cheek, beautied with plastering art,
Is not more ugly to the thing that helps it
Than is my deed to my most painted word:
O heavy burden!
55 POLONIUS: I hear him coming: let's withdraw, my lord.

(Exeunt King and Polonius.)

(Enter Hamlet.)

HAMLET: To be, or not to be,—that is the question:
Whether 'tis nobler in the mind to suffer
The slings and arrows of outrageous fortune,
Or to take arms against a sea of troubles,
60 And by opposing end them?—To die,—to sleep,—
No more; and by a sleep to say we end
The heart-ache and the thousand natural shocks
That flesh is heir to,—'tis a consummation
Devoutly to be wish'd. To die,—to sleep;—
65 To sleep! perchance to dream:—ay, there's the rub;
For in that sleep of death what dreams may come,
When we have shuffled off this mortal coil,
Must give us pause: there's the respect
That makes a calamity of so long life;

70 For who would bear the whips and scorns of time,
The oppressor's wrong, the proud man's contumely,
The pangs of déspis'd love, the law's delay,
The insolence of office, and the spurns
That patient merit of the unworthy takes,
75 When he himself might his quietus make
With a bare bodkin?[2] who would fardels[3] bear,
To grunt[4] and sweat under a weary life,
But that the dread of something after death,—
The undiscover'd country, from whose bourn[5]
80 No traveler returns,—puzzles the will,
And makes us rather bear those ills we have
Than to fly to others that we know not of?
Thus conscience does make cowards of us all;
And thus the native hue of resolution
85 Is sicklied o'er with the pale cast of thought;
And enterprises of great pith and moment,
With this regard, their currents turn awry,
And lose the name of action.—Soft you now!
The fair Ophelia.—Nymph, in thy orisons[6]
90 Be all my sins remember'd.

OPHELIA: Good my lord,
How does your honor for this many a day?

HAMLET: I humbly thank you; well, well, well.

OPHELIA: My lord, I have remembrances of yours,
That I have longed long to re-deliver;
95 I pray you, now receive them.

HAMLET: No, not I;
I never gave you aught.

OPHELIA: My honor'd lord, you know right well you did;
And with them, words of so sweet breath compos'd
As made the things more rich: their perfume lost,
100 Take these again; for to the noble mind
Rich gifts wax poor when givers prove unkind.
There, my lord.

HAMLET: Ha, ha! are you honest?

OPHELIA: My lord?

105 HAMLET: Are you fair?

OPHELIA: What means your lordship?

---

[2] *bodkin:* stiletto.
[3] *fardels:* burdens.
[4] *grunt:* groan.
[5] *bourn:* boundary.
[6] *orisons:* prayers.

HAMLET: That if you be honest and fair, your honesty should admit
    no discourse to your beauty.

OPHELIA: Could beauty, my lord, have better commerce than with
110   honesty?

HAMLET: Ay, truly; for the power of beauty will sooner transform
    honesty from what it is to a bawd than the force of honesty can
    translate beauty into his likeness: this was sometime a paradox,
    but now the time gives it proof. I did love you once.

115 OPHELIA: Indeed, my lord, you made me believe so.

HAMLET: You should not have believed me; for virtue cannot so
    inoculate our old stock but we shall relish of it: I loved you not.

OPHELIA: I was the more deceived.

HAMLET: Get thee to a nunnery: why wouldst thou be a breeder of
120   sinners? I am myself indifferent[7] honest; but yet I could accuse me
    of such things that it were better my mother had not borne me: I
    am very proud, revengeful, ambitious; with more offences at my
    beck than I have thoughts to put them in, imagination to give
    them shape, or time to act them in. What should such fellows as I
125   do crawling between heaven and earth? We are arrant knaves, all;
    believe none of us. Go thy ways to a nunnery. Where's your father?

OPHELIA: At home, my lord.

HAMLET: Let the doors be shut upon him, that he may play the fool
    nowhere but in's own house. Farewell.

130 OPHELIA: O, help him, you sweet heavens!

HAMLET: If thou dost marry, I'll give thee this plague for thy
    dowry,—be thou as chaste as ice, as pure as snow, thou shalt not
    escape calumny. Get thee to a nunnery, go: farewell. Or, if thou
    wilt needs marry, marry a fool; for wise men know well enough
135   what monsters you make of them. To a nunnery, go; and quickly
    too. Farewell.

OPHELIA: O heavenly powers, restore him!

HAMLET: I have heard of your paintings too, well enough; God has
    given you one face and you make yourselves another: you jig, you
140   amble, and you lisp, and nickname God's creatures, and make your
    wantonness your ignorance. Go to, I'll no more on't; it hath made
    me mad. I say, we will have no more marriages: those that are
    married already, all but one, shall live; the rest shall keep as they are.
    To a nunnery, go. *(Exit.)*

145 OPHELIA: O, what a noble mind is here o'erthrown!
    The courtier's, soldier's, scholar's eye, tongue, sword:
    The expectancy and rose of the fair state,
    The glass of fashion and the mould of form,
    The observ'd of all observers,—quite, quite down!
150   And I, of ladies most deject and wretched

---

[7] *indifferent:* tolerably.

That suck'd the honey of his music vows,
Now see that noble and most sovereign reason,
Like sweet bells jangled, out of tune and harsh;
That unmatch'd form and feature of blown[8] youth

155 Blasted with ecstasy: O, woe is me,
To have seen what I have seen, see what I see!

(Re-enter King and Polonius.)

KING: Love! his affections do not that way tend;
Nor what he spake, though it lack'd form a little,
Was not like madness. There's something in his soul

160 O'er which his melancholy sits on brood;
And I do doubt[9] the hatch and the disclose
Will be some danger: which for to prevent,
I have in quick determination
Thus set it down:—he shall with speed to England

165 For the demand of our neglected tribute:
Haply, the seas and countries different,
With variable objects, shall expel
This something-settled matter in his heart;
Whereon his brains still beating puts him thus

170 From fashion of himself. What think you on't?
POLONIUS: It shall do well: but yet do I believe
The origin and commencement of his grief
Sprung from neglected love.—How now, Ophelia!
You need not tell us what Lord Hamlet said;

175 We heard it all.—My lord, do as you please;
But if you hold it fit, after the play,
Let his queen mother all alone entreat him
To show his grief: let her be round with him;
And I'll be plac'd, so please you, in the ear

180 Of all their conference. If she finds him not,[10]
To England send him; or confine him where
Your wisdom best shall think.
KING: It shall be so:
Madness in great ones must not unwatch'd go.

(Exeunt.)

---

[8] *blown:* full-blown.
[9] *doubt:* fear.
[10] *she . . . not:* does not find him out.

SCENE 2

A hall in the castle.

(Enter Hamlet and certain Players.)

HAMLET: Speak the speech, I pray you, as I pronounced it to you, trippingly on the tongue: but if you mouth it, as many of your players do, I had as lief the town-crier spoke my lines. Nor do not saw the air too much with your hand, thus; but use all gently: for
5   in the very torrent, tempest, and, as I may say, the whirlwind of passion, you must acquire and beget a temperance that may give it smoothness. O, it offends me to the soul, to hear a robustious periwigpated fellow tear a passion to tatters, to very rags, to split the ears of the groundlings, who, for the most part, are capable of
10   nothing but inexplicable dumb shows and noise: I could have such a fellow whipped for o'erdoing Termagant;[1] it out-herods Herod:[2] pray you, avoid it.

1ST PLAYER: I warrant your honor.

HAMLET: Be not too tame neither, but let your own discretion be
15   your tutor; suit the action to the word, the word to the action; with this special observance, that you o'erstep not the modesty of nature: for anything so overdone is from the purpose of playing, whose end, both at the first and now, was and is, to hold, as 'twere, the mirror up to nature; to show virtue her own feature,
20   scorn her own image, and the very age and body of the time his form and pressure. Now, this overdone or come tardy off, though it make the unskilful laugh, cannot but make the judicious grieve; the censure of the which one must, in your allowance, o'erweigh a whole theater of others. O, there be players that I have seen
25   play,—and heard others praise, and that highly,—not to speak it profanely, that, neither having the accent of Christians, nor the gait of Christian, pagan, nor man, have so strutted and bellowed that I have thought some of nature's journeymen had made men, and not made them well, they imitated humanity so abominably.
30 1ST PLAYER: I hope we have reformed that indifferently with us, sir.

HAMLET: O, reform it altogether. And let those that play your clowns speak no more than is set down for them: for there be of them that will themselves laugh, to set on some quantity of barren spectators to laugh too; though, in the meantime, some necessary question of
35   the play be then to be considered: that's villainous, and shows a most pitiful ambition in the fool that uses it. Go, make you ready.

(Exeunt Players.)

---

[1] *Termagant:* a violent pagan deity, supposedly Mohammedan.
[2] *out-herods Herod:* outrants the ranting Herod, who figures in medieval drama.

(Enter Polonius, Rosencrantz, and Guildenstern.)

How now, my lord! will the king hear this piece of work?
POLONIUS: And the queen, too, and that presently.
HAMLET: Bid the players make haste.

(Exit Polonius.)

40   Will you two help to hasten them?
ROSENCRANTZ and GUILDENSTERN: We will, my lord. *(Exeunt.)*
HAMLET: What, ho, Horatio!

(Enter Horatio.)

HORATIO: Here, sweet lord, at your service.
HAMLET: Horatio, thou art e'en as just a man
45   As e'er my conversation cop'd withal.
HORATIO: O, my dear lord,—
HAMLET: Nay, do not think I flatter;
For what advancement may I hope from thee,
That no revénue hast, but thy good spirits,
To feed and clothe thee? Why should the poor be flatter'd?
50   No, let the candied tongue lick ábsurd pomp;
And crook the pregnant hinges of the knee
Where thrift may follow fawning. Dost thou hear?
Since my dear soul was mistress of her choice,
And could of men distinguish, her election
55   Hath seal'd thee for herself: for thou hast been
As one, in suffering all, that suffers nothing;
A man that Fortune's buffets and rewards
Hast ta'en with equal thanks: and bless'd are those
Whose blood and judgment are so well commingled
60   That they are not a pipe for Fortune's finger
To sound what stop she please. Give me that man
That is not passion's slave, and I will wear him
In my heart's core, ay, in my heart of heart,
As I do thee.—Something too much of this.—
65   There is a play to-night before the king;
One scene of it comes near the circumstance
Which I have told thee of my father's death:
I pr'ythee, when thou see'st that act a-foot,
Even with the very comment of thy soul
70   Observe mine uncle: if this his occulted guilt
Do not itself unkennel in one speech,
It is a damned ghost that we have seen;
And my imaginations are as foul
As Vulcan's stithy.[3] Give him heedful note:

――――――――

[3] *stithy*: smithy.

75   For I mine eyes will rivet to his face;
    And, after, we will both our judgments join
    In censure of his seeming.
HORATIO: Well, my lord:
    If he steal aught the whilst this play is playing,
    And 'scape detecting, I will pay the theft.
80 HAMLET: They are coming to the play; I must be idle:[4]
    Get you a place.

(Danish march. A flourish. Enter King, Queen, Polonius, Ophelia, Rosencrantz, Guildenstern, and others.)

KING: How fares our cousin Hamlet?
HAMLET: Excellent, i'faith; of the chameleon's dish:[5] I eat the air,
    promise-crammed: you cannot feed capons so.
85 KING: I have nothing with this answer, Hamlet; these words are not
    mine.
HAMLET: No, nor mine now. *(To Polonius)* My lord, you played once
    i' the university, you say?
POLONIUS: That did I, my lord, and was accounted a good actor.
90 HAMLET: And what did you enact?
POLONIUS: I did enact Julius Caesar: I was killed i' the Capitol; Brutus
    killed me.
HAMLET: It was a brute part of him to kill so capital a calf there.—Be
    the players ready.
95 ROSENCRANTZ: Ay, my lord; they stay upon your patience.
QUEEN: Come hither, my good Hamlet, sit by me.
HAMLET: No, good mother, here's metal more attractive.
POLONIUS: O, ho! do you mark that? *(To the King)*
HAMLET: Lady, shall I lie in your lap? *(Lying down at Ophelia's feet)*
100 OPHELIA: No, my lord.
HAMLET: I mean, my head upon your lap?
OPHELIA: Ay, my lord.
HAMLET: Do you think I meant country matters?
OPHELIA: I think nothing, my lord.
105 HAMLET: That's a fair thought to lie between maids' legs.
OPHELIA: What is, my lord?
HAMLET: Nothing.
OPHELIA: You are merry, my lord.
HAMLET: Who, I?
110 OPHELIA: Ay, my lord.
HAMLET: O, your only jig-maker. What should a man do but be
    merry? for, look you, how cheerfully my mother looks, and my father
    died within's two hours.

---

[4] *idle:* foolish.
[5] *chameleon's dish:* chameleons were supposed to live on air.

OPHELIA: Nay, 'tis twice two months, my lord.

115 HAMLET: So long? Nay, then, let the devil wear black, for I'll have a
suit of sables. O heavens! die two months ago, and not forgotten
yet? Then there's hope a great man's memory may outlive his life
half a year: but, by'r lady, he must build churches, then; or else shall
he suffer not thinking on, with the hobby-horse, whose epitaph is,
120 *For, O, for, O, the hobby-horse is forgot.*

(Trumpets sound. The dumb show enters.)

*(Enter a King and a Queen, very lovingly; the Queen embracing him and he her.
She kneels, and makes show of protestation unto him. He takes her up, and
declines his head upon her neck: lays him down upon a bank of flowers: she, seeing
him asleep, leaves him. Anon comes in a fellow, takes off his crown, kisses it, and
pours poison in the King's ears, and exit. The Queen returns; finds the King dead,
and makes passionate action. The Poisoner, with some two or three Mutes, comes
in again, seeming to lament with her. The dead body is carried away. The Poisoner
woos the Queen with gifts: she seems loth and unwilling awhile, but in the end
accepts his love.)*

(Exeunt.)

OPHELIA: What means this, my lord?
HAMLET: Marry, this is miching mallecho;[6] it means mischief.
OPHELIA: Belike this show imports the argument of the play.

(Enter Prologue.)

HAMLET: We shall know by this fellow: the players cannot keep counsel;
125 they'll tell all.
OPHELIA: Will he tell us what this show meant?
HAMLET: Ay, or any show that you'll show him: be not you ashamed
to show, he'll not shame to tell you what it means.
OPHELIA: You are naught, you are naught: I'll mark the play.
130 PROLOGUE:

> For us, and for our tragedy,
> Here stooping to your clemency,
> We beg your hearing patiently.

HAMLET: Is this a prologue, or the posy[7] of a ring?
OPHELIA: 'Tis brief, my lord.
135 HAMLET: As woman's love.

(Enter a King and a Queen.)

PROLOGUE KING: Full thirty times hath Phoebus' cart gone round
Neptune's salt wash and Tellus' orbed ground,[8]

---

[6] *miching mallecho:* a sneaking misdeed.
[7] *posy:* motto or inscription.
[8] *Neptune's . . . ground:* the globe.

And thirty dozen moons with borrow'd sheen
About the world have times twelve thirties been,

140 Since love our hearts, and Hymen did our hands
Unite commutual in most sacred bands.

PROLOGUE QUEEN: So many journeys may the sun and moon
Make us again count o'er ere love be done!
But, woe is me, you are so sick of late,

145 So far from cheer and from your former state
That I distrust you.[9] Yet, though I distrust,
Discomfort you, my lord, it nothing must:
For women's fear and love holds quantity,[10]
In neither aught, or in extremity.

150 Now, what my love is, proof hath made you know;
And as my love is siz'd, my fear is so:
Where love is great, the littlest doubts are fear;
Where little fears grow great, great love grows there.

PROLOGUE KING: Faith, I must leave thee, love, and shortly too;

155 My operant powers their functions leave[11] to do:
And thou shalt live in this fair world behind,
Honor'd, belov'd; and haply one as kind
For husband shalt thou,—

PROLOGUE QUEEN: O, confound the rest!
Such love must needs be treason in my breast:

160 In second husband let me be accurst!
None wed the second but who kill'd the first.

HAMLET: *(Aside)* Wormwood, wormwood.

PROLOGUE QUEEN: The instances that second marriage move
Are base respects of thrift, but none of love:

165 A second time I kill my husband, dead,
When second husband kisses me in bed.

PROLOGUE KING: I do believe you think what now you speak;
But what we do determine oft we break.
Purpose is but the slave to memory;

170 Of violent birth, but poor validity:
Which now, like fruit unripe, sticks on the tree;
But fall unshaken when they mellow be.
Most necessary 'tis that we forget
To pay ourselves what to ourselves is debt:

175 What to ourselves in passion we propose,
The passion ending, doth the purpose lose.
The violence of either grief or joy
Their own enactures with themselves destroy:

---

[9] *distrust you:* worry about you.
[10] *holds quantity:* correspond in degree.
[11] *leave:* cease.

Where joy most revels grief doth most lament;
180 Grief joys, joy grieves, on slender accident.
This world is not for aye; nor 'tis not strange
That even our loves should with our fortunes change;
For 'tis a question left us yet to prove
Whether love lead fortune or else fortune love.
185 The great man down, you mark his favorite flies;
The poor advanc'd makes friends of enemies.
And hitherto doth love on fortune tend:
For who not needs shall never lack a friend;
And who in want a hollow friend doth try,
190 Directly seasons him his enemy.
But, orderly to end where I begun,—
Our wills and fates do so contrary run
That our devices still are overthrown;
Our thoughts are ours, their ends none of our own:
195 So think thou wilt no second husband wed;
But die thy thoughts when thy first lord is dead.
PROLOGUE QUEEN: Nor earth to me give food, nor heaven light!
Sport and repose lock from me day and night!
To desperation turn my trust and hope!
200 An anchor's[12] cheer in prison be my scope!
Each opposite, that blanks the face of joy,
Meet what I would have well, and it destroy!
Both here and hence, pursue me lasting strife,
If, once a widow, ever I be wife!
205 HAMLET: If she should break it now! *(To Ophelia)*
PROLOGUE KING: 'Tis deeply sworn. Sweet, leave me here awhile;
My spirits grow dull, and fain I would beguile
The tedious day with sleep. *(Sleeps)*
PROLOGUE QUEEN: Sleep rock thy brain,
And never come mischance between us twain! *(Exit.)*
210 HAMLET: Madam, how like you this play?
QUEEN: The lady doth protest too much, methinks.
HAMLET: O, but she'll keep her word.
KING: Have you heard the argument? Is there no offence in't?
HAMLET: No, no, they do but jest, poison in jest; no offence i' the
215   world.
KING: What do you call the play?
HAMLET: The Mouse-trap. Marry, how? Tropically.[13] This play is the
image of a murder done in Vienna: Gonzago is the duke's name:
his wife, Baptista: you shall see anon; 'tis a knavish piece of work:
220   but what o' that? your majesty, and we that have free souls, it
touches us not: let the galled jade wince, our withers are unwrung.

---

[12] *anchor's:* anchorite's, or hermit's.
[13] *Tropically:* figuratively, or metaphorically; by means of a "trope."

(Enter Lucianus.)

This is one Lucianus, nephew to the king.

OPHELIA: You are a good chorus, my lord.

HAMLET: I could interpret between you and your love, if I could see
225   the puppets dallying.

OPHELIA: You are keen, my lord, you are keen.

HAMLET: It would cost you a groaning to take off my edge.

OPHELIA: Still better, and worse.

HAMLET: So you must take your husbands.—Begin, murderer; pox,
230   leave thy damnable faces and begin. Come:—*The croaking raven*
doth bellow for revenge.

LUCIANUS: Thoughts black, hands apt, drugs fit, and time agreeing;
    Confederate season, else no creature seeing;
    Thou mixture rank, of midnight weeds collected,
235   With Hecate's ban[14] thrice blasted, thrice infected,
    Thy natural magic and dire property
    On wholesome life usurp immediately.

(Pours the poison into the sleeper's ears.)

HAMLET: He poisons him i' the garden for's estate. His name's Gonzago:
    the story is extant, and writ in choice Italian: you shall see anon how
240   the murderer gets the love of Gonzago's wife.

OPHELIA: The king rises.

HAMLET: What, frighted with false fire!

QUEEN: How fares my lord?

POLONIUS: Give o'er the play.
245 KING: Give me some light:—away!

ALL: Lights, lights, lights!

(Exeunt all but Hamlet and Horatio.)

HAMLET: Why, let the stricken deer go weep,
    The hart ungalled play;
    For some must watch, while some must sleep:
250   So runs the world away.—
    Would not this, sir, and a forest of feathers, if the rest of my fortunes
    turn Turk with me, with two Provencial roses on my razed shoes, get
    me a fellowship in a cry[15] of players, sir?
255 HORATIO: Half a share.

HAMLET: A whole one, I.

               For thou dost know, O Damon dear,
                   This realm dismantled was

---

[14] *Hecate's ban:* the spell of the goddess of witchcraft.

[15] *cry:* company.

260   Of Jove himself; and now reigns here
                      A very, very—pajock.[16]

HORATIO: You might have rhymed.

HAMLET: O good Horatio, I'll take the ghost's word for a thousand
     pound. Didst perceive?

HORATIO: Very well, my lord.

265 HAMLET: Upon the talk of the poisoning,—

HORATIO: I did very well note him.

HAMLET: Ah, ha!—Come, some music! come, the recorders!—
     For if the king like not the comedy,
     Why, then, belike,—he likes it not, perdy.

270   Come, some music!

(Re-enter Rosencrantz and Guildenstern.)

GUILDENSTERN: Good my lord, vouchsafe me a word with you.

HAMLET: Sir, a whole history.

GUILDENSTERN: The king, sir,—

HAMLET: Ay, sir, what of him?

275 GUILDENSTERN: Is, in his retirement, marvelous distempered.

HAMLET: With drink, sir?

GUILDENSTERN: No, my lord, rather with choler.

HAMLET: Your wisdom should show itself more richer to signify this
     to his doctor; for, for me to put him to his purgation would perhaps

280   plunge him into far more choler.

GUILDENSTERN: Good my lord, put your discourse into some frame,
     and start not so wildly from my affair.

HAMLET: I am tame, sir:—pronounce.

GUILDENSTERN: The queen, your mother, in most great affliction of

285   spirit, hath sent me to you.

HAMLET: You are welcome.

GUILDENSTERN: Nay, good my lord, this courtesy is not of the right
     breed. If it shall please you to make me a wholesome answer, I will
     do you mother's commandment: if not, your pardon and my return

290   shall be the end of my business.

HAMLET: Sir, I cannot.

GUILDENSTERN: What, my lord?

HAMLET: Make you a wholesome answer; my wit's diseas'd: but, sir,
     such answer as I can make, you shall command; or, rather, as you

295   say, my mother: therefore no more, but to the matter: my mother,
     you say,—

ROSENCRANTZ: Then thus she says: your behavior hath struck her into
     amazement and admiration.

HAMLET: O wonderful son, that can so astonish a mother!—But is

300   there no sequel at the heels of this mother's admiration?

---

[16] *pajock:* peacock.

ROSENCRANTZ: She desires to speak with you in her closet[17] ere you
   go to bed.
HAMLET: We shall obey, were she ten times our mother. Have you any
   further trade with us?
305 ROSENCRANTZ: My lord, you once did love me.
HAMLET: So I do still, by these pickers and stealers.[18]
ROSENCRANTZ: Good, my lord, what is your cause of distemper? you
   do, surely, bar the door upon your own liberty if you deny your
   griefs to your friend.
310 HAMLET: Sir, I lack advancement.
ROSENCRANTZ: How can that be, when you have the voice of the king
   himself for your succession in Denmark?
HAMLET: Ay, but *While the grass grows,*—the proverb is something
   musty.

(Re-enter the Players, with recorders.)

315   O, the recorders:—let me see one.—To withdraw with you:—why
   do you go about to recover the wind of me, as if you would drive
   me into a toil?
GUILDENSTERN: O, my lord, if my duty be too bold, my love is too
   unmannerly.
320 HAMLET: I do not well understand that. Will you play upon this pipe?
GUILDENSTERN: My lord, I cannot.
HAMLET: I pray you.
GUILDENSTERN: Believe me, I cannot.
HAMLET: I do beseech you.
325 GUILDENSTERN: I know no touch of it, my lord.
HAMLET: 'Tis as easy as lying: govern these ventages[19] with your finger
   and thumb, give it breath with your mouth, and it will discourse
   most eloquent music. Look you, these are the stops.
GUILDENSTERN: But these cannot I command to any utterance of
330   harmony; I have not the skill.
HAMLET: Why, look you now, how unworthy a thing you make of me!
   You would play upon me; you would seem to know my stops; you
   would pluck out the heart of my mystery; you would sound me
   from my lowest note to the top of my compass: and there is much
335   music, excellent voice, in this little organ; yet cannot you make it
   speak. 'Sblood, do you think that I am easier to be played on than
   a pipe? Call me what instrument you will, though you can fret me
   you cannot play upon me.

(Enter Polonius.)

---

[17] *closet:* boudoir.
[18] *pickers and stealers:* fingers.
[19] *ventages:* holes.

God bless you, sir!
340 POLONIUS: My lord, the queen would speak with you, and
presently.
HAMLET: Do you see yonder cloud that's almost in shape of a camel?
POLONIUS: By the mass, and 'tis like a camel indeed.
HAMLET: Methinks it is like a weasel.
345 POLONIUS: It is backed like a weasel.
HAMLET: Or like a whale?
POLONIUS: Very like a whale.
HAMLET: Then will I come to my mother by and by.—They fool me
to the top of my bent.—I will come by and by.
350 POLONIUS: I will say so.
HAMLET: By and by is easily said.

(Exit Polonius.)

Leave me, friends.

(Exeunt Rosencrantz, Guildenstern, Horatio, and Players.)

'Tis now the very witching time of night,
When churchyards yawn, and hell itself breathes out
355 Contagion to this world: now could I drink hot blood,
And do such bitter business as the day
Would quake to look on. Soft! now to my mother.—
O heart, lose not thy nature; let not ever
The soul of Nero[20] enter this firm bosom:
360 Let me be cruel, not unnatural:
I will speak daggers to her, but use none;
My tongue and soul in this be hypocrites,—
How in my words soever she be shent,
To give them seals never, my soul, consent! *(Exit.)*

SCENE 3

A room in the castle.

(Enter King, Rosencrantz, and Guildenstern.)

KING: I like him not; nor stands it safe with us
To let his madness range. Therefore prepare you;
I your commission with forthwith despatch,
And he to England shall along with you:
5 The terms of our estate may not endure
Hazard so dangerous as doth hourly grow
Out of his lunacies.

---

[20] *soul of Nero:* Nero killed his mother, a crime of which Hamlet does not want to be
guilty.

GUILDENSTERN: We will ourselves provide:
    Most holy and religious fear it is
    To keep those many many bodies safe
10   That live and feed upon your majesty.
ROSENCRANTZ: The single and peculiar life is bound,
    With all the strength and armor of the mind,
    To keep itself from 'noyance; but much more
    That spirit upon whose weal depend and rest
15   The lives of many. The cease of majesty
    Dies not alone; but like a gulf doth draw
    What's near it with it: it is a massy wheel,
    Fix'd on the summit of the highest mount,
    To whose huge spokes ten thousand lesser things
20   Are mortis'd and adjoin'd; which, when it falls,
    Each small annexment, petty consequence,
    Attends the boisterous ruin. Never alone
    Did the king sigh, but with a general groan.
KING: Arm you, I pray you, to this speedy voyage;
25   For we will fetters put upon this fear,
    Which now goes too free-footed.
ROSENCRANTZ and GUILDENSTERN: We will haste us.

(Exeunt Rosencrantz and Guildenstern.)

(Enter Polonius.)

POLONIUS: My lord, he's going to his mother's closet:
    Behind the arras I'll convey myself
    To hear the process; I'll warrant she'll tax him home:[1]
30   And, as you said, and wisely was it said,
    'Tis meet that some more audience than a mother,
    Since nature makes them partial, should o'erhear
    The speech, of vantage. Fare you well, my liege:
    I'll call upon you ere you go to bed,
35   And tell you what I know.
KING: Thanks, dear my lord.

(Exit Polonius.)

    O, my offence is rank, it smells to heaven;
    It hath the primal eldest curse upon't,—
    A brother's murder!—Pray can I not,
    Though inclination be as sharp as will:
40   My stronger guilt defeats my strong intent;
    And, like a man to double business bound,
    I stand in pause where I shall first begin,
    And both neglect. What if this cursed hand

---

[1] *tax him home:* reprove him properly.

Were thicker than itself with brother's blood,—
45   Is there not rain enough in the sweet heavens
To wash it white as snow? Whereto serves mercy
But to confront the visage of offence?
And what's in prayer but this twofold force,—
To be forestalled ere we come to fall,
50   Or pardon'd being down? Then I'll look up;
My fault is past. But, O, what form of prayer
Can serve my turn? Forgive me my foul murder?—
That cannot be; since I am still possess'd
Of those effects for which I did the murder,—
55   My crown, mine own ambition, and my queen.
May one be pardon'd and retain the offence?[2]
In the corrupted currents of this world
Offence's gilded hand may shove by justice;
And oft 'tis seen the wicked prize itself
60   Buys out the law: but 'tis not so above;
There is no shuffling,—there the action lies
In his true nature; and we ourselves compell'd,
Even to the teeth and forehead of our faults,
To give in evidence. What then? what rests?[3]
65   Try what repentance can: what can it not?
Yet what can it when one can not repent?
O wretched state! O bosom black as death!
O limed[4] soul, that, struggling to be free,
Art more engag'd! Help, angels! make assay:
70   Bow, stubborn knees; and, heart, with strings of steel,
Be soft as sinews of the new-born babe!
All may be well. *(Retires and kneels)*

(Enter Hamlet.)

HAMLET: Now might I do it pat, now he is praying;
And now I'll do't—and so he goes to heaven;
75   And so am I reveng'd:—that would be scann'd:
A villain kills my father; and for that,
I, his sole son, do this same villain send
To heaven.
O, this is hire and salary, not revenge.
80   He took my father grossly, full of bread;
With all his crimes broad blown, as flush as May;
And how his audit stands who knows save heaven?
But in our circumstance and course of thought
'Tis heavy with him: and am I, then, reveng'd,

---

[2] *offence:* that is, the gains won by the offence.
[3] *rests:* remains.
[4] *limed:* snared.

85   To take him in the purging of his soul,
    When he is fit and season'd for his passage?
    No.
    Up, sword; and know thou a more horrid hent:[5]
    When he is drunk, asleep, or in his rage;
90   Or in the incestuous pleasure of his bed;
    At gaming, swearing; or about some act
    That has no relish of salvation in't;—
    Then trip him, that his heels may kick at heaven;
    And that his soul may be as damn'd and black
95   As hell, whereto it goes. My mother stays:
    This physic but prolongs thy sickly days. *(Exit.)*

(The King rises and advances.)

King: My words fly up, my thoughts remain below:
    Words without thoughts never to heaven go. *(Exit.)*

SCENE 4

Another room in the castle.

(Enter Queen and Polonius.)

Polonius: He will come straight. Look you lay home to him:
    Tell him his pranks have been too broad to bear with,
    And that your grace hath screen'd and stood between
    Much heat and him. I'll silence me e'en here.
5   Pray you, be round with him.
Hamlet: *(Within)* Mother, mother, mother!
Queen: I'll warrant you:
    Fear me not:—withdraw, I hear him coming.

(Polonius goes behind the arras.)

(Enter Hamlet.)

Hamlet: Now, mother, what's the matter?
Queen: Hamlet, thou hast thy father much offended.
10 Hamlet: Mother, you have my father much offended.
Queen: Come, come, you answer with an idle tongue.
Hamlet: Go, go, you question with a wicked tongue.
Queen: Why, how now, Hamlet!
Hamlet: What's the matter now?
Queen: Have you forgot me?
Hamlet: No, by the rood, not so:

---

[5] *hent:* opportunity.

15 You are the queen, your husband's brother's wife;
  And,—would it were not so!—you are my mother.
 QUEEN: Nay, then, I'll set those to you that can speak.
 HAMLET: Come, come, and sit you down; you shall not budge;
  You go not till I set you up a glass
20 Where you may see the inmost part of you.
 QUEEN: What wilt thou do? thou wilt not murder me?—
  Help, help, ho!
 POLONIUS: *(Behind)* What, ho! help, help, help!
 Hamlet: How now! a rat? *(Draws)*
  Dead, for a ducat, dead! *(Makes a pass through the arras)*
25 POLONIUS: *(Behind)* O, I am slain! *(Falls and dies.)*
 QUEEN: O me, what hast thou done?
 HAMLET: Nay, I know not:
  Is it the king? *(Draws forth Polonius)*
 QUEEN: O, what a rash and bloody deed is this!
 HAMLET: A bloody deed!—almost as bad, good mother,
30 As kill a king and marry with his brother.
 QUEEN: As kill a king!
 HAMLET: Ay, lady, 'twas my word.—
  Thou wretched, rash, intruding fool, farewell! *(To Polonius)*
  I took thee for thy better: take thy fortune;
  Thou find'st to be too busy is some danger.—
35 Leave wringing of your hands: peace; sit you down,
  And let me wring your heart: for so I shall,
  If it be made of penetrable stuff;
  If damned custom have not braz'd it so
  That it is proof and bulwark against sense.
40 QUEEN: What have I done, that thou dar'st wag thy tongue
  In noise so rude against me?
 HAMLET: Such an act
  That blurs the grace and blush of modesty;
  Calls virtue hypocrite; takes off the rose
  From the fair forehead of an innocent love,
45 And sets a blister there; makes marriage-vows
  As false as dicers' oaths: O, such a deed
  As from the body of contraction plucks
  The very soul, and sweet religion makes
  A rhapsody of words: heaven's face doth glow;
50 Yea, this solidity and compound mass,
  With tristful[1] visage, as against the doom,
  Is thought-sick at the act.
 QUEEN: Ah me, what act,
  That roars so loud, and thunders in the index?
 HAMLET: Look here upon this picture and on this,—

---

[1] *tristful:* gloomy.

55   The counterfeit presentment of two brothers.
     See what grace was seated on this brow;
     Hyperion's curls; the front of Jove himself;
     An eye like Mars, to threaten and command;
     A station like the herald Mercury
60   New-lighted on a heaven-kissing hill;
     A combination and a form, indeed,
     Where every god did seem to set his seal,
     To give the world assurance of a man:
     This was your husband.—Look you now, what follows:
65   Here is your husband, like a mildew'd ear
     Blasting his wholesome brother. Have you eyes?
     Could you on this fair mountain leave to feed,
     And batten on this moor? Ha! have you eyes?
     You cannot call it love; for at your age
70   The hey-day in the blood is tame, it's humble,
     And waits upon the judgment: and what judgment
     Would step from this to this? Sense, sure, you have,
     Else could you not have motion: but sure that sense
     Is apoplex'd: for madness would not err;
75   Nor sense to ecstasy was ne'er so thrill'd
     But it reserv'd some quantity of choice
     To serve in such a difference. What devil was't
     That thus hath cozen'd you at hoodman-blind?[2]
     Eyes without feeling, feeling without sight,
80   Ears without hand or eyes, smelling sans all,
     Or but a sickly part of one true sense
     Could not so mope.
     O shame! where is thy blush! Rebellious hell,
     If thou canst mutine in a matron's bones,
85   To flaming youth let virtue be as wax,
     And melt in her own fire: proclaim no shame
     When the compulsive ardor gives the charge,
     Since frost itself as actively doth burn,
     And reason panders[3] will.

QUEEN: O Hamlet, speak no more:
90   Thou turn'st mine eyes into my very soul;
     And there I see such black and grained spots
     As will not leave their tinct.[4]

HAMLET: Nay, but to live
     In the rank sweat of an enseamed bed,
     Stew'd in corruption, honeying and making love

---

[2] *cozen'd . . . hoodman-blind:* tricked you at blindman's bluff.
[3] *panders:* becomes subservient to.
[4] *As . . . tinct:* as will not yield up their colour.

95   Over the nasty sty,—

QUEEN: O, speak to me no more;

These words like daggers enter in mine ears;

No more, sweet Hamlet.

HAMLET: A murderer and a villain;

A slave that is not twentieth part the tithe

Of your precedent lord; a vice of kings;[5]

100   A cutpurse of the empire and the rule,

That from a shelf the precious diadem stole,

And put it in his pocket!

QUEEN: No more.

HAMLET: A king of shreds and patches,—

(Enter Ghost.)

Save me, and hover o'er me with your wings,

105   You heavenly guards!—What would your gracious figure?

QUEEN: Alas, he's mad!

HAMLET: Do you not come your tardy son to chide,

That, laps'd in time and passion, lets go by

The important acting of your dread command?

110   O, say!

GHOST: Do not forget: this visitation

Is but to whet thy almost blunted purpose.

But, look, amazement on thy mother sits:

O, step between her and her fighting soul,—

115   Conceit in weakest bodies strongest works,—

Speak to her, Hamlet.

HAMLET: How is it with you, lady?

QUEEN: Alas, how is't with you,

That you do bend your eye on vacancy,

And with the incorporal air do hold discourse?

120   Forth at your eyes your spirits wildly peep;

And, as the sleeping soldiers in the alarm,

Your bedded hair, like life in excrements,[6]

Starts up and stands on end. O gentle son,

Upon the heat and flame of thy distemper

125   Sprinkle cool patience. Whereon do you look?

HAMLET: On him, on him! Look you, how pale he glares!

His form and cause conjoin'd, preaching to stones,

Would make them capable.—Do not look upon me;

Lest with this piteous action you convert

130   My stern effects: then what I have to do

Will want true color; tears perchance for blood.

---

[5] *a vice of kings:* a buffoon among kings; the "Vice" in morality plays.

[6] *excrements:* in outgrowths or extremities.

QUEEN: To whom do you speak this?

HAMLET: Do you see nothing there?

QUEEN: Nothing at all; yet all that is I see.

HAMLET: Nor did you nothing hear?

135   QUEEN: No, nothing but ourselves.

HAMLET: Why, look you there! look, how it steals away!

      My father, in his habit as he liv'd!

      Look, where he goes, even now, out at the portal!

(Exit Ghost.)

QUEEN: This is the very coinage of your brain:

140   This bodiless creation ecstasy

      Is very cunning in.

HAMLET: Ecstasy!

      My pulse, as yours, doth temperately keep time.

      And makes as healthful music: it is not madness

      That I have utter'd: bring me to the test,

145   And I the matter will re-word; which madness

      Would gambol from. Mother, for love of grace,

      Lay not that flattering unction to your soul,

      That not your trespass, but my madness speaks:

      It will but skin and film the ulcerous place,

150   Whilst rank corruption, mining all within,

      Infects unseen. Confess yourself to Heaven;

      Repent what's past; avoid what is to come;

      And do not spread the compost on the weeds,

      To make them ranker. Forgive me this my virtue;

155   For in the fatness[7] of these pursy times

      Virtue itself of vice must pardon beg,

      Yea, curb and woo for leave to do him good.

QUEEN: O Hamlet, thou hast cleft my heart in twain.

HAMLET: O, throw away the worser part of it,

160   And live the purer with the other half.

      Good-night: but go not to mine uncle's bed;

      Assume a virtue, if you have it not.

      That monster custom, who all sense doth eat,

      Of habits devil, is angel yet in this,—

165   That to the use of actions fair and good

      He likewise gives a frock or livery

      That aptly is put on. Refrain to-night;

      And that shall lend a kind of easiness

      To the next abstinence: the next more easy;

170   For use almost can change the stamp of nature,

      And either curb the devil, or throw him out

---

[7] *fatness:* corruption.

With wondrous potency. Once more, good-night:
And when you are desirous to be bless'd,
I'll blessing beg of you.—For this same lord *(Pointing to Polonius)*
175 I do repent: but Heaven hath pleas'd it so,
To punish me with this, and this with me,
That I must be their[8] scourge and minister.
I will bestow him, and will answer well
The death I gave him. So, again, good-night.—
180 I must be cruel only to be kind:
Thus bad begins and worse remains behind.—
One word more, good lady.

QUEEN: What shall I do?

HAMLET: Not this, by no means, that I bid you do:
Let the bloat king tempt you again to bed;
185 Pinch wanton on your cheek; call you his mouse;
And let him, for a pair of reechy kisses,
Or paddling in your neck with his damn'd fingers,
Make you to ravel all this matter out,
That I essentially am not in madness,
190 But mad in craft. 'Twere good you let him know;
For who that's but a queen, fair, sober, wise,
Would from a paddock,[9] from a bat, a gib,[10]
Such dear concernings hide? who would do so?
No, in despite of sense and secrecy,
195 Unpeg the basket on the house's top,
Let the birds fly, and, like the famous ape,
To try conclusions, in the basket creep,
And break your own neck down.

QUEEN: Be thou assur'd, if words be made of breath
200 And breath of life, I have not life to breathe
What thou hast said to me.

HAMLET: I must to England; you know that?

QUEEN: Alack,
I had forgot: 'tis so concluded on.

HAMLET: There's letters seal'd: and my two school-fellows,—
205 Whom I will trust as I will adders fang'd,
They bear the mandate; they must sweep my way,
And marshal me to knavery. Let it work;
For 'tis the sport to have the éngineer
Hoist with his own petard: and't shall go hard
210 But I will delve one yard below their mines,
And blow them at the moon: O, 'tis most sweet,
When in one line two crafts directly meet.—

---

[8] *their:* Heaven's, or the heavens'.
[9] *paddock:* toad.
[10] *gib:* tomcat.

This man shall set me packing:
I'll lug the guts into the neighbor room.—
215   Mother, good-night.—Indeed, this counsellor
Is now most still, most secret, and most grave,
Who was in life a foolish prating knave.
Come, sir, to draw toward an end with you:—
Good-night, mother.

(Exeunt severally; Hamlet dragging out Polonius.)

ACT IV
SCENE 1

A room in the castle.

(Enter King, Queen, Rosencrantz, and Guildenstern.)

KING: There's matter in these sighs, these prófound heaves:
    You must translate: 'tis fit we understand them.
    Where is your son?
QUEEN: Bestow this place on us a little while. *(To Rosencrantz and*
        Guildenstern, who go out)
5   Ah, my good lord, what have I seen to-night!
KING: What, Gertrude? How does Hamlet?
QUEEN: Mad as the sea and wind, when both contend
    Which is the mightier: in his lawless fit,
    Behind the arras hearing something stir,
10   He whips his rapier out, and cries, *A rat, a rat!*
    And, in this brainish apprehension,[1] kills
    The unseen good old man.
KING: O heavy deed!
    It had been so with us had we been there:
    His liberty is full of threats to all;
15   To you yourself, to us, to every one.
    Alas, how shall this bloody deed be answer'd?
    It will be laid to us, whose providence
    Should have kept short, restrain'd, and out of haunt
    This mad young man: but so much was our love,
20   We would not understand what was most fit;
    But, like the owner of a foul disease,
    To keep it from divulging, let it feed
    Even on the pith of life. Where is he gone?
QUEEN: To draw apart the body he hath kill'd:
25   O'er whom his very madness, like some ore
    Among a mineral of metals base,
    Shows itself pure; he weeps for what is done.

---

[1] *brainish apprehension:* mad notion.

KING: O Gertrude, come away!
    The sun no sooner shall the mountains touch
30   But we will ship him hence: and this vile deed
    We must, with all our majesty and skill,
    Both countenance and excuse.—Ho, Guildenstern!

(Enter Rosencrantz and Guildenstern.)

    Friends both, go join you with some further aid:
    Hamlet in madness hath Polonius slain,
35   And from his mother's closet hath he dragg'd him:
    Go seek him out; speak fair, and bring the body
    Into the chapel. I pray you, haste in this.

(Exeunt Rosencrantz and Guildenstern.)

    Come, Gertrude, we'll call up our wisest friends;
    And let them know both what we mean to do
40   And what's untimely done: so haply slander,—
    Whose whisper o'er the world's diameter,
    As level as the cannon to his blank,
    Transports his poison'd shot,—may amiss our name,
    And hit the woundless air.—O, come away!
45   My soul is full of discord and dismay.

(Exeunt.)

SCENE 2

Another room in the castle.

(Enter Hamlet.)

HAMLET: Safely stowed.
ROSENCRANTZ and GUILDENSTERN: *(Within)* Hamlet! Lord Hamlet!
HAMLET: What noise? who calls on Hamlet? O, here they come.

(Enter Rosencrantz and Guildenstern.)

ROSENCRANTZ: What have you done, my lord, with the dead body?
5 HAMLET: Compounded it with dust, whereto 'tis kin.
ROSENCRANTZ: Tell us where 'tis, that we may take it thence,
    And bear it to the chapel.
HAMLET: Do not believe it.
ROSENCRANTZ: Believe what?
10 HAMLET: That I can keep your counsel, and not mine own. Besides, to
    be demanded of a sponge!—what replication should be made by the
    son of a king?
ROSENCRANTZ: Take you me for a sponge, my lord?
HAMLET: Ay, sir; that soaks up the king's countenance, his rewards,
15   his authorities. But such officers do the king best service in the

end: he keeps them, like an ape, in the corner of his jaw; first
mouthed, to be last swallowed: when he needs what you have
gleaned, it is but squeezing you, and, sponge, you shall be dry
again.

20 ROSENCRANTZ: I understand you not, my lord.

HAMLET: I am glad of it: a knavish speech sleeps in a foolish ear.

ROSENCRANTZ: My lord, you must tell us where the body is, and go
with us to the king.

HAMLET: The body is with the king, but the king is not with the
25 body. The king is a thing,—

GUILDENSTERN: A thing, my lord!

HAMLET: Of nothing: bring me to him. Hide fox, and all after.

(Exeunt.)

SCENE 3

Another room in the castle.

(Enter King, attended.)

KING: I have sent to seek him, and to find the body.
How dangerous is it that this man goes loose!
Yet must not we put the strong law on him:
He's lov'd of the distracted multitude,
5 Who like not in their judgment, but their eyes;
And where 'tis so, the offender's scourge is weigh'd,
But never the offence. To bear all smooth and even,
This sudden sending him away must seem
Deliberate pause: diseases desperate grown
10 By desperate appliance are reliev'd,
Or not at all.

(Enter Rosencrantz.)

How now! what hath befallen!

ROSENCRANTZ: Where the dead body is bestow'd, my lord,
We cannot get from him.

KING: But where is he?

15 ROSENCRANTZ: Without, my lord; guarded, to know your pleasure.

KING: Bring him before us.

ROSENCRANTZ: Ho, Guildenstern! bring in my lord.

(Enter Hamlet and Guildenstern.)

KING: Now, Hamlet, where's Polonius?

HAMLET: At supper.

20 KING: At supper! where?

HAMLET: Not where he eats, but where he is eaten: a certain
convocation of politic worms are e'en at him. Your worm is your

only emperor for diet: we fat all creatures else to fat us, and we fat
ourselves for maggots: your fat king and your lean beggar is but
25   variable service,—two dishes, but to one table: that's the end.

KING: Alas, alas!

HAMLET: A man may fish with the worm that hath eat of a king, and
eat of the fish that hath fed of that worm.

KING: What does thou mean by this?

30 HAMLET: Nothing but to show you how a king may go a progress
    through the guts of a beggar.

KING: Where is Polonius?

HAMLET: In heaven; send thither to see: if your messenger find him
not there, seek him i' the other place yourself. But, indeed, if you
35   find him not within this month, you shall nose him as you go up
    the stairs into the lobby.

KING: Go seek him there. (*To some Attendants*)

HAMLET: He will stay till ye come.

(Exeunt Attendants.)

KING: Hamlet, this deed, for thine especial safety,—
40   Which we do tender, as we dearly grieve
    For that which thou hast done,—must send thee hence
    With fiery quickness: therefore prepare thyself;
    The bark is ready, and the wind at help,
    The associates tend, and everything is bent
45   For England.

HAMLET: For England!

KING: Ay, Hamlet.

HAMLET: Good.

KING: So is it, if thou knew'st our purposes.

HAMLET: I see a cherub that sees them.—But, come; for England!—
    Farewell, dear mother.

KING: Thy loving father, Hamlet.

50 HAMLET: My mother: father and mother is man and wife; man and
    wife is one flesh; and so, my mother.—Come, for England! *(Exit.)*

KING: Follow him at foot; tempt him with speed aboard;
    Delay it not; I'll have him hence to-night:
    Away! for everything is seal'd and done
55   That else leans on the affair, pray you, make haste.

(Exeunt Rosencrantz and Guildenstern.)

    And, England, if my love thou hold'st at aught,—
    As my great power thereof may give thee sense,
    Since yet thy cicatrice looks raw and red
    After the Danish sword, and thy free awe
60   Pays homage to us,—thou mayst not coldly set
    Our sovereign process; which imports at full,

By letters conjuring to that effect,
The present death of Hamlet. Do it, England;
For like the hectic in my blood he rages,
65 And thou must cure me: till I know 'tis done,
Howe'er my haps, my joys will ne'er begin. *(Exit.)*

Scene 4

A plain in Denmark.

(Enter Fortinbras, and Forces marching.)

FORTINBRAS: Go, from me greet the Danish king:
Tell him that, by his license, Fortinbras
Craves the conveyance of a promis'd march
Over his kingdom. You know the rendezvous,
5 If that his majesty would aught with us,
We shall express our duty in his eye,
And let him know so.
CAPTAIN: I will do't, my lord.
FORTINBRAS: Go softly on.

(Exeunt Fortinbras and Forces.)

(Enter Hamlet, Rosencrantz, Guildenstern, &c.)

HAMLET: Good sir, whose powers are these?
10 CAPTAIN: They are of Norway, sir.
HAMLET: How purpos'd, sir, I pray you?
CAPTAIN: Against some part of Poland.
HAMLET: Who commands them, sir?
CAPTAIN: The nephew to old Norway, Fortinbras.
15 HAMLET: Goes it against the main of Poland, sir,
Or for some frontier?
CAPTAIN: Truly to speak, and with no addition,
We go to gain a little patch of ground
That hath in it no profit but the name.
20 To pay five ducats, five, I would not farm it;
Nor will it yield to Norway or the Pole
A ranker[1] rate should it be sold in fee.
HAMLET: Why, then the Polack never will defend it.
CAPTAIN: Yes, it is already garrison'd.
25 HAMLET: Two thousand souls and twenty thousand ducats
Will not debate the question of this straw:
This is the imposthume[2] of much wealth and peace,
That inward breaks, and shows no cause without

---

[1] *ranker:* dearer.
[2] *imposthume:* ulcer.

Why the man dies.—I humbly thank you, sir.
30 CAPTAIN: God b' wi' you, sir. *(Exit.)*
ROSENCRANTZ: Will't please you go, my lord?
HAMLET: I'll be with you straight. Go a little before.

(Exeunt all but Hamlet.)

How all occasions do inform against me,
And spur my dull revenge! What is a man,
35 If his chief good and market of his time
Be but to sleep and feed? a beast, no more.
Sure he that made us with such large discourse,[3]
Looking before and after, gave us not
That capability and godlike reason
40 To fust[4] in us unus'd. Now, whether it be
Bestial oblivion or some craven scruple
Of thinking too precisely on the event,—
A thought which, quarter'd, hath but one part wisdom
And ever three parts coward,—I do not know
45 Why yet I live to say, *This thing's to do;*
Sith[5] I have cause, and will, and strength, and means
To do't. Examples, gross as earth, exhort me:
Witness this army, of such mass and charge,
Led by a delicate and tender prince;
50 Whose spirit, with divine ambition puff'd,
Makes mouths at the invisible event;
Exposing what is mortal and unsure
To all that fortune, death, and danger dare,
Even for an egg-shell. Rightly to be great
55 Is not to stir without great argument,
But greatly to find quarrel in a straw
When honor's at the stake. How stand I, then,
That have a father kill'd, a mother stain'd,
Excitements of my reason and my blood,
60 And let all sleep? while, to my shame, I see
The imminent death of twenty thousand men,
That, for a fantasy and trick of fame,
Go to their graves like beds; fight for a plot
Whereon the numbers cannot try the cause,
65 Which is not tomb enough and continent[6]
To hide the slain?—O, from this time forth,
My thoughts be bloody, or be nothing worth! *(Exit.)*

---

[3] *discourse:* reasoning faculty.
[4] *fust:* grow musty.
[5] *Sith:* since.
[6] *continent:* container.

SCENE 5

Elsinore. A room in the castle.

(Enter Queen and Horatio.)

QUEEN: I will not speak with her.
HORATIO: She is importunate; indeed, distract:
    Her mood will needs be pitied.
QUEEN: What would she have?
HORATIO: She speaks much of her father; says she hears
5   There's tricks i' the world; and hems, and beats her heart;
    Spurns enviously at straws; speaks things in doubt,
    That carry but half sense: her speech is nothing,
    Yet the unshapéd use of it doth move
    The hearers to collection; they aim at it,
10   And botch the words up fit to their own thoughts;
    Which, as her winks, and nods, and gestures yield them,
    Indeed would make one think there might be thought,
    Though nothing sure, yet much unhappily.
    'Twere good she were spoken with; for she may strew
15   Dangerous conjectures in ill-breeding minds.
QUEEN: Let her come in.

(Exit Horatio.)

    To my sick soul, as sin's true nature is,
    Each toy seems prologue to some great amiss:
    So full of artless jealousy is guilt,
20   It spills itself in fearing to be spilt.

(Re-enter Horatio and Ophelia.)

OPHELIA: Where is the beauteous majesty of Denmark?
QUEEN: How now, Ophelia!
OPHELIA: *(Sings)*

                How should I your true love know
                    From another one?
25   By his cockle hat and staff,
                    And his sandal shoon.

QUEEN: Alas, sweet lady, what imports this song?
OPHELIA: Say you? nay, pray you, mark.

(Sings)

                He is dead and gone, lady,
30   He is dead and gone;
                At his head a grass green turf,
                  At his heels a stone.

QUEEN: Nay, but, Ophelia,—

OPHELIA: Pray you, mark.

(Sings)

        White his shroud as the mountain snow,

(Enter King.)

35 QUEEN: Alas, look here, my lord.
OPHELIA: *(Sings)*

           Larded with sweet flowers;
           Which bewept to the grave did go
           With true-love showers.

KING: How do you, pretty lady?
40 OPHELIA: Well, God 'ild[1] you! They say the owl was a baker's daughter.
    Lord, we know what we are, but know not what we may be.
    God be at your table!
KING: Conceit upon her father.
OPHELIA: Pray you, let's have no words of this; but when they ask
45   you what it means, say you this:

(Sings)

         To-morrow is Saint Valentine's day
         All in the morning betime,
         And I a maid at your window,
         To be your Valentine.

50   Then up he rose, and donn'd his clothes,
         And dupp'd the chamber-door;
         Let in the maid, that out a maid
         Never departed more.

KING: Pretty Ophelia!
55 OPHELIA: Indeed, la, without an oath, I'll make an end on't;

(Sings)

         By Gis[2] and by Saint Charity,
         Alack, and fie for shame!
         Young men will do't, if they come to't;
         By cock, they are to blame.

60   Quoth she, before you tumbled me,
         You promis'd me to wed.
         So would I ha' done, by yonder sun,
         An thou hadst not come to my bed.

KING: How long hath she been thus?

---

[1] *'ild:* yield you—that is, reward you.
[2] *By Gis:* a contraction for "by Jesus."

65 OPHELIA: I hope all will be well. We must be patient: but I cannot
choose but weep, to think they should lay him i' the cold ground.
My brother shall know of it: and so I thank you; for your good
counsel.—Come, my coach!—Good-night, ladies; good-night,
sweet ladies; good-night, good-night. *(Exit.)*
70 KING: Follow her close; give her good watch, I pray you.

(Exit Horatio.)

O, this is the poison of deep grief; it springs
All from her father's death. O Gertrude, Gertrude,
When sorrows come, they come not single spies,
But in battalions! First, her father slain:
75 Next, your son gone; and he most violent author
Of his own just remove: the people muddied,
Thick and unwholesome in their thoughts and whispers
For good Polonius' death; and we have done but greenly
In hugger-mugger[3] to inter him: poor Ophelia
80 Divided from herself and her fair judgment,
Without the which we are pictures, or mere beasts:
Last, and as much containing as all these,
Her brother is in secret come from France;
Feeds on his wonder, keeps himself in clouds,
85 And wants not buzzers to infect his ear
With pestilent speeches of his father's death;
Wherein necessity, of matter beggar'd,
Will nothing stick our person to arraign
In ear and ear. O my dear Gertrude, this,
90 Like to a murdering piece,[4] in many places
Gives me superfluous death.

(A noise within.)

QUEEN: Alack, what noise is this?
KING: Where are my Switzers?[5] let them guard the door.

(Enter a Gentleman.)

What is the matter?
GENTLEMAN: Save yourself, my lord:
The ocean, overpeering of his list,
95 Eats not the flats with more impetuous haste
Than young Laertes, in a riotous head,
O'erbears your officers. The rabble call him lord;
And, as the world were now but to begin,

---

[3] *In hugger-mugger:* in great secrecy and haste.

[4] *piece:* a cannon.

[5] *Switzers:* bodyguard of Swiss mercenaries.

Antiquity forgot, custom not known,
100 The ratifiers and props of every word,
They cry, *Choose we, Laertes shall be king!*
Caps, hands, and tongues applaud it to the clouds,
Laertes shall be king, Laertes king!
QUEEN: How cheerfully on the false trail they cry!
105 O, this is counter, you false Danish dogs!
KING: The doors are broke.

(Noise within.)

(Enter Laertes armed; Danes following.)

LAERTES: Where is this king?—Sirs, stand you all without.
DANES: No, let's come in.
LAERTES: I pray you, give me leave.
DANES: We will, we will. *(They retire without the door.)*
110 LAERTES: I thank you:—keep the door.—O thou vile king,
Give me my father!
QUEEN: Calmly, good Laertes.
LAERTES: That drop of blood that's calm proclaims me bastard;
Cries cuckold to my father; brands the harlot
Even here, between the chaste unsmirched brow
115 Of my true mother.
KING: What is the cause, Laertes,
That thy rebellion looks so giant-like?—
Let him go, Gertrude; do not fear our person:
There's such divinity doth hedge a king,
That treason can but peep to what it would,
120 Acts little of his will.—Tell me, Laertes,
Why thou art thus incens'd.—Let him go, Gertrude:—
Speak, man.
LAERTES: Where is my father?
KING: Dead.
QUEEN: But not by him.
KING: Let him demand his fill.
125 LAERTES: How came he dead? I'll not be juggled with:
To hell, allegiance! vows, to the blackest devil!
Conscience and grace, to the profoundest pit!
I dare damnation:—to this point I stand,—
That both the worlds I give to negligence,
130 Let come what comes; only I'll be reveng'd
Most thoroughly for my father.
KING: Who shall stay you?
LAERTES: My will, not all the world:
And for my means, I'll husband them so well,
They shall go far with little.
KING: Good Laertes,

135   If you desire to know the certainty
      Of your dear father's death, is't writ in your revenge
      That, sweepstake, you will draw both friend and foe,
      Winner or loser?
    LAERTES: None but his enemies.
    KING: Will you know them, then?
140   LAERTES: To his good friends thus wide I'll ope my arms;
      And, like the kind life-rendering pelican,[6]
      Repast them with my blood.
    KING: Why, now you speak
      Like a good child and a true gentleman.
      That I am guiltless of your father's death,
145   And am most sensible in grief for it,
      It shall as level to your judgment pierce
      As day does to your eye.
    DANES: *(Within)*   Let her come in.
    LAERTES: How now! what noise is that?

(Re-enter Ophelia, fantastically dressed with straws and flowers.)

      O heat, dry up my brains! tears seven times salt
150   Burn out the sense and virtue of mine eyes!—
      By heaven, thy madness shall be paid by weight
      Till our scale turn the beam. O rose of May!
      Dear maid, kind sister, sweet Ophelia!—
      O heavens! is't possible a young maid's wits
155   Should be as mortal as an old man's life!
      Nature is fine in love; and where 'tis fine
      It sends some precious instance of itself
      After the thing it loves.
    OPHELIA: *(Sings)*
                 They bore him barefac'd on the bier;
160   Hey no nonny, nonny, hey nonny;
                And on his grave rain'd many a tear,—
                Fare you well, my dove!

    LAERTES: Hadst thou thy wits, and didst persuade revenge,
      It could not move thus.
165   OPHELIA: You must sing, *Down-a-down, an you call him a-down-a.* O,
      how the wheel becomes it! It is the false steward, that stole his
      master's daughter.
    LAERTES: This nothing's more than matter.
    OPHELIA: There's rosemary, that's for remembrance; pray, love,
170   remember: and there is pansies that's for thoughts.
    LAERTES: A document in madness,—thoughts and remembrance fitted.
    OPHELIA: There's fennel for you, and columbines:—there's rue for

---

[6] *life-rendering pelican:* the pelican mother was believed to draw blood from itself to feed its young.

you; and here's some for me:—we may call it herb-grace o' Sundays:—
O, you must wear your rue with a difference.—There's a
175 daisy:—I would give you some violets, but they withered all when
my father died:—they say, he made a good end,—

(Sings)

For bonny sweet Robin is all my joy,—

LAERTES: Thoughts and affliction, passion, hell itself,
She turns to favor and to prettiness.

OPHELIA: *(Sings)*

180 And will he not come again?
And will he not come again?
No, no, he is dead,
Go to thy death-bed,
He never will come again.

185 His beard was as white as snow
All flaxen was his poll:
He is gone, he is gone,
And we cast away moan:
God ha' mercy on his soul!

190 And of all Christian souls, I pray God.—God b' wi' ye. *(Exit.)*

LAERTES: Do you see this, O God?

KING: Laertes, I must commune with your grief,
Or you deny me right. Go but apart,
Make choice of whom your wisest friends you will,
195 And they shall hear and judge 'twixt you and me:
If by direct or by collateral hand
They find us touch'd, we will our kingdom give,
Our crown, our life, and all that we call ours,
To you in satisfaction; but if not,
200 Be you content to lend your patience to us,
And we shall jointly labor with your soul
To give it due content.

LAERTES: Let this be so;
His means of death, his obscure burial,—
No trophy, sword, nor hatchment[7] o'er his bones
205 No noble rite nor formal ostentation,—
Cry to be heard, as 'twere from heaven to earth,
That I must call't in question.

KING: So you shall;
And where the offence is, let the great axe fall.
I pray you, go with me.

(Exeunt.)

---

[7] *hatchment*: a tablet with coat of arms.

SCENE 6

Another room in the castle.

(Enter Horatio and a Servant.)

HORATIO: What are they that would speak with me?
SERVANT: Sailors, sir: they say they have letters for you.
HORATIO: Let them come in.—

(Exit Servant.)

> I do not know from what part of the world
5 > I should be greeted, if not from Lord Hamlet.

(Enter Sailors.)

1ST SAILOR: God bless you, sir.
HORATIO: Let him bless thee too.
1ST SAILOR: He shall, sir, an't please him. There's a letter for you, sir;
  it comes from the ambassador that was bound for England; if your
10 name be Horatio, as I am let to know it is.
HORATIO: *(Reads) Horatio, when thou shalt have overlooked this, give these*
  fellows some means to the king: they have letters for him. Ere we were
  two days old at sea, a pirate of very warlike appointment gave us chase.
  Finding ourselves too slow of sail, we put on a compelled valor; and in
15 *the grapple I boarded them; on the instant they got clear of our ship; so I*
  alone became their prisoner. They have dealt with me like thieves of
  mercy: but they knew what they did; I am to do a good turn for them.
  Let the king have the letters I have sent; and repair thou to me with as
  much haste as thou wouldst fly death. I have words to speak in thine ear
20 *will make thee dumb; yet are they much too light for the bore of the*
  matter. These good fellows will bring thee where I am. Rosencrantz and
  Guildenstern hold their course for England: of them I have much to tell
  thee. Farewell. He that thou knowest thine. Hamlet
  Come, I will give you way for these your letters;
25 And do't the speedier, that you may direct me
  To him from whom you brought them.

(Exeunt.)

SCENE 7

Another room in the castle.

(Enter King and Laertes.)

KING: Now must your conscience my acquittance seal,
  And you must put me in your heart for friend,
  Sith you have heard, and with a knowing ear,
  That he which hath your noble father slain
5 Pursu'd my life.
LAERTES: It well appears:—but tell me

Why you proceeded not against these feats,
So crimeful and so capital in nature.
As by your safety, wisdom, all things else,
You mainly were stirr'd up.

KING: O, for two special reasons;
10   Which may to you, perhaps, seem much unsinew'd,
But yet to me they are strong. The queen his mother
Lives almost by his looks; and for myself,—
My virtue or my plague, be it either which,—
She's so conjunctive to my life and soul,
15   That, as the star moves not but in his sphere,
I could not but by her. The other motive,
Why to a public count I might not go,
Is the great love the general gender bear him;
Who, dipping all his faults in their affection,
20   Would, like the spring that turneth wood to stone,
Convert his gyves to graces; so that my arrows,
Too slightly timber'd for so loud a wind,
Would have reverted to my bow again,
And not where I had aim'd them.
25 LAERTES: And so have I a noble father lost;
A sister driven into desperate terms,—
Whose worth, if praises may go back again,
Stood challenger on mount of all the age
For her perfections:—but my revenge will come.
30 KING: Break not your sleeps for that: you must not think
That we are made of stuff so flat and dull
That we can let our beard be shook with danger,
And think it pastime. You shortly shall hear more:
I lov'd your father, and we love ourself;
35   And that, I hope, will teach you to imagine,—

(Enter a Messenger.)

How now! what news?
MESSENGER: Letters, my lord, from Hamlet:
This to your majesty; this to the queen.
KING: From Hamlet! Who brought them?
MESSENGER: Sailors, my lord, they say; I saw them not:
40   They were given me by Claudio,—he receiv'd them
Of him that brought them.
KING: Laertes, you shall hear them.—Leave us.

(Exit Messenger.)

*(Reads) High and mighty,—You shall know I am set naked on your
kingdom. To-morrow shall I beg leave to see your kingly eyes: when I shall,
45   first asking your pardon thereunto, recount the occasions of my sudden
and more strange return.*
                                                                    Hamlet

What should this mean? Are all the rest come back?
Or is it some abuse,[1] and no such thing?
LAERTES: Know you the hand?
50 KING: 'Tis Hamlet's character:[2]—*Naked,*—
And in a postscript here, he says, *alone.*
Can you advise me?
LAERTES: I am lost in it, my lord. But let him come;
It warms the very sickness in my heart,
55 That I shall live, and tell him to his teeth,
Thus diddest thou.
KING: If it be so, Laertes,—
As how should it be so? how otherwise?—
Will you be rul'd by me?
LAERTES: Ay, my lord:
So you will not o'errule me to a peace.
60 KING: To thine own peace. If he be now return'd,—
As checking at his voyage, and that he means
No more to undertake it,—I will work him
To an exploit, now ripe in my device,
Under the which he shall not choose but fall:
65 And for his death no wind of blame shall breathe;
But even his mother shall uncharge the practice
And call it accident.
LAERTES: My lord, I will be rul'd;
The rather if you could devise it so
That I might be the organ.
KING: It falls right.
70 You have been talk'd of since your travel much,
And that in Hamlet's hearing, for a quality
Wherein they say you shine: your sum of parts
Did not together pluck such envy from him
As did that one; and that, in my regard,
75 Of the unworthiest siege.
LAERTES: What part is that, my lord?
KING: A very riband in the cap of youth,
Yet needful too; for youth no less becomes
The light and careless livery that it wears
Than settled age his sables and his weeds,
80 Importing health and graveness.—Two months since,
Here was a gentleman of Normandy,—
I've seen myself, and serv'd against, the French,
And they can well on horseback: but this gallant
Had witchcraft in't; he grew unto his seat;

---

[1] *abuse:* ruse.
[2] *character:* handwriting.

85 And to such wondrous doing brought his horse,
As he had been incorps'd and demi-natur'd[3]
With the brave beast: so far he topp'd my thought,
That I, in forgery of shapes and tricks,[4]
Come short of what he did.
LAERTES: A Norman was't?
90 KING: A Norman.
LAERTES: Upon my life, Lamond.
KING: The very same.
LAERTES: I know him well: he is the brooch, indeed,
And gem of all the nation.
KING: He made confession of you;
95 And gave you such a masterly report
For art and exercise in your defence,
And for your rapier most especially,
That he cried out, 'twould be a sight indeed
If one could match you: the scrimers[5] of their nation,
100 He swore, had neither motion, guard, nor eye,
If you oppos'd them. Sir, this report of his
Did Hamlet so envenom with his envy,
That he could nothing do but wish and beg
Your sudden coming o'er, to play with him.
105 Now, out of this,—
LAERTES: What out of this, my lord?
KING: Laertes, was your father dear to you?
Or are you like the painting of a sorrow,
A face without a heart?
LAERTES: Why ask you this?
KING: Not that I think you did not love your father;
110 But that I know love is begun by time;
And that I see, in passages of proof,[6]
Time qualifies the spark and fire of it.
There lives within the very flame of love
A kind of wick or snuff that will abate it;
115 And nothing is at a like goodness still;
For goodness, growing to a pleurisy,[7]
Dies in his own too much: that we would do
We should do when we would; for this *would* changes,
And hath abatements and delays as many
120 As there are tongues, or hands, or accidents;

---

[3] *incorps'd and demi-natur'd:* made as one body and formed into half man, half horse—or centaur.
[4] *in . . . tricks:* in imagining tricks of horsemanship.
[5] *scrimers:* fencers.
[6] *passages of proof:* the evidence of experience.
[7] *pleurisy:* plethora, an excess of blood.

And then this *should* is like a spendthrift sigh
That hurts by easing. But to the quick o' the ulcer:
Hamlet comes back: what would you undertake
To show yourself your father's son in deed
125 More than in words?

LAERTES: To cut his throat i' the church.

KING: No place, indeed, should murder sanctuarize;
Revenge should have no bounds. But, good Laertes,
Will you do this, keep close within your chamber.
Hamlet return'd shall know you are come home:
130 We'll put on those shall praise your excellence,
And set a double varnish on the fame
The Frenchman gave you; bring you, in fine, together,
And wager on your heads: he, being remiss,[8]
Most generous, and free from all contriving,
135 Will not peruse the foils; so that, with ease,
Or with a little shuffling, you may choose
A sword unbated, and, in a pass of practice,
Requite him for your father.

LAERTES: I will do't it:
And, for that purpose, I'll anoint my sword.
140 I bought an unction of a mountebank,
So mortal that but dip a knife in it,
Where it draws blood no cataplasm so rare,[9]
Collected from all simples that have virtue
Under the moon, can save the thing from death
145 That is but scratch'd withal: I'll touch my point
With this contagion, that, if I gall him slightly,
It may be death.

KING: Let's further think of this;
Weigh what convenience both of time and means
May fit us to our shape: if this should fail,
150 And that our drift look through our bad performance,
'Twere better not assay'd: therefore this project
Should have a back or second, that might hold
If this should blast in proof. Soft! let me see:—
We'll make a solemn wager on your cunnings,—
155 I ha't:
When in your motion you are hot and dry,—
As make your bouts more violent to that end,—
And that he calls for drink, I'll have prepar'd him
A chalice for the nonce;[10] whereon but sipping,
160 If he by chance escape your venom'd stuck
Our purpose may hold there.

---

[8] *remiss:* unguarded and free from suspicion.
[9] *Where . . . rare:* no poultice, however remarkably efficacious.
[10] *nonce:* purpose.

(Enter Queen.)

How now, sweet queen!

QUEEN: One woe doth tread upon another's heel,
So fast they follow:—your sister's drown'd, Laertes.

LAERTES: Drown'd! O, where?

165 QUEEN: There is a willow grows aslant a brook,
That shows his hoar leaves in the glassy stream;
There with fantastic garlands did she come
Of crowflowers, nettles, daisies, and long purples,
That liberal shepherds give a grosser name,
170 But our cold maids do dead men's fingers call them.
There, on the pendant boughs her coronet weeds
Clambering to hang, an envious[11] sliver broke;
When down her weedy trophies and herself
Fell in the weeping brook. Her clothes spread wide;
175 And, mermaid-like, awhile they bore her up:
Which time she chanted snatches of old tunes;
As one incapable of her own distress,
Or like a creature native and indu'd
Unto that element: but long it could not be
180 Till that her garments, heavy with their drink,
Pull'd the poor wretch from her melodious lay
To muddy death.

LAERTES: Alas, then, she is drown'd?

QUEEN: Drown'd, drown'd.

LAERTES: Too much of water hast thou, poor Ophelia,
185 And therefore I forbid my tears: but yet
It is our trick; nature her custom holds,
Let shame say what it will: when these are gone,
The woman will be out.[12]—Adieu, my lord:
I have a speech of fire, that fain would blaze,
190 But that this folly douts it.[13] *(Exit.)*

KING: Let's follow, Gertrude;
How much I had to do to calm his rage!
Now fear I this will give it start again;
Therefore let's follow.

(Exeunt.)

---

[11] *envious:* malicious.
[12] *The . . . out:* that is, "I shall be ruthless."
[13] *douts it:* drowns it.

ACT V

SCENE 1

A churchyard.

(Enter two Clowns[1] with spades, &c.)

1ST CLOWN: Is she to be buried in Christian burial that wilfully seeks her own salvation?

2ND CLOWN: I tell thee she is; and therefore make her grave straight: the crowner[2] hath sat on her, and finds it Christian burial.

5 1ST CLOWN: How can that be, unless she drowned herself in her own defence?

2ND CLOWN: Why, 'tis found so.

1ST CLOWN: It must be *se offendendo*,[3] it cannot be else. For here lies the point: if I drown myself wittingly, it argues an act: and an act

10 hath three branches; it is to act, to do, and to perform: argal,[4] she drowned herself wittingly.

2ND CLOWN: Nay, but hear you, goodman delver,—

1ST CLOWN: Give me leave. Here lies the water; good: here stands the man; good: if the man go to this water and drown himself, it is,

15 will he, nill he, he goes,—mark you that: but if the water come to him and drown him, he drowns not himself: argal, he that is not guilty of his own death shortens not his own life.

2ND CLOWN: But is this law?

1ST CLOWN: Ay, marry, is't; crowner's quest law.

20 2ND CLOWN: Will you ha' the truth on't? If this had not been a gentlewoman she should have been buried out of Christian burial.

1ST CLOWN: Why, there thou say'st: and the more pity that great folks should have countenance in this world to drown or hang themselves more than their even-Christian.[5]—Come, my spade. There is

25 no ancient gentlemen but gardeners, ditchers, and grave-makers; they hold up Adam's profession.

2ND CLOWN: Was he a gentleman?

1ST CLOWN: He was the first that ever bore arms.

2ND CLOWN: Why, he had none.

30 1ST CLOWN: What, art a heathen? How dost thou understand the Scripture? The Scripture says, Adam digged: could he dig without arms? I'll put another question to thee: if thou answerest me not to the purpose, confess thyself,[6]—

2ND CLOWN: Go to.

---

[1] *Clowns:* rustic fellows.

[2] *crowner:* coroner.

[3] *se offendendo:* in self-offence; he means *se defendendo*, in self-defence.

[4] *argal:* he means *ergo*, therefore.

[5] *even-Christian:* fellow Christian.

[6] *confess thyself:* "Confess thyself an ass," perhaps.

35 1ST CLOWN: What is he that builds stronger than either the mason,
the shipwright, or the carpenter?

2ND CLOWN: The gallows-maker; for that frame outlives a thousand
tenants.

1ST CLOWN: I like thy wit well, in good faith: the gallows does well;
40 but how does it well? it does well to those that do ill: now thou
dost ill to say the gallows is built stronger than the church: argal,
the gallows may do well to thee. To't again, come.

2ND CLOWN: Who builds stronger than a mason, a shipwright, or a
carpenter?

45 1ST CLOWN: Ay, tell me that, and unyoke.

2ND CLOWN: Marry, now I can tell.

1ST CLOWN: To't.

2ND CLOWN: Mass, I cannot tell.

(Enter Hamlet and Horatio, at a distance.)

1ST CLOWN: Cudgel thy brains no more about it, for your dull ass will
50 not mend his pace with beating; and when you are asked this
question next, say a grave-maker; the houses that he makes last till
doomsday. Go, get thee to Yaughan: fetch me a stoup of liquor.

(Exit Second Clown.)

(Digs and sings.)

> In youth, when I did love, did love,
> Methought it was very sweet,
55 > To contract, O, the time, for, ah, my behove,[7]
> O, methought there was nothing meet.

HAMLET: Has this fellow no feeling of his business, that he sings at
grave-making?

HORATIO: Custom hath made it in him a property of easiness.

60 HAMLET: 'Tis e'en so: the hand of little employment hath the daintier
sense.

1ST CLOWN: *(Sings)*

> But age, with his stealing steps,
> Hath claw'd me in his clutch,
> And hath shipp'd me intil the land,
65 > As if I had never been such.

(Throws up a skull)

HAMLET: That skull had a tongue in it, and could sing once: how the
knave joels[8] it to the ground, as if it were Cain's jawbone, that did
the first murder! This might be the pate of a politician, which this
ass now o'erreaches; one that would circumvent God, might it not?

---

[7] *behove:* behoof, or advantage.
[8] *joels:* throws.

70 HORATIO: It might, my lord.

HAMLET: Or of a courtier; which could say, *Good-morrow, sweet lord!*
How dost thou, good lord? This might be my lord such-a-one, that
praised my lord such-a-one's horse, when he meant to beg it,—
might it not?

75 HORATIO: Ay, my lord.

HAMLET: Why, e'en so: and now my Lady Worm's; chapless,[9] and
knocked about the mazard[10] with a sexton's spade: here's fine
revolution, an we had the trick to see't. Did these bones cost no
more the breeding but to play at loggats[11] with 'em? Mine ache
80 to think on't.

1ST CLOWN: *(Sings)*

A pick-axe and a spade, a spade,
For and a shrouding sheet:
O, a pit of clay for to be made
For such a guest is meet.

(Throws up another.)

85 HAMLET: There's another: why may not that be the skull of a lawyer?
Where be his quiddits[12] now, his quillets,[13] his cases, his tenures,
and his tricks? why does he suffer this rude knave now to knock
him about the sconce with a dirty shovel, and will not tell him of
his action of battery? Hum! This fellow might be in's time a great
90 buyer of land, with his statutes, his recognizances, his fines, his
double vouchers, his recoveries: is this the fine of his fines, and the
recovery of his recoveries, to have his fine pate full of fine dirt?
will his vouchers vouch him no more of his purchases, and double
ones too, than the length and breadth of a pair of indentures? The
95 very conveyances of his lands will hardly lie in this box; and must
the inheritor himself have no more, ha?

HORATIO: Not a jot more, my lord.

HAMLET: Is not parchment made of sheep-skins?

HORATIO: Ay, my lord, and of calf-skins too.

100 HAMLET: They are sheep and calves which seek out assurance in that.
I will speak to this fellow.—Whose grave's this, sir?

1ST CLOWN: Mine, sir.—*(Sings)*

O, a pit of clay for to be made
For such a guest is meet.

105 HAMLET: I think it be thine indeed; for thou liest in't.

1ST CLOWN: You lie out on't, sir, and therefore it is not yours: for my
part, I do not lie in't, and yet it is mine.

---

[9] *chapless:* without a lower jaw.
[10] *mazard:* head.
[11] *loggats:* a game in which small pieces of wood are hurled at a stake.
[12] *quiddits:* "whatnesses"—that is, hair-splittings.
[13] *quillets:* quibbling distinctions.

HAMLET: Thou dost lie in't, to be in't, and say it is thine: 'tis for the
    dead, not for the quick; therefore thou liest.

110 1ST CLOWN: 'Tis a quick lie, sir: 'twill away again from me to you.

HAMLET: What man dost thou dig it for?

1ST CLOWN: For no man, sir.

HAMLET: What woman, then?

1ST CLOWN: For none, neither.

115 HAMLET: Who is to be buried in't?

1ST CLOWN: One that was a woman, sir; but, rest her soul, she's dead.

HAMLET: How absolute the knave is! we must speak by the card, or
    equivocation will undo us. By the Lord, Horatio, these three years I
    have taken note of it; the age is grown so picked[14] that the toe of
120   the peasant comes so near the heel of the courtier, he galls his
    kibe.[15]—How long hast thou been a grave-maker?

1ST CLOWN: Of all the days i' the year, I came to't that day that our
    last King Hamlet o'ercame Fortinbras.

HAMLET: How long is that since?

125 1ST CLOWN: Cannot you tell that? every fool can tell that: it was the
    very day that young Hamlet was born,—he that is mad, and sent
    into England.

HAMLET: Ay, marry, why was he sent into England?

1ST CLOWN: Why, because he was mad: he shall recover his wits there;
130   or, if he do not, it's no great matter there.

HAMLET: Why?

1ST CLOWN: 'Twill not be seen in him there; there the men are as mad
    as he.

HAMLET: How came he mad?

135 1ST CLOWN: Very strangely, they say.

HAMLET: How strangely?

1ST CLOWN: Faith, e'en with losing his wits.

HAMLET: Upon what ground?

1ST CLOWN: Why, here in Denmark: I have been sexton here, man
140   and boy, thirty years.

HAMLET: How long will a man lie i' the earth ere he rot?

1ST CLOWN: Faith, if he be not rotten before he die,—as we have many
    pocky corses now-a-days, that will scarce hold the laying in,—he
    will last you some eight year or nine year: a tanner will last you nine
145   year.

HAMLET: Why he more than another?

1ST CLOWN: Why, sir, his hide is so tanned with his trade that he will
    keep out water a great while; and your water is a sore decayer of
    your whoreson dead body. Here's a skull now; this skull has lain in
150   the earth three-and-twenty years.

---

[14] *picked:* refined or educated.

[15] *he . . . kibe:* rubs and irritates the chilblain sore on the courtier's heel.

HAMLET: Whose was it?

1ST CLOWN: A whoreson mad fellow's it was: whose do you think
it was?

HAMLET: Nay, I know not.

155 1ST CLOWN: A pestilence on him for a mad rogue! 'a poured a flagon
of Rhenish on my head once. This same skull, sir, was Yorick's
skull, the king's jester.

HAMLET: This?

1ST CLOWN: E'en that.

160 HAMLET: Let me see. *(Takes the skull)*—Alas, poor Yorick!—I knew
him, Horatio; a fellow of infinite jest, of most excellent fancy: he
hath borne me on his back a thousand times; and now, how abhorred
in my imagination it is! my gorge rises at it. Here hung
those lips that I have kissed I know not how oft. Where be your
165 gibes now? your gambols? your songs? your flashes of merriment,
that were wont to set the table on a roar? Not one now, to mock
your own grinning? quite chap-fallen? Now get you to my lady's
chamber, and tell her, let her paint an inch thick, to this favor[16]
she must come; make her laugh at that.—Pr'ythee, Horatio, tell me
170 one thing.

HORATIO: What's that, my lord?

HAMLET: Dost thou think Alexander looked o' this fashion i' the earth?

HORATIO: E'en so.

HAMLET: And smelt so? pah! *(Throws down the skull)*

175 HORATIO: E'en so, my lord.

HAMLET: To what base uses we may return, Horatio! Why may not
imagination trace the noble dust of Alexander till he find it stopping
a bung-hole?

HORATIO: 'Twere to consider too curiously to consider so.

180 HAMLET: No, faith, not a jot; but to follow him thither with modesty
enough, and likelihood to lead it: as thus; Alexander died, Alexander
was buried, Alexander returneth into dust; the dust is earth; of earth
we make loam; and why of that loam whereto he was converted
might they not stop a beer-barrel?

185   Imperious Caesar, dead and turn'd to clay,
          Might stop a hole to keep the wind away:
        O, that that earth which kept the world in awe
          Should patch a wall to expel the winter's flaw!—

But soft! but soft! aside.—Here comes the king.

*(Enter Priests, &c., in procession; the corpse of Ophelia, Laertes and Mourners fol-
lowing; King, Queen, their Trains, &c.)*

190 The queen, the courtiers: who is that they follow?
And with such maimed rites? This doth betoken

---

[16] *favor:* face.

The corse they follow did with desperate hand
Fordo its own life: 'twas of some estate.
Couch we awhile and mark. *(Retiring with Horatio)*
195 LAERTES: What ceremony else?
HAMLET: That is Laertes,
A very noble youth: mark.
LAERTES: What ceremony else?
1ST PRIEST: Her obsequies have been as far enlarg'd
As we have warrantise: her death was doubtful,
200 And, but that great command o'ersways the order,
She should in ground unsanctified have lodg'd
Till the last trumpet; for charitable prayers,
Shards, flints, and pebbles, should be thrown on her,
Yet here she is allowed her virgin rites,
205 Her maiden strewments, and the bringing home
Of bell and burial.
LAERTES: Must there no more be done?
1ST PRIEST: No more be done:
We should profane the service of the dead
To sing a *requiem,* and such rest to her
210 As to peace-parted souls.
LAERTES: Lay her i' the earth;—
And from her fair and unpolluted flesh
May violets spring!—I tell thee, churlish priest,
A ministering angel shall my sister be
When thou liest howling.
HAMLET: What, the fair Ophelia!
215 QUEEN: Sweets to the sweet: farewell! *(Scattering flowers)*
I hop'd thou shouldst have been my Hamlet's wife;
I thought thy bride-bed to have deck'd, sweet maid,
And not have strew'd thy grave.
LAERTES: O, treble woe
Fall ten times treble on that cursed head
220 Whose wicked deed thy most ingenious sense
Depriv'd thee of!—Hold off the earth awhile,
Till I have caught her once more in mine arms:

(Leaps into the grave.)

Now pile your dust upon the quick and dead,
Till of this flat a mountain you have made,
225 To o'er-top old Pelion[17] or the skyish head
Of blue Olympus.
HAMLET: *(Advancing)* What is he whose grief
Bears such an emphasis? whose phrase of sorrow

---

[17] *Pelion:* a mountain in Greece.

Conjures the wandering stars, and makes them stand
230   Like wonder-wounded hearers? this is I, Hamlet the
Dane. *(Leaps into the grave)*
LAERTES: The devil take thy soul! *(Grappling with him)*
HAMLET: Thou pray'st not well.
I pr'ythee, take thy fingers from my throat;
235   For, though I am not splenitive[18] and rash,
Yet have I in me something dangerous,
Which let thy wiseness fear: away thy hand.
KING: Pluck them asunder.
QUEEN: Hamlet! Hamlet!
ALL: Gentlemen,—
HORATIO: Good my lord, be quiet.

(The Attendants part them, and they come out of the grave.)

240 HAMLET: Why, I will fight with him upon this theme
Until my eyelids will no longer wag.
QUEEN: O my son, what theme?
HAMLET: I lov'd Ophelia; forty thousand brothers
Could not, with all their quantity of love,
245   Make up my sum.—What wilt thou do for her?
KING: O, he is mad, Laertes.
QUEEN: For love of God, forbear him.
HAMLET: 'Swounds, show me what thou'lt do:
Woul't weep? woul't fight? woul't fast? woul't tear thyself?
250   Woul't drink up eisel?[19] eat a crocodile?
I'll do't.—Dost thou come here to whine?
To outface me with leaping in her grave?
Be buried quick[20] with her, and so will I:
And, if thou prate of mountains, let them throw
255   Millions of acres on us, till our ground,
Singeing his pate against the burning zone,[21]
Make Ossa[22] like a wart! Nay, an thou'lt mouth,
I'll rant as well as thou.
QUEEN: This is mere madness:
And thus awhile the fit will work on him;
260   Anon, as patient as the female dove,
When that her golden couplets are disclos'd,[23]
His silence will sit drooping.
HAMLET: Hear you, sir;

---

[18] *splenitive:* hot-tempered.
[19] *eisel:* vinegar.
[20] *quick:* alive.
[21] *burning zone:* the fiery zone of the celestial sphere.
[22] *Ossa:* a high mountain in Greece.
[23] *golden . . . disclos'd:* when the golden twins are hatched.

What is the reason that you use me thus?
I lov'd you ever: but it is no matter;
265   Let Hercules himself do what he may,
The cat will mew, and dog will have his day. *(Exit.)*
KING: I pray thee, good Horatio, wait upon him.—

(Exit Horatio.)

(To Laertes) Strengthen your patience in our last night's speech;
We'll put the matter to the present push.—
270   Good Gertrude, set some watch over your son.—
This grave shall have a living monument:
An hour of quiet shortly shall we see;
Till then, in patience our proceeding be.

(Exeunt.)

SCENE 2

A hall in the castle.

(Enter Hamlet and Horatio.)

HAMLET: So much for this, sir: now let me see the other;
You do remember all the circumstance?
HORATIO: Remember it, my lord!
HAMLET: Sir, in my heart there was a kind of fighting
5   That would not let me sleep: methought I lay
Worse than the mutines in the bilboes.[1] Rashly,
And prais'd be rashness for it,—let us know,
Our indiscretion sometimes serves us well,
When our deep plots do fail: and that should teach us
10   There's a divinity that shapes our ends,
Rough-hew them how we will.
HORATIO: This is most certain.
HAMLET: Up from my cabin,
My sea-gown scarf'd about me, in the dark
Grop'd I to find out them: had my desire;
15   Finger'd their packet; and, in fine, withdrew
To mine own room again: making so bold,
My fears forgetting manners, to unseal
Their grand commission; where I found, Horatio,
O royal knavery! an exact command,—
20   Larded with many several sorts of reasons,
Importing Denmark's health and England's too,
With, ho! such bugs[2] and goblins in my life,—
That, on the supervise, no leisure bated,

---

[1] *bilboes:* mutineers in the iron stocks on board ship.
[2] *bugs:* bugbears.

No, not to stay the grinding of the axe,
25 My head should be struck off.

HORATIO: Is't possible?

HAMLET: Here's the commission: read it at more leisure.
    But wilt thou hear me how I did proceed?

HORATIO: I beseech you.

HAMLET: Being thus benetted round with villainies,—
30 Ere I could make a prologue to my brains,
    They had begun the play,—I sat me down;
    Devis'd a new commission; wrote it fair:
    I once did hold it, as our statists do,
    A baseness to write fair, and labor'd much
35 How to forget that learning; but, sir, now
    It did me yeoman's service. Wilt thou know
    The effect of what I wrote?

HORATIO: Ay, good my lord.

HAMLET: An earnest conjuration from the king,—
    As England was his faithful tributary;
40 As love between them like the palm might flourish;
    As peace should still her wheaten garland wear
    And stand a comma[3] 'tween their amities;
    And many such like as's of great charge,—
    That, on the view and know of these contents,
45 Without debatement further, more or less,
    He should the bearers put to sudden death,
    Not shriving-time allow'd.

HORATIO: How was this seal'd?

HAMLET: Why, even in that was heaven ordinant.
    I had my father's signet in my purse,
50 Which was the model of that Danish seal:
    Folded the writ up in form of the other;
    Subscrib'd it; gav't the impression; plac'd it safely,
    The changeling never known. Now, the next day
    Was our sea-fight; and what to this was sequent
55 Thou know'st already.

HORATIO: So Guildenstern and Rosencrantz go to't.

HAMLET: Why, man, they did make love to this employment;
    They are not near my conscience; their defeat
    Does by their own insinuation[4] grow:
60 'Tis dangerous when the baser nature[5] comes
    Between the pass and fell[6] incensed points
    Of mighty opposites.

---

[3] *comma:* link.

[4] *Does . . . insinuation:* by their own "sticking their noses" into the business.

[5] *baser nature:* men of lower rank.

[6] *fell:* fierce.

HORATIO: Why, what a king is this!

HAMLET: Does it not, think'st thee, stand me now upon,[7]

      He that hath kill'd my king and whor'd my mother;

65   Popp'd in between the election and my hopes;

      Thrown out his angle for my proper life,

      And with such cozenage,[8]—is't not perfect conscience

      To quit him with this arm? and is't not to be damn'd,

      To let this canker of our nature come

70   In further evil?

HORATIO: It must be shortly known to him from England

      What is the issue of the business there.

HAMLET: It will be short: the interim is mine;

      And a man's life's no more than to say One.

75   But I am very sorry, good Horatio,

      That to Laertes I forgot myself;

      For by the image of my cause I see

      The portraiture of his: I'll court his favors:

      But, sure, the bravery[9] of his grief did put me

      Into a towering passion.

80 HORATIO: Peace; who comes here?

(Enter Osric.)

OSRIC: Your lordship is right welcome back to Denmark.

HAMLET: I humbly thank you, sir.—Dost know this water-fly?

HORATIO: No, my good lord.

HAMLET: Thy state is the more gracious; for 'tis a vice to know him.

85   He hath much land, and fertile: let a beast be lord of beasts, and

      his crib shall stand at the king's mess: 'tis a chough;[10] but, as I say,

      spacious in the possession of dirt.

OSRIC: Sweet lord, if your lordship were at leisure, I should impart a

      thing to you from his majesty.

90 HAMLET: I will receive it with all diligence of spirit. Put your bonnet

      to his right use; 'tis for the head.

OSRIC: I thank your lordship, 'tis very hot.

HAMLET: No, believe me, 'tis very cold; the wind is northerly.

OSRIC: It is indifferent cold, my lord, indeed.

95 HAMLET: Methinks it is very sultry and hot for my complexion.

OSRIC: Exceedingly, my lord; it is very sultry,—as't were,—I cannot

      tell how.—But, my lord, his majesty bade me signify to you that he

      has laid a great wager on your head. Sir, this is the matter,—

HAMLET: I beseech you, remember,—

---

[7] *Does . . . upon:* that is, "Don't you think it is my duty?"

[8] *cozenage:* deceit.

[9] *bravery:* ostentation.

[10] *his . . . chough:* He shall have his trough at the king's table: he is a chattering fool.

(Hamlet moves him to put on his hat.)

100 OSRIC: Nay, in good faith; for mine ease, in good faith. Sir, here is
newly come to court Laertes; believe me, an absolute gentleman, full
of most excellent differences, of very soft society and great showing:
indeed, to speak feelingly of him, he is the card or calendar of gentry,
for you shall find in him the continent of what part a gentleman
105 would see.

HAMLET: Sir, his definement suffers no perdition in you;—though, I
know, to divide him inventorially would dizzy the arithmetic of
memory, and yet but yaw neither, in respect of his quick sail. But,
in the verity of extolment, I take him to be a soul of great article;
110 and his infusion of such dearth[11] and rareness as, to make true
diction of him, his semblable is his mirror; and who else would
trace him, his umbrage,[12] nothing more.

OSRIC: Your lordship speaks most infallibly of him.

HAMLET: The concernancy, sir? why do we wrap the gentleman in our
115 more rawer breath?

OSRIC: Sir?

HORATIO: Is't not possible to understand in another tongue? You will
do't sir, really.

HAMLET: What imports the nomination[13] of this gentleman?

120 OSRIC: Of Laertes?

HORATIO: His purse is empty already; all's golden words are spent.

HAMLET: Of him, sir.

OSRIC: I know, you are not ignorant,—

HAMLET: I would you did, sir; yet, in faith, if you did, it would not
125 much approve me.[14]—Well, sir.

OSRIC: You are not ignorant of what excellence Laertes is,—

HAMLET: I dare not confess that, lest I should compare with him in
excellence; but to know a man well were to know himself.

OSRIC: I mean, sir, for his weapon; but in the imputation laid on him
130 by them, in his meed he's unfellowed.[15]

HAMLET: What's his weapon?

OSRIC: Rapier and dagger.

HAMLET: That's two of his weapons: but, well.

OSRIC: The king, sir, hath wagered with him six Barbary horses:
135 against the which he has imponed,[16] as I take it, six French rapiers
and poniards, with their assigns, as girdle, hangers, and so: three

---

[11] *dearth:* rareness, or excellence.

[12] *umbrage:* shadow.

[13] *nomination:* naming.

[14] *I . . . me:* If you, who are a fool, thought me not ignorant, that would not be particularly to my credit.

[15] *in . . . unfellowed:* In his worth he has no equal.

[16] *imponed:* staked.

of the carriages, in faith, are very dear to fancy, very responsive to
the hilts, most delicate carriages, and of very liberal conceit.

HAMLET: What call you the carriages?

140 HORATIO: I knew you must be edified by the margent ere you had
done.[17]

OSRIC: The carriages, sir, are the hangers.

HAMLET: The phrase would be more germane to the matter if we could
carry cannon by our sides: I would it might be hangers till then.

145 But, on: six Barbary horses against six French swords, their assigns,
and three liberal conceited carriages; that's the French bet against
the Danish: why is this imponed, as you call it?

OSRIC: The king, sir, hath laid, that in a dozen passes between you
and him he shall not exceed you three hits: he hath laid on twelve

150 for nine; and it would come to immediate trial if your lordship
would vouchsafe the answer.

HAMLET: How if I answer no?

OSRIC: I mean, my lord, the opposition of your person in trial.[18]

HAMLET: Sir, I will walk here in the hall: if it please his majesty, it is

155 the breathing time of day with me: let the foils be brought, the
gentleman willing, and the king hold his purpose, I will win for him
if I can; if not, I will gain nothing but my shame and the odd hits.

OSRIC: Shall I re-deliver you[19] e'en so?

HAMLET: To this effect, sir; after what flourish your nature will.

160 OSRIC: I commend my duty to your lordship.

HAMLET: Yours, yours.

(Exit Osric.)

He does well to commend it himself; there are no tongues else for's
turn.

HORATIO: This lapwing runs away with the shell on his head.[20]

165 HAMLET: He did comply with his dug before he sucked it.[21] Thus has
he,—and many more of the same bevy, that I know the drossy age
dotes on,—only got the tune of the time, and outward habit of
encounter; a kind of yesty collection,[22] which carries them through
and through the most fanned and winnowed opinions; and do but

170 blow them to their trial, the bubbles are out.

(Enter a Lord.)

---

[17] *edified . . . done:* informed by a note in the margin of your instructions.

[18] *I . . . trial:* that is, the presence of your person as Laertes' opponent in the fencing contest.

[19] *re-deliver you:* carry back your answer.

[20] *This . . . head:* This precocious fellow is like a lapwing that starts running when it is barely out of the shell.

[21] *He . . . it:* He paid compliments to his mother's breast before he sucked it.

[22] *yesty collection:* yeasty or frothy affair.

LORD: My lord, his majesty commended him to you by young Osric, who brings back to him that you attend him in the hall: he sends to know if your pleasure hold to play with Laertes, or that you will take longer time.

175 HAMLET: I am constant to my purposes; they follow the king's pleasure: if his fitness speaks, mine is ready; now or whensoever, provided I be so able as now.

LORD: The king and queen and all are coming down.

HAMLET: In happy time.

180 LORD: The queen desires you to use some gentle entertainment to Laertes before you fall to play.

HAMLET: She well instructs me.

(Exit Lord.)

HORATIO: You will lose this wager, my lord.

HAMLET: I do not think so; since he went into France I have been in
185 continual practice: I shall win at the odds. But thou wouldst not think how ill all's here about my heart: but it is no matter.

HORATIO: Nay, good my lord,—

HAMLET: It is but foolery; but it is such a kind of gain-giving[23] as would perhaps trouble a woman.

190 HORATIO: If your mind dislike anything, obey it: I will forestall their repair hither, and say you are not fit.

HAMLET: Not a whit, we defy augury: there's a special providence in the fall of a sparrow. If it be now, 'tis not to come; if it be not to come, it will be now; if it be not now, yet it will come: the readiness
195 is all. Since no man has aught of what he leaves, what is't to leave betimes?[24]

(Enter King, Queen, Laertes, Lords, Osric, and Attendants with foils, &c.)

KING: Come, Hamlet, come, and take this hand from me.

(The King puts Laertes' hand into Hamlet's.)

HAMLET: Give me your pardon, sir: I have done you wrong:
But pardon't, as you are a gentleman.
200 This presence knows, and you must needs have heard,
How I am punish'd with sore distraction.
What I have done,
That might your nature, honor, and exception
Roughly awake, I here proclaim was madness.
205 Was't Hamlet wrong'd Laertes? Never Hamlet:
If Hamlet from himself be ta'en away,
And when he's not himself does wrong Laertes,

---

[23] *gain-giving*: misgiving.
[24] *what . . . betimes?*: What does an early death matter?

Then Hamlet does it not, Hamlet denies it.
Who does it, then? His madness: if't be so,
210 Hamlet is of the faction that is wrong'd;
His madness is poor Hamlet's enemy.
Sir, in this audience,
Let my disclaiming from a purpos'd evil
Free me so far in your most generous thoughts
215 That I have shot mine arrow o'er the house
And hurt my brother.
LAERTES: I am satisfied in nature,
Whose motive, in this case, should stir me most
To my revenge: but in my terms of honor
I stand aloof; and will no reconcilement
220 Till by some elder masters of known honor
I have a voice and precedent of peace
To keep my name ungor'd. But till that time
I do receive your offer'd love like love,
And will not wrong it.
HAMLET: I embrace it freely;
225 And will this brother's wager frankly play.[25]—
Give us the foils; come on.
LAERTES: Come, one for me.
HAMLET: I'll be your foil, Laertes; in mine ignorance
Your skill shall, like a star in the darkest night,
Stick fiery off indeed.
LAERTES: You mock me, sir.
230 HAMLET: No, by this hand.
KING: Give them the foils, young Osric.
Cousin Hamlet,
You know the wager?
HAMLET: Very well, my lord;
Your grace hath laid the odds o' the weaker side.
235 KING: I do not fear it; I have seen you both;
But since he's better'd, we have therefore odds.
LAERTES: This is too heavy, let me see another.
HAMLET: This likes me well. These foils have all a length?

(They prepare to play.)

OSRIC: Ay, my good lord.
240 KING: Set me the stoups of wine upon that table,—
If Hamlet give the first or second hit,
Or quit in answer of the third exchange,
Let all the battlements their ordnance fire;

---

[25] *And . . . play:* fence with a heart free from resentment.

The king shall drink to Hamlet's better breath;
245 And in the cup an union[26] shall he throw,
Richer than that which four successive kings
In Denmark's crown have worn. Give me the cups;
And let the kettle[27] to the trumpet speak,
The trumpet to the cannoneer without,
250 The cannons to the heavens, the heavens to earth,
Now the king drinks to Hamlet.—Come, begin;—
And you, the judges, bear a wary eye.

HAMLET: Come on, sir.
LAERTES: Come, my lord.

(They play.)

HAMLET: One.
LAERTES: No.
HAMLET: Judgment.
OSRIC: A hit, a very palpable hit.
LAERTES: Well;—again.
255 KING: Stay, give me a drink.—Hamlet, this pearl is thine;
Here's to thy health.—

(Trumpets sound, and cannon shot off within.)

Give him the cup.
HAMLET: I'll play this bout first; set it by awhile.—
Come.—Another hit; what say you?

(They play.)

260 LAERTES: A touch, a touch, I do confess.
KING: Our son shall win.
QUEEN: He's fat, and scant of breath.—
Here, Hamlet, take my napkin, rub thy brows:
The queen carouses to thy fortune, Hamlet.
HAMLET: Good madam!
KING: Gertrude, do not drink.
265 QUEEN: I will, my lord; I pray you, pardon me.
KING: *(Aside)* It is the poison'd cup; it is too late.
HAMLET: I dare not drink yet, madam; by and by.
QUEEN: Come, let me wipe thy face.
LAERTES: My lord, I'll hit him now.
KING: I do not think't.
270 LAERTES: *(Aside)* And yet 'tis almost 'gainst my conscience.
HAMLET: Come, for the third, Laertes: you but dally;
I pray you, pass with your best violence:

---

[26] *an union:* a pearl.
[27] *kettle:* kettledrum.

I am afeard you make a wanton of me.
LAERTES: Say you so? come on.

(They play.)

275 OSRIC: Nothing, neither way.
LAERTES: Have at you now!

(Laertes wounds Hamlet; then, in scuffling, they change rapiers, and Hamlet wounds Laertes.)

KING: Part them; they are incens'd.
HAMLET: Nay, come, again.

(The Queen falls.)

OSRIC: Look to the queen there, ho!
HORATIO: They bleed on both sides.—How is it, my lord?
OSRIC: How is't, Laertes?
280 LAERTES: Why, as a woodcock to my own springe, Osric;
  I am justly kill'd with mine own treachery.
HAMLET: How does the queen?
KING: She swoons to see them bleed.
QUEEN: No, no, the drink, the drink,—O my dear Hamlet,—
  The drink, the drink!—I am poison'd. *(Dies.)*
285 HAMLET: O villainy!—Ho! let the door be lock'd:
  Treachery! seek it out.

(Laertes falls.)

LAERTES: It is here, Hamlet: Hamlet, thou art slain;
  No medicine in the world can do thee good;
  In thee there is not half an hour of life;
290 The treacherous instrument is in thy hand,
  Unbated and envenom'd: the foul practice
  Hath turn'd itself on me; lo, here I lie,
  Never to rise again: thy mother's poison'd:
  I can no more:—the king, the king's to blame.
295 HAMLET: The point envenom'd too!—
  Then venom to thy work. *(Stabs the King)*
OSRIC and LORDS: Treason! treason!
KING: O, yet defend me, friends; I am but hurt.
HAMLET: Here, thou incestuous, murderous, damned Dane,
300 Drink off this potion.—Is thy union here?
  Follow my mother.

(King dies.)

LAERTES: He is justly serv'd;
  It is a poison temper'd by himself.—
  Exchange forgiveness with me, noble Hamlet:
305 Mine and my father's death come not upon thee,

Nor thine on me! *(Dies.)*
HAMLET: Heaven make thee free of it! I follow thee.—
I am dead, Horatio.—Wretched queen, adieu!—
You that look pale and tremble at this chance,
310   That art but mutes or audience to this act,
Had I but time,—as this fell sergeant, death,
Is strict in his arrest,—O, I could tell you,—
But let it be.—Horatio, I am dead;
Thou liv'st; report me and my cause aright
315   To the unsatisfied.[28]
HORATIO: Never believe it:
I am more an antique Roman than a Dane,—
Here's yet some liquor left.
HAMLET: As thou'rt a man,
Give me the cup; let go; by heaven, I'll have't.—
O good Horatio, what a wounded name,
320   Things standing thus unknown, shall live behind me!
If thou didst ever hold me in thy heart,
Absent thee from felicity awhile,
And in this harsh world draw thy breath in pain,
To tell my story.—

(March afar off, and shot within.)

What warlike noise is this?
325   OSRIC: Young Fortinbras, with conquest come from Poland,
To the ambassadors of England gives
This warlike volley.
HAMLET: O, I die, Horatio;
The potent poison quite o'er-crows my spirit:
I cannot live to hear the news from England;
330   But I do prophesy the election lights
On Fortinbras: he has my dying voice;
So tell him, with the occurrents, more and less,
Which have solicited.[29]—The rest is silence. *(Dies)*
HORATIO: Now cracks a noble heart.—Good-night, sweet prince,
335   And flights of angels sing thee to thy rest!
Why does the drum come hither?

(March within. Enter Fortinbras, the English Ambassadors, and others.)

FORTINBRAS: Where is this sight?
HORATIO: What is it you would see?
If aught of woe or wonder, cease your search.
FORTINBRAS: This quarry cries on havoc.[30]—O proud death,
340   What feast is toward in thine eternal cell,

---

[28] *unsatisfied:* the uninformed.

[29] *So . . . solicited:* So tell him, together with the events, more or less, that have brought
on this tragic affair.

[30] *This . . . havoc:* This collection of dead bodies cries out havoc.

That thou so many princes at a shot
So bloodily hast struck?

1ST AMBASSADOR: The sight is dismal;
And our affairs from England come too late:
The ears are senseless that should give us hearing,

345   To tell him his commandment is fulfill'd,
That Rosencrantz and Guildenstern are dead:
Where should we have our thanks?

HORATIO: Not from his mouth,
Had it the ability of life to thank you:
He never gave commandment for their death.

350   But since, so jump[31] upon this bloody question,
You from the Polack wars, and you from England,
Are here arriv'd, give order that these bodies
High on a stage be placed to the view;
And let me speak to the yet unknowing world

355   How these things came about: so shall you hear
Of carnal, bloody, and unnatural acts;
Of accidental judgments, casual slaughters;
Of deaths put on by cunning and forc'd cause;
And, in this upshot, purposes mistook

360   Fall'n on the inventors' heads: all this can I
Truly deliver.

FORTINBRAS: Let us haste to hear it,
And call the noblest to the audience.
For me, with sorrow I embrace my fortune:
I have some rights of memory in this kingdom,[32]

365   Which now to claim my vantage doth invite me.

HORATIO: Of that I shall have also cause to speak,
And from his mouth whose voice will draw on more:
But let this same be presently perform'd,
Even while men's minds are wild: lest more mischance

370   On plots and errors happen.

FORTINBRAS: Let four captains
Bear Hamlet like a soldier to the stage;
For he was likely, had he been put on,[33]
To have prov'd most royally: and, for his passage,
The soldier's music and the rites of war

375   Speak loudly for him.—
Take up the bodies.—Such a sight as this
Becomes the field, but here shows much amiss.
Go, bid the soldiers shoot.

(A dead march)

(Exeunt, bearing off the dead bodies: after which a peal of ordnance is shot off.)

---

[31] *jump:* opportunely.

[32] *I . . . kingdom:* I have some unforgotten rights to this kingdom.

[33] *had . . . on:* tested by succession to the throne.

READING AND REACTING

1. What are Hamlet's most notable character traits?

2. Review each of Hamlet's **soliloquies.** Judging from his own words, do you believe his assessments of his own problems are accurate? Are his assessments of other characters' behaviour accurate? Point to examples from the soliloquies that reveal Hamlet's insight (or lack of insight).

3. Is Hamlet a sympathetic character? Where (if anywhere) do you find yourself growing impatient with him or disagreeing with him?

4. What is the emotional impact on the audience of having Hamlet behave so cruelly toward Ophelia after his "To be or not to be" soliloquy?

5. What do other characters' comments reveal about Hamlet's character *before* the key events in the play begin to unfold? For example, in what way has he changed since he returned to the castle and found out about his father's death?

6. Claudius is presented as the play's villain. Is he all bad, or does he have any redeeming qualities?

7. List those in the play whom you believe to be **flat characters.** Why do you characterize each individual in this way? What does each of these flat characters contribute to the play?

8. Is Fortinbras simply Hamlet's **foil,** or does he have another essential role? Explain.

9. Each of the play's major characters makes one or more errors that influence plot development. What specific errors do you see made by Claudius, Gertrude, Polonius, Laertes, Ophelia, and Hamlet himself? How does each error contribute to the play's action?

10. Why doesn't Hamlet kill Claudius as soon as the Ghost tells him what Claudius did? Why doesn't he kill him when he has the chance in act 3? What words or actions reveal his motivation for hesitating? What are the implications of his failure to act?

11. Why does Hamlet pretend to be insane? Why does he arrange for the "play within a play" to be performed? Why does he agree to the duel with Laertes? In each case, what words or actions reveal his motivation to the audience?

12. Is the Ghost an essential character, or could the information he reveals and the reactions he arouses come from another source? Explain. (Keep in mind that the ghost is a **stock character** in Elizabethan drama.)

13. Describe Hamlet's relationship with his mother. Do you consider this a typical mother/son relationship? Why or why not?

14. In the graveyard scene (act 5, scene 1), the gravediggers make many ironic comments. In what way do these comments shed light on the events taking place in the play?

15. **JOURNAL ENTRY** Both Gertrude and Ophelia are usually seen as weak women, firmly under the influence of the men in their lives.

Do you think this characterization of them as passive and dependent is accurate? Explain.

16. **CRITICAL PERSPECTIVE** In a 1951 book, *The Meaning of Shakespeare,* Harold Goddard reads *Hamlet* as, in part, a play about war, with a grimly ironic conclusion in that "all the Elder Hamlet's conquests have been for nothing—for less than nothing. Fortinbras, his former enemy, is to inherit the kingdom! Such is the end to which the Ghost's thirst for vengeance has led." He goes on to describe the play's ending:

> The dead Hamlet is borne out "like a soldier" and the last rites over his body are to be the rites of war. The final word of the text is "shoot." The last sounds we hear are a dead march and the reverberations of ordnance being shot off. The end crowns the whole. The sarcasm of fate could go no further. Hamlet, who aspired to nobler things, is treated at death as if he were the mere image of his father: a warrior. Shakespeare knew what he was about in making the conclusion of his play martial. Its theme has been war as well as revenge. It is the story of the Minotaur over again, of that monster who from the beginning of human strife has exacted his annual tribute of youth. No sacrifice ever offered to it was more precious than Hamlet. But he was not the last.
>
> If ever a play seems expressly written for the twentieth century, it is *Hamlet.* It should be unnecessary to underscore its pertinence to an age in which, twice within three decades, the older generation has called on the younger generation to settle a quarrel with the making of which it had nothing to do. So taken, *Hamlet* is an allegory of our time. Imagination or violence, Shakespeare seems to say, there is no other alternative.

Can you find other evidence in the play to support the idea that one of its major themes is war? Do you agree that the play is "an allegory of our time"?

Related Works: "Young Goodman Brown" (p. 307), *Oedipus the King* (p. 1293)

◊ **MICHEL TREMBLAY** (1942–   ) has set most of his plays and novels in the Plateau Mont-Royal neighbourhood of Montreal where he was born and raised. He studied graphic arts after high school and worked as a printer like his father and brother. His first attempt as a playwright, *Le Train* (1959), won first prize in a contest sponsored by Radio-Canada, the French-language division of the CBC, when it was first produced in 1964. But it was with *Les Belles Soeurs*, written in 1965 and produced in 1968, that he broke through on the world stage. He has published nearly twenty plays and works of short fiction. Among some of his other works in translation are *Forever Yours, Marie-Lou* (1975), *Sainte-Carmen of the Main* (1976), *Stories for Late-Night Drinkers* (1977, a collection of short stories), *The First Quarter of the Moon* (1994, a novel), and *Remember Me* (1984).

◊ ◊ ◊

MICHEL TREMBLAY

Les Belles Soeurs
(1965)

CHARACTERS

GERMAINE LAUZON
LINDA LAUZON, *her daughter*

GABRIELLE JODOIN
ROSE OUIMET } *sisters of Germaine Lauzon*
PIERRETTE GUÉRIN

THÉRÈSE DUBUC, *sister-in-law of Germaine Lauzon*
OLIVINE DUBUC, *Thérèse Dubuc's mother-in-law*

MARIE-ANGE BROUILLETTE
YVETTE LONGPRÉ
LISETTE DE COURVAL
DES-NEIGES VERRETTE } *neighbours*
RHÉAUNA BIBEAU
ANGÉLINE SAUVÉ

GINETTE MENARD
LISE PAQUETTE } *friends of Linda Lauzon*

VOICE OF NEIGHBOUR

The action takes place in the kitchen of Germaine Lauzon.

ACT I

Linda Lauzon enters. She sees four boxes in the middle of the kitchen.

LINDA: God, what's that? Ma!
GERMAINE: Is that you, Linda?
LINDA: Yeah! What are all these boxes in the kitchen?
GERMAINE: They're my stamps.
5 LINDA: Already? Jeez, that was fast.

Germaine Lauzon enters.

GERMAINE: Yeah, it surprised me too. They came this morning right after you left. The doorbell rang. I went to answer it and there's this big fellow standing there. Oh, you'd have liked him, Linda. Just your type. About twenty-two, twenty-three, dark curly hair. Nice little moustache. Real handsome. Anyway, he says to me, "Are you the lady of the house, Mme. Germaine Lauzon?" I said, "Yes that's me." And he says, "Good, I've brought your stamps." Linda, I was so excited. I didn't know what to say. Next thing I knew, two guys are bringing in the boxes and the other one's giving me this speech. Linda, what a talker. And such manners. I'm sure you would have liked him.

LINDA: So, what did he say?

GERMAINE: I can't remember. I was so excited. He told me the company he works for was real happy I'd won the million stamps. That I was real lucky . . . Me, I was speechless. I wish your father had been here, he could have talked to him. I don't even know if I thanked him.

LINDA: That's a lot of stamps to glue. Four boxes! One million stamps, that's no joke!

10 GERMAINE: There's only three boxes. The other one's booklets. But I had an idea, Linda. We're not gonna do all this alone! You going out tonight?

LINDA: Yeah, Robert's supposed to call me . . .

GERMAINE: You can't put it off til tomorrow? Listen, I had an idea. I phoned my sisters, your father's sister and I went to see the neighbours. And I've invited them all to come and paste stamps with us tonight. I'm gonna give a stamp-pasting party. Isn't that a great idea? I bought some peanuts, and your little brother went out to get some Coke . . .

LINDA: Ma, you know I always go out on Thursdays! It's our night out. We're gonna go to a show.

GERMAINE: You can't leave me alone on a night like this. I've got fifteen people coming . . .

15 LINDA: Are you crazy! You'll never get fifteen people in this kitchen! And you can't use the rest of the house. The painters are here. Jesus, Ma! Sometimes you're really dumb.

GERMAINE: Sure, that's right, put me down. Fine, you go out, do just as you like. That's all you ever do anyway. Nothing new. I never have any pleasure. Someone's always got to spoil it for me. Go ahead Linda, you go out tonight, go to your goddamned show. Jesus Christ Almighty, I'm so fed up.

LINDA: Come on, Ma, be reasonable . . .

GERMAINE: I don't want to be reasonable, I don't want to hear about it! I kill myself for you and what do I get in return? Nothing! A big fat nothing! You can't even do me a little favour! I'm warning you, Linda, I'm getting sick of waiting on you, you and everyone else. I'm not your servant, you know. I've got a million stamps to paste and I'm not about to do it myself. Besides, those stamps are for the whole family, which means everybody's gotta do their share. Your father's working tonight but if we don't get done he says he'll help tomorrow. I'm not asking for the moon. Help me for a change, instead of wasting your time with that jerk.

LINDA: Robert is not a jerk.

20 GERMAINE: Sure, he's a genius! Boy, I knew you were stupid, but not that stupid. When are you going to realize your Robert is a bozo? He doesn't even make sixty bucks a week. All he can do is take you to the local movie house Thursday nights. Take a mother's advice, Linda, keep hanging around with that dope and you'll end up just like him. You want to marry a shoe-gluer and be a strapper all your life?

Linda: Shut up, Ma! When you get sore, you don't know what you're saying. Anyway, forget it. . . . I'll stay home . . . Just stop screaming, okay? And by the way, Robert's due for a raise soon and he'll be making lot's more. He's not as dumb as you think. Even the boss told me he might start making big money 'cause they'll put him in charge of something. You wait. Eighty bucks a week is nothing to laugh at. Anyway . . . I'm gonna go phone him and tell him I can't go to the show . . . . Hey, why don't I tell him to come and glue stamps with us?

Germaine: Mother of God, I just told you I can't stand him and you want to bring him home tonight. Where the hell are your brains? What did I do to make God in heaven send me such idiots? Just this afternoon, I send your brother to get me a bag of onions and he comes home with a quart of milk. It's unbelievable! You have to repeat everything ten times around here. No wonder I lose my temper. I told you, Linda. The party's for girls. Just girls. Your Robert's not queer, is he?

Linda: Okay ma, okay, don't flip your wig. I'll tell him not to come. Jesus, you can't do a thing around here. You think I feel like gluing stamps after working all day.

Linda starts to dial a number.

Why don't you go dust in the living room, eh? You don't have to listen to what I'm going to say . . . "Hello, may I speak to Robert? . . . When do you expect him? . . . Okay, will you tell him Linda phoned? . . . Fine, Mme. Bergeron, and you? . . . That's good . . . Okay, thanks a lot. Bye."

She hangs up. The phone rings right away.

"Hello?" . . . Ma, it's for you.

Germaine: *(entering)* Twenty years old and you still can't say "One moment please" when you answer a phone.

25 Linda: It's only Aunt Rose. Why should I be polite to her?

Germaine: *(putting her hand over the receiver)* Will you be quiet! What if she heard you?

Linda: Who gives a shit?

Germaine: "Hello? Oh, it's you, Rose . . . Yeah, they're here . . . How 'bout that? A million of 'em! They're sitting right in front of me and I still can't believe it. One million! One million! I don't know how much that is, but who cares. A million's a million. . . . Sure, they sent a catalogue. I already had one but this one's for this year, so it's a lot better. The old one was falling apart . . . They've got the most beautiful stuff, wait til you see it. It's unbelievable! I think I'll be able to take everything they've got. I'll re-furnish the whole house. I'm gonna get a new stove, new fridge, new kitchen table and chairs. I think I'll take the red one with the gold stars. I don't think you've seen that one. . . . Oh, it's so beautiful, Rose. I'm getting new pots, new cutlery, a full set of dishes, salt and pepper shakers . . . Oh, and you know those glasses with the 'caprice' design. Well, I'm taking a set of those, too. Mme. de Courval got a set last year and she paid a fortune for them, but mine will be free. She'll be mad as hell . . . What? . . . Yeah, she'll be here tonight. They've got those chrome tins for flour and sugar, coffee and stuff . . . I'm taking it all. I'm getting a Colonial bedroom suite with full accessories. There's curtains, dresser-covers, one of those things you put on the floor beside the bed . . . No, dear, not that . . . New wallpaper . . . Not the floral, Henri can't sleep with flowers . . . I'm telling you Rose, it's gonna be one beautiful bedroom. And the living room! Wait till you hear this . . . I've got a big TV with a built-in stereo, a synthetic nylon carpet, real paintings . . . You know those Chinese paintings I've always wanted, the ones with the velvet? . . . Aren't they though? Oh, now get a load of this . . . I'm gonna have the same crystal platters as your sister-in-law, Aline! I'm not sure, but I think mine are even nicer. There's ashtrays and lamps . . . I guess that's about it for the living room . . . there's an electric razor for Henri to shave with, shower curtains. So what? We'll put one in. It all comes with the stamps. There's a sunken bathtub, a new sink, bathing suits for everyone . . . No, Rose, I am not too fat. Don't get smart. Now listen, I'm gonna re-do the kid's room, completely. Have you seen what they've got for kids' bedrooms? Rose, it's fabulous! They've got Mickey Mouse all over everything. And for Linda's room . . . Okay, sure, you can just look at the catalogue. But come over right away, the others will be here any minute. I told them to come early. I mean it's gonna take forever to paste all those stamps."

Marie-Ange Brouillette enters.

"Okay, I've gotta go, Mme. Brouillette's just arrived. Okay, yeah . . . Yeah . . . Bye!"

MARIE-ANGE: Mme. Lauzon, I just can't help it, I'm jealous.

30 GERMAINE: Well, I know what you mean. It's quite an event. But excuse me for a moment, Mme. Brouillette, I'm not quite ready. I was talking to my sister, Rose. We can see each other across the alley, it's handy.

MARIE-ANGE: Is she gonna be here?

GERMAINE: You bet! She wouldn't miss this for love nor money. Here, have a seat and while you're waiting look at the catalogue. You won't believe all the lovely things they've got. And I'm getting them all, Mme. Brouillette. The works! The whole catalogue.

Germaine goes into her bedroom.

MARIE-ANGE: You wouldn't catch me having luck like that. Fat chance. My life is shit and it always will be. A million stamps! A whole house. If I didn't bite my tongue, I'd scream. Typical. The ones with all the luck least deserve it. What did Mme. Lauzon do to deserve this, eh? Nothing. Absolutely nothing! She's no better looking than me. In fact, she's no better period. These contests shouldn't be allowed. The priest the other day was right. They ought to be abolished. Why should she win a million stamps and not me? Why? It's not fair. I work too, I've got kids, too, I have to wipe their asses, just like her. If anything, my kids are cleaner than hers. I work like a slave, it's no wonder I'm all skin and bones. Her, she's fat as a pig. And now, I'll have to live next door to her and the house she gets for free. It burns me up, I can't stand it. What's more, there'll be no end to her smart-assed comments 'cause it'll all go straight to her head. She's just the type, the loud-mouthed bitch. We'll be hearing about her goddamned stamps for years. I've a right to be angry. I don't want to die in this shit while madame Fatso here goes swimming in velvet! It's not fair! I'm sick of knocking myself out for nothing! My life is nothing. A big fat zero. And I haven't a cent to my name. I'm fed up. I'm fed up with this stupid, rotten life.

During the monologue, Gabrielle Jodoin, Rose Ouimet, Yvette Longpré, and Lisette de Courval have entered. They take their places in the kitchen without paying attention to Marie-Ange. The five women get up and turn to the audience.

THE FIVE WOMEN: *(together)* This stupid, rotten life! Monday!

35 LISETTE: When the sun with his rays starts caressing the little flowers in the fields and the little birdies open wide their little beaks to send forth their little cries to heaven . . .

THE OTHERS: I get up and I fix breakfast. Toast, coffee, bacon, eggs. I nearly go nuts trying to get the others out of bed. The kids leave for school, my husband goes to work.

MARIE-ANGE: Not mine, he's unemployed. He stays in bed.

THE FIVE WOMEN: Then I work. I work like a demon. I don't stop til noon. I wash . . . Dresses, shirts, stockings, sweaters, pants, underpants, bras. The works. I scrub it, wring it out, scrub it again, rinse it . . . My hands are chapped. My back is sore. I curse like hell. At noon, the kids come home. They eat like pigs, they wreck the house, they leave. In the afternoon I hang out the wash, the biggest pain of all. When that's finished, I start the supper. They all come home. They're tired and grumpy. We all fight. But at night, we watch TV. Tuesday.

LISETTE: When the sun with his rays . . .

40 THE OTHERS: I get up and I fix breakfast. The same goddamn thing. Toast, coffee, bacon, eggs. I drag the others out of bed and I shove them out the door. Then it's the ironing. I work, I work, I work and I work. It's noon before I know it and the kids are mad because lunch isn't ready. I make 'em baloney sandwiches. I work all afternoon. Suppertime comes, we all fight. But at night, we watch TV. Wednesday . . . Shopping day. I walk all day, I break my back carrying parcels this big, I come back home exhausted. But I've still got to make supper. When the others get home I look like I'm dead. I am. My husband bitches, the kids scream. We all fight. But at night, we watch TV. Thursday and Friday . . . Same thing . . . . I work. I slave. I kill myself for my pack of

morons. Then I spend the day Saturday tripping over the kids and we all fight. But at night, we watch TV. Sunday we go out, the whole family, we get on the bus and go for supper with the mother-in-law. I have to watch the kids like a hawk, laugh at the old man's jokes, eat the old lady's food, which everyone says is better than mine . . . At night, we watch TV. I'm fed up with this stupid, rotten life! This stupid, rotten life! This stupid, rotten life. This stup . . .

They sit down suddenly.

LISETTE: On my last trip to Europe . . .
ROSE: There she goes with her Europe again. We're in for it now. Once she gets started, there's no shutting her up!

Des-Neiges Verrette comes in. Discreet little greetings are heard.

LISETTE: I only wished to say that in Europe they don't have stamps. I mean, they have stamps, but not like these ones. Only letter stamping stamps.
DES-NEIGES: That's no fun! So they don't get presents like us? Sounds pretty dull to me, Europe.
45 LISETTE: Oh no, it's very nice despite that . . .
MARIE-ANGE: Mind you, I've got nothing against stamps, they're useful. If it weren't for the stamps, I'd still be waiting for that thing to grind my meat with. What I don't like is the contests.
LISETTE: But why? They can make families happy.
MARIE-ANGE: Maybe, but they're a pain in the ass for the people next door.
LISETTE: Mme. Brouillette, your language! I speak properly, and I'm none the worse for it.
50 MARIE-ANGE: I talk the way I talk, and I say what I got to say. I never went to Europe, so I can't afford to talk like you.
ROSE: Hey, you two, cut it out! We didn't come here to fight. You keep it up, I'm crossing the alley and going home.
GABRIELLE: What's taking Germaine so long? Germaine!
GERMAINE: *(from the bedroom)* Be there in a minute. I'm having a hard time getting into my . . . Well, I'm having a hard time . . . Is Linda there?
GABRIELLE: Linda! Linda! No, she's not here.
55 MARIE-ANGE: I think I saw her go out a while ago.
GERMAINE: Don't tell me she's snuck out, the little bugger.
GABRIELLE: Can we start pasting stamps in the meantime?
GERMAINE: No wait! I'm going to tell you what to do. Don't start yet, wait till I get there. Chat for a bit.
GABRIELLE: "Chat for a bit?" What are we going to chat about . . .

The telephone rings.

60 ROSE: My God, that scared me! "Hello . . . No, she's out, but if you want to wait I think she'll be back in a few minutes."

She puts the receiver down, goes out on the balcony and shouts.

"Linda! Linda, telephone!"

LISETTE: So, Mme. Longpré how does marriage agree with your daughter Claudette?

YVETTE: Oh, she loves it. She's having a ball. She told me about her honeymoon, you know.

GABRIELLE: Where did they go to?

YVETTE: Well, he won a trip to the Canary Islands, eh? So you see, they had to put the wedding ahead a bit. . . .

65 ROSE: *(laughing)* The Canary Islands! A honeymoon in bird shit, eh?

GABRIELLE: Come on, Rose!

ROSE: What?

DES-NEIGES: The Canary Islands, where's that?

LISETTE: We stopped by there, my husband and I, on our last trip to Europe. It's a real . . . It's a very pleasant country. The women only wear skirts.

70 ROSE: The perfect place for my husband!

LISETTE: And I'm afraid the natives are not very clean. Of course, in Europe, people don't wash.

DES-NEIGES: It shows, too. Look at those Italians next door to me. You wouldn't believe how that woman stinks.

They all burst out laughing.

LISETTE: *(insinuating)* Did you ever notice her clothesline, on Monday?

DES-NEIGES: No, why?

75 LISETTE: Well, all I know is this. . . . Those people don't have any underwear.

MARIE-ANGE: You're kidding!

ROSE: I don't believe it!

YVETTE: You gotta be joking!

LISETTE: It's the God's truth! Take a look for yourselves next Monday. You'll see.

80 YVETTE: No wonder they stink.

MARIE-ANGE: Maybe she's too modest to hang them outside.

The others laugh.

LISETTE: Modest! A European? They don't know what it means. Just look at their movies you see on TV. It's appalling. They stand right in the middle of the street and kiss. On the mouth, too! It's in their blood, you know. Take a look at that Italian's daughter when she brings her friends around. . . . Her boyfriends, that is. . . . It's disgusting what she does, that girl. She has no shame! Which reminds me, Mme. Ouimet. I saw your Michel the other day . . .

ROSE: Not with that slut, I hope!

LISETTE: I'm afraid so.

85 ROSE: You must be mistaken. It couldn't have been him.

LISETTE: I beg your pardon, but the Italians are my neighbours, too. The two of them were on the front balcony . . . I suppose they thought no one could see them . . .

DES-NEIGES: It's true, Mme. Ouimet, I saw them myself. I tell you, they were necking like crazy.

ROSE: The little bastard! As if one pig in the family's not enough. By pig I mean my husband. Can't even watch a girl on TV without getting a. . . . Without getting worked up. Goddamn sex! They never get enough, those Ouimets. They're all alike, they . . .

GABRIELLE: Rose, you don't have to tell the whole world . . .

90 LISETTE: But we're very concerned . . .

DES-NEIGES AND MARIE-ANGE: Yes, we are . . .

YVETTE: To get back to my daughter's honeymoon . . .

GERMAINE: *(entering)* Here I am, girls!

Greetings, "how are you's," etc.

So, what have you all been talking about?

ROSE: Oh, Mme. Longpré was telling us about her daughter Claudette's honeymoon. . . .

95 GERMAINE: Really? (to Yvette) Hello, dear . . . (to Rose) And what was she saying?

ROSE: Sounds like they had a great trip. They met all these people. They went on a boat. They were visiting islands, of course, The Canary Islands . . . They went fishing and they caught fish this big. They ran into some couples they knew. . . . Old friends of Claudette's. Then they came back together and, oh yes, they stopped over in New York. Mme. Longpré was giving us all the details . . .

YVETTE: Well . . .

ROSE: Eh, Mme. Longpré, isn't that right?

YVETTE: Well, as a matter of fact . . .

100 GERMAINE: You tell your daughter, Mme. Longpré, that I wish her all the best. Of course, we weren't invited to the wedding, but we wish her well anyway.

There is an embarrassed silence.

GABRIELLE: Hey! It's almost seven! The rosary!

GERMAINE: Dear God, my novena for Ste.-Thérèse. I'll get Linda's radio.

She goes out.

ROSE: What does she want with Ste.-Thérèse, especially after winning all that?

DES-NEIGES: Maybe she's having trouble with her kids. . . .

105 GABRIELLE: No, she would have told me. . . .

GERMAINE: *(from the bedroom)* Goddamn it! Where did she put that frigging radio?

ROSE: I don't know, Gaby. Our sister usually keeps things to herself.
GABRIELLE: Not with me. She tells me everything. You, you're such a blabbermouth. . . .
ROSE: You've got a lot of nerve! What do you mean, blabbermouth? Gabrielle Jodoin! My mouth's no bigger than yours.
110 GABRIELLE: Come off it, you know you can't keep a secret!
ROSE: Well, I never . . . If you think . . . .
LISETTE: Wasn't it you, Mme. Ouimet, who just said we didn't come here to quarrel?
ROSE: Hey, you mind your own business. Besides, I didn't say "quarrel." I said "fight."

Germaine comes back in with a radio.

GERMAINE: What's going on? I can hear you at the other end of the house!
115 GABRIELLE: Nothing, it's our sister again . . .
GERMAINE: Settle down, Rose. You're supposed to be the life of the party . . . No fighting tonight.
ROSE: You see! In our family we say "fight."

Germaine turns on the radio. We hear a voice saying the rosary. All the women get down on their knees. After a few "Hail Marys" a great racket is heard outside. The women scream and run to the door.

GERMAINE: Oh my god! My sister-in-law Thérèse's mother-in-law just fell down three flights of stairs!
ROSE: Did you hurt yourself, Mme. Dubuc?
120 GABRIELLE: Rose, shut up! She's probably dead!
THÉRÈSE: *(from a distance)* Are you all right, Mme. Dubuc? *(A faint moan is heard.)* Wait a minute. Let me get the wheelchair off you. Is that better? Now I'm gonna help you get back in your chair. Come on, Mme. Dubuc, make a little effort. Don't be so limp! Ouch!
DES-NEIGES: Here, Mme. Dubuc. Let me give you a hand.
THÉRÈSE: Thanks Mlle. Verrette. You're so kind.

The other women come back into the room.

ROSE: Germaine, shut off the radio. I'm a nervous wreck!
125 GERMAINE: What about my novena?
ROSE: How far have you gotten?
GERMAINE: I'm only up to seven, but I promised to do nine.
ROSE: So, pick it up tomorrow and you'll be finished on Saturday.
GERMAINE: It's not for nine days, it's for nine weeks.

Thérèse Dubuc and Des-Neiges Verrette enter with Olivine Dubuc, who is in a wheelchair.

My God, she wasn't hurt bad, I hope.
130 THÉRÈSE: No, no, she's used to it. She falls out of her chair ten times a day. Whew! I'm all out of breath. It's no joke, hauling this thing up three flights of stairs. You got something to drink, Germaine?

GERMAINE: Gaby, give Thérèse a glass of water.

She approaches Olivine Dubuc.

And how are you today, Mme. Dubuc?

THÉRÈSE: Don't get too close, Germaine. She's been biting lately.

In fact, Olivine Dubuc tries to bite Germaine's hand.

GERMAINE: My god, you're right! She's dangerous! How long has she been doing that?

THÉRÈSE: Shut off the radio, Germaine, it's getting on my nerves. I'm too upset after what's happened.

Germaine reluctantly shuts off the radio.

135 GERMAINE: It's alright, Thérèse, I understand.

THÉRÈSE: Honestly, you don't know what it's like, I'm at the end of my tether! You can't imagine my life since I got stuck with my mother-in-law. It's not that I don't love her, the poor woman, I pity her. But she's sick, and so temperamental. I've gotta watch her like a hawk!

DES-NEIGES: How come she's out of the hospital?

THÉRÈSE: Well, you see, Mlle. Verrette, three months ago my husband got a raise, so welfare stopped paying for his mother. If she'd stayed there, we would have had to pay all the bills ourselves.

MARIE-ANGE: My, my, my . . .

140 YVETTE: That's awful.

DES-NEIGES: Dreadful!

During Thérèse's speech, Germaine opens the boxes and distributes the stamps and books.

THÉRÈSE: We had to bring her home. It's some cross to bear, believe me! Don't forget, that woman's ninety-three years old. It's like having a baby in the house. I have to dress her, undress her, wash her . . .

DES-NEIGES: God forbid!

YVETTE: You poor thing.

145 THÉRÈSE: No, it's no fun. Why only this morning, I said to Paul . . . he's my youngest . . . "Maman's going shopping, so you stay here and take good care of Granny." Well, when I got home, Mme. Dubuc had dumped a quart of molasses all over herself and was playing in it like a kid. Of course, Paul was nowhere to be seen. I had to clean the table, the floor, the wheelchair . . .

GERMAINE: What about Mme. Dubuc?

THÉRÈSE: I left her like that for the rest of the afternoon. That'll teach her. If she's gonna act like a baby, I'll treat her like one. Do you realize I have to spoon feed her?

GERMAINE: My poor Thérèse. How I feel for you.

DES-NEIGES: You're too good, Thérèse.

150 GABRIELLE: Much too good, I agree.

THÉRÈSE: What can you do, we all have our crosses to bear.

MARIE-ANGE: If you ask me, Thérèse, you've got a heavy one!

THÉRÈSE: Oh well, I don't complain. I just tell myself that our Lord is good and he's gonna help me get through.

LISETTE: I can't bear it, it makes me want to weep.

155 THÉRÈSE: Now, Mme. de Courval, don't overdo it.

DES-NEIGES: All I can say Mme. Dubuc, is you're a real saint.

GERMAINE: Well now that you've got stamps and booklets, I'll put a little water in some saucers and we can get started, eh? We don't want to spend the night yacking.

She fills a few saucers and passes them around. The women start pasting stamps in the books. Germaine goes out on the balcony.

If Linda were here, she could help me! Linda! Linda! Richard, have you seen Linda? I don't believe it! She's got the nerve to sit and drink Coke while I'm slaving away! Be an angel, will you, and tell her to come home right away? Come see Mme. Lauzon tomorrow and she'll give you some peanuts and candy, if there's any left, okay? Go on, Sweetie, and tell her to get home this minute!

She comes back inside.

The little bitch. She promised to stay home.

MARIE-ANGE: Kids are all the same.

THÉRÈSE: You can say that again! They got no respect.

160 GABRIELLE: You're telling me. At our house, it's unbearable. Ever since my Raymond started his *cours classique* he's changed something awful . . . We don't recognize him! He walks around with his nose in the air like he's too good for us. He speaks Latin, at the table! We have to listen to his awful music. Can you imagine, classical music in the middle of the afternoon? And when we don't want to watch his stupid TV concerts, he throws a fit. If there's one thing I hate it's classical music.

ROSE: Ah! You're not the only one.

THÉRÈSE: I agree. It drives me crazy. Clink! Clank! Bing, Bang, Bong!

GABRIELLE: Of course, Raymond says we don't understand it. As if there's something to understand! Just because he's learning all sorts of nonsense at school, he thinks he can treat us like dirt. I've got half a mind to yank him out and put him to work.

ALL THE WOMEN: Kids are so ungrateful! Kids are so ungrateful!

165 GERMAINE: Be sure to fill those books, eh, girls? Stamps on every page.

ROSE: Relax, Germaine, you'd think we'd never done it before.

YVETTE: Isn't it getting a little warm in here? Maybe we could open the window a bit . . .

GERMAINE: No, no, not with the stamps. It'll make a draft.

ROSE: Come on, Germaine, they're not birds. They won't fly away. Oh, speaking of birds, last Sunday I went to see Bernard, my oldest. Well, you've never seen so many birds in one house. The house is one big bird cage. And it's her doing, you know. She's nuts about birds! And she doesn't want to kill any. Too soft-hearted, but surely to God there's a limit. Listen to this, it's a scream.

Spotlight on Rose Ouimet.

I'm telling you the woman's nuts. I joke about it but really, it's not funny. Anyway, last Easter, Bernard picked up this bird cage for the two kids. Some guy at the tavern needed money, so he sold it to him cheap. . . . Well, the minute he got it in the house, she went bananas. Fell head over heels in love with his birds. No kidding. She took better care of them than she did her kids. Of course, in no time at all the females were laying eggs . . . And when they started to hatch, Manon thought they were so cute. She didn't have the heart to get rid of them. You've got to be crazy, eh? So she kept them! The whole flock! God knows how many she's got. I never tried to count 'em . . . But, believe me, every time I set foot in the place I nearly go out of my mind! But wait, you haven't heard anything yet. Every day around two, she opens up the cage and out come her stupid birds. What happens? They fly all over the house. They shit all over everything, including us, and we run after them cleaning it all up. Of course, when it's time to get them back in the cage, they don't want to go. They're having too much fun! So Manon starts screaming at the kids, "Catch Maman's little birdies, Maman's too tired." So the kids go charging after the birds and the place is a frigging circus. Me, I get the hell out! I go sit on the balcony and wait till they've all been caught.

The women laugh.

And those kids! God, what brats! Oh, I like them okay, they're my grandchildren. But Jesus, do they drive me nuts. Our kids weren't like that. Say what you like. Young people today, they don't know how to bring up their kids.

170 GERMAINE: You said it!

YVETTE: That's for sure.

ROSE: I mean, take the bathroom. Now we wouldn't have let our kids play in there. Well, you should have seen it on Sunday. The kids went in there like they were just going about their business and in no time flat they'd turned the place upside down. I didn't say a word! Manon always says I talk too much. But I could hear them alright and they were getting on my nerves. You know what they were doing? They took the toilet paper, and they unrolled the whole goddamn thing. Manon just yelled "Look, you kids, Maman's gonna get angry." A lot of good that did. They didn't pay any attention. They kept right on going. I would've skinned them alive, the little buggers. And were they having a ball! Bruno, the youngest . . . Can you imagine calling a kid "Bruno"? . . . Anyway, Bruno climbed into the bathtub fully dressed and all rolled up in toilet paper and turned on the water. Listen, he was laughing so hard he nearly drowned! He was making boats out of soggy paper and the water was running all over the place. A real flood! Well, I had to do something. I mean, enough is enough, so I gave them a licking and sent them off to bed.

Yvette: That's exactly what they needed!

Rose: Their mother raised a stink, of course, but I'll be damned if I was gonna let them carry on like that. Manon, the dim-wit, she just sits there peeling potatoes and listening to the radio. Oh, she's a winner, that one! But I guess she's happy. The only thing she worries about is her birds. Poor Bernard! At times I really feel sorry for him, being married to that. He should have stayed home with me. He was a lot better off . . .

She bursts out laughing.

175 Yvette: Isn't she a riot! There's no stopping her.

Gabrielle: Yeah, there's never a dull moment with Rose.

Rose: I always say, when it's time to laugh, might as well have a good one. Every story has a funny side, you know? Even the sad ones . . .

Thérèse: You're damn lucky if you can say that, Mme. Ouimet. It's not everyone . . .

Des-Neiges: We understand, dear. It must be hard for you to laugh with all your troubles. You're far too good, Mme. Dubuc! You're always thinking of others . . .

180 Rose: That's right, you should think of yourself sometimes. You never go out.

Thérèse: I don't have time! When would you have me go out? I have to take care of her . . . Ah! If only that was all . . .

Germaine: Thérèse, don't tell me there's more.

Thérèse: If you only knew! Now that my husband's making some money the family thinks we're millionaires. Why only yesterday, a sister-in-law of my sister-in-law's came to the door with her hand out. Well, you know me. When she told me her story it just broke my heart. So I gave her some old clothes I didn't need anymore . . . Ah, she was so happy . . . weeping with gratitude . . . she even kissed my hands.

Des-Neiges: I'm not surprised. You deserve it!

185 Marie-Ange: Mme. Dubuc, I really admire you.

Thérèse: Oh, don't say that . . .

Des-Neiges: No, no, no. You deserve it.

Lisette: You certainly do, Mme. Dubuc. You deserve our admiration and I assure you, I shan't forget you in my prayers.

Thérèse: Well, I always say, "If God put poor people on this earth, they gotta be encouraged."

190 Germaine: When you're through filling your books there, instead of piling them on the table, why don't we put them back in the box? . . . Rose, give me a hand. We'll take out the empty books and put in the full ones.

ROSE: Good idea. My God! Look at all these books. We gotta fill all them tonight?

GERMAINE: Sure, why not? Besides, everyone's not here yet, so we . . .

DES-NEIGES: Who else is coming, Mme. Lauzon?

GERMAINE: Rhéauna Bibeau and Angéline Sauvé are supposed to come by after the funeral parlour. One of Mlle. Bibeau's old girlfriends has a daughter whose husband died. His name was . . . Baril, I think . . .

195　YVETTE: Not Rosaire Baril.

GERMAINE: Yeah, I think that's it . . .

YVETTE: But I knew him well! I used to go out with him for Godsake. How do you like that! I'd have been a widow today.

GABRIELLE: Guess what, girls? I got the eight mistakes in last Saturday's paper. It's the first time I ever got 'em all and I've been trying for six months . . . I sent in the answer . . .

YVETTE: Did you win anything yet?

200　GABRIELLE: Do I look like someone who's ever won anything?

THÉRÈSE: Hey, Germaine, what are you going to do with all these stamps?

GERMAINE: Didn't I tell you? I'm going to re-decorate the whole house. Wait a minute . . . Where did I put the catalogue? . . . Ah, here it is. Look at that, Thérèse. I'm gonna have all that for nothing.

THÉRÈSE: For nothing! You mean it's not going to cost you a cent?

GERMAINE: Not a cent! Aren't these contests wonderful?

205　LISETTE: That's not what Mme. Brouillette said a while ago . . .

GERMAINE: What do you mean?

MARIE-ANGE: Mme. de Courval, really!

ROSE: Well, come on, Mme. Brouillette. Don't be afraid to say what you think. You said earlier you don't like these contests because only one family wins.

MARIE-ANGE: Well, it's true! All these lotteries and contests are unfair. I'm against them.

210　GERMAINE: Just because you never won anything.

MARIE-ANGE: Maybe, maybe, but they're still not fair.

GERMAINE: Not fair, my eye! You're jealous, that's all. You said so yourself the minute you walked in. Well, I don't like jealous people, Mme. Brouillette. I don't like them one bit! In fact, if you really want to know, I can't stand them!

MARIE-ANGE: Well! In that case, I'm leaving!

GERMAINE: No, no don't go! Look I'm sorry . . . I'm all nerves tonight. I don't know what I'm saying. We'll just forget it, okay? You have every right to your opinions. Every right. Just sit back down and keep pasting.

215　ROSE: Our sister's afraid of losing one of her workers.

GABRIELLE: Shut up, Rose! You're always sticking your nose where it don't belong.

ROSE: What's eating you? I can't even open my mouth?

MARIE-ANGE: Alright, I'll stay. But I still don't like them.

From this point on, Marie-Ange Brouillette will steal all the books she fills. The others will see what she's doing right from the start, except for Germaine, obviously, and they will decide to follow suit.

LISETTE: Well, I figured out the mystery charade in last month's Chatelaine. It was very easy . . . My first syllable is a Persian king . . .

220 ROSE: Onassis?

LISETTE: No, a *Persian* king . . . It's a "shah" . . .

ROSE: That's a Persian?

LISETTE: Why, of course . . .

ROSE: *(laughing)* That's his tough luck!

225 LISETTE: My second is for killing bugs . . . No one? . . . Oh, well, "Raid" . . .

ROSE: My husband's a worm, do you think it would work on him? . . . She's really nuts with all this stuff, eh?

LISETTE: And the whole thing is a social game . . .

ROSE: Spin the bottle!

GABRIELLE: Rose, will you shut up for Godsake! *(to Lisette)* Scrabble?

230 LISETTE: Oh, come now, it's simple . . . Shah-raid . . . Charade!

YVETTE: Ah . . . What's a charade?

LISETTE: Of course, I figured it out in no time . . . It was so easy . . .

YVETTE: So, did you win anything?

LISETTE: Oh, I didn't bother to send it in. I just did it for the challenge . . . Besides, do I look like I need to win things?

235 ROSE: Well, I like mystery words, hidden words, crosswords, turned-around words, bilingual words. All that stuff with words. It's my specialty. I'm a champ, you know, I've broken all the records! Never miss a contest . . . Costs me two bucks a week just for stamps!

YVETTE: So did you win yet?

ROSE: *(looking at Germaine)* Do I look like somebody who's ever won anything?

THÉRÈSE: Mme. Dubuc, will you let go of my saucer? . . . There, now you've done it! You've spilled it! That's the last straw!

She socks her mother-in-law on the head and the latter settles down a little.

GABRIELLE: Wow! You don't fool around! Aren't you afraid you'll hurt her?

240 THÉRÈSE: No, no. She's used to it. It's the only way to shut her up. My husband figured it out. If you give her a good bash on the head, it seems to knock her out a while. That way she stays in her corner and we get some peace.

Blackout.

Spotlight on Yvette Longpré.

YVETTE: When my daughter Claudette got back from her honeymoon, she gave me the top part of her wedding cake. I was so proud! It's such a lovely piece. A miniature sanctuary all made of icing. It's got a red velvet stairway leading up to a platform and on top of the platform stand the bride and groom. Two little dolls all dressed up like newly-weds. There's even a priest to bless them and behind him there's an altar. It's all icing. I've never seen anything so beautiful. Of course, we paid a lot for the cake. After all, six levels! It wasn't all cake though. That would have cost a fortune. Just the first two levels were cake. The rest was wood. But it's amazing, eh? You'd never have guessed. Anyway, when my daughter gave me the top part, she had it put under this glass bell. It looked so pretty, but I was afraid it would spoil . . . you know, without air. So I took my husband's glass knife . . . He's got a special knife for cutting glass . . . And I cut a hole in the top of the bell. Now the air will stay fresh and the cake won't go bad.

DES-NEIGES: Me too. I took a stab at a contest a few weeks ago. You had to find a slogan for some bookstore . . . I think it was Hachette or something . . . Anyway, I gave it a try . . . I came up with "Hachette will chop the cost of your books." Not bad, eh?

YVETTE: Yeah, but did you win anything?

DES-NEIGES: Do I look like somebody who's ever won anything?

245 GERMAINE: By the way, Rose, I saw you cutting your grass this morning. You should buy a lawn-mower.

ROSE: What for? I get along fine with scissors. Besides it keeps me in shape.

GERMAINE: You were puffing away like a steam engine.

ROSE: I'm telling you, it's good for me. Anyway, I can't afford a lawn-mower. Even if I could, that's the last thing I'd buy.

GERMAINE: I'll be getting a lawn-mower with my stamps . . .

250 DES-NEIGES: Her and her stamps, she's starting to get on my nerves!

She hides a booklet in her purse.

ROSE: What are you gonna do with a lawn-mower on the third floor?

GERMAINE: You never know, it might come in handy. And who knows, we might move someday.

DES-NEIGES: I suppose she's going to tell us she needs a new house for all the stuff she's gonna get with her lovely stamps.

GERMAINE: You know, we probably will need a bigger place for all the stuff I'm gonna get with my stamps.

Des-Neiges Verrette, Marie-Ange Brouillette, and Thérèse Dubuc all hide two or three books each.

Rose, if you want, you can borrow my lawn-mower.

255 ROSE: No way! I might bust it. I'd be collecting stamps for the next two years just to pay you back.

The women laugh.

GERMAINE: Don't be smart.

MARIE-ANGE: Isn't she something! Can you beat that!

THÉRÈSE: Hey, I forgot to tell you. I guessed the mystery voice on the radio
. . . It was Duplessis . . . My husband figured it out 'cause it was an old
voice. I sent in twenty-five letters just to be sure they'd get it. And for
extra luck, I signed my youngest boy's name, Paul Dubuc . . .

YVETTE: Did you win anything yet?

260 THÉRÈSE: *(looking to Germaine)* Do I look like someone who's ever won anything?

GABRIELLE: Say, do you know what my husband's gonna get me for my
birthday?

ROSE: Same as last year. Two pairs of nylons.

GABRIELLE: No sir-ee! A fur coat. Of course, it's not real fur, but who cares? I
don't think real fur's worth buying anymore. The synthetics they make
nowadays are just as nice. In fact, sometimes nicer.

LISETTE: Oh, I disagree . . .

265 ROSE: Sure, we all know who's got a fat mink stole!

LISETTE: Well, if you ask me, there's no substitute for authentic, genuine
fur. Incidentally, I'll be getting a new stole in the autumn. The one I
have now is three years old and it's starting to look . . . Well, a bit
ratty. Mind you, it's still mink, but . . .

ROSE: Shut your mouth, you bloody liar! We know goddamn well your
husband's up to his ass in debt because of your mink stoles and trips
to Europe! She's got no more money than the rest of us and she thinks
her farts smell like perfume!

LISETTE: Mme. Jodoin, if your husband wants to buy my stole, I'll sell it to
him cheap. Then you'll have a real mink. After all, between friends . . .

YVETTE: You know the inflated objects game in the paper, the one where
you're supposed to guess what the objects are? Well, I guessed them.
There was a screw, a screw-driver and some kind of bent up hook.

270 THE OTHERS: So . . .

Yvette sits down.

GERMAINE: You know Daniel, Mme. Robitaille's little boy? He fell off the
second floor balcony the other day. Not even a scratch! How 'bout
that?

MARIE-ANGE: Don't forget he landed on Mme. Turgeon's hammock. And
Monsieur Turgeon was in it at the time . . .

GERMAINE: That's right. He's in hospital for three months.

DES-NEIGES: Speaking of accidents, I heard a joke the other day . . .

275 ROSE: Well, aren't you gonna tell us?

DES-NEIGES: Oh, I couldn't. It's too racy . . .

ROSE: Come on, Mlle. Verrette! We know you've got a stack of them . . .

DES-NEIGES: No. I'm too embarrassed. I don't know why, but I am . . .

GABRIELLE: Don't be such a tease, Mlle. Verrette. You know darn well you're
gonna tell us anyway . . .

280 DES-NEIGES: Well . . . Alright . . . There was this nun who got raped in an
   alley . . .

ROSE: Sounds good!

DES-NEIGES: And the next morning they found her lying in the yard, a real
   mess, her habit pulled over her head, moaning away . . . so this
   reporter comes running over and he says to her, "Excuse me, Sister, but
   could you tell us something about this terrible thing that's happened
   to you?" Well, she opens her eyes, looks up at him and in a very small
   voice she says, "Again, please."

*All the women burst out laughing except for Lisette de Courval who appears scan-
dalized.*

ROSE: Christ Almighty, that's hysterical! I haven't heard such a good one
   for ages. I'm gonna pee my pants! Mlle. Verrette, where in the world
   do you get them?

GABRIELLE: You know where, from her travelling salesman . . .

285 DES-NEIGES: Mme. Jodoin, please!

ROSE: That's right too. Her travelling salesman . . .

LISETTE: I don't understand.

GABRIELLE: Mme. Verrette has a travelling salesman who comes to sell her
   brushes every month. I think she likes him more than his brushes.

DES-NEIGES: Mme. Jodoin, honestly!

290 ROSE: One thing's for sure, Mlle. Verrette has more brushes than anyone in
   the parish. Hey, I saw your boyfriend the other day . . . He was sitting
   in the restaurant . . . He must have been to see you, eh?

DES-NEIGES: Yes, he was—but I assure you, there's nothing between us.

ROSE: That's what they all say.

DES-NEIGES: Really, Mme. Ouimet, you're always twisting things to make
   people look bad. Monsieur Simard is a very nice man.

ROSE: Yeah, but who's to say you're a nice lady? Now, now, Mlle. Verrette,
   don't get angry. I'm only pulling your leg.

295 DES-NEIGES: Then don't say things like that. Of course, I'm a nice lady, a
   thoroughly respectable one, too. By the way, the last time he was over,
   Henri . . . 'Er . . . Monsieur Simard was telling me about a project he
   has in mind . . . And he asked me to extend you all an invitation. He
   wants me to organize a demonstration next week . . . At my house. He
   chose me because he knows my house . . . It'd be for a week Sunday,
   right after the rosary. I need at least ten people if I'm gonna get my
   gift . . . You know, they give away those fancy cups to the one who
   holds the demonstration . . . Fantasy Chinaware . . . You should see
   them, they're gorgeous. They're souvenirs he brought back from
   Niagara Falls . . . They must have cost a fortune.

ROSE: You bet, we'll go, eh, girls? I love demonstrations! Any door prizes?

DES-NEIGES: I don't know. I suppose. Maybe . . . Anyway, I'll provide snacks . . .

ROSE: That's more than you get around here. We'll be lucky to see a glass
   of water!

Olivine Dubuc tries to bite her daughter-in-law.

THÉRÈSE: Mme. Dubuc, if you don't stop that I'm gonna lock you in the bathroom and you can stay there for the rest of the evening.

Blackout. Spotlight on Des-Neiges Verrette.

300 DES-NEIGES: The first time I saw him I thought he was ugly . . . it's true. He's not good-looking. When I opened the door he took off his hat and said, "Would you be interested in buying some brushes, Madame?" I slammed the door in his face. I never let a man in the house! Who knows what might happen . . . The only one who gets in is the paper boy. He's still too young to get any wrong ideas. Well, a month later my friend with the brushes came back. There was a horrible snowstorm outside, so I let him stand in the hall. Once he was in the house, I was frightened, but I told myself he didn't look dangerous, even if he wasn't good looking . . . He's always well-dressed . . . Not a hair out of place . . . He's a real gentleman . . . And so polite! Well, he sold me a couple of brushes and then he showed me his catalogue. There was one that I wanted, but he didn't have it with him, so he said I could place an order. Ever since then, he's come back once a month. Sometimes I don't buy a thing. He just comes in and we chat for a while. He's such a nice man. When he speaks, you forget he's ugly. And he knows so many interesting things! The man must travel all over the province! I think . . . I think I'm in love with him . . . I know it's crazy. I only see him once a month, but it's so nice when we're together. I'm so happy when he comes. I've never felt this way before. Never. Men never paid much attention to me. I've always been . . . unattached. But he tells me about his trips, and all kinds of stories . . . Sometimes they're a bit risqué, but honestly, they're so funny! I must admit, I've always liked stories that are a bit off-colour . . . And it's good for you to tell them sometimes. Not all his jokes are dirty, mind you. Lots of them are clean. And it's only lately that he's been telling me the spicy ones. Sometimes they're so dirty I blush! The last time he came he took my hand when I blushed. I nearly went out of my mind. My insides went all funny when he put his big hand on mine. I need him so badly! I don't want him to go away! Sometimes, just sometimes, I dream about him. I dream . . . that we're married. I need him to come and see me. He's the first man that ever cared about me. I don't want to lose him! I don't want to! If he goes away, I'll be all alone again, and I need . . . someone to love . . .

She lowers her eyes and murmurs.

I need a man.

The lights come on again. Linda Lauzon, Ginette Menard, and Lise Paquette enter.

GERMAINE: Ah, there you are!

LINDA: I was at the restaurant.

GERMAINE: I know you were at the restaurant. You keep hanging around there, you're gonna end up like your Aunt Pierrette . . . In a whore house.

LINDA: Lay off, Ma! You're making a stink over nothing.

305 GERMAINE: I asked you to stay home . . .

LINDA: Look, I went to get cigarettes and I ran into Lise and Ginette . . .

GERMAINE: That's no excuse. You knew I was having company, why didn't you come right home. You do it on purpose, Linda. You do it just to make my blood boil. You want me to blow my stack in front of my friends? Is that it? You want me to swear in public? Well, Jesus Christ Almighty, you've succeeded! But don't think you're off the hook yet, Linda Lauzon. I'll take care of you later.

ROSE: This is no time to bawl her out, Germaine!

GABRIELLE: Rose, you mind your own business.

310 LINDA: So, I'm a little late, my God, it's not the end of the world!

LISE: It's our fault, Mme. Lauzon.

GINETTE: Yeah, it's our fault.

GERMAINE: I know it's your fault. And I've told Linda a hundred times not to run around with tramps. But you think she gives a damn? Sometimes I'd like to strangle her!

ROSE: Now, Germaine . . .

315 GABRIELLE: Rose, I told you, stay out of this! You got that? It's their business. It's nothing to do with you.

ROSE: Hey, get off my back! What's with you anyway? Linda's getting bawled out and she hasn't done a goddamn thing!

GABRIELLE: It's none of our business!

LINDA: Leave her alone, Aunt Gaby. She's only trying to defend me.

GABRIELLE: Don't you tell me what to do! I'm your Godmother!

320 GERMAINE: You see what she's like! Day in and day out! I never brought her up to act this way.

ROSE: Now that you mention it, how do you bring up your kids?

GERMAINE: Hah! You should talk! . . . Your kids . . .

LINDA: Go on, Aunt Rose, tell her. You're the only one who can give it to her good.

GERMAINE: So, you're siding with your Aunt Rose now are you? You've forgotten what you said when she phoned a while ago, eh? You've forgotten about that? Come on, Linda, tell Aunt Rose what you said about her.

325 LINDA: That was different . . .

ROSE: Why, what did she say?

GERMAINE: Well, she answered the phone when you called, right? And she was too rude to say, "One moment, please," so I told her to be more polite with you. . . .

LINDA: Will you shut up, Ma! That has nothing to do with it.

ROSE: I want to know what you said, Linda.

330 LINDA: It's not important, I was mad at her.

GERMAINE: She said, "It's only Aunt Rose. Why should I be polite to her?"

ROSE: I don't believe it . . . You said that?

LINDA: I told you, I was mad at her!

ROSE: I never thought that of you, Linda. There, you've let me down. You've really let me down.

335 GABRIELLE: Let them fight it out themselves, Rose.

ROSE: You bet I'll let 'em fight. Go on, Germaine. Knock her silly, the little brat! You wanna know something, Linda? Your mother's right. If you're not careful, you'll end up like your Aunt Pierrette. I've got a good mind to slap your face!

GERMAINE: Just you try it! You don't lay a hand on my kids! If they need a beating, I'll do it. Nobody else!

THÉRÈSE: Will you please stop bickering, I'm tired!

DES-NEIGES: Lord, yes, you're wearing us out.

340 THÉRÈSE: You'll wake up my mother-in-law and get her going again.

GERMAINE: She's your problem, not mine! Why didn't you leave her at home?

THÉRÈSE: Germaine Lauzon!

GABRIELLE: Well, she's right. You don't go out to parties with a ninety-three year old cripple.

LISETTE: Mme. Jodoin, didn't I just hear you tell your sister to mind her own business?

345 GABRIELLE: Keep your big nose out of this, you stuck up bitch! Shut your yap and keep pasting or I'll shut it for you.

Lisette de Courval gets up.

LISETTE: Gabrielle Jodoin!

Olivine Dubuc spills the saucer she has been playing with.

THÉRÈSE: Mme. Dubuc, for Godsake!

GERMAINE: Aw, shit, my tablecloth!

ROSE: She's soaked me, the old bag!

350 THÉRÈSE: That's not true! You weren't even close!

ROSE: Sure, call me a liar right to my face!

THÉRÈSE: Rose Ouimet, you are a liar!

GERMAINE: Look out, she's falling out of her chair!

DES-NEIGES: Oh, no, she's on the floor, again!

355 THÉRÈSE: Somebody give me a hand.

ROSE: Not me, no way!

GABRIELLE: Pick her up yourself.

DES-NEIGES: Here, I'll help you, Mme. Dubuc.

THÉRÈSE: Thank you, Mlle. Verrette.

360 GERMAINE: And you, Linda, you watch your step for the rest of the evening.

LINDA: I feel like going back to the restaurant.

GERMAINE: Do that and you won't set foot in this house again, you hear?

LINDA: Sure, I've heard it a thousand times.

LISE: Can it, Linda . . .

365 THÉRÈSE: For Godsake, Mme. Dubuc, make a little effort. You go limp like
that on purpose.

MARIE-ANGE: I'll hold the chair.

THÉRÈSE: Thank you . . .

ROSE: If it was me, I'd take that lousy chair and . . .

GABRIELLE: Rose, don't start again!

370 THÉRÈSE: Whew! What I go through. . . .

GABRIELLE: Hey, will you get a load of de Courval, still pasting her stamps
. . . The bloody snob. As if nothing had happened! I guess we're not
good enough for her.

Blackout.

Spotlight on Lisette de Courval.

LISETTE: It's like living in a barnyard. Léopold told me not to come and he
was right. I should have stayed home. We don't belong with these
people. Once you've tasted life on an ocean liner and have to return to
this, well . . . It's enough to make you weep . . . I can still see myself,
stretched out on the deck chair, a Book-of-the-Month in my lap . . .
And that lieutenant who was giving me the eye . . . My husband says
he wasn't, but he didn't see what I saw . . . Mmmmm . . . That was
some man. Maybe I should have encouraged him a little more . . . *(She
sighs)* . . . And Europe! Everyone there is so refined! So much more
polite than here. You'd never meet a Germaine Lauzon in Europe.
Never! Only people of substance. In Paris, you know, everyone speaks
so beautifully and there they talk real French . . . Not like here . . . I
despise everyone of them. I'll never set foot in this place again!
Léopold was right about these people. These people are cheap. We
shouldn't mix with them. Shouldn't talk about them . . . They should
be hidden away somewhere. They don't know how to live! We broke
away from this and we must never, ever go back. Dear God, they make
me so ashamed!

The lights come back up.

LINDA: I've had it. I'm leaving . . .

GERMAINE: The hell you are! I'm warning you Linda! . . .

375 LINDA: "I'm warning you, Linda!" Is that all you know how to say?

LISE: Linda, don't be stupid.

GINETTE: Let's stay.

LINDA: No, I'm leaving. I've listened to enough crap for one night.

GERMAINE: Linda, I forbid you to leave!

380 VOICE OF A NEIGHBOUR: Will you stop screaming up there. We can't hear
ourselves think!

Rose goes out on the balcony.

ROSE: Hey, you! Get back in your house.

NEIGHBOUR: I wasn't talking to you!

ROSE: Oh yes, you were. I'm just as loud as the rest of them!

GABRIELLE: Rose, get in here!

385 DES-NEIGES: *(referring to the neighbour)* Don't pay any attention to her.

NEIGHBOUR: I'm gonna call the cops!

ROSE: Go right ahead, we need some men up here.

GERMAINE: Rose Ouimet, get back in this house! And you, Linda . . .

LINDA: I'm leaving. See ya!

She goes out with Ginette and Lise.

390 GERMAINE: She's gone! Gone! Walked right out! I don't believe it! That kid will be the death of me. I'm gonna smash something. I'm gonna smash something!

ROSE: Germaine, control yourself.

GERMAINE: Making a fool of me in front of everyone! *(She starts sobbing.)* My own daughter . . . I'm so ashamed!

GABRIELLE: Come on, Germaine. It's not that bad . . .

LINDA'S VOICE: Hey, if it isn't Mlle. Sauvé. How are you doing?

395 ANGÉLINE'S VOICE: Hello, sweetheart, how are you?

ROSE: Germaine, they're here. Blow your nose and stop crying.

LINDA'S VOICE: Not bad, thanks.

RHÉAUNA'S VOICE: Where are you off to?

LINDA'S VOICE: I was gonna go to the restaurant, but now that you're here, I think I'll stay.

Linda, Ginette, and Lise enter with Angéline and Rhéauna.

400 ANGÉLINE: Hello, everybody.

RHÉAUNA: Hello.

THE OTHERS: Hello, hello. Come on it, how have you been . . . *(etc.)*

RHÉAUNA: What an awful climb, Mme. Lauzon. I'm all out of breath.

GERMAINE: Well, have a seat . . .

405 ROSE: You're out of breath? Don't worry, my sister's getting an elevator with her stamps.

They all laugh except Rhéauna and Angéline who don't understand.

GERMAINE: Very funny, Rose! Linda, go get some more chairs . . .

LINDA: Where? There aren't any more.

GERMAINE: Go ask Mme. Bergeron if she'll lend us some . . .

LINDA: *(to the girls)* Come on guys . . .

410 GERMAINE: *(low to Linda)* We make peace for now, but wait til the others have gone . . .

LINDA: I'm not scared of you. If I came back it's because Mlle. Sauvé and Mlle. Bibeau showed up, not because of you.

Linda goes out with her friends.

DES-NEIGES: Here, take my seat, Mlle. Bibeau . . .

THÉRÈSE: Yes, come and sit next to me . . .

MARIE-ANGE: Sit down here, Mlle. Bibeau . . .

415 ANGÉLINE AND RHÉAUNA: Thank you. Thanks very much.

RHÉAUNA: I see you're pasting stamps.

GERMAINE: We sure are. A million of 'em!

RHÉAUNA: Dear God, a million! How are you getting on?

ROSE: Not bad . . . But my tongue's paralyzed.

420 RHÉAUNA: You've been doing it with your tongue?

GABRIELLE: Of course not, she's just being smart.

ROSE: Good old Bibeau. Sharp as a tack!

ANGÉLINE: Why don't we give you a hand?

ROSE: Okay. As long as you don't give us some tongue!

She bursts out laughing.

425 GABRIELLE: Rose, don't be vulgar!

GERMAINE: So, how was the funeral parlour?

Black out. Spotlight on Angéline and Rhéauna.

RHÉAUNA: I tell you, it came as a shock . . .

ANGÉLINE: But I thought you hardly knew him.

RHÉAUNA: I knew his mother. So did you. Remember, we went to school
together. I watched that man grow up . . .

430 ANGÉLINE: Such a shame. Gone, just like that. And us, we're still here.

RHÉAUNA: Ah, but not for long . . .

ANGÉLINE: Rhéauna, please . . .

RHÉAUNA: I know what I'm talking about. You can tell when the end is
near. I've suffered. I know.

ANGÉLINE: Ah, when it comes to that, we've both had our share. I've suffered, too.

435 RHÉAUNA: I've suffered a lot more that you, Angéline. Seventeen operations! A lung, a kidney, one of my breasts . . . Gone! I'm telling you,
there's not much left.

ANGÉLINE: And me with my arthritis that won't let up. But Mme. . . . What
was her name . . . You know, the wife of the deceased . . . She gave me
a recipe . . . She says it works wonders.

RHÉAUNA: But you've tried everything. The doctors have all told you,
there's nothing you can do. There's no cure for arthritis.

ANGÉLINE: Doctors, doctors! . . . I've had it with doctors. All they think
about is money. They bleed you to death and go to California for the
winter. You know, Rhéauna, the doctor said he'd get well, Monsieur . . .
What was his name again? The one who died?

RHÉAUNA: Monsieur Baril . . .

440 ANGÉLINE: That's it. I can never remember it. It's easy enough, too.
Anyhow, the doctor told Monsieur Baril that he had nothing to worry
about . . . And look what happened . . . Only forty years old . . .

RHÉAUNA: Forty years old! That's young to die.

ANGÉLINE: He sure went fast . . .

RHÉAUNA: She told me how it happened. It's so sad . . .

ANGÉLINE: Really? I wasn't there. How did it happen?

445 RHÉAUNA: When he got home from work on Monday night, she thought
he was looking a bit strange. He was white as a sheet, so she asked him
how he felt. He said he felt okay and they started supper . . . Well,
now, the kids were making a fuss at the table and Monsieur Baril got
mad and had to punish Rolande. That's his daughter . . . of course,
after that, he looked like he was ready to drop . . . she didn't take her
eyes off him for a second . . . But she told me later that it happened so
fast she didn't have time to do a thing. All of a sudden he said he felt
funny and over he went . . . His face right in the soup. That was it!

ANGÉLINE: Lord, have mercy. So sudden! I tell you, Rhéauna, it's frightening. It gives me the shivers.

RHÉAUNA: Isn't it the truth? We never know when God's going to come for
us. He said it Himself, "I'll come like a thief."

ANGÉLINE: Don't talk like that, it scares me. I don't want to die that way. I
want to die in my bed . . . have time to make my confession . . .

RHÉAUNA: Oh, God forbid that I should die before confessing! Angéline,
promise me you'll call the priest the minute I'm feeling weak. Promise
me that.

450 ANGÉLINE: You know I will. You've asked me a hundred times. Didn't I get
him there for your last attack? You had Communion and everything.

RHÉAUNA: I'm so afraid to die without the last rites.

ANGÉLINE: But what do you have to confess, Rhéauna?

RHÉAUNA: Don't say that, Angéline. Don't ever say that! We're never too
old to sin.

ANGÉLINE: If you ask me, Rhéauna, you'll go straight to heaven. You've got
nothing to worry about. Hey! Did you notice Baril's daughter? The way
she's changed! She looks like a corpse.

455 RHÉAUNA: Isn't it the truth. Poor Rolande. She's telling everyone that she
killed her father. It's because of her that he got mad, you see, at supper
. . . Oh I feel sorry for her . . . And her mother. What a tragedy! Such a
loss for everyone. They'll miss him so. . . .

ANGÉLINE: You're telling me . . . The father. Mind you, it's not as bad as the
mother, but still . . .

RHÉAUNA: True. Losing the mother is worse. You can't replace a mother.

ANGÉLINE: Did you see how nice he looked? . . . Like a young man. He was
even smiling. . . . I could have sworn he was asleep. But I still think
he's better off where he is . . . You know what they say, it's the ones
who stay behind who most deserve the pity. Him, he's fine now . . .
Ah, I still can't get over how good he looked. Almost like he was
breathing.

RHÉAUNA: Yeah! But he wasn't.

460 ANGÉLINE: But I can't imagine why they put him in that suit . . .

RHÉAUNA: What do you mean?

ANGÉLINE: Didn't you notice? He was wearing a blue suit. You don't do that
when you're dead. A blue suit is much too light. Now, navy-blue

would be okay, but powder blue . . . Never! When you're dead, you
wear a black suit.

RHÉAUNA: Maybe he didn't have one. They're not that well off, you know.

ANGÉLINE: Dear God, you can rent a black suit! And look at Mme. Baril's
sister! In green! At a funeral parlour! And did you notice how much
she's aged? She looks years older than her sister . . .

465 RHÉAUNA: She is older.

ANGÉLINE: Don't be silly, Rhéauna, she's younger.

RHÉAUNA: No, she isn't.

ANGÉLINE: Why sure, Rhéauna, listen! Mme. Baril is at least thirty-seven,
but her sister . . .

RHÉAUNA: She's well over forty!

470 ANGÉLINE: Rhéauna, she isn't!

RHÉAUNA: She's at least forty-five . . .

ANGÉLINE: That's what I'm telling you. She's aged so much, she looks a lot
older than she is . . . Listen, my sister-in-law, Rose-Aimée, is thirty-six
and the two of them went to school together. . . .

RHÉAUNA: Well, anyway, it doesn't surprise me she's aged so fast . . . What
with the life she leads . . .

ANGÉLINE: I'm not sure they're true, all those stories.

475 RHÉAUNA: They must be! Mme. Baril tries to hid it 'cause it's her sister . . .
But the truth always comes out. It's like Mme. Lauzon and her sister,
Pierrette. Now, if there's one person I can't stand, it's Pierrette Guérin.
A shameless hussy! Nothing but shame to her whole family. I tell you,
Angéline, I wouldn't want to see her soul. It must be black as coal.

ANGÉLINE: You know, Rhéauna, deep down inside, Pierrette isn't all bad.

Spotlight on Germaine Lauzon.

GERMAINE: My sister, Pierrette, I've had nothing to do with her for a long
time. Not after what she did. When she was young, she was so good, and
so pretty. But now, she's nothing but a whore. My sisters and I were nuts
about her. We spoiled her rotten. And look what it got us . . . I don't
understand. I don't understand. Papa used to call her his pepper pot. He
was so crazy about his little Pierrette. When he'd put her on his knee,
you could tell he was happy. And the rest of us weren't even jealous . . .

ROSE: We'd say, "She's the youngest. It's always that way, it's the youngest
who gets the attention." When she started school, we dressed her like
a princess. I was already married, but I remember as if it were yesterday. Oh, she was so pretty! Like Shirley Temple! And so quick at
school. A lot better than me, that's for sure. I was lousy at school . . . I
was the class clown, that's all I was ever good for . . . . But her, the little
bugger, always coming home with prizes. First in French, first in
Arithmetic, first in Religion . . . Yeah, Religion! She was pious as a nun,
that kid. I tell you, the Sisters were nuts about her! But to see her
today . . . I almost feel sorry for her. She must need help sometimes
. . . She must get so lonely. . . .

GABRIELLE: When she finished school, we asked her what she wanted to do. She wanted to be a teacher. She was all set to begin her training. . . . And then she met her Johnny.

480 THE THREE SISTERS: Goddamn Johnny! He's a devil out of hell! It's all his fault she turned out the way she did. Goddamn Johnny! Goddamn Johnny!

RHÉAUNA: What do you mean, not all bad! You've got to be pretty low to do what she did. Do you know what Mme. Longpré told me about her?

ANGÉLINE: No, what?

THÉRÈSE: Ow!!!

The lights come back up. Thérèse Dubuc gives her mother-in-law a sock on the head.

GERMAINE: Beat her brains out, if you have to Thérèse but do something!

485 THÉRÈSE: Sure, beat her brains out! Look, I'm doing all I can to keep her quiet. I'm not about to kill her just to make you happy.

ROSE: If it was up to me, I'd shove her off the balcony . . . .

THÉRÈSE: What? Say that again, Rose. I didn't hear you!

ROSE: I was talking to myself.

THÉRÈSE: You're scared, eh?

490 ROSE: Me, scared?

THÉRÈSE: Yes, Rose. Scared!

MARIE-ANGE: Don't tell me there's gonna be another fight.

ANGÉLINE: Has there been a fight?

RHÉAUNA: Oh, who was fighting?

495 ANGÉLINE: We should have come sooner.

THÉRÈSE: I won't stand for that. She insulted my mother-in-law! My husband's mother!

LISETTE: There they go again!

ROSE: She's so old! She's useless!

GERMAINE: Rose!

500 GABRIELLE: Rose, that's cruel! Aren't you ashamed?

THÉRÈSE: Rose Ouimet, I'll never forgive you for those words! Never!

ROSE: Ah, piss off!

ANGÉLINE: Who had a fight?

ROSE: You want to know everything, eh, Mademoiselle Sauvé? You want all the gory details?

505 ANGÉLINE: Mme. Ouimet!

ROSE: So you can blab it all over town, eh? Isn't that it?

RHÉAUNA: Rose Ouimet, I don't lose my temper often, but I will not allow you to insult my friend.

MARIE-ANGE: *(to herself)* I'll just grab a few more while no one's looking.

GABRIELLE: *(who has seen her)* What are you doing there, Mme. Brouillette?

510 ROSE: Fine, I've said enough. I'll shut up.

MARIE-ANGE: Shhhh! Take these and keep quiet!

Linda, Ginette, and Lise arrive with the chairs. There is a great hullabalou. All the women change places, taking advantage of the occasion to steal more stamps.

Don't be afraid, take them!

DES-NEIGES: Aren't you overdoing it?

THÉRÈSE: Hide these in your pocket, Mme. Dubuc, . . . No! Damn it! Hide them!

GERMAINE: You know that guy who runs the meat shop, what a thief!

The door opens suddenly and Pierrette Guérin comes in.

515 PIERRETTE: Hi, everybody!

THE OTHERS: Pierrette!

LINDA: Great! It's Aunt Pierrette!

ANGÉLINE: Oh my God, Pierrette!

GERMAINE: What are you doing here? I told you I never wanted to see you again.

520 PIERRETTE: I heard that my big sister, Germaine, had won a million stamps, so I decided to come over and have a look. *(She sees Angéline)* Well, I'll be goddamned! Angéline! What are you doing here?

Everyone looks at Angéline.

Blackout.

ACT II

The second act begins with Pierrette's entrance. Hence the last six lines of Act One are repeated now. The door opens suddenly and Pierrette Guérin comes in.

PIERRETTE: Hi, everybody!

THE OTHERS: Pierrette!

LINDA: Great! It's Aunt Pierrette!

ANGÉLINE: Oh my God, Pierrette!

5 GERMAINE: What are you doing here? I told you I never wanted to see you again.

PIERRETTE: I heard that my big sister, Germaine, had won a million stamps, so I decided to come over and have a look. *(She sees Angéline)* Well, I'll be goddamned! Angéline! What are you doing here?

Everyone looks at Angéline.

ANGÉLINE: My God! I'm caught.

GERMAINE: What do you mean, Angéline?

GABRIELLE: How come you're talking to Mlle. Sauvé?

10 ROSE: You oughta be ashamed!

PIERRETTE: Why? We're real good friends, eh, Géline?

ANGÉLINE: Oh! I think I'm going to faint!

Angéline pretends to faint.

RHÉAUNA: Good heavens, Angéline!

ROSE: She's dead!

15 RHÉAUNA: What?

GABRIELLE: Don't be ridiculous! Rose, you're getting carried away again.

PIERRETTE: She hasn't even fainted. She's only pretending.

Pierrette approaches Angéline.

GERMAINE: Don't you touch her!

PIERRETTE: Mind your own business! She's my friend.

20 RHÉAUNA: What do you mean, your friend?

GERMAINE: Don't try to tell us Mlle. Sauvé is a friend of yours!

PIERRETTE: Of course she is! She comes to see me at the club almost every
    Friday night.

ALL THE WOMEN: What!

RHÉAUNA: That's impossible.

25 PIERRETTE: Ask her! Hey, Géline, isn't it true what I'm saying? Come on,
    stop playing dead and answer me. Angéline, we all know you're faking!
    Tell them. Isn't it true you come to the club?

ANGÉLINE: *(after a silence)* Yes, it's true.

RHÉAUNA: Oh, Angéline! Angéline!

SOME OF THE WOMEN: Dear God, this is dreadful!

SOME OTHER WOMEN: Dear God, this is horrible!

30 LINDA, GINETTE, AND LISE: Holy shit, that's great!

The lights go out.

RHÉAUNA: Angéline! Angéline!

Spotlight on Angéline and Rhéauna.

ANGÉLINE: Rhéauna, you must understand . . .

RHÉAUNA: Don't you touch me! Get away!

THE WOMEN: Who would have thought . . . Such a horrible thing!

35 RHÉAUNA: I'd never have thought this of you. You, in a club. And every
    Friday night! It's not possible. It can't be true.

ANGÉLINE: I don't do anything wrong, Rhéauna. All I have is a Coke.

THE WOMEN: In a club! In a night club!

GERMAINE: God only knows what she does there.

ROSE: Maybe she tries to get picked up.

40 ANGÉLINE: But I tell you, I don't do anything wrong!

PIERRETTE: It's true. She doesn't do anything wrong.

ROSE, GERMAINE, AND GABRIELLE: Shut up, you demon. Shut up!

RHÉAUNA: You're no longer my friend, Angéline. I don't know you.

ANGÉLINE: Listen to me, Rhéauna, you must listen! I'll explain everything
    and then you'll see!

45 ROSE, GERMAINE, AND GABRIELLE: A club! the fastest road to hell!

ALL THE WOMEN: *(except the girls)* The road to hell, the road to hell! If you
    go there, you'll lose your soul! Cursed drink, cursed dancing! That's

the place where our men go wrong and spend their money on women of sin!

ROSE, GERMAINE, AND GABRIELLE: Women of sin like you, Pierrette!

ALL THE WOMEN: *(except the girls)* Shame on you, Angéline Sauvé, to spend your time in this sinful way!

RHÉAUNA: But Angéline, a club! It's worse than hell!

50 PIERRETTE: *(laughing heartily)* If hell's anything like the club I work in, I wouldn't mind eternity there!

ROSE, GERMAINE, AND GABRIELLE: Shut up, Pierrette. The devil has your tongue!

LINDA, GINETTE, AND LISE: The devil? Come on! Get with the times! The clubs are not the end of the world! They're no worse than any place else. They're fun! They're lots of fun. The clubs are lots of fun.

THE WOMEN: Ah! Youth is blind! Youth is blind! You're gonna lose your-selves and then you'll come crying to us. But it'll be too late! It'll be too late! Watch out! You be careful of these cursed places! We don't always know when we fall, but when we get back up, it's too late!

LISE: Too late! It's too late! Oh my God, it's too late!

55 GERMAINE: I hope at least you'll go to confession, Angéline Sauvé!

ROSE: And to think that every Sunday I see you at Communion . . . Communion with a sin like that on your conscience!

GABRIELLE: A mortal sin!

ROSE, GERMAINE, AND GABRIELLE: How many times have we been told . . . It's a mortal sin to set foot in a club!

ANGÉLINE: That's enough. Shut up and listen to me!

60 THE WOMEN: Never! You've no excuse!

ANGÉLINE: Rhéauna, will you listen to me! We're old friends. We've been together for thirty-five years. You mean a lot to me, but there are times when I want to see other people. You know how I am. I like to have fun. I grew up in church basements and I want to see other things. Clubs aren't all bad, you know. I've been going for four years and I never did anything wrong. And the people who work there, they're no worse than us. I want to meet people, Rhéauna! Rhéauna, I've never laughed in my life!

RHÉAUNA: There are better places to laugh. Angéline, you're going to lose your soul. Tell me you won't go back.

ANGÉLINE: Listen, Rhéauna, I can't! I like to go there, don't you understand. I like it!

RHÉAUNA: You must promise or I'll never speak to you again. It's up to you. It's me or the club. If you only knew how much that hurts, my best friend sneaking off to a night club. How do you think that looks, Angéline? What will people say when they see you going there? Especially where Pierrette works. It's the lowest of them all! You must never go back, Angéline, you hear? If you do, it's finished between us. Finished! You ought to be ashamed!

65 ANGÉLINE: Rhéauna, you can't ask me not to go back . . . Rhéauna, answer me!

RHÉAUNA: Until you promise, not another word!

The lights come up. Angéline sits in a corner. Pierrette joins her.

ANGÉLINE: Why did you have to come here tonight?

PIERRETTE: Let them talk. They love to get hysterical. They know damn well you don't do anything wrong at the club. In five minutes, they'll forget all about it.

ANGÉLINE: You think so, eh? Well, what about Rhéauna? You think she'll forgive me just like that? And Mme. de Courval who's in charge of recreation for the parish, also President of the Altar Society at Our Lady of Perpetual Help! You think she'll continue speaking to me? And your sisters who can't stand you because you work in a club! I'm telling you it's hopeless! Hopeless!

70 GERMAINE: Pierrette!

PIERRETTE: Listen, Germaine, Angéline feels bad enough. So let's not fight, eh? I came here to see you and paste stamps and I want to stay. And I don't have the plague, okay? Just leave us alone. Don't worry. The two of us'll stay out of your way. After tonight, if you want, I'll never come back again. But I can't leave Angéline alone.

ANGÉLINE: You can leave if you want, Pierrette . . .

PIERRETTE: No, I want to stay.

ANGÉLINE: Okay, then I'll go.

75 LISETTE: Why don't they both leave!

Angéline gets up.

ANGÉLINE: *(to Rhéauna)* Are you coming?

Rhéauna doesn't answer.

Okay. I'll leave the door unlocked . . .

She goes towards the door. The lights go out. Spotlight on Angéline Sauvé.

It's easy to judge people. It's easy to judge them, but you have to look at both sides of the coin. The people I've met in the club are my best friends. No one has ever treated me so well . . . Not even Rhéauna. I have fun with those people. I can laugh with them. I was brought up by nuns in the parish halls who did the best they could, poor souls, but knew nothing. I was fifty-five years old when I learned to laugh. And it was only by chance. Because Pierrette took me to her club one night. Oh, I didn't want to go. She had to drag me there. But, you know, the minute I got in the door, I knew what it was to go through life without having any fun. I suppose clubs aren't for everyone, but me, I like them. And of course, it's not true that I only have a Coke. Of course, I drink liquor! I don't have much, but still, it makes me happy. I don't do anyone any harm and I buy myself two hours of pleasure every week. But this was bound to happen someday. I knew I'd get caught sooner or later. I knew it. What am I going to do now? Dear

God, what am I going to do? (*Pause.*) Damn it all! Everyone deserves to
get some fun out of life! (*Pause.*) I always said that if I got caught I'd
stop going . . . But I don't know if I can . . . And Rhéauna will never go
along with that. (*Pause.*) Ah, well, I suppose Rhéauna is worth more
than Pierrette. (*She gives a long sigh.*) I guess the party's over . . .

She goes off. Lights out. Spotlight on Yvette Longpré.

YVETTE: Last week, my sister-in-law, Fleur-Ange, had a birthday. They had a
real nice party for her. There was a whole gang of us there. First there
was her and her family, eh? Oscar David, her husband, Fleur-Ange
David, that's her, and their seven kids: Raymonde, Claude, Lisette,
Fernand, Réal, Micheline and Yves. Her husband's parents, Aurèle
David and his wife, Ozéa David, were there too. Next, there was my
sister-in-law's mother, Blanche Tremblay. Her father wasn't there 'cause
he's dead . . . Then there were the other guests: Antonio Fournier, his
wife Rita, Germaine Gervais, also, Wilfred Gervais, Armand Campeau,
Daniel Lemoyne and his wife, Rose-Aimée, Roger Joly, Hormidas Guay,
Simmone Laflamme, Napoléon Gauvin, Anne-Marie Turgeon, Conrad
Joanette, Léa Liasse, Jeanette Landreville, Nona Laplante, Robertine
Portelance, Gilbert Morrissette, Lilianne Beaupré, Virginie Latour,
Alexandre Thibodeau, Ovila Gariépy, Roméo Bacon and his wife
Juliette, Mimi Bleau, Pit Cadieux, Ludger Champagne, Rosaire Rouleau,
Roger Chabot, Antonio Simard, Alexandrine Smith, Philemon Langlois,
Eliane Meunier, Marcel Morel, Grégoire Cinq-Mars, Théodore Fortier,
Hermine Héroux and us, my husband, Euclide, and me. And I think
that's just about everyone. . . .

The lights come back up.

GERMAINE: Okay, now let's get back to work, eh?
ROSE: On your toes, girls. Here we go!
80 DES-NEIGES: We're not doing badly, are we? Look at all I've pasted . . .
MARIE-ANGE: What about all you've stolen . . .
LISETTE: You want to hand me some more stamps, Mme. Lauzon.
GERMAINE: Sure . . . coming right up . . . Here's a whole bunch.
RHÉAUNA: Angéline! Angéline! It can't be true!
85 LINDA: *(to Pierrette)* Hi, Aunt Pierrette.
PIERRETTE: Hi! How're you doing?
LINDA: Oh, not too hot. Ma and I are always fighting and I'm really getting
sick of it. She's always bitching about nothing, you know? I'd sure like
to get out of here.
GERMAINE: The retreats will be starting pretty soon, eh?
ROSE: Yeah! That's what they said last Sunday.
90 MARIE-ANGE: I hope we won't be getting the same priest as last year . . .
GERMAINE: Me too! I didn't like him either. What a bore.
PIERRETTE: Well, what's stopping you? You could come and stay with me . . .
LINDA: Are you kidding? They'd disown me on the spot!

LISETTE: No, we've got a new one coming this year.

95 DES-NEIGES: Oh yeah? Who's it gonna be?

LISETTE: A certain Abbé Rochon. They say he's excellent. I was talking to l'Abbé Gagné the other day and he tells me he's one of his best friends . . .

ROSE: *(to Gabrielle)* There she goes again with her l'Abbé Gagné. We'll be hearing about him all night! You'd think she was in love with him. L'Abbé Gagné this, l'Abbé Gagné that. Well, if you want my opinion, I don't like l'Abbé Gagné.

GABRIELLE: I agree. He's too modern for me. It's okay to take care of parish activities, but he shouldn't forget he's a priest! A man of God!

LISETTE: Oh, but the man is a saint . . . You should get to know him, Mme. Dubuc. I'm sure you'd like him . . . When he speaks, you'd swear it was the Lord himself talking to us.

100 THÉRÈSE: Don't overdo it . . .

LISETTE: And the children! They adore him. Oh, that reminds me, the children in the parish are organizing a variety night for next month. I hope you can all make it because it should be very impressive. They've been practising for ages . . .

DES-NEIGES: What's on the programme?

LISETTE: Well, it's going to be very good. There'll be all sorts of things. Mme. Gladu's little boy is going to sing . . .

ROSE: Again! I'm getting sick of that kid. Besides, since he went on television, his mother's got her nose in the air. She thinks she's a real star!

105 LISETTE: But the child has a lovely voice.

ROSE: Oh yeah? Well, he looks like a girl with his mouth all puckered up like a turkey's ass.

GABRIELLE: Rose!

LISETTE: Diane Aubin will give a demonstration of aquatic swimming . . . We'll be holding the event next door to the city pool, it will be wonderful . . .

ROSE: Any door prizes?

110 LISETTE: Oh yes, lots. And the final event of the evening will be a giant bingo.

THE OTHER WOMEN: *(except the girls)* A bingo!

Blackout.

When the lights come back up, the women are all at the edge of the stage.

LISETTE: Ode to Bingo!

While Rose, Germaine, Gabrielle, Thérèse, and Marie-Ange recite the Ode to Bingo, the four other women call out bingo numbers in counterpoint.

ROSE, GERMAINE, GABRIELLE, THÉRÈSE, AND MARIE-ANGE: Me, there's nothing in the world I like more than bingo. Almost every month we have one in the parish. I get ready two days ahead of time; I'm all wound up, I can't sit still, it's all I can think of. And when the big day arrives, I'm so excited, housework's out of the question. The minute supper's over, I get all dressed up, and a team of wild horses couldn't hold me back. I love playing bingo! I adore playing bingo! There's nothing in the world can beat bingo! When we arrive at the apartment where we're going to play we take off our coats and head straight for the tables. Sometimes it's the living room the lady's cleared, sometimes it's the kitchen. Sometimes it's even the bedroom. We sit at the tables, distribute the cards, set up the chips and the game begins!

The women who are calling the numbers continue alone for a moment.

I'm so excited, I go bananas. I get all mixed up, I sweat like a pig, screw up the numbers, put my chips in the wrong squares, make the caller repeat the numbers, I'm in an awful state! I love playing bingo! I adore playing bingo! There's nothing in the world can beat bingo! The game's almost over. I've got three more tries. Two down and one across. I'm missing the B14! I need the B14! I want the B14! I look at the others. Shit, they're as close as I am. What am I gonna do? I've gotta win! I've gotta win! I've gotta win!

LISETTE: B14!

115　THE OTHERS: Bingo! Bingo! I've won! I knew it! I knew I couldn't lose! I've won! Hey, what did I win?

LISETTE: Last month we had Chinese dog door stops. But this month, this month, we've got ashtray floor lamps!

THE OTHERS: I love playing bingo! I adore playing bingo! There's nothing in the world beats bingo! What a shame they don't have 'em more often. The more they have, the happier it makes me! Long live the Chinese dogs! Long live the ashtray floor lamps! Long live bingo!

Lights go normal.

ROSE: I'm getting thirsty.

GERMAINE: Oh, God, I forgot the drinks! Linda, get out the Cokes.

120　OLIVINE: Coke . . . Coke . . . Yeah . . . Yeah, Coke . . .

THÉRÈSE: Relax, Mme. Dubuc. You'll get your Coke like everyone else. But drink it properly! No spilling it like last time.

ROSE: She's driving me up the wall with her mother-in-law . . .

GABRIELLE: Forget it, Rose. There's been enough fighting already.

GERMAINE: Yeah! Just keep quiet and paste. You're not doing a thing!

Spotlight on the refrigerator. The following scene takes place by the refrigerator door.

125　LISE: *(to Linda)* I've got to talk to you, Linda . . .

LINDA: I know, you told me at the restaurant . . . But it's hardly a good time . . .

LISE: It won't take long and I've got to tell somebody, I can't hide it much longer. I'm too upset. And Linda, you're my best friend . . . Linda, I'm going to have a baby.

LINDA: What! But that's crazy! Are you sure?

LISE: Yes, I'm sure. The doctors told me.

130 LINDA: What are you gonna do?

LISE: I don't know. I'm so depressed! I haven't told my parents yet. My father'll kill me, I know he will. When the doctor told me, I felt like jumping off the balcony . . .

PIERRETTE: Listen, Lise . . .

LINDA: You heard?

PIERRETTE: Yeah! I know you're in a jam, kid, but . . . I might be able to help you . . .

135 LISE: Yeah? How?

PIERRETTE: Well, I know a doctor . . .

LINDA: Pierrette, she can't do that!

PIERRETTE: Come on, it's not dangerous . . . He does it twice a week, this guy.

LISE: I've thought about it already, Linda . . . But I didn't know anyone . . . And I'm scared to try it alone.

140 PIERRETTE: Don't ever do that! It's too dangerous! But with this doctor . . . I can arrange it, if you like. A week from now you'll be all fixed up.

LINDA: Lise, you can't do that!

LISE: What else can I do? It's the only way out. I don't want the thing to be born. Look what happened to Manon Belair. She was in the same boat and now her life's all screwed up because she's got that kid on her hands.

LINDA: What about the father? Can't he marry you?

LISE: Are you kidding! I don't even know where he is. He just took off somewhere. Sure, he promised me the moon. We were gonna be happy. He was raking it in, I thought everything was roses. One present after another. No end to it. It was great while it lasted . . . but Goddamn it, this had to happen. It just had to. Why is it always me who ends up in the shit? All I ever wanted was a proper life for myself. I'm sick of working at Kresge's. I want to make something of myself, you know, I want to be somebody. I want a car, a decent place to live, nice clothes. My uniforms for the restaurant are all I own, for Chrissake. I never have any money, I always have to scrounge, but I want that to change. I don't want to be cheap anymore. I came into this world by the back door, but by Christ I'll go out by the front! Nothing's gonna stop me. Nothing. You watch, Linda, you'll see I was right. Give me two or three years and you'll see that Lise Paquette is a somebody. And money, she's gonna have it, okay?

145 LINDA: You're off to a bad start.

LISE: That's just it! I've made a mistake and I want to correct it. After this I'll start fresh. You understand, don't you, Pierrette?

PIERRETTE: Sure, I do. I know what it is to want to be rich. Look at me. When I was your age, I left home because I wanted to make some money. But I didn't start by working in a dime store. Oh, no! I went straight to the club. Because that's where the money was. And it won't be long now before I hit the jackpot. Johnny's promised me . . .

ROSE, GERMAINE, AND GABRIELLE: Goddamn Johnny! Goddamn Johnny!

GINETTE: What's going on over here?

150 LISE: Nothing, nothing. *(to Pierrette)* We'll talk about it later . . .

GINETTE: Talk about what?

LISE: Forget it. It's nothing!

GINETTE: Can't you tell me?

LISE: Look, will you leave me alone?

155 PIERRETTE: Come on, we can talk over here . . .

GERMAINE: What's happening to those Cokes?

LINDA: Coming, coming . . .

The lights come back up.

GABRIELLE: Hey, Rose, you know that blue suit of yours? How much did you pay for it?

ROSE: Which one?

160 GABRIELLE: You know, the one with the white lace around the collar?

ROSE: Oh, that one . . . I got it for $9.98.

GABRIELLE: That's what I thought. Imagine, today I saw the same one at Reitmans for $14.98.

ROSE: No kidding! I told you I got it cheap, eh?

GABRIELLE: I don't know how you do it. You always find the bargains.

165 LISETTE: My daughter Micheline just found a new job. She's started to work with those F.B.I. machines.

MARIE-ANGE: Oh yeah! I hear those things are tough on the nerves. The girls who work them have to change jobs every six months. My sister-in-law, Simonne's daughter, had a nervous breakdown over one. Simonne just called today to tell me about it.

ROSE: Oh my God, I forgot, Linda, you're wanted on the phone!

Linda runs to the phone.

LINDA: "Hello? Robert? How long have you been waiting?"

GINETTE: Tell me.

170 LISE: No. Beat it, will you? I want to talk to Pierrette . . . Go on, get lost!

GINETTE: Okay, I get the message! You're happy to have me around when there's nobody else, eh? but when someone more interesting comes along . . .

LINDA: "Listen, Robert, how many times do I have to tell you, it's not my fault! I just found out!"

THÉRÈSE: Here, Mme. Dubuc, hide these!

ROSE: How are things at your place, Ginette?

175 GINETTE: Oh, same as usual, they fight all day long . . . Nothing new. My mother still drinks . . . And my father gets mad . . . And they go on fighting . . .

ROSE: Poor kid . . . And your sister?

GINETTE: Suzanne? Oh, she's still the brainy one. She can't do anything wrong, you know? "Now there's a girl who uses her head. You should be more like her, Ginette. She's making something of her life" . . . Nobody else even counts, especially me. But they always did like her best. And, of course, now she's a teacher, you'd think she was a saint or something.

ROSE: Hey, come on, Ginette. Isn't that a bit much?

GINETTE: No, I'm serious . . . My mother's never cared about me. It's always, "Suzanne's the prettiest. Suzanne's the nicest," . . . Day in, day out till I'm sick of it! Even Lise doesn't like me anymore!

180 LINDA: *(on the phone)* "Oh, go to hell! If you're not gonna listen, why should I talk? Call me back when you're in a better mood!"

She hangs up.

For Chrissake, Aunt Rose, why didn't you tell me I was wanted on the phone? Now he's pissed off at me!

ROSE: Isn't she polite! You see how polite she is?

Spotlight on Pierrette.

PIERRETTE: When I left home, I was head over heels in love, I couldn't even see straight. No one existed for me but Johnny. He made me waste ten years of my life, the bastard. I'm only thirty now and I feel like sixty. The things that guy got me to do! And me, the idiot, I listened to him. Did I ever. Ten years I worked his club for him. I was a looker, I brought in the customers, and that was fine as long as it lasted . . . But now . . . now I'm fucked. I feel like jumping off a bridge. All I got left is the bottle. And that's what I've been doing since Friday. Poor Lise, she thinks she's done for just 'cause she's pregnant. She's young, I'll give her my doctor's name . . . He'll fix her up. It'll be easy for her to start over. But not me. Not me. I'm too old. A girl who's been at it for ten years is washed up. Finished. And try telling that to my sisters. They'll never understand. I don't know what I'm gonna do now. I don't know.

LISE: I don't know what I'm gonna do now. I don't know. An abortion, that's serious. I've heard enough stories to know that. But I guess I'm better off going to see Pierrette's doctor than trying to do it myself. Ah, why do these things always happen to me? Pierrette, she's lucky. Working in the same club for ten years, making a bundle . . . And she's in love! I wouldn't mind being in her shoes. Even if her family can't stand her, at least she's happy on her own.

PIERRETTE: He dumped me, just like that! "It's finished," he said. "I don't need you anymore. You're too old and ugly. So pack your bags and beat it." That son-of-a-bitch! He didn't leave me a nickel! Not a god-damn nickel! After all I did for him. Ten years! Ten years for nothing. That's enough to make anyone pack it in. What am I gonna do now, eh? What? Become a waitress at Kresge's like Lise? No thanks! Kresge's is fine for kids and old ladies, but not for me. I don't know what I'm gonna do. I just don't know. And here I've gotta pretend everything's great. But I can't tell Linda and Lise I'm washed up. *(Silence.)* Yeah . . . I guess there's nothing left but booze . . . good thing I like that . . .

185 LISE: *(interspersed throughout Pierrette's last speech)* I'm scared, dear God, I'm scared!

She approaches Pierrette.

Are you sure this'll work, Pierrette? If you only knew how scared I am!
PIERRETTE: *(laughing)* 'Course it will. It'll be fine, kid. You'll see . . .

The lights come back up.

MARIE-ANGE: It's not even safe to go to the show anymore. I went to the Rex the other day to see Belmondo in something, I forget what. I went alone, cause my husband didn't wanna go. Well, all of a sudden, right in the middle of the show this smelly old bum sits down next to me and starts grabbing my knee. You can imagine how embarrassed I was but that didn't stop me. I stood up, took my purse and smashed him right in his ugly face.
DES-NEIGES: Good for you, Mme. Brouillette! I always carry a hat pin when I go to the show. You never know what'll happen. And the first one who tries to get fresh with me . . . But I've never used it yet.
ROSE: Hey, Germaine, these Cokes are pretty warm.
190 GERMAINE: When are you gonna stop criticizing, eh? When?
LISE: Linda, you got a pencil and paper?
LINDA: I'm telling you, Lise, don't do it!
LISE: I know what I'm doing. I've made up my mind and nothing's gonna make me change it.
RHÉAUNA: *(to Thérèse)* What are you doing there?
195 THÉRÈSE: Shh! Not so loud! You should take some, too. Two or three books, she'll never know.
RHÉAUNA: I'm not a thief!
THÉRÈSE: Come on, Mlle. Bibeau, it's not a question of stealing. She got these stamps for nothing and there's a million of 'em. A million!
RHÉAUNA: Say what you will, she invited us here to paste her stamps and we've got no right to steal them!
GERMAINE: *(to Rose)* What are those two talking about? I don't like all this whispering . . .

She goes over to Rhéauna and Thérèse.

200 THÉRÈSE: *(seeing her coming)* Oh . . . Yeah . . . You add two cups of water and stir.

RHÉAUNA: What? *(Noticing Germaine)*. Oh! Yes! She was giving me a recipe.

GERMAINE: A recipe for what?

RHÉAUNA: Doughnuts!

THÉRÈSE: Chocolate pudding!

205 GERMAINE: Well, which is it? Doughnuts or chocolate pudding?

She comes back to Rose.

Listen, Rose, there's something fishy going on around here.

ROSE: *(who has just hidden a few books in her purse)* Don't be silly . . . You're imagining things . . .

GERMAINE: And I think Linda's spending too much time with Pierrette. Linda, get over here!

LINDA: In a minute, Ma . . .

GERMAINE: I said come here! That means now. Not tomorrow!

210 LINDA: Okay! Don't get in a flap . . . so, what do you want?

GABRIELLE: Stay with us a bit . . . You've been with your Aunt long enough.

LINDA: So what?

GERMAINE: What's going on between her and Lise there?

LINDA: Oh . . . Nothing . . .

215 GERMAINE: Answer when you're spoken to!

ROSE: Lise wrote something down a while ago.

LINDA: It was just an address . . .

GERMAINE: Not Pierrette's, I hope! If I ever find out you've been to her place, you're gonna hear from me, got that?

LINDA: Will you leave off! I'm old enough to know what I'm doing!

She goes back to Pierrette.

220 ROSE: Maybe it's none of my business, Germaine, but . . .

GERMAINE: Why, what's the matter now?

ROSE: Your Linda's picking up some pretty bad habits . . .

GERMAINE: You can say that again! But don't worry, Rose, I can handle her. She's gonna straighten out fast. And as for Pierrette, it's the last time she'll set foot in this house. I'll throw her down the goddamn stairs!

MARIE-ANGE: Have you noticed Mme. Bergeron's daughter lately? Wouldn't you say she's been putting on weight?

225 LISETTE: Yes, I've noticed that . . .

THÉRÈSE: *(insinuating)* Strange, isn't it? It's all in her middle.

ROSE: I guess the sap's running a bit early this year.

MARIE-ANGE: She tries to hide it too. It's beginning to show, though.

THÉRÈSE: And how! I wonder who could have done it?

230 LISETTE: It's probably her step-father . . .

GERMAINE: Wouldn't surprise me in the least. He's been after her ever since he married her mother.

THÉRÈSE: It must be awful in that house. I feel sorry for Monique. She's so young . . .

ROSE: Maybe so, but you must admit, she's been looking for it, too. Look how she dresses. Last summer, I was embarrassed to look at her! And you know me, I'm no prude. Remember those red shorts she had on, those short shorts? Well, I said it then, and I'll say it again, "Monique Bergeron is gonna turn out bad." She's got the devil in her, that girl, a real demon. Besides, she's a redhead . . . No, you can say what you like, those unwed mothers deserve what they get and I got no sympathy for 'em.

Lise starts to get up.

PIERRETTE: Take it easy, kid!

235 ROSE: It's true! It's their own damn fault! I'm not talking about the ones who get raped. That's different. But an ordinary girl who gets herself knocked up, uh! uh! . . . She gets no sympathy from me. It's too goddamn bad! I tell you, if my Carmen ever came home like that, she'd go sailing right through the window! Not that I'm worried about her, mind you. She's not that kind of girl . . . Nope, for me unwed mothers are all the same. A bunch of depraved sluts. You know what my husband calls 'em, eh? Cockteasers!

LISE: I'll kill her if she doesn't shut up!

GINETTE: Why? If you ask me, she's right.

LISE: You shut your trap and get out of here!

PIERRETTE: Isn't that a bit much, Rose?

240 ROSE: Listen, Pierrette, we know you're an expert on these matters. We know you can't be shocked. Maybe you think it's normal, but we don't. There's one way to prevent it . . .

PIERRETTE: *(laughing)* There's lots of ways. Ever heard of the pill?

ROSE: It's no use talking to you! That's not what I meant! I'm against free love! I'm a Catholic! So leave us alone and stay where you belong, filthy whore!

LISETTE: I think perhaps you exaggerate, Mme. Ouimet. There are occasions when girls can get themselves in trouble and it's not entirely their fault.

ROSE: You! You believe everything they tell you in those stupid French movies!

245 LISETTE: What have you got against French movies?

ROSE: Nothing. I like English ones better, that's all. French movies, they're too realistic, too far-fetched. You shouldn't believe what they say. They always make you feel sorry for the girl who gets pregnant. It's never anyone else's fault. Well, do you feel sorry for tramps like that? I don't! A movie's a movie and life's life!

LISE: I'll kill her, the bitch! Stupid fucking jerk! She goes around judging everyone and she's got the brains of a . . . And as for her Carmen. Well, I happen to know her Carmen and believe me, she does a lot more than tease! She oughta clean her own house before she shits on everyone else.

Spotlight on Rose Ouimet.

ROSE: That's right. Life is life and no goddamn Frenchman ever made a
movie about that! Sure, any old actress can make you feel sorry for her
in a movie. Easy as pie! And when she's finished work, she can go
home to her big fat mansion and climb into her big fat bed that's twice
the size of my bedroom, for Chrissake! But the rest of us, when we get
up in the morning . . . when I wake up in the morning he's lying there
staring at me . . . Waiting. Every morning, I open my eyes and there
he is, waiting! Every night, I get into bed and there he is, waiting! He's
always there, always after me, always hanging over me like a vulture.
Goddamn sex! It's never that way in the movies, is it? Oh no, in the
movies it's always fun! Besides, who cares about a woman who's gotta
spend her life with a pig just 'cause she said yes to him once? Well, I'm
telling you, no fucking movie was ever this sad. Because movies don't
last a lifetime! *(Silence.)* Why did I ever do it? Why? I should have said
no. I should have yelled no at the top of my lungs and stayed an old
maid. At least I'd have had some peace. I was so ignorant in those
days. Christ, I didn't know what I was in for. All I could think was "the
Holy State of Matrimony!" You gotta be stupid to bring up your kids
like that, knowing nothing. My Carmen won't get caught like that.
Because I've been telling her for years what men are really worth. She
won't be able to say I didn't warn her! *(On the verge of tears.)* She won't
end up like me, forty-four years old, with a two year old kid and
another one on the way, with a stupid slob of a husband who can't
understand a thing, who demands his "rights" at least twice a day,
three hundred and sixty-five days a year. When you get to be forty and
you realize you've got nothing behind you and nothing ahead of you,
it makes you want to dump everything and start all over . . . But
women . . . women can't do that . . . They get grabbed by the throat,
and they stay that way, right to the end!

The lights come back up.

GABRIELLE: Well, I like French movies. They sure know how to make 'em
good and sad. They make me cry every time. And you must admit,
Frenchmen are a lot better looking than Canadians. They're real men!
250 GERMAINE: Now wait just a minute! That's not true.
MARIE-ANGE: Come on! The little peckers don't even come up to my
shoulder. And they act like girls! Of course, what do you expect?
They're all queer!
GABRIELLE: I beg your pardon. Some of them are men! And I don't mean
like our husbands.
MARIE-ANGE: After our husbands anything looks good.
LISETTE: You don't mix serviettes with paper napkins.
255 GERMAINE: Okay, so our husbands are rough, but our actors are just as good
and just as good-looking as any one of those French fairies from
France.

GABRIELLE: Well, I wouldn't say no to Jean Marais. Now there's a real man!

OLIVINE: Coke . . . Coke . . . More . . . Coke . . .

ROSE: Hey, can't you shut her up? It's impossible to work! Shove a Coke in her mouth, Germaine. That'll keep her quiet.

GERMAINE: I think I've run out.

260 ROSE: Jesus, you didn't buy much, did you? Talk about cheap!

RHÉAUNA: *(as she steals some stamps)* Oh, what the heck. Three more books and I can get my chrome dustpan.

Angéline comes in.

ANGÉLINE: Hello . . . *(to Rhéauna)* I've come back . . .

THE OTHERS: *(coldly)* Hello . . .

ANGÉLINE: I went to see Father Castelneau . . .

265 PIERRETTE: She didn't even look at me!

MARIE-ANGE: What does she want with Mlle. Bibeau?

DES-NEIGES: I'm sure it's to ask forgiveness. After all, Mlle. Sauvé is a good person and she knows what's right. It'll all work out for the best, you'll see.

GERMAINE: While we're waiting, I'm gonna see how many books we've filled.

The women sit up in their chairs. Gabrielle hesitates, then speaks.

GABRIELLE: Oh, Germaine, I forgot to tell you. I found a corsetmaker. Her name's Angélina Giroux. Come over here, I'll tell you about her.

270 RHÉAUNA: I knew you'd come back to me, Angéline. I'm very happy. You'll see, we'll pray together and the Good Lord will forget all about it. God's not stupid, you know.

LISE: That's it, Pierrette, they've made up.

PIERRETTE: I'll be goddamned!

ANGÉLINE: I'll just say goodbye to Pierrette and explain . . .

RHÉAUNA: No, you'd best not say another word to her. Stay with me and leave her alone. That chapter's closed.

275 ANGÉLINE: Whatever you say.

PIERRETTE: Well, that's that. She's won. Makes me want to puke. Nothing left for me to do here. I'm getting out of here.

GERMAINE: Gaby, you're terrific. I'd almost given up hope. It's not everyone can make me a corset. I'll go see her next week.

She goes over to the box that is supposed to hold the completed books. The women follow her with their eyes.

My God, there isn't much here! Where are all the booklets? There's no more than a dozen in the box. Maybe they're . . . No, the table's empty!

Silence. Germaine looks at all the women.

What's going on here?

THE OTHERS: Well . . . Ah . . . I don't know . . . Really . . .

They pretend to search for the books. Germaine stations herself in front of the door.

GERMAINE: Where are my stamps?

280   ROSE: I don't know, Germaine. Let's look for them.

GERMAINE: They're not in the box and they're not on the table. I want to know what's happened to my stamps!

OLIVINE: *(pulling stamps out from under her clothes)* Stamps? Stamps . . . Stamps . . .

She laughs.

THÉRÈSE: Mme. Dubuc, hide that . . . Goddamn it, Mme. Dubuc!

MARIE-ANGE: Holy Ste.-Anne!

285   DES-NEIGES: Pray for us!

GERMAINE: But her clothes are full of them! What the . . . She's got them everywhere! Here . . . And here . . . Thérèse . . . Don't tell me it's you.

THÉRÈSE: Heavens, no! I swear, I had no idea!

GERMAINE: Let me see your purse.

THÉRÈSE: Really, Germaine, if that's all the faith you have in me.

290   ROSE: Germaine, don't be ridiculous!

GERMAINE: You too, Rose. I want to see your purse. I want to see all your purses. Every one of them!

DES-NEIGES: I refuse! I've never been so insulted!

YVETTE: Me neither.

LISETTE: I'll never set foot in here again!

Germaine grabs Thérèse's bag and opens it. She pulls out several books.

295   GERMAINE: Ahah! I knew it! I bet it's the same with all of you! You bastards! You won't get out of here alive! I'll knock you to kingdom come!

PIERRETTE: I'll help you, Germaine. Nothing but a pack of thieves! And they look down their noses at me!

GERMAINE: Show me your purses.

She grabs Rose's purse.

Look at that . . . And that!

She grabs another purse.

More here. And look, still more! You too, Mlle. Bibeau? There's only three, but even so!

ANGÉLINE: Oh, Rhéauna, you too!

GERMAINE: All of you, thieves! The whole bunch of you, you hear me? Thieves!

300   MARIE-ANGE: You don't deserve all those stamps.

DES-NEIGES: Why you more than anyone else?

ROSE: You've made us feel like shit with your million stamps!

GERMAINE: But those stamps are mine!

LISETTE: They ought to be for everyone!

305 THE OTHERS: Yeah, everyone!

GERMAINE: But they're mine! Give them back to me!

THE OTHERS: No way!

MARIE-ANGE: There's lots more in the boxes. Let's help ourselves.

DES-NEIGES: Good idea.

310 YVETTE: I'm filling my purse.

GERMAINE: Stop! Keep your hands off!

THÉRÈSE: Here, Mme. Dubuc, take these! Here's some more.

MARIE-ANGE: Come on, Mlle. Verrette. There's tons of them. Here. Give me
a hand.

PIERRETTE: Let go of that!

315 GERMAINE: My stamps! My stamps!

ROSE: Help me, Gaby, I've got too many!

GERMAINE: My stamps! My stamps!

*A huge battle ensues. The women steal all the stamps they can. Pierrette and
Germaine try to stop them. Linda and Lise stay seated in the corner and watch
without moving. Screams are heard as some of the women begin fighting.*

MARIE-ANGE: Give me those, they're mine!

ROSE: That's a lie, they're mine!

320 LISETTE: *(to Gabrielle)* Will you let go of me! Let me go!

*They start throwing stamps and books at one another. Everybody grabs all they can
get their hands on, throwing stamps everywhere, out the door, even out the window.
Olivine Dubuc starts cruising around in her wheelchair singing "O Canada." A few
women go out with their loot of stamps. Rose and Gabrielle stay a bit longer than
the others.*

GERMAINE: My sisters! My own sisters!

*Gabrielle and Rose go out. The only ones left in the kitchen are Germaine, Linda,
and Pierrette. Germaine collapses into a chair.*

My stamps! My stamps!

Pierrette puts her arms around Germaine's shoulders.

PIERRETTE: Don't cry, Germaine.

GERMAINE: Don't talk to me. Get out! You're no better than the rest of
them!

PIERRETTE: But . . . .

325 GERMAINE: Get out! I never want to see you again!

PIERRETTE: But I tried to help you! I'm on your side, Germaine!

GERMAINE: Get out and leave me alone! Don't speak to me. I don't want to
see anyone!

Pierrette goes out slowly. Linda also heads towards the door.

LINDA: It'll be some job cleaning all that up!

GERMAINE: My God! My God! My stamps! There's nothing left! Nothing! Nothing! My beautiful new home! My lovely furniture! Gone! My stamps! My stamps!

She falls to her knees beside the chair, picking up the remaining stamps. She is crying very hard. We hear all the others outside singing "O Canada." As the song continues, Germaine regains her courage. She finishes "O Canada" with the others, standing at attention, with tears in her eyes. A rain of stamps falls slowly from the ceiling . . .

READING AND REACTING

1. With which character in the play do you most identify? Why?
2. Is Germaine a likable character? What words and actions—both Germaine's and those of other characters—help you form your conclusion?
3. How does the existence of Pierrette affect your overall impression of Germaine and the other characters? What does Pierrette reveal about the others?
4. What does Germaine's attitude toward her daughter indicate about her character?
5. Does the play have a hero? A villain? Explain.
6. The dialogue between Angéline and Rhéauna in act 2 reveals many of their differences. List some of the differences between these two characters.
7. In the absence of a narrator, what devices does Tremblay use to provide exposition—basic information about character and setting?
8. In numerous remarks Germaine expresses her ideas about religion and sexuality. Summarize some of her key ideas. How realistic do you think these ideas are? How dependent are these ideas on the setting of the play?
9. What do the stamps represent apart from their physical properties?
10. Does the play trivialize women by showing them as gossiping, conniving creatures, or is Tremblay getting at another issue?
11. How important is it to consider that the characters are minority residents in their own country?
12. While there are no male characters in the play, men are certainly significant. Explain.
13. Why is the title of the play not translated from its original French in the English version?
14. What expectations do the characters have about family? Does the squabbling among the family members possibly symbolize the disruptions between French and English Canada?

15. **JOURNAL ENTRY** Do you think Germaine is an innocent victim of the society in which she lives, or do you believe there are flaws in her character that make her at least partially responsible for her own misfortune? Explain.

16. **CRITICAL PERSPECTIVE** In *Canadian Drama and the Critics*, Carol Corbeil commented:

> The specific meaning of any work of art changes, often radically, as the cultural context of the society it originally addressed changes. In the case of *Les Belles-Soeurs*, the context is pointed. Not only did this play prove to be a turning point in the history of Quebec theatre, it also sent shock waves into the very consciousness of Quebec society.

Tremblay's play was first performed in French in 1968 and in English in 1973. What is the difference between Quebec society then and now? What has changed? What elements of the play may have less relevance for today's audience, but which still retain their historical significance?

Related Works: "A Rose for Emily" (p. 90), "Speak White" (p. 806), *The Rez Sisters* (p. 1248)

◈ WRITING SUGGESTIONS: CHARACTER

1. In *Les Belles Soeurs,* characters attempt to pursue their life's dream. Choose two characters, define their idea of their dream, and explain how each tries to make the dream a reality. Consider the obstacles the characters encounter, and try to account for their success or lack of success.

2. The female characters in this chapter's plays—Mrs. Popov, Gertrude, Ophelia, Germaine Lauzon (and the other women in the play)—are all in one way or another in conflict with men. Focusing on the women in two different plays, define each conflict, and consider whether or not it is resolved in the play. (If you like, you may discuss a female character in one of the plays in another chapter.)

3. Minor characters are often flat characters; in many cases their sole function is to advance the plot or to highlight a particular trait in a major character. Sometimes, however, minor characters may be of more than minor importance. Choose one minor character from *Hamlet* or *Les Belles Soeurs* (or from a play in another chapter), and write a paper in which you discuss how the play would be different without this character.

4. Review the explanation of tragedy in Chapter 20, "Understanding Drama." Using the discussion of the tragic hero as your guide, write an essay in which you discuss either Germaine Lauzon or Hamlet (or another character from a play in this text) as a tragic hero.

CHAPTER 24

Staging

◊ ◊ ◊

In reading a play rather than witnessing it on stage, we . . . have to imagine what it might look like in performance, projecting in our mind's eye an image of the setting and the props, as well as the movements, gestures, facial expressions, and vocal intonations of the characters. . . . And we—like the director, designers, and actors—must develop our understanding of the play and our idea of the play in performance primarily from a careful reading of the dialogue, as well as from whatever stage directions and other information the dramatist might provide about the characters and the setting.

CARL H. KLAUS, MIRIAM GILBERT, AND BRAFORD S. FIELD, JR., *Stages of Drama*

Why the stage? For me the reason is that this oral tradition [Cree, Ojibway, and Mohawk] translates most easily and most effectively into a three dimensional medium. In a sense it's like taking the "stage" that lives inside the mind, the imagination, and transposing it—using words, actors, lights, sound—onto a stage in a theatre. For me, it is really a matter of taking a mythology as extraordinary and as powerful as the human imagination itself and reworking it to fit, snugly and comfortably, the medium of the stage.

TOMSON HIGHWAY, "On Native Mythology"

Whether the director sees . . . a play as tragedy, comedy or even farce will have an immediate and very practical effect on his handling of the production: it will influence his casting, the design of the set and costumes, the tone, rhythm and pacing of the performance. And, above all, the style in which it is to be acted.

MARTIN ESSLIN, *An Anatomy of Drama*

The argument is sometimes advanced that the complete verisimilitude of the movies is more enjoyable than the necessarily limited illusionism of the live theater. Hollywood producers evidently believe the public in general holds such an opinion. Yet accepting conventions can be a source of pleasure for its own sake, just as children have always had fun putting on shows in the cellar by ignoring the steampipe or else turning it into the Brooklyn Bridge.

THELMA ALTSHULER AND RICHARD PAUL JENARO, *Responses to Drama*

◊ ◊ ◊

Staging refers to the elements of a play's production that determine how the play looks and sounds to an audience. It encompasses the **stage settings,** or **sets**—scenery and props—as well as the costumes, lighting, sound effects, and music that bring the play to life on the stage. In short, staging is everything that goes into making a written script a play.

Most contemporary staging in the West has concentrated on re-creating the outside world. This concept of staging, which has dominated Western theatrical productions for centuries, would seem alien in many non-Western theatres. Japanese kabuki dramas and No plays, for example, depend on staging conventions that make no attempt to mirror reality or everyday speech. Scenery and costumes are largely symbolic, and often actors wear highly stylized makeup or masks. Although some European and North American playwrights have been strongly influenced by non-Western staging, the majority of plays being produced in the West still try to create the illusion of reality.

STAGE DIRECTIONS

◈ ◈ ◈

Usually a playwright presents instructions for the staging of a play in **stage directions**—notes that comment on the scenery, the movements of the performers, the lighting, and the placement of props. (In the absence of detailed stage directions, dialogue can provide information about staging.) Sometimes these stage directions are quite simple, leaving much to the imagination of the director. Consider how little specific information about the setting of the play is provided in these stage directions from Samuel Beckett's 1952 absurdist play *Waiting for Godot:*

ACT I

A country road. A tree. Evening.

Often, however, playwrights furnish much more detailed information about staging. Consider these notes from Anton Chekhov's *The Cherry Orchard:*

ACT I

A room, which has always been called the nursery. One of the doors leads into Anya's room. Dawn, sun rises during the scene. May, the cherry trees in flower, but it is cold in the garden with the frost of the early morning. Windows closed.

Enter Dunyasha with a candle and Lopahin with a book in his hand.

These comments indicate that the first act takes place in a room with more than one door and that several windows reveal cherry trees in bloom. They also specify that the lighting should simulate the sun rising at dawn and that certain characters should enter carrying particular props. Still, Chekhov leaves it up to those staging the play to decide on the costumes for the characters and on the furniture that will be placed around the room.

Some stage directions are even more specific. George Bernard Shaw's long, complex stage directions are legendary in the theatre. Note the degree of detail he provides in these stage directions from his comedy *The Doctor's Dilemma:*

> *The consulting-room has two windows looking on Queen Anne Street. Between the two is a marble-topped console, with haunched gilt legs ending in sphinx claws. The huge pier-glass [a long narrow mirror that fits between two windows] which surmounts it is mostly disabled from reflection by elaborate painting on its surface of palms, ferns, lilies, tulips, and sunflowers. The adjoining wall contains the fireplace, with two arm-chairs before it. As we happen to face the corner we see nothing of the other two walls. On the right of the fireplace, or rather on the right of any person facing the fireplace, is the door. On the left is the writing-table at which Redpenny [a medical student] sits. It is an untidy table with a microscope, several test tubes, and a spirit lamp [an alcohol burner] standing up through its litter of papers. There is a couch in the middle of the room, at right angles to the console, and parallel to the fireplace. A chair stands between the couch and the window. Another in the corner. Another at the other end of the windowed wall. . . . The wallpaper and carpets are mostly green. . . . The house, in fact, was so well furnished in the middle of the XIXth century that it stands unaltered to this day and is still quite presentable.*

Not only does Shaw describe the furniture to be placed on stage, but he also includes a good deal of detail—specifying, for example, "gilt legs ending in sphinx claws" and "test tubes and a spirit lamp" that clutter the writing table. In addition, he defines furniture placement and specifies colour.

Regardless of how detailed the stage directions are, they do not eliminate the need for creative interpretations on the part of the producer, director, set designers, and actors (see "Actors' Interpretations," p. 1078). Stage directions—and, for that matter, the entire script—are the foundation on which to construct the play that the audience finally sees. Many directors, in fact, see stage directions as suggestions, not requirements, and some even consider them more confusing than helpful. Therefore, directors may choose to interpret a play's stage directions quite loosely—or even to ignore them entirely.

THE USES OF STAGING
◆ ◆ ◆

Staging is a key element of drama, and details that the audience sees and hears—such as costumes, props, scenery, lighting, and music and sound effects—communicate important information about characters and their motivation as well as about the play's theme.

COSTUMES

Costumes not only establish the historical period in which a play is set but also provide insight into the character who wears them. When he first appears, Hamlet is profoundly disillusioned and quite melancholy. This fact was immediately apparent to Shakespeare's audience because Hamlet is dressed in black, which to the Elizabethans signified a melancholy nature. In Tomson Highway's *The Rez Sisters* (p. 1248), the costumes reveal the characters' sense of themselves and their roles on the reserve.

PROPS

Props (short for *properties*)—pictures, furnishings, objects, and the like—can also help audiences to interpret a play's characters and themes. For example, the handkerchief in Shakespeare's *Othello* gains significance as the play progresses. It begins as an innocent object and ends as the piece of evidence that convinces Othello his wife is committing adultery. Sometimes props can have symbolic significance. During the Renaissance, for example, flowers had symbolic meaning. In act 4 of *Hamlet*, Ophelia, who is mad, gives flowers to various characters. In a note to the play the critic Thomas Parrott points out the symbolic significance of her gifts: to Claudius, the murderer of Hamlet's father, she gives fennel and columbines, which signify flattery and ingratitude; to the Queen, she gives rue and daisies, which symbolize sadness and unfaithfulness. Although modern audiences probably do not understand the full implications of the flowers, many people in Shakespeare's Elizabethan audience would have been aware of their meaning.

The furnishings in a room can also reveal a lot about a play's characters and themes. In *The Rez Sisters*, for example, Philomena's delight in her new bathroom with its toilet that makes her feel like "the Queen" reveals class distinctions within her own family.

SCENERY AND LIGHTING

Playwrights often use scenery and lighting to create imaginative stage settings. In Michel Tremblay's *Les Belles Soeurs* (p. 1196), spotlights draw our attention to various objects and characters. A spotlight can be used to focus on a character delivering a soliloquy, such as Angéline's in act 2.

Innovation can be created by the use of a *scrim*, a curtain that when illuminated from the front appears solid but when illuminated from the back becomes transparent. Contemporary playwrights often use sets that combine realistic and nonrealistic elements. In his 1988 Tony Award–winning play *M. Butterfly*, for example, David Henry Hwang employs not only scrims but also a large red lacquered ramp that runs from the bottom to the top of the stage. The action takes place beneath, on, and above the ramp, creating an effect not unlike that created by Shakespeare's multiple stages. At several points in the play, a character who acts as the narrator sits beneath the ramp, addressing the audience, while at the same time a character on top of the ramp acts out the narrator's words.

MUSIC AND SOUND EFFECTS

Staging involves more than visual elements such as costumes and scenery; it also involves music and sound effects. The stage directions for *The Rez Sisters* include numerous references to country music, drum beats when the women are frantically trying to raise money, and Emily's own song performed at the Anchor Inn. The mournful quality of country music is central to the desire of the women for more than they have.

Sound effects play an important part in Henrik Ibsen's *A Doll House* (p. 1013). At the end of the play, after his wife has left him, Torvald Helmer sits alone on the stage. Notice in the following stage directions how the final sound effect cuts short Helmer's attempt at self-deluding optimism:

> **HELMER:** *(sinks down on a chair by the door, face buried in his hands)* Nora! Nora! *(Looking about and rising.)* Empty. She's gone. *(A sudden hope leaps in him.)* The greatest miracle—?
>
> *From below, the sound of a door slamming shut.*

When you read a play, it may be difficult to appreciate the effect that staging can have on a performance. As you read, pay particular attention to the stage directions, and use your imagination to visualize the scenes the playwright describes. In addition, try to imagine the play's sights and sounds, and consider the options for staging that are suggested as characters speak to one another. Although even such careful reading cannot substitute for actually seeing a play performed, it can help you imagine the play as it might appear on the stage.

A FINAL NOTE

◊ ◊ ◊

Because of a play's limited performance time, and because of space and financial limitations, not every action or event can be represented on stage. Frequently, incidents that would involve many actors or require elaborate scenery are only suggested. For example, a violent political riot may be suggested by a single scuffle, a full-scale wedding by the kiss between bride and groom, a gala evening at the opera by a well-dressed group in box seats, and a trip to an exotic locale by a departure scene. Other events are simply said to occur offstage, with the roar of a crowd suggesting an athletic event, for instance.

✓ CHECKLIST: WRITING ABOUT STAGING

- ✓ What information about staging is contained in the stage directions of the play?
- ✓ What information about staging is suggested by the play's dialogue?
- ✓ What information about staging is left to the imagination?
- ✓ How might different decisions about staging change the play?
- ✓ Do the stage directions provide information about how characters are supposed to look or behave?
- ✓ What costumes are specified? In what ways do costumes give insight into the characters who wear them?
- ✓ What props play an important part in the play? Do these props have symbolic meaning?
- ✓ Is the scenery used in the play special or unusual in any way?
- ✓ What kind of lighting is specified by the stage directions? In what way does this lighting affect your reaction to the play?
- ✓ In what ways are music and sound effects used in the play? Are musical themes associated with any characters? Do music and sound effects heighten the emotional impact of certain lines?
- ✓ How does staging help to communicate the play's themes?
- ✓ What events occur offstage? Why? How are they suggested?

◊ **TOMSON HIGHWAY** (1951–   ) was born on a trapline in northern Manitoba. He spoke only Cree until age six when he was separated from his mother, father, and eleven brothers and sisters to attend a Catholic boarding school in The Pas. A gifted pianist, he studied music at the University of Western Ontario, from which he graduated with degrees in music and English literature in 1976.

Increasingly disenchanted with the treatment of Native peoples in Canada, Highway soon rejected what he called "the white man's game" and worked with Native organizations across Canada for the next several years. His first play, *The Rez Sisters* (1988), brought Highway into the national spotlight. Where *The Rez Sisters* is humorous, touching, and irreverent, Highway's second play, *Dry Lips Oughta Move to Kapuskasing* (1990), explores the cultural collision between Native and non-Native worlds in a darker, more turbulent setting. The play was an unprecedented commercial success. Among Highway's talents is his adeptness at incorporating Native themes and mythical characters in conventional Western art forms. In 1998,

Highway's reputation as a writer was enhanced with the successful publication of his novel *Kiss of the Fur Queen*. He became a Member of the Order of Canada in 1994.

⟩ ⟩ ⟩

TOMSON HIGHWAY

The Rez Sisters
(1988)

PRODUCTION NOTES

The role of Nanabush in The Rez Sisters *is to be played by a male dancer—modern, ballet, or traditional. Stage directions for this mostly silent Nanabush are indicated very sparingly in this script. Only his most "essential" appearances are explicitly set out.*

The music for The Rez Sisters, *in its first productions, was provided by a musician who played at least 30 different percussion instruments from drum kit to bells to rattles, etc. This is the way I find the "soundscape" and the rhythm of this piece to be most effectively underlined.*

Both Cree and Ojibway are used freely in this text for the reasons that these two languages, belonging to the same linguistic family, are very similar and that the fictional reserve of Wasaychigan Hill has a mixture of both Cree and Ojibway residents.

A NOTE ON NANABUSH

The dream world of North American Indian mythology is inhabited by the most fantastic creatures, beings, and events. Foremost among these beings is the "Trickster," as pivotal and important a figure in the Native world as Christ is in the realm of Christian mythology. "Weesageechak" in Cree, "Nanabush" in Ojibway, "Raven" in others, "Coyote" in still others, this Trickster goes by many names and many guises. In fact, he can assume any guise he chooses. Essentially a comic, clownish sort of character, he teaches us about the nature and the meaning of existence on the planet Earth; he straddles the consciousness of man and that of God, the Great Spirit.

Some say that "Nanabush" left this continent when the whiteman came. We believe he is still here among us—albeit a little the worse for wear and tear—having assumed other guises. Without him—and without the spiritual health of this figure—the core of Indian culture would be gone forever.

CAST OF CHARACTERS

PELAJIA PATCHNOSE, 53
PHILOMENA MOOSETAIL, 49, *sister of Pelajia*
MARIE-ADELE STARBLANKET, 39, *half-sister of Pelajia & Philomena*
ANNIE COOK, 36, *sister of Marie-Adele & half-sister of the other two*
EMILY DICTIONARY, 32, *sister of Annie & ditto*
VERONIQUE ST. PIERRE, 45, *sister-in-law of all the above*
ZHABOONIGAN PETERSON, 24, *mentally disabled adopted daughter of Veronique*
NANABUSH—*who plays the* SEAGULL *(the dancer in white feathers), the* NIGHTHAWK
(the dancer in dark feathers), and the BINGO MASTER.

TIME: *Late summer, 1986.*
PLACE: *The Wasaychigan Hill Indian Reserve, Manitoulin Island, Ontario. (Note:
"Wasaychigan" means "window" in Ojibway.)*

ACT ONE

*It is mid-morning of a beautiful late August day on the Wasaychigan Hill Indian
Reserve, Manitoulin Island, Ontario. Pelajia Patchnose is alone on the roof of her
house, nailing shingles on. She wears faded blue denim men's cover-alls and a
baseball cap to shade her eyes from the sun. A brightly colored square cushion
belonging to her sister, Philomena Moosetail, rests on the roof beside her. The
ladder to the roof is offstage.*

PELAJIA: Philomena. I wanna go to Toronto.
PHILOMENA: *(From offstage.)* Oh, go on.
PELAJIA: Sure as I'm sitting away up here on the roof of this old house. I
   kind of like it up here, though. From here, I can see half of Manitoulin
   Island on a clear day. I can see the chimneys, the tops of apple trees,
   the garbage heap behind Big Joey's dumpy little house. I can see the
   seagulls circling over Marie-Adele Starblanket's white picket fence.
   Boats on the North Channel I wish I was on, sailing away somewhere.
   The mill at Espanola, a hundred miles away . . . and that's with just a
   bit of squinting. See? If I had binoculars, I could see the superstack in
   Sudbury. And if I were Superwoman, I could see the CN Tower in
   Toronto. Ah, but I'm just plain old Pelajia Rosella Patchnose and I'm
   here in plain, dusty, boring old Wasaychigan Hill . . . Wasy . . . waiting
   . . . waiting . . . nailing shining shingles with my trusty silver hammer
   on the roof of Pelajia Rosella Patchnose's little two-bedroom welfare
   house. Philomena. I wanna go to Toronto.

*Philomena Moosetail comes up the ladder to the roof with one shingle and obvi-
ously hating it. She is very well dressed, with a skirt, nylons, even heels, completely
impractical for the roof.*

PHILOMENA: Oh, go on.

5 PELAJIA: I'm tired, Philomena, tired of this place. There's days I wanna leave so bad.

PHILOMENA: But you were born here. All your poop's on this reserve.

PELAJIA: Oh, go on.

PHILOMENA: You'll never leave.

PELAJIA: Yes, I will. When I'm old.

10 PHILOMENA: You're old right now.

PELAJIA: I got a good 30 years to go . . .

PHILOMENA: . . . and you're gonna live every one of them right here beside me . . .

PELAJIA: . . . maybe 40 . . .

PHILOMENA: . . . here in Wasy. *(Tickles Pelajia on the breasts.)* Chiga-chiga-chiga.

15 PELAJIA: *(Yelps and slaps Philomena's hand away.)* Oh, go on. It's not like it used to be.

PHILOMENA: Oh, go on. People change, places change, time changes things. You expect to be young and gorgeous forever?

PELAJIA: See? I told you I'm not old.

PHILOMENA: Oh, go on. You.

PELAJIA: "Oh, go on. You." You bug me like hell when you say that.

20 PHILOMENA: You say it, too. And don't give me none of this "I don't like this place. I'm tired of it." This place is too much inside your blood. You can't get rid of it. And it can't get rid of you.

PELAJIA: Four thirty this morning, I was woken by . . .

PHILOMENA: Here we go again.

PELAJIA: . . . Andrew Starblanket and his brother, Matthew. Drunk. Again. Or sounded like . . .

PHILOMENA: Nothing better to do.

25 PELAJIA: . . . fighting over some girl. Heard what sounded like a baseball bat landing on somebody's back. My lawn looks like the shits this morning.

PHILOMENA: Well, I like it here. Myself, I'm gonna go to every bingo and I'm gonna hit every jackpot between here and Espanola and I'm gonna buy me that toilet I'm dreaming about at night . . . big and wide and very white . . .

PELAJIA: Aw-ni-gi-naw-ee-dick.[1]

PHILOMENA: I'm good at bingo.

PELAJIA: So what! And the old stories, the old language. Almost all gone . . . was a time Nanabush and Windigo and everyone here could rattle away in Indian fast as Bingo Betty could lay her bingo chips down on a hot night.

30 PHILOMENA: Pelajia Rosella Patchnose. The sun's gonna drive you crazy. *(And she descends the ladder.)*

---

[1] Oh, go on. (Ojibway)

PELAJIA: Everyone here's crazy. No jobs. Nothing to do but drink and screw each other's wives and husbands and forget about our Nanabush.

From offstage Philomena screams. She fell down the ladder.

Philomena! *(As she looks over the edge of the roof.)* What are you doing down there?

PHILOMENA: What do you think? I fell.

PELAJIA: Bring me some of them nails while you're down there.

PHILOMENA: *(Whining and still from offstage, from behind the house.)* You think I can race up and down this ladder? You think I got wings?

35 PELAJIA: You gotta wear pants when you're doing a man's job. See? You got your skirt ripped on a nail and now you can see your thighs. People gonna think you just came from Big Joey's house.

PHILOMENA: *(She comes up the ladder in a state of disarray.)* Let them think what they want. That old cow Gazelle Nataways . . . always acting like she thinks she's still a spring chicken. She's got them legs of hers wrapped around Big Joey day and night . . .

PELAJIA: Philomena. Park your tongue. My old man has to go the hundred miles to Espanola just to get a job. My boys. Gone to Toronto. Only place educated Indian boys can find decent jobs these days. And here I sit all broken-hearted.

PHILOMENA: Paid a dime and only farted.

PELAJIA: Look at you. You got dirt all over your backside. *(Turning her attention to the road in front of her house and standing up for the first and only time.)* And dirt roads! Years now that old chief's been making speeches about getting paved roads "for my people" and still we got dirt roads all over.

40 PHILOMENA: Oh, go on.

PELAJIA: When I win me that jackpot next time we play bingo in Espanola . . .

PHILOMENA: *(Examining her torn skirt, her general state of disarray, and fretting over it.)* Look at this! Will you look at this! Ohhh!

PELAJIA: . . . I'm gonna put that old chief to shame and build me a nice paved road right here in front of my house. Jet black. Shiny. Make my lawn look real nice.

PHILOMENA: My rib-cage!

45 PELAJIA: And if that old chief don't wanna make paved roads for all my sisters around here . . .

PHILOMENA: There's something rattling around inside me!

PELAJIA: . . . I'm packing my bags and moving to Toronto. *(Sits down again.)*

PHILOMENA: Oh, go on. *(She spies Annie Cook's approach a distance up the hill.)* Why, I do believe that cloud of dust over there is Annie Cook racing down the hill, Pelajia.

PELAJIA: Philomena. I wanna go to Toronto.

50 PHILOMENA: She's walking mighty fast. Must be excited about something.

PELAJIA: Never seen Annie Cook walk slow since the day she finally lost Eugene to Marie-Adele at the church 19 years ago. And even then she was walking a little too fast for a girl who was supposed to be broken-heart . . . *(Stopping just in time and laughing)* . . . . heart-broken.

Annie Cook pops up the top of the ladder to the roof.

ANNIE: *(All cheery and fast and perky.)* Halloooo! Whatchyou doing up here?

PELAJIA: There's room for only so much weight up here before we go crashing into my kitchen, so what do you want?

ANNIE: Just popped up to say hi.

55 PELAJIA: And see what we're doing?

ANNIE: Well . . .

PELAJIA: Couldn't you see what we're doing from up where you were?

ANNIE: *(Confidentially, to Philomena.)* Is it true Gazelle Nataways won the bingo last night?

PHILOMENA: Annie Cook, first you say you're gonna come with me and then you don't even bother showing up. If you were sitting beside me at that bingo table last night you would have seen Gazelle Nataways win that big pot again with your own two eyes.

60 ANNIE: Emily Dictionary and I went to Little Current to listen to Fritz the Katz.

PELAJIA: What in God's name kind of a band might that be?

ANNIE: Country rock. My favorite. Fritz the Katz is from Toronto.

PELAJIA: Fritzy . . . ritzy . . . Philomena! Say something.

PHILOMENA: My record player is in Espanola getting fixed.

65 ANNIE: That's nice.

PHILOMENA: Good.

ANNIE: Is it true Gazelle Nataways plans to spend her bingo money to go to Toronto with . . . with Big Joey?

PHILOMENA: Who wants to know? Emily Dictionary?

ANNIE: I guess so.

70 PELAJIA: That Gazelle Nataways gonna leave all her babies behind and let them starve to death?

ANNIE: I guess so. I don't know. I'm asking you.

PELAJIA AND PHILOMENA: We don't know.

ANNIE: I'm on my way to Marie-Adele's to pick her up.

PELAJIA: Why? Where you gonna put her down?

Pelajia and Philomena laugh.

75 ANNIE: I mean, we're going to the store together. To the post office. We're going to pick up a parcel. They say there's a parcel for me. They say it's shaped like a record. And they say it's from Sudbury. So it must be from my daughter, Ellen . . .

PELAJIA AND PHILOMENA: . . . "who lives with this white guy in Sudbury" . . .

ANNIE: How did you know?

PHILOMENA: Everybody knows.

ANNIE: His name is Ray<u>mond</u>. Not <u>Ray</u>mond. But Ray<u>mond</u>. Like in Bon Bon.

Philomena tries out "bon bon" to herself.

    He's French.

80 PELAJIA: Oh?

ANNIE: Garage mechanic. He fixes cars. And you know, talking about Frenchmen, that old priest is holding another bingo next week and when I win . . . *(To Philomena.)* Are you going?

PELAJIA: Does a bear shit in the woods?

ANNIE: . . . when I win, I'm going to Espanola and play the bingo there. Emily Dictionary says that Fire Minklater can give us a ride in her new car. She got it through Ray<u>mond</u>'s garage. The bingo in Espanola is bigger. And it's better. And I'll win. And then I'll go to Sudbury, where the bingos are even bigger and better. And then I can visit my daughter, Ellen . . .

PELAJIA: . . . "who lives with this white guy in Sudbury" . . .

85 ANNIE: . . . and go shopping in the record stores and go to the hotel and drink beer quietly—not noisy and crazy like here—and listen to the live bands. It will be so much fun. I hope Emily Dictionary can come with me.

PHILOMENA: It's true. I've been thinking . . .

PELAJIA: You don't say.

PHILOMENA: It's true. The bingos here are getting kind of boring . . .

ANNIE: That old priest is too slow and sometimes he gets the numbers all mixed up and the pot's not big enough.

90 PHILOMENA: And I don't like the way he calls the numbers. *(Nasally.)* B 12, O 64.

ANNIE: When Little Girl Manitowabi won last month . . .

PHILOMENA: She won just enough to take a taxi back to Buzwah.

ANNIE: That's all.

Both Annie and Philomena pause to give a quick sigh of yearning.

PHILOMENA: Annie Cook, I want that big pot.

95 ANNIE: We all want big pots.

PELAJIA: Start a revolution!

PHILOMENA AND ANNIE: Yes!

ANNIE: All us Wasy women. We'll march up the hill, burn the church hall down, scare the priest to death, and then we'll march all the way to Espanola, where the bingos are bigger and better . . .

PHILOMENA: We'll hold big placards!

100 ANNIE: They'll say: "Wasy women want bigger bingos!"

PELAJIA: And one will say: "Annie Cook Wants Big Pot!"

PHILOMENA: . . . and the numbers at those bingos in Espanola go faster and the pots get bigger by the week. Oh, Pelajia Patchnose, I'm getting excited just thinking about it!

ANNIE: I'm going.

PELAJIA: You are, are you?

105 ANNIE: Yes. I'm going. I'm running out of time. I'm going to Marie-Adele's house and then we'll walk to the store together to pick up the parcel—I'm sure there'll be a letter in it, and Marie-Adele is expecting mail, too—and we'll see if Emily Dictionary is working today and we'll ask her if Fire Minklater has her new car yet so we can go to Espanola for that big pot. *(She begins to descend the ladder.)*

PELAJIA: Well, you don't have much to do today, do you?

ANNIE: Well. Toodle-oo! *(And she pops down the ladder and is gone.)*

PELAJIA: Not bad for someone who was in such a hurry to get her parcel. She talks faster than she walks. *(Noticing how dejected and abandoned Philomena looks, she holds up her hammer.)* Bingo money. Top quality. $24.95.

PHILOMENA: It's true. Bingos here in Wasy are getting smaller and smaller all the time. Especially now when the value of the dollar is getting lesser and lesser. In the old days, when Bingo Betty was still alive and walking these dirt roads, she'd come to every single bingo and she'd sit there like the Queen of Tonga, big and huge like a roast beef, smack-dab in the middle of the bingo hall. One night, I remember, she brought two young cousins from the city—two young women, dressed real fancy, like they were going to Sunday church—and Bingo Betty made them sit one on her left, with her three little bingo cards, and one on her right, with her three little ones. And Bingo Betty herself sat in the middle with 27 cards. Twenty seven cards! Amazing.

Pelajia starts to descend the ladder, and Philomena, getting excited, steps closer and closer to the edge of the roof.

And those were the days when they still used bingo chips, not these dabbers like nowadays, and everyone came with a little margarine container full of these bingo chips. When the game began and they started calling out the numbers, Bingo Betty was all set, like a horse at the race-track in Sudbury, you could practically see the foam sizzling and bubbling between her teeth. Bingo Betty! Bingo Betty with her beady little darting eyes, sharp as needles, and her roly-poly jiggledy-piggledy arms with their stubby little claws would go: chiga-chiga-chiga-chiga-chiga-chiga arms flying across the table smooth as angel's wings chiga-chiga-chiga-chiga-chiga-chiga-woosh! Cousin on the left chiga-chiga, cousin on the right chiga, chiga-eeee! *(She narrowly misses falling off the roof and cries out in terror.)*

110 PELAJIA: Philomena!

PHILOMENA: *(Scrambling on hands and knees to Pelajia, and coming to rest in this languorous pose, takes a moment to regain her composure and catch her breath.)* And you know, to this very day, they say that on certain nights at the bingo here in Wasy, they say you can see Bingo Betty's ghost, like a mist, hovering in the air above the bingo tables, playing bingo like it's never been played before. Or since.

PELAJIA: Amazing! She should have gone to Toronto.

Black-out.

The same day, same time, in Wasaychigan Hill. Marie-Adele Starblanket is standing alone outside her house, in her yard, by her 14-post white picket fence. Her house is down the hill from Pelajia Patchnose's, close to the lake. A seagull watches her from a distance away. He is the dancer in white feathers. Through this whole section, Nanabush (i.e., Nanabush in the guise of the seagull), Marie-Adele, and Zhaboonigan play "games" with each other. Only she and Zhaboonigan Peterson can see the spirit inside the bird and can sort of (though not quite) recognize him for who he is. A doll belonging to a little girl lies on the porch floor. Marie-Adele throws little stones at the seagull.

MARIE-ADELE: Awus! Wee-chee-gis. Ka-tha pu-g'wun-ta oo-ta pee-weesta-ta-gu-mik-si. Awus! Neee. U-wi-nuk oo-ma kee-tha ee-tee-thi-mi-soo-yin holy spirit chee? Awus! Hey, maw ma-a oop-mee tay-si-thow u-wu seagull bird. I-goo-ta poo-goo ta-poo. Nu-gu-na-wa-pa-mik. Nu-gu-na-wa-pa-mik.

NANABUSH: As-tum.

115 MARIE-ADELE: Neee. Moo-tha ni-gus-kee-tan tu-pi-mi-tha-an. Moo-tha oo-ta-ta-gwu-na n'tay-yan. Chees-kwa. *(Pause.)* Ma-ti poo-ni-mee-see i-goo-ta wee-chi-gi-seagull bird come shit on my fence one more time and you and anybody else look like you cook like stew on my stove. Awus![2]

Veronique St. Pierre "passes by" with her adopted daughter Zhaboonigan Peterson.

VERONIQUE: Talking to the birds again, Marie-Adele Starblanket?

MARIE-ADELE: Aha. Veronique St. Pierre. How are you today?

VERONIQUE: Black Lady Halked's sister-in-law Fire Minklater, Fire Minklater's husband, just bought Fire Minklater a car in Sudbury.

MARIE-ADELE: New?

120 VERONIQUE: Used. They say he bought it from some Frenchman, some garage. Cray-<u>on.</u>

MARIE-ADELE: Ray<u>mond</u>.

---

[2] MARIE-ADELE: Go away! You stinking thing. Don't come messing around here for nothing. Go away! Neee. Who the hell do you think you are, the Holy Spirit? Go away! Hey, but he won't fly away, this seagull bird. He just sits there. And watches me. Watches me.

NANABUSH: Come.

MARIE-ADELE: Neee. I can't fly away. I have no wings. Yet. *(Pause.)* Will you stop shitting all over the place you stinking seagull bird, *etc.* (Cree)

(Note: "Neee" is a very common Cree expression with the approximate meaning of "Oh you.")

VERONIQUE: These Frenchmen are forever selling us their used cars. And I'm sure that's why Black Lady Halked has been baring those big yellow teeth of hers, smiling all over the reserve recently. She looks like a hound about to pounce on a mouse, she smiles so hard when she smiles. I'd like to see her smile after plastic surgery. Anyway. At the bingo last night she was hinting that it wouldn't be too long before she would be able to go to the bingo in Espanola more frequently. Unfortunately, a new game started and you know how Black Lady Halked has to concentrate when she plays bingo—her forehead looks like corduroy, she concentrates so hard—so I didn't get a chance to ask her what she meant. So. Fire Minklater has a used car. Imagine! Maybe I can make friends with her again. NO! I wouldn't be caught dead inside her car. Not even if she had a brand-new Cadillac. How are your children? All 14 of them.

MARIE-ADELE: Okay, I guess.

VERONIQUE: Imagine. And all from one father. Anyway. Who will take care of them after you . . . ahem . . . I mean . . . when you go to the hospital?

125 MARIE-ADELE: Eugene.

ZHABOONIGAN: Is he gentle?

MARIE-ADELE: Baby-cakes. How are you?

ZHABOONIGAN: Fine. *(Giggles.)*

VERONIQUE: She's fine. She went berry-picking yesterday with the children.

130 ZHABOONIGAN: Where's Nicky?

MARIE-ADELE: Nicky's down at the beach.

ZHABOONIGAN: Why?

MARIE-ADELE: Taking care of Rose-Marie.

ZHABOONIGAN: Oh.

135 MARIE-ADELE: Yup.

ZHABOONIGAN: Me and Nicky, ever lots of blueberries!

MARIE-ADELE: Me and Nicky picked lots of blueberries.

ZHABOONIGAN: I didn't see you there.

MARIE-ADELE: When?

140 ZHABOONIGAN: Before today.

MARIE-ADELE: How come Nicky didn't come home with any?

ZHABOONIGAN: Why?

Marie-Adele shrugs. Zhaboonigan imitates this, and then pretends she is stuffing her mouth with berries.

MARIE-ADELE: Aw, yous went and made pigs of yourselves.

ZHABOONIGAN: Nicky's the pig.

145 MARIE-ADELE: Neee.

ZHABOONIGAN: Are you going away far?

MARIE-ADELE: I'm not going far.

ZHABOONIGAN: Oh. Are you pretty?

Marie-Adele, embarrassed for a moment, smiles and Zhaboonigan smiles, too.

MARIE-ADELE: You're pretty, too.

Zhaboonigan tugs at Marie-Adele's shoelaces.

Oh, Zhaboonigan. Now you have to tie it up. I can't bend too far cuz I get tired.

Zhaboonigan tries to tie the shoelaces with great difficulty. When she finds she can't she throws her arms up and screams.

150 ZHABOONIGAN: Dirty trick! Dirty trick! *(She bites her hand and hurts herself.)*
MARIE-ADELE: Now, don't get mad.
VERONIQUE: Stop it. Stop it right now.
ZHABOONIGAN: No! No!
MARIE-ADELE: Zha. Zha. Listen. Listen.
155 ZHABOONIGAN: Stop it! Stop it right now!
MARIE-ADELE: Come on, Zha. You and I can name the koo-koos-suk.[3] All 14 of them.
ZHABOONIGAN: Okay. Here we go.

Marie-Adele leads Zhaboonigan over to the picket fence and Veronique follows them.

ZHABOONIGAN: *(To Veronique.)* No.

Veronique retreats, obviously hurt.

MARIE-ADELE: *(Taking Zhaboonigan's hand and counting on the 14 posts of her white picket fence.)* Simon, Andrew, Matthew, Janie, Nicky, Ricky, Ben, Mark, Ron, Don, John, Tom, Pete, and Rose-Marie. There.

Underneath Marie-Adele's voice, Zhaboonigan has been counting.

160 ZHABOONIGAN: One, two, three, four, five, six, seven, eight, nine, ten, eleven, twelve, thirteen, fourteen. *(Giggles.)*
MARIE-ADELE: Ever good counter you, Zhaboonigan.
ZHABOONIGAN: Yup.
VERONIQUE: This reserve, sometimes I get so sick of it. They laugh at me behind my back, I just know it. They laugh at me and Pierre St. Pierre because we don't have any children of our own. "Imagine," they say, "she's on her second husband already and she still can't have children!" They laugh at Zhaboonigan Peterson because she's crazy, that's what they call her. They can't even take care of their own people, they'd rather laugh at them. I'm the only person who would take Zhaboonigan after her parents died in that horrible car crash near Manitowaning on Saturday November 12 1964 may they rest in peace *(She makes a quick sign of the cross without skipping a beat.)* I'm the only one around here who is kind enough. And they laugh at me. Oh, I wish I had a new stove, Marie-Adele. My stove is so old and broken

---

[3] The little pigs. (Cree)

down, only two elements work anymore and my oven is starting to talk back at me.

MARIE-ADELE: Get it fixed.

165 VERONIQUE: You know that Pierre St. Pierre never has any money. He drinks it all up. *(She sighs longingly.)* Some day! Anyway. Zhaboonigan here wanted to go for a swim so I thought I'd walk her down—drop by and see how you and the children are doing—it will do my weak heart good, I was saying to myself.

MARIE-ADELE: Awus!

As she throws a pebble at the seagull on the stone, Veronique, for a second, thinks it's her Marie-Adele is shooing away. There is a brief silence broken after a while by Zhaboonigan's little giggle.

VERONIQUE: Anyway. I was walking down by that Big Joey's shameless little shack just this morning when guess who pokes her nose out the window but Gazelle Nataways—the nerve of that woman. I couldn't see inside but I'm sure she was only half-dressed, her hairdo was all mixed up and she said to me: "Did you know, Veronique St. Pierre, that Little Girl Manitowabi told me her daughter, June Bug McLeod, just got back from the hospital in Sudbury where she had her tubes tied and told her that THE BIGGEST BINGO IN THE WORLD is coming to Toronto?"

MARIE-ADELE: When?

VERONIQUE: I just about had a heart attack.

170 MARIE-ADELE: When?

VERONIQUE: But I said to Gazelle anyway: Is there such a thing as a BIGGEST BINGO IN THE WORLD? And she said: Yes. And she should know about these things because she spends all her waking and sleeping hours just banging about in bed with the biggest thing on Manitoulin Island, I almost said.

MARIE-ADELE: This bingo. When?

VERONIQUE: She didn't know. And now that I think of it, I don't know whether to believe her. After all, who should believe a woman who wrestles around with dirt like Big Joey all night long leaving her poor babies to starve to death in her empty kitchen? But if it's true, Marie-Adele, if it's true that THE BIGGEST BINGO IN THE WORLD is coming to Toronto, I'm going and I want you to come with me.

MARIE-ADELE: Well . . .

175 VERONIQUE: I want you to come shopping with me and help me choose my new stove after I win.

MARIE-ADELE: Hang on . . .

VERONIQUE: They have good stoves in Toronto.

MARIE-ADELE: Let's find out for sure. Then we start making plans.

VERONIQUE: Maybe we should go back and ask that Gazelle Nataways about this. If she's sure.

180 MARIE-ADELE: Maybe we should go and ask June Bug McLeod herself.

VERONIQUE: We can't walk to Buzwah and I'm too old to hitch-hike.

MARIE-ADELE: There's Eugene's van. He'll be home by six.

VERONIQUE: I want to find out NOW. But what if people see us standing at Big Joey's door?

MARIE-ADELE: What do you mean? We just knock on the door, march right in, ask the bitch, and march right out again.

185 VERONIQUE: Zhaboonigan dear, wait for me over there. *(She waits until Zhaboonigan is safely out of earshot and then leans over to Marie-Adele in a conspiratorial whisper.)* Anyway. You must know, Marie-Adele, that there's all kinds of women who come streaming out of that house at all hours of the day and night. I might be considered one of them. You know your youngest sister, Emily Dictionary, was seen staggering out of that house in the dead of night two nights ago?

MARIE-ADELE: Veronique St. Pierre, what Emily Dictionary does is Emily's business.

Annie Cook enters, walking fast, and comes to a screeching halt.

ANNIE: Hallooooo! Whatchyou doin'?

VERONIQUE: *(Giving Annie the baleful eye.)* How are you?

ANNIE: High as a kite. Just kidding. Hi, Zha.

190 ZHABOONIGAN: Hi. *(Giggles. She runs toward Marie-Adele, bumping into Annie en route.)*

ANNIE: Hey, Marie-Adele.

ZHABOONIGAN: Marie-Adele. How's your cancer? *(Giggles and scurries off laughing.)*

VERONIQUE: Shkanah, Zhaboonigan, sna-ma-bah . . . [4]

MARIE-ADELE: Come on, before the post office closes for lunch.

195 VERONIQUE: You didn't tell me you were going to the store.

ANNIE: Well, we are. *(To Marie-Adele.)* Hey, is Simon in? I'm sure he's got my Ricky Skaggs album. You know the one that goes *(Sings.)* "Honeee!" *(Calling into the house.)* Yoo-hoo, Simon!

MARIE-ADELE: He's in Espanola with Eugene.

VERONIQUE: Expecting mail, Annie Cook?

ANNIE: A parcel from my daughter, Ellen, who lives with this white guy in Sudbury . . .

200 VERONIQUE: So I've heard.

ANNIE: And my sister here is expecting a letter, too.

VERONIQUE: From whom?

ANNIE: From the doctor, about her next check-up.

VERONIQUE: When?

205 MARIE-ADELE: We don't know when. Or where. Annie, let's go.

ANNIE: They say it's shaped like a record.

---

[4] Shush, Zhaboonigan, don't say that. (Ojibway)

VERONIQUE: Maybe there'll be news in that parcel about THE BIGGEST BINGO IN THE WORLD! *(Shouts toward the lake, in a state of great excitement.)* Zhaboonigan! Zhaboonigan! We're going to the store!

ANNIE: THE BIGGEST BINGO IN THE WORLD?

VERONIQUE: In Toronto. Soon. Imagine! Gazelle Nataways told me. She heard about it from Little Girl Manitowabi over in Buzwah who heard about it from her daughter June Bug McLeod who just got back from the hospital in Sudbury where she had her tubes tied I just about had a heart attack!

210 ANNIE: Toronto?

MARIE-ADELE: We gotta find out for sure.

ANNIE: Right.

MARIE-ADELE: We could go to Big Joey's and ask Gazelle Nataways except Veronique St. Pierre's too scared of Gazelle.

VERONIQUE: I am not.

215 ANNIE: You are too.

MARIE-ADELE: We could wait and borrow Eugene's van . . .

VERONIQUE: I am not.

ANNIE: . . . drive over to Buzwah . . .

MARIE-ADELE: . . . and ask June Bug McLeod . . .

220 ANNIE: . . . but wait a minute! . . .

MARIE-ADELE AND ANNIE: Maybe there IS news in that parcel about this BIGGEST BINGO IN THE WORLD!

MARIE-ADELE: Come on.

VERONIQUE: *(Shouting toward the lake.)* Zhaboonigan! Zhaboonigan!

ANNIE: And here I was so excited about the next little bingo that old priest is holding next week. Toronto! Oh, I hope it's true!

225 VERONIQUE: Zhaboonigan! Zhaboonigan! Zhaboonigan! Dammit! We're going to the store!

And the "march" to the store begins, during which Nanabush, still in the guise of the seagull, follows them and continues to play tricks, mimicking their hand movements, the movement of their months, etc. The three women appear each in her own spot of light at widely divergent points on the stage area.

ANNIE: When I go to THE BIGGEST BINGO IN THE WORLD, in Toronto, I will win. For sure, I will win. If they shout the B 14 at the end, for sure I will win. The B 14 is my lucky number after all. Then I will take all my money and I will go to every record store in Toronto. I will buy every single one of Patsy Cline's records, especially the one that goes *(Sings.)* "I go a-walking, after midnight," oh I go crazy every time I hear that one. Then I will buy a huge record player, the biggest one in the whole world. And then I will go to all the taverns and all the night clubs in Toronto and listen to the live bands while I drink beer quietly—not noisy and crazy like here—I will bring my daughter Ellen and her white guy from Sudbury and we will sit together. Maybe I will call Fritz the Katz and he will take me out. Maybe he will hire me as one of his singers and I can (*Sings.*) "Oooh," in the background while my feet go (*Shuffles her feet from side to side.*) while Fritz the Katz is singing and the lights are flashing and the people are drinking beer and smoking cigarettes and dancing. Ohhh, I could dance all night with that Fritz the Katz. When I win, when I win THE BIGGEST BINGO IN THE WORLD!

MARIE-ADELE: When I win THE BIGGEST BINGO IN THE WORLD, I'm gonna buy me an island. In the North Channel, right smack-dab in the middle—eem-shak min-stik[5]—the most beautiful island in the world. And my island will have lots of trees—great big bushy ones— and lots and lots and lots of sweetgrass. MMMMM! And there's gonna be pine trees and oak trees and maple trees and big stones and little stonelets—neee—and, oh yeah, this real neat picket fence, real high, long and very, very, very white. No bird shit. Eugene will live there and me and all my Starblanket kids. Yup, no more smelly, stinky old pulp and paper mill in Espanola for my Eugene—pooh!—my 12 Starblanket boys and my two Starblanket girls and me and my Eugene all living real nice and comfy right there on Starblanket Island, the most beautiful incredible goddamn island in the whole goddamn world. Eem-shak min-stik! When I win THE BIGGEST BINGO IN THE WORLD!

VERONIQUE: Well, when I win THE BIGGEST BINGO IN THE WORLD. No! After I win THE BIGGEST BINGO IN THE WORLD, I will go shopping for a brand-new stove. In Toronto. At the Eaton Centre. A great big stove. The kind Madame Benoit has. The kind that has the three different compartments in the oven alone. I'll have the biggest stove on the reserve. I'll cook for all the children on the reserve. I'll adopt all of Marie-Adele Starblanket's 14 children and I will cook for them. I'll even cook for Gazelle Nataways' poor starving babies while she's lolling around like a pig in Big Joey's smelly, sweaty bed. And Pierre St. Pierre can drink himself to death for all I care. Because I'll be the best cook on all of Manitoulin Island! I'll enter competitions. I'll go to Paris and meet what's-his-name Cordon Bleu! I'll write a cookbook called "The Joy of Veronique St. Pierre's Cooking" and it will sell in the millions! And I will become rich and famous! Zhaboonigan Peterson will wear a mink while she eats steak tartare-de-frou-frou! Madame Benoit will be so jealous she'll suicide herself. Oh, when I win THE BIGGEST BINGO IN THE WORLD!

Zhaboonigan comes running in from swimming, "chasing" after the other three women, counting to herself and giggling.

ZHABOONIGAN: One, two, three, four, five, six, seven, eight, nine, ten, eleven, twelve, thirteen, fourteen.

---

[5] A great big island. (Cree)

At the store. Annie Cook, Marie-Adele Starblanket, Veronique St. Pierre, and Zhaboonigan Peterson have arrived. Emily Dictionary makes a sudden appearance, carrying a huge bag of flour on her shoulder. She is one tough lady, wearing cowboy boots, tight blue jeans, a black leather jacket—all three items worn to the seams— and she sports one black eye.

230 EMILY: *(In a loud, booming voice that paralyzes all movement in the room while she speaks.)* Zhaboonigan Peterson! What in Red Lucifer's name ever possessed you to be hangin' out with a buncha' dizzy old dames like this?

Bag of flour hits the floor with a "doof."

MARIE-ADELE: Emily. Your eye.

EMILY: Oh, bit of a tussle.

VERONIQUE: With who?

EMILY: None of your goddamn business.

235 MARIE-ADELE: Emily, please.

ANNIE: *(Following Emily about the store while Veronique tries, in vain, to hear what she can.)* I wasn't able to find out from Pelajia Patchnose or Philomena Moosemeat if Gazelle Nataways is going to Toronto this weekend with . . . Big Joey . . . they didn't know . . . Gazelle did win the bingo last night though.

EMILY: Aw shit. Veronique St. Pierre, you old bag. Is it true Gazelle Nataways is takin' off for Toronto with that hunk Big Joey?

VERONIQUE: It WAS you coming out of that house two nights ago. I walked by as quickly as I could . . .

EMILY: . . . shoulda come out and nailed your big floppy ears to the door . . .

240 VERONIQUE: . . . and I would have called the police but I was too scared Big Joey might come after me and Zhaboonigan later . . .

EMILY: . . . yeah, right.

ZHABOONIGAN: Yeah, right.

VERONIQUE: . . . and I have a weak heart, you know? Who hit you? Big Joey? Or Gazelle Nataways?

EMILY: The nerve of this woman.

245 VERONIQUE: Well?

EMILY: *(Calls Zhaboonigan, who is behind the counter, on the floor, playing with the merchandise.)* Zhaboonigan Peterson! Where in Red Lucifer's name is that dozy pagan?

VERONIQUE: You keep hanging around that house and you're gonna end up in deep trouble. You don't know how wicked and vicious those Nataways women can get. They say there's witchcraft in their blood. And with manners like yours, Emily Dictionary, you'd deserve every hex you got.

EMILY: Do I know this woman? Do I know this woman?

VERONIQUE: *(During this speech, Marie-Adele and Annie sing "Honeee" tauntingly.)* I'm sorry I have to say this in front of everyone like this but this woman has just accused my daughter of being a pagan. I didn't call her Zhaboonigan. The people on this reserve, who have nothing better to do with their time than call each other names, they called her that. Her name is Marie-Adele. Marie-Adele Peterson. You should talk. I should ask you where in Red . . . Red . . . whatever, you got a circus of a name like Emily Dictionary.

Emily grabs Veronique and throws her across the room. Veronique goes flying right into Pelajia, who has entered the store during the latter part of this speech.

250 PELAJIA: Veronique St. Pierre! Control yourself or I'll hit you over the head with my hammer.

VERONIQUE: *(Blows a "raspberry" in Pelajia's face.)* Bleah!

ANNIE: No, Pelajia, no.

EMILY: Go ahead, Pelajia. Make my day.

ANNIE: Down, put it down.

255 PHILOMENA: *(As she comes scurrying into the store.)* I have to use the toilet. *(Running to Emily.)* I have to use your toilet. *(And goes scurrying into the toilet.)*

ANNIE: *(To Pelajia.)* Remember, that's Veronique St. Pierre and if you get on the wrong side of Veronique St. Pierre she's liable to spread rumors about you all over kingdom come and you'll lose every bit of respect you got on this reserve. Don't let those pants you're wearing go to your head.

PELAJIA: *(Catching Annie by the arm as she tries to run away.)* Annie Cook! You got a mouth on you like a helicopter.

ANNIE: Veronique's mad at you, Emily, because you won't tell her what happened the other night at Big Joey's house. And she's jealous of Gazelle Nataways because Gazelle won the bingo again last night and she hopes you're the one person on this reserve who has the guts to stand up to Gazelle.

VERONIQUE: *(Making a lunge at Annie, who hides behind Emily.)* What's that! What's that! Ohhh! Ohhh!

260 ANNIE: Leave me alone, you old snoop. All I wanna know is this big bingo really happening in Toronto.

VERONIQUE: Annie Cook. You are a little suck.

EMILY: *(To Veronique.)* Someday, someone oughta stick a great big piece of shit into that mouth of yours.

PELAJIA: *(To Emily.)* And someday, someone ought to wash yours out with soap.

PHILOMENA: *(Throwing the toilet door open, she sits there in her glory, panties down to her ankles.)* Emily Dictionary. You come back to the reserve after all these years and you strut around like you own the place. I know Veronique St. Pierre is a pain in the ass but I don't care. She's your elder and you respect her. Now shut up, all of you, and let me shit in peace.

And slams the washroom door. Veronique, scandalized by this, haughtily walks through toward the door, bumping into Pelajia en route.

265 PELAJIA: Philomena. Get your bum out here. Veronique St. Pierre is about to lose her life. *(She raises her hammer at Veronique.)*
VERONIQUE: *(To Pelajia.)* Put that hammer away. And go put a skirt on, for heaven's sake, you look obscene in those tight pants.
ANNIE: Hit her. Go on. Hit the bitch. One good bang is all she needs.
EMILY: Yeah, right. A gang-bang is more like it.

And a full-scale riot breaks out, during which the women throw every conceivable insult at each other. Emily throws open the toilet door and Philomena comes stomping out, pulling her panties on and joining the riot. All talk at the same time, quietly at first, but then getting louder and louder until they are all screaming.

PHILOMENA: *(To Annie.)* What a slime. Make promises and then you go do something else. And I always have to smile at you. What a slime. *(To Emily.)* All that tough talk. I know what's behind it all. You'll never be big enough to push me around. *(To Marie-Adele.)* Fourteen kids! You look like a wrinkled old prune already. *(To Pelajia.)* At least I'm a woman. *(To Veronique.)* Have you any idea how, just how offensive, how obnoxious you are to people? And that halitosis. Pooh! You wouldn't have it if you didn't talk so much.
270 EMILY: *(To Philomena.)* So damned bossy and pushy and sucky. You make me sick. Always wanting your own *way.* *(To Veronique.)* Goddamned trouble-making old crow. *(To Pelajia.)* Fuckin' self-righteous old bitch. *(To Marie-Adele.)* Mental problems, that's what you got, princess. I ain't no baby. I'm the size of a fuckin' church. *(To Annie.)* You slippery little slut. Brain the size of a fuckin' pea. Fuck, man, take a Valium.
VERONIQUE: *(To Emily.)* You have no morals at all. You sick pervert. You should have stayed where you came from, where all the other perverts are. *(To Pelajia.)* Slow turtle. Talk big and move like Jell-O. *(To Annie.)* Cockroach! *(To Philomena.)* You big phony. Flush yourself down that damned toilet of yours and shut up. *(To Marie-Adele.)* Hasn't this slimy little reptile *(Referring to Annie.)* ever told you that sweet little Ellen of hers is really Eugene's daughter? Go talk to the birds in Sudbury and find out for yourself.
PELAJIA: *(To Veronique.)* This reserve would be a better place without you. I'm tired of dealing with people like you. Tired. *(To Marie-Adele.)* You can't act that way. This here's no time to be selfish. You spoiled brat. *(To Philomena.)* You old fool. I thought you were coming back to help me and here you are all trussed up like a Thanksgiving turkey, putting on these white lady airs. *(To Annie.)* Annie Cook. Move to Kapuskasing! *(To Emily.)* "Fuck, fuck, fuck!" Us Indian women got no business talking like that.
MARIE-ADELE: *(To Pelagia.)* You don't have all the answers. You can't fix everything. *(To Annie.)* White guys. Slow down a minute and see how stupid you look. *(To Emily.)* Voice like a fog-horn. You ram through

everything like a truck. You look like a truck. *(To Veronique.)* Some kind of insect, sticking insect claws into everybody's business. *(To Philomena.)* Those clothes. You look like a giant Kewpie doll. You make me laugh.

ANNIE: *(To Marie-Adele.)* You always make me feel so . . . small . . . like a little pig or something. You're no better than me. *(To Philomena.)* Why can't you go to bingo by yourself, you big baby? At least I got staying power. Piss off. *(To Veronique.)* Sucking off everybody else's life like a leech because you got nothing of your own. Pathetic old coot. Just buzz off. *(To Emily.)* You call me names. I don't call you names. You think you're too smart. Shut up. *(To Pelajia.)* "Queen of the Indians," you think that's what you are. Well, that stupid hammer of yours doesn't scrab me. Go away. Piss me off.

Then Pelajia lifts her hammer with a big loud "Woah"! And they come to a sudden dead stop. Pause. Then one quick final volley, all at once, loudest of all.

275 PHILOMENA: *(To Annie.)* You slimy buck-toothed drunken worm!
EMILY: *(To Veronique.)* Fuckin' instigator!
VERONIQUE: *(To Marie-Adele.)* Clutching, clinging vine!
PELAJIA: *(To Veronique.)* Evil no-good insect!
MARIE-ADELE: *(To Veronique.)* Maggot-mouthed vulture!
280 ANNIE: *(To Philomena.)* Fat-assed floozy, get off the pot!

Marie-Adele, stung to the quick, makes a vicious grab for Veronique by the throat. In a split-second, all freeze. Lights out in store interior. Lights on on Zhaboonigan, who has run out in fright during the riot, outside the store. Nanabush, still in his guise as the seagull, makes a grab at Zhaboonigan. Zhaboonigan begins talking to the bird.

ZHABOONIGAN: Are you gentle? I was not little. Maybe. Same size as now. Long ago it must be? You think I'm funny? Shhh. I know who you are. There, there. Boys. White boys. Two. Ever nice white wings, you. I was walking down the road to the store. They ask me if I want ride in car. Oh, I was happy I said, "Yup." Took me far away. Ever nice ride. Dizzy. They took all my clothes off me. Put something up inside me here. *(Pointing to her crotch, underneath her dress.)* Many, many times. Remember. Don't fly away. Don't go. I saw you before. There, there. It was a. Screwdriver. They put the screwdriver inside me. Here. Remember. Ever lots of blood. The two white boys. Left me in the bush. Alone. It was cold. And then. Remember. Zhaboonigan. Everybody calls me Zhaboonigan. Why? It means needle. Zhaboonigan. Going-through-thing. Needle Peterson. Going-through-thing Peterson. That's me. It was the screwdriver. Nice. Nice. Nicky Ricky Ben Mark. *(As she counts, with each name, feathers on the bird's wing.)* Ever nice. Nice white birdie you.

During this last speech, Nanabush goes through agonizing contortions. Then lights change instantly back to the interior of the store. The six women spring back into action. Philomena stomps back into the toilet.

MARIE-ADELE: *(To Veronique.)* Fine. And the whole reserve knows the only reason you ever adopted Zhaboonigan is for her disability cheque.

ANNIE: You fake saint.

Annie, Marie-Adele, and Emily start pushing Veronique, round-robin, between the three of them, laughing tauntingly until Veronique is almost reduced to tears.

VERONIQUE: *(Almost weeping.)* Bastards. The three of you.

Marie-Adele grabs Veronique by the throat and lifts her fist to punch her in the face. But the exertion causes her body to weaken, almost to the point of collapse, from her illness. At this point, Philomena emerges from the toilet.

285 PHILOMENA: *(Crinkling her nose.)* Emily. Your toilet.

WOMEN: Shhhh.

MARIE-ADELE: *(Holding her waist, reeling, barely audible.)* Oh, Shit.

PHILOMENA: I can't get it to flush.

WOMEN: Shhhh.

290 PELAJIA: *(Rushing to Marie-Adele.)* Marie-Adele. You're not well.

MARIE-ADELE: *(Screams.)* Don't touch me.

Complete silence from all while Marie-Adele weaves and struggles to keep herself from collapsing. Annie scurries offstage, to the back part of the store, where the post office would be.

EMILY: *(To Veronique.)* You f'in' bitch!

PHILOMENA: What did I just tell you? Who did that to your eye?

VERONIQUE: Big Joey.

295 EMILY: *(To Veronique.)* Look here, you old buzzard. I'll tell you a few things. You see this fist? You see these knuckles? You wanna know where they come from? Ten years. Every second night for 10 long ass-fuckin' years that goddamn Yellowknife asshole Henry Dadzinanare come home to me so drunk his eyes was spittin' blood like Red Lucifer himself and he'd beat me purple.

VERONIQUE: I wish I'd been there to see it all.

EMILY: Yeah, scumbag. I wish you'd been there to watch me learn to fight back like you've never seen a woman fight for her life before. Take a look at this eye. I earned it, Veronique St. Pierre, I earned it.

PHILOMENA: Henry Dadzinanare, Big Joey. They're all the same. Emily, use your brains.

EMILY: Use my brains. Yeah, right. I used them alright the night he came at me with an axe and just about sank it into my spine, I grabbed one bag, took one last look at the kids and walked out of his life forever.

300 ANNIE: *(From offstage.)* And she took the bus to San Francisco.

PHILOMENA: And gets herself mixed up with a motorcycle gang, for God's sake.

EMILY: *(Now addressing all in the room.)* Rosabella Baez, Hortensia Colorado, Liz Jones, Pussy Commanda. And me. The best. "Rose and the Rez Sisters," that's us. And man, us sisters could weave knuckle magic.

VERONIQUE: So why did you bother coming back?

PHILOMENA: You stay out of this.

305 EMILY: Come back to the Rez for a visit, get all wedged up with that hunk Big Joey one night . . . *(Grunts.)*

PHILOMENA: I give up.

EMILY: . . . and I was hooked. Couldn't leave. Settlin' back on a coupla beers with Big Joey the other night when Gazelle Nataways come sashayin' in like she's got half the Rez squished down the crack of her ass. She was high. I was high. Hell, we were all high. Get into a bit of a discussion, when she gets me miffed and I let fly, she let fly, Big Joey let fly, misses that nympho and lands me one in the eye instead.

VERONIQUE: So it was Big Joey.

EMILY: Damn rights. And that's as close as he got cuz I put him out for the night right then and there. Just one of these. *(Brandishing her fist.)* One. That's all it took.

Veronique runs off to look for Zhaboonigan.

310 ANNIE AND PHILOMENA: Emily Dictionary. *(Philomena with exasperation, Annie with adulation, from offstage.)*

ANNIE: You're amazing!

EMILY: Not Dictionary. Dadzinanare. Henry Dadzinanare. The man who made me learn to fight back. Never let a man raise one dick hair against me since.

VERONIQUE: *(Calling out to Zhaboonigan.)* Zhaboonigan. Don't you be talking to the birds like that again. You're crazy enough as it is.

ANNIE: *(As she comes running back in from the post office with her parcel, already unwrapped, and two letters, one for herself, already unfolded, and one still in its envelope.)* See? I told you. It's a record. Patsy Cline.

315 PHILOMENA: Never mind Patsy Cline.

ANNIE: *(As she hands Marie-Adele the letter in the envelope.)* Hey, Marie-Adele.

EMILY: Read your friggin' letter, Annie Cook.

ANNIE: Listen to this.

Zhaboonigan walks back in as Annie reads her own letter very haltingly.

Dear Mom: Here is the record you wanted. I thought you'd like the picture of Patsy Cline on the cover. *(Annie shows off her record.)* See? It's Patsy Cline. *(Returns to her letter.)* I also thought you might like to know that there is a bingo called THE BIGGEST BINGO IN THE WORLD. Can you fu . . . ture that?

EMILY: *(Who has been looking over Annie's shoulder.)* Feature. Feature.

320 ANNIE: Can you . . . feature . . . that? . . . that's coming to Toronto. The jackpot is $500,000. It's on Saturday, September 8. Raymond's Mom was in Toronto. Aunt Philomena will hit the roof when she hears this. Much love, your daughter Ellen.

Annie announces once more.

There is a brief electric silence followed by an equally electric scream from all the women. Even Zhaboonigan screams. Excitement takes over completely.

VERONIQUE: So it's true! It's true!

PHILOMENA: The Espanola bingo. Piffle. Mere piffle.

VERONIQUE: My new stove!

PHILOMENA: My new toilet! White! Spirit white!

325 EMILY: *(Grabbing Zhaboonigan and dancing around the room with her.)* I'd take the money, come back to the Rez, beat the shit out of Gazelle Nataways and take you down to Frisco with me. Whaddaya think?

ZHABOONIGAN: Yup.

MARIE-ADELE: *(In the background, where she has been reading her letter quietly to herself.)* September 10.

ANNIE: *(Taking the letter from Marie-Adele.)* Look, Pelajia. Marie-Adele's tests are in Toronto just two days after THE BIGGEST.

There is a brief embarrassed silence.

MARIE-ADELE: Kill two birds with one stone. *(To Nanabush.)* I wanna go. *(To Pelajia and Philomena.)* I wanna go.

330 VERONIQUE: Goood!

EMILY: *(Mimicking Veronique.)* Goood! Now how the hell are you guys gonna get down to Toronto? You're all goddamn welfare cases.

ANNIE: Fire Minklater.

VERONIQUE: Mary, mother of Jesus! I refuse, I absolutely refuse to be seen anywhere near that sorceress! We'll chip in and rent a car.

EMILY: Zhaboonigan Peterson here gonna chauffeur you down?

335 ZHABOONIGAN: Yup.

VERONIQUE: Don't you make fun of my daughter.

EMILY: What kind of stove you gonna buy, Veronique St. Pierre? Westinghouse? Electrolux? Yamaha? Kawasaki?

VERONIQUE: Oh my god, Marie-Adele, I never thought about it. They will have so many stoves in Toronto, I'll get confused.

ANNIE: If you go to Toronto and leave Wasy for even one day, Emily, you'll lose Big Joey forever . . .

340 VERONIQUE: To that witch!

ANNIE: . . . and then whose thighs will you have to wrestle around with in the dead of night? You'll dry up, get all puckered up and pass into ancient history.

EMILY: Annie Cook. I don't know what the fuck you're yatterin' on about now but I'd like to hear you say two words of French to that white guy in Sudbury you're so damn proud of.

ANNIE: Oh my god, Marie-Adele, she's right. I won't know what to say to this Raymond. I've never met him. I can't speak French. All I can say in French is Raymond and Bon Bon and I don't even know what that means. I can't go and live with them, not even after I win THE

BIGGEST BINGO IN THE WORLD. What am I gonna do? *(She collapses on the floor and rolls around for a bit.)*

EMILY: And Philomena Moosemeat's so fulla shit she'd need five toilets to get it all out.

345 PHILOMENA: *(Going at Emily.)* And just who do you think you're talking to, Miss Dictionary, just who the hell do you think you're talking to?

With a resounding belly butt from Emily, they begin to wrestle.

PELAJIA: *(Banging her hammer on the counter.)* Alright, alright. It's obvious we've got a problem here.

EMILY: *(Throwing Philomena off to the side.)* I'll say.

MARIE-ADELE: It's true. None of us has any money.

But Veronique, standing behind Pelajia, winks at the others and makes a hand motion indicating that Pelajia, for one, does have money. All the other women slowly surround Pelajia. But Pelajia catches the drift and quickly collects herself to meet the onslaught. During Pelajia's speech, the women respond at periodic intervals with a "yoah" and "hmmm," etc., as when a chief speaks at a council meeting.

PELAJIA: I say we all march down to the Band Office and ask the Band Council for a loan that will pay for the trip to this bingo. I know how to handle that tired old chief. He and I have been arguing about paved roads for years now. I'll tell him we'll build paved roads all over the reserve with our prize money. I'll tell him the people will stop drinking themselves to death because they'll have paved roads to walk on. I'll tell him there'll be more jobs because the people will have paved roads to drive to work on. I'll tell him the people will stop fighting and screwing around and Nanubush will come back to us because he'll have paved roads to dance on. There's enough money in there for everyone, I'll say. And if he doesn't lend us the money, I'll tell him I'm packing my bags and moving to Toronto tomorrow.

350 EMILY: That oughta twist his arm but good.

PELAJIA: And if he still says no, I'll bop him over the head with my hammer and we'll attack the accountant and take the money ourselves. Philomena, we're going to Toronto!

The seven women have this grand and ridiculous march to the band office, around the set and all over the stage area, with Pelajia leading them forward heroically, her hammer just a-swinging in the air. Nanabush trails merrily along in the rear of the line. They reach the "band office"—standing in one straight line square in front of the audience. The "invisible" chief "speaks": cacophonous percussion for about seven beats, the women listening more and more incredulously. Finally, the percussion comes to a dead stop.

PELAJIA: No?

Pelajia raises her hammer to hit the "invisible" chief, Nanabush shrugs a "don't, ask me, I don't know," Emily fingers a "fuck you, man." Black-out. End of Act One.

Act Two

All seven women are holding a meeting in the basement of Pelajia Patchnose's house. This is a collection of chairs and stools off to the side of the stage area. The only light comes from an old, beat-up trilight pole lamp. Some have tea, Emily and Annie a beer.

VERONIQUE: We should have met at the priest's house.

PELAJIA: No! We're gonna work this out on our own. Right here. Emily Dictionary, you chair. *(And she lends Emily her hammer.)*

VERONIQUE: She's good at ordering people around.

PHILOMENA: Shut up.

5 EMILY: First. When are we leaving? *(She bangs the hammer regularly throughout the meeting.)*

VERONIQUE: How much is the trip going to cost?

EMILY: When are we leaving?

PHILOMENA: How long to Toronto?

ANNIE: Four hours.

10 EMILY: When are we leaving?

PHILOMENA: The only human being who can make it in four hours is Annie Cook.

VERONIQUE: I'm not dying on the highway.

PHILOMENA: Eight hours.

PELAJIA: No way we're gonna stop at every toilet on the highway.

15 MARIE-ADELE: Six hours. Eugene's driven there.

VERONIQUE: Maybe we can borrow his van.

ANNIE: Maybe we can borrow Big Joey's van. *(A quick little aside to Pelajia.)* Hey, can I have another beer?

PELAJIA: No.

VERONIQUE: What about Gazelle Nataways?

20 EMILY: We're gonna borrow his van, not his buns, for Chris'sakes.

MARIE-ADELE: The only thing we have to pay for is gas.

ANNIE: Philomena's got gas.

EMILY: Right! Six hours. Eugene's van.

MARIE-ADELE: We still don't know when we're leaving.

25 PHILOMENA: Bingo's on Saturday night.

ANNIE: Leave Saturday morning.

VERONIQUE: Oh! I'll be so tired for the bingo. I'll get confused. Wednesday. Rest on Thursday.

ANNIE: And rest again on Friday? Too much resting. I can't go for that.

PELAJIA: And we can't afford such a long stay.

30 PHILOMENA: Where are we gonna stay?

EMILY: Whoa!

Pause.

PELAJIA: Friday night.

EMILY: Right. Leave Friday night. Next.

PHILOMENA: Coming home right after the bingo.
35 MARIE-ADELE: And leave me behind? Remember my tests Monday morning.
EMILY: Right. Monday noon, we come back. Next.
VERONIQUE: Don't go so fast. My mind is getting confused.
EMILY: Goood! Next.
MARIE-ADELE: Where are we gonna stay?
40 ANNIE: The Silver Dollar!
MARIE-ADELE: You can't stay there.
ANNIE: There's rooms upstairs.
PELAJIA: You wanna sleep in a whorehouse?
VERONIQUE: Zhaboonigan! Don't listen to this part.
45 PELAJIA: There's room at my son's.
PHILOMENA: Two washrooms! He's got a wonderful education.
EMILY: Next.
VERONIQUE: Who's going to drive?
ANNIE: Emily. She can drive anything.
50 VERONIQUE: I believe it.
ANNIE: But I can drive, too.
VERONIQUE: Oh my god.
ANNIE: Long as I don't have to drive in the city. You drive the city.
VERONIQUE: Me?
55 ANNIE AND MARIE-ADELE: No!
PELAJIA: Long as you don't drive too fast, Annie Cook.
PHILOMENA: And we'll pack a lunch for the trip and then eat in restaurants. Chinese.
PELAJIA: Can't afford it. We chip in, buy groceries and cook at my son's.
VERONIQUE: I'll give $10.
60 EMILY: You old fossil. You want us to starve?
PHILOMENA: $50 a day. Each.
EMILY: Philomena Moosemeat! That's $50 times seven people times four days. That's over $1,000 worth of groceries.
VERONIQUE: Imagine!
MARIE-ADELE: Okay. Veronique St. Pierre. You cook. $20 apiece. Right?
65 EMILY: Right. Next.
PHILOMENA: Anybody writing this down?
ANNIE: I'm gonna go to Sam the Recordman.
MARIE-ADELE: I'll make the grocery list.
PELAJIA: How much for gas?
70 VERONIQUE: *(Still in dreamland over the groceries.)* $1,000!
PHILOMENA: *(Flabbergasted.)* Nooo! You goose.
ANNIE: $40.
EMILY: $150. Period. Next.
PELAJIA: We got 10 days to find this money.
75 MARIE-ADELE: What's it cost to get into the bingo?
VERONIQUE: All the Indians in the world will be there!
PHILOMENA: $50.

ANNIE: And we're gonna be the only Indians there.
PELAJIA: Silence.

There is a long, thoughtful silence, broken only after a while by a scream from Zhaboonigan. Nanabush has knocked her off her stool. The women laugh.

    Can't think of anything else.
80 PHILOMENA: Add it up. *(She hands a pencil to Emily.)*
EMILY: *(Calculates.)* $1,400. You guys need $200 each.
VERONIQUE: Where am I going to get $400?
EMILY: Make it. End of meeting.

And the women start their fundraising activities with a vengeance. The drive is underlined by a wild rhythmic beat from the musician, one that gets wilder and wilder with each successive beat, though always underpinned by this persistent, almost dance-like pulse. The movement of the women covers the entire stage area, and like the music, gets wilder and wilder, until by the end it is as if we are looking at an insane eight-ring circus, eight-ring because through all this, Nanabush, as the seagull, has a holiday, particularly with Marie-Adele's lines of laundry, as Marie-Adele madly strings one line of laundry after another all over the set, from Pelajia's roof to Emily's store, etc. For the garage sale, Annie sells off Pelajia's lamp, chairs, etc., so that Pelajia's "basement" simply dissolves into the madness of the fundraising drive.

Beat one.

Pelajia is hammering on the roof.

Emily is at the store cash register and rings up each sale as Annie, Philomena, Marie-Adele, Zhaboonigan, and Veronique stand shoulder to shoulder and pass the following from one side of the stage to the other:

seven large sacks marked "FLOUR"

two giant tubs marked "LARD"

one bushel of apples

Beat two.

Zhaboonigan brings small table on and puts it stage left.

Annie brings table on and puts it stage right.

Philomena brings a basket full of beer bottles to center and empties it. She has a baby attached to her.

Veronique comes on with cloth and Windex and starts "cleaning windows" rhythmically, listening to whatever gossip she can hear.

Marie-Adele strings two lines of clothing across the stage.

Pelajia hammers on her roof.

Emily brings on several empty beer cases and fills them with Philomena's bottles.

Beat three.

Zhaboonigan brings in six quarts of blueberries and then takes over window cleaning from Veronique.

Annie brings on a basket of old clothes and a broken kitchen chair.

Philomena brings on another basket full of beer bottles, empties it. She now has two babies attached to her, like a fungus.

Emily fills beer cases rapidly, expertly.

Pelajia gets down off roof, hammering everything until she is on hands and knees, hammering the floor.

Marie-Adele strings third and fourth lines of laundry across the stage.

Veronique comes in burdened with seven apple pies and puts them on Annie's table.

Beat four.

Pelajia hammers as she crawls across the floor.

Zhaboonigan washes windows like a person possessed.

Emily runs and rings up a sale on the cash register and then brings on more empty beer cases and loads them up.

Philomena brings on a third load of bottles. Three babies are now attached to her.

Annie brings on an old trilight pole lamp and an old record player, which she opens and stacks alongside the rest of her stuff.

Annie and Emily sing a line of their song with very bad harmony.

Marie-Adele strings fifth and sixth lines of laundry across stage.

Veronique comes on with seven loaves of bread and puts them neatly by the pies.

Beat five.

Pelajia hammers as she crawls across the floor, hammering everything in sight. The women protect their poor feet.

Zhaboonigan washes windows even faster; she's starting to cry.

Emily and Philomena work together filling the empty beer cases as fast as they can. Emily runs to the register, rings in seven sales and sings a bit of song with Annie, better this time. Philomena now has four kids attached to her body.

Annie comes on with a small black and white TV with rabbit ears and an old toaster.

Veronique comes on with six dozen buns and dumps them out of their tins all over the table.

Pelajia hammers faster and faster.

Zhaboonigan is now working like a maniac and is sobbing.

Marie-Adele strings seventh and eighth lines of laundry across stage.

Beat six.

Emily goes to cash register and tallies their earnings; she works the register with tremendous speed and efficiency all this beat.

Zhaboonigan continues washing windows.

Philomena sticks a sign in beer bottles: World's Biggest Bottle Drive. She now has five babies attached to her.

Veronique sticks a sign on her table: World's Biggest Bake Sale.

Annie sticks a sign up around her stuff: World's Biggest Garage Sale.

Marie-Adele sticks a sign up on Zha's table: Big Blueberries and Laundry While You Wait.

Pelajia begins hammering the air. She may have lost her marbles.

Beat Seven.

EMILY: Whoa!

The "music" comes to a sudden stop. The women all collapse. The women look at each other. They then quickly clear the stage of everything they've brought on as Pelajia speaks, consulting her list. By the end of Pelajia's speech, the stage area is clear once more, except for a microphone stand that one of the women has brought on as part of the "clean-up" activities.

85 PELAJIA: Bottle drive. Ten cents a bottle, 24 bottles a case, equals two dollars and 40 cents. 777 bottles collected divided by 24 is 32 cases and nine singles that's 32 times $2.40 equals $77.70. Blueberries equals $90. Good pickin' Zha and the Starblanket kids. Washing windows at $5.00 a house times 18 houses. Five eights are 40, carry the four and add the five is 90 bucks less two on account of that cheap Gazelle Nataways only gave three dollars. That's $88. Household repairs is four roofs including the Chief's and one tiled floor is $225. Garage sale brung in $246.95, the bake sale equals $83 after expenses, we make 110 bucks on doing laundry, 65 bucks babysitting, 145 from Emily doing a double shift at the store and I have generously donated $103 from my savings. That brings us to a grand total of $1233.65. So!

Emily and Annie move forward as the music starts up. They are lit only by tacky floor flood-lighting, and are, in effect, at the Anchor Inn, Little Current. Emily speaks into the microphone.

EMILY: Thank-you. Thank-you, ladies and gentlemen. I thank you very much. And now for the last song of the night, ladies and gents, before we hit the road. A song that's real special to me in my heart. A song I wrote in memory of one Rosabella Baez, a Rez Sister from way back. And Rose baby, if you're up there tonight, I hope you're listenin' in. Cuz it's called: "I'm Thinkin' of You." Here goes . . .

Emily and Annie grab their microphones; Emily sings lead, Annie sings backup. And it's "country" to the hilt.

> I'm thinkin' of you every moment,
> As though you were here by my side;
> I'll always remember the good times,
> So darlin' please come back to me.
>
> I'm dreamin' of you every night,
> That we were together again;
> If time can heal up our partin'
> Then love can remove all this pain.

Instrumental—dance break

> If love is the secret of livin',
> Then give me that love, shinin' light;
> When you are again by my side,
> Then livin' will once more be right.

The audience claps. Emily says, "Thank-you." And then she and Annie join the other women, who have, during the song, loaded themselves, their suitcases, and their lunches into the "van." This van consists of three battered old van seats stuck to the walls of the theater, on either side and up high. The back seat is on the "stage left" side of the theater and the other two are on the other side, the middle seat of the van towards the back of the theater, the front seat, complete with detachable steering wheel, just in front and "stage right" of the stage area. Each seat is lit by its own light.

EMILY: How much did me and Annie take in singin' at the Anchor Inn?
PELAJIA: $330 at the door.
MARIE-ADELE: Solid packed house, eh? Shoulda charged more.
90 ANNIE: Fifty bucks for the oom-chi-cha machine. Twenty bucks for Ronnie's guitar. That's our only costs.
EMILY: Ha! We're laughin'.

A capella reprise of a verse of their song, which fades into highway sounds, and they drive, for a few moments, in silence.

In the van, driving down the highway to Toronto, at night. The women have intimate conversations, one on one, while the rest are asleep or seated at the other end of the van. Annie is driving. Emily sits beside her listening to her Walkman, while Marie-Adele is "leaning" over Annie's shoulder from her place in the middle seat. Veronique sits beside Marie-Adele, sleeping. Pelajia and Philomena are in the very back seat with Zhaboonigan between them.

MARIE-ADELE: Nee, Annie, not so fast.

Pause. Annie slows down.

So. You couldn't get Ellen and Raymond to come along? I'd like to meet this Raymond someday.
ANNIE: *(Angrily insisting on the correct pronunciation.)* Ray<u>mond</u>! Ellen says he's got a whole library full of cassette tapes.
MARIE-ADELE: Annie. You ever think about getting married again?
95 ANNIE: Not really. I can hear the band at the Silver Dollar already.
MARIE-ADELE: Do you still think about . . . Eugene?
ANNIE: What're you talkin' about? Of course, I think about him, he's my brother-in-law, ain't he?
MARIE-ADELE: He made his choice.
ANNIE: Yeah. He picked you.
100 MARIE-ADELE: Annie. I never stole him off you.
ANNIE: Drop dead. Shit! I forgot to bring that blouse. I mean. In case I sing. Shit.

MARIE-ADELE: If I'm gone and Eugene if he starts drinkin' again. I see you going for him.

ANNIE: Why would I bother? I had my chance 20 years ago. Christ!

MARIE-ADELE: Twenty years ago, I was there.

105 ANNIE: Why would I want 14 kids for?

MARIE-ADELE: That's exactly what I'm scared of. I don't want them kids to be split up. You come near Eugene you start drinking messing things up me not here I come back and don't matter where you are . . .

ANNIE: I don't want him. I don't want him. I don't want him. I don't want him. I don't want him.

EMILY: Put us all in the fuckin' ditch!

PELAJIA: Hey, watch your language up there.

110 ANNIE: Shit! I don't care. There's nothing more to say about it. Why don't you take your pills and go to sleep.

Pelajia and Philomena begin talking.

PHILOMENA: September 8 again.

PELAJIA: Hmmm? What about September 8?

PHILOMENA: You don't remember?

PELAJIA: What?

115 PHILOMENA: How could you?

PELAJIA: Mama died?

PHILOMENA: No! Remember?

PELAJIA: I can't remember. Got so much on my mind. So many things to forget.

ZHABOONIGAN: *(To Philomena.)* You like me?

120 PHILOMENA: Yes, Zhaboonigan. I like you.

ZHABOONIGAN: I like the birdies.

PHILOMENA: You like talking to the birdies?

ZHABOONIGAN: Yup. *(She falls asleep.)*

PHILOMENA: Zhaboonigan . . . sometimes I wonder . . .

125 PELAJIA: It's dark . . . warm . . . quiet . . .

PHILOMENA: Toronto. Had a good job in Toronto. Yeah. Had to give it all up. Yeah. Cuz mama got sick. Philomena Margaret Moosetail. Real live secretary in the garment district. He'd come in and see my boss. Nice man, I thought. That big, red, fish-tail Caddy. Down Queen Street. He liked me. Treated me like a queen. Loved me. Or I thought he did. I don't know. Got pregnant anyway. Blond, blue-eyed, six foot two. And the way he smelled. God! His wife walks in on us. *(Long silence.)* He left with her. *(Long silence.)* I don't even know to this day if it was a boy or a girl. I'm getting old. That child would be . . . 28 . . . 28 years old. September 8. You know what I'm gonna do with that money if I win? I'm gonna find a lawyer. Maybe I can find that child. Maybe I wouldn't even have to let him . . . her . . . know who I am. I just . . . want to see . . . who . . .

PELAJIA: I hope you win.

Annie and Emily, at the front of the van with Annie driving, are laughing and singing, "I'm a little Indian who loves fry bread." From time to time, they sneak each other a sip of this little bottle of whiskey Annie has hidden away inside her purse.

> I'm a little Indian who loves fry bread,
> Early in the morning and when I go to bed;
> Some folks say I'm crazy in the head,
> Cuz I'm a little Indian who loves fry bread.
>
> Now, some folks say I've put on a pound or two,
> My jeans don't fit the way they used to do;
> But I don't care, let the people talk,
> Cuz if I don't get my fry bread, you'll hear me squawk.

ANNIE: So tell me. What's it like to go to a big bar like . . . I mean like . . . the Silver Dollar.

EMILY: Lotta Nishnawbs.[6]

130 ANNIE: *(Disappointed.)* Yeah? Is the music good?

EMILY: Country rock.

ANNIE: *(Screams gleefully.)* Yee-haw! Maybe the band will ask me up to sing, eh? I'll sing something fast.

EMILY: You would, too.

ANNIE: *(Sings, real fast.)* "Well, it's 40 below and I don't give a fuck, got a heater in my truck and I'm off to the rodeo. Woof!" Something like that.

135 EMILY: Yup. That's pretty fast.

ANNIE: Hey. Maybe Fritz the Katz will be there. Never know. Might get laid, too, eh? Remember Room 20 at the Anchor Inn? Oh, that Fritz! Sure like singin' with him. Crazy about the way . . .

EMILY: *(Starts singing Patsy Cline's famous "Crazy . . . crazy for feelin' so lonely . . ." all the way through Annie's next speech.)*

ANNIE: . . . he stands there with his guitar and his 10-gallon hat. Is that what you call them hats? You know the kind you wear kind of off to the side like this? That's what he does. And then he winks at me. *(Sings.)* "Crazy . . ." Oooh, I love, just love the way the lights go woosh woosh in your eyes and kinda wash all over your body. Me standing there shuffling my feet side to side, dressed real nice and going *(Sings.)* "Oooh darlin' . . ." with my mike in my hand just so. Oh! And the sound of that band behind me. And Fritz. *(Sings.)* "Crazy, crazy for feelin' so lonely . . ."

EMILY: Yeah. You look good on stage.

140 ANNIE: Yeah?

EMILY: How come you're so keen on that guy anyway?

---

[6] Indians. (Ojibway)

ANNIE: Sure Veronique St. Pierre isn't just pretending to be asleep back there?

Emily and Marie-Adele check Veronique in the middle seat.

MARIE-ADELE: Nah. Out like a lamp.

EMILY: Hey! We'll get her drunk at the Silver Dollar and leave her passed out under some table. Take two beers to do that.

145 ANNIE: Hey. Too bad Big Joey had to come back from Toronto before we got there, eh?

EMILY: Man! That dude's got buns on him like no other buns on the face of God's entire creation. Whooo! Not to mention a dick that's bigger than a goddamn breadbox.

Annie screams gleefully.

How about Fritz? What's his look like?

ANNIE: *(After an awkward pause.)* He's Jewish, you know.

EMILY: *(Laughing raucously.)* World's first Jewish country singer!

ANNIE: Don't laugh. Those Jews make a lot of money, you know.

150 EMILY: Not all of them.

ANNIE: Fritz buys me jeans and things. I'm gonna be one of them Jewish princesses.

EMILY: What's wrong with being an Indian princess?

ANNIE: Aw, these white guys. They're nicer to their women. Not like Indian guys. Screw you, drink all your money, and leave you flat on your ass.

EMILY: Yeah, right. Apple Indian Annie. Red on the outside. White on the inside.

155 ANNIE: Emily!

EMILY: Keep your eye on the road.

ANNIE: Good ol' highway 69.

EMILY: Hey. Ever 69 with Fritz?

MARIE-ADELE: Neee.

160 ANNIE: White guys don't make you do things to them. You just lie there and they do it all for you. Ellen's real happy with her Raymond. You can tell the way she sounds on the phone. Maybe someday I'll just take off with a guy like Fritz.

EMILY: Then what? Never come back to the rez?

Annie is cornered. Emily then slaps her playfully on the arm.

Hey. Know what?

Sings.

> When I die, I may not go to heaven,
> I don't know if they let Indians in;
> If they don't, just let me go to Wasy, lord,
> Cuz Wasy is as close as I've been.

ANNIE: Lots of white people at this Silver Dollar?

EMILY: Sometimes. Depends.

ANNIE: How much for beer there?

165 EMILY: Same as up here. Nah! Don't need money, Annie Cook. You just
gotta know how to handle men. Like me and the Rez Sisters down in
Frisco.

ANNIE: Yeah?

EMILY: I'll take care of them.

ANNIE: Maybe we can find a party, eh? Maybe with the band.

EMILY: Whoa! Slow down, Annie Cook! Easy on the gas!

170 MARIE-ADELE: Annie!

Pow. Black-out. They have a flat tire.

The flat tire. Everything now happens in complete darkness.

VERONIQUE: Bingo!

PHILOMENA: What was that? What happened?

ANNIE: I don't know. Something just went "poof"!

EMILY: Alright. Everybody out. We got a fuckin' flat.

They all climb out of the van.

175 VERONIQUE: Oh my god! We'll never get to the bingo.

ZHABOONIGAN: Pee pee.

PELAJIA: I can't fix a flat tire.

ANNIE: Emily can.

PELAJIA: Get the jack. Spare tire.

180 ANNIE: Philomena's wearing one.

ZHABOONIGAN: Pee pee.

PHILOMENA: This is all your fault, Annie Cook.

MARIE-ADELE: It's in the back.

ANNIE: So what do we do?

185 PELAJIA: What's the matter with Zha?

PHILOMENA: Gotta make pee pee.

VERONIQUE: I knew there was something wrong with this van the moment
I set eyes on it. I should have taken the bus.

PHILOMENA: Oh shut up. Quack, quack, quack.

ANNIE: Don't look at me. It's not my fault the tires are all bald.

190 PHILOMENA: Nobody's blaming you.

ANNIE: But you just did.

PHILOMENA: Quack, quack, quack.

VERONIQUE: Where are we?

ANNIE: The Lost Channel. This is where you get off.

195 VERONIQUE: *(Groans.)* Ohhh!

EMILY: Yeah, right.

PHILOMENA: Shhh!

PELAJIA: Jack's not working too well.

EMILY: Okay. Everybody. Positions.

200 VERONIQUE: Not me. My heart will collapse.

EMILY: You wanna play bingo?

VERONIQUE: *(Groans.)* Ohhhh!

ANNIE: Hurry up! Hurry up!

EMILY: Okay. One, two, three lift.

Everybody lifts and groans.

205 PELAJIA: Put the jack in there.

All lift, except Marie-Adele and Zha, who wander off into the moonlit darkness. Dim light on them.

ZHABOONIGAN: Ever dark.

MARIE-ADELE: You'll be fine, Zhaboonigan.

Suddenly, a nighthawk—Nanabush, now in dark feathers—appears, darting in the night.

ZHABOONIGAN: The birdies!

MARIE-ADELE: Yes, a birdie.

210 ZHABOONIGAN: Black wings!

Marie-Adele begins talking to the bird, almost if she were talking to herself. Quietly, at first, but gradually—as the bird begins attacking her—growing more and more hysterical, until she is shrieking, flailing, and thrashing about insanely.

MARIE-ADELE: Who are you? What do you want? My children? Eugene? No! Oh no! Me? Not yet. Not yet. Give me time. Please. Don't. Please don't. Awus! Get away from me. Eugene! Awus! You fucking bird! Awus! Awus! Awus! Awus! Awus! *(And she has a total hysterical breakdown.)*

Zhaboonigan, at first, attempts to scare the bird off by running and flailing her arms at it. Until the bird knocks her down and she lies there on the ground, watching in helpless astonishment and abject terror. Underneath Marie-Adele's screams, she mumbles to herself, sobbing.

ZHABOONIGAN: One, two, three, four, five, six, seven . . . Nicky Ricky Ben Mark . . . eight, nine, ten, eleven, twelve . . .

Until the other women come running. Total darkness again.

EMILY: What the . . .

ANNIE: Marie-Adele!

215 PELAJIA: Stop her! Hold her!

VERONIQUE: What's happening?

PHILOMENA: Marie-Adele. Now, now . . . come . . . come . . .

EMILY: *(In the background.)* Stop that fucking screaming will ya, Marie-Adele!

PHILOMENA: Emily. There's no need to talk to her like that now.

220 PELAJIA: Help us get her in the van.

PHILOMENA: Come . . . come, Marie-Adele . . . everything's fine . . . you'll be fine . . . come . . . shhh . . . shhh . . .

And they ease Marie-Adele back into the van. Once all is beginning to settle down again:

PELAJIA: Everything okay now?

PHILOMENA: Yes. She's fine now.

PELAJIA: Emily, take over.

225 VERONIQUE: Yes. I don't trust that Annie Cook. Not for one minute.

EMILY: All set?

MARIE-ADELE: What time is it?

PELAJIA: Twenty after four.

ANNIE: Oh! We're over two hours behind schedule. Hurry up. Hurry up.

230 VERONIQUE: I'll be exhausted for the bingo tomorrow night. Maybe I should just take 15 cards.

EMILY: You can rest your heart. And your mouth. All day tomorrow. All set?

And she starts up the van. The van lights come back on.

The dialogues resume. Marie-Adele now sits in the front with Emily, who is driving. Zhaboonigan sits between them. Pelajia and Philomena are now in the middle seat, Annie and Veronique in the back.

EMILY: You scared the shit out of me out there. *(Silence.)* Don't do that again. *(Silence.)* Feeling better now? *(Silence.)*

MARIE-ADELE: I could be really mad, just raging mad just wanna tear his eyes out with my nails when he walks in the door and my whole body just goes "k-k-k-k" . . . . . He doesn't talk, when something goes wrong with him, he doesn't talk, shuts me out, just disappears. Last night he didn't come home. Again, it happened. I couldn't sleep. You feel so ugly. He walks in this morning. Wanted to be alone, he said. The curve of his back, his breath on my neck, "Adele, ki-sa-gee-ee-tin oo-ma,"[7] making love, always in Indian, only. When we still could. I can't even have him inside me anymore. It's still growing there. The cancer. Pelajia, een-pay-seek-see-yan.[8]

PELAJIA: You know one time, I knew this couple where one of them was dying and the other one was angry at her for dying. And she was mad because he was gonna be there when she wasn't and she had so much left to do. And she'd lie there in bed and tell him to do this and do that and he'd say "Okay, okay." And then he'd go into the kitchen and say to me, "She's so this and she's so that and she's so damned difficult." And I watched all this going on. That house didn't have room for two such angry people. But you know, I said to her, "You

_____
[7] Adele, I love you. (Cree)
[8] Pelajia, I'm scared to death. (Cree)

gotta have faith in him and you gotta have faith in life. He loves you very much but there's only so much he can do. He's only human." There's only so much Eugene can understand, Marie-Adele. He's only human.

235 EMILY: Fuckin' right. Me and the Rez Sisters, okay? Cruisin' down the coast highway one night. Hum of the engine between my thighs. Rose. That's Rosabella Baez, leader of the pack. We were real close, me and her. She was always thinkin' real deep. And talkin' about bein' a woman. An Indian woman. And suicide. And alcohol and despair and how fuckin' hard it is to be an Indian in this country. *(Marie-Adele shushes her gently.)* No goddamn future for them, she'd say. And why, why, why? Always carryin' on like that. Chris'sakes. She was pretty heavy into the drugs. Guess we all were. We had a fight. Cruisin' down the coast highway that night. Rose in the middle. Me and Pussy Commanda off to the side. Big 18-wheeler come along real fast and me and Pussy Commanda get out of the way. But not Rose. She stayed in the middle. Went head-on into that truck like a fly splat against a windshield. I swear to this day I can still feel the spray of her blood against my neck. I drove on. Straight into daylight. Never looked back. Had enough gas money on me to take me far as Salt Lake City. Pawned my bike off and bought me a bus ticket back to Wasy. When I got to Chicago, that's when I got up the nerve to wash my lover's dried blood from off my neck. I loved that woman, Marie-Adele, I loved her like no man's ever loved a woman. But she's gone. I never wanna go back to San Francisco. No way, man.

MARIE-ADELE: *(Comforting the crying Emily.)* You should get some rest. Let Annie take over.

EMILY: I'll be fine. You go to sleep. Wake you up when we get to Toronto.

Emily puts her Walkman on and starts to sing along quietly to "Blue Kentucky Girl" by Emmylou Harris with its "I swear I love you . . ." while Marie-Adele leans her head against the "window" and falls asleep.

After a few moments, Zhaboonigan, who has been dozing off between Emily and Marie-Adele in the front seat, pokes her head up and starts to sing along off-key. Then she starts to play with Emily's hair.

EMILY: *(Shrugging Zhaboonigan's hand off.)* Don't bug me. My favorite part's comin' up.

Initiated by Zhaboonigan, they start playing "slap." The game escalates to the point where Emily almost bangs Zhaboonigan over the head with her elbow.

EMILY: Yeah, right. You little retard.

Mad at this, Zhaboonigan hits Emily in the stomach.

Don't hit me there, you little. . . . Hey, man, like ummm . . . I'm sorry, Zha.

240 ZHABOONIGAN: Sorry.

EMILY: *(Emily feels her belly thoughtfully. After a brief silence)* You gonna have kids someday, Zha?

ZHABOONIGAN: Ummm . . . buy one.

EMILY: Holy! Well, kids were alright. Aw geez, Zha, that man treated me real bad. Ever been tied to a bed post with your arms up like this? Whoa! *(Grabbing the steering wheel.)* Maybe you should drive.

ZHABOONIGAN: Scary.

245 EMILY: Aw, don't be scared. Fuck.

ZHABOONIGAN: Fuck.

EMILY: Zhaboonigan Peterson! Your ma'll give me a black eye.

Zhaboonigan turns her head toward the back seat, where Veronique sits sleeping, and says one more time, really loud.

ZHABOONIGAN: Fuck!

EMILY: Shhh! Look, Zha. You don't let any man bother you while we're down in T.O. You just stick close to me.

250 ZHABOONIGAN: Yup.

EMILY: We're sisters, right? Gimme five.

They slap hands.

Alright. Bingo!!!

Instantly, the house lights come on full blast. The Bingo Master—the most beautiful man in the world—comes running up center aisle, cordless mike in hand, dressed to kill: tails, rhinestones, and all. The entire theater is now the bingo palace. We are in: Toronto!!!!

BINGO MASTER: Welcome, ladies and gentlemen, to the biggest bingo the world has ever seen! Yes, ladies and gentlemen, tonight, we have a very, very special treat for you. Tonight, ladies and gentlemen, you will be witness to events of such gargantuan proportions, such cataclysmic ramifications, such masterly and magnificent manifestations that your minds will reel, your eyes will nictitate, and your hearts will palpitate erratically.

Because tonight, ladies and gentlemen, you will see the biggest, yes, ladies and gentlemen, the very biggest prizes ever known to man, woman, beast, or appliance. And the jackpot tonight? The jackpot, ladies and gentlemen, is surely the biggest, the largest, the hugest, and the most monstrous jackpot ever conceived of in the entire history of monstrous jackpots as we know them. $500,000! Yes, ladies and gentlemen, $500,000 can be yours this very night! That's half a million—A HALF MILLION SMACKEROOS!!! IF you play the game right.

And all you have to do, ladies and gentlemen, is reach into your programs and extract the single bingo card placed therein. Yes, ladies and gentlemen, the single bingo card placed therein, which bingo card will entitle you to one chance at winning the warm-up game for a prize of $20. $20! And all you have to do is poke holes in that single bingo card. Yes, ladies and gentlemen, just poke holes in that single bingo card and bend the numbers backward as the numbers are called. And don't forget the free hole in the middle of the card. Twenty dollars, ladies and gentlemen, that's one line in any direction. That means, of course, ladies and gentlemen, that the first person to form one line, just one straight line in any direction on their card, will be the very lucky winner of the $20 prize. $20! Are you ready, ladies and gentlemen? Are you ready? Then let the game begin! Under the G 56. *Etc.* . . .

The audience plays bingo, with the seven women, who have moved slowly into the audience during the Bingo Master's speech, playing along. Until somebody in the audience shouts, "Bingo!"

BINGO MASTER: Hold your cards, ladies and gentlemen, bingo has been called.

The Bingo Master and the assistant stage manager check the numbers and the prize money is paid out.

BINGO MASTER: And now for the game you've all been waiting for, ladies and gentlemen. Now for the big game. Yes, ladies and gentlemen, get ready for THE BIGGEST BINGO IN THE WORLD! For the grand jackpot prize of $500,000! Full house, ladies and gentlemen, full house! Are you ready? Are you ready? Then let the game begin!

The house lights go out. And the only lights now are on the bingo balls bouncing around in the bingo machine—an eery, surreal sort of glow—and on the seven women who are now playing bingo with a vengeance on centerstage, behind the Bingo Master, where a long bingo table has magically appeared with Zhaboonigan at the table's center banging a crucifix Veronique has brought along for good luck. The scene is lit so that it looks like "The Last Supper."

The women face the audience. The bingo table is covered with all the necessary accoutrements: bags of potato chips, cans of pop, ashtrays (some of the women are smoking), etc. The Bingo Master calls out number after number—but not the B 14—with the women improvising responses. These responses—Philomena has 27 cards!—grow more and more raucous: "B 14? Annie Cook? One more number to go! The B 14! Where is that B 14?! Gimme that B 14! Where the fuck is that B 14?!!!" etc. Until the women have all risen from the table and come running downstage, attacking the bingo machine and throwing the Bingo Master out of the way. The women grab the bingo machine with shouts of: "Throw this fucking machine into the lake! It's no damn good!" etc. And they go running down center aisle with it and out of the theater. Bingo cards are flying like confetti. Total madness and mayhem. The music is going crazy.

And out of this chaos emerges the calm, silent image of Marie-Adele waltzing romantically in the arms of the Bingo Master. The Bingo Master says "Bingo" into her ear. And the Bingo Master changes, with sudden bird-like movements, into the nighthawk, Nanabush in dark feathers. Marie-Adele meets Nanabush.

During this next speech, the other women, one by one, take their positions around Marie-Adele's porch, some kneeling, some standing. The stage area, by means of "lighting magic," slowly returns to its Wasaychigan Hill appearance.

255　MARIE-ADELE: U-wi-nuk u-wa? U-wi-nuk u-wa? Eugene? Neee. U-wi-nuk ma-a oo-ma kee-tha? Ka. Kee-tha i-chi-goo-ma so that's who you are . . . at rest upon the rock . . . the master of the game . . . the game . . . it's me . . . nee-tha . . . come . . . come . . . don't be afraid . . . as-tum . . . come . . . to . . . me . . . ever soft wings . . . beautiful soft . . . soft . . . dark wings . . . here . . . take me . . . as-tum . . . as-tum . . . pee-na-sin . . . wings . . . here . . . take me . . . take . . . me . . . with . . . pee-na-sin . . .[9]

As Nanabush escorts Marie-Adele into the spirit world, Zhaboonigan, uttering a cry, makes a last desperate attempt to go with them. But Emily rushes after and catches her at the very last split second. And the six remaining women begin to sing the Ojibway funeral song. By the beginning of the funeral song, we are back at the Wasaychigan Hill Indian Reserve, at Marie-Adele's grave.

WOMEN:
　Wa-kwing, wa-kwing,
　Wa-kwing nin wi-i-ja;
　Wa-kwing, wa-kwing,
　Wa-kwing nin wi-i ja.[10]

At Marie-Adele's grave. During Pelajia's speech, the other women continue humming the funeral song until they fade into silence. Pelajia drops a handful of earth on the grave.

PELAJIA: Well, sister, guess you finally hit the big jackpot. Best bingo game we've ever been to in our lives, huh? You know, life's like that, I figure. When all is said and done. Kinda' silly, innit, this business of living? But. What choice do we have? When some fool of a being goes and puts us Indians plunk down in the middle of this old earth, dishes out this lot we got right now. But. I figure we gotta make the most of it while we're here. You certainly did. And I sure as hell am giving it one

---

[9] MARIE-ADELE: Who are you? Who are you? Eugene? Neee. Then who are you really? Oh. It's you, so that's who you are . . . at rest upon the rock . . . the master of the game . . . the game . . . it's me . . . me . . . come . . . come . . . don't be afraid . . . come . . . come . . . to . . . me . . . ever soft wings . . . beautiful soft . . . soft . . . dark wings . . . here . . . take me . . . come . . . come . . . come and get me . . . wings . . . here . . . take me . . . take . . . me . . . with . . . come and get me . . . (Cree)

[10] WOMEN: Heaven, heaven, heaven, I'm going there; Heaven, heaven, heaven, I'm going there. (Ojibway)

good try. For you. For me. For all of us. Promise. Really. See you when that big bird finally comes for me. *(Whips out her hammer one more time, holds it up in the air and smiles.)* And my hammer.

Back at the store in Wasaychigan Hill. Emily is tearing open a brand-new case of the small cans of Carnation milk, takes two cans out and goes up to Zhaboonigan with them.

EMILY: See, Zha? The red part up here and the white part down here and the pink flowers in the middle?
ZHABOONIGAN: Oh.
260 EMILY: Carnation milk.
ZHABOONIGAN: Carnation milk.
EMILY: And it goes over here where all the other red and white cans are, okay?
ZHABOONIGAN: Yup.

Zhaboonigan rushes to Emily and throws her arms around her affectionately. Emily is embarrassed and struggles to free herself. Just then, Annie enters. She's lost some of her speed and frenetic energy. There's obviously something wrong with her.

ANNIE: Hallooo! Whatchyou doing.
265 EMILY: Red Lucifer's whiskers! It's Annie Cook.
ANNIE: Well, we seem to have survived the biggest bingo in the world, eh? Well . . . ummm . . . not all of us . . . not Marie-Adele . . . but she knew she was . . . but we're okay. *(Laughs.)* . . . us? . . .
EMILY: Annie Cook. Sometimes you can be so goddamn ignorant. *(Pause.)* Too bad none of us won, eh.
ANNIE: Philomena Moosemeat won $600. That's something.
EMILY: Yup. That's one helluva jazzy toilet she's got there, eh?
270 ANNIE: She's got eight-ply toilet paper. Dark green. Feels like you're wiping your ass with moss!
EMILY: Holy!
ANNIE: I'm singing back-up for Fritz weekends. 25 bucks a gig. That's something, eh?
EMILY: Katz's whore . . .
ANNIE: What?
275 EMILY: You heard me.
ANNIE: The Katz's what?
EMILY: Chris'sakes. Wake up.
ANNIE: I love him, Emily.
EMILY: You been drinkin'.
280 ANNIE: Please, come with me tonight.
EMILY: Have to wait for the old buzzard to come pick up this dozy daughter of hers and that's not 'til seven.
ANNIE: Okay?
EMILY: Alright. But we're comin' right back to the Rez soon as the gig's over. Hear?

ANNIE: Thanks. Any mail today?

285 EMILY: Sorry.

ANNIE: That's okay. See you at seven.

And she exits.

ZHABOONIGAN: Why . . . why . . . why do you call me that?

EMILY: Call you what?

ZHABOONIGAN: Dozy dotter.

Awkward silence, broken after a while by Zhaboonigan's little giggle.

290 EMILY: Look, Zha. Share a little secret with you, okay?

ZHABOONIGAN: Yup.

EMILY: Just you and me, promise?

ZHABOONIGAN: Yup.

EMILY: Gazelle Nataways'll see fit to kill . . . but I'm gonna have a baby.

295 ZHABOONIGAN: *(Drops the Carnation milk cans she's been holding all this time and gasps.)* Ohhh! Big Joey!

EMILY: *(In exasperation.)* This business of having babies . . .

And the last we see of them is Zhaboonigan playfully poking Emily in the belly and Emily slapping Zhaboonigan's hand away.

At Eugene Starblanket's house. Veronique St. Pierre is sitting on the steps, glowing with happiness, looking up at the sky as though looking for seagulls. She sees none so she picks up the doll that lies under her chair and cradles it on her lap as though it were a child. At this point, Annie Cook enters.

ANNIE: Hellooo! *(Surprised to see Veronique sitting there.)* Veronique St. Pierre. What are you doing here?

VERONIQUE: Annie Cook. Haven't you heard I'm cooking for Eugene and the children these days? It's been four days since the funeral as you know may she rest in peace *(Makes a quick sign of the cross without missing beat.)* but I was the only person on this reserve who was willing to help with these 14 little orphans.

ANNIE: That's nice. But I came to see if Simon Star . . .

300 VERONIQUE: The stove is so good. All four elements work and there is even a timer for the oven. As I was saying to Black Lady Halked at the bingo last night, "Now I don't have to worry about burning the fried potatoes or serving the roast beef half-raw."

ANNIE: Well, I was about to . . .

VERONIQUE: Yes, Annie Cook. I bought a roast beef just yesterday. A great big roast beef. Almost 16 pounds. It's probably the biggest roast beef that's been seen on this reserve in recent years. The meat was so heavy that Nicky, Ricky, Ben, and Mark had to take turns carrying it here for me. Oh, it was hard and slippery at first, but I finally managed to wrestle it into my oven. And it's sitting in there at this very moment just sizzling and bubbling with the most succulent and delicious

juices. And speaking of succulent and delicious juices, did you come to
call on Eugene? Well, Eugene's not home.

ANNIE: Yeah, right. I came to see if Simon had that new record.

VERONIQUE: Why?

305 ANNIE: I'm singing in Little Current tonight and I gotta practice this one
song.

VERONIQUE: *(Contemptuously.)* That Ritzie Ditzie character.

ANNIE: It's Fritz the Katz, Veronique St. Pierre. FREDERICK STEPHEN KATZ.
He's a very fine musician and a good teacher.

VERONIQUE: Teacher?! Of what?! As I was saying to Little Girl Manitowabi
and her daughter June Bug McLeod at the bingo last night, "You never
know about these non-Native bar-room types." I said to them, "We
have enough trouble right here on this reserve without having our
women come dragging these shady white characters into the picture."
Before you know it, you will end up in deep trouble and bring shame
and disrespect on the name of Pelajia Patchnose and all your sisters,
myself included.

ANNIE: Myself included, my ass! Veronique St. Pierre. I wish you would
shut that great big shitty mouth of yours at least once a year!

310 VERONIQUE: *(Stunned into momentary silence. Then.)* Simon Starblanket is not
home. *(With this, she bangs the doll down viciously.)*

ANNIE: Good day, Veronique St. Pierre. *(And exits.)*

*Veronique, meanwhile, just sits there in her stunned state, mouth hanging open
and looking after the departing Annie.*

*On Pelajia Patchnose's roof. As at the beginning of the play, Pelajia is alone,
nailing shingles on. But no cushion this time.*

PELAJIA: Philomena. Where are those shingles?

PHILOMENA: *(From offstage.)* Oh, go on. I'll be up in just a minute.

PELAJIA: *(Coughs.)* The dust today. It's these dirt roads. Dirt roads all over.
Even the main street. If I were chief around here, that's the very first
thing I would do is . . .

315 PHILOMENA: *(Coming up the ladder with one shingle and the most beautiful
pink, lace-embroidered, heart-shaped pillow you'll ever see.)* Oh, go on.
You'll never be chief.

PELAJIA: And why not?

PHILOMENA: Because you're a woman.

PELAJIA: Bullshit! If that useless old chief of ours was a woman, we'd see a
few things get done around here. We'd see our women working, we'd
see our men working, we'd see our young people sober on Saturday
nights, and we'd see Nanabush dancing up and down the hill on shiny
black paved roads.

Annie Cook pops up at the top of the ladder.

ANNIE: Pelajia for chief! I'd vote for you.

320   PHILOMENA: Why, Annie Cook. You just about scared me off the edge of this roof.

PELAJIA: Someday, we'll have to find you a man who can slow you down. So what do you want this time, Annie Cook?

ANNIE: Well, to tell you the truth, I came to borrow your record player, Philomena Moosemeat . . . I mean, Moosetail. I'm going to practice this one song for tonight. Emily Dictionary is coming to Little Current to watch me sing with the band.

PELAJIA: It's back from Espanola.

PHILOMENA: *(To Pelajia.)* Pelajia Rosella Patchnose! *(To Annie.)* It's still not working very well. There's a certain screeching, squawking noise that comes out of it every time you try to play it.

325   PELAJIA: That's okay, Philomena. There's a certain screechy, squawky noise that comes out of Annie Cook every time she opens her mouth to sing anyway.

PHILOMENA: Yes, Annie Cook. You can borrow it. But only for one night.

ANNIE: Good. Hey, there's a bingo in Espanola next week and Fire Minklater is driving up in her new car. There might be room. *(To Philomena.)* Would you like to go?

PELAJIA: Does a bear shit in the woods?

PHILOMENA: *(Glares at Pelajia first.)* Yes. *(Then quickly to Annie.)* Make . . . make sure you don't leave me behind.

330   ANNIE: I'll make sure. Well. Toodle-oo! *(And she pops down the ladder again, happy, now that she's finally got her record player.)*

PELAJIA: That Annie Cook. Records and bingo. Bingo and records.

PHILOMENA: You know, Pelajia, I'd like to see just what this Fritz looks like. Maybe he IS the man who can slow her down, after all.

PELAJIA: Foolishness! Annie Cook will be walking fast right up until the day she dies and gets buried beside the two of us in that little cemetery beside the church.

PHILOMENA: Oh, go on. *(Pause. As Philomena sits down beside her sister, leaning with her elbow on her heart-shaped pillow.)* So, Pelajia Patchnose. Still thinking about packing your bags and shipping off to Toronto?

335   PELAJIA: Well . . . oh . . . sometimes. I'm not so sure I would get along with him if I were to live down there. I mean my son Tom. He was telling me not to play so much bingo.

PHILOMENA: His upstairs washroom. Mine looks just like it now.

PELAJIA: Here we go again.

PHILOMENA: Large shining porcelain tiles in hippity-hoppity squares of black and white . . . so clean you can see your own face, like in a mirror, when you lean over to look into them. It looks so nice. The shower curtains have a certain matching blackness and whiteness to them—they're made of a rich, thick plasticky sort of material—and they're see-through in parts. The bathtub is beautiful, too. But the best, the most wonderful, my absolute most favorite part is the toilet bowl itself. First of all, it's elevated, like on a sort of . . . pedestal, so that it makes you feel like . . . the Queen . . . sitting on her royal throne, ruling her Queendom with a firm yet gentle hand. And the bowl itself—white, spirit white—is of such a shape, such an exquisitely soft, perfect oval shape that it makes you want to cry. Oh!!! And it's so comfortable you could just sit on it right up until the day you die!

After a long, languorous pause, Philomena snaps out of her reverie when she realizes that Pelajia, all this time, has been looking at her disbelievingly and then contemptuously. Pelajia cradles her hammer as though she'd like to bang Philomena's head with it. Philomena delicately starts to descend the ladder. The last we see of her is her Kewpie-doll face. And beside it, the heart-shaped pillow, disappearing like a setting sun behind the edge of the roof. Once she's good and gone, Pelajia dismisses her.

PELAJIA: Oh, go on!

Then she pauses to look wistfully at the view for a moment.

Not many seagulls flying over Eugene Starblanket's house today.

And returns once more to her hammering on the roof as the lights fade into blackout. Split seconds before complete black-out, Nanabush, back once more in his guise as the seagull, "lands" on the roof behind the unaware and unseeing Pelajia Patchnose. He dances to the beat of the hammer, merrily and triumphantly.

END OF PLAY

READING AND REACTING

1. *The Rez Sisters* has the setting of the mythical Wasaychigan Hill Indian Reserve. In what additional locations could Tomson Highway have set the play's action? What might be gained or lost by changing the setting?
2. What lighting and sound effects does the play call for? In what way do these effects advance the action of the play? In what ways—if any—do they help communicate the play's theme(s)?
3. Although most of the play is in English, the characters frequently speak Cree or Ojibway. What are the advantages of this use of Cree and Ojibway? Are there any drawbacks?
4. What function do the references to Nanabush serve in the play?
5. What conflicts develop among the characters as the play proceeds? In what way might these conflicts represent the problems of the Cree and Ojibway (and other Aboriginal nations) in Canada?

6. Why is bingo the focus?
7. What does the play suggest about the role of women in the reserve society and in Canadian society at large?
8. Could this play be seen as an **allegory?** What is the value of seeing it this way?
9. **JOURNAL ENTRY** Are you able to empathize with any of the characters? If so, which one? Why?
10. **CRITICAL PERSPECTIVE** In a 1998 article in the *New York Times*, theatre critic Brooks Atkinson said, "Nothing is better for good actors than a stage with no scenery." Do you think this remark could be applied to the staging of *The Rez Sisters*?
11. **CRITICAL PERSPECTIVE** Anne Nothof argues that "Tomson Highway places in violent juxtaposition the cultural and spiritual values of Native and non-Native Canadians. Although there is in some respects a cultural accommodation and a positive integration of some of the materialistic products of a White capitalist society, the negative consequences of cultural collision are played out in the lives of the women and men who constitute the Native community of Wasaychigan Hill Indian Reserve[.]" (*Studies in Canadian Literature* 20.2 [199]).

    Do you agree with Nothof's assessment? Why or why not? Use specific examples in your argument.

Related Works: "The Loons" (p. 249), *Les Belles Soeurs* (p. 1196), *The Ecstasy of Rita Joe* (p. 1376)

◈ **SOPHOCLES** (496–406 B.C.), along with Aeschylus and Euripides, is one of the three great Greek tragic dramatists. He lived during the great flowering and subsequent decline of fifth-century Athens—the high point of Greek civilization. Born as Greece struggled against the Persian empire and moved to adopt democracy, he lived as an adult under Pericles in the Golden Age of Athens and died as it became clear that Athens would lose the Peloponnesian War. Sophocles was an active participant in the public life of Athens, serving as a collector of tribute from Athenian subjects and later as a general. Though he wrote at least one hundred and twenty plays, only seven have survived, including three plays about Oedipus: *Oedipus the King* (c. 430 B.C.), *Oedipus at Colonus* (411? B.C.), and *Antigone* (441 B.C.).

Oedipus the King, or *Oedipus Rex* (sometimes called *Oedipus the Tyrant*), was performed shortly after a great plague in Athens (probably in 429 or 425 B.C.) and as Athens was falling into decline; the play opens with the account of a plague in Thebes, Oedipus's kingdom. Over the years, *Oedipus the King* has attracted impressive critical attention, from Aristotle's use of it as a model for his definition of tragedy to Freud's use of its power as evidence of the validity of the so-called Oedipus complex.

SOPHOCLES

Oedipus the King*
(C. 430 B.C.)

Translated by Thomas Gould

CHARACTERS

OEDIPUS,[1] *the King of Thebes*
PRIEST OF ZEUS, *leader of the suppliants*
CREON, *Oedipus's brother-in-law*
CHORUS, *a group of Theban elders*
CHORAGOS, *spokesman of the Chorus*
TIRESIAS, *a blind seer or prophet*

JOCASTA, *the queen of Thebes*
MESSENGER, *from Corinth, once a shepherd*
HERDSMAN, *once a servant of Laius*
SECOND MESSENGER, *a servant of Oedipus*

MUTES

SUPPLIANTS, *Thebans seeking Oedipus's help*
ATTENDANTS, *for the Royal Family*
SERVANTS, *to lead Tiresias and Oedipus*
ANTIGONE, *daughter of Oedipus and Jocasta*
ISMENE, *daughter of Oedipus and Jocasta*

The action takes place during the day in front of the royal palace in Thebes. There are two altars (left and right) on the proscenium and several steps leading down to the orchestra. As the play opens, Thebans of various ages who have come to beg Oedipus for help are sitting on these steps and in part of the orchestra. These suppliants are holding branches of laurel or olive which have strips of wool[2] wrapped around them. Oedipus enters from the palace (the central door of the skene).

PROLOGUE

OEDIPUS: My children, ancient Cadmus'[3] newest care,
    why have you hurried to those seats, your boughs
    wound with the emblems of the suppliant?
    The city is weighed down with fragrant smoke,
5   with hymns to the Healer[4] and the cries of mourners.
    I thought it wrong, my sons, to hear your words

---

* Note that individual lines are numbered in the following play. When a line is shared by two or more characters, it is counted as one line.

[1] *Oedipus:* the name means "swollen foot." It refers to the mutilation of Oedipus's feet done by his father, Laius, before the infant was sent to Mount Cithaeron to be put to death by exposure.

[2] *wool:* branches wrapped with wool are traditional symbols of prayer or supplication.

[3] *Cadmus:* Oedipus's great-great-grandfather (although he does not know this) and the founder of Thebes.

[4] *Healer:* Apollo, god of prophecy, light, healing, justice, purification, and destruction.

> through emissaries, and have come out myself,
> I, Oedipus, a name that all men know.

(Oedipus addresses the Priest.)

> Old man—for it is fitting that you speak
> 10   for all—what is your mood as you entreat me,
> fear or trust? You may be confident
> that I'll do anything. How hard of heart
> if an appeal like this did not rouse my pity!

PRIEST: You, Oedipus, who hold the power here,
> 15   you see our several ages, we who sit
> before your altars—some not strong enough
> to take long flight, some heavy in old age,
> the priests, as I of Zeus,[5] and from our youths
> a chosen band. The rest sit with their windings
> 20   in the markets, at the twin shrines of Pallas,[6]
> and the prophetic embers of Ismēnos.[7]
> Our city, as you see yourself, is tossed
> too much, and can no longer lift its head
> above the troughs of billows red with death.
> 25   It dies in the fruitful flowers of the soil,
> it dies in its pastured herds, and in its women's
> barren pangs. And the fire-bearing god[8]
> has swooped upon the city, hateful plague,
> and he has left the house of Cadmus empty.
> 30   Black Hades[9] is made rich with moans and weeping.
> Not judging you an equal of the gods,
> do I and the children sit here at your hearth,
> but as the first of men, in troubled times
> and in encounters with divinities.
> 35   You came to Cadmus' city and unbound
> the tax we had to pay to the harsh singer,[10]
> did it without a helpful word from us,

---

[5] *Zeus:* father and king of the gods.

[6] *Pallas:* Athena, goddess of wisdom, arts, crafts, and war.

[7] *Ismēnos:* a reference to the temple of Apollo near the river Ismēnos in Thebes. Prophecies were made here by "reading" the ashes of the altar fires.

[8] *fire-bearing god:* contagious fever viewed as a god.

[9] *Black Hades:* refers to both the underworld where the spirits of the dead go and the god of the underworld.

[10] *harsh singer:* the Sphinx, a monster with a woman's head, a lion's body, and wings. The "tax" that Oedipus freed Thebes from was the destruction of all the young men who failed to solve the Sphinx's riddle and were subsequently devoured. The Sphinx always asked the same riddle: "What goes on four legs in the morning, two legs at noon, and three legs in the evening, and yet is weakest when supported by the largest number of feet?" Oedipus discovered the correct answer—man, who crawls in infancy, walks in his prime, and uses a stick in old age—and thus ended the Sphinx's reign of terror. The Sphinx destroyed herself when Oedipus answered the riddle. Oedipus's reward for freeing Thebes of the Sphinx was the throne and the hand of the recently widowed Jocasta.

with no instruction; with a god's assistance
you raised up our life, so we believe.
40 Again now Oedipus, our greatest power,
we plead with you, as suppliants, all of us,
to find us strength, whether from a god's response,
or learned in some way from another man.
I know that the experienced among men
45 give counsels that will prosper best of all.
Noblest of men, lift up our land again!
Think also of yourself; since now the land
calls you its Savior for your zeal of old,
oh let us never look back at your rule
50 as men helped up only to fall again!
Do not stumble! Put our land on firm feet!
The bird of omen was auspicious then,
when you brought that luck; be that same man again!
The power is yours; if you will rule our country,
55 rule over men, not in an empty land.
A towered city or a ship is nothing
if desolate and no man lives within.
OEDIPUS: Pitiable children, oh I know, I know
the yearnings that have brought you. Yes, I know
60 that you are sick. And yet, though you are sick,
there is not one of you so sick as I.
For your affliction comes to each alone,
for him and no one else, but my soul mourns
for me and for you, too, and for the city.
65 You do not waken me as from a sleep,
for I have wept, bitterly and long,
tried many paths in the wanderings of thought,
and the single cure I found by careful search
I've acted on: I sent Menoeceus' son,
70 Creon, brother of my wife, to the Pythian
halls of Phoebus,[11] so that I might learn
what I must do or say to save this city.
Already, when I think what day this is,
I wonder anxiously what he is doing.
75 Too long, more than is right, he's been away.
But when he comes, then I shall be a traitor
if I do not do all that the god reveals.
PRIEST: Welcome words! But look, those men have signaled
that it is Creon who is now approaching!
80 OEDIPUS: Lord Apollo! May he bring Savior Luck,
a Luck as brilliant as his eyes are now!

---

[11] *Pythian . . . Phoebus:* the temple of Phoebus, Apollo's oracle or prophet at Delphi.

PRIEST: His news is happy, it appears. He comes,
    forehead crowned with thickly berried laurel.[12]
OEDIPUS: We'll know, for he is near enough to hear us.

(Enter Creon along one of the parados.)

85   Lord, brother in marriage, son of Menoeceus!
    What is the god's pronouncement that you bring?
CREON: It's good. For even troubles, if they chance
    to turn out well, I always count as lucky.
OEDIPUS: But what was the response? You seem to say
90   I'm not to fear—but not to take heart either.
CREON: If you will hear me with these men present,
    I'm ready to report—or go inside.

(Creon moves up the steps toward the palace.)

OEDIPUS: Speak out to all! The grief that burdens me
    concerns these men more than it does my life.
95 CREON: Then I shall tell you what I heard from the god.
    The task Lord Phoebus sets for us is clear:
    drive out pollution sheltered in our land,
    and do not shelter what is incurable.
OEDIPUS: What is our trouble? How shall we cleanse ourselves?
100 CREON: We must banish or murder to free ourselves
    from a murder that blows storms through the city.
OEDIPUS: What man's bad luck does he accuse in this?
CREON: My Lord, a king named Laius ruled our land
    before you came to steer the city straight.
105 OEDIPUS: I know. So I was told—I never saw him.
CREON: Since he was murdered, you must raise your hand
    against the men who killed him with their hands.
OEDIPUS: Where are they now? And how can we ever find
    the track of ancient guilt now hard to read?
110 CREON: In our own land, he said. What we pursue,
    that can be caught; but not what we neglect.
OEDIPUS: Was Laius home, or in the countryside—
    or was he murdered in some foreign land?
CREON: He left to see a sacred rite, he said;
115   He left, but never came home from his journey.
OEDIPUS: Did none of his party see it and report—
    someone we might profitably question?
CREON: They were all killed but one, who fled in fear,
    and he could tell us only one clear fact.
120 OEDIPUS: What fact? One thing could lead us on to more
    if we could get a small start on our hope.

---

[12] *laurel:* Creon is wearing a garland of laurel leaves, sacred to Apollo.

CREON: He said that bandits chanced on them and killed him—
    with the force of many hands, not one alone.
OEDIPUS: How could a bandit dare so great an act—
125   unless this was a plot paid off from here!
CREON: We thought of that, but when Laius was killed,
    we had no one to help us in our troubles.
OEDIPUS: It was your very kingship that was killed!
    What kind of trouble blocked you from a search?
130 CREON: The subtle-singing Sphinx asked us to turn
    from the obscure to what lay at our feet.
OEDIPUS: Then I shall begin again and make it plain.
    It was quite worthy of Phoebus, and worthy of you,
    to turn our thoughts back to the murdered man,
135   and right that you should see me join the battle
    for justice to our land and to the god.
    Not on behalf of any distant kinships,
    it's for myself I will dispel this stain.
    Whoever murdered him may also wish
140   to punish me—and with the selfsame hand.
    In helping him I also serve myself.
    Now quickly, children: up from the altar steps,
    and raise the branches of the suppliant!
    Let someone go and summon Cadmus' people:
145   say I'll do anything.

(Exit an Attendant along one of the parados.)

             Our luck will prosper
    if the god is with us, or we have already fallen.
PRIEST: Rise, my children; that for which we came,
    he has himself proclaimed he will accomplish.
    May Phoebus, who announced this, also come
150   as Savior and reliever from the plague.

(Exit Oedipus and Creon into the palace. The Priest and the Suppliants exit left and right along the parados. After a brief pause, the Chorus (including the Choragos) enters the orchestra from the parados.)

PARADOS

STROPHE 1[13]
CHORUS: Voice from Zeus,[14] sweetly spoken, what are you
    that have arrived from golden
    Pytho[15] to our shining

---

[13] *Strophe, Antistrophe:* probably refer to the direction in which the Chorus danced while reciting specific stanzas. Strophe may have indicated dance steps to stage left, antistrophe to stage right.
[14] *Voice from Zeus:* a reference to Apollo's prophecy. Zeus taught Apollo how to prophesy.
[15] *Pytho:* Delphi.

155 Thebes? I am on the rack, terror
　　shakes my soul.
Delian Healer,[16] summoned by "iē!"
I await in holy dread what obligation, something new
or something back once more with the revolving years,
　　you'll bring about for me.
160 Oh tell me, child of golden Hope,
　　deathless Response!

ANTISTROPHE 1

I appeal to you first, daughter of Zeus,
　　deathless Athena,
and to your sister who protects this land,
165 Artemis,[17] whose famous throne is the whole circle
　　of the marketplace,
and Phoebus, who shoots from afar: iō!
Three-fold defenders against death, appear!
If ever in the past, to stop blind ruin
170 　　sent against the city,
you banished utterly the fires of suffering,
　　come now again!

STROPHE 2

Ah! Ah! Unnumbered are the miseries
I bear. The plague claims all
175 our comrades. Nor has thought found yet a spear
by which a man shall be protected. What our glorious
earth gives birth to does not grow. Without a birth
from cries of labor
　　do the women rise.
180 One person after another
　　you may see, like flying birds,
faster than indomitable fire, sped
to the shore of the god that is the sunset.[18]

ANTISTROPHE 2

And with their deaths unnumbered dies the city.
185 Her children lie unpitied on the ground,
spreading death, unmourned.
Meanwhile young wives, and gray-haired mothers with them,
on the shores of the altars, from this side and that,
suppliants from mournful trouble,
190 　　cry out their grief.

---

[16] *Delian Healer:* Apollo.
[17] *Artemis:* goddess of virginity, childbirth, and hunting.
[18] *god . . . sunset:* Hades, god of the underworld.

A hymn to the Healer shines,
    the flute a mourner's voice.
Against which, golden goddess, daughter of Zeus,
    send lovely Strength.

STROPHE 3

195   Causing raging Ares[19]—who,
    armed now with no shield of bronze,
burns me, coming on amid loud cries—
to turn his back and run from my land,
with a fair wind behind, to the great
200   hall of Amphitritē,[20]
or to the anchorage that welcomes no one,
Thrace's troubled sea!
If night lets something get away at last,
    it comes by day.
205   Fire-bearing god . . .
    you who dispense the might of lightning,
Zeus! Father! Destroy him with your thunderbolt!

(Enter Oedipus from the palace.)

ANTISTROPHE 3

Lycēan Lord![21] From your looped
    bowstring, twisted gold,
210   I wish indomitable missiles might be scattered
and stand forward, our protectors; also fire-bearing
radiance of Artemis, with which
    she darts across the Lycian mountains.
I call the god whose head is bound in gold,
215   with whom this country shares its name,
Bacchus,[22] wine-flushed, summoned by "euoi!,"
    Maenads' comrade,
to approach ablaze
    with gleaming . . .
220   pine, opposed to that god-hated god.

EPISODE 1

OEDIPUS: I hear your prayer. Submit to what I say
and to the labors that the plague demands
and you'll get help and a relief from evils.
I'll make the proclamation, though a stranger
225   to the report and to the deed. Alone,

---

[19] *Ares:* god of war and destruction.
[20] *Amphitritē:* the Atlantic Ocean.
[21] *Lycēan Lord:* Apollo.
[22] *Bacchus:* Dionysus, god of fertility and wine.

had I no key, I would soon lose the track.
Since it was only later that I joined you,
to all the sons of Cadmus I say this:
whoever has clear knowledge of the man
230 who murdered Laius, son of Labdacus,
I command him to reveal it all to me—
nor fear if, to remove the charge, he must
accuse himself: his fate will not be cruel—
he will depart unstumbling into exile.
235 But if you know another, or a stranger,
to be the one whose hand is guilty, speak:
I shall reward you and remember you.
But if you keep your peace because of fear,
and shield yourself or kin from my command,
240 hear you what I shall do in that event:
I charge all in this land where I have throne
and power, shut out that man—no matter who—
both from your shelter and all spoken words,
nor in your prayers or sacrifices make
245 him partner, nor allot him lustral[23] water.
All men shall drive him from their homes: for he
is the pollution that the god-sent Pythian
response has only now revealed to me.
In this way I ally myself in war
250 with the divinity and the deceased.[24]
And this curse, too, against the one who did it,
whether alone in secrecy, or with others:
may he wear out his life unblest and evil!
I pray this, too: if he is at my hearth
255 and in my home, and I have knowledge of him,
may the curse pronounced on others come to me.
All this I lay to you to execute,
for my sake, for the god's, and for this land
now ruined, barren, abandoned by the gods.
260 Even if no god had driven you to it,
you ought not to have left this stain uncleansed,
the murdered man a nobleman, a king!
You should have looked! But now, since, as it happens,
It's I who have the power that he had once,
265 and have his bed, and a wife who shares our seed,
and common bond had we had common children
(had not his hope of offspring had bad luck—
but as it happened, luck lunged at his head);

---

[23] *lustral:* purifying.
[24] *the deceased:* Laius.

because of this, as if for my own father,
270 I'll fight for him, I'll leave no means untried,
to catch the one who did it with his hand,
for the son of Labdacus, of Polydōrus,
of Cadmus before him, and of Agēnor.[25]
This prayer against all those who disobey:
275 the gods send out no harvest from their soil,
nor children from their wives. Oh, let them die
victims of this plague, or of something worse.
Yet for the rest of us, people of Cadmus,
we the obedient, may Justice, our ally,
280 and all the gods, be always on our side!
CHORAGOS: I speak because I feel the grip of your curse:
the killer is not I. Nor can I point
to him. The one who set us to this search,
Phoebus, should also name the guilty man.
285 OEDIPUS: Quite right, but to compel unwilling gods—
no man has ever had that kind of power.
CHORAGOS: May I suggest to you a second way?
OEDIPUS: A second or a third—pass over nothing!
CHORAGOS: I know of no one who sees more of what
290 Lord Phoebus sees than Lord Tiresias.
My Lord, one might learn brilliantly from him.
OEDIPUS: Nor is this something I have been slow to do.
At Creon's word I sent an escort—twice now!
I am astonished that he has not come.
295 CHORAGOS: The old account is useless. It told us nothing.
OEDIPUS: But tell it to me. I'll scrutinize all stories.
CHORAGOS: He is said to have been killed by travelers.
OEDIPUS: I have heard, but the one who did it no one sees.
CHORAGOS: If there is any fear in him at all,
300 he won't stay here once he has heard that curse.
OEDIPUS: He won't fear words: he had no fear when he did it.

(Enter Tiresias from the right, led by a Servant and two of Oedipus's Attendants.)

CHORAGOS: Look there! There is the man who will convict him!
It's the god's prophet they are leading here,
one gifted with the truth as no one else.
305 OEDIPUS: Tiresias, master of all omens—
public and secret, in the sky and on the earth—
your mind, if not your eyes, sees how the city
lives with a plague, against which Thebes can find
no Saviour or protector, Lord, but you.
310 For Phoebus, as the attendants surely told you,

---

[25] *Son . . . Agēnor:* refers to Laius by citing his genealogy.

returned this answer to us: liberation
from the disease would never come unless
we learned without a doubt who murdered Laius—
put them to death, or sent them into exile.

315 Do not begrudge us what you may learn from birds
or any other prophet's path you know!
Care for yourself, the city, care for me,
care for the whole pollution of the dead!
We're in your hands. To do all that he can

320 to help another is man's noblest labor.

TIRESIAS: How terrible to understand and get
no profit from the knowledge! I knew this,
but I forgot, or I had never come.

OEDIPUS: What's this? You've come with very little zeal.

325 TIRESIAS: Let me go home! If you will listen to me,
You will endure your troubles better—and I mine.

OEDIPUS: A strange request, not very kind to the land
that cared for you—to hold back this oracle!

TIRESIAS: I see your understanding comes to you

330 inopportunely. So that won't happen to me . . .

OEDIPUS: Oh, by the gods, if you understand about this,
don't turn away! We're on our knees to you.

TIRESIAS: None of you understands! I'll never bring
my grief to light—I will not speak of yours.

335 OEDIPUS: You know and won't declare it! Is your purpose
to betray us and to destroy this land!

TIRESIAS: I will grieve neither of us. Stop this futile
cross-examination. I'll tell you nothing!

OEDIPUS: Nothing? You vile traitor! You could provoke

340 a stone to anger! You still refuse to tell?
Can nothing soften you, nothing convince you?

TIRESIAS: You blamed anger in me—you haven't seen.
The kind that lives with you, so you blame me.

OEDIPUS: Who wouldn't fill with anger, listening

345 to words like yours which now disgrace this city?

TIRESIAS: It will come, even if my silence hides it.

OEDIPUS: If it will come, then why won't you declare it?

TIRESIAS: I'd rather say no more. Now if you wish,
respond to that with all your fiercest anger!

350 OEDIPUS: Now I am angry enough to come right out
with this conjecture: you, I think, helped plot
the deed; you did it—even if your hand,
cannot have struck the blow. If you could see,
I should have said the deed was yours alone.

355 TIRESIAS: Is that right! Then I charge you to abide
by the decree you have announced: from this day

say no word to either these or me,
for you are the vile polluter of this land!

OEDIPUS: Aren't you appalled to let a charge like that
360 come bounding forth? How will you get away?
TIRESIAS: You cannot catch me. I have the strength of truth.
OEDIPUS: Who taught you this? Not your prophetic craft!
TIRESIAS: You did. You made me say it. I didn't want to.
OEDIPUS: Say what? Repeat it so I'll understand.
365 TIRESIAS: I made no sense? Or are you trying me?
OEDIPUS: No sense I understood. Say it again!
TIRESIAS: I say you are the murderer you seek.
OEDIPUS: Again that horror! You'll wish you hadn't said that.
TIRESIAS: Shall I say more, and raise your anger higher?
370 OEDIPUS: Anything you like! Your words are powerless.
TIRESIAS: You live, unknowing, with those nearest to you
in the greatest shame. You do not see the evil.
OEDIPUS: You won't go on like that and never pay!
TIRESIAS: I can if there is any strength in truth.
375 OEDIPUS: In truth, but not in you! You have no strength,
blind in your ears, your reason, and your eyes.
TIRESIAS: Unhappy man! Those jeers you hurl at me
before long all these men will hurl at you.
OEDIPUS: You are the child of endless night; it's not
380 for me or anyone who sees to hurt you.
TIRESIAS: It's not my fate to be struck down by you.
Apollo is enough. That's his concern.
OEDIPUS: Are these inventions Creon's or your own?
TIRESIAS: No, your affliction is yourself, not Creon.
385 OEDIPUS: Oh success!—in wealth, kingship, artistry,
in any life that wins much admiration—
the envious ill will stored up for you!
to get at my command, a gift I did not
seek, which the city put into my hands,
390 my loyal Creon, colleague from the start,
longs to sneak up in secret and dethrone me.
So he's suborned this fortuneteller—schemer!
deceitful beggar-priest!—who has good eyes
for gains alone, though in his craft he's blind.
395 Where were your prophet's powers ever proved?
Why, when the dog who chanted verse[26] was here,
did you not speak and liberate this city?
Her riddle wasn't for a man chancing by
to interpret; prophetic art was needed,

26 *dog . . . verse:* the Sphinx.

but you had none, it seems—learned from birds
or from a god. I came along, yes I,
400 Oedipus the ignorant, and stopped her—
by using thought, not augury from birds.
And it is I whom you now wish to banish,
so you'll be close to the Creontian throne.
You—and the plot's concocter—will drive out
405 pollution to your grief: you look quite old
or you would be the victim of that plot!

CHORAGOS: It seems to us that this man's words were said
in anger, Oedipus, and yours as well.
Insight, not angry words, is what we need,
410 the best solution to the god's response.

TIRESIAS: You are the king, and yet I am your equal
in my right to speak. In that I too am Lord.
for I belong to Loxias,[27] not you.
415 I am not Creon's man. He's nothing to me.
Hear this, since you have thrown my blindness at me:
Your eyes can't see the evil to which you've come,
nor where you live, nor who is in your house.
Do you know your parents? Not knowing, you are
420 their enemy, in the underworld and here.
A mother's and a father's double-lashing
terrible-footed curse will soon drive you out.
Now you can see, then you will stare into darkness.
What place will not be harbor to your cry,
425 or what Cithaeron[28] not reverberate
when you have heard the bride-song in your palace
to which you sailed? Fair wind to evil harbor!
Nor do you see how many other woes
will level you to yourself and to your children.
430 So, at my message, and at Creon, too,
splatter muck! There will never be a man
ground into wretchedness as you will be.

OEDIPUS: Am I to listen to such things from him!
May you be damned! Get out of here at once!
435 Go! Leave my palace! Turn around and go!

(Tiresias begins to move away from Oedipus.)

TIRESIAS: I wouldn't have come had you not sent for me.

OEDIPUS: I did not know you'd talk stupidity,
or I wouldn't have rushed to bring you to my house.

---

27 *Loxias:* Apollo.
28 *Cithaeron:* reference to the mountain on which Oedipus was to be exposed as an infant.

440 TIRESIAS: Stupid I seem to you, yet to your parents
    who gave you natural birth I seemed quite shrewd.
OEDIPUS: Who? Wait! Who is the one who gave me birth?
TIRESIAS: This day will give you birth,[29] and ruin too.
OEDIPUS: What murky, riddling things you always say!
445 TIRESIAS: Don't you surpass us all at finding out?
OEDIPUS: You sneer at what you'll find has brought me greatness.
TIRESIAS: And that's the very luck that ruined you.
OEDIPUS: I wouldn't care, just so I saved the city.
TIRESIAS: In that case I shall go. Boy, lead the way!
450 OEDIPUS: Yes, let him lead you off. Here, underfoot,
    you irk me. Gone, you'll cause no further pain.
TIRESIAS: I'll go when I have said what I was sent for.
    Your face won't scare me. You can't ruin me.
    I say to you, the man whom you have looked for
455   as you pronounced your curses, your decrees
    on the bloody death of Laius—he is here!
    A seeming stranger, he shall be shown to be
    a Theban born, though he'll take no delight
    in that solution. Blind, who once could see,
460   a beggar who was rich, through foreign lands
    he'll go and point before him with a stick.
    To his beloved children, he'll be shown
    a father who is also brother; to the one
    who bore him, son and husband; to his father,
465   his seed-fellow and killer. Go in
    and think this out; and if you find I've lied,
    say then I have no prophet's understanding!

(Exit Tiresias, led by a Servant. Oedipus exits into the palace with his Attendants.)

STASIMON 1

STROPHE 1
CHORUS: Who is the man of whom the inspired
    rock of Delphi[30] said
470   he has committed the unspeakable
      with blood-stained hands?
    Time for him to ply a foot
    mightier than those of the horses
      of the storm in his escape;
475   upon him mounts and plunges the weaponed
    son of Zeus,[31] with fire and thunderbolts,
    and in his train the dreaded goddesses
    of Death, who never miss.

---

[29] *give you birth:* that is, identify your parents.
[30] *rock of Delphi:* Apollo's oracle at Delphi.
[31] *son of Zeus:* Apollo.

ANTISTROPHE 1

The message has just blazed,
480   gleaming from the snows
of Mount Parnassus: we must track
      everywhere the unseen man.
He wanders, hidden by wild
forests, up through caves
485   and rocks, like a bull,
anxious, with an anxious foot, forlorn.
He puts away from him the mantic[32] words come from earth's
navel,[33] at its center, yet these live
forever and still hover round him.

STROPHE 2

490   Terribly he troubles me,
      the skilled interpreter of birds![34]
I can't assent, nor speak against him.
      Both paths are closed to me.
I hover on the wings of doubt,
495   not seeing what is here nor what's to come.
What quarrel started in the house of Labdacus[35]
or in the house of Polybus,[36]
      either ever in the past
      or now, I never
500   heard, so that . . . with this fact for my touchstone
I could attack the public
      fame of Oedipus, by the side of the Labdaceans
an ally, against the dark assassination.

ANTISTROPHE 2

No, Zeus and Apollo
505   understand and know things
mortal; but that another man
      can do more as a prophet than I can—
for that there is no certain test,
      though, skill to skill,
510   one man might overtake another.
No, never, not until
      I see the charges proved,
when someone blames him shall I nod assent.
For once, as we all saw, the winged maiden[37] came
515   against him: he was seen then to be skilled,

---

[32] *mantic:* prophetic.
[33] *earth's navel:* Delphi.
[34] *interpreter of birds:* Tiresias. The Chorus is troubled by his accusations.
[35] *house of Labdacus:* the line of Laius.
[36] *Polybus:* Oedipus's foster father.
[37] *winged maiden:* the Sphinx.

proved, by that touchstone, dear to the people. So,
never will my mind convict him of the evil.

EPISODE 2

(Enter Creon from the right door of the skene and speaks to the Chorus.)

CREON: Citizens, I hear that a fearful charge
 is made against me by King Oedipus!
520 I had to come. If, in this crisis,
 he thinks that he has suffered injury
 from anything that I have said or done,
 I have no appetite for a long life—
 bearing a blame like that! It's no slight blow
525 the punishment I'd take from what he said:
 it's the ultimate hurt to be called traitor
 by the city, by you, by my own people!
CHORAGOS: The thing that forced that accusation out
 could have been anger, not the power of thought.
530 CREON: But who persuaded him that thoughts of mine
 had led the prophet into telling lies?
CHORAGOS: I do not know the thought behind his words.
CREON: But did he look straight at you? Was his mind right
 when he said that I was guilty of this charge?
535 CHORAGOS: I have no eyes to see what rulers do.
 But here he comes himself out of the house.

(Enter Oedipus from the palace.)

OEDIPUS: What? You here? And can you really have
 the face and daring to approach my house
 when you're exposed as its master's murderer
540 and caught, too, as the robber of my kingship?
 Did you see cowardice in me, by the gods,
 or foolishness, when you began this plot?
 Did you suppose that I would not detect
 your stealthy moves, or that I'd not fight back?
545 It's your attempt that's folly, isn't it—
 tracking without followers or connections,
 kingship which is caught with wealth and numbers?
CREON: Now wait! Give me as long to answer back!
 Judge me for yourself when you have heard me!
550 OEDIPUS: You're eloquent, but I'd be slow to learn
 from you, now that I've seen your malice toward me.
CREON: That I deny. Hear what I have to say.
OEDIPUS: Don't you deny it! You are the traitor here!
CREON: If you consider mindless willfulness
555 a prized possession, you are not thinking sense.

NEL

OEDIPUS: If you think you can wrong a relative
　　　and get off free, you are not thinking sense.
CREON: Perfectly just, I won't say no. And yet
　　　what is this injury you say I did you?
560　OEDIPUS: Did you persuade me, yes or no, to send
　　　someone to bring that solemn prophet here?
CREON: And I still hold to the advice I gave.
OEDIPUS: How many years ago did your King Laius . . .
CREON: Laius! Do what? Now I don't understand.
565　OEDIPUS: Vanish—victim of a murderous violence?
CREON: That is a long count back into the past.
OEDIPUS: Well, was this seer then practicing his art?
CREON: Yes, skilled and honored just as he is today.
OEDIPUS: Did he, back then, ever refer to me?
570　CREON: He did not do so in my presence ever.
OEDIPUS: You did inquire into the murder then.
CREON: We had to, surely, though we discovered nothing.
OEDIPUS: But the "skilled" one did not say this then? Why not?
CREON: I never talk when I am ignorant.
575　OEDIPUS: But you're not ignorant of your own part.
CREON: What do you mean? I'll tell you if I know.
OEDIPUS: Just this: if he had not conferred with you
　　　he'd not have told about my murdering Laius.
CREON: If he said that, you are the one who knows.
580　　But now it's fair that you should answer me.
OEDIPUS: Ask on! You won't convict me as the killer.
CREON: Well then, answer. My sister is your wife?
OEDIPUS: Now there's a statement that I can't deny.
CREON: You two have equal power in this country?
585　OEDIPUS: She gets from me whatever she desires.
CREON: And I'm a third? The three of us are equals?
OEDIPUS: That's where you're treacherous to your kinsman!
CREON: But think about this rationally, as I do.
　　　First look at this: do you think anyone
590　　prefers the anxieties of being king
　　　to untroubled sleep—if he has equal power?
　　　I'm not the kind of man who falls in love
　　　with kingship. I am content with a king's power.
　　　And so would any man who's wise and prudent.
595　　I get all things from you, with no distress;
　　　as king I would have onerous duties, too.
　　　How could the kingship bring me more delight
　　　than this untroubled power and influence?
　　　I'm not misguided yet to such a point
600　　that profitable honors aren't enough.
　　　As it is, all wish me well and all salute;
　　　those begging you for something have me summoned,

for their success depends on that alone.
Why should I lose all this to become king?
605 A prudent mind is never traitorous.
Treason's a thought I'm not enamored of;
nor could I join a man who acted so.
In proof of this, first go yourself to Pytho[38]
and ask if I brought back the true response.
610 Then, if you find I plotted with that portent
reader,[39] don't have me put to death by your vote
only—I'll vote myself for my conviction.
Don't let an unsupported thought convict me!
It's not right mindlessly to take the bad
615 for good or to suppose the good are traitors.
Rejecting a relation who is loyal
is like rejecting life, our greatest love.
In time you'll know securely without stumbling,
for time alone can prove a just man just,
620 though you can know a bad man in a day.
CHORAGOS: Well said, to one who's anxious not to fall.
Swift thinkers, Lord, are never safe from stumbling.
OEDIPUS: But when a swift and secret plotter moves
against me, I must make swift counterplot.
625 If I lie quiet and await his move,
he'll have achieved his aims and I'll have missed.
CREON: You surely cannot mean you want me exiled!
OEDIPUS: Not exiled, no. Your death is what I want!
CREON: If you would first define what envy is . . .
630 OEDIPUS: Are you still stubborn? Still disobedient?
CREON: I see you cannot think!
OEDIPUS: For me I can.
CREON: You should for me as well!
OEDIPUS: But you're a traitor!
CREON: What if you're wrong?
OEDIPUS: Authority must be maintained.
CREON: Not if the ruler's evil.
OEDIPUS: Hear that, Thebes!
635 CREON: It is my city too, not yours alone!
CHORAGOS: Please don't, my Lords! Ah, just in time, I see
Jocasta there, coming from the palace.
With her help you must settle your quarrel.

(Enter Jocasta from the palace.)

---

[38] *Pytho:* Delphi.
[39] *portent reader:* Apollo's oracle or prophet.

JOCASTA: Wretched men! What has provoked this ill-
640   advised dispute? Have you no sense of shame,
        with Thebes so sick, to stir up private troubles?
        Now go inside! And Creon, you go home!
        Don't make a general anguish out of nothing!
CREON: My sister, Oedipus your husband here
645   sees fit to do one of two hideous things:
        to have me banished from the land—or killed!
OEDIPUS: That's right: I caught him, Lady, plotting harm
        against my person—with a malignant science.
CREON: May my life fail, may I die cursed, if I
650   did any of the things you said I did!
JOCASTA: Believe his words, for the god's sake, Oedipus,
        in deference above all to his oath
        to the gods. Also for me, and for these men!

KOMMOS[40]

STROPHE 1
CHORUS: Consent, with will and mind,
655   my king, I beg of you!
OEDIPUS: What do you wish me to surrender?
CHORUS: Show deference to him who was not feeble in time past
        and is now great in the power of his oath!
OEDIPUS: Do you know what you're asking?
CHORUS: Yes.
OEDIPUS: Tell me then.
660 CHORUS: Never to cast into dishonored guilt, with an unproved
        assumption, a kinsman who has bound himself by curse.
OEDIPUS: Now you must understand, when you ask this,
        you ask my death or banishment from the land.

STROPHE 2
CHORUS: No, by the god who is the foremost of all gods,
665   the Sun! No! Godless,
            friendless, whatever death is worst of all,
        let that be my destruction, if this
            thought ever moved me!
        But my ill-fated soul
670   this dying land
        wears out—the more if to these older troubles
        she adds new troubles from the two of you!
OEDIPUS: Then let him go, though it must mean my death,
        or else disgrace and exile from the land.

---

[40] *Kommos:* a dirge or lament sung by the Chorus and one or more of the chief characters.

675 My pity is moved by your words, not by his—
he'll only have my hate, wherever he goes.
CREON: You're sullen as you yield; you'll be depressed
when you've passed through this anger. Natures like yours
are hardest on themselves. That's as it should be.
680 OEDIPUS: Then won't you go and let me be?
CREON: I'll go.
Though you're unreasonable, they know I'm righteous.

(Exit Creon.)

ANTISTROPHE 1
CHORUS: Why are you waiting, Lady?
Conduct him back into the palace!
JOCASTA: I will, when I have heard what chanced.
685 CHORUS: Conjectures—words alone, and nothing based on thought.
But even an injustice can devour a man.
JOCASTA: Did the words come from both sides?
CHORUS: Yes.
JOCASTA: What was said?
CHORUS: To me it seems enough! enough! the land already troubled,
that this should rest where it has stopped.
690 OEDIPUS: See what you've come to in your honest thought,
in seeking to relax and blunt my heart?

ANTISTROPHE 2
CHORUS: I have not said this only once, my Lord.
That I had lost my sanity,
without a path in thinking—
695 be sure this would be clear
if I put you away
who, when my cherished land
wandered crazed
with suffering, brought her back on course.
700 Now, too, be a lucky helmsman!
JOCASTA: Please, for the god's sake, Lord, explain to me
the reason why you have conceived this wrath?
OEDIPUS: I honor you, not them,[41] and I'll explain
to you how Creon has conspired against me.
705 JOCASTA: All right, if that will explain how the quarrel started.
OEDIPUS: He says I am the murderer of Laius!
JOCASTA: Did he claim knowledge or that someone told him?
OEDIPUS: Here's what he did: he sent that vicious seer
so he could keep his own mouth innocent.

---

[41] *them:* the Chorus.

710 JOCASTA: Ah then, absolve yourself of what he charges!
    Listen to this and you'll agree, no mortal
    is ever given skill in prophecy.
    I'll prove this quickly with one incident.
    It was foretold to Laius—I shall not say
715   by Phoebus himself, but by his ministers—
    that when his fate arrived he would be killed
    by a son who would be born to him and me.
    And yet, so it is told, foreign robbers
    murdered him, at a place where three roads meet.
720   As for the child I bore him, not three days passed
    before he yoked the ball-joints of its feet,[42]
    then cast it, by others' hands, on a trackless mountain.
    That time Apollo did not make our child
    a patricide, or bring about what Laius
725   feared, that he be killed by his own son.
    That's how prophetic words determined things!
    Forget them. The things a god must track
    he will himself painlessly reveal.
  OEDIPUS: Just now, as I was listening to you, Lady,
730   what a profound distraction seized my mind!
  JOCASTA: What made you turn around so anxiously?
  OEDIPUS: I thought you said that Laius was attacked
    and butchered at a place where three roads meet.
  JOCASTA: That is the story, and it is told so still.
735 OEDIPUS: Where is the place where this was done to him?
  JOCASTA: The land's called Phocis, where a two-forked road
    comes in from Delphi and from Daulia.
  OEDIPUS: And how much time has passed since these events?
  JOCASTA: Just prior to your presentation here
740   as king this news was published to the city.
  OEDIPUS: Oh, Zeus, what have you willed to do to me?
  JOCASTA: Oedipus, what makes your heart so heavy?
  OEDIPUS: No, tell me first of Laius' appearance,
    what peak of youthful vigor he had reached.
745 JOCASTA: A tall man, showing his first growth of white.
    He had a figure not unlike your own.
  OEDIPUS: Alas! It seems that in my ignorance
    I laid those fearful curses on myself.
  JOCASTA: What is it, Lord? I flinch to see your face.
750 OEDIPUS: I'm dreadfully afraid the prophet sees.
    But I'll know better with one more detail.
  JOCASTA: I'm frightened too. But ask: I'll answer you.

---

[42] *ball-joints of its feet:* the ankles.

OEDIPUS: Was his retinue small, or did he travel
with a great troop, as would befit a prince?
755 JOCASTA: There were just five in all, one a herald.
There was a carriage, too, bearing Laius.
OEDIPUS: Alas! Now I see it! But who was it,
Lady, who told you what you know about this?
JOCASTA: A servant who alone was saved unharmed.
760 OEDIPUS: By chance, could he be now in the palace?
JOCASTA: No, he is not. When he returned and saw
you had the power of the murdered Laius,
he touched my hand and begged me formally
to send him to the fields and to the pastures,
765 so he'd be out of sight, far from the city.
I did. Although a slave, he well deserved
to win this favor, and indeed far more.
OEDIPUS: Let's have him called back in immediately.
JOCASTA: That can be done, but why do you desire it?
770 OEDIPUS: I fear, Lady, I have already said
too much. That's why I wish to see him now.
JOCASTA: Then he shall come; but it is right somehow
that I, too, Lord, should know what troubles you.
OEDIPUS: I've gone so deep into the things I feared
775 I'll tell you everything. Who has a right
greater than yours, while I cross through this chance?
Polybus of Corinth was my father,
my mother was the Dorian Meropē.
I was first citizen, until this chance
780 attacked me—striking enough, to be sure,
but not worth all the gravity I gave it.
This: at a feast a man who'd drunk too much
denied, at the wine, I was my father's son.
I was depressed and all that day I barely
785 held it in. Next day I put the question
to my mother and father. They were enraged
at the man who'd let this fiction fly at me.
I was much cheered by them. And yet it kept
grinding into me. His words kept coming back.
790 Without my mother's or my father's knowledge
I went to Pytho. But Phoebus sent me away
dishonoring my demand. Instead, other
wretched horrors he flashed forth in speech.
He said that I would be my mother's lover,
795 show offspring to mankind they could not look at,
and be his murderer whose seed I am.[43]

---

[43] *be . . . am:* that is, murder my father.

When I heard this, and ever since, I gauged
the way to Corinth by the stars alone,
running to a place where I would never see
800   the disgrace in the oracle's words come true.
But I soon came to the exact location
where, as you tell of it, the king was killed.
Lady, here is the truth. As I went on,
when I was just approaching those three roads,
805   a herald and a man like him you spoke of
came on, riding a carriage drawn by colts.
Both the man out front and the old man himself[44]
tried violently to force me off the road.
The driver, when he tried to push me off,
810   I struck in anger. The old man saw this, watched
me approach, then leaned out and lunged down
with twin prongs[45] at the middle of my head!
He got more than he gave. Abruptly—struck
once by the staff in this my hand—he tumbled
815   out, head first, from the middle of the carriage.
And then I killed them all. But if there is
a kinship between Laius and this stranger,
who is more wretched than the man you see?
Who was there born more hated by the gods?
820   For neither citizen nor foreigner
may take me in his home or speak to me.
No, they must drive me off. And it is I
who have pronounced these curses on myself!
I stain the dead man's bed with these my hands,
825   by which he died. Is not my nature vile?
Unclean?—if I am banished and even
in exile I may not see my own parents,
or set foot in my homeland, or else be yoked
in marriage to my mother, and kill my father,
830   Polybus, who raised me and gave me birth?
If someone judged a cruel divinity
did this to me, would he not speak the truth?
You pure and awful gods, may I not ever
see that day, may I be swept away
835   from men before I see so great and so
calamitous a stain fixed on my person!
CHORAGOS: These things seem fearful to us, Lord, and yet,
until you hear it from the witness, keep hope!

---

[44] *old man himself:* Laius.
[45] *lunged . . . prongs:* Laius strikes Oedipus with a two-pronged horse goad, or whip.

OEDIPUS: That is the single hope that's left to me,
840   to wait for him, that herdsman—until he comes.
JOCASTA: When he appears, what are you eager for?
OEDIPUS: Just this: if his account agrees with yours
      then I shall have escaped this misery.
JOCASTA: But what was it that struck you in my story?
845 OEDIPUS: You said he spoke of robbers as the ones
      who killed him. Now: if he continues still
      to speak of many, then I could not have killed him.
      One man and many men just do not jibe.
      But if he says one belted man, the doubt
850   is gone. The balance tips toward me. I did it.
JOCASTA: No! He told it as I told you. Be certain.
      He can't reject that and reverse himself.
      The city heard these things, not I alone.
      But even if he swerves from what he said,
855   he'll never show that Laius' murder, Lord,
      occurred just as predicted. For Loxias
      expressly said my son was doomed to kill him.
      The boy—poor boy—he never had a chance
      to cut him down, for he was cut down first.
860   Never again, just for some oracle
      will I shoot frightened glances right and left.
OEDIPUS: That's full of sense. Nonetheless, send a man
      to bring that farm hand here. Will you do it?
JOCASTA: I'll send one right away. But let's go in.
865   Would I do anything against your wishes?

(Exit Oedipus and Jocasta through the central door into the palace.)

STASIMON 2

STROPHE 1

CHORUS: May there accompany me
      the fate to keep a reverential purity in what I say,
      in all I do, for which the laws have been set forth
      and walk on high, born to traverse the brightest,
870   highest upper air; Olympus[46] only
      is their father, nor was it
      mortal nature
      that fathered them, and never will
      oblivion lull them into sleep;
875   the god in them is great and never ages.

---

[46] *Olympus:* Mount Olympus, home of the gods, treated as a god.

ANTISTROPHE 1

The will to violate, seed of the tyrant,
if it has drunk mindlessly of wealth and power,
without a sense of time or true advantage,
mounts to a peak, then
880 plunges to an abrupt . . . destiny,
where the useful foot
is of no use. But the kind
of struggling that is good for the city
I ask the god never to abolish.
885 The god is my protector: never will I give that up.

STROPHE 2

But if a man proceeds disdainfully
in deeds of hand or word
and has no fear of Justice
or reverence for shrines of the divinities
890 (may a bad fate catch him
for his luckless wantonness!),
if he'll not gain what he gains with justice
and deny himself what is unholy,
or if he clings, in foolishness, to the untouchable
895 (what man, finally, in such an action, will have strength
enough to fend off passion's arrows from his soul?),
if, I say, this kind of
deed is held in honor—
why should I join the sacred dance?

ANTISTROPHE 2

900 No longer shall I visit and revere
Earth's navel,[47] the untouchable,
nor visit Abae's[48] temple,
or Olympia,[49]
if the prophecies are not matched by events
905 for all the world to point to.
No, you who hold the power, if you are rightly called
Zeus the king of all, let this matter not escape you
and your ever-deathless rule,
for the prophecies to Laius fade . . .
910 and men already disregard them;
nor is Apollo anywhere
glorified with honors.
Religion slips away.

---

[47] *Earth's navel:* Delphi.
[48] *Abae:* a town in Phocis where there was another oracle of Apollo.
[49] *Olympia:* site of the oracle of Zeus.

Episode 3

(Enter Jocasta from the palace carrying a branch wound with wool and a jar of incense. She is attended by two women.)

JOCASTA: Lords of the realm, the thought has come to me
915   to visit shrines of the divinities
     with suppliant's branch in hand and fragrant smoke.
     For Oedipus excites his soul too much
     with alarms of all kinds. He will not judge
     the present by the past, like a man of sense.
920   He's at the mercy of all terror-mongers.

(Jocasta approaches the altar on the right and kneels.)

     Since I can do no good by counseling,
     Apollo the Lycēan!—you are the closest—
     I come a suppliant, with these my vows,
     for a cleansing that will not pollute him.
925   For when we see him shaken we are all
     afraid, like people looking at their helmsman.

(Enter a Messenger along one of the parados. He sees Jocasta at the altar and then addresses the Chorus.)

MESSENGER: I would be pleased if you would help me, stranger.
     Where is the palace of King Oedipus?
     Or tell me where he is himself, if you know.
930 CHORUS: This is his house, stranger. He is within.
     This is his wife and mother of his children.
MESSENGER: May she and her family find prosperity,
     if, as you say, her marriage is fulfilled.
JOCASTA: You also, stranger, for you deserve as much
935   for your gracious words. But tell me why you've come.
     What do you wish? Or what have you to tell us?
MESSENGER: Good news, my Lady, both for your house and husband.
JOCASTA: What is your news? And who has sent you to us?
MESSENGER: I come from Corinth. When you have heard my news
940   you will rejoice, I'm sure—and grieve perhaps.
JOCASTA: What is it? How can it have this double power?
MESSENGER: They will establish him their king, so say
     the people of the land of Isthmia.[50]
JOCASTA: But is old Polybus not still in power?
945 MESSENGER: He's not, for death has clasped him in the tomb.
JOCASTA: What's this? Has Oedipus' father died?
MESSENGER: If I have lied then I deserve to die.

---

[50] *land of Isthmia:* Corinth, which was on an isthmus.

JOCASTA: Attendant! Go quickly to your master,
and tell him this.

(Exit an Attendant into the palace.)

Oracles of the gods!
950   Where are you now? The man whom Oedipus
fled long ago, for fear that he should kill him—
he's been destroyed by chance and not by him!

(Enter Oedipus from the palace.)

OEDIPUS: Darling Jocasta, my beloved wife,
Why have you called me from the palace?
955 JOCASTA: First hear what this man has to say. Then see
what the god's grave oracle has come to now!
OEDIPUS: Where is he from? What is this news he brings me?
JOCASTA: From Corinth. He brings news about your father:
that Polybus is no more! that he is dead!
960 OEDIPUS: What's this, old man? I want to hear you say it.
MESSENGER: If this is what must first be clarified,
please be assured that he is dead and gone.
OEDIPUS: By treachery or by the touch of sickness?
MESSENGER: Light pressures tip agéd frames into their sleep.
965 OEDIPUS: You mean the poor man died of some disease.
MESSENGER: And of the length of years that he had tallied.
OEDIPUS: Aha! Then why should we look to Pytho's vapors,[51]
or to the birds that scream above our heads?[52]
If we could really take those things for guides,
970 I would have killed my father. But he's dead!
He is beneath the earth, and here am I,
who never touched a spear. Unless he died
of longing for me and I "killed" him that way!
No, in this case, Polybus, by dying, took
975 the worthless oracle to Hades with him.
JOCASTA: And wasn't I telling you that just now?
OEDIPUS: You were indeed. I was misled by fear.
JOCASTA: You should not care about this anymore.
OEDIPUS: I must care. I must stay clear of my mother's bed.
980 JOCASTA: What's there for man to fear? The realm of chance
prevails. True foresight isn't possible.
His life is best who lives without a plan.
This marriage with your mother—don't fear it.
How many times have men in dreams, too, slept

---

[51] *Pytho's vapors:* the prophecies of the oracle at Delphi.
[52] *birds . . . heads:* the prophecies derived from interpreting the flights of birds.

985   with their own mothers! Those who believe such things
       mean nothing endure their lives most easily.
    OEDIPUS: A fine, bold speech, and you are right, perhaps,
       except that my mother is still living,
       so I must fear her, however well you argue.
990 JOCASTA: And yet your father's tomb is a great eye.
    OEDIPUS: Illuminating, yes. But I still fear the living.
    MESSENGER: Who is the woman who inspires this fear?
    OEDIPUS: Meropē, Polybus' wife, old man.
    MESSENGER: And what is there about her that alarms you?
995 OEDIPUS: An oracle, god-sent and fearful, stranger.
    MESSENGER: Is it permitted that another know?
    OEDIPUS: It is. Loxias once said to me
       I must have intercourse with my own mother
       and take my father's blood with these my hands.
1000   So I have long lived far away from Corinth.
       This has indeed brought much good luck, and yet,
       to see one's parents' eyes is happiest.
    MESSENGER: Was it for this that you have lived in exile?
    OEDIPUS: So I'd not be my father's killer, sir.
1005 MESSENGER: Had I not better free you from this fear,
       my Lord? That's why I came—to do you service.
    OEDIPUS: Indeed, what a reward you'd get for that!
    MESSENGER: Indeed, this is the main point of my trip,
       to be rewarded when you get back home.
1010 OEDIPUS: I'll never rejoin the givers of my seed![53]
    MESSENGER: My son, clearly you don't know what you're doing.
    OEDIPUS: But how is that, old man? For the gods' sake, tell me!
    MESSENGER: If it's because of them you won't go home.
    OEDIPUS: I fear that Phoebus will have told the truth.
1015 MESSENGER: Pollution from the ones who gave you seed?
    OEDIPUS: That is the thing, old man, I always fear.
    MESSENGER: Your fear is groundless. Understand that.
    OEDIPUS: Groundless? Not if I was born their son.
    MESSENGER: But Polybus is not related to you.
1020 OEDIPUS: Do you mean Polybus was not my father?
    MESSENGER: No more than I. We're both the same to you.
    OEDIPUS: Same? One who begot me and one who didn't?
    MESSENGER: He didn't beget you any more than I did.
    OEDIPUS: But then, why did he say I was his son?
1025 MESSENGER: He got you as a gift from my own hands.

---

[53] *givers of my seed:* that is, my parents. Oedipus still thinks Meropē and Polybus are his
   parents.

OEDIPUS: He loved me so, though from another's hands?

MESSENGER: His former childlessness persuaded him.

OEDIPUS: But had you bought me, or begotten me?

MESSENGER: Found you. In the forest hallows of Cithaeron.

1030 OEDIPUS: What were you doing traveling in that region?

MESSENGER: I was in charge of flocks which grazed those mountains.

OEDIPUS: A wanderer who worked the flocks for hire?

MESSENGER: Ah, but that day I was your savior, son.

OEDIPUS: From what? What was my trouble when you took me?

1035 MESSENGER: The ball-joints of your feet might testify.

OEDIPUS: What's that? What makes you name that ancient trouble?

MESSENGER: Your feet were pierced and I am your rescuer.

OEDIPUS: A fearful rebuke those tokens left for me!

MESSENGER: That was the chance that names you who you are.

1040 OEDIPUS: By the gods, did my mother or my father do this?

MESSENGER: That I don't know. He might who gave you to me.

OEDIPUS: From someone else? You didn't chance on me?

MESSENGER: Another shepherd handed you to me.

OEDIPUS: Who was he? Do you know? Will you explain!

1045 MESSENGER: They called him one of the men of—was it Laius?

OEDIPUS: The one who once was king here long ago?

MESSENGER: That is the one! The man was shepherd to him.

OEDIPUS: And is he still alive so I can see him?

MESSENGER: But you who live here ought to know that best.

1050 OEDIPUS: Does any one of you now present know
   about the shepherd whom this man has named?
   Have you seen him in town or in the fields? Speak out!
   The time has come for the discovery!

CHORAGOS: The man he speaks of, I believe, is the same
1055   as the field hand you have already asked to see.
   But it's Jocasta who would know this best.

OEDIPUS: Lady, do you remember the man we just
   now sent for—is that the man he speaks of?

JOCASTA: What? The man he spoke of? Pay no attention!
1060   His words are not worth thinking about. It's nothing.

OEDIPUS: With clues like this within my grasp, give up?
   Fail to solve the mystery of my birth?

JOCASTA: For the love of the gods, and if you love your life,
   give up this search! My sickness is enough.

1065 OEDIPUS: Come! Though my mothers for three generations
   were in slavery, you'd not be lowborn!

JOCASTA: No, listen to me! Please! Don't do this thing!

OEDIPUS: I will not listen; I will search out the truth.

JOCASTA: My thinking is for you—it would be best.

1070 OEDIPUS: This "best" of yours is starting to annoy me.

JOCASTA: Doomed man! Never find out who you are!

OEDIPUS: Will someone go and bring that shepherd here?
    Leave her to glory in her wealthy birth!
JOCASTA: Man of misery! No other name
1075   shall I address you by, ever again.

(Exit Jocasta into the palace after a long pause.)

CHORAGOS: Why has your lady left, Oedipus,
    hurled by a savage grief? I am afraid
    disaster will come bursting from this silence.
OEDIPUS: Let it burst forth! However low this seed
1080   of mine may be, yet I desire to see it.
    She, perhaps—she has a woman's pride—
    is mortified by my base origins.
    But I who count myself the child of Chance,
    the giver of good, shall never know dishonor.
1085   She is my mother,[54] and the months my brothers
    who first marked out my lowness, then my greatness.
    I shall not prove untrue to such a nature
    by giving up the search for my own birth.

STASIMON 3

STROPHE
CHORUS: If I have mantic power
1090   and excellence in thought,
    by Olympus,
        you shall not, Cithaeron, at tomorrow's
    full moon,
    fail to hear us celebrate you as the countryman
1095   of Oedipus, his nurse and mother,
    or fail to be the subject of our dance,
        since you have given pleasure
    to our king.
    Phoebus, whom we summon by "iē!,"
1100   may this be pleasing to you!

ANTISTROPHE
    Who was your mother, son?
    which of the long-lived nymphs
    after lying with Pan,[55]
        the mountain roaming . . . Or was it a bride
1105   of Loxias?[56]

---

[54] *She . . . mother:* Chance is my mother.
[55] *Pan:* god of shepherds and woodlands, half man and half goat.
[56] *Loxias:* Apollo.

> For dear to him are all the upland pastures.
> Or was it Mount Cyllēnē's lord,[57]
> or the Bacchic god,[58]
>> dweller of the mountain peaks,
1110
> who received you as a joyous find
> from one of the nymphs of Helicon,
> the favorite sharers of his sport?

EPISODE 4

OEDIPUS: If someone like myself, who never met him,
    may calculate—elders, I think I see
1115
    the very herdsman we've been waiting for.
    His many years would fit that man's age,
    and those who bring him on, if I am right,
    are my own men. And yet, in real knowledge,
    you can outstrip me, surely: you've seen him.

(Enter the old Herdsman escorted by two of Oedipus's Attendants. At first, the Herdsman will not look at Oedipus.)

1120 CHORAGOS: I know him, yes, a man of the house of Laius,
    a trusty herdsman if he ever had one.
OEDIPUS: I ask you first, the stranger come from Corinth:
    is this the man you spoke of?
MESSENGER: That's he you see.
OEDIPUS: Then you, old man. First look at me! Now answer:
1125
    did you belong to Laius' household once?
HERDSMAN: I did. Not a purchased slave but raised in the palace.
OEDIPUS: How have you spent your life? What is your work?
HERDSMAN: Most of my life now I have tended sheep.
OEDIPUS: Where is the usual place you stay with them?
1130 HERDSMAN: On Mount Cithaeron. Or in that district.
OEDIPUS: Do you recall observing this man there?
HERDSMAN: Doing what? Which is the man you mean?
OEDIPUS: This man right here. Have you had dealings with him?
HERDSMAN: I can't say right away. I don't remember.
1135 MESSENGER: No wonder, master. I'll bring clear memory
    to his ignorance. I'm absolutely sure
    he can recall it, the district was Cithaeron,
    he with a double flock, and I, with one,
    lived close to him, for three entire seasons,
1140
    six months along, from spring right to Arcturus.[59]
    Then for the winter I'd drive mine to my fold,

---

[57] *Mount Cyllēnē's lord:* Hermes, messenger of the gods.
[58] *Bacchic god:* Dionysus.
[59] *Arcturus:* a star that is first seen in September in the Grecian sky.

and he'd drive his to Laius' pen again.
Did any of the things I say take place?
HERDSMAN: You speak the truth, though it's from long ago.
1145 MESSENGER: Do you remember giving me, back then,
a boy I was to care for as my own?
HERDSMAN: What are you saying? Why do you ask me that?
MESSENGER: There, sir, is the man who was that boy!
HERDSMAN: Damn you! Shut your mouth! Keep your silence!
1150 OEDIPUS: Stop! Don't you rebuke his words.
Your words ask for rebuke far more than his.
HERDSMAN: But what have I done wrong, most royal master?
OEDIPUS: Not telling of the boy of whom he asked.
HERDSMAN: He's ignorant and blundering toward ruin.
1155 OEDIPUS: Tell it willingly—or under torture.
HERDSMAN: Oh god! Don't—I am old—don't torture me!
OEDIPUS: Here! Someone put his hands behind his back!
HERDSMAN: But why? What else would you find out, poor man?
OEDIPUS: Did you give him the child he asks about?
1160 HERDSMAN: I did. I wish that I had died that day!
OEDIPUS: You'll come to that if you don't speak the truth.
HERDSMAN: It's if I speak that I shall be destroyed.
OEDIPUS: I think this fellow struggles for delay.
HERDSMAN: No, no! I said already that I gave him.
1165 OEDIPUS: From your own home, or got from someone else?
HERDSMAN: Not from my own. I got him from another.
OEDIPUS: Which of these citizens? What sort of house?
HERDSMAN: Don't—by the gods!—don't, master, ask me more!
OEDIPUS: It means your death if I must ask again.
1170 HERDSMAN: One of the children of the house of Laius.
OEDIPUS: A slave—or born into the family?
HERDSMAN: I have come to the dreaded thing, and I shall say it.
OEDIPUS: And I to hearing it, but hear I must.
HERDSMAN: He was reported to have been—his son.
1175 Your lady in the house could tell you best.
OEDIPUS: Because she gave him to you?
HERDSMAN: Yes, my lord.
OEDIPUS: What was her purpose?
HERDSMAN: I was to kill the boy.
OEDIPUS: The child she bore?
HERDSMAN: She dreaded prophecies.
OEDIPUS: What were they?
HERDSMAN: The word was that he'd kill his parents.
1180 OEDIPUS: Then why did you give him up to this old man?
HERDSMAN: In pity, master—so he would take him home,
to another land. But what he did was save him
for this supreme disaster. If you are the one
he speaks of—know your evil birth and fate!

1185 OEDIPUS: Ah! All of it was destined to be true!
Oh light, now may I look my last upon you,
shown monstrous in my birth, in marriage monstrous,
a murderer monstrous in those I killed.

(Exit Oedipus, running into the palace.)

STASIMON 4

STROPHE 1
CHORUS: Oh generations of mortal men,
1190 while you are living, I will
appraise your lives at zero!
What man
comes closer to seizing lasting blessedness
than merely to seize its semblance,
1195 and after living in this semblance, to plunge?
With your example before us,
with your destiny, yours,
suffering Oedipus, no mortal
can I judge fortunate.

ANTISTROPHE 1
1200 For he,[60] outranging everybody,
shot his arrow[61] and became the lord
of wide prosperity and blessedness,
oh Zeus, after destroying
the virgin with the crooked talons,[62]
1205 singer of oracles; and against death,
in my land, he arose a tower of defense.
From which time you were called my king
and granted privileges supreme—in mighty
Thebes the ruling lord.

STROPHE 2
1210 But now—whose story is more sorrowful than yours?
Who is more intimate with fierce calamities,
with labors, now that your life is altered?
Alas, my Oedipus, whom all men know:
one great harbor[63]—
1215 one alone sufficed for you,

---

[60] *he:* Oedipus.
[61] *shot his arrow:* took his chances; made a guess at the Sphinx's riddle.
[62] *virgin . . . talons:* the Sphinx.
[63] *one great harbor:* metaphorical allusion to Jocasta's body.

as son and father,
when you tumbled,[64] plowman[65] of the woman's chamber.
How, how could your paternal
    furrows, wretched man,
1220 endure you silently so long.

ANTISTROPHE 2

Time, all-seeing, surprised you living an unwilled life
and sits from of old in judgment on the marriage, not a marriage,
where the begetter is the begot as well.
Ah, son of Laius . . . ,
1225 would that—oh, would that
I had never seen you!
I wail, my scream climbing beyond itself
from my whole power of voice. To say it straight:
    from you I got new breath—
1230 but I also lulled my eye to sleep.[66]

EXODOS

(Enter the Second Messenger from the palace.)

SECOND MESSENGER: You who are first among the citizens,
    what deeds you are about to hear and see!
    What grief you'll carry, if, true to your birth,
    you still respect the house of Labdacus!
1235 Neither the Ister nor the Phasis river
    could purify this house, such suffering
    does it conceal, or soon must bring to light—
    willed this time, not unwilled. Griefs hurt worst
    which we perceive to be self-chosen ones.
1240 CHORAGOS: They were sufficient, the things we knew before,
    to make us grieve. What can you add to those?
SECOND MESSENGER: The thing that's quickest said and quickest heard:
    our own, our royal one, Jocasta's dead.
CHORAGOS: Unhappy queen! What was responsible?
1245 SECOND MESSENGER: Herself. The bitterest of these events
    is not for you, you were not there to see,
    but yet, exactly as I can recall it,
    you'll hear what happened to that wretched lady.
    She came in anger through the outer hall,
1250 and then she ran straight to her marriage bed,
    tearing her hair with the fingers of both hands.

---

[64] *tumbled:* were born and had sex.
[65] *plowman:* plowing is used here as a sexual metaphor.
[66] *I . . . sleep:* I failed to see the corruption you brought.

Then, slamming shut the doors when she was in,
she called to Laius, dead so many years,
remembering the ancient seed which caused
1255   his death, leaving the mother to the son
to breed again an ill-born progeny.
She mourned the bed where she, alas, bred double—
husband by husband, children by her child.
From this point on I don't know how she died,
1260   for Oedipus then burst in with a cry,
and did not let us watch her final evil.
Our eyes were fixed on him. Wildly he ran
to each of us, asking for his spear
and for his wife—no wife: where he might find
1265   the double mother-field, his and his children's.
He raved, and some divinity then showed him—
for none of us did so who stood close by.
With a dreadful shout—as if some guide were leading—
he lunged through the double doors; he bent the hollow
1270   bolts from the sockets, burst into the room,
and there we saw her, hanging from above,
entangled in some twisted hanging strands.
He saw, was stricken, and with a wild roar
ripped down the dangling noose. When she, poor woman,
1275   lay on the ground, there came a fearful sight:
he snatched the pins of worked gold from her dress,
with which her clothes were fastened: these he raised
and struck into the ball-joints of his eyes.[67]
He shouted that they would no longer see
1280   the evils he had suffered or had done,
see in the dark those he should not have seen,
and know no more those he once sought to know.
While chanting this, not once but many times
he raised his hand and struck into his eyes.
1285   Blood from his wounded eyes poured down his chin,
not freed in moistening drops, but all at once
a stormy rain of black blood burst like hail.
These evils, coupling them, making them one,
have broken loose upon both man and wife.
1290   The old prosperity that they had once
was true prosperity, and yet today,
mourning, ruin, death, disgrace, and every
evil you could name—not one is absent.
CHORAGOS: Has he allowed himself some peace from all this grief?

---

[67] *ball-joints of his eyes:* his eyeballs. Oedipus blinds himself in both eyes at the same time.

1295 SECOND MESSENGER: He shouts that someone slide the bolts and show
to all the Cadmeians the patricide,
his mother's—I can't say it, it's unholy—
so he can cast himself out of the land,
not stay and curse his house by his own curse.

1300 He lacks the strength, though, and he needs a guide,
for his is a sickness that's too great to bear.
Now you yourself will see: the bolts of the doors
are opening. You are about to see
a vision even one who hates must pity.

(Enter the blinded Oedipus from the palace, led in by a household Servant.)

1305 CHORAGOS: Terrifying suffering for men to see,
more terrifying than any I've ever
come upon. Oh man of pain
what madness reached you? Which god from far off,
surpassing in range his longest spring,

1310   struck hard against your god-abandoned fate?
Oh man of pain,
I cannot look upon you—though there's so much
I would ask you, so much to hear,
so much that holds my eyes—

1315   such is the shudder you produce in me.
OEDIPUS: Ah! Ah! I am a man of misery.
Where am I carried? Pity me! Where
is my voice scattered abroad on wings?
     Divinity, where has your lunge transported me?

1320 CHORAGOS: To something horrible, not to be heard or seen.

KOMMOS

STROPHE 1
OEDIPUS: Oh, my cloud
of darkness, abominable, unspeakable as it attacks me,
not to be turned away, brought by an evil wind!
Alas!

1325 Again alas! Both enter me at once:
the sting of the prongs,[68] the memory of evils!
CHORUS: I do not marvel that in these afflictions
you carry double griefs and double evils.

ANTISTROPHE 1
OEDIPUS: Ah, friend,
1330 so you at least are there, resolute servant!
Still with a heart to care for me, the blind man.

---

[68] *prongs:* refers to both the whip that Laius used and the two gold pins Oedipus used to
blind himself.

Oh! Oh!
I know that you are there. I recognize
even inside my darkness, that voice of yours.

1335 CHORUS: Doer of horror, how did you bear to quench
your vision? What divinity raised your hand?

STROPHE 2

OEDIPUS: It was Apollo there, Apollo, friends,
who brought my sorrows, vile sorrows to their perfection,
these evils that were done to me.

1340 But the one who struck them with his hand,
that one was none but I, in wretchedness.
For why was I to see
when nothing I could see would bring me joy?

CHORUS: Yes, that is how it was.

1345 OEDIPUS: What could I see, indeed,
or what enjoy—what greeting
is there I could hear with pleasure, friends?
Conduct me out of the land
as quickly as you can!

1350 Conduct me out, my friends,
the man utterly ruined,
supremely cursed,
the man who is by gods
the most detested of all men!

1355 CHORUS: Wretched in disaster and in knowledge:
oh, I could wish you'd never come to know!

ANTISTROPHE 2

OEDIPUS: May he be destroyed, whoever freed the savage shackles
from my feet when I'd been sent to the wild pasture,
whoever rescued me from murder

1360 and became my savior—
a bitter gift:
if I had died then,
I'd not have been such grief to self and kin.

CHORUS: I also would have had it so.

1365 OEDIPUS: I'd not have returned to be my father's
murderer; I'd not be called by men
my mother's bridegroom.
Now I'm without a god,
child of a polluted parent,

1370 fellow progenitor with him
who gave me birth in misery.
If there's an evil that
surpasses evils, that
has fallen to the lot of Oedipus.

1375   CHORAGOS: How can I say that you have counseled well?
       Better not to be than live a blind man.
     OEDIPUS: That this was not the best thing I could do—
       don't tell me that, or advise me any more!
       Should I descend to Hades and endure
1380   to see my father with these eyes? Or see
       my poor unhappy mother? For I have done,
       to both of these, things too great for hanging.
       Or is the sight of children to be yearned for,
       to see new shoots that sprouted as these did?
1385   Never, never with these eyes of mine!
       Nor city, nor tower, nor holy images
       of the divinities! For I, all-wretched,
       most nobly raised—as no one else in Thebes—
       deprived myself of these when I ordained
1390   that all expel the impious one—god-shown
       to be polluted, and the dead king's son![69]
       Once I exposed this great stain upon me,
       could I have looked on these with steady eyes?
       No! No! And if there were a way to block
1395   the source of hearing in my ears, I'd gladly
       have locked up my pitiable body,
       so I'd be blind and deaf. Evils shut out—
       that way my mind could live in sweetness.
       Alas, Cithaeron,[70] why did you receive me?
1400   Or when you had me, not killed me instantly?
       I'd not have had to show my birth to mankind.
       Polybus, Corinth, halls—ancestral,
       they told me—how beautiful was your ward,
       a scar that held back festering disease!
1405   Evil my nature, evil my origin.
       You, three roads, and you, secret ravine,
       you oak grove, narrow place of those three paths
       that drank my blood[71] from these hands, from him
       who fathered me, do you remember still
1410   the things I did to you? When I'd come here,
       what I then did once more? Oh marriages! Marriages!
       You gave us life and when you'd planted us
       you sent the same seed up, and then revealed
       fathers, brothers, sons, and kinsman's blood,
1415   and brides, and wives, and mothers, all the most
       atrocious things that happen to mankind!

---

[69] *I . . . son:* Oedipus refers to his own curse against the murderer as well as his sins of patricide and incest.

[70] *Cithaeron:* the mountain on which the infant Oedipus was supposed to be exposed.

[71] *my blood:* that is, the blood of my father, Laius.

One should not name what never should have been.
Somewhere out there, then, quickly, by the gods,
cover me up, or murder me, or throw me
1420   to the ocean where you will never see me more!

(Oedipus moves toward the Chorus and they back away from him.)

Come! Don't shrink to touch this wretched man!
Believe me, do not be frightened! I alone
of all mankind can carry these afflictions.

(Enter Creon from the palace with Attendants.)

CHORAGOS: Tell Creon what you wish for. Just when we need him
1425   he's here. He can act, he can advise you.
He's now the land's sole guardian in your place.
OEDIPUS: Ah! Are there words that I can speak to him?
What ground for trust can I present? It's proved
that I was false to him in everything.
1430 CREON: I have not come to mock you, Oedipus,
nor to reproach you for your former falseness.
You men, if you have no respect for sons
of mortals, let your awe for the all-feeding
flames of lordy Hēlius[72] prevent
1435   your showing unconcealed so great a stain,
abhorred by earth and sacred rain and light.
Escort him quickly back into the house!
If blood kin only see and hear their own
afflictions, we'll have no impious defilement.
1440 OEDIPUS: By the gods, you've freed me from one terrible fear,
so nobly meeting my unworthiness:
grant me something—not for me; for you!
CREON: What do you want that you should beg me so?
OEDIPUS: To drive me from the land at once, to a place
1445   where there will be no man to speak to me!
CREON: I would have done just that—had I not wished
to ask first of the god what I should do.
OEDIPUS: His answer was revealed in full—that I,
the patricide, unholy, be destroyed.
1450 CREON: He said that, but our need is so extreme,
it's best to have sure knowledge what must be done.
OEDIPUS: You'll ask about a wretched man like me?
CREON: Is it not time you put your trust in the god?
OEDIPUS: But I bid you as well, and shall entreat you.
1455   Give her who is within what burial
you will—you'll give your own her proper rites;
but me—do not condemn my fathers' land

---

[72] *Hēlius:* the sun.

1460

1465

1470

1475

to have me dwelling here while I'm alive,
but let me live on mountains—on Cithaeron
famed as mine, for my mother and my father,
while they yet lived, made it my destined tomb,
and I'll be killed by those who wished my ruin!
And yet I know: no sickness will destroy me,
nothing will: I'd never have been saved
when left to die unless for some dread evil.
Then let my fate continue where it will!
As for my children, Creon, take no pains
for my sons—they're men and they will never lack
the means to live, wherever they may be—
but my two wretched, pitiable girls,
who never ate but at my table, never
were without me—everything that I
would touch, they'd always have a share of it—
please care for them! Above all, let me touch
them with my hands and weep aloud my woes!
Please, my Lord!
Please, noble heart! Touching with my hands,
I'd think I held them as when I could see.

(Enter Antigone and Ismene from the palace with Attendants.)

1480

What's this?
Oh gods! Do I hear, somewhere, my two dear ones
sobbing? Has Creon really pitied me
and sent to me my dearest ones, my children?
Is that it?
CREON: Yes, I prepared this for you, for I knew
you'd feel this joy, as you have always done.
OEDIPUS: Good fortune, then, and, for your care, be guarded
far better by divinity than I was!
Where are you, children? Come to me! Come here
to these my hands, hands of your brother, hands
of him who gave you seed, hands that made
these once bright eyes to see now in this fashion.

1485

1490

(Oedipus embraces his daughters.)

1495

He, children, seeing nothing, knowing nothing,
he fathered you where his own seed was plowed.
I weep for you as well, though I can't see you,
imagining your bitter life to come,
the life you will be forced by men to live.
What gatherings of townsmen will you join,
what festivals, without returning home
in tears instead of watching holy rites?

NEL

1500 And when you've reached the time for marrying,
where, children, is the man who'll run the risk
of taking on himself the infamy
that will wound you as it did my parents?
What evil is not here? Your father killed
1505 his father, plowed the one who gave him birth,
and from the place where he was sown, from there
he got you, from the place he too was born.
These are the wounds: then who will marry you?
No man, my children. No, it's clear that you
1510 must wither in dry barrenness, unmarried.

(Oedipus addresses Creon.)

Son of Menoeceus! You are the only father
left to them—we two who gave them seed
are both destroyed: watch that they don't become
poor, wanderers, unmarried—they are your kin.
1515 Let not my ruin be their ruin, too!
No, pity them! You see how young they are,
bereft of everyone, except for you.
Consent, kind heart, and touch me with your hand!

(Creon grasps Oedipus's right hand.)

You, children, if you had reached an age of sense,
1520 I would have counseled much. Now, pray you may live
always where it's allowed, finding a life
better than his was, who gave you seed.
CREON: Stop this now. Quiet your weeping. Move away, into the house.
OEDIPUS: Bitter words, but I obey them.
CREON: There's an end to all things.
1525 OEDIPUS: I have first this request.
CREON: Tell me. I shall judge when I will hear it.
OEDIPUS: Banish me from my homeland.
CREON: You must ask that of the god.
OEDIPUS: But I am the gods' most hated man!
CREON: Then you will soon get what
you want.
OEDIPUS: Do you consent?
CREON: I never promise when, as now, I'm ignorant.
OEDIPUS: Then lead me in.
CREON: Come. But let your hold fall from your
children.
1530 OEDIPUS: Do not take them from me, ever!
CREON: Do not wish to keep all of the
power.
You had power, but that power did not follow you through life.

(Oedipus's daughters are taken from him and led into the palace by Attendants. Oedipus is led into the palace by a Servant. Creon and the other Attendants follow. Only the Chorus remains.)

CHORUS: People of Thebes, my country, see: here is that Oedipus—
he who "knew" the famous riddle, and attained the highest power,
whom all citizens admired, even envying his luck!
1535   See the billows of wild troubles which he has entered now!
Here is the truth of each man's life: we must wait, and see his end,
scrutinize his dying day, and refuse to call him happy
till he has crossed the border of his life without pain.

(Exit the Chorus along each of the parados.)

READING AND REACTING

1. The ancient Greeks used no scenery in their theatrical productions. In the absence of scenery, how is the setting established at the beginning of *Oedipus the King*?

2. In order not to detract from the language of *Oedipus the King*, some contemporary productions use very simple costumes. Do you agree with this decision? If so, why? If not, what kind of costumes would you use?

3. In some recent productions of *Oedipus the King*, actors wear copies of ancient Greek masks. What are the advantages and disadvantages of using such masks in a contemporary production of the play?

4. In the ancient Greek theatre, the *strophe* and *antistrophe* were sung or chanted by the chorus as it danced back and forth across the stage. If you were staging the play today, would you retain the chorus or do away with it entirely? What would be gained or lost with each alternative?

5. Why does Sophocles have Oedipus blind himself offstage? What would be the effect of having Oedipus perform this act in full view of the audience?

6. In what ways does Sophocles observe the unities of time, place, and action described on page 916? How does Sophocles manage to present information about what happened years before the action of the play while still maintaining the three unities?

7. The ancient Greek audience that viewed *Oedipus the King* was familiar with the plot of the play. Given this situation, how does Sophocles create suspense? What are the advantages and disadvantages of using a story that the audience already knows?

8. At the end of the play, what has Oedipus learned about himself? About the gods? About the quest for truth? Is he a tragic or a pathetic figure? (See pages 914–16 for a discussion of these terms.)

9. Today, some directors employ *colour-blind casting*—that is, they cast an actor in a role without regard to his or her race. Do you think this practice could be used in casting *Oedipus the King*?

10. **JOURNAL ENTRY** Do you think Oedipus deserves his fate? Why or why not?

11. **CRITICAL PERSPECTIVE** In "On Misunderstanding the *Oedipus Rex*," F. R. Dodds argues that Sophocles did not intend that Oedipus's tragedy be seen as rising from a "grave moral flaw." Neither, says Dodds, was Oedipus a "mere puppet" of the gods. Rather, "what fascinates us is the spectacle of a man freely choosing, from the highest motives, a series of actions which lead to his own ruin":

> Oedipus is great, not in virtue of a great worldly position—for his worldly position is an illusion which will vanish like a dream—but in virtue of his inner strength: strength to pursue the truth at whatever personal cost, and strength to accept and endure it when found. . . . Oedipus is great because he accepts the responsibility for *all* his acts, including those which are objectively most horrible, though subjectively innocent.

Do you agree with Dodds's arguments? Do you see Oedipus as someone who has inner strength or as a morally flawed victim of the gods?

Related Works: "Barn Burning" (p. 234), " 'Out, Out—' " (p. 721), "Ulysses" (p. 886)

♦ WRITING SUGGESTIONS: STAGING

1. Discuss the problems the original staging in *Oedipus the King* poses for contemporary audiences.

2. Suppose you are the set designer for *The Rez Sisters*. Decide whether you want to use a realistic, surrealistic, or minimalist set for the production. Then, write a letter to the play's director in which you present and defend your proposal. Be sure to include specific references to the play.

3. Discuss and analyze the staging techniques used in a play that is not in this chapter—for example, *Trifles* (p. 948) or *The Shape of a Girl* (p. 1348).

4. Choose a short story that appears in this anthology, and explain how you would stage it if it were a play. What props, costumes, lighting, and sound effects would you choose? What events would occur offstage? Possible subjects for this paper might include "A&P" (p. 122), "The Story of an Hour" (p. 77), or "The Boat" (p. 447).

5. What scenery, props, and costumes would you use to transform the setting of *Oedipus the King* to a contemporary drama?

CHAPTER 25

Theme

◇ ◇ ◇

Plays are like doors to me. They can be as massive and ornate as cathedrals or as small and intimate as keyholes. They can be as real as the kitchen sink or as ephemeral as dreams. When we read them in the quiet or sit in a darkened theatre space and listen we step over the threshold of the door that the playwright has opened for us. We walk into their secret garden or jungle and hopefully we are taken on an adventurous odyssey.

MARSHA MASON, *Women Playwrights*

[D]rama is one of the things that makes possible a solution to the problem of socializing people. In other words, we are born private, and we die private, but we live of necessity in direct relation to other people, even if we live alone. And dramatic conflict of significance always verges on and deals with the way men live together. And this is incomprehensible to Man as a private person. He is always trying to find out where he stands in his society, whether he uses those terms or not. He always wants to know whether his life has a meaning, and that meaning is always in relation to others. It is always in relation to his society, it's always in relation to his choices, to the absence of his choices, which are dominated by other people. I think that when we speak of dramatic significance we're really talking about, either openly or unknowingly, about the dilemma of living together, of living a social existence, and the conflict is endless between Man and his fellows and between his own instincts and the social necessity.

ARTHUR MILLER, *The Playwrights Speak*

I can't even count how many times I've heard the line, "Where did the idea for this play come from?" . . . Ideas emerge from plays—not the other way around. . . . I think explanation destroys [a play] and makes it less than it is.

SAM SHEPARD, *Fool for Love and Other Plays*

◇ ◇ ◇

Like a short story or a novel, a play is open to interpretation. Readers' reactions are influenced by the language of the text, and audiences' reactions are influenced by the performance on stage. Just as in fiction, every element of a play—its title, its conflicts, its dialogue, its characters, and its staging, for instance—can shed light on its themes.

TITLES

◊ ◊ ◊

The title of a play can provide insight into themes. The ironic title of Susan Glaspell's *Trifles* (p. 948), for example, suggests that women's concern with "trifles" may get to the heart of the matter more effectively than the preoccupations of self-important men do. Wendy Wasserstein's *Tender Offer* (p. 1341) is another title that offers clues to a theme of the play. It not only suggests the father's preoccupation with business (a company makes a *tender offer* when it wants to buy another company), but also makes the point that parents need to take the time to relate (make tender offers) to their children. Finally, Anton Chekhov's *The Brute* (p. 1081) effectively calls attention to the play's ideas about male-female relationships. The title may refer to Smirnov, who says that he has never liked women—whom he characterizes as "creatures of poetry and romance." Or it may refer to Mrs. Popov's late husband, to whose memory she has dedicated her life despite the fact that he was repeatedly unfaithful. Either alternative reinforces the play's tongue-in-cheek characterization of men as "brutes."

CONFLICTS

◊ ◊ ◊

The unfolding plot of a play—especially the conflicts that develop—can also reveal the play's themes. In Henrik Ibsen's *A Doll House* (p. 1013), for example, at least three major conflicts are present: one between Nora and her husband Torvald, one between Nora and Krogstad (an old acquaintance), and one between Nora and society. Each of these conflicts sheds light on the themes of the play.

Through Nora's conflict with Torvald, Ibsen examines the constraints placed on women and men by marriage in the nineteenth century. Both Nora and Torvald are imprisoned within their respective roles: Nora must be passive and childlike, and Torvald must be proper and always in control. Nora, therefore, expects her husband to be noble and generous and, in a crisis, to sacrifice himself for her. When he fails to live up to her expectations, she is profoundly disillusioned.

Nora's conflict with Krogstad underscores Ibsen's criticisms of the class system in nineteenth-century Norway. At the beginning of the play, Nora finds it "immensely amusing: that we—that Torvald has so much power over . . . people." Krogstad, a bank clerk who is in the employ of Torvald, visits Nora in act 1 to enlist her aid in saving his job. It is clear that she sees him as her social inferior. When Krogstad questions her about a woman with whom he has seen her, she replies, "What makes you think you can cross-examine me, Mr. Krogstad—you, one of my husband's employees?" Nora does not realize that she and Krogstad are, ironically, very much alike: both occupy subordinate positions and therefore have no power to determine their own destinies.

Finally, through Nora's conflict with society Ibsen examines an important theme of his play: the destructive nature of the forces that subjugate women. Nineteenth-century society was male-dominated. Married women could not borrow money without their husband's signatures, own real estate in their own names, or enter into contracts. In addition, all their assets—including inheritances and trust funds—automatically became the property of their husbands at the time of marriage. As a result of her sheltered life, Nora at the beginning of the play is completely innocent of the consequences of her actions. Most readers share Dr. Rank's confusion when he asks Nora, "Why do you laugh at that? Do you have any idea of what society is?" It is Nora's disillusionment at finding out that Torvald and the rest of society are not what she has been led to believe they are that ultimately causes her to rebel. By walking out the door at the end of the play, Nora rejects not only her husband and her children (to whom, incidentally, she has no legal right once she leaves), but also society and its laws.

These conflicts, then, underscore many of the themes that dominate *A Doll House.* First, the conflicts show that marriage in the nineteenth century imprisons both men and women in narrow, constricting roles. Next, the conflicts show that middle-class Norwegian society is narrow, smug, and judgmental. (Krogstad, for example, is looked down upon for a crime years after he committed it, and Nora is looked down upon because she borrows money to save her husband's life.) Finally, the conflicts show that society does not offer individuals—especially women—the freedom to lead happy and fulfilling lives. Only when the social and economic conditions that govern society change, Ibsen suggests, can women and men live together in mutual esteem.

DIALOGUE
◊ ◊ ◊

The dialogue of a play can also give insight into its themes. Sometimes a character will suggest—or even explicitly state—a theme. In act 3 of *A Doll House,* for example, Nora's friend, Mrs. Linde, comes as close as any character to expressing a central concern of the play when she says, "Helmer's got to learn everything; this dreadful secret has to be aired; those two have to come to a full understanding; all these lies can't go on." As the play goes on to demonstrate, the lies that exist both in marriage and in society are obstacles to love and happiness.

One of the main themes of George Ryga's *The Ecstasy of Rita Joe* (p. 1376)—the dehumanizing and isolating effects of racism—is developed by the play's dialogue. The issue of race is made explicit by Rita's words about her sister Eileen Joe who tried to earn a living as a seamstress:

> "Two weeks, and not one white woman came to her to leave an order or old clothes for her to fix. No work at all for two weeks, an' her money ran out . . . . Isn't that funny?"

The difficulty of finding a decent job—in the city or home on the reserve— means that Rita Joe and her people are in a constant state of displacement, both physical and emotional. And at the root is racism.

Characters
◇ ◇ ◇

Because a dramatic work focuses on a central character, or protagonist, the development of this character can shed light on a play's themes. Braidie in Joan MacLeod's *The Shape of a Girl* (p. 1348), for example, is developed in great detail. At the beginning of the play, Braidie reveals her confusion over her own circle of friends at school, and mixed in with that confusion is her understanding of the murder of a teenage girl by other teenagers, in partic- ular another girl. (The play is loosely based on the murder of Reena Virk, which took place in Victoria, British Columbia, in 1997.) Braidie moves through various states of mind in her monologue, largely addressed to her brother, Trevor. The horror of what happened to Reena (unnamed but iden- tifiable by details in the play) is explored by Braidie, who comes to the con- clusion that what happened was not so unusual—that Braidie and her friends have participated in bullying as well. By the end of the play Braidie's essential goodness reasserts itself, and she realizes that she will have to try to protect Sofie, both by an act of friendship toward Sofie and an act of betrayal toward Adrienne, who has been the chief malevolent force against Sofie. Cruelty, Braidie demonstrates, is prevalent in the lives of girls, and while she understands how easy it is to fall into the trap of bullying, she also learns that the destructive actions must be stopped—if not by her, then by adults in power. Her growth into responsibility forms the basis of the play.

Nora, the main character in *A Doll House*, changes a great deal during the course of the play. At the beginning of the play, she is more her husband's possession than an adult capable of determining her own destiny. Nora's status becomes apparent in the first act when Torvald gently scolds his "little spendthrift" and refers to her as his "little lark" and his "squirrel." She is reduced to childish deceptions, such as hiding her macaroons from her husband when he enters the room. After Krogstad accuses her of committing forgery and threatens to expose her, she expects her husband to rise to the occasion and take the blame for her. When Torvald instead accuses her of being a hypocrite, a liar, and a criminal, Nora's neat little world comes crashing down. As a result of this experience, Nora changes; no longer is she the submissive and obedient wife. Instead, she becomes confident and assertive, ultimately telling Torvald that their marriage is a sham and that she can no longer stay with him. This abrupt shift in Nora's personality gives the audience a clear understanding of the major themes of the play.

Unlike Braidie and Nora, Horatio in *Hamlet* (p. 1093) is a character who changes very little, if at all, during the course of the play. Horatio is initially depicted as intelligent, educated, and loyal. He remains so throughout the play, even to the point of wishing to accompany Hamlet in death. But Hamlet requests that Horatio remain alive to tell the story, and Horatio—ever loyal to the Prince—complies.

STAGING

◊ ◊ ◊

Scenery and props may also convey the themes of a play. For example, in Edward Albee's absurdist drama *The Sandbox*, the stage is relatively bare. Containing only two chairs and a sandbox, this bare stage suggests the play's frightening emptiness, a quality Albee believes characterizes the lives of all human beings. In Michel Tremblay's *Les Belles Soeurs* (p. 1196), the stamps, which are nearly always visible, ironically underscore the futility of Germaine's efforts to achieve success. Lighting effects and music can also suggest a play's themes, as in *Les Belles Soeurs* with the specialized use of lighting and spotlights to illuminate characters and actions, such as the bingo game.

A FINAL NOTE

◊ ◊ ◊

As you read, your values and beliefs will influence your interpretation of a play's themes. For instance, your interest in feminism could lead you to focus your attention on the roles of women in various plays. Remember, however, that the details of a play, not just your own feelings or assumptions, must support your interpretation.

CHECKLIST: WRITING ABOUT THEME

✓ What is the central theme of the play?

✓ What other themes can you identify?

✓ Does the title of the play suggest a theme?

✓ What conflicts exist in the play? In what way do they shed light on the themes of the play?

✓ Do any characters' statements express or imply a theme of the play?

✓ Do any characters change during the play? How do these changes suggest the play's themes?

✓ Do certain characters resist change? How does their failure to change suggest a theme of the play?

✓ Do scenery and props help to communicate the play's themes?

✓ Does music reinforce certain ideas in the play?

✓ Does lighting underscore the themes of the play?

⟩ **WENDY WASSERSTEIN** (1950–2006) was born in Brooklyn, New York. She failed to gain entry into law school and business school, but she went on to become a Tony Award– and Pulitzer Prize–winning dramatist known for plays about educated women and the challenges they face. The characters in her plays often struggle to define themselves in relation to (and sometimes in opposition to) the stereotypical roles of wife, mother, and career woman.

Her plays include *Uncommon Women and Others* (1977), her Yale School of Drama thesis; *Isn't It Romantic* (1983), the story of a budding writer; and *The Heidi Chronicles* (1988), for which she won both a Tony Award and a Pulitzer Prize. Her first book of essays, *Bachelor Girls* (1991), is openly autobiographical, and her novel, *An American Daughter* (1998), chronicles a woman's struggles with politics and fame. In plays, essays, and prose fiction, Wasserstein's work conveys its themes through realistic dialogue, through realistic situations, and, most of all, through humour.

WENDY WASSERSTEIN

Tender Offer
(1983)

CHARACTERS
LISA
PAUL

A girl of around nine is alone in a dance studio. She is dressed in traditional leotards and tights. She begins singing to herself, "Nothing Could be Finer Than to Be in Carolina." She maps out a dance routine, including parts for the chorus. She builds to a finale. A man, Paul, around thirty-five, walks in. He has a sweet, though distant, demeanor. As he walks in, Lisa notices him and stops.

PAUL: You don't have to stop, sweetheart.
LISA: That's okay.
PAUL: Looked very good.
LISA: Thanks.
5 PAUL: Don't I get a kiss hello?
LISA: Sure.
PAUL: *(embraces her)* Hi, Tiger.
LISA: Hi, Dad.
PAUL: I'm sorry I'm late.
10 LISA: That's okay.
PAUL: How'd it go?
LISA: Good.
PAUL: Just good?
LISA: Pretty good.
15 PAUL: "Pretty good." You mean you got a lot of applause or "pretty good" you could have done better.
LISA: Well, Courtney Palumbo's mother thought I was pretty good. But you know the part of the middle when everybody's supposed to freeze and the big girl comes out. Well, I think I moved a little bit.
PAUL: I thought what you were doing looked very good.
LISA: Daddy, that's not what I was doing. That was tap-dancing. I made that up.
PAUL: Oh. Well it looked good. Kind of sexy.
20 LISA: Yuch!
PAUL: What do you mean "yuch"?
LISA: Just yuch!
PAUL: You don't want to be sexy?
LISA: I don't care.
25 PAUL: Let's go Tiger. I promised your mother I'd get you home in time for dinner.
LISA: I can't find my leg warmers.

PAUL: You can't find your what?

LISA: Leg warmers. I can't go home till I find my leg warmers.

PAUL: I don't see you looking for them.

30 LISA: I was waiting for you.

PAUL: Oh.

LISA: Daddy.

PAUL: What?

LISA: Nothing.

35 PAUL: Where do you think you left them?

LISA: Somewhere around here. I can't remember.

PAUL: Well, try to remember, Lisa. We don't have all night.

LISA: I told you. I think somewhere around here.

PAUL: I don't see them. Let's go home now. You'll call the dancing school
tomorrow.

40 LISA: Daddy, I can't go home till I find them. Miss Judy says it's not
professional to leave things.

PAUL: Who's Miss Judy?

LISA: She's my ballet teacher. She once danced the lead in *Swan Lake,* and
she was a June Taylor dancer.

PAUL: Well, then, I'm sure she'll understand about the leg warmers.

LISA: Daddy, Miss Judy wanted to know why you were late today.

45 PAUL: Hmmmmmmmm?

LISA: Why were you late?

PAUL: I was in a meeting. Business. I'm sorry.

LISA: Why did you tell Mommy you'd come instead of her if you knew you
had business?

PAUL: Honey, something just came up. I thought I'd be able to be here. I
was looking forward to it.

50 LISA: I wish you wouldn't make appointments to see me.

PAUL: Hmmmmmmmm.

LISA: You shouldn't make appointments to see me unless you know you're
going to come.

PAUL: Of course I'm going to come.

LISA: No, you're not. Talia Robbins told me she's much happier living
without her father in the house. Her father used to come home late
and go to sleep early.

55 PAUL: Lisa, stop it. Let's go.

LISA: I can't find my leg warmers.

PAUL: Forget your leg warmers.

LISA: Daddy.

PAUL: What is it?

60 LISA: I saw this show on television, I think it was WPIX Channel 11. Well,
the father was crying about his daughter.

PAUL: Why was he crying? Was she sick?

LISA: No. She was at school. And he was at business. And he just missed
her, so he started to cry.

PAUL: What was the name of this show?

LISA: I don't know. I came in in the middle.

65 PAUL: Well, Lisa, I certainly would cry if you were sick or far away, but I know that you're well and you're home. So no reason to get maudlin.

LISA: What's maudlin?

PAUL: Sentimental, soppy. Frequently used by children who make things up to get attention.

LISA: I am sick! I am sick! I have Hodgkin's disease and a bad itch on my leg.

PAUL: What do you mean you have Hodgkin's disease? Don't say things like that.

70 LISA: Swoosie Kurtz, she had Hodgkin's disease on a TV movie last year, but she got better and now she's on *Love Sidney*.

PAUL: Who is Swoosie Kurtz?

LISA: She's an actress named after an airplane. I saw her on *Live at Five*.

PAUL: You watch too much television; you should do your homework. Now, put your coat on.

LISA: Daddy, I really do have a bad itch on my leg. Would you scratch it?

75 PAUL: Lisa, you're procrastinating.

LISA: Why do you use words I don't understand? I hate it. You're like Daria Feldman's mother. She always talks in Yiddish to her husband so Daria won't understand.

PAUL: Procrastinating is not Yiddish.

LISA: Well, I don't know what it is.

PAUL: Procrastinating means you don't want to go about your business.

80 LISA: I don't go to business. I go to school.

PAUL: What I mean is you want to hang around here until you and I are late for dinner and your mother's angry and it's too late for you to do your homework.

LISA: I do not.

PAUL: Well, it sure looks that way. Now put your coat on and let's go.

LISA: Daddy.

85 PAUL: Honey, I'm tired. Really, later.

LISA: Why don't you want to talk to me?

PAUL: I do want to talk to you. I promise when we get home we'll have a nice talk.

LISA: No, we won't. You'll read the paper and fall asleep in front of the news.

PAUL: Honey, we'll talk on the weekend, I promise. Aren't I taking you to the theater this weekend? Let me look. (*He takes out an appointment book.*) Yes. Sunday. *Joseph and the Amazing Technicolor Raincoat* with Lisa. Okay, Tiger?

90 LISA: Sure. It's Dreamcoat.

PAUL: What?

LISA: Nothing. I think I see my leg warmers. (*She goes to pick them up, and an odd-looking trophy.*)

PAUL: What's that?

LISA: It's stupid. I was second best at the dance recital, so they gave me this thing. It's stupid.

95 PAUL: Lisa.

LISA: What?

PAUL: What did you want to talk about?

LISA: Nothing.

PAUL: Was it about my missing your recital? I'm really sorry, Tiger. I would have liked to have been here.

100 LISA: That's okay.

PAUL: Honest?

LISA: Daddy, you're prostrastinating.

PAUL: I'm procrastinating. Sit down. Let's talk. How's school?

LISA: Fine.

105 PAUL: You like it?

LISA: Yup.

PAUL: You looking forward to camp this summer?

LISA: Yup.

PAUL: Is Daria Feldman going back?

110 LISA: Nope.

PAUL: Why not?

LISA: I don't know. We can go home now. Honest, my foot doesn't itch anymore.

PAUL: Lisa, you know what you do in business when it seems like there's nothing left to say? That's when you really start talking. Put a bid on the table.

LISA: What's a bid?

115 PAUL: You tell me what you want and I'll tell you what I've got to offer. Like Monopoly. You want Boardwalk, but I'm only willing to give you the Railroads. Now, because you are my daughter I'd throw in Water Works and Electricity. Understand, Tiger?

LISA: No. I don't like board games. You know, Daddy, we could get Space Invaders for our home for thirty-five dollars. In fact, we could get an Osborne System for two thousand. Daria Feldman's parents . . .

PAUL: Daria Feldman's parents refuse to talk to Daria, so they bought a computer to keep Daria busy so they won't have to speak in Yiddish. Daria will probably grow up to be a homicidal maniac lesbian prostitute.

LISA: I know what the word prostitute means.

PAUL: Good. *(Pause.)* You still haven't told me about school. Do you still like your teacher?

120 LISA: She's okay.

PAUL: Lisa, if we're talking try to answer me.

LISA: I am answering you. Can we go home now, please?

PAUL: Damn it, Lisa, if you want to talk to me . . . Talk to me!

LISA: I can't wait till I'm old enough so I can make my own money and never have to see you again. Maybe I'll become a prostitute.

125 PAUL: Young lady, that's enough.

LISA: I hate you, Daddy! I hate you! *(She throws her trophy into the trash bin.)*

PAUL: What'd you do that for?

LISA: It's stupid.

PAUL: Maybe I wanted it.

130 LISA: What for?

PAUL: Maybe I wanted to put it where I keep your dinosaur and the picture you made of Mrs. Kimbel with the chicken pox.

LISA: You got mad at me when I made that picture. You told me I had to respect Mrs. Kimbel because she was my teacher.

PAUL: That's true. But she wasn't my teacher. I liked her better with the chicken pox. *(Pause.)* Lisa, I'm sorry. I was very wrong to miss your recital, and you don't have to become a prostitute. That's not the type of profession Miss Judy has in mind for you.

LISA: *(mumbles)* No.

135 PAUL: No. *(Pause.)* So Talia Robbins is really happy her father moved out?

LISA: Talia Robbins picks open the eighth-grade lockers during gym period. But she did that before her father moved out.

PAUL: You can't always judge someone by what they do or what they don't do. Sometimes you come home from dancing school and run upstairs and shut the door, and when I finally get to talk to you, everything is "okay" or "fine." Yup or nope?

LISA: Yup.

PAUL: Sometimes, a lot of times, I come home and fall asleep in front of the television. So you and I spend a lot of time being a little scared of each other. Maybe?

140 LISA: Maybe.

PAUL: Tell you what. I'll make you a tender offer.

LISA: What?

PAUL: I'll make you a tender offer. That's when one company publishes in the newspaper that they want to buy another company. And the company that publishes is called the Black Knight because they want to gobble up the poor little company. So the poor little company needs to be rescued. And then a White Knight comes along and makes a bigger and better offer so the shareholders won't have to tender shares to the Big Black Knight. You with me?

LISA: Sort of.

145 PAUL: I'll make you a tender offer like the White Knight. But I don't want to own you. I just want to make a much better offer. Okay?

LISA: *(sort of understanding)* Okay. *(Pause. They sit for a moment.)* Sort of, Daddy, what do you think about? I mean, like when you're quiet what do you think about?

PAUL: Oh, business usually. If I think I made a mistake or if I think I'm doing okay. Sometimes I think about what I'll be doing five years from now and if it's what I hoped it would be five years ago. Sometimes I think about what your life will be like, if Mount Saint Helen's will erupt again. What you'll become if you'll study penmanship or word processing. If you speak kindly of me to your psychiatrist when you are in graduate school. And how the hell I'll pay for your graduate school. And sometimes I try and think what it was I thought about when I was your age.

LISA: Do you ever look out your window at the clouds and try to see which kinds of shapes they are? Like one time, honest, I saw the head of Walter Cronkite in a flower vase. Really! Like look don't those kinda look like if you turn it upside down, two big elbows or two elephant trunks dancing?

PAUL: Actually still looks like Walter Cronkite in a flower vase to me. But look up a little. See the one that's still moving? That sorta looks like a whale on a thimble.

150 LISA: Where?

PAUL: Look up to your right.

LISA: I don't see it. Where?

PAUL: The other way.

LISA: Oh, yeah! There's the head and there's the stomach. Yeah! *(Lisa picks up her trophy.)* Hey, Daddy.

155 PAUL: Hey, Lisa.

LISA: You can have this thing if you want it. But you have to put it like this, because if you put it like that it is gross.

PAUL: You know what I'd like? So I can tell people who come into my office why I have this gross stupid thing on my shelf, I'd like it if you could show me your dance recital.

LISA: Now?

PAUL: We've got time. Mother said she won't be home till late.

160 LISA: Well, Daddy, during a lot of it I freeze and the big girl in front dances.

PAUL: Well, how 'bout the number you were doing when I walked in?

LISA: Well, see, I have parts for a lot of people in that one, too.

PAUL: I'll dance the other parts.

LISA: You can't dance.

165 PAUL: Young lady, I played Yvette Mimieux in a *Hasty Pudding Show.*[1]

LISA: Who's Yvette Mimieux?

PAUL: Watch more television. You'll find out. *(Paul stands up.)* So I'm ready. *(He begins singing.)* "Nothing could be finer than to be in Carolina."

LISA: Now I go. In the morning. And now you go. Dum-da.

PAUL: *(obviously not a tap dancer)* Da-da-dum.

170 LISA: *(whines)* Daddy!

PAUL: *(mimics her)* Lisa! Nothing could be finer . . . .

---

[1] Shows put on by the Hasty Pudding Club of Harvard University at the Hasty Pudding Theatre in Harvard Square. A 150-year-old tradition, the shows are famous for their use of a completely male cast, with female roles being played by men dressed as women.

LISA: That looks dumb.

PAUL: Oh, yeah? You think they do this better in *The Amazing Minkcoat?* No way! Now you go—da da da dum.

LISA: Da da da dum.

175 PAUL: If I had Aladdin's lamp for only a day, I'd make a wish . . .

LISA: Daddy, that's maudlin!

PAUL: I know it's maudlin. And here's what I'd say:

LISA and PAUL: I'd say that "nothing could be finer than to be in Carolina in the moooooooooooornin'."

READING AND REACTING

1. How would you describe the relationship between Paul and his daughter? Does this relationship change during the course of the play?

2. How would you characterize Paul? Would you describe him as loving? Arrogant? Distant? Preoccupied? Or would you describe him in some other way?

3. During the first half of the play, Lisa wants to have a conversation, and her father doesn't. At what point does the situation change? What do you think causes this change?

4. Do you find any of Paul's comments to Lisa—for example, his telling her that her tap dance looked "kind of sexy"— inappropriate or unusual? How would you explain these remarks?

5. What is the main point of this play? What other points are developed?

6. At one point in the play, Paul says that he performed in a Hasty Pudding Club show, suggesting that he attended Harvard University. This, along with his preoccupation with business, would seem to suggest that he and his family are privileged. What else suggests the family's social status? Does the main point of this play apply primarily to affluent families, or can it apply to all families, regardless of income level?

7. What is the significance of the play's title? In what way does it express the play's main theme?

8. Do any of the characters change during the course of the play? If so, what is the significance of these changes?

9. What is the central conflict of the play? In what way is it resolved?

10. The play begins with Lisa dancing alone and ends with Paul and Lisa dancing together. What is the significance of this ending? Can you think of another ending that would be more effective?

11. **JOURNAL ENTRY** Do you think the relationship between Paul and Lisa will be better in the future? Or, after all is said and done, will it remain the same?

12. **Critical Perspective** According to playwright Arthur Miller, "drama is one of the things that makes possible a solution to the problem of socializing people." In other words, drama addresses the "dilemma of living together" and helps people resolve the conflict between their "own instincts and the social necessity."

In what way does *Tender Offer* address the conflict between instincts and social necessity? Is this conflict resolved?

Related Works: "Barn Burning" (p. 234), "Daddy" (p. 712), *The Shape of a Girl* (p. 1348)

◊ **Joan MacLeod** (1954–   ) was born in North Vancouver, British Columbia, where she has lived most of her life. She studied at the University of Victoria and the University of British Columbia before working as a writer in residence at Toronto's Tarragon Theatre. Her plays have been performed extensively and translated into five languages. MacLeod is active in sponsoring and resettling refugees, and aspects of this concern are seen in her writing, including in her Governor General's Award–winning *Amigo's Blue Guitar*, which premiered at the Tarragon Theatre in 1990. Her latest play, *Homechild*, is the story of a dysfunctional family told in the present day and in flashbacks. It premiered in January 2006 in Toronto. Joan MacLeod is a professor in the Department of Writing, University of Victoria.

JOAN MACLEOD

The Shape of a Girl
(2001)

The Shape of a Girl is a one act, one character play. Braidie is a fifteen-year-old female. The running time is approximately eighty minutes; there is no intermission.

The original set was a gravel beach with a large and beautiful driftwood tree upstage.

Darkness, a bell sounds from the distance, spot up on Braidie, she speaks to her absent brother Trevor.

BRAIDIE: I woke up this morning to this sound. This sound that feels far away one second then from right inside my gut the next. Very pure with the potential to be extremely creepy. But before I've even opened my eyes this other thing worms its way in and wreaks its usual havoc: the voice of mum.

I tell you Trevor, she's gotten even worse since you left. She is yelling that THIS *is* IT. What IT is I still haven't figured out. At this point in my life being kicked out would be incredible. All I know is her voice chiseled, no burrowed into my brain before I was fully conscious. By the time I'm actually awake the voice of mum has reached this pitch that is making the panelling beside my bed vibrate. *Braidie—I have had* IT!

And then I remembered that day, that truly outstanding day Trevor when you told mum that in another life her voice is going to come back as an ear wig. I was thinking of that exact thing when that sound comes again and this time I know what it is. The blind are back, back at their summer camp across the bay—which is highly weird because it's hardly April. That sound is the gong that tells the blind folks to get up or come for porridge. It just seems like it's really close, sound carrying across water and all that.

And for some reason today, on this particular morning, at this particular point in time, after living on this stupid island my whole life, I am acutely aware for the first time that sound carries across water BOTH ways. Did that ever dawn on you? Did you ever have this really ugly image of mum's voice snaking around the blind camp? There they are: lying on their bunk beds, innocent as pie. *You're your own worst enemy!* That'll get them sitting up or worse yet shuffling off to the cook shack, mum's voice attacking them from above like some crow gone nuts. *Keep your shoulders back! You are walking like an ape!*

5   I am thinking of all these things Trevor and how I wish I could talk to you about it. I wish you were here, asleep in your room. You, big brother, with the unparalleled ability to sleep until three in the afternoon three months in a row; you who can drive all the way to your place in Whistler using only your peripheral vision. I am thinking of all this stuff then all of a sudden this seaplane lands, right outside the deck. I pretend, just like we always did, that the plane is here to kill us. BAM! BAM! BAM!—it'll dive-bomb the whole island. Bullets will explode the mattress around me, outline my arms, my legs.

That is how my day begins, that is how I greet the morning. And from across the water the gong from the camp sounds again. I think, briefly, very briefly, about actually going to school. I also contemplate apologizing to mum for the basic snarkiness of my disposition—all inherited of course—but she's already left for work. Then I'm pretending we're all Muslims or Buddhist monks or anything except who we are. And that the gong is calling us to prayer or at least ending this round.

That the sound means—STOP, don't move a muscle, help is on the way.

*

I watch the school bus come and go. I haven't been to school in a
week now. Adrienne always waits until the last minute to climb
aboard. She looks tall and grumpy. Mum says I need to make more
friends. She reminds me that in grade five I almost had a heart attack
because Adrienne and I had different teachers for the first time, the
first time since preschool. In preschool Annie made a point of trying
to let other kids sit beside Adrienne at circle and I'd just freak. And
Annie and me, we'd have to go off together for a quiet time in her
rocking chair. She smelled like play dough. I'd bury my head in her
shirt and I'd blubber all over Annie. The world was ending. I love
Adrienne so much I used to worry I was a lesbian and when dad would
say stuff like *you two sure are joined at the hip!* I thought he was worried
that I was a lesbian too.

If Adrienne jumped off the Lions Gate Bridge would you? All over the
world, parents have been posing this question to their children forever.
I used to think I'd want to be dead if mum or dad died. Now I actually
imagine them dead so that I'll be able to stay out late and do what I
want. If Adrienne jumped off the Lions Gate I wouldn't follow BUT—I
would spend the rest of my life writing poems about her short one.
And explaining the devastating effect that her death had on, well, her
obviously. And me. I'm not the suicidal type. Even if I was a complete
mess and my brain had turned to jello I wouldn't want anyone pulling
the plug.

10   Mum would pull the plug on me in a second. Remember that
Trevor. Make sure mum doesn't pull the plug.

So the bus is gone and mum is gone and even though it is my
intention to at least try and write a poem I end up flipping on the TV.
I watch one of those really bad shows about really bad things that
happen to really depressingly normal people. We're still not allowed
cable so the reception is just rancid—everybody's foreheads have gone
alien and bodies all shivery—like when you'd try to zap down
something racy from Pay. The show's called MOST DANGEROUS AND
AWFUL MOMENTS EVER.

They're showing this speedboat, this speedboat in Florida
somewhere and it's heading full speed, dead ahead, for this big
bleacher full of spectators. God knows what the problem with the boat
is but the guy driving it is yelling and waving his hands, warning the
people in the stands to get the hell out of the way. The boat smashes
right into the crowd—chaos. I tell you—blood and guts and totally
nuts.

And I was thinking of this poet, this poet I have recently
discovered called Stevie Smith. Not a guy Stevie, a girl Stevie. I was
thinking of this thing she said that I loved, that reminded me of my

friends and me. This thing about not waving but drowning. I was thinking of that when the rabbit ears sort of shake, almost like they're one of those divining things and all of a sudden the whole scene changes on the TV.

And there we are. A group of girls—just like me and Adrienne and Jackie and Amber. A group of girls with hair and jeans and jackets. *They are not waving, they are drowning.* And this group of girls on the TV starts waving, right on cue. Weird I'm thinking. This is highly weird.

15   And what feels even stranger is that the picture is actually clear for once, from the neck down at least. But their faces are blurry, smudged, almost as though someone has taken an eraser and tried to rub them out.

And then I realize who these girls are. They are supposed to look distorted because they are young offenders and we aren't allowed to see who they are. They are accused of assault, accused of murder, accused of killing another girl—a fourteen-year-old girl. One is wearing these big high heel runners like Amber's. They are all standing out front of the courthouse while the judge is taking a break. They are laughing like maniacs. Me and Adrienne often laugh like maniacs. Honestly, totally unprovoked.

Then the news guy starts talking about how one saw her dad murdered when she was six. And another girl's dad was also murdered. And I feel stupid to have ever thought we have anything in common. In fact it pisses me off that they are trying to pass themselves off as normal. And even though it's illegal to do so, I can imagine their faces: slutty eyes, chapped lips. Then one girl waves again and yells *hi* and you just know she's making goofy faces just like Adrienne and me did when we saw the Canucks, when we thought we were making our debut on national television.

I don't know why I have to find out more about those girls, I just do. They are all over the news. Always in a group, always from the back or with their jackets pulled over their heads. I don't want to look at the victim, it's too depressing. But she is everywhere too—as a baby with her dad, as a regular weird kid on holiday, then one of those blown up yearbook pictures that always mean someone is either a movie star or dead.

And then that gong across the bay starts ringing again. Except this time it sounds like a summons, like someone is calling me.

Lights up on set—Braidie is on a beach, perhaps leaning against a log, looking out at the water, she is wearing jeans, a warm jacket, a tangle of blackberry vines and bush rise up steeply on the bank behind.

20   Hello! I'm here . . . Attention: Braidie has landed.

Braidie looks upstage.

But up at the camp the shutters are all still up, the flag pole is bare, not a blind guy in sight. And you know that gong? It's just the same old bell. I was expecting something out of Tarzan. So it's me, solo. Braidie on the beach. Remember how much we used to love coming here to spy?

Braidie holds her arms, straight out in front.

Trevor, let's be blind.

Shutting her eyes.

Shut your eyes and you can hear the summer. The little kids arriving, so wired up. And the older ones with their dogs, those outstanding dogs. I love Buster but I've always felt he was an inferior species of animal. I mean I've never seen a seeing-eye dog eating goose shit or sniffing up another retriever.

A bell rings softly in the distance, Braidie opens her eyes and looks up the bank, watching a memory from years ago.

Trevor? Did you hear that? Do you see? It's Sofie, twelve years old. The camp is deserted like now. It's winter. I am below her, also twelve. Adrienne is up the hill beside Sofie, always nearly one year older. Sofie wants to ring the bell because she thinks Adrienne might kill her and I think Adrienne might kill Sofie too. I watch Adrienne watching Sofie. Adrienne is so mad her mouth is shaking. Sofie is watching me. She has no idea my body has turned to concrete. I can't move and I can't shout. All I can do is see.

*

Braidie goes back in time, she is eight years old, she gallops around until she falls over, exhausted and happy.

25   We are in love, we are all forever in love. We spend hours drawing them. We call ourselves by our new names in secret: Rainbow Rider, Lucky Lady, Thunder. We cram our pockets and lunchkits with them— piles and piles of ponies. Little brushes for their tiny pink manes, their purple tails.

Sofie is the new girl in grade two. Her horse name is Trotter and Toto and Lala and Gypsy. Because Sofie doesn't just fall in love with horses and have a horse name like the rest of us. Sofie becomes a horse or sometimes an entire herd of horses. She gallops out to the playground for recess; she trots down the halls. She talks by doing whinnies and stomping her feet. She even eats her lunch like it's a feedbag, without using her hands.

We are amazed by Sofie, how she can spend hours, entire afternoons, down there on all fours. How she never cares about who sees. *Good little horsie.* That's what Adrienne says and then Adrienne is flying, having been bucked by Sofie the horse onto the couch. And then Rachel has a turn on Sofie's back and Sofie sends her flying too. We love Sofie the horse. We make tiny braids all over her head; we paint rainbows on her cheeks.

And then one day, one normal un-special day Adrienne comes to school and announces that it's penalty day. We don't know what penalty day is. Adrienne explains that on penalty day one girl is chosen and everyone is mean to that one girl for the whole day. *Why?* Adrienne doesn't know. It's just a part of school. Adrienne offers to go first. We get to be mean to her first. I want to go first too.

At first penalty day is hard to figure out. There are a lot of rules. The person we have to be mean to has fleas of course. Everyone has to write FP for flea proof on their hand.

Braidie, as a teenager again.

30   You know something Trevor? By the end of grade four penalty day had become as complex as World War Two. But who the enemy was had become entirely simple. Now all the girls had FP written on their hands, all the girls but one. I don't know why it was Sofie. It just was.

*

It is the next day, Braidie is settling in on the beach.

THE VOICE OF MUM came in weak today, this annoying little signal that was barely registering. I believe I told her I was sick—perhaps I surfaced long enough to tell her school was out of the question. I sense she senses that school and myself are on our last legs. Maybe I'll be like you, try homeschooling. Maybe I'll move up to Whistler too.

Mum and me did have a big blow out last night, a major blow out. She says to me, all weird and cheery—*the teen centre is having a dance this weekend. Why don't you go?* I point out I went last time and that it was BEYOND repulsive.

She points out that I never actually went inside, that I hung out with Adrienne in the parking lot. How does she know?

Because she drove by—MORE than once. She cruised the teen centre like an undercover cop or a pervert. Life with her is unbearable, a lesson in indignity.

35   In today's papers there are no pictures of those young offenders. I tell you—it's almost a relief. You remember when the girl was killed Trevor, you were still living here. How she was beat up by a group of girls and this guy and then finished off a few minutes later by that boy and this one girl who went back for more. The ones that watched the girl get beat up, they aren't accused of anything. To be accused you have to have gotten in there, down and dirty. I suppose that to be a teenager, even to be a little kid, is to often see very hideous behaviour from your peers.

If you reported everyone you would certainly have to watch your back at all times and look no one in the face, ever. You would have to go through your entire life using only your peripheral vision.

The girls who beat her up, the girls who are on trial for assault, they used to hang out at Walmart. They also hang out UNDER COVER. This sounds cooler than it is. Because under cover really is just that—a covered area at the school just like we had for playing hopscotch when it rained. But these really are tough girls. They make like they are a gang and that they're all hooked up with the gangs in New York and L.A.

On Granville Mall once Adrienne and me were followed by some tough girls, these wipe out girls. They wanted us to give them some money and Adrienne said no way. They said they were going to get us. One gobbed on the back of Adrienne's jeans. But we weren't afraid of them. We just thought they were idiots.

These girls in Victoria, they're a mess. Some are in foster care, some have been doing the McFamily thing for a long long time. Some have already been up on charges, one for lighting fire to another girl's hair. The fight with the dead girl starts when someone butts out a cigarette on her forehead. This is terrible enough in itself but it also opens a door. *Look what I did? Now just watch, just wait and see . . .* It's surreal. And that's not fair to say because it's exactly the opposite—it's totally real. I mean it happened. And what scares me, what freaks me right out Trevor is that I know the way in. I don't know how else to put it. I know the way in.

40   The human body is what? Eighty percent water? That kills me. We're like these melons with arms and legs. Well eighty percent of the female brain is pure crap. We're constantly checking each other out, deciding who goes where, who's at the bottom.

When I look at her picture, when I look at the picture of the dead girl in the paper, part of me gets it. And I hate it that I do; I hate to be even partly composed of that sort of information. But right now, if you put me in a room filled with girls, girls my age that I've never seen before in my life—I could divide them all up. I could decide who goes where and just where I fit in without anyone even opening their mouth. They could be from this island, they could be from Taiwan. It doesn't matter. Nobody would have to say a word. You know something Trevor? I could have divided up a room like that when I was in grade two. Grade fucking two.

*

When the lights come up Braidie is ten years old, being Adrienne, perhaps standing up the bank, up high.

No one is to have contact of any kind with IT *from first period until lunch. If you have to address* IT *do so during homeroom. On the school bus* IT *has to sit on the fourth seat on the left. If IT talks to any boys it will be dealt with by me. ITS lunch today will be divided between Amber, Braidie and Jackie. Case closed. IT will make no comments and will not be allowed to look at me anymore as of now.*

Braidie leaps down.

Adrienne then turns her back on Sofie, to show us she means business. Adrienne always means business. So the five of us sit there, waiting for the school bus.

Yesterday means nothing now; it means nothing that we spent all day Sunday together and had a good time. There is a brand new code every day. I spend most of my time trying to figure out what the code is.

—*What if she . . .*
—*IT.*
—*What if IT has to go to the bathroom.*

45   This is Amber interjecting when she shouldn't. Adrienne ignores her. Adrienne often ignores what isn't important. And it works.

Yesterday we let ourselves into one of the houses Adrienne's mum is trying to sell. *Let's take off our tops.* Adrienne is lifting up her teeshirt. She is wearing a white bra covered with tiny pink flowers. Mine is identical. Sofie yanks up her blouse. She is wearing a rolled up undershirt.

—*IT'S A SPORTS BRA, says Sofie.*
—*IT thinks that's a bra.*
—*DON'T CALL ME THAT.*
—*Don't call me that.*

The house is freezing. The beds are all bare. The mattresses and the ocean silver. Something shitty's going to happen. Something shitty could happen here. *Tell IT to get us something from the fridge.* And Sofie does. She comes back with a box of baking soda and a jar of relish. The lousy food is Sofie's fault. Maybe she should've broken in early and stocked the fridge. I would've. I would've done that if I was in her position. But Sofie doesn't have a clue. She has no sense of how to avoid anything.

A sports bra, says Adrienne, is a defense against guys. The really high end sports bras repel guys, totally impenetrable. A good sports bra will catapult guys across the room. THAT is NOT a sports bra. It's a little Miss Undie Undie shirt.

Ha ha. Another one of Sofie's bad habits, ha-ha-ing all the time. She sticks her fingers into the jar of relish. *Ooohhhh Gross.* Adrienne practically has a heart attack. It is gross. Sofie slopping up a jar of hamburger relish. Except now Adrienne also finds it funny. And all of a sudden everyone is laughing and Sofie is allowed to be our friend again.

So we sit there all afternoon in our bras or our phony bras, fingers in the relish. Last year we took off all our clothes and sat together in a dry bathtub. I don't know why. We just did.

—You have to swim across this lake to get there. Then you'll come to a little door in the side of a tree.

50   This is Adrienne, doing what we always do. Designing a place, a home for the four of us. A dream house where we will all live together forever.

My dream house always looks the same—one big room that is divided by gauzy white curtains, sort of like a swishy hospital ward. There are no mothers and our dads will show up with supplies only when we want them to. Boys are banished. We do not want boys like the ones we see now, getting on the school bus. Adrienne, Sofie, Amber and me are first picked up and last home everyday on the school bus.

Braidie, as a teenager again.

You were there too Trevor. At the back with the boys: throwing pencil cases and shoes and sweaters out the window. You had a handmade sling shot that was the envy of everyone. And a pocketful of smooth black stones. You were always pummeling each other, always mouthing off to Gustaf the driver. So you probably didn't notice how we sat around Sofie. And how still she was, with her eyes straight ahead. Behind her Jackie was kicking her calves, something was smeared in her hair. The girls across from her were chanting but you'd have to listen hard to hear it. While you boys in the back were slugging it out we were in the front, almost still, always the good little girls.

*

A few days later.

The voice of mum and I went out for dinner last night. As usual Dad— also known as Planet Dad—is away on business, so it's going to be, and I quote—*just us girls.*

One would think that dinner would mean ordering food, eating food, paying for food. Not so. Mum insists, first, that we sit at the same table. Two, that I don't read. Three, four, and five that I get my hair out of my face, sit up properly and stop looking as though I'm planning my escape. And six, she wants us to *reconnect*, have ourselves a little chat. I explain, patiently, that I'd rather be shot from a cannon than hang around and see what she really has up her stupid sleeve.

55   And so it comes out: the school has phoned her at work. They are seeking an explanation for my unexplained absences. I explain, patiently, that I am now homeschooling.

     All apparently news to mum. And news to the school.

     I am part way through stating just what I think homeschooling should be when the voice of mum jumps to her feet and starts doing the famous whisper-shriek. *This is the last straw, the end of the road, the end of the rope, the absolute limit.* Then she goes. Leaves me sitting there alone with Terry the cook. Terry leers from the kitchen. He cleans his teeth with a business card and winks at me.

     The Braidie Institute Of Higher Learning. Lesson One—Current Events.

Braidie holds up a newspaper.

Girls Turning On Each Other
Bullied To Death
Girls Killing Girls

     These are the headlines, these are what put us on the map. Like the Stanley Cup riots only worse, way worse.

60   The articles go on and on about how girls are getting meaner. The attacks more vicious. I look at those girls. I look at the pictures of those young offenders until the newspaper goes all squirrelly. If you look at them in bits they are regular girls: these lips, that hair, those kind of jeans.

     If someone could invent a laser to zap the rotten parts they would be entirely normal. Young offenders. *Sorry—I didn't mean to offend you!* Adrienne and me would run into people on purpose on the ferry so that we could say that. *Ooops! No offense . . .* We thought that was hysterical.

A girl in the shape of a monster
A monster in the shape of a girl

     That, Trevor, is poetry. It is also a riddle that gets played out in Victoria. Because that's how they treat her—like a monster. Only they're the monsters, get it? Because they phoned her up. *Guess what we're doing? Wanna come?* It's like wolves pretending to be some animal that's hurt, maybe a little calf or a goat. This wasn't a case of someone in the wrong place at the wrong time. This was planned, organized.

     And the girl, she knows they're one scary bunch but she goes. Maybe she is pleased that someone phoned, someone wanted her to do something. *Let's meet here . . .* She even brings her pyjamas. Her pyjamas and diary and Charlie perfume are buckled into her back pack.

Braidie goes back in time, she is twelve years old.

Sofie walks like a cripple, little quarters of blood on her heel, soaking into her white socks. Sofie wears her runners too small because her feet are too big. She is accused of watching the girls get undressed in gym. But I watch too. I want to see who else has hair under their arms or who has thighs as big as mine. I talked to her after volley ball. I told her, I did the best I could.

—*Sofie don't go on the field trip.* See—I said it: in plain English.
—*Why?*
—*Just don't.*
—*But we have to write an essay.*

65   This is pure Sofie, putting homework ahead of life or death. I tell you—she's an extremely exasperating person. We are all going to see *Hamlet* for the field trip, at a theatre in town. It's not the real *Hamlet;* it's a phony version for kids.

FOR EMERGENCY ONLY—SORTIE DU SECOURS. I have studied that sign ever since I can remember. It is written over top of some windows in the bus. I sit three rows down from Sofie. Jackie and Adrienne are behind me.

Sofie is sitting with Lorna. Lorna's dad owns the store on our island; sometimes she works there. We don't know Lorna. We don't even think of Lorna as an actual person.

The ocean shrinks and glitters as we head over the Lions Gate. You can see where we live, lying out there in the strait, all wrapped up in mist. It looks uninhabited, prehistoric. Adrienne and Lorna have switched places. Adrienne is whispering something to Sofie. Sofie is looking dead ahead. Adrienne leans into Sofie so that Sofie is squished up against the side. Sofie's face turns grey.

FOR EMERGENCY ONLY. Sofie pushes the window on the bus. It fans out unnaturally from the bottom. Sofie hoists herself up, her head is out. Sofie is going to jump out the window. The ocean is hundreds of feet below.

70   I shut my eyes. And Sofie is falling, cannon-balling over the side of the bridge, her clothes parachute around her, a gigantic flower. I open my eyes. Sofie hasn't gone over the side of anything. Her bum is stuck in the window of the bus.

Amber and Adrienne and me and Jackie—we laugh so hard we nearly puke. Sofie is all weird and breathing heavy. Then she pushes out a sound that is hardly human. *Ha-ha.*

The bus driver is grabbing Sofie by the sweater. He pulls her in. *What the hell do you think you're doing?* Adrienne watches Sofie. *Nothing,* Sofie says. *Fooling around.*

Sofie isn't allowed to see the play. We watch Ophelia load herself up with flowers and sail off to meet her maker. We make burp noises except when Hamlet's around. Hamlet's cute.

When Hamlet gets going on one of his long speeches we go *oh oh oh oh* like we are Hamlet's own girlfriend. Then this lady usher comes and tells us we have to be quiet. She's a total bitch.

*

A few days later.

75 The first week is now history at the Braidie Institute. Two weeks now without Adrienne.

This is me without my friends. I am nothing, zero, zip. A black mark on the horizon.

If I had to I could live on this beach for a long time—live on berries and fish and kelp. Trevor, remember how we'd plant ourselves up there in the bank? The perfect camouflage—we would spy on the blind just doing their everyday stuff: the little kids going ballistic, the old guys sucking back the lemonade. Remember them swimming? Bobbing around in their lifejackets, unaware that the sun is descending in some spectacular fashion. They had that way of turning their faces up to the sky—all weird and happy.

It floored me Trevor. I mean I'm sure their lives are usually even more dull and shitty and hideous than the rest of us but I used to imagine myself blind—how careful I would be. For my eighteenth birthday I would be given a dog. I would call him Henry. *There goes Henry and Braidie.* I never think about all the stuff I wouldn't be able to do, what I wouldn't be able to see. For once I am focusing on only the positive. The voice of mum would be proud of me.

Braidie goes back in time, she is twelve years old.

We are blind: Adrienne, Amber, Jackie and me. We have made a huge pile of sand and leaves. We cover our eyes with a pair of old panty hose and leap off the bank. We turn each other around and around to see if we can point in the right direction—at the beach, the mountains, each other. We feel each other's faces, stomachs, breasts. *Definitely Braidie.* If it wasn't winter I would swim away, swim blind into the middle of the sea.

80 *This is boring.* Adrienne takes off her blind fold. We take off ours. We climb up the bank and hide in the laurel leaves. We think about going to the store to steal something: gum, matches, bath oil bubbles that squish in our pockets and leak all over our shirts. Sometimes Adrienne steals change and cans of beer from the people she baby-sits for. I confine my crimes to the General Store and believe I am a slightly less bad person.

Adrienne goes to light a smoke then stops. *Look . . . .* And we look out on the beach and there is Sofie. *What is It doing?* We haven't seen Sofie in ages. *God, look at* IT! Adrienne makes it sound as if Sofie is out there killing something. I squint in on her but Sofie is just hunched over a little book. Maybe Sophie still draws pictures of horses. Maybe she also likes trying to write poems and stories. The possibility that Sofie and I might have even one thing in common makes a little shift in me.

I'm going to get It. Adrienne is climbing down the vines. Sofie looks up and in the wrong direction: pure Sofie. And Adrienne is right there, grabbing Sofie by the ponytail.

What do you think you're doing?

Nothing. Sofie slams her book shut, she examines her feet.

85   *What's in the book?*

Nothing.

And Sofie tries to run, to bolt down the beach. Adrienne still has a hold of her hair, she pushes Sofie down. Sofie's head makes a little smack sound on the rock. It sounds phony—like a slap in the movies. And then her head is bleeding and the blood looks phony too. And then we are all around Sofie. This is it. Adrienne is going to do something. And we are going to see. Then Adrienne is holding a covered elastic and a tangle of Sofie's hair.

Sofie is gone, running. And then everybody is running after her, someone is yelling *No No No . . .* It isn't me.

Sofie mashes open her jeans falling on the barnacles. She starts climbing back up the blackberries and Adrienne is right there, grabbing on to her ankle.

90   I understand too now what Sofie wants to do. Sofie is going to ring the bell at the blind camp. You can hear that bell all over the island. But then Adrienne screams and we all stop breathing.

We watch Adrienne slide down the bank while Sofie scrambles away. We peer down at Adrienne on the sand, all curled up and quiet. *She's dead,* Amber announces.

Braidie, as a teenager again.

But I knew Adrienne had just been stalled, shot, hit by a smooth black stone. And that you were there, you were with us Trevor, up in the maple tree. How much did you know all along? How much did you see? Adrienne came back from the dead a moment later. *Your brother is such an asshole.* Adrienne knew it was you but somehow it becomes Sofie's fault too. *Sofie and Trevor probably do it together, do it twenty times a day.*

We all lay there on the sand, joined at the head, spokes in a wheel. In my pocket, a pink plastic diary and a key. Of course it belonged to Sofie. I didn't show it to anyone. But I felt entitled, I found it, it was mine to keep and mine to see.

What was Sofie doing as we lay there on the beach? Were the others thinking about her too? How she might be stumbling in the back door of her house, trying to keep the blood and the dirt from getting over everything. *I fell, I slipped, I whacked my head on an alder tree.* We all understand that Sofie telling the truth isn't even a remote possibility.

Braidie goes back in time, she is twelve years old.

95   Jackie shifts down, rests her head on my stomach. I place my head on Adrienne's. We make a chain. First Amber laughs then Jackie, all around the circle. I can feel the laughter and the skin of Adrienne's body, warm against my ear. And then, I'm laughing too and when we stop there's just our breath, rising and falling. I match my breath to Adrienne's perfectly.

*

The next day.

Mum comes thundering down the stairs last night to announce she has given up. I point out, as calmly as possible—*If you're going to give up on someone you just give up. You don't tell them about it.* Mum goes berserk. All this screaming and crying and gnashing of teeth. Then she notices the pictures, some of the newspaper clippings tacked up around my room. *I'm studying.*

And then she's screaming—*Cut the lip! Cut all the nonsense about homeschooling.* And she is inside my room, mine, for the first time in a year and a half. A complete violation of my rights. *What is this stuff?* She is looking at this cover from the Vancouver Province. *At least* SHE *has a nice haircut.*

She's a killer—I tell her.

And mum takes me by the shoulders—*Look.* She stares right into me, then her eyes fill up and she touches my cheek. *Braidie?* It's worse than anything, the voice of mum trying to be my buddy, trying to be half-way sweet.

100   *Get out.* Her hands drop to her side. *This is my room.* But she isn't moving. She gets me so pissed off I just start flailing.

—*Braidie use your words.*
—*All right. Fuck you mother.*

And she gets it, she finally gets it. She slams the door behind her. She's giving up on me.

I look at the girl, the picture of the girl who did it. The one in Victoria who held her head underwater until all was quiet. The one who held a smoke in one hand and held the girl under with the other, her foot on her back. She bragged about it. Maybe she made the telling of it into a joke because she doesn't know how else to try it out. *Did you hear the one about . . .* Maybe she just snapped. I do that. I look at the picture again: she's a regular girl.

And she's hanging out on a Friday night in November, 1997—the moon is full, the air is clear. Usually the stars get lost in winter here. But on this night the stars are out, everyone is out, *under cover*, passing a joint, drinking vodka and sprite mixed in a can. Some are watching the sky and waiting because a Russian satellite is going to break through the earth's atmosphere tonight, right over Victoria. It will explode, light up all that black.

But this girl, this regular girl and one other girl are waiting for something else; they are waiting to teach someone a lesson. They've already phoned her up, they've called her out.

105 Because she is big, because she likes *that* boy. Because she is brown and she lost their book; because she doesn't fit and she lies. Because they can.

The girl they're going to get is miserable, that much is clear. Four different schools and two different foster homes in the past year. She keeps returning to family—her parents, her grandma and grandpa. And she keeps running away. And she doesn't know, doesn't get the plot, doesn't understand her part. So it starts.

The ones who watched, maybe they thought it wasn't real. Maybe as they yelled out or laughed they were actually frozen. Maybe they were so glad to not be that girl—whose hair is being held up to a lighter now— that they don't even know how to imagine shouting *stop*. Maybe they think that silence is the ticket, the only way to never end up like the girl.

Even the ones who didn't watch, who just heard about what happened, they carry the silence too—a dark present, passed hand to hand. When they get home maybe they will dream about being blind. Because they can't stand the replays anymore—how the girl looked up and begged for help.

Or maybe it's that boy in Burnaby last winter, how he wrote his goodbye note and climbed the rails on the Putallo Bridge.

110 Or maybe it's Sofie. Because just when you think it was all ancient history it starts again.

Trevor—remember how I went through the first five years of life hiding behind mum's bum whenever we were out in public? That's the trouble with staying silent. I can't move, even when I want to. And I start thinking Adrienne acts for me.

*

Braidie goes back in time, she is fourteen years old.

It is dark now by 4:30. We miss the school bus on purpose so that we can hang out longer in town. *Mum—I'll be on the 6:30 ferry, pick me up . . .* I'm doing what I do everyday after school, what I did practically every day in grade eight and in grade nine too. I am in the parking lot behind the school and I am waiting for Adrienne. High School is just like how movie stars describe making movies—there's a lot of waiting around.

It's raining hard; my hair is soaking wet—unbelievably ugly. There are about thirty of us hanging out. Some of the older guys have cars. These little pools of light—vibrating with music and bodies and smoke. And with Adrienne.

Right now she is in Justin Hannah's dodge Caravan. She loves Justin and Justin, of course, treats her terribly. I think Justin is sort of an idiot. In fact I find a lot of Adrienne's guys are fairly gross.

115 Across from the parking lot everyone else lines up for the bus—shoving and smoking and fooling around. Except for one still shape, holding on to the bus sign like it's some sort of anchor. Sofie always has her hood up, rain or shine. From the back she looks like this giant version of ET. Sofie is something Adrienne seems to have forgotten. At lunch Sofie doesn't go to the cafeteria or behind the gym or the parking lot like the rest of us. She slinks along the edges of the halls; she walks away from the school. She walks around and around. She often eats lunch in a bus shelter, six blocks from our school. She doesn't hang out with other kids. She is certainly doing her very best to be invisible.

I have no idea why I feel I have to keep tabs on Sofie. I just do. Sometimes I follow her around. She has no idea; she has always been a fairly clued out individual. I go to the bus shelter after she's left to check it out. There are little rocks lined up along the sides and she's carved her initials—S.G.—into the seat. No doubt it all is charged with meaning in the weird world of Sofie. Maybe I'll give back her diary. I keep it at the back of my locker, just on the verge of handing it over. I never even finished reading the whole thing. It was too boring—just a regular girl. She doesn't let anyone in on anything.

I watch Sofie board the bus, always first on so that she can sit directly behind the driver. I watch the bus pull away just as Adrienne gets out of Justin's van.

Adrienne lights a cigarette and glares at me. Justin was supposed to give us a ride to the ferry but apparently now this is completely and totally out of the question. We walk—two and a half miles. I get home four hours late, the voice of mum waiting on the dock to tear a strip off of me.

*

A girl in the shape of a monster
A monster in the shape of a girl

It all starts again just three weeks ago, in the girls' bathroom. Right after home room. I walk in. I'm not doing anything, I'm minding my own business, I just have to pee. Sofie is there. Applying this goofy blue eye-liner in a goofy blue line. Then guess-who comes kicking her way out of the end cubicle. Adrienne's been crying; her eyes are rabbity pink. No doubt there has been some new atrocity between her and Justin. *Let's go.* That's me, trying to head her off but Adrienne has already seen Sofie.

—*What are you looking at?* Sofie goes blank. She turns and fixes her sights on the tampax machine. *I asked you a question.* But Sofie is still in statue mode, uninhabited. No doubt Sofie's entire school life is an out of body experience.

120   Adrienne drops her Atlas on Sofie's foot. Sofie doesn't blink.

—*Pick it up.*
—*Let's go.*
—*I said pick it up.*

Do something, say something, anything, fight. Do something, say something, anything, fight . . .

But Sofie just bends over. And I hate her. As soon as she does it I know she's lost. Adrienne kicks Sofie down on all fours. All the work she'd put into being invisible, down the drain. Sofie is entirely visible—her legs are pink, her underwear covered in little blue circles.

Lovely. Sofie the horse. Sofie tries to get up and Adrienne's boot comes down in the centre of Sofie's back. *Did I say you could get up?* Sofie tries to turn her head around but Adrienne grabs her by the shirt. *Maybe the horse needs a drink of water.* Adrienne pulls Sofie over to the toilet.

And yes, finally, Sofie's head is turning, twisting away from Adrienne and . . . turning toward me. *Braidie please.*

You do what you have to do.
You look down.
Like this.

125   And then you navigate your way to the door using only your peripheral vision.

When I walk down the hall, I feel all weird and pukey. I feel like everyone is staring at me. I don't go to English; I just walk around. And then I don't go to Math or P.E. At lunch I go looking for Sofie. I go to the bus shelter. S.G. still carved into the bench. Why wouldn't it be?

After school, when I get on the bus, Adrienne is waiting, waiting for me.

—*Adrienne. What happened?* But she doesn't know what I'm talking about, can't remember, just a regular day. *What happened to Sofie?*
—*Nothing happened.* I see the empty seat behind the driver on the bus, Sofie's seat. A tremor starts, way down low on the floor of the ocean. *With someone like Sofie you never have to actually DO anything.* My hands are shaking, the bus pulls out. *Shut up* says Adrienne. *Stop breathing like a pervert.*

But Adrienne seems miles away now, deflated, her face behind her hair all white and skinny.

And she's gone. The friend I loved is gone. All that's left is the shape of a girl.

130   FOR EMERGENCY ONLY. I push out the window and it fans out from the bottom unnaturally. I puke all down the side of the bus. The driver lets me off. I walk back to school. I go right into the girls' bathroom. I wash my face. When I turn off the tap I hear a sound, from the last cubicle.

Sofie is sitting on the lid of the toilet. Her lips all puffed up and purple. When she sees who it is, she covers her head. *Don't worry . . .* She's acting like I'm going to hit her, which is so crazy. *I never did anything.* I bet she wishes you were there Trevor, hiding out behind the tampax machine, waiting to get off a good shot at me.

Sofie rocks back and forth then all of a sudden she smashes her head into the side of the stall.

We did a good job. Even Sofie hates Sofie.

*

A bell sounds as in the beginning.

Sound carries across water. On that full moon night, in Victoria, the word goes out that a girl was killed, that girl. Maybe there are groups of kids in schoolyards, malls . . . *Really?* And by the time her body is found—hundreds of kids know and hundreds of kids don't tell. Who is the one who told the unthinkable to their mum or their teacher? Who marched into the police station and said *see here, enough is enough?* I'll bet you a million dollars everyone thinks it wasn't a girl.

*

135   I always thought it was the voice of mum that made you escape Trevor. But I'm wondering now if you moved to Whistler to get away from me. In fact you might be ecstatic to know I am well on my way to becoming the official island outcast. I just wanted you to know one thing. One tiny thing that'll probably be the end of me.

Mum is forcing me to abandon homeschooling. I agreed, on the condition that the voice of mum no longer speak to me. So yesterday the now defunct Braidie Institute went on our first and last field trip— to the Island Community Preschool. Remember preschool? Remember what a big deal it was?

They have this snazzy new building now. I'm hanging out at the fence like some kind of psycho. Watching all these kids smash into each other on their trikes and kicking around in the mud puddles. All these nutty four-year-olds doing their usual things. And Annie comes out. Her hair is all grey now. But she is still the same because this boy is hanging off her arm by his teeth and she doesn't even notice. You can tell she still thinks all kids are just dandy.

Then Annie spots me. *Braidie!* You'd think I was God or something. You'd think I was the greatest thing she's ever seen. And Annie comes running over. She smells like play dough. She opens the gate for me.

A spot shines brightly in front of Braidie, she steps into the light.

And I understand for the first time what I have to say and how long I've been practicing.

I wish to report the behaviour of . . .
I fear for . . .
I'm scared. Scared for the safety of another girl. That she might do some-thing crazy. Her name is Sofie. She has been treated in a despicable way by many people . . . including me.

140   Annie doesn't say anything. For the longest time she just nods. And then when she finally does speak it's in this weird whisper because she probably hates me. She will go with me to my school, to the principal. I tell her—*okay.*

She holds me tightly. Maybe she thinks I'm going to escape. Her arms still fit around me.

*

A bell sounds again, then Braidie looks up.

Sound carries across water. The girl in Victoria is discovered after eight days, her body seen floating from the air above. The stories were end-less, the stories about how it all happened. Most of them weren't true. The only real story is the one told by her body, silently. This bruising beneath her eyes, the black nose and cheeks. The broken arm and the star burnt into her forehead.

A bell sounds fourteen times.

Sometimes I dream she got away, swam straight out into the ocean, maybe floated off on a log boom. Where? Not south to the States, not here. I don't know how to imagine it; I don't know where her safe place might be. I only know how to go backwards.

Braidie goes back in time, she is eight years old.

We are eight years old. We are all planting our toes in the edge of the water. We're at the blind beach, it's summer, the water is foamy and brown around our feet. We are all wearing life jackets. Adrienne,

Amber, Sofie and me. The jackets make us feel like we can go anywhere, do anything—deep water, waves, you name it, all these possibilities.

145   We are brave, we are perfect—girls.

READING AND REACTING

1. *The Shape of a Girl* begins with minimal stage directions: the set is "a gravel beach with a large and beautiful driftwood tree upstage." Why is the set so simple? How does it help MacLeod to convey her theme(s)?
2. In what way would you characterize the relationship between Braidie and her mother?
3. How would you describe the relationship between Braidie and Trevor?
4. Is it important to know that the death of the teenage girl in the play is based on an actual event (the murder of Reena Virk in 1997)? What effect does knowing about the event have on you?
5. What is the significance of the play's title? How does it shed light on the play's theme(s)?
6. Throughout the play, Braidie uses flashbacks to explain her long-term friendships. What do these incidents tell us about Braidie, Sofie, and Adrienne?
7. *The Shape of a Girl* is a monologue: only Braidie speaks, although she does reproduce conversations. What does the play gain or lose (if anything) by being a monologue?
8. **JOURNAL ENTRY** Are Braidie's descriptions of the bullying realistic? What about her reasons or lack of reasons for why the bullying occurs?

Related Works: "Simple Recipes" (p. 45), "Stones" (p. 135), "Barn Burning" (p. 234), *Trifles* (p. 948)

◊ **SAMUEL BECKETT** (1906–1989) was born in Dublin to an upper-class Protestant family. He attended Trinity College, Dublin, and after graduation went to Paris, where he became friends with James Joyce. His first novel, *Murphy* (1937), was rejected by 41 publishers. He settled permanently in Paris in 1937 and wrote mainly in French after that date. During World War II, Beckett worked with the French Resistance, and he was awarded the Croix de Guerre and the Médaille de la Résistance. Beckett's greatest novels are the trilogy *Molloy, Malone Dies*, and *The Unnameable* (1951–1953); his most famous play is *Waiting for Godot* (1952), which breaks with all dramatic tradition. Beckett was awarded the Nobel Prize for literature in 1969.

SAMUEL BECKETT

Krapp's Last Tape

(1960)

A late evening in the future.

Krapp's den.

Front centre a small table, the two drawers of which open towards the audience.

Sitting at the table, facing front, i.e. across from the drawers, a wearish old man: Krapp.

Rusty black narrow trousers too short for him. Rusty black sleeveless waistcoat, four capacious pockets. Heavy silver watch and chain. Grimy white shirt open at neck, no collar. Surprising pair of dirty white boots, size ten at least, very narrow and pointed.

White face. Purple nose. Disordered grey hair. Unshaven.

Very near-sighted (but unspectacled). Hard of hearing.

Cracked voice. Distinctive intonation.

Laborious walk.

On the table a tape-recorder with microphone and a number of cardboard boxes containing reels of recorded tapes.

Table and immediately adjacent area in strong white light. Rest of stage in darkness.

Krapp remains a moment motionless, heaves a great sigh, looks at his watch, fumbles in his pockets, takes out an envelope, puts it back, fumbles, takes out a small bunch of keys, raises it to his eyes, chooses a key; gets up and moves to front of table. He stoops, unlocks first drawer, peers into it, feels about inside it, takes out a reel of tape, peers at it, puts it back, locks drawer, unlocks second drawer, peers into it, feels about inside it, takes out a large banana, peers at it, locks drawer, puts keys back in his pocket. He turns, advances to edge of stage, halts, strokes banana, peels it, drops skin at his feet, puts end of banana in his mouth and remains motionless, staring vacuously before him. Finally he bites off the end, turns aside and begins pacing to and fro at edge of stage, in the light, i.e. not more than four or five paces either way, meditatively eating banana. He treads on skin, slips, nearly falls, recovers himself, stoops and peers at skin and finally pushes it, still stooping, with his foot over edge of stage into pit. He resumes his pacing, finishes banana, returns to table, sits down, remains a moment motionless, heaves a great sigh, takes keys from his pockets, raises them to his eyes, chooses key, gets up and moves to front of table, unlocks second drawer, takes out a second large banana, peers at it, locks drawer, puts back keys in his pocket, turns, advances to edge of stage, halts, strokes banana, peels it, tosses skin into pit, puts end of banana in his mouth and remains motionless, staring vacuously before him. Finally he has an idea, puts banana in his waistcoat pocket, the end emerging, and goes with all the speed he can muster backstage into darkness. Ten seconds. Loud pop of cork. Fifteen seconds. He comes back into light carrying an old ledger and sits down at table. He lays ledger on table, wipes his mouth, wipes his hands on the front of his waistcoat, brings them smartly together and rubs them.

KRAPP (*briskly*): Ah! (*He bends over ledger, turns the pages, finds the entry he wants, reads.*) Box . . . thrree . . . spool . . . five. (*He raises his head and stares front. With relish.*) Spool . . . (*Pause.*) Spooool! (*Happy smile. Pause. He bends over table, starts peering and poking at the boxes.*) Box . . . thrree . . . thrree . . . four . . . two . . . (*with surprise*) nine! good God! . . . seven . . . ah! the little rascal! (*He takes up box, peers at it.*) Box thrree. (*He lays it on table, opens it and peers at spools inside.*) Spool . . . (*he peers at ledger*) . . . five . . . (*he peers at spools*) . . . five . . . five . . . ah! the little scoundrel! (*He takes out a spool, peers at it.*) Spool five. (*He lays it on table, closes box three, puts it back with the others, takes up the spool.*) Box thrree, spool five. (*He bends over the machine, looks up. With relish.*) Spooool! (*Happy smile. He bends, loads spool on machine, rubs his hands.*) Ah! (*He peers at ledger, reads entry at foot of page.*) Mother at rest at last. . . . Hm. . . . The black ball. . . . (*He raises his head, stares blankly front. Puzzled.*) Black ball? . . . (*He peers again at ledger, reads.*) The dark nurse. . . . (*He raises his head, broods, peers again at ledger, reads.*) Slight improvement in bowel condition. . . . Hm. . . . Memorable . . . what? (*He peers closer.*) Equinox, memorable equinox. (*He raises his head, stares blankly front. Puzzled.*) Memorable equinox? . . . (*Pause. He shrugs his shoulders, peers again at ledger, reads.*) Farewell to—(*he turns page*)—love. (*He raises his head, broods, bends over machine, switches on and assumes listening posture, i.e. leaning forward, elbows on table, hand cupping ear towards machine, face front.*)

TAPE (*strong voice, rather pompous, clearly Krapp's at a much earlier time*): Thirty-nine today, sound as a—(*Settling himself more comfortably he knocks one of the boxes off the table, curses, switches off, sweeps boxes and ledger violently to the ground, winds tape back to beginning, switches on, resumes posture.*) Thirty-nine today, sound as a bell, apart from my old weakness, and intellectually I have now every reason to suspect at the . . . (*hesitates*) . . . crest of the wave—or thereabouts. Celebrated the awful occasion, as in recent years, quietly at the Winehouse. Not a soul. Sat before the fire with closed eyes, separating the grain from the husks. Jotted down a few notes, on the back of an envelope. Good to be back in my den, in my old rags. Have just eaten I regret to say three bananas and only with difficulty refrained from a fourth. Fatal things for a man with my condition. (*Vehemently.*) Cut'em out! (*Pause.*) The new light above my table is a great improvement. With all this darkness round me I feel less alone. (*Pause.*) In a way. (*Pause.*) I love to get up and move about in it, then back here to . . . (*hesitates*) . . . me. (*Pause.*) Krapp.

(*Pause.*)

The grain, now what I wonder do I mean by that, I mean . . . (*hesitates*) . . . I suppose I mean those things worth having when all the dust has— when all *my* dust has settled. I close my eyes and try and imagine them.

(*Pause. Krapp closes his eyes briefly.*)

Extraordinary silence this evening, I strain my ears and do not hear a sound. Old Miss McGlome always sings at this hour. But not tonight. Songs of her girlhood, she says. Hard to think of her as a girl. Wonderful woman though. Connaught,[1] I fancy. (*Pause.*) Shall I sing when I am her age, if I ever am? No. (*Pause.*) Did I sing as a boy? No. (*Pause.*) Did I ever sing? No.

(*Pause.*)

Just been listening to an old year, passages at random. I did not check in the book, but it must be at least ten or twelve years ago. At that time I think I was still living on and off with Bianca in Kedar Street. Well out of that, Jesus yes! Hopeless business. (*Pause.*) Not much about her, apart from a tribute to her eyes. Very warm. I suddenly saw them again. (*Pause.*) Incomparable! (*Pause.*) Ah well? (*Pause.*) These old P.M.s are gruesome, but I often find them—(*Krapp switches off, broods, switches on.*)—a help before embarking on a new . . . (*hesitates*) . . . retrospect. Hard to believe I was ever that young whelp. The voice! Jesus! And the aspirations! (*Brief laugh in which Krapp joins.*) And the resolutions! (*Brief laugh in which Krapp joins.*) To drink less, in particular. (*Brief laugh of Krapp alone.*) Statistics. Seventeen hundred hours, out of the preceding eight thousand odd, consumed on licensed premises[2] alone. More than 20 per cent, say 40 per cent of his waking life. (*Pause.*) Plans for a less . . . (*hesitates*) . . . engrossing sexual life. Last illness of his father. Flagging pursuit of happiness. Unattainable laxation.[3] Sneers at what he calls his youth and thanks to God that it's over. (*Pause.*) False ring there. (*Pause.*) Shadows of the opus . . . magnum.[4] Closing with a—(*brief laugh*)—yelp to Providence. (*Prolonged

---

[1] A province in northwestern Ireland.

[2] Pubs licensed to sell alcohol.

[3] Movement of the bowels.

[4] A "magnum opus" is a great work; a magnum is a large wine bottle.

laugh in which Krapp joins.) What remains of all that misery? A girl in a shabby green coat, on a railway-station platform? No?

(Pause.)

When I look—

(Krapp switches off, broods, looks at his watch, gets up, goes backstage into darkness. Ten seconds. Pop of cork. Ten seconds. Second cork. Ten seconds. Third cork. Ten seconds. Brief burst of quavering song.)

KRAPP *(sings):* Now the day is over,
　　　　　　　 Night is drawing nigh-igh,
　　　　　　　 Shadows—

(Fit of coughing. He comes back into light, sits down, wipes his mouth, switches on, resumes his listening posture.)

TAPE: —back on the year that is gone, with what I hope is perhaps a glint of the old eye to come, there is of course the house, on the canal where mother lay a-dying, in the late autumn, after her long viduity *(Krapp gives a start)* and the—*(Krapp switches off, winds back tape a little, bends his ear closer to machine, switches on)*—a-dying, after her long viduity, and the—

(Krapp switches off, raises his head, stares blankly before him. His lips move in the syllables of "viduity." No sound. He gets up, goes backstage into darkness, comes back with an enormous dictionary, lays it on table, sits down and looks up the word.)

5　KRAPP *(reading from dictionary):* State—or condition—of being—or remaining—a widow—or widower. *(Looks up. Puzzled.)* Being—or remaining? . . . *(Pause. He peers again at dictionary. Reading.)* "Deep weeds of viduity" . . . Also of an animal, especially a bird . . . the vidua or weaver-bird. . . . Black plumage of male. . . . *(He looks up. With relish.)* The vidua-bird!

(Pause. He closes dictionary, switches on, resumes listening posture.)

TAPE: —bench by the weir from where I could see her window. There I sat, in the biting wind, wishing she were gone. *(Pause.)* Hardly a soul, just a few regulars, nursemaids, infants, old men, dogs. I got to know them quite well—oh by appearance of course I mean! One dark young beauty I recollect particularly, all white and starch, incomparable bosom, with a big black hooded perambulator, most funereal thing. Whenever I looked in her direction she had her eyes on me. And yet when I was bold enough to speak to her—not having been introduced—she threatened to call a policeman. As if I had designs on her virtue! *(Laugh. Pause.)* The face she had! The eyes! Like . . . *(hesitates)* . . . chrysolite![5] *(Pause.)* Ah well. . . . *(Pause.)* I was there

---

[5] Green gemstone.

when—(*Krapp switches off, broods, switches on again.*)—the blind went down, one of those dirty brown roller affairs, throwing a ball for a little white dog as chance would have it. I happened to look up and there it was. All over and done with, at last. I sat on for a few moments with the ball in my hand and the dog yelping and pawing at me. (*Pause.*) Moments. Her moments, my moments. (*Pause.*) The dog's moments. (*Pause.*) In the end I held it out to him and he took it in his mouth, gently, gently. A small, old, black, hard, solid rubber ball. (*Pause.*) I shall feel it, in my hand, until my dying day. (*Pause.*) I might have kept it. (*Pause.*) But I gave it to the dog.

(*Pause.*)

Ah well. . . .

(*Pause.*)

Spiritually a year of profound gloom and indigence until that memorable night in March, at the end of the jetty, in the howling wind, never to be forgotten, when suddenly I saw the whole thing. The vision at last. This I fancy is what I have chiefly to record this evening, against the day when my work will be done and perhaps no place left in my memory, warm or cold, for the miracle that . . . (*hesitates*) . . . for the fire that set it alight. What I suddenly saw then was this, that the belief I had been going on all my life, namely—(*Krapp switches off impatiently, winds tape forward, switches on again*)—great granite rocks the foam flying up in the light of the lighthouse and the wind-gauge spinning like a propeller, clear to me at last that the dark I have always struggled to keep under is in reality my most—(*Krapp curses, switches off, winds tape forward, switches on again*)—unshatterable association until my dissolution of storm and night with the light of the understanding and the fire—(*Krapp curses louder, switches off, winds tape forward, switches on again*)—my face in her breasts and my hand on her. We lay there without moving. But under us all moved, and moved us, gently, up and down, and from side to side.

(*Pause.*)

Past midnight. Never knew such silence. The earth might be uninhabited.

(*Pause.*)

Here I end—

(*Krapp switches off, winds tape back, switches on again.*)

—upper lake, with the punt,[6] bathed off the bank, then pushed out into the stream and drifted. She lay stretched out on the floorboards

---

[6] A small, flat-bottomed boat.

with her hands under her head and her eyes closed. Sun blazing down, bit of a breeze, water nice and lively. I noticed a scratch on her thigh and asked her how she came by it. Picking gooseberries, she said. I said again I thought it was hopeless and no good going on and she agreed, without opening her eyes. (*Pause.*) I asked her to look at me and after a few moments—(*Pause.*)—after a few moments she did, but the eyes just slits, because of the glare. I bent over her to get them in the shadow and they opened. (*Pause. Low.*) Let me in. (*Pause.*) We drifted in among the flags[7] and stuck. The way they went down, sighing, before the stem! (*Pause.*) I lay down across her with my face in her breasts and my hand on her. We lay there without moving. But under us all moved, and moved us, gently, up and down, and from side to side.

(*Pause.*)

Past midnight. Never knew—

(*Krapp switches off, broods. Finally he fumbles in his pockets, encounters the banana, takes it out, peers at it, puts it back, fumbles, brings out envelope, fumbles, puts back envelope, looks at his watch, gets up and goes backstage into darkness. Ten seconds. Sound of bottle against glass, then brief siphon. Ten seconds. Bottle against glass alone. Ten seconds. He comes back a little unsteadily into light, goes to front of table, takes out keys, raises them to his eyes, chooses key, unlocks first drawer, peers into it, feels about inside, takes out reel, peers at it, locks drawer, puts keys back in his pocket, goes and sits down, takes reel off machine, lays it on dictionary, loads virgin reel on machine, takes envelope from his pocket, consults back of it, lays it on table, switches on, clears his throat and begins to record.*)

KRAPP: Just been listening to that stupid bastard I took myself for thirty years ago, hard to believe I was ever as bad as that. Thank God that's all done with anyway. (*Pause.*) The eyes she had! (*Broods, realizes he is recording silence, switches off, broods. Finally.*) Everything there, everything, all the— (*Realizes this is not being recorded, switches on.*) Everything there, everything on this old muckball, all the light and dark and famine and feasting of . . . (*hesitates*) . . . the ages! (*In a shout.*) Yes! (*Pause.*) Let that go! Jesus! Take his mind off his homework! Jesus! (*Pause. Weary.*) Ah well, maybe he was right. (*Pause.*) Maybe he was right. (*Broods. Realizes. Switches off. Consults envelope.*) Pah! (*Crumples it and throws it away. Broods. Switches on.*) Nothing to say, not a squeak. What's a year now? The sour cud and the iron stool.[8] (*Pause.*) Revelled in the word spool. (*With relish.*) Spooool! Happiest moment of the past half million. (*Pause.*) Seventeen copies sold, of which eleven at trade price to free circulating libraries beyond the seas. Getting known. (*Pause.*) One pound six and something, eight I have little doubt. (*Pause.*) Crawled out once or twice, before the summer was cold. Sat

---

[7] Reeds.

[8] Indigestion and constipation.

shivering in the park, drowned in dreams and burning to be gone. Not a soul. (*Pause.*) Last fancies. (*Vehemently.*) Keep 'em under! (*Pause.*) Scalded the eyes out of me reading *Effie*[9] again, a page a day, with tears again. Effie. . . . (*Pause.*) Could have been happy with her, up there on the Baltic, and the pines, and the dunes. (*Pause.*) Could I? (*Pause.*) And she? (*Pause.*) Pah! (*Pause.*) Fanny came in a couple of times. Bony old ghost of a whore. Couldn't do much, but I suppose better than a kick in the crutch. The last time wasn't so bad. How do you manage it, she said, at your age? I told her I'd been saving up for her all my life. (*Pause.*) Went to Vespers[10] once, like when I was in short trousers. (*Pause. Sings.*)

Now the day is over,
Night is drawing nigh-igh,
Shadows—(*coughing, then almost inaudible*)—of the evening
Steal across the sky.

(*Gasping.*) Went to sleep and fell off the pew. (*Pause.*) Sometimes wondered in the night if a last effort mightn't—(*Pause.*) Ah finish your booze now and get to your bed. Go on with this drivel in the morning. Or leave it at that. (*Pause.*) Leave it at that. (*Pause.*) Lie propped up in the dark—and wander. Be again in the dingle[11] on a Christmas Eve, gathering holly, the red-berried. (*Pause.*) Be again on Croghan[12] on a Sunday morning, in the haze, with the bitch, stop and listen to the bells. (*Pause.*) And so on. (*Pause.*) Be again, be again. (*Pause.*) All that old misery. (*Pause.*) Once wasn't enough for you. (*Pause.*) Lie down across her.

(*Long pause. He suddenly bends over machine, switches off, wrenches off tape, throws it away, puts on the other, winds it forward to the passage he wants, switches on, listens staring front.*)

TAPE: —gooseberries, she said. I said again I thought it was hopeless and no good going on and she agreed, without opening her eyes. (*Pause.*) I asked her to look at me and after a few moments—(*Pause.*)—after a few moments she did, but the eyes just slits, because of the glare. I bent over her to get them in the shadow and they opened. (*Pause. Low.*) Let me in. (*Pause.*) We drifted in among the flags and stuck. The way they went down, sighing, before the stem! (*Pause.*) I lay down across her with my face in her breasts and my hand on her. We lay there without moving. But under us all moved, and moved us, gently, up and down, and from side to side.

---

[9] Theodor Fontane's sentimental novel *Effi Briest* (1895).
[10] Evening church service.
[11] Valley.
[12] Mountain in County Wicklow in southeastern Ireland.

(Pause. Krapp's lips move. No sound.)

Past midnight. Never knew such silence. The earth might be uninhabited.

(Pause.)

Here I end this reel. Box—*(Pause.)*—three, spool—*(Pause.)*—five. *(Pause.)* Perhaps my best years are gone. When there was a chance of happiness. But I wouldn't want them back. Not with the fire in me now. No, I wouldn't want them back.

(Krapp motionless staring before him. The tape runs on in silence.)

CURTAIN

READING AND REACTING

1. How does the tape recording contribute to the plot and theme of the play?
2. What is the effect of the stage directions? Can you distinguish between what you would understand when you read the play and what you would understand when you attend a performance?
3. The technology of the tape recording can be considered a memory aid. What is the role of memory? Does it fix a point in time or is memory constantly being reconstructed, with or without technology?
4. A performance of the play is available from the Smithsonian Institution Press, in the *Beckett Directs Beckett* series. If possible, watch the play and try to focus on the humour and how it is generated.
5. **JOURNAL ENTRY** Write the transcription of your own last tape. Pay attention to how the mind moves between time frames and details. What sensory perceptions are the strongest?
6. **CRITICAL PERSPECTIVE** Beckett said, "To find a form that accommodates the mess, that is the task of the artist now." Do you agree? Do you think Beckett achieves his own goal in *Krapp's Last Tape*?

◆ **GEORGE RYGA** (1932–1987) was born in northern Alberta in the Ukrainian community of Deep Creek. His formal education was limited: seven years of school and a brief stint at the University of Texas in 1949. In 1962 he moved with his wife and children to Summerland, British Columbia, where he lived until his death. Ryga worked in several genres, and *The Ecstasy of Rita Joe* (1967) is his best-known work. It was commissioned by the Vancouver Playhouse for Canada's centennial. It was the first play in English produced at the National Arts Centre, Ottawa (1969). When the play was first performed in Vancouver, several of the Native actors were arrested on the street—indicating the real problems the play grapples with. Ryga's attention to the underprivileged, especially the racism facing Natives in Canada, came at a time when Native groups across Canada and the United States were gaining momentum in their ability to reveal the inequities of the political and social system.

Ryga's technique in the play combines various elements from realism to surrealism. Music and dance contribute to explorations of culture, and the movement between past and present aids in the overall construction of a play that confronts colonialism.

◈ ◈ ◈

GEORGE RYGA

The Ecstasy of Rita Joe
(1967; pub. 1970)

CHARACTERS

RITA JOE	EILEEN JOE	WITNESS; MURDERER
JAIMIE PAUL	OLD INDIAN WOMAN	WITNESS; MURDERER
FATHER, DAVID JOE	TEACHER, MISS DONOHUE	YOUNG INDIAN MEN
MAGISTRATE	POLICEMAN	GUITARIST-SINGER
MR. HOMER	SCHOOL BOARD CLERK	
PRIEST, FATHER ANDREW	WITNESS; MURDERER	

ACT ONE

A circular ramp beginning at floor level stage left and continuing downward below floor level at stage front, then rising and sweeping along stage back at two-foot elevation to disappear in the wings of stage left. This ramp dominates the stage by wrapping the central and forward playing area. A short approach ramp, meeting with the main ramp at stage right, expedites entrances from the wings of stage right.

The Magistrate's chair and representation of court desk are situated at stage right, enclosed within the sweep of the ramp. At the foot of the desk is a lip on stage right side. The Singer sits here, turned away from the focus of the play. Her songs and accompaniment appear almost accidental. She has all the reactions of a white liberal folklorist with a limited concern and understanding of an ethnic dilemma which she touches in the course of her research and work in compiling and writing folk songs. She serves too as an alter ego to Rita Joe.

No curtain is used during the play. At the opening, intermission and conclusion of the play, the curtain remains up. The onus for isolating scenes from the past and present in Rita Joe's life falls on highlight lighting.

Backstage, there is a mountain cyclorama. In front of the cyclorama there is a darker maze curtain to suggest gloom and confusion, and a cityscape.

The house lights and stage work lights remain on. Backstage, cyclorama, and maze curtains are up, revealing wall back of stage, exit doors, etc.

Cast, Singer enter offstage singly and in pairs from the wings, the exit doors at the back of the theatre, and from the auditorium side doors. The entrances are work-manlike and untheatrical. When all the Cast is on stage, they turn to face the audience momentarily. The house lights dim.

The cyclorama is lowered into place. The maze curtain follows. This creates a sense of compression of stage into the auditorium. Recorded voices are heard in a jumble of mutterings and throat clearings. The Magistrate enters as the Clerk begins.

CLERK: *(recorded)* This court is in session. All present will rise . . .

The shuffling and scraping of furniture is heard.

The Cast repeat "Rita Joe, Rita Joe." A Policeman brings on Rita Joe.

MAGISTRATE: Who is she? Can she speak English?
POLICEMAN: Yes.
MAGISTRATE: Then let her speak for herself! *(He speaks to the audience firmly and with reason.)* To understand life in a given society, one must understand laws of that society. All relationships . . .
5 CLERK: *(recorded)* Man to man . . . man to woman . . . man to property . . . man to the state . . .
MAGISTRATE: . . . are determined and enriched by laws that have grown out of social realities. The quality of the law under which you live and function determines the real quality of the freedom that was yours today.

The rest of the Cast slowly move out.

    Your home and your well-being were protected. The roads of the city are open to us. So are the galleries, libraries, the administrative and public buildings. There are buses, trains . . . going in and coming out. Nobody is a prisoner here.
RITA: *(with humour, almost a sad sigh)* The first time I tried to go home I was picked up by some men who gave me five dollars. An' then they arrested me.

The Policeman retreats into the shadows. The Singer crosses down.

MAGISTRATE: Thousands leave and enter the city everyday . . .
RITA: It wasn't true what they said, but nobody'd believe me . . .
10 SINGER: *(Singing a recitivo searching for a melody)*
    Will the winds not blow
    My words to her
    Like the seeds
    Of the dandelion?
MAGISTRATE: *(smiles, as at a private joke)* Once . . . I saw a little girl in the Cariboo country. It was summer then and she wore only a blouse and skirt. I wondered what she wore in winter.

The Murderers hover in background on the upper ramp. One whistles and one lights a cigarette—an action which will be repeated at the end of the play.

RITA: *(moving to him, but hesitating)* You look like a good man. Tell them to let me go, please!

The Magistrate goes to his podium.

MAGISTRATE: Our nation is on an economic par with the state of Arkansas . . . We are a developing country, but a buoyant one. Still . . . the summer report of the Economic Council of Canada predicts a reduction in the gross national product unless we utilize our manpower for greater efficiency. Employed, happy people make for a prosperous, happy nation . . .

RITA: *(exultantly)* I worked at some jobs, mister!

The Magistrate turns to face Rita Joe. The Murderers have gone.

15 MAGISTRATE: Gainful employment. Obedience to the law . . .

RITA: *(to the Magistrate)* Once I had a job . . .

He does not relate to her. She is troubled. She talks to the audience.

Once I had a job in a tire store . . . an' I'd worry about what time my boss would come . . . He was always late . . . and so was everybody. Sometimes I got to thinkin' what would happen if he'd not come. And nobody else would come. And I'd be all day in this big room with no lights on an' the telephone ringing an' people asking for other people that weren't there . . . What would happen?

As she relates her concern, she laughs. Towards the end of her dialogue she is so amused by the absurdity of it all that she can hardly contain herself.

Lights fade on the Magistrate who broods in his chair as he examines his court papers.

Lights up on Jaimie Paul approaching on the backstage ramp from stage left. He is jubilant, his laughter blending with her laughter. At the sound of his voice, Rita Joe runs to him, to the memory of him.

JAIMIE: I seen the city today and I seen things today I never knew was there, Rita Joe!

RITA: *(happily)* I seen them too, Jaimie Paul!

He pauses above her, his mood light and childlike.

JAIMIE: I see a guy on top of a bridge, talkin' to himself . . . an' lots of people on the beach watchin' harbour seals . . . Kids feet popcorn to seagulls . . . an' I think to myself . . . Boy! Pigeons eat pretty good here!

20 RITA: In the morning, Jaimie Paul . . . very early in the morning . . . the air is cold like at home . . .

JAIMIE: Pretty soon I seen a little woman walkin' a big black dog on a rope
. . . Dog is mad . . . Dog wants a man!

Jaimie Paul moves to Rita Joe. They embrace.

RITA: Clouds are red over the city in the morning. Clara Hill says to me if
you're real happy . . . the clouds make you forget you're not home . . .

*They laugh together. Jaimie Paul breaks from her. He punctuates his story with
wide, sweeping gestures.*

JAIMIE: I start singin' and some hotel windows open. I wave to them, but
nobody waves back! They're watchin' me, like I was a harbour seal! *(He
laughs.)* So I stopped singin'!
RITA: I remember colours, but I've forgot faces already . . .

*Jaimie Paul looks at her as her mood changes. Faint light on the Magistrate
brightens.*

A train whistle is white, with black lines . . . A sick man talkin' is
brown like an overcoat with pockets torn an' string showin' . . . A sad
woman is a room with the curtains shut . . .
25 MAGISTRATE: Rita Joe?

*She becomes sobered, but Jaimie Paul continues laughing. She nods to the
Magistrate, then turns to Jaimie Paul.*

RITA: Them bastards put me in jail. They're gonna do it again, they said . . .
Them bastards!
JAIMIE: Guys who sell newspapers don't see nothin' . . .
RITA: They drive by me, lookin' . . .
JAIMIE: I'm gonna be a carpenter!
30 RITA: I walk like a stick, tryin' to keep my ass from showin' because I know
what they're thinkin' . . . Them bastards!
JAIMIE: I got myself boots an' a new shirt . . . See!
RITA: *(worried now)* I thought their jail was on fire . . . I thought it was
burning.
JAIMIE: Room I got costs me seven bucks a week . . .
RITA: I can't leave town. Everytime I try, they put me in jail.

A Policeman enters with a file folder.

35 JAIMIE: They say it's a pretty good room for seven bucks a week . . .

*Jaimie Paul begins to retreat backwards from her, along the ramp to the wings of
stage left. She is isolated in a pool of light away from the Magistrate. The light isolation between her and Jaimie Paul deepens, as the scene turns into the courtroom
again.*

MAGISTRATE: Vagrancy . . . You are charged with vagrancy.
JAIMIE: *(with enthusiasm, boyishly)* First hundred bucks I make, Rita Joe . . .
I'm gonna buy a car so I can take you everyplace!

RITA: *(moving after him)* Jaimie!

He retreats, dreamlike, into the wings. The spell of memory between them is broken. Pools of light between her and the Magistrate spread and fuse into a single light area. She turns to the Magistrate, worried and confused.

MAGISTRATE: *(reading the documents in his hand)* The charge against you this morning is vagrancy . . .

The Magistrate continues studying the papers he holds. She looks up at him and shakes her head helplessly, then blurts out to him . . .

40   RITA: I had to spend last night in jail . . . Did you know?
MAGISTRATE: Yes. You were arrested.
RITA: I didn't know when morning came . . . There was no windows . . . The jail stinks! People in jail stink!
MAGISTRATE: *(indulgently)* Are you surprised?
RITA: I didn't know anybody there . . . People in jail stink like paper that's been in the rain too long. But a jail stinks worse. It stinks of rust . . . an' old hair . . .

The Magistrate looks down at her for the first time.

45   MAGISTRATE: You . . . are Rita Joe?

She nods quickly. A faint concern shows in his face. He watches her for a long moment.

    I know your face . . . yet . . . it wasn't in this courtroom. Or was it?
RITA: I don't know . . .
MAGISTRATE: *(pondering)* Have you appeared before me in the past year?
RITA: *(turning away from him, shrugging)* I don't know. I can't remember . . .

The Magistrate throws his head back and laughs. The Policeman joins in.

MAGISTRATE: You can't remember? Come now . . .
50   RITA: *(laughing with him and looking to the Policeman)* I can't remember . . .
MAGISTRATE: Then I take it you haven't appeared before me. Certainly you and I would remember if you had.
RITA: *(smiling)* I don't remember . . .

The Magistrate makes some hurried notes, but he is watching Rita Joe, formulating his next thought.

She speaks naively . . .

    My sister hitchhiked home an' she had no trouble like I . . .
MAGISTRATE: You'll need witnesses, Rita Joe. I'm only giving you eight hours to find witnesses for yourself . . .
RITA: Jaimie knows . . .

She turns to where Jaimie Paul had been, but the back of the stage is in darkness. The Policeman exits suddenly.

Jamie knew . . .

Her voice trails off pathetically. The Magistrate shrugs and returns to studying his notes. Rita Joe chaffs during the silence which follows. She craves communion with people, with the Magistrate.

My sister was a dressmaker, mister! But she only worked two weeks in the city . . . An' then she got sick and went back to the reserve to help my father catch fish an' cut pulpwood. *(She smiles.)* She's not coming back . . . that's for sure!

55 MAGISTRATE: *(with interest)* Should I know your sister? What was her name?
RITA: Eileen Joe.

Eileen Joe appears spotlit behind, a memory crowding in.

MAGISTRATE: Eileen . . . that's a soft, undulating name.
RITA: Two weeks, and not one white woman came to her to leave an order or old clothes for her to fix. No work at all for two weeks, an' her money ran out . . . Isn't that funny?

The Magistrate again studies Rita Joe, his mind elsewhere.

MAGISTRATE: Hmmmmm . . .

Eileen Joe disappears.

60 RITA: So she went back to the reserve to catch fish an' cut pulpwood!
MAGISTRATE: I do know your face . . . Yes! And yet . . .
RITA: Can I sit someplace?
MAGISTRATE: *(excited)* I remember now . . . Yes! I was on holidays three summers back in the Cariboo country . . . driving over this road with not a house or field in sight . . . just barren land, wild and windblown. And then I saw this child beside the road, dressed in a blouse and skirt, barefooted . . .
RITA: *(looking around)* I don't feel so good, mister.
65 MAGISTRATE: My God, she wasn't more than three or four years old . . . walking towards me beside the road. When I'd passed her, I stopped my car and then turned around and drove back to where I'd seen her, for I wondered what she could possibly be doing in such a lonely country at that age without her father or mother walking with her . . . Yet when I got back to where I'd seen her, she had disappeared. She was nowhere to be seen. Yet the land was flat for over a mile in every direction . . . I had to see her. But I couldn't . . . *(He stares down at Rita Joe for a long moment.)* You see, what I was going to say was that this child had your face! Isn't that strange?
RITA: *(with disinterest)* Sure, if you think so, mister . . .
MAGISTRATE: Could she have been . . . your daughter?
RITA: What difference does it make?
MAGISTRATE: Children cannot be left like that . . . It takes money to raise children in the woods as in the cities . . . There are institutions and people with more money than you who could . . .

70   RITA: Nobody would get my child, mister!

She is distracted by Eileen Joe's voice in her memory. Eileen's voice begins in darkness, but as she speaks, a spotlight isolates her in front of the ramp, stage left. Eileen is on her hands and knees, two buckets beside her. She is picking berries in mime.

EILEEN: First was the strawberries an' then the blueberries. After the frost . . .
    we picked the cranberries . . . . *(She laughs with delight.)*
RITA: *(pleading with the Magistrate, but her attention on Eileen)* Let me go,
    mister . . .
MAGISTRATE: I can't let you go. I don't think that would be of any use in
    the circumstances. Would you like a lawyer?

Even as he speaks, Rita Joe has entered the scene with Eileen picking berries.

The Magistrate's light fades on his podium.

RITA: You ate the strawberries an' blueberries because you were always a
    hungry kid!
75   EILEEN: But not cranberries! They made my stomach hurt.

Rita Joe goes down on her knees with Eileen.

RITA: Let me pick . . . You rest. *(She holds out the bucket to Eileen.)* Mine's full
    already . . . Let's change. You rest . . .

During the exchange of buckets, Eileen notices her hands are larger than Rita Joe's. She is both delighted and surprised by this.

EILEEN: My hands are bigger than yours, Rita . . . Look! *(She takes Rita Joe's
    hands in hers.)* When did my hands grow so big?
RITA: *(wisely and sadly)* You've worked so hard . . . I'm older than you,
    Leenie . . . I will always be older.

The two sisters are thoughtful for a moment, each watching the other in silence. Then Rita Joe becomes animated and resumes her mime of picking berries in the woods.

    We picked lots of wild berries when we were kids, Leenie!

They turn away from their work and lie down alongside each other, facing the front of the stage.

The light on them becomes summery, warm.

    In the summer, it was hot an' flies hummed so loud you'd go to sleep
    if you sat down an' just listened.
EILEEN: The leaves on the poplars used to turn black an' curl together with
    the heat . . .
80   RITA: One day you and I were pickin' blueberries and a big storm came . . .

A sudden crash of thunder and a lightning flash. The lights turn cold and blue. The three Murderers stand in silhouette on a riser behind them. Eileen cringes in fear, afraid of the storm, aware of the presence of the Murderers behind them.

Rita Joe springs to her feet, her being attuned to the wildness of the atmosphere. Lightning continues to flash and flicker.

EILEEN: Oh, no!

RITA: *(shouting)* It got cold and the rain an' hail came . . . the sky falling!

EILEEN: *(crying in fear)* Rita!

RITA: *(laughing, shouting)* Stay there!

A high flash of lightning, silhouetting the Murderers harshly. They take a step forward on the lightning flash. Eileen dashes into the arms of Rita Joe. She screams and drags Rita Joe down with her.

Rita Joe struggles against Eileen.

85 RITA: Let me go! What in hell's wrong with you? Let me go!

MAGISTRATE: I can't let you go.

The lightning dies, but the thunder rumbles off into the distance. Eileen subsides and pressing herself into the arms of Rita Joe as a small child to her mother, she sobs quietly.

RITA: There, there . . . *(With infinite tenderness.)* You said to me, "What would happen if the storm hurt us an' we can't find our way home, but are lost together so far away in the bush?"

Eileen looks up, brushing away her tears and smiling at Rita Joe.

RITA & EILEEN: *(in unison)* Would you be my mother then?

RITA: Would I be your mother?

Rita Joe releases Eileen who looks back fearfully to where the Murderers had stood. They are gone. She rises and, collecting the buckets, moves hesitantly to where they had been. Confident now, she laughs softly and nervously to herself and leaves the stage.

Rita Joe rises and talks to Eileen as she departs.

We walked home through the mud an' icy puddles among the trees. At first you cried, Leenie . . . and then you wanted to sleep. But I held you up an' when we got home you said you were sure you would've died in the bush if it hadn't been for us being together like that.

Eileen disappears from the stage. The Magistrate's light comes up. Rita Joe shakes her head sadly at the memory, then comes forward to the apron of the stage. She is proud of her sister and her next speech reveals this pride.

She made a blouse for me that I wore everyday for one year, an' it never ripped at the armpits like the blouse I buy in the store does the first time I stretch . . . *(She stretches languidly.)* I like to stretch when I'm happy! It makes all the happiness go through me like warm water . . .

The Priest, the Teacher, and a Young Indian Man cross the stage directly behind her. The Priest wears a Roman collar and a check bush-jacket of a worker-priest. He pauses before passing Rita Joe and goes to meet her.

90 PRIEST: Rita Joe? When did you get back? How's life?

Rita Joe shrugs noncommittally.

RITA: You know me, Father Andrew . . . Could be better, could be worse . . .
PRIEST: Are you still working?

Rita Joe is still noncommittal. She smiles at him. Her gestures are not definite.

RITA: I live.
PRIEST: *(serious and concerned)* It's not easy, is it?
95 RITA: Not always.

The Teacher and the Young Indian Man exit.

PRIEST: A lot of things are different in the city. It's easier here on the reserve . . . Life is simpler. You can be yourself. That's important to remember.
RITA: Yes, Father . . .

The Priest wants to ask and say more, but he cannot. An awkward moment between them and he reaches out to touch her shoulder gently.

PRIEST: Well . . . be a good girl, Rita Joe . . .
RITA: *(without turning after him)* Goodbye, Father.
100 MAGISTRATE: *(more insistently)* Do you want a lawyer?

The Priest leaves stage right. As he leaves, cross light to where a happy Jaimie Paul enters from stage left. Jaimie Paul comes down to join Rita Joe.

JAIMIE: This guy asked me how much education I got, an' I says to him, "Grade six. How much education a man need for such a job?" . . . An' the bum, he says it's not enough! I should take night school. But I got the job, an' I start next Friday . . . Like this . . .

Jaimie Paul does a mock sweeping routine as if he was cleaning a vast office building. He and Rita Joe are both laughing.

Pretty good, eh?
RITA: Pretty good.
JAIMIE: Cleaning the floors an' desks in the building . . . But it's a government job, and that's good for life. Work hard, then the government give me a raise . . . I never had a job like that before . . .

RITA: When I sleep happy, I dream of blueberries an' sun an' all the nice things when I was a little kid, Jaimie Paul.

The sound of an airplane is heard. Jaimie Paul looks up. Rita Joe also stares into the sky of her memory. Jaimie Paul's face is touched with pain and recollection. The Teacher, Rita Joe's Father, an Old Woman, four Young Indian Men and Eileen Joe come into the background quietly, as if at a wharf watching the airplane leave the village. They stand looking up until the noise of the aircraft begins to diminish.

105 JAIMIE: That airplane . . . a Cessna . . . *(He continues watching the aircraft and turns, following its flight path.)* She said to me, maybe I never see you again, Jaimie Paul.

There is a faint light on the Magistrate in his chair. He is thoughtful, looking down at his hands.

MAGISTRATE: Do you want a lawyer?
RITA: *(to Jaimie Paul)* Who?
JAIMIE: Your mother . . . I said to her, they'll fix you up good in the hospital. Better than before. . . . It was a Cessna that landed on the river an' took her away . . . Maybe I never see you again, Jaimie, she says to me. She knew she was gonna die, but I was a kid and so were you . . . What the hell did we know? I'll never forget . . . *(Jaimie Paul joins the village group on the upper level.)*
SINGER: *(singing an indefinite melody developing into a square-dance tune)*
There was a man in a beat-up hat
Who runs a house in the middle of town,
An' round his stove-pipe chimney house
The magpies sat, just a-lookin' round.

The Indian village people remain in the back of the stage, still watching the airplane which has vanished.

Jaimie Paul, on his way, passes Mr. Homer, a white citizen who has the hurried but fulfilled appearance of the socially responsible man. Mr. Homer comes to front of the stage beside Rita Joe. He talks directly to the audience.

110 MR. HOMER: Sure, we do a lot of things for our Indians here in the city at the Centre . . . Bring 'em in from the cold an' give them food . . . The rest . . . Well, the rest kinda take care of itself.

Rita Joe lowers her head and looks away from him. Mr. Homer moves to her and places his hand on her shoulders possessively.

When your mother got sick we flew her out . . . You remember that, Rita Joe?
RITA: *(nodding, looking down)* Yes, Mr. Homer . . . Thank you.
MR. HOMER: And we sent her body back for the funeral . . . Right, Rita Joe?

The people of the village leave except for the Young Indian Men who remain and mime drinking.

> And then sometimes a man drinks it up an' leaves his wife an' kids and the poor dears come here for help. We give them food an' a place to sleep . . . Right, Rita?

RITA: Yes.

MR. HOMER: Clothes too . . . White people leave clothes here for the Indians to take if they need 'em. Used to have them all up on racks over there . . . just like in a store . . . *(He points.)* But now we got them all on a heap on a table in the basement.

He laughs and Rita Joe nods with him.

> Indian people . . . 'specially the women . . . get more of a kick diggin' through stuff that's piled up like that . . . *(Mr. Homer chuckles and shakes his head.)*

There is a pale light on the Magistrate, who is still looking down at his hands.

115 MAGISTRATE: There are institutions to help you . . .

Mr. Homer again speaks to audience, but now he is angry over some personal beef.

MR. HOMER: So you see, the Centre serves a need that's real for Indians who come to the city . . . *(He wags his finger at the audience angrily.)* It's the do-gooders burn my ass, you know! They come in from television or the newspaper . . . hang around just long enough to see a drunken Indian . . . an' bingo!

JAIMIE: Bingo!

MR. HOMER: That's their story! Next thing, they're seeing some kind of Red Power . . .

The Young Indian Men laugh and Rita Joe gets up to join them.

> . . . or beatin' the government over the head! Let them live an' work among the Indians for a few months . . . then they'd know what it's really like . . .

The music comes up sharply.

SINGER:
> Round and round the cenotaph,
> The clumsy seagulls play.
> Fed by funny men with hats
> Who watch them night and day.

The four Young Indian Men join with Rita Joe and dance. Leading the group is Jaimie Paul. He is drunk, disheveled.

Light spreads before them as they advance onstage. They are laughing rowdily.

Rita Joe moves to them.

120 **RITA:** Jaimie Paul?

Mr. Homer leaves. Jaimie Paul is overtaken by two of his companions who take him by the arms, but he pushes them roughly away.

JAIMIE: Get the hell outa my way! . . . I'm as good a man as him any time
. . . *(Jaimie Paul crosses downstage to confront a member of the audience.)*
You know me? . . . You think I'm a dirty Indian, eh? Get outa my way!
(He puts his hands over his head and continues staggering away.)
Goddamnit, I wanna sleep . . .

The Young Indian Men and Jaimie Paul exit. Rita Joe follows after Jaimie Paul, reaching out to touch him, but the Singer stands in her way and drives her back, singing . . .

Music up tempo and volume.

SINGER:
Oh, can't you see that train roll on,
Its hot black wheels keep comin' on?
A Kamloops Indian died today.
Train didn't hit him, he just fell.
Busy train with wheels on fire!

The music dies. A Policeman enters.

POLICEMAN: Rita Joe! *(He repeats her name many times.)*

The Teacher enters ringing the school handbell and crosses through.

TEACHER: *(calling)* Rita Joe! Rita Joe! Didn't you hear the bell ring? The class
is waiting . . . The class is always waiting for you. *(The Teacher exits.)*

125 **MAGISTRATE & POLICEMAN:** *(sharply, in unison)* Rita Joe!

The Policeman grabs and shakes Rita Joe to snap her out of her reverie.

Light up on the Magistrate who sits erect, with authority.

MAGISTRATE: I ask you for the last time, Rita Joe . . . Do you want a lawyer?
RITA: *(defiantly)* What for? . . . I can take care of myself.
MAGISTRATE: The charge against you this morning is prostitution. Why did
you not return to your people as you said you would?

The light on the backstage dies. Rita Joe stands before the Magistrate and the Policeman. She is contained in a pool of light before them.

RITA: *(nervous, with despair)* I tried . . . I tried . . .

The Magistrate settles back into his chair and takes a folder from his desk, which he opens and studies.

130 MAGISTRATE: Special Constable Eric Wilson has submitted a statement to the effect that on June 18th he and Special Constable Schneider approached you on Fourth Avenue at nine-forty in the evening . . .

POLICEMAN: We were impersonating two deck-hands newly arrived in the city . . .

MAGISTRATE: You were arrested an hour later on charges of prostitution.

The Magistrate holds the folder threateningly and looks down at her. Rita Joe is defiant.

RITA: That's a goddamned lie!

MAGISTRATE: *(sternly, gesturing to the Policeman)* This is a police statement. Surely you don't think a mistake was made?

135 RITA: *(peering into the light above her, shuddering)* Everything in this room is like ice . . . How can you stay alive working here? . . . I'm so hungry I want to throw up . . .

MAGISTRATE: You have heard the statement, Rita Joe . . . Do you deny it?

RITA: I was going home, trying to find the highway . . . I knew those two were cops the moment I saw them . . . I told them to go f . . . fly a kite! They got sore then an' started pushing me around . . .

MAGISTRATE: *(patiently now, waving down the objections of the Policeman)* Go on.

RITA: They followed me around until a third cop drove up. An' then they arrested me.

140 MAGISTRATE: Arrested you . . . Nothing else?

RITA: They stuffed five dollar bills in my pockets when they had me in the car . . . I ask you, mister, when are they gonna charge cops like that with contributing to . . .

POLICEMAN: Your Worship . . .

MAGISTRATE: *(irritably, indicating the folder on the table before him)* Now it's your word against this! You need references . . . People who know you . . . who will come to court to substantiate what you say . . . today! That is the process of legal argument!

RITA: Can I bum a cigarette someplace?

145 MAGISTRATE: No. You can't smoke in court.

The Policeman smiles and exits.

RITA: Then give me a bed to sleep on, or is the sun gonna rise an' rise until it burns a hole in my head?

Guitar music cues softly in the background.

MAGISTRATE: Tell me about the child.

RITA: What child?

MAGISTRATE: The little girl I once saw beside the road!

150 RITA: I don't know any girl, mister! When do I eat? Why does an Indian wait even when he's there first thing in the morning?

The pool of light tightens around Magistrate and Rita Joe.

MAGISTRATE: I have children . . . two sons . . .
RITA: *(nodding)* Sure. That's good.

The Magistrate gropes for words to express a message that is very precious to him.

MAGISTRATE: My sons can go in any direction they wish . . . Into trades or
  university . . . But if I had a daughter, I would be more concerned . . .
RITA: What's so special about a girl?
155 MAGISTRATE: I would wish . . . Well, I'd be concerned about her choices . . .
  Her choices of living, school . . . friends . . . These things don't come
  as lightly for a girl. For boys it is different . . . But I would worry if I
  had a daughter . . . Don't hide your child! Someone else can be found
  to raise her if you can't!

Rita Joe shakes her head, a strange smile on her face.

  Why not? There are people who would love to take care of it.
RITA: Nobody would get my child . . . I would sooner kill it an' bury it first!
  I am not a kind woman, mister judge!
MAGISTRATE: *(at a loss)* I see . . .
RITA: *(a cry)* I want to go home . . .

Quick up-tempo music is heard. Suddenly, the lights change.

*Jaimie Paul and the Young Indian Men sweep over the backstage ramp, the light
widening for them. Rita Joe moves into this railway station crowd. She turns from
one man to another until she sees Jaimie Paul.*

Eileen Joe and an Old Woman enter.

RITA: Jaimie!
160 EILEEN: *(happily, running to him)* Jaimie Paul! God's sakes . . . When did you
  get back from the north? . . . I thought you said you wasn't coming
  until breakup . . .

Jaimie Paul turns to Eileen.

JAIMIE: I was comin' home on the train . . . had a bit to drink and was
  feeling pretty good . . . Lots of women sleeping in their seats on the
  train . . . I'd lift their hats an' say, "Excuse me, lady . . . I'm lookin' for
  a wife!" *(He turns to the Old Woman.)* One fat lady got mad, an' I says
  to her, "That's alright, lady . . . You got no worries . . . You keep
  sleepin'!"

Laughter.

Jaimie Paul and the Old Woman move away.

Eileen sees Rita Joe who is standing watching.

EILEEN: Rita! . . . Tom an' I broke up . . . Did I tell you?

RITA: No, Leenie . . . You didn't tell me!

EILEEN: He was no good . . . He stopped comin' to see me when he said he would. I kept waiting, but he didn't come . . .

165 RITA: I sent you a pillow for your wedding!

EILEEN: I gave it away . . . I gave it to Clara Hill.

RITA: *(laughing bawdily and miming pregnancy)* Clara Hill don't need no pillow now!

JAIMIE: *(smiling, crossing by her and exiting)* I always came to see you, Rita Joe . . .

Rita Joe looks bewildered.

OLD WOMAN: *(exiting)* I made two Saskatoon pies, Rita . . . You said next time you came home you wanted Saskatoon pie with lots of sugar . . .

Eileen and the Old Woman drift away.

Jaimie Paul moves on to the shadows.

The Three Murderers enter in silhouette; one whistles. Rita Joe rushes to the Young Indian Men in stagefront.

170 RITA: This is me, Rita Joe, God's sakes . . . We went to the same school together . . . Don't you know me now, Johnny? You remember how tough you was when you was a boy? . . . We tied you up in the Rainbow Creek and forgot you was there after recess . . . An' after school was out, somebody remembered . . . *(She laughs.)* And you was blue when we got to you. Your clothes was wet to the chin, an' you said, "That's a pretty good knot . . . I almost give up trying to untie it!"

The music continues. Rita Joe steps among the Young Indian Men and they mime being piled in a car at a drive-in.

Steve Laporte? . . . You remember us goin' to the drive-in and the cold rain comin' down the car windows so we couldn't see the picture show anyhow?

She sits beside Steve Laporte. They mime the windshield wipers.

A cold white light comes up on playing area directly in front of the Magistrate's chair. A Male Witness of disheveled, dirty appearance steps into light and delivers testimony in a whining, defensive voice. He is one of the Murderers, but apart from the other two, he is nervous.

WITNESS: I gave her three bucks . . . an' once I got her goin' she started yellin' like hell! Called me a dog, pig . . . some filthy kind of animal . . . So I slapped her around a bit . . . Guys said she was a funny kind of bim . . . would do it for them standing up, but not for me she wouldn't . . . So I slapped her around . . .

The Magistrate nods and makes a notation. The light on the Witness dies.

Rita Joe speaks with urgency and growing fear to Steve Laporte.

RITA: Then you shut the wipers off an' we were just sitting there, not knowing what to do . . . I wish . . . we could go back again there an' start livin' from that day on . . . Jaimie!

Rita Joe looks at Steve Laporte as at a stranger. She stands and draws away from him. Jaimie Paul enters behind Rita Joe.

There is a cold light before the Magistrate again and another Male Witness moves into the light, replacing the first Witness. He too is one of the Murderers.

This Witness testifies with full gusto.

WITNESS: Gave her a job in my tire store . . . took her over to my place after work once . . . She was scared when I tried a trick, but I'm easy on broads that get scared, providin' they keep their voices down . . . After that, I slipped her a fiver . . . Well, sir, she took the money, then she stood in front of the window, her head high an' her naked shoulders shakin' like she was cold. Well, sir, she cried a little an' then she says, "Goddamnit, but I wish I was a school teacher . . ."

He laughs and everyone onstage joins in the laughter.

The light dies out on the Witness. Jaimie Paul enters and crosses to Rita Joe. They lie down and embrace.

RITA: You always came to see me, Jaimie Paul . . . The night we were in the cemetery . . . You remember, Jaimie Paul? I turned my face from yours until I saw the ground . . . an' I knew that below us . . . they were like us once, and now they lie below the ground, their eyes gone, the bones showin' . . . They must've spoke and touched each other here . . . like you're touching me, Jaimie Paul . . . an' now there was nothing over them, except us . . . an' wind in the grass an' a barbwire fence creaking. An' behind that, a hundred acres of barley.

Jaimie Paul stands.

That's something to remember, when you're lovin', eh?

The sound of a train whistle is heard. Jaimie Paul goes and the lights onstage fade.

The music comes up and the Singer sings. As Jaimie Paul passes her, the Singer pursues him up the ramp, and Rita Joe runs after them.

175 SINGER:
　　Oh, can't you see that train roll on,
　　Gonna kill a man, before it's gone?
　　Jaimie Paul fell and died.
　　He had it comin', so it's alright.
　　Silver train with wheels on fire!

The music dies instantly. Rita Joe's words come on the heels of music as a bitter extension of song.

She stands before the Magistrate, again in the court, but looks back to where Jaimie Paul had been in the gloom. The Policeman enters where Jaimie Paul has exited, replacing him, for the fourth trial scene.

RITA: Jaimie, why am I here? . . . Is it . . . because people are talkin' about me and all them men . . . Is that why? I never wanted to cut cordwood for a living . . . *(With great bitterness.)* Never once I thought . . . it'd be like this . . .

MAGISTRATE: What are we going to do about you, Rita Joe? This is the seventh charge against you in one year . . . Laws are not made to be violated in this way . . . Why did you steal?

RITA: I was hungry. I had no money.

MAGISTRATE: Yet you must have known you would be caught?

180 RITA: Yes.

MAGISTRATE: Are you not afraid of what is happening to you?

RITA: I am afraid of a lot of things. Put me in jail. I don't care . . .

MAGISTRATE: *(with forced authority)* Law is a procedure. The procedure must be respected. It took hundreds of years to develop this process of law.

RITA: I stole a sweater . . . They caught me in five minutes!

She smiles whimsically at this. The Magistrate is leafing through the documents before him. The Policeman stands to one side of him.

185 MAGISTRATE: The prosecutor's office has submitted some of the past history of Rita Joe . . .

POLICEMAN: She was born and raised on a reservation. Then came a brief period in a public school off the reservation . . . at which time Rita Joe established herself as something of a disruptive influence . . .

RITA: What's that mean?

MAGISTRATE: *(turning to her, smiling)* A troublemaker!

Rita Joe becomes animated, aware of the trap around her closing even at moments such as this.

RITA: Maybe it was about the horse, huh? . . . *(She looks up at the Magistrate who is still smiling, offering her no help.)* There was this accident with a horse . . . It happened like this . . . I was riding a horse to school an' some of the boys shot a rifle an' my horse bucked an' I fell off. I fell in the bush an' got scratched . . . The boys caught the horse by the school and tried to ride him, but the horse bucked an' pinned a boy against a tree, breaking his leg in two places . . . *(She indicates the place the leg got broken.)* They said . . . an' he said I'd rode the horse over him on purpose!

190 MAGISTRATE: Well . . . Did you?

RITA: It wasn't that way at all, I tell you! They lied!

The Policeman and the Singer laugh.

MAGISTRATE: Why should they lie, and Rita Joe alone tell the truth? . . . Or are you a child enough to believe the civilization of which we are a part . . . *(He indicates the audience as inclusive of civilization from his point of view.)* . . . does not understand Rita Joe?

RITA: I don't know what you're saying.

MAGISTRATE: *(with a touch of compassion)* Look at you, woman! Each time you come before me you are older. The lines in your face are those of . . .

195 RITA: I'm tired an' I want to eat, mister! I haven't had grub since day before yesterday . . . This room is like a boat on water . . . I'm so dizzy . . . What the hell kind of place is this won't let me go lie down on grass? *(She doubles over to choke back her nausea.)*

MAGISTRATE: This is not the reservation, Rita Joe. This is another place, another time . . .

RITA: *(straining to remember, to herself)* I was once in Whitecourt, Alberta. The cops are fatter there than here. I had to get out of Whitecourt, Alberta . . .

MAGISTRATE: Don't blame the police, Rita Joe! The obstacles to your life are here . . . *(He touches his forefinger to his temples.)* . . . in your thoughts . . . possibly even in your culture . . .

Rita Joe turns away from him, searching the darkness behind her.

What's the matter?

RITA: I want to go home!

200 MAGISTRATE: But you can't go now. You've broken a law for which you will have to pay a fine or go to prison . . .

RITA: I have no money.

MAGISTRATE: *(with exasperation)* Rita Joe . . . It is against the law to solicit men on the street. You have to wash . . .

Rita Joe begins to move away from him, crossing the front of the stage along the apron, her walk cocky.

The light spreads and follows her.

You can't walk around in old clothes and running shoes made of canvas . . . You have to have some money in your pockets and an address where you live. You should fix your hair . . . perhaps even change your name. And try to tame that accent that sounds like you have a mouthful of sawdust . . . There is no peace in being extraordinary!

The light dies on the Magistrate and the Policeman.

Rita Joe is transported into another memory. Jaimie Paul enters and slides along the floor, left of centre stage. He is drunk, counting the fingers on his outstretched hands.

Mr. Homer has entered with a wagon carrying hot soup and mugs. Four Young Indian Men come in out of the cold. Mr. Homer speaks to audience in a matter-of-fact informative way.

Mr. Homer: *(dispensing soup to the Young Indian Men)* The do-gooders make something special of the Indian . . . There's nothing special here . . . At the centre here the quick cure is a bowl of stew under the belt and a good night's sleep.

Jaimie: Hey, Mister Homer! How come I got so many fingers? Heh? *(He laughs.)*

Mr. Homer ignores Jaimie Paul and continues talking to the audience.

205 **Mr. Homer:** I wouldn't say they were brothers or sisters to me . . . No sir! But if you're . . .

Jaimie Paul gets up and embraces Rita Joe.

Jaimie: I got two hands an' one neck . . . I can kill more than I can eat . . . If I had more fingers I would need mittens big as pie plates . . . Yeh?

Mr. Homer: *(to Jaimie Paul)* Lie down, Jaimie Paul, an' have some more sleep. When you feel better, I'll get you some soup.

Rita Joe laughs. Jaimie Paul weaves his way uncertainly to where Mr. Homer stands.

Jaimie: *(laughing)* I spit in your soup! You know what I say? . . . I say I spit in your soup, Mister Homer . . . *(He comes to Mr. Homer and seems about to do just what he threatens.)*

Mr. Homer: *(pushing him away with good humour)* I'll spit in your eyeball if you don't shut up!

210 **Jaimie:** *(breaking away from Mr. Homer, taunting)* You . . . are not Mister Homer!

Mr. Homer: I'm not what?

Jaimie: You're not Mister Homer . . . You're somebody wearing his pants an' shirt . . . *(He stumbles away.)* But you're not Mister Homer . . . Mister Homer never gets mad . . . No sir, not Mister Homer!

Mr. Homer: I'm not mad . . . What're you talkin' about?

Jaimie Paul turns and approaches the Young Indian Men. He threatens to fall off the apron of the stage.

Jaimie: No . . . not Mister Homer! An' I got ten fingers . . . How's that?

215 **Mr. Homer:** For Chris' sake, Jaimie . . . Go to sleep.

Jaimie Paul stops and scowls, then grins knowingly. He begins to mime a clumsy paddler paddling a boat.

Jaimie: *(laughing again)* I know you . . . Hey? I know you! . . . I seen you up Rainbow Creek one time . . . I seen you paddling! *(He breaks up with laughter.)*

MR. HOMER: *(amused, tolerant)* Oh, come on . . . I've never been to Rainbow Creek.

Jaimie Paul controls his laughter.

JAIMIE: Sure you been to Rainbow Creek . . . *(He begins to mime paddling again.)* Next time you need a good paddler, you see me. I have a governmen' job, but screw that. I'm gonna paddle! I seen you paddle . . . *(Again he breaks up in laughter as he once more demonstrates the quality of paddling he once saw.)*

Rita Joe is fully enjoying the spectacle. So are the Young Indian Men. Mr. Homer is also amused by the absurdity of the situation. Jaimie Paul turns, but chokes up with laughter after saying . . .

I have seen some paddlers . . . but you! *(Jaimie Paul turns and waves his hand derisively, laughing.)*

MR. HOMER: It must've been somebody else . . . I've never been to Rainbow Creek.

220 JAIMIE: Like hell, you say!

Jaimie Paul paddles the soup wagon out. Guitar music comes in with an upbeat tempo. Rita Joe and the Young Indian Men dance to the beat. The Young Indian Men then drift after Mr. Homer.

The light fades slowly on centre stage and the music changes.

Rita Joe, happy in her memory, does a circling butch walk in the fading light to the song of the Singer. At the conclusion of the song, she is on the apron, stage right, in a wash of light that includes the Magistrate and the Singer.

SINGER:
    I woke up at six o'clock
    Stumbled out of bed,
    Crash of cans an' diesel trucks
    Damned near killed me dead.

    Sleepless hours, heavy nights,
    Dream your dreams so pretty.
    God was gonna have a laugh
    An' gave me a job in the city!

Rita Joe is still elated at her memory of Jaimie Paul and his story. With unusual candour, she turns girlishly before the Magistrate, and in mild imitation of her own moment of drunkenness, begins telling him a story.

Faint guitar music in the background continues.

RITA: One night I drank a little bit of wine, an' I was outside lookin' at the stars . . . thinking . . . when I was a little girl how much bigger the trees were . . . no clouds, but suddenly there was a light that made the whole sky look like day . . .

Guitar out.

> . . . just for a moment . . . an' before I got used to the night . . . I saw animals, moving across the sky . . . two white horses . . . A man was takin' them by the halters, and I knew the man was my grandfather . . . *(She stares at the Magistrate, unsure of herself now.)*

Magistrate: Yes! Is that all?

Rita: No . . . But I never seen my grandfather alive, and I got so sad thinkin' about it I wanted to cry. I wasn't sure it was him, even . . . *(She begins to laugh.)* I went an' telephoned the police and asked for the chief, but the chief was home and a guy asks what I want.

225 Magistrate: *(mildly amused)* You . . . called the police?

Rita: I told the guy I'd seen God, and he says, "Yeh? What would you like us to do about it?" An' I said, "Pray! Laugh! Shout!"

Magistrate: Go on . . .

Rita: He . . . asked where I'd seen God, an' I told him in the sky. He says you better call this number . . . It's the Air Force. They'll take care of it!

She laughs and the Magistrate smiles.

> I called the number the guy gave me, but it was nighttime and there was no answer! If God was to come at night, after office hours, then . . .

A terrible awkwardness sets in. There is a harsh light on her. She turns away, aware that she is in captivity.

The Magistrate stirs with discomfort.

Rita: *(with great fear)* How long will this be? Will I never be able to . . .

230 Magistrate: *(annoyed at himself, at her)* There is nothing here but a record of your convictions . . . Nothing to speak for you and provide me with any reason to moderate your sentence! What the hell am I supposed to do? Violate the law myself because I feel that somehow . . . I've known and felt . . . No! *(He turns from her.)* You give me no alternative . . . No alternative at all! *(The Magistrate packs up his books.)*

Rita: I'll go home . . . jus' let me go home. I can't get out of jail to find the highway . . . or some kind of job!

The Magistrate stands.

Magistrate: Prison and fines are not the only thing . . . Have you, for instance, considered that you might be an incurable carrier? There are people like that . . . They cannot come into contact with others without infecting them. They cannot eat from dishes others may use . . . They cannot prepare or touch food others will eat . . . The same with clothes, cars, hospital beds! *(The Magistrate exits.)*

Rita Joe shakes her head with disbelief. The idea of perpetual condemnation is beyond her comprehension. She falls to the floor.

Guitar music is heard in the background.

She turns away from the Magistrate and the light comes up over the ramp at the back of the stage.

Another light comes up on centre stage left. Here, Eileen Joe and the Old Woman are miming clothes washing using a scrubbing board and placing the wash into woven baskets. The woman and the girl are on their knees, facing each other.

On the ramp above them, Jaimie Paul is struggling with a Policeman who is scolding him softly for being drunk, abusive and noisy. Jaimie Paul is jocular; the Policeman, harassed and worried. They slowly cross the ramp from stage left.

SINGER:
> Four o'clock in the morning,
> The sailor rides the ship
> An' I ride the wind!
>
> Eight o'clock in the morning,
> My honey's scoldin' the sleepyheads
> An' I'm scoldin' him.

JAIMIE: *(to the Policeman)* On the Smoky River . . . four o'clock in the
morning . . . Hey? There was nobody . . . just me . . . You know that?
235 POLICEMAN: No, I don't. Come on. Let's get you home.

Jaimie Paul moves forward and embraces the Policeman.

JAIMIE: You wanna see something? *(Jaimie Paul takes out a coin to do a trick.)*
OLD WOMAN: *(to Eileen)* Your father's been very sick.
EILEEN: He won't eat nothing . . .
OLD WOMAN: Jus' sits and worries . . . That's no good.

Jaimie Paul finishes his coin trick.

240 JAIMIE: You like that one? Hey, we both work for the government, eh?

They exit laughing.

> Watch the rough stuff . . . Just don't make me mad.
OLD WOMAN: If Rita Joe was to come and see him . . . maybe say goodbye
to him . . .
RITA: *(calling from her world to the world of her strongest fears)* But he's not
dying! I saw him not so long ago . . .

The women in her memory do not hear her. They continue discussing her father.

OLD WOMAN: He loved her an' always worried . . .

RITA: I didn't know he was sick!

245 OLD WOMAN: You were smart to come back, Eileen Joe.

RITA: *(again calling over the distance of her soul)* Nobody told me!

SINGER:
> Nine o'clock in the evening,
> Moon is high in the blueberry sky
> An' I'm lovin' you.

JAIMIE: *(now passing along the apron beside Rita Joe, talking to the Policeman)* You seen where I live? Big house with a mongolia in front . . . Fancy place! You wanna see the room I got?

POLICEMAN: *(gruffly, aware that Jaimie Paul can become angry quickly)* When I get holidays, we'll take a tour of everything you've got . . . but I don't get holidays until September!

From the apron they cross to the stage rear diagonally, between the Old Woman with Eileen, and Rita Joe.

250 JAIMIE: You're a good man . . . Good for a laugh. I'm a good man . . . You know me!

POLICEMAN: Sure, you're first class when you're sober!

JAIMIE: I got a cousin in the city. He got his wife a stove an' washing machine! He's a good man . . . You know my cousin maybe?

Fading off.

They leave the stage.

The Old Woman has risen from her knees and wearily collected one basket of clothes. She climbs the ramp and moves to the wings, stage right. Eileen is thoughtful and slower, but she also prepares her clothes wash and follows.

OLD WOMAN: Nothing in the city I can see . . . only if you're lucky. A good man who don't drink or play cards . . . that's all.

EILEEN: And if he's bad?

255 OLD WOMAN: Then leave him. I'm older than you, Eileen . . . I know what's best.

The Old Woman exits. The guitar music dies out. Jaimie Paul's laughter and voice is heard offstage.

JAIMIE: *(offstage, loud, boisterous)* We both work for the gov'ment! We're buddies, no? . . . You think we're both the same?

Laughter.

The lights on the ramp and centre stage die.

RITA: *(following Jaimie Paul's laughter)* Good or bad, what difference? So long as he's a livin' man!

Rita Joe and Eileen giggle.

The light spreads around her into pale infinity.

The Teacher enters on the ramp. She rings a handbell and stops a short distance from wings to peer around. She is a shy, inadequate woman who moves and behaves jerkily, the product of incomplete education and poor job placement.

TEACHER: *(in a scolding voice)* Rita! Rita Joe!

The bell rings.

The class is waiting for you. The class is always waiting.

Rita Joe is startled to hear the bell and see the woman. She comes to her feet, now a child before the Teacher, and runs to join Eileen. Jaimie Paul and the Young Indian Men have entered with the bell and sit cross-legged on the floor as school children.

RITA: The sun is in my skin, Miss Donohue. The leaves is red and orange, and the wind stopped blowin' an hour ago.

The Teacher has stopped to listen to this. Rita Joe and Eileen, late again, slip into class and sit on the floor with the others.

260 TEACHER: Rita! What is a noun?

No answer. The kids poke Rita Joe to stand up.

Did you hear what I asked?
RITA: *(uncertain)* No . . . Yes?
TEACHER: There's a lot you don't know . . . That kind of behaviour is exhibitionism! We are a melting pot!
RITA: A melting pot?
TEACHER: A melting pot! Do you know what a melting pot is?
265 RITA: It's . . . *(She shrugs)* . . . a melting pot!

The class laughs.

TEACHER: Precisely! You put copper and tin into a melting pot and out comes bronze . . . It's the same with people!
RITA: Yes, Miss Donohue . . . out comes bronze . . .

Laughter again.

The Teacher calls Rita Joe over to her. The light fades on the other children.

TEACHER: Rita, what was it I said to you this morning?
RITA: You said . . . wash my neck, clean my fingernails . . .
270 TEACHER: *(cagey)* No, it wasn't, Rita!
RITA: I can't remember. It was long ago.
TEACHER: Try to remember, Rita.

RITA: I don't remember, Miss Donohue! I was thinkin' about you last night, thinkin' if you knew some . . .

TEACHER: You are straying off the topic! Never stray off the topic!

275 RITA: It was a dream, but now I'm scared, Miss Donohue. I've been a long time moving about . . . trying to find something! . . . I must've lost . . .

TEACHER: No, Rita. That is not important.

RITA: Not important?

TEACHER: No, Rita . . . Now you repeat after me like I said or I'm going to have to pass you by again. Say after me . . .

RITA: Sure. Say after you . . .

280 TEACHER: Say after me . . . "A book of verse underneath the spreading bough . . ."

RITA: "A book of verse underneath the spreading bough . . ."

TEACHER: "A jug of wine, a loaf of bread and thou beside me . . . singing in the wilderness."

RITA: *(the child spell broken, she laughs bawdily)* Jaimie said, "To heck with the wine an' loaf . . . Let's have some more of this here thou!" *(Her laughter dies. She wipes her lips, as if trying to erase some stain there.)*

TEACHER: *(peevish)* Alright, Rita . . . Alright, let's have none of that!

285 RITA: *(plaintively)* I'm sorry, Miss Donohue . . . I'm sure sorry!

TEACHER: That's alright.

RITA: I'm sorry!

TEACHER: Alright . . .

RITA: Sorry . . .

290 TEACHER: You will never make bronze! Coming from nowhere and going no place! Who am I to change that?

Rita Joe grips the edge of the desk with both hands, holding on tightly.

RITA: No! They said for me to stay here, to learn something!

TEACHER: *(with exasperation)* I tried to teach you, but your head was in the clouds, and as for your body . . . Well! I wouldn't even think what I know you do! *(The Teacher crosses amongst the other children.)*

RITA: I'm sorry . . . please! Let me say it after you again . . . *(Blurting it out)* . . . "A book of verse underneath the spreading . . ."

TEACHER: Arguing . . . always trying to upset me . . . and in grade four . . . I saw it then . . . pawing the ground for men like a bitch in heat!

295 RITA: *(dismayed)* It . . . isn't so!

TEACHER: You think I don't know? I'm not blind . . . I can see out of the windows.

The Teacher marches off into wings and the class runs after her leaving Rita Joe alone onstage.

RITA: That's a lie! For God's sake, tell the judge I have a good character . . . I am clean an' honest . . . Everything you said is right, I'm never gonna argue again . . . I believe in God . . . an' I'm from the country and lost like hell! Tell him! *(She shakes her head sadly, knowing the extent of her betrayal.)* They only give me eight hours to find somebody who knows me . . . An' seven and a half hours is gone already!

The light on the scene dies.

SINGER: *(recitivo)*
Things that were . . .
Life that might have been . . .

A pale backlight on the back of the ramp comes up.

Recorded sounds of crickets and the distant sound of a train whistle are heard.

Rita Joe's Father and Jaimie Paul enter on the ramp from stage left. The Father leads the way. Jaimie Paul is behind, rolling a cigarette. They walk slowly, thoughtfully, following the ramp across and downstage. Rita Joe stands separate, watching.

The blue evening of the first
Warm day
Is the last evening.
There'll not be another
Like it.

JAIMIE: No more handouts, David Joe . . . We can pick an' can the berries ourselves.

300 FATHER: We need money to start a cooperative like that.

JAIMIE: Then some other way!

The old man listens, standing still, to the sounds of the train and night.

FATHER: You're a young man, Jaimie Paul . . . young an' angry. It's not good to be that angry.

JAIMIE: We're gonna work an' live like people . . . Not be afraid all the time . . . Stop listening to an old priest an' Indian department guys who're working for a pension!

FATHER: You're young man, Jaimie Paul . . .

305 JAIMIE: I say stop listening, David Joe! . . . In the city they never learned my name. It was "Hey, fella" . . . or "You, boy" . . . That kind of stuff.

Pause. The sound of the train whistle is heard.

FATHER: A beautiful night, Jaimie Paul.

JAIMIE: We can make some money. The berries are good this year! *(Jaimie Paul is restless, edgy, particularly on the train whistle sound.)*

FATHER: Sometimes . . . children . . . You remember everyday with them . . . Never forget you are alive with children.

Jaimie Paul turns away and begins to retrace his steps.

JAIMIE: You want us all to leave an' go to the city? Is that what you want?

The Father shakes his head. He does not wish for this, but the generation spread between them is great now. Jaimie Paul walks away with a gesture of contempt.

The sounds die.

The light dies and isolates the Father and Rita Joe.

310 RITA: You were sick, an' now you're well.

FATHER: *(in measured speech, turning away from Rita Joe, as if carefully recalling something of great importance)* You left your father, Rita Joe . . . never wrote Eileen a letter that time . . . Your father was pretty sick man that time . . . pretty sick man . . . June ninth he got the cold, an' on June twenty he . . .

RITA: But you're alive! I had such crazy dreams I'd wake up laughing at myself!

FATHER: I have dreams too . . .

Rita Joe moves forward to him. She stops talking to him, as if communicating thoughts rather than words. He remains standing where he is, facing away from her.

RITA: I was in a big city . . . so many streets I'd get lost like nothin' . . . When you got sick I was on a job . . .

315 FATHER: June ninth I got the cold . . .

RITA: Good job in a tire store . . . Jaimie Paul's got a job with the government, you know?

FATHER: Pretty sick man, that time . . .

RITA: A good job in a tire store. They was gonna teach me how to file statements after I learned the telephone. Bus ticket home was twenty dollars . . . But I got drunk all the same when I heard an' I went in and tried to work that day . . . *(She smiles and shakes her head.)* Boy, I tried to work! Some day that was!

FATHER: I have dreams . . . Sometimes I'm scared . . .

They finally look at each other.

320 RITA: *(shuddering)* I'm so cold . . .

FATHER: Long dreams . . . I dream about Rita Joe . . . *(Sadly.)* Have to get better. I've lived longer, but know nothing . . . Nothing at all. Only the old stories.

Rita Joe moves sideways to him. She is smiling happily.

RITA: When I was little, a man came out of the bush to see you. Tell me why again!

The Father hesitates, shaking his head, but he is also smiling.

The light of their separate yearnings fades out and the front of the stage is lit with the two of them together.

The Father turns and comes forward to meet her.

FATHER: You don't want to hear that story again.

He sits on the slight elevation of the stage apron. Rita Joe sits down in front of him and snuggles between his knees. He leans forward over her.

RITA: It's the best story I ever heard!

325 FATHER: You were a little girl . . . four years old already . . . an' Eileen was getting big inside your mother. One day it was hot . . . sure was hot. Too hot to try an' fish in the lake, because the fish was down deep where the water was cold.

RITA: The dog started to bark . . .

FATHER: The dog started to bark . . . How!

FATHER & RITA: *(in unison)* How! How! How!

FATHER: Barking to beat hell an' I says to myself why . . . on such a hot day? Then I see the bushes moving . . . somebody was coming to see us. Your mother said from inside the house, "What's the matter with that dog?" An' I says to her, "Somebody coming to see me." It was big Sandy Collins, who ran the sawmill back of the reserve. Business was bad for big Sandy then . . . but he comes out of that bush like he was being chased . . . his clothes all wet an' stickin' to him . . . his cap in his hands, an' his face black with the heat and dirt from hard work . . . He says to me, "My little Millie got a cough last night an' today she's dead." . . . "She's dead," big Sandy says to me. I says to him, "I'm sorry to hear that, Sandy . . . Millie is the same age as my Rita." And he says to me, "David Joe . . . Look, you got another kid coming . . . Won't make much difference to you . . . Sell me Rita Joe like she is for a thousand dollars!"

Rita Joe giggles. The Father raises his hand to silence her.

"A thousand dollars is a lot of money, Sandy," I says to him . . . "lots of money. You got to cut a lot of timber for a thousand dollars." Then he says to me, "Not a thousand cash at once, David Joe. First I give you two-hundred-fifty dollars . . . When Rita Joe comes ten years old and she's still alright, I give you the next two-hundred-fifty . . . An' if she don't die by fifteen, I guarantee you five-hundred dollars cash at once!"

Rita Joe and the Father break into laughter.

He reaches around her throat and draws her close.

So you see, Rita Joe, you lose me one thousand dollars from big Sandy Collins!

They continue laughing.

A harsh light on the Magistrate, who enters and stands on his podium.

330 MAGISTRATE: Rita Joe, when was the last time you had dental treatment?

Rita Joe covers her ears, refusing to surrender this moment of security in the arms of her Father.

RITA: I can't hear you!
MAGISTRATE: *(loudly)* You had your teeth fixed ever?

Rita Joe comes to her feet and turns on him.

RITA: Leave me alone!
MAGISTRATE: Have you had your lungs X-rayed recently?
335 RITA: I was hungry, that's all!
MAGISTRATE: *(becoming staccato, machine-like in his questions)* When was your
    last Wasserman taken?
RITA: What's that?

*Rita Joe hears the Teacher's voice. She turns to see the approaching Teacher give the
Magistrate testimony.*

The stage is lit in a cold blue light now.

TEACHER: *(crisply, to the Magistrate as she approaches, her dialogue a reading)*
    Dear Sir . . . In reply to your letter of the twelfth, I cannot in all
    sincerity provide a reference of good character for one Rita Joe . . .

*The Witnesses do not see her and the testimony takes on the air of a nightmare for
Rita Joe. She is baffled and afraid. The Teacher continues to quietly repeat her testimony.*

Rita Joe appeals to the Magistrate.

RITA: Why am I here? What've I done?
340 MAGISTRATE: You are charged with prostitution.

*Her Father stands and crosses upstage to the ramp to observe. He is joined by Eileen
Joe, the Old Woman and the Priest. Mr. Homer approaches briskly from stage left.*

MR. HOMER: She'd been drinking when she comes into the centre . . .
    Nothing wrong in that I could see, 'specially on a Friday night. So I
    give her some soup an' a sandwich. Then all of a sudden in the middle
    of a silly argument, she goes haywire . . . an' I see her comin' at me . . .
    I'll tell you, I was scared! I don't know Indian women that well!
MAGISTRATE: Assault!

*Rita Joe retreats from him, and the Teacher and Mr. Homer now stand before the
Magistrate as if they were frozen. Mr. Homer repeats his testimony under the main
dialogue. Jaimie Paul staggers in from stage right, over the ramp, heading to the
wings of lower stage left.*

JAIMIE: *(to himself)* What the hell are they doing?
RITA: *(running to him)* Say a good word for me, Jaimie!
345 JAIMIE: They fired me yesterday . . . What the hell's the use of living?

*Jaimie Paul leaves the stage as the School Board Clerk enters to offer further testi-
mony to the Magistrate.*

School Board Clerk: I recommended in a letter that she take school after grade five through correspondence courses from the Department of Education . . . but she never replied to the form letter the school division sent her . . .

Rita: *(defending herself to the Magistrate)* That drunken bastard Mahoney used it to light fire in his store . . . He'd never tell Indians when mail came for us!

School Board Clerk: I repeat . . . I wish our position understood most clearly . . . No reply was ever received in this office to the letter we sent to Rita Joe!

Rita: One letter . . . one letter for a lifetime?

350 Teacher: Say after me! "I wandered lonely as a cloud, that floats on high o'er vales and hills . . . when all at once I saw a crowd . . . a melting pot . . ."

A Policeman and a Male Witness enter. The Priest crosses downstage. The testimonies are becoming a nightmare babble.

Rita Joe is stung, stumbles backward from all of them as they face the Magistrate with their condemnations.

Policeman: We were impersonating two deck-hands . . .

The Priest is passing by Rita Joe. He makes the sign of the cross and offers comfort in a thin voice, lost in the noise.

Priest: Be patient, Rita . . . The young are always stormy, but in time, your understanding will deepen . . . There is an end to all things.

Witness: I gave her a job, but she was kind of slow . . . I can't wait around, there's lots of white people goin' lookin' for work . . . so I figure, to hell with this noise . . .

Magistrate: *(loudly over the other voices)* Have your ears ached?

355 Rita: No!

Magistrate: Have you any boils on your back? Any discharge? When did you bathe last?

The Murderers appear and circle Rita Joe.

Answer me! Drunkenness! Shoplifting! Assault! Prostitution, prostitution, prostitution, prostitution!

Rita: *(her voice shrill, cutting over the babble)* I don't know what happened . . . but you got to listen to me and believe me, mister!

The babble ceases abruptly.

Pleading with them as best she knows.

You got rules here that was made before I was born . . . I was hungry when I stole something . . . an' I was hollerin' I was so lonely when I started whoring . . .

The Murderers come closer.

MAGISTRATE: Rita Joe . . . Has a doctor examined you? . . . I mean, really examined you? Rita Joe . . . You might be carrying and transmitting some disease and not aware of it!

RITA: *(breaking away from the Murderers)* Bastards! *(To the Magistrate.)* Put me in jail . . . I don't care . . . I'll sign anything. I'm so goddamn hungry I'm sick . . . Whatever it is, I'm guilty! *(She clutches her head and goes down in a squat of defeat.)*

360 MAGISTRATE: Are you free of venereal disease?

RITA: I don't know. I'm not sick that way.

MAGISTRATE: How can you tell?

RITA: *(lifting her face to him)* I know . . . A woman knows them things . . .

Pause.

MAGISTRATE: Thirty days!

The Policeman leads Rita Joe off and the house lights come up.

The Actors and the Singer walk off the stage, leaving emptiness as at opening of the act.

ACT TWO

The house lights dim.

A Policeman brings Rita Joe in downstage centre. She curls up in her jail cell and sleeps.

Rita Joe's Father enters on the ramp and crosses down to the audience.

The stage work lights die down. Lights isolate Rita Joe's Father. Another light with prison bar shadows isolates Rita Joe in her area of the stage.

FATHER: *(looking down on Rita Joe)* I see no way . . . no way . . . It's not clear like trees against snow . . . . not clear at all . . . *(To the audience.)* But when I was fifteen years old, I leave the reserve to work on a threshing crew. They pay a dollar a day for a good man . . . an' I was a good strong man. The first time I got work there was a girl about as old as I . . . She'd come out in the yard an' watch the men working at the threshing machine. She had eyes that were the biggest I ever seen . . . like fifty-cent pieces . . . an' there was always a flock of geese around her. Whenever I see her I feel good. She used to stand an' watch me, an' the geese made a helluva lot of noise. One time I got off my rick an' went to get a drink of water . . . but I walked close to where she was watching me. She backed away, and then ran from me with the geese chasin' after her, their wings out an' their feet no longer touching the ground . . . They were white geese . . . The last time Rita

Joe come home to see us . . . the last time she ever come home . . . I watched her leave . . . and I seen geese running after Rita Joe the same way . . . white geese . . . with their wings out an' their feet no longer touching the ground. And I remembered it all, an' my heart got so heavy I wanted to cry . . . .

The light fades to darkness on the Father, as he exits up the ramp and off. Rita Joe wakes from her dream, cold, shaking, desperate.

SINGER:
The blue evening of the
First warm day
Is the last evening.
There's not be another
Like it.

The Priest enters from darkness with the Policeman. He is dressed in a dark suit which needs pressing. He stops in half shadow outside Rita Joe's prison light.

The scene between them is played out in the manner of two country people meeting in a time of crisis. Their thoughts come slowly, incompletely. There is both fear and helplessness in both characters.

PRIEST: I came twice before they'd let me see you . . .

Rita Joe jumps to her feet. She smiles at him.

RITA: Oh, Father Andrew!
5 PRIEST: Even so, I had to wait an hour.

A long pause.

He clumsily takes out package of cigarettes and matches from his pocket and hands them to her, aware that he is possibly breaking a prison regulation.

I'm sorry about this, Rita.

Rita Joe tears the package open greedily and lights a cigarette. She draws on it with animal satisfaction.

RITA: I don't know what's happening, Father Andrew.
PRIEST: They're not . . . hurting you here?
RITA: No.
PRIEST: I could make an appointment with the warden if there was something . . .
10 RITA: What's it like outside? . . . Is it a nice day outside? . . . I heard it raining last night . . . Was it raining?
PRIEST: It rains a lot here . . .
RITA: When I was a kid, there was leaves an' a river . . . Jaimie Paul told me once that maybe we never see those things again.

A long pause. The Priest struggles with himself.

PRIEST: I've never been inside a jail before . . . They told me there was a chapel . . .

He points indefinitely back.

RITA: What's gonna happen to me? . . . That judge sure got sore . . . *(She laughs.)*

15 PRIEST: *(with disgust, yet unsure of himself)* Prostitution this time?

RITA: I guess so . . .

PRIEST: You know how I feel . . . City is no place for you . . . nor for me . . . I've spent my life in the same surroundings as your father!

RITA: Sure . . . but you had God on your side!

She smiles mischievously. The Priest angers.

PRIEST: Rita, try to understand . . . Our Lord Jesus once met a woman such as you beside the well . . . He forgave her!

20 RITA: I don't think God hears me here . . . Nobody hears me now, nobody except cops an' pimps an' bootleggers!

PRIEST: I'm here. I was there when you were born.

RITA: You've told me lots of times . . . I was thinkin' about my mother last night . . . She died young . . . I'm older than she was . . .

PRIEST: You mother was a good, hard-working woman. She was happy . . .

A pause between them.

RITA: There was frost on the street at five o'clock Tuesday morning when they arrested me . . . Last night, I remembered things flyin' an' kids runnin' past me trying to catch a chocolate wrapper that's blowin' in the wind . . . *(She presses her hands against her bosom.)* It hurts me here to think about them things!

25 PRIEST: I worry about you . . . Your father worries too . . . I baptized you . . . I watched you and Leenie grow into women!

RITA: Yes . . . I seen God in what you said . . . In your clothes! In your hair!

PRIEST: But you're not the woman I expected you to be . . . Your pride, Rita . . . your pride . . . may bar you from heaven.

RITA: *(mocking him)* They got rules there too . . . in heaven?

PRIEST: *(angry)* Rita! . . . I'm not blind . . . I can see! I'm not deaf . . . I know all about you! So does God!

30 RITA: My uncle was Dan Joe . . . He was dyin' and he said to me, "Long ago the white man come with Bibles to talk to my people, who had the land. They talk for hundred years . . . then we had all the Bibles, an' the white man had our land . . ."

PRIEST: Don't blame the Church! We are trying to help . . .

RITA: *(with passion)* How? I'm looking for the door . . .

PRIEST: *(tortured now)* I . . . will hear your confession . . .

RITA: But I want to be free!

35 PRIEST: *(stiffly)* We learn through suffering, Rita Joe . . . We will only be free if we become humble again.

Pause.

Will you confess, Rita Joe?

A long pause.

I'm going back on the four o'clock bus.

He begins walking away into the gloom.

I'll tell your father I saw you, and you looked well.

He is suddenly relieved.

RITA: *(after him as he leaves)* You go to hell!

The Priest turns sharply.

Go tell your God . . . when you see him . . . . Tell him about Rita Joe an' what they done to her! Tell him about yourself too! . . . That you were not good enough for me, but that didn't stop you tryin'! Tell him that!

The Priest hurries away.

Guitar in. Rita Joe sits down, brooding.

SINGER:
I will give you the wind and a sense of wonder
As the child by the river, the reedy river.
I will give you the sky wounded by thunder
And a leaf on the river, the silver river.

A light comes up on the ramp where Jaimie Paul appears, smiling and waving to her.

JAIMIE: *(shouts)* Rita Joe! I'm gonna take you dancing after work Friday . . .
That job's gonna be alright!

Rita Joe springs to her feet, elated.

RITA: Put me back in jail so I can be free on Friday!

A sudden burst of dance music. The stage lights up and Jaimie Paul approaches her. They dance together, remaining close in the front centre stage.

40 SINGER:
Round an' round the cenotaph,
The clumsy seagulls play.
Fed by funny men with hats
Who watch them night and day.

Sleepless hours, heavy nights,
Dream your dreams so pretty.
God was gonna have a laugh
An' gave me a job in the city!

The music continues for the interlude.

Some Young Indian Men run onto the stage along the ramp and join Jaimie Paul and Rita Joe in their dance. The Murderers enter and elbow into the group, their attention specifically menacing towards Jaimie Paul and Rita Joe. A street brawl begins as a Policeman passes through on his beat. The Murderers leave hastily.

> I woke up at six o'clock,
> Stumbled out of bed.
> Crash of steel and diesel trucks
> Damned near killed me dead
>
> Sleepless hours, heavy nights,
> Dream your dreams so pretty.
> God was gonna have a laugh
> An' gave me a job in the city!

Musical interlude.

Rita Joe and Jaimie Paul continue dancing languidly. The Young Indian Men exit.

> I've polished floors an' cut the trees,
> Fished and stocked the wheat.
> Now "Hallelujah, Praise the Lord,"
> I sing before I eat!
>
> Sleepless hours, heavy nights,
> Dream your dreams so pretty.
> God was gonna have a laugh
> An' gave me a job in the city!

Musical interlude.

The music dies as the Young Indian Men wheel in a brass bed, circle it around and exit.

The stage darkens except for a pool of light where Rita Joe and Jaimie Paul stand, embracing. Jaimie Paul takes her hand and leads her away.

JAIMIE: Come on, Rita Joe . . . you're slow.
RITA: *(happy in her memories, not wishing to forget too soon, hesitating)* How much rent . . . for a place where you can keep babies?
JAIMIE: I don't know . . . maybe eighty dollars a month.
RITA: That's a lot of money.
45 JAIMIE: It costs a buck to go dancin' even . . .

They walk slowly along the apron to stage left, as if following a street to Jaimie Paul's rooming house.

It's a good place . . . I got a sink in the room. Costs seven bucks a
week, that's all!

RITA: That's good . . . I only got a bed in my place . . .

JAIMIE: I seen Mickey an' Steve Laporte last night.

RITA: How are they?

JAIMIE: Good . . . We're goin' to a beer parlour Monday night when I get
paid . . . the same beer parlour they threw Steve out of! Only now
there's three of us goin' in!

They arrive at and enter his room.

A spot illuminates the bed near the wings of stage left. It is old, dilapidated.

*Jaimie Paul and Rita Joe enter the area of light around the bed. He is aware that
the room is more drab than he would wish it.*

How do you like it . . . I like it!

50 RITA: *(examining room critically)* It's . . . smaller than my place.

JAIMIE: Sit down.

She sits on edge of the bed and falls backward into a springless hollow.

*He laughs nervously. He is awkward and confused. The ease they shared walking
to his place is now constricted.*

I was gonna get some grub today, but I was busy . . . Here . . .

*He takes a chocolate bar out of his shirt pocket and offers it to her. She opens it,
breaks off a small piece, and gives the remainder to him. He closes the wrapper and
replaces the bar in his pocket. She eats ravenously. He walks around the bed nervously.*

No fat d.p.'s gonna throw me or the boys out of that beer parlour or
he's gonna get this!

*He holds up a fist in a gesture that is both poignant and futile. She laughs and he
glowers at her.*

I'm tellin' you!

RITA: If they want to throw you out, they'll throw you out.

JAIMIE: Well, this is one Indian guy they're not pushing around no more!

RITA: God helps them who help themselves.

55 JAIMIE: That's right! *(He laughs.)* I was lookin' at the white shirts in Eaton's
and this bugger comes an' says to me, you gonna buy or you gonna
look all day?

RITA: *(looking around her)* It's a nice room for a guy, I guess . . .

JAIMIE: It's a lousy room!

Rita Joe lies back lengthwise in the bed. Jaimie Paul sits on the bed beside her.

RITA: You need a good job to have babies in the city . . . Clara Hill gave
   both her kids away they say . . .

JAIMIE: Where do kids like that go?

60 RITA: Foster homes, I guess.

JAIMIE: If somebody don't like the kid, back they go to another foster
   home?

RITA: I guess so . . . Clara Hill don't know where her kids are now.

Jaimie Paul twists sharply in his anger.

JAIMIE: Goddamnit!

RITA: My father says . . .

Jaimie Paul rises, crosses round the bed to the other side.

65 JAIMIE: *(harshly)* I don't want to hear what your father got to say! He's like
   . . . like the kind of Indian a white man likes! He's gonna look wise and
   wait forever . . . For what? For the kids they take away to come back?

RITA: He's scared . . . I'm scared . . . We're all scared, Jaimie Paul.

Jaimie Paul lies face down and mimes a gun through the bars.

JAIMIE: Sometimes I feel like takin' a gun and just . . . *(He waves his hand as
   if to liquidate his environment and all that bedevils him. He turns over on
   his back and lies beside Rita Joe.)* I don't know . . . Goddamnit, I don't
   know what to do. I get mad an' then I don't know what I'm doing or
   thinkin' . . . I get scared sometimes, Rita Joe.

RITA: *(tenderly)* We're scared . . . everybody . . .

JAIMIE: I'm scared of dyin' . . . in the city. They don't care for one another
   here . . . You got to be smart or have a good job to live like that.

70 RITA: Clara Hill's gonna have another baby . . .

JAIMIE: I can't live like that . . . A man don't count for much here . . .
   Women can do as much as a man . . . There's no difference between
   men and women. I can't live like that.

RITA: You got to stop worrying, Jaimie Paul. You're gonna get sick worryin'.

JAIMIE: You can't live like that, can you?

RITA: No.

75 JAIMIE: I can't figure out what the hell they want from us!

RITA: *(laughing)* Last time I was in trouble, the judge was asking me what I
   wanted from him! I could've told him, but I didn't!

They both laugh. Jaimie Paul becomes playful and happy.

JAIMIE: Last night I seen television in a store window. I seen a guy on
   television showing this knife that cuts everything it's so sharp . . . He
   was cutting up good shoes like they were potatoes . . . That was sure
   funny to see!

*Again they laugh in merriment at the idea of such a demonstration. Jaimie Paul
continues with his story, gesturing with his hands.*

Chop . . . chop . . . chop . . . A potful of shoes in no time! What's a guy gonna do with a potful of shoes? Cook them?

They continue laughing and lie together again. Then Jaimie Paul sobers. He rises from the bed and walks around it. He offers his hand to Rita Joe, who also rises.

Drily.

Come on. This is a lousy room!
SINGER: *(reprise)*
God was gonna have a laugh,
And gave me a job in the city!

The light goes down on Rita Joe and Jaimie Paul. The Young Indian Men clear the bed.

Cross fade the rear ramp off the stage. Rita Joe's Father and the Priest enter and cross the stage.

PRIEST: She got out yesterday, but she wouldn't let me see her. I stayed an extra day, but she wouldn't see me.
80 FATHER: *(sadly)* I must go once more to the city . . . I must go to see them.
PRIEST: You're an old man . . . I wish I could persuade you not to go.
FATHER: You wouldn't say that if you had children, Andrew . . .

The lights go down on them.

The lights come up on centre stage front. Three Young Indian Men precede Mr. Homer, carrying a table between them. Mr. Homer follows with a hamper of clothes under his arm.

MR. HOMER: Yeh . . . right about there is fine, boys. Got to get the clutter out of the basement . . . There's mice coming in to beat hell.

Mr. Homer empties the clothes hamper on the table. The Young Indian Men step aside and converse in an undertone.

On the ramp, a Young Indian Man weaves his way from stage left and down to centre stage where the others have brought the table. He is followed by Jaimie Paul and Rita Joe, who mime his intoxicated progress.

Mr. Homer speaks to the audience . . .

The Society for Aid to the Indians sent a guy over to see if I could recommend someone who'd been . . . Well, through the mill, like they say . . . An' then smartened up an' taken rehabilitation. The guy said they just wanted a rehabilitated Indian to show up at their annual dinner. No speeches or fancy stuff . . . just be there.

The Young Indian Man lies down carefully to one side of Mr. Homer.

Hi, Louie. Not that I would cross the street for the Society . . . They're nothing but a pack of do-gooders out to get their name in the papers . . .

The Young Indian Man begins to sing a tuneless song, trailing off into silence.

Keep it down, eh, Louie? I couldn't think of anybody to suggest to this guy . . . so he went away pretty sore . . .

Rita Joe begins to rummage through the clothes on the table. She looks at sweaters and holds a red one thoughtfully in her hands.

Jaimie Paul is in conversation with the Young Indian Men to one side of the table.

Mr. Homer turns from audience to see Rita Joe holding the sweater.

Try it on, Rita Joe . . . That's what the stuff's there for.

Jaimie Paul turns. He is in a provocative mood, seething with rebellion that makes the humour he triggers both biting and deceptively innocent. The Young Indian Men respond to him with strong laughter. Jaimie Paul takes a play punch at one of them.

JAIMIE: Whoops! Scared you, eh? *(He glances back at Mr. Homer, as if talking to him.)* Can't take it, eh? The priest can't take it. Indian Department guys can't take it . . . Why listen to them? Listen to the radio if you want to hear something.

The Young Indian Men laugh.

Or listen to me! You think I'm smart?

85 YOUNG INDIAN MAN: You're a smart man, Jaimie Paul.

JAIMIE: Naw . . . I'm not smart . . . *(He points to another Young Indian Man.)* This guy here . . . calls himself squaw-humper . . . He's smart! . . . . Him . . . he buys extra big shirts . . . more cloth for the same money . . . That's smart!

Laughter.

I'm not smart.

Seriously.

You figure we can start a business an' be our own boss?

YOUNG INDIAN MAN: I don't know about that . . .

Jaimie Paul leaves them and goes to lean over the Young Indian Man who is now asleep on the floor.

JAIMIE: Buy a taxi . . . Be our own boss . . .

He shakes the sleeping Young Indian Man, who immediately begins his tuneless song.

Aw, he's drunk . . .

Jaimie Paul goes over to the table and stares at the Young Indian Man beyond the table.

Soberly.

> Buy everything we need . . . Don't be bums! Bums need grub an'
> clothes . . . Bums is bad for the country, right, Mr. Homer?
>
> MR. HOMER: *(nods)* I guess so . . .

To Rita Joe who is now wearing the old sweater.

> Red looks good on you, Rita Joe . . . Take it!

Jaimie Paul goes over and embraces Rita Joe, then pushes her gently away.

90 JAIMIE: She looks better in yellow. I never seen a red dandelion before.

He and the Young Indian Men laugh, but the laughter is hollow.

> MR. HOMER: Come on, Jaimie! Leave the girl alone. That's what it's here for
> . . . Are you working?
>
> JAIMIE: *(evasive, needling)* Yeh! . . . No! . . . "Can you drive?" the guy says to
> me. "Sure, I can drive," I says to him. "Okay," he says, "then drive this
> broom until the warehouse is clean."

They all laugh.

> MR. HOMER: That's a good one . . . Jaimie, you're a card . . . Well, time to
> get some food for you lot . . .

Mr. Homer leaves. Rita Joe feels better about the sweater. She looks to one of the Young Indian Men for approval. Jaimie Paul becomes grim-faced.

> RITA: Do you like it?

95 YOUNG INDIAN MAN: Sure. It's a nice sweater . . . Take it.

> JAIMIE: Take it where? Take it to hell . . . Be men!

He points after Mr. Homer.

> He's got no kids . . . Guys like that get mean when they got no kids . . .
> We're his kids an' he means to keep it that way! Well, I'm a big boy
> now!

To Rita Joe.

> I go to the employment office. I want work an' I want it now. "I'm not
> a goddamned cripple," I says to him. An' he says he can only take my
> name! If work comes he'll call me! "What the hell is this," I says to
> him. "I'll never get work like that . . . There's no telephone in the
> house where I got a room!"

Mr. Homer returns pushing a wheeled tray on which he has some food for sandwiches, a loaf of bread and a large cutting knife. He begins to make some sandwiches.

RITA: *(scolding Jaimie Paul)* You won't get work talking that way, Jaimie
Paul!

JAIMIE: Why not? I'm not scared. He gets mad at me an' I say to him . . .
"You think I'm some stupid Indian you're talkin' to? Heh? You think
that?"

*Jaimie Paul struts and swaggers to demonstrate how he faced his opponent at the
employment office.*

MR. HOMER: *(cutting bread)* You're a tough man to cross, Jaimie Paul.

100   JAIMIE: *(ignoring Mr. Homer, to the Young Indian Men)* Boy, I showed that
bastard who he was talkin' to!

RITA: Did you get the job?

JAIMIE: *(turns to her, laughing boyishly)* No! He called the cops an' they threw
me out!

*They all laugh. The Young Indian Men go to the table now and rummage through
the clothes.*

MR. HOMER: Take whatever you want, boys . . . there's more clothes comin'
tomorrow.

*Jaimie Paul impulsively moves to the table where the Young Indian Men are fin-
gering the clothes. He pushes them aside and shoves the clothes in a heap leaving
a small corner of table clean. He takes out two coins from his pockets and spits in
his hands.*

JAIMIE: I got a new trick . . . Come on, Mister Homer . . . I'll show you! See
this! *(He shows the coins, then slams his hands palms down on the table.)*
Which hand got the coins?

105   MR. HOMER: Why . . . one under each hand . . .

JAIMIE: Right! *(He turns up his hands.)* Again? *(He collects the coins and slaps
his hands down again.)* Where are the coins now? Come on, guess!

*Mr. Homer is confident now and points to right hand with his cutting knife. Jaimie
Paul laughs and lifts his hands.*

The coins are under his left hand.

MR. HOMER: Son of a gun.

JAIMIE: You're a smart man.

*He puts coins in his pockets and laughing, turns to Rita Joe, who stands uncer-
tainly dressed in the red sweater. She likes the garment, but she is aware Jaimie
Paul might resent her taking it. The Young Indian Men again move to the table,
and Mr. Homer returns to making sandwiches.*

MR. HOMER: There's a good pair of socks might come in handy for one of
you guys!

A Young Indian Man pokes his thumbs through the holes in the socks, and laughs.

110 JAIMIE: Sure . . . Take the socks! Take the table! *(He slaps the table with his hands and laughs.)* Take Mister Homer cutting bread! Take everything!

MR. HOMER: Hey, Jaimie!

JAIMIE: Why not? There's more comin' tomorrow, you said!

RITA: Jaimie!

MR. HOMER: You're sure in a smart-assed mood today, aren't you?

115 JAIMIE: *(pointing to the Young Indian Man with the socks, but talking to Mr. Homer)* Mister, friend Steve over there laughs lots . . . He figures . . . the way to get along an' live is to grab his guts an' laugh at anything anybody says. You see him laughing all the time. A dog barks at him an' he laughs . . .

Laughter from the Young Indian Man.

Laughs at a fence post fallin' . . .

Laughter.

Kids with funny eyes make him go haywire . . .

Laughter.

Can of meat an' no can opener . . .

Mr. Homer watches the Young Indian Men and grins at Jaimie Paul.

MR. HOMER: Yeh . . . He laughs quite a bit . . .

JAIMIE: He laughs at a rusty nail . . . Nice guy . . . laughs all the time.

MR. HOMER: *(to Jaimie Paul, holding the knife)* You wanted mustard on your bread or just plain?

JAIMIE: I seen him cut his hand and start laughin' . . . Isn't that funny?

The Young Indian Men laugh, but with less humour now.

120 MR. HOMER: *(to Jaimie Paul)* You want mustard? . . . I'm talkin' to you!

JAIMIE: I'm not hungry.

The Young Indian Men stop laughing altogether. They become tense and suspicious of Jaimie Paul, who is watching them severely.

MR. HOMER: Suit yourself. Rita?

She shakes her head slowly, her gaze on Jaimie Paul's face.

RITA: I'm not hungry.

Mr. Homer looks from Rita Joe to Jaimie Paul, then to the Young Indian Men. His manner stiffens.

MR. HOMER: I see . . .

Jaimie Paul and Rita Joe touch hands and come forward to sit on the apron of the stage front. A pale light is on the two of them.

The stage lights behind them fade. A low light that is diffused and shadowy remains on the table where Mr. Homer has prepared the food. The Young Indian Men move slowly to the table and begin eating the sandwiches Mr. Homer offers to them. The light on the table fades very low.

Jaimie Paul hands a cigarette to Rita Joe and they smoke.

Light comes up over the rear ramp. Rita Joe's Father enters onto the ramp from the wings of stage right. His step is resolute. The Priest follows behind him a few paces. They have been arguing. Both are dressed in work clothes of heavy trousers and windbreakers.

125 JAIMIE: When I'm laughing, I got friends.
RITA: I know, Jaimie Paul . . .
PRIEST: That was the way I found her, that was the way I left her.
JAIMIE: *(bitterly)* When I'm laughing, I'm a joker . . . A funny boy!
FATHER: If I was young . . . I wouldn't sleep. I would talk to people . . . let them all know!
130 JAIMIE: I'm not dangerous when I'm laughing . . .
PRIEST: You could lose the reserve and have nowhere to go!
FATHER: I have lost more than that! Young people die . . . young people don't believe me . . .
JAIMIE: That's alright . . . that's alright . . .

The light dies out on Jaimie Paul and Rita Joe. The light also dies out on Mr. Homer and Young Indian Men.

PRIEST: You think they believe that hot-headed . . . that troublemaker?
135 FATHER: *(turning to face the Priest)* Jaimie Paul is a good boy!
PRIEST: David Joe . . . you and I have lived through a lot. We need peace now, and time to consider what to do next.
FATHER: Eileen said to me last night . . . she wants to go to the city. I worry all night . . . What can I do?
PRIEST: I'll talk to her, if you wish.
FATHER: *(angry)* And tell her what? . . . . Of the animals there . . . *(He gestures to the audience.)* Who sleep with sore stomachs because . . . they eat too much?
140 PRIEST: We mustn't lose the reserve and the old life, David Joe . . . Would you . . . give up being chief on the reserve?
FATHER: Yes!
PRIEST: To Jamie Paul?
FATHER: No . . . To someone who's been to school . . . Maybe university . . . who knows more.
PRIEST: *(relieved by this, but not reassured)* The people here need your wisdom and stability, David Joe. There is no man here who knows as much about hunting and fishing and guiding. You can survive . . . What does a youngster who's been away to school know of this?

145 FATHER: *(sadly)* If we only fish an' hunt an' cut pulpwood . . . pick
strawberries in the bush . . . for a hundred years more, we are dead. I
know this, here . . . *(He touches his breast.)*

The light dies on the ramp.

*A light rises on stage front, on Jaimie Paul and Rita Joe sitting at the apron of the
stage. Mr. Homer is still cutting bread for sandwiches. The three Young Indian Men
have eaten and appear restless to leave. The fourth Young Indian Man is still asleep
on the floor.*

Rita Joe has taken off the red sweater, but continues to hold it in her hand.

JAIMIE: *(to Mr. Homer)* One time I was on a trapline five days without grub.
I ate snow an' I walked until I got back. You think you can take it like
me?

Mr. Homer approaches Jaimie Paul and holds out a sandwich to him.

MR. HOMER: Here . . . have a sandwich now.

Jaimie Paul ignores his hand.

RITA: Mister Homer don't know what happened, Jaimie Paul.

Mr. Homer shrugs and walks away to his sandwich table.

JAIMIE: Then he's got to learn . . . Sure he knows! *(To Mr. Homer.)* Sure he
knows! He's feedin' sandwiches to Indian bums . . . He knows. He's the
worst kind!

The Young Indian Men freeze and Mr. Homer stops.

150 MR. HOMER: *(coldly)* I've never yet asked a man to leave this building.

*Rita Joe and Jaimie Paul rise to their feet. Rita Joe goes to the clothes table and
throws the red sweater back on the pile of clothes. Jaimie Paul laughs sardonically.*

To Rita Joe.

Hey, not you, girl . . . You take it!

She shakes her head and moves to leave.

RITA: I think we better go, boys.

*The sleeping Young Indian Man slowly raises his head, senses there is something
wrong, and is about to be helped up, when . . .*

JAIMIE: After five days without grub, the first meal I threw up . . . stomach
couldn't take it . . . But after that it was alright . . . *(To Mr. Homer, with
intensity.)* I don't believe nobody . . . No priest nor government . . .
They don't know what it's like to . . . to want an' not have . . . to stand
in line an' nobody sees you!

MR. HOMER: If you want food, eat! You need clothes, take them. That's all
. . . But I'm runnin' this centre my way, and I mean it!

JAIMIE: I come to say no to you . . . That's all . . . that's all!

*He throws out his arms in a gesture that is both defiant and childlike. The gesture
disarms some of Mr. Homer's growing hostility.*

155   MR. HOMER: You've got that right . . . No problems. There's others come
through here day an' night . . . No problem.

JAIMIE: I don't want no others to come. I don't want them to eat here! *(He
indicates his friends.)* If we got to take it from behind a store window,
then we break the window an' wait for the cops. It's better than . . .
than this! *(He gestures with contempt at the food and the clothes on the
table.)*

MR. HOMER: Rita Joe . . . where'd you pick up this . . . this loudmouth
anyway?

RITA: *(slowly, firmly)* I think . . . Jaimie Paul's . . . right.

*Mr. Homer looks from face to face. The three Young Indian Men are passive, staring
into the distance. The fourth is trying hard to clear his head. Jaimie Paul is cold,
hostile. Rita Joe is determined.*

MR. HOMER: *(decisively)* Alright! You've eaten . . . looked over the clothes
. . . Now clear out so others get a chance to come in! Move!

*He tries to herd everyone out and the four Young Indian Men begin to move away.
Jaimie Paul mimics the gestures of Mr. Homer and steps in front of the Young
Indian Men, herding them back in.*

160   JAIMIE: Run, boys, run! Or Mister Homer gonna beat us up!

Rita Joe takes Jaimie Paul's hand and tries to pull him away to leave.

RITA: Jaimie Paul . . . you said to me no trouble!

*Jaimie Paul pulls his hand free and jumps back of the clothes table. Mr. Homer
comes for him, unknowingly still carrying the slicing knife in his hand. An absurd
chase begins around the table. One of the Young Indian Men laughs, and stepping
forward, catches hold of Mr. Homer's hand with the knife in it.*

YOUNG INDIAN MAN: Hey! Don't play with a knife, Mister Homer!

*He gently takes the knife away from Mr. Homer and drops it on the food table
behind. Mr. Homer looks at his hand, an expression of shock on his face.*

*Jaimie Paul gives him no time to think about the knife and what it must have
appeared like to the Young Indian Men. He pulls a large brassiere from the clothes
table and mockingly holds it over his breasts, which he sticks out enticingly at Mr.
Homer. The Young Indian Men laugh. Mr. Homer is exasperated and furious. Rita
Joe is frightened.*

RITA: It's not funny, Jaimie!

JAIMIE: It's funny as hell, Rita Joe. Even funnier this way!

Jaimie Paul puts the brassiere over his head, with the cups down over his ears and the straps under his chin. The Young Indian Men are all laughing now and moving close to the table. Mr. Homer makes a futile attempt at driving them off.

Suddenly Jaimie Paul's expression turns to one of hatred. He throws the brassiere on the table and gripping its edge, throws the table and clothes over, scattering the clothes. He kicks at them. The Young Indian Men all jump in and, picking up the clothes, hurl them over the ramp.

Rita Joe runs in to try and stop them. She grips the table and tries lifting it up again.

165 MR. HOMER: *(to Jaimie Paul)* Cut that out, you sonofabitch!

Jaimie Paul stands watching him. Mr. Homer is in a fury. He sees Rita Joe struggling to right the table. He moves to her and pushes her hard.

You slut! . . . You breed whore!

Rita Joe recoils.

With a shriek of frustration, she attacks Mr. Homer, tearing at him. He backs away, then turns and runs.

Jaimie Paul overturns the table again. The others join in the melée with the clothes.

A Policeman enters and grabs Jaimie Paul. Rita Joe and the four Young Indian Men exit, clearing away the tables and remaining clothes.

A sharp, tiny spotlight comes up on the face and upper torso of Jaimie Paul. He is wild with rebellion as the Policeman forces him, in an arm lock, down towards the audience.

JAIMIE: *(screaming defiance at the audience)* Not jus' a box of cornflakes! When I go in, I want the whole store! That's right . . . the whole goddamned store!

Another sharp light on the Magistrate standing on his podium looking down at Jaimie Paul.

MAGISTRATE: Thirty days!
JAIMIE: *(held by Policeman)* Sure, sure . . . Anything else you know?
MAGISTRATE: Thirty days!
170 JAIMIE: Gimme back my truth!
MAGISTRATE: We'll get larger prisons and more police in every town and city across the country!
JAIMIE: Teach me who I really am! You've taken that away! Give me back the real me so I can live like a man!

MAGISTRATE: There is room for dialogue. There is room for disagreement and there is room for social change . . . but within the framework of institutions and traditions in existence for that purpose!

JAIMIE: *(spits)* Go to hell! . . . I can die an' you got nothing to tell me!

175 MAGISTRATE: *(in a cold fury)* Thirty days! And after that, it will be six months! And after that . . . God help you!

The Magistrate marches off his platform and offstage.

Jaimie Paul is led off briskly in the other direction offstage.

The lights change.

Rita Joe enters, crossing the stage, exchanging a look with the Singer.

SINGER:
    Sleepless hours, heavy nights,
    Dream your dreams so pretty.
    God was gonna have a laugh
    An' gave me a job in the city!

Rita Joe walks the street. She is smoking a cigarette. She is dispirited.

The light broadens across the stage.

Rita Joe's Father and Jaimie Paul enter the stage from the wings of centre stage left.

They walk slowly towards where Rita Joe stands.

At the sight of her Father, Rita Joe moans softly and hurriedly stamps out her cigarette. She visibly straightens and waits for the approaching men, her expression one of fear and joy.

FATHER: I got a ride on Miller's truck . . . took me two days . . .

JAIMIE: It's a long way, David Joe.

The Father stops a pace short of Rita Joe and looks at her with great tenderness and concern.

FATHER: *(softly)* I come . . . to get Rita Joe.

180 RITA: Oh . . . I don't know . . .

She looks to Jaimie Paul for help in deciding what to do, but he is sullen and uncommunicative.

FATHER: I come to take Rita Joe home . . . We got a house an' some work sometime . . .

JAIMIE: She's with me now, David Joe.

RITA: *(very torn)* I don't know . . .

JAIMIE: You don't have to go back, Rita Joe.

Rita Joe looks away from her Father with humility. The Father turns to Jaimie Paul.

He stands ancient and heroic.

185 FATHER: I live . . . an' I am afraid. Because . . . I have not done everything. When I have done everything . . . know that my children are safe . . . then . . . it will be alright. Not before.

JAIMIE: *(to Rita)* You don't have to go. This is an old man now . . . He has nothing to give . . . nothin' to say!

Rita Joe reacts to both men, her conflict deepening.

FATHER: *(turning away from Jaimie Paul to Rita Joe)* For a long time . . . a very long time . . . she was in my hands . . . like that! *(He cups his hands into shape of a bowl.)* Sweet . . . tiny . . . lovin' all the time and wanting love . . . *(He shakes his head sadly.)*

JAIMIE: *(angrily)* Go tell it to the white men! They're lookin' for Indians that stay proud even when they hurt . . . just so long's they don't ask for their rights!

The Father turns slowly, with great dignity, to Jaimie Paul. His gestures show Jaimie Paul to be wrong, the old man's spirit was never broken. Jaimie Paul understands and looks away.

FATHER: You're a good boy, Jaimie Paul . . . A good boy . . . *(To Rita Joe, talking slowly, painfully.)* I once seen a dragonfly breakin' its shell to get its wings . . . It floated on water an' crawled up on a log where I was sitting . . . It dug its feet into the log an' then it pulled until the shell bust over its neck. Then it pulled some more . . . an' slowly its wings slipped out of the shell . . . like that! *(He shows with his hands how the dragonfly got his freedom.)*

190 JAIMIE: *(angered and deeply moved by the Father)* Where you gonna be when they start bustin' our heads open an' throwing us into jails right across the goddamned country?

FATHER: Such wings I never seen before . . . folded like an accordion so fine, like thin glass an' white in the morning sun . . .

JAIMIE: We're gonna have to fight to win . . . there's no other way! They're not listenin' to you, old man! Or to me.

FATHER: It spread its wings . . . so slowly . . . an' then the wings opened an' began to flutter . . . Just like that . . . see! Hesitant at first . . . then stronger . . . an' then the wings beatin' like that made the dragonfly's body quiver until the shell on its back falls off . . .

JAIMIE: Stop kiddin' yourself! We're gonna say no pretty soon to all the crap that makes us soft an' easy to push this way . . . that way!

195 FATHER: . . . An' the dragonfly . . . flew up . . . up . . . up . . . into the white sun . . . to the green sky . . . to the sun . . . faster an' faster . . . Higher . . . Higher!

The Father reaches up with his hands, releasing the imaginary dragonfly into the sun, his final words torn out of his heart.

Rita Joe springs to her feet and rushes against Jaimie Paul, striking at him with her fists.

RITA: *(savagely)* For Chris' sakes, I'm not goin' back! . . . Leave him alone . . . He's everything we got left now!

Jaimie Paul stands, frozen by his emotion which he can barely control. The Father turns. Rita Joe goes to him.

The Father speaks privately to Rita Joe in Indian dialect. They embrace.

He pauses for a long moment to embrace and forgive her everything. Then he goes slowly offstage into the wings of stage left without looking back.

FATHER: Goodbye, Rita Joe . . . Goodbye, Jaimie Paul . . .
RITA: Goodbye, Father.

Jaimie Paul watches Rita Joe who moves away from him to the front of the stage.

JAIMIE: *(to her)* You comin'?

She shakes her head to indicate no, she is staying.

Suddenly Jaimie Paul runs away from her diagonally across to the wings of rear stage left. As he nears the wings, the four Young Indian Men emerge, happily on their way to a party.

They stop him at his approach. He runs into them, directing them back, his voice breaking with feelings of love and hatred intermingling.

Shouting at them.

> Next time . . . in a beer parlour or any place like that . . . I'll go myself or you guys take me home . . . No more white buggers pushin' us out the door or he gets this!

He raises his fist.

The group of Young Indian Men, elated by their newly found determination, surround Jaimie Paul and exit into the wings of the stage. The light dies in back and at stage left. The Magistrate enters.

There is a light on Rita Joe where she stands. There is also a light around the Magistrate. The Magistrate's voice and purpose are leaden. He has given up on Rita Joe. He is merely performing the formality of condemning her and dismissing her from his conscience.

200 **MAGISTRATE:** I sentence you to thirty days in prison.
RITA: *(angry, defiant)* Sure, sure . . . Anything else you know?
MAGISTRATE: I sentence you to thirty days in prison, with a recommendation you be examined medically and given all necessary

treatment at the prison clinic. There is nothing . . . there is nothing I can do now.

RITA: *(stoically)* Thank you. Is that right? To thank you?

MAGISTRATE: You'll be back . . . always be back . . . growing older . . . tougher . . . filthier . . . looking more like stone and prison bars . . . the lines in your face will tell everyone who sees you about prison windows and prison food.

205 RITA: No child on the road would remember you, mister!

The Magistrate comes down to stand before her. He has the rambling confidence of detached authority.

MAGISTRATE: What do you expect? We provide schools for you and you won't attend them because they're out of the way and that little extra effort is too much for you! We came up as a civilization having to . . . yes, claw upwards at times . . . There's nothing wrong with that . . . We give you X-ray chest clinics . . . *(He turns away from her and goes to the apron of the stage and speaks directly to the audience.)* We give them X-ray chest clinics and three-quarters of them won't show up . . . Those that do frequently get medical attention at one of the hospitals . . .

RITA: *(interjecting)* My mother died!

He does not hear her.

MAGISTRATE: But as soon as they're released they forget they're chronically ill and end up on a drinking party and a long walk home through the snow . . . Next thing . . . they're dead!

RITA: *(quietly)* Oh, put me in jail an' then let me go.

210 MAGISTRATE: *(turning to her)* Some of you get jobs . . . There are jobs, good jobs, if you'd only look around a bit . . . and stick with them when you get them. But no . . . you get a job and promise to stay with it and learn, and two weeks later you're gone for three, four days without explanation . . . Your reliability record is ruined and an employer has to regard you as lazy, undependable . . . What do you expect?

RITA: I'm not scared of you now, bastard!

MAGISTRATE: You have a mind . . . you have a heart. The cities are open to you to come and go as you wish, yet you gravitate to the slums and skid rows and the shanty-town fringes. You become a whore, drunkard, user of narcotics . . . At best, dying of illness or malnutrition . . . At worst, kicked or beaten to death by some angry white scum who finds in you something lower than himself to pound his frustrations out on! What's to be done? You Indians seem to be incapable of taking action to help yourselves. Someone must care for you . . . Who? For how long?

RITA: You don't know nothin'!

MAGISTRATE: I know . . . I know . . . It's a struggle just to stay alive. I know . . . I understand. That struggle is mine, as well as yours, Rita Joe! The jungle of the executive has as many savage teeth ready to go for the throat as the rundown hotel on the waterfront . . . Your days and hours are numbered, Rita Joe . . . I worry for the child I once saw . . . I have already forgotten the woman!

He turns away from her and exits into the wings of stage right.

The lights on Rita Joe fade.

Lights of cold, eerie blue wash the backdrop of the stage faintly.

Rita Joe stands in silhouette for a long moment.

Slowly, ominously, the three Murderers appear on the ramp backstage, one coming from the wings of stage right; one from the wings of stage left; and one rising from the back of the ramp, climbing it. One of the Murderers is whistling a soft nervous noise throughout their scene onstage.

Rita Joe whimpers in fear, and as the Murderers loom above her, she runs along the apron to stage left.

Here she bumps into Jaimie Paul who enters. She screams in fear.

215 JAIMIE: Rita Joe!
RITA: *(terrorized)* Jaimie! They're comin'. I seen them comin'!
JAIMIE: Who's coming? What's the matter, Rita Joe?
RITA: Men I once dreamed about . . . . I seen it all happen once before . . . an' it was like this . . . .

Jaimie Paul laughs and pats her shoulders reassuringly. He takes her hand and tries to lead her forward to the apron of the stage, but Rita Joe is dead, her steps wooden.

JAIMIE: Don't worry . . . I can take care of myself!

A faint light on the two of them.

220 RITA: You been in jail now too, Jaimie Paul . . .
JAIMIE: So what? Guys in jail was saying that they got to put a man behind bars or the judge don't get paid for being in court to make the trial . . . Funny world, eh, Rita Joe?
RITA: *(nods)* Funny world.

The light dies on them. They come forward slowly.

JAIMIE: I got a room with a hot plate . . . We can have a couple of eggs and some tea before we go to the movie.
RITA: What was it like for you in jail?
225 JAIMIE: So so . . .

Jaimie Paul motions for Rita Joe to follow him and moves forward from her.

The distant sound of a train approaching is heard.

She is wooden, coming slowly after him.

RITA: It was different where the women were . . . It's different to be a woman . . . Some women was wild . . . and they shouted they were riding black horses into a fire I couldn't see . . . There was no fire there, Jaimie!

JAIMIE: *(turns to her, takes her arm)* Don't worry . . . We're goin' to eat and then see a movie . . . Come on, Rita Joe!

She looks back and sees the Murderers rise and slowly approach from the gloom. Her speech becomes thick and unsteady as she follows Jaimie Paul to the front of the ramp.

RITA: One time I couldn't find the street where I had a room to sleep in . . . Forgot my handbag . . . had no money . . . An old man with a dog said hello, but I couldn't say hello back because I was worried an' my mouth was so sticky I couldn't speak to him . . .

JAIMIE: Are you comin?

230 RITA: When you're tired an' sick, Jaimie, the city starts to dance . . .

JAIMIE: *(taking her hand, pulling her gently along)* Come on, Rita Joe.

RITA: The street lights start rollin' like wheels an' cement walls feel like they was made of blanket cloth . . .

The sound of the train is closer now. The lights of its lamps flicker in back of the stage.

Rita Joe turns to face the Murderers, one of whom is whistling ominously. She whimpers in fear and presses herself against Jaimie Paul.

Jaimie Paul turns and sees the Murderers hovering near them.

JAIMIE: Don't be scared . . . Nothing to be scared of, Rita Joe . . .

To the Murderers.

What the hell do you want?

One of the Murderers laughs. Jaimie Paul pushes Rita Joe back behind himself. He moves towards the Murderers.

Taunting them.

You think I can't take care of myself?

With deceptive casualness, the Murderers approach him. One of them makes a sudden lurch at Jaimie Paul as if to draw him into their circle. Jaimie Paul antici-pates the trap and takes a flying kick at the Murderer, knocking him down.

They close around Jaimie Paul with precision, then attack. Jaimie Paul leaps, but is caught mid-air by the other two. They bring him down and put the boots to him.

Rita Joe screams and runs to him. The train sound is loud and immediate now.

One of the Murderers has grabbed Rita Joe. The remaining two raise Jaimie Paul to his feet and one knees him viciously in the groin. Jaimie Paul screams and doubles over.

The lights of the train are upon them. The Murderers leap off the ramp leaving Jaimie Paul in the path of the approaching train. Jaimie Paul's death cry becomes the sound of the train horn. As the train sound roars by, the Murderers return to close in around Rita Joe.

One Murderer springs forward and grabs Rita Joe. The other two help to hold her, with nervous fear and lust.

Rita Joe breaks free of them and runs to the front of the stage. The three Murderers come after her, panting hard.

They close in on her leisurely now, playing with her, knowing that they have her trapped.

Recorded and overlapping voices . . .

CLERK: The court calls Rita Joe . . .
235 MAGISTRATE: Who is she? . . . Let her speak for herself . . .
RITA: In the summer it was hot, an' flies hummed . . .
TEACHER: A book of verse, a melting pot . . .
MAGISTRATE: Thirty days!
FATHER: Barkin' to beat hell . . . How! How!
240 JAIMIE: *(laughter, defiant, taunting)* You go to hell!
PRIEST: A confession, Rita Joe . . .

Over the voices she hears, the Murderers attack.

Dragging her down backwards, they pull her legs open and one Murderer lowers himself on her.

RITA: Jaimie! Jaimie! Jaimie!

Rita Joe's head lolls over sideways. The Murderers stare at her and pull back slightly.

MURDERER: *(thickly, rising off her twisted, broken body)* Shit . . . She's dead . . . We hardly touched her.

He hesitates for a moment, then runs, joined by second Murderer.

SECOND MURDERER: Let's get out of here!

They run up onto the ramp and watch as the third Murderer piteously climbs onto the dead Rita Joe.

Sounds of a funeral chant. Mourners appear on riser backstage. Rita Joe's Father enters from the wings of stage left, chanting an ancient Indian funeral chant, carrying the body of Jaimie Paul.

The Murderer hesitates in his necrophillic rape and then runs away.

The Young Indian Men bring the body of Jaimie Paul over the ramp and approach. The body is placed down on the podium, beside Rita Joe's.

All the Indians, young and old, kneel around the two bodies. The Father continues his death chant. The Priest enters from the wings of stage right reciting a prayer. The Teacher, Singer, Policeman and Murderers come with him, forming the outside perimeter around the Indian funeral.

245 PRIEST: Hail Mary, Mother of God . . . Pray for us sinners now and at the
     hour of our death . . .

Repeated until finally Eileen Joe slowly rises to her feet and turning to the Priest and White Mourners, says softly . . .

EILEEN: *(over the sounds of chanting and praying)* No! . . . No! . . . No more!

The Young Indian Men rise one after another, facing the outer circle defiantly and the Cast freezes onstage, except for the Singer.

SINGER:
     Oh, the singing bird
     Has found its wings
     And it's soaring!

     My God, what a sight!
     On the cold fresh wind of morning! . . .

During the song, Eileen Joe steps forward to the audience and as the song ends, says . . .

EILEEN: When Rita Joe first come to the city, she told me . . . The cement
     made her feet hurt.

READING AND REACTING

1. The play was first produced in 1967. Does it have any relevance
   for today's audience?
2. Does the guitarist-singer add to the play? If so, in what ways?
3. What is the significance of the little girl the magistrate sees?
4. Explain how the set works. Does the ramp provide sufficient dif-
   ferentiation of time and space?

5. What suggestions does the Father have for the future of his people? What gives him hope?

6. Do you agree with the magistrate when he says, "It's a struggle just to stay alive. I know . . . I understand. That struggle is mine, as well as yours, Rita Joe! The jungle of the executive has as many savage teeth ready to go for the throat as the rundown hotel on the waterfront"?

7. How does the word *Ecstasy* function in the title?

8. What does the flock of white geese symbolize?

9. **Journal Entry** Imagine you are Rita Joe or Jaimie Paul and write about the feelings you have trying to survive in the city.

10. **Critical Perspective** In a review of James Hoffman's *The Ecstasy of Resistance: A Biography of George Ryga*, Len Falkenstein notes: "As a non-Native playwright whose two best-known dramas, *Rita Joe* and *Indian*, centre on Native characters, Ryga has become the target of charges of cultural appropriation and stereotyping." Do you think such charges are valid? Why or why not?

Related Works: "The Loons" (p. 249), "My Ledders" (p. 845), *The Rez Sisters* (p. 1248)

◆ Writing Suggestions: Theme

1. One of the topics of *The Shape of a Girl* is friendship and what that means. Compare the depiction of friendship in *The Shape of a Girl* to that in one other play in this book—for example, *Hamlet* or *The Rez Sisters*.

2. Both *The Shape of a Girl* and *The Ecstasy of Rita Joe* deal with the challenges presented by being female. How are females viewed by themselves and by others in these plays? You could write an essay on one of these plays and this issue or compare the two plays.

3. Technology in the form of a tape recorder is important in the staging of Beckett's *Krapp's Last Tape,* as well as its thematic concerns regarding memory. How does the tape help convey the complexities of memory, and how does the play connect memory and identity?

4. Three of the plays in this chapter move between the present and past. Analyze how the past is conveyed in these plays and how the present and future differ for Braidie, Krapp, and Rita Joe. Consider why life is different for the three characters.

5. Both *The Shape of a Girl* and *Krapp's Last Tape* use monologue. How do the plays overcome the limitations of monologue while conveying the importance of the single voice?

6. Analyze the significance of music and dance in *The Ecstasy of Rita Joe*. How does the play use music and dance to develop theme(s)? Could either music or dance be eliminated from the play?

◊ ◊ ◊

Documenting Sources

Documentation is the acknowledgment of information from an outside source that you use in a paper. In general, you should document your sources whenever you quote, paraphrase, summarize, or in any other way incorporate borrowed information or ideas into your work. Not to do so—on purpose or by accident—is to commit **plagiarism,** to appropriate the intellectual property of others. By following accepted conventions of documentation, you avoid plagiarism and at the same time show your readers that your research has been done with care and precision. In addition, you enable them to distinguish your ideas from those of your sources and, if they wish, to consult the sources you cite.

Not all ideas from your sources need to be documented. **Common knowledge**—facts that can be found in a number of different encyclopedias, textbooks, newspapers, magazines, and dictionaries—need not be documented as long as you do not use the exact wording of your source. However, all direct quotations, as well as information that is in dispute or that is the original contribution of a particular person, *must* be documented. You need not, for example, document the fact that Arthur Miller's *Death of a Salesman* was first performed in 1949 or that it won a Pulitzer Prize for drama. (You could find this information in any current encyclopedia.) You would, however, have to document a quotation from a critic's interpretation of a performance, and you would have to document a scholar's analysis of an early draft of the play—even if you do not use your source's exact words.

Students writing about literature use the documentation style recommended by the Modern Language Association of America (MLA), a professional organization of more than 25,000 teachers and students of English and other languages. This style of documentation, the one that you should use any time you write a literature paper, has three components: *parenthetical references in the text, a list of works cited,* and *explanatory notes.*

PARENTHETICAL REFERENCES
IN THE TEXT

◊ ◊ ◊

MLA documentation style uses parenthetical references within the text that refer to an alphabetical list of works cited at the end of the paper. A typical **parenthetical reference** consists of the author's last name and a page number.

> Gwendolyn Brooks uses the sonnet form to create poems that
> have a wide social and aesthetic range (Williams 972).

If you use more than one source by the same author, include a shortened
title in the parenthetical reference.

> Brooks knows not only Shakespeare, Spenser, and Milton,
> but also the full range of African-American poetry
> (Williams, "Brooks's Way" 972).

If you mention the author's name or the title of the work in your paper, only
a page reference is needed.

> According to Gladys Margaret Williams in "Gwendolyn
> Brooks's Way with the Sonnet," Brooks combines a
> sensitivity to poetic forms with a depth of emotion
> appropriate for her subject matter (972–73).

✓ GUIDELINES FOR PUNCTUATING PARENTHETICAL REFERENCES

◊ *Paraphrases and summaries*

Place the parenthetical reference after the last word of the sentence
and before the final punctuation:

> In her works, Brooks combines the pessimism of Modernist
> poetry with the optimism of the Harlem Renaissance
> (Smith 978).

◊ *Direct quotations run in with the text*

Place the parenthetical reference after the quotation marks and
before the final punctuation:

> According to Gary Smith, Brooks's A Street in
> Bronzeville "conveys the primacy of suffering in the
> lives of poor Black women" (980).

> According to Gary Smith, the poems in A Street in
> Bronzeville "served notice that Brooks had learned her
> craft . . ." (978).

> Along with Thompson we must ask, "Why did it take so
> long for critics to acknowledge that Gwendolyn Brooks is
> an important voice in twentieth-century American poetry"
> (123)?

◊ *Quotations set off from the text*

Omit the quotation marks and place the parenthetical reference one space after the final punctuation. (For guidelines for setting off long quotations, see p. 36.)

For Gary Smith, the identity of Brooks's African-American women is inextricably linked with their sense of race and poverty:

> For Brooks, unlike the Renaissance poets, the victimization of poor Black women becomes not simply a minor chord but a predominant theme of <u>A Street in Bronzeville</u>. Few, if any, of her female characters are able to free themselves from a web of poverty that threatens to strangle their lives. (980)

SAMPLE REFERENCES

An entire work

David French's play <u>Jitters</u> is a sophisticated comedy of manners satirizing Canadian theatre.

When citing an entire work, state the name of the author in your paper instead of in a parenthetical reference.

A work by two or three authors

Myths cut across boundaries and cultural spheres and reappear in strikingly similar forms from country to country (Feldman and Richardson 124).

The effect of a work of literature depends on the audience's predispositions that derive from membership in various social groups (Hovland, Janis, and Kelley 87).

A work by more than three authors

Hawthorne's short stories frequently use a combination of allegorical and symbolic methods (Guerin et al. 91).

The abbreviation *et al.* is Latin for "and others."

A work in an anthology

> In his essay "Flat and Round Characters" E. M. Forster
> distinguishes between one-dimensional characters and those
> that are well developed (Stevick 223-31).

The parenthetical reference cites the anthology (edited by Stevick) that contains Forster's essay; full information about the anthology appears in the list of works cited.

A work with volume and page numbers

> Critics consider The Zoo Story to be one of Albee's best
> plays (Eagleton 2:17).

An indirect source

> Wagner observed that myth and history stood before him
> "with opposing claims" (qtd. in Winkler 10).

The abbreviation *qtd. in* (quoted in) indicates that the quoted material was not taken from the original source.

A play with numbered lines

> "Give thy thoughts no tongue," says Polonius, "Nor any
> unproportion'd thought his act" (Ham. 1.3.59-60).

The parentheses contain the act, scene, and line numbers, separated by periods. When included in parenthetical references, titles of the books of the Bible and well-known literary works are often abbreviated—*Gen.* for *Genesis* and *Ado* for *Much Ado about Nothing,* for example.

A poem

> "I muse my life-long hate, and without flinch / I bear it
> nobly as I live my part," says Claude McKay in his
> bitterly ironic poem "The White City" (3-4).

Notice that a slash (/) is used to separate lines of poetry run in with the text. The parenthetical reference cites the lines quoted.

THE LIST OF WORKS CITED

◇ ◇ ◇

Parenthetical references refer to a **Works Cited** list that includes all the sources you refer to in your paper. Begin the Works Cited list on a new page,

INFORMAL DOCUMENTATION

Sometimes, when you are writing a paper that includes quotations from a single source that the entire class has read or if all your sources are from your textbook, your instructor may give you permission to use *informal documentation*. Because both the instructor and the class are familiar with the sources, you supply the authors' last names and page numbers in parentheses and omit a Works Cited list.

continuing the page numbers of the paper. For example, if the text of the paper ends on page 6, the Works Cited section will begin on page 7.

Centre the title *Works Cited* 2.5 cm from the top of the page. (If your list includes all the works consulted, whether you cite them or not, use the title *Works Consulted*.) Arrange entries alphabetically, according to the last name of each author (or the first word of the title if the author is unknown). Articles—*a, an,* and *the*—at the beginning of a title are not considered first words. In order to conserve space, publishers' names are abbreviated—for example, *Norton* for *W.W. Norton & Company*. Double-space the entire Works Cited list between and within entries. Begin typing each entry at the left margin, and indent subsequent lines five spaces. Each Works Cited entry has three divisions—author, title, and publishing information—separated by periods.*

A book by a single author

> Strube, Cordelia. <u>Milton's Elements</u>. Toronto:
> HarperCollins, 1995.

A book by two or three authors

> Feldman, Burton, and Robert D. Richardson. <u>The Rise of
> Modern Mythology</u>. Bloomington: Indiana UP, 1972.

Notice that only the *first* author's name is in reverse order.

A book by more than three authors

> Guerin, Wilfred, et al., eds. <u>A Handbook of Critical
> Approaches to Literature</u>. 3rd. ed. New York: Harper,
> 1992.

Instead of using *et al.*, you may list all the authors' names in the order in which they appear on the title page.

---

* The *MLA Handbook for Writers of Research Papers* shows a single space after all end punctuation.

Two or more works by the same author

> Novoa, Juan-Bruce. <u>Chicano Authors: Inquiry by Interview</u>.
> Austin: U of Texas P, 1980.

> ---. "Themes in Rudolfo Anaya's Work." Address given at
> New Mexico State University, Las Cruces. 11 Apr.
> 1987.

List two or more works by the same author in alphabetical order by title. Include the author's full name in the first entry; use three unspaced hyphens followed by a period to take the place of the author's name in second and subsequent entries.

An edited book

> Karpinski, Eva C., ed. <u>Pens of Many Colours: A Canadian
> Reader</u>. 3rd ed. Toronto: Nelson, 2002.

Notice that the abbreviation *ed.* stands for *editor.*

A book with a volume number

> Rothenberg, Jerome, and Pierre Joris, eds. <u>Poems for the
> Millennium</u>. Vol. 1. Berkeley: U of California P, 1995.

All volumes in the entry above have the same title.

> Durant, Will, and Ariel Durant. <u>The Age of Napoleon: A
> History of European Civilization from 1789 to 1815</u>.
> New York: Simon, 1975.

Each volume has a different title. *The Age of Napoleon* is volume 2 of *The Story of Civilization.*

A short story, poem, or play in a collection of the author's work

> Munro, Alice. "Family Furnishings." <u>Hateship, Friendship,
> Courtship, Loveship, Marriage</u>. Toronto: McClelland,
> 2001. 111-27.

A short story in an anthology

> Salinas, Marta. "The Scholarship Jacket." <u>Nosotros: Latina
> Literature Today</u>. Ed. Maria del Carmen Boza, Beverly
> Silva, and Carmen Valle. Binghamton: Bilingual, 1986.
> 68-70.

The inclusive page numbers follow the year of publication. Note that here the abbreviation *Ed.* stands for *Edited by.*

A poem in an anthology

> Rossetti, Christina G. "At Home." <u>Victorian Women Poets:</u>
> <u>An Anthology</u>. Ed. Angela Leighton and Margaret
> Reynolds. Oxford: Blackwell, 1995. 372-73.

A play in an anthology

> Hughes, Langston. <u>Mother and Child</u>. <u>Black Drama Anthology</u>.
> Ed. Woodie King and Ron Miller. New York: NAL, 1986.
> 399-406.

An article in an anthology

> Foucault, Michel. "What Is an Author?" <u>The Art of Art</u>
> <u>History: A Critical Anthology</u>. Ed. Donald Preziosi.
> New York: Oxford UP, 1998. 299-314.

More than one selection from the same anthology

If you are using more than one selection from an anthology, cite the anthology in a separate entry. Also, list each individual selection separately, including the author and title of the selection, the anthology editor's last name, and the inclusive page numbers.

> Kirszner, Laurie G., Stephen R. Mandell, and Candace
> Fertile, eds. <u>Literature: Reading, Reacting, Writing</u>.
> 2nd Can. ed. Toronto: Nelson, 2007.

> Rich, Adrienne. "Diving into the Wreck." Kirszner,
> Mandell, and Fertile 800-02.

A translation

> Freud, Sigmund. <u>Totem and Taboo: Some Points of Agreement</u>
> <u>between the Mental Lives of Savages and Neurotics</u>.
> Trans. James Strachey. New York: Norton, 1989.

An article in a journal with continuous pagination in each issue

> Le Guin, Ursula K. "American Science Fiction and the
> Other." <u>Science Fiction Studies</u> 2 (1975): 208-10.

An article with separate pagination in each issue

> Grossman, Robert. "The Grotesque in Faulkner's 'A Rose for
> Emily.'" <u>Mosaic</u> 20.3 (1987): 40-55.

[*20.3* signifies volume 20, issue 3.]

An article in a magazine

```
Johnson, Brian D. "Beowulf Rides Again." Maclean's 13
     March 2006: 76-78.

Unwin, Peter. "The Pen and the Sword." The Beaver
     Feb./March 2006: 28-33.

"Solzhenitsyn: An Artist Becomes an Exile." Time 25 Feb.
     1974: 34+.
```

34+ indicates that the article appears on pages that are not consecutive; in this case, the article begins on page 34 and then continues on page 37. An article with no listed author is entered by title on the Works Cited list.

An article in a daily newspaper

```
Armstrong, Jane. "FLQ on CBC (English only)." The Globe
     and Mail 18 Feb. 2006: R1+.
```

R1+ indicates that the article begins on page 1 of Section R and continues on a subsequent page.

An article in a reference book

```
"Croatia." The New Encyclopaedia Britannica: Micropaedia.
     1991.
```

You do not need to include publication information for well-known reference books.

```
Grimstead, David. "Fuller, Margaret Sarah." Encyclopedia
     of American Biography. Ed. John A. Garraty. New
     York: Harper, 1974.
```

You must include publication information when citing reference books that are not well known.

Like print sources, the purpose of including references to electronic media sources is so your reader can locate the information you have used. Unlike print sources, however, electronic sources are dynamic. In order to enable your reader to track this information, electronic works citations must provide more information than print citations. For example, an electronic source may require two and sometimes more publication dates. Because electronic sources are often updated frequently, the information that students collect on a specific date may differ from information collected before or after the student's date of collection. Therefore, electronic citations contain the date that the document was published and the date when the researcher accessed the document. If a document was originally published as a print source, then three dates are required: the date of the original print source; the date of the document online; and the date that the student retrieved the document.

Another important component to any electronic source is the Web site address or URL (universal resource locator). URLs allow the reader of a student's paper to track down the information he or she has included. Unfortunately, URLs change frequently so it is important for students to take special care when copying the URL onto the Works Cited page. It is a good idea to either download or print the material you use because sometimes Web pages disappear altogether. All URLs should be enclosed in angled brackets (<>) in your document.

Finally, be sure to cite as much information as possible from a URL. However, if the URL of a document is very long or complex, include the site's or database's search page instead; the reader can link to or search for the document.

—Joseph Gibaldi, *MLA Handbook for Writers of Research Papers,* 6th ed., New York: MLA, 2003, pp. 207–08, 211–12.

A professional/personal site

> Canadian Literature Archive. U of Manitoba. 16 March 2006
>   <http://www.umanitoba.ca/canlit/>.

If the Web site has no author listed, then begin your entry with the name of the Web site. The date listed in this entry is the date of retrieval. No date of publication was listed on the site.

> Mabillard, Amanda. Shakespeare Online. 16 March 2006
>   <http://www.shakespeare-online.com>.

> Theology and Religion Collection Homepage. 5 Oct. 2004.
>   Thomas Fisher Rare Book Library. U of Toronto. 16
>   March 2006
>   <http://www.library.utoronto.ca/fisher/collections/
>   theology-religion.html>.

The first date listed in the above entry is the date that the Web site was last updated. The second date listed is the date of retrieval. In all cases, the date of retrieval appears nearest to the URL.

An online book

> Austen, Jane. Pride and Prejudice. Ed. H. Churchyard.
>   1996. 16 March 2006 <http://www.pemberley.com/
>   janeinfo/pridprej.html>.

An article in an online newspaper

> Chalmers, Ron. "Future is Now, Business Students Learn."
>   Edmonton Journal 15 March 2006. 16 March 2006
>   <http://www.canada.com/edmontonjournal/news/
>   business/story.html?id=20f352ad-81ba-41f7-b2f2-
>   531b17e95dcc>.

An article in an online magazine

> Newman, Peter C. "Canada: Peaceable Kingdom No More."
>   Maclean's 15 March 2006. 16 March 2006
>   <http://www.macleans.ca/topstories/canada/
>   article.jsp?content=20060320_123546_123546>.

If the Web site address is too long to fit on one line, the address can extend over as many lines as required, but you should break the Web site address at a slash where possible.

An online review

> Johnston, Elizabeth. Rev. of The Pagan Nuptials of Julia:
>   And Other Stories, by Keith Henderson. The Globe and
>   Mail 10 March 2006. 16 March 2006 <http://www.
>   theglobeandmail.com/servlet/story/RTGAM.20060310.
>   bknupt0311/BNStory/SpecialEvents/home>.

An online source: Entry with a print version

> Machosky, Brenda. "Fasting at the Feast of Literature."
>   Comparative Literature Studies 42.2 (2005): 288-305.
>   18 March 2006 <http://muse.jhu.edu/journals/
>   comparative_literature_studies/v042/42.2machosky.html>.

When you cite information with a print version from an online source, include the publication information for the printed source, the number of pages or the number of paragraphs (if available), and the date of access. Information from a commercial computer service—America Online, Pro Quest Direct, Prodigy, and InfoTrac, for example—will not have an electronic address.

> O'Hara, Sandra. "Reexamining the Canon." Time 13 May 1994:
>   27. America Online. 22 Aug. 1994.

An online source: Entry with no print version

> "Romanticism." Academic American Encyclopedia. Prodigy. 6
>   Nov. 2001.

This entry shows that the material was accessed on November 6, 2001.

An online source: Public posting

> Peters, Olaf. "Studying English through German." Online
>   posting. 29 Feb. 1996. Foreign Language Forum, Multi
>   Language Section. CompuServe. 15 Mar. 1996.

> Gilford, Mary. "Dog Heroes in Children's Literature." 4
>   Oct. 1996. Newsgroup alt.animals.dogs. America
>   Online. 23 Mar. 1996.

WARNING: Using information from online forums and newsgroups in papers for your college or university courses is risky. Contributors are not necessarily experts, and frequently they are incorrect and misinformed. Unless you can be certain that the information you are receiving from these sources is reliable, do not use it.

An online source: Electronic text

> Twain, Mark. <u>The Adventures of Huckleberry Finn</u>. From <u>The</u>
>   <u>Writing of Mark Twain</u>. Vol. 13. New York: Harper,
>   1970. <u>Wiretap.spies</u>. 13 Jan. 1996
>   <http://www.sci.dixie.edu/DixieCollege/Ebooks/
>   huckfin.html>.

This electronic text was originally published by Harper. The name of the repository for the electronic edition is Wiretap.spies.

An online source: E-mail

> Adkins, Camille. E-mail to the author. 8 June 2006.

A CD-ROM: Entry with a print version

> Zurbach, Kate. "The Linguistic Roots of Three Terms."
>   <u>Linguistic Quarterly</u> 37 (1994): 12-47. <u>Infotrac:</u>
>   <u>Magazine Index Plus</u>. CD-ROM. Information Access.
>   Jan. 1996.

When you cite information with a print version from a CD-ROM, include the publication information, the underlined title of the database (<u>Infotrac: Magazine Index Plus</u>), the publication medium (CD-ROM), the name of the company that produced the CD-ROM (Information Access), and the electronic publication date.

A CD-ROM: Entry with no print version

> "Surrealism." <u>Encarta 1996</u>. CD-ROM. Redmond: Microsoft,
>   1996.

If you are citing a part of a work, include the title in quotation marks.

> <u>A Music Lover's Multimedia Guide to Beethoven's 5th</u>. CD-
> ROM. Spring Valley: Interactive, 1993.

If you are citing an entire work, include the underlined title.

An interview

> Ondaatje, Michael. Interview. <u>Essays on Canadian Writing</u>
> 53 (1994): 238-49.

A lecture, a speech, an address, or a reading

> Atwood, Margaret. "Silencing the Scream." Boundaries of
> the Imagination Forum. MLA Convention. Royal York
> Hotel, Toronto. 29 Dec. 1993.

> Leggatt, Alexander. Interpretation of Shakespeare's <u>King</u>
> <u>Lear</u>. Lecture. University of Toronto, Toronto. 31
> Jan. 2001.

If you do not know the title of the lecture, then use an appropriate descriptive label, neither underlined nor enclosed in quotation marks.

A film or videocassette

> <u>The Burning Times</u>. Videotape. Dir. Donna Reed. Narr.
> Martha Henry. National Film Board of Canada, 1990.

In addition to the title, the director, and the year, include other pertinent information such as the principal performers or narrator.

CONTENT NOTES

◇ ◇ ◇

Use **content notes,** indicated by a superscript (a raised number) in the text, to cite several sources at once or to provide commentary or explanations that do not fit smoothly into your paper. The full text of these notes appears on the first numbered page following the last page of the paper. (If your paper has no content notes, the Works Cited page follows the last page of the paper.) Like Works Cited entries, content notes are double-spaced within and between entries. However, the first line of each explanatory note is indented five spaces, with subsequent lines flush with the left-hand margin.

TO CITE SEVERAL SOURCES

In the paper

> Surprising as it may seem, there have been many attempts to define literature.[1]

In the note

> [1] For an overview of critical opinion, see Arnold 72; Eagleton 1-2; Howe 43-44; and Abrams 232-34.

TO PROVIDE EXPLANATIONS

In the paper

> In recent years, gothic novels have achieved great popularity.[3]

In the note

> [3] Gothic novels, works written in imitation of medieval romances, originally relied on supernatural occurrences. They flourished in the late eighteenth and early nineteenth centuries.

SAMPLE LITERATURE PAPERS WITH MLA DOCUMENTATION

◆ ◆ ◆

The two research papers that follow, written for introduction to literature courses, use MLA documentation style.

Daniel Collins

English 201

Professor Smith

30 October 2007

And Again She Makes the Journey: Character

and Act in Eudora Welty's "A Worn Path"

Over the past fifty years, Eudora Welty's "A Worn Path," the tale of an elderly black woman, Phoenix Jackson, travelling to the city to obtain medicine for her sick grandson, has been the subject of much critical interpretation. Critics have speculated on the meaning of the many death and rebirth symbols, including the scarecrow, which the old woman believes is a ghost; the buzzard who watches her travel; the skeleton-like branches that reach out to slow her; and her first name, Phoenix. From the study of these symbols, various critics have concluded that "A Worn Path" represents either a "heroic act of sacrifice," "a parable for the journey of life," or "a religious pilgrimage" (Keys 354). It is certainly true, as these interpretations imply, that during her journey Phoenix Jackson struggles through difficult terrain and encounters many dangers and that despite these obstacles, she does not abandon her quest. However, it is neither the symbols associated with the quest nor the quest itself that is the story's primary focus; what is most important is Phoenix Jackson's character and her act of making the journey.

Eudora Welty discusses the characterization of Phoenix Jackson in a videotaped interview. Here, Welty

Collins 2

acknowledges that Jackson's first name refers to a mythical bird that dies and is reborn every five hundred years. She explains, however, that despite her character's symbolic name, Phoenix Jackson is a complex being with human frailties and emotions (Henley).

Phoenix Jackson has a number of physical problems that challenge her ability to perform daily tasks. Because of her age, she has failing eyesight, which distorts her perception of the objects she encounters during her journey. For instance, Phoenix mistakes a patch of thorns for "a pretty little green bush," and she believes a scarecrow is the ghost of a man (Welty 398–99). Likewise, she has difficulty walking, so she must use a cane; at one point, she is unable to bend and tie her own shoes. Because of these physical disabilities, readers might expect her to fail in her attempt to reach town, because "the journey is long; the path, though worn, is difficult" (Keys 354). So what gives Phoenix Jackson the energy and endurance for the journey? The question can best be answered by looking at the inner qualities of the woman: although Jackson's body is weak, she has great spiritual and emotional strength.

Phoenix Jackson's spiritual strength comes from her oneness with nature and her belief in God. This oneness with nature, claims James Saunders, helps her overcome the challenges that she encounters (67). Because Phoenix Jackson is "a child of nature," her impaired vision, although it slows her journey, does not stop it, because as Saunders explains, "mere human

Collins 3

vision would not have been sufficient for the journey"
(67). Instead of allowing her failing vision to
restrict her actions, Phoenix Jackson relies on her
spiritual connection with nature; thus, she warns various animals to "Keep out from under these feet" (Welty
397). Additionally, her spiritual strength comes from
her belief in God--a quality seen when she refers to
God watching her steal the hunter's nickel.

Phoenix Jackson's spiritual strength is comple-
mented by her emotional strength. Her love for her
grandson compels her to endure any difficulty and to
defy any personal danger. Thus, throughout her
journey, she demonstrates fearlessness and selfless-
ness. For example, when the hunter threatens her with
his gun, she tells him that she has faced worse dangers. Even after stealing and accepting nickels, she
does not consider replacing her own worn shoes, but
instead remains intent upon buying a paper windmill
for her grandson.

In her video interview, Eudora Welty explains how
she came to create the paradoxical Phoenix Jackson--
outwardly frail and inwardly strong. Welty tells how
she noticed an "old lady" slowly making her way across
a "silent horizon,"[1] driven by an overwhelming determination to reach her destination; as Welty says, "she
had a purpose" (Henley). Welty created Phoenix Jackson
in the image of this determined woman. In order to
emphasize the character's strength, Welty had her
make the journey to Natchez to get medication for
her grandson. Because the act had to be performed

Collins 4

repeatedly, the journey became a ritual that had to
be completed at all costs. Thus, as Welty explains in
her interview, the act of making the journey is the
most important element in the story (Henley).

In order to convey the significance of the
journey, Welty focuses her story on the process of the
journey. For this reason, readers receive little information about the daily life of the boy and his grandmother or about the illness for which the boy is being
treated. Regardless of the boy's condition--or even
whether he is alive or dead--Jackson must complete her
journey (Henley). The nurse's statement--"The doctor
said as long as you came to get it [the medicine], you
could have it" (Welty 403)--reinforces the ritualistic
nature of Jackson's journey, a journey that Bartel suggests is a "subconscious" act (289). Thus, Phoenix
Jackson cannot answer the nurse's questions because she
does not consciously know what compels her to make the
journey. According to Welty, the character's silence
and disorientation can also be attributed to her relief
and disillusionment upon completing the ritualistic
journey (Henley). Nevertheless, next Saturday, Phoenix
Jackson will again walk "miles and miles, and will continue to do so, regardless of the difficulties facing
her, along the worn path that leads through the wilderness of the Natchez Trace, cheerfully performing her
labor of love" (Howard 84).

Clearly, the interaction of character (Phoenix
Jackson) and act (the ritual journey in search of
medication) is the most important element of Welty's

Collins 5

story. By relying heavily on the characterization of Phoenix Jackson and by describing her difficult encounters during her ritual journey to town, Welty emphasizes how spiritual and emotional strength can overcome physical frailty and how determination and fearlessness can overcome any danger. These moral messages become clear by the time Phoenix reaches the doctor's office. The image of the elderly woman determinedly walking across the horizon, the image that prompted Welty's writing of the story, remains in the minds of the readers, and significantly, it is the final image of the videotaped version of "A Worn Path."

Collins 6

Note

[1] Unlike the written version of "A Worn Path,"
the video of the short story ends not at the doctor's
office but with a vision similar to the one that
inspired Welty to write the story--the elderly black
woman silently walking along the horizon at dusk.

Collins 7

Works Cited

Bartel, Roland. "Life and Death in Eudora Welty's 'A Worn Path.'" <u>Studies in Short Fiction</u> 14 (1977): 288–90.

Henley, Beth. <u>Interview with Eudora Welty</u>. Dir. John Reid and Claudia Velasco. Videocassette. Harcourt, 1994.

Howard, Zelma Turner. <u>The Rhetoric of Eudora Welty's Short Stories</u>. Jackson: UP of Mississippi, 1973.

Keys, Marilyn. "'A Worn Path': The Way of Dispossession." <u>Studies in Short Fiction</u> 16 (1979): 354–56.

Saunders, James Robert. "'A Worn Path': The Eternal Quest of Welty's Phoenix Jackson." <u>Southern Literary Journal</u> 25.1 (Fall 1992): 62–73.

Welty, Eudora. "A Worn Path." <u>Literature: Reading, Reacting, Writing</u>. 2nd Can. ed. Ed. Laurie G. Kirszner, Stephen R. Mandell, and Candace Fertile. Toronto: Nelson, 2007. 397–403.

"<u>A Worn Path</u>." By Eudora Welty. Dir. John Reid and Claudia Velasco. Perf. Cora Lee Day and Conchita Ferrell. Videocassette. Harcourt, 1994.

Akingbola 1

Agnes Akingbola

Professor Michael Trussler

ENGL2001

9 December 2007

"Just a Girl": Gender Segregation

in Alice Munro's "Boys and Girls"

The parental characters that Alice Munro portrays in "Boys and Girls" are similar to those parents in many of her stories. Georgeann Murphy states
that while "fathers in Munro's stories are often
strong, courageous, traditionally masculine," the
mothers are "dreadful housekeepers, visibly constrained by poverty and family obligations" (13-14).
It is no wonder, then, that the young female protagonist in the short story is disconcerted when she
realizes that she must follow in her mother's footsteps and no longer work with her father. This story,
however, deals in subtle ways with the opposition and
separation of gender. The protagonist must confront
the stereotypes that her parents and her community
hold of women. She must also come to terms with the
emotional changes that she is experiencing. Tracing
the segregation of gender roles in this story will not
only show the internal conflict that the protagonist
experiences but also will demonstrate that the protagonist surreptitiously rises above the gender constraints by which her family feels she must abide.

At the very start of the story, the lives of the
men dominate. The narrator begins with the line, "My

father was a fox farmer" (Munro 111). A gory description of his work follows as the narrator and her brother Laird watch fascinated as the foxes are skinned in the basement. This is the only time that the outside world of the men's work encroaches on the domestic sphere, and the narrator's mother, who commands the domestic sphere, despises the fact that the "pelting operation" takes place at all. The men's work is the only work that the narrator feels is valuable. The value that she places on the men's work keeps her from revealing her gender to the reader. She does not mention that she is a girl until a third of the way into the story. In fact, the narrator is not the one who reveals her gender--it is revealed by a salesman who comments, "She's only a girl" (116)--which further suggests that it is a characteristic that she would like to ignore. The fact that the male characters dominate the start of the story coupled with the narrator's desire to hide her "girliness" shows that the world that she admires is that located in the male sphere.

The violence that the protagonist watches on the farm as she helps her father does not bother her at the start of the story. Indeed, the smell of the skinned foxes is "reassuringly seasonal, like the smell of oranges and pine needles" (112). In fact, it is the inside space that causes the narrator worry, for it is the inside space that does not feel "safe." Unlike the "tidy and ingenious" order of her father's workspace, the children's bedroom is full of cast-offs that terrify them when they are sent to bed. As her mother prepares preserves in the autumn, the narrator comments that "sweat trickled over her face and she was always counting under her breath, pointing at jars, dumping cups of sugar" (117). When juxtaposed with the "ritualistically important" work on her father's farm, the housework certainly appears both strenuous and ugly. The respective value that the narrator places on the work of the father and mother determines the value that she places on them as individuals. And although her father can enter into the domestic sphere to skin the foxes, when the protagonist's mother comes near the barn, she is an obvious outsider. She appears "out of place, with her bare lumpy legs, not touched by the sun" (116).

This fear of the domestic sphere can be linked to the narrator's hesitation to be bound by the constraints of femininity. She is always already categorized as "just a girl" by those in her community, and her greatest fear is to be categorized in this way by her father. Because her mother has already defined her in this way, the narrator is suspicious of what she says and claims that her mother is "her enemy" (117). Ultimately, the narrator knows that even though her mother has no economic power in the house, the power that she does hold is not clearly apparent. She knows that her mother has the power to determine where and how she will work. This manifests itself in the narrator's eyes as a distrust of her mother: "She was kinder than my father and more easily fooled, but you could not depend on her, and the real reasons for the things she said and did were not to be known" (117).

Akingbola 4

As her mother's power becomes apparent to the narrator, we can see subtle changes in how the narrator perceives herself. When she looks in the mirror and wonders whether she will be pretty when she grows up, we can see that her greatest struggle is that she feels caught between two identities--that of the androgynous child who accompanies her father as his hired hand and that of the young woman who recognizes that she will be defined, as all women are, by her sexuality. Certainly the way in which her fantasies change as the story progresses hints at this realization. Initially, she dreams of saving people from the perils of animal attack, but by the end of the story the fantasies she creates are ones in which she is rescued. The transformation from proactive participant to docile damsel has taken place. Although the protagonist does not state outright the cause of this transformation, she suggests that it is caused by the narrow definitions of how women are perceived. She eventually understands that she is just a girl.

This realization gains a certain acceptance by the narrator when she sets Flora free. In fact, the narrator is clearly aligned with Flora. To illustrate this alignment, the narrator uses language to describe Flora that others use to define her. The protagonist is told that she is "just a girl" (emphasis added). Flora is defined as "just an old driver" (emphasis added 124). And yet Flora's behaviour indicates that despite her age and seeming worthlessness, she is able to be feisty and fight against the fate to which she has been assigned. Although the narrator realizes the power of

Akingbola 5

language itself when she learns the real meaning of the word girl (119), witnessing Flora's behaviour makes her realize that nothing can be completely prescribed by language. In fact, although she claims not to know the reasons for her actions, it is this realization that prompts her to set Flora free. After all, Flora's feistiness reminds her of her own stubbornness that she displays when her grandmother and mother insist that she sit like a girl. She also helps Flora to escape because she knows that by doing so there remains hope for her own future. She realizes that despite the imprisonment that domestic life holds for her, there is the possibility that she can transcend, if only in small ways, the insignificant definition that is destined for her. Although the narrator realizes that her attempt to set Flora free may be futile in the end, she knows that she gave her one last gasp at freedom, a freedom that she hopes one day she may attain.

At the end of the story, the narrator feels the need to clearly demarcate her own physical space from that of the brother's. She puts up a barricade between her brother's bed and her own. When she sees whom her brother has turned into--someone who is no longer emotionally impacted by the slaughter of the horses--she decides that this so-called masculinity is not a trait that she desires.

Certainly at the end of the story the narrator is upset by the fact that her important role as her father's helper is no longer her own--she has been usurped by her brother. But she gives up this role willingly. She cries at the end of the story not only because her father no longer trusts her and dismisses her but also because she now knows that her desire to be like him is an impossible one to fulfill. The uniqueness of the character of the protagonist, however, is that she has gained a freedom to question and oppose her father's will and the role expectations imposed on her gender--a lesson that Laird will probably never learn. Moreover, before she knows that she has lost her father's trust, she feels that "there was a new wariness, a sense of holding-off, in my attitude to my father and his work" (124). Like the way she felt toward her mother's work at the start of the story, she now questions her father's motives. When her father dismisses her by saying that "she's only a girl," the narrator can finally accept this and concedes, "Maybe it was true" (127).

Critical interpretations of this story have stated that Munro attempts to show the constraints that gender roles can hold for women. Beverly Rasporich has stated that "the narrator comes to see that the social standing of girls and women is dependent on that of their fathers and husbands in the community" (37). But the narrator learns much more than this. She learns that women are dependent on men for their social standing, but that men can be defied. And for the narrator in "Boys and Girls" defiance is always better than complaisance.

Akingbola 7

Works Cited

Munro, Alice. "Boys and Girls." <u>Dance of the Happy Shades</u>. Toronto: Ryerson Press, 1968. 111–27.

Murphy, Georgeann. "The Art of Alice Munro: Memory, Identity, and the Aesthetics of Connection." <u>Canadian Women Writing Fiction</u>. Ed. Mickey Pearlmann. Jackson: Mississippi UP, 1993. 12–27.

Rasporich, Beverly J. <u>Dance of the Sexes</u>. Edmonton: U of Alberta P, 1990.

◇ ◇ ◇

Using Literary Criticism in Your Writing

As you become aware of various schools of literary criticism, you see new ways to think—and to write—about fiction, poetry, and drama. Just as you value the opinions of your peers and your professors, you also will find that the ideas of literary critics can enrich your own reactions to and evaluations of literature. Keep in mind that no single school of literary criticism offers the "right" way of approaching what you read; no single critic provides the definitive analysis of any short story, poem, or play. As you become aware of the richly varied possibilities of literary criticism, you will begin to ask new questions and discover new insights about the works you read.

FORMALISM

◇ ◇ ◇

Formalism stresses the importance of literary form to the meaning of a work. Formalist scholars consider each work of literature in isolation. They consider biographical, historical, and social matters to be irrelevant to the real meaning of a play, short story, novel, or poem. For example, a formalist would see the relationship between Adam and Eve in *Paradise Lost* as entirely unrelated to John Milton's own marital concerns, and they would view theological themes in the same work as entirely separate from Milton's deep involvement with the Puritan religious and political cause in seventeenth-century England. Formalists also would regard Milton's intentions and readers' responses to the epic poem as irrelevant. Instead, formalists would read the text closely, paying attention to organization and structure, to verbal nuances (suggested by word choice and use of figurative language), and to multiple meanings (often created through the writer's use of paradox and irony). The formalist critic tries to reconcile the tensions and oppositions inherent in the text in order to develop a unified reading.

The formalist movement in English-language criticism began in England with I. A. Richards's *Practical Criticism* (1929). To explain and introduce his theory, Richards asked students to interpret famous poems without telling them the poets' names. This strategy encouraged close reading of the text rather than reliance on information about a poet's reputation, the details of a poet's life, or historical context. The American formalist movement, called **New Criticism**, was made popular by college instructors who realized that formalist criticism provided a useful way for students to work along with an instructor in interpreting a literary work rather than passively listening to a lecture on biographical, literary, and historical influences. The New Critical theorists Cleanth Brooks and Robert Penn Warren put together a series of textbooks (*Understanding Poetry, Understanding Fiction,* and *Understanding Drama,* first published in the late 1930s) that were used in colleges for years. After the 1950s, many New Critics began to reevaluate their theories and to broaden their approaches. Although few scholars currently maintain a strictly formalist approach, nearly every critical movement, including feminist, Marxist, psychoanalytic, structuralist, and deconstructionist criticism, owes a debt to the close reading techniques introduced by the formalists.

◊ ◊ ◊

KATE CHOPIN

The Storm
(1898)

A Sequel to "The 'Cadian Ball"

I

The leaves were so still that even Bibi thought it was going to rain. Bobinôt, who was accustomed to converse on terms of perfect equality with his little son, called the child's attention to certain sombre clouds that were rolling with sinister intention from the west, accompanied by a sullen, threatening roar. They were at Friedheimer's store and decided to remain there till the storm had passed. They sat within the door on two empty kegs. Bibi was four years old and looked very wise.

"Mama'll be 'fraid, yes," he suggested with blinking eyes.

"She'll shut the house. Maybe she got Sylvie helpin' her this evenin'," Bobinôt responded reassuringly.

"No; she ent got Sylvie. Sylvie was helpin' her yistiday," piped Bibi.

5   Bobinôt arose and going across to the counter purchased a can of shrimps, of which Calixta was very fond. Then he returned to his perch on the keg and sat stolidly holding the can of shrimps while the storm burst. It shook the wooden store and seemed to be ripping great furrows in the distant field. Bibi laid his little hand on his father's knee and was not afraid.

II

Calixta, at home, felt no uneasiness for their safety. She sat at a side window sewing furiously on a sewing machine. She was greatly occupied and did not notice the approaching storm. But she felt very warm and often stopped to mop her face on which the perspiration gathered in beads. She unfastened her white sacque at the throat. It began to grow dark, and suddenly realizing the situation she got up hurriedly and went about closing windows and doors.

Out on the small front gallery she had hung Bobinôt's Sunday clothes to air and she hastened out to gather them before the rain fell. As she stepped outside, Alcée Laballière rode in at the gate. She had not seen him very often since her marriage, and never alone. She stood there with Bobinôt's coat in her hands, and the big rain drops began to fall. Alcée rode his horse under the shelter of a side projection where the chickens had huddled and there were plows and a harrow piled up in the corner.

"May I come and wait on your gallery till the storm is over, Calixta?" he asked.

"Come 'long in, M'sieur Alcée."

His voice and her own startled her as if from a trance, and she seized Bobinôt's vest; Alcée, mounting to the porch, grabbed the trousers and snatched Bibi's braided jacket that was about to be carried away by a sudden gust of wind. He expressed an intention to remain outside, but it was soon apparent that he might as well have been out in the open: the water beat in upon the boards in driving sheets, and he went inside, closing the door after him. It was even necessary to put something beneath the door to keep the water out.

"My! what a rain! It's good two years since it rain' like that," exclaimed Calixta as she rolled up a piece of bagging and Alcée helped her to thrust it beneath the crack.

She was a little fuller of figure than five years before when she married; but she had lost nothing of her vivacity. Her blue eyes still retained their melting quality; and her yellow hair, dishevelled by the wind and rain, kinked more stubbornly than ever about her ears and temples.

The rain beat upon the low, shingled roof with a force and clatter that threatened to break an entrance and deluge them there. They were in the dining room—the sitting room—the general utility room. Adjoining was her bed room, with Bibi's couch along side her own. The door stood open, and the room with its white, monumental bed, its closed shutters, looked dim and mysterious.

Alcée flung himself into a rocker and Calixta nervously began to gather up from the floor the lengths of a cotton sheet which she had been sewing.

15 "If this keeps up, *Dieu sait* if the levees goin' to stan' it!" she exclaimed.

"What have you got to do with the levees?"

"I got enough to do! An' there's Bobinôt with Bibi out in that storm—if he only didn' left Friedheimer's!"

"Let us hope, Calixta, that Bobinôt's got sense enough to come in out of a cyclone."

She went and stood at the window with a greatly disturbed look on her face. She wiped the frame that was clouded with moisture. It was stiflingly hot. Alcée got up and joined her at the window, looking over her shoulder. The rain was coming down in sheets obscuring the view of far-off cabins and enveloping the distant wood in a gray mist. The playing of the lightning was incessant. A bolt struck a tall chinaberry tree at the edge of the field. It filled all visible space with a blinding glare and the crash seemed to invade the very boards they stood upon.

20 Calixta put her hands to her eyes, and with a cry, staggered backward. Alcée's arm encircled her, and for an instant he drew her close and spasmodically to him.

"*Bonté!*" she cried, releasing herself from his encircling arm, and retreating from the window, "the house'll go next! If I only knew w'ere Bibi was!" She would not compose herself; she would not be seated. Alcée clasped her shoulders and looked into her face. The contact of her warm, palpitating body when he had unthinkingly drawn her into his arms, had aroused all the old-time infatuation and desire for her flesh.

"Calixta," he said, "don't be frightened. Nothing can happen. The house is too low to be struck, with so many tall trees standing about. There! aren't you going to be quiet? say, aren't you?" He pushed her hair back from her face that was warm and steaming. Her lips were as red and moist as pomegranate seed. Her white neck and a glimpse of her full firm bosom disturbed him powerfully. As she glanced up at him the fear in her liquid blue eyes had given place to a drowsy gleam that unconsciously betrayed a sensuous desire. He looked down into her eyes and there was nothing for him to do but to gather her lips in a kiss. It reminded him of Assumption.

"Do you remember—in Assumption, Calixta?" he asked in a low voice broken by passion. Oh! she remembered; for in Assumption he had kissed her and kissed and kissed her; until his senses would well nigh fail, and to save her he would resort to a desperate flight. If she was not an immaculate dove in those days, she was still inviolate; a passionate creature whose very defenselessness had made her defense, against which his honor forbade him to prevail. Now—well, now—her lips seemed in a manner free to be tasted, as well as her round, white throat and her whiter breasts.

They did not heed the crashing torrents, and the roar of the elements made her laugh as she lay in his arms. She was a revelation in that dim, mysterious chamber; as white as the couch she lay upon. Her firm, elastic flesh that was knowing for the first time its birthright was like a creamy lily that the sun invites to contribute its breath and perfume to the undying life of the world.

25 The generous abundance of her passion, without guile or trickery, was like a white flame which penetrated and found response in depths of his own sensuous nature that had never yet been reached.

When he touched her breasts they gave themselves up in quivering ecstasy, inviting his lips. Her mouth was a fountain of delight. And when he possessed her, they seemed to swoon together at the very borderland of life's mystery.

He stayed cushioned upon her, breathless, dazed, enervated, with his heart beating like a hammer upon her. With one hand she clasped his head, her lips lightly touching his forehead. The other hand stroked with a soothing rhythm his muscular shoulders.

The growl of the thunder was distant and passing away. The rain beat softly upon the shingles, inviting them to drowsiness and sleep. But they dared not yield.

The rain was over; and the sun was turning the glistening green world into a palace of gems. Calixta, on the gallery, watched Alcée ride away. He turned and smiled at her with a beaming face; and she lifted her pretty chin in the air and laughed aloud.

III

30   Bobinôt and Bibi, trudging home, stopped without at the cistern to make themselves presentable.

"My! Bibi, w'at will yo' mama say! You ought to be ashame'. You oughtn' put on those good pants. Look at 'em! An' that mud on yo' collar! How you got that mud on yo' collar, Bibi? I never saw such a boy!" Bibi was the picture of pathetic resignation. Bobinôt was the embodiment of serious solicitude as he strove to remove from his own person and his son's the signs of their tramp over heavy roads and through wet fields. He scraped the mud off Bibi's bare legs and feet with a stick and carefully removed all traces from his heavy brogans. Then, prepared for the worst—the meeting with an over-scrupulous housewife, they entered cautiously at the back door.

Calixta was preparing supper. She had set the table and was dripping coffee at the hearth. She sprang up as they came in.

"Oh, Bobinôt! You back! My! but I was uneasy. W'ere you been during the rain? An' Bibi? he ain't wet? he ain't hurt?" She had clasped Bibi and was kissing him effusively. Bobinôt's explanations and apologies, which he had been composing all along the way, died on his lips as Calixta felt him to see if he were dry, and seemed to express nothing but satisfaction at their safe return.

"I brought you some shrimps, Calixta," offered Bobinôt, hauling the can from his ample side pocket and laying it on the table.

35   "Shrimps! Oh, Bobinôt! you too good fo' anything!" and she gave him a smacking kiss on the cheek that resounded. *J'vous réponds*, we'll have a feas' to night! umph-umph!"

Bobinôt and Bibi began to relax and enjoy themselves, and when the three seated themselves at table they laughed much and so loud that anyone might have heard them as far away as Laballière's.

IV

Alcée Laballière wrote to his wife, Clarisse, that night. It was a loving letter, full of tender solicitude. He told her not to hurry back, but if she and the babies liked it at Biloxi, to stay a month longer. He was getting on nicely; and though he missed them, he was willing to bear the separation a while longer—realizing that their health and pleasure were the first things to be considered.

V

As for Clarisse, she was charmed upon receiving her husband's letter. She and the babies were doing well. The society was agreeable; many of her old friends and acquaintances were at the bay. And the first free breath since her marriage seemed to restore the pleasant liberty of her maiden days. Devoted as she was to her husband, their intimate conjugal life was something which she was more than willing to forego for a while.

So the storm passed and every one was happy.

A Formalist Reading: Kate Chopin's "The Storm"

If you were to apply formalist criticism to Chopin's "The Storm," you might begin by noting the story's distinctive sections. What relationship do the sections bear to one another? What do we learn from the word choice, the figures of speech, and the symbols in these sections? And, most important, how do these considerations lead readers to a unified view of the story?

In the first section of "The Storm," readers meet Bobinôt and his son Bibi. The description of the approaching clouds as "sombre," "sinister," and "sullen" suggests an atmosphere of foreboding, yet the alliteration of these words also introduces a poetic tone. The conversation between father and son in the final part of this section contrasts, yet does not conflict with, the rather formal language of the introduction. Both Bobinôt and Bibi speak in Cajun dialect, suggesting their humble origins, yet their words have a rhythm that echoes the poetic notes struck in the description of the storm. As the section closes, Bobinôt, thinking of his wife, Calixta, at home, buys a can of the shrimp he knows she likes and holds the treasure "stolidly," ironically suggesting the protection he cannot offer his wife in his separation from her during the coming storm.

The long second section brings readers to the story's central action. Calixta, as she watches the rain, sees her former lover, Alcée, riding up to seek shelter. As in the first section, the language of the narrator is somewhat formal and always poetic, filled with sensuous diction and images. For instance, we see Calixta "unfasten[ing] her white sacque at the throat" and, later, Alcée envisions her lips "as red and moist as pomegranate seed." Again, paralleling the first section, the conversation of the characters is carried on in dialect, suggesting their lack of sophistication and their connection to the powerful natural forces that surround them. The lovemaking that follows, then, seems both natural and poetic. There is nothing sordid about this interlude and, as the final sections of the story suggest through their rather ordinary, matter-of-fact language, nothing has been harmed by Calixta and Alcée's yielding to passion.

In section 3, Bobinôt brings home the shrimp, symbol of his love for Calixta, and, although we recognize the tension between Bobinôt's shy, gentle approach and Alcée's passion, readers can accept the final sentence as literal rather than ironic. The "storms" (both the rain and the storm of passion) have passed, and no one has been hurt. The threat suggested in the opening sentences has been diffused; both the power and the danger evoked by the poetic diction of the first two sections have disappeared, to be replaced entirely by the rhythms of daily life and speech.

FOR FURTHER READING: FORMALISM

Brooks, Cleanth. *The Well Wrought Urn*. 1947.
Empson, William. *Seven Types of Ambiguity*. 1930.
Hartman, Geoffrey H. *Beyond Formalism*. 1970.
Stallman, Robert W. *Critiques and Essays in Criticism, 1920–1948*. 1949.
Wellek, René. *A History of Modern Criticism*. Vol. 6. 1986.
Wimsatt, W. K. *The Verbal Icon*. 1954.

READER-RESPONSE CRITICISM
◊ ◊ ◊

Reader-response criticism suggests a critical view that opposes formalism, seeing the reader's interaction with the text as central to interpretation. Unlike formalists, reader-response critics do not believe that a work of literature exists as a separate, closed entity. Instead, they consider the reader's contribution to the text as essential. A poem, short story, novel, or play is not a solid piece of fabric but rather a series of threads separated by gaps that readers must fill in, drawing on their own experiences and knowledge.

As we read realistic fiction (fiction in which the world of the text closely resembles what we call reality), we may not notice that we are contributing our interpretation. As we read one sentence and then the next, we develop expectations; and, in realistic stories, these expectations are generally met. Nevertheless, nearly every reader supplies personal meanings and observations, making each reader's experience with a work unique and distinctive from every other reader's experience with the same work. For example, imagine Shakespeare's *Romeo and Juliet* as it might be read by a fourteen-year-old high school student and by her father. The young woman, whose age is the same as Juliet's, is almost certain to identify closely with the female protagonist and to "read" Lord Capulet, Juliet's father, as overbearing and rigid. The young reader's father, however, may be drawn to the poignant passage where Capulet talks with a prospective suitor, urging that he wait while Juliet has time to enjoy her youth. Capulet describes the loss of his other children and calls Juliet "the hopeful lady of my earth." Although the young woman reading this line may interpret it as yet another indication of Capulet's possessiveness, her father may see it as a sign of love and even generosity. The twenty-first-century father may "read" Capulet as a man willing to risk offending a friend in order to keep his daughter safe from the rigours of early marriage (and early childbearing). Whose interpretation is correct? Reader-response theorists would say that both readings are entirely possible and therefore equally "right."

The differing interpretations produced by different readers can be seen as simply the effect of the different personalities (and personal histories) involved in constructing meaning from the same series of clues. Not only does the reader "create" the work of literature, in large part, but the literature itself may work on the reader as he or she reads, altering the reader's experience and thus the reader's interpretation. For example, the father reading *Romeo and Juliet* may alter his sympathetic view of Capulet as he continues through the play and observes Capulet's later, angry exchanges with Juliet.

Reader-response theorists believe in the importance of *recursive reading*—that is, reading and rereading with the idea that no interpretation is carved in stone. A second or third interaction with the text may well produce a new interpretation. This changing view is particularly likely when the rereading takes place significantly later than the initial reading. For example, if the young woman just described reread *Romeo and Juliet* when she was middle-aged and herself the mother of teenage children, her reaction to Capulet would quite likely be different from her reaction when she read the work at age fourteen.

In one particular application of reader-response theory, called *reception theory*, the idea of developing readings is applied to the general reading public rather than to individual readers. Reception theory, as proposed by Hans Robert Jauss ("Literary History as a Challenge to Literary Theory," *New Literary History*, Vol. 2 [1970–71]), suggests that each new generation reads the same works of literature differently. Because each generation of readers has experienced different historical events, read different books, and been aware of different critical theories, each generation will view the same works very differently from its predecessors. (Consider, for example, the changing views toward Shakespeare from the seventeenth century to the present.)

Reader-response criticism has received serious attention since the 1960s, when Norman Holland formulated the theory in *The Dynamics of Literary Response* (1968). The German critic Wolfgang Iser (*The Implied Reader*, 1974) argued that in order to be an effective reader, one must be familiar with the conventions and "codes" of writing. This, then, is one reason for studying literature in a classroom, not to produce approved interpretations but to develop strategies and information that will make sense of a text. Stanley Fish, an American critic, goes even further, arguing that there may not be any "objective" text at all (*Is There a Text in This Class?*, 1980). Fish says that no two readers read the same book, though readers can be trained to have relatively similar responses to a text if they have had relatively similar experiences. For instance, readers who went to college and took an introduction to literature course in which they learned to respond to the various elements of literature, such as character, theme, irony, and figurative language, are likely to have similar responses to a text.

READER-RESPONSE READINGS: KATE CHOPIN'S "THE STORM"

To demonstrate possible reader-response readings, we can look at the same story previously considered from a formalist perspective. (Of course, if several formalist critics read the story, they too would each write a somewhat different interpretation.)

Written by a twenty-five-year-old man who has studied American literature

In Kate Chopin's "The Storm," attention must be paid to the two adult male characters, Bobinôt and Alcée. Usually, in a love triangle situation, one man is portrayed more sympathetically than the other. But Chopin provides us with a dilemma. Alcée is not a cavalier seducer; he genuinely cares for Calixta. Neither is he a brooding hero. There is nothing gruff or angry about Alcée, and he returns to his family home with no apparent harm done following the passionate interlude. On the other hand, Bobinôt is not a cruel or abusive husband. We can see no clear reason for Calixta's affair except for her desire to fulfill a sexual longing for Alcée.

Written by an eighteen-year-old male student in a first-year literature course

Bibi doesn't seem to be a very important character in the story, but we should pay attention to him as a reflection of his father. At the beginning of the story, Bibi worries about his mother and he expresses his concern to his father. Bobinôt tries to reassure his son, but he gets up and buys a treat for Calixta as much to comfort himself as to get something for her. Then Bibi sits with his father, and it seems as if he has transferred all his worries to Bobinôt. In the third section of the story, after Calixta and Alcée have had their love affair, Bibi and Bobinôt come home. They both seem like children, worried about how Calixta will react. She, of course, is nice to them because she feels so guilty. At the end of section 3, both father and son are happy and enjoying themselves. You can't help but feel great sympathy for them both because they are so loving and simple and because they have been betrayed by Calixta, who has not behaved the way a loving mother and wife should.

Written by a forty-five-year-old woman who has studied Kate Chopin's life and work

A decade after the controversial novel *The Awakening* was published in 1899, one critic protested, "To think of Kate Chopin, who once contented herself with mild yarns about genteel Creole life . . . blowing us a hot blast like that!" (qtd. in Gilbert and Gubar 981). This literary observer was shocked, as one might expect from an early-twentieth-century reader, by Chopin's frank picture of sexual relations, and particularly of the sexual feelings of the novel's heroine. One cannot help but wonder, however, whether the scandalized reader was really widely acquainted with Chopin.

Certainly he could not have read "The Storm." This short story is surprising for many reasons, but primarily because it defies the sexual mores of the late nineteenth century by showing a woman who is neither evil nor doomed enjoying, even glorying in, her sexuality. Calixta is presented as a good wife and loving mother, concerned about her husband and son who are away from home during the storm. Yet her connection to Bobinôt and Bibi does not keep her from passionately enjoying her interlude with Alcée. She goes to his arms unhesitatingly, with no false modesty or guilt (feigned or real) to hold her back. Somehow, this scenario does not seem to fit the definition of "a mild yarn about genteel Creole life."

FOR FURTHER READING: READER-RESPONSE CRITICISM

Bleich, David. *Subjective Criticism*. 1978.
Fish, Stanley. *Is There a Text in This Class?* 1980.
Holland, Norman. *The Dynamics of Literary Response*. 1968.
Iser, Wolfgang. *The Implied Reader*. 1974.
———. *The Act of Reading: A Theory of Aesthetic Response*. 1978.
Rosenblatt, Louise. *The Reader, the Text, the Poem*. 1978.
Sulleiman, Susan, and Inge Crosman, eds. *The Reader in the Text*. 1980.
Tomkins, Jane P., ed. *Reader-Response Criticism*. 1980.

SOCIOLOGICAL CRITICSM

⟡ ◇ ◇ ◇

Like reader-response criticism, **sociological criticism** takes issue with formalism. Sociological theorists maintain that the literary work cannot be separated from the social context in which it was created, insisting that literature reflects society and derives its essential existence and significance from the social situations to which it responds. Sociological critics speculate about why a particular work might have been written and explore the ways in which it reacts to a specific situation.

For instance, a sociological literary scholar might note with interest that Shakespeare's history plays about Richard II, Henry IV, and Henry V deal with the consequences of uncertain royal succession and usurpation. These dramas were written during the final years of the reign of Queen Elizabeth I, a monarch who had not produced an heir and refused to designate one. Although the plays cited were set considerably before Elizabeth's time, a sociological critic might conclude that they reflect the English concern about the threat of monarchic chaos should Elizabeth die with no clear line of succession.

In the twentieth century, two strong arms of sociological criticism emerged as dominant: **feminist criticism** and **Marxist criticism**. They remain particularly forceful theories because most of their practitioners have a strong commitment to these ideologies, which they apply as they read literature. Although Feminism and Marxism share a concern with segments of society that have been underrepresented and often ignored, scholars working in these fields do not necessarily agree on what constitutes the best response to the issues highlighted by sociological critiques. Both of these views are supported by modern critical theories such as the reader-response idea of gaps in the text that must be filled in through the reader's own experience and knowledge. In addition, the techniques of New Criticism (in particular, close reading of the text), psychoanalysis, and structuralism have allowed sociological critics to focus on what had been overlooked or skewed in traditional readings and to analyze how the experience of marginal and minority groups has been represented in literature. Sociological critics have also employed poststructuralist strategies to reveal and question the assumptions made within their disciplines and to analyze the cultural contexts of their own work.

The late twentieth century also saw the rise of a third group of theorists, who focus on the relationship between marginalization and ideology. **Postcolonialists**, **multiculturalists**, and **race theorists** share with other sociological critics a concern with underrepresented and ignored populations, but these schools of criticism focus on representations of ethnic and racial difference. Scholars working from a multicultural perspective seek to develop a more inclusive attitude toward literature, highlighting the contributions of authors working in non-white and non-Western traditions. Although both multiculturalist and postcolonialist critics study the social implications of interactions between members of different cultures, postcolonial criticism (like that of the influential critic Edward Said in his landmark text *Orientalism*) analyzes the effects of imperialist discourses on colonized peoples. Race theorists also examine the relationship between literary discourses and racial and ethnic identities in specific political and social contexts, as reflected in the work of bell hooks and Henry Louis Gates, Jr. The differences between these branches of criticism are sometimes difficult to articulate, however, as the scholars working in these fields often employ similar strategies of interpretation and analysis.

FEMINIST CRITICISM
◆ ◆ ◆

Throughout the nineteenth century, women such as the Brontë sisters, George Eliot (Mary Ann Evans), Elizabeth Barrett Browning, and Christina Rossetti struggled for the right to be taken as seriously as their male counterparts. In addition, in 1929 Virginia Woolf, an experimental novelist and literary critic, published *A Room of One's Own,* which described the difficulties that women writers faced and defined a tradition of literature written by women.

Feminist criticism emerged as a defined approach to literature in the late 1960s. Modern feminist criticism began with works such as Mary Ellman's *Thinking about Women* (1968), which focuses on the negative female stereotypes in books authored by men and points out alternative feminine characteristics suggested by women authors. Another pioneering feminist work was Kate Millet's *Sexual Politics* (1969), which analyzes the societal mechanisms that perpetuate male domination of women. Since that time, feminist writings, though not unified in one theory or methodology, have appeared in ever-growing numbers. Some feminist critics have adapted psychoanalytic, Marxist, or other poststructuralist theories, and others have broken new ground. In general, feminist critics take the view that our culture—and by extension our literature—is primarily patriarchal (controlled by males).

According to feminist critics, what is at issue is not anatomical sex, but gender. As Simone de Beauvoir explained, a person is not born feminine, as our society defines it, but rather becomes so because of cultural conditioning. According to feminist critics, paternalist Western culture has defined the feminine as "other" to the male, as passive and emotional in opposition to the dominating and rational masculine.

Feminist critics claim that paternalist cultural stereotypes pervade works of literature in the **canon**—those works generally acknowledged to be the best and most significant. Feminists point out that the canon consists of works almost exclusively written by males and about male experiences. Female characters, when they do appear, are often subordinate to male characters. A female reader of these works must either identify with the male protagonist or accept a marginalized role.

One response of feminist critics is to reinterpret works in the traditional canon. As Judith Fetterley explains in *The Resisting Reader* (1978), the reader "revisions" the text, focusing on the covert sexual bias in a literary work. For example, a feminist scholar studying Shakespeare's *Macbeth* might look closely at the role played by Lady Macbeth and argue that she was not simply a cold-hearted villain but a victim of the circumstances of her time: women in her day were not permitted to follow their own ambitions but were relegated to supporting roles, living their lives through the achievements of their husbands and sons.

A second focus of feminist scholars has been the redefinition of the canon. By seeking out, analyzing, and evaluating little-known works by women, feminist scholars have rediscovered women writers who were ignored or shunned by the reading public and by critics of their own times. Thus, writers such as Kate Chopin and Charlotte Perkins Gilman (see "The Yellow Wall-Paper," p. 189), who wrote during the late nineteenth and early twentieth centuries, are now recognized as worthy of study and consideration.

A FEMINIST READING: TILLIE OLSEN'S "I STAND HERE IRONING"

To approach Tillie Olsen's "I Stand Here Ironing" (p. 181) from a feminist perspective, you might focus on the passages in which the narrator describes her relationships and encounters with men.

> Some readings of Tillie Olsen's "I Stand Here Ironing" suggest that the narrator made choices that doomed her oldest daughter to a life of confusion. If we look at the narrator's relationships with the men in her life, however, we can see that she herself is the story's primary victim.

At nineteen, the narrator was a mother abandoned by her husband, who left her a note saying that he "could no longer endure . . . sharing want" (182) with his wife and infant daughter. This is the first desertion we hear about in the narrator's life, and although she agonizingly describes her painful decisions and the mistakes she made with her daughter Emily, we cannot help but recognize that she was the one who stayed and tried to make things right. Her actions contrast sharply with those of her husband, who ran away, implying that his wife and daughter were burdens too great for him to bear.

The second abandonment is more subtle than the first but no less devastating. After the narrator remarried, she was again left alone to cope with a growing family when her second husband went off to war. True, this desertion was for a "noble" purpose and probably was not voluntary, but the narrator, nevertheless, had to seek one of the low-paying jobs available to women to supplement her allotment cheques. She was again forced to leave her children because her husband had to serve the needs of the male-dominated military establishment.

The narrator was alone at crucial points in Emily's life and had to turn away from her daughter in order to survive. Although she has been brought up in a world that teaches women to depend on men, she learns that she is ultimately alone. Although the desertions she endured were not always intentional, she had to bear the brunt of circumstances that were not her choice but were foisted on her by the patriarchal society in which she lives.

For Further Reading: Feminist Criticism

Benstock, Shari, ed. *Feminist Issues in Literary Scholarship.* 1987.

Engleton, Mary, ed. *Feminist Issues in Literary Theory: A Reader.* 1986.

Gilbert, Sandra, and Susan Gubar. *The Madwoman in the Attic.* 1979.

———. *No Man's Land.* 3 vols. 1988, 1989, 1994.

———, eds. *The Norton Anthology of Literature by Women.* 1985.

Heilbrun, Carolyn G. *Hamlet's Mother and Other Women.* 1990.

Jacobus, Mary. *Reading Woman: Essays in Feminist Criticism.* 1986.

Miller, Nancy K., ed. *The Poetics of Gender.* 1986.

———. *Subject to Change.* 1988.

Showalter, Elaine. *A Literature of Their Own.* 1977.

———. *Sister's Choice: Tradition and Change in American Women's Writing.* 1991.

Marxist Criticism

◈ ◈ ◈

Scholars influenced by Marxist criticism base their readings of literature on the social and economic theories of Karl Marx (*Das Kapital*, 1867–94) and his colleague and coauthor Friedrich Engels (*The Communist Manifesto*, 1884). Marx and Engels believed that the dominant capitalist middle class would eventually be challenged and overthrown by the working class. In the meantime, however, middle-class capitalists would exploit the working class, who produce excess products and profits yet do not share in the benefits of their labour. Marx and Engels further regarded all parts of the society in which they lived—religious, legal, educational, governmental—as tainted by what they saw as the corrupt values of middle-class capitalists.

Marxist critics apply these views about class struggle to their readings of poetry, fiction, and drama. They tend to analyze the literary works of any historical era as products of the ideology, or network of concepts, that supports the interests of the cultural elite and suppresses those of the working class. Some Marxist critics see all Western literature as distorted by the privileged views of the elite class, but most believe that a few creative writers reject the distorted views of their society and see clearly the wrongs to which working-class people have been subjected. For example, George Lukacs, a Hungarian Marxist critic, proposed that great works of literature create their own worlds and reflect life with clarity. These great works, though not written by Marxists, can be studied for their revealing examples of class conflict and other Marxist concerns. A Marxist critic would look with favour on Charles Dickens, who in nearly every novel pointed out inequities in the political, legal, and educational establishments of his time. Readers who remember Oliver Twist's pitiful plea for "more" workhouse porridge (refused by evil Mr. Bumble, who skims money from funds intended to feed the impoverished inmates) cannot help but see fertile ground for the Marxist critic, who would certainly applaud Dickens's scathing criticism of Victorian social and economic inequality.

Marxist criticism developed in the 1920s and 1930s in Germany and the Soviet Union. Since 1960, British and American Marxism has received greatest attention, with works such as Raymond Williams's *Culture and Society, 1780–1950* (1960) and Terry Eagleton's *Criticism and Ideology* (1976).

A MARXIST READING: TILLIE OLSEN'S "I STAND HERE IRONING"

In a Marxist reading of Tillie Olsen's "I Stand Here Ironing," you might concentrate on events that demonstrate how the narrator's and Emily's fates have been directly affected by the capitalist society of the United States.

> Tillie Olsen's "I Stand Here Ironing" stands as a powerful indictment of the capitalist system. The narrator and her daughter, Emily, are repeatedly exploited and defeated by the pressures of the economic system in which they live.
>
> The narrator's first child, Emily, is born into the world of the 1930s Depression—an economic disaster brought on by the excesses and greed of Wall Street. When the young mother is deserted by her first husband, there are no government programs in place to help her. She says it was the "pre-relief, pre-WPA world of the depression" that forced her away from her child and into "a job hashing at night" (182). Although she is willing to work, she is paid so poorly that she must finally send Emily

to live with her husband's family. Raising the money to bring Emily back takes a long time; and after this separation, Emily's health, both physical and emotional, is precarious.

When Emily gets the measles, we get a hard look at what the few social programs that existed during the Depression were like. The child is sent—at the urging of a government social worker—to a convalescent home. The narrator notes bitterly, "They still send children to that place. I see pictures on the society page of sleek young women planning affairs to raise money for it, or dancing at the affairs, or decorating Easter eggs or filling Christmas stockings for the children" (184). The privileged class basks in the artificial glow of their charity work for the poor, yet the newspapers never show pictures of the hospitalized children who are kept isolated from everyone they loved and forced to eat "runny eggs . . . or mush with lumps" (184). Once again the mother is separated from her daughter by a system that discriminates against the poor. Because the family cannot afford private treatment, Emily is forced to undergo treatment in a public institution that not only denies her any contact with her family but also cruelly forbids her to save the letters she receives from home. Normal family relationships are severely disrupted by an uncaring economic structure that only grudgingly offers aid to the poor.

It is clear that the division between mother and daughter is created and worsened by the social conditions in which they live. Because they are poor, they are separated at crucial times and, therefore, never get to know each other fully. Thus, neither can truly understand the ordeals the other has been forced to endure.

For Further Reading: Marxist Criticism

Agger, Ben. *The Discourse of Domination.* 1992.

Bullock, Chris, and David Peck, eds. *Guide to Marxist Literary Criticism.* 1980.

Eagleton, Terry. *Marxism and Literary Criticism.* 1976.

Frow, John. *Marxism and Literary History.* 1986.

Holub, Renate, and Antonio Gramsci. *Beyond Marxism and Postmodernism.* 1992.

Jameson, Fredric. *Marxism and Form.* 1971.

Lentricchia, Frank. *Criticism and Social Change.* 1983.

Ohmann, Richard M. *Politics of Letters.* 1987.

Strelka, Joseph P., ed. *Literary Criticism and Sociology.* 1973.

Williams, Raymond. *Culture and Society, 1780–1950.* 1960.

———. *Marxism and Literature.* 1977.

New Historicism

◊ ◊ ◊

New Historicist critics relate a text to the historical and cultural contexts of the period in which it was created and the periods in which it was critically evaluated. These contexts are not considered simply as "background" but as integral parts of a text. According to the New Historicists, history is not objective facts; rather, like literature, history is subject to interpretation and reinterpretation depending on the power structure of a society. Louis Althusser, for example, suggests that ideology intrudes in the discourse of an era, subjecting readers to the interests of the ruling establishment. Michel Foucault reflects that the discourse of an era defines the nature of "truth" and what behaviours are acceptable, sane, or criminal. "Truth," according to Foucault, is produced by the interaction of power and the systems in which the power flows, and it changes as society changes. Mikhail Bakhtin suggests that all discourse is dialogic, containing within it many independent and sometimes conflicting voices.

Literature, in the opinion of the New Historical critics, cannot be interpreted without reference to the time and place in which it was written. Criticism likewise cannot be evaluated without reference to the time and place in which it was written. A flaw of much criticism, according to the New Historicists, is the consideration of a literary text as if it were an organic whole. Such an approach ignores the diversity of conflicting voices in a text and in the cultural context in which a text is embedded. Indeed, Stephen Greenblatt prefers the term "cultural poetics" to New Historicism because it acknowledges the integral role that literature and art play in the culture of any era. Works of art and literature, according to Greenblatt, actively foster subversive elements or voices but somehow constrain those forces in ways that defuse challenges to the dominant culture.

New Historicists also point out that readers, like texts, are influenced and shaped by the cultural context of their eras and that a thoroughly objective "reading" of a text is therefore impossible. Acknowledging that all readers to some degree "appropriate" a text, some New Historicists present their criticism of texts as "negotiations" between past and present contexts. Thus, criticism of a particular work of literature would draw from both the cultural context of the era in which the text was written and the critic's present cultural context, and the critic would acknowledge how the latter context influences interpretation of the former.

Since the early 1970s, feminist critics have adopted some New Historicist positions, focusing on male-female power conflicts. And critics interested in multicultural texts have stressed the role of the dominant white culture in suppressing or marginalizing the texts of non-whites. Marxist critics, including Raymond Williams, have adopted the term "cultural materialism" in discussing their mode of New Historicism, which focuses on the political significance of a literary text.

A New Historicist Reading: Charlotte Perkins Gilman's "The Yellow Wall-Paper"

A New Historicist scholar might write an essay about "The Yellow Wall-Paper" as an illustration of the destructive effects of the patriarchal culture of the late nineteenth century on women. This reading would be vastly different from that of most nineteenth-century critics, who interpreted the story as a harrowing case study of female mental illness. Even some early-twentieth-century readings posited that the narrator's mental illness is the result of her individual psychological problems. In a New Historicist reading, however, you might focus on the social conventions of the time, which produced conflicting discourses that drove the narrator to madness.

The female narrator of "The Yellow Wall-Paper," who is writing in her private journal (which is the text of the short story), explains that her husband, a physician, has diagnosed her as having a "temporary nervous depression—a slight hysterical tendency" (189). She says she should believe such a physician "of high standing" (189) and cooperate with his treatment, which is to confine her to a room in an isolated country estate and compel her to rest and have no visitors and not to write. The "cure" is intended to reduce her nervousness, she further explains. But as the story unfolds, the narrator reveals that she suspects the treatment will not cure her because it leaves her alone with her thoughts without even her writing to occupy her mind. Her husband's "cure" forces her into a passive role and eliminates any possibility of asserting her own personality. However, she guiltily suggests that her own lack of confidence in her husband's diagnosis may be what is preventing her cure.

The text of "The Yellow Wall-Paper" can be divided into at least two conflicting discourses: (1) the masculine discourse of the husband, who has the authority both of a highly respected physician and of a husband, two positions reinforced by the patriarchal culture of the time; and (2) the feminine discourse of the narrator, whose hesitant personal voice contradicts the masculine voice but undermines itself because it keeps reminding her that women should obey their husbands and their physicians. A third discourse underlies the two dominant ones—that of the gothic horror tale, a popular genre of the late nineteenth century. The narrator in "The Yellow Wall-Paper" is isolated against her will in a room with barred windows in an almost deserted palatial country mansion she describes as "The most beautiful place!" (190). She is at the mercy of her captor, in this case her husband. She is not sure whether she is hallucinating, and she thinks the mansion may be haunted. She does not know whom to trust, not being sure whether her husband really wants to "cure" her or to punish her for expressing her rebellion.

The narrator learns to hide her awareness of the conflicting discourses. She avoids mentioning her thoughts and fears about her illness or her fancies about the house being haunted, and she hides her writing. She speaks reasonably and in "a very quiet voice" (197). But this inability to speak freely to anyone is a kind of torture, and alone in her room with the barred windows, she takes up discourse with the wallpaper. At first she describes it as "One of those sprawling flamboyant patterns committing every artistic sin" (190). But she is fascinated by the pattern, which has been distorted by mildew and by the tearing away of some sections. The narrator begins to strip off the wallpaper to free a woman she thinks is trapped inside; and, eventually, she visualizes herself as that woman, trapped yet freed by the destruction of the wallpaper. The narrator retreats, or escapes into madness, driven there by the multiple discourses she cannot resolve.

FOR FURTHER READING: NEW HISTORICIST CRITICISM

Brook, Thomas. *The New Historicism and Other Old Fashioned Topics.* 1991.
Coates, Christopher. "What Was the New Historicism?" *Centennial Review* 32.2 (Spring 1993): 267–80.
Geertz, Clifford. "Thick Description: Toward an Interpretive Theory of Culture." *The Interpretation of Cultures.* By Clifford Geertz. 1973.
Greenblatt, Stephen, ed. *Representing the English Renaissance.* 1988.
Levin, David. "American Historicism: Old and New." *American Literary History* 6.3 (Fall 1994): 527–38.
Rabinov, Paul, ed. *The Foucault Reader.* 1986.
Veeser, H. Aram, ed. *The New Historicism.* 1989.

PSYCHOANALYTIC CRITICISM
◇ ◇ ◇

Psychoanalytic criticism focuses on a work of literature as an expression in fictional form of the inner workings of the human mind. The premises and procedures used in psychoanalytic criticism were developed by Sigmund Freud (1846–1939), though some critics disagree strongly with his conclusions and their therapeutic and literary applications. Feminists, for example, take issue with Freud's notion that women are inherently masochistic.

Some of the major points of Freud's theories depend on the idea that much of what is most significant to us does not take place in our conscious life. Freud believed that we are forced (mostly by the rigours of having to live in harmony with other people) to repress much of our experience and many of our desires in order to coexist peacefully with others. Some of this repressed experience Freud saw as available to us through dreams and other unconscious structures. He believed that literature could often be interpreted as the reflection of our unconscious life.

Freud was among the first psychoanalytic critics, often using techniques developed for interpreting dreams to interpret literature. Among other analyses, he wrote an insightful study of Dostoevsky's *The Brothers Karamazov* as well as brief commentaries on several of Shakespeare's plays, including *A Midsummer Night's Dream, Macbeth, King Lear,* and *Hamlet.* The study of Hamlet may have inspired a classic of psychoanalytic criticism: Ernest Jones's *Hamlet and Oedipus* (1949), in which Jones explains Hamlet's strange reluctance to act against his uncle Claudius as resulting from Hamlet's unresolved longings for his mother and subsequent drive to eliminate his father. Because Hamlet's own father is dead, Jones argues, Claudius becomes, in the young man's subconscious mind, a father substitute. Hamlet, then, cannot make up his mind to kill his uncle because he sees not a simple case of revenge (for Claudius's murder of his father) but rather a complex web that includes incestuous desire for his own mother (now wed to Claudius). Jones extends his analysis to include the suggestion that Shakespeare himself experienced such a conflict and reflected his own Oedipal feelings in *Hamlet*.

A French psychoanalyst, Jacques Lacan (1901–1981), combined Freudian theories with structuralist literary theories to argue that the essential alienating experience of the human psyche is the acquisition of language. Lacan believed that once you can name yourself and distinguish yourself from others, you enter the difficult social world that requires you to repress your instincts. Like Lacan, who modified and adapted psychoanalytic criticism to connect it to structuralism, many twentieth-century literary scholars, including Marxists and feminists, have found useful approaches in psychoanalytic literary theory (see, for example, Mary Jacobus's *Reading Woman: Essays in Feminist Criticism*, 1986).

Psychoanalytic Terms

To fully appreciate psychoanalytic criticism, readers need to understand the following terms:

◊ *id*—The part of the mind that determines sexual drives and other unconscious compulsions that urge individuals to unthinking gratification.

◊ *ego*—The conscious mind that strives to deal with the demands of the id and to balance its needs with messages from the superego.

◊ *superego*—The part of the unconscious that seeks to repress the demands of the id and to prevent gratification of basic physical appetites. The superego is a sort of censor that represents the prohibitions of society, religion, family beliefs, and so on.

◊ *condensation*—A process that takes place in dreams (and in literature) when several elements from the repressed unconscious are linked together to form a new yet disguised whole.

◊ *symbolism*—Use of representative objects to stand for forbidden (often sexual) objects. This process takes place in dreams and in literature. For instance, a pole, knife, or gun may stand for the penis.

◊ *displacement*—Substitution of a socially acceptable desire for a desire that is not acceptable. This process takes place in dreams or in literature. For example, a woman who experiences sexual desires for her son may instead dream of being intimate with a neighbour who has the same first name as (or who looks like) her son.

◊ *Oedipus complex*—Repressed desire of a son to unite sexually with his mother and kill his father. According to Freud, all young boys go through this stage, but most resolve these conflicts before puberty.

◊ *projection*—Defence mechanism in which people mistakenly see in others antisocial impulses they fail to recognize in themselves.

◊ *subject*—The term used in Lacanian theory to designate a speaking person, or a person who has assumed a position within language. The Lacanian subject of language is split, or characterized by unresolvable tension between the conscious perception of the self (Freud's ego) and the unconscious desires that motivate behaviour.

A PSYCHOANALYTIC READING: EDGAR ALLAN POE'S "THE CASK OF AMONTILLADO"

Edgar Allan Poe died in 1849, six years before Freud was born, so Poe could not possibly have known Freud's work. Nevertheless, psychoanalytic critics argue that the principles discovered by Freud and those who followed him are inherent in human nature. Therefore, they believe it is perfectly plausible to use modern psychiatric terms when analyzing a work written before their invention. If you approached Poe's "The Cask of Amontillado" (p. 227) from a psychoanalytic perspective, you might write the following interpretation.

> Montresor, the protagonist of Poe's "The Cask of Amontillado," has long fascinated readers who have puzzled over his motives for the story's climactic action when he imprisons his rival, Fortunato, and leaves him to die. Montresor claims that Fortunato insulted him and dealt him a "thousand injuries" (227). Yet when we meet Fortunato, although he appears something of a pompous fool, none of his actions—or even his comments—seems powerful enough to motivate Montresor's thirst for revenge.
>
> If, however, we consider a defence mechanism, first named "projection" and described by Sigmund Freud, we gain a clearer picture of Montresor. Those who employ projection are often people who experience antisocial impulses yet are not conscious of these impulses. It seems highly likely that Fortunato did not persecute Montresor; rather, Montresor himself experienced the impulse to act in a hostile manner toward Fortunato. We know, for instance, that Fortunato belongs to the exclusive Order of Masons because he gives Montresor the secret Masonic sign. Montresor's failure to recognize the sign shows that he is a mason only in the grimmest literal sense. Montresor clearly resents Fortunato's high standing and projects onto Fortunato all of his own hostility toward those who (he thinks) have more or know more than he does. Thus, he imagines that Fortunato's main business in life is to persecute and insult him.
>
> Montresor's obsessive behaviour further indicates his pathology. He plans Fortunato's punishment with the cunning one might ordinarily reserve for a major battle, cleverly figuring out a way to keep his servants from the house and to lure the ironically named Fortunato to his death. Each step of the revenge is carefully plotted. This is no sudden crime of passion but rather the diabolically planned act of a deeply disturbed mind.

If we understand Montresor's need to take all of the hatred and anger that is inside himself and to rid himself of those socially unacceptable emotions by projecting them on to someone else, then we can see how he rationalizes a crime that seems otherwise nearly unmotivated. By killing Fortunato, Montresor symbolically kills the evil in himself. It is interesting to note that the final lines of the story support this reading. Montresor observes that "For the half of a century no mortal has disturbed" the bones. In other words, the unacceptable emotions have not again been aroused. His last words, a Latin phrase from the Mass for the Dead meaning "rest in peace," suggest that only through his heinous crime has he found release from the torment of his own hatred.

FOR FURTHER READING: PSYCHOANALYTIC CRITICISM

Freud, Sigmund. *The Interpretation of Dreams*. 1900.
Gardner, Shirley N., ed. *The (M)other Tongue: Essays in Feminist Psychoanalytic Interpretation*. 1985.
Hartman, Geoffrey H., ed. *Psychoanalysis and the Question of the Text*. 1979.
Kris, Ernst. *Psychoanalytic Explorations in Art*. 1952.
Kristeva, Julia. *Desire in Language*. 1980.
Nelson, Benjamin, ed. *Sigmund Freud on Creativity and the Unconscious*. 1958.
Wright, Elizabeth. *Psychoanalytic Criticism: Theory in Practice*. 1984.

STRUCTURALISM

◊ ◊ ◊

Structuralism, a literary movement with roots in linguistics and anthropology, concentrates on literature as a system of signs that have no inherent meaning except in their agreed-upon or conventional relation to one another. Structuralism is usually described by its proponents not as a new way to interpret literary works but rather as a way to understand how works of literature come to have meaning. Because structuralism developed from linguistic theory, some structuralists use linguistic approaches to literature. When they talk about literary texts, they use the terms (such as *morpheme* and *phoneme*) that linguists use as they study the nature of language. Many structuralists, however, use the linguistic model as an analogy. To understand the analogy, you need to know a bit of linguistic theory.

The French linguist Ferdinand de Saussure (*Course in General Linguistics*, 1915) suggested that the relationship between an object and the name we use to designate it is purely arbitrary. What, for example, makes "C-A-T" signify a small, furry animal with pointed ears and whiskers? Only our learned expectation makes us associate cat with the family feline pet. Had we grown up in France, we would make the same association with *chat,* or in Mexico with *gato.* The words we use to designate objects (linguists call these words *signs*) make sense only within the large context of our entire language system and will not be understood as meaningful by someone who does not know that language system. Further, Saussure pointed out, signs become truly useful only when we use them to designate difference. For instance, the word *cat* becomes useful when we want to differentiate a small furry animal that meows from a small furry animal that barks. Saussure was interested in how language, as a structure of conventions, worked. He asked intriguing questions about the underlying rules that allow this made-up structure of signs to work, and, as a result, his pioneering study caught the interest of scholars in many fields.

Many literary scholars saw linguistic structuralism as analogous to the study of literary works. Literary structuralism leads readers to think of poems, short stories, novels, and plays not as self-contained and individual entities that have some kind of inherent meaning but rather as part of a larger literary system. To fully appreciate and analyze the work, the reader must understand the system within which it operates. Like linguistic structuralism, literary structuralism focuses on the importance of difference. We must, for example, understand the difference between the structure of poetry and the structure of prose before we can make sense of a sentence like this:

so much depends
upon
a red wheel
barrow

WILLIAM CARLOS WILLIAMS, "The Red Wheelbarrow" (p. 686)

* * *

Readers unacquainted with the conventions of poetry would find those lines meaningless and confusing, although if they knew the conventions of prose, they would readily understand this sentence:

So much depends upon a red wheelbarrow.

The way we interpret any group of "signs," then, depends on how they are structured and on the way we understand the system that governs their structure.

Structuralists believe that literature is basically artificial because although it uses the same "signs" as everyday language, whose purpose is to give information, the purpose of literature is *not* primarily to relay data. For example, a poem like Dylan Thomas's "Do Not Go Gentle into That Good Night" (p. 571) is written in the linguistic form of a series of commands, yet the poem goes much further than that. Its meaning is created not only by our understanding the lines as a series of commands but also by our recognition of the poetic form, the rhyming conventions, and the figures of speech that Thomas uses. We can only fully discuss the poem within the larger context of our literary knowledge.

Structuralism also provides the foundation for poststructuralism, a theoretical movement that informs the fields of deconstructionist and New Historicist criticism and has influenced the work of many psychoanalytic and sociological critics. Although structuralists claim that language functions by arbitrarily connecting words (signifiers) to ideas (signifieds), poststructuralists develop the implications of this claim, arguing that because the connection of a word to an idea is purely arbitrary, any operation of language is inherently unstable. Poststructuralists believe that to study a literary text is to study a continuously shifting set of meanings.

A STRUCTURALIST READING: WILLIAM FAULKNER'S "BARN BURNING"

A structuralist reading tries to bring to light some of the assumptions about language and form that we are likely to take for granted. Looking at the opening paragraph of Faulkner's "Barn Burning" (p. 234), from the point of view of structuralist criticism, you might first look at an interpretation that reads the passage as a stream of Sarty's thoughts. The structuralist critic might then consider the assumptions a reader would have to make to see what Faulkner has written as the thoughts of an illiterate child. Next, the structuralist might look at evidence to suggest the language in this section operates outside the system of language that would be available to Sarty and that, therefore, "Barn Burning" opens not with a simple recounting of the main character's thoughts but rather with something far more complex.

The opening paragraph of William Faulkner's "Barn Burning" is often read as an excursion into the mind of Sarty, the story's young protagonist. When we read the passage closely, however, we note that a supposedly simple consciousness is represented in a highly complex way. For Sarty—uneducated and illiterate—the "scarlet devils" and "silver curve of fish" on the labels of food tins serve as direct signs appealing to his hunger. It is unlikely, however, that Sarty could consciously understand what he sees and express it as metaphor. We cannot, then, read this opening passage as a recounting of the thoughts that pass through Sarty's mind. Instead, these complex sentences and images offer possibilities that reach beyond the limits of Sarty's linguistic system.

Because our own knowledge is wider than Sarty's, the visual images the narrator describes take on meanings for us that are unavailable to the young boy. For example, like Sarty, we know that the "scarlet devils" stand for deviled ham. Yet the devils also carry another possible connotation. They may indicate evil and thus serve to emphasize the despair and grief Sarty feels are ever present. So we are given images that flash through the mind of an illiterate young boy, apparently intended to suggest his poverty and ignorance (he cannot read the words on the labels), yet we are led to see a highly complicated set of meanings. When we encounter later in the passage Sarty's articulated thought, "*our enemy . . . ourn! mine and hisn both! . . .,*" his down-to-earth dialect shows clearly the sharp distinction between the system of language the narrator uses to describe Sarty's view of the store shelves and the system of language Sarty uses to describe what he sees and feels.

FOR FURTHER READING: STRUCTURALISM

Barthes, Roland. *Critical Essays.* 1964.
Culler, Jonathan. *Structuralist Poetics.* 1975.
Greimas, A. J. *Structured Semantics: An Attempt at a Method.* Trans. McDowell, Schleifer, and Velie. 1983.
Hawkes, Terence. *Structuralism and Semiotics.* 1977.
Lentricchia, Frank. *After the New Criticism.* 1980.
Pettit, Philip. *The Concept of Structuralism: A Critical Analysis.* 1975.
Scholes, Robert. *Structuralism in Literature: An Introduction.* 1974.

DECONSTRUCTION

◈ ◈ ◈

Deconstruction is a literary movement developed from structuralism. Deconstructionists argue that every text contains within it some ingredient undermining its purported system of meaning. In other words, the structure that seems to hold the text together is unstable because it depends on the conclusions of a particular ideology (for instance, the idea that women are inferior to men or that peasants are content with their lowly position in life), conclusions that are not really as natural or inevitable as the text may pretend. The practice of finding the point at which the text falls apart because of these internal inconsistencies is called deconstruction.

Deconstructive theorists share with formalists and structuralists a concern for the work itself rather than for biographical, historical, or ideological influences. Like formalists, deconstructionists focus on possibilities for multiple meanings within texts. However, while formalists seek to explain paradox by discovering tensions and ironies that can lead to a unified reading, deconstructionists insist on the primacy of multiple possibilities. They maintain that any given text is capable of yielding many divergent readings, all of which are equally valid yet may in some way undermine and oppose one another.

Like structuralists, deconstructionists see literary texts as part of larger systems of discourse. A key structuralist technique is identifying opposites in an attempt to show the structure of language used in a work. Having identified the opposites, the structuralist rests the case. Deconstructionists, however, go further. Jacques Derrida, a French philosopher, noticed that these oppositions do not simply reflect linguistic structures but are the linguistic response to the way people deal with their beliefs (their ideologies). For instance, if you believe strongly that democracy is the best possible form of government, you tend to lump other forms of government into the category "nondemocracies." If a government is nondemocratic, that—not its other distinguishing characteristics—would be significant to you. This typical ideological response operates in all kinds of areas of belief, even ones we are not aware of. Deconstructionists contend that texts tend to give away their ideological biases by means of this opposition.

Derrida called this distinction between "A" and "Not-A" (rather than between "A" and "B") *différance,* a word he coined to suggest a concept represented by the French verb *différer,* which has two meanings: "to be different" and "to defer." (Note that in Derrida's new term an "a" is substituted for an "e"—a distinction that can be seen in writing but not heard in speaking.) When a deconstructionist uncovers *différance* through careful examination of a text, he or she also finds an (often unwitting) ideological bias. Deconstructionists argue that the reader must transcend such ideological biases and must instead acknowledge contradictory possibilities as equally worthy of consideration. No one meaning can or should be designated as correct.

Deconstruction, then, is not really a system of criticism (and, in fact, deconstructionists resist being labelled as a school of criticism). Rather, deconstruction offers a way to take apart a literary text and thereby reveal its separate layers. Deconstructionists often focus on the metaphorical nature of language, claiming that all language is basically metaphoric because the sign we use to designate any given object or action stands apart from the object itself. In fact, deconstructionists believe that all writing is essentially literary and metaphorical because language, by its very nature, can only *stand for* what we call reality or truth; it cannot *be* reality or truth.

A major contribution of deconstructive critics lies in their playful approach to language and to literary criticism. They refuse to accept as absolute any one way of reading poetry, fiction, or drama, and they guard against what they see as the fixed conclusions and arbitrary operating assumptions of many schools of criticism.

A DECONSTRUCTIONIST READING: FLANNERY O'CONNOR'S "A GOOD MAN IS HARD TO FIND"

A deconstructionist reading of Flannery O'Connor's "A Good Man Is Hard to Find" (p. 280) might challenge the essentially religious interpretations the author offered of her own stories in essays and letters. If you were applying deconstructionist criticism to the story, you might argue that the author's reading of the story is no more valid than anyone else's, and that the story can just as legitimately be read as an investigation of the functions of irony in language.

> Flannery O'Connor explained that the grotesque and violent aspects of her stories are intended to shock the reader into recognizing the inhospitable nature of the world and thereby the universal human need for divine grace. The last sentence of "A Good Man Is Hard to Find" is spoken by The Misfit, who has just murdered a family of travellers: "It's no real pleasure in life." However, the language of O'Connor's stories is

extremely ironic—that is, her narrators and characters often say one thing but mean another. So it is possible that their statements are not empirically true but are representations of a persona or elements of a story they have created using language.

The Grandmother, for example, lives almost entirely in fictions—newspaper clippings, stories for the grandchildren, her belief that The Misfit is a good man. In contrast, The Misfit is more literal than the Grandmother in his perception of reality. He knows, for example, whether the car turned over once or twice. But he too is posing, at first as the tough guy who rejects religious and societal norms by saying, ". . . it's nothing for you to do but enjoy the few minutes you got left the best way you can—by killing somebody or burning down his house or doing some other meanness to him. No pleasure but meanness. . . ." Finally, he poses as the pessimist—or, according to O'Connor's reading, the Christian—who claims, "It's no real pleasure in life." The contradictions in The Misfit's language make it impossible to tell which of these façades is "real."

For Further Reading: Deconstruction

Abrams, M. H. "Rationality and the Imagination in Cultural History." *Critical Inquiry* 2 (1976): 447–64. (Abrams claims deconstructionists are parasites who depend on other critics to come up with interpretations that can be deconstructed.)

Arac, Jonathan, Wlad Godzich, and Wallace Martin, eds. *The Yale Critics: Deconstruction in America.* 1983.

Berman, Art. *From the New Criticism to Deconstruction.* 1988.

Culler, Jonathan. *On Deconstruction: Theory and Criticism after Structuralism.* 1982.

Jefferson, Ann. "Structuralism and Post-Structuralism." *Modern Literary Theory: A Comparative Introduction.* 1982.

Johnson, Barbara. *The Critical Difference: Essays in the Contemporary Rhetoric of Reading.* 1980.

Leitsch, Vincent B. *Deconstructive Theory and Practice.* 1982.

Lynn, Steven. "A Passage into Critical Theory." *College English* 52 (1990): 258–71.

Miller, J. Hillis. "The Critic as Host." *Deconstruction and Criticism.* Ed. Harold Bloom et al. 1979. (a response to Abrams's article, listed above)

Norris, Christopher. *Deconstruction: Theory and Practice.* 1982.

Acknowledgments

CHINUA ACHEBE, "Dead Man's Path" reprinted by permission of Harold Ober Associates Incorporated. Copyright © 1972, 1973 by Chinua Achebe.

MARGARET ATWOOD, "Death by Landscape" taken from *Wilderness Tips* by Margaret Atwood. Used by permission of McClelland & Stewart Ltd. "Variations on the Word *Love*", "Death of a Young Son by Drowning" and "The Animals in That Country" from *Selected Poems 1966–1984*. Copyright © 1990 by Margaret Atwood. Reprinted with the permission of Oxford University Press. "The City Planners" from *The Circle Game* by Margaret Atwood. Copyright © 1966. Reprinted with the permission of the House of Anansi, Toronto, Ontario. "You Fit into Me" from *Power Politics* by Margaret Atwood. Reprinted with the permission of the House of Anansi, Toronto, Ontario.

W.H. AUDEN, "Stop All The Clocks", "The Unknown Citizen", "As I Walked Out One Evening" and "Musée des Beaux Arts", copyright 1940 and renewed © 1968 by W.H. Auden, from COLLECTED POEMS by W.H. Auden. Reprinted by permission of Random House, Inc. "The Shield of Achilles" copyright 1952 by W.H. Auden, from COLLECTED POEMS by W.H. Auden. Reprinted by permission of Random House, Inc.

MARGARET AVISON, "The Swimmer's Moment" reprinted from *Always Now, The Collected Poems* (in three volumes) by Margaret Avison, The Porcupine's Quill, 2003, by permission of the publisher.

MATSUO BASHO, Five haiku by Matsuo Basho from *The Penguin Book of Japanese Verse* translated by Geoffrey Bownas and Anthony Thwaite (Penguin Books, 1964). Translation copyright © Geoffrey Bownas and Anthony Thwaite, 1964. Reproduced by permission.

SAMUEL BECKETT, *Krapp's Last Tape* from THE COLLECTED SHORTER PLAYS of Samuel Beckett. Copyright © 1958 by Samuel Beckett. Used by permission of Grove/Atlantic, Inc.

EARLE BIRNEY, "Bushed" taken from *Ghost in the Wheels* by Earle Birney. Used by permission of McClelland & Stewart Ltd.

ELIZABETH BISHOP, "Sestina" from THE COMPLETE POEMS 1927–1979 by Elizabeth Bishop. Copyright © 1979, 1983 by Alice Helen Methfessel. *Reprinted by permission of Farrar, Straus and Giroux, LLC.*

ROO BORSON, "After a Death" by Roo Borson, reprinted by permission of the author.

TIM BOWLING, "Hamlet" from *Darkness and Silence* by Tim Bowling, Nightwood Editions, 2001. Reprinted by permission of the publisher.

DIONNE BRAND, "Tamarindus Indica" by Dionne Brand extracted from *In the Full and Change of the Moon* by Dionne Brand. Copyright © 1999 by Dionne Brand. Reprinted with permission of Knopf Canada. "Blues Spiritual for Mammy Prater" taken from *No Language Is Neutral* by Dionne Brand. Used by permission, McClelland & Stewart Ltd.

RICHARD BRAUTIGAN, "Widow's Lament" from THE PILL VERSUS THE SPRINGHILL MINE DISASTER by Richard Brautigan. Copyright © 1968 by Richard Brautigan. Reprinted by permission of Houghton Mifflin Company. All rights reserved.

ROBERT BRINGHURST, "For the Bones of Josef Mengele, Disinterred June 1985" taken from *The Calling: Selected Poems, 1970–1995* by Robert Bringhurst. Used by permission of McClelland & Stewart Ltd.

GWENDOLYN BROOKS, "Sadie and Maud", "First Fight. Then Fiddle" and "We Real Cool" from *Blacks* by Gwendolyn Brooks. Copyright © by Third World Press, Chicago. *Reprinted by Consent of Brooks Permissions.*

CHARLES BUKOWSKI, "Dog Fight" from WHAT MATTERS MOST IS HOW WELL YOU WALK THROUGH THE FIRE by CHARLES BUKOWSKI. Copyright © 1999 by Linda Lee Bukowski. Reprinted by permission of HarperCollins Publishers.

RAYMOND CARVER, "Photograph of My Father in His Twenty-Second Year" from *Fires* by Raymond Carver. Copyright © 1983 by Raymond Carver; 1989 to the present by Tess Gallagher, most recent publication in ALL OF US, published by Knopf. By permission of Tess Gallagher. "Cathedral" from CATHEDRAL by Raymond Carver, copyright © 1981–1988 by Raymond Carver; 1989–2005 by Tess Gallagher. Used by permission of Alfred A. Knopf, a division of Random House, Inc.

ANTON CHEKOV, "THE BRUTE" by Anton Chekov. Translated by Eric Bentley. Copyright © 1958 by Eric Bentley. Caution: Professionals and amateurs are hereby warned that *The Brute* being fully protected under the copyright laws of the United States of America, the British Commonwealth countries, including Canada, and the other countries of the Copyright Union, is subject to a royalty. All rights, including professional, amateur, motion picture, recitation, public reading, radio, television and cable broadcasting, and the rights to translation into foreign languages, are strictly reserved. Any inquiry regarding the availability of performance rights, or the purchase of individual copies of the authorized acting edition, must be directed to Samuel French Inc., 45 West 25 Street, NY, NY 10010 with other locations in Hollywood and Toronto, Canada.

MICHÈLE LALONDE, "Speak White" by Michele Lalonde, reprinted by permission of the translator, D.G. Jones.

PATRICK LANE, "Albino Pheasants" by Patrick Lane from *15 Canadian Poets × 3*, edited by Gary Geddes, Oxford University Press Canada, 2001. Reprinted by permission of the author. "Fathers and Sons" reprinted by permission of the author.

PHILIP LARKIN, "Aubade" from *Collected Poems of Philip Larkin*. Copyright © 1988, 1989 by the Estate of Philip Larkin. Reprinted by permission of Faber and Faber Limited.

EVELYN LAU, "My Tragic Opera" by Evelyn Lau from *In the House of Slaves* by Evelyn Lau. Reprinted by permission of the author.

MARGARET LAURENCE, "The Loons" taken from *A Bird in the House* by Margaret Laurence. Used by permission of McClelland & Stewart Ltd.

IRVING LAYTON, "Whatever Else Poetry Is Freedom" and "Keine Lazarovitch 1870–1959" taken from *A Wild Peculiar Joy: Selected Poems 1945–89* by Irving Layton. Used by permission of McClelland & Stewart Ltd.

URSULA LE GUIN, "The Ones Who Walk Away from Omelas" by Ursula Le Guin, Copyright © 1973, 2001 by Ursula K. Le Guin; first appeared in *New Dimensions 3;* reprinted by permission.

DENISE LEVERTOV, "What Were They Like?" by Denise Levertov, from POEMS 1960–1967, copyright © 1966 by Denise Levertov. Reprinted by permission of New Directions Publishing Corp.

TIM LILBURN, "Pumpkins" reprinted with permission of the author.

DOROTHY LIVESAY, "Green Rain", "Bartok and the Geranium" and "The Three Emilys" from *Collected Poems: the Two Seasons* (Toronto: McGraw-Hill Ryerson, 1972). Reprinted by permission of Jay Stewart, Literary Executrix for the Estate of Dorothy Livesay.

BILLIE LIVINGSTON, "Letter from Lucy" by Billie Livingston from *The Chick at the Back of the Church* by Billie Livingston, Nightwood Editions, 2001. Reprinted with permission of the publisher.

AUDRE LORDE, "Rooming Houses Are Old Women". Copyright © 1973, 1970, 1968 by Audre Lorde, from *Chosen Poems: Old and New* by Audre Lorde. Used by permission of W.W. Norton & Company, Inc.

ROBERT LOWELL, "For the Union Dead" from FOR THE UNION DEAD by Robert Lowell. Copyright © 1959 by Robert Lowell. Copyright renewed 1987 by Harriet Lowell, Caroline Lowell, and Sheridan Lowell. *Reprinted by permission of Farrar, Straus and Giroux, LLC.*

PAT LOWTHER, "Wanting" from *Milk Stone* by Pat Lowther (Borealis Press 1974). Reprinted by permission of Borealis Press.

GWENDOLYN MACEWEN, "A Breakfast for Barbarians" from *Magic Animals: Selected Poetry of Gwendolyn MacEwen* (Toronto: Macmillian, 1996). Permission for use granted by the author's family.

ARCHIBALD MACLEISH, "Ars Poetica" from COLLECTED POEMS, 1917–1982 by Archibald MacLeish. Copyright © 1985 by The Estate of Archibald MacLeish. Reprinted by permission of Houghton Mifflin Company. All rights reserved.

ALISTAIR MACLEOD, "The Boat" taken from *Island* by Alistair MacLeod. Used by permission of McClelland & Stewart Ltd.

JOAN MACLEOD, *The Shape of a Girl* reprinted with permission of Talonbooks.

WILLIAM MEREDITH, "In Memory of Donald A. Stauffer" and "Dreams of Suicide" reprinted from *Effort at Speech: New and Selected Poems* by William Meredith, published by TriQuarterly Books/Northwestern University Press in 1997. Copyright © 1997 by William Meredith. All rights reserved; used by permissions of Northwestern University Press and the author.

CZESLAW MILOSZ, "Christopher Robin" from ROAD SIDE DOG by Czeslaw Milosz. Copyright © 1998 by Czeslaw Milosz. Reprinted by permission of Farrar, Straus and Giroux, LLC.

JANICE MIRIKITANI, "Suicide Note" reprinted with permission from *Shredding Silence* by Janice Mirikitani. Copyright © 1987 by Janice Mirikitani, Celestial Arts, a division of Ten Speed Press, Berkeley, CA. www.tenspeed.com.

ROHINTON MISTRY, "Swimming Lessons" from *Tales from Firozsha Baag* by Rohinton Mistry. Used by permission, McClelland & Stewart Ltd.

N. SCOTT MOMADAY, "Comparatives" from *In the Presence of the Sun* by N. Scott Momaday. Copyright © 1992 by the author and reprinted by permission of St. Martin's Press, LLC.

SHANI MOOTOO, "A Garden of Her Own" from *Out on Main Street and Other Stories* by Shani Mootoo (Press Gang, an imprint of Raincoast Books 1993) copyright 1993 Shani Mootoo. Reprinted by permission of Raincoast Books.

ERIN MOURÉ, "It Is Only Me" from *Wanted Alive* Copyright © 1983 Erin Moure. Reprinted with permission of House of Anansi Press.

ALICE MUNRO, "How I Met My Husband", Copyright © 1974 by Alice Munro. Reprinted by permission of William Morris Agency, LLC on behalf of the Author. "Boys and Girls" from *Dance of the Happy Shades*. Copyright © 1968 Alice Munro. Used by permission of McGraw-Hill Ryerson Ltd.

OGDEN NASH, "The Lama", Copyright © 1931 by Ogden Nash, renewed. Reprinted by permission of Curtis Brown, Ltd.

PABLO NERUDA, "The United Fruit Company" by Pablo Neruda translated by Robert Bly. Reprinted by permission.

bp Nichol, "Blues" and excerpt from "The Captain Poetry Poems" by bp Nichol, reprinted by permission of the Estate of bp Nichol.

Marlene Nourbese Philip, "Blackman Dead" from *Thorns* (Toronto: Williams-Wallace, 1980). Reprinted by permission of the author.

Alden Nowlan, "The Bull Moose" and "Britain Street" reprinted with permission.

Tim O'Brien, "The Things They Carried" from THE THINGS THEY CARRIED by Tim O'Brien. Copyright © 1990 by Tim O'Brien. Reprinted by permission of Houghton Mifflin Company. All rights reserved.

Flannery O'Connor, "A Good Man Is Hard to Find" by Flannery O'Connor from A GOOD MAN IS HARD TO FIND AND OTHER STORIES, copyright 1953 by Flannery O'Connor and renewed © 1981 by Regina O'Connor. Reprinted by permission of Harcourt, Inc.

Sharon Olds, "Rite of Passage" from THE DEAD AND THE LIVING by Sharon Olds, copyright © 1987 by Sharon Olds. Used by permission of Alfred A. Knopf, a division of Random House, Inc.

Tillie Olsen, "I Stand Here Ironing," copyright © 1956, 1957, 1960, 1961 by Tillie Olsen. From *Tell Me a Riddle* by Tillie Olsen, Introduction by John Leonard. Used by permission of Elaine Markson Literary Agency.

Michael Ondaatje, "Dates" from *The Cinnamon Peeler* by Michael Ondaatje. Copyright © 1989 by Michael Ondaatje. Reprinted by permission of Ellen Levine Literary Agency/Trident Media Group. "Letters & Other Worlds" and "The Cinnamon Peeler" from *The Cinnamon Peeler*. Copyright © by Michael Ondaatje. Reprinted by permission of the author.

P.K. Page, "After Reading *Albino Pheasants* by Patrick Lane" reprinted from *The Hidden Room: Collected Poems* (in two volumes) by P.K. Page by permission of The Porcupine's Quill. "The Stenographers" from *The Hidden Room* (in two volumes) (The Porcupine's Quill, 1997) Copyright P.K. Page. Reprinted with permission of the author.

Dorothy Parker, "General Review of the Sex Situation," copyright 1926, renewed © 1954 by Dorothy Parker, from THE PORTABLE DOROTHY PARKER by Dorothy Parker. Used by permission of Viking Penguin, a division of Penguin Group (USA) Inc.

Linda Pastan, "Ethics" from WAITING FOR MY LIFE by Linda Pastan. Copyright © 1981 by Linda Pastan. Used by permission of W.W. Norton & Company, Inc.

Marge Piercy, "The Secretary Chant" and "Barbie Doll" from CIRCLES ON THE WATER by Marge Piercy. Copyright © 1982 by Marge Piercy. Used by permission of Alfred A. Knopf, a division of Random House, Inc.

Sylvia Plath, "Wreath for a Bridal" by Sylvia Plath from *Collected Poems* by Sylvia Plath, edited by Ted Hughes. Copyright © 1960, 1965, 1971, 1981 by the Estate of Sylvia Plath. Copyright renewed. Reprinted by permission of Faber and Faber Limited. "Daddy" from *Ariel* by Sylvia Plath. Copyright © 1963 by Ted Hughes. Copyright renewed. Reprinted by permission of Faber and Faber Limited.

Ezra Pound, Excerpt from "Canto LXXVI" by Ezra Pound from THE CANTOS OF EZRA POUND, copyright © 1934, 1937, 1940, 1948, 1956, 1959, 1962, 1963, 1966, and 1968 by Ezra Pound. Reprinted by permission of New Directions Publishing Corp. "In a Station of the Metro" and "The River Merchant's Wife: A Letter" from PERSONAE, copyright © 1926 by Ezra Pound. Reprinted by permission of New Directions Publishing Corp.

E.J. Pratt, "The Prize Cat" from *E.J. Pratt: Complete Poems*, edited by Sandra Djwa and R.G. Moyles. Copyright © 1989 by University of Toronto Press. Reprinted with permission of the publisher.

Al Purdy, "The Cariboo Horses" from Beyond Remembering: The Collected Poems of Al Purdy, Harbour Publishing, 2000. Reprinted with permission. "Lament of the Dorsets" and "The Country North of Belleville" from Beyond Remembering: The Collected Poems of Al Purdy, Harbour Publishing, 2000. Reprinted with permission.

Henry Reed, "Naming of Parts" from *Collected Poems*, edited by Jon Stallworthy, 1991. Copyright The Executor of Henry Reed's Estate. Reprinted by permission of Oxford University Press.

Adrienne Rich, "A Woman Mourned by Daughters" by Adrienne Rich. Copyright © 1993, 1967, 1963 by Adrienne Rich, from COLLECTED EARLY POEMS: 1950–1970 by Adrienne Rich. Used by permission of the author and W.W. Norton & Company, Inc. "Living in Sin" and "Aunt Jennifer's Tigers" copyright © 2002, 1955 by Adrienne Rich. "Diving into the Wreck" Copyright © 2002 by Adrienne Rich. Copyright © 1973 by W.W. Norton & Company, Inc., from THE FACT OF THE DOORFRAME: SELECTED POEMS 1950–2001 by Adrienne Rich. Used by permission of the author and W.W. Norton & Company, Inc.

Ríos, Alberto Alvaro, "Nani" from Whispering to Fool the Wind. © 1982 by Alberto Ríos. Reprinted by permission of the author.

Hélène Rioux, "Opening Night," translated by Diane Schomperlen, from *Parallel Voices* edited by Andre Carpentier and Matt Cohen. Reprinted by permission of Quarry Press.

Theodore Roethke, "My Papa's Waltz," copyright 1942 by Hearst Magazines, Inc., "I Knew a Woman," copyright 1954 by Theodore Roethke, "The Waking," copyright 1953 by Theodore Roethke, "Night Crow," copyright 1944 by Saturday Review Association, Inc., from THE COLLECTED POEMS OF THEODORE ROETHKE by Theodore Roethke. Used by permission of Doubleday, a division of Random House, Inc.

SINCLAIR ROSS, "A Field of Wheat" taken from *The Lamp at Noon and Other Stories* by Sinclair Ross. Used by permission of McClelland & Stewart Ltd.

ARMAND GARNET RUFFO, "Creating a Country" from *Opening in the Sky,* Theytus Books (1994). Reprinted with permisssion of the author.

JANE RULE, "Inland Passage" from *Inland Passage* (Toronto: Lester and Orpen Dennys, 1985). Reprinted by permission of Key Porter Books.

GEORGE RYGA, *The Ecstasy of Rita Joe* by George Ryga, Talonbooks, 1970. Reprinted by permission of the publisher.

JIM SAGEL, "Baca Grande" by Jim Sagel, from *Hispanics in the U.S.: An Anthology of Creative Literature,* Vol. 2, 1982. Reprinted by permission of Bilingual press/Editorial Bilingue (Arizona State University, Tempe, AZ).

CARL SANDBURG, "Fog" from CHICAGO POEMS by Carl Sandburg, copyright 1916 by Holt, Rinehart and Winston and renewed 1944 by Carl Sandburg, reprinted by permission of Harcourt, Inc.

F.R. SCOTT, "Laurentian Shield" from *The Collected Poems of F.R. Scott,* edited by John Newlove. Reprinted with the permission of William Toye, Literary Executor for the Estate of F.R. Scott.

SIPHO SEPAMLA, "Words, Words, Words" by Sipho Sepamla.

VIKRAM SETH, "Work and Freedom" by Vikram Seth from ALL YOU WHO SLEEP TONIGHT by Vikram Seth, copyright © 1990 by Vikram Seth. Used by permission of Alfred A. Knopf, a division of Random House, Inc.

ANNE SEXTON, "Cinderella" from TRANSFORMATIONS by Anne Sexton. Copyright © 1971 by Anne Sexton. Reprinted by permission of Houghton Mifflin Company. All rights reserved.

CAROL SHIELDS, "Scenes" by Carol Shields from *Ink Lake,* edited by Michael Ondaatje, Random House of Canada, 1992. Copyright © 2006 Carol Shields Literary Trust. Reprinted by permission.

BORIS SLUTSKY, "How Did They Kill My Grandmother?" from *Post-War Russian Poetry,* translated by Elaine Feinstein. Copyright © 1974. Reprinted by permission of Elaine Feinstein.

STEVIE SMITH, "Not Waving but Drowning" by Stevie Smith, from COLLECTED POEMS OF STEVIE SMITH. Copyright © 1972 by Stevie Smith. Reprinted by permission of New Directions Publishing Corp.

GARY SNYDER, "Some Good Things to Be Said for the Iron Age" reprinted by permission of the author.

SOPHOCLES, *Oedipus the King,* translated by Thomas F. Gould © 1970. Reprinted by permission.

WOLE SOYINKA, "Future Plans" from A SHUTTLE IN THE CRYPT by Wole Soyinka. Copyright © 1972 by Wole Soyinka. *Reprinted by permission of Hill and Wang, a division of Farrar, Straus and Giroux, LLC.* "Telephone Coversation" copyright Wole Soyinka. Reprinted by permission of the author.

WILLIAM STAFFORD, "Traveling through the Dark" copyright 1962, 1998 by the Estate of William Stafford. Reprinted from *The Way It Is: New & Selected Poems* by William Stafford with the permission of Graywolf Press, Saint Paul, Minnesota.

ANDREW SUKNASKI, "The Bitter Word" from *Wood Mountain Poems* by Andrew Suknaski. Copyright © 1976 by Andrew Suknaski. Reprinted by permission of Andrew Suknaski.

MAY SWENSON, "Women" by May Swenson. Used with permission of the Literary Estate of May Swenson.

SHARON THESEN, "Animals" by Sharon Thesen from *15 Canadian Poets × 3,* edited by Gary Geddes, Oxford University Press Canada, 2001. Reprined by permission of the author.

MADELEINE THIEN, "Simple Recipes" taken from *Simple Recipes* by Madeline Thien. Used by permission of McClelland & Stewart Ltd.

MICHEL TREMBLAY, *Les Belles Soeurs,* translated by John Van Burek and Bill Glassco. Reprinted with permission of Talonbooks.

JOHN UPDIKE, "A&P" by John Updike from PIGEON FEATHERS AND OTHER STORIES, copyright © 1962 and renewed 1990 by John Updike. Published by Alfred A. Knopf, a division of Random House, Inc.

LUISA VALENZUELA, "All About Suicide" from STRANGE THINGS HAPPEN HERE: TWENTY SIX SHORT STORIES AND A NOVEL BY LUISA VALENZUELA, copyright © 1975 by Ediciones de la Flor, English translation by Helen Lane copyright © 1979 by Harcourt, Inc., reprinted by permission of the publisher.

MIRIAM WADDINGTON, "How I Spent the Year Listening to the Ten O'Clock News" from *Collected Poems* by Miriam Waddington. Copyright Miriam Waddington 1986. Reprinted with permission.

DEREK WALCOTT, "Sea Grapes" from SEA GRAPES by Derek Walcott. Copyright © 1976 by Derek Walcott. Reprinted by permission of Farrar, Straus and Giroux, LLC.

ALICE WALKER, "Everyday Use" by Alice Walker from IN LOVE & TROUBLE: STORIES OF BLACK WOMEN, copyright © 1973 by Alice Walker. Reprinted by permission of Harcourt, Inc. "Women" from REVOLUTIONARY PETUNIAS & OTHER POEMS, copyright © 1970 and renewed 1998 by Alice Walker, reprinted by permission of the publisher.

BRONWEN WALLACE, "A Simple Poem for Virginia Woolf" is reprinted from *Common Magic* by permission of Oberon Press.

WENDY WASSERSTEIN, *Tender Offer* copyright © 1983. Reprinted by permission of International Creative Management.

SHEILA WATSON, "Antigone" by Sheila Watson. Reprinted by permission.

TOM WAYMAN, "Wayman in Love" by Tom Wayman. Reprinted by permission of Harbour Publishing. "Did I Miss Anything?" from *Did I Miss Anything?* by Tom Wayman (1993). Reprinted by permission of Harbour Publishing.

PHYLLIS WEBB, "Cornflowers and Saffron Robes Belittle the Effort" from *Selected Poems* by Phyllis Webb. Reprinted by permission of Talonbooks.

EUDORA WELTY, "A Worn Path" by Eudora Welty from A CURTAIN OF GREEN AND OTHER STORIES, Copyright 1941 and renewed 1969 by Eudora Welty, reprinted by permission of Harcourt, Inc.

RICHARD WILBUR, "For the Student Strikers" from THE MIND-READER. Copyright © 1971 by Richard Wilbur, reprinted by permission of Harcourt, Inc. "Sleepless at Crown Point" from THE MIND-READER. Copyright © 1973 by Richard Wilbur, reprinted by permission of Harcourt, Inc. "A Sketch" from THE MIND-READER. Copyright © 1975 by Richard Wilbur, reprinted by permission of Harcourt, Inc.

WILLIAM CARLOS WILLIAMS, "The Red Wheelbarrow", "The Great Figure" and "Spring and All" by William Carlos Williams, from COLLECTED POEMS: 1909–1939, Volume I, copyright © 1938 by New Directions Publishing Corp. Reprinted by permission of New Directions Publishing Corp. "The Dance", from COLLECTED POEMS: 1939–1962, Volume II. Copyright © 1944 by William Carlos Williams. Reprinted by permission of New Directions Publishing Corp.

JIM WONG-CHU, "old chinese cemetery kamloops july 1977" from *Chinatown Ghosts* (1986). Reprinted by permission of Arsenal Press.

JAN ZWICKY, "Border Station" from *Songs for Relinquishing the Earth* by Jan Zwicky. Reprinted by permission of Brick Books.

Index of Authors, Titles, and First Lines of Poetry

INDEX OF KEY TERMS

action, 946
active reading, 18, 600, 924
allegorical figure, 305, 798
allegorical framework, 305, 798
allegory, 44, 305–306, 404, 600, 798–799, 1292
alliteration, 261, 744, 756, 771
allusion, 265, 600, 721, 803–805
anapest, 734
annotating, 22–23, 52–53, 601–603, 924–925
antagonist, 73
antihero, 920
antistrophe, 907
apostrophe, 725
archetype, 303, 794
arena stage, 912
aside, 904, 1075
assonance, 746, 756
atmosphere, 171, 685
aubade, 566
audience, 23

ballad, 565, 762
ballad stanza, 565, 762
beast fable, 305
beginning rhyme, 747
black comedy, 920
blank verse, 735, 761
box set, 911
brainstorming, 26, 54, 926–927

cacophony, 743
caesura, 738
Canadian theatre (English), 912–914
canon, literary, 6–7, 1469
caricature, 120
carpe diem theme, 566, 653
catharsis, 915
chamber, 908
character, 41, 43, 118–119, 352, 353, 923, 1070–1076, 1338–1339
characterization, 118
chorus, 905–906
cliché, 351
climax, 74, 944
closed form, 759–774
closet drama, 904
colonnade, 906
comedy, 917–920
comedy of humours, 919

comedy of manners, 919
common knowledge, 1431
common measure, 762
conceit, 711
conclusion, 34–35
concrete poetry, 786–787
conflict, 73, 353, 944, 1336–1337
connotation, 657–658, 685
content note, 1442–1443
convention, 23
conventional symbol, 303, 793
cosmic irony, 915
costumes, 1245
couplet, 761
crisis, 74
critical thinking, 9–16

dactyl, 734
dark comedy, 920
deconstruction, 1481–1483
denotation, 657–658
denouement, 74, 944
deus ex machina, 74
dialogue, 904, 1070–1072, 1337–1338
dialogue with instructor, 31
diction, 262–263, 599, 666–671
dimeter, 735
documentation, 35–36, 1431–1457
double rhyme, 747
drama, identified, 904
dramatic irony, 213, 640, 915, 1075
dramatic monologue, 566, 624, 642
dramatic point of view, 216
dynamic character, 120, 1070

editing, 37–38
elegy, 566, 736
Elizabethan theatre, 907–910
emblem poem, 786–787
end rhyme, 747
end-stopped line, 738
enjambment, 738
environmental staging, 912
envoi, 767
epic, 40, 565
epigram, 632, 736, 772
epiphany, 42
episodia, 907
euphony, 743
exodos, 907
exposition, 73–74, 944

expressionism, 911
eye rhyme, 747

fairy tale, 41
falling action, 944
falling metre, 734
falling rhyme, 747
farce, 919, 1092
feminine rhyme, 747
feminist criticism, 1467–1470
figurative language, 264–265, 1072–1073
figures of speech, 264, 600, 700–729, 1072
first-person point of view, 212–214
fixed form, 759–774
flashback, 75, 946–947
flat character, 119, 1070, 1194
foil, 120, 1070, 1194
folktale, 41
foot, 734–735, 738
foreshadowing, 75, 947
form, 600, 759–790
formal diction, 262, 667–668, 1072
formalism, 1458–1459, 1463–1464
free verse, 760, 775–778

genres, 4
geographical setting, 170–171
Greek theatre, ancient, 905–907
groundlings, 908

haiku, 692, 773–774
hamartia, 915
heavens, 908
hell, 908
heptameter, 735
heroic couplets, 750, 761
hexameter, 735
high comedy, 920
highlighting, 19–20, 52–53, 601–603, 924–925
historical setting, 169–170
hubris, 915
humour, 918–920
huts, 908
hyperbole, 265, 712

iamb, 734–735
iambic pentameter, 735, 761
imagery, 263–264, 599, 685–699
imaginative literature, 3–5